RESEARCH COMPANION TO ORGANIZATIONAL HEALTH PSYCHOLOGY

NEW HORIZONS IN MANAGEMENT

Series Editor: Cary L. Cooper, *CBE, Professor of Organizational Psychology and Health, Lancaster University Management School, Lancaster University, UK*

This important series makes a significant contribution to the development of management thought. This field has expanded dramatically in recent years and the series provides an invaluable forum for the publication of high quality work in management science, human resource management, organisational behaviour, marketing, management information systems, operations management, business ethics, strategic management and international management.

The main emphasis of the series is on the development and application of new original ideas. International in its approach, it will include some of the best theoretical and empirical work from both well-established researchers and the new generation of scholars.

Titles in the series include:

The Handbook of Human Resource Management Policies and Practices in Asia-Pacific Economics
Volume One
Michael Zanko

The Handbook of Human Resource Management Policies and Practices in Asia-Pacific Economics
Volume Two
Michael Zanko and Matt Ngui

Human Nature and Organization Theory
On the Economic Approach to Institutional Organization
Sigmund Wagner-Tsukamoto

Organizational Relationships in the Networking Age
Edited by Willem Koot, Peter Leisink and Paul Verweel

Research Companion to Organizational Health Psychology

Edited by

Alexander-Stamatios G. Antoniou

Consultant in the Department of Occupational and Industrial Hygiene, National School of Public Health, Athens, and Research Centre of Psychophysiology and Education, University of Athens, Greece

and

Cary L. Cooper, CBE

Professor of Organizational Psychology and Health, Lancaster University Management School, Lancaster University, UK

New Horizons in Management

Edward Elgar
Cheltenham, UK • Northampton, MA, USA

© Alexander-Stamatios G. Antoniou and Cary L. Cooper 2005

All rights reserved. No part of this publication may be reproduced, stored in a retrieval system or transmitted in any form or by any means, electronic, mechanical or photocopying, recording, or otherwise without the prior permission of the publisher.

Published by
Edward Elgar Publishing Limited
Glensanda House
Montpellier Parade
Cheltenham
Glos GL50 1UA
UK

Edward Elgar Publishing, Inc.
136 West Street
Suite 202
Northampton
Massachusetts 01060
USA

A catalogue record for this book
is available from the British Library

ISBN 1 84376 624 8 (cased)

Printed and Bound in Great Britain by MPG Books Ltd, Bodmin, Cornwall

Contents

List of contributors ix
Foreword xiv
Preface xvi

PART I CONCEPTUALIZATION AND THEORETICAL FRAMEWORK

1 The role of event characteristics and situational appraisals in the prediction of employee adjustment to change and change implementation success 3
   Nerina L. Jimmieson

2 Constructions of occupational stress: nuisances, nuances or novelties? 20
   Dianna Kenny and Dennis McIntyre

3 Psychosocial risk factors and work-related stress: state of the art and issues for future research 59
   Michiel A.J. Kompier and Toon W. Taris

4 Biological basis of stress-related diseases 70
   Maria-Alexandra Magiakou and George P. Chrousos

5 The relationship between ethnicity and work stress 87
   Grace V.F. Miller and Cheryl J. Travers

6 Eustress and attitudes at work: a positive approach 102
   Debra L. Nelson and Bret L. Simmons

7 Stress and strain at work: how much is there, who has most and are things changing? 111
   Roy L. Payne

8 Stress, alienation and shared leadership 122
   Marc J. Schabracq

9 Job demands, job control, strain and learning behavior: review and research agenda 132
   Toon W. Taris and Michiel A.J. Kompier

10 The seeds of stress in the organizations of tomorrow: the impact of new technology and working methods 151
   Ashley Weinberg

PART II STRESS MANAGEMENT ISSUES

11 Stress and individual differences: implications for stress management 163
   Susan Cartwright and Lynne C. Whatmore

12	Work-related stress: the risk management paradigm *Stavroula Leka, Amanda Griffiths and Tom Cox*	174
13	Coping with stress through reason *Edwin A. Locke*	188
14	An organizational approach to stress management *Valerie J. Sutherland*	198
15	Prevention perspectives in occupational health psychology *Lois E. Tetrick, James Campbell Quick and Jonathan D. Quick*	209
16	Emotional intelligence and coping with occupational stress *Moshe Zeidner*	218

PART III   STRESS IN SPECIFIC GROUPS

17	Study and student counselling in higher education: an incentive towards a practice-relevant vision *Eric Depreeuw*	243
18	Stress and unemployment: a comparative review of female and male managers *Sandra L. Fielden and Marilyn J. Davidson*	254
19	Stress in veterinary surgeons: a review and pilot study *Howard Kahn and Camilla V.J. Nutter*	293
20	Structural work change and health: studies of long spells of sick leave and hospitalization among working men and women during a period of marked changes in the Swedish labour market *Gabriel Oxenstierna, Hugo Westerlund, Jane Ferrie, Martin Hyde, Jan Hagberg and Töres Theorell*	304
21	Role-related stress experienced by temporary employees *Ellen I. Shupe*	314

PART IV   STRESS, WELL-BEING AND HEALTH

22	The role of psychosocial factors in the development of periodontal disease *Alexander-Stamatios G. Antoniou, Diamanto Komboli, John Vrotsos and Zacharias Mantzavinos*	335
23	Work–family conflict and stress *Paula Brough and Michael O'Driscoll*	346
24	Workaholism in organizations: work and well-being consequences *Ronald J. Burke*	366
25	The healthy organization *Jane Henry*	382

26	Health care and subjective well-being in nations *Bruce Kirkcaldy, Adrian Furnham and Ruut Veenhoven*	393
27	New technology, the global economy and organizational environments: effects on employee stress, health and well-being *Janice Langan-Fox*	413
28	The effects of effort–reward imbalance at work on health *Johannes Siegrist, Bianca Falck and Ljiljana Joksimovic*	430
29	Occupational stress and health *Charles D. Spielberger and Eric C. Reheiser*	441
30	The role of emotions in cardiovascular disorders *Juan José Miguel-Tobal and Héctor González-Ordi*	455
31	The impact of short business travels on the individual, the family and the organization *Mina Westman*	478

PART V PROFESSIONAL BURNOUT

32	Burnout and emotions: an underresearched issue in search of a theory *Dirk Enzmann*	495
33	Proactive coping, resources and burnout: implications for occupational stress *Esther R. Greenglass*	503
34	Burnout and wornout: concepts and data from a national survey *Lennart Hallsten*	516
35	'Burning in' – 'burning out' in public: aspects of the burnout process in community-based psychiatric services *Thomas Hyphantis and Venetsanos Mavreas*	537
36	A mediation model of job burnout *Michael P. Leiter and Christina Maslach*	544
37	Love and work: the relationships between their unconscious choices and burnout *Ayala Malach Pines*	565
38	Unconscious influences on the choice of a career and their relationship to burnout: a psychoanalytic existential approach *Ayala Malach Pines*	579
39	Does burnout affect physical health? A review of the evidence *Arie Shirom and Samuel Melamed*	599
40	Rediscovering meaning and purpose at work: the transpersonal psychology background of a burnout prevention programme *Dirk van Dierendonck, Bert Garssen and Adriaan Visser*	623

PART VI EMOTIONAL INTELLIGENCE AT WORK

41 Emotional intelligence and transformational leadership 633
    Alexander-Stamatios G. Antoniou

42 Developing leadership through emotional intelligence 656
    Richard E. Boyatzis

Index 671

Contributors

Alexander-Stamatios G. Antoniou, Research Centre of Psychophysiology and Education, University of Athens, and Department of Occupational and Industrial Hygiene, National School of Public Health, Athens, Greece

Richard E. Boyatzis, Professor of Organizational Behavior, Weatherheard School of Management, Case Western Reserve University, USA

Paula Brough, Lecturer, School of Applied Psychology, Griffith University, Australia

Ronald J. Burke, Professor of Organisational Behaviour/Industrial Relations, Schulich School of Business, York University, Canada

Susan Cartwright, Senior Lecturer in Organisational Psychology, Manchester School of Management, UMIST, UK

George Chrousos, First Department of Pediatrics, Athens University Medical School and Pediatric and Reproductive Endocrinology Branch, Bethesda, USA

Cary L. Cooper, CBE, Professor of Organizational Psychology and Health, Lancaster University Management School, Lancaster University, UK

Tom Cox, Professor, Institute of Work, Health and Organisations, University of Nottingham, UK

Marilyn J. Davidson, Professor of Managerial Psychology, Manchester School of Management, UMIST, UK

Eric Depreeuw, Professor, Research Center for Motivation and Time Perspective, Catholic University Brussels, Belgium

Dirk Enzmann, Institute of Criminal Sciences, Department of Criminology, University of Hamburg

Bianca Falck, Department of Medical Sociology, University of Dusseldorf, Germany

Jane Ferrie, Senior Research Fellow, Department of Epidemiology and Public Health, University College London, UK

Sandra L. Fielden, Lecturer in Organizational Psychology, Centre for Diversity and Work Psychology, Manchester School of Management, UMIST, UK

Contributors

Adrian Furnham, Professor of Psychology, Department of Psychology, University College London, UK

Bert Garssen, Helen Dowling Institute, Utrecht, The Netherlands

Héctor González-Ordi, Faculty of Psychology, Complutense University of Madrid, Spain

Esther R. Greenglass, Professor of Psychology, Department of Psychology, York University, Canada

Amanda Griffiths, Professor of Occupational Health Psychology, Institute of Work, Health and Organisations, University of Nottingham, UK

Jan Hagberg, Department of Statistics, Stockholm University, Stockholm, Sweden

Lennart Hallsten, Assistant Professor, National Institute for Working Life, Stockholm, Sweden

Jane Henry, Chair of Creativity, Innovation and Change Programme, Open University, Milton Keynes, UK

Martin Hyde, Department of Epidemiology and Public Health, University College, London, UK

Thomas Hyphantis, Assistant Professor of Psychiatry, University of Ioannina Medical School, Ioannina, Greece

Nerina L. Jimmieson, School of Psychology, University of Queensland, Australia

Ljiljana Joksimovic, Department of Medical Sociology, University of Dusseldorf, Germany

Howard Kahn, Senior Lecturer, School of Management, Heriot-Watt University, UK

Dianna Kenny, Associate Professor, School of Behavioural and Community Health Sciences, The University of Sydney, Australia

Bruce Kirkcaldy, Professor, International Centre for the Study of Occupational and Mental Health, Düsseldorf, Germany

Diamanto Komboli, Associate Professor, Department of Periodontology, School of Dentistry, University of Athens, Greece

Michiel A.J. Kompier, Professor, Department of Work and Organisational Psychology, University of Nijmegen, The Netherlands

Janice Langan-Fox, Department of Psychology, University of Melbourne, Australia

Michael P. Leiter, Centre for Organizational Research and Devlopment, Acadia University, Canada

Stavroula Leka, Institute of Work, Health and Organisations, University of Nottingham, UK

Edwin A. Locke, Dean's Professor (Emeritus) of Leadership and Motivation, R.H. Smith School of Business at the University of Maryland, College Park, USA

Maria-Alexandra Magiakou, Assistant Professor of Pediatric Endrocrinology, University of Athens, Greece

Ayala Malach Pines, Professor, Ben-Gurion University of the Negev, Israel

Zacharias Mantzavinos, Department of Periodontology, School of Dentistry, University of Athens, Greece

Christina Maslach, Department of Psychology, University of California, Berkeley, USA

Venetsanos Mavreas, Assistant Professor of Psychiatry, University of Ioannina Medical School, Ioannina, Greece

Dennis McIntyre, School of Behavioural and Community Health Sciences, The University of Sydney, Australia

Samuel Melamed, Bar Ilian University, Israel

Juan José Miguel-Tobal, Professor, Faculty of Psychology, Complutense University of Madrid, Spain

Grace V.F. Miller, The Business School, University of Loughborough, UK

Debra L. Nelson, Department of Management, Oklahoma State University, USA

Camilla V.J. Nutter, Heriot-Watt University, UK

Michael O'Driscoll, Professor of Psychology, Department of Psychology, Waikato University, New Zealand

Gabriel Oxenstierna, National Institute for Psychosocial Medicine, Stockholm, Sweden and Division for Psychosocial Factors and Health, Department of Public Health Sciences, Karolinska Institutet, Stockholm, Sweden

Roy L. Payne, Professor, Institute of Work Psychology, Sheffield University, UK

James Campbell Quick, Professor of Organizational Behaviour, Department of Management, University of Texas at Arlington, USA

Jonathan D. Quick, World Health Organisation

Eric C. Reheiser, Center for Research in Behavioral Medicine and Health Psychology, University of South Florida, Tampa, USA

Marc J. Schabracq, Independent Management Consultant and Department of Work and Organization Psychology, University of Amsterdam, The Netherlands

Arie Shirom, Professor, The Leon Racanti Graduate School of Business Administration, Tel Aviv University, Israel

Ellen I. Shupe, Assistant Professor, Department of Psychology, Grand Valley State University, USA

Johannes Siegrist, Professor and Director, Department of Medical Sociology, University of Dusseldorf, Germany

Bret L. Simmons, Assistant Professor, Department of Management, College of Business Administration, North Dakota State University, USA

Charles Spielberger, Professor, Center for Research in Behavioral Medicine and Health Psychology, University of South Florida, Tampa, USA

Valerie J. Sutherland, Business Psychology Research Unit, UMIST, UK

Toon W. Taris, Department of Work and Organizational Psychology, University of Nijmegen, The Netherlands

Lois E. Tetrick, Professor and Director of Industrial Organizational Training, Department of Psychology, University of Houston, USA

Töres Theorell, Professor, National Institute for Psychosocial Medicine, Stockholm, Sweden and Division for Psychosocial Factors and Health, Department of Public Health Sciences, Karolinska Institutet, Stockholm, Sweden

Cheryl J. Travers, The Business School, University of Loughborough, UK

Dirk van Dierendonck, Assistant Professor, University of Amsterdam, The Netherlands

Ruut Veenhoven, Professor of Social Conditions for Human Happiness, Department of Social Sciences, Erasmus University Rotterdam, and Professor of Humanism, University of Utrecht, The Netherlands

Adriaan Visser, Helen Dowling Institute, Utrecht, The Netherlands

John Vrotsos, Professor, Department of Periodontology, School of Dentistry, University of Athens, Greece

Ashley Weinberg, Senior Lecturer in Psychology, School of Community, Health Sciences and Social Care, Salford University, UK

Hugo Westerlund, National Institute for Psychosocial Medicine, Stockholm, Sweden and Division for Psychosocial Factors and Health, Department of Public Health Sciences, Karolinska Institutet, Stockholm, Sweden

Mina Westman, Faculty of Management, Tel Aviv University, Israel

Lynne C. Whatmore, Manchester School of Management, UMIST, UK

Moshe Zeidner, Professor, University of Haifa, Israel

Foreword

There is ample scientific evidence that working (and other organizational) life and its conditions are powerful determinants of health, for better or for worse. The relationship works both ways. Work affects health but health, more often than not, also affects a person's productivity and earning capacity as well as his or her social and family relationships. Needless to say, this holds true for all aspects of health, both physical and mental (Levi, 2002).

The many causes and consequences of work-related and other organizational exposures are widespread in the 15 European Union member states. Over half of the EU's 160 million workers report working at very high speeds (56 per cent), and to tight deadlines (60 per cent). More than a third have no influence on task order. Forty per cent report having monotonous tasks. Such work-related 'stressors' are likely to have contributed to the present spectrum of ill health: 15 per cent of the workforce complain of headaches, 23 per cent of neck and shoulder pains, 23 per cent of fatigue, 28 per cent of 'stress', and 33 per cent of backache (European Foundation, 2001), plus a host of other illnesses, including life-threatening ones, such as depressive disorders. Such disorders are the fourth biggest cause of the global disease burden.

It is further likely that sustained work-related stress is an important determinant of metabolic syndrome (Folkow, 2001; Björntorp, 2001), probably contributing to ischaemic heart disease and Diabetes Type 2 morbidity.

In these ways, virtually every aspect of work-related health and disease can be affected. Such influences can also be mediated through emotional, and/or cognitive misinterpretation of work conditions as threatening, even when they are not, and/or trivial symptoms and signs occurring in one's own body as manifestations of serious illness. All this can lead to a wide variety of disorders, diseases, loss of well-being – and loss of productivity.

According to the European Union's Framework Directive, employers have a 'duty to ensure the safety and health of workers in every aspect related to the work'. The Directive's principles of prevention include 'avoiding risks', 'combating the risks at source', and 'adapting the work to the individual'. In addition, the Directive indicates the employers' duty to develop 'a coherent overall prevention policy'.

The short- and long-term outcomes of such interventions then need to be evaluated, in terms of (a) stressor exposures, (b) stress reactions, (c) incidence and prevalence of ill health, (d) indicators of wellbeing, and (e) productivity with regard to the quality and quantity of goods or services. Also to be considered are (f) the costs and benefits in economic terms. If the interventions have no effects, or negative ones in one or more respects, the stakeholders may wish to rethink what should be done, how, when, by whom and for whom. If, on the other hand, outcomes are generally positive, they may wish to continue or expand their efforts along similar lines. It simply means systematic learning from experience. If they do so over a longer perspective, the workplace becomes an example of organizational learning (Levi and Levi, 2000).

To be cost-effective, such learning should be based both on a conceptual framework and on empirical evidence. In addition, its possible impact should be evaluated across societal sectors and scientific disciplines. This is why this volume has an important role to play, as a basis for research but also for implementation and evaluation of the results of such research.

This volume's 42 theoretical and empirical chapters are grouped into six parts covering conceptualization, theoretical framework, stress management, stress in specific groups, stress as related to health and well-being, professional burnout and emotional intelligence.

The 72 distinguished contributors from over 50 different institutions provide a multi-faceted picture of an important area mainly to an academic and post-graduate student audience of Psychology and Medicine. I am pleased to recommend it for perusal, implementation and evaluation.

Lennart Levi, M.D., Ph.D.
November 2003
Emeritus Professor of Psychosocial Medicine
Karolinska Institutet
Stockholm, Sweden

References

Björntorp, P. (2001), 'Heart and Soul: Stress and the Metabolic Syndrome', *Scandinavian Cardiovascular Journal*, **35**, 172–77.

European Foundation, P. Paoli and D. Merllié (2001), *Third European Survey on Working Conditions*, Dublin: European Foundation.

Folkow, B. (2001), 'Mental Stress and its Importance for Cardiovascular Disorders; Physiological Aspects, "from-mice-to-man"', *Scandinavian Cardiovascular Journal*, **35**, 165–72.

Levi, L. (2002), 'The European Commission's Guidance on Work-Related Stress: From Words to Action', *TUTB Newsletter*, **19–20**, 12–17.

Levi, L. and I. Levi (2000), *Guidance on Work-Related Stress. Spice of Life, or Kiss of Death?*, Luxembourg: Office for Official Publications of the European Communities.

Preface

For slaves, there is no leisure, (Aristotle, *Politics*, 1334a 21)

The rapid change in the economy and technology along with the strong competition worldwide has changed the way that we perceive the world and, consequently our life style. Working hours are becoming longer and technological changes taking place every day demand high levels of adaptability and flexibility. Jobs are no longer for life and the modern family has been transformed from a one to a two-earner structure, creating a situation where individuals are expected to balance work and home commitments. The question which arises at this point is: who shall survive this process? One could answer it is the 'fittest' employee who has the ability to adjust adequately to these rapid changes and can remain undistracted from external factors. Furthermore such a person manages to avoid the experience or to cope with the negative effects of stress.

Organizational health psychology has its share in contributing to the understanding of healthy behaviours within working environments and identifying parameters that can be the cause of health problems. For example, stress in the workplace can contribute to individual and organizational skill effectiveness but it is also an aspect which, in most cases, leads to undesirable effects. In general, organizational stress is by definition an unpleasant state of being that affects employees' creativity and work pleasure, while its results on physical and psychological well-being are evident. The undesirable effects of job-related stress occur when this acts as a barrier to employees' adjustment to the work setting. In addition to the impact of occupational stress on the individual's well-being, the consequences for organizations are particularly important: poor individual functioning, compensation claims, accidents, absenteeism, medical expenses and the reduction of workplace satisfaction and productivity. These are some of the most important factors which relate to workplace stress and affect the workers' psychosomatic status as well as the organizations in terms of productivity and effectiveness.

Although organizational stress constitutes only one of the major topics in the field of organizational health psychology, the need to raise awareness of this problem is emphasized worldwide with the aim of adopting direct measures to protect employees' hygiene and safety and advance their mental health cost-effectively for organizations. With the pressures of the competitive world market on working standards, workers are subjected to heavy workloads and pressing schedules. The recent redesigning of the traditional work structure is the cause of an increase in work rates, a boost in productivity, 'downsizing', underpromotion and job insecurity. Nevertheless individuals are expected to respond to these demanding and ever changing conditions in a positive and creative way.

The Greek philosopher Aristotle, in his acclaimed work *Politics*, states that work is inevitable and people need to find the appropriate means to ease their heavy workload. Organizational health psychology can make a significant contribution in this direction by setting out the conditions for creative and 'healthy' jobs. (It is worth noticing that, in the Greek language the words 'job' and 'slavery' are identical apart from the intonation, perhaps reminding us that without the right conditions there is a high risk that these two concepts will be misconstrued.) In our day, it has been demonstrated that the modern employee needs to determine a reasonable hierarchy of his or her life's values. According to Emmanuel Kant, individuals themselves are the purpose, not the means, and they are the reference point of other means and values. Accordingly, a job should be the means of serving people's needs and developing the values which will determine their principles and ethos. What needs to be achieved now is a solid theoretical framework for future research and systematic approaches towards practical actions and interventions applied to working environments.

Following this direction, this volume is an edited collection of theoretical and empirical papers, across 42 chapters which fall into six parts, written by distinguished academics working in Europe, the USA and Australia. Even though the majority of the contributions refer to stress-related issues (current theories of stress, stress management, stress in specific occupational groups, the relation of stress to well-being), the reader can also find leading-edge topics on the area of organizational health psychology such as professional burnout, workaholism and emotional intelligence. With a strong international framework (72 academics and professionals from over 50 different institutions) this volume is aimed mainly at an academic and postgraduate student readership from psychology and medicine, and is of value to researchers interested in the main study areas of organizational health psychology.

We would like to express our sincere thanks to all contributors to this volume who very eagerly agreed to participate in this project and to cooperate during the period of its preparation.

Alexander-Stamatios G. Antoniou
Cary L. Cooper

PART I

CONCEPTUALIZATION AND THEORETICAL FRAMEWORK

1 The role of event characteristics and situational appraisals in the prediction of employee adjustment to change and change implementation success

Nerina L. Jimmieson

Organizational change is typically activated by a relevant environmental shift that, once recognized by the organization, leads to an intentionally generated response (Porras and Silvers, 1991). In this respect, organizational change is intended to alter key organizational variables that then have an impact on the members of the organization and their work-related behaviors. Similarly, Van de Ven and Poole (1995) described change as an empirical observation of difference in form or state over time in an organizational entity. The entity may be a product or service, an individual's job, a work group, or the overall strategy for an organization. Thus organizational change can be viewed as a critical event, which has the potential to evoke stress reactions and other negative consequences in employees. In this respect, employees are confronted with a unique set of workplace stressors resulting from a changing work environment. As organizational change by its very nature is not linear, the most frequent psychological state resulting from organizational change is that of uncertainty (see Ashford, 1988; Begley, 1998; Callan, 1993; Carnall, 1986; Gemmil and Smith, 1985; Jick, 1985; Nelson *et al.*, 1995; Olson and Tetrick, 1988; Sagie and Koslowsky, 1994; Schweiger and Ivancevich, 1985; Sverke *et al.*, 1997).

Employees are likely to experience uncertainty about many different facets of their job during times of organizational change. For instance, Shaw *et al.*, (1993) argue that role stress is likely to result from uncertainty associated with organizational change. Role conflict may be particularly prevalent during organizational change as the expectations of the new organization may be in direct contrast to the expectations of the old organization. Similarly role ambiguity may occur when the expectations applicable to the old organization have not been replaced by clear expectations set by the new organization. Employees also may experience role overload when too many tasks are assigned in a given time period or when new job duties go beyond employees' current knowledge, skills and abilities. In addition to experiencing uncertainty over the nature of present and future job responsibilities, employees may perceive organizational change as a major source of threat to their personal career paths and financial well-being (Callan, 1993). Employees also may experience the loss of many intangible features associated with their work environment, such as power and prestige, and a sense of community at work (Ashford, 1988; Callan, 1993; Greenhalgh and Rosenblatt, 1984; Kanter, 1983). Given that the experience of organizational change and the uncertainty it creates is likely to be a stressful event for many employees, the primary aim of this chapter is to highlight how a stress and coping perspective provides a useful theoretical framework for understanding of how organizational change can be managed to facilitate employee adjustment and better change implementation success.

Role of information provision during organizational change
In light of the previous discussion, one of the managerial challenges facing organizations is the effective implementation of organizational change programs that minimize feelings of uncertainty and associated threat. As discussed by Milliken (1987), uncertainty in the work context points to the crucial need for the provision of information. Indeed Sutton and Kahn (1986) argue that, when profound organizational change is imminent, employees go through a process of sense making in which they need information to help them establish a sense of prediction (for example, the time frame for organizational change) and understanding (for example, the need for organizational change). Thus feelings of workplace uncertainty can be reduced by providing employees with timely and accurate information concerning the organizational change process, through either formal or informal communication channels (see also Ashford, 1988). In the context of organizational change, there is a growing body of research examining the role of a range of information-related constructs as predictors of employee adjustment. Generally studies of this nature have shown that better reactions to organizational change (in terms of reduced anxiety and heightened satisfaction and commitment) are observed when employees are provided with realistic communications about various features of the organizational change process (for example, Brockner *et al.*, 1990; Miller and Monge, 1985; Schweiger and DeNisi, 1991).

Role of employee participation during organizational change
Another change management strategy that is important for determining employee adjustment during times of organizational change is employee participation. Although workplace interventions designed to increase levels of employee participation can take a variety of forms, the employee participation construct traditionally has been defined as the amount of involvement employees have in the decision-making processes of the organization. Employee participation is one potential strategy that helps to create a sense of personal control among employees. In this respect, involvement in decision-making processes gives employees the opportunity to adopt direct behavioral efforts to control significant work-related events, thereby achieving desired outcomes. Empirical evidence attesting to the importance of employee participation during times of organizational change also has spanned several decades of research. For example, Korunka *et al.* (1995) found that employees who perceived high levels of participation during the implementation of new technologies in their workplace reported lower levels of psychosomatic health complaints and job dissatisfaction than those employees who perceived low levels of involvement throughout the change process. Sagie and Koslowsky (1994) also found that employee participation in decisions concerning the organizational change process (for example, mode of implementation) was related to a variety of positive change outcomes, including job satisfaction (see also Sagie and Koslowsky, 1996).

A stress and coping approach to organizational change
In light of empirical support for the role of information provision and employee participation in determining adjustment for employees undergoing specific organizational

change events, an important avenue for future research is to examine the cognitive mechanisms through which such processes are related to employee adjustment. In this chapter, three studies that have examined the extent to which information provision and employee participation engender a sense of change-related self-efficacy and readiness for change among employees experiencing organizational change are reviewed. The cognitive–phenomenological model of stress and coping provides an appropriate theoretical framework for research of this nature (Lazarus and Folkman, 1984; Lazarus, 1990). This model proposes that an understanding of how individuals adjust to stressful life events requires a consideration of the dual role of event characteristics and coping resources in shaping one's appraisal of the situation. More recently Terry and Callan (2000) used this approach to develop a model of employee adjustment to organizational change. They proposed that the way in which organizational change is implemented represents the characteristics of the event that are likely to have a strong impact on subsequent stress and coping processes for employees. Key event characteristics include the effectiveness of the leadership provided, the extent to which the implementation process is consultative, and how much information is communicated to employees. Coping resources are relatively stable characteristics of employees' dispositions and refer to what is available to them when they develop their coping responses.

Next, to understand how employees adjust to organizational change, Terry and Callan noted that it is necessary to consider, not only event characteristics and coping resources, but also how employees cognitively construe the situation. This is referred to as 'situational appraisal' and consists of both primary appraisal and secondary appraisal processes. Primary appraisal reflects the individual's subjective judgment of the relevance of the situation to his or her level of well-being, whereas secondary appraisal reflects the individual's assessment of what can be done to manage the situation. Terry and Callan reviewed evidence to suggest that secondary appraisal comprises a number of judgments, related to appraisals of control, efficacy and uncertainty. Of particular interest in this chapter is the notion of an employee's expectancies of self-efficacy. Employees who appraise the impending organizational change as a situation in which they have the ability to cope with the demands of the situation are more likely to experience better adjustment. A number of interrelationships among event characteristics, coping resources and situational appraisals can be derived from this model to predict employee adjustment to change. In particular, event characteristics and coping resources are hypothesized to be directly related to situational appraisals of self-efficacy. In addition positive situational appraisals are expected to facilitate the use of more effective coping strategies and higher levels of employee adjustment.

Change-related self-efficacy
A key element in Bandura's (1977) theory of social learning, self-efficacy refers to an individual's belief in his or her capability to execute a course of action needed to meet the demands of a situation. Bandura noted that self-efficacy should not be conceptualized and measured in terms of generalized feelings of mastery but rather with reference to handling a specific situation or performing a specific behavior. Thus, in the context of organizational change, change-related self-efficacy can be defined as an employee's perceived ability to function well on the job, despite the demands of a changing work

environment (see Ashford, 1988; Wanberg and Banas, 2000). Employees who doubt their ability to respond to the demands of a specific organizational change event are likely to focus attention on their feelings of incompetence, which will be accompanied by feelings of psychological distress, and a failure to deal with the situation (Bandura, 1977). In contrast, employees who have high levels of change-related efficacy are unlikely to be distressed by feelings of inadequacy and, for this reason, are expected to persist in their efforts to manage the organizational change process.

Bandura (1977) identified several sources of information that may engender perceptions of self-efficacy. These include internal cues drawn from an individual's own state of physiological arousal, verbal persuasion aimed at convincing an individual of his or her capability to perform a task, vicarious experience by way of behavior modeling, and enactive mastery through repeated performance accomplishments. Although Bell and Staw (1989) argued that opportunities for more direct forms of employee involvement, such as participation in work-related decisions, are likely to be stronger determinants of self-efficacy expectations, they suggested that self-efficacy expectations also are likely to mediate the effects of information on employee adjustment. Some initial evidence in support of this proposition comes from research conducted in an experimental setting. For instance, Pond and Hay (1989) found that self-efficacy expectations increased for university students who received information designed to familiarize them with the type of job performed by customs inspectors prior to processing the paperwork for 16 import shipments. Earley (1986) also speculated that the influence of his strategic information manipulation on goal acceptance and subsequent task performance for employees working in two tire manufacturing companies would be through an enhancement of employees' self-efficacy expectations. However research of this nature has not been extended to applied settings undergoing specific organizational change initiatives. Thus, in this chapter, a series of studies are reviewed that have been undertaken to address specifically the extent to which information provision and employee participation create a belief among employees that they have the ability to meet the situational demands of organizational change (that is, change-related self-efficacy).

Readiness for change
An additional dimension on which events can be appraised, and one that is likely to be relevant to the context of organizational change, is the notion of readiness for change. Indeed several researchers have recently turned their attention to the notion of readiness for change as an aspect of the change situation that is considered by employees (Eby *et al.*, 2000; Yousef, 2000). Readiness for change can be defined as the extent to which employees hold positive views about the need for organizational change (that is, change acceptance) as well as the extent to which employees believe that such changes are likely to have positive implications for themselves and the organization (Miller *et al.*, 1994; see also Armenakis *et al.*, 1999; Armenakis *et al.*, 1993). As Armenakis *et al.* have noted, readiness for change is the cognitive precursor to employee behaviors that either support or resist a specific organizational change event. Armenakis *et al.* also went on to speculate that a variety of change management strategies (such as persuasive communication) are important for building up readiness for change perceptions. Similarly, drawing on theories of psychological ownership, Dirks *et al.* (1996) proposed that employees are more likely to

promote organizational change when conditions are created that allow them to maintain a sense of control and involvement.

Theoretical propositions of this nature have received some empirical attention in the organizational change literature. For instance, Miller *et al.* (1994) examined the predictive utility of several information-related variables (for example, amount of general information, amount of change-related information, quality of change-related information) as predictors of readiness for change for 168 employees in a national insurance company that was about to introduce team-based methods of working. Results indicated that quality of change-related information was the strongest precursor to readiness for change perceptions. Although anxiety levels were assessed in this study, the mediating role of readiness for change in the relationship between the informational environment and employee adjustment was not explored. More recently Wanberg and Banas (2000) found that pre-implementation measures of several context-specific variables (which included information and participation) were predictive of readiness for change (assessed two months later) for 130 employees working in a public housing association undergoing large-scale restructuring. There also was some evidence to suggest that readiness for change was related to the delayed measures of work irritation, job satisfaction and turnover intentions. Given that information and participation were not predictive of the employee adjustment measures in this study, tests for a mediational relationship between the context-specific variables, readiness for change and employee adjustment were not possible. In the review of studies that follows, the extent to which readiness for change mediates the relationship between effective change management strategies (that is, information provision and employee participation) and employee adjustment to organizational change is examined.

Introduction of a new pay scheme in a corporatized public utility
Aims of the study
In a preliminary test of the mediating role of situational appraisals in the relationship between event characteristics and employee adjustment in the context of organizational change, Jimmieson and Griffiths (2001) examined the extent to which positive change management strategies (that is, information provision and employee participation) led to appraisals that are specific to the organizational change event (that is, change-related self-efficacy and readiness for change), thereby heightening levels of employee adjustment (that is psychological well-being and job satisfaction). These propositions were tested for a group of senior managers experiencing the introduction of a new pay scheme. Specifically it was hypothesized that both information provision and employee participation would be indirectly related to better psychological well-being and job satisfaction, via their positive effects on change-related self-efficacy. In addition, it was anticipated that senior managers who felt that they received information about the impending changes and were able to participate in related decision making would report higher levels of readiness for change which, in turn, would predict levels of psychological well-being and job satisfaction.

Organizational context and sample
Participants in this study were senior managers employed in a corporatized public utility responsible for water and waste management in Sydney, Australia. This organization was undergoing changes in relation to a new pay scheme that would directly link the payment

of annual bonuses to the performance of their business unit. Given that pay transitions send strong messages to employees about strategic shifts in the organization and the consequences for their immediate job responsibilities, several authors have highlighted the importance of creating change readiness among employees in this context (for example Marquardt and Meehan, 1995; Saunier and Gallo, 1994; Zingheim and Schuster, 1995).

Questionnaires were sent to 199 senior managers. A total of 167 employees provided data, an acceptable response rate of 84 per cent. Employees ranged in age from 27 to 65 years, with a mean of 47 years ($SD = 7.20$). Education levels included secondary school qualifications (4 per cent), TAFE qualifications at either the certificate (14 per cent) or diploma (4 per cent) level, as well as trade qualifications (1 per cent). The majority of participants had some form of tertiary education, either at the undergraduate (31 per cent) or postgraduate (40 per cent) level. Total remuneration packages ranged from $70 000 to $157 600, with a mean of $92 246 ($SD = $17 220). The senior managers in this sample were represented throughout a variety of business units providing either professional (20 per cent) or technical (70 per cent) services.

Measures
Perceptions of information provision were measured with three items designed to assess the extent to which employees felt they had been provided with sufficient information about the organizational changes. Perceptions of employee participation were measured with three items designed to assess the extent to which senior managers felt they had been given opportunities to influence the implementation process for the new pay scheme. Levels of change-related self-efficacy were measured with three items asking staff to make generalized judgments of self-mastery about the organizational changes. Readiness for change was operationalized as the extent to which senior managers were feeling positive about, and supportive of, the proposed changes to the pay scheme (see Miller *et al.*, 1994). Levels of psychological well-being were measured with the 12-item version of the General Health Questionnaire (GHQ) (Goldberg, 1972). Job satisfaction was assessed with four items adapted from the scale developed by Caplan *et al.*, (1980). Each item was designed to assess individuals' global level of satisfaction with their job.

Findings and discussion
To test the proposed model, structural equation modeling (SEM) was performed using LISREL 8.3 (Jöreskog and Sörbom, 2000). The null model that tests the hypothesis that the constructs are unrelated to one another was rejected, $\chi^2 (14) = 142.29, p < 0.001$. Next the proposed model was tested. The proposed model provided an adequate fit to the data, $\chi^2 (6) = 14.60, p < 0.05$; RMR = 0.07; NNFI = 0.88; CFI (Bentler, 1990) = 0.95; GFI = 0.97; AGFI = 0.89. A chi-square difference test indicated a significant improvement in fit between the null model and the proposed model. To rule out the possibility of main effect relationships between information provision and employee participation with the outcomes variables of psychological well-being and job satisfaction, a further model was tested. While this alternative model provided an adequate fit to the data, $\chi^2 (2) = 5.22$, $p > 0.05$; RMR = 0.03; CFI (ibid.) = 0.98; NNFI = 0.85; GFI = 0.99; AGFI = 0.88, the direct effect paths were not significant. Therefore the proposed model was retained. Post hoc modifications were undertaken on the proposed model in an attempt to develop a

better fitting model. Using the Wald test, two paths were deleted. These paths were employee participation to change-related self-efficacy, and change-related self-efficacy to psychological well-being, each of which produced minimal change in the chi-square value. The resulting final model fitted the data well, χ^2 (8) = 14.86, $p < 0.05$, RMR = 0.05; CFI (ibid.) = 0.96; NNFI = 0.91; GFI = 0.97; AGFI = 0.91.

The results from the final model indicated that change-related self-efficacy mediated the positive relationship between information provision and job satisfaction (standardized coefficient for indirect effect = 0.13, $p < 0.01$). However these results were not replicated in the prediction of psychological well-being. Inconsistent with expectations, employee participation was not a predictor of change-related efficacy. Thus it appeared that the provision of information during times of organizational change had a stronger impact on employees self-efficacy beliefs than opportunities for change-related decision making. Although this pattern of results is somewhat inconsistent with theories of self-efficacy that typically suggest that more active ways of involving employees in organizational processes are likely to have the most salient impact on self-efficacy perceptions (see Bell and Staw, 1989), it does point towards some important practical implications. In this respect, strategies for providing accurate and timely information during times of organizational change are potentially more easily implemented than interventions designed to afford employees greater participation, especially if the change event is largely not under the control of employees.

Perceptions of readiness of change were found to play an important role in the final model. Senior managers who perceived high levels of information provision reported higher levels of readiness for change which, in turn, were related to better psychological well-being (standardized coefficient for indirect effect = 0.12, $p < 0.01$) and job satisfaction (standardized coefficient for indirect effect = 0.13, $p < 0.01$). In addition, respondents who felt that they had had opportunities to participate in the implementation process reported higher levels of psychological well-being (standardized coefficient for indirect effect = 0.09, $p < 0.01$) and job satisfaction (standardized coefficient for indirect effect = 0.06, $p < 0.05$), an effect that was mediated via change readiness perceptions. Overall these findings contribute to recent research that has begun to examine the antecedents and consequences of employees readiness for change perceptions (Eby *et al.*, 2000; Wanberg and Banas, 2000; Yousef, 2000).

Introduction of multi-disciplinary work teams in midwifery hospitals
Aims of the study
In an attempt to replicate the pattern of findings reported in the study conducted by Jimmieson and Griffiths (2001), an additional test of the mediating role of situational appraisals in the relationship between positive change management strategies and levels of employee adjustment to organizational change was conducted with a group of nurses undergoing a process of job redesign that involved a move to team-based methods of working (see Jimmieson, 2002). A similar set of hypotheses were examined involving the relationship among event characteristics (that is, information provision and employee participation), situational appraisals (that is, efficacy and readiness) and employee adjustment. Given the situationally specific nature of self-efficacy, this study made a distinction between the broader construct of change-related self-efficacy and a more specific form of

self-efficacy related to the nature of the changes taking place in the organizations who participated in the research. Given that the hospitals were introducing team-based methods of working, a measure of team-related self-efficacy was developed for use in this study. The extent to which information provision and employee participation helped to develop employees' confidence about working in teams was examined, in addition to the broader construct of change-related self-efficacy. Lastly the range of employee adjustment measures considered in this particular study was extended to include organizational commitment and (low) turnover intentions.

Organizational setting and sample
The change context for this research was three maternity hospitals in Australia, each of which was about to introduce a new model of maternity care based on the principle of continuity of care. One of the major vehicles for achieving this initiative was the implementation of multidisciplinary work teams each of which would be responsible for the care of a designated group of women and their families throughout all three phases of maternity care (antenatal care, labour and birth, and postnatal care). Thus the team-based method of working had significant implications for the roles and responsibilities of staff, most of whom were about to undertake intensive training to prepare them for the multi faceted nature of this more holistic approach to midwifery care. Completed questionnaires were received from 281 midwifery nurses (representing a response rate of 78 per cent) across each of the three hospitals. As to be expected, the majority of the respondents were females ($n = 269$). Age ranged from 23 to 65 years ($M = 40.68$, $SD = 9.35$). Both full-time (36 per cent) and part-time (63 per cent) employees were represented in the sample.

Measures
Perceptions of information provision were measured with five items designed to assess the extent to which employees felt they had been provided with sufficient information about the organizational changes. Perceptions of employee participation were measured with five items designed to assess the extent to which nurses felt they had been given opportunities to influence the way in which the organizational changes were implemented. Levels of change-related self-efficacy were measured with five items asking nurses how confident they felt in their ability to deal with the changes planned for their workplace. Team-related self-efficacy was measured with ten items designed to assess the extent to which employees felt confident in their ability to carry out a variety of teamwork requirements. Items were developed using the taxonomy of knowledge, skills and abilities (KSAs) required for successful teamwork developed by Stevens and Campion (1994). Items reflected KSAs of both an interpersonal nature (for example, conflict resolution) and a self-management nature (for example, goal-setting and performance management). Levels of readiness for change were measured with 11 items designed to assess the extent to which nurses were feeling supportive of the organizational changes (adapted from items developed by Miller *et al.*, 1994).

Four indicators of employee adjustment were assessed in this study. Psychological wellbeing was measured with the GHQ-12 (Goldberg, 1972) which asked respondents how their health had been, in general, over the last few weeks. Job satisfaction was measured with five items designed to assess individuals' global level of satisfaction with their job (Caplan *et al.*, 1980). Levels of organizational commitment were assessed with four items designed to measure the extent to which employees identified with the values of their organization (Allen and Meyer, 1990). Lastly, (low) turnover intentions were assessed with three items asking employees if they seriously intended to seek a job, transfer, resign from their job or enter a different occupation during the next three months (Mobley, 1977).

Findings and discussion
Four sets of hierarchical multiple regression analyses were performed to examine the main and mediating effects of the focal variables on each of the dependent variables. Given that age was found to be positively correlated with three of the indicators of employee adjustment, the effects of age were statistically controlled on the first step of the analyses. Other demographic variables (such as organizational type, job status and tenure) were found to be unrelated to the variables and were therefore not included in subsequent analyses. Entry of the event characteristics (that is, information provision and employee participation) into the second step of the hierarchical multiple regression analyses accounted for a significant increment of variance in psychological well-being, R^2ch. = 0.06, $p < 0.01$, job satisfaction, R^2ch. = 0.10, $p < 0.01$, organizational commitment, R^2ch. = 0.06, $p < 0.01$ and (low) turnover intentions, R^2ch. = 0.04, $p < 0.01$. There was evidence to suggest that information provision emerged as a significant positive predictor of psychological well-being, job satisfaction, and (low) turnover intentions, whereas employee participation was only predictive of organizational commitment.

Entry of the situational appraisals (that is, the efficacy variables and readiness for change) at the third also accounted for an additional increment of variance in psychological well-being, R^2ch. = 0.08, $p < 0.01$, job satisfaction, R^2ch. = 0.04, $p < 0.01$, organizational commitment, R^2ch. = 0.03, $p < 0.05$, and (low) turnover intentions, R^2ch. = 0.06, $p < 0.01$. Perceptions of change-related self-efficacy were found to be positively related to levels of psychological well-being (but not the other indicators of employee adjustment assessed in this study). Team-related self-efficacy was not significantly related to any of the employee adjustment measures. However there was consistent support for the proposal that readiness for change would be related to better employee adjustment. Nurses who reported that they felt a sense of change readiness also reported higher levels of psychological well-being, job satisfaction, organizational commitment and (low) turnover intentions.

These analyses also permitted an examination of the extent to which the event characteristics exerted a positive indirect effect on employee adjustment, via their effects on employees' situational appraisals of efficacy and readiness. To provide evidence of a mediating model, it is necessary to demonstrate that the observed positive main effects of information provision are no longer significant when the effects of the mediating variables (that is, change-related self-efficacy, team-related self-efficacy and readiness for change) are controlled on the subsequent step (see Baron and Kenny, 1986). Entry of the situational appraisals into the third step of the hierarchical multiple regression analyses provided some support for this proposition. When these variables were in the equation, the observed positive main effect of information provision was no longer significant when predicting psychological well-being and (low) turnover intentions. Closer examination of the results revealed that change-related self-efficacy mediated the positive relationship between information provision and psychological well-being. Readiness for change also mediated the effects of information provision on both psychological well-being and (low) turnover intentions. This pattern of findings was further supported in follow-up analyses in which the situational appraisals were entered into the equation prior to the event characteristics. After the effects of change-related self-efficacy and readiness for change were controlled, information provision failed to add significantly to scores in psychological well-being and (low) turnover intentions.

Several methodological limitations of the studies just presented should be considered when interpreting the results reported in this research. In particular the reliance on contemporaneous self-report data from a single source is problematic because temporal relationships specified in the theoretical framework presented in this study cannot be established. Furthermore significant relationships may reflect the confounding influence of common method variance, thereby resulting in spuriously high intercorrelations (Bagozzi and Yi, 1990; Glick et al., 1986; Williams et al., 1989). Thus there is a need to employ longitudinal research designs that can help to clarify the extent to which change management strategies and employees' appraisals of the change event have any long-term implications for well-being. It is also important to extend the range of outcome variables typically assessed in this type of organizational change research to include variables related to change implementation success. Clearly measures of success will be dependent on the nature of the specific organizational change taking place. In the next study, involving the introduction of a new information system, the extent to which reshaping capabilities (that promote information provision and employee participation) created change readiness perceptions among employees just prior to the change implementation were examined. The extent to which change readiness at Time 1 (T1) was predictive of user satisfaction and system usage at Time 2 (T2) also was explored.

Introduction of a new information system in a state government department
Aims of the study
In this final study it was hypothesized that employees who report high, rather than low, levels of organizational reshaping capabilities within their workplace would also perceive heightened levels of readiness for change which, in turn, would be predictive of change implementation (see Jones et al., 2002). Based on the findings of the two studies just presented, it was argued that readiness for change is an important mediating variable to consider in understanding employee adjustment to organizational change and, similarly, would be a relevant concept to consider in relation to implementation outcomes. Given that the change event involved the implementation of a new information system, change implementation success was operationalized as user satisfaction and system usage, both of which are key indicators of successful information system implementation (Guimaraes et al., 1992; Pinto, 1994; Santhanam et al., 2000). User satisfaction is defined by Ives et al., (1983) as the extent to which users believe the system meets their needs and is probably the most widely used measure of success in this context (DeLone and McLean, 1992). System usage is defined by Lee et al., (1995) as the amount of effort expended by users interacting with the information system or, more simplistically, the amount of time per day spent utilizing the system. Together user satisfaction and system usage provide a more complete picture of success than if either measure was utilized alone. The first is based on beliefs and attitudes, whereas the second is based on behaviors (Haines and Petit, 1997).

In this last study, a different approach was taken to the measurement of employees' perceptions of the way in which organizational change was managed in their workplace. In this respect, this study examined the extent to which employees who rated their workplace as having adequate organizational capabilities relevant to the management of change (that is reshaping capabilities) also reported higher levels of change readiness and, subsequently, better user satisfaction and system usage. The capabilities required for successful change have been specifically addressed by Turner and Crawford (1998), who proposed a taxonomy of reshaping capabilities that consisted of engagement, development and performance management capabilities. Engagement is based on informing and involving organizational members in an attempt to encourage a sense of motivation and commitment to the goals and objectives of the organization. These capabilities are similar to the notions of information provision and employee participation considered in the previous two studies. Development involves developing all resources and systems needed to achieve the organization's future directions, whereas proactively managing the factors that drive the organization's performance to ensure it consistently and effectively achieves the intended change is referred to as 'performance management'.

Miller and Chen (1994) claimed that successful change implementation will be the result of the development of reshaping capabilities. Indeed, in an analysis of 243 cases of organizational change, Turner and Crawford (1998) found that, as the strength of reshaping capabilities rises, so too do the rates of change implementation success, leading them to conclude that reshaping capabilities are needed whenever organizational change is needed. However the potential to draw strong conclusions about these findings is limited, given that few studies have examined the direct relationship between reshaping capabilities and change implementation success. Furthermore no studies to date have examined the extent to which reshaping capabilities help to foster a sense of readiness for change among employees. Indeed, as shown in the previous two studies, readiness for change perceptions may be the mediating variable that helps to explain the positive relationship between reshaping capabilities and a range of change-related outcomes for both the employee and the organization.

Organizational context and sample
This study involved a state government department in Queensland, Australia about to implement an end-user information system. The end-user information system was an extension of the existing Human Resource Information System (HRIS) that was implemented a year earlier, with the implementation of the HRIS affecting only the data entry personnel at that time. The implementation of the end-user information system would now affect all employees within the organization, as they would need to access the system for viewing payroll information, requesting annual leave and applying for training courses. The outcome of implementing a new information system is not just a change in technology, but also a change in structures, duties, tasks and personnel. In addition Bjorn-Anderson (1988) and Hirscheim and Newman (1988) claim that managers and users of information systems often remain resistant throughout the implementation process, despite the disappearance of most technical barriers. Understanding and creating the workplace conditions under which employees embrace such challenges remains a high-priority research issue (Vankatesh and Davis, 2000).

14 *Conceptualization and theoretical framework*

Questionnaires were posted to all employees in the pilot group ($N = 580$) via the organization's internal dispatch system. Employees were asked to return the questionnaire directly to the researchers in the reply-paid envelope provided. Despite a range of tactics to maximize response rates, only 156 employees provided data at T1, providing a response rate of 27 per cent. Ninety-eight employees returned the T2 questionnaire. However employees who completed both the T1 and T2 questionnaires amounted to 43 per cent of the T1 sample ($n = 67$). Analyses were performed only for employees who provided data at both points in time. The T2 sample consisted of a relatively equal proportion of male (41 per cent) and female (57 per cent) respondents; 2 per cent of employees failed to specify their gender. Employees ranged in age from 20 to 65 years, with a mean of 37 years ($SD = 11.08$). The majority of participants were either administrative officers (58 per cent) or professional officers (38 per cent), whereas 4 per cent of employees occupied other roles in the organization.

Research design and measures
As just noted, a temporal research design was used in which employee perceptions of reshaping capabilities and readiness for change were measured just prior to the introduction of the new HRIS in the workplace. To measure reshaping capabilities, ten items were developed based on Turner and Crawford's (1998) taxonomy of engagement, development and performance management. Items were also selected from a similar scale developed by Waldersee *et al.* (2003). Readiness for change was measured with seven items designed to assess the extent to which employees were feeling positive about the implementation of the new HRIS (Miller *et al.*, 1994). The measures of user satisfaction and system usage were assessed in a second wave of data collection (at T2) once the implementation process had been finalized, approximately five weeks after the collection of the T1 data. At this point, employees had been using the new HRIS for a period of one month. Levels of user satisfaction were measured with the End-User Computing Satisfaction Instrument (Doll and Torkzadeh, 1988). Consisting of 34 items, exploratory factor analytic procedures resulted in four usable factors for use in this study: satisfaction with accuracy, content, formatting and user-friendliness. Measurement of system usage consisted of a single item (that is 'In a typical week, how many times do you utilize the system?').

Findings and discussion
Multiple hierarchical regression analyses were used to test the proposal that employees' perceptions of reshaping capabilities at T1 would be associated with higher levels of user satisfaction and system usage at T2, and that this relationship would be mediated by pre-implementation perceptions of change readiness. These analyses revealed support for this proposition in relation to system usage, but not for any of the dimensions of user satisfaction. At Step 1, T1 reshaping capabilities exerted a positive main effect on T2 system usage, $\beta = 0.28$; $p < 0.05$, $R^2 = 0.08$, $F(1, 63) = 5.29$, $p < 0.05$. At Step 2, T1 readiness for change accounted for a significant increment of variance, $R^2\text{ch.} = 0.13$, $F(2, 62) = 8.11$, $p < 0.01$ and, as anticipated, was positively related to this dependent variable, $\beta = 0.38$; $p < 0.01$. In line with Baron and Kenny's (1986) procedures for testing mediating models, it was found that the positive main effect of T1 reshaping capabilities on T2 system usage was no longer significant when the effects of the mediating variable (that is,

readiness for change) were controlled on the subsequent step. Furthermore subsequent analyses in which T1 readiness for change was entered into the equation prior to T1 reshaping capabilities demonstrated that, once the effects of T1 readiness for change were controlled, employees' perceptions of T1 reshaping capabilities did not add significantly to the prediction of system usage. Therefore the results provided support for a mediated relationship between T1 reshaping capabilities and T2 system usage, via T1 readiness for change. Although T1 readiness for change was not found to mediate the relationship between T1 reshaping capabilities and user satisfaction, T1 readiness for change was found to exert a positive main effect on several of the dimensions of user satisfaction. Employees who felt positive about the impending organizational changes at T1 reported higher levels of satisfaction with the accuracy of the system, the system's formatting functions, and the user-friendly nature of the system at T2.

Overall this study presents some encouraging results of importance to the organizational change literature, and more specifically to the literature on the implementation of information technology. However these results should be interpreted with caution, owing to several issues. First, the limited sample size has the potential to jeopardize the generalizability of the results to the rest of the population. Although it was established that those who failed to respond at T2 were not significantly different from those who responded at both points in time, it is important to consider those employees who did not respond at all. Generalizability is further diminished as the results were derived from an investigation of employees in a single organization, more importantly, a public sector organization. Second, only five weeks elapsed between the collection of the T1 and T2 data. This was a relatively short period and may have captured initial impressions only. It would be valuable to measure user satisfaction and system usage again, perhaps six months after the implementation, in order to examine the long-term effects of culture and capabilities on satisfaction and usage. Third, the indicators of change implementation success were limited to self-report measures obtained from employees. Future research should incorporate more objective measures such as electronic records of system usage.

Conclusion
The series of studies reviewed in this chapter provides consistent evidence to suggest that the use of effective change management strategies facilitates positive change outcomes for employees because of their indirect effects on employees' levels of change-related self-efficacy and readiness for change. First, the results indicated that change-related self-efficacy mediated the relationship between information provision and psychological well-being for a group of senior managers undergoing changes to the way in which they were remunerated. Second, nurses who perceived that they had received sufficient information throughout the introduction of multidisciplinary work teams reported higher levels of job satisfaction, and this effect was mediated through enhanced levels of change-related self-efficacy. Given that perceptions of opportunity and threat derive significantly from personal perceptions of situational competence, these findings suggest that self-efficacy is likely to be influential in helping employees to view organizational change as an opportunity rather than as a threat (Krueger and Dickson, 1993). Interestingly, as noted earlier, information provision emerged as a stronger predictor of change-related self-efficacy than opportunities to participate in the implementation of organizational

change. This pattern of findings suggests that the provision of information may play an important compensatory role in determining adjustment among employees whose jobs are undergoing changes over which they may have little control or influence. Determining the extent to which the effects of information provision and employee participation are interactive in nature provides an avenue for future research.

In relation to readiness for change, results from the studies showed that information provision predicted change readiness which, in turn, was related to heightened levels of psychological well-being (see studies 1 and 2), job satisfaction (see study 1) and (low) turnover intentions (see study 2). In addition, readiness for change mediated the positive effects of employee participation on levels of employee adjustment (see study 1). In the study involving the implementation of a new information system, a pre-implementation measure of readiness of change mediated the positive effects of T1 reshaping capabilities (as rated by employees) on the amount of system usage at T2. In addition employees who perceived high levels of T1 readiness for change reported higher levels of satisfaction with the new HRIS one month after implementation. Overall these results highlight the importance of assessing the determinants of readiness for change as premature implementation may not produce intended outcomes simply because employees are not psychologically ready. This pattern of findings also reinforces the importance of undertaking pre-implementation assessments of readiness for change. Such assessments should help change agents to make specific choices about strategies and tactics that are needed to help foster employee enthusiasm for specific change events

In conclusion, it is suggested that a stress and coping perspective provides a useful framework for considering the direct and indirect relationships between event characteristics, situational appraisals and employee adjustment in the context of organizational change. Given the consistent evidence linking event characteristics and situational appraisals to employee adjustment, efforts that both counter the belief that the situation is threatening and help to foster a sense of psychological readiness should serve to maintain employee well-being during the very common experience of organizational change. In addition future research that explores the utility of stress-based models of employee adjustment to organizational change may help to clarify the psychological processes that act as precursors to more long-term outcomes that are indicative of change implementation success.

References

Allen, N.J. and J.P. Meyer (1990), 'The measurement and antecedents of affective, continuance, and normative commitment', *Journal of Occupational Psychology*, **63**, 1–18.
Armenakis, A.A., S.G. Harris and H.S. Feild (1999), 'Making change permanent: a model for institutionalizing change interventions', in W.A. Pasmore and R.W. Woodman (eds), *Research in Organizational Development and Change*, Stamford, CT: JAI Press, pp. 97–128.
Armenakis, A.A., S.G. Harris and K.W. Mossholder (1993), 'Creating readiness for organizational change', *Human Relations*, **46**, 681–703.
Ashford, S.J. (1988), 'Individual strategies for coping with stress during organizational transitions', *The Journal of Applied Behavioral Science*, **24**, 19–36.
Bagozzi, R.P. and Y. Yi (1990), 'Assessing method variance in multitrait–multimethod matrices: the case of self-reported affect and perceptions at work', *Journal of Applied Psychology*, **75**, 547–60.
Bandura, A. (1977), 'Self-efficacy: toward a unified theory of behavioral change', *Psychological Review*, **84**, 191–215.
Baron, R.M. and D.A. Kenny (1986), 'The moderator – mediator distinction in social psychological research: conceptual, strategic, and statistical considerations', *Journal of Personality and Social Psychology*, **51**, 1173–82.
Begley, T.M. (1998), 'Coping strategies as predictors of employee distress and turnover after an organizational

consolidation: a longitudinal analysis', *Journal of Occupational and Organizational Psychology*, **71**, 305–29.
Bell, N.E. and B.M. Staw (1989), 'People as sculptors versus sculpture: the roles of personality and personal control in organizations', in M.B. Arthur, D.T. Hall and B.S. Lawrence (eds), *Handbook of Career Theory*, Cambridge: Cambridge University Press, pp. 232–51.
Bentler, P.M. (1990), 'Comparative fit indexes in structural models', *Psychological Bulletin*, **107**, 238–46.
Bjorn-Anderson, N. (1988), 'Are human factors human?', *The Computer Journal*, **31**, 386–90.
Brockner, J., R.L. DeWitt, S. Grover and T. Reed (1990), 'When it is especially important to explain why: factors affecting the relationship between managers' explanations of a layoff and survivors' reactions to the layoff', *Journal of Experimental Social Psychology*, **26**, 389–407.
Callan, V.J. (1993), 'Individual and organizational strategies for coping with organizational change', *Work and Stress*, **7**, 63–75.
Caplan, R.D., S. Cobb, J.R.P. French, R.V. Harrison and S.R. Pinneau (1980), *Job Demands and Worker Health*, Ann Arbor, MI: University of Michigan, Institute for Social Research.
Carnall, C.A. (1986), 'Managing strategic change: an integrated approach', *Long Range Planning*, **19**, 105–15.
DeLone, W. and R. McLean (1992), 'Information system success: the quest for the dependent variable', *Information Systems Research*, **3**, 60–95.
Dirks, K.T., L.L. Cummings and J.L. Pierce (1996), 'Psychological ownership in organizations: conditions under which individuals promote and resist change', *Research in Organizational Change and Development*, **9**, 1–23.
Doll, W. and G. Torkzadeh (1988), 'The measurement of end-user computing satisfaction', *MIS Quarterly*, June, 259–74.
Earley, P.C. (1986), 'Supervisors and shop stewards as sources of contextual information in goal setting: a comparison of the United States with England', *Journal of Applied Psychology*, **71**, 111–17.
Eby, L.T., D.M. Adams, J.E.A. Russell and S.H. Gaby (2000), 'Perceptions of organizational readiness for change: factors related to employees' reactions to the implementation of team-based selling', *Human Relations*, **53**, 419–42.
Gemmil, G. and C. Smith (1985), 'A dissipative structure model of organization transformation', *Human Relations*, **38**, 751–66.
Glick, W., G. Jenkins and N. Gupta (1986), 'Method versus substance: how strong are underlying relationships between job characteristics and attitudinal outcomes?', *Academy of Management Journal*, **29**, 441–64.
Goldberg, D. (1972), *The detection of Psychiatric Illness by Questionnaire*, London: Oxford University Press.
Greenhalgh, L. and Z. Rosenblatt (1984), 'Job insecurity: toward conceptual clarity', *Academy of Management Review*, **9**, 438–48.
Guimaraes, T., M. Igbaria and L. Ming-Te (1992), 'The determinants of DSS success: an integrated model', *Decision Sciences*, **23**, 409–30.
Haines, V. and A. Petit (1997), 'Conditions for successful human resource information systems', *Human Resource Management*, **36**, 261–75.
Hirscheim, R. and M. Newman (1988), 'Information systems and user resistance: theory and practice', *The Computer Journal*, **31**, 398–408.
Ives, B., M. Olson and J. Baroudi (1983), 'The measurement of user information satisfaction', *Communications of the ACM*, **26**, 785–93.
Jick, T.D. (1985), 'As the axe falls: budget cuts and the experience of stress on organizations', in T.A. Beehr and R.S. Bhagat (eds), *Human Stress and Cognition in Organizations*, New York: Wiley, pp. 83–114.
Jimmieson, N.L. (2002), 'Predicting employee adjustment to organizational change among maternity care workers: a stress and coping perspective', paper presented at the 23rd International Conference of the Stress and Anxiety Research Society, Melbourne, Australia, 14–17 July.
Jimmieson, N.L. and A. Griffiths (2001), 'The role of coping resources in creating employee adjustment during organizational change', 4th Australian Industrial and Organizational Psychology Conference, Sydney, Australia, 22–24 June.
Jones, R.A., N.L. Jimmieson and A. Griffiths (in press), 'The impact of organizational culture and reshaping capabilities on change implementation success: the mediating role of readiness for change', *Journal of Management Studies*.
Jöreskog, K.G. and D. Sörbom (2000), *LISREL 8.3: Structural Equation Modeling with SIMPLIS Command Language*, Chicago: Scientific Software.
Kanter, R.M. (1983), *The Change Masters: Transformations in the American Corporate Environment 1860–1980s*, New York: Simon & Schuster.
Korunka, C., A. Weiss, K.H. Huemer and B. Karetta (1995), 'The effect of new technologies on job satisfaction and psychosomatic complaints', *Applied Psychology: An International Review*, **44**, 123–42.

Krueger, N.F. and P.R. Dickson (1993), 'Perceived self-efficacy and perceptions of opportunity and threat', *Psychological Reports*, **72**, 1235–40.
Lazarus, R.S. (1990), 'Theory based stress management', *Psychological Inquiry*, **1**, 3–13.
Lazarus, R.S. and S. Folkman (1984), *Stress, Appraisal and Coping*, New York: Springer.
Lee, S., Y. Kim and J. Lee (1995), 'An empirical study of the relationships among end-user information systems acceptance, training, and effectiveness', *Journal of Management Information Systems*, **12**, 189–201.
Marquardt, E.P. and R.H. Meehan (1995), 'A slight alteration of fit: managing compensation plan change', *Journal of Compensation and Benefits*, **10**, 27–34.
Miller, D. and M. Chen (1994), 'Sources and consequences of competitive inertia', *Administrative Science Quarterly*, **39**, 1–15.
Miller, K.I. and P.R. Monge (1985), 'Social information and employee anxiety about organizational change', *Human Communication Research*, **11**, 365–86.
Miller, V.D., J.R. Johnson and J. Grau (1994), 'Antecedents to willingness to participate in a planned organizational change', *Journal of Applied Communication Research*, **22**, 59–80.
Milliken, F.J. (1987), 'Three types of perceived uncertainty about the environment: state, effect, and response uncertainty', *Academy of Management Review*, **12**, 133–43.
Mobley, W.H. (1977), 'Intermediate linkages in the relationship between job satisfaction and employee turnover', *Journal of Applied Psychology*, **62**, 237–40.
Nelson, A., C.L. Cooper and P.R. Jackson (1995), 'Uncertainty amidst change: the impact of privatization on employee job satisfaction and well-being', *Journal of Occupational and Organizational Psychology*, **68**, 57–71.
Olson, D.A. and L.E. Tetrick (1988), 'Organizational restructuring: the impact on role perceptions, work relationships, and satisfaction', *Group and Organization Studies*, **13**, 374–88.
Pinto, J. (1994), *Successful Information System Implementation: The Human Side*, Upper Darby: Project Management Institute.
Pond, S.B. and M.S. Hay (1989), 'The impact of task preview information as a function of recipient self-efficacy', *Journal of Vocational Behavior*, **35**, 17–29.
Porras, J.I. and R.C. Silvers (1991), 'Organization development and transformation', *Annual Review of Psychology*, **42**, 51–78.
Sagie, A. and M. Koslowsky (1994), 'Organizational attitudes and behaviors as a function of participation in strategic and tactical change decisions: an application of path–goal theory', *Journal of Organizational Behavior*, **15**, 37–47.
Sagie, A. and M. Koslowsky (1996), 'Decision type, organizational control, and acceptance of change: an integrative approach to participative decision-making', *Applied Psychology: An International Review*, **45**, 85–92.
Santhanam, R., T. Guimaraes and J. George (2000), 'An empirical investigation of ODSS impact on individuals and organizations', *Decision Support Systems*, **30**, 51–72.
Saunier, A.M. and D.D. Gallo (1994), 'Use focus groups to support compensation change initiatives', *Journal of Compensation and Benefits*, **9**, 12–19.
Schweiger, D.M. and A.S. DeNisi (1991), 'Communication with employees following a merger: a longitudinal field experiment', *Academy of Management Journal*, **34**, 110–35.
Schweiger, D.M. and J.M. Ivancevich (1985), 'Human resources: the forgotten factor in mergers and acquisitions', *Personnel Administrator*, **30**, 47–61.
Shaw, J.B., M.W. Fields, J.W. Thacker and C.D. Fisher (1993), 'The availability of personal and external coping resources: their impact on job stress and employee attitudes during organizational restructuring', *Work and Stress*, **7**, 229–46.
Stevens, M.J. and M.A. Campion (1994), 'The knowledge, skill, and ability requirements for teamwork: implications for human resource management', *Journal of Management*, **20**, 503–30.
Sutton, R.I. and R.L. Kahn (1986), 'Prediction, understanding, and control as antidotes to organizational stress', in J. Lorsch (ed.), *Handbook of Organizational Behavior*, Englewood Cliffs, CA: Prentice-Hall, pp. 272–85.
Sverke, M., J. Hellgren and J. Öhrming (1997), 'Hospital corporatization: how are nurses' job perceptions and work-related attitudes affected?', *Reports from the Department of Stockholm*, **819**, 1–26.
Terry, D.J. and V.J. Callan (2000), 'Employee adjustment to an organizational change: a stress and coping perspective', in P. Dewe, M. Leiter and T. Cox (eds), *Coping, Health and Organizations*, London: Taylor and Francis, pp. 259–76.
Turner, D. and M. Crawford (1998), *Change Power: Capabilities that Drive Corporate Renewal*, Warriewood, NSW: Business and Professional Publishing.
Van de Ven, A.H. and M.S. Poole (1995), 'Explaining development and change in organizations', *Academy of Management Review*, **20**, 510–40.
Vankatesh, V. and F. Davis (2000), 'A theoretical extension of the technology acceptance model: four longitudinal field studies', *Management Science*, **46**, 186–204.

Waldersee, R., A. Griffiths and J. Lai (2003), 'Predicting organizational change success: matching organization type, change type, and capabilities', Journal of Applied Management and Entrepreneurship, **8**, 66–81.

Wanberg, C.R. and J.T. Banas (2000), 'Predictors and outcomes of openness to changes in a reorganizing workplace', *Journal of Applied Psychology*, **85**, 132–42.

Williams, L.J., J.A. Cote and M.R. Buckley (1989), 'Lack of method variance in self-reported affect and perceptions at work: reality or artifact?', *Journal of Applied Psychology*, **74**, 462–8.

Yousef, D.A. (2000), 'Organizational commitment as a mediator of the relationship between Islamic work ethic and attitudes towards organizational change,' *Human Relations*, **53**(4), 513–37.

Zingheim, P.K. and J.R. Schuster (1995), 'Exploring three pay transition tools: readiness assessment, benchmarking, and piloting', *Compensation and Benefits Review*, July–August, 40–45.

2 Constructions of occupational stress: nuisances, nuances or novelties?

Dianna Kenny and Dennis McIntyre

We should make everything as simple as possible, but not simpler. (Albert Einstein)

Overview

The concept of stress is as elusive as it is pervasive. Discourses of stress in general and occupational stress in particular are so powerful that they are 'seemingly written into and all over our daily lives' (Newton, 1995, p. 1). But what is stress? Is it a stimulus or a response? Is it an objective, quantifiable, environmental demand or a subjective cognitive appraisal of environmental conditions? Is stress universal or personal? Does stress need 'managing' and, if so, is it a public responsibility or a private concern? In order to answer some of these questions, it is necessary to deconstruct the concept and find its core. This is no easy matter. Heisenberg (1958) reminds us that even 'natural science does not simply describe and explain nature; it is part of the interplay between nature and ourselves; it describes nature as exposed to our method of questioning'. A construct like occupational stress has been shaped not only by our method of questioning, but by powerful political, cultural, social and economic forces in which work occurs and in which people respond to their work experiences. In this chapter, we will briefly review the major ways of constructing occupational stress, with particular focus on emergent issues, problematic areas, and less used paradigms, before attempting a synthesis of this difficult and complex field.

Occupational stress was initially explained and managed within a psychomedical model. This model focused on personal attributes such as personality traits (Type A behavior pattern, neuroticism, negative affectivity, extraversion, introversion, hardiness, locus of control) and coping styles (active, passive, problem or emotion focused and so on) rather than job and organizational characteristics. This construction of work stress made it a 'personal trouble' rather than a 'public concern' and several professions (medicine, psychology, psychiatry, human resource management) have greatly benefited from such an approach. In this model personality deficits or vulnerabilities were considered to be causal, or at least precursors to the experience of occupational stress. On the other hand, the stressor and strain approach attributed the cause of psychological and behavioral strain to work stressors. This view of occupational stress was adopted by the Scandinavian school (see for, example, Levi, 1999). It focuses primarily on work characteristics and the epidemiology of occupational health. Rather than treating the individual, the focus of intervention is work reform. Research into the role of organizational factors in the etiology of occupational stress has followed a similar trajectory to the psychomedical model. Ever lengthening lists of putative factors have been identified. In two early reviews of occupational stress, Cooper (1983; 1985) summarized and categorized six groups of organizational variables, outlined below, that may cause stress in the workplace:

1. factors intrinsic to the job (heat, noise, chemical fumes, shift work);
2. relationships at work (conflict with co-workers or supervisors, lack of social support);
3. role in the organization (for example, role ambiguity);
4. career development (lack of status, lack of prospects for promotion, lack of a career path, job insecurity);
5. organizational structure and climate (lack of autonomy, lack of opportunity to participate in decision making, lack of control over the pace of work);
6. home and work interface (conflict between domestic and work roles; lack of spousal support for remaining in the workforce).

While increased worker participation in decision making, job enlargement and enrichment, redesign of jobs and working environment, and creation of a more supportive work environment through a range of human resource management interventions have demonstrable effects on a number of personal and work indicators (Cooper *et al.*, 1996), many organizations are deterred from such global changes as a means of preventing stress, owing to the cost and disruption of implementing such strategies and the relatively small numbers of employees manifesting stress conditions that impair occupational functioning at any one time in any one workplace (Cooper and Payne, 1992). Many employees work under similar conditions of stress; why, then, do only a few succumb to occupational stress (however defined) in any given organization, and which of this subgroup of individuals will subsequently make a claim for workers' compensation?

Recent theorizing has recognized that occupational stress is a complex, multilayered phenomenon that requires a systemic or ecological analysis using multiple perspectives. To attempt lesser explanations would make things simpler than is possible. Even as recently as 1999, established definitions of occupational stress, such as that presented by the National Institute for Occupational Safety and Health (NIOSH, 1999) as the 'harmful physical and emotional responses that occur when the requirements of the job do not match the capabilities, resources or needs of the worker' does not encompass, for example, causes located in the organization of production, dysfunctional organizations, problematic interpersonal relationships or workplace inequities.

The ecological view of humans is one of living systems dependent upon a healthy relationship with their environment, defined in its broadest sense to incorporate the physical and social milieu and both proximal and distal influences. The ecological view argues that social structures and processes affect people through psychological processes and that there is a dynamic reciprocal influence of social and psychological processes. In the remaining sections of the chapter, we will summarize and critique each of the main approaches to understanding occupational stress – the intrapersonal, interpersonal, organizational and transactional, cybernetic and systemic, and labor process analysis – before offering the promised synthesis.

Intrapersonal constructions of occupational stress
Approaches to understanding occupational stress as a private concern that is a problem that resides within individuals rather than in the organization of work, organizational climate or the structure of power and authority in industry (Bohle, 1993), have located the cause of the problem in the personality, cognitions (cognitive appraisals) and (coping)

behaviors of individual workers. Despite the huge research effort in these areas, the compelling intuitive appeal of personality as explanation for behavior, and the research evidence attesting to its importance in accounting for individual variations in response to stressors, its contribution to understanding and ameliorating occupational stress has been modest. This is a paradoxical state of affairs that has not been explicitly acknowledged within the research community. It may well be that the problem resides substantially in one place (that is, the individual) but the solution resides substantially in another (the organization of work and the organizational climate of the workplace). Alternatively, both the source and solution may lie in the unique interpersonal space between individual worker and his/her actual and/or perceived work environment, a space that interpersonal and cybernetic theories address.

Personality
Personality has long been considered a major mediator/moderator of stress reactivity, although there have been recent challenges to the view that people differ in their reactions to stress on the basis of individual differences in their psychological traits (Bright, 2001). Personality theories attempt to explain the fact that sensitivity to stressors varies between individuals. Although certain events, such as extreme physical threats, are regarded as normatively stressful, (coping) responses to ego threats are related to personality differences (Eysenck, 1988). Most theories of occupational functioning agree that personality makes a significant contribution to performance and well-being, while acknowledging that the relationship between personality and environmental factors is dynamic and complex. For example, Work Adjustment Theory (Rounds *et al.*, 1987) is founded on the notion that stable cognitive, behavioral and emotional dispositions underpin work adjustment, but that situational influences have an impact upon these stable dispositions for adaptation and change, in both positive and negative ways. Similarly, Headey and Wearing (1992) found that enduring personality characteristics, such as neuroticism and extraversion, determine people's daily work experiences, use of coping strategies, and levels of psychological distress and well-being. From a series of studies on government employees, university academics, police officers (Hart, Wearing and Headey, 1993), and schoolteachers (Hart, 1994), Hart and colleagues concluded that personality characteristics were the strongest determinants of psychological responses to work in all these occupational groups. Others have also identified the significant relationship between extraversion and subjective well-being (Costa and McCrae, 1980), while introversion and neuroticism have been consistently associated with increased stress (Fontana and Abouserie, 1993), emotional exhaustion and depersonalization (Piedmont, 1993).

Objective circumstances rarely account for more than 20 per cent of the explained variance in well-being and personality factors are now considered to be the most important contributors (DeNeve and Cooper, 1998), with neuroticism the most powerful and consistent contributor (Creed and Evans, 2002). Kozma *et al.* (1999), in a study exploring the relationship between stability in well-being and stability in the environment, found that stability in the environment contributed least and personality factors contributed most to stability in well-being. However, while neuroticism appears to be a very strong determinant of occupational distress, it exerts very little impact on performance outcomes (Barrick and Mount, 1991) and there is no evidence to indicate that those high in neuroticism or distress are more likely to have elevated sick leave or workers' compensation claims for occupational stress (Hart *et al.*, in press).

Hobfoll *et al.* (1994), reacting to what they perceived to be a growing overemphasis on environmental factors, urged a reconsideration of the role of personality in the etiology of occupational stress. They stated that we could no longer pretend that there was an objective way to define stress at the level of environmental conditions without reference to the character of the person (p. 24). In similar vein, Roskies *et al.* (1993) concluded that 'personality can cushion as well as aggravate the impact of occupational stress' (pp. 616–17); with negative personality dispositions transforming stressors into strains and strains into symptoms. The relationship between role stress and role distress has been found to be moderated by a range of personality characteristics including intolerance of ambiguity, dependence, strong affiliation needs, low risk propensity (Siegall and Cummings, 1995) and high self-focused attention (Frone *et al.*, 1991). On the positive side, humor and optimism significantly moderate the relationship between daily hassles, self-esteem maintenance, emotional exhaustion and physical illness (Fry, 1995).

Negative affectivity (NA) has received a great deal of attention in the recent literature. Synonymous with Eysenck's construct of neuroticism, it was first defined by Watson and Clark (1984) as a summary for individual differences in negative emotionality (distress, discomfort, dissatisfaction) and poor self-esteem. NA has been associated with interpersonal conflict (Spector and O'Connell, 1994), negative emotions (Chen and Spector, 1991), psychological distress, physical symptoms (Watson *et al.*, 1986), Type A behavior pattern (Payne, 1988) and job strain (Decker and Borgen, 1993). Negative affectivity has also been found to influence job satisfaction directly through its influence on relationships at work, increased sensitivity to negative job events and the propensity to experience less pleasure in positive work experiences (Brief and Weiss, 2002). However it is almost a tautology to argue that those individuals high in negative affectivity are more likely to experience greater depressed mood, anxiety and stress in the workplace than those with high positive affect, since dispositional characteristics are to a large extent defined by their concomitant affective states. Schaubroeck *et al.* (1992) concluded that negative affectivity was a nuisance in the analysis of job stress because it inflates relationships between self-reports of stressors and strains. The implication of this confound model is that 'changing the work environment will be of little benefit if self-report of work stressors and strains are surrogate measures of NA' (Bright 2001, p. 68). Two major types of research indicate support for the confound model: research showing that strain measures remain consistent over time and across career/job change and research that indicates that NA is a predictor neither of long-term health nor of health related behaviors (diet, exercise and so on). Research by Brief *et al.* (1988) showed that stress–strain relationships disappeared after controlling for NA. However, support for the alternative vulnerability model (that is, NA as a moderator of the stress–strain relationship) has also been found. Individuals high in NA are consistently more reactive to stressors than those low in NA, but the relationship is very weak in occupational stress research (Cooper, 2002).

Using a latent deprivation model, Jahoda (1982) asserted that employment contributes manifest (financial) and latent benefits (time structure, regular enforced activity, social contact, identity, and shared effort) to individuals that enhance their well-being. Loss of either form of benefit will lead to a reduction in well-being. However, Creed and Evans (2002) found that personality accounted for an additional significant amount of the explained variance in well-being over and above that contributed by the latent and manifest benefits of employment.

Despite the converging evidence that personality characteristics make significant contributions to the experience of occupational stress, much of the research has been atheoretical or exploratory, and it is difficult to formulate workplace practices or occupational stress interventions based on findings that a small or even moderate amount of variance in the experience of occupational stress is accounted for by a particular personality characteristic. Researchers working within this framework would perhaps recommend that interventions be aimed at increasing humour, optimism and tolerance of ambiguity and decreasing negative trait affectivity, neuroticism and dependence. However, personality characteristics are notoriously difficult to modify (McCrae and Costa, 1994). Even if it were possible to change personality in the desired direction, it is not certain that workplace difficulties would improve without simultaneously attending to extrinsic organizational factors that may be operating. Brief and Weiss (2002) argued that, while personality research had demonstrated the self-evident personality–affect linkage, it had not contributed to the identification of modifiable stressors in the workplace. They point to the crucial role of organizational factors such as the quality of leadership, work group characteristics, the physical setting in which the work is performed and organizational rewards and punishments that have an impact upon affect in the workplace. They drew the important distinction between the relative impact of personality on mood as opposed to emotion, citing evidence of the link between personality and mood but not personality and emotion. We will return to this point later in the discussion of the interpersonal constructions of occupational stress.

While personality traits may be fixed to some extent, their place in the system as antecedents or consequences of occupational stress will depend on the nature of the interaction between individual and environmental systems, and on any changes that may occur within that system. Using structural equation modeling to assess the role of personality as an antecedent to job stressors, Cooper and Baglioni (1988) found that personality both preceded and determined the perception of job stressors. Hart and Wearing (1995) developed the dynamic equilibrium theory to account for the synergies between personality characteristics, organizational factors and operational demands in determining both psychological distress and well-being in the workplace. They concluded that, while personality characteristics are the primary determinants of psychological responses to work, positive and negative work experiences contributed separately to psychological distress and morale, and that a supportive organizational climate could mitigate the effects of negative work experiences.

Most of the research on personality and work assumes that personality shapes or even causes particular reactions to the job. Far fewer studies consider the potential influence of job characteristics in shaping personality and behavior inside and outside work. Kohn and Schooler (1982), for example, demonstrated that the complexity of one's work predicted personality characteristics such as intellectual flexibility, non-authoritarianism, and other behaviors such as intellectually demanding leisure time activities. Similarly, Karasek and Theorell (1990) demonstrated a relationship between changes in the active–passive dimension of work and changes in the degree to which workers participated in political and leisure activities. Kipnis (1997) has also argued that variations in the degree to which work is automated can predict changes in mental states. For example, when the outcome of work depends more on a person's skill and effort than on the machinery that they operate, feelings of competence and job satisfaction are greater. Taylorism, a form of work organization that reduces worker skill and influence in production has been strongly associated with passivity, learned helplessness and lack of participation at work.

A similar argument, that is, that changing social and work conditions shapes or changes behavior/personality has been proposed by Mahony (2001b). She traced the historical development of the 'stress' discourse and found that the original motivation for the research into the so called Type A personality arose from society's concerns early in the 20th century with the growing metropolis, change in the pace of life, and increased competition. Interestingly, the original research focused on behavior, not innate personality traits. Rosenman (1988) argued that changed living circumstances led to behavioral (mal) adaptations in the direction that subsequently became known as the Type A personality. (Behavioral changes have also been observed in rats as a result of overcrowding: Calhourn, 1962.) Transmuting an emergent behavioral pattern into an immutable personality trait effectively removed the nexus between behavior and the workplace and located the source of the problem (in the case of Type A personality, an increased propensity to cardiovascular disease) within the individual. Thus the psychology of occupational stress was born. Mahony explained this shift in terms of its economic and political utility. If the problem is personal, there is no obligation on the employer to change the organization of work.

The now seminal work of Michael Marmot provided support for Rosenman's observations. In what has become a landmark series of studies known as the *Whitehall studies*, Marmot (1986) demonstrated that British civil servants followed a *social gradient* in mortality and morbidity: the lower the grade of employment, the higher the mortality from coronary heart disease, from all causes, and from most other causes of death. The degree of control in the job corresponded to the position on the social hierarchy, and demonstrated that control was 'an important predictor of the risk of cardiovascular disease and that it had an important role in accounting for the social gradient in coronary heart disease and depression' (Marmot et al., 1991). Both Mahony (2001b) and McIntyre (1994) argue that theories and research that link alienating work to the experience of occupational stress and illness have never been afforded the status they deserve because there are vested interests in maintaining the focus on 'who is at risk' rather than on 'who or what is imposing the risk'. In support of their position, Winefield (1995) found that leaving highly stressful or dissatisfying work could result in an immediate improvement in well-being, even during periods of subsequent unemployment.

Although the construct of a Type A behavior pattern is well-entrenched in both the scholarly literature and lay language, it continues to be controversial. Because it is 'taken for granted', problems with definition and measurement have been neglected. For example, the three most widely used measures of Type A (Bortner, Framingham, and Jenkins Activity Survey) show low intercorrelations, although all are significantly related to the development of coronary heart disease. Low correlations point to differences in underlying constructs, measurement error and multidimensionality (Edwards *et al.*, 1990). Evidence indicates that a Type A behavior pattern is more strongly associated with physiological risk factors than psychological or work–related distress (Ganster et al., 1991). Further, research assessing Type A behavior as both a mediator (Caplan and Jones, 1975) and a moderator (Hurrell, 1985) of stress has failed to confirm its role. Subsequent work has identified hostility as the salient factor in Type A, particularly as it has an impact on coronary heart disease (Gidron et al., 1999). A new subset of Type A, labeled 'Type D' behavior, is typified by 'chronically angry, suspicious, and mistrustful behaviors and greater proneness to cardiovascular conditions' (cited in Robbins et al., 1994, p. 345). Type D is now held to be the 'toxic core' of Type A (see Rice, 1999, pp. 107–9).

Coping
As stated earlier, personality and coping are closely related concepts. Some theories of coping ascribe dispositional status to coping styles; for example, Miller (1992) described 'monitors' and 'blunters'; Rotter (1966) 'internals' and 'externals'; Carver et al. (1989) 'optimists' and 'pessimists'. Current conceptualizations posit that personality characteristics, especially optimism (Carver and Scheier, 1999), neuroticism and extraversion (McCrae and Costa, 1991), exert a significant impact on coping behaviors. In addition to personality dispositions or traits, coping is also influenced by the actual or appraised characteristics of the stressful environment, particularly its controllability and predictability, and by the social resources available to the individual in the coping enterprise (Folkman and Moskowitz, 2000). These latter two characteristics of coping are also closely tied to personality dispositions. To the optimist, the glass is half full; to the pessimist it is half empty. Of course, coping styles and strategies are interdependent and situation-specific.

Coping has unfortunately assumed an amorphous, multivariate dichotomous character. The recent literature is replete with studies comparing problem-focused and emotion-focused coping (Lazarus and Folkman, 1984); direct and indirect coping (Parkes, 1994); active and passive coping (Peter and Siegrist, 1997); behavioral and avoidance coping (Cushway and Tyler, 1994); positive and negative coping (Burke and Greenglass, 2000); and meaning-based coping, dichotomized into situational and global meaning (Folkman and Moskowitz, 2000). Are all these forms of coping describing different coping constructs? Which classification of coping is better, and how do we decide? Each of these forms of coping have been associated with a formidable array of equally nebulous and ill-defined, global, non-specific adaptational outcomes (Weber, 1997) such as negative affect, psychological distress and stress levels, some of which could be argued to be tautological since, for example, negative affect is both a determinant of coping style and an outcome of coping. It is not surprising that a number of researchers have declared the field to be disappointing, if not barren, sterile (Snyder, 1999) and trivial (Lazarus, 1999) in terms of its theoretical and clinical contributions to psychological adaptation under conditions of stress. One of the main reasons for this is the coping literature's primary focus on the individual and its neglect of the social context in which individuals operate, although situational determinants of coping have been acknowledged (Lazarus, 1993); and more recently, attention has been given to the 'relational meaning that an individual constructs from the person – environment relationship' (Lazarus, 2000, p. 665).

Somerfield and McCrae (2000) argue that, since people have spent their lives learning particular adaptational or coping strategies to deal with intrapersonal and environmental challenges, it may be unrealistic to expect further yield from attempts to change an individual's coping behaviors. Since coping behaviors are highly correlated with personality characteristics (Eysenck, 1988, defined personality as a function of coping style) and since the latter are resistant to change, it follows that coping behaviors will also be difficult to change. Paraphrasing Pealin (1991), Somerfield and McCrae (2000) state, 'certain of life's problems cannot be resolved by the efforts of individuals . . . stress arising in the context of a bureaucratized workplace [is] an example of a situation in which the individual may have few coping options . . . group coping and organization-level coping strategies may be the only avenue for reducing the strains caused by job stress' (p. 623). Otto (1985) maintained that the best medicine for stress was a strike, because the strikers consider that they, albeit temporally, have taken control of the situation. The strike essentially acts as a 'safety valve', tensions are released, and activity returns to 'normal'.

It has often been assumed in the occupational stress literature that coping mediates the relationship between employees' work experiences and psychological well-being. A strong corpus of evidence now exists that work experiences, in general, and organizational climate (recognition, co-worker interaction, goal congruency, opportunities for development, participative decision making, role clarity and supportive leadership) in particular, mediate the relationship between coping and occupational well-being (Hart and Cotton, 2002). Even in this role, coping was shown to exert minimal impact on the experience of occupational well-being, calling into question the use of stress management training programs that teach coping strategies. Otto (1985) provided a damming critique of stress management programs almost 20 years ago. Judging from the proliferation of stress management programs it would appear that this critique has been ignored.

Finally, the stress and coping literature has neglected the impact of unconscious processes on human behavior and adaptation. In other areas, there has been a re-emergence of interest in unconscious mental processes, particularly with respect to the impact of unconscious memories (Greenwald, 1992), selective attention (see Paulhus *et al.*, 1997 for a review), self-deception (Baumeister *et al.*, 1998), positive illusions (Taylor and Brown, 1994), and the repression or denial of impaired attachment (Fonagy *et al.*, 1991) on coping and adaptation. Cramer (1998) cogently argues that both coping (conscious and intentional processes) and defense mechanisms (unconscious and unintentional processes) are adaptational processes of equal status in determining the outcomes of responses to stressors, and should assume equal status in explanatory models.

Kipnis (1994, 1997) takes an opposing stance, and argues that the study of the relationship between individuals' psychological states or processes, whether conscious or unconscious, and social behavior has run its course, and that future research should focus on the relationships between systems and social behavior. Kipnis (1997) contends that attempts at classification of psychological states obfuscates rather than enlightens, firstly because there are no procedures currently available to verify these states, and secondly, because there are many ways of classifying the same states, as has just been demonstrated with coping, with each classification failing to include the full range of characteristics (however determined). One test of a worthwhile classification system is the number and quality of predictions that arise and the inferences regarding behavior that can be made from knowing to which class the individual belongs (for example, negative or positive affect; problem or emotion–focused coping). Kipnis (1997) and others before him (including Marx and Marxist sociologists – to paraphrase Marx, the world is not determined by our consciousness; rather our consciousness is determined by our world) argue that more can be inferred and understood from an examination of objective changes in the social fabric brought about by, for example, technology, than can be understood from further exploration of individual psychological states. We might conclude from this argument that a more useful way to seek explanations for occupational stress is to examine the objective changes in the workplace and in the organization of work than in the subjective contents of and changes in individual workers' consciousness (that is, mental states).

Of course, this approach is probably as incomplete as the mental states explanation for (coping) behavior (captured by Carl Jung in his statement, 'It all depends on how we look at things, not on how they are in themselves'), since it does not account for individual differences in responses to changes in the workplace and in the organization of work. We all know that individuals differ significantly in their vulnerability and resilience to the environment and to change, and no social theory will have sufficient explanatory power without accounting in some way for individual variation.

Finally, we still know little about how coping processes operate (Folkman and Moskowitz, 2000) and whether they are helpful in dealing with stress (Snyder, 1999). Specifically, in the work setting, coping outcome studies cannot specify which aspects of the job or work environment should be modified, since individuals appraise their social and work contexts in individual ways. Thus the lack of interventions, therapeutic programs or clinical benefits arising from the coping literature is problematic for the field (Coyne and Racioppo, 2000).

Interpersonal constructions of occupational stress
Interpersonal conflict in the workplace, increasingly recognized as a major contributor to occupational stress and work disability, has a complex etiology. While personal factors such as dissatisfaction with life, daily stress, negative affectivity, neuroticism and hostility are significant risk factors for interpersonal conflict at work for both men and women (Appelberg et al., 1991), this section will focus on the social factors that enhance risk of interpersonal conflict in the workplace. A number of theories have been proposed to explain the interpersonal dimensions of occupational stress. These include job burnout theory, equity theory, and organizational justice theory.

Job burnout
Burnout is defined as the prolonged response to chronic emotional and interpersonal stressors in the job, and is characterized by physical and emotional exhaustion, cynicism (depersonalization) and inefficacy (Maslach et al., 2001). Job burnout theory is probably the first interpersonal theory of occupational stress. Formulated initially for people working in the care-giving and human service occupations (Freudenberger, 1975), it describes a pattern of distancing responses of workers to their clients and the workplace whose function was believed to be a way of protecting oneself from intense emotional arousal created by interactions between workers and their clients or family members, or between workers and their co-workers. These relationships were posited to be sources of both emotional strains and rewards. The initial clinical and social psychology interpretation of the concept of burnout was subsequently modified to include industrial and organizational psychology approaches that expanded the concept to take account of its

relationship to occupational stress, job satisfaction, organizational commitment and turnover. The Maslach Burnout Inventory (MBI) (Maslach and Jackson, 1982), originally designed for use in human service occupations, was modified for use with teachers, and later a general form of the inventory was developed in the recognition that the constellation of factors first described in human service workers could occur in other types of occupations. While exhaustion was viewed as the individual stress dimension of burnout that with continued work overload and social conflict in the workplace led to cynicism, inefficacy was perceived to originate in organizational deficits such as inadequate resources (Maslach *et al.*, 2001).

Bakker *et al.* (2000) examined the discriminant validity of burnout and concluded that while burnout is a distinct work-related and situation-specific construct (compared to the more pervasive nature of depression), workers high in neuroticism (that is, more depression prone) were at greater risk of burnout. Much of the recent work on burnout has focused on identifying its temporal characteristics and its personality, job, occupational, situational, organizational and transactional (workload, control, reward, fairness and values) determinants. Maslach and Leiter (1997) argued that the transactional determinants formed the basis of the (implicit) psychological contract between workers and employers and that any actual or perceived violation of the psychological contract with respect to these transactional dimensions placed the worker at risk of burnout.

Burnout has consistently been associated with reduced commitment and job satisfaction, increased interpersonal conflict, 'contagion' (to other workers), lower productivity, absenteeism and job turnover. Since burnout seems to be more strongly related to situational factors, and can arise in previously psychologically healthy workers, Maslach *et al.*, (2001) concluded that burnout is more a social phenomenon arising in particular workplaces than a psychological construct arising in the personal vulnerabilities of workers, although those with low hardiness, poor self-esteem, external locus of control, avoidant coping style (Semmer, 1996) and high neuroticism (Piedmont, 1993) are more prone to experience job stress in general and burnout in particular (Maslach *et al.*, 2001). Indeed, Piedmont (1993) demonstrated in a large longitudinal study that neuroticism was a much stronger predictor of burnout than demographic and work climate variables, calling into question the assertion that situational factors are the principal determinants of burnout. A more detailed treatment of burnout can be found in Shirom (2003, this volume).

Finally, burnout can be theorized as a *double bind* situation. Owing to an initial overidentification with clients and/or tasks, the alleged sufferer is on the one hand complimented for their diligence and later cautioned for being over-zealous.

Equity theory
Adams (1965) devised equity theory to account for differences in pay satisfaction. Equity theory states that people compare outcomes with the amount of effort they have invested and the relative efforts of others. If the effort/outcome ratios are not proportional, then inequity arises. Adams and others (Sweeney *et al.*, 1990; Martin and Bennett, 1996) found that pay satisfaction is related to perceptions of distributive justice (that is, perceived fairness of the outcome) and that perceptions of distributive justice are better predictors of pay satisfaction than perceptions of procedural justice (that is, perceived fairness of procedures used to determine outcomes) (Tremblay *et al.*, 2000). Perceived

inequity is considered to be a key driver of counterproductive and withdrawal behaviors in the workplace. Examples of responses to perceived inequity include, in the first instance, decreased engagement and commitment to the job and workplace, the consequences of which include lateness, absenteeism, organizational cynicism, turnover and, in some cases, workers' compensation claims.

The principles of equity theory are applicable at all levels of interpersonal exchange – between co-workers, between workers and their supervisors and between workers and their organizations. Rousseau (1995) argued that the current economic climate of organizational instability brought about by corporation failures, downsizings, mergers, and sales of government instrumentalities to private companies, has resulted in a change in the psychological contract, based on reciprocal exchange, between workers and their employers. Workers perceive that they give more (time, effort, skills, flexibility) and receive less (job security, career opportunities). It is arguable that increases in workers' compensation claims for occupational stress may be an attempt by workers to redress the perceived inequity.

Organizational justice theory

> Nothing is more unequal than the equal treatment of unequals. (Vincent Lombardi, football coach)

The performance of an organization is at least partly related to the commitment of its employees, which in turn is a precursor to cooperative behavior (Tremblay et al., 2000). Although justice matters in all organizational settings, concerns about organizational justice are triggered only under certain circumstances, for example, when workers are the recipients of negative outcomes or perceive themselves to be treated disrespectfully. Justice concerns are also more likely to be triggered during times of organizational change, when resources are scarce, or when the power balance between workers is unequal (Greenberg, 2001).

Justice theory proposes that perceived injustice, or unfair treatment, underlies counterproductive or retaliatory behaviors in groups, including workplaces. Organizational justice theory, expanding on equity theory, identifies three types of justice:

1. distributive justice, defined as the perceived fairness of outcomes (ends) (cf equity theory);
2. procedural justice, defined as the perceived fairness of the processes leading to outcomes (means to an end);
3. interactive justice, defined as perceived interpersonal quality between people in power positions, for example, whether the person feels that they have been treated with care and respect (Cropanzano, 1993; Weiss and Cropanzano, 1996; Kenny, 1995a, 1995b).

A number of studies demonstrate that the promotion of procedural justice in organizations reduces theft and turnover and increases job satisfaction and commitment. Many perceived procedural injustices arise from workers' perceptions that their supervisors are disrespectful and uncaring, arbitrary in their decision making, and uncommunicative.

Training managers to delegate, communicate and show concern to their employers yields significant organizational benefits (Greenberg, 2001).

Roberts and Markel (2001), in a test of the predictive validity of justice theory with respect to workers' compensation claims for occupational overuse injuries, found that issues related to interpersonal quality in claimants' relationships with their managers and supervisors (interactive justice) had a significant impact on their decision to lodge a claim. Although not tested with occupational stress claims, there is indirect evidence that similar forces may be at work in employees' decisions to lodge claims for occupational stress. Karasek and Theorell (1990) viewed occupational stress as a strategic communication of distress related to perceptions of unfair treatment. During the second Whitehall study (Marmot et al., 1991) the researchers revisited a department of the British Public Service. During the course of the investigation, the closure/privatization of the department was announced and the 'stress' claims increased dramatically. Toohey (1993, 1995) expanded this notion into a model of functional communication. In this model, dissatisfaction at the workplace may be expressed through illness behavior such as occupational stress, which is assessed as 'a safe and acceptable manner in which to communicate distress' (Toohey, 1995, p. 57). It is certainly debatable as to how expressing one's distress in this way is either safe or acceptable in a workplace context, especially given the social stigma attached both to mental illness and to workers' compensation claims generally. However, these methods are obviously more acceptable than outbursts of anger, physical violence or criminal acts such as theft or destruction of property.

In legislative attempts to curb the avalanche of stress claims in the late 1980s and early 1990s in Australia, significant changes to the definition of occupational stress were made to limit the grounds for claims. These limits were stated in the amendments to the Western Australia Workers Compensation and Rehabilitation Bill (1993). Stress claims were to be excluded:

> where stress arises wholly or predominantly from matters involving dismissal, retrenchment, demotion, discipline, transfer, redeployment, non-promotion or reclassification, or the non-granting of leave of absence or other benefit.

In response to such legislation, David Biggins, an Australian occupational health researcher, exclaimed, 'What can one say . . . except that management/government has a clear understanding of the major causes of stress' (personal communication reported in McIntyre, 2002, p. 197). Each of the 'matters' referred to in this Bill could readily be interpreted by aggrieved workers as breaches of one or more of distributive, procedural or interactive forms of justice described by justice theory. Defensive interpretations such as those provided by justice theory externalize the problem for the worker. However, corporate managers and/or governments (especially when their practices are driven by the ideology of neoliberalism) have contended that it is easier for workers to attribute their non-promotion or dismissal to unjust treatment than to misconduct or incompetence.

Organizational and transactional constructions of occupational stress
Organizational and transactional theories of occupational stress attempt to explain the amount of occupational stress experienced by assessing both the characteristics of the

person and job and/or organizational characteristics of the work and workplace. Different theories place different emphases on different characteristics and some of these are discussed briefly below.

Person–environment fit theories
Person–Environment (P–E) fit theories (Caplan and Harrison, 1993; Furnham and Schaeffer, 1984) account for job strain in terms of discrepancies between the abilities and motives (participation, income, self-utilization) of workers and the demands of the job. Caplan (1987) suggested that recollections of past, present and anticipated P–E fit might influence well-being as well as performance. In a major test of the P–E fit model, 2010 workers across 23 occupations were assessed (Caplan and Jones, 1975). The main stressors identified were excessive workloads, inappropriate job complexity (compared to perceived ability) and unwanted overtime. However, the specific P–E fit measures accounted for only 2–14 per cent of additional variance over and above the main effects of environment and person (Baker, 1985). Most P–E fit theories are static and failed to address the ongoing, reciprocal influences of environment and person (Kulik *et al.*, 1987).

Demand–control–support (DCS) model
The demand–control model (Karasek, 1979) focuses on the joint effects of job demands and job control on worker well-being. Demand is subdivided into work load, work hazards, physical and emotional demands and role conflict. Control refers to the complexity of the work, administrative control, control of outcomes, skill discretion, supervision, decision authority and ideological control (Söderfeldt *et al.*, 1996). Based on the dimensions of demand and control, jobs were classified into four categories: high strain jobs (high demands/low control); low strain jobs (low demands/high control); active jobs (high demands/high control); and passive jobs (low demands/low control) (Landsbergis *et al.*, 1993). According to Karasek (1990), psychological distress is predicted by high demand/low control combinations. Conversely an increase in control is positively correlated with job satisfaction (Murphy, 1988). According to the theory, control buffers the effects of demands, such that high demand jobs will only produce adverse stress reactions among those workers who simultaneously experience low control. High strain occupations such as machine-paced work, service-based occupations such as cooks and waiters, and those tied to strict timetables like bus drivers are hypothesized by the model to place workers at higher risk of stress and its deleterious health effects. By contrast, executives and professionals may have higher demands placed upon them, but they also have greater control to self-regulate both the demands and the pace of work. Empirical support for the model has been demonstrated, both for the main effects of demand and control (Melamed *et al.*, 1991) and for the hypothesized interactions between demand and control (Schnall *et al.*, 1994). There is also qualified support (six of ten longitudinal studies of male workers) for the relationship between high demand, low control (both objective and perceived) jobs and cardiovascular disease (Belkic *et al.*, 2000). Terry and Jimmieson (1999) are somewhat less convinced of the buffering effects of control over demand. Spector (2002) speculates that the concept of control may be too non-specific, and that in order for control to buffer strain, the control must be over the particular stress-producing element of the work and not some other aspect unrelated to strain. Control or the perception of control can be experienced over a number

of aspects of the job; for example, organization, timing, pacing, or location. Intervention studies designed to enhance control are needed to assess its impact on well-being.

Control has also been implicated in occupational stress arising from organizational change processes, where control is conceptualized as a stress antidote (Sutton and Kahn, 1986). The perception of control has also been linked to personality factors, such as locus of control and private self-consciousness (Frone and McFarlin, 1989; Kivimaki and Lindstrom, 1995).

Johnson and Hall (1988) expanded the DCS model to include a support component incorporating coworker and supervisor social support. Social support has positive effects on well-being and buffers the impact of occupational stressors on psychological distress (Karasek et al., 1982). Low social support has been associated with greater symptomatology, and a significant interaction with demand and control has been observed for job dissatisfaction (Landsbergis et al., 1993). Uchino et al. (1996) in a review of 81 studies of the impact of social support found that it reliably protected against cardiovascular, endocrine and immune dysfunction. Thus high demand, low control and low social support combinations produce the greatest risk to workers.

Although primarily concerned with job characteristics rather than personality characteristics, the majority of studies of the DCS model rely on the self-report of workers to determine the degree of demand and control in their jobs. Clearly, the appraisal process required to complete such questionnaires may bias the reporting of the actual or objective job characteristics. Attempts to redress this problem have been made with some success using the imputation method (see Schwartz et al., 1988, for an explanation of the method), expert observers and the job exposure matrix (see Johnson and Stewart, 1993). Findings using these objective methods of assessing job characteristics have produced substantially the same findings as studies relying on self-report.

Cooper (2002) expressed more serious concerns regarding the continuing utility of the DCS model. He argued, firstly, that two- or three-dimensional models are inadequate to account for the complexities of job-related strain outcomes; and secondly, that the changing nature of work, which simultaneously affords workers more control but less job security, make the basic assumptions of the DCS no longer current. Conversely, Dollard (2001) points out that low demand jobs are disappearing as work environments become more competitive, so that Karasek's two-by-two matrix of job classification may reduce to high or low control jobs, all with high demands. This is probably an overstatement of the actual work situation. A recent Australian study reported that workers waste the equivalent of 90 working days per year on cigarette and coffee breaks, chatting with colleagues, and private email and phone calls. Inadequate management (24 per cent), poor work morale (9 per cent) and inappropriately qualified workforce (9 per cent) contributed to the time wasting. Other factors included computers crashing, people waiting for meetings to start and task duplication (Proudfoot Consulting, 2002).

Control
Since control is the central tenet of the DCS model, it is worthwhile to examine this concept a little more critically as it is understood more broadly in psychology. 'Relegated to the graveyard of epiphenomena' (Shapiro et al., 1996, p. 1213) by Skinner (1953, 1971), control did not regain the attention of researchers until about 50 years ago. Since that

time, a number of theoretical constructs have been proposed to distinguish between people on this dimension; for example, locus of control (Rotter, 1966), personal control (Peterson and Stunkard, 1989) and self-efficacy (Bandura, 1982). A relationship between perceived control and physical (Blumenthal *et al.*, 1994) and mental (Baltes and Baltes, 1986) health has been repeatedly demonstrated. The degree of perceived control also reliably distinguishes normal from clinical populations, with clinical groups reporting a greater sense of feeling out of control of their lives (Shapiro *et al.*, 1996). However, the relationship between control and health may not be linear, since those demonstrating both excessively low and excessively high control show increased risk for cardiovascular disease (Brown and Smith, 1992). Evans *et al.* (1993), citing over 60 studies, demonstrated the importance of the fit between the amount of control wanted by the individual and the amount of control required by the job. Mismatches between the person's desire for control and the amount of control afforded, active attempts to control situations that are actually uncontrollable, illusory control (Shedler *et al.*, 1994) and over-control have all been shown to be damaging to health and well-being (Shapiro *et al.*, 1996). A new concept, 'controllability awareness' has been proposed by Todrank *et al.* (2002) to 'describe the extent to which an individual's responses to life situations reflect attention to distinctions between controllable and uncontrollable aspects of potential outcomes. The construct distinguishes four aspects of controllability: personal control of outcomes, shared control of outcomes, others in responsibility, and uncontrollable/unpredictable outcomes' (p. 883). In a test of the relationship between this construct and stress tolerance, Todrank *et al.* (2002) found that those with greater awareness reported better health, more functional problem solving and less stress than those with low controllability awareness. Simple, uni-dimensional theories of control are no longer adequate and greater clarity and specificity are needed in the definition of the concept. It may be necessary for the occupational stress literature to take note of the research on control in the broader psychological sciences to advance the development of theories relating control to occupational stress and other health outcomes in the work environment.

Sociologists are more specific about the meaning of control. Scambler and Higgs (1999) conceptualize control in the workplace as command over capital and/or command over labour power. These are objective criteria and individuals either do or do not have control over the resources that shape life chances. Ritzer (1993) maintains that there is now more management control (Taylorism and Fordism) than ever before due to the 'McDonaldization' of hospitals, banks, universities and call centres, among others. Yet, at the same time, workers may experience greater freedom because they experience less loyalty to their employers with the lowered expectation of reciprocity in contemporary employer–employee relationships.

Effort–reward imbalance (ERI) model
Siegrist's (1996) Effort–Reward Imbalance (ERI) model of occupational stress is both an interpersonal and a transactional theory and, although it shares some commonalities with the DCS model, it also differs in significant ways. For example, while control is the central dimension in the DCS model, the ERI model focuses on rewards, specifically on the threats to or violations of (perceived) legitimate rewards. Unlike the DCS model which focuses exclusively on the psychosocial work environment, the ERI model is concerned

with both the work environment and the personal characteristics of workers, in particular the coping style described as overcommitment. In this way it is aligned with both the interpersonal theories described earlier and the labor process analysis of occupational stress that is covered in detail later in the chapter. All three models incorporate the sociological dimensions of fairness, distributive justice and reciprocity in social exchange.

The ERI model states that people exchange effort for rewards (money, self-esteem, job security/career opportunities). Imbalance arises when there is a lack of reciprocity between costs and gains and this imbalance results in emotional distress that creates physiological arousal (arousal of the autonomic nervous system) and job strain. In an increasingly precarious and fragmented working environment, a third factor that Siegrist (1996) calls overcommitment and that Cooper (1998) calls 'presenteeism' (characterized by excessive striving, diligence and need for approval) has an impact on the balance sheet. Occupational stress arises from an imbalance between (high) extrinsic effort and (low) extrinsic reward, and/or from a high level of overcommitment. These imbalances are compounded when labor market forces such as fewer jobs (that is lack of alternative options for employment) and risk of redundancy lead workers to accept unfair job arrangements to maintain their employment.

The occupational health and stress outcomes of these circumstances vary according to occupational and sociodemographic factors. In a 6.5 year prospective, longitudinal study of 416 male German factory workers, Siegrist and Klein (1990) found that the odds ratio (OR) for combined clinical and subclinical coronary heart disease for those experiencing effort–reward imbalances was 6.2. Status inconsistency (OR = 4.4), job insecurity (OR = 3.4), work pressure (OR = 3.4) and immersion (OR = 4.5) each independently predicted myocardial infarction or sudden cardiac death after adjusting for other behavioral and somatic risk factors. Effort–reward imbalances also predicted hypertension in male middle managers (OR = 6.8) (Siegrist, 1996).

Unlike the personality and coping literature on occupational stress, both the ERI and DCS models have exerted a major impact on international policy in occupational health and work stress (for example, Luxembourg Declaration, 1997; Tokyo Declaration, 1998). A detailed account of the ERI model can be found in Siegrist (this volume).

Dynamic equilibrium theory
Headey and Wearing (1992), Hart et al. (1993), and Hart and Wearing (1995) challenged the engineering (stressor-strain) model of stress as the force exerted on a structure, which shows signs of strain in response to that force (Cannon, 1929; Selye, 1975). Dynamic equilibrium theory focuses on the characteristics that create susceptibility to strain, either through innate personality traits, behaviors, resources or organizational factors. According to the theory, stress is not defined as a demand, a response or a process, but as a state of disequilibrium that arises when a change occurs that affects the individual's normal levels of psychological distress and well-being. To understand the cause of this change, it is necessary to assess separately the impact of personality, organization, coping processes and both positive and negative work experiences, noting that people may respond with both positive and negative affect to the same environment (Diener and Emmons, 1985). Hart and colleagues found that psychological well-being is determined by the balance between separate positive factors (such as extraversion, salutogenic life events) and

negative factors (such as neuroticism, adverse life events) each one of which has its own unique set of causes and consequences (Hart, 1994). Hart and Wearing (1995) argued that both stable personality characteristics and the dynamic interplay between coping and daily work experiences together accounted for changes in levels of psychological distress and well-being. They demonstrated that psychological distress and morale operate as separate dimensions and make independent contributions to the quality of work life: positive work experiences have an impact upon morale, and negative work experiences have an impact upon psychological distress. This suggests that morale may be improved by increasing positive work experiences and that psychological distress can be reduced by decreasing negative work experiences. In addition, research with teachers and police officers has indicated that these professional groups are not stressed so much by the nature of their work, but by the organizational context in which the work occurs (Headey and Wearing, 1992). The implication of this finding is that intervention should focus on developing a supportive organizational climate that enables workers to cope more adaptively with operational work demands, rather than to direct change efforts at the nature of the work per se. A core set of organizational factors, among them staff relationships and leadership quality, is related to both psychological distress and morale. Other factors, such as excessive work demands, are negative and relate only to psychological distress, while factors such as opportunities for advancement are positive and relate only to morale (Hart et al., 1993). Accordingly, strain occurs when excess elements (for example, demands) threaten one need and deficit elements (for example, lack of communication or support) threaten another. Careful analysis of both positive and negative organizational characteristics is therefore needed before intervening to ameliorate identified problems. Cotton (2002) has provided a simplified schematic that encapsulates the theory (see Figure 2.1). It should be noted that this conceptualization is remarkably similar to the model provided by Beehr (1998) in his organizational psychology meta-model of occupational stress.

The key elements in organizational climate are: supportive leadership, goal alignment, co-worker interaction, role clarity, appraisal and recognition, decision making, work demands, professional development, workplace distress and workplace morale. Research is converging on the importance of organizational climate in employee satisfaction and well-being. Using structural equation modeling on large samples of public sector employees, Hart and Cotton (2002) have found that organizational climate is a major contributor to individual morale (0.51), workplace morale (0.85), and workplace distress (−0.60) when compared with positive (0.28) and negative work experiences (−0.18) and personality factors (0.30). Emotionality (neuroticism) (0.67) was most closely associated with individual distress; organizational climate was the second major contributor (−0.36). Positive and negative work experiences made small significant contributions, but emotion-focused coping did not contribute to any of the dimensions of satisfaction. Conversely, the key drivers in withdrawal behaviors such as making a claim for workers' compensation were emotionality (0.55) and individual morale (−0.28); organizational climate still made a significant contribution (−0.26) (Note: numbers in parentheses represent standardized beta coefficients.)

Despite the elegance and intuitive appeal of this model, recent research has shown that a 10 per cent improvement in organizational climate leads to a 3.6 per cent decrease in distress, a 4.9 per cent improvement in morale, a 5.4 per cent improvement in quality of

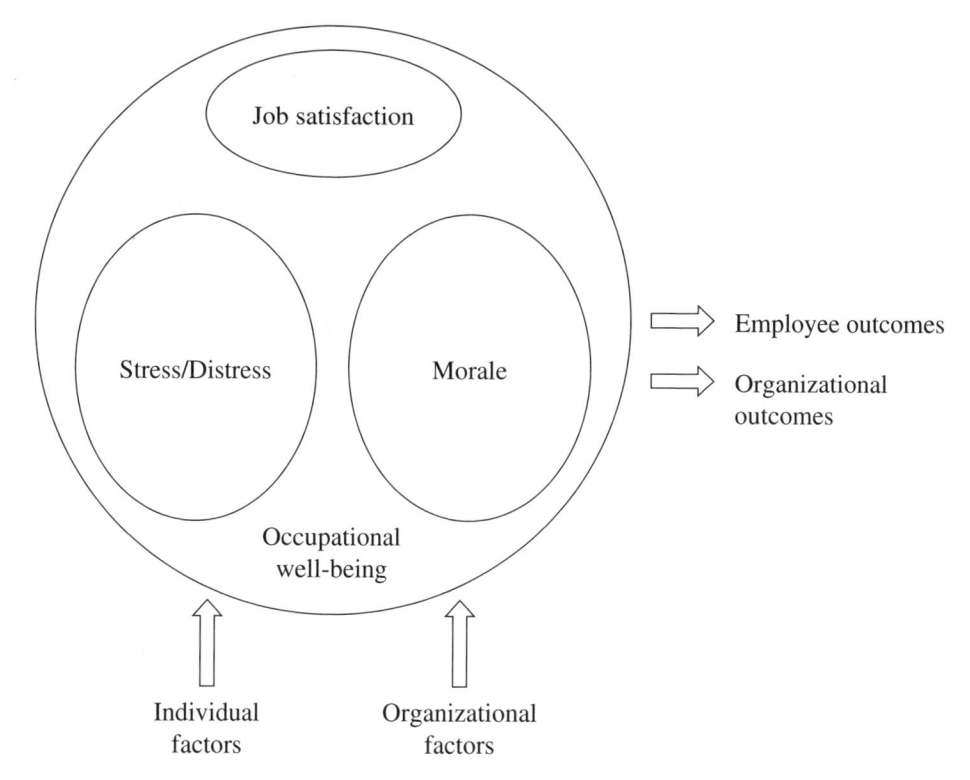

Figure 2.1 Schematic representation of dynamic equilibrium theory

work life and a 3.2 per cent decrease in a range of withdrawal behaviors (ibid.). It is difficult to imagine how these percentages would translate into a tangible change in the individual worker, his work or the organization.

Cybernetics and systems theory
Cybernetics is a theory that explains the functioning of self-regulating systems. It is neither an interpersonal theory nor a transactional theory and, while containing elements of both, it also transcends them. Cybernetics and general systems theory were developed concurrently and are based on similar theoretical principles. Social systems theory emphasizes wholeness, the interaction of component parts, and organization as unifying principles (Goldenberg and Goldenberg, 1985, p. 28), incorporates non-linear theories of causation (Cottone, 1991) and is based on a circular epistemology (Hoffman, 1981). This means that information and feedback direct behavior and that this behavior informs subsequent behavior. It stands in contrast to theories based on linear causality, such as the psychomedical model. The basic assumptions of each of these orientations are presented in Table 2.1.

In cybernetic theory, the concept of feedback is the pivotal process. Feedback describes a process whereby the system initiates homeostatic mechanisms based on information received. Hoffman (1981) describes feedback loops as either deviation amplifying or deviation counteracting, whereby a system either stabilizes, moving to a state of

Table 2.1 Basic assumptions

Dimensions	Psychomedical	Systemic
1. Theoretical foundation	psychology and medicine	social systems theory
2. Focus of study	unitary: the individual	unitary: relationships in context
3. View of the nature	reality is composed of things	reality is composed of relationships
4. Scientific viewpoint	reductionistic	holistic
5. Role of counsellor	diagnostician or remediator	trans-systemic intellectual
6. Focus of assessment	individual traits and skills	relationship dynamics
7. Goal of services	individual adjustment	social fit
8. Locus of responsibility	individual	social system
9. Causality	linear factors affect the person in an 'A causes B' way	circular factors affect persons simultaneously through relationships

Source: Adapted from Cottone (1991).

equilibrium, or destabilizes, moving to a state of disequilibrium. According to a cybernetic analysis, systems or organizations may undergo first- or second-order change. In first-order change, negative feedback is the process whereby systems maintain their organization through deviation-counteracting mechanisms such as homeostasis, morphostasis and self-correction (Sluzki, 1985). In second-order change, positive feedback loops amplify deviation; that is, they create change rather than maintain stasis.

Feedback loops are initiated when an individual identifies a discrepancy between a perceived current state that creates imbalance and discomfort, and another desired psychological and/or physiological state (Frone and McFarlin, 1989). The individual then assigns significance (importance) to the discrepancy (Carver and Scheier, 1981; Cummings and Cooper, 1979; Edwards, 1992). The importance or meaning accorded this discrepancy determines whether a feedback mechanism is initiated (Edwards 1992). In cybernetic theory, stress is defined as a relational concept, in contrast to the stimulus (environment as stress) and response (behavioral outcome) definitions. In an interesting variation of this theme, Buunk and Ybema (1997) have proposed that experiencing occupational stress, or any form of uncertainty, instigates a desire for social comparison information, that is, a need to discover how other people feel about the situation. Contact with similar others may lead the individual to adapt his/her stress response to those of other group members. Such a process may account, in part, for particular patterns (or contagion) of occurrence of occupational stress or illness that have been identified (Willis, 1994).

Consistent with circular causality and the mutability of causal direction in relation to key variables, coping is defined as discrepancy reduction behavior (Frone and McFarlin, 1989), an outcome of the stress process (Edwards, 1992), as a component of the intrapersonal variables that make up personality, which influence both the initial susceptibility to perceived stressors (variables such as ego strength, hardiness and so on) and the ability to respond to the threat to homeostasis in systemic terms (or the discrepancy occurring between perceived and desired states in cybernetic theory). The application of a circular epistemology resolves current disagreement over the function and consequences of coping as either a mediator of the stress–strain relationship or as a moderator (stress buffer) of the relationship (O'Driscoll and Cooper, 1994). Edwards (1992) describes stress explicitly as a discrepancy between perceptions and desires, rather than a conflict between demands and abilities, as in Selye's model (Selye, 1975), which Edwards views as predictors of coping efficacy, rather than as stress per se (p. 246). Coping entails one of four actions: changing the perceptions and desires involved in the discrepancy; changing the importance associated with the discrepancy; changing the situation (problem-focused coping); or cognitively restructuring the stress-producing event (repressing, denying, distorting, reframing).

Although the parallel is rarely drawn, there is a strong philosophical relationship between the concept of 'discrepancy' in systems theory, Karl Marx's theory of 'alienation' (circa 1844), Emile Durkheim's theory of 'anomie.' (circa 1897) and Max Weber's theory of 'rationality' (circa 1905). In essence the early sociologists (Marx, Durkheim and Weber), via their various investigations of the *modernity* process, produced a range of theories about social malaise that were deleterious to the essential nature of human beings. Susan Sontag (1978) conceived of 'illness as metaphor' within sociological theorizing at about the same time that psychologists and family therapists were embracing the notion of the symptom in the identified patient as a metaphor of family dysfunction (Bowen, 1978; Haley, 1964; Minuchin, 1974; Palazzoli et al., 1978). Similar analogies have been offered subsequently, for example, Willis's (1994) analysis of repetitive strain injury (RSI) as a metaphor for alienation. Applying these concepts to the occupational stress arena, one could argue that occupational stress arises when, through either individual or organizational change processes, a discrepancy occurs between the personal values of the worker and the values of the organization to which he or she belongs. Because managers and supervisors are key representatives of organizational culture, it is most often within the relationship between the individual and the supervisor that the individual will become aware of alienation (McIntyre, 1998).

The experience of occupational stress and one of its concrete manifestations, the lodging of a workers' compensation claim, is the functional communication of distress brought about by alienation (Karasek and Theorell, 1990). In Edward's (1992) theory, alienation may be understood in terms of thwarted desires, which produce negative emotions such as anger, disillusionment or the desire for retribution or revenge. Compensation may represent an effort to offset job dissatisfaction by investing energy in an alternative domain (for example, leisure or family) (ibid.). Decreased worker morale, in dynamic equilibrium theory (Hart and Wearing, 1995), may be conceptualized as a precursor to alienation if steps are not taken to remedy the morale problem early in the cycle. Similarly, Kenny (1995a; 1995b) argued that the failure of some injured workers to return to work following workplace injury was due, at least in part, to a failure of management to either believe that the injury was genuine or to show care, concern and respect to the injured worker. These failures set up a negative feedback loop in which workers experienced a narcissistic injury that resulted in anger, hostility and a desire for revenge against management, which of course, leads to an awareness of the 'true' nature of the relationship between worker and management. Marxist sociologists would argue that the structural conditions of alienation were already present in the contradictory interests of labor and capital and that the antagonisms became visible during a crisis. In organizational justice theory, this process is conceptualized as a violation in interactive justice. There are clearly strong linkages between justice theory and cybernetics; cybernetics is more process-oriented and therefore more difficult to test empirically in large samples and this may account for its neglect in the mainstream occupational stress literature (Edwards, 1992).

Interpreting occupational stress within a labor process analysis

> Men [*sic*] make their own history but they do not make it just as they please; they do not make it under circumstances chosen by themselves, but under circumstances directly encountered, given and transmitted from the past. The tradition of all the dead generations weighs like a nightmare on the brain of the living. (Karl Marx, 1954, p. 10)

A labor process approach to occupational health and illness (occupational stress in this instance) is concerned with the social, economic and political context in which paid work is performed. Although use is made of empirical data such as the physical and ergonomic aspects of work, the pace and timing of production (timetables, shiftwork, breaks, overtime arrangements), technology, management styles (for example, Taylorism or managerialism), the investigation is largely concerned with class relations at the actual workplace (the *relations in production*). There is also concern with *relations of production* (class relations in the wider society) and the relationship between the relations *in* and *of* production are crucial to understanding the labor process. This approach is radically different to all of the previous approaches discussed above, since it is in no way based on an assessment of individual characteristics. In a labour process analysis, the atomized individual has been removed from the equation and the focus is on social formations (groups with interests in common) and patterns of statistical regularity.

A labor process perspective has informed recent Australian research into occupational stress (see Peterson, 1994, 1999; McIntyre, 1994, 2002; Mahony, 2000, 2001a; Mahony and McIntyre, 2002). This research found that the origins of occupational stress exist at more sites than just the point of production, and that managerial control of the labor process is also dispersed into civil society and institutions of the state. Thus the way we carry out the production of goods and services is inexorably linked to the organization of the society in which we live, and in conjunction with the production of goods and services there is the production of occupational illness.

It was Karl Marx and Frederick Engels who (in the mid-19th century) first investigated and analyzed the labor process under capitalism and the emergence of alienated labor as a specific form of social pathology. Kitay (1997) has identified three waves of labor process analysis: Marxist, radical Weberian and post-structuralist. The following truncated account of the labor process is from a Marxist perspective, and the three key concepts that underpin the discussion are alienation, valorization of labor power and managerial prerogative.

From alienation to stress

During the 20th century, sets of symptoms (physiological, psychological and later behavioral) which had been labeled as 'worker fatigue' (physical and mental exhaustion) or 'nervous exhaustion' were redefined as 'occupational stress'. But although worker fatigue and its attendant symptoms were linked to Taylorism (scientific management) by the early members of the Human Relations School (for example, Elton Mayo), who attempted to improve production by blending the interests of labor and capital, the concept 'alienated labor' was never in their tool-box. Marx, who was androcentric, wrote in *Capital*:

> Within the capitalist system all methods for raising the social productiveness of labor are brought about at the cost of the individual laborer; all means for the development of production transform themselves into means of domination over, and exploitation of the producer; they mutilate the laborer into a fragment of a man [*sic*], degrade him to the level of an appendage of a machine, destroy every remnant of charm in his work and turn it into a hated toil; they estrange him from the intellectual potentialities of the labor process in the same proportion as science is incorporated in it as an independent power. (Marx, quoted in Fromm, 1966, p. 52)

By the late 1980s, occupational stress in addition to now being a 'rag bag' collection of symptoms had also become a metaphor for having a 'bad day' or a single unpleasant experience, rather than an expression of *alienated labor*. Stress had taken on a normative meaning: hence the expression 'stressed out'. To quote Marx again, this time from the *Economic and Philosophical Manuscripts of 1844*, 'It [alienated labor] alienates man from his own body, external nature, his mental life and his human life' (Marx, quoted in Fromm, 1966, p. 53).

In essence, the Marxian theory of alienation asserted that, in capitalist society, workers are alienated in four distinct ways. They are estranged from the product of their labor, from work itself as an area of fulfillment, from co-workers, and from their essential species nature as a human being. Finally, it was maintained that alienation could be overcome by changing conditions rather than consciousness (Ollman, 1971). What demarcated the human species from animals is that animals merely adapt to their environment, whereas human beings consciously strive to master theirs. Expecting workers just to adapt is to deny them their species being and to reduce them to the status of animals (Schacht, 1971, pp. 259–66).

Alienation is one of the oldest concepts in the social sciences, yet it has been borrowed, reworked and distorted to such an extent that it has been emptied of its explanatory usefulness. Today, according to the mass media, everyone is alienated. The list includes school children, serial murderers and film stars, in addition to alienated laborers (wageworkers).

The valorization of labor power
Karl Marx made the distinction between labor power and labor. Labor is the actual application of intellectual and physical capacity to produce goods or services. Labor power is the human capacity to do useful work which adds value to commodities (items which have an exchange value in a market). It is labor power which workers sell to capitalists for a wage.

In a capitalist labor process, the means of production (which includes labor) are purchased in a market. The capitalist buys labor (wage–effort bargain), in order to extract labor power (the actual not the potential application of effort), because it is only labor, not technology (as capital), which is capable of producing goods and services. It is the workers at Ford, not the assembly line, that produces automobiles. Buses do not drive themselves – they require an operator.

When capital purchases labor, only a potential capacity to work is acquired. This has always been the problem for management. To ensure profitable production, management must organize production to its own advantage, but workers may have different interests such as higher wages, shorter working hours, job security, mateship and so forth.

For Marx it was productive labor, not exchange in a market, which was the essence of the capitalist labor process: hence the importance of the labor theory of value and the centrality of surplus value. According to Meikle (1995, p. 193), 'If you had to say in a one-liner what Marx thought history was all about, you would have to say: It's all about extracting the surplus.' The surplus is pivotal to Marx's theory of history:

> The surplus is whatever is produced beyond what is needed to sustain the population. 'Surplus labor time' is the time spent producing it, and the time spent producing what is required for present needs is called 'necessary labor time'. Something has to be done with a surplus in a society that is productive enough to produce one, and decisions must be taken about its use. Decisions must also be taken about what it should consist of, and how the efforts of the direct producers should be allocated in order to produce those things in the required proportions. A society which produces a surplus must allocate its labor time and administer its surplus, and it has to have some way of making these decisions and some institutions to make them. (Meikle, 1995, p. 189)

A surplus is the basis of class society. A surplus requires allocation and administration. That is, occupations can become separate from actual production. A society divides into classes: a class which produces the surplus value and a class which controls and allocates the production of the surplus. To Marx, this relationship was the key to class society irrespective of its form, whether slave, feudal, capitalist or so-called 'socialist'.

Following Marx (d.1883) and Engels (d.1895) there was little Marxist analysis of the capitalist labor process until the 1970s, when Harry Braverman raised the question of the labor process in *monopoly capitalism* (the form of capitalism that had largely deposed the competitive capitalism of Marx's time). Braverman (1974) argued that monopoly capitalism contains a logic of deskilling manifested in Taylorism, that control was the central concept of all management systems, and proletarianization was a general trend (see Kitay, 1997, pp. 1–2). The Braverman thesis (1974) reinstated the labor process as a central concept for understanding the organization of work in capitalist enterprises. To Braverman, paid work was a relationship of power, nuanced by relationships of domination and subordination, exploitation and alienation. The relationship was constructed by the logic and dynamics of capitalism. Accumulation was the logic, exploitation and valorization were the dynamics. It was in the labor process, not the market place, that the generation of surplus value, and the quest to maximize the extraction of surplus value (valorization) took place. The rise of monopoly capitalism, accompanied by the emergence of managers (the separation of ownership and control), effected changes in the labor process but not in the fundamental relationship between labor and capital, and the embodiment of these formations as workers and managers.

It thus becomes essential for the capitalist that control over the labor process pass from the hands of the worker into his own. This transition presents itself in history as the *progressive alienation of the process of production* (emphasis in original) from the worker; to the capitalist, it presents itself as the problem of management (Braverman, 1974, p. 58).

Managers mediated the relationship between labor and capital through the design and implementation of new methods of valorization, based on principles of scientific management (Taylorism) and technological innovation. For Braverman the capitalist labor process, in all its forms, was the product of a class society. Notions of management, technology, skill and efficiency were not neutral; they had their basis in class relations. Management, irrespective of how it was performed, was about control of the labor process. Managers (mental workers) were engaged in the process of working out what, when and how work ought to be done; that is, managing the surplus extraction process.

Managers, though generally not owners of capital themselves (a 'new' middle class), commanded the labor power of other employees and enjoyed superior control over their own work, including the freedom to use creative talent. Managers had access to better pay and conditions, and were less exposed to alienation.

The managerial prerogative

Managerial prerogatives refer to the right of managers to manage. Brown (1992, pp. 229–41), characterized work organizations as negotiated orders in which organizational structures are continually (re)created by the actions and interactions of their members. The negotiated order reflects the continuing process of conflict, negotiation and the temporary resolution of differences (cf. cybernetics and systems theory). The key issue for 'negotiation' revolved around the regulation of the employment contract, which is necessary if work is to be done. Even though all members of an organization can negotiate their conditions to some extent, there are some who are more powerful than others, and can draw on sources of power (material and/or ideological) from sites external to the organization (professional associations, trade unions and the state). Campbell (1993, p. 14) argues that the greater the call for labor market flexibility, the greater the demand for enhancing managerial prerogative.

Navarro (1986, pp. 103–40) has provided a Marxist account of the relationship between the labor process and occupational health and illness. This account acknowledges the structural relationship between injury and the labor process in which labor is viewed as a commodity; health is sold and injury and death are compensated. Marxist labor process theorists maintain that it is the extraction of surplus labor power from alienated labor that shapes social, economic and political relationships and, that the symptomatology of occupational stress is an empirical reflection of these relationships.

Stress as a discourse

How do you find a lion that has swallowed you? (Carl Jung)

Carl Jung, in addition to interpreting dreams, has also (posthumously) interpreted the post-structuralist project in one sentence. In Australia since the late 1980s, post-structuralist theory, influenced by the ideas of Michel Foucault, has been increasingly applied to understanding the ways in which language, knowledge and power interact to produce and reproduce ways of experiencing identity, our bodies and the social and material worlds. Post-structuralist theory has questioned many of the domain assumptions held by medicine and psychology (and the social sciences), especially the claim that knowledge about disease and illness is built upon the accumulation of scientific facts. A fundamental challenge posed to the medical and health sciences by post-structuralist theory is that as all knowledge is socially constructed, so-called 'objective knowledge' (scientific knowledge) is not neutral (apolitical) but embodies meanings, values and practices. That is, discourses have truth effects. In Foucauldian terms, the right of management to define efficiency and control the labor process (the managerial prerogative) is a discourse.

Foucault's method was to use the past in order to problematize the present by challenging the way that knowledge, as a claim to 'truth', is taken for granted by human beings in constructing their understandings of reality; human beings do not have access to reality outside their own understandings of it. Thus, if reality cannot be known, only human understandings of it, the major concern of the investigator should be with these understandings (Finch, 1993, p. 5). Foucault maintains that these understandings of reality are organized into discourses that involve the classification of a body of knowledge, and the identification of who, and in what circumstances and/or locations, can make knowledge claims. Foucault's project was to identify and trace changes in these discourses, which privilege or marginalize particular kinds of knowledge (Philp, 1990, pp. 68–9).

Thus occupational stress can be viewed as a discourse, and being encapsulated in a discourse is like trying to find a lion that has swallowed you. According to Petersen and Lupton (1996, p. 112) stress 'has become a popular way of describing a sense of malaise, fatigue, depression, anxiety or tenseness in individuals in contemporary Western societies'. The concept relies on images of human beings struggling to cope with the unnatural demands created by modern industrial society.

Stress/risk discourses, be they in medicine, psychology or public health, or reported in the media, maintain that stress is the inevitable consequence of modern living, a risk factor that can be managed by the individual. For instance, in October 1997 the Australian Council of Trade Unions (ACTU) released the results of a stress survey (5000 public sector workers) and the president of the ACTU (Jennie George) recommended that workers counter stress by taking a 'stress-free day' (that is, a holiday). The same media report reinforced the hegemonic stress/risk discourse by publishing a mandatory list of tips for a stress-free working day, commencing with 'Stress is part of everyday life. How you respond to stress is the key. Be proactive, not reactive.' Then came the time-management, self-talk and therapeutic activities (cooking, music, art, exercise, sport, yoga, meditation, massage and so on) and finally, 'If all else fails, you could take a holiday' (*Australian*, 22 October 1997, p. 15). In short, research commissioned by the peak trade union organization in Australia conformed to the hegemonic stress discourse. The solutions and, hence, the problem were related to the characteristics of the individual and were perceived to be external to the labor process.

This brief engagement with discourses serves to illustrate certain insights and limitations that come with the post-structuralist approach. By deconstructing the stress and risk discourses it can be demonstrated that 'stress' and 'risk' are vague concepts which serve to obscure rather than explain social relations. Stress, in its popular conception, is represented as a risk inherent in living in modern society, and as a consequence no individual or group is considered responsible for creating the risk – it comes with the territory. At the same time, however, individuals are charged with the task of risk avoidance, especially those who have been constructed as being more 'at risk', usually owing to another inherent, but individualized trait, their personality. There are multiplicities of stress/risk discourses, but the above discourse is not only the hegemonic discourse, is also presented as the truth. There is no space for the labor process in this discourse. Moreover the hegemonic discourse does not question the managerial prerogative to define efficiency and control the labor process. Nor does the hegemonic discourse treat occupational stress as a social process.

Occupational stress as a social process
By the early 1990s, the reporting of occupational stress in Australia was claimed to have reached epidemic proportions (Toohey, 1995; Auditor-General, 1997). The same claim was made about repetitive strain injury (RSI) in the 1980s. 'A spectre is haunting Australian business life – the epidemic of repetition strain injuries (RSI) which is undermining the viability of many business enterprises' (Willis, 1994, p. 133).

Willis (1994) demonstrated how RSI could be understood as a social process by drawing upon a framework developed by Figlio (1982) in his examination of the miners' nystagmus epidemic in the United Kingdom (UK) at the beginning of the 20th century. Willis, like Figlio, was interested in the way illness mediates social relations; how the changing social relations of production produce both discontent and increased reporting of sickness by workers, and how, in the mediation process, the illness/injury itself becomes an object of negotiation.

In essence miners' nystagmus, RSI and occupational stress have a common heritage in the history of occupational health. Firstly, they may be understood as an expression of a devalued state, an illness that has acquired a (stigmatized) label. Secondly, some of the vital symptoms for each condition (for instance, visual disorientation with miners' nystagmus, wrist and arm pain with RSI and anxiety/depression with occupational stress) are difficult to match with an objective pathology (disease). Thirdly, even when a relationship between illness (the presentation of symptoms) and disease (for example, cancer) can be demonstrated, there is – especially when compensation is involved – a political struggle around establishing that the etiology of the disease was located in the workplace. Finally, the emergence of all three epidemics coincided with changes in the social relations of production. On one hand there had been changes in the various Workers' Compensation and/or OH&S Acts (1906 in the UK, 1983 in NSW, and 1988 in the Commonwealth) in which the legal liability of employers to ensure the health and safety of their workers had been emphasized. At the same time, however, there had been changes to the labor process.

Irrespective of whether the changes were technological (mechanization in mining, computers in data processing) or organizational (reduced staffing and faster paced work in word-processing offices) the outcome was comparable for each condition. A changed labor process engendered intensification in the pace of production, increased surveillance and discipline of the workforce, and was accompanied by workplace hazards. For instance, and they are straightforward examples of risk imposition, in mining there was an increased exposure to noise and dust; with data entry, operators were unable to keep pace with the speed of electronic data-processing systems; and, in public sector employment, it was becoming increasingly difficult for workers to maintain services without cutting corners, thereby increasing the risk of interpersonal conflict with both co-workers and clients/customers. The occupational stress epidemic in general, especially when related to the public sector (state and federal), appeared to emerge in conjunction with legislative changes (corporatization and privatization) that have led to the 'withering away of the Australian state' (see Fairbrother et al., 1997).

Figlio's argument (codified by Willis, 1994, p. 136), 'is that the mediation of the social relations of production by illness, occurs as a three-stage process: (a) the appearance of the disease or injury, represented as a set of symptoms; (b) the appearance of observers of the disease or injury who set in operation various medical, legal and administrative apparatuses to 'cope' with the disease or injury; (c) negotiation of the socioeconomic and political meaning of the disease or injury: at its most basic this is workers' compensation, paid in place of wages, but the negotiation goes much further than the redefinition of disease (see Willis, 1994, p. 136).

What has been termed the RSI debate was joined by an eclectic range of disciplines and experts (see Quinlan and Bohle, 1991, ch.4). Practitioners in medicine, ergonomics, psychiatry, psychology and sociology provided explanations and putative solutions to the phenomenon. The debate was polarized, with worker organizations (unions) arguing that, as organizational factors (such as the design of work) were the cause of the problem, management had the responsibility for the problem. Employers and insurance providers conversely argued that the source of the problem resided in the sufferer (for example, personality characteristics such as neurosis), or that factors outside of the workplace (such as heightened awareness of compensation) could have contributed to the problem. Quinlan and Bohle (ibid., p. 136) maintained that health professionals tried to occupy the middle ground (if that is possible), but aspects of their work were often selectively used to support the ideological position of either labor or management.

The same range of experts also entered the occupational stress debate: is stress an illness and, if so, what are the stressors and to what extent are they intrinsic to the occupation or generated by the labor process? Hopkins (1990) argued that RSI was an epidemic of reporting rather than of actual incidence. Could the same case be made for occupational stress? Willis (1994) argued that the reporting of occupational illness/injury was like the tip of an iceberg, with the visible part changing in accord with the economic and political climate. One major dimension of this climate was class. Until the 1980s, 'work stress' was class-specific: only the members of professional and managerial occupations presented episodes of work stress (see Cooper, 1981, ch.9). 'Helping professionals' (such as in nursing, social work, teaching) were deemed to be suffering from burnout due to overwork brought on by overidentification with the client and/or task (Zastrow, 1984). With burnout came the sick role and an injunction to slow down. And just when some researchers (such as the Scandinavian School of the Social Psychology of Work) were arguing that there was an inverse relationship between work stress and work autonomy (more autonomy equals less stress), the restructuring of the economy and labor markets accelerated (driven by the dual ideologies of managerialism and neoliberalism). Today there are no injunctions to slow down. Workers and managers are urged to 'work smarter not harder', but how smarter or harder do you need to work to produce surplus value?

The third stage in the process described by Figlio (1982) and Willis (1994), the negotiation of the socioeconomic and political meaning of the disease or injury, was completed by 1997 in the federal sphere of the public sector. The Auditor-General reported (1997, p. xiii) that Comcare was winning the battle against stress in the Australian Public Service, and recent changes in claims management had resulted in a decline in the rate of approvals for stress claims. Changes included amendments to the Safety, Rehabilitation and Compensation Act 1988 'to redefine "disease" so as to require a high degree of association between employment and a claimed medical condition' (ibid., p. 11). That is, occupational stress, like RSI, had been redefined by a political process, and had effectively become a set of symptoms in search of a disease.

Other changes in the labor process have been held responsible for increased occupational stress and ill health. For example, Quinlan *et al.* (2001) argue that the increase in precarious or unstable employment (part-time, casual, contract, seasonal) has profound consequences for occupational health. In a recent review of the international literature on this subject, they state:

> the growth of precarious employment commonly leads to more pressured work processes and more disorganized work settings and in so doing creates challenges for which existing regulatory regimes are ill prepared. Despite the pervasive language of 'management systems', 'performance standards' and the like that marks government and business circles, the reality is a substantial and sustained growth of disorganized work settings. In large organizations making extensive use of outsourcing and temporary workers, or with a demoralized 'post-restructuring' core workforce, extensive documents attesting to a coherent system may constitute little more than 'paper compliance'. [...] It is arguable that the growth of precarious employment has reduced both the direct and indirect scope for worker involvement in management decisions on working conditions and, indeed, is conducive to the development of more despotic forms of labor management. [...] Further, the scope for managing adverse outcomes through conventional OHS regulatory regimes is open to serious question. [...] Although the precise interrelationship of business and employment laws varies between countries, the subordination of employment standards and OHS laws to business/competition laws at the national level, is a trend across countries. (Quinlan *et al.*, 2001, p. 367)

It has been argued that work intensity and job insecurity have adverse consequences for the physical health, psychological well-being and occupational safety of workers. While it would be difficult to sustain a thesis that precarious employment is not linked to the incidence of occupational stress, it is likely that workers who are precariously employed would be less rather than more likely to report occupational stress (Cooper, 1998). In such circumstances, one could argue that only the reporting, not the incidence, of occupational stress had declined. Other labor process changes, such as commercialization, corporatization, and privatization, leading as they do to downsizing, outsourcing, redundancies and terminations, all contribute to heightened occupational stress in affected workers.

Could it be that miners' nystagmus, RSI, occupational stress, Post-traumatic Stress Disorder (PTSD) and epidemics yet to emerge (such as harassment and bullying) are really consequences of alienated labor? If so, as the Marxist labor process theorists would argue, the focus of investigation needs to be the capitalist labor process. The fundamental structural contradictions between labor and capital (represented by shareholders, directors and senior management) have not been resolved because the relations in production (at the workplace) and the relations of production (the wider society and now globally) have remained unequal. In fact, it could be argued that class relations have become more polarized. Some managers, perhaps the majority, are supportive and try to ameliorate the situation, but at great personal cost as they, like tightrope walkers, try to balance a duty of care with the demands of production. Managers are also part of the labor process which they help to reproduce, and the manager who allows sentiment to subordinate the valorization of labor power will have a short career as a manager.

Or perhaps these phenomena are not, and never have been, 'epidemics'. In NSW, Australia, workers' compensation claims for occupational stress occupy a very small proportion of total claims, less than 2.5 per cent of all claims over the period 1991–6 (WorkCover Authority of NSW, 1997), the period claimed to represent the epidemic in occupational stress and the explosion in occupational stress claims. Of course one can always resort to the argument that this is a matter of reporting, not a matter of incidence, an issue with no satisfactory resolution. But as Willis (1994) reminds us, the identification and labeling of the illness and its designation as an 'epidemic' are social processes. It should also be remembered that all stakeholders (including academics) were quite prolific in their use of 'stress epidemic'. Moreover, we have to be careful when talking about the social construction of occupational illness because it could be misconstrued as meaning a product of the mind (imagination), when in fact a stressed worker by any name is still a stressed worker.

Like many compensable conditions, occupational stress has been abused by some as a source of (secondary) gain (income without work, payback, malingering, restricted duties and medical retirement). The outcome of this abuse is that the real stressed worker can now only seek redress once he or she has developed a condition that has an objective pathology (such as heart disease). You may have met the real stressed worker. The worst cases of occupational stress just vanish – they often do not even claim the wages owed to them. The sufferer, being in a psychologically weakened state, finds that the process of having to engage with medical specialists, insurance doctors, psychologists, lawyers, rehabilitation providers, rehabilitation counsellors and so on (and some will be hostile) is an extra burden to be avoided.

Perhaps the labor process debate has never had a central role because, like some other theories outlined in this chapter, the arguments are not matched by sufficient evidence. The Marxist theory of the labor process has only been applied to a handful of empirical studies into occupational illness; internal and external validity has been demonstrated and none of these studies has been discredited. They are simply ignored. We live in an age of evidence-based medicine (and this is laudable), but it depends on what evidence is selected.

Towards a synthesis of constructions of occupational stress

Although Freud's contention that an illness phenomenon rarely vanishes unless the core causes have been addressed has been challenged by behaviorists and others, there is evidence that, at a systemic level, phenomena do re-emerge in another time or place, and/or with a different symptomatology and label. Occupational stress has been (legislatively) replaced by ASD (Acute Stress Disorder) and PTSD (Post-traumatic Stress Disorder). There is emerging sociological research into PTSD. Mahony (2000) has argued that ambulance officers present with PTSD (formerly occupational stress) because it is more acceptable and legitimate, than claiming that the source of stress is organizational restructuring. If everyone is feeling the impact of workplace restructuring, why should ambulance officers expect special consideration unless they have a special case? Extracting bodies from crash or building wreckage is heroic, visible and taken for granted as an intrinsic stressor of the job. Thus PTSD in this 'heroic' profession is unchallenged by management and the general public. Mahony (2001a) has also argued that even stressors thought to be intrinsic to the core work of ambulance officers have an organizational dimension.

Of course, all the same controversies surrounding the more generic concept of occupational stress have reappeared in the more clinically focused labels of ASD and PTSD. How can these phenomena be defined? Does the labor process provide any explanatory utility? What are the boundaries of these definitions and how do we prevent definitional creep, which makes researching the concepts and addressing the issues problematic (McNally, 2003)? What are the underlying causes? Is personality the best predictor of ASD and PTSD? What role does the stressor play? What are the most effective interventions? With whom should we intervene? These familiar questions in the occupational stress literature are now being recycled in their new guise.

Perhaps it might be useful if we stopped talking and writing about 'occupational stress' because there is no such disease state. Moreover, in some jurisdictions the label has been legislated out of existence and now has as much legitimacy as 'masturbatory insanity' or RSI. Focusing on occupational stressors would make far more sense, because there is a point where even the most resilient worker will break down. The current research into worker fatigue shows some promise and at the same time reveals a paradox. Stress studies originated with worker fatigue (munitions workers, circa 1915); the wheel is turning full circle and there is much at stake for the big players in the (occupational) stress industry.

The diligent reader will no doubt by now have detected both the substantive differences and the compelling synergies between the different theories of occupational stress presented in this chapter. Kuhn (1962) alerts us to the 'incommensurability of paradigms' that exists because the holders of one paradigm may not only speak a language that is

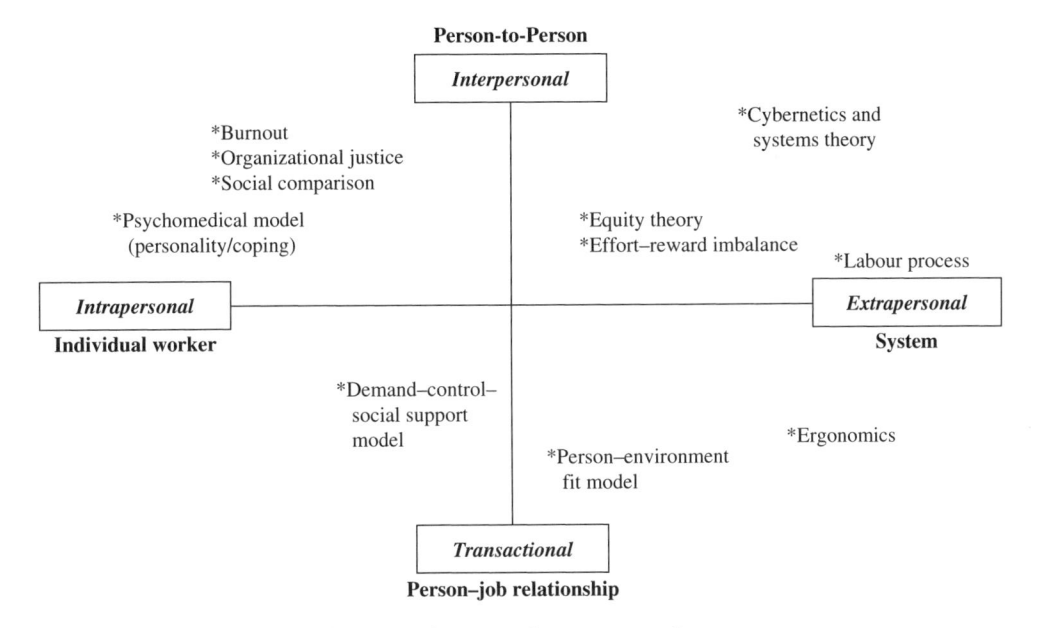

Figure 2.2 Relationships between theories of occupational stress

50 *Conceptualization and theoretical framework*

fundamentally different to that of the holders of another paradigm, but they are also bearers of different assumptions about the world and the nature of knowledge (epistemology). In short, the holders of various scientific paradigms can actually lack the capacity to speak to each other. A paradigm is similar to a subculture. For this reason, material interests notwithstanding, it does help if you have some idea about the view of the world from the other side of the paradigm divide. Accordingly, we present below an attempt to connect the paradigms, to be inclusive and communicative across paradigms.

Figure 2.2 places these theories in two-dimensional space on the continua ranging from intrapersonal (individual) to extrapersonal (system) and from interpersonal (person-to-person) to transactional (person-to-job). Even those theories at greatest distance have commonalities that could form the basis of a unified meta-theory. Figure 2.3 integrates the main features of each theory into a unified system that attempts to account for both

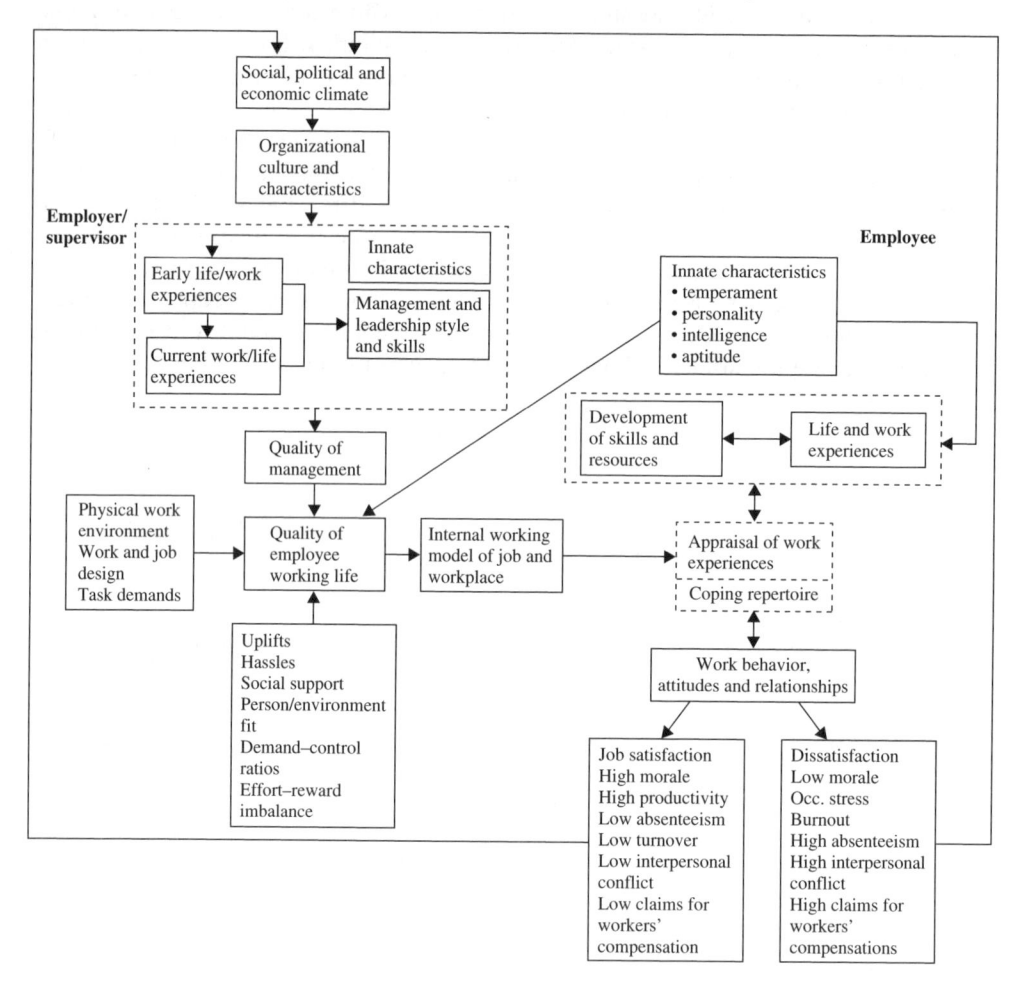

Figure 2.3   *A model of the quality of working life, integrating the dominant theories of occupational stress*

universal commonalities and individual differences in the experience of occupational stress and to take account of occupational stressors and the labor process. Each theory has made a unique contribution to our understanding of occupational stress. Emphases and recommended change processes differ, and it is now time to attempt a synthesis about the future focus of this field.

References

Adams, J.S. (1965), 'Inequity in social exchange', in L. Berkowitz (ed.), *Advances in Experimental Social Psychology*, **2**, 267–99, New York: Academic Press.

Appelberg, K., K. Romanov, M.L. Honkasalo and M. Koskenvuo (1991), 'Interpersonal conflicts at work and psychosocial characteristics of employees', *Social Science and Medicine*, **32**(9), 1051–6.

Auditor-General (1997), *The Management of Occupational Stress in Commonwealth Employment*, Canberra: Australian National Audit Office.

Baker, D. (1985), 'Occupational stress', *Annual Review of Public Health*, **6**, 367–81.

Bakker, A.B., W.B. Schaufeli, H.J. Sixma, W. Bosveld and D. Van Dierendonck (2000), 'Patient demands, lack of reciprocity, and burnout: A five-year longitudinal study among general practioners', *Journal of Organizational Behavior*, **21**, 425–41.

Baltes, M.M. and P.B. Baltes (eds) (1986), *The Psychology of Control and Aging*, Hillsdale, NJ: Erlbaum.

Bandura, A. (1982), 'Self-efficacy mechanism in human agency', *American Psychologist*, **37**, 122–47.

Barrick, M.R. and M.K. Mount (1991), 'The Big Five personality dimensions and job performance: a meta-analysis', *Personnel Psychology*, **44**, 1–26.

Baumeister, R.F., K. Dale and K.L. Sommer (1998), 'Freudian defense mechanisms and empirical findings in modern social psychology: reaction formation, projection, displacement, undoing, isolation, sublimation and denial', *Journal of Personality*, **66**, 1081–1124.

Beehr, T.A. (1998), 'An organizational psychology meta-model of occupational stress', in C.L. Cooper (ed.), *Theories of Organizational Stress*, Oxford: Oxford University Press, pp. 6–27.

Belkic, K.L., P.L. Schnall, P.A. Landsbergis and D.B. Baker (2000), 'The workplace and cardiovascular health: conclusions and thoughts for a future agenda', in P.L. Schnall, K.L. Belkic, P.A. Landsbergis and D.B. Baker (eds), *State of the Art Reviews, Occupational Medicine, The Workplace and Cardiovascular Disease*, **15**(1), Philadelphia: Hanley & Belfus, 307–21.

Blumenthal, S.J., K. Matthews and S.M. Weiss (1994), 'New research frontiers and behavioral medicine: proceedings of the national conference' (NIH Publication no. 94-3772), US Printing Office, Washington, DC.

Bohle, P. (1993), 'Work psychology and the management of occupational health and safety: an historical overview', in M. Quinlan and P. Bohle (eds), *Work and Health: The Origins, Management and Regulation of Occupational Illness*, Melbourne: Macmillan.

Bowen, M. (1978), *Family Therapy in Clinical Practice*, New York: Aronson.

Braverman, H. (1974), *Labor and Monopoly Capital: The Degradation of Work in the Twentieth Century*, New York: Monthly Review Press.

Brief, A.P. and H.M. Weiss (2002), 'Organizational behavior: affect in the workplace', *Annual Review of Psychology*, **53**, 279–307.

Brief, A.P., M.J. Burke, J.M. George, B.S. Robinson and J. Webster (1988), 'Should negative affectivity remain an unmeasured variable in the study of job stress?', *Journal of Applied Psychology*, **73**, 193–8.

Bright, J. (2001), 'Individual difference factors and stress: a case study paper', NOHSC Symposium on the OHS Implications of Stress, 58–79.

Brown, P.C. and T.W. Smith (1992), 'Social influences, marriage, and the heart: cardiovascular consequences of interpersonal control in husbands and wives', *Health Psychology*, **11**, 88–96.

Brown, R. (1992), *Understanding Industrial Organisations: Theoretical Perspectives in Industrial Sociology*, London: Routledge.

Burke, R.J. and E.R. Greenglass (2000), 'Organizational restructuring: identifying effective hospital downsizing processes,' in R.J. Burke and C.L. Cooper (eds), *The Organization in Crisis*, London: Blackwell, pp. 284–303.

Buunk, B.P. and J.F. Ybema (1997), 'Social comparisons and occupational stress: the identification–contrast model', in B.P. Buunk and F.X. Gibbons (eds), *Health, Coping and Well-being: Perspectives from Social Comparison Theory*, Mahwah, NJ: Lawrence Erlbaum Associates, pp. 359–88.

Calhoun, J.B. (1962), *The Ecology and Sociology of the Norway Rat*, US Department of Health, Education and Welfare Public Health Service Monograph, 1008.

Campbell, I. (1993), 'Labour market flexibility in Australia: enhancing management prerogative', *Labour and Industry*, **5**(3), 1–32.

Cannon, W.B. (1929), 'Organisation for physiological homeostasis', *Physiological Reviews*, **9**, 399–431.
Caplan, R.D. (1987), 'Person–environment fit theory and organizations: commensurate dimensions, time perspectives and mechanisms', *Journal of Vocational Behavior*, **31**, 248–67.
Caplan, R.D. and R.V. Harrison (1993), 'Person–environment fit theory: some history, recent developments and future directions', *Journal of Social Issues*, **49**(4), 253–75.
Caplan, R.D. and K.W. Jones (1975), 'Effects of work load, role ambiguity and Type A personality on anxiety, depression and heart rate', *Journal of Applied Psychology*, **60**(6), 713–19.
Carver, C.S. and M.F. Scheier (1981), *Attention and Self-regulation: A Control Theory Approach to Human Behavior*, New York: Springer-Verlag.
Carver, C.S. and M.F. Scheier (1999), 'Optimism', in C.R. Snyder (ed.), *Coping: The Psychology of What Works*, New York: Oxford University Press, pp. 182–204.
Carver, C.S., M.F. Scheier and J.K. Weintraub (1989), 'Assessing coping strategies: a theoretically based approach', *Journal of Personality and Social Psychology*, **56**, 267–83.
Chen, P.Y. and P.E. Spector (1991), 'Negative affectivity as the underlying cause of correlations between stressors and strains', *Journal of Applied Psychology*, **76**(3), 398–407.
Cooper, C.L. (1981), 'Sources of stress on managers at work', in C.L. Cooper (ed.), *Psychology and Management: A Text for Managers and Trade Unionists*, London: Macmillan.
Cooper, C.L. (1983), 'Identifying stressors at work: recent research developments', *Journal of Psychosomatic Research*, **27**(5), 369–76.
Cooper, C.L. (1985), 'The stress of work: an overview', *Aviation, Space and Environmental Medicine*, **56**(7), 627–32.
Cooper, C.L. (1987), 'Stress-prone behavior: Type A pattern', in R. Kalimo, M.A. El-Batawi and C.L. Cooper (eds), *Psychosocial Factors at Work*, Geneva: World Health Organization, pp. 134–8.
Cooper, C.L. (1998), *Theories of Organizational Stress*, Oxford: Oxford University Press.
Cooper, C.L. (2002), 'The changing psychological contract at work', *Occupational and Environmental Medicine*, **59**(6), 355.
Cooper, C.L. and A.J. Baglioni (1988), 'A structural model approach toward the development of a theory of the link between stress and mental health', *British Journal of Medical Psychology*, **61**(1), 87–102.
Cooper, C.L. and S. Cartwright (1994), 'Healthy mind, healthy organization', *Human Relations*, **47**(4), 455–71.
Cooper, C.L. and R.L. Payne (1992), 'International perspectives on research into work, well being and stress management', in J.C. Quick, L.R. Murphy and J.J. Hurrell Jr (eds), *Stress and Wellbeing at Work*, Washington, DC: American Psychology Association.
Cooper, C.L., P. Liukkonen and S. Cartwright (1996), *Stress Prevention in the Workplace*, Dublin: European Foundation for the Improvement of Living and Working Conditions.
Costa, P.T. and R.R. McCrae (1980), 'Influence of extroversion and neuroticism on subjective well-being', *Journal of Personality and Social Psychology*, **38**, 668–78.
Cotton, P. (2002), 'Challenges in the assessment and management of psychological/psychiatric injuries: a research-based perspective, paper presented at the LexisNexis Butterworths 'Psychological and Psychiatric Trauma: Approaches to Injury Management' Conference, Sydney, Australia, 16–17 May.
Cottone, R. (1991), 'Counselor roles according to two counseling worldviews', *Journal of Counseling and Development*, **69**, 398–401.
Coyne, J.C. and M.W. Racioppo (2000), 'Never the twain shall meet? Closing the gap between coping research and clinical intervention research', *American Psychologist*, **55**, 655–64.
Cramer, J. (1998), 'Freshman to senior year: a follow-up study of identity, narcissism and defense mechanisms', *Journal of Research in Personality*, **32**, 156–72.
Creed, P.A. and B.M. Evans (2002), 'Personality, well-being and deprivation theory', *Personality and Individual Differences*, **33**(7), 1045–54.
Cropanzano, R. (ed.) (1993), *Justice in the Workplace: Approaching Fairness in Human Resource Management*, Hillsdale, NJ: Lawrence Erlbaum Associates.
Cummings, T.G. and C.L. Cooper (1979), 'A cybernetic framework for studying occupational stress', *Human Relations*, **72**, 395–418.
Cushway, D. and P.A. Tyler (1994), 'Stress and coping in clinical psychologists', *Stress Medicine*, **10**, 35–42.
Decker, P.J. and F.H. Borgen (1993), 'Dimensions of work appraisal: stress, strain, coping, job satisfaction and negative affectivity', *Journal of Counseling Psychology*, **40**(4), 470–78.
DeNeve, K.M. and H. Cooper (1998), 'The happy personality: a meta-analysis of 137 personality traits and subjective well-being', *Psychological Bulletin*, **124**(2), 197–230.
Diener, E. and R.A. Emmons (1985), 'The independence of positive and negative affect', *Journal of Personality and Social Psychology*, **47**, 1105–17.
Dollard, M. (2001), 'Work stress theory and interventions: from evidence to policy', *NOHSC Symposium on the OHS Implications of Stress*, 2–57.

Edwards, J.R. (1992), 'A cybernetic theory of stress, coping, and well being in organizations', *Academy of Management Review*, **17**(2), 238–74.
Edwards, J.R., A.J. Baglioni and C.L. Cooper (1990), 'Stress, Type-A, coping, and psychological and physical symptoms: a multi-sample test of alternative models', *Human Relations*, **43**, 919–56.
Evans, G.E., D.H. Shapiro and M. Lewis (1993), 'Specifying dysfunctional mismatches between different control dimensions', *British Journal of Psychology*, **84**, 255–73.
Eysenck, H.J. (1988), 'Personality, stress and cancer: prediction and prophylaxis', *British Journal of Medical Psychology*, **61**, 57–75.
Fairbrother, P., S. Svensen and J. Teicher (1997), 'The withering away of the Australian state: privatisation and its implications for labour', *Labour and Industry*, **8**(2), 1–29.
Figlio, K. (1982), 'How does illness mediate social relations? Workmen's compensation and medico-legal practices, 1890–1940', in P. Wright and A. Treacher (eds), *The Problem of Medical Knowledge, Examining the Social Construction of Medicine*, Edinburgh: Edinburgh University Press.
Finch, L. (1993), *The Classing Gaze*, Sydney: Allen and Unwin.
Folkman, S. and, J.T. Moskowitz (2000), 'Positive affect and the other side of coping', *American Psychologist*, **55**, 647–54.
Fonagy, P., H. Steele and M. Steele (1991), 'Maternal representations of attachment during pregnancy predict the organization of infant–mother attachment at one year of age', *Child Development*, **62**, 891–905.
Fontana, D. and R. Abouserie (1993), 'Stress levels, gender and personality factors in teachers', *British Journal of Educational Psychology*, **63**, 261–70.
Freudenberger, H.J. (1975), 'The staff burnout syndrome in alternative institutions', *Psychotherapy: Theory, Research and Practice*, **12**, 72–82.
Fromm, E. (1966), *Marx's Concept of Man*, New York: Frederick Ungar Publishing Co.
Frone, M.R. and D.B. McFarlin (1989), 'Chronic occupational stressors, self-focused attention and well-being: testing a cybernetic model of stress', *Journal of Applied Psychology*, **74**(6), 876–83.
Frone, M.R., M. Russell and M.L. Cooper (1991), 'Relationship of work and family stressors to psychological distress: the independent moderating influence of social support, mastery, active coping and self-focused attention', *Journal of Social Behavior and Personality*, **6**(7), 227–50.
Fry, P.S. (1995), 'Perfectionism, humour and optimism as moderators of health outcomes and determinants of coping styles of women executives', *Genetic, Social and General Psychology Monographs*, **121**(2), 211–45.
Furnham, A. and R. Schaeffer (1984), 'Person–environment fit, job satisfaction and mental health', *Journal of Occupational Psychology*, **57**, 295–307.
Ganster, D.C., J.S. Schaubroeck, E. Wesley and B.T. Mayes (1991), 'The nomological validity of the Type A personality among employed adults', *Journal of Applied Psychology*, **76**(1), 143–68.
Gidron, Y., K. Davidson and I. Bata (1999), 'The short-term effects of a hostility reduction intervention in CHD patients', *Health Psychology*, **18**, 416–20.
Goldenberg, I. and H. Goldenberg (1985), *Family Therapy: An Overview*, Monterey, CA: Brooks/Cole.
Greenberg, J. (2001), 'The seven loose can(n)ons of organizational justice', in J. Greenberg and R. Cropanzano (eds), *Advances in Organizational Justice*, Stanford, CA: Stanford University Press, pp. 245–72.
Greenwald, A.G. (1992), 'Unconscious cognition reclaimed', *American Psychologist*, **47**, 766–79.
Haley, J. (1964), *Strategies of Psychotherapy*, New York: Grune and Stratton.
Hart, P.M. (1994), 'Teacher quality of work life: integrating work experiences, psychological distress and morale', *Journal of Occupational and Organization Psychology*, **67**, 109–32.
Hart, P.M. and P. Cotton (2002), 'Conventional wisdom is often misleading: police stress within an organizational health framework', in M.F. Dollard, A.H. Winefield and H.R. Winefield (eds), *Occupational Stress in the Service Professions*, London: Taylor & Francis.
Hart, P.M. and A.J. Wearing (1995) 'Occupational stress and well-being: a systematic approach to research, policy and practice', in P. Cotton (ed.), *Psychological Health in the Workplace*, Victoria: The Australian Psychological Society.
Hart, P. M., P. Cotton, A.J. Wearing and C.L. Cooper (forthcoming), 'Stress in the public service: a test of the organizational health framework', manuscript in preparation, University of Melbourne.
Hart, P.M., A.J. Wearing and B. Headey (1993), 'Assessing police work experiences: development of the police daily hassles and uplifts scales', *Journal of Criminal Justice*, **21**, 553–72.
Hart, P.M., M. Conn, N.L. Carter and A.J. Wearing (1993), 'Development of the School Organisational Health Questionnaire: a measure for assessing teacher morale and school organisational climate', paper presented at the Annual Conference of the Australian Association for Research in Education, Fremantle, Western Australia, November.
Headey, B. and A.J. Wearing (1992), *Understanding Happiness: A Theory of Subjective Well-being*, Melbourne: Longman Cheshire.
Heisenberg, W. (1958), *The Physicist's Conception of Nature*, New York: Harcourt, Brace & Company.

Hobfoll, S.E., C.L. Dunahoo, Y. Ben-Porath and J. Monnier (1994), 'Gender and coping: the dual-axis model of coping', *American Journal of Community Psychology*, **22**, 49–82.
Hoffman, L. (1981), *Foundations of Family Therapy*, New York: Basic Books.
Hopkins, A. (1990), 'The social recognition of repetition strain injuries: an Australian/American comparison', *Social Science and Medicine*, **30**(3), 365–72.
Hurrell, J.J. (1985), 'Machine-paced work and the Type A behaviour pattern', *journal of Occupational Psychology*, **58**(1), 15–25.
Jahoda, M. (1982), *Employment and Unemployment: A Social–psychological Analysis*, Cambridge: Cambridge University Press.
Johnson, J.V. and E.M. Hall (1988), 'Job strain, work place social support and cardiovascular disease: a cross-sectional study of a random sample of the Swedish working population', *American Journal of Public Health*, **78**, 1336–42.
Johnson, J.V. and W. Stewart (1993), 'Measuring work organization exposure over the life course with a job-exposure matrix', *Scandinavian Journal of Work, Environment and Health*, **15**, 271–9.
Karasek, R. (1979), 'Job demands, job decision latitude and mental strain: implications for job redesign', *Administrative Science Quarterly*, **24**, 285–308.
Karasek, R. (1990), 'Health risk with increased job control among white-collar workers', *Journal of Organizational Behavior*, May, **11**(3), 171–85.
Karasek, R. and T. Theorell (1990), *Healthy Work: Stress, Productivity and the Reconstruction of Working Life*, New York: Basic Books.
Karasek, R., K. Triantis and S. Chaudry (1982), 'Work group and supervisor support as moderators of association between task characteristics and mental strain', *Journal of Occupational Behavior*, **3**, 181–200.
Kenny, D.T. (1994), 'Determinants of time lost from workplace injury: the impact of the injury, the injured, the industry, the intervention and the insurer', *International Journal of Rehabilitation Research*, **17**(4), 333–42.
Kenny, D.T. (1995a), 'Failures in occupational rehabilitation: a case study analysis', *Australian Journal of Rehabilitation Counselling*, **1**(1), 33–45.
Kenny, D.T. (1995b), 'Case management in occupational rehabilitation: would the real case manager please stand up?', *Australian Journal of Rehabilitation Counselling*, **1**(2), 104–17.
Kipnis, D. (1994), 'Accounting for the use of behavior technologies in social psychology', *American Psychologist*, **49**, 165–72.
Kipnis, D. (1997), 'Ghosts, taxonomies and social psychology', *American Psychologist*, **52**(3), 205–11.
Kitay, J. (1997), 'The labour process: Still stuck? Still a perspective? Still useful?', *EJROT*, **3**(1), 1–8.
Kivimaki, M. and K. Lindstrom (1995), 'Effects of private self-consciousness and control on the occupational stress–strain relationship', *Stress Medicine*, **11**, 7–16.
Kohn, M.L. and C. Schooler (1982), 'Job conditions and personality: a longitudinal assessment of their reciprocal effects', *American Journal of Sociology*, **87**, 1257–86.
Kottage, B.E. (1992), 'Stress in the workplace', *Professional Safety*, **37**(August), 24–6.
Kozma, A., S. Stone and M.J. Stones (1999), 'Stability in components and predictors of subjective well-being (SWB): implications for SWB structure', *Journal of Personality and Social Psychology*, **69**(1), 152–61.
Kuhn, T.S. (1962), *The Structure of Scientific Revolutions*, enlarged 1970 edn, Chicago, University of Chicago Press.
Kulik, C.T., G.R. Oldman and J.R. Hackman (1987), 'Work design as an approach to person–environment fit', *Journal of Vocational Behavior*, **31**, 278–96.
Landsbergis, P.A., S. Schurman, B. Israel, P.L. Schnall, M. Hugentobler, J. Cahill and D. Baker (1993), 'Job stress and heart disease: evidence and strategies for prevention', *New Solutions*, **3**(3), 42–58.
Lazarus, R.S. (1987), 'Individual susceptibility and resistance to psychological stress', in R. Kalimo, M.A. El-Batawi and C. L. Cooper (eds), *Psychosocial Factors at Work*, Geneva: World Health Organization, pp. 127–33.
Lazarus, R.S. (1993), 'Coping theory and research: past, present, and future', *Psychosomatic Medicine*, **55**, 234–47.
Lazarus, R.S. (1999), 'The cognition–emotion debate: a bit of history', in T. Dalgliesh and M.J. Power (eds), *Handbook of Cognition and Emotion*, Chichester, England: Wiley, pp. 3–19.
Lazarus, R.S. (2000), 'Toward better research on stress and coping', *American Psychologist*, **55**(6), 665–73.
Lazarus, R.S. and S. Folkman (1984), *Stress, Appraisal, and Coping*, New York: Springer.
Levi, L. (1999), 'Stress management and prevention on a European community level: options and obstacles', in D.T. Kenny, J.G. Carlson, F.J. McGuigan and J.L. Sheppard (eds), *Stress and Health: Research and Applications*, Australia: Harwood Academic, pp. 229–42.
Mackay, C.J. and C.L. Cooper (1987), Occupational Stress and Health: Some Current Issues, In C.L. Cooper

and I.T. Robertson (eds), *International Review of Industrial and Organizational Psychology*, Chichester, U.K.: John Wiley & Sons.

Mahony, K.L. (2000), 'The multi-causality of occupational stress experienced by on-road ambulance personnel', International Conference on Pre-Hospital Emergency Care 2000, Conrad Jupiters, Gold Coast, Queensland.

Mahony, K.L. (2001a), 'Management and the creation of stressors in an Australian and a UK ambulance service', *Australian Health Review*, **24**(4), 135–45.

Mahony, K.L. (2001b), 'What can we believe in? How a scientific community only got it half wrong in the aetiology of occupational stress', *Electronic Journal of Radical Organisation Theory*, **7**(1), 1–11.

Mahony, K.L. and D. McIntyre (2002), 'From alienation to occupational stress: the case of a corporised ambulance service', XV World Congress of Sociology, paper ID 2668 from <www.sociology2002.com>, Brisbane, Australia.

Marmot, M. (1986), 'Social inequalities in mortality; the social environment', in R. Wilkinson (ed.), *Class and Health: Research and Longitudinal Data*, London: Tavistock.

Marmot, M., G. Davey Smith, S. Stansfeld, C. Patel, F. North, J. Head, I. White, E. Brunner and A. Feeney (1991), 'Health inequalities among British civil servants: the Whitehall II study', *The Lancet*, **337**, 1387–93.

Martin, C.L. and N. Bennett (1996), 'The role of justice judgments in explaining the relationship between job satisfaction and organizational commitment', *Group & Organization Management*, **21**(1), 84–104.

Marx, K. (1954), *The Eighteenth Brumaire of Louis Bonaparte*, 3rd rev. edn, Moscow: Progress Publishers.

Maslach, C. and S. Jackson (1982), 'Burnout in health professionals: a social psychological analysis', in G. Sanders and J. Suls (eds), *Social Psychology of Health and Illness*, Hillsdale, NJ: Erlbaum, pp. 227–51.

Maslach, C. and M.P. Leiter (1997), *The Truth about Burnout*, San Franscisco, CA: Jossey-Bass.

Maslach, C., W.B. Schaufeli and M.P. Leiter (2001), 'Job burnout', *Annual Review of Psychology*, **52**, 397–422.

McCrae, R.R. and P.T. Costa (1991), 'Adding liebe & arbeit: the full five factor model and well-being', *Bulletin of Personality and Social Psychology*, **17**, 227–32.

McCrae, R.R. and P.T. Costa (1994), 'The stability of personality: observations and evaluations', *Current Directions in Psychological Science*, **3**(6), 173–5.

McIntyre, D. (1994), 'Occupational stressors: an insidious form of assault', in C. Waddell and A.R. Petersen (eds), *Just Health: Inequality in Illness, Care and Prevention*, Melbourne: Churchill Livingstone, pp. 61–72.

McIntyre, D. (1998), 'Ontological assumptions about the nature of occupational health research', unpublished conference paper, TASA '98 sociology conference, University of Technology, Queensland.

McIntyre, D. (2002), 'The politics of occupational health: the fate of a stress study that was informed by a labour process perspective', unpublished PhD thesis, The University of Newcastle, NSW, Australia.

McNally, R.J. (2003), 'Progress and controversy in the study of posttraumatic stress disorder', *Annual Review of Psychology*, **54**(1), 1–24.

Meikle, S. (1995), 'Marx and the Stalinist history textbook', *Critique*, **27**, 181–201.

Melamed, S., T. Kushnir and E. Meir (1991), 'Attenuating the impact of job demands: additive vs. interactive effects of perceived control and social support', *Journal of Vocational Behavior*, **39**, 40–53.

Miller, S.M. (1992), 'Individual differences in the coping process: what to know and when to know it', in B.N. Carpenter (ed.), *Personal Coping: Theory, Research and Application*, Westport, CN: Praeger.

Minuchin, S. (1974), *Families and Family Therapy*, Cambridge, MA: Harvard University Press.

Murphy, L.R. (1988), 'Workplace interventions for stress reduction and prevention', in C.L. Cooper and R.L. Payne (eds), *Causes, Coping and Consequences of Stress at Work*, Chichester: Wiley & Sons.

Navarro, V. (1986), *Crisis, Health and Medicine: A Social Critique*, London: Tavistock.

Newton, T. (1995), *Managing Stress: Emotion and Power at Work*, London: Sage.

NIOSH (1999), *Stress at Work* (DHHS Publication No. 99-101), Cincinnati, OH: Author.

O'Driscoll, M.P. and C.L. Copper (1994), 'Coping with work-related stress: a critique of existing measures and proposal for an alternative methodology', *Journal of Occupational and Organizational Psychology*, **67**(4), 343–54.

Ollman, B. (1971), *Alienation: Marx's Conception of Man in Capitalist Society*, Cambridge: Cambridge University Press.

Otto, R. (1985), 'Health damage through work stress: is stress management the answer?', *New Doctor*, **35**(March), 13–15.

Palazzoli, M., L. Boscolo, G. Cecchin and G. Prata (1978), *Paradox and Counter Paradox*, New York: Jason Aronson.

Parkes, K.R. (1994), 'Personality and coping as moderators of work stress processes: models, methods and measures', *Work and Stress*, **8**(2), 110–29.

Patton, M.Q. (1990), *Qualitative Evaluation and Research Methods*, California: Sage Publications.

Paulhus, D.L., B. Fridhandler and S. Hayes (1997), 'Psychological defense: contemporary theory and research', in R. Hogan, J. Johnson and S. Briggs (eds), *Handbook of Personality*, New York: Guilford Press, pp. 236–59.

Payne, R.L., M.M. Jabri and A.W. Pearson (1998), 'On the importance of knowing the affective meaning of job demands', *Journal of Organizational Behavior*, **9**(2), 149–58.
Pearlin, L.I. (1991), 'The study of coping: an overview of problems and directions', in J. Eckenrode (ed.), *The Social Context of Coping*, New York: Plenum Press, pp. 261–76.
Peter, R. and J. Siegrist (1997), 'Chronic work stress, sickness absence, and hypertension in middle managers: general or specific sociological explanations?', *Social Science Medicine*, **45**, 1111–20.
Petersen, A. and D. Lupton (1996), *The New Public Health: Health and Self in the Age of Risk*, Sydney: Allen & Unwin.
Peterson, C.L. (1994), 'Work factors and stress: a critical review', *International Journal of Health Services*, **24**(3), 495–519.
Peterson, C.L. (1999), *Stress At Work: A Sociological Perspective*, Amityville, NY: Baywood Publishing Company.
Peterson, C. and A.J. Stunkard (1989), 'Personal control and health promotion', *Social Scientific Medicine*, **28**(8), 819–28.
Philp, M. (1990), 'Michael Foucault', in Q. Skinner (ed.), *The Return of Grand Theory in the Human Sciences*, Cambridge: Cambridge University Press.
Piedmont, R.L. (1993), 'A longitudinal analysis of burnout in the health care setting: the role of personal dispositions', *Journal of Personality Assessment*, **61**(3), 457–73.
Powell, S. (1997), 'Stress: the distressing news', *The Australian, Features*, 22 October, p. 15.
Proudfoot Consulting (2002), 'Workers slack off – bosses to blame (Jim O'Rourke), *Sun Herald*, 20 October, p. 43.
Quinlan, M. and P. Bohle (1991), *Managing Occupational Health and Safety in Australia: A Multidisciplinary Approach*, Melbourne: Macmillan Education.
Quinlan, M., C. Mayhew and P. Bohle (2001), 'The global expansion of precarious employment, work disorganization and consequences for occupational health: a review of recent research', *International Journal of Health Services*, **31**(2), 335–414.
Reddy, V.S. and P.V. Ramamurti (1991), 'The relation between stress experience on the job, age, personality and general ability', *Psychological Studies*, **36**(2), 87–95.
Rees, D.W. and C.L. Cooper (1992), 'Occupational stress in health workers in the UK', *Stress Medicine*, **8**(2), 79–90.
Remenyi, A. (1992), 'The workplace as a rehabilitating environment', *Proceedings of the First National Australian Society of Rehabilitation Counsellors Conference*, Sydney, Australia: Commonwealth Rehabilitation Service, pp. 1–7.
Rice, P.L. (1999), *Stress and Health*, 3rd edn, Pacific Grove, California: Brooks/Cole.
Ritzer, G. (1993), *The McDonaldization of Society*, Newbury Park, Pine Forge Press.
Robbins, P., T. Waters-Marsh, R. Cacioppe and B. Millett (1994), *Organisational Behavior: Concepts, Controversies and Applications*, Sydney: Prentice-Hall.
Roberts, K. and K.S. Markel (2001), 'Claiming in the name of fairness: organizational justice and the decision to file for workplace injury compensation', *Journal of Occupational Health Psychology*, **6**(4), 332–47.
Rosenman, R.H., G.E. Swan and D. Carmelli (1998), 'Some recent findings relative to the relationship of Type A behavior pattern to coronary heart disease', in S. Maes, C.D. Spielberger, P.B. Defares and I.G. Sarason (eds), *Topics in Health Psychology*, Chichester, New York: John Wiley, pp. 21–9.
Roskies, E., C. Louis-Guerin and C. Fournier (1993), 'Coping with job insecurity: how does personality make a difference?', *Journal of Organizational Behavior*, **14**(7), 617–30.
Rotter, J.B. (1966), 'Generalized expectancies for internal versus external control of reinforcement', *Psychological Monographs*, **80**, 1–28.
Rounds J.B., R.V. Dawis and L.H. Laofquist (1987), 'Measurement of person-environment fit and prediction of satisfaction in the theory of work adjustment', *Journal of Vocational Behavior*, **31**(3), 279–318.
Rousseau, D.M. (1995), *Psychological Contracts in Organizations: Understanding Written and Unwritten Agreements*, Thousand Oaks, CA: Sage.
Scambler, G. and P. Higgs (1999), 'Stratification, class and health: class relations and health inequalities in high modernity', *Sociology*, **33**(2), 275–96.
Schacht, R. (1971), *Alienation*, London: George Allen & Unwin Ltd.
Schaubroeck, J., D. Ganster and M. Fox (1992), 'Dispositional affect and work-related stress', *Journal of Applied Psychology*, **77**(3), 322–35.
Schnall, P., P. Landsbergis and D. Baker (1994), 'Job strain an cardiovascular disease', *Annual Review of Public Health*, **15**, 381–411.
Schwartz, J.E., C.F. Piper and R.A. Karasek (1988), 'A procedure for linking psychosocial job characteristics data to health surveys', *American Journal of Public Health*, **78**, 904–9.
Selye, H. (1975), *The Stress of Life*, rev. edn, New York: McGraw-Hill.

Semmer, N. (1996), 'Individual differences, work stress and health', in M.J. Schabracq *et al.* (eds), *Handbook of Work and Health Psychology*, Chichester: Wiley, pp. 51–86.
Shapiro Jr, D.H., C.E. Schwartz and J.A. Astin (1996), 'Controlling ourselves, controlling our world: psychology's role in understanding positive and negative consequences of seeking and gaining control', *American Psychologist*, **51**(12), 1213–30.
Shedler, J., M. Manis and M. Mayman (1994), 'More illusions', *American Psychologist*, **49**, 975–6.
Siegall, M. and L.L. Cummings (1995), 'Stress and organizational role conflict', *Genetic, Social and General Psychology Monographs*, **121**(1), 65–95.
Siegrist, J. (1996), 'Adverse health effects of high effort–low reward conditions', *Journal of Occupational Health Psychology*, **1**, 27–41.
Siegrist, J. and D. Klein (1990), 'Occupational stress and cardiovascular reactivity in blue-collar workers', *Work & Stress*, **4**, 295–304.
Skinner, B.F. (1953), *Science and Human Behavior*, New York: Macmillan.
Skinner, B.F. (1971), *Beyond Freedom and Dignity*, New York: Knopf.
Sluzki, C.E. (1985), 'A minimal map of cybernetics', *Networker*, May–June, 26.
Snyder, C.R. (1999), 'Coping: where are you going?', in C.R. Snyder (ed.), *Coping: The Psychology of What Works*, New York: Oxford University Press, pp. 324–33
Söderfeldt, B., M. Söderfeldt, C. Muntaner, P. O'Campo, L-E. Warg and C-G. Ohlson (1996), 'Psychosocial work environment in human service organizations: A conceptual analysis and development of the demand-control model', *Social Science and Medicine*, **42**(9), 1217–26.
Somerfield, M.R. and R.R. McCrae (2000), 'Stress and coping research', *American Psychologist*, **55**, 620–25.
Sontag, S. (1978), *Illness as Metaphor*, Harmondsworth: Penguin.
Spector, P.E. (2002), 'Employee control and occupational stress', *Current Directions in Psychological Science*, **11**(4), 128–32.
Spector, P.E. and B.J. O'Connell (1994), 'The contribution of personality traits, negative affectivity, locus of control and Type A to the subsequent reports of job stressors and job strains', *Journal of Occupational and Organizational Psychology*, **67**(1), 1–12.
Spielberger, C.D. and E.C. Reheiser (1994), 'The Job Stress Survey: measuring gender differences in occupational stress', *Journal of Social Behavior and Personality*, **9**(2), 199–218.
Spillane, R. (1984), 'Psychological aspects of occupational stress and workers' compensation', *Journal of Industrial Relations*, **25**(4), 496–503.
Sutherland, V.J. (1993), 'The use of a stress audit', *Leadership and Organization Development Journal*, **14**(1), 22–8.
Sweeney, P.D., D.B. McFarlin and E.J. Inderrieden (1990), 'Using relative deprivation theory to explain satisfaction with income and pay level: a multistudy evaluation', *Academy of Management Journal*, **33**, 423–36.
Taylor, H. and C.L. Cooper (1989), 'The stress-prone personality: a review of the research in the context of occupational stress', *Stress Medicine*, **5**(1), 17–27.
Taylor, S.E. and J.D. Brown (1994), 'Positive illusions and well-being revisited: separating fact from fiction', *Psychological Bulletin*, **116**, 21–7.
Terry, D.J. and N.L. Jimmieson (1999), 'Work control and employee well-being: a decade review', in C.L. Cooper and I.T. Robertson (eds), *International Review of Industrial and Organizational Psychology*, Chichester, UK: John Wiley, pp. 95–148.
Todrank J., G. Heth and E. Somer (2002), 'Characterizing stress tolerance: a new approach to controllability and its relationship to perceived stress and reported health', *Personality and Individual Differences*, **33**(6), 883–95.
Toohey, J. (1993), *Quality of Working Life Project: a Study of Occupational Stress in Commonwealth Government Agencies*, Canberra, Australia: Comcare.
Toohey, J. (1995), 'Managing the stress phenomenon at work', in P. Cotton (ed.), *Psychological Health in the Workplace*, Melbourne: The Australian Psychological Society.
Tremblay, M., B. Sire and D.B. Balkin (2000), 'The role of organizational justice in pay and employee benefit satisfaction, and effects on work attitudes', *Group & Organization Management*, **25**, 269–90.
Uchino, B.N., J.T. Cacioppo and J.K. Kiecolt-Glaser (1996), 'The relationship between social support and physiological processes: a review with emphasis on underlying mechanisms and implications for health', *Psychological Bulletin*, **119**, 488–531.
Watson, D. and L.A. Clark (1984), 'Negative affectivity: the disposition to experience aversive emotional states', *Psychological Bulletin*, **96**, 465–90.
Watson, D., J.W. Pennebaker and R. Folger (1986), 'Beyond negative affectivity: measuring stress and satisfaction in the workplace', *Journal of Organizational Behavior Management*, **8**(2), 141–57.
Weber, H. (1997), 'Sometimes more complex, sometimes more simple', *Journal of Health Psychology*, **2**, 170–71.

Weiss, H.M. and R. Cropanzano (1996), 'Affective events theory: a theoretical discussion of the structure, causes and consequences of affective experiences at work', *Research in Organizational Behavior*, **18**, 1–74.

Willis, E. (1994), 'RSI as a social process', *Illness and Social Relations: Issues in the Sociology of Health Care*, Sydney: Allen & Unwin, pp. 133–50.

Winefield, A.H. (1995), 'Unemployment: its psychological costs', in C.L.Cooper and I.T. Robertson (eds), *International Review of Industrial and Organizational Psychology*, London: Wiley, pp. 169–212.

WorkCover Authority of New South Wales (1997), 'Statistics on Occupational Diseases Claims due to Mental Disorder in NSW, 1991–1996', Sydney: Author.

Zastrow, C. (1984). 'Understanding and preventing burnout', *British Journal of Social Work*, **14**, 141–55.

3 Psychosocial risk factors and work-related stress: state of the art and issues for future research
Michiel A.J. Kompier and Toon W. Taris

Introduction
Every year the results of hundreds, if not thousands, of studies into work stress and its causes and consequences are published. Many of these studies provide interesting insights into the nature of stress at work, and some even present important new insights. On the other hand we believe that many other manuscripts do not make a real contribution to furthering knowledge. In this chapter we will discuss the current status in this research area and issues for future research. It presents our, perhaps somewhat idiosyncratic, ideas as stress researchers, journal editors and reviewers.

The objectives of this chapter are twofold. The first aim is to provide a brief overview of what is known with respect to the psychosocial work environment and stress. We will look at the changing nature of work and at its increasing psychosocial workload. We will also characterize the major risk factors for stress in the psychosocial work environment and comment on the role of individual characteristics and behavioural styles in the interplay between work characteristics, work behaviour and work performance and health outcomes. Legal issues with respect to the psychosocial work environment will also be introduced. On the basis of this overview, the second aim of this chapter is to assess the implications of this 'state of the knowledge' especially for research, but also for policy and practice. The question we will address is, 'where should research in this domain be heading?', simultaneously dealing with the question regarding the directions that we feel should *not* be chosen.

In the context of this chapter it is neither possible nor our intention to provide full answers to these questions. We will sketch what we consider to be the most important lines and, by doing this, try to point out some knowledge-based directions for future research in occupational health psychology.

Current knowledge: where we are now
Stress and the changing nature of work and employment
In the occupational arena, the most striking development over the last decades has been the changing nature of work itself and its increasing psychosocial workload. This development is mirrored in a recent study among 21 500 European employees (Merllie and Paoli, 2000). This study by the European Foundation for the Improvement of Living and Working Conditions provides a recent picture of the prevalence of work-related stress and of some important risk factors. It shows that 27 per cent of these employees report that their health and safety are at risk because of their work. The most common work-related health problems are backache (33 per cent), stress (28 per cent) and fatigue (23 per cent). Today, the same study shows, most European employees work at very high speed (56 per cent) or to

tight deadlines (60 per cent) more than 50 per cent of the time. These percentages are higher when compared with those of 1990 and 1995 (Paoli, 1992, 1997). As most workers are nowadays employed in the service sector, this work pace is primarily dependent on direct demands from clients (67 per cent) and colleagues (48 per cent). Of the employees who continuously work to tight deadlines, 40 per cent report stress and 42 per cent report backache (against 20 per cent and 27 per cent, respectively, of the employees who never work to tight deadlines). From the same study it appears that large numbers of European employees have little job control and autonomy in their work: 36 per cent have no choice over the order of their tasks, 29 per cent have no choice over the pace of their work and 30 per cent have no choice over their methods of work.

These figures do not merely reflect a European phenomenon. Comparable figures are found in a representative sample of 3000 American employees (Bond et al., 1998), where 26 per cent felt emotionally drained from their work, and 26 per cent felt burned out and stressed by their work. This US study also points at another prominent psychosocial risk factor, that is job insecurity and the risk of unemployment. Some 29 per cent of the respondents found it somewhat or very likely that they would lose their current job in the next couple of years. Bond and colleagues also asked questions with regard to work–home interaction, that is the way the work situation influences private life, and vice versa. Whereas 7 per cent of the employees mentioned that family or personal life drained them of the energy they needed to do their job (often or very often), 28 per cent reported having no energy to do things with family or other important people in their lives because of their job (often, very often). This finding, which is quite robust in the literature (see Geurts and Demerouti, 2003, for an overview), suggests that the negative impact of work on one's private life is more powerful than the other way around.

Which developments in the world of work and organizations are behind these figures? Over recent decades the world of work has undergone remarkable changes, and these changes have certainly influenced the psychosocial work environment and, thereby, affected stress at work (see also Sauter et al., 2002; Landsbergis, 2003). Among these developments are the increased utilization of information and communication technology, the rapid expansion of the service sector, the globalization of the economy, the changing structure of the workforce (more women, fewer young, and more highly educated employees), the increasing flexibilization of work, the creation of the 24-hour economy and the utilization of new production concepts (for example, team-based work, telework, downsizing, outsourcing, subcontracting, lean production). Compared with workers 20 years ago, modern employees increasingly work in offices (and less in industry or in agriculture) with information or clients (and less with tangible objects), in teams (and less in isolation), and with less job security. The most striking development is the changing nature of work itself and its increased psychosocial workload. Largely work has changed from manual to mental in nature. Today, for many employees, work poses primarily mental and emotional demands. This change explains why mismatches between work and the worker are increasingly manifested in psychological dysfunctioning and psychosomatic diseases.

Risk factors

Now which factors in work are major risk factors for stress and its consequences for ill-health? There is a wealth of theories and empirical studies on work, stress, motivation and performance. Recent overviews are provided by Cox and colleagues (2000) and by Kompier (2003). Kompier distinguishes seven important theoretical approaches in the field of stress and well-being, job satisfaction and job design:

1. job characteristics model (Hackman and Oldham, 1975);
2. Michigan organization stress model (Caplan *et al.*, 1975; Kahn *et al.*, 1964);
3. job demand control model (Karasek, 1998);
4. sociotechnical approach (for example, De Sitter, 1989; Cherns, 1987);
5. action-theoretical approach (Hacker, 1998; Frese and Zapf, 1994);
6. effort–reward imbalance model (Siegrist, 1996); and
7. vitamin model (Warr, 1996).

With regard to each of these theories, Kompier (2002) discusses (a) the content, that is, the way it relates job characteristics to stress and/or well-being, and/or job satisfaction, (b) the level of analysis (task, position, group or organization), (c) possible principles of job (re)design, and (d) the empirical status and (methodological) criticisms. These theories stem from different schools and research traditions. As a general conclusion it can be stated that substantial support has been found for all seven theories. Although there are also clear differences between them, there is a remarkable overlap between these approaches when it comes to identifying critical job features, that is the factors in the psychosocial work environment that may either cause stress or promote motivation or learning. These critical job characteristics are job demands (six out of seven theories), autonomy (six out of seven theories) and skill variety (six out of seven theories). Other important psychosocial job characteristics are social support (or strongly related concepts) (four out of seven theories), feedback (three), task identity (three) and job future ambiguity (or related constructs such as job insecurity – also part of three theories). Pay (money rewards, availability of money) as an aspect of terms of employment is an important factor in two theories.

These theories teach us that stress and motivation can be regarded as two sides of the same coin. If work provides the right mix of work characteristics (that is, high but not too high demands, skill variety, autonomy, social support and feedback, task identity, not too much job future ambiguity, and proper pay) work stimulates motivation and mental health as well as productive performance. Consequently, healthy work is often also *productive* work. When work does not provide a proper configuration of these work characteristics (for example, too many demands, too little autonomy), it may provoke stress reactions. Stress may be defined as an individual, psychophysiological and subjective state, characterized by the combination of high arousal and displeasure (Kristensen *et al.*, 1998). There is now strong evidence that, in a process of chronic exposure to such risk factors, and insufficient recovery, these reactions (behavioural, psychological, physiological) may lead to serious illness.

Individual characteristics, stress and health
As in other occupational health areas, individual characteristics and behavioural styles of employees do play a role in the complex and dynamic interplay between combinations of work characteristics, work behaviour and health outcomes. It is obvious that the

pathway between the exposure to (combinations of) psychosocial work characteristics and health goes via the individual appraisal of these characteristics. It is also true that people differ in their knowledge, skills, abilities and in their attitudes and preferences. Some people may be more vulnerable to stress than others. Some personality characteristics, such as hardiness, may even have a certain protective value against stressful working conditions. Individual characteristics are often conceptualized as determinants of stress, that is as independent variables or causal factors. They may also strengthen or reduce the impact of psychosocial risk factors on stress reactions and ill-health, that is act as an intervening (moderator) factor. Finally individual characteristics may be conceptualized as an outcome (that is act as a dependent variable) of working in a certain work environment. As is emphasized in two of the aforementioned theories (the job demand control model and action theory) one's personality is at least partly shaped by what we do, and for many people what we do is for an important part of the day performing tasks in the work situation. To give an example, self-efficacy, a much studied personality issue in this field, may not only be an independent factor that influences stress reactions, it may also be the effect of working in stimulating and challenging working conditions. Finally, notwithstanding the fact that there are differences between employees (and therefore stress starts with an individual reaction), we should not forget that there are factors in work that are threatening to most people most of the time. These factors may be regarded as collective stressors and have been discussed above on the basis of the scientific literature.

Legislation on work stress
Given that we now know that particular work characteristics may have an adverse impact on worker stress and health, there is a need for clear legislation regarding psychosocial factors at work. Several European countries have indeed introduced legislation in this respect. The most prominent legal regulation on the quality of working life is the European framework directive on health and safety at work (89/391/EEC, 1993). This framework states, among other things, that the employer has a duty to ensure the safety and health of workers in every aspect related to the work, following general principles of prevention: avoiding risks, evaluating risks which cannot be avoided, combating the risks at source, adapting the work to the individual, especially as regards the design of workplaces, the choice of work equipment and the choice of work and production methods, with a view, in particular, to alleviating monotonous work and work at a predetermined work rate and to reducing their effects on health, and developing a coherent overall prevention policy which covers technology, organization of work, working conditions, social relationships and the influence of factors related to the working environment. This directive also applies to psychosocial job design and work-related well-being (see Levi, 2000, p. 28). A few years ago, the European Parliament took a clear and comparable stand (European Parliament's Resolution A4-0050/99 of 25 February 1999). It considered that work must be adapted to people's abilities and needs and not vice versa, and noted that, by preventing a disparity from arising between the demands of work and the capacities of the workers, it is possible to retain employees until retirement age; it considered that new technologies should be used in order to achieve these aims, drew attention to the problems resulting from a lack of autonomy at the workplace, monotonous and repetitive

work and work with a narrow variety of content, all features which are typical of women's work in particular, and called for attention to be paid to the importance of ergonomics to the improvement of health and safety conditions at the workplace. We may conclude that such national and international legislation underlines the importance of risk assessment and risk management (making work less stressful: that is primary prevention) (Levi, 2000).

Work stress: what do we know?
Let us now try to provide answers to our first question: what is known with respect to the psychosocial work environment and stress? We feel that the general situation is well characterized by Cox and colleagues (2000, p. 10), who conclude that there is a wealth of scientific data on work stress, its causes and effects, and some of the mechanisms underpinning the relationships among these. We may draw four conclusions:

1. occupational stress is a major problem in modern organizations, for both individual employees and for management;
2. we do have good general models on the relations between work factors, personal characteristics and short- and long-term consequences for the individual and the organization;
3. we do know which factors in work are major risk factors for stress and its consequences for ill-health; and
4. there is national and international legislation that underlines the importance of risk assessment and risk management (primary prevention).

Now what could be the implications of these conclusions for future research?

Where should research not be heading?
Before we try to answer the question of where research should be heading, we will first discuss which directions we prefer *not* to be chosen. The four conclusions drawn in the previous section lead us to take three interrelated positions. First, more general research is not needed as it adds little to current knowledge. Second, further expansion of the number of cause–effect studies that are based on cross-sectional study designs and on employees' self-reports adds little to current knowledge. Third, we should not try to compensate for weak study designs by increasing the number of sophisticated statistical analyses; merely substituting (good) statistics for bad ideas adds little to current knowledge.

More general research is not needed
With respect to the first point we can be brief. We argue that new general models on the relations between work, stress and health are often just variations of existing models: old wine in new bottles. There is now enough general knowledge and we do not need more of the same (see also Cox *et al.*, 2000, p. 10). Of course it is always possible to make finer distinctions between, say, different sorts of job demands (for example, emotional demands, time demands and physical demands) or job resources (for example, support from

64 Conceptualization and theoretical framework

colleagues, superiors and friends). While it is not unlikely that fine-tuning the models that are currently available results in somewhat higher percentages of explained variance in the outcome variables than their parent models, it is unlikely that such models lead to any important shift in our understanding of the effects of work characteristics on worker stress and health.

Methodological issues
Our two other points are discussed here in more detail. General stress models are often tested in a cross-sectional study design. As early as 1987, Kasl emphasized the pitfalls of this type of data collection: The sheer volume of studies which has been generated by cross-sectional retrospective designs, in which only self-reports of independent, intervening and outcome variables are correlated to each other, is so enormous that they have created their own standard of acceptable methodology. Journal editors (presumably quite aware of methodological limitations) may be reluctant to put a moratorium on a methodology which was acceptable only yesterday (Kasl, 1987, p. 308). In 1978, the same author demonstrated even less appreciation of cross-sectional study designs, commenting on the plethora of hopeless cross-sectional studies which attack extremely complex issues with the weakest of research designs (Kasl, 1978, p. 3).

Correlation is no causation. Kasl points to the fact that a statistical association between high perceived work demands and self-reported health complaints is usually interpreted as bad work causing bad health (normal causation, from left to right). However people with health complaints may have more problems in coping with their work demands and accordingly report higher demands (reverse causation, from right to left). Both mechanisms may play a role (bidirectional or reciprocal relations). A third variable such as a personality trait may cause both. The association may even be artificial and trivial and a matter of content overlap (work demands: my work is often very demanding; health complaints: I am often tired).

Twenty-five years later, papers of this type are still submitted and many of them are published. What does many an author do? Usually in the manuscripts discussion section, by way of cliché, some standard remarks are made: (1) this research was cross-sectional and based on self-reports; (2) therefore we cannot draw causal inferences; (3) replication using longitudinal data is necessary. In the remainder of the text the author often tends to ignore these restrictions, stating that one variable leads to, has effect on, causes or predicts the other. What the researcher does not admit is that, given the design of the study, it is quite possible that all arrows in his or her research model point from right to left instead of from left to right. In fact, each model that is empirically tested on cross-sectional data is often at least as plausible as the alternative model in which all arrows are reversed. When confronted with these critical remarks, researchers often reply that their model is theory-based, and that the fit indexes are satisfactory. Many researchers tend to ignore the fact that it is often quite possible to think of various other theoretically derived path models, that from a theoretical point of view are just as plausible, but are not tested.

Thirdly, and related to the previous point, we criticize the tendency to correct or even rescue weak study designs by increasing the number of sophisticated statistical analyses. It is a popular myth that sophisticated statistical analyses may compensate for weak study designs. It is interesting to note how methodological semantics has contributed to this present status. Structural equation modelling, for example, quite popular among psychological stress researchers, has originally been labelled 'causal modelling' (Brannick, 1995). Path analysis presupposes the notion of direction, that is from point *a* to point *b*. The assumption is thus temporal ordering, but this assumption is not met in a cross-sectional study design.

Again what does many an author do? Without providing a simple correlation table and a comparison of the average scores on the various scales with reference scores, a lot of fashionable highbrow statistics is presented. In part this is caused by editors and reviewers who demand that simpler methods be replaced by the latest, cutting-edge methods, as if this in and of itself represents advancement of our science (Spector, 2001, p. 24). Many statistical packages are now easily accessible and user-friendly, and sometimes the reader gets the impression that little theoretical, methodological and statistical knowledge is required to try them.

Such concerns about misuse and poor use of methodology in psychology in general (Spector, 2001, p. 23) have led to a report by a special task force on statistical inference of the American Psychological Association (APA, 1996). The committee points out the importance of the analytical parsimony principle: use the simplest methodology that is necessary to meet the research objective. The APA committee argues that the simplest methods have the fewest and least restrictive assumptions, are less prone to error, and that results of simple analyses are easier to communicate. Since the goal of publication is to communicate, this should be a concern (Spector, 2001, p. 24).

In addition to this principle, the APA committee calls for the adoption of three others that should be the basis for everyone's personal research practice: (a) avoid potential misrepresentation of findings (at a minimum the basic statistics: means, standard deviations, ranges and correlations among variables under study should be shown); (b) avoid the use of premature theory (the committee calls for an equal emphasis and respect for descriptive/exploratory versus confirmatory studies); (c) be competent in a computer program before using it (it is recommended that researchers do not use computer programs without understanding the statistical method they are using).

It is a common misunderstanding that scientific progress first and foremost stems from applying methodological designs, standard statistical procedures and variations on a research theme, rather than from clever thinking. It seems that many researchers put the emphasis on a particular methodological context, on examining already existing questions and on refining already existing findings from different angles, instead of taking a fresh look and generating and testing novel ideas. We also do need to bear in mind that *it is the way that the study is designed and the way that the data are collected*, and not the statistical tools, that may permit us to make (causal) inferences. Better knowledge in occupational health psychology is much more likely to come about from simple analyses of good data than from increasingly sophisticated analyses of poor data (see Brannick, 1995, p. 210). This is not to say that, in the field of work, stress and health cross-sectional designs are inherently of little scientific value. That of course depends on the question under study. Aetiological and causality questions cannot be answered with such designs. On the other hand, prevalence questions may well be answered by such cross-sectional designs (see the next section).

Where should research be heading?

Now that we have stressed where we should *not* go, in which directions do we think that research in the field of work, stress and health should go? We feel that there are at least three important directions for future research: aetiology and causality, prevalence and impact, and prevention and intervention.

Aetiology and causality: how questions and micro-processes
In order to better understand the complex and dynamic interplay between work characteristics, personal characteristics, behaviour and health outcomes, we think there is a need for good thinking and original ideas. We also think that there is a need for better designs and better data. Better designs will often be longitudinal and (quasi)-experimental designs.

Longitudinal research, preferably using a full panel design that measures both the independent and the dependent variables at various theoretically chosen points, provides the opportunity to investigate three types of causation: normal, reversed and reciprocal. We should bear in mind that longitudinal designs have their problems too (for example attrition; the process under study may have started before the chosen time span: there always is a Time 0 minus 1), and applying them is in itself no guarantee for making causal inferences We would like longitudinal studies to provide answers to innovative questions, that is, to focus on new insights that may be obtained using such designs. Three possibly interesting and interrelated notions that can be tested using such designs are the effects of prolonged exposure to particular job-related conditions, the issue of subgroup analysis and the issue of reciprocal effects. As regards the first point, longitudinal research in occupational health psychology typically aims to explain the Time 2 score on a particular variable from the Time 1 scores on that variable and other variables, without controlling the amount of exposure to the explanatory variables before Time 1 (that is, the history preceding the Time 1 scores). There seems little interest in work, stress and health research in the effects of prolonged exposure to particular (job-related) conditions, despite the prominent role that chronic or day-to-day exposure plays in most psychosocial theories. Whereas in occupational medicine it is common to include an estimate of the cumulative amount of exposure to X in examining the effects of X on Y (for example, the number of exposure years), as yet such practices are rarely applied in psychosocial longitudinal research.

The second issue relates to studying the total group of employees versus theoretically specified subgroups analysis. Employed workers mostly constitute a relatively healthy subset of the total population. While most employees do not face high levels of adverse working conditions (peak loads), some may face day-to-day working conditions that are tolerable for one day but not for a lifetime. It is probably the long-term, everyday exposure, combined with insufficient coping possibilities and insufficient recovery, that causes disease. This implies that neither the average work score nor the average health score of a large group of (intrinsically healthy) employees will change much over a particular time lag (for example, one year). Indeed, Time 1 and Time 2 overall sample scores may well be interpreted as test–retest scores in such a design, with the test–retest correlation being dependent on the length of the time interval. However this bland impression may conceal the fact that for at least some participants some change may have occurred. At the aggregate level such change may remain undetected; changes occurring for one participant may compensate changes occurring for another. It would thus seem particularly rewarding to focus on specific subgroups of the total sample. Potentially interesting subgroups include participants whose psychosocial work environment changed and participants reporting a change in the dependent variable (for example, a change in health status) and/or independent variables (for example, a change from a low-demand to a high-demand job or vice versa). Other interesting subgroups would include participants reporting long-term exposure to unfavourable job conditions or participants reporting high levels of strain. It would seem likely that closer examination of these (and other) groups would yield more insight into the processes that underlie change in the outcome variables.

The third issue is the current lack of interest in reciprocal effects. Much research in this area examines the effects of job characteristics (as explanatory variables) on health (the outcome variable). However it is often conceivable that health status also affects the (perception of the) characteristics of one's job. Workers may be unable to retain good job conditions because of bad health, or they may perceive their job differently (for example, people may judge their job as more taxing because their resources have been depleted). There is some limited evidence for such effects, but more evidence on the possible effects of health on work characteristics is certainly needed.

More detailed (both experimental and quasi-experimental) studies into work–person–stress–health aetiology may shed more light on various links and loops in the chain. Such (quasi) experimental studies may take place in laboratory and in field settings. We expect that adequate research programmes will increasingly combine laboratory and field studies. Better data means triangulation, that is collecting data from several sources (such as self reports, performance data, psychophysiological data). It is important for future research to combine psychological, behavioural and physiological measures. Leading principles here are triangulation, plausible rival hypothesis, converging and diverging evidence (Kompier and Kristensen, 2000). The inclusion of physiological measures and measures of cognitive functioning is needed to understand better the various pathways between the exposure to certain work characteristics and health outcomes.

Through such longitudinal and more experimental designs and data, and in addition to the existing general stress models, we believe that researchers should focus more on more specific 'how' questions and micro-processes. Such questions may be the following: How, that is via which mechanisms and through which links, do work characteristics influence health? How does actual work behaviour and situation-specific coping influence this relation? How is actual work behaviour influenced in such a process? Such better designed studies may also focus on the positive effects of work on health and performance. Preferably they will treat personality factors not only as independent or moderator variables but also as dependent variables.

Prevalence and impact of changes in the psychosocial work environment
Until now we have argued against a further expansion of cross-sectional study designs as a means to the further increase of expertise on aetiology and causality. We have also noticed that the psychosocial work environment is changing rapidly, and have argued that cross-sectional studies may be adequate for the monitoring of psychosocial working conditions, and for studying prevalence (trends and changes).

In this context we agree with NORA (National Occupational Research Agenda), a research team headed by Sauter (Sauter *et al.*, 2002). Sauter and colleagues conclude that an important future research line should encompass the further development of improved surveillance mechanisms to track better how the organization of work is changing, and to investigate the health and safety implications of these changes in the organization of work. We need to improve the study of changes in the exposure to risk factors. There is a need to study systematically major trends in new forms of work organization, the ways they influence job characteristics (for example, job demands, job control) and their impact on health and performance. We need more detailed accounts on several levels of aggregation: for various countries, for various branches of industry and for various subgroups of workers (males, females, temporary workers and so on). For example, despite growing concern that inexperience resulting from variable and short-term job assignments may place temporary workers at increased risk of illness and injury, few data exist on safety and health outcomes among these workers (ibid., p. vii). We believe that one of the assignments of occupational health psychology should be to fill these gaps.

Prevention and intervention
Finally there is a need to transform the existing body of knowledge in prevention and intervention research. There is a strong need for well-designed and well-implemented prevention and intervention studies. What is the current status with respect to prevention and intervention? Such programmes are predominantly reactive and aimed at individuals. This is surprising and disappointing in view of all that is known on the relationships between the psychosocial work environment and health, and in view of working conditions legislation that puts the emphasis on primary prevention. More recently, though, there is a clear increase in well-documented intervention studies in the psychosocial work environment that aim at improving job design through improving job features. Evidence is growing that interventions do have the potential to be beneficial for both the employee and the company, if they combine a thorough risk assessment, measures that include both the task and the social work environment, ways to deal with stress and a careful approach to implementation (Semmer, 2003).

Acknowledgment
Parts of this chapter are based on two editorials the author(s) wrote in the *Scandinavian Journal of Work, Environment and Health* (SJWEH, 2002, **28**(1), 1–4; SJWEH, 2003, **29**(1), 1–4).

References
American Psychological Association (1996), 'Task Force on Statistical Inference Initial Report' (online available: http://www.apa.org/science/tsfi.html>) 20 October.
Bond, T., E. Galinsky and J.E. Swanberg (1998), *The 1997 National Study of the Changing Workforce*, New York: Families and Work Institute.
Brannick, M. (1995), 'Critical comments on applying covariance structural modeling', *Journal of Organizational Behavior*, **16**, 201–13.
Caplan, R., S. Cobb, J. French and R. Harrison (1975), *Job Demands and Worker Health, Main Effects and Occupational Differences*, Washington: NIOSH.
Cherns, A.B. (1987), 'Principles of sociotechnical design revisited', *Human Relations*, **40**, 153–62.
Cox, T., A. Griffiths and R. Rial Gonzalez (2000), *Research on Work-related Stress*, Bilbao: European Agency for Safety and Health at Work.

Frese, M. and D. Zapf (1994), 'Action as the core of work psychology: a German approach', in H.C. Triandis, M.D. Dunnette and L.M. Hough (eds), *Handbook of Industrial and Organizational Psychology*, volume 4, 2nd edn, Palo Alto, CA: Consulting Psychologists Press, pp. 271–340.
Geurts, S. and E. Demerouti (2003), 'Work/non-work interface: a review of theories and findings', in M. Schabracq, J. Winnubst and C. Cooper (eds), *Handbook of Work and Health Psychology*, Chichester: Wiley, pp. 279–312.
Hacker, W. (1998), *Allgemeine Arbeits- und Ingenieurspsychologie*, Berlin: Deutscher Verlag der Wissenschaften.
Hackman, J.R. and G.R. Oldham (1975), 'Development of the job diagnostic survey', *Journal of Applied Psychology*, **60**, 159–70.
Kahn, R.L., D. Wolfe, R. Quinn, J. Snoek and R. Rosenthal (1964), *Organizational Stress: Studies in Role Conflict and Ambiguity*, New York: Wiley.
Karasek, R.A. (1998), 'Demand/control model: a social, emotional and physiological approach to stress risk and active behaviour development', in J. Stellman (ed.), *Encyclopaedia of Occupational Health and Safety*, Geneva: International Labour Office, 34.6–34.14.
Kasl, S.V. (1978), 'Epidemiological contributions to the study of work stress', in C.L. Cooper and R. Payne (eds), *Stress at Work*, New York: Wiley, pp 3–48.
Kasl, S.V. (1987), 'Methodologies in stress and health: past difficulties, present dilemmas, future directions', in S.V. Kasl and C.L. Cooper (eds), *Stress and Health: Issues in Research and Methodology*, Chichester: John Wiley, pp. 307–18.
Kompier, M. (2003), 'Job design and well-being', in M. Schabracq, J. Winnubst and C. Cooper (eds), *Handbook of Work and Health Psychology*, Chichester: Wiley, pp. 429–54.
Kompier, M. and T.S. Kristensen (2000), 'Organizational work stress interventions in a theoretical, methodological and practical context', in J. Dunham (ed.), *Stress in the Workplace: Past, Present and Future*, London: Whurr Publishers, pp. 164–90.
Kristensen, T.S., M. Kornitzer and L. Alfredson (1998), *Social Factors, Work, Stress and Cardiovascular Disease Prevention in the European Union*, Brussels: The European Heart Network.
Landsbergis, P. (2003), 'The changing organization of work and the safety and health of working people: a commentary', *Journal of Occupational and Environmental Medicine*, **45**(1), 61–72.
Levi, L. (2000), *Guidance on Work-related Stress. Spice of Life or Kiss of Death?*, Luxembourg: Office for Official Publications of the European Communities.
Merllie, D. and P. Paoli (2000), *Ten Years of Working Conditions in the European Union*, Dublin: European Foundation for the Improvement of Living and Working Conditions, Loughlinstown House.
Paoli, P. (1992), *First European Survey on the Work Environment 1991–1992*, Dublin: European Foundation for the Improvement of Living and Working Conditions, Loughlinstown House.
Paoli, P. (1997), *Second European Survey on the Work Environment 1991–1992*, Dublin: European Foundation for the Improvement of Living and Working Conditions, Loughlinstown House.
Sauter, S. et al. (2002), *The Changing Organization of Work and the Safety and Health of Working People*, Cincinnati: NIOSH.
Semmer, N. (2003), 'Job stress interventions and organization of work', in J.C. Quick and L.E. Tetrick (eds), Handbook of Occupational Health Psychology, Washington DC: American Psychological Association, pp. 325–53.
Siegrist, J. (1996), 'Adverse health effects of high effort–low reward conditions at work', *Journal of Occupational Health Psychology*, **1**, 27–43.
Sitter, L.U. de (1989), 'Moderne sociotechniek' (Modern sociotechnics), *Gedrag en Organisatie*, **2**, 222–51.
Spector, P.E. (2001), 'Research methods in industrial and organizational psychology: data collection and data analysis with specific consideration to international issues', in N. Anderson, D.S. Ones, H.D. Sinangil and C. Viswesvaran (eds), *Handbook of Industrial, Work & Organizational Psychology*, London: Sage, pp. 10–26.
Warr, P. (1996), 'Employee well-being', in P. Warr (ed.), *Psychology at Work*, 4th edn, London: Wiley.

4 Biological basis of stress-related diseases
Maria-Alexandra Magiakou and George P. Chrousos

Introduction
'Stress' is a state of disharmony or threatened homeostasis. The concepts of stress and homeostasis can be traced back to ancient Greek history, however, the integration of these notions with related physiological and pathophysiological mechanisms and their association with specific illnesses are much more recent (Chrousos and Gold, 1992).

Life exists by maintaining a complex dynamic equilibrium or homeostasis that is constantly challenged by intrinsic or extrinsic adverse forces, the stressors (Chrousos and Gold, 1992). Under favorable conditions and under the influence of controllable stressors, individuals can be involved in pleasurable functions that enhance their emotional and intellectual growth and development and the survival of their species. In contrast, activation of the stress response during threatening situations that are beyond the control of the individual can be associated with dysphoria and eventually mental and/or somatic disease (Chrousos, 1992; Tsigos and Chrousos, 1994, 2002).

Both physical and emotional stressors set into motion central and peripheral physiological responses designed to preserve homeostasis (Table 4.1) (Chrousos and Gold, 1992). Hence every element of the stress response, including that originating from an inflammatory/immune reaction, must briskly respond to restraining forces, otherwise these responses will lose their adaptive quality and contribute to the process of pathological change.

Stress system physiology and regulation of the stress response
The stress system is defined as a discrete, dedicated system evolved specifically for the coordination of the general adaptation response. Its two principal components are the corticotrophin-releasing hormone (CRH) and the locus ceruleus-norepinephrine (LC-NE)/ autonomic (sympathetic) nervous systems and their peripheral effectors, the pituitary – adrenal axis and the limbs of the autonomic system (Chrousos and Gold, 1992). The brain circuits that intitiate and maintain the stress response are illustrated in Figure 4.1, which is a simplified, heuristic representation of the central and peripheral components of the stress system, their functional interrelations and their relations to other central systems involved in the stress response. The hypothalamic corticotropin-releasing hormone (CRH) neuron in the paraventricular nucleus and the centers of the arousal and autonomic systems in the brain stem represent major centers of this system connected anatomically and functionally to each other. Solid lines indicate stimulation and dashed lines indicate inhibition.

The central control stations of the stress system are located in the hypothalamus and the brain stem and include the parvocellular CRH and arginine-vasopressin (AVP) neurons of the paraventricular nuclei (PVN) of the hypothalamus, and the (LC-NE)

Table 4.1 Behavioral and physical adaptation during stress

Behavioral Adaptation

Adaptive redirection of behavior
Acute facilitation of adaptive and inhibition of nonadaptive neural pathways
   Increased arousal, alertness
   Increased cognition, vigilance and focused attention on stressor
   Suppression of feeding behavior, digestion
   Suppression of reproductive behavior
   Containment of the stress response

Physical Adaptation

Adaptive redirection of energy
   Oxygen and nutrients directed to the central nervous system and stressed body site (s)
   Altered cardiovascular tone, increased blood pressure and heart rate
   Increased respiratory rate
   Increased gluconeogenesis and lipolysis
   Increased colonic activity
   Detoxification from toxic products
   Inhibition of growth and reproductive systems
   Containment of the stress response
   Containment of the inflammatory/immune response

Source: Adapted from Chrousos and Gold (1992).

autonomic nervous system. The hypothalamic-pituitary-adrenal (HPA) axis, together with the efferent sympathetic/adrenomedullary system, represent the effector limbs, via which the brain influences all body organs during exposure to threatening stimuli (Figure 4.1) (Chrousos, 1992; Tsigos and Chrousos, 1994, 2002).

The hypothalamus controls the secretion of corticotropin (ACTH) from the anterior pituitary which, in turn, stimulates the secretion of glucocorticoids by the adrenal cortex. The principal hypothalamic stimulus to the pituitary–adrenal axis is CRH, a 41 amino acid peptide first isolated and sequenced by W. Vale *et al.* in 1981. AVP acts synergistically with CRH in stimulating ACTH secretion; however, it has little ACTH secretagogue activity alone (Lambert *et al.*, 1984). Furthermore it appears that there is a reciprocal positive interaction between CRH and AVP at the level of the hypothalamus, with each neuropeptide stimulating the secretion of the other.

In nonstressful situations, both CRH and AVP are secreted in the portal system in a circadian, pulsatile fashion, with a frequency of about two to three secretory episodes per hour (Engler *et al*., 1989). Under resting conditions, the amplitude of the CRH and AVP pulses increases in the early morning hours. These diurnal variations are perturbed by changes in lighting, feeding schedules and activity and are disrupted by stress. During acute stress, the amplitude and synchronization of the CRH and AVP pulsations in the hypophyseal portal system markedly increase, resulting in increases of ACTH and cortisol secretory episodes (Tsigos and Chrousos, 1994, 2002). Depending on the type of stress,

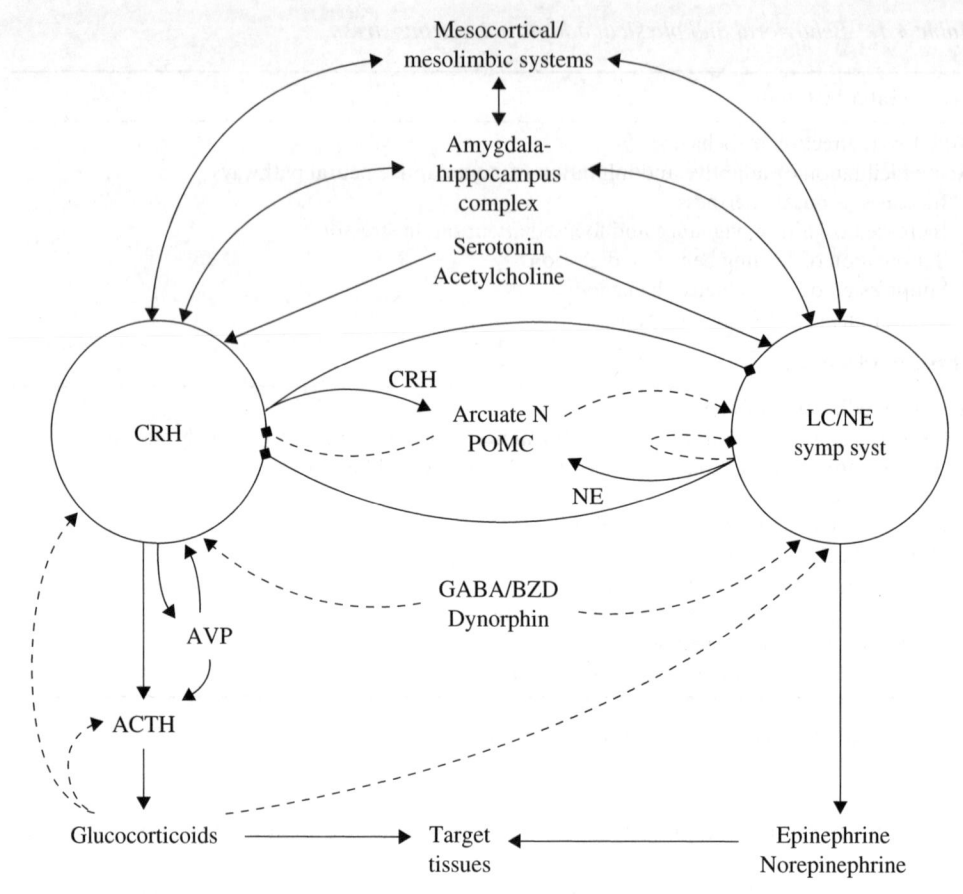

72 *Conceptualization and theoretical framework*

Notes: POMC: proopiomelanocortin; LC/NE symp syst: locus ceruleus-norepinephrine/ sympathetic system; AVP: arginine vasopressin; GABA: γ-aminobutyric acid, BZD: benzodiazepine; ACTH: corticotropin.

Source: Adapted from Chrousos and Gold (1992).

Figure 4.1   Brain circuits

other factors such as AVP of magnocellular neuron origin, angiotensin II and various cytokines and lipid mediators of inflammation are secreted and act on hypothalamic, pituitary and/or adrenal components of the HPA axis, potentiating its activity (Philips, 1987).

Shortly after its isolation, it became apparent that CRH was implicated in several components of the stress response, such as arousal and autonomic activity. Supportive evidence was derived from intracerebroventricular or selective brain administration of CRH in rodents and nonhuman primates, which precipitated several coordinated responses characteristic of stress (Shibasaki *et al.*, 1993), whereas brain administration of CRH peptide antagonists suppressed many aspects of the stress response. Finally CRH type 1 receptor knockout mice had a marked deficiency in mounting an effective stress response (Smith et al., 1998).

CRH and its receptors were found in many sites in the brain outside the hypothalamus, including parts of the limbic system and the central arousal sympathetic systems (LC-sympathetic systems) in the brain stem and spinal cord (Turnbull and Rivier, 1997). Stress activates CRH release from the hypothalamus and some extrahypothalamic sites through still unclear mechanisms (Chrousos, 1998). CRH-binding sites were also found in various peripheral tissues, such as the adrenal medulla, heart, prostate, gut, liver, kidney, uterus, ovaries and testes (Chrousos et al., 1998). The CRH receptors belong to the G-protein-coupled receptor superfamily, and two distinct subtypes have been characterized: CRH-R1 found mainly in the anterior pituitary and also widely distributed in the brain, and CRH-R2 expressed mainly in the heart, the peripheral vasculature and also in subcortical structures in the brain (Turnbull and Rivier, 1997; Wong et al., 1994).

The locus ceruleus and other noradrenergic cell groups of the medulla and pons are collectively known as the locus ceruleus-norepinephrine (LC-NE) system. Brain epinephrine serves globally as an alarm system that decreases neurovegetative functions, such as eating and sleeping, and contributes to accompanying increases in autonomic and neuroendocrine responses to stress, including HPA axis activation (Chrousos, 1998). NE also activates the amygdala, the principal brain locus for fear-related behaviors, and enhances the long-term storage of aversively charged emotional memories in sites such as the hippocampus and striatum.

There are many potential sites of interaction among the different components of the stress system shown in Figure 4.1. Reciprocal neural connections exist between the CRH and LC-NE neurons of the central stress system, with CRH and norepinephrine stimulating each other, the latter primarily through α1-noradrenergic receptors (Chrousos, 1998; Tsigos and Chrousos, 1994). There is an ultra-short autoregulatory negative feedback loop on the CRH neurons exerted by CRH itself, just like a similar loop in the LC-NE neurons, by way of presynaptic CRH and a2-noradrenergic receptors, respectively. There is also parallel regulation of both central components of the stress system by other stimulatory and inhibitory neuronal pathways. Several neurotransmitters, including serotonin and acetylcholine, excite CRH and the LC/NE neurons (Chrousos, 1998). The negative feedback controls, include glucocorticoids, γ-amino-butyric acid (GABA), corticotropin and several opioid peptides, which inhibit both the CRH and LC-NE neurons (Calogero et al., 1988).

Three major brain systems are activated by the stress system and, in turn, influence its activity (Figure 4.1). First, the mesocortical and mesolimbic dopamine systems are activated by the LC-NE/sympathetic systems during stress. The former innervates the prefrontal cortex, a brain region involved in anticipatory phenomena and cognitive function, and the latter is closely linked to the nucleus accumbens, which plays a principal role in motivational/reinforcement/reward phenomena. Second, the amygdala/ hippocampus complex is activated during stress, primarily by noradrenergic neurons or by an incoming 'emotional' stressor (for example fear). Activation of the amygdala by the LC-NE/sympathetic system is important for retrieval and emotional analysis of information pertinent to the stressor and, if the stressor is emotional, for stimulation of the activity of the PVN/CRH and LC-NE/sympathetic systems. The hippocampus has a major inhibitory influence on the activity of the amygdala and the PVN/CRH system.

Third, activation of CRH neurons in the PVN leads to activation of arcuate proopiomelanocortin neurons that send projections to the PVN and brain stem and other brain areas to counterregulate CRH neuron and LC-NE/sympathetic system activity, induce opioid receptor-mediated stress-related analgesia, and, perhaps, influence the emotional tone (Chrousos and Gold, 1992; Tsigos and Chrousos, 2002).

The peripheral effectors of the stress system are the pituitary–adrenal axis and the limbs of the autonomic system. Circulating ACTH is the key regulator of glucocorticoid secretion by the adrenal cortex. Other hormones or cytokines, either originating from the adrenal medulla or coming from the systemic circulation, as well as neuronal information from the autonomic innervation of the adrenal cortex, may also participate in the regulation of cortisol secretion (Hinson, 1990; Ottenweller, 1982). Glucocorticoids participate in the control of whole body homeostasis and the organism's response to stress, and play a key regulatory role in the basal activity of the HPA axis and on the termination of the stress response, by acting at extrahypothalamic centers, the hypothalamus and the pituitary gland (de Kloet, 1991). The inhibitory glucocorticoid feedback on the ACTH secretory response acts to limit the duration of the total tissue exposure to glucocorticoids, minimizing the catabolic, antireproductive and immunosuppressive effects of these hormones. Glucocorticoids exert their effects through their ubiquitous cytoplasmic receptors (Smith and Toft, 1993).

The autonomic nervous system provides a rapidly responsive mechanism to control a wide range of functions (Tsigos and Chrousos, 1994, 2002). Cardiovascular, respiratory, gastrointestinal, renal, endocrine and other systems are regulated by the sympathetic or the parasympathetic nervous system or both (Gilbey and Spyer, 1993). Interestingly the parasympathetic system may assist sympathetic functions by withdrawing and can antagonize them by increasing its activity. Sympathetic innervation of peripheral organs is derived from the efferent preganglionic fibers, whose cell bodies lie in the intermediolateral column of the spinal cord. These nerves synapse in the bilateral chains of sympathetic ganglia with postganglionic sympathetic neurons that richly innervate the smooth muscle of the vasculature, the heart, skeletal muscles, kidney, gut, fat and many other organs. The preganglionic neurons are cholinergic, whereas the postganglionic ones are mostly noradrenergic.

The sympathetic system provides most of the circulating epinephrine and some of the norepinephrine from the adrenal medulla. In addition to the classic neurotransmitters acetylcholine and norepinephrine, both sympathetic and parasympathetic subdivisions of the autonomic nervous system contain several subpopulations of target-selective and neurochemically coded neurons that express a variety of neuropeptides and, in some cases, ATP, nitric oxide (Benaroch, 1994), or lipid mediators of inflammation. Interestingly CRH, neuropeptide Y (NPY) and somatostatin are colocalized in noradrenergic vasoconstrictive neurons. Transmission in sympathetic ganglia is also modulated by neuropeptides released from preganglionic fibers and short interneurons (for example enkephalin, neurotensin), as well as from primary afferent collaterals (for example substance P) (Elfvin et al., 1993).

Body systems' responses to stress
Interactions of the HPA axis with gonadal, growth and thyroid axes
The systems responsible for reproduction, growth and thyroid function are directly linked to the stress system, and each is profoundly influenced by the effectors of the stress response. See Figure 4.2, which is a simplified heuristic representation of the interactions between the hypothalamic–pituitary–adrenal axis and other neuroendocrine systems including the reproductive axis (A), the growth and thyroid axis (B), and the immune system (C). Solid lines indicate stimulation and dashed lines indicate inhibition. The reproductive axis is inhibited at all levels by various components of the HPA axis (Chrousos et al., 1998). (Figure 4.2A). Either directly or via β-endorphin, CRH suppresses the luteinizing hormone-releasing hormone (LHRH) neuron of the arcuate nucleus of the hypothalamus. Glucocorticoids, on the other hand, exert inhibitory effects at the level of the LHRH neuron, the pituitary gonadotroph, and the gonad itself and render target tissues of sex steroids resistant to these hormones (Chrousos and Gold, 1992; Tsigos and Chrousos, 2002). Suppression of gonadal function caused by chronic HPA axis activation has been demonstrated in highly trained athletes of both sexes, ballet dancers and individuals with anorexia nervosa or starvation. During inflammatory stress, cytokines suppress reproductive function directly and indirectly by activating hypothalamic secretion of CRH and POMC-derived peptides, as well as by peripheral elevations of glucocorticoids and inhibition of steroidogenesis at both ovaries and testes (Rivier and Rivest, 1991).

The interaction between CRH and the gonadal axis appears to be bidirectional. Thus the presence of estrogen-responsive elements has been demonstrated in the promoter area of the CRH gene, and direct stimulatory estrogen effects have been demonstrated on CRH gene expression (Vamvakopoulos and Chrousos, 1993).The growth axis is also inhibited at many levels during stress (Figure 4.2B). Although an acute elevation of growth hormone (GH) concentration is usually observed during the onset of the stress response in man, prolonged activation of the stress system leads to suppression of GH secretion and inhibition of somatomedin C and other growth factor effects on their target tissues. Increases in somatostatin secretion stimulated by CRH, with resultant inhibition of GH secretion, as well as direct glucocorticoid effects – acutely stimulatory but chronically inhibitory – on GH secretion have been implicated as potential mechanisms for the stress-related suppression of GH secretion (Burguera et al., 1990; Casanueva et al., 1990; Dieguez et al., 1988; Magiakou et al., 1994a, b; Magiakou and Chrousos, 2002; Ono et al., 1984; Rivier and Vale, 1985; Unterman and Phillips, 1985).

A corollary phenomenon to growth axis suppression is the stress-related inhibition of thyroid axis function. Stress is associated with decreased production of thyroid-stimulating hormone (TSH) and inhibition of conversion of the relatively inactive thyroxine to the more biologically active triiodothyronine in peripheral tissues (the 'euthyroid sick' syndrome). Both phenomena may be caused by the increased levels of glucocorticoids and may serve to conserve energy during stress (Benker et al., 1990; Stratakis et al., 1997). Inhibition of TRH and TSH secretion by CRH-stimulated increases in somatostatin might also participate in the central component of thyroid axis suppression during stress. In the case of inflammatory stress, inhibition of TSH secretion might in part be due to the action of cytokines both on the hypothalamus and on the pituitary (Tsigos et al., 1997).

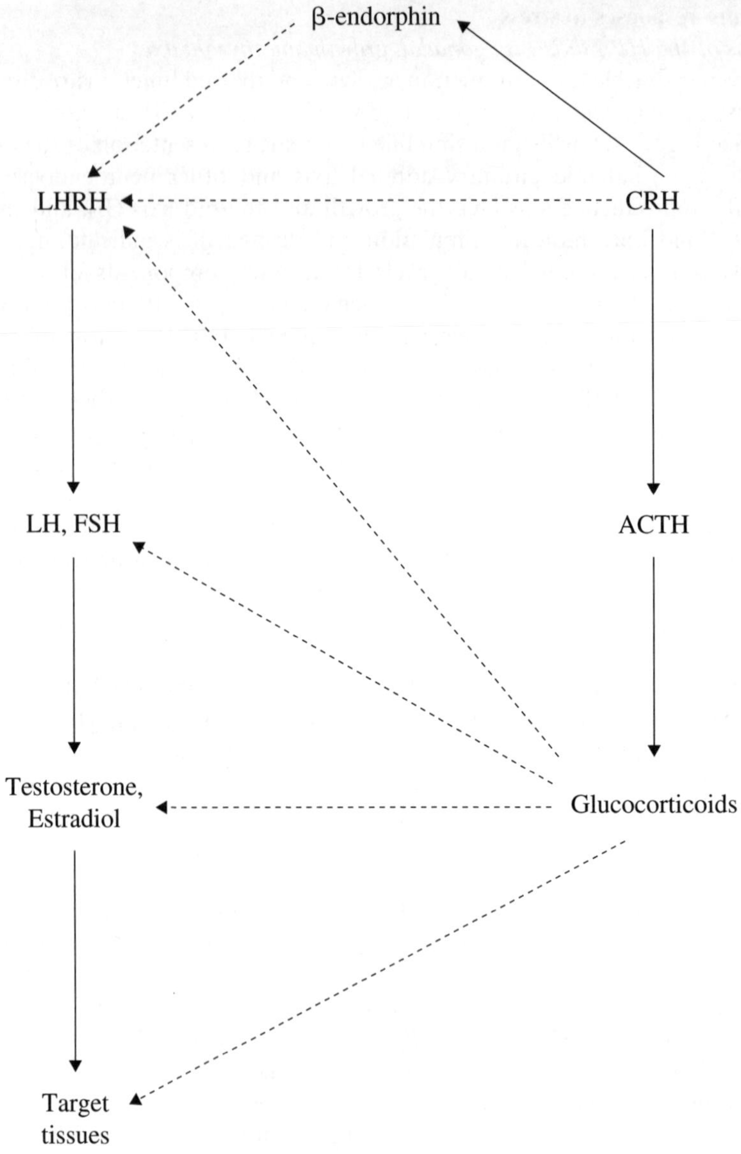

76   *Conceptualization and theoretical framework*

```
                    β-endorphin
                   ↙          ↖
              LHRH ◀------------------- CRH
               │  ↖
               │    ╲
               ▼     ╲
            LH, FSH   ╲
               │  ◀╌╌╌ ╲            ACTH
               │        ╲            │
               │         ╲           │
               ▼          ╲          ▼
          Testosterone, ◀╌╌╌╌╌╌╌╌╌ Glucocorticoids
            Estradiol              ╱
               │                  ╱
               ▼                 ╱
            Target ◀╌╌╌╌╌╌╌╌╌╌╌
            tissues
```

Notes: LHRH: luteinizing hormone-releasing hormone; CRH: corticotropin-releasing hormone; LH: luteinizing hormone; FSH: follicle-stimulating hormone; ACTH: corticotropin.

Source: Adapted from Chrousos and Gold (1992).

Figure 4.2A   Reproduction

Biological basis of stress-related diseases 77

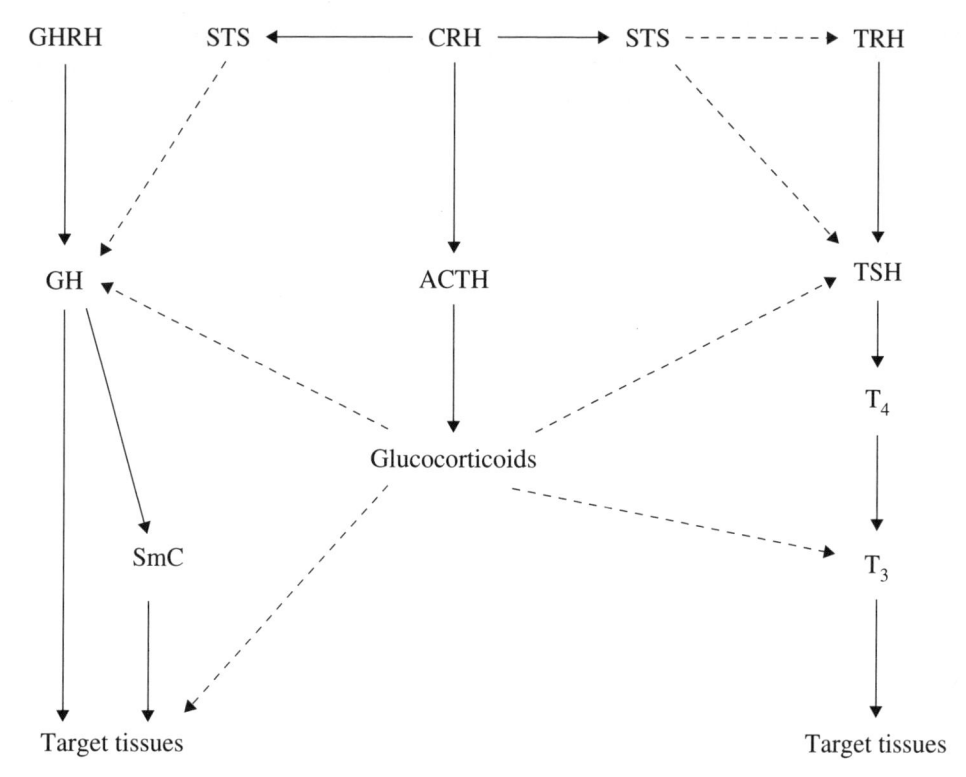

```
GHRH        STS ←————— CRH —————→ STS -------→ TRH
  │        ╱                                      ╲
  │       ╱                                        ╲
  ↓      ╱                                          ↓
  GH ←--                    ACTH                   TSH
  │ ╲                        │                      │
  │  ╲                       │                      ↓
  │   ╲                      ↓                     T₄
  │    ╲              Glucocorticoids               │
  ↓     ╲          ╱              ╲                 │
  SmC    ╲--------                  ------→        T₃
  │                                                 │
  ↓                                                 ↓
Target tissues                               Target tissues
```

Notes: CRH: corticotropin-releasing hormone; ACTH: corticotropin; GHRH: growth hormone-releasing hormone; STS: somatostatin; TRH: thyrotropin-releasing hormone; GH: growth hormone; TSH: thyroid-stimulating hormone; T4: thyroxine; SmC: somatomedin C; T3: triiodothyronine.

Source: Adapted from Chrousos and Gold (1992).

Figure 4.2B Growth and thyroid function

Interactions of the HPA axis with the immune system
It has been shown for several decades that stress is associated with concurrent activation of the HPA axis. In the early 1990s it also became apparent that cytokines and other humoral mediators of inflammation are potent activators of the central stress response, constituting the afferent limb of the feedback loop through which the immune/inflammatory system and the CNS communicate (Chrousos, 1995).

Most stimulatory effects from the immune system are exerted by the inflammatory cytokines tumor necrosis factor-α (TNFα), interleukin 1β (IL-1β), and IL-6, or by mediators of inflammation such as several eicosanoids, platelet-activating factor and serotonin on hypothalamic CRH secretion via auto/paracrine and/or endocrine effects (Bernardini *et al.*, 1989a, b; Bernardini *et al.*, 1990; Chrousos, 1995; Naito *et al.*, 1988; Sapolsky *et al.*, 1987). All three inflammatory cytokines can cause stimulation of the HPA axis alone, or in synergy with each other, and IL-6 is believed to play the major role in the immune stimulation of the axis (Chrousos, 1995; Tsigos *et al.*, 1997). Some of the activating effects of

78 *Conceptualization and theoretical framework*

cytokines on the HPA axis may be exerted indirectly by stimulation of the central catecholaminergic pathways. Also activation of peripheral nociceptive, somatosensory and visceral afferent fibers would lead to stimulation of both the catecholaminergic and CRH neuronal systems via ascending spinal pathways. Direct effects of the three inflammatory cytokines and the other mediators of inflammation on adrenal glucocorticoid secretion might also be present.

Conversely activation of the HPA axis has profound inhibitory effects on the inflammatory/immune response because virtually all the components of the immune response are inhibited by cortisol (Figure 4.2C). Alterations of leucocyte traffic and function, decreases in production of cytokines and mediators of inflammation, and inhibition of the latter's effects on target tissues are among the main immunosuppressive effects of

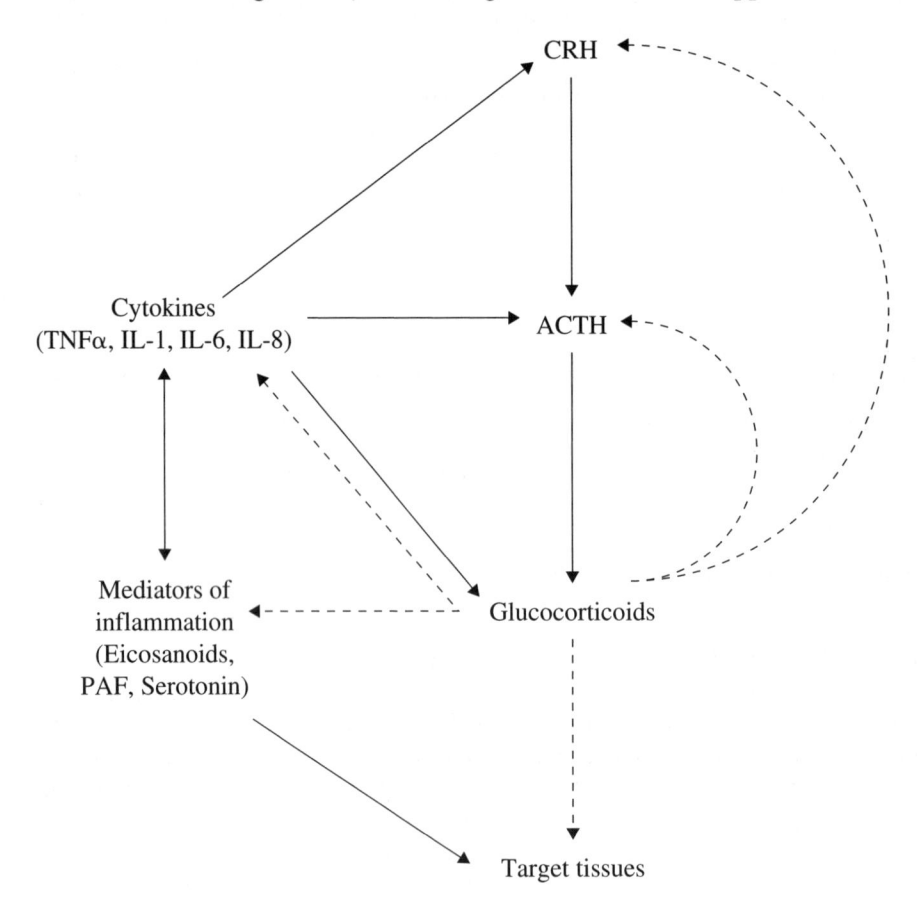

Notes: CRH: corticotropin-releasing hormone; ACTH: corticotropin; IL-1: interleukin 1; IL-6: interleukin 6; TNF: tumor necrosis factor; PAF: platelet-activating factor.

Source: Adapted from Chrousos and Gold (1992).

Figure 4.2C Immune function

glucocorticoids (Chrousos, 1995; Munck and Guyre, 1986; Munck et al., 1984; Tsigos et al., 1997).

The efferent sympathetic/adrenomedullary system apparently participates in a major fashion in the interactions of the HPA axis and the immune/inflammatory reaction by being reciprocally connected with the CRH system, by receiving and transmitting humoral and nervous immune signals from the periphery, by densely innervating both primary and secondary lymphoid oprgans and by reaching all sites of inflammation via the post-ganglionic sympathetic neurons (Elenkov et al., 1999). When activated during stress, the autonomic system exerts its own direct effects on immune organs, which can be immunosuppressive, or both immunopotentiating and anti-inflammatory.

The influence of the HPA axis on metabolism
Glucocorticoids directly inhibit pituitary GH, gonadotropin and thyrotropin secretion and make the target tissues of sex steroids and growth factors resistant to these hormones. Thus glucocorticoids antagonize the beneficial actions of GH and sex steroids on fat tissue (lipolysis) and muscle and bone anabolism (Chrousos, 2000). Chronic activation of the stress system would be expected to increase visceral adiposity, decrease lean body (muscle and bone) mass, and suppress osteoblastic activity (Figure 4.3). Interestingly the phenotype of central obesity and decreased lean body mass is present in patients with Cushing syndrome and some patients with the combined diagnosis of melancholic depression or chronic anxiety disorder and the metabolic syndrome (visceral adiposity, insulin resistance, dyslipidemia, hypertension) or 'pseudo-Cushing syndrome' (Chrousos, 2000).

Also, since glucocorticoids induce insulin resistance, and increased hepatic gluconeogenesis is a characteristic feature of the stress response, activation of the HPA axis may contribute to the poor control of diabetic patients during periods of emotional stress, or those with inflammatory and other diseases (Roy et al., 1993; Tsigos et al., 1997).

Obese subjects with psychiatric manifestations ranging from those of melancholic depression to anxiety with perception of 'uncontrollable' stress frequently have mild hypercortisolism, while carefully screened obese subjects without such manifestations are eucortisolemic (Tsigos and Chrousos, 1994). The former may have stress-induced glucocorticoid-mediated visceral obesity and metabolic syndrome manifestations, which in the extreme may be called a pseudo-Cushing state that needs to be differentiated from frank Cushing syndrome (Papanicolaou et al., 1998; Yanovski et al., 1993). Stress-induced hypercortisolism and visceral obesity and their cardiovascular and other sequelae increase the all-cause mortality risk of affected subjects by two to three times and curtail their life expectancy by several years (Tsigos and Chrousos, 2002).

Pathophysiology of the stress system
Generally the stress response is meant to be acute or at least of a limited duration. The time-limited nature of this process renders its accompanying antianabolic, catabolic and immunosuppressive effects temporarily beneficial and with no adverse consequences. Chronicity and excessiveness of stress system activation, on the other hand, would lead to the syndromal state that Selye described in 1936 (Selye, 1936). Because CRH coordinates behavioral, neuroendocrine and autonomic adaptation during stressful situations,

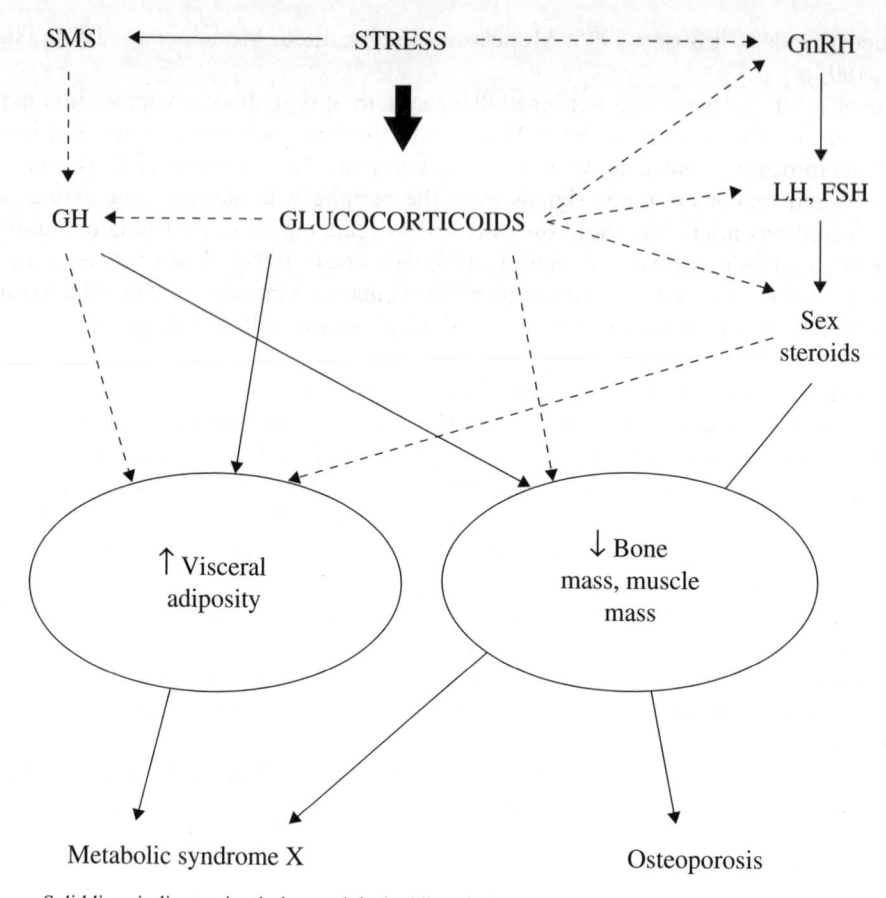

80 *Conceptualization and theoretical framework*

Notes: Solid lines indicate stimulation and dashed lines indicate inhibition.

Source: Adapted from Tsigos and Chrousos (2002).

Figure 4.3 Detrimental effect of chronic stress on adipose tissue, metabolism and bone mass

increased and prolonged production of CRH could explain the pathogenesis of the syndrome (Chrousos, 1998).

The disorders associated with dysregulation of the stress system (hyper- or hypo activation of the HPA axis) are shown in Table 4.2. The prototypic example of chronic hyperactivation of the stress system (both HPA axis and LC-NE system) is manifested in melancholic depression, with dysphoric hyperarousal and relative immunosuppression (Gold and Chrousos, 2002; Gold *et al.*, 1988a, b). In this situation cortisol excretion is increased and plasma ACTH response to exogenous CRH decreased. Hypersecretion of CRH has been shown in melancholic depression and suggests that CRH may participate in the initiation or perpetuation of a vicious cycle. Owing to chronically hyperactive stress, patients with melancholic depression may sustain several severe somatic sequelae, such as osteoporosis, metabolic syndrome features, varying degrees of atherosclerosis, innate and

Table 4.2 *Disorders associated with dysregulation of the stress system*

Increased stress system activity	Decreased stress system activity
Severe chronic disease	Atypical depression
Anorexia nervosa	Seasonal depression
Melancholic depression	Chronic fatigue syndrome
Panic disorder	Premenstrual tension syndrome
Obsessive–compulsive disorder	Postpartum depression
Chronic active alcoholism	Climacteric depression
Alcohol and narcotic withdrawal	Fibromyalgia
Chronic excessive exercise	Hypothyroidism
Malnutrition	Nicotine withdrawal
Hyperthyroidism	Obesity ('hyposerotonergic' forms)
Vulnerability to addiction (rats)	Posttraumatic stress disorder
	Vulnerability to inflammatory disease (Lewis rat)
	Rheumatoid arthritis
	Adrenal suppression

Source: Adapted from Chrousos and Gold (1992).

T-helper 1-directed immunosuppression and certain infectious and neoplastic diseases (Elenkov and Chrousos, 1999). When not treated, these patients have a compromised life expectancy curtailed by 15–20 years after excluding suicides (Chrousos, 1998).

Also a wide spectrum of other conditions may be associated with increased and prolonged activation of the HPA axis (Table 4.2), including anorexia nervosa with or without malnutrition, obsessive–compulsive disorder, panic anxiety, chronic active alcoholism, alcohol and narcotic withdrawal, excessive exercising, poorly controlled diabetes mellitus, childhood sexual abuse, hyperthyroidism and the premenstrual tension syndrome (Chrousos and Gold, 1992; Tsigos and Chrousos, 2002).

Another group of states is characterized by hypoactivation of the stress system, rather than sustained activation, in which chronically reduced secretion of CRH may result in pathological hypoarousal (Table 4.2). Patients with atypical depression, the chronic fatigue syndrome, fibromyalgia and hypothyroidism fall in this category (Chrousos, 1998; Gold and Chrousos, 2002). Also nicotine withdrawal has been associated with decreased cortisol and catecholamine secretion. The decreased CRH secretion in the early period of nicotine abstinence could explain the increased appetite and weight gain frequently observed in these patients. Similarly, in Cushing syndrome, the clinical picture of atypical depression, hyperphagia, weight gain, fatigue and anergia is consistent with suppression of the CRH neuron by the associated hypercortisolism. The periods after cure of hypercortisolism or following cessation of chronic stress and the postpartum period are also associated with atypical depression, suppressed CRH secretion and decreased HPA axis activity (Chrousos, 1998).

In the case of inflammatory stimuli, an excessive HPA axis response to them would mimic the stress of hypercortisolemic state and would lead to increased susceptibility of the individual to a host of infectious agents or tumors as a result of T-helper-1 suppression, but enhanced resistance to autoimmune/inflammatory disease (Elenkov et al., 1999). In contrast, a defective HPA axis response to such stimuli would reproduce the glucocorticoid-deficient state and would lead to relative resistance to infections and neoplastic disease, but increased susceptibility to autoimmune/inflammatory disease, such as Hashimoto's thyroiditis or rheumatoid arthritis (Chrousos, 1995). It is strongly suggested that patients with rheumatoid arthritis have a mild form of central hypocortisolism (Chikanza et al., 1992). Indeed dysfunction of the HPA axis may actually play a role in the development or perpetuation of autoimmune disease, rather than being an epiphenomenon. The same rationale may explain the high incidence of autoimmune disease in the period after cure of hypercortisolism, the postpartum period, as well as in glucocorticoid underreplaced adrenal insufficiency (Elenkov and Chrousos, 1999; Elenkov et al., 2001).

The biological basis of stress related diseases and future therapeutic perspectives
Dysregulation of the stress system, expressed either as hyperfunction or as hypofunction, involves, as already mentioned, a number of human health problems of enormous impact on society (Table 4.2). It is quite difficult to distinguish between cause and effect in such dysregulation, since this system is, to a large extent, 'nonspecific' and meant to interact with internal or external perturbations in a quite similar manner. Thus inappropriate adaptational responses could be maladaptive and act as stressors themselves, feeding into a sustained vicious cycle (Chrousos and Gold, 1992). The magnitude or duration of the stressor, the critical timing of the event, the actual genetic vulnerability and makeup of the individual and the influences of her or his social environment (modifiers of coping and social support) might, thus, ultimately determine the pathogenesis of a syndrome related to dysregulation of the stress system (Bouchard et al., 1990; Chrousos and Gold, 1992; Kagan et al., 1988a, b; Werner, 1989).

Based on the information presented on the physiological regulation of the stress system, one could postulate a number of potential biochemical defects that could, theoretically, lead to basal or stressor-induced hyperactivity or hypoactivity of this system (Figure 4.1). Thus increased CRH peptidergic, serotonergic, cholinergic, catecholaminergic or thyroid hormone-mediated stimulatory activity, or decreased inhibitory activity of the CRH-peptidergic, γ-aminobutyric acid/benzodiazepine, glucocorticoid-mediated, and opioid- or corticotropin peptidergic influences on the stress system could result in diseases characterized by increased stress system activity. The converse biochemical changes, on the other hand, would be expected in diseases characterized by hypoactivity of the stress system. We may be quite far from definitively elucidating the molecular defects responsible for a disease potentially attributable to a dysregulated stress system, such as the ones mentioned above. Moreover it is likely that a combination of molecular defects and/or environmental events may be required for the expression of each of these illnesses.

However it is nowadays certain that a dysregulation of the stress system leads to human disease, with the potential for improved understanding, diagnosis and treatment of these disorders. Therapeutically CRH antagonists may be useful in human pathologic states, such as melancholic depression and chronic anxiety, associated with chronic hyperactivity of the stress system, along with predictable behavioral, neuroendocrine, metabolic and immune changes, based on the interrelations outlined above (Grammatopoulos and Chrousos, 2002; Habib *et al.*, 2000; Webster *et al.*, 1996, 2002). Early studies with the nonpeptidic antagonist antalarmin are quite promising (Gabry *et al.*, 2002). Conversely, potentiators of CRH secretion/action may be useful to treat atypical depression, postpartum depression and the fibromyalgia/chronic fatigue syndromes, all characterized by low hypothalamic–pituitary–adrenal axis and LC-NE activity, fatigue, depressive symptomatology, hyperalgesia and increased immune/inflammatory responses to stimuli.

References

Benarroch, E.E., (1994), 'Neuropeptides in the sympathetic system: presence, plasticity, modulation and implications, *Annals of Neurology*, **36**, 6–13.

Benker, G., M. Raida, T. Olbricht, R. Wagner, W. Reinhardt and D. Reinwein (1990), 'TSH secretion in Cushing's syndrome: relation to glucocorticoid excess, diabetes, goitre, and the "sick euthyroid syndrome", *Clinical Endocrinology (Oxford)*, **33**, 777–86.

Bernardini, R., A. Chiarenza, A.E. Calogero, P.W. Gold and G.P. Chrousos (1989a), 'Arachidonic acid metabolites modulate rat hypothalamic corticotropin releasing hormone secretion in vitro', *Neuroendocrinology*, **50**, 708–15.

Bernardini, R., A.E. Calogero, Y.H. Ehlich, T. Brucke, G.P. Chrousos and P.W. Gold (1989b), 'The alkyl-ether phospholipid platelet-activating factor is a stimulator of the hypothalamic–pituitary–adrenal axis in the rat', *Endocrinology*, **125**, 1067–73.

Bernardini, R., T.C. Kamilaris, A.E. Calogero, E.O. Johnson, P.W. Gold and G.P. Chrousos (1990), 'Interactions between tumor necrosis factor-α, hypothalamic corticotropin- releasing hormone and adrenocorticotropin secretion in the rat', *Endocrinology*, **126**, 2876–81.

Bouchard, T.J. Jr, D.T. Lykken, M. McGue, N.L. Segal and A. Tellegen (1990), 'Sources of human psychological differences: the Minnesota study of twins reared apart', *Science*, **250**, 223–50.

Burguera, B., C. Muruais, A. Penalva, C. Dieguez and F. Casanueva (1990), 'Dual and selective actions of glucocorticoids upon basal and stimulated growth hormone release in man', *Neuroendocrinology*, **51**, 51–8.

Calogero, A.E., W.T. Gallucci, P.W. Gold and G.P. Chrousos (1988), 'Multiple feedback regulatory loops upon rat hypothalamic corticotropin-releasing hormone secretion', *The Journal of Clinical Investigation*, **82**, 767–74.

Casanueva, F.F., B. Burguera, C. Muruais and C. Dieguez (1990), 'Acute administration of corticosteroids: a new and peculiar stimulus of growth hormone secretion in man', *The Journal of Clinical Endocrinology and Metabolism*, **70**, 234–7.

Chikanza, I.C., P. Petrou, G.P. Chrousos, O. Kingsley and G. Panayi (1992), 'Defective hypothalamic response to immune/inflammatory stimuli in patients with rheumatoid arthritis', *Arthritis Rheumatology*, **35**, 1281–88.

Chrousos, G.P. (1992), 'Regulation and dysregulation of the hypothalamic–pituitary–adrenal axis: the corticotropin-releasing hormone perspective', *Endocrinology and Metabolism Clinics of North America*, **21**, 833–58.

Chrousos, G.P. (1995), 'The hypothalamic–pituitary–adrenal axis and immune-mediated inflammation', *The New England Journal of Medicine*, **332**, 1351–62.

Chrousos, G.P. (1998), 'Stressors, stress, and neuroendocrine integration of the adaptive response. The 1997 Hans Selye Memorial Lecture', *Annals of the New York Academy of Sciences*, **851**, 311–35.

Chrousos, G.P. (2000), 'The role of stress and the hypothalamic–pituitary–adrenal axis in the pathogenesis of the metabolic syndrome: neuroendocrine and target tissue-related causes', *International Journal of Obesity and Related Metabolic Disorders*, **24**, suppl. 2, S50–55.

Chrousos, G.P. and P.W. Gold (1992), 'The concepts of stress system disorders: overview of behavioral and physical homeostasis', *Journal of the American Medical Association*, **267**, 1244–52.

Chrousos, G.P., D.J. Torpy and P.W. Gold (1998), 'Interactions between the hypothalamic–pituitary–adrenal axis and the female reproductive system: clinical implications', *Annals of Internal Medicine*, **129**, 229–40.

de Kloet, R. (1991), 'Brain corticosteroid receptor balance and homeostatic control', *Frontiers in Neuroendocrinology*, **12**, 95–164.

Dieguez, C., M.D. Page and M.F. Scanlon (1988), 'Growth hormone neuroregulation and its alterations in disease states', *Clinical Endocrinology (Oxford)*, **28**, 109–43.

Elenkov, I.J. and G.P. Chrousos (1999), 'Stress hormones, Th1/Th2 patterns, pro/anti-inflammatory cytokines and susceptibility to disease', *Trends Endocrinology and Metabolism*, **10**, 359–68.

Elenkov, I.J., E.L. Webster, D.J. Torpy and G.P. Chrousos (1999), 'Stress, corticotropin-releasing hormone, glucocorticoids, and the immune/inflammatory response: acute and chronic effects', *Annals of the New York Academy of Sciences*, **876**, 1–11; discussion 11–13.

Elenkov, I.J., R.L. Wilder, V.K. Bakalov, A.A. Link, M.A. Dimitroy, S. Fisher, M. Crane, K.S. Kanik and G.P. Chrousos (2001), 'IL-12, TNF-alpha, and hormonal changes during late pregnancy and early postpartum: implications for autoimmune disease activity during these times', *The Journal of Clinical Endocrinology and Metabolism*, **86**, 4933–8.

Elfvin, L.G., B. Lindh and T. Hokfelt (1993), 'The chemical neuroanatomy of sympathetic ganglia', *Annual Review of Neuroscience*, **16**, 471–507.

Engler, O., T. Pham, M.J. Fullenon, G. Ooi, J.W. Funder and I.J. Clarke (1989), 'Studies of the secretion of corticotropin releasing factor and arginine vasopressin into hypophyseal portal circulation of the conscious sheep', *Neuroendocrinology*, **49**, 367–81.

Gabry, K.E., G.P. Chrousos, K.C. Rice, R.M. Mostafa, E. Sternberg, A.B. Negrao, E.L. Webster, S.M. McCann and P.W. Gold (2002), 'Marked suppression of gastric ulcerogenesis and intestinal responses to stress by a novel class of drugs', *Molecular Psychiatry*, **7**, 474–83.

Gilbey M.P. and K.M. Spyer (1993), 'Essential organization of the sympathetic nervous system', *Bailliere's Clinical Endocrinology and Metabolism*, **7**, 259–78.

Gold, P.W., F. Goodwin and G.P. Chrousos (1988a), 'Clinical and biochemical manifestations of depression: relationship to the neurobiology of stress, Part 1', *The New England Journal Medicine*, **319**, 348–53.

Gold, P.W., F. Goodwin and G.P. Chrousos (1988b), 'Clinical and biochemical manifestations of depression: relationship to the neurobiology of stress, Part 2', *The New England Journal Medicine*, **319**, 413–20.

Gold, P.W. and G.P. Chrousos (2002), 'Organization of the stress system and its dysregulation in melancholic and atypical depression: high vs low CRH/NE states', *Molecular Psychiatry*, **7**, 254–75.

Grammatopoulos, D.K. and G.P. Chrousos (2002), 'Functional characteristics of CRH receptors and potential clinical applications of CRH-receptor antagonists', *Trends in Endocrinology and Metabolism*, **13**, 436–44.

Habib, K.E., K.P. Weld, K.C. Rice, J. Pushkas, M. Champoux, S. Listwak, E.L. Webster, A.J. Atkinson,. J. Schulkin, C. Contoreggi,. G.P. Chrousos, S.M. McCann, S.J. Suomi, J.D. Higley and P.W. Gold (2000), 'Oral administration of a corticotrophin-releasing hormone receptor antagonist significantly attenuates behavioral, neuroendocrine and autonomic responses to stress in primates', *Proceedings of the National Academy of Sciences of the United States of America*, **97**, 6079–84.

Hinson, J.P. (1990), 'Paracrine control of adrenocortical function: A new role for the medulla?', *The Journal of Endocrinology*, **124**, 7–9.

Kagan, J., J.S. Reznick and N. Snidman (1998a), 'Biological bases of childhood shyness', *Science*, **240**, 167–71.

Kagan, J., J.S. Reznick and N. Snidman (1988b), 'Temperamental influences on reactions to unfamiliarity and challenge', in G.P. Chrousos, D.L. Loriaux and P.W. Gold (eds), Mechanisms of Physical and Emotional Stress, New York: Plenum Press, pp. 319–39.

Lamberts, S.W.J., T. Verleun, R. Oosterom, P. DeJong and W.H.L. Hackeng (1984), 'Corticotropin releasing factor and vasopressin exert a synergistic effect on adrenocorticotropin release in man', *The Journal of Clinical Endiocrinology and Metabolism*, **58**, 298–303.

Magiakou, M.A., G. Mastorakos and G.P. Chrousos (1994a), 'Final stature in patients with endogenous Cushing's syndrome', *The Journal of Clinical Endocrinology and Metabolism*, **79**, 1082–5.

Magiakou, M.A., G. Mastorakos, M.T. Gomez, S.R. Rose and G.P. Chrousos (1994b), 'Suppressed spontaneous and stimulated growth hormone secretion in patients with Cushing's disease before and after surgical cure', *The Journal of Clinical Endocrinology and Metabolism*, **78**, 131–7.

Magiakou, M.A. and G.P. Chrousos (2002), 'Cushing's syndrome in children and adolescents: current diagnostic and therapeutic strategies,' *Journal of Endocrinological Investigation*, **25**, 181–94.

Munck, A., P.M. Guyre and N.J. Holbrook (1984), 'Physiological functions of glucocorticoids in stress and their relation to pharmacological actions', *Endocrine Reviews*, **5**, 25–44.

Munck, A. and P.M. Guyre (1986), 'Glucocorticoid physiology, pharmacology and stress', in G.P. Chrousos, D.L. Loriaux and M.B. Lipsett (eds), Steroid Hormone Resistance: Mechanisms and Clinical Aspects, New York: Plenum Press, pp. 81–96.

Naito, Y., J. Fukata and T. Tominaga et al. (1998), 'Interleukin 6 stimulates the secretion of adrenocortico-tropic hormone in conscious, freely moving rats', *Biochemical Biophysical Research Communication*, **155**, 1459–63.

Ono, N., M.D. Lumpkin, W.K. Samson, J.K. McDonald and S.M. McCann (1984), 'Intrahypothalamic action of corticotropin-releasing factor to inhibit growth hormone and LH release in the rat', *Life Sciences*, **35**, 1117–23.

Ottenweller, J.E. and A.H. Meier (1982), 'Adrenal innervation may be an extrapituitary mechanism able to regulate adrenocortical rhythmicity in rats', *Endocrinology*, **111**, 1334–8.
Papanicolaou, D.A., J.A. Yanovski, G.B. Cutler, Jr, G.P. Chrousos and L.K. Nieman (1998), 'A single midnight serum cortisol measurement distinguishes Cushing's syndrome from pseudo-Cushing states', *The Journal of Clinical Endocrinology and Metabolism*, **83**, 1163–7.
Phillips, M.I. (1987), 'Functions of angiotensin in the central nervous system', *Annual Review of Physiology*, **49**, 413–35.
Rivier, C. and W. Vale (1985), 'Involvement of corticotrophin-releasing factor and somatostatin in stress-induced inhibition of growth hormone secretion in the rat', *Endocrinology*, **117**, 2478–82.
Rivier, C. and S. Rivest (1991), 'Effect of stress on the activity of the hypothalamic–pituitary–gonadal axis: peripheral and central mechanisms', *Biology of Reproduction*, **45**, 523–32.
Roy, M.S., A. Roy, W.T. Gallucci, B. Collier, K. Young, T.C. Kamilaris and G.P. Chrousos (1993), 'The ovine corticotrophin-releasing hormone-stimulation test in type I diabetic patients and controls: suggestion of mild chronic hypercortisolism', *Metabolism*, **42**, 696–700.
Sapolsky, R., C. Rivier, G. Yamamoto, P. Plotsky and W. Vale (1987), 'Interleukin 1 stimulates the secretion of hypothalamic corticotropin-releasing factor', *Science*, **238**, 522–4.
Selye, H. (1936), 'A syndrome produced by diverse nocuous agents', *Nature*, **138**, 32–6.
Shibasaki, T., T. Imaki, M. Hotta, N. Ling and H. Demura (1993), 'Psychological stress increases arousal through brain corticotropin-releasing hormone without significant increase in adrenocorticotropin and catecholamine secretion', *Brain Research*, **618**, 71–5.
Smith, D.F. and D.O. Toft (1993), 'Steroid receptors and their associated proteins', *Molecular Endocrinology*, **7**, 4–11.
Smith, G.W., J.M. Aubry, F. Dellu, A. Contarino, L.M. Bilezikjian, L.H. Gold, R. Chen, Y. Marchuk, C. Hauser, C.A. Bentley, P.E. Sawchenko, G.F. Koob, W. Vale and K.F. Lee (1998), 'Corticotropin releasing factor receptor 1-deficient mice display decreased anxiety, impaired stress response and aberrant neuroendocrine development', *Neuron*, **20**, 1093–1102.
Stratakis, C.A., G. Mastorakos, M.A. Magiakou, E. Papavasiliou, E.H. Oldfield and G.P. Chrousos (1997), 'Thyroid function in children with Cushing's disease before and after transsphenoidal surgery', *Journal of Pediatrics*, **131**, 905–9.
Tsigos, C. and Chrousos G.P. (1994), 'Physiology of the hypothalamic–pituitary–adrenal axis in health and dysregulation in psychiatric and autoimmune disorders', *Endocrinology and Metabolism Clinics of North America*, **23**, 451–66.
Tsigos, C. and Chrousos G.P. (2002), 'Hypothalamic–pituitary–adrenal axis, neuroendocrine factors and stress', *Journal of Psychossomatic Research*, **53**(4), 865–71.
Tsigos, C. D.A. Papanicolaou, R. Defensor, C.S. Mitsiadis, I. Kyrou and G.P. Chrousos (1997a), 'Dose-effects of recombinant human interleukin-6 on anterior pituitary hormone secretion and thermogenesis', *Neuroendocrinology*, **66**, 54–62.
Tsigos, C., D.A. Papanicolaou, I. Kyrou, R. Defensor, C.S. Mitsiadis and G.P. Chrousos (1997b), 'Dose-dependent effects of recombinant human interleukin-6 on glucose regulation', *The Journal of Clinical Endocrinology and Metabolism*, **82**, 4167–70.
Turnbull, A.V. and C. Rivier (1997), 'Corticotropin-releasing factor (CRF) and endocrine responses to stress: CRF receptors, binding protein, and related peptides', *Proceedings of the Society for Experimental Biology and Medicine*, **215**, 1–10.
Unterman, T.G. and L.S. Phillips (1985), 'Glucocorticoid effects on somatomedins and somatomedin inhibitors', *The Journal of Clinical Endocrinology and Metabolism*, **61**, 618–26.
Vale, W.W., S. Spiess, C. Rivier and J. Rivier (1981), 'Characterization of a 41-residue ovine hypothalamic peptide that stimulates secretion of corticotropin and β-endorphin', *Science*, **213**, 1394–97.
Vamvakopoulos, N.C. and G.P. Chrousos (1993), 'Evidence of direct estrogen regulation of human corticotropin releasing hormone gene expression: potential implications for the sexual dimorphism of the stress response and immune/inflammatory reaction', *The Journal of Clinical Investigation*, **92**, 1896–1902.
Webster, E.L., D.B. Lewis, D.J. Torpy, E.K. Zachman, K.C. Rice and G.P. Chrousos (1996), 'In vivo and in vitro characterization of antalarmin, a nonpeptidic corticotropin-releasing hormone (CRH) receptor antagonist in suppression of pituitary ACTH release and peripheral inflammation', *Endocrinology*, **137**, 5747–50.
Webster, E.L., R.M. Barrientos, C. Contoreggi, M.G. Isaac, S. Ligier, K.E. Gabry, G.P. Chrousos, E.F. McCarthy, K.C. Rice, P.W. Gold and E.M. Sternberg (2002), 'Corticotropin-releasing hormone (CRH) antagonist attenuates adjuvant induced arthritis: role of CRH in peripheral inflammation', *Journal of Rheumatology*, **29**, 1252–61.
Werner, E.E. (1989), 'Children of the garden island', *Scientific American*, **260**, 106–11.
Wong, M.L., J. Licinio, K.I. Pasternak and P.W. Gold (1994), 'Localization of corticotropin-releasing hormone

(CRH) receptor mRNA in adult rat brain by in situ hybridization histochemistry', *Endocrinology*, **135**, 2275–78.

Yanovski, J.A., G.B. Cutler, Jr, G.P. Chrousos and L.K. Nieman (1993), 'Corticotropin-releasing hormone stimulation following low-dose dexamethasone administration. A new test to distinguish Cushing's syndrome from pseudo-Cushing's states', *Journal of the American Medical Association*, **269**, 2232–8.

5 The relationship between ethnicity and work stress
Grace V.F. Miller and Cheryl J. Travers

The present research has identified one area which clearly requires further study, namely investigation of occupational stress in different ethnic groups. It has categorized the most prevalent type of reported occupational stress and this can be labelled 'social group II' stress. This is clearly very different from the social gradient health effects that have been widely studied and it requires further investigation. (Smith *et al.*, 2000 p. 60)

Introduction
Cooper *et al.* (1988) suggest that workload, the position within the organization, the relationships that are formed, career progression, the structure of the organization and the atmosphere within that structure can be major sources of stress. Others have identified a relationship with work stress and demographic variables such as age, gender and position (Travers and Cooper, 1996, 1998; Travers, 2001). However no studies to date have found a significant link between stress and ethnicity or have explored the possible effects of ethnicity on stress. Until recently studies have either identified a gap in the ethnicity research upon analysis of the data from their stress surveys (Smith *et al.*, 2000), or have focused primarily upon the overall experiences of minority ethnic women managers (Davidson, 1997). This chapter argues that individual ethnic identity may be just as important or more important in determining the amount of stress an individual may suffer at work. Ethnicity as a demographic variable may seem like any other demographic variable as a contributory factor in the experience of stress. However the lack of research into this area is made more pressing by studies (Primatesta *et al.*, 2000; Bhugra and Jones, 2001) suggesting that people from minority ethnic groups may be more vulnerable to certain stress-related health outcomes. In particular their vulnerability is made distinct by their exposure to environments where they are in the minority, environments such as the workplace, where economic necessity may counteract intention to leave behaviour. This chapter will consider the nature of ethnicity, the measurement and value of ethnicity, and will explore its relationship with stress and the risk factors associated with stress.

The nature of ethnicity
Modern usage of the term 'ethnic' describes those who are distinguishable from the indigenous people (Guirdham, 1999). It seems to be the term preferred to 'race' as the latter implies a biological conception of identity based purely on phenotypic features (Fenton, 1999; Modood *et al.*, 2002). The *Oxford English Dictionary* definition of ethnicity is 'the fact or state of belonging to a social group that has a common national or cultural tradition' (Hanks and Pearsall, 2001 p. 632). Its conceptualization has extended the traditional boundaries to include commonalties such as shared language, origin, religion, history and culture (Anthias, 1992, 2001; Law, 1996). Likewise the present-day term

'minority ethnic' seems preferable to the historical term 'ethnic minority', as the latter term implies that populations such as the indigenous people cannot be defined on the basis of their ethnicity (sharing the same cultural values and identity) or that their ethnicity is consistently in the majority. It also suggests that ethnic groups who are in the minority are somewhat less important than ethnic groups who are in the majority (Parekh, 2002).

Ethnic self-identification
Ethnicity is a complex and changeable phenomenon that is evolving through the subjectivity and perception of an individual (Law, 1996; Bhopal and Rankin, 1999). It relies on the contextual framework with which the individual identifies (Bhopal, 1997), such as origins, religious affiliation and the colour of the skin (Senior and Bhopal, 1994; Modood, 1997b). It is no longer possible to categorize an individual at face value, on the notion of homogeneity, or to assign them to a group on the basis of ethnic family values, as was historically the case. It is more appropriate to allow freedom in the development of an individual's self-identification. This rather complicated process, it is suggested, is influenced by the dualistic role of agency (accepted individuality) and structure (socioeconomic position) in the identification of an ethnic identity (Nazroo, 2001). Karlsen and Nazroo (2002a) suggest five dimensions that are both interrelated and influential in the completeness of self-identification. The first is nominal. This relates to the nationality or country of origin of the individual or indeed their skin colour. The virtual dimension relates to the perception of what it is to be that chosen identity. The influence of the traditional dimension can be seen in the choice of clothes and language, and could also refer to the development of an inner awareness of individuality, as well as the opinion of the individual towards mixed relationships. The internal dimension relates to the participation of that individual within the community that may be influenced by the extent of exclusion by society, or by the desire to be a member of a chosen group. Lastly the external dimension refers to the perception of the phenomenology of racial discrimination.

These dimensions were derived from factoral analysis of the data from the Fourth National Survey of Ethnic Minorities (Modood *et al.*, 1997).

Measuring ethnicity
The complex nature of this process has implications for the production of a quantitative map of ethnic identities such as the Fourth National Survey of Ethnic Minorities and the Censuses. The first Census to recognize the various ethnic groups was produced in 1991, as previous Census surveys recorded only the respondent's nationality and country of birth (Nazroo, 2001). This was viewed as an unreliable method of measurement (Berthoud *et al.*, 1997). The categories of note were 'White; Black-Caribbean; Black-African; Black Other (please describe); Indian; Pakistani; Bangladeshi; Chinese; Any Other Ethnic group (please describe)' (p. 5). These categories were considered to be incomplete (Fenton, 1996) and insensitive (Aspinall, 2001), as no account was taken of individuals who were the children from mixed parentage. The limited categories also seemed to support the misconception that any individual whose ethnic identity is in the minority is an immigrant.

In order to overcome the incompleteness and insensitivity of the measure the Office of National Statistics (ONS) introduced what they called an option of choice, incorporating the 'cultural background' (Aspinall, 2000) of the individual. This gives the individual the chance to make known their individual identity and their phenotype (Aspinall, 2001). The categories have been extended to meet the challenges of self-identification and mixed parentage (for example, with Mixed as the heading: tick one group from White and Black Caribbean; White and Black African; White and Asian). However it could be argued these changes do not go far enough. Although the subcategories are broken down (for example Black or Black British) and headed in this manner, individuals are required to tick a box from a choice of Caribbean, African and Any Other Black background. No dichotomized distinction is made between the Black and Black British, so that everyone who is Black is put into the same category. For example, a Black person who emigrated from Kenya as an adult has the same ethnic identity as a Black person who was born and has resided continuously in England whose grandparents were born in Nigeria.

The prevalence of minority ethnic workers
There are now nearly 6 million minority ethnic people living in the UK, nearly 11 per cent of the entire population (Parekh, 2002), who make up 6.6 per cent of the UK working population (Pathak, 2000). This ethnic compilation is now mostly made up of people who are African, African–Caribbean, Bangladeshi, Chinese, Indian, Irish, Pakistani or White (other than Irish) or who are the children, grandchildren or great-grandchildren of the first immigrants who arrived in the UK nearly 50 years ago. Owing to the complex composition of the UK population there becomes a need for an appropriate, coherent and dependable classification method, not only to emphasize disparities or similarities in the workplace, but also to dispel unfounded suppositions about intellectual capacity and/or physical ability. A coherent classification method can also lead to the identification of new risk factors in specific ethnic groups; 'most importantly it leads to specific prevention strategies that are appropriately tailored to the major ethnic groups' (Anand, 1999, p. 244).

The effect of ethnicity in the working environment has become more pressing recently because of the growing mix of ethnic groups that are consistently being increased as a result of the overseas recruitment initiatives in medicine, nursing and teaching. This chapter draws on examples from the nursing and teaching professions because of the high levels of stress found in those sectors, and also because of the increase in minority ethnic workers due to the overseas recruitment strategies. During 2001 the UK issued 6000 work permits to teachers outside the EU (Baker, 2002). In addition, the overseas registration of nurses rose from 3621 in 1998/1999 to 8403 in 2000/2001 (RCN, 2002a), also from countries outside the EU. However this type of recruitment is not a new phenomenon (Sheffield et al., 1999). The first major labour migration to the UK occurred during the 1950s and 1960s, from post-colonial countries, such as Jamaica and India. This phenomenon was due in part to the economic growth at that time. The government of the day was extremely keen to stem the resultant labour shortages, mostly within the manufacturing industry, and decided that recruitment abroad could prove to be mutually beneficial. With what seemed to be a recruitment success, the majority of these immigrants were not only hopeful of securing some form of unskilled employment but also of realizing some form of career (Smaje, 1995).

However employment is not without its disparities. Over the last decade the unemployment rate amongst some of the UK's minority ethnic working population has nearly doubled that of the majority working population (Thomas, 1998). By 1998, 24.9 per cent of the majority working population was unemployed, as opposed to 65 per cent Bangladeshi and 59 per cent Pakistani with the overall average of minority ethnic people unemployed at 43 per cent (Parekh, 2002, p. 194). Two major factors are suggested to account for these high levels of unemployment: poor educational attainment (Modood, 1997a) and discrimination (Blackaby et al., 1999) that could be based on stereotypical misconceptions (Dale et al., 2002). Although racial discrimination still exists, the employment position of some minority ethnic employees has been partially improved (Iganski et al., 2001), but in reality professions such as teaching and nursing are still experiencing major recruitment and retention problems that could be due to a variety of organizational barriers (Sheffield et al., 1999). It is shown in the underrepresentation of minority ethnic groups (Holmes and Robinson, 1999) in the teaching profession where the government, in partnership with the Teacher Training agency, are making efforts to recruit teachers from minority ethnic backgrounds. A range of strategies are being used, such as advertising in minority ethnic mediums, consultations with community organizations, and the offering of taster courses for underrepresented ethnic groups (Carrington et al., 2001).

Historical approaches to ethnic disparities

The first Race Relations Act was introduced in 1965 as a deterrent against 'racial hatred' (Sloane and Mackay, 1997). It was subsequently updated in 1968 to outlaw discrimination in employment and housing, as many of the immigrants were unable to secure adequate accommodation or, indeed, gainful employment. A new act was established in 1976 alongside the Commission for Racial Equality (CRE). It was amended in the year 2000 against a backdrop of extensive and probing media coverage into institutional racism from the findings of the Macpherson Report into the murder of Stephen Lawrence (CRE, 1999; McKenzie, 1999). The brief for the implementation of these new Acts was to provide significant legislative power to counteract the discriminatory loopholes exhibited in the practices of organizations and public services through a variety of indirect discriminatory acts (Berthoud et al., 1997). Organization-specific equal opportunity policies are now commonplace, and are an initiative following on from the Race Relations Act (1976) reinforced by the Race Relations (Amendment) Act 2000. They can be seen as the organizations attempt to regulate and eliminate discriminatory practices concerning recruitment, training and promotion (Noon and Hoque, 2001). However, as organizations are not under any legal obligation to have an equal opportunities policy, the practice is not officially regulated or inspected by a regulatory body. Therefore organizations still have the opportunity to mislead employees and potential employees by paying lip service to the policy while continuing to undermine the management of diversity. However researchers (Noon and Hoque, 2001; Shields and Wheatley Price, 2002) found that minority ethnic employees received equal treatment when compared to their majority counterparts in organizations where an equal opportunities policy was in practice. Nevertheless Singh Ghuman (1995) found a correlation between stress and discrimination from his qualitative survey of 64 Asian teachers. An overseas teacher who secured employment relates her experience:

I wore a sari or a suit to work. They used to call me a Paki *[who?]*, the white colleagues, or 'you coloured' etc. They would call me a Paki teacher... nobody used my name. Sometimes Madrasi currey and papadom. I used to take it. If you are a second-class citizen, you learn to live with it, otherwise you can't teach. My tension got worse, I couldn't swallow food ... My male colleagues criticised my accent, my practical work and a lot of pressure was put on me. (Singh Ghumanh, 1995, p. 27)

A relationship between discrimination and stress was also found in the studies conducted in the USA by Contrada *et al.* (2000, 2001), and in UK organizations by Davidson (1997), discussed later in the chapter.

The causes of stress
Defining stress
The origin of stress research is significant for the definitions of stress. Selye (1956) introduced the response-based approach to stress. The author suggested that stress was the non-specific response to the demands placed upon the body, thus producing physical degeneration. The approach is based on his General Adaptation Syndrome (GAS) theory, which is 'the manifestation of stress in the whole body, as they develop in time. The general adaptation syndrome evolves in three distinct stages: alarm reaction, stage of resistance, stage of exhaustion' (Selye, 1974, p. 139). The stimulus-based approach to stress theorizes that an individual is assailed by environmental stimuli. The individual learns to cope with these stimuli. The problem occurs when one event elicits an interruption in the coping regime and can be seen as 'the straw that breaks the camel's back' (Sutherland and Cooper, 2000, p. 53). An amalgamation of the response-based and the stimulus-based approaches is reflected in the interactive model of stress (Sutherland and Cooper, 2000), one example being 'the person–environment fit' (Van Harrison, 1978). Alternatively, Cox and Mackay (1981) suggests that the transactional model of stress embodies the complex process that an individual can undergo, and their reaction to difficulties. They posit that 'stress is an individual phenomenon; it is the result of a transaction between the person and his situation' (p. 101).

A variety of approaches to the understanding of stress have been presented, but, in the context of this chapter, the transactional approach is taken, where there is interaction between the environment (workplace) and the individual (ethnic identity). As suggested earlier by Cooper *et al.* (1988), the universal aetiological causes of stress are the amount of workload, the individuals' role within the organization, the relationships with colleagues, management and subordinates, promotional prospects and the environment and structure of the organization. These causes can be applied to the general population holistically. However some researchers (Fielden and Cooper, 2001; Fielden and Davidson, 2001) have identified particular groups that may be especially susceptible to stress, for example women. They found 'additional sources of stress arising as a direct result of discrimination and prejudice in the workplace' (Fielden and Davidson, 2001, p. 124). These general and gender-specific causes still apply to ethnic groups who are in the minority but there may also be additional stressors due to the ethnic identity of the employee. It is suggested that this situation can result in a double-blind paradigm, 'of racism and sexism' (Davidson, 1997, p. 78), adversely influencing the progression of employees. Sparks *et al.* (2001, p. 504) maintain, 'individuals from ethnic-minority groups may be more prone to stress'. The authors argue that this could be due to problems resulting from interpersonal and institutional discrimination and racism. These issues not only lead to the marginalization of minority ethnic employees but can also lead to 'ethnicity-related stress' (Contrada *et al.*, 2001). The authors describe ethnicity-related stress as 'the outcome of a person–situation interaction in which perception of features of the social environment, in light of knowledge of one's ethnicity, leads either to the anticipation of psychological and/or physical harm, or to the belief that such harm has already occurred' (p. 4).

Ethnic-specific causes of stress
The research seems to show that the amount of stress experienced will depend on your ethnic identity, the visual perception by others of your identity, and whether you are in the minority. Also the self-identification matrix and the level of acculturation as perceived by others can lead to the minority ethnic individual being on the receiving end of discriminatory acts. These can be viewed as ethnic-related stressors. In the working environment these can take the form of 'racist "jokes", banter, insults, taunts, gibes, literature, and graffiti; shunning people because of their race, colour, nationality or ethnic background, excluding them from conversations; making racist insinuations; being condescending or deprecating about the way they dress or speak; picking on them unnecessarily' (CRE, 1995, p. 8). Ethnic discrimination relates to the experience of inequitable behaviour that an individual can put down to their background (Contrada *et al.*, 2000). There are numerous *a priori* assumptions of the types and experiences of ethnic discrimination. Karlsen and Nazroo (2002b) posit that ethnic discrimination is multifaceted, and is manifested via two means of expression, interpersonal discrimination and institutional discrimination, sometimes perceived to be direct and indirect, respectively. Interpersonal discrimination denotes individuals' inequitable behaviour towards another individual, such as being suspected as a shoplifter by the store detective, or by being spat on in the street. In contrast institutional discrimination symbolizes a collective organizational ideology that is portrayed through organizational practices such as recruitment, training and promotion.

Ethnic discrimination   Contrada *et al.* (2001) have extended the dichotomized theory of ethnic discrimination and suggest there are seven forms of discrimination specifically aimed at the individual because of their ethnicity. From the study the authors found that verbal rejection, avoidance, exclusion, denial of equal treatment, disvaluing action, threat of aggression and aggression were the factors involved. Conversely, and from the perspective of the perpetrator, Bhugra and Ayonrinde (2001) suggest a number of individual and institutional ways in which discriminatory behaviour is manifested against the personal or group identity. They found that the perpetrator reconciled the discriminatory behaviour on the basis of their perceptions, opinions and fears. Another type of discrimination is racism. It is unlike ethnic discrimination, in that an individual receives unfair treatment because of their background. Racism is attributed to individual differences that are visually apparent, such as skin colour or type of dress. It is defined as 'a form of discrimination that stems from the belief that groups should be treated differently according to phenotypic difference' (Chakraborty and McKenzie, 2002, p. 475).

These forms of discrimination can occur in an employment environment either individually or institutionally and can be manifested through promotion, pay, harassment, bullying and training. Noon and Hoque (2001, p. 112) posit, 'both ethnic minority men and women receive poorer treatment than their white counterparts'. They found this from analysing the data from the 1998 Workplace Employment Relations Survey (WERS 98), which they used to examine the treatment of minority ethnic employees at work. In reality Karlsen and Nazroo (2002b, p. 630) note:

> Reported experienced interpersonal racism and perceived institutional discrimination have each been shown to have independent health effects, which, based on their consistency across a range of quite different health indicators, would seem to persist over and above any immediate physical injury caused by an incident itself. The role of racism in the relation between ethnicity and health has been ignored for too long.

Krieger (1990), to explore the impact of racial and gender discrimination on health, conducted more than 100 qualitative interviews. She found that the majority of Black respondents had experienced discrimination more than once in their lives and the most reported environment (53 per cent) was the workplace. Discrimination as a stress factor was revealed to Davidson (1997) in her quantitative study on 30 Black and minority ethnic woman managers. She found that the most cited source of stress for these women was performance pressures. They felt that they had to justify their positions continually and perform at an exceptional rate in order for their position and achievements to be recognized and accredited. These stressful situations are attributed to racial and gender issues. She concludes, 'more than 80% of the sample reported negative psychosocial and health outcomes which were related to sexism and racism at work – racism being the most often quoted as being the major cause' (p. 77). Shields and Wheatley Price (2002, p. 7) suggest that 'attributes, deterrence and exposure' are the three main factors that are likely to affect the level of discrimination the minority ethnic worker will be subjected to within their work environment. From their study they found that ethnic discrimination at work held stress related implications for the mental well-being of the minority employee. Bhugra and Ayonrinde (2001) believe that ethnic discrimination at either the individual or the institutional level is 'likely to act as a chronic stress' (p. 347).

Migration and acculturation The act of migration exposes an individual to new types of environments and therefore could be an aetiological factor behind recently explored health risks, such as the effect of urbanization on hypertension (van Rooyen *et al.*, 2000). Migration is the progression of change an individual will undergo in order to move from one country to another, either to live permanently or for an extended period of time (Bhugra and Jones, 2001). The authors suggest that this type of upheaval can have serious implications for an individual's mental well-being, such as post-traumatic stress disorder. The disorder is likely to manifest itself when the individual is placed within the unfamiliar social and cultural framework of their host country. This provokes the issue of acculturation theory and the complete acceptance of the new cultural values to the detriment of the native values. The reconciliation of this quandary as suggested by Bhugra and Ayonrinde (2001) is likely to invoke more stress on the individual. Acculturation is concerned with the artefacts from the meeting of two cultures and the effects of this meeting upon the basic values of both cultures (Bhagat and London, 1999).

It is suggested that 'perfect acculturation' can occur, but only when an individual adopts the culture of the host country and the adoption is made visible by a change in their ethnic identity (Pires and Stanton, 2000), such as a change in their style of dress. However it is suggested that an outcome of this change is likely to be high levels of stress brought on by perceptions of alienation and marginality, not only from members of the host country, but also from members of the native country (Berry and Annis, 1974). Acculturation stress can be defined as the insecurities perceived and experienced by an individual when adjusting to and assimilating the values of a new culture (Bhagat and London, 1999). These insecurities are suggested as artefacts from the difficulties faced throughout the acculturation process, such as disconnection and nonconformity. The earlier sections of this chapter referred to the overseas recruitment of professionals such as teachers and nurses. These new opportunities, based on acculturation, can produce additional stresses for the overseas professional such as 'demand, opportunity and constraints' (Bhagat and London, 1999, p. 354). Demand and opportunity stresses are the complex working conditions that can prevent or present career opportunities to individuals. The constraint stressor is the work situation that can restrict or limit the desired career progression.

The impact of stress on health
The financial cost of work stress to employers is around £381 million per year. The cost to society in relation to medical treatment is in the region of £4 billion per year, resulting from approximately 6.5 million workdays being lost to stress-related illnesses (HSE, 2002). The recent stress survey commissioned by the Communication Workers Union (CWU, 2001) found that over the previous 12 months, 15 per cent (400 employees) of the respondents had taken at least one sick day off work that they considered to be stress-induced. The Royal College of Nursing believes that at least 14 days per nurse, per year are lost through stress-related illness, totalling nearly £1000 per nurse (RCN, 2002b). The Association of Teachers and Lecturers has further highlighted the problems in the teaching profession. Over a period of two years, calls to 'Teacherline', a support network for teachers, revealed that over 200 000 teachers had experienced stress, and 40 000 of them had suffered illnesses as a result of the stress. Similarly Nash (2000), from his survey into the management of stress in schools, found that 4000 teachers called the Teacherline advice network with complaints of stress, anxiety and depression. A significant proportion was displaying very high levels of distress, and 30 per cent of them had visited their GP before contact. He concludes, 'as a result of our research . . . these figures considerably understate the problems of stress, anxiety and depression' (p. 22). Unfortunately these results cannot be broken down by ethnic group or compared, as Teacherline does not record the ethnicity of the teachers.

As well as the impact on employers and society there is also the cost of stress to the individual that eventually can have an impact on the organization. Arnold et al. (1998) suggest that stress is manifested in a variety of ways, both individually and organizationally, and is linked to potentially adverse health outcomes. The authors also note such individual symptoms as raised blood pressure, depressed mood, excessive drinking, irritability and chest pains, and such organizational symptoms as high absenteeism and labour turnover, industrial relations difficulties and poor quality control. The individual symptoms can sometimes lead to 'caseness', defined by the Royal College of Nursing (RCN,

2002b) as a level of mental distress sufficient to be considered a minor psychiatric disorder, such as depression or anxiety. The study by Borrill *et al.* (1998) of 12 000 staff across 19 NHS trusts found a mean level of 'caseness' of 27 per cent; whereas the level of 'caseness' in the general working population is 18 per cent, nurses were found to have a score of 28.5 per cent.

Other studies (Travers and Cooper, 1996, 1998; Troman and Woods, 2000; Travers, 2001) also note similar findings within the teaching profession. Rose (2000), upon analysis of several data sets (Workplace Employee Relations Survey, British Household Panel Survey, Social Change and Economic Life, and Employment in Britain Survey), maintains, 'teaching professionals make up a bigger [5.6 per cent] block even than health professions of employment in the entire sample, and in the real economy itself. Arguably they lie at the core of national stress problems'. When the levels of stress were measured and compared against demographic variables, Smith *et al.* (2000) made a significant discovery when ethnicity was compared. They found that 29 per cent of non-white employees indicated that they were suffering high stress and 70.9 per cent low stress as opposed to 18.3 per cent and 81.7 per cent, respectively for their majority counterparts. They claim that 'this effect was reliable over time, related to potentially stressful working conditions and associated with impaired physical and mental health. These effects of occupational stress could not be attributed to life stress or negative affectivity' (p. 1).

Internationally this stress-related vulnerability has been correlated to raised blood pressure and hypertension among populations in the USA (Light *et al.*, 1995; Goldstein *et al.*, 1999), as also when the effects of work stress were measured in the Netherlands and France (Vrijkotte *et al.*, 2000; Fauvel *et al.*, 2001). Studies from Finland and the USA have found a relationship between stress and carotid atherosclerosis in men and women (Kamarck *et al.*, 1997; Matthews *et al.*, 1998) and, more significantly, Finnish studies have linked the progression of the disease to workplace demands (Everson *et al.*, 1997; Lynch *et al.*, 1997). The UK study conducted by Bosma *et al.* (1997) supports the theory of work-related stress as an aetiological factor of coronary heart disease that could be induced by psychosocial work characteristics (Hemingway and Marmot, 1999), or by low job control (Macleod *et al.*, 2002). In this connection, an individual's personality can have a significant impact on their susceptibility to stress and therefore stress-related illnesses. Travers and Cooper (1996), from their study of the teaching profession, found that individuals displaying Type A coronary-prone behaviours reported more pressure that those displaying Type B behaviours. Type A is a set of overt behaviours involving 'hostility, aggressiveness, competitiveness and a sense of time urgency' (p. 65) and is significantly related to coronary heart disease (Hemingway and Marmot, 1999).

Ethnicity and health
When researchers looked at gender as a demographic variable of note, no differences were identified within some comparative stress-related illness literature (Bosma *et al.*, 1997; Matthews *et al.*, 2000). Only when high-effort coping strategies were observed with women who had a high-status job did the readings reveal that they had higher blood pressure than men (Light *et al.*, 1995). Also women who used healthier coping mechanisms (who drank less alcohol and had a healthy diet) were observed to have lower blood pressure readings (Lindquist *et al.*, 1997). However Fielden and Davidson (2001) maintain that women with

high-status jobs such as managerial positions 'tend to report significantly poorer mental well-being' (p. 124) than their male counterparts. The trend may be underreported as women tend 'to normalize [sic] their mental health problems' (Fielden and Cooper, 2001, p. 9) because of the belief that poor mental health is a reflection of a weak nature.

Among ethnic groups, Primatesta et al. (2000) noted that the highest rates of hypertension were found amongst the sample of Black men and women living in England, whereas the readings from the South Asian women were similar to those of the White women in the sample. Further studies from the UK and the USA (Stewart et al., 1999; Jones et al., 2000; Hajat et al., 2001) have used comparative methods to investigate the incidence of stroke between ethnic groups. They found that Blacks had the highest incident rate, and greater severity of stroke, than did their majority counterparts. Other differences were found in the areas of psychosis and schizophrenia in the minority ethnic population (Bhugra and Jones, 2001). It was found more prevalent among the UK African–Caribbean population (Sharpley et al., 2001) and it seemed to become more prevalent within environments where the ethnic identity was in the minority (Boydell et al., 2001).

Coping strategies
A strategy for coping with stress is essential to reduce the risk to health. Sutherland and Cooper (2000) suggest a tripartite model to manage stress. It consists of identifying and reducing the situation that is causing the stress, instructing the individual on the best way to cope with stress, and assisting those individuals who are experiencing poor health outcomes from their exposure to stress. However coping strategies are interpersonal and subjective, so strategies should be applied on an individual basis according to the situation, as using the most effective strategy could change 'the relationship between the individual and the environment' (Green and Ross, 1996, p. 316). Bunce and Stephenson (2000), upon analysis of 27 published stress management intervention (SMI) reports, are even more sceptical: they argue, 'at present the quality of reporting and research design is such that it is difficult to form an impression of what type of SMI is appropriate to whom, and in what circumstances' (p. 197). This type of intervention strategy is said to aid in the prevention of distress (Neves de Jesus and Conboy, 2001) and has been used to help individual teachers develop strategies consisting of direct action and palliative techniques (Kyriacou, 1998, 2001). Direct action or problem-focused techniques are aimed at managing the self more effectively, whilst the palliative techniques, that can be emotion-focused, are aimed at lessening the feelings of stress and can include adverse factors such as drinking or smoking in excess.

Previous research into teacher stress has shown that personality variables (Chakravorty, 1989; Travers and Cooper, 1996) can have a mediating effect on the way teachers cope, as it was found that 'teachers have a tendency to exhibit Type A behaviour, which has implications for the experience of stress' (p. 164). Gender differences in coping were found by Fielden and Davidson (2001). The authors suggest that the preferred coping strategies for women were emotion-based through social support, whilst the preferred method of coping for men was problem-based, addressing the situation as it occurs. Other forms of coping strategies are cognitive and behavioural, used 'to manage the demands faced by an individual as a result of their situation' (Fielden and Davidson, 2001, p. 121). Griffith et al. (1999) suggest, 'the application of both cognitive and behavioural disengagement are coping strategies which can be implemented directly, without the help of others and with immediate consequences'. They are individual-based and can be used immediately as the stressful situations arise.

Ethnicity and coping
In her study, Davidson (1997) found that 40 per cent of the minority ethnic sample felt that they were inadequately equipped to cope with work stress because of their lack of confidence, partly attributed to their individual personality and to their ethnic identity. Owing to the subtle nature of some discriminatory acts, minority ethnic employees are often unclear as to whether some behaviours are unacceptable (Contrada *et al.*, 2001) this having an influence on whether they report the incident or not. Studies by Krieger (1990) and Krieger and Sidney (1996) suggest that individuals' health outcomes are moderated by the strategies used to cope with a discriminatory event, displayed either cognitively or behaviourally (Contrada *et al.*, 2001). The cognitive response can be seen as denial of the event, reinterpretation of the event or placation of the perpetrator, whilst the behavioural response, it is suggested, is demonstrated by confronting the offender, complaining about the offence and retaliating. The risk to health therefore, is diminished by the immediate behavioural response (Krieger and Sidney, 1996).

Conclusion
The research suggests that an individual's ethnic identity is an important issue in the experience of stress that is open to influence from one's working environment, and whether one's ethnicity is in the minority. The research also proposes that minority ethnic employees are more likely to suffer poorer physiological and psychological health outcomes as a result of stress than their majority counterparts. This may be due to a variety of factors, such as acculturation, ethnic discrimination and racism. It is only relatively recently that the debate about ethnicity has gathered pace, and the link to health has only become the focus of research of late, the more so in the USA than in the UK. In the teaching profession an implication of this can be seen in the form of vigorous recruitment campaigns to attract minority ethnic teachers. Other implications are that minority ethnic employees, when compared with their majority counterparts, have higher percentages for poorer health outcomes such as high blood pressure, stroke and schizophrenia.

Researchers need to be proactive in their approach to research, especially in the areas of ethnicity and health, and the effect on health of discrimination at work. Although Davidson (1997) has qualitatively studied the experiences of minority ethnic women managers, there is a need for further qualitative and quantitative research. This should be carried out by researchers from various ethnic groups to explore and compare the perceptions and experiences of work stress, the effect of acculturation, ethnic discrimination and racism, to measure the impact on health. Particular focus should comparatively explore similarities and disparities between minority ethnic employees and their majority counterparts, and highlight the relationship between work stress and ethnicity to test empirically the proposition that a direct relationship exists.

References
Anand, S. (1999), 'Using ethnicity as a classification variable in health research: perpetuating the myth of biological determinism, serving socio-political agendas or making valuable contributions to medical sciences?', *Ethnicity and Health*, **4**(4), 241–4.

Anthias, F. (1992), *Ethnicity, Class, Gender and Migration: Greek-Cypriots in Britain*, Aldershot: Avebury.
Anthias, F. (2001), 'The material and the symbolic in theorizing social stratification: issues of gender, ethnicity and class', *British Journal of Sociology*, **52**(3), 367–90.
Arnold, J., C.L. Cooper and I.T. Robertson (1998), *Work Psychology: Understanding Human Behaviour in the Workplace*, London: Financial Times Pitman Publishing.
Aspinall, P.J. (2000), 'The new 2001 census question set on cultural characteristics: is it useful for the monitoring of the health status of people from ethnic groups in Britain?', *Ethnicity and Health*, **5**(1), 33–40.
Aspinall, P.J. (2001), 'Operationalising the collection of ethnicity data in studies of the sociology of health and illness', *Sociology of Health and Illness*, **23**(6), 829–62.
Baker, M. (2002), 'UK "poaching" Jamaican teachers', Education, London, BBC News.
Berry, J.W. and R.C. Annis (1974), 'Acculturation stress: the role of ecology, culture and differentiation', *Journal of Cross-Cultural Psychology*, **5**, 382–406.
Berthoud, R., T. Modood and P. Smith (1997), 'Introduction', in [T. Modood, R. Berthoud, J. Lakey, J. Nazroo, P. Smith, S. Virdee and S. Beishon] (eds), *Ethnic Minorities in Britain: Diversity and Disadvantage*, London: Policy Studies Institute.
Bhagat, R.S. and M. London (1999), 'Getting started and getting ahead: career dynamics of immigration', *Human Resource Management Review*, **9**(3), 349–65.
Bhopal, R. (1997), 'Is research into ethnicity and health racist, unsound, or important science?', *British Medical Journal*, **314**, 1751.
Bhopal, R. and J. Rankin (1999), 'Concepts and terminology in ethnicity, race and health: be aware of the ongoing debate', *British Dental Journal*, **186**(10), 483–4.
Bhugra, D. and O. Ayonrinde (2001), 'Racism, racial life events and mental ill health', *Advances in Psychiatric Treatment*, **7**, 343–9.
Bhugra, D. and P. Jones (2001), 'Migration and mental illness', *Advances in Psychiatric Treatment*, **7**, 216–23.
Blackaby, D., D. Leslie, P. Murphy and N. O'Leary (1999), 'Unemployment among Britain's ethnic minorities', *The Manchester School*, **67**(1), 1–20.
Borrill, C.S., T.D. Wall, M.A. West, G.E. Hardy, D.A. Shapiro, C.E. Haynes, C.B. Stride, D. Woods and A.J. Carter (1998), 'Stress among staff in NHS Trusts', Institute of Work Psychology, University of Sheffield and Psychological Therapies Research Centre, University of Leeds.
Bosma, H., M. Marmot, H. Hemingway, A.C. Nicholson, E. Brunner and S.A. Stansfeld (1997), 'Low job control and risk of coronary heart disease in Whitehall II (prospective cohort) study', *British Medical Journal*, **314**, 558.
Boydell, J., J. van Os, K. McKenzie, J. Allardyce, R. Goel, R.G. McCreadie and R.M. Murray (2001), 'Incidence of schizophrenia in ethnic minorities in London: ecological stgudy into interaction with environment', *British Medical Journal*, **323**, 1–4.
Brunner, E. (1997), 'Socioeconomic determinants of health: stress and the biology of inequality', *British Medical Journal*, **314**, 1472.
Bunce, D. and K. Stephenson (2000), 'Statistical considerations in the interpretation of research on occupational stress management interventions', *Work and Stress*, **14**(3), 197–212.
Carrington, B., A. Bonnett, J. Demaine, I. Hall, A. Nayak, G. Short, C. Skilton, F. Smith and R. Tomlin (2001), 'Ethnicity and the professional socialisation of teachers', Teacher Training Agency, London.
Chakraborty, A. and K. McKenzie (2002), 'Does racial discrimination cause mental illness?', *British Journal of Psychiatry*, **180**, 475–477.
Chakravorty, B. (1989), 'Mental health among school teachers', in M. Cole and S. Walker (eds), *Teaching and Stress*, Milton Keynes, Open University Press.
Contrada, R.J., R.D. Ashmore, M.L. Gary, E. Coups, J.D. Egeth, A. Sewell, K. Ewell, T.M. Goyal and V. Chasse (2000), 'Ethnicity-related sources of stress and their effects on well-being', *Current Directions in Psychological Science*, **9**(4), 136–9.
Contrada, R .J., R.D. Ashmore, M.L. Gary, E. Coups, J.D. Egeth, A. Sewell, K. Ewell, T.M. Goyal and V. Chasse (2001), 'Measures of ethnicity-related stress: psychometric properties, ethnic group differences, and associations with well-being', *Journal of Applied Social Psychology*, **31**(9), 1775–1820.
Cooper, C.L., R.D. Cooper and L.H. Eaker (1988), *Living With Stress*, London: Harmondsworth.
Cox, T. and C. Mackay (1981), 'A transactional approach to occupational stress.E.N. Corlett and J. Richardson Stress', *Work Design, and Productivity*, London: John Wiley and Sons.
CRE (1995), *Racial Harassment At Work: What Employers Can Do About It*, London: Commission For Racial Equality.
CRE (1999), *The Stephen Lawrence Inquiry: Implications For Racial Equality*, London: Commission For Racial Equality.
CWU (2001), *Stress Survey*, London: Labour Research Department, Health Safety and Environment Committe, Communication Workers Union.

Dale, A., N. Shaheen, E. Fieldhouse and V. Kalra (2002), 'The labour market prospects for Pakistani and Bangladeshi women', Work, *Employment and Society*, **16**(1), 5–25.
Davidson, M.J. (1997), *The Black and Ethnic Minority Woman Manager: Cracking the Concrete Ceiling*, London: Paul Chapman Publishing.
Everson, S.A., J.W. Lynch, M.A. Chesney, G.A. Kaplan, D.E. Goldberg, S.B. Shade, R.D. Cohen, R. Salonen and J.T. Salonen (1997), 'Interaction of workplace demands and cardiovascular reactivity in progression of carotid atherosclerosis: population-based study', *British Medical Journal*, **314**, 553.
Fauvel, J.P., P. Quelin, M. Ducher, H. Rakotomalala and M. Laville (2001), 'Perceived job stress but not individual cardiovascular reactivity to stress is related to higher blood pressure at work', *Hypertension*, **38**, 71–5.
Fenton, S. (1996), 'Counting ethnicity: social groups and official categories', in R. Levitas and W. Guy (eds), *Interpreting Official Statistics*, London: Routledge.
Fenton, S. (1999), *Ethnicity, Racism, Class and Culture*, London: Macmillan Press.
Fielden, S.L. and C.L. Cooper (2001), 'Women managers and stress: a critical analysis', *Equal Opportunities International*, **20**(1/2), 3–16.
Fielden, S.L. and M.J. Davidson (2001), 'Stress and the woman manager', in J. Dunham (ed.), *Stress in the Workplace: Past, Present and Future*, London: Whurr Publishers.
Goldstein, I.B., D. Shapiro, A. Chicz-Demet and D. Guthrie (1999), 'Ambulatory blood pressure, heart rate, and neuroendocrine responses in women nurses during work and off work days', *Psychosomatic Medicine*, **61**, 387–96.
Green, S.B. and M.E. Ross (1996), 'A theory-based measure of coping strategies used by teachers: the problems in teaching scale', *Teaching and Teacher Education*, **12**(3), 315–25.
Griffith, J., A. Steptoe and M. Cropley (1999), 'An investigation of coping strategies associated with job stress in teachers', *British Journal of Educational Psychology*, **69**, 517–31.
Guirdham, M. (1999), *Communicating Across Cultures*, London: Macmillan Press.
Hajat, C., R. Dundas, J.A. Stewart, E. Lawrence, A.G. Rudd, R. Howard and C.D.A. Wolfe (2001), 'Cerebrovascular risk factors and stroke subtypes: differences between ethnic groups', *Stroke*, **32**, 37–42.
Hanks, P. and J. Pearsall (eds) (2001), *The New Oxford Dictionary of English*, Oxford: Oxford University Press.
Hemingway, H. and M. Marmot (1999), 'Psychosocial factors in the aetiology and prognosis of coronary heart disease: systematic review of prospective cohort studies', *British Medical Journal*, **318**, 1460–67.
Holmes, L. and G. Robinson (1999), 'The making of Black managers: unspoken issues of identity formation', International Conference on Critical Management Studies, UMIST.
HSE (2002), 'Occupational stress statistics information sheet', Health and Safety Executive: 1/02/EMSU, Sudbury.
Iganski, P., G. Payne and J. Roberts (2001), 'Inclusion or Exclusion? Reflections on the evidence of declining racial disadvantage in the British labour market', *International Journal of Sociology and Social Policy*, **21**(4/5/6), 184–211.
Jones, M.R., R.D. Horner, L.J. Edwards, J. Hoff, S.B. Armstrong, C.A. Smith-Hammond, D.B. Matchar and E.Z. Oddone (2000), 'Racial variation in initial stroke severity', *Stroke*, **31**, 563–7.
Kamarck, T.W., S.A. Everson, G.A. Kaplan, S.B. Manuck, R. Jennings, R. Salonen and J.T. Salonen (1997), 'Exaggerated blood pressure responses during mental stress are associated with enhanced carotid atherosclerosis in middle-aged Finnish men', *Circulation*, **96**, 3842–8.
Karlsen, S. and J.Y. Nazroo (2002a), 'Agency and structure: the impact of ethnic identity and racism on the health of ethnicity minority people', *Sociology of Health and Illness*, **24**(1), 1–20.
Karlsen, S. and J.Y. Nazroo (2002b), 'Relation between racial discrimination, social class and health among ethnic minority groups', *American Journal of Public Health*, **92**(4), 624–31.
Krieger, N. (1990), 'Racial and gender discrimination: risk factors for high blood pressure?', *Social Science and Medicine*, **30**, 1273–81.
Krieger, N. and S. Sidney (1996), 'Racial discrimination and blood pressure: the CARDIA study of young black and white adults', *American Journal of Public Health*, **86**, 1370–78.
Kyriacou, C. (1998), 'Teacher stress: past and present', J. Dunham and V. Varma (eds), *Stress in Teachers: Past, Present and Future*, London, Whurr Publishers.
Kyriacou, C. (2001), 'Teacher stress: directions for future research', *Educational Review*, **53**(1), 27–35.
Law, I. (1996), *Racism, Ethnicity and Social Policy*, London: Prentice-Hall/Harvester Wheatsheaf.
Light, K.C., K.A. Brownley, J.R. Turner, A.L. Hinderliter, S.S. Girdler, A. Sherwood and N.B. Anderson (1995), 'Job status and high-effort coping influence work blood pressure in women and Blacks', *Hypertension*, **25**, 554–9.
Lindquist, T.L., L.J. Beilin and M.W. Knuiman (1997), 'Influence of lifestyle, coping, and job stress on blood pressure in men and women', *Hypertension*, **29**, 1–7.
Lynch, J., N. Krause, G.A. Kaplan, R. Salonen and J.T. Salonen (1997), 'Workplace demands, economic reward, and progression of carotid atherosclerosis', *Circulation*, **96**, 302–7.

Macleod, J., G. Davey Smith, P. Heslop, C. Metcalfe, D. Carroll and C. Hart (2002), 'Limitations of adjustment for reporting tendency in observational studies of stress and self reported coronary heart disease', *Journal of Epidemiology and Community Health*, **56**, 76–7.

Matthews, K.A., J.F. Owens, L.H. Kuller, K. Sutton-Tyrrell, H.C. Lassila and S.K. Wolfsonm (1998), 'Stress-induced pulse pressure change predicts women's carotid atherosclerosis', *Stroke*, **29**, 1525–30.

Matthews, K.A., K. Raikkonen, S.A. Everson, J.D. Flory, C.A. Marco, J.F. Owens and C.E. Lloyd (2000), 'Do the daily experiences of healthy men and women vary according to occupational prestige and work strain?', *Psychosomatic Medicine*, **62**, 346–53.

McKenzie, K. (1999), 'Something borrowed from the blues?', *British Medical Journal*, **318**, 616–17.

Modood, T. (1997a), 'Qualifications and English language', in T. Modood, R. Berthoud, J. Lakey, J. Nazroo, P. Smith, S. Virdee and S. Beishon (eds), *Ethnic Minorities in Britain: Diversity and Disadvantage*, London: Policy Studies Institute.

Modood, T. (1997b), 'Culture and Identity', in T. Modood, R. Berthoud, J. Lakey, J. Nazroo, P. Smith, S. Virdee, and S. Beishon (eds), *Ethnic Minorities in Britain: Diversity and Disadvantage*, London, Policy Studies Institute.

Modood, T., R. Berthoud and J. Nazroo (2002), 'Race, racism and ethnicity: a response to Ken Smith', *Sociology*, **36**(2), 419–27.

Modood, T., R. Berthoud, J. Lakey, J. Nazroo, P. Smith, S. Virdee and S. Beishon (eds) (1997), *Ethnic Minorities in Britain: Diversity and Disadvantage*, London: Policy Studies Institute.

Nash, P. (2000), 'Managing stress in schools', Teacherline: First Report, London.

Nazroo, J. (2001), *Ethnicity, Class and Health*, London: Policy Studies Institute.

Neves de Jesus, S. and J. Conboy, (2001), 'A stress management course to prevent teacher distress', *The International Journal of Educational Management*, **15**(3), 131–7.

Noon, M. and K. Hoque (2001), 'Ethnic minorities and equal treatment: the impact of gener, equal opportunities policies and trade unions', *National Institute Economic Reivew*, **176**, 105–16.

Parekh, B. (2002), *The Future of Multi-Ethnic Britain*, London: Profile Books.

Pathak, S. (2000), *Race Research for the Future: Ethnicity in Education, Training and the Labour Market*, London: Department for Education and Employment (now known as the Department for Education and Skills).

Pires, G.D. and P.J. Stanton (2000), 'Ethnicity and acculturation in a culturally diverse country: identifying ethnic markets', *Journal of Multilingual and Multicultural Development*, **21**(1), 42–57.

Primatesta, P., L. Bost and N.R. Poulter (2000), 'Blood pressure levels and hypertension status among ethnic groups in England', *Journal of Human Hypertension*, **14**, 143–8.

RCN (2002a), 'Congress items report', Royal College of Nursing.

RCN (2002b), 'Dealing with stress', Royal College of Nursing.

Rose, M. (2000), 'Future tense? Are growing occupations more stressed out and depressive?', University of Bath, ESRC working paper 3, Work Centrality and Careers Project.

Selye, H. (1956), *The Stress of Life*, New York: McGraw-Hill.

Selye, H. (1974), *Stress Without Distress*, London, Hodder and Stoughton.

Senior, P.A. and R. Bhopal (1994), 'Ethnicity as a variable in epidemiological research', *British Medical Journal*, **309**, 327–30.

Sharpley, M., G. Hutchinson, K. McKenzie and R.M. Murray (2001), 'Understanding the excess of psychosis among the African–Caribbean population in England', *British Journal of Psychiatry*, **178**(suppl. 40), s60–s68.

Sheffield, J., A. Hussain and P. Coleshill (1999), 'Organisational barriers and ethnicity in the Scottish NHS', *Journal of Management in Medicine*, **13**(4), 263–84.

Shields, M.A. and S. Wheatley Price (2002), 'The determinants of racial harassment at the workplace: evidence from the British nursing profession', *British Journal of Industrial Relations*, **40**(1), 1–21.

Singh Ghuman, P.A. (1995), *Asian Teachers in British Schools: A Study of Two Generations*, Clevedon: Multilingual Matters Ltd.

Sloane, P.J. and D. Mackay (1997), 'Employment equity and minority legislation in the UK after two decades: a review', *International Journal of Manpower*, **18**(7), 597–626.

Smaje, C. (1995), *Health 'Race' and Ethnicity: Making Sense of the Evidence*, London: King's Fund Institute.

Smith, A., C. Brice, A. Collins, V. Matthews and R. McNamara (2000), 'The scale of occupational stress: a further analysis of the impact of demographic factors and type of job', Contract Research Report 311/2000, Health and Safety Executive.

Sparks, K., B. Faragher and C.L. Cooper (2001), 'Well-being and occupational health in the 21st century workplace', *Journal of Occupational and Organizational Psychology*, **74**, 489–509.

Stewart, J.A., R. Dundas, R.S. Howard, A.G. Rudd and C.D.A. Wolfe (1999), 'Ethnic differences in incidence of stroke: prospective study with stroke register', *British Medical Journal*, **318**, 967–71.

Sutherland, V.J. and C.L. Cooper (2000), *Strategic Stress Management: An Organizational Approach*, London: Macmillan Press.
Taylor, S.E., R.L. Repetti and T. Seeman (1997), 'Health psychology: what is an unhealthy environment and how does it get under the skin?', *Annual Review of Psychology*, **48**, 411–47.
Thomas, J.M. (1998), 'Who feels it knows it: work attitudes and excess non-white unemployment in the UK', *Ethnic and Racial Studies*, **21**(1), 138–50.
Travers, C.J. (2001), 'Stress in teaching: past, present and future', in J. Dunham (ed.), *Stress in the Workplace: Past, Present and Future*, London: Whurr Publishers.
Travers, C.J. and C.L. Cooper (1996), *Teachers Under Pressure: Stress in the Teaching Profession*, London: Routledge.
Travers, C.J. and C.L. Cooper (1998), 'Increasing costs of occupational stress for teachers', in J. Dunham and V. Varma (eds), *Stress in Teachers: Past, Present and Future*, London: Whurr Publishers.
Troman, G. and P. Woods (2000), 'Careers under stress: teacher adaptations at a time of intensive reform', *Journal of Educational Change*, **1**, 253–75.
Van Harrison, R. (1978), 'Person–environment fit and job stress', in C.L. Cooper and R. Payne (eds), *Stress at Work*. Chichester: John Wiley and Sons.
van Rooyen, J.M., H.S. Kruger, H.W. Huisman, M.P. Wissing, B.M. Margetts, C.S. Venter and H.H. Vorster (2000), 'An epidemiological study of hypertension and its determinants ina a population in transition: the THUSA study', *Journal of Human Hypertension*, **14**, 779–87.
Vrijkotte, T.G.M., L.J.P. van Doornen and E.J.C. de Geus (2000), 'Effects of work stress on ambulatory blood pressure, heart rate, and heart rate variability', *Hypertension*, **35**, 880–86.

6 Eustress and attitudes at work: a positive approach
Debra L. Nelson and Bret L. Simmons

Studies of work stress have proliferated in the past twenty years, and a solid research base has been built that focuses on the identification of stressors, the individual stress response and the consequences of distress. This research has been built upon a tradition of preventing the negative; that is, preventing the noxious aspects of stress at work and treating the symptoms. Organizational interventions have been proposed, and individual characteristics have been identified that predispose people either to cope less well with stressors or to be particularly vulnerable to the deleterious health outcomes of excessive or mismanaged distress.

Our own research is a part of this tradition. We see it as an integral part of stress management, yet there is an overlooked aspect of the management of work stress that remains to be explored. While some scholars mention eustress, and even offer definitions of it, we have yet to see evidence of studies that focus on the positive response to demands. Intuitively, however, we know that some people flourish under stress. We propose that there are two pathways to the positive in terms of managing work stress. One pathway is the more familiar preventing or reframing the negative, as in the bulk of work stress research as we know it. The second pathway, more hazy and unfamiliar, is the promotion of the positive, recognizing and generating eustress at work. This is indeed a new perspective in occupational health.

In this chapter, we develop the construct of eustress and present two studies of nurses that shed some light on the possibilities for understanding eustress and incorporating it into our research. We begin by briefly describing the positive psychology and positive organizational behavior backdrops that serve to frame our mode of inquiry. We then develop a theoretical framework for eustress, its definition, and a review of the research evidence that supports eustress as the positive response to stressors. Next we present two studies of nurses that identified the potential indicators of eustress, its relationship with health and well-being, and the work attitudes associated with it. Finally we explore the practical and research implications of a more positive approach to work stress.

Health, positive psychology and positive organizational behavior
The idea that health is more than the absence of infirmity has been around for years, but this idea has been no more than an idea. Ryff and Singer (1998) reviewed philosophy's focus on the positive in terms of human thriving and flourishing. Aristotle put forth the notion of eudaemonia, the realization of the individual's true potential (Rothman, 1993). Russell (1930) articulated the causes of happiness as zest and affection, along with work. Antonovsky (1987), in the description of sense of coherence, noted its relationship with salutogenesis, the development of health and well-being (as opposed to pathogenesis, development of disease or disorder). Many writers, including Ryff and Singer (1998), in their proposition of positive human health, lamented that researchers and practitioners,

while paying homage to the idea of health as the presence of the positive, have not adopted this positive approach to health. Based on their philosophical analysis, Ryff and Singer further proposed that the goods that are essential for positive human health include purpose in life, quality connections to others, self-regard and mastery, and that examining the physiological processes underlying the relationship between these goods and health constitutes the most important research endeavor. They called for a more comprehensive treatment of health to directly include wellness and the mind–body interaction.

Along with this more positive view of health have come calls for a more positive psychology. Seligman and Csikszentmihalyi (2000), as champions of positive psychology, highlighted psychology's focus on pathology as a product of history, including World War II, and its appropriate emphasis was on healing human suffering. They noted, however, that even during WWII there were individuals who retained their integrity and purpose in those chaotic times. Human characteristics such as courage, optimism and capacity for flow acted as buffers against mental and physical illnesses normally associated with trauma. These authors called for positive psychology to be a 'science of positive subjective experience,' investigating positive individual characteristics and positive institutions. Like Ryff and Singer (1998), Seligman and Csikszentmihalyi noted the need to understand the neurochemistry and anatomy of positive experiences and traits.

Much of the focus in positive psychology has been on the identification of traits that promote health and well-being. Some of the individual characteristics investigated include positive affect (Folkman and Moskowitz, 2000), optimism (Peterson, 2000), self-determination (Ryan and Deci, 2000) and hope (Snyder, 2002). Positive psychology is not an entirely new paradigm, but merely a shift in focus. It has much in common with the view of health as the presence of positive states, and the study of human resilience and flourishing.

Organizational behaviorists and occupational health psychology researchers have joined the positive science movement, bringing the movement into the world of work. Luthans (2002a, 2002b) called for a positive approach to organizational behavior (POB), to emphasize strengths rather than trying to fix weaknesses. Specifically he defined positive organizational behavior as 'the study and application of positively oriented human resource strengths and psychological capacities that can be measured, developed and effectively managed for performance improvement in today's workplace (Luthans, 2002a, p. 59). Luthans contended that the most fruitful approach for POB is to identify states that are positive psychological capacities, which additionally should be validly measured and amenable to development in order to improve performance. He also suggested that confidence, hope and resiliency are states that meet these critieria.

Turner *et al.* (2002) asserted that healthy work means promoting both psychological and physical well-being. They present a model of healthy work in which work redesign, teamwork and transformational leadership are practices that help employees develop more flexible role orientations, in turn leading to employee resilience and optimism. These practices can also indirectly affect positive outcomes through trust, interpersonal justice and organizational commitment. The authors conclude that an understanding of healthy work is a critical element of positive psychology.

In a study of military personnel deployed on a peace-keeping mission, Britt *et al.* (2001) investigated the relationship between the meaning of work and hardiness. As a disposition, hardiness is the tendency to find meaning in events, especially stressors that challenge individuals. Soldiers were surveyed midway through a year-long deployment, and again several months after. Results indicated that hardiness was associated with engagement in meaningful work, which in turn was associated with deriving benefits from the deployment long after it ended. Soldiers who were hardy identified with their peace-keeping role, believed in the importance of their mission and were personally engaged in that mission. This study illustrated that individuals confronted by stressful situations can derive positive outcomes, and that certain individual characteristics (for example hardiness) can facilitate this process. Other characteristics that can promote health and well-being include self-reliance (Quick *et al.*, 1987) and character (Quick, 2002).

In this vein, and following the lineage of positive health, positive psychology and positive organizational behavior, we sought to develop a more positive view of stress. The next section summarizes what we have learned about the concept of eustress and the development of our approach to studying it.

Eustress: a positive approach
Some researchers have alluded to the concept of eustress or included it in their writings. Edwards and Cooper (1988), for example, contended that eustress could be associated with well-being directly through hormonal and biochemical changes or indirectly by facilitating effort and abilities directed toward coping with existing distress. In reviewing the scant evidence concerning eustress, the authors examined a variety of sources, including anecdotal evidence, laboratory experiments and studies of positive life events and job satisfaction. They found *preliminary* evidence for the direct effect of eustress on health. Little research, in contrast, has focused on the relationship of eustress and coping with existing distress; thus there is a dearth of evidence for the proposed indirect benefits of eustress. Sales (1969) indicated that eustress is associated with an *improvement* in physiological functioning rather than merely a reduction in physiological damage. Edwards and Cooper (1988) concluded that, if we are to better understand the beneficial effects of eustress, researchers much attend to the methodological issues of measurement, design and analysis.

Along those lines, how can eustress be most appropriately measured? According to Edwards and Cooper (1988), the most promising approach to the measurement of eustress entails the assessment of positive psychological states. The major concern in this undertaking is *establishing the presence of positive psychological states*, rather than merely the absence of negative states. The authors state that, rather than representing opposite ends of a single continuum, positive (eustress) and negative (distress) states may represent two distinct constructs, which would require separate multivariate indices for their measurement.

Our approach to the study of eustress has its roots in the cognitive appraisal theory of stress, in which the interpretation of stressors, rather than stressors *per se*, determines how individuals respond. According to this approach, two individuals with significantly different perceptions of the same stressor (or a single individual with differing interpretations at different times) would respond differently. Likewise two individuals with similar perceptions of the same (or different) stressors would experience similar responses (Roseman, 1984). Thus perception, or cognitive appraisal, is the key to the response.

Richard Lazarus (1966) and his colleagues pioneered a cognitive appraisal approach. The essence of this approach is that individuals manifest different responses to stressors they encounter, depending on whether they appraise a relevant stressor as positive or negative. Lazarus did acknowledge the existence of positive responses; however, like many stress researchers, he focused his research almost exclusively on negative responses.

In accordance with cognitive appraisal, a person encounters a stressor and then she or he *evaluates* the encounter with respect to its significance for well-being. If a stressor is not appraised as irrelevant, Lazarus and Folkman (1984) assert that appraisals can be complex and mixed, depending on person factors and the situational context. They essentially describe two types of appraisals and associated response patterns: positive and stressful. Positive appraisals 'occur if the outcome of an encounter is construed as positive; that is, if it preserves or enhances well-being or promises to do so' (ibid., p. 32). As indicators of positive appraisals, they suggest looking for the presence of positive or pleasurable psychological states such as exhilaration.

Stressful, negative appraisals include harm/loss, threat and challenge. In harm/loss appraisals, some damage to the person has already occurred (for example, injury, illness, loss of a loved one, damage to self-esteem). Threat involves harms or losses that have not yet occurred but are anticipated. Challenge appraisals occur if the outcome of an encounter holds the potential for gain or growth. As indicators of challenge appraisals, the authors suggest looking for some of the same positive or pleasurable psychological states they identify as indicators of the positive response.

An important factor in cognitive appraisal theory is that its authors, Lazarus and Folkman (1984) do not view challenge and threat as poles of a single continuum. They believe that challenge and threat responses can occur simultaneously, as the result of the same stressor, and should be considered as separate but related constructs. While threat is clearly a negative appraisal, challenge is better thought of as a positive appraisal (they share the same indicators). Therefore positive and negative responses can occur simultaneously, as a result of the same stressor, and should be considered separate but related constructs. For any given stressor, an individual can have both a degree of positive and a degree of negative response. This is consistent with Lazarus and Folkman's (1984) view that any psychophysiological theory of stress or emotion which views the response as unidimensional disequilibrium or arousal is grossly incomplete. They support this with research on emotions and autonomic nervous system activity (Elkman *et al.*, 1983) as well as research of hormonal response to arousing conditions (Mason, 1974; Frankenhauser *et al.*, 1978).

Although most stress research has focused on the negative, Rose's (1987) longitudinal study of air traffic controllers (ATCs) provides a rare glimpse of the positive stress response. Over a three-year period, the cortisol values of 201 men were measured every 20 minutes for five hours on three or more days and compared to both objective and subjective assessments of workload. Cortisol is a hormone secreted by the hypothalamic–pituitary–adrenal system that has been found to be responsive to a variety of different environmental challenges. Cortisol acts on a variety of the body's organs, but its primary effect is to increase the supply of glucose and fatty acids in the bloodstream. Cortisol can also have harmful effects on the body's digestion, immune response and muscular–skeletal system (Quick *et al.*, 1997).

While the increases in cortisol for all levels of workload were slight, the men who showed the highest increase in cortisol to increased work reported themselves as more satisfied and were regarded by peers as more competent. These high-cortisol responders also showed less frequent illness than those with lower cortisol levels, who for any given level of work tended to have more minor health problems. Rose described the men whose cortisol increased in response to challenging work as *engaged* rather than stressed. Elsewhere the happiness derived from engagement in mindful challenge has been termed 'flow' (Csikszentmihalyi, 1990). In their review of Rose's study, Ganster and Schaubroek (1991) described the healthy state of physiological arousal experienced by the engaged workers as 'eustress'.

On the basis of the cognitive appraisal theory, and in an effort to provide a more holistic representation of stress, we define eustress as follows: a positive psychological response to a stressor, as indicated by the presence of positive psychological states. Accordingly distress is the negative psychological response to a stressor, as indicated by the presence of negative psychological states.

In our next section we present two studies conducted within the nursing profession that represent preliminary evidence for the efficacy of studying eustress and its relationship with positive attitudes at work.

Two studies of nurses

Nurses, given their line of work, are in a good position to report experiences of eustress and distress. Theirs is an experience of highs and lows, characterized by both new beginnings such as births and transitions such as deaths. Death, for example, could be appraised by a nurse as both positive and negative. When caring for an individual who has experienced a prolonged illness, death may represent a relief and peace, while there is still the attendant sense of loss and sadness. Some of the primary stressors for hospital nurses are work overload, dealing with death and dying patients, poor communication with colleagues, shift work, inadequate preparation, conflict with doctors or other supervisory personnel, uncertainty over authority, political and union issues, financial resources and increasing bureaucracy (Tyler and Ellison, 1994). Some of the most apparent outcomes of work-related distress in nurses are absenteeism, turnover and injuries (Hemingway and Smith, 1999). We will briefly describe two studies of nurses within the positive science tradition. The first study focuses on eustress and well-being among nurses.

Study one: nurses and eustress

Among the important outcome variables associated with the study of work stress are health and well-being (Quick *et al.*, 1987, 1997; Ganster and Schaubroeck, 1991). While we do include distress, the primary focus of this study is the relationship between a positive response to work demands and the health of the health care provider, specifically nurses. This is important because the health of the health care provider can affect the quality of health care delivery (Cox and Leitter, 1992). In order for the nurse to deliver the optimum service, she must herself be healthy. Because nurses provide the majority of the care for hospital patients, and the perception of how they were treated while in the hospital is as important to patients as the technical quality of the care, nurses that respond positively to the demands of the job can have a substantial impact on the image of a hospital within the community. The direct assessment of eustress in nurses and its positive association with their health is the primary contribution of this study. Using the research literature presented earlier in this chapter, we formed two hypotheses:

H1: there is a positive relationship between eustress and an individual's perception of health.

H2: there is a negative relationship between distress and an individual's perception of health.

Method Research sites were two hospitals in the southwestern United States, one a for-profit corporation with 303 beds and another a nonprofit corporation with 550 beds. Nurses completed a self-report survey while at work, depositing their surveys in a collection box at each site. A total of 450 nurses were surveyed, with a response rate of 47 per cent, which yielded a sample of 158 nurses. Most of the nurses were female (92 per cent) and half worked in critical care areas, while the other half practices in various areas of the hospital.

Measures included in the study were control variables, indicators of eustress and an outcome variable. The stressors used as control variables were role ambiguity, work overload and death/dying. Indicators of eustress were hope, positive affect and meaningfulness. The indicator of distress was negative affect. The outcome variable was the nurse's perception of his/her health. (For additional details of the study, please consult Simmons and Nelson, 2001b.)

Results All measures showed acceptable psychometric properties. Regression was used to analyze the relationships among the variables. The control variables were entered, followed by NA, and then the indicators of eustress (PA, meaningfulness and hope). Hope was the single variable that had a significant relationship with perceptions of health. This indicates partial support for H1. Interestingly post hoc analyses showed that nurses in critical care had higher levels of hope than those working in other areas of the hospital.

Discussion Study one showed that eustress can indeed be differentiated from distress, and that hope is a sound indicator of eustress. Despite the demanding nature of their work, nurses reported high levels of the positive psychological state of hope. They remained actively engaged in their work, and this positive response to demands (eustress) was related to their perceptions of their own well-being. This suggests that hope, defined in our study as the ability to focus on the most essential parts of the job, may bring about active engagement in even the most demanding work.

Study two: attitudes among nurses
In this study we explored differences in attitudes among nurses in two different work settings: hospitals and home health care. Home health care is among the fastest growing professions, in part owing to perceptions of advantages of practicing in homes as opposed to hospitals. Home health care affords the opportunity to provide one-on-one care, to conduct health education with patients and their families, and the ability to work autonomously as a primary case manager. We wanted to determine whether these perceived advantages extended to differences in attitudes between nurses in the two different settings. Attitudes, as state indicators of eustress and distress, might allow us to

108 Conceptualization and theoretical framework

make comparisons as to whether hospital nurses or home health nurses were more eustressed or distressed than the other group. Our proposition was that home health care nurses would experience more eustress and less distress than their hospital counterparts.

Method The hospital nurses participating in Study one, described earlier, were subjects in this study (145 RNs). In addition surveys were mailed to 950 home health nurses in the same southwestern state, and a total of 175 were returned and used in the analysis.

Measures used in the study were stressors and indicators of the stress response. Stressors included role ambiguity, work overload and death/dying. Indicators of eustress were hope, positive affect, meaningfulness, manageability, satisfaction and trust. Indicators of distress were negative affect, anger, job alienation and frustration. (For additional details of the study, please consult Simmons & Nelson, 2001a.)

Results Data were analyzed using multivariate anova (MANOVA). In both groups of nurses, workload and role ambiguity were related to almost all of the attitudinal variables, showing negative relationships with the positive attitudes and positive relationships with the negative attitudes. Interestingly death/dying was positively related to the eustress indicators trust, hope and positive affect. Contrary to what we had expected, there were no differences between hospital and home health nurses on any of the positive indicators for eustress. Home health nurses reported lower levels of two distress indicators, anger and frustration with the system. In terms of the stressors, home health nurses reported lower levels of role ambiguity and workload conflicts than did hospital nurses.

Discussion Our study indicated that home health nurses can be considered less distressed than hospital nurses, but both groups appeared equally eustressed. For both groups of nurses, the strongest positive attitudes were meaningfulness and hope, important indicators of eustress. Nurses thus have a strong emotional attachment to their work (meaningfulness) and, in the face of great challenges, find the will and the way to care for their patients (hope).

Through these two studies we can conclude that eustress is an important construct to include in a more holistic examination of stress at work. It can be measured by using state-like, attitudinal indicators, as can distress, its counterpart. Even in a demanding profession such as nursing, with stressors such as overload and death and dying, individuals who find their work meaningful and who believe they have the will and the way to accomplish their goals can glean positive experiences and related health benefits.

Implications for practice
The results of our studies provide some interesting insights for managers. Even in demanding and changing environments, such as those faced by nurses, people can have a positive response (eustress) to work, which is in turn related to health.

Meaningfulness and hope are important positive attitudes that may promote the experience of eustress at work. Eustress is related to health and well-being, which in turn are related to work performance. It makes sense, therefore, that helping employees find meaning and hope at work are important activities for managers. One way to accomplish this is by reinforcing the importance of the work employees perform (meaningfulness) and equipping employees with ways of actively engaging in work (hope).

The ability to generate hope in today's work environment, which is fraught with change and ambiguity, represents a major challenge for managers. If individuals believe that their actions can lead to positive results, they will be more willing to take on new and difficult challenges at work. Managers can assist workers in developing hope by establishing meaningful, challenging goals, and by providing workers with the resources necessary for meeting these goals. Frequent, meaningful, inspirational dialogue can go a long way toward the development of hope.

Another important challenge for managers is identifying the aspects of work that employees find most meaningful and engaging. Active engagement in work is an important factor in hope, and therefore in eustress.

Implications for research
Consistent with recent calls for a more positive psychology, and a focus on the positive rather than the negative, our research provides support for the importance of positive work attitudes and eustress. Researchers face several opportunities in further enhancing our knowledge of eustress at work.

A primary challenge is developing the theory by examining other indicators of eustress. While our studies focused on hope, meaningfulness, manageability, positive affect, satisfaction and trust, there are many other indicators that may be a part of eustress. Identifying these indicators is important if we are to define and operationalize eustress adequately.

In addition researchers are challenged to employ longitudinal designs in modeling both the positive and negative aspects of the stress response. Most studies (ours included) have consisted of cross-sectional, self-report data collection methods. A more holistic approach would include not only both the positive and the negative response, but also a full range of both positive and negative outcomes of the stress process. These would include psychological, behavioral and physiological outcomes, and particularly focus on performance at work.

Finally we propose a focus on eustress generation to complement the well-developed focus on distress prevention. We must know more about how to generate eustress at work, the individual characteristics that predispose individuals to seek out and savor eustress, and the organizational conditions that encourage eustress at work.

Conclusion
Our hope in this chapter is to generate some excitement and motivate other researchers to join us in turning toward a more positive approach to work stress. The challenges in studying eustress are many. We need more evidence of the indicators of eustress so we may offer a more complete understanding of the construct. We also need to know more about the biochemical differences between the positive and negative responses to work stress, and the pathways that these responses follow. In addition we need to explore more fully the management actions that can create and sustain eustressful conditions at work. All of these endeavors should keep researchers eustressed for quite some time. The ultimate aim is the creation of healthy work, with health defined as the presence of the positive rather than the absence of the negative.

References

Antonovsky, A. (1987), *Unraveling the mystery of health*, San Francisco: Jossey-Bass.
Britt, T.W., A.B. Adler and P.T. Bartone (2001), 'Deriving benefits from stressful events: the role of engagement in meaningful work and hardiness', *Journal of Occupational Health Psychology*, **6**, 53–63.
Cox, T., and M. Leitter (1992), 'The health of health care organizations', *Work & Stress*, **6**, 219–27.
Csikszentmihalyi, M. (1990). *Flow: The Psychology of Optimal Experience*, New York: Harper and Row.
Edwards, J.R. and C.L. Cooper (1988), 'The impacts of positive psychological states on physical health: a review and theoretical framework', *Social Science Medicine*, **27**, 1147–59.
Elkman, P., R.W. Levenson and W.V. Friesen (1983), 'Autonomic nervous system activity distinguishes among emotions', *Science*, **221**, 1208–10.
Folkman, S. and J.T. Moskowitz (2000), 'Positive affect and the other side of coping', *American Psychologist*, **55**, 647–54.
Frankenhauser, M., M.R. Von Wright, A. Collins, J. Von Wright, G. Sedvall and C.G. Swahn (1978), 'Sex differences in psychoendocrine reactions to examination stress', *Psychosomatic Medicine*, **40**, 334–343.
Ganster, D.C. and J. Schaubroeck (1991), 'Work stress and employee health', *Journal of Management*, **17**, 235–71.
Hemingway, M.A. and C.S. Smith (1999), 'Organizational climate and occupational stressors as predictors of withdrawal behaviors and injuries in nurses', *Journal of Occupational and Organizational Psychology*, **72**, 285–99.
Lazarus, R.S. (1966), *Psychological Stress and the Coping Process*, New York: McGraw-Hill.
Lazarus, R.S. and S. Folkman (1984), *Stress, Appraisal and Coping*, New York: Springer Publishing.
Luthans, F. (2002a), 'The need for and meaning of positive organizational behavior', *Journal of Organizational Behavior*, **23**(6), 695–706.
Luthans, F. (2002b), 'Positive organizational behavior: developing and managing psychological strength', *Academy of Management Executive*, **16**, 57–72.
Mason, J.W. (1974), 'Specificity in the organization response profiles', in P. Seeman and G. Brown (eds), *Frontiers in Neurology and Neuroscience Research*, Toronto: University of Toronto.
Peterson, C. (2000), 'The future of optimism', *American Psychologist*, **55**, 44–55.
Quick, J.C. (2002), 'Self-reliance: the implications of character in building effective networking', presentation at the Academy of Management annual meeting, Denver, CO.
Quick, J.C., D.L. Nelson and J.D. Quick (1987), 'Successful executives: how independent?', *Academy of Management Executive*, **1**, 139–45.
Quick, J.C., J.D. Quick, D.L. Nelson and J.J. Hurrell (1997), *Preventive Stress Management in Organizations*, Washington, DC: American Psychological Association.
Rose, R.M. (1987), 'Neuroendocrine effects of work stress', in J.C. Quick, R.S. Bhagal, J.E. Dalton and J.D. Quick (eds), *Work Stress: Health Care Systems in the Workplace*, New York: Praeger, pp. 130–47.
Roseman, I.J. (1984), 'Cognitive determinants of emotion: a structural theory', in P. Shaver (ed.), *Review of Personality and Social Psychology: Emotions, Relationships and Health*, Beverly Hills, CA: Sage, pp. 11–36.
Rothman, J.C. (1993), 'Aristotle's eudaepomnia, terminal illness, and the question of life support', *American University Studies (Series V, vol. 141)*, New York: P. Lang.
Ryan, R.M. and E.L. Deci (2000), 'Self-determination theory and the facilitation of intrinsic motivation, social development, and well-being', *American Psychologist*, **55**, 68–78.
Ryff, C.D. and P.C. Hill (2001), 'The virtues of positive psychology: the rapprochement and challenges of an affirmative postmodern perspective', *Journal for the Theory of Social Behavior*, **31**, 241–60.
Sales, S.M. (1969), 'Organizational role as a risk factor in coronary disease', *Administrative Science Quarterly*, **14**, 325–36.
Seligman, M.E.P. and M. Csikszentmihalyi (2000), 'Positive psychology', *American Psychologist*, **55**, 5–14.
Simmons, B.L. and D.L. Nelson (2001a), 'A comparison of the positive and negative work attitudes of home health care and hospital nurses', *Health Care Management Review* (Summer), 63–74.
Simmons, B.L. and D.L. Nelson (2001b), 'Eustress at work: the relationship between hope and health in hospital nurses', *Health Care Management Review*, **26**(4), 7–18.
Snyder, C.R. (2002), *Handbook of Hope*, San Diego: Academic Press.
Turner, N., J. Barling and A. Zacharatos (2002), 'Positive psychology at work', in C. Snyder and S.J. Lopez (eds), *Handbook of Positive Psychology*, New York: Oxford University Press, pp.715–728.
Tyler, P.A. and R.N. Ellison (1994), 'Sources of stress and psychological well-being in high-dependency nursing', *Journal of Advanced Nursing*, **19**, 469–76.

7 Stress and strain at work: how much is there, who has most and are things changing?
Roy L. Payne

In 1979 two colleagues and I published a short paper entitled 'Exploding the myth of executive stress' (Fletcher *et al.*, 1979). Encouraged by academic books such as *The failure of success* (Morrow, 1963) and the classic *Organizational Stress: Studies in Role Conflict and Ambiguity* (Kahn *et al.*, 1964) and highly successful novels such as *Something Happened* by Joseph Heller, the media of the 1960s and 1970s did much to promote the idea that executive life was highly stressful and that executives were the unsung super heroes of western societies (well, protestant ethic-driven societies anyway). Our paper, based on the following sorts of data, tried to dispel this myth.

Table 7.1 shows data derived from a survey of 1 per cent of the community based in a town in South Australia. The paper was published in 1977 but the survey was carried out in 1972 (Finlay-Jones and Burville, 1977). The table contains data for the 12-item version of the General Health Questionnaire (Goldberg, 1972) and it shows the percentage of people classified as 'cases of minor psychological distress' broken down by social class. Note that the sample is of people residing in the community, so it does not include severely ill people in mental hospitals and so on. A person is classified as a 'case' if they report having three or more of the 12 symptoms assessed by the GHQ-12. Social class is based on education, income and occupation. Social class 1 includes those in the higher and better paid professions and wealthy owners of businesses or properties. Social class 2 includes moderately well paid people who are well educated and in slightly less prestigious professions. Social class 3 consists largely of white-collar workers who are less well trained/educated than those in social class 2. Social class 4 contains craftsmen and well trained, reasonably paid blue-collar workers. Social class 5 houses the semi-skilled and unskilled, and social class 6 includes the least advantaged, including the unemployed. It is evident from Table 7.1 that there is not a great deal of difference in psychological strain for social classes 1 to 4, but the percentage of 'cases' almost doubles amongst those in social classes 5 and 6. There is no evidence here that the upper and middle classes are particularly psychologically strained.

Table 7.2 contains data on absence from work due to illness or injury and is also broken down by social class. The data are taken from the UK General Health Survey, 1971 and are based on people's answer to the question, 'How much time off work have you had in

Table 7.1 Prevalence of minor psychiatric morbidity in a healthy community, GHQ-12

Social class	1	2	3	4	5	6
With 'minor psychological distress' (%)	9.7	12.5	12.2	10.7	19.8	17.0

Table 7.2 Absence due to illness or injury, by social class

Social class	1	2	3	4	5	6
Average working days lost per man year	3.9	7.2	6.7	9.3	11.5	18.4

the last 2 weeks?' Since people are interviewed in their own homes there is a reasonably good chance that these self-reports of sickness absence are reasonably accurate although, as Johns (1997) has shown, there is a tendency for people to underreport their own absence levels and inflate their colleagues' levels. Accepting these data at face value, there is obviously a strong effect of social class on sickness absence: the higher one's social class the less one is absent from work because of sickness or injury.

A major assumption in the stress literature is that exposure to long-term stress will affect health, with some diseases being more affected than others (for example, ulcers, cardiovascular diseases, psychiatric conditions such as anxiety and depression). Ultimately such stresses might lead to premature death. Table 7.3 presents data on standardized mortality ratios for UK males aged 15–64 (that is, of employable ages). These too are broken down by social class and for ten different causes of death. Death from all causes is shown in the last line of the table. The standardized mortality ratio (SMR) is defined as the number of deaths observed divided by the number of deaths expected to be observed multiplied by 100. For the total population the observed and expected are the same, so the SMR is by definition 100. If death rates were equally distributed across the social classes then the figure for all causes would be 100 in each column. As is evident from Table 7.3, there are many fewer deaths in social class 1 than would be expected given their prevalence in the total population (SMR = 77). The opposite applies in social class 6, where there are many more deaths (SMR = 137). Indeed the SMRs get larger the lower the social class. This relationship applies to all causes of death except suicide, including the so-called 'executive disease', heart disease.

Table 7.3 Standardized mortality ratios, by major causes and social class, 1970–72, for UK males aged 15–64

Social class	1	2	3	4	5	6
Trachea, bronchus, lung cancer	53	68	84	118	123	143
Prostate cancer	91	89	99	115	106	115
Ischaemic heart disease	88	91	114	107	108	111
Other heart disease	69	75	94	100	121	157
Cerebrovascular disease	80	86	98	106	111	136
Pneumonia	41	53	78	92	115	195
Bronchitis, asthma	36	51	82	113	128	188
Accidents (not motor)	58	64	53	97	128	225
Motor vehicle accidents	77	83	89	105	120	174
Suicide	110	89	113	77	117	184
All causes	77	81	99	106	114	137

I am not claiming these differences are just due to differences in occupation of course. There are differences in diet, lifestyle (smoking, alcohol and so on), information about health, access to health care, quality of cars driven and so forth that will all affect death rates, but exposure to working conditions and the stresses they create will also have some effect on health and mortality. Chandola and Jenkinson (2000) analysed data from the Oxford Health Lifestyle Survey, with the sample made up of adult men and women aged 18–64, and data were obtained for 6454 subjects. The authors related social class to measures of physical and mental health and found the moderately strong relationship reported above. However, when they controlled for differences in lifestyle, housing and neighbourhood conditions, the relationship of health to social class disappeared; all these variables are related to social class of course.

Whilst the bulk of the evidence during this period shows that higher levels of strain and illness occur amongst people in the lowest-level jobs/occupations there is at least one study that found the opposite. Cherry (1978) asked 1415 men who were all 26 years old at the time (1972) to indicate whether in their work they experienced 'little or no nervous strain', 'some nervous strain' or 'severe nervous strain'. Thirty-eight per cent reported experiencing some nervous strain at work but only 4 per cent reported it was severe. Amongst this cohort of young men, however, the highest proportion experiencing at least 'some nervous strain' was amongst the professionals and non-manual workers (about 55 per cent) with the skilled manual workers having about 30 per cent and the semi-skilled about 15 per cent. The fact that they were all 26 years of age, however, makes this a very odd sample, since the young professionals will be at the bottom of their learning curve and the well trained and experienced manual workers well along theirs. The other key point is that this is a report of *'nervous strain' at work only*, whilst the GHQ, for example, is not specific about the place where the strain is experienced, and covers a much wider range of stress-related symptoms. The amount of stress in the total life-space of these different occupational groups may still have been more in favour of the professionals.

The final piece of evidence, quoted in Fletcher *et al.*, was on job satisfaction. Table 7.4 ranks various occupational groups according to their self-rated job satisfaction. These data are taken from the US Department of Labour Survey (1974). The most satisfying occupations are again professional and managerial and the least satisfying are in semi-skilled and unskilled jobs. This is unlikely to come as a great surprise to most people when one considers the differences in pay and rewards for these different groups, but the myth

Table 7.4 Job satisfaction, by occupational group

Professional and technical	25
Managers and similar occupational groups	19
Sales	11
Craftsmen and foremen	8
Service workers	−11
Clerical workers	−14
Operatives	−35
Non-farm labourers	−42

of executive stress persisted in the 1970s despite these very obvious differences. The question I wish to ask now is, 'Is the myth still a myth?'

Before embarking on this question, and to draw attention to the title of this chapter, it should be pointed out that the evidence quoted above is all about the outcomes of being stressed: the data all indicate the strain people have experienced rather than the stress that has been 'causing' that strain. A later part of this chapter will examine some data relating to whether ratings of stress have changed during the last three or four decades, and whether the direction of change is the same as that for data on strain.

Is the myth of executive stress still a myth?
Strictly speaking, the question is, 'Is the myth of executive strain still a myth?' Fortunately the GHQ-12 has continued to be used as a measure of strain and Table 7.5 contains data from two very large studies that both used it. The NHS sample is drawn from studies of National Health Service staff, carried out by the Institute of Work Psychology at Sheffield University. The studies have involved the staff from 21 hospital trusts in the UK and staff have been surveyed in 1996 and 1998. In each case questionnaires measuring both stress and strain were completed by over 11 000 staff from all occupations and levels in the NHS. The details of the studies are in Borrill *et al.* (1998).

The BHPS sample is derived from the British Household Panel Survey (Taylor *et al.*, 1995). This survey is carried out in people's homes and covers a random sample of British households. The data in Table 7.5 shows the percentage of adults who scored four or more on the GHQ-12 for both the NHS sample (N=11 005) and the BHPS sample for 1996/7 (N=5216). Note that in the Finlay-Jones and Burville survey (Table 7.1) people were classified as a case if they scored three or more, so this is a more stringent criterion. In Table 7.5 the percentages for the BHPS study are broken down by occupation as defined by the Standard Occupational Classification (SOC). The staff from the NHS sample have been classified into the occupational categories in the SOC into which they would be classified by that system to enable comparisons to be made between the two studies.

Given that a more stringent criterion was used, the most obvious change is the percentage of people that are 'cases'. In the early 1970s the percentages of cases in social classes 1–4 were about 10–12 per cent and for social classes 5 and 6 about 19 per cent (Table 7.1). As is evident from Table 7.5, the percentage of cases in all levels of NHS staff are greater than 20 per cent and the same applies to the BHPS sample except for the two 'blue-collar' occupations, where they are between 11 per cent and 14 per cent. These last two percentages are not too different from the 1970s figures but for all the white-collar, managerial and professional groups the percentages have nearly doubled. Furthermore, on this evidence, executive stress (strain) is no longer a myth, for the highest percentages are amongst the managers (nearly 33 per cent in the NHS) and the professionals, though in the BHPS study all groups except the blue-collar groups are around 20 per cent. The NHS staff is particularly highly strained, being higher than the BHPS sample for every occupational category.

Another author who has used the BHPS data sets is Rose (2002), who also presents data using the GHQ classified by SOC, but he uses only one question, which is whether people have recently felt 'constantly under strain'. With this single question, the craft and manufacturing occupations have about 23 per cent saying 'yes' and the sales, managers and

Table 7.5 GHQ-12 'case' rates by, occupation for, NHS and BHPS samples

Occupational Gp	NHS N	Sample %	SOC Occup. Gp	BHPS N	Sample %
Managers	934	32.8	Managers	809	21.3
Doctors	1235	24.6	Prof. occupations	555	18.6
Nurses	4236	27.6	Assoc. prof. and tech.	469	19.0
Prof. allied to med.	1502	26.8	Assoc. prof. and tech.	565	20.0
Prof. and tech. staff	730	25.8	Assoc. prof. and tech.	565	20.0
Admin. staff	1801	23.5	Clerical and secretarial	893	19.8
Ancillary staff	567	23.1	Other occupations	270	21.9
			Sales	336	21.1
			Craft occupations	669	11.5
			Plant and machine	464	14.2

professional groups have between 31 per cent and 38 per cent, with the managerial group scoring 34 per cent. Rose also examines the expressed happiness of the different occupational groups and it is the craft and manufacturing groups that are the happiest, with sales being the least happy and managers and professionals in between. The myth appears to be becoming reality.

In an attempt to understand the possible causes of 'feeling constantly under strain' Rose plotted the percentages for the years 1991 to 1998 and for each year compared the rates for people in industries that were growing with those that were declining. The percentages showed a rise from the early 1990s (about 27 per cent) to the late 1990s about 31 per cent and for three years (1994, 95 and 98) the percentages were higher for occupations experiencing growth (29 per cent versus 32 per cent).

Rose also examined the percentages of people who were positively satisfied with their jobs and again compared different occupational groups. The least satisfied occupations are plant and manufacturing (31 per cent) and craft and related occupations (32 per cent satisfied with material aspects and 36 per cent with quality aspects). Managers and professionals have about 44 per cent satisfied and they are slightly more satisfied with their material aspects (47 per cent). The most satisfied are the personal and protective occupations that score particularly highly on quality aspects of satisfaction (51 per cent).

This general pattern, however, is very different from the psychological strain data. The least satisfied occupations are the lower-level ones and the more satisfied are the managerial ones, which is more like the pattern found in the 1970s (Table 7.4). Whilst the data are not directly comparable, the percentage satisfied has fallen considerably in the three decades, for over 75 per cent of people used to report positive satisfaction with most facets of their jobs (Lawler, 1973). Andrews and Withey (1976) wrote a book about the perceived quality of life of people in the USA. On three questions about how people felt about their jobs that asked about 'the job itself, the people they worked with, and the work they actually did', they found only about 15 per cent reported any kind of dissatisfaction whatsoever. Herzberg et al. (1959) reported the percentage dissatisfied with their jobs annually between 1947 and 1953 and showed that this fell from 21 per cent to only 13 per cent over that six-year period. The percentage of people satisfied with their jobs in the 1960s and 1970s is clearly much higher than it is in the late 1990s and the early years of the 21st century, though the positive difference between those in higher-level jobs and those in lower-level jobs remains, even though the absolute levels of satisfaction have fallen.

In trying to get a precise estimate of the amount of strain in the working population, Warr and Payne (1983) interviewed a random sample of British workers (over 1100) and asked them to say how much job-related strain they had experienced on the previous day. Fifteen per cent of men reported feeling unpleasant emotional strain from their job at least 'sometime' on the previous day. The figure was 10 per cent for full-time employed women. When the data were analysed by occupation, however, the figures were 9 per cent for male skilled and semi-skilled workers and 18 per cent for managerial, professional and administrative workers. When asked to report how much pleasure they had experienced from their job the previous day, however, the pattern is reversed: 25 per cent of managerial, professional and administrative workers reported that they had experienced pleasure and only 17 per cent of the skilled and semi-skilled workers did.

This pattern is paralleled by UK data on absence from work. Table 7.6 presents data from the Household survey for 2001. The data are broken down into three broad occupational groups. The lost worktime rate is the hours absent as a percentage of hours usually worked. As can be seen, there is a very small difference between the lost worktime rates of the white-collar workers in the middle category and the service and largely blue-collar workers (farming and so on excluded), with the latter category having the higher absence. The difference is larger when they are compared with the managers, executives and professionals in the group at the top of the table. This pattern of results is very similar to those quoted for the early 1970s (Table 7.4), where absence rates were higher amongst the lower social classes.

Finally let us turn to the ultimate absence, death rates: have they changed over recent decades? Table 7.7 shows standardized mortality ratios, by major causes, for males aged

Table 7.6 Absence from work, by occupational group

Occupation	Lost Worktime Rate			
	Total employed	Total	Illness or injury	Other reasons
Manag and prof speciality	32 231	1.5	0.9	0.6
Exec and admin	15 881	1.3	0.9	0.5
Prof speciality	16 350	1.6	0.9	0.7
Tech, sales, admin	28 047	2.0	1.4	0.6
Technicians and support	3 755	2.0	1.4	0.6
Sales	10 128	1.6	1.1	0.5
Admin and clerical	14 165	2.3	1.6	0.8
Service occupations	11 034	2.3	1.7	0.6
Precision prod'n, craft	12 006	1.8	1.3	0.5
Operators, labourers	14 685	2.5	2.0	0.4
Farming, forestry, fishing	1 505	1.5	1.2	0.3

Table 7.7 Standardized mortality ratios, by major causes and social class, 1991–3, for males aged 20–64

Social class	1	2	3	4	5	6
Trachea, bronchus, lung cancer	45	61	87	138	132	206
Prostate cancer	111	103	108	120	103	132
Ischaemic heart disease	63	73	107	125	121	182
Cerebrovascular disease	70	67	96	118	125	219
Pneumonia	58	69	106	93	108	197
Bronchitis	44	43	81	125	137	268
Asthma	51	55	90	128	114	229
Accidents (not motor)	54	57	74	107	106	226
Accidents (motor)	66	65	86	113	101	185
Suicide	55	63	87	96	107	215
All causes	66	72	100	117	116	189

20–64, broken down by social class for the years 1991–3. These are the latest figures available and were published in 1997. The very strong effect of social class on death rates is once again seen in the last row of the table, showing deaths from all causes. Many more working-age men are dying in the lower social classes than would be expected by their prevalence, and vice versa for the upper social classes. The pattern remains as in 1972 for most causes of death. The one obvious exception is death from prostate cancer, which is similar across all social classes. There is no evidence here that heart disease is an executive disease. One change from 1972 is that deaths by suicide in the early 1990s are much more strongly related to social class. Since suicide is strongly related to depression, this again suggests that people in the higher social classes are not suffering from depression as much as those in the lower social classes are.

The answer to the question, 'Is the myth of executive stress still a myth?' is not at all straightforward. People in managerial and professional jobs are reporting a lot more psychological strain than they were, and a lot more than those in blue-collar and lower-level white-collar jobs. On the other hand these managers and professionals are having less absence from work due to sickness, they are more satisfied with their jobs, and they are living much longer than one would expect from their prevalence in the population. What might be causing these changes and differences? Is there more stress at work (which may be causing higher levels of strain and lower levels of job satisfaction) and is it related to occupational level?

Levels of perceived stress over the last few decades

Obtaining data on this topic is very difficult. The main stressors in the workplace are things such as workload or job demands, sometimes measured as role overload. Others include role conflict and role ambiguity. Role overload, role ambiguity and role conflict are concepts originally created by Kahn *et al.* (1964) and have been used by other researchers over the decades, but different researchers have measured them in different ways, so it becomes difficult to compare them over time. Another problem is that, even when the same measures have been used (for example, the ones used by Karasek, 1979, to measure job demands and job decision latitude, and subsequently used by many other researchers) many authors fail to publish means and standard deviations as they are only interested in testing predictive models. Indeed, there are no means and standard deviations quoted in the original Karasek paper. The same applies to meta-analyses such as those by Jackson and Schuler (1985) and Tubre and Collins (2000) on measures of role conflict and role ambiguity – correlations are quoted, but not means.

Haynes et al. (1999), for example, measured both role conflict and role ambiguity. The measure of role ambiguity used five of the six items originally designed by Rizzo et al. (1970) but they were measured on a five-point scale instead of a seven-point scale and the scale was reversed so that it measured role clarity. Haynes et al. found a mean score of just under 4 for over 11 000 hospital personnel and job level/occupation accounted for less than 1 per cent of the variance. Reversing the scale suggests the mean score on role ambiguity (as opposed to role clarity) is therefore about 1.2. Using the seven-point scale version in the early 1970s, Schuler et al. (1977) reported studies on seven different groups of workers. The mean ambiguity scores on the seven-point scale varied from 4.03 to 1.23 with the median being 3.2. Comparing this to the mean of 1.2 on the five-point scales in the 1990s suggests they are not too different and if anything the mean of 1.2 is relatively slightly smaller. Whilst the evidence is not unambiguous it appears that role ambiguity has not increased and that it does not differ much by occupation either. The Haynes et al. measure of role conflict bears no resemblance to that of the Rizzo et al. measure, so comparison there is impossible.

Caplan et al. (1975) surveyed over 2300 workers from 23 different occupations, which ranged from forklift drivers and assembly line workers to physicians, professors and scientists. They obtained ratings on many variables but included workload, role conflict and role ambiguity. Role conflict was assessed by three items measured on a four-point scale, with 2 meaning 'sometimes' and 3 'fairly often'. Mean scores ranged from 1.37 (professor) to 2.01 (dispatcher), indicating relatively low conflict. Role ambiguity was measured by four items on a five-point scale, with the middle category being 'sometimes'. The lowest score was 1.6 (physicians) and the highest accountants (2.41) which again suggests that ambiguity was not a major stressor. Physicians reported the highest mean scores on workload which was measured by ten items rated on five-point scales, with 'sometimes' being the middle category. The physicians scored 4.14, the administrative professors 4.07, the forklift drivers 3.58, and assembly line workers 3.40. The physicians earned five times as much as the latter two groups of workers, worked far more hours (58 versus 40) and were the least dissatisfied. Clearly the overall stress in a job is determined by a balance of factors, so that long hours can be compensated for by the positive experiences the job provides and the rewards that go with it that help to make life outside work more enjoyable too. Unfortunately I know of no studies that have used these same measures in more recent times.

Haynes et al. (1999) measured role conflict with four items rated on five-point scales, with 'moderate amount' being the central category. In their study of over 11 000 NHS personnel, the largest mean was 2.47 (managers) and the smallest 2.13 for administrators and 2.11 for professions allied to medicine. These data suggest that perceived levels of conflict are not particularly high amongst any occupational group in the late 1990s and no more

Table 7.8   Percentage of people reporting they have more effort and stress and greater pace of work than a year ago

	Effort		Stress		Pace	
	More	Same	More	Same	More	Same
Mgrs and admin. staff	68	28	62	32	52	44
Professionals	63	33	62	32	57	44
Para-professionals	62	33	61	32	50	46
Trade persons	54	42	44	49	40	55
Clerks	62	34	51	41	50	45
Salespersons/personal services	58	38	42	49	47	50
Plant and machine ops	56	41	44	50	36	59
Labourers etc	52	44	50	51	36	57

Note: N=19 155 Australian workers in 1995.

than in the early 1970s (though the measures and samples are different, so caution needs to be exercised).

Table 7.8 shows the results of a large study of over 19 000 Australian workers drawn from over 2 000 different organizations. Amongst the many questions asked, the survey included ones about changes in perceived stressors over the previous year. The three stressors were about effort, stress and pace of working. The table shows the percentage of people from different occupational groups who have reported the change is towards 'more' or there is no change (same). The table shows that, for all three stressors, getting close to 40 per cent or more of every occupational group has reported that the demand has gone up in the last year. The table also shows that the largest increases have been experienced by the managerial and professional workers. This work is published in Moorehead *et al.* (1997).

In Britain, at least, another major contributor to the higher levels of strain reported above may be the sheer number of hours being worked. One in six employees is now working over 60 hours a week and only two years ago it was one in eight. This overtime culture and the costs of the stress associated with it to British industry alone (£370 million per annum) has inspired the government to launch a campaign to improve the work–life balance (*The Guardian*, 30 August 2002, p. 6). Certainly perceived workload appears to be the biggest stressor in the data reported above. However, as is now reasonably well established, senior managers can also reduce strain by improving social support and optimizing the degree of autonomy available to all workers (Van der Doef and Maes, 1999).

Conclusion
Executive (professional/administrative/technical) strain is no longer a myth, but the patterns of stress that can cause it are obviously quite complex, and the patterns of events/environments that influence one's overall experience of work (satisfaction, challenge, commitment, alienation and so on) are even more so. In an informative article entitled 'Working 61 hours plus a week: why do managers do it?' Brett and Stroh (2003) provide references on the work hours of US managers, who work 137 more hours per year

than Japanese managers, 260 more than the British and 449 more than the French. They also report an empirical study of 595 male managers and 301 female managers, all of whom worked more than 35 hours per week. The average hours for males was 56 hours per week and for females it was 52 hours. Almost 29 per cent of males worked 61 hours plus and the figure for females was 11 per cent. The authors also measured 19 other variables covering background variables, perceptions of work and its benefits, family circumstances and so on. Regressing these on hours of work, they found that amount of financial compensation for men *and* women was one of the best predictors (standardized beta was 0.31 for females and 0.26 for males). The biggest predictor for males was work stress (beta = 0.31 followed by age (−0.15), job involvement (0.14) and family stress (−0.13). The additional significant predictors for females managers were family stress (−0.36), family alienation (0.33) and family satisfaction (0.28). It appears that managers who work long hours provide good support for their families, either through a non-employed spouse or by extra care providers, leading them to report lower levels of family stress. Despite this apparent positive outcome a meta analysis of hours of work and health has shown that longer hours lead to poorer health (Sparks *et al.*, 1997). The Brett and Stroh article ends with a call for strategies for reducing hours of work for US managers. A meta-analysis of interventions for work-related stress can be found in Van der Klink *et al.* (2001) and the authors conclude that they are effective, but the cognitive–behavioural interventions are more effective than organizational, relaxation and multi-modal interventions.

Another explanation for the rise in strain is offered by Twenge (2000), who has analysed large amounts of data on self-reported trait anxiety for both college students and children in the USA. These impressive analyses show that trait anxiety rose considerably from the 1950s to the 1990s. 'The average respondent from 1993 would score at the 84th percentile on a distribution of self-reports of anxiety collected in the 1950s' (p. 1018). These increases in self-reported anxiety are highly correlated with changes in the degree of 'social connectedness' in society and feelings of threat and lack of trust, but not changes in economic conditions. Where the data presented above are at odds with such findings is that scores on strain have risen for people at the top and middle of organizations but not those at the lower levels. Again, whilst the levels of strain are higher, the levels of satisfaction are higher and sickness absence is lower for those in the higher echelons. Trait anxiety is a strong predictor of GHQ and societal increases in it may be part of the explanation, but as far as work stress is concerned other factors are also at play, as has been shown by Payne and Morrison (2002). The major research implication of this chapter is the need for longitudinal studies that contain good measures of both subjective and objective stress as well as measures of psychological strain and well-being.

References

Andrews, F.M and S.B. Withey (1976), *Social Indicators of Well-being: Americans' Perceptions of Life Quality*, New York: Plenum Press.

Borrill, C.S., T.D. Wall, M.A. West, G.E. Hardy, D.A. Shapiro, C.E. Haynes, C.B. Stride, D. Woods and A.J. Carter, (1998), 'Stress amongst staff in NHS Trusts', Final Report, Institute of Work Psychology, University of Sheffield.

Brett, J.M. and L.K. Stroh, (2003), 'Working 61 hours plus per week: why do managers do it?' *Journal of Applied Psychology*, **88** (1), 67–78.

Caplan, R.D., S. Cobb, J.R.P. French, Jr., R. Van Harrison and S.R. Pinneau, Jr. (1975), 'Job demands and worker health: main effects and occupational differences', Institute for Social Research, University of Michigan.

Chandola, T. and C. Jenkinson, (2000), 'The new UK national statistics socioeconomic classification (NS-SEC): investigating social class differences in self-reported health status', *Journal of Public Health Medicine*, **22**(2), 182–90.

Cherry, N. (1978), 'Stress, anxiety and work: a longitudinal study', *Journal of Occupational Psychology*, **51**, 259–70.

Finlay-Jones, R.A. and P.W. Burville, (1977), 'The prevalence of minor psychiatric morbidity in the community', *Psychological Medicine*, **7**, 475–89.

Fletcher, B., D. Gowler and R. Payne, (1979), 'Exploding the myth of executive stress', *Personnel Management*, May, 30–4.

Goldberg, D.P. (1972), *The Detection of Minor Psychiatric Illness by Questionnaire*, Oxford: Oxford University Press.

Haynes, C.E., T.D. Wall, R.I. Bolden and J.D. Rick, (1999), 'Measures of perceived work characteristics for health services research: test of a measurement model and normative data', *British Journal of Health Psychology*, **4**, 257–75.

Herzberg, F., B. Mausner and B. Snyderman, (1959), *The Motivation to Work*, New York: John Wiley.

Jackson, S.E. and R.S. Schuler, (1985), 'A meta-analysis and conceptual critique of research on role ambiguity and role conflict in work settings', *Organizational Behavior and Human Decision Processes*, **36**, 16–78.

Johns, G. (1997), 'Contemporary research on absence from work: correlates, causes and consequences', *International Review of Industrial and Organizational Psychology*, **12**, 115–74.

Kahn, R.L., D.M. Wolfe, R.P. Quinn, J.D. Snoek and R.A. Rosenthal, (1964), *Organizational Stress; Studies in Role Conflict and Ambiguity*, New York: John Wiley.

Karasek, R.A. (1979), 'Job demands, job decision latitude, and mental strain: implications for job redesign', *Administrative Science Quarterly*, **24**, 285–308.

Lawler, E.E. (1973), *Motivation in Work Organizations*, Belmont, CA: Wadsworth.

Moorehead, A., A. Steele, M. Alexander and L. Duffin, (1997), Changes at Work: The 1995 Australian *Workplace Industrial Relations Survey*, Melbourne: Addison-Wesley Longman.

Morrow, E. (1963), *The Failure of Success*, Washington: American Management Association.

Payne, R.L. and D. Morrison, (2002), 'The differential effects of negative affectivity on measures of well-being versus job satisfaction and organizational commitment', *Anxiety, Stress and Coping*, 1–13.

Rizzo, J.R., R.J. House and S.I. Lirtzman, (1970), 'Role conflict and ambiguity in complex organizations', *Administrative Science Quarterly*, **15**, 150–63.

Rose, M. (2002), 'Future tense: are growing occupations more stressed out and depressive?' (www.bath.ac.uk/~hssmjr/fow/wp3/wp3_text.htm).

Schuler, R.S., R.J. Aldag and A.P. Brief, (1977), 'Role conflict and ambiguity: a scale analysis', *Organizational Behaviour and Human Performance*, **20**, 111–28.

Sparks, K., C.L. Cooper, Y. Fried and A. Shirom, (1997), 'The effects of hours of work on health: a meta-analysis review, *Journal of Occupational and Organizational Psychology*, **70**, 391–409.

Taylor, M., J. Brice and N. Buck, (1995), *British Household Panel Survey User Manual*, Colchester: University of Essex.

Tubre, T.C. and J.M. Collins, (2000), 'Jackson and Schuler (1985) revisited: a meta-analysis of the relationships between role ambiguity, role conflict, and job performance', *Journal of Management*, **26**, 155–69.

Twenge, J.M. (2000), 'The age of anxiety? Birth cohort change in anxiety and neuroticism, 1952–1993', *Journal of Personality and Social Psychology*, **79**(6), 1007–21.

Van der Doef, M. and S. Maes, (1999), 'The job demand-control (-support) model and psychological well-being: a review of 20 years' empirical research', *Work and Stress*, **13**, 87–114.

Van der Klink, J.J.L., R.W.B. Blank, A.H. Schene and F.J.H. Van Dijk, (2001), 'The benefits of interventions for work-related stress', *American Journal of Public Health*, **19**, 270–6.

Warr, P.B. and R.L. Payne, (1983), 'Affective outcomes of paid employment in a random sample of British workers', *Journal of Occupational Behaviour*, **4**, 91–104.

8 Stress, alienation and shared leadership
Marc J. Schabracq

Introduction
This chapter is about the possible role of good leadership in preventing and counteracting alienation and stress. First, the main antecedents of stress and alienation are described, namely everyday reality in organizations, and the concepts of stress and alienation are further examined as disturbances of that everyday reality. Then leadership is described as 'realizing' in both of its meanings (generating reality and reflecting about it) and leadership tasks are explicated. Having described what abilities and qualities good leaders must have, it is concluded that, in many cases, this may be too much for one person. So the concept of shared leadership is introduced and its advantages and disadvantages are discussed. Finally, a scenario for implementation of shared leadership is described.

Everyday reality
To most of us everyday reality is a predictable and comfortable place. Essentially this is a strange way to experience a world full of violence, disaster, illness and death. It suggests that everyday reality as we experience it is something else: not the grim chaos outside, but our set of habits to deal with that world. So our everyday reality consists of our habitual ways of doing things in our familiar niches, with their familiar steps and limited horizons, which are so familiar to us. We experience these routines, as well as our own feelings and sensations resulting from this repetition, as a familiar, seemingly continuous, background to our functioning. Such a self-made background we trust as a solid reality. This way of organizing one's life affords one the luxury of nice megalomaniac sayings such as 'the psyche is everything', as Aristotle used to state (in Delfgauw, 1988) and 'about which one cannot speak: one should be silent' (Wittgenstein, 1961).

Elsewhere (Schabracq, 1991, 2002a), I have described in more detail how one generates and maintains such a reality. Here I give only the bare essentials. First, this is a matter of selecting and designing a small niche to live in, keeping it that way and taking care of it. Then it involves relentless repetition of familiar patterns of behaviour. In addition it takes strict attention discipline, that is, attending to some items, mostly those related to the familiar behaviour patterns, and ignoring the rest (see also Goffman, 1963, 1971). Lastly, by following culturally shared representations in doing all this (Moscovici, 1984), one signifies and explicates what one does, to the relevant others as well as to oneself, in order to prevent their and one's own alienation. All in all, keeping up everyday reality costs us a lot of work.

For instance, by allowing our attention to be determined by familiar working tasks, we time after time synchronize our functioning with the task structure, as well as with the organization and its further environment (Schutz, 1970). In the reality resulting from this task performance, we know what to do, what to think and what to feel. As long as everything goes well, we submit ourselves to the situational rules without a thought and, more or less automatically, get into the corresponding state of consciousness as well. Behaving in the right way, we 'slide' from one situation into the next: our attention is systematically *not* directed to places where, from a task perspective, there is nothing to focus on.

So reality is something like a journey through a landscape of realistically looking coulisses. It is as if a competent and attentive magician seems to go out of his way to make sure that our attention is diverted into an intended direction each time that it is about to be focused on something that is incompatible with task performance (Schabracq, 1987). Of course we ourselves are the magicians here. The most important point, however, is that this actually works: most of us feel that we inhabit a solid reality. As a result, we can experience ourselves also as real persons: we exist as persons and, because we are continuously more or less the same, we experience ourselves and our environment as quite normal.

By working, we also make our surroundings, as shaped by our own activities, real and normal, to ourselves as well as to others. In this way, we also contribute to the reality of the organization, within which we perform our tasks. Though to a smaller degree, this applies to the society at large of which the organization is a part. So work adds to the possibility of inhabiting a familiar and shared reality.

Many people dislike this idea of reality. It is just not attractive and appealing to them. Though most people actually are leading a life of continuous repetition, it sounds to them as more a punishment, the sad fate of slaves and prisoners, than a truthful description of their own normal way of living. After all, is one not free and creative, can people not choose what they want? Many people just love excitement and like to think that they are leading challenging lives. However, maybe one just does not notice the repetition in one's life because is it so omnipresent, so common and normal. Is not the fish the last to detect the water?

Maintaining reality implies much work, but there is also much that can go wrong. Reality is not permanent. It can be disturbed and brought down altogether. One's particular niche and its surroundings can change. One can alter one's behaviour and other people can alter theirs. New social representations, for example from other cultures, may appear. And one can simply change one's division of attention, for instance by fixating a certain object, closing the eyes or repeating a certain word for some time, techniques well-known for their power to bring about so-called 'altered states of consciousness'. This does not mean that reality is only an illusion, as is often stated. It just implies that reality is not always there.

Alienation and stress

Disturbance or breakdown of reality leads to alienation and stress. From this point of view, it is even much easier to produce alienation and stress than to bring about normality. This is only a matter of slightly changing the very same factors that bring about normality. In principle, all changes in work tasks and the work environment can bring this about.

Following Schabracq (2003), two kinds of alienation are distinguished, designated as primary and secondary alienation. Primary alienation refers to an experience or feeling that something is different from normal, so primary alienation is an experience or feeling of difference. Secondary alienation, on the other hand, is about the absence of an experience or feeling about something abnormal, where one is expected – by others – to experience or feel something. In this way, secondary alienation is about a difference in experience or feeling.

As already suggested by the terms 'primary' and 'secondary', the second form of alienation may ensue from the first, though not necessarily so. Both forms of alienation refer to a disturbance in a relationship, either between a person and his environment or within the person himself, that is, being alienated from a part of oneself or one's activities. Both terms therefore represent an insufficiency, a state of being less than ideal, as a consequence of a change. Alienation is often considered to be the opposite of 'engagement', commitment and involvement (Kanungo, 1982; Maslach *et al.*, 2001; Goffman, 1963; 1971), though this clearly is not a one-dimensional opposition. Moreover alienation always implies a lack or loss of control (Seeman, 1983; Blauner, 1964). Typical objects of alienation are the physical environment as designed and made by ourselves, other people, norms and values, and one's own activities, a categorization which goes back to Marx (Ollman, 1971; see also Schabracq *et al.*, 2001; Schabracq, 2002b). All in all, secondary alienation acts – at the level of experience – as a common final path in the second stage of a human stress process, which corresponds to the maintenance stage of the 'general adaptation syndrome' described by Selye (1956).

Work stress is taken to be a response to a loss or lack of control over our work performance. It evolves when we must do something that we are not able and/or willing to do. In a work context, this is related to the appropriateness of the work and its environment, that is the degree on which we are able and want to attend on the work and be involved in it. In general, it can be stated that work and work environments that make it too hard to keep our attention on the work lead to stress. In everyday practice, this appropriateness is a kind of middle zone between too much and too little challenge (Schabracq *et al.*, 2001; Schabracq, 2002a, 2002b).

Work that becomes too challenging demands more knowledge, skills and abilities than we can mobilize. It becomes impossible to deal with the task in a systematic and orderly way. Chaos takes over, our involvement vanishes and task performance breaks down. As we lose control over our task performance, having to perform the task anyhow then becomes a serious source of stress. This activates, to a certain degree, a primordial response pattern (fight, flight or freezing), which is only appropriate in situations that quickly demand intensive bodily activity.

On the other hand, work that offers too little challenge to keep us involved (Goffman, 1963), while we must do it anyhow, demands from us that we force ourselves to stay involved. This soon becomes very tiring and we can go on in this way only for a limited time. Our attention wanders. We become bored and drowsy, and sometimes somewhat irritated. The work becomes less and less manageable, and this too can give rise to stress, though of a different quality from the kind of stress discussed above.

Both kinds of stress processes can initially be accompanied by more or less explicit feelings of primary alienation of differing duration, which sooner or later turn into secondary alienation. When the source of stress cannot be taken away or neutralized, the two kinds of stress enter a common final path, corresponding more or less to the second stage of the 'general adaptation syndrome', the maintenance stage, described by Selye (1956), in which the stressor is ignored as much as possible.

As described elsewhere (for example Schabracq *et al.*, 2001, 2002), alienation and stress can have severe negative consequences for the individual employees involved as well as for the organization as a whole. One important way to prevent and cure phenomena such as alienation and stress is good leadership.

Good leadership
What is good leadership? Compared to management, it is more about developing a vision, in the long and short term, and designing the organization, and less about controlling the everyday course of affairs. Leadership is about 'realizing', in both of its senses: making things happen as well as reflecting about them. In this second meaning, leadership is about learning, wisdom and a clear moral perspective. Actualizing a functional reality, its first meaning, implies that the resulting organization is, or should be, relatively free from alienation and stress. In order to develop a real organization, four functions have to be realized (Smit, 1997; Parsons, 1937). Seen from this perspective, good leadership is a matter of developing good solutions for the following four issues.

The first issue is setting (and adjusting) goals for the organization. What needs of the outer world, so essential that they would justify the existence of the organization, does the organization want to fulfil? What real problems can it help to solve, or what substantial improvements can it bring about, and how can this be done as effectively and efficiently as possible? These are questions about the mission and vision of the organization (Collins and Porras, 1994; Hamel and Pralahad, 1994). As long as the goal is viable, a good leader holds on to it. This demands much persistence and effort, as well as sufficient professional knowledge. Of course this is about goals that conform to the law and the usual ethical norms, while they also must contribute sufficiently to the goal and needs of the employees. Does the work offer sufficient meaning, challenge, possibilities for development and pleasure? All questions ask for diverse leadership qualities. Poor solutions impair the reality and survival of the resulting organization and may lead to alienation and stress.

The second issue concerns the question how the organization is able to attune itself successfully to and embed itself in its environment. How do you become a self-evident, accessible and trusted partner to your environment? How do you make enough money by this to be able to flourish? How do you earn respect, prestige and legitimacy? This is about connecting with customers, suppliers and organizations of the same branch, as well as attuning oneself to the government and its legislation. How do you build strong, self-evident relations with all these parties? How do you make it for them more pleasurable, easier and cheaper to do business with you? This can be a matter of integrating activities in a joint production process with partner organizations that take care of other parts of the process, in order to serve the final customer as well as possible (Hammer, 2001). In addition it concerns developing and maintaining processes to gather information about changes in the environment that demand timely adaptations from the organization. Of course poor solutions in all of these respects endanger organizational survival and also may lead to alienation and stress.

The third matter is about optimizing the internal cooperation in order to deal with the first two issues as well as possible. This is about cooperation both between and within different departments. It is also about creating 'processes' to serve the customer optimally (ibid.), so that employees can work effectively and pleasurably, without unnecessary alienation and stress, while adaptations and changes can be implemented in a supple way too. This demands that the common interest comes first and conflicts are prevented. This results in a pleasurable and effective working climate, where all involved are available to each other and help each other if needed.

The last issue is seeing to it that that the first three issues are actually dealt with and that everything sinks into a self-evident, everyday way of doing things, free from stress or alienation. This is a matter of repetition (building up automatisms and routine) and discipline of attention, minding what should be minded and giving the least possible attention to other matters. Put differently, an everyday reality should be created that enables those involved to lose themselves in their work without unnecessary disturbances or distractions. Though a leader cannot act upon this directly – after all, this is a matter of learning by employees – leaders can influence a number of its preconditions (see Schabracq, 2002b, for a more elaborated description). This is, for example, about manageable tasks, as well as functional physical worksites, which make it possible to work effectively and efficiently. Another point is a functional social structure, which prevents unnecessary conflicts and provides sufficient possibilities for identification, making a mark and belonging, as well as for personal contacts and stable relations. Finally, it is important that the values and goals of those involved remain compatible with the organizational ones, though overidentification in this respect should be avoided too, as this may lead to loss of personal limits.

Successful execution of all these tasks generates a safe reality with minimal stress and alienation. The other way around, frequent occurrence of stress and alienation somewhere in the organization serves as a signal that something has gone wrong that needs the special attention of the leader (Schabracq et al., 2001). Radical changes can undermine the self-evidence of this reality and this too calls for the leader's special attention. All in all, the leader is facing such a great number of diverse tasks that it is questionable whether this is not too much for one person.

What qualities and abilities must an ideal leader bring along?
First, an ideal leader must have sufficient mastery of all the above-mentioned tasks, including the design and implementation of necessary changes. Apart from great professional knowledge and social skill, this calls for much wisdom, self-knowledge, sophistication, savoir faire and self-confidence. Somebody like that must also be able to develop a compelling and morally sound vision, as well as to communicate this so convincingly that all involved accept it as a logical point of departure and guideline for their own actions. Moreover this vision must be appropriate in the short as well as the long term and be able to adapt to changes.

Another crucial point is that an ideal leader always puts the organizational interest before his own need for power and should not short-change or otherwise mistreat anybody. This demands a clear moral consciousness and habitual testing of decisions by moral standards. Essentially this is about standards that stem from the familiar principal virtues and cardinal sins such as were expounded in antiquity. This involves, for instance, striving for wisdom and love for your fellowmen and not falling into pride, anger and greed. Such an attitude prevents unnecessary conflicts and needless exhaustion of environmental resources.

The effects of unethical acts, often inconsequential in the case of somebody in a lower position, are always magnified in the case of a leader, also because power itself often corrupts the one involved even more. There are plenty of examples of strong leaders who did not have or apply this moral consciousness and in this way have had a devastating effect on their organization and further environment.

Lastly, a leader should dispose of sufficient energy actually to execute all tasks, as well as of tenacity when it comes to vision and ethical consciousness. This becomes especially acute in times of setbacks, ambiguity and uncertainty (Bennis, 1998). Leadership, then, is not so much a matter of following a map or itinerary as of using one's own compass (Bennis and Thomas, 2002).

Toward a new division of roles
Can all this be accomplished by one person? As morally infallible people who know it all and do not make mistakes are hard to find, the chances are that, in our search for an ideal leader, we get stuck with a psychopath, a gifted narcissist who succeeds in drawing the needed media attention to feed our eager imagination. For many organizations, leadership by one person is no longer feasible. The world has become simply too complicated for that. Leadership then becomes a matter of a team, each of whose members executes different tasks and who complement and supervise each other in a predetermined fashion. The team size and division of tasks can receive its own interpretation in each organization. An example of such a construction is the committee of group directors at Shell, though in this case there is still a 'primus inter pares' (Nieuwenhuis, 1995). However one can imagine that such a role, of the one who acts as the leader to the outside world, may be a leadership role like any other, without extra power or influence.

Advantages
One of the most important advantages of shared leadership is that each leadership task can be optimally executed, namely by someone who has a special affinity for that specific task. Besides the fact that in this way fewer tasks are skipped, it also offers the possibility of spending more time on difficult or important questions which otherwise would get too little attention. This can lead to more satisfied customers, better cooperation with other parties, higher sales and higher profit. Within the organization it may result in more attention to the daily course of events and the cooperation of departments, as well as to the development and well-being of employees. This, in its turn, can foster the organizational climate, synergy, social support and quality of production and contribute to better coping with changes and stress.

Striving for personal power and office politics are often an important cause of poor performance and decline of organizations. Shared leadership is a good approach, though of course not a perfect one, to prevent such problems. It helps also to moderate the effects of the psychopathic traits of some leaders. Keeping yourself and each other alert in the case of opposition between personal and common interest by testing all decisions by agreed criteria is in the end the only viable option.

Another advantage is that team members can now occupy themselves first and foremost with the matters with which they want to occupy themselves and which enable them to use their talents fully. Besides this leading to better solutions, it benefits their individual development as well.

Shared leadership also opens up the option of 'normal' working hours and perhaps even a part-time assignment. This also makes leadership more attractive to many women. In addition, it creates the option to employ the better human resource (HR) officers more effectively and contribute to policies for management development and employability.

Disadvantages
Though shared leadership is attractive at first view and many people in organizations pay lip service to it – this is only logical – it is still a rare phenomenon. Moreover most people paying this lip service also say that it is not really an option in their own organization.

Primarily this is a matter of the status quo: when something is arranged in a certain way, it cannot be arranged in another way just like that. To that effect, the status quo is too entangled with individual interests. When there is one clear leader, and that one wants to keep it this way, implementation of shared leadership is no real option. To the other management members it also implies a breach with the past, whose consequences they cannot size up. Perhaps, also, it goes against their values and even endangers their position. All in all, implementation of shared leadership demands substantial adaptations from all involved, something people usually only want to do when they see their importance and usefulness, which often is not the case. Sometimes implementation of shared leadership even demands that one or more team members be replaced.

Of course shared leadership is no panacea. For some organizations and persons it is even completely useless. This applies for instance to small organizations where the leadership tasks have little meaning, organizations that are managed in a completely hierarchical way and organizations in which personal power and prestige are very important. Furthermore the success of shared leadership is of course a matter of careful implementation. This is above all a matter of sufficient attention, time and information (Doeglas and Schabracq, 1992) and not ignoring individual objections and feelings.

Besides problems with the implementation, there are also problems inherent in the practice of shared leadership. A self-evident problem is the possibility of a power struggle, personal differences of opinion and being played off against each other. This is often a matter of sliding back into 'old' familiar forms of functioning, certainly when these fit in with the usual opinions in the organization and basic individual needs. The only remedy consists of more reflection about one's own performance and its effect on the common interest, honesty in this respect and better communication with each other, with or without the help of an external facilitator.

When shared leadership has been implemented successfully at last and appropriate ways found to deal with conflicts and personal power, the main pitfall is that team members may spare each other too much and interact in too friendly a manner. Problems then might be ignored which would affect organizational decisiveness (Nieuwenhuis, 1995).

Implementation
Before implementing shared leadership in an organization, a thorough analysis should be made of the status quo, the immediate past and the opportunities and pitfalls for shared leadership. The reasons and particular occasion for implementation that are mentioned

should be examined as well. Other points for attention are the way the present management team is functioning, possibilities for synergy, possible overlaps and lacunas, forms of resistance and the individual interests of team members, as well as potential mutual differences of opinions and conflicts. So it is crucial to determine to what degree the different leadership tasks mentioned above are actually and appropriately executed. All of this must then lead, by way of a force field analysis (that is, an analysis of all the forces pro and contra) and a workshop, to a decision whether to implement or not. Next a plan with a time path can be made. Methods to be used at this stage include a quick scan of the organizational culture and the way the management team functions. Important instruments here are interviews, a checklist regarding abuse of power, as well as observation and video feedback focusing on the relational and non-verbal aspects of management team meetings.

A subsequent step is a group programme for the management team to get an idea of the contributions that each member is able and willing to give. What path will each have to follow in order to participate optimally in this team? This involves maturity and getting to know yourself better, in order to realize in the end what you yourself will, can, may and must do, as well as how the others can complement and help you in this respect. What are your basic motives, moral guidelines and goals? Do you admit your own feelings and intuitions and do you make use of them? How do you sabotage yourself? How can you become a more effective model and a better conductor? Who can help you and whom can you help? All of this makes for a collective 'rite of passage', which enables you, free from the everyday demands and distractions, to identify and develop personal themes and motives, in order to determine each member's place in the team. Ultimately this must lead for all team members to a form of self-management, focusing also on their own well-being.

A third step may consist of a collective training programme which brings the cognitive functioning of the team and its members onto a higher level. Leadership is after all also a matter of wisdom. Apart from awareness of members' own thoughts and feelings, this is about empathy, curiosity, reflection, moral consciousness and learning to use mental quiet. Other important elements are developing abilities such as changing of perspectives, tracing and adjusting one's own presuppositions, learning to see something as part of a greater whole, thinking in alternatives, intentionally applying different time perspectives, reformulating problems, learning to tolerate uncertainty and making use of dilemmas to generate win–win solutions. This is a great deal, maybe enough for half a lifetime, but it is good to experience the fact that all of this is important, as well as (to an important degree) trainable.

Developing together a vision for the organization, step four, is the vehicle used for actually installing shared leadership. This step focuses on the integration of individual ideas and motives in a desirable and rewarding image of the organizational future. To this end, the suppositions of the team members on each point of difference must be made explicit, in order to use them as building blocks for win–win solutions that can be subscribed by all team members. On the one hand, the vision concerns a meaningful goal for the organization and a promising niche in the environment, as well as an effective, pleasurable and creative way to organize all of this internally. On the other hand, it is about dividing team roles in order to attain maximal synergy and developing ways to supervise and support each other in such a way that individual responsibilities become completely clear.

The next step is then actually working as a leadership team as a form of 'learning-by-doing' and 'action learning'. Learning here occurs by trying out, exercising, making errors, asking yourself the right questions and 'intervision', that is, talking and reflecting together about this. The first task of the team then consists of translating the vision to the shop floor. All employees involved must actively participate in this, because this is the best possible way to generate a functional reality, which does not invoke feelings of alienation and insecurity and makes it easy to execute the work task. Here too, goals, a place in the surrounding environment and internal adjustment play a role again. Of course, at this stage, extra attention should be paid to an appropriate division of roles and cooperation within the team. Lastly it is also important to record and document all of this – mission, vision, procedures, rules of thumb, guidelines, criteria – appropriately.

A last step concerns the decision making about, as well as the design and implementation of, changes. This involves internalizing a scenario with fixed steps and a division of roles, which prevents unnecessary changes and enables us to deal with necessary changes in a more or less unchanging way. At each stage, this scenario focuses attention on what needs to be attended to and specifies possible pitfalls and criteria for success. It is thus directed to the joint optimization of the effects of the change: maximizing effectiveness, motivation and creativity, as well as minimizing stress and alienation.

References

Bennis, W.G. (1998), *On Becoming a Leader*, New York: Perseus.
Bennis, W.G. and R.J. Thomas (2002), *Geeks and Geezers*, Boston: Harvard Business School Press.
Blauner, R. (1964), *Alienation and Freedom: The Factory Worker and His Industry*, Chicago and London: University of Chicago Press.
Collins, J.C. and J.I. Porras (1994), *Built to Last*, New York: Harper Business.
Delfgauw, B. (1988), *Filosofie van de vervreemding als vervreemding van de filosofie* (Philosophy of Alienation as Alienation of Philosophy), Kampen: Kok Agora.
Doeglas, J.D.A. and M.J. Schabracq (1992), 'Transitiemanagement' (Transition Management), *Gedrag en Organisatie* (Behaviour and Organization), **5**, 448–66.
Goffman, E. (1963), *Behavior in Public Places*, Glencoe, IL: Free Press.
Goffman, E. (1971), *Relations in Public*, New York: Harper & Row.
Hamel, G. and C.K. Pralahad (1994), *Competing for the Future*, Boston: Harvard Business School Press.
Hammer, M. (2001), *The Agenda*, New York: Crown Business.
Kanungo, R.N. (1982), *Work Alienation: An Integrative Approach*, New York: Praeger Publishers.
Maslach, C., W.B. Schaufeli and M.P. Leiter (2001), 'Job burnout', *Annual Review of Psychology*, **52**, 397–422.
Moscovici, S. (1984), 'The phenomenon of social representation', in R.M. Farr and S. Moscovici (eds), *Social Representations*, Cambridge: Cambridge University Press, pp. 3–69.
Nieuwenhuis, F. (1995), *Monseigneurs en managers. De kerk van Rome en Shell vergeleken* (Monsignors and Managers. The Church of Rome and Shell Compared), Rotterdam: Ad Donker.
Ollman, B. (1971), *Alienation. Marx's Conception of Man in Capitalist Society*, London: Cambridge University Press.
Parsons, T. (1937), *The Structure of Social Action*, New York: McGraw-Hill.
Schabracq, M.J. (1987), 'Betrokkenheid en onderlinge gelijkheid in sociale interacties' (Involvement and Mutual Similarity in Social Interaction), dissertation, UvA, Amsterdam.
Schabracq, M.J. (1991), *De inrichting van de werkelijkheid* (The Design of Reality), Amsterdam/Assen: Boom.
Schabracq, M.J. (2002a), 'Everyday well-being and stress in work and organisations', in M.J. Schabracq, J.A.M. Winnubst and C.L. Cooper (eds), *Handbook of Work and Health Psychology*, 2nd rev. edn, Chichester: Wiley, pp. 9–36.
Schabracq, M.J. (2002b), 'Organisational culture, stress and change', in M.J. Schabracq, J.A.M. Winnubst and C.L. Cooper (eds), *Handbook of Work and Health Psychology*, 2nd rev. edn, Chichester: Wiley, pp. 37–62.
Schabracq, M.J. (2003), 'To be me or not to be me. About alienation', *Counselling Psychology Quarterly*, **16**, 53–79.

Schabracq, M.J., J.A.M. Winnubst and C.L. Cooper (eds) (2002), *Handbook of Work and Health Psychology*, 2nd rev. edn, Chichester: Wiley.
Schabracq, M.J., C.L. Cooper, C. Travers and D. van Maanen (2001), *Occupational Health Psychology: The Challenge of Workplace Stress*, Leicester: British Psychological Society.
Schutz, A. (1970), *On Phenomenology and Social Relations*, Chicago: University of Chicago Press.
Seeman, M. (1983), 'Alienation motifs in contemporary theorizing: the hidden continuity of the classic themes', *Social Psychology Quarterly*, **46**, 171–84.
Selye, H. (1956), *The Stress of Life*, New York: McGraw-Hill.
Smit, I. (1997), 'Patterns of Coping', dissertation, Utrecht University.
Wittgenstein, L. (1961), *Tractatus Logico-Philosophicus*, London: Routledge & Kegan Paul.

9 Job demands, job control, strain and learning behavior: review and research agenda
Toon W. Taris and Michiel A.J. Kompier

Over the last 25 years Karasek's (1979) job demand–control (JDC) model has been a leading work stress model in occupational health psychology. One of its basic assumptions is that the combination of high job demands with high job control has positive effects on employee motivation for learning new behavior patterns. To date, very little research has addressed this interesting and potentially practically important assumption. The current chapter first provides a short introduction to the JDC model. Then the results of a systematic literature review on worker activation and learning in the context of this model are presented. Based on this review, shortcomings of this research and knowledge gaps are identified. It will be concluded that, while the results of the research currently available are suggestive, actually no firm conclusions regarding the effects of work characteristics on employee active learning behavior can be drawn owing to methodological and conceptual flaws. We end with an inventory of issues to be addressed in future research on the active learning hypothesis in the JDC model.

The job demand–control model
At the heart of the JDC model lies the assumption that a work environment can be described in terms of the combination of two dimensions: the psychological demands of the work situation and the amount of control workers have to meet these demands, usually measured in terms of worker decision latitude (referring to the amount of say workers have over their work, the methods they apply and the order in which they handle their tasks) and skill discretion (the degree to which workers make full use of their skills). Crossing these two dimensions leads to four basic quadrants, each corresponding to a particular job type (see Figure 9.1):

1. In high demands/low control jobs high levels of strain will occur, because workers have insufficient control to respond optimally to the demands of the work situation. Because of this low control, workers cannot experiment with different ways of meeting the demands, meaning that they have little opportunity for learning and personal growth. High demands/low control jobs are often referred to as 'high strain jobs', but this label confuses the job content (that is, high demands and low control) with one of its presumed outcomes (high strain).
2. If high job demands occur in conjunction with high job control ('active jobs', again confusing job content with its presumed outcome), workers will be able to deal effectively with these demands, which will thus protect them from excessive strain. Learning and feelings of mastery will result.

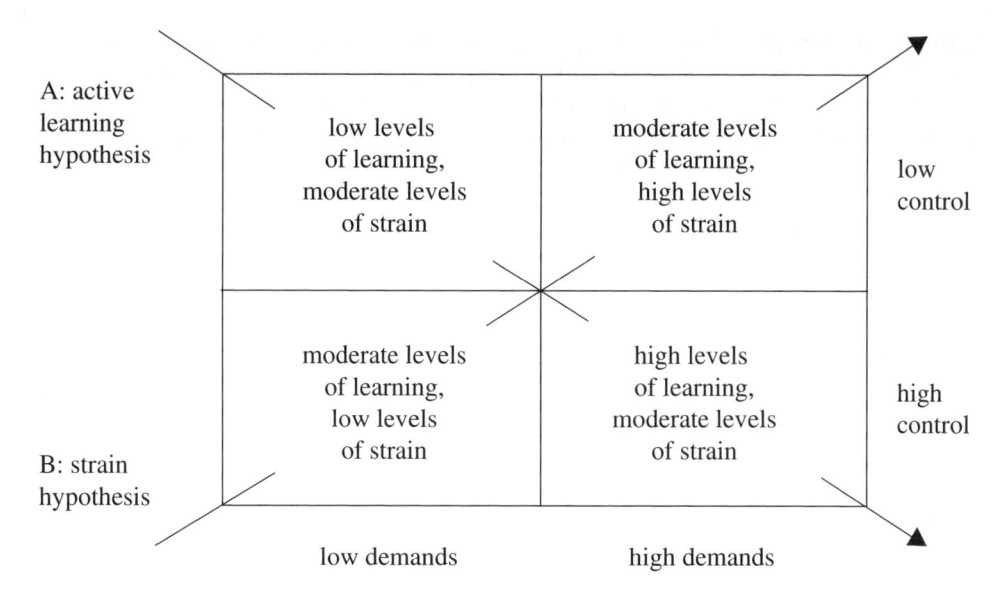

Figure 9.1 The four Karasek job types and their implications for learning and strain

3. Incumbents of low demands/low control jobs (or 'passive jobs'), will experience low levels of strain, in spite of the fact that they have little opportunity to influence their work situation. These jobs are presumed to offer little opportunity for learning and personal development.
4. Finally, in low demand/high control jobs ('low strain jobs') low levels of strain are expected because incumbents have sufficient possibilities of coping with situational demands. As job demands are low, workers in such jobs can explore different ways of dealing with the demands of the job which is conducive to learning (Bandura, 1997).

A large body of research has focused on the *strain hypothesis* of the JDC model, juxtaposing high demand/low control jobs with low demand/high control jobs (axis B in Figure 9.1). The overall conclusion of this research is that high job demands and low control tend to adversely effect psychological and physiological health (De Jonge and Kompier, 1997; De Lange *et al.*, 2003; Van der Doef and Maes, 1999, for reviews). Conversely, the *active learning hypothesis* of the JDC model, focusing on the distinction between low control/low demands (or 'passive') versus high control/high demands ('active') jobs (axis A in Figure 9.1), has received surprisingly little attention. The paucity of research addressing the learning-oriented outcomes of the JDC model is quite surprising, especially since many current management practices and philosophies emphasize the organization's interest in having self-managing and development-oriented employees (Parker and Sprigg, 1999).

Work characteristics and active learning: what we know – and what not
It must be noted that Karasek has never been clear about the precise nature of the active learning concept. What do we talk about when we talk about active learning? Karasek and Theorell (1990) speak of 'learning motivation to develop new behavior patterns' (p. 32),

'learning and increased motivation' (p. 38), 'additions to competence' (p. 92), 'feeling of mastery' (p. 99), and so on. Karasek (1981) tested his active learning hypothesis in terms of a spillover effect from the work to the nonwork context, focusing on participation in leisure activities (which seems the initial focus of his JDC model; cf. Karasek, 1976). Karasek (1998) mentions 'active/passive behavioral correlates of jobs' and 'motivation processes of high performance work' (34.6), 'effective problem-solving', 'growth and learning' and 'the individual's repertoire of coping strategies' (34.7), and 'behavioral outcomes of work activity' (34.9). Clearly many different concepts seem relevant for testing the active learning hypothesis (motivation, coping, problem solving abilities, learning, personal growth, performance, mastery, competence, to mention just a few), but how should the concept encompassing all these aspects be defined? Perhaps the best candidate for such a definition is 'the motivation for developing new behavior patterns and competences', which would seem to cover most of the aspects mentioned above. Feelings of mastery and competence (Karasek and Theorell, 1990) may then be construed as outcomes of the learning process.

Similarly Karasek is not very explicit about which pattern of results is required to conclude that the active learning hypothesis is supported. Karasek and Theorell (1990) suggest that it is sufficient that incumbents of high demands/high control jobs report the highest levels of learning, compared to incumbents of low demands/low control jobs. This leaves unresolved whether a statistical interaction between job demands and job control is needed in order to confirm the learning hypothesis, or that two main effects of demands and control suffice. We propose that *any* situation in which incumbents of high demands/high control jobs report the highest and incumbents of low demands/low control jobs the lowest levels of learning supports Karasek and Theorell's (1990) learning hypothesis, irrespective of whether this is due to two main effects of job demands and job control, or to a demand–control interaction effect (cf. De Lange *et al.*, 2003).

In order to shed more light on the degree to which the active learning hypothesis is supported, studies dealing with the active learning hypothesis were identified through a computer-based search in the Medline and PsycInfo data bases, as available in January 2003. Key words used in this search were 'demands', 'control', 'work', 'employment', 'active', 'passive', 'activation', 'learning' and 'Karasek', in various combinations. Further more publications of known experts on the JDC model were scrutinized for possible relevance. Studies were considered relevant if the abstract revealed that measures of both job demands and job control were included in the study. This resulted in 11 studies explicitly dealing with the active learning hypothesis. Consistent with the lack of clarity on the 'right' measurement of active learning behavior, previous research on the activation hypothesis has focused on a broad range of outcomes, including job satisfaction, job involvement and commitment, self-efficacy and job challenge. Table 9.1 presents descriptive information on these studies, including information on the nature and size of the samples used, the results thereof and whether the findings support the active learning hypothesis.

Job satisfaction and job involvement/commitment
Seven studies examined job satisfaction and/or job involvement/commitment in the context of the active learning hypothesis (job satisfaction was examined by Dollard *et al.*, 2000; De Jonge *et al.*, 2000; De Jonge *et al.*, 1999; Landsbergis *et al.*, 1992; Dollard and Winefield, 1998; job involvement and commitment were examined by Landsbergis *et al.*,

Table 9.1 Review of studies on Karasek's active learning hypothesis

Outcome variable/study	Sample	Results	Support for JDC(S) model
Job satisfaction			
De Jonge et al. (1999)	1489 human service workers	satisfaction highest in high demand/high control jobs	+
De Jonge et al. (2000)	2485 human service workers	satisfaction highest in high demand/high control jobs	+
Landsbergis et al. (1992)	297 healthy men, various occupations	dissatisfaction lowest in low demand/high control jobs	−
Dollard et al. (2000)	813 human service workers	satisfaction highest in high demand/high control jobs	+
Dollard and Winefield (1998)	419 correctional officers	dissatisfaction highest in high demand/low control jobs	−
Work and organizational commitment			
Demerouti et al. (2001)	381 employees of insurance company	high control associated with higher commitment; demands irrelevant	−
De Jonge et al. (1996)	249 nurses and nurses' aids	high control associated with higher commitment; demands irrelevant	−
Landsbergis et al. (1992)	297 healthy men, various occupations	commitment highest in high demand/high control jobs	+
Work challenge			
De Jonge et al. (1996)	249 nurses and nurses' aids	high job control associated with grater job challenge, job demands irrelevant	−
De Jonge et al. (1999)	1489 human service workers	highest level of challenge in high demand/high control jobs	+
Dollard et al. (2000)	813 human service workers	highest level of challenge in high demand/high control jobs	+
Dollard and Winefield (1998)	419 correctional officers	highest level of challenge in high demand/high control jobs	+
Van Yperen and Hagedoorn (2003)	555 nurses	intrinsic motivation highest in high demand/high control jobs with low social support	+

Table 9.1 (continued)

Outcome variable/study	Sample	Results	Support for JDC(S) model
Work related efficacy and mastery			
Dollard et al. (2000)	813 human service workers	highest level of personal accomplishment in high demand/high control jobs	+
Demerouti et al. (2001)	381 employees of insurance company	highest level of personal accomplishment in high demand/high control jobs	+
Holman and Wall (2002)	774 call center employees	job demands irrelevant; efficacy and skill utilization highest in high control jobs	–
Parker and Sprigg (1999)	268 production workers	role breadth self-efficacy highest in high demand/high control jobs; perceived mastery highest in low demand/high control jobs	+/–
Other outcomes			
Dollard and Winefield (1998)	419 correctional officers	level of feedback-seeking behavior highest in high demand/high control jobs	+
Karasek (1981)	1451 Swedish males	participation in active leisure behaviors and political activities highest in high demand/high control jobs	+

Note: + = active learning hypothesis supported; – = active learning hypothesis not supported.

1992; De Jonge et al., 1996; and Demerouti et al., 2001). Four of these provided support for the active learning hypothesis in the form of two main effects of job demands and job control and/or a demand by control interaction effect, such that incumbents of high demand/high control jobs reported higher levels of satisfaction, commitment and/or involvement than incumbents of low demand/low control jobs. In the other studies the active learning hypothesis was not or only in part supported.

Although the evidence presented in the studies mentioned above is usually at least partly supportive of the active learning hypothesis, it should be noted that the validity of job satisfaction and job commitment/involvement as representing Karasek and Theorell's (1990) active learning has been questioned. Parker and Sprigg (1999) rightly argue that being satisfied with one's job may actually be a quite passive state of mind (that is, a state of 'resigned satisfaction', Feldman, 1981). Furthermore it is not immediately clear how job satisfaction relates to the motivation for learning new behavior patterns or new coping strategies. Perhaps job satisfaction is best construed as a distant outcome of learning, in the sense that learning may allow workers to achieve higher goals (or to achieve the same goals with less effort), which in turn may be conducive to satisfaction. But this link seems quite weak and indirect, depending on extra (usually untested) hypotheses that may not be tenable.

Similar reservations apply to studies employing job involvement and commitment; here, too, the link between active learning and involvement/commitment is weak and indirect. Of course it is certainly possible that workers who learn much in their jobs perform well, which may in turn lead to elevated levels of satisfaction and commitment; it seems equally plausible, however, that workers *dislike* their job and organization, precisely because they must learn so much to be fit for the job. Thus it is questionable whether studies using these and similar criterion variables bear much relevance for testing the active learning hypothesis.

Efficacy, mastery and job challenge
Two other clusters of outcome variables seem more appropriate for testing the active learning hypothesis. Efficacy and mastery refer to feelings of self-confidence, having effective coping strategies and adequate performance at work. Karasek and Theorell (1990) explicitly mention feelings of mastery and competence as possible outcomes of a process of active learning. The concept of job challenge can be defined as the degree to which workers consider their jobs challenging, motivating and stimulating, conditions that are conducive to learning. In support of the active learning hypothesis, Dollard et al. (2000), Demerouti et al. (2001) and Parker and Sprigg (1999) found that incumbents of high demands/high control jobs reported the highest levels of mastery and efficacy, whereas Holman and Wall (2002) found a main effect of control only. Similarly Dollard and Winefield (1998), De Jonge et al. (1999, 2000) and Van Yperen and Hagedoorn (2003) found that incumbents of high demand/high control jobs reported high levels of motivation and/or perceived their jobs as challenging. Only De Jonge et al.'s (1996) study did not offer unequivocal support for the active learning hypothesis; their study revealed a positive main effect of job control on motivation only.

Other outcomes
Two studies employed other outcome variables. Dollard and Winefield (1998) found that incumbents of high demand/high control jobs sought more actively for feedback on their

performance than others. Seeking feedback may be considered to tap an aspect of the motivation to learn new behavior patterns. Finally Karasek (1981) examined whether incumbents of high demand/high control jobs were also more active regarding their leisure activities. He reported that incumbents of such jobs were relatively active in terms of their participation in recreational and political activities.

Evaluation of past research
As Table 9.1 shows, the studies discussed above seem reasonably supportive of the active learning hypothesis at first sight. However this research suffers from several limitations. The following four problems stand out as being especially important.

Construct validity of the measures used is questionable   In many cases the construct validity of the measures representing active learning behavior seems questionable. This applies especially to studies with job satisfaction and job involvement/commitment as the outcome variable, meaning that the results of these studies are largely irrelevant as regards the validation of the active learning hypothesis. None of the studies mentioned above measured learning behavior directly; past research has confined itself to examining antecedents of learning behavior (motivation, job challenge) or (sometimes very) distant outcomes of such behavior (satisfaction and commitment). Obviously the larger the conceptual gap between what is measured and what should be measured, the greater the chances of distorted results and incorrect conclusions.

Causal direction of effects unknown   Virtually all studies mentioned here (with the notable exceptions of Holman and Wall, 2002, and Karasek, 1981) employed a *cross-sectional design*. Whereas cross-sectional designs can be used to compare levels of active learning across the four Karasek job types, they are largely uninformative concerning the process that generated possible differences in active learning. Unfortunately many processes may produce positive correlations between job demands, job control and active learning behavior, and the process described by the JDC model is only one of these. For example, it would seem possible that high job control generates high levels of active learning and motivation; highly motivated workers, however, may generate their own high job demands (for example, Machlowitz, 1980, noted that workaholics – high-motivation workers per definition – tend to increase the complexity of the projects they are working on, only for the fun of working on the problems to create for themselves. It is not surprising, then, that workaholics usually report high levels of job demands and strain, see Burke, this volume, and Taris *et al.*, in press, for reviews).

Analyses often not tailored to testing the learning hypothesis   Most studies to date have not exclusively (or even primarily) tested Karasek and Theorell's (1990) *activation* hypothesis, but rather Karasek's (1979) *strain* hypothesis. This shows in the type of outcome variable that is considered; as shown above, often the outcome variables in these studies are often not the best conceivable representatives of the active–passive dimension. More importantly the lack of attention for the active learning hypothesis also shows in the analyses that are conducted, focusing on juxtaposing high demands/low control jobs to other job types, thus not presenting appropriate statistical tests for examining the active learning hypothesis. But even studies explicitly designed to test the active learning hypothesis may not present sufficient information to judge whether this hypothesis is actually confirmed. For example, researchers may focus on the contrast between high demands/high control jobs versus other job types, conveniently ignoring the possibility that levels of learning may actually be higher in, say, low demands/high control jobs than in high demands/high control jobs.

Relationship between strain and learning is seldomly addressed   It is noteworthy that few studies have addressed the relationships between active learning and strain (with the exceptions of Holman and Wall, 2002; Parker and Sprigg, 1999). Karasek and Theorell (1990) and Karasek (1998) hold that the two phenomena influence each other, so that high levels of strain inhibit learning and high levels of learning inhibit strain. If this is correct, full understanding of the links between work characteristics and strain (or learning) requires that employee learning (or strain) be recognized as a factor that plays a potentially important role in this process.

Taking these four limitations into account, it would seem fair to conclude that as yet the evidence supporting the active learning hypothesis is quite weak. Research explicitly dealing with this hypothesis is scarce, employed poor measures of active learning and/or designs that are inadequate to study causal relationships and across-time development, and largely failed to consider the reciprocal effects between strain and learning. Fortunately, recently several studies dealing with these issues have been conducted. These are discussed in more detail below. The next section deals with the temporal development of learning as a function of demands and control, providing evidence on the causal effects of these work characteristics on learning. Then the interrelations between learning and strain are discussed.

The temporal effects of work characteristics on learning

As noted earlier, previous research on the active learning hypothesis has suggested that levels of active learning are relatively high in high demands/high control jobs. Although this is consistent with the active learning hypothesis, it does not follow that job demands and job control are *causally* related to active learning, in the sense that changes in job characteristics 'produce' corresponding changes in active learning behavior. Two types of designs may yield insight in such causal relationships. The 'natural experiments' centered upon interventions and changes in the demand/control structure of a particular task provide windows of opportunity to examine the causal effects of demands and control on learning. The same applies to longitudinal survey studies, involving multiple measurements of the same set of variables on multiple occasions for the same set participants (Taris, 2000).

Temporal effects of job characteristics on learning
The JDC model proposes that high levels of learning will occur in high demands/high control jobs and low levels of learning will occur for low demands/low control jobs. For the two other job types intermediary levels of learning are expected (Karasek and Theorell, 1990). This implies that workers experiencing a change in job characteristics such that they move closer to the high demands/high control quadrant, will develop more

learning behavior in time. Thus a change from low demands to high demands and/or low control to high control should lead to an increase in learning behavior. From the perspective of German action theory, demands provide goals to overcome (Frese and Zapf, 1994; Hacker, 1998). Thus increases in job demands make the environment more challenging, offering more opportunities for the development and use of skills. An increase in job control implies that workers obtain more opportunities to experiment with different ways of meeting their demands, which may result in the development of new skills (Bandura, 1997). People who have control can do better than others because they can pick strategies that are adequate for dealing with the situation; they can plan ahead and they are more flexible if anything goes wrong (Frese and Zapf, 1994).

The reverse applies when workers experience a change in job characteristics that takes them closer to the low demands/low control quadrant. As their job environment becomes less challenging and provides fewer opportunities for learning, these workers are expected to develop less learning motivation and fewer feelings of efficacy and competence in time.

Note that a change in work characteristics is not necessary for producing a change in learning behavior. According to Karasek and Theorell (1990), incumbents of 'high demands/high control jobs develop feelings of mastery and confidence. These help the person to cope with the inevitable strain-inducing situations of the job. The result is reduced residual strain and thus increased capacity to accept still more learning . . . *ad infinitum*' (p. 103, italics ours). Thus a prolonged stay in this job quadrant should result in higher levels of learning, simply because the adverse impact of stress on learning decreases. A similar (but negative) development is expected for workers in low demands/low control jobs. Karasek (1998) argues that such jobs lead to '"negative learning" or gradual loss of previously acquired skill', (34.7), which leads him to conclude that 'The passive job setting is [a] major psychosocial problem . . . lost skills, lack of job challenges, and environmentally rigid restrictions preventing workers from testing their own ideas for improving the work process can only mean an extremely unmotivating job setting and result in long term loss of work motivation and productivity' (Karasek and Theorell, 1990, p. 38).

Karasek and Theorell (1990) do not discuss the implications of a prolonged stay in either low demands/high control or high demands/low control jobs for learning. Presumably the beneficial effects of having much of one job characteristic make up for the harmful effects of being short on the other. Thus it would seem likely that no changes in learning behavior occur for these jobs, irrespective of the time workers are exposed to this particular condition.

Effects of changes in job demands and control
To what degree do the predictions regarding the development of learning as a function of changes in demands and control hold water? In a carefully designed study among 144 call center employees, Holman and Wall (2002) examined the lagged effects of job control on skill utilization (a three-item scale tapping the degree to which the participants made full use of their current skills and could develop new skills). Job demands were not included in their study, because an earlier cross-sectional analysis employing a larger sample suggested that this concept was irrelevant in predicting learning behavior among this sample. Holman and Wall found that Time 1 job control had a lagged positive effect on Time 2

skill utilization, after controlling Time 1 skill utilization; participants reporting high levels of control were more likely to report high levels of skill utilization as well, which agrees with the assumption that high control is conducive to learning.

Similar results were obtained in a longitudinal study among 998 teachers (Taris *et al.*, 2003); teachers reporting high job control at the first wave were more likely to report high levels of job-related efficacy (as measured with the personal accomplishment scale of Maslach *et al.*'s, 1996, Maslach Burnout Inventory – Educators Survey) and learning behavior (a three-item scale measuring whether the participants were actively looking for new challenges in their job, whether they invested much time and effort in keeping up with new developments and whether their job offered them good opportunities for developing new skills) in the second wave of the study, which was conducted one year later. Whereas this result confirmed Holman and Wall's (2002) findings, the finding that job demands had a lagged *negative* effect on learning and efficacy was not in agreement with the active learning hypothesis. Thus, in Taris *et al.*'s (2003) study the highest levels of learning occurred in low demands/high control jobs rather than in high demands/high control jobs. In fact the average level of learning/efficacy reported by teachers in the low demands/low control did not differ significantly from that reported by teachers in high demands/high control jobs, which casts serious doubts on the tenability of the active learning hypothesis. Although these results seemed quite surprising, similar findings were obtained by Parker and Sprigg (1999) in a cross-sectional study among 268 production employees. They also found that the highest levels of 'mastery' (a measure tapping work-related efficacy) occurred for low demands/high control jobs and not for high demands/high control jobs, whereas 'moderate' levels of learning were obtained for both the low demands/low control jobs and the high demands/high control jobs.

Thus, whereas the expected positive effects of high job control on the across-time development of learning have been confirmed in two independent longitudinal studies, it is questionable at best whether high job demands have a similar positive effect on learning behavior. Indeed the evidence presented here suggests that high job demands *impede* the development of learning.

Effects of prolonged exposure to particular demand/control combinations
The JDC model predicts not only that changes in job demands/job control lead to corresponding changes in learning behavior, but also that the *absence* of change in (that is, prolonged exposure to) work characteristics may produce changes in learning behavior. The Taris *et al.* (2003) study discussed above deals with this issue as well. However little change in learning behavior and/or efficacy was observed for any of the four stable groups across the one-year interval. Only for learning behavior was a prolonged stay in the low demands/low control quadrant associated with the expected decrease in learning behavior. Although the absence of change is partly in agreement with the expectations discussed above (that is, prolonged stay in the low demands/high control and high demands/low control will not lead to changes in learning behavior), it contradicts the hypothesis that prolonged exposure to high demands/high control or low demands/low control will lead to higher (lower) levels of learning, at least not for a one-year interval.

Taris and Feij (in press) addressed the same issue in a two-year three-wave prospective cohort study among newcomers. The advantage of this particular sample is that all par-

142   *Conceptualization and theoretical framework*

ticipants entered the labor market at the same time, meaning that possible differences in labor market experience did not influence the across-time development of the outcome variables. In this case the outcome variable was the degree to which participants engaged in various behaviors that were aimed at further skill development (for example, seeking advice from co-workers and supervisors about additional training or skills needed for improving one's future work prospects; see Backman, 1978). Only participants who reported no change in job demands/job control across time and who were in the same job across the observed period were included in the analysis (total $N = 311$, minimum group size was 77).

Figure 9.2 shows the group-level scores on this concept as a function of the four stable job demands/job control combinations across time. First it is interesting to see that at each wave of the study incumbents of high demands/high control jobs received the highest scores and incumbents of low demands/low control the lowest scores, which is consistent with the active learning hypothesis. The scores of the other two groups are at all waves in between these two extreme groups, with the low demands/high control group obtaining

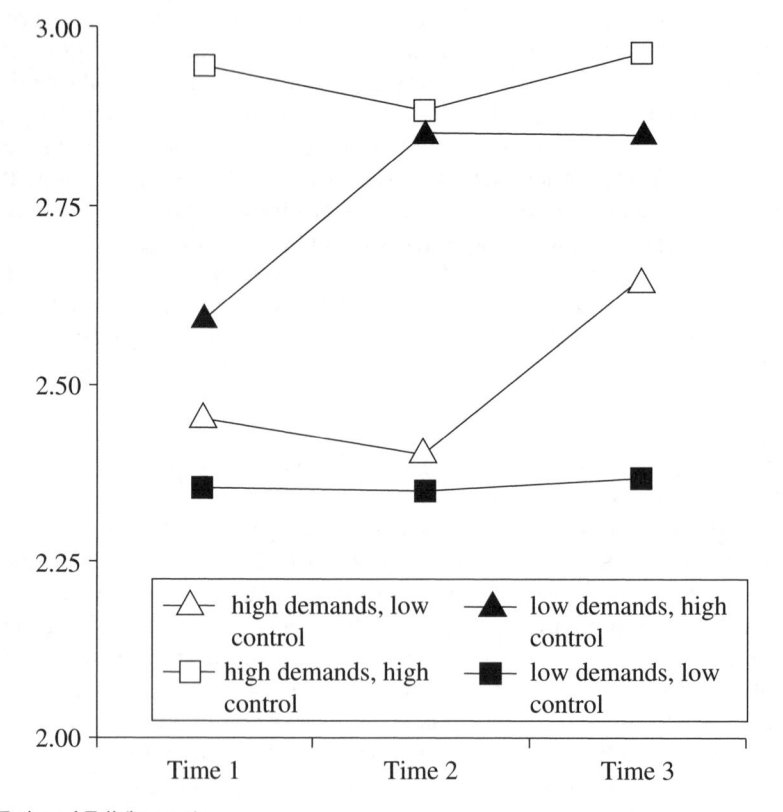

Source: Taris and Feij (in press).

Figure 9.2   Learning among newcomers as a function of prolonged exposure to particular combinations of demands and control

higher scores than the high demands/low control group. Thus, on each separate occasion, the two high control groups obtain higher scores than the low control groups; the effects of demands seem less clear. Even more interesting is the across-time development of the scores of the four groups. Whereas no statistically significant changes over time occur for the low demands/low control and high demands/high control groups (thus contradicting the expectations that in these two groups learning would deteriorate and grow, respectively; cf. Karasek, 1998; Karasek and Theorell, 1990), the two groups in time approach the level of the high demands/high control group, suggesting that these groups ultimately reach the level of motivated learning initially reported by incumbents of the high demands/high control group. In contrast the absence of any change for the low demands/low control group is striking: no change in learning motivation is observed for incumbents of this group.

The results reported above provide partial support for the active learning hypothesis. The beneficial effect of having high control on the development of learning behavior is confirmed. The effects of demands on learning seem less clear. Contrary to the results reported in the preceding section concerning the effects of change in job characteristics on learning, having high job demands does not seem a major obstacle to developing active learning behavior: only the *low* demands/low control group lags behind in developing such behaviors.

Learning and strain
Another major issue that has seldomly been addressed is how learning and strain influence each other. Karasek and Theorell (1990) argued that high levels of strain inhibit learning, whereas high levels of learning inhibit stress. Holman and Wall (2002) discussed the evidence for both assumptions. Evidence for the effects of strain on learning and learning-oriented outcomes such as efficacy, mastery and skill utilization comes largely from studies conducted from cognitive, clinical and educational perspectives. Experimental work has shown that anxiety (a major dimension of strain: Warr, 1990) reduces the effectiveness of information processing, which is crucial in the early stages of skill acquisition. Furthermore attending to anxiety provokes nontask activities and inhibits understanding and experimenting with new ideas, thus reducing learning (Warr and Downing, 2000). Studies in educational settings have shown that there is a negative relationship between anxiety and outcomes such as test scores (ibid.) and skill acquisition (Colquitt et al., 2000). Similar findings have been obtained for the effects of depression (another major dimension of strain) on learning. Conversely there is also some reason to expect that learning inhibits stress. Greater knowledge, skill and efficacy enable the individual to deal more effectively with work tasks and problems therein, thus reducing strain (cf. Lazarus and Folkman, 1984). There is some evidence for these assumptions. For example, individuals with high self-efficacy are less likely to suffer from depression and anxiety (Saks, 1994), and feel more able to cope with challenging situations (Ozer and Bandura, 1990).

Given the empirical evidence for both assumptions, it would seem plausible that strain and learning influence each other. As discussed earlier on, the dynamic interplay between learning and strain is a major element in the JDC model. However, as little research addressed the learning hypothesis, it should come as no surprise that even fewer studies deal with the interrelations between strain and learning. In their seminal cross-sectional study on the relations between job demands, job control and learning-oriented outcomes such as self-efficacy and mastery, Parker and Sprigg (1999) examined the associations between these outcomes and job strain (a measure tapping the degree to which participants had felt tense, anxious, relaxed and so on in the past month). Higher levels of mastery were associated with lower levels of strain, albeit not strongly (r was -0.24, $p < 0.001$); for efficacy no significant association was found.

Holman and Wall (2002) tested various models for the associations between job characteristics, learning and strain (including models in which learning mediated or moderated the effects of job demands and job control on strain, and vice versa). Their study provided some support for both the 'strain inhibits learning' and the 'learning inhibits strain' hypotheses, showing that the effects of control on learning and strain were mediated through strain and learning, respectively.

Finally, in their study of 311 newcomers introduced above, Taris and Feij (in press) found that strain (measured using Goldberg's, 1972, 12-item General Health Questionnaire) had a lagged, albeit weak, negative effect on learning. Participants reporting high levels of strain reported relatively low levels of learning at the next wave of the study, controlling previous levels of learning. Thus strain inhibited learning in their study, while the reverse effect, learning inhibits strain, was not supported.

The last three studies described above provide some evidence for the assumption that high levels of strain have adverse effects on learning. The reverse effect, that high levels of learning lead to lower levels of strain, received less support. The evidence here is sparse, however. Whereas the evidence available so far suggests that there is an association between learning and strain, considerably more (preferably longitudinal) evidence is needed to draw firm conclusions on the structure of the causal process that links work characteristics, learning and strain.

Active learning: where should we go?
The aim of this contribution was to discuss the effects of two particular job characteristics (job demands and job control) on worker learning. According to the active learning hypothesis in Karasek's (1979) JDC model, incumbents of high demands/high control jobs would experience high levels of learning, while low levels of learning would occur in low demands/low control jobs. Although few studies explicitly addressed this hypothesis, at first sight the evidence collected so far seems reasonably in accordance with this hypothesis. It should be noted, however, that the construct validity of some well-used outcome variables (most notably job satisfaction and commitment) is questionable; that longitudinal designs are virtually absent in this area, meaning that causal interpretation of the findings is impossible; that it is often difficult to judge whether past results actually support the active learning hypothesis; and that few studies have addressed the interplay of strain and learning. The latter issue is important, as the JDC model holds that the same job characteristics that are responsible for learning also influence levels of strain, while strain and learning are assumed to influence each other.

Our discussion of several recent studies dealing with the latter two issues revealed no unequivocal support for the active learning hypothesis. Longitudinal research revealed that high job control predicted increases in learning behavior, which supports the active learning hypothesis. The effects of job demands are still unclear: current evidence suggests that high job demands are either unrelated or negatively related to learning behavior, rather than positively, as argued by Karasek and Theorell (1990). Further, while high levels of strain seem to inhibit learning, the reverse relationship (learning inhibits strain) could not be confirmed in one of the studies discussed here. All in all, these findings strongly suggest that more research on the activation hypothesis is necessary before firm conclusions can be drawn. Future research should especially address the following issues.

1. *Measurement of learning.* Our literature review made it clear that current measures of learning behavior differ widely, in terms of both their content and their construct validity as a measure of learning behavior. This is partly due to the fact that Karasek is unclear about the 'correct' operationalization of learning-at-work; he initially construed learning as affecting non-work behavior (that is, leisure activities), rather than behavior at work. Conversely current research on active learning primarily focuses on work-related outcomes. In the absence of any guidance from the founder of the JDC model, no straightforward and valid operationalization of the active learning concept, defined as the motivation for developing new work-related behavior patterns and competences, has emerged.

    One important venue for future research would thus be to develop such a measure. This measure may focus on the degree to which the work environment automatically 'invites' workers to develop new skills and competences and make full use of their skills. However one important problem with such a measure would be that it would overlap significantly with Karasek's (1985) measure of job control, encompassing items measuring 'skill discretion'. For example, the positive associations between job control and skill utilization reported by Holman and Wall (2002) may have been inflated because at the operational level Karasek's concept of job control encompasses skill discretion, a concept that strongly resembles Holman and Wall's skill utilization. One possible avenue to resolve this problem is to omit the skill discretion scale from the measurement of job control (cf. De Jonge and Kompier, 1997). While this solution solves *operationally* the overlap between job control and active learning behavior, it also deals with the *conceptual* problem of measuring job control as an amalgamate of worker decision latitude and skill discretion. The latter concept does not seem to reflect job control (defined as the amount of say workers have over their job) adequately; previous research has suggested that this concept be omitted from the measure of job control (see Schreurs and Taris, 1998, for a review).

2. *Longitudinal designs.* Previous research has mostly used cross-sectional designs for studying the effects of job demands and job control on learning. Whereas such designs may provide evidence showing that these concepts are associated, conclusions concerning the causal direction of effects cannot be drawn. In order to enhance our understanding of the process generating the associations between demands, control and learning (and, perhaps, strain), longitudinal research is indispensable.

3. *Strain and learning.* One of the most intriguing aspects of the JDC model is its proposition that job strain and learning interact. Few studies have addressed this issue; consequently little can be said about the degree to which this proposition can be retained. Again future research should examine the cross-relations between strain

and learning, preferably using a longitudinal design. The evidence that is currently available suggests that learning is largely a function of strain (so that high strain inhibits learning). For example, incumbents of high-strain jobs may simply lack the time to learn new skills (for example, to master new computer programs, to learn new production methods). The absence of effects of learning on strain may be explained by assuming that a job is an 'open system', such that job demands vary positively with the level of skills of the employee. That is, the job demands of skilled and well-performing employees may more or less increase automatically as they may take on new assignments (either voluntarily, or because their superior feels they are ready for a (qualitatively or quantitatively) more demanding task). Thus increased skills due to active learning may *not* lead to lower job demands.

A related problem regarding the interrelation between strain and learning is that it is conceivable that this relationship is curvilinear rather than linear: while high levels of strain may inhibit learning, jobs that result in exceedingly low levels of strain will presumably offer little challenge as well. Thus optimal levels of active learning behavior may occur for jobs offering moderate levels of strain.

Finally research does not unequivocally support the hypothesis that the highest levels of learning occur for high demand/high control jobs. At least two studies (Parker and Sprigg, 1999, and Taris *et al.*, 2003) revealed that active learning behavior was highest among incumbents of low demand/high control jobs. Indeed the results of the latter study on learning were fully consistent with what would have been predicted for the strain hypothesis: high levels of learning in low demands/high control jobs, and low levels of learning in high demands/low control jobs. Thus the effects of demands and control on strain and learning are similar, questioning the hypothesis that we are dealing with two statistically and conceptually independent dimensions.

Although it would seem likely that there is an association between strain and learning, the structure of the process generating this association is largely unknown, as findings tend to contradict each other. More research on the interrelationships between strain and learning is desperately needed; as yet the empirical data base is too small to draw any firm conclusions regarding these relationships.

4. *Dealing with strain is dealing with learning.* Research on learning behavior in the context of the JDC model is likely to have implications for practice (that is, organizational interventions). The findings so far suggest that employee learning is at least partly a function of strain. If this is correct (and future research has yet to confirm previous findings), organizations that would like to improve opportunities for employee learning should deal with work stress and strain as well. Stated differently, it would seem that programs designed for reducing work stress may have the added effect of optimizing employee learning as well. Note that *some* strain may actually be conducive to learning (see our previous point), but given the current high levels of stress and effectiveness of most current stress intervention programs it would seem unlikely that any such intervention will result in a work context that offers no challenge at all.

5. *Extending the JDC model with social support.* The basic JDC model distinguishes between just two task characteristics: job demands and job control. However the model has been extended in several respects. Karasek and Theorell (1990) added social

support as a major work characteristic, assuming that the strain-related predictions of the JDC model would be especially salient for low-support jobs. As yet it is unclear how inclusion of social support relates to the learning-related predictions of the model: more (theoretical and empirical) work is necessary in this respect.

6. *Personality, job characteristics and learning.* Parker and Sprigg (1999) suggested that worker personality (that is, the proactive personality) is a key factor in understanding the effects of work characteristics on learning. This points to a more general problem with the JDC model. The model only considers the effects of work characteristics on learning and strain, excluding personal factors such as personality. This may turn out to be a serious omission. It seems plausible that, while searching for employment, workers will choose a job that fits their own preferences and needs (compare Schneider, 1998). Employees who are unwilling to learn may choose jobs offering low learning opportunities (that is, low demands, low control), while those who are highly motivated may choose jobs that offer plenty of such opportunities (that is, high demand/high control jobs). Thus the association between particular job characteristics and active learning behavior (or strain) may at least partly be due to third factors. To the degree that these third factors are temporally stable (as is often assumed for personality factors), this issue would seem extremely salient in cross-sectional research, presenting yet another threat to the validity of current findings on the relationship between work characteristics and learning behavior. However this issue is certainly not completely irrelevant for longitudinal research on active learning behavior, especially since job characteristics are presumed to mould workers' personal characteristics (motivation, efficacy, active coping strategies, personal initiative and the like). One as yet largely unexplored a venue thus concerns the possibly mutual relationships between work characteristics and worker characteristics (Taris, 1999).

7. *Job demands and job control: specific effects?* De Jonge et al. (2000) suggested that it is important to distinguish between various types of job demands and job control in examining their effects on learning. The effects of these task characteristics may be contingent on the degree to which they correspond to the precise demands and control in a particular occupation. Stated differently, emotional demands may be much more salient than time demands, depending on the occupational context, implying that the general measures proposed by Karasek (1985) will not always capture the 'right' elements of a particular job. This, in turn, might lead to relatively low proportions of explained variance in the outcome variables. Future research may indicate to what degree research using general measures of demands and control has underestimated their effects on learning and strain.

8. *Job characteristics, self-regulatory processes and learning motivation.* One final issue that would deserve further consideration is the degree to which self-regulatory processes mediate the relationship between job characteristics and active learning. If anything, active learning is a form of motivational behavior. This implies that self-regulatory motivational processes such as goal setting may play an important role in the development of workers' skills and their personal growth (Pomaki and Maes, 2002). Consistent with this reasoning, Pomaki et al. (2004) showed that workers reporting high control and low demands were more likely to report that they could attain self-set work goals such as 'increase knowledge and expertise' and 'improve my

job performance'. In turn, attainment of these goals was positively related to feelings of self-efficacy. These findings could be due to individual difference variables such as level of ambition, conscientiousness, openness to experience and the like, but they can also be interpreted as evidence for the assumption that combinations of job characteristics differentially influence the degree to which workers can set and achieve their own learning-related outcomes. Although the evidence is only preliminary, these findings suggest that research into the role of self-regulatory processes in the process that links work characteristics to active learning is worth pursuing.

Summarizing, although the evidence concerning the effects of job demands and job control on learning is largely inconclusive as yet, the evidence that is currently available suggests that more attention to this idea may have important implications for workplace (re-)design. Additional research into the processes that facilitate employee on-the-job learning should focus on several important issues, including methodological issues (better measurement of learning behavior, better – longitudinal – designs, ruling out third variable explanations, specific versus general measures for job demands and control) and conceptual issues (conceptualization and measurement of decision latitude, relationship with personal factors, self-regulatory processes, extending the JDC model with social support, and the interrelation with strain). Although the JDC model now ranks among the classic work stress models, the above inventory of issues for further research suggests that this framework can still generate interesting and challenging research questions, questions we intend to take up in the near future, and which we hope will stimulate others to do the same.

References

Backman, J. (1978), *Adolescence to Adult Change and Stability in the Lives of Young Men*, Ann Arbor: University of Michigan.
Bandura, A. (1997), *Self-efficacy: The exercise of control*, New York: Freeman.
Colquitt, J.A., J.A. LePine and R.A. Noe (2000), 'Toward an integrative theory of training motivation: a meta-analytic path analysis of 20 years of research', *Journal of Applied Psychology*, 85, 678–707.
De Jonge, J. and M.A.J. Kompier (1997), 'A critical examination of the Demand–Control–Support Model from a work psychological perspective', *International Journal of Stress Management*, 4, 235–58.
De Jonge, J., P.P.M. Janssen and G.J.P. Van Breukelen (1996), 'Testing the demand–control–support model among health-care professionals: a structural equation model', *Work & Stress*, 10, 209–24.
De Jonge, J., G.J.P. Van Breukelen, J.A. Landeweerd and F.J.N. Nijhuis (1999), 'Comparing group and individual level assessments of job characteristics on testing the job demands–control model: a multilevel approach', *Human Relations*, 52, 95–122.
De Jonge, J., M.F. Dollard, C. Dormann, P.M. Leblanc and I.L.D. Houtman (2000), 'The demand–control model: specific demands, specific control and well-defined groups', *International Journal of Stress Management*, 7, 269–87.
De Lange, A.H., T.W. Taris, M.A.J. Kompier, I.L.D. Houtman and P.M. Bongers (2003), 'The very best of the millennium: longitudinal research on the job demands–control model', *Journal of Occupational Health Psychology*, 8, 282–305.
Demerouti, E., A.B. Bakker, J. De Jonge, P.P.M. Janssen and W.B. Schaufeli (2001), 'Burnout and engagement at work as a function of demands and control', *Scandinavian Journal of Work, Environment and Health*, 27, 279–86.
Dollard, M.F. and A.H. Winefield (1998), 'A test of the demand–control/support model of work stress in correctional officers', *Journal of Occupational Health Psychology*, 3, 243–64.
Dollard, M.F., H.R. Winefield, A.H. Winefield and J. De Jonge (2000), 'Psychosocial job strain and productivity in human service workers: a test of the demand–control–support model', *Journal of Occupational and Organizational Psychology*, 73, 501–10.

Feldman, D.C. (1981), 'The multiple socialization of organization members', *Academy of Management Review*, **6**, 309–18.
Frese, M. and D. Zapf (1994), 'Action as the core of work psychology: a German approach', in H.C. Triandis, M.D. Dunnette and L.M. Hough (eds), *Handbook of Industrial and Organizational Psychology*, vol. 4, Palo Alto, CA: Consulting Psychologists Press, pp. 271–340.
Goldberg, D. (1972), *The Detection of Mental Illness by Questionnaire*, London: Oxford University Press.
Hacker, W. (1998), *Allgemeine Arbeitspsychologie: Psychische Regulation von Arbeitstätigkeiten*, Berne: Verlag Hans Huber.
Holman, D.J. and T.D. Wall (2002), 'Work characteristics, learning-related outcomes and strain: a test of competing direct effects, mediated and moderated models', *Journal of Occupational Health Psychology*, **7**, 283–301.
Karasek, R.A. (1976), *The Impact of the Work Environment on Life outside the Job*, Stockholm: Institutet för Social Forskning.
Karasek, R.A. (1979), 'Job demands, job decision latitude and mental strain: implications for job design', *Administrative Science Quarterly*, **24**, 285–308.
Karasek, R.A. (1981), 'Job socialization and job strain: the implications of two related psychosocial mechanisms for job design', in B. Gardell and G. Johansson (eds), *Working life: A Social Science Contribution to Work Reform*, Chichester: Wiley, pp. 75–94
Karasek, R.A. (1985), *Job Content Instrument: Questionnaire and User's Guide, rev. 1.1*, Los Angeles: University of Southern California.
Karasek, R. (1998), 'Demand–Control Model: A Social, Emotional and Physiological Approach to Stress Risk and Active Behaviour Development', in J.M. Stellmann (ed.), *Encyclopaedia of occupational health and safety*, 4th edn, Geneva: International Labour Office, pp. 34.6–34.14.
Karasek, R.A. and T. Theorell (1990), *Healthy work: Stress, Productivity and the Reconstruction of Working Life*, New York: Basic Books.
Landsbergis, P.A., P.L. Schnall, D. Deitz, R. Friedman and T. Pickering (1992), 'The patterning of psychological job attributes and distress by "job strain" and social support in a sample of working men', *Journal of Behavioral Medicine*, **15**, 379–405.
Lazarus, R.S. and S. Folkman (1984), *Stress, Appraisal and Coping*, New York: Springer.
Machlowitz, M. (1980), *Workaholics: Living with Them, Working with Them*, New York: Simon & Schuster.
Maslach, C., S.E. Jackson and R.L. Schwab (1996), 'Maslach Burnout Inventory – Educators Survey (MBI-ES)', in C. Maslach, S.E. Jackson and M.P. Leiter (eds), *Maslach Burnout Inventory*, 3rd edn, Palo Alto, CA: Consulting Psychologists Press.
Ozer, E.M. and A. Bandura (1990), 'Mechanisms governing empowerment effects: a self-efficacy analysis', *Journal of Personality and Social Psychology*, **58**, 472–86.
Parker, S.K. and C.A. Sprigg (1999), 'Minimizing strain and maximizing learning: the role of job demands, job control and proactive personality', *Journal of Applied Psychology*, **84**, 925–39.
Pomaki, G. and S. Maes (2002), 'Predicting quality of work life: from work conditions to self-regulation', in E. Gullone and R.A. Cummins (eds), *The Universality of Subjective Well-being Indicators*, Dordrecht, Kluwer, pp. 151–73.
Pomaki, G., S. Maes and L. Ter Doest (2004), 'Work conditions and employees' self-set goals: goal processes enhance prediction of psychological distress and well-being', *Personality and Social Psychology Bulletin*, **30**, 685–94.
Saks, A.M. (1994), 'Moderating effects of self-efficacy for the relationship between training method and anxiety and stress reactions of newcomes', *Journal of Organizational Behavior*, **15**, 639–54.
Schnall, P.L., J.E. Schwartz, P.A. Landsbergis, K. Warren and T.G. Pickering (1998), 'A longitudinal study of job strain and ambulatory blood pressure: results from a three year follow-up', *Psychosomatic Medicine*, **60**, 697–706.
Schneider, B. (1998), 'Personality and organizations: a test of the homogeneity of personality hypothesis', *Journal of Applied Psychology*, **83**, 462–70.
Schreurs, P.J.G. and T.W. Taris (1998), 'Construct validity of the demand–control model: a double cross-validation approach', *Work & Stress*, **12**, 66–84.
Taris, T.W. (1999), 'The mutual effects between job resources and mental health: a prospective study among Dutch youth', *Genetic, Social and General Psychology Monographs*, **125**, 433–50.
Taris, T.W. (2000), *A Primer in Longitudinal Data Analysis*, London: Sage.
Taris, T.W. and J.A. Feij (in press), 'Learning and strain among newcomers: a three-wave study on the effects of job demands and job control', *Journal of Psychology*.
Taris, T.W., W.B. Schaufeli and L.C. Verhoeven (in press), 'Workaholism in the Netherlands: measurement and implications for job strain and work–nonwork conflict', *Applied Psychology: An International Review*.
Taris, T.W., M.A.J. Kompier, A.H. De Lange, W.B. Schaufeli and P.J.G. Schreurs (2003), 'Learning new behavior patterns: a longitudinal test of Karasek's active learning hypothesis among Dutch teachers', *Work & Stress*, **17**, 1–20.

Theorell, T. and R.A. Karasek (1996), 'Current issues relating to psychosocial job strain and cardiovascular disease research', *Journal of Occupational Health Psychology*, **1**, 9–26.

Van der Doef, M.P. and S. Maes (1999), 'The Job Demand–Control(–Support) Model and psychological well-being: a review of 20 years of empirical research', *Work & Stress*, **13**, 87–114.

Van Yperen, N.W. and M. Hagedoorn (2003), 'Do high job demands increase intrinsic motivation or fatigue or both?', *Academy of Management Journal*, **46**, 339–48.

Warr, P.B. (1990), 'The measurement of well-being and other aspects of mental health', *Journal of Occupational Psychology*, **63**, 193–210.

Warr, P.B. and J. Downing (2000), 'Learning strategies, learning anxiety and knowledge acquisition', *British Journal of Psychology*, **91**, 311–33.

10 The seeds of stress in the organizations of tomorrow: the impact of new technology and working methods
Ashley Weinberg

What is new technology?
Anything which can be seen as a machine-operated innovation has the right to be given this label. Hence all computer or microchip-run machines, communications systems from mobile phones to videoconferencing facilities and transport systems from the wheel to time travel are all eligible for the title of new technology. The adjective 'new' is continually revised of course, but this simply highlights the pace of change. Tape recorders were relatively new technology not so long ago, but within 20 years have been superseded by compact disc players. The advent of email and the Internet has made the world more accessible for those with access to computers, while the invention of the pocket-sized mobile phone means that we can contact others around the world at any time, regardless of where we are.

All of this means that the flow of information in our world has quickened and with it the expectations we have of each other have also been raised. As information is provided in a speedier manner than before, it is expected that we will respond to it equally speedily. Within the workplace this means that not only has new technology changed the way we work, but so have the expectations held by employers and organizations of their employees. This means we can be told to respond more quickly to the demands of the workplace and in theory we can be available to our employers at any time. Taken to its logical conclusion, this can lead to wider social changes where teams and offices can be virtual, linked across geographical space, and the working week becomes a 'waking week' instead (Parker *et al.*, 2001). These developments pose threats to personal control, which in turn can lead to damaged psychological health (Sparks *et al.*, 2001).

This chapter sets out to scrutinize the psychological impact of new technology on the employees who are expected to work with it and the organizations which employ them. The main focus will be on the new battle for control of the workplace which has resulted from technological change. Within this the relationship between new technological innovations, the way in which work is changing and the health implications for employees will be highlighted.

How did we get here?
Since the industrial revolution the history of the workplace has been about control: control over the activities of individuals, the management of groups of employees and the power to direct organizations. This has been reflected in a continuing battle between workers and their employers, sometimes fought over seemingly trivial issues, to see who could exert control over the workplace. This has often led to conflict between governments

and trade unions or bands of workers. The Luddites were early representatives of this struggle. They were anti-technology protestors who set out to destroy manufacturing machinery in the UK, burning factories and smashing their contents. In part the protests of the Luddites were symptoms of anger against the rapid advance of new technology which had been changing the nature of work and eroding the rural lifestyles of many of the population. Anyone who has sat helplessly in front of their computer as it failed to work properly might understand some of this frustration.

When the Labour Prime Minister Harold Wilson encouraged Britain in the 1970s to embrace the 'white heat of technology', he envisaged that new inventions would change the way we work for the better. However the question of whether such change would actually improve our working lives has not been satisfactorily answered. Instead new technology has been taken for granted as a sign of progress. Governments tend to focus on the fairness of the economic exchange which takes place between employers and employees, but there is still no broad framework for assessing the impact of new technology on our employees and the wider public. To take Harold Wilson's reference to the white heat of technology, we all know that it is accompanied by the ability to burn and destroy, as well as to forge new and exciting materials.

Perhaps we do not want to be left behind in our own adaptive drive to survive, and certainly examples of our willingness to use new technology are all around. If this is true of individuals, it also applies at the level of the organization. New technology appeals to business operations as it can appear to lead to increased productivity, to improve longer-term flexibility and also to cutbacks on labour costs (Arnold, *et al.*, 1998). Yet, in reality, it is thought that less than half of projects effectively combine technology with desired business outcomes (Clegg *et al.*, 1996). In fact more than half of systems development programmes fail, either in part or completely. If this is the organizational picture, the range of emotions experienced by individual employees is likely to include puzzlement, frustration, anger and resentment. Taken objectively, workers are having to respond to the change which new technology has had on the characteristics of the work. Mostly this serves to simplify jobs, or more rarely to enrich them (Arnold *et al.*, 1998).

What has changed?
An example of everyday use of new technology highlights how life has changed and with it the expectations of people, both inside and outside work. The act of purchasing a newspaper or magazine is as common today as it was 30 years ago, and the financial transaction with the shopkeeper continues to be a major feature. However changes have occurred at a range of levels throughout all the processes involved. Scrutiny of these will help to highlight the role of new technology, including both the advantages and disadvantages for the consumer and the employees engaged in production.

Let us begin with the production of the newspaper. This usually starts with the collection of news. While travelling overnight to carry out an interview, a news reporter might get a mobile phone call or text message with vital information about another story. Having arrived at the destination and gathered the rest of the relevant information, he or she can write the news article using a laptop computer before it is emailed to the news office. The newspaper editor can then amend the article on the desktop computer and shape the page layout. Following this the whole publication is emailed to a specialist firm who rely on computer-aided design and advanced manufacturing technology to make the finished product. Any difficulties may be resolved via a videoconference link, which saves time on travelling to meetings. The printed publication is mass-produced overnight using laser printing technology and then transported to distribution outlets where the quantity of papers and magazines will be logged on to the shops' stocktaking software. In this way retailers can track how many newspapers have been sold and how many are left in stock, as well as calculating revenue from sales.

The time taken for the above to happen should be a fraction of the time once taken to produce a newspaper, when communication relied on landlines rather than mobile phones, on postal services rather than email and networked computers, on manual typesetting rather than laser printing, and on stocktaking by hand rather than via the computerized till. For the employees engaged in the above production process, including journalists, printers and retailers, one would expect that the job tasks are made easier. For the customer there is also change in how they purchase the newspaper. They may decide to download the publication from the Internet or pay for it using a bank card which immediately transfers money from their bank account to that of the shop. These innovations mean that the behaviour of the consumer, the shop worker and the banker is also affected by new technology. This smooth process is how new technology was imagined in the 1970s.

In a less than perfect world
In the above example new technology worked according to expectations and meant that less time was spent carrying out work than would have been the case only a few years before. However, where technology may give us the capability to achieve new heights, it can also work against us. Taking a slightly different view of the above example, there is the potential for the journalist's mobile phone to fail or be out of range, for the computer software to crash, for the videoconference to convey ambiguous messages or for a computer virus or electrical fault to halt the production or purchase of the newspaper. This sort of bad technical luck may seem unlikely, but there are many other reasons why the new technology involved in the above process might not work; nearly all of these are likely to be human and a large proportion can be traced to the way in which we work, that is, not like machines.

Taking from the above example each of the commonly used aspects of new technology in turn, it is possible to understand how people utilize it and how the tussle for control is acted out.

Mobile phones
A fertile area for future research surrounds the use of mobile phones. In theory a mobile phone can make us available to the workplace at all times. It has the ability to blur the boundaries between our work and non-work lives. Anyone receiving a phone call or text message outside working hours or hundreds of miles from the office will testify to this. On the one hand this increases the individual's perception that they are 'on call' and therefore subject to the control of their line manager, while on the other the receiver may perceive the call as a form of social support depending on who is making the call. Karasek's (1979) demands–control model highlights the importance of workload and control for psychological outcomes at work, in conjunction with social support. Further analysis of mobile phone use based on this model is needed. Another potential cause for concern, given the

prevalence of mobile phone use across the population, is the emerging research on the impact on physical health (for example Wilen *et al.*, 2002). Research in this area is already being examined within the field of bioelectromagnetics, but the scope for multidisciplinary approaches remains to be realized.

Concerns about the psychosocial impact of the mobile phone in employment situations may be offset by positive characteristics associated with its use at work. These include the potential for greater flexibility for the employee and the opportunity to optimize their use of time, for example utilizing what would otherwise be 'waiting time'. This type of task-related control can act as a buffer against experiences of stress (Terry and Jimmieson, 1999). Because of our fairly ingrained and conditioned response to the phone, we are subject to feeling that we should deal with whoever is at the other end. This conditioned response is reinforced by subsequent interactions, but with mobile phones there can be the added factor of 'self-importance' for the receiver of the call, which is imbued by taking that call while in a public place, such as a train. The attention which the receiver attracts by talking out loud in a social situation, when they are the subject of the conversation, may be a positive factor. This may provide one explanation why mobile phone use has been recognized as habit-forming, even to the point that it can become a positive addiction (Cassidy, 2002).

Visual display terminals

Laptop and desktop computers have been a tremendous aid to the preparation of written material, at least where there have been no electrical or networking problems. However there is a need for much more research in this area. This is emphasized by indications of a long-term negative impact on employees who are seated for prolonged periods at computer terminals. These range from musculoskeletal difficulties (Aaras *et al.*, 2000) to psychological stress (Ekberg *et al.*, 1995). Where computers have been introduced to an office environment, clerical employees have reported raised workloads, with one-third experiencing increased symptoms of stress (Liff, 1990).

Email has made the distribution of documents easy and the process of written communication much speedier than postal mail. This is ensured of course when the person who is in receipt of the message has time to switch on their machine and can distinguish the significance of key messages from that of the other 20 they received that same morning. Furthermore the nature of their reply is subject to the time at their disposal, their ability to write in a socially acceptable manner, the ability of their system to decode any attached documents and the visibility of their computer screen or its contents to co-workers and line management. Electronic performance monitoring (EPM), where managers can see what is on the employee's screen, represents a new battleground for control between employees and their organizations. Situations have already arisen in the UK where an employee has been fired from their job for sending emails which the organization has deemed inappropriate. Research has claimed that EPM can result in positive or negative outcomes. Stanton (2000) claims that it can provide feedback for employees on their work, while Cararyon (1994) predicts decreased privacy and increased workloads.

It is natural that employees will develop a range of strategies for maintaining their level of control over their work. One method for dealing with the weight of information channelled to employees via email and the Internet is simply to ignore much of the information available (Finholt and Sproull, 1990), yet this increases the likelihood of vital knowledge being missed (Symon, 2000). The potential for increased autonomy for workers linked via an electronic network is exemplified by the use of email to serve the needs of various subgroups of employees. On the other hand, the network can equally be used to disempower employees, by encouraging them to work from home to carry out more routine computerized tasks, where they are physically isolated from their colleagues (Symon, 2000).

Teleworking or telecommuting (working from computers at home), is on the increase, with around 5 per cent of UK and US employees operating in this way (Chapman *et al.*, 1995). With this comes the potential for more challenges to employee control over their work and over other workers. A range of difficulties may be endured by the individual employee, including technological breakdowns, conflict at the home–work interface and social isolation from colleagues. It has been suggested as a positive factor that there will be a reduced need for face-to-face meetings. However teleworking is likely to have an impact on the number of people involved in organizational decisions and thereby has an implication for the exercise of control in the workplace (Arnold *et al.*, 1998).

However control is exercised and by whom, it is the case that social interaction via email is different from such interaction in person. A range of social signals, including non-verbal cues, cannot be transmitted and this can lead to the removal of inhibitions (Arnold *et al.*, 1998) or simple misunderstandings (Symon, 2000). The apparent absence of social barriers to sending certain types of communication can create in managers and employees alike a sense of false security, which makes them feel comfortable about emailing what they would not normally say. The quality of interaction can also suffer, so much so that one UK city council felt obliged to introduce an email-free day each week, to encourage the employees to talk to one another, even within the same office. If we can actually see the person down the line, via a videoconference for example, this can help build the communication on a more human level. While this is closer to a more usual interaction, it can be subject to time delays and a range of assumptions about the other person which are quite unlike face-to-face encounters.

Advanced manufacturing technology
Advanced manufacturing technology (AMT) can mean computer-numerically controlled machinery, robots or software applications in design and manufacturing. These might be involved in the mass production of an item such as a newspaper, or in retail stocktaking and banking procedures. AMT has been seen as producing speedier and more flexible working (Chmiel, 1998), with the added value for the organization of saving labour and guaranteeing standardized products and quality. However this implies again that the new technology, driven by management concerns, moulds the working lives of those responsible for the daily operation of the machinery. Once again this is an example of striving for control. When newspaper printing in the UK was moved from Fleet Street to Wapping in the 1980s, to facilitate the introduction of new technology, there were large-scale and violent industrial disputes. As has been noted, the introduction of new technology often results in failure of the new system as the role of the employees has not been adequately consulted or considered. The following list highlights some of the issues of control which deserve scrutiny.

1. The perception of new technology by the employees on the shopfloor or on the frontline. It may not be the actual change in working practice which creates hostility, rather it is more likely to be the workers' perception of the underlying motives of the management (Arnold *et al.*, 1998): is this another of management's bright ideas which have helped someone gain promotion, will my working life become easier or, more importantly, is this the end of my job?
2. The lack of involvement in the design or implementation of technology of those workers who are supposed to use it. Training may well be provided, but the parameters of the technology have already been set by that stage and workers are obliged to work within its confines. Wall and Davids (1992) highlight the link between poorer psychological health and jobs entailing high cognitive demand for monitoring new technology.
3. Lack of autonomy for employees who use the technology, including the ability to fix the technology or 'trouble shoot' problems for themselves. This in turn leads to increased downtime and decreased satisfaction. Where increased control over the new technology is encouraged, these trends are reversed (Jackson and Wall, 1991). In fact, where autonomous work groups take responsibility for new technology, increases in sales of almost one-fifth have been recorded (Batt, 1999).

Much of the research has tended to show that AMT has produced job simplification (Kelly, 1982), rather than enrichment (Arnold *et al.*, 1998), yet the above studies clearly support the logic that new technology will improve organizational efficiency where there is greater freedom for employees to take control. However, as the 20th century dawned, Frederick Winslow Taylor was championing the introduction of 'scientific management', whereby work was divided into its component tasks, thus ensuring savings in workforce pay and training. Taylorism spawned the assembly lines, including those at Ford, which dominated mass production operations for the next hundred years. However recognition of the impact of AMT on the social and psychological features of work inspired attempts to optimize jointly the psychosocial needs of the employee and the requirements of working with new technology (for example Trist and Bamforth, 1951). The clear route to avoid the failure of new technological implementation is to ensure that an appropriate work design accompanies it (Waterson *et al.*, 1999 in Parker *et al.*, 2001). Despite this recognition, the attraction of Taylorism remains, as it so clearly ensures that control over almost all of the processes in the workplace is retained by management. In fact the approach which was designed to promote AMT has been imported to manage the human interaction element of many retail and sales functions.

Mass production of human interaction
Work within call centres represents the clearest example of standardization of human social behaviour. The 'conversation' of the employee is often scripted so that certain questions are asked and often in a particular manner. Furthermore calls are timed, recorded and sampled by management to ensure that the script is being followed and that the service is standardized. This parallels the job simplification seen on the assembly lines dedicated to mass production and tends to ensure that employees have very little control over their job tasks. It is perhaps not surprising that call centres have been labelled the 21st century

equivalent of the 'dark, satanic mills' of the industrial revolution (Sparks et al., 2001). Given that, as human beings, we will tend to resist moves to deprive us of freedom, it is not surprising that call centre employees regain some level of control by identifying and exploiting gaps in the surveillance systems established by management (Bain and Taylor, 2000). On occasion this can be as simple as departing from the script to be rude to a customer (Taylor, 1998).

The phenomenon of managing one's behaviour to create an image which is consistent with the goals of the organization is known as 'emotional labour'. This was first observed in the airline industry (see Hochschild, 1983) and can be seen in many jobs in the service sector, including fast food outlets, where scripts are often issued to employees. One could argue that the introduction of this kind of job simplification or new technology without consideration of the psychological needs of the employee has led to increased control for management and resulted in a greater emotional, as well as physical, distance between the employee, manager and consumer. The distance between the customer and the organization has the potential to grow ever wider and with it the ability to build meaningful consumer relationships. The move by banks in the UK towards more automated procedures and Internet-based accounts has demonstrated this. Labour costs are reduced, but, as branches close and communities are deprived of focal points, it is also the business which stands to lose, as customers gravitate towards organizations with a 'friendly face'. The consumer–company gap can only be bridged if one can get through the computer-run call options and the scripted phone transactions with customer relations staff. However, given the Taylorist design of their jobs, they are often not empowered to take the action the customer asks. Here again the personal control of the employee is threatened.

Conclusion
The crux of the impact of new technology and job simplification on employees and organizations rests on where the control is held in the workplace. This chapter has taken as its premise that control underpins effective employee functioning, in line with a considerable amount of occupational research (for example Sparks et al., 2001). Whether this is control over when and how tasks are carried out, or over the machinery and the relevant employees (Arnold et al., 1998), scrutiny of examples of commonly used new technology has shown that there can be both positive and negative outcomes. The balance for the individual employee seems to tilt towards a negative effect of new technology, where little or no personal control has been shown to harm psychological health (Evans and Carrere, 1991). However this can depend on the individual worker's need for autonomy (Sparks et al., 2001), and further research is needed on this point. Social support can act as a buffer against stress where employees' control over their work is not optimal (van der Doef et al., 2000) and new technology, in the case of mobile phones and email, can be used by employees to draw upon it.

At the level of the organization the attraction of new technology has been recognized in lower production and employee costs and increased flexibility. Nevertheless the approaches to introducing and utilizing systems have tended to emphasize the distance between the management and the employee and increase the distance between the organization and the customer. The psychological contract which describes the unwritten expectations between the employee and employer (Robinson and Rousseau, 1994) has undergone massive change and has not been properly re-established (Herriot and Pemberton, 1995) in the light of new technological change. One consequence of this is a lack of communication with the relevant employees prior to introduction of new technology, resulting in unrealistic expectations of what a system can deliver, or its operators achieve. Greater care is needed to ensure that employees' control matches the psychological demands placed upon them, otherwise there is an increased risk of stress-related problems (Houtman, 1999). Where new technology fails, this is due, not to the technology, but to the lack of an accompanying appropriate job design (Parker et al., 2001).

An examination of the production and purchase of a newspaper – an everyday item which is taken for granted – helps to illustrate the impact of new technology on jobs. Whilst one might not want to return to the days before mobile phones, email and assembly lines, as would-be Luddites might wish, the challenges to employees' personal control over their behaviour strike a chord within all of us and emphasize the need to optimize the match between organizational and individual needs. To engage in and maintain this two-way communication process, a new world must also be a brave one.

References

Aaras, A., G. Horgen and O. Ro (2000), 'Work with the display unit: health consequences', *International Journal of Human–Computer Interaction*, **12**, 107–34.
Arnold, J., C.L. Cooper and I.T. Robertson (1998), *Understanding Human Bheaviour in the Workplace*, 3rd edn, Harlow: Prentice-Hall.
Bain, P. and P. Taylor (2000), 'Trapped by the "electronic panoptician"? Worker resistance in the call centre', *New Technology, Work and Employment*, **15**, 2–18.
Batt, R. (1999), 'Work organization, technology and performance in customer service sales', *Industrial and Labour Relations Review*, **52**, 539–64.
Cararyon, P. (1994), 'Effects of electronic performance monitoring on job design and worker stress: results of two studies', *International Journal of Human–Computer Interaction*, **6**, 177–90.
Cassidy, S. (2002), 'A social psychological perspective on mobile phone use', *Proceedings of the British Psychological Society*, **11**(1).
Chapman, A.J., N.P. Sheehy, S. Heywood, B. Dooley and S.C. Collins (1995), 'The organizational implications of teleworking', in C.L. Cooper and I.T. Robertson (eds), *International Review of Industrial and Organizational Psychology*, vol. 10, Chichester: Wiley.
Chmiel, N. (1998), *Jobs Technology and People*, London: Routledge.
Clegg, C., P. Coleman, P. Hornby, R. McClaren, J. Robson, N.Carey and G. Symon (1996), 'Tools to incorporate some psychological and organizational issues during the development of computer-based systems', *Ergonomics*, **39**, 482–511.
Ekberg, K., J. Eklund, M. Tuvesson, R. Oertengren, P. Odenrick and M. Ericson (1995), 'Psychological stress and muscle activity data entry at visual display units', *Work and Stress*, **9**, 475–90.
Evans, G.W. and S. Carrere (1991), 'Traffic congestion, perceived control, and psychophysiological stress among urban bus drivers', *Journal of Applied Psychology*, **76**, 658–63.
Finholt, T. and L. Sproull (1990), 'Electronic groups at work', *Organization Science*, **1**, 41–64.
Herriot, P. and C. Pemberton (1995), *New Deals*, Chichester: Wiley.
Hochschild, A.R. (1983), *The Managed Heart*, Berkeley: University of California Press.
Houtman, I.L.D. (1999), 'The changing workplace', in *Work, stress and health 1999: organization of work in a global economy*, Conference Proceedings, March, APA and NIOSH.
Jackson, P.R. and T.D. Wall (1991), 'How does operator control enhance performance of advanced manufacturing technology?', *Ergonomics*, **34**, 1301–11.
Karasek, R.A. (1979), 'Job demands, job decision latitude and mental strain: implications for job design', *Administrative Science Quarterly*, **24**, 285–308.
Kelly, J. (1982), *Scientific Management, Job Redesign and Work Performance*, London: Academic Press.
Liff, S. (1990), 'Clerical workers and information technology; gender relations and occupational change', *New Technology, Work and Employment*, **5**, 44–55.
Parker, S.K., T.D. Wall and J.L. Cordery (2001), 'Future work design research and practice: towards an elaborated model of work design', *Journal of Occupational and Organizational Psychology*, **74**, 413–40.

Robinson, S.L. and D.M. Rousseau (1994), 'Violating the psychological contract: not the exception but the norm', *Journal of Organizational Behaviour*, **15**, 245–59.
Sparks, K., B. Faragher and C.L. Cooper (2001), 'Well-being and occupational health in the 21st century workplace', *Journal of Occupational and Organizational Psychology*, **74**, 489–509.
Stanton, J.M. (2000), 'Reactions to employee performance monitoring: framework, review and research directions', *Human Performance*, **13**, 85–113.
Symon, G. (2000), 'Information and communication technologies and the network organisation: a critical analysis', *Journal of Occupational and Organizational Psychology*, **73**, 389–414.
Taylor, S. (1998), 'Emotional Labour and the New Workplace', in P. Thompson and C. Warhurst (eds), *Workplaces of the Future*, Basingstoke: Macmillan.
Terry, J. and N.L. Jimmieson (1999), 'Work Control and Well-being: a Decade Review', in C.L. Cooper and I.T. Robertson (eds), *International Review of Industrial and Organizational Psychology*, vol. 14, Chichester: Wiley.
Trist, E. and K. Bamforth (1951), 'Some social and psychological consequences of the longwall method of coal-getting', *Human Relations*, **4**, 3–38.
Van der Doef, M., S. Maes and R. Dieksra (2000), 'An examination of a job–demand–control–support model with various occupational strain indicators', *Anxiety, Stress and Coping*, **13**, 165–85.
Wall, T.D. and K. Davids (1992), 'Shopfloor work organization and advanced manufacturing technology', in C.L. Cooper and I.T. Robertson (eds), *International Review of Industrial and Organizational Psychology*, vol. 7, Chichester: Wiley.
Waterson, P.E., C.W. Clegg, R. Bolden, K. Pepper, P.B. Warr and T.D. Wall (1999), 'The use and effectiveness of modern manufacturing practices: a survey of UK industry', *International Journal of Production Research*, **37**, 2271–92.
Wilen, J., M. Sandstrom and K. Hansson Mild (2002), 'Subjective symptoms among mobile phone users – a consequence of absorption of radiofrequency fields?', Bioelectromagnetics Society 24th Annual Meeting, Quebec.

PART II

STRESS MANAGEMENT ISSUES

11 Stress and individual differences: implications for stress management
Susan Cartwright and Lynne C. Whatmore

Introduction
Stress has been identified as a major factor in ill-health, particularly psychological health. Workplace surveys (Cartwright and Cooper, 1997; Worral and Cooper, 2001) consistently report that employees consider that stress at work is a significant factor which affects their health and well-being. As a consequence many organizations are implementing stress management interventions in order to reduce stress levels, help employees cope more effectively with experienced stress and to reduce sickness absence costs. At the same time such activities are perceived to be effective in demonstrating a sense of organizational care and concern and a desire to improve employee morale (Sigman, 1992).

The potential sources of stress in the workplace are many and various and differ between occupational groups and job status (Gibson *et al.*, 1988; Cooper and Cartwright, 1994). However organizational change and reorganization have been increasingly cited as significant, and potentially universal, factors responsible for high stress levels amongst employees (Callan, 1993; Saksvik, 1996). Tackling the environmental sources of stress, described as 'primary level interventions' (Murphy, 1988), is widely argued as the most effective, yet less common, strategy for reducing workplace stress.

The transactional model of stress (Cox and MacKay, 1976) emphasizes the subjective nature of stress as 'an individual perceptual phenomenon rooted in psychological processes'. Consistent with the view that individual factors play a significant role in the appraisal and experience of stress as well as influencing the way in which individuals subsequently cope with stress, most interventions are aimed at the individual (Norvell *et al.*, 1987). Individually selected interventions, for example health promotion activities and skills training, have value in helping individuals develop techniques to improve their resilience and capabilities to deal more effectively with stressful situations which they encounter both at work and in their personal life (Dewe, 1989). From an organizational viewpoint, individually selected interventions are favoured over more fundamental organizational interventions because they are considered less disruptive, less expensive and much easier to implement (Murphy, 1988).

While the debate about the efficacy of selective and organizational level interventions is an important one, this chapter will confine its focus to individual differences which influence and moderate the stress response and consider the implications for stress management.

Individual factors in the stress–strain relationship
Researchers have investigated a wide range of individual and behavioural characteristics believed to be involved in the relationship between stressors and resultant strain.

164 Stress management issues

Traditionally the key factors which influence an individual's vulnerability to stress are considered to include the following:

- their personality and lifestyle,
- their coping strategies,
- age,
- gender,
- attitudes,
- training,
- past experiences,
- their perceptions of control,
- the degree of social support which is available to them from family, friends and work colleagues.

For convenience, these variable are commonly grouped into three categories: personality or dispositional factors, situational, and social (Cooper *et al.*, 2001). However these categorical distinctions are not always clear-cut. For example, the notion that coping is a stable dispositional characteristic is strongly debated (Lazarus, 1991). Similarly the concept of locus of control (Rotter, 1966) is frequently classified as a dispositional variable, yet some research evidence (Cartwright *et al.*, 2000) suggests that it may be situational, that is state rather than trait.

While by no means exhaustive, this chapter will now consider a number of important individual variables: those which have been well researched and those which are emerging as interesting avenues for future research.

Type A behaviour pattern (TABP)

Originally identified in the 1950s as a personality type associated with increased risks of coronary artery disease (Friedman and Rosenman, 1959), TABP has been extensively researched as a predictor of strain and strain-related outcomes. TABP is characterized by a set of behaviours that reflect an individual's strong sense of time urgency, competitive drive and sense of hostility. These behaviours manifest themselves in the work environment as a tendency to work long hours, cut short holidays, report excessive workloads, feel misunderstood and to display frustration and irritability when dealing with work colleagues.

The renowned Western Collaborative Group prospective study conducted amongst a male population in the United States during the 1960s (Rosenman *et al.*, 1964) confirmed the link between Type A behaviour and an increased incidence of chronic heart disease (CHD), as well as increased risk factors for CHD compared to the more relaxed males classified as Type B. By the end of the study, Type A males were found to be twice as likely to suffer from CHD, even after controlling for traditional factors such as age, smoking, blood cholesterol, blood pressure and familial heart disease.

Since then, numerous researchers have investigated the links between TABP, stress and health (for example Ivancevich *et al.*, 1982; Sharpley *et al.*, 1995). In the Sharpley *et al.* (1995) study conducted among almost 2000 staff in an Australian university, those categorized as Type A reported significantly higher levels of anxiety, daily hassles and job stress than their Type B colleagues. Additionally they reported significantly poorer levels of physical health, along with more injuries, accidents and illness. Of several predictor variables included in the study (cognitive hardiness, coping behaviour and social support), TABP was the strongest predictor of ill-health assessed by number of days absent, frequency of illness, visits to a medical practitioner and self-rating of physical health.

In a review (Parkes, 1994) of several moderator variables, it was concluded that Type A individuals create additional stress for themselves through their actions and attitudes. However the precise relationship between TABP and stress remains controversial and the subject of continuing research (Rhodewalt and Zone, 1991). The majority of studies have used global measures of TABP, which have produced conflicting results. Spector and O'Connell (1994) have argued that TABP is multidimensional, rather than unidimensional, and that researchers need to examine the moderating effects of specific components of TABP. In particular it would seem that it is the anger/hostility aspects of TABP which may account for increased stress levels and strain outcomes. In a longitudinal prospective study (Spector and O'Connell, 1994) it was found that impatience/irritability was correlated with stressors (constraints and interpersonal conflicts) and with somatic symptoms but not with job satisfaction, anxiety or frustration. Achievement/striving correlated with job stressors (role ambiguity, role conflict and workload) but not with strains.

Implications for stress management
Sharpley *et al.* (1995) suggest that, because TABP is a psychological characteristic, it can be modified by awareness programmes, cognitive–behavioural and health promotion strategies to enhance health and well-being. Friedman and Rosenman (1974) have devised a number of behavioural drills which Type As can follow to modify their behaviour, based on positive/negative reinforcement theory. They have successfully used such techniques amongst clinical populations. Given the potential importance of the anger/hostility component of TABP, anger management programmes may also be useful in helping Type A individuals manage stress more effectively.

In common with other forms of cognitive–behavioural therapy, programmes to modify Type A behaviour may not easily transfer from a clinical setting to a workplace environment (Saunders *et al.*, 1996). Organizations may need to examine the extent to which the type of work environment they create and the practices they promote serve to encourage and reward Type A behaviour. By monitoring working hours and ensuring that employees take their full holiday entitlement, organizations can modify environmental factors which enhance Type A behaviour. While exercise programmes have been found to be an effective universal strategy for reducing stress (Whatmore *et al.*, 1998), some caution may be appropriate in terms of their applicability to Type As. Certain types of exercise (for example those conducted in group settings) may actually increase competiveness and aggression.

Locus of control
Locus of control (LOC) refers to the beliefs that individuals have over events in their lives. An individual with an internal LOC perceives himself or herself as being able to influence what happens to them, through their own actions and decisions. Someone with an external LOC believes that he or she has little influence over events and situations and that what

happens to them is largely due to luck, chance, fate or other people (Rotter, 1966). The relationship with stress is that LOC acts as a moderator between stress and strain; individuals with an external LOC report higher levels of job stress and appear to experience more psychological ill-effects than those with internal LOCs (for example Spector, 1982; Cummins, 1988). More recent research by Horner (1996) demonstrated that individuals with an external LOC were more vulnerable to illness than those with internal LOCs. The 'externals' reported higher levels of distressing emotions, made fewer attempts to exert control over their experiences, resorted to self-blame tactics and avoidance behaviour such as sleeping and watching television, and generally perceived life to be stressful. A meta-analysis conducted by Spector (1986) concluded that LOC was significantly correlated with both job stressors and job strains.

Rahim (1997) goes so far as to suggest that 'internals' should be selected for managerial jobs that involve a high level of stress. On the basis of a study of 288 managers, Rahim examined the moderating effects of both LOC and social support on job stress (defined as role conflict, overload, ambiguity and insufficiency) and on strain (measured as a composite of depression, anxiety, cognitive disturbance and anger). Rahim found significant inverse relationships of locus of control to both stress and strain: the internal managers were able to cope with role overload more effectively than externals. LOC was found to be more important than social support in explaining both stress and strain and in moderating the relationship between the two. Similarly, Spector and O'Connell (1994) in their prospective study found that, compared with externals, internals reported lower stress and anxiety levels and were more satisfied with their jobs. However an extreme internal LOC score can itself bring problems. If such individuals find themselves in situations that are beyond their control, they can actually experience a greater degree of stress than 'externals' (Cooper et al., 1988). Indeed Krause and Stryker (1994) found that men with a moderately high LOC score coped better with work stressors than did those with an extremely internal or external score.

Implications for stress management
Again cognitive–behavioural techniques such as rational–emotive behaviour therapy (Ellis, 1962) may prove useful in helping individuals with an external LOC to challenge the irrationality of their beliefs and promote a greater sense of personal control. Similarly organizations can increase perceptions of individual influence in the workplace by increased employee involvement and consultation, particularly in situations involving organizational change.

Emotional intelligence
Recent developments in the study of emotions at work (Payne and Cooper, 2001) have highlighted that central to all behaviour is the overriding drive by the individual to reduce aversive emotional experiences and stress and to maintain a sense of integrated self. There is considerable controversy surrounding the concept of emotional intelligence as to whether it is a true form of intelligence, a set of competencies or a cluster of personality traits (Davies et al., 1998). However it is accepted that the essence of what is regarded as emotional intelligence is the ability of individuals to be aware, recognize and effectively integrate emotions with thoughts and behaviours, and that, importantly, individuals differ

in their emotional aptitudes to do this. Bar-on (1997), who has developed a measure of emotional intelligence, defines the concept as 'a multifactorial array of interrelated emotional, personal and social abilities that influence our overall ability to actively and effectively cope with demands and pressures'.

Slaski and Cartwright (2002) have provided research evidence to support the relationship between emotional intelligence and stress, health and performance. In a study of 225 retail managers it was found that those who scored higher in emotional intelligence demonstrated less stress and had significantly better health and well-being. In addition they enjoyed a better quality of working life and were rated by their line managers as significantly higher performers. Emotional intelligence is also being considered a selection criterion for highly stressful jobs which demand particularly high levels of understanding and empathy, such as nursing (Cadman and Brewer, 2001).

Implications for stress management
Unlike cognitive intelligence (IQ), which remains more or less fixed throughout adult life, emotional intelligence can be developed through training. Slaski and Cartwright (2003) introduced emotional intelligence training into a large retail organization. Sixty managers participated in the training and pre- and post-measures of emotional intelligence, health and stress were taken. For comparison, measures were also taken from a matched control group. The results showed a significant increase in emotional intelligence scores pre- and post-training. Furthermore stress and health levels improved. As a new technique in improving individual resilience to stress, emotional intelligence training may present an important and effective strategy and at the same time have the additional benefit of improving managerial style and leadership skills (Barling *et al.*, 2000; Palmer *et al.*, 2000).

Other personality/dispositional variables
Researchers have also considered other variables such as negative affectivity (NA), which closely approximates neuroticism and relates to the tendency of individuals to focus differently on negative aspects of themselves, others and the world in general. Although there is some evidence to suggest that high NA individuals report more distress than low NA individuals (Watson and Clark, 1984; Spector and O'Connell, 1994), research in this area still remains inconclusive as to the direction of the stressor–strain relationship. This is largely due to methodological problems, particularly the issue of common-method variance.

Concepts such as hardiness (Kobosa, 1982), optimism, self-esteem and self-efficacy (Cohen and Edwards, 1989) have also been considered as individual factors implicated in the stress–strain relationship but again, to date, research findings remain equivocal and more research is needed.

Situational factors
Research by Karasek (1979) has highlighted that employee perceptions of control are strongly influenced by organizational circumstances and job characteristics rather than the general disposition of the individual. Jobs which are highly demanding, and yet at the same time afford the individual little discretion to exercise personal control and influence, have been linked to high levels of stress, poor health outcomes and potential burnout (Fox *et al.*, 1993).

Stress management issues

Implications for stress management
The aim of most selective stress management programmes is to help the individual assume responsibility for stress reduction and to take control over their circumstances and exercise greater personal influence. However any benefits gained from such programmes will rapidly disappear if the individual does not feel able to transfer that learning into the workplace because the environment is too restrictive and controlling. Work by Brady (1992) has demonstrated that performance management systems and techniques can contribute significantly to stress.

Social support
Leavy (1983) defines social support as 'the availability of helping relationships and the quality of those relationships'. Research has demonstrated that social support has a direct effect upon psychological strain and interacts with other variables, to mediate the negative effects of stress (O'Driscoll and Cooper, 1996). In a study of three large Finnish organizations, Kinnunen *et al.* (2000) found that social support significantly moderated the adverse impact of job insecurity on employee well-being.

According to House (1981) social support has four components: (a) giving direct help (instrumental support), (b) showing care and understanding (emotional support), (c) giving helpful information (informational support), and (d) providing feedback that may enhance self-esteem (appraisal support). Individuals differ in terms of the frequency with which they are likely to seek social support and the nature and amount of support they perceive they have from others around them, particularly in the workplace.

Implications for stress management
Attendance on stress management programmes can encourage individuals to seek social support and at the same time, through interaction with other participants, increase their support networks. One of the perceived benefits of in-house stress management courses is that they provide a common understanding and a shared language for openly discussing the problems of stress and that this reduces the stigma often associated with admissions of stress. Moyle (1998) found that managerial support during organizational change influenced job satisfaction and psychological health. Organizations can positively promote social support at work by encouraging social activities, management training and mentoring schemes.

Organizations can provide employee counselling services as a means of acquiring professional support when other sources of social support are inappropriate or unavailable.

Coping strategies
Social support is a potential coping resource, but there are many other ways in which individuals cope with stress. Lazarus (1991) considers that coping strategies can be either problem-focused and directed at dealing with the stressful encounter or emotion-focused and directed at managing the resultant emotional disturbance of that encounter. Generally problem-focused coping is considered more effective than emotion-focused coping.

Individuals vary in terms of the number and variety of coping strategies they use to deal with stress. Some of the ways in which individuals cope with stress are maladaptive and increase the risks of ill-health (cigarette smoking, increased alcohol consumption, overeating and so on). The problem with such strategies is that they are often a habitual quick fix solution which provides some temporary relief but has harmful effects in the longer term.

Implications for stress management
Stress management programmes can be useful in extending the individual's repertoire of coping behaviours by introducing them to new techniques. Lifestyle information and health promotion activities can encourage the individual to abandon poor stress-related lifestyle habits which account for almost half of all premature deaths in the UK alone. Organizations can support such programmes in various ways, for example by providing on-site exercise facilities, setting aside designated quiet areas where employees can relax and providing healthy menus in workplace restaurants.

Stress management training programmes

Stress management training (SMT) programmes can vary considerably in terms of content, duration and foci. Some programmes focus exclusively on a single technique, for example relaxation training; others are multimodular in their approach, combining educational activities with a range of different cognitive and behavioural methods. Typically the content of SMT programmes might include the following:

- stress awareness and education,
- relaxation techniques,
- cognitive coping strategies, for example rational emotive behavioural therapy (REBT),
- biofeedback,
- meditation,
- exercise,
- lifestyle advice and health promotion activities,
- interpersonal skills training such as time management and assertiveness training.

The company-wide 'Building Better Health' programme introduced in the US organization Home Depot in 1982 (Schmidt *et al.*, 2000) included elements of lifestyle advice and health promotion activities as well as services relating to child and elder care, family leave and community volunteering activities. The 'Managing Pressure' programme offered by the UK based retailer, Marks & Spencer, to its employees varies in duration from four hours to a more extensive day and a half event for store managers (Williams and McElearney, 2000). The content of the courses provides stress awareness and stress education and includes some basic exercise physiology, dietary advice and simple relaxation techniques. While both organizations intend to evaluate the effectiveness of these programmes, such data are not yet available.

In common with most training programmes, the potential benefits of SMT are largely accepted as an act of faith, rather than based on systematic evaluation studies. Niven and Johnson (1989) suggest that SMT programmes are unlikely to prove successful because invariably they are too short in duration and do not allow sufficient practice time.

Certainly there is considerable evidence to suggest that any measured benefits decay rapidly over time and are rarely maintained beyond six months post training (Reynolds and Shapiro, 1991; Bunce and West, 1996).

Because company-wide programmes are based on 'broad-brush', 'one size fits all' principles (Murphy and Cooper, 2000), little account has been taken of the differential effects of different types of training and/or traditional behavioural and attitudinal characteristics which may affect individual responsiveness. Contrary to previous evidence (Conrad, 1987), it was found more recently (Whatmore et al., 1998) that volunteers for SMT, far from being the 'worried well', tend to present higher levels of ill-health symptoms than non-volunteers and that multi-session programmes record high attrition rates, particularly in the early stages. In their study, comparing the differential effects of three types of training (stress awareness, REBT and exercise), Whatmore et al. (1998) also found that individuals with extremely elevated stress levels were more likely to 'drop out' of programmes than those whose stress levels were moderately high. This suggests that highly stressed employees may benefit more from a one-to-one counselling approach than more generic group training initiatives. The study concluded that exercise was a more effective individual strategy in stress reduction than cognitive techniques, probably because it was a less complex strategy to implement and was perceived as providing more immediate physical and psychological benefits. This finding is consistent with many other studies which have investigated the benefits of exercise. In a review of research studies, Ashton (1993) concluded that regular exercise reduces the risk of a number of physical problems, including various forms of cancer, as well as reducing the incidence of depression, stress, fatigue and aggression.

Conclusion

Kahn and Byosiere (1992) asserts that personality and individual differences must be one of the 'oldest insights into the complexities of human behaviour'. Although individual variables such as TABP and LOC have been extensively researched in terms of their relationship with stress and ill-health, the influence of such variables as differentiating between individuals who respond to SMT generally, and specific types of training and those who do not, has been little investigated.

One of the shortcomings of SMT may be that insufficient attention to individual factors and existing stress levels has been taken into account in the design and delivery of such programmes. Consequently there is little baseline knowledge by which to evaluate effectiveness.

It is widely recognized (Cooper and Cartwright, 1994) that employees performing different functions and at different levels in an organization are likely to experience different environmental sources of stress, which require different organizational solutions. In the same way, different organizational populations may benefit from different forms and types of SMT which are more tailored to suit their individual needs, characteristics and preferences. Therefore one could question the efficacy of broad-based company-wide SMT programmes, particularly when they operate in isolation from a more holistic integrated approach to stress reduction. In providing specific interventions, organizations might better consider abandoning the traditional instructive methods of the training room in favour of more flexible interactive learning programmes which enable individuals to select and tailor the training to suit their personal requirements. Such programmes are available, using CD Rom technology (Cartwright and Cooper, 2002) which provides opportunities for the individual to select the structure and content of their learning based on individual self-assessment. Technological advances mean that this form of SMT can present a lower-cost alternative to more conventional forms of training and delivery.

In terms of the future research agenda, research into the field of individual differences and stress still remains an important area as the results of studies into many of the possible moderating variables remain inconclusive. Emotional intelligence appears to be an interesting emergent area, but one in which as yet there has been little research.

References

Ashton, D. (1993), 'Exercise: health benefits and risks', European Occupational Health Series no.7, World Health Organisation, Copenhagen.
Bar-On, R. (1997), 'Bar-On Emotional Quotient Inventory: a measure of emotional intelligence', technical manual, Multi Health Systems, Toronto.
Barling, J., F. Slater and F. Kelloway (2000), 'Transformational leadership and EQ', *Leadership and Organisation Development Journal*, **21**, 145–50.
Brady, T. (1992), 'Handling the disappointing performance appraisal', *Supervisory Management*, **37**(9), 3.
Bunce, D. and M.A. West (1996), 'Stress management and innovation interventions at work', *Human Relations*, **49**(2), 209–32.
Cadman, C. and J. Brewer (2001), 'Emotional Intelligence: a vital prerequisite for recruitment in nursing', *Journal of Nursing Management*, **9**, 321–4.
Callan, V.J. (1993), 'Individual and organizational strategies for coping with organizational change', *Work and Stress*, **7**(1), 63–78.
Cartwright, S. and C.L. Cooper (1997), *Managing Workplace Stress*, Thousand Oaks: Sage.
Cartwright, S. and C.L. Cooper (2002), *Under Pressure*, London: BDP Media.
Cartwright, S., C.L. Cooper and L. Whatmore (2000), 'Improving communications and health in a government department', in L.R. Murphy and C.L. Cooper (eds), *Healthy and Productive Work: An International Perspective*, London: Taylor & Francis.
Cohen, S. and J. Edwards (1989), 'Personality characteristics as moderators of the relationship between stress and disorder', in W. Neufeld (ed.), *Advances in the Investigation of Psychological Stress*, New York: John Wiley.
Conrad, P. (1987), 'Who comes to Worksite Wellness Programs? A preliminary review', *Journal of Occupational Medicine*, **29**(4), 317–20.
Cooper, C.L. and S. Cartwright (1994), 'Stress management inventions in the workplace: stress counselling and stress audits', *British Journal of Guidance and Counselling*, **22**(1), 65–73.
Cooper, C.L., R.D. Cooper and L. Eaker (1988), *Living with Stress*, London: Penguin.
Cooper, C.L., P. Dewe and M. O'Driscoll (2001), *Organizational Stress: A Review and Critique of Theory, Research and Application*, Thousand Oaks: Sage.
Cox, T. and C. MacKay (1976), 'Transactional Model of Stress', in T. Cox (ed.), *Stress*, Basingstoke: Macmillan.
Cummins, R.C. (1988), 'Perceptions of social support, receipt of supportive behaviours and locus of control as moderators of the effects of chronic stress', *American Journal of Community Psychology*, **16**, 685–99.
Davies, M., L. Stankov and R.D. Roberts (1998), 'Emotional Intelligence: in search of an elusive contract', *Journal of Personality and Social Psychology*, **75**, 989–1015.
Dewe, P. (1989), 'Examining the nature of work stress: individual evaluations of stressful experiences and coping', *Human Relations*, **42**, 993–1013.
Ellis, A. (1962), *Reason and Emotion in Psychotherapy*, Secaucus NJ: Citadel.
Fox, M., D. Dwyer and D. Ganster (1993), 'Effects of stressful job demands and control of physiological and attitudinal outcomes in a hospital setting', *Academy of Management Journal*, **36**, 289–318.
Friedman, M. and R.H. Rosenman (1959), 'Associations of a specific behaviour pattern with increases in blood cholesterol, blood clotting time, incidence of arcus senilis, and clinical coronary artery disease', *Journal of American Medical Association*, **169**, 1286–96.
Friedman, M. and R.H. Rosenman (1974), *Type A Behavior and Your Heart*, New York: Knopf.
Gibson, J., J. Ivancevich and J. Donnelly, Jnr (1988), *Organizations: Behaviour, Structure, Processes*, 6th edn, Plano, Texas: Business Publications.

House, J.S. (1981), *Work Stress and Social Support*, Reading, MA: Addison-Wesley.
Ivancevich, J.M., M.T. Matteson and C. Preston (1982), 'Occupational stress Type A behaviour and physical well being', *Academy of Management Journal*, **25**(2), 373–91.
Kahn, R.L. and P. Byosiere (1992), 'Stress in Organizations', in M.D. Dunnette and L.M. Hough (eds), *Handbook of Industrial and Organizational Psychology*, 2nd edn, vol.3.
Karasek, R. (1979), 'Job demands, job decision latitude and mental strain: implications for job redesign', *Administrative Science Quarterly*, **24**, 285–308.
Kinnunen, U., S. Mauno, J. Natti and M. Happonen (2000), 'Organizational antecedents and outcomes of job insecurity: a longitudinal study in three organizations in Finland', *Journal of Organizational Behaviour*, **21**, 443–59.
Kobosa, S. (1982), 'The hardy personality: towards a social psychology of stress and health', in G. Sanders and J. Suls (eds), *Social Psychology of Health and Illness*, Hillsdale, NJ: Lawrence Erlbaum.
Krause, N. and S. Stryker (1994), 'Stress and well being: the buffering role of locus of control beliefs', *Social Science and Medicine*, **18**, 783–90.
Lazarus, R.S. (1966), *Psychological Stress and the Coping Process*, New York: McGraw-Hill.
Lazarus, R.S. (1991), 'Psychological stress in the workplace', *Journal of Social Behaviour and Personality*, **6**, 1–13.
Leavy, R.I. (1983), 'Social support and psychological disorder: a review', *Journal of Community Psychology*, **11**, 3–21.
Moyle, P. (1998), 'Longitudinal influences on managerial support on employee well being', *Work and Stress*, **12**(1), 29–49.
Murphy, L.R. (1988), 'Workplace interventions for stress reduction and prevention', in C.L. Cooper and R. Payne (eds), *Causes, Coping and Consequences of Stress at Work*, London: John Wiley.
Murphy, L.R. and C.L. Copper (2000), *Healthy and Productive Work*: An International Perspective, London: Taylor & Francis.
Niven, N. and D. Johnson (1989), 'Taking the lid off stress management', *Industrial and Commercial Training*, **21**, 8–11.
Norvell, N., D. Belles, S. Brody and A. Freund (1987), 'Worksite stress management for medical care personnel: results from a pilot program', *Journal for Specialists in Group Work*, **12**(3), 118–26.
O'Driscoll, M.P. and C.L. Cooper (1996), 'Sources and management of excessive job stress and burnout', in P. Warr (ed.), *Psychology at Work*, 4th edn, London: Penguin.
Palmer, B., M.B. Walls, Z. Burgess and C. Stough (2000), 'Emotional intelligence and effective leadership', *Leadership & Organisation Development Journal*, **22**, 5–11.
Parkes, K.R. (1994), 'Personality and coping as moderators of work stress processes: models, methods and measures', *Work and Stress*, **8**(2), 110–29.
Payne, R.L. and C.L. Cooper (2001), *Emotions at work: Theory, research and applications in management*, New York: John Wiley & Sons.
Rahim, M.A. (1997), 'Relationships of stress, locus of control and social support to psychiatric symptoms and prosperity to leave a job', *Journal of Business and Psychology*, **12**(2), 159–74.
Reynolds, S. and D.A. Shapiro (1991), 'Stress reduction in transition: conceptual problems in the design, implementation and evaluation of worksite stress management interventions', *Human Relations*, **44**(7), 717–33.
Rhodewalt, F. and J. Zone (1991), 'Appraisal of life change, depression and illness in hardy and non hardy women', *Journal of Personality and Social Psychology*, **56**, 81–8.
Rosenman, R., M. Friedman, R. Straus, M. Wurm, R. Kositchek, W. Hahn and N. Werthessen (1964), 'A predictive study of coronary heart disease', *Journal of the American Medical Association*, **189**, 15–22.
Rotter, J.B. (1966), 'Generalized expectancies for internal versus external control of reinforcement', *Psychological Monographs*, **30**(1), 1–26.
Saksvik, P.O. (1996), 'Attendance pressure during organizational change', *International Journal of Stress Management*, **3**(1), 47–59.
Saunders, T., J.E. Driskell, J.H. Johnston and E. Salas (1996), 'The effect of stress inoculation training on anxiety and performance', *Journal of Occupational Health Psychology*, **1**(2), 170–86.
Schmidt, W.C., L. Welch and M.G. Wilson (2000), 'Individual and organizational activities to build better health', in L.R. Murphy and C.L. Cooper (eds), *Health and Productive Work: An International Perspective*, London: Taylor Francis.
Sharpley, C.F., J.K. Dua, R. Reynolds and A. Acosta (1995), 'The direct and relative efficacy of cognitive hardiness, Type A behaviour pattern, coping behaviour and social support as predictors of stress and ill health', *Scandinavian Journal of Behaviour Therapy*, **24**, 15–29.
Sigman, A. (1992), 'The state of corporate healthcare', *Personnel Management*, February, 24–31.

Slaski, M. and S. Cartwright (2002), 'Health performance and emotional intelligence: an exploratory study of retail managers', *Stress and Health*, **18**(2), 63–9.
Slaski, M. and S. Cartwright (2003), 'Emotional intelligence training and its implications for stress, health and performance', *Stress and Health*, **19**, 233–9.
Spector, P.E. (1982), 'Behavior in organisations as a determinant of employee's locus of control', *Psychological Bulletin*, **91**, 482–92.
Spector, P.E. (1986), 'Perceived control by employees: a meta analysis of studies concerning autonomy and participation at work', *Human Relations*, **39**, 1005–16.
Spector, P.E. and B.J. O'Connell (1994), 'The contribution of personality traits, negative affectivity, locus of control and Type A to the subsequent reports of job stressors and job strain', *Journal of Occupational and Organizational Psychology*, **67**(1), 1–12.
Watson, D. and L. Clerk (1984), 'Negative affectivity: the disposition to experience negative aversive emotional states', *Psychological Bulletin*, **96**, 465–98.
Worrall, L. and C.L. Cooper (2001), *The Quality of Working Life Survey*, London: Institute of Management.
Whatmore, L., S. Cartwright, and C.L. Cooper (1998), 'Stress interventions in the UK: an evaluation of a stress management programme in the public sector', in M. Kompier and C.L. Cooper (eds), *Improving Work Health and Productivity*, London: Routledge.
Williams, S. and N. McElearney (2000), 'Designing and implementing a managing pressure program at Marks & Spencer plc', in L.R. Murphy and C.L. Cooper (eds), *Healthy and Productive Work: An International Perspective*, London: Taylor Francis.

12 Work-related stress: the risk management paradigm
Stavroula Leka, Amanda Griffiths and Tom Cox

In 1994 Hernberg argued that 'the fact that classical occupational diseases still occur does not automatically mean that more research is needed . . . what it really means is that we have failed to implement already existing knowledge'. One year earlier, Cox (1993) had stated that we knew enough then about work-related stress to act to reduce the associated risk to employees' health: he argued that we needed to be able to translate that existing knowledge into practice and suggested that the risk management paradigm offered an appropriate vehicle for doing this.

Background
An unwavering commitment to protect and promote the safety and health of working people should be a defining characteristic of any civilized society. Over the last decade it has become obvious to all but the ill-informed and ideologically prejudiced that work-related stress now presents one of the major challenges to the safety and health of such people. In the European Union this challenge has been recognized by the governments of most member states and by the Commission and its agencies, and has prompted concerted effort to develop a practical methodology for managing work-related stress within the framework of existing safety and health legislation. For many applied researchers and practitioners, managers, trades unionists and policy makers, the obvious way forward was the development of an evidence-based problem-solving process through our cumulative knowledge of risk management. This chapter describes an example of such an approach, developed by the Institute of Work, Health & Organisations in Nottingham with the support of the British Health and Safety Executive, several European bodies and a wide variety of private and public sector organizations. It discusses the background to and nature of the Nottingham approach and also some of the general issues that have been raised in relation to such approaches.

The evidence for work-related stress
The starting point for the development of any new problem-solving methodology is the evidence that a problem exists. Harvesting, collating and evaluating such evidence, however, is not a straightforward or simple matter. The definition of what is and what is not acceptable evidence will in large part determine the outcome of such a review and this question of definition is, in turn, rooted in the purpose of the overall exercise. If that purpose is to produce a research methodology to promote knowledge (and careers) through the publication process then the ideal or the perfect will take precedence over the adequate. If the purpose is to produce a practical methodology capable of supporting action in work situations to protect and promote safety and health – making a difference – then the adequate

takes precedence over the ideal. The criteria for what is acceptable by way of evidence are naturally different in the two cases. In the former case, strict criteria based on ideal science (often experimental science) can be used to reduce uncertainty and avoid false positives in drawing conclusions. However this approach is extremely conservative and results in very slow progress. This is not always acceptable in the face of possible hazards of significance. Where such hazards may exist, a more eclectic approach to evidence is indicated, one where there is a role for informed judgment. The imperative is to avoid false negatives in drawing conclusions about such hazards and, within the framework of the precautionary principle, to quickly develop and test solutions to these problems. This difference in approach is obvious when recent reviews of the literature on work-related stress are compared. Here the more eclectic approach is adopted.

European data from a variety of national and transnational surveys of those in work, or who have recently worked, have identified stress-related problems as among the most commonly reported sources of work-related ill-health (Cox, 2003). For example, the European Foundation's 1996 survey of working conditions in the European Union revealed that 57 per cent of the workers questioned believed that their work affected their health. The work-related health problems most frequently mentioned were musculoskeletal complaints (30 per cent) and stress (28 per cent). In England and Wales, similar data can be drawn from the trailer to the 1990 Labour Force Survey, appended by the Health & Safety Executive, and from the subsequent follow-up survey in 1995 of self-reported work-related illness. Broadly comparable data from the most recent survey (2001/2002) clearly indicate a marked increase in the incidence of work-related stress. This unwelcome finding is supported by data from other occupational health surveillance systems such as ODIN.

The data from the 1990 and 1995 surveys in England and Wales suggested stress and stress-related illness was second only to musculoskeletal disorders as the major cause of work-related ill-health (Hodgson *et al.*, 1993; Jones *et al.*, 1998). At that time, it was estimated that these stress-related problems resulted in about 6.5 million working days lost to industry and commerce each year. In terms of annual costs, estimated using the 1995–6 economic framework, the financial burden to society was £ 3.7–3.8 billion.

Survey data such as those referred to above are available from a variety of European (and other) countries across at least a ten-year window and gathered using a variety of instruments. These data are supplemented by at least two other sources: empirical data from more focused studies on particular work groups and occupations, again across a wide variety of countries and sectors using an equal variety of approaches and instruments, and practice data from both occupational and primary health care specialists. While the purist may painstakingly dismiss each individual survey and study on the grounds that it is not methodologically perfect, there is a more pragmatic argument. After rejecting the more ridiculous, taking such studies and surveys together, the weight of evidence provided can tell a reliable enough story to support action. Doing this, it becomes obvious that work-related stress now presents one of the major challenges to the health of working people.

Solving the problem of work-related stress
In a review of the scientific literature on work-related stress commissioned by the British Health and Safety Executive, Cox (1993) formally suggested that the risk management

paradigm, used to good effect in dealing with physical hazards, be applied to the problem of work-related stress. Over the last decade, the Institute of Work, Health and Organisations, University of Nottingham, has been committed to a programme of research and development designed to produce a usable and useful risk management methodology for work-related stress. The focus of the approach is upstream and on the design and management of work. It is largely preventive. It works best when applied to particular and defined working groups, workplaces or functions.

The major objective of the work conducted at Nottingham was the development and proving of a practical risk management methodology that can be used with different groups (and so on) in different organizations across sectors and countries. As a necessary result, the methodology is process-based and requires a manageable degree of tailoring for use in any particular situation. It is the process that is transferable. The question of whether the outcomes resulting from the application of the process can be generalized across situations is an empirical one. This is an important point. It often translates into a debate as to whether standard off-the-shelf instruments can be used instead of the recommended tailored approach. The former are often instruments developed for purposes of research into stress and not for purposes of risk assessment. It is arguable whether they will prove adequate for the latter as they will, by their very nature, both miss situation-specific problems and include those that are irrelevant to any particular situation. Avoiding these sources of error is one of the purposes of the tailoring process.

The answer to this debate, and to several of the others referred to in this chapter, is framed by the existing safety and health legislation. This is briefly reviewed below.

The Law
In 1989 the European Commission published the 'Council Framework Directive on the Introduction of Measures to Encourage Improvements in the Safety and Health of Workers at Work'. The duties imposed by this directive had to be 'transposed' into each of the member states of the European Union within their respective national legislative frameworks and within a specified time frame. The directive required employers to avoid risks to the safety and health of their employees, to evaluate the risks that cannot be avoided, to combat those risks at source (Article 6:2), to keep themselves informed of the 'latest advances in technology and scientific findings concerning workplace design' (Article 10:1) and to 'consult workers and/or their representatives and allow them to take part in discussions on all questions relating to safety and health at work' (Article 11:1). Employers were also charged to develop a 'coherent overall prevention policy which covers technology, organisation of work, working conditions [and] social relationships' (Article 6:2). In addition, employers were required to 'be in possession of an assessment of the risks to safety and health at work' and to 'decide on the protective measures to be taken' (Article 9:1).

In Britain many of these provisions had already been enacted through the Health and Safety at Work etc Act 1974 (Health and Safety Executive, 1990) but some of the 1989 requirements, such as the duty to undertake assessments for *all* risks to health, had to be introduced in the *Management of Health and Safety at Work Regulations 1992* (Health and Safety Commission, 1992) and their revision (Health and Safety Commission, 1999). Employers were advised to consider work-related stress when undertaking their general risk assessments (Health and Safety Executive, 1995). In terms of the law, a risk assessment involves a systematic examination of all aspects of the work undertaken to consider what could cause injury or harm, whether the hazards could be eliminated and, if not, what preventive or protective measures are, or should be, in place to control the risks (European Commission, 1996). In other words, employers in the European Union have a responsibility to take reasonable steps to protect their employees from those aspects of work or the working environment that are foreseeably detrimental to safety and health. What is being described in this safety and health legislation is the risk management approach with risk assessment as the initial step. It is easy to see from such descriptions that risk management is essentially a problem-solving methodology.

Adapting the risk management paradigm for work-related stress
The challenge has been to adapt the risk management approach to deal with work-related stress in line with existing European legislation. The use of risk management in health and safety has a substantive history, and there are many texts that present and discuss its general principles and variants (Cox and Tait, 1998; Hurst, 1998; Stranks, 1996) and that discuss its scientific and sociopolitical contexts (Bate, 1997). Most models incorporate five important elements or principles: (i) a declared focus on a defined work population, workplace, set of operations or particular type of equipment, (ii) an assessment of risks, (iii) the design and implementation of actions designed to remove or reduce those risks, (iv) the evaluation of those actions, and (v) the active and careful management of the process. Perhaps to these should be added a sixth: organizational learning and training. All of these fundamental elements and principles have been incorporated into the Nottingham process.

It has been argued that there cannot be an exact point-by-point translation of models designed for the management of more tangible and physical risks to situations involving psychosocial and organizational risks and the experience of work stress. This is not a matter of real debate, nor is it a problem, as there is already a wide variety of effective risk management models in existence both across and within different areas of health and safety. The lack of any felt need to agree on one single model has not hampered progress in health and safety management – quite the reverse. Furthermore the adaptation of the traditional risk management paradigm to deal with work-related stress does not have to aim at an exhaustive, precisely measured account of all possible stressors for all individuals and all health outcomes. The overriding objective is to produce a reasoned account of the most important stress-related hazards for a particular and defined working group, grounded in evidence. The account simply needs to be good enough to enable employers and employees to move forward in solving the associated problems and comply with their legal duty of care. The notion of 'good enough' is used here to mean fit and sufficient for purpose. In other words this is not an activity carried out for the benefit of researchers, but one pursued with the aim of making a difference to working conditions within organizations (Griffiths, 1995).

Psychosocial hazards and work-related stress
Central to the Nottingham approach is the concept of 'psychosocial and organizational hazards'. Building on the model offered by the International Labour Office (ILO, 1986),

these have been defined by Cox and Griffiths (1996) as 'those aspects of work design and the organization and management of work, and their social and environmental context, that have the potential for causing psychological, social or physical harm'. The question is, what is the relationship between such psychosocial and organizational hazards, on the one hand, and work-related stress and health, on the other?

The present authors suggest that work-related stress is essentially an explanatory variable that mediates between employees' exposure to certain types of work hazards and their effects on health. There is an interesting supplementary question here as to whether work-related stress is simply a convenient and powerful hypothetical construct or a real experience rooted in the person's emotional architecture and processes. Put simply, in what sense does stress exist: in our data or in our experience? For the millions of working people who answered the survey questions about stress referred to earlier in this chapter, the answer is clear: stress is a real experience.

There appear to be two types of hazard whose effects on health might be mediated by the experience of work-related stress: those physical hazards that evoke anxiety or fear (World Health Organization, 1995) and those hazards that are psychosocial or organizational in nature (Cox, 1993). These psychological, social and organizational aspects of work have been the object of scientific interest since the early 1950s (Barling and Griffiths, 2002; Johnson, 1996). Initially the focus of research was employees' adaptation to their work and work environments, and individual differences in that process of adaptation and coping (Gardell, 1982). However, during the 1960s, the focus of interest had begun to move away from how individuals coped towards a concern for the design and management of their work as a source of their stress-related problems (Leka et al., 2003). This shift in focus has facilitated the development of the risk management approach.

The risk management approach to work-related stress draws on existing taxonomies of the psychosocial and organizational characteristics of work (Cooper and Marshall, 1976; Warr, 1992; Cox, 1993; Cox, Griffiths and Rial-González, 2000; Cox, Griffiths et al., 2000). In his 1993 review, Cox identified nine categories of psychosocial and organizational aspects of work that had been shown to be associated with the experience of stress and/or poor health outcomes. These he labelled 'psychosocial and organisational hazards'. They relate both to the content of work and to its social and organizational context. They are summarized, together with examples, in Table 12.1.[1] There is a good consensus in the literature on the nature of psychosocial and organizational hazards but it should be noted that new forms of work give rise to new hazards, not all of which will yet be represented in scientific publications. This is an important point and has been discussed in more detail elsewhere (Cox, 2003).

In the present authors' experience, it is often very context-specific factors that prove to be associated with poor health. The quality of appraisal systems and consultation with senior managers are two examples (Griffiths, 1998). Factors such as performance visibility (where errors are highly visible), production responsibility (where the cost of errors is great) or employee interdependence may also prove to be problematic (Parker and Wall, 1998). Job insecurity, excessive working hours and a bullying managerial style have also been suggested as imminent concerns for many employees (Sparks et al., 2001). Any assessment of a particular group's work situation needs flexibility in order to allow for the discovery of new psychosocial factors (Griffiths, 1998).

Table 12.1   Psychosocial hazards

Job content	Lack of variety or short work cycles, fragmented or meaningless work, underuse of skills, high uncertainty, continuous exposure to people through work
Workload & work pace	Work overload or underload, machine pacing, high levels of time pressure, continually subject to deadlines
Work schedule	Shift working, night shifts, inflexible work schedules, unpredictable hours, long or unsociable hours
Control	Low participation in decision making, lack of control over workload, pacing, shift working
Environment & equipment	Inadequate equipment availability, suitability or maintenance; poor environmental conditions such as lack of space, poor lighting, excessive noise
Organizational culture & function	Poor communication, low levels of support for problem solving and personal development, lack of definition of, or agreement on, organizational objectives
Interpersonal relationships at work	Social or physical isolation, poor relationships with superiors, interpersonal conflict lack of social support
Role in organization	Role ambiguity, role conflict and responsibility for people
Career development	Career stagnation and uncertainty, underpromotion or overpromotion, poor pay, job insecurity, low social value to work
Home-work interface	Conflicting demands of work and home, low support at home, dual career problems

Source: Adapted from Cox (1993).

While most risk assessments for work-related stress clearly focus on psychosocial and organizational hazards, it is important to note that physical hazards also need consideration in relation to the experience of stress (Cox, 1993). As already stated, anxiety or fear in relation to physical hazards is a source of stress and can, in part, mediate the effects of those hazards on health.

Exposure to different types of hazard can contribute to different forms of harm. For example, exposure to organic solvents may have a psychological effect on the person through their direct effects on the brain, through the unpleasantness of their smell or through fear that such exposure might be harmful (Levi, 1981). Physical hazards can affect health through psychophysiological as well as physicochemical pathways (Levi, 1984). Psychosocial and organizational hazards affect health largely but not exclusively through psychophysiological pathways. For example, violence, as a psychosocial hazard, may have a direct physical effect on its victim in addition to any psychological trauma or social distress that it causes. Both physical and psychosocial and organizational hazards have the potential for detrimentally affecting social and psychological health as well as physical health. One should not make the mistake of thinking about psychosocial and organizational hazards solely as risks to psychological health (Cox, 1993).

```
┌─────────────────────────────────────────────────────────┐
│                    EVALUATION                           │
│  ┌──────────────┐                   ┌──────────────┐    │
│  │    RISK      │                   │    RISK      │    │
│  │ ASSESSMENT   │──▶ TRANSLATION ──▶│  REDUCTION   │    │
│  │(including    │                   │              │    │
│  │  AUDIT)      │                   │              │    │
│  └──────┬───────┘        ▲          └──────┬───────┘    │
│         │                │                 │            │
└─────────┼────────────────┼─────────────────┼────────────┘
          │                │                 │  FEEDBACK
          │                │                 │
          │         ┌──────┴───────────┐     │
          └─────────│  ORGANIZATIONAL  │◀────┘
                    │    LEARNING &    │
                    │    TRAINING      │
                    └──────────────────┘
```

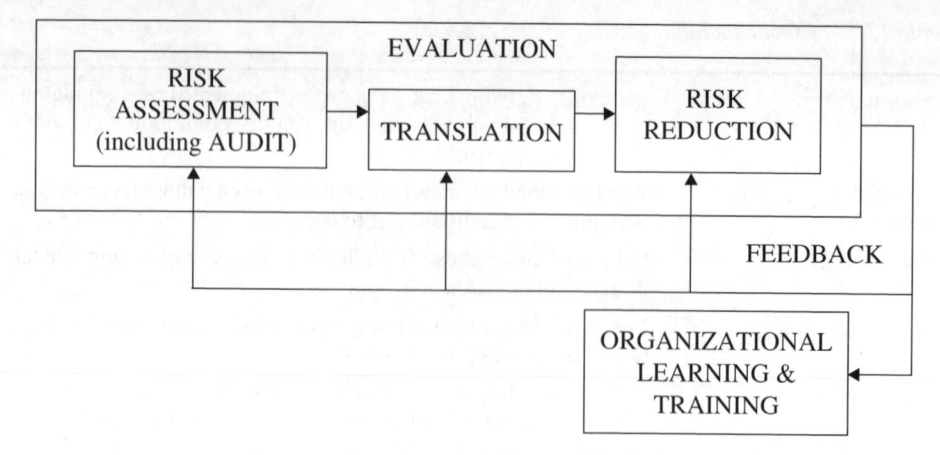

Figure 12.1 A framework model of risk management for work-related stress

Furthermore significant interactions can occur both between hazards and in their effects on health.

The risk management model for work-related stress

At the heart of most risk management models are two distinct but intimately related cycles of activity: risk assessment and risk reduction. This is implicit in the European Commission's *Guidance on Risk Assessment at Work* (European Commission, 1996): risk management involves a systematic examination of all aspects of the work undertaken to consider what could cause injury or harm, whether the hazards could be eliminated and, if not, what preventive or protective measures are, or should be, in place to control the risks.

The risk assessment and risk reduction cycles form the basic building blocks for the Nottingham model described here (see Figure 12.1). They are linked by the processes involved in translating the output of the former into an input to the latter: translation. The model also includes consideration of 'evaluation' and 'organizational learning and training'. Because all aspects of the risk management process should be evaluated – and not just the outcomes of the risk reduction stage – the evaluation stage is treated as supra-ordinate to the other stages. The risk reduction stage, in practice, tends to involve not only prevention but also actions more oriented towards individual health.

Risk assessment for work-related stress

The initial stage, risk assessment, is designed to identify for a defined employee group, with some certainty and in sufficient detail, significant sources of stress relating to its work and working conditions that can be shown to be associated with an impairment of the health of that group. Several issues follow from this definition of risk assessment that have implications not only for the design and use of the assessment procedure but also for the overall risk management process. These are presented in Table 12.2.

Table 12.2 Key principles of risk assessment and management

Work with defined groups	Each risk assessment is carried out within a defined work group, workplace or function
Focus on working conditions, not individuals	Risk assessments are executed in order to identify the aspects of work that give rise to the experience of stress and challenges to health and not the individuals experiencing stress
Focus on big issues: significant sources of stress	The focus is on the problems that affect the majority of staff, not on individual complaints
Provide evidence of effects of working conditions on health	The process is evidence-driven
Use valid and reliable measures	All methods of data collection should be both reliable and valid; employees' expertise provides an important source of information
Maintain confidentiality of information	The confidentiality of information given by individuals must be guaranteed; individual information must be stored securely and not disclosed
Focus on risk reduction as the goal	The risk assessment is designed with risk reduction in mind; risk assessment tools are designed to provide sufficient detail and context-specific information to allow for control measures to be taken; the emphasis is primarily on prevention and organization-level interventions
Involve employees	The use of participative methods and employee involvement are critical to success

Stepwise process for risk assessment
The logic underpinning risk assessment can be operationalized through a six-step process:

1. *Hazard identification*: reliably identify the stressors which exist in relation to the design and management of work and of working conditions, for specified groups of employees, and make an assessment of the degree of exposure. Since many of the problems that give rise to the experience of stress at work are chronic in nature, the proportion of employees reporting a particular aspect of work as stressful may be a 'good enough' group exposure statistic. There are various ways of measuring and presenting the strength of such consensus.
2. *Assessment of harm*: harvest and evaluate evidence that exposure to such stressors is associated with impaired health in the group being assessed. This validation exercise should consider the possible detrimental effects of work-related stress in relation to a wide range of health-related outcomes, including symptoms of general malaise and

specific disorders, and of organizational and health-related behaviours such as smoking and drinking, and sickness absence.
3. *Identification of likely risk factors*: logically or statistically explore the associations between exposure to stressors and measures of harm to identify likely risk factors at the group level, and to make some estimate of their size and significance.[2]
4. *Description of underlying mechanisms*: understand and describe the possible mechanisms by which exposure to the stressors is associated with damage to the health of the assessment group or to the organization.
5. *Audit existing management control and employee support systems* (AMSES): identify and assess all existing management systems both in relation to the control of stressors and the experience of work-related stress and in relation to the provision of support for employees experiencing problems.
6. *Draw conclusions about residual risk*: taking existing management control and employee support systems into account, make recommendations on the residual risk associated with the likely risk factors related to work-related stress.

This process is represented diagrammatically in Figure 12.2, which provides a schematic summary of the risk assessment strategy.

Much of the information used in the risk assessment is based on the expert judgments of working people aggregated to the group level. However such judgments are sometimes labelled as 'self-report' data and this is taken as grounds for dismissal. However there is some evidence to suggest that, for research into work-related stress, it is more appropriate to measure work and working conditions as perceived rather than objectively assessed by supervisors, colleagues, and so on (Spector, 1987; Jex and Spector, 1996; Bosma et al., 1997). From a theoretical perspective, perceptions of work and working conditions may, in fact, be a better predictor of behaviour and health than more objective measures.

It is important to understand clearly that referring to perceived problems of work and working conditions does not place a value or ontological judgment on those problems: perceptions can be accurate as well as inaccurate and moderated by other factors (for example, individual differences: see below). The reliability, validity and accuracy of

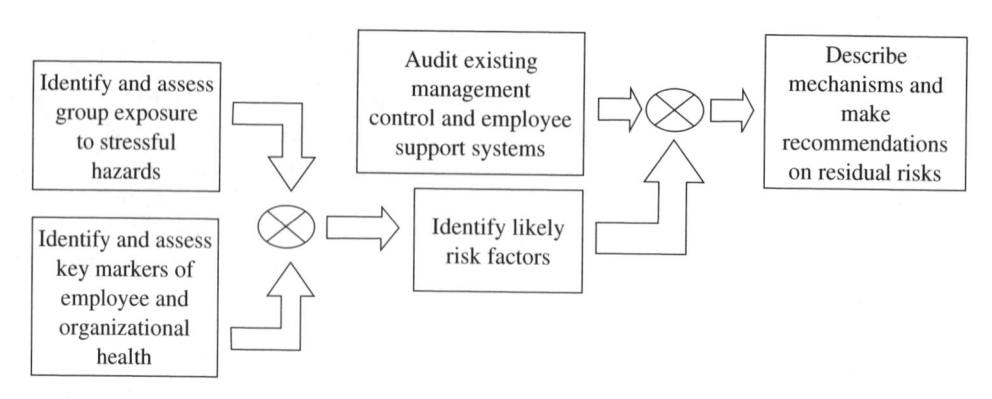

Figure 12.2 The risk assessment strategy

perceptions and self-report data are empirical questions and, as such, can themselves be the subject of investigation. For example, social desirability effects (a common source of bias) can be tested for and screened out at several stages in the development of the risk assessment (Ferguson and Cox, 1993). Respondents' patterns of reporting can be examined for halo effects: any evidence of differential effects would reduce the likelihood of the assessment data being driven by halo or similar effects (for example, negative affectivity). The use of different measurement techniques and different sources of data (triangulation) should reduce the likelihood of common method variance (Jick, 1979; Cox, Griffiths, Barlow *et al.*, 2000). It would be interesting to apply this level of questioning to some of the more objective measures used in stress research. What, for example, is the reliability of a measure of blood pressure taken with an electronic sphygmometer? What are its accuracy and its validity as a predictor of heart disease?

The estimation of risk at the group level is effectively the estimation of risk for the average employee and can be contrasted with the estimation of risk for any specified individual. Where there is much difference between the two, individual differences obviously exist. There are several points to note here. First, the individual differences that exist can only operate through the person's interaction with their work environment. There is no other logical pathway by which their effects can be made manifest. Second, there is no evidence that the individual differences that exist in respect to the effects of stressors on health are any greater (or less) than those that exist in relation to other health hazards. Therefore the existence of individual differences does not negate the overall assessment exercise. Rather it adds an important extra dimension, and opens up questions about moderators of the stressor–health relationship. It should be noted here that, despite these arguments and the fact of any group-based risk assessments, employers still have a duty of care to the individual.

Translation and action planning for risk reduction
The processes by which the information provided by the risk assessment is discussed, explored and used to develop interventions has been termed 'translation' (Cox *et al.*, 2002). In other models of risk management, such processes have often been ignored or underestimated in their importance.

Usually the discussion and exploration of the likely risk factors identified in the risk assessment lead to the discovery of underlying organizational pathologies. In turn their recognition often facilitates the design of economical action plans where those organizational pathologies are the target, rather than their manifestations or symptoms (likely risk factors). Translation often takes some time to accomplish satisfactorily. The development of an action plan for risk reduction involves deciding upon what is to be the target, the methods used, their integration, those responsible, the proposed time schedule, the resources required and how these interventions will be evaluated. The emphasis in the Nottingham process is on prevention and organization-led interventions.

The interventions required by any action plan can often be integrated into current management activites and otherwise planned change. They need not be treated as different from other management practices. Indeed prevention in relation to work-related stress is largely about good management practice. It is about achieving well designed, organized and managed work in well designed, organized and managed workplaces and organizations. Many interventions are simply examples of ensuring good management practice. Examples might be the introduction of regular team meetings or open forums, developing staff newsletters, reviewing administrative procedures, introducing effective appraisal systems or adjusting rotas. Others, such as increasing staffing levels or installing new equipment, may incur extra costs, but may pay off through improved attendance at work or reduced staff turnover, increased productivity and quality or improved creativity and innovation. Preventing the loss of one key member of staff, for example, may save the organisation considerable disruption, recruitment and training costs. Detailed examples of interventions that have resulted from risk assessment work carried out in organizations by the authors and their coleagues are provided elsewhere (Cox, Griffiths, Barlow *et al.*, 2000; Griffiths *et al.*, 2003).

Evaluation and organizational learning
The key question in any evaluation phase is, did the action plan and interventions achieve what was intended? However evaluation is also a thread that runs though the entire risk management process and questions should also be asked about that process as a whole.

While the evaluation of organization-led interventions is not straightforward (Griffiths, 1995), it is manageable. The authors have explored various methods of evaluating organization-led interventions, with the stated aim of identifying a method that is good enough, yet also straightforward enough, for non-researchers to use. As well as measuring quantitative change in key outcomes, qualitative approaches such as stakeholder interviews may offer cost-effective and satisfactory sources of evaluation data. In considering outcomes, it is also useful to assess the extent to which any planned action was actually implemented and whether or not it reached its intended audience. Exploring variations in implementation and organizational penetration can provide a useful technique for evaluation research (Randall *et al.*, 2001).

Three methods of data collection for evaluation purposes are interviews with management and trade union representatives, interviews with a sample of the staff involved, and surveys of the entire population of those staff. Together these three methods of data collection can yield considerable information about the interventions and their impact and the appropriateness and effectiveness of the overall process. Data collected at the intervention evaluation stage can be compared with data collected from the survey at the initial risk assessment stage. Information from staff involved in specific interventions can be compared with that from staff not involved in those interventions either by design or owing to lack of penetration of the intervention. Together these aspects of evaluation design and measurement facilitate a clearer picture of what has happened. The use of qualitative data from interviews can sometimes enable apparently conflicting results from the questionnaire survey to be resolved. Such information also provides valuable material for the design of future interventions within the organization.

Although the evaluation of interventions is important, it is often overlooked or deliberately avoided. Not to evaluate is to miss an opportunity. Evaluation not only tells the organization the extent to which actions have worked but also why they have worked in that way. It also allows the reassessment of the 'at risk' situation and the methods of assessment used. In all, it provides the basis for organizational learning and establishes a process for continuous improvement. Managing work-related stress is not a one-off activity but part of a continuing cycle of good management at work and the effective management of health and safety.

The Nottingham process in perspective
There are parallels between the risk management process developed at Nottingham, and described above, and organizational intervention processes developed by other researchers worldwide. When looking at the potential health effects of work design and management, and particularly when attempting to go further and intervene, many applied psychologists have independently formulated somewhat problem-solving approaches and have identified issues that have proved to be common (for example Hugentobler *et al.*, 1992; Israel *et al.*, 1996; Goldenhar *et al.*, 2001; Israel *et al.*, 1998; Kompier *et al.*, 1998; Kompier and Kristensen, 2000; Landsbergis and Vivona-Vaughn, 1995; Lindström, 1995; Nytrø *et al.*, 2000; Schurman and Israel, 1995). One major development inherent in the Nottingham approach is that it deliberately attempts to construct a process based on the integration of European legal requirements and sound applied science.

Final comments
The complex aetiology of work-related stress presents us with an interesting challenge. Its mechanisms and causes may never be completely understood in their finest detail, but there is a moral, as well as scientific and legal, imperative to act to reduce the harm caused by work-related stress. The risk management paradigm provides a framework for positive action, focused on prevention and on organization-led interventions. It has already proved successful in a wide range of organizational settings. Using this approach, employers may be able to develop more effectively working conditions in relation to employee health, to provide opportunities for wider organizational development, to reduce the likelihood of claims against organizations for breach of their duty of care, to improve their defence against such claims, and to strengthen the organization's position with regard to employer liability insurance. They may be able to achieve all these things in a way that involves their employees and improves their lot in working life. A 'win–win' situation and an exciting future may be at hand.

Notes
1. A hazard is an event or situation that has the potential for causing harm. Work hazards can be broadly divided into the physical, which include, among others, the biological, biomechanical, chemical, mechanical and radiological, and the psychosocial.
2. Transforming the exposure and health measures to provide binary data at the group level and then relating those measures using frequency-based statistics such as Odds Ratios offers one statistical way forward that is consistent with the logic of a group-based risk assessment.

References
Barling, J. and A. Griffiths (2002), 'A history of occupational health psychology', in J.C. Quick and L.Tetrick (eds), *Handbook of Occupational Health Psychology*, Washington, DC: American Psychological Association.
Bate, R. (1997), *What Risk?*, Oxford: Butterworth-Heinemann.
Bosma, H., M.G. Marmot, H. Hemingway, A.C. Nicholson, E. Brunner and S.A. Stansfeld (1997), 'Low job control and risk of coronary heart disease in Whitehall II (prospective cohort) study', *British Medical Journal*, **314**, 70–80.
Cooper, C.L. and J. Marshall (1976), 'Occupational sources of stress: a review of the literature relating to coronary heart disease and mental ill health', *Journal of Occupational Psychology*, **49**, 11–28.

Cox, S. and R. Tait (1998), *Safety, Reliability and Risk Management*, Oxford: Butterworth-Heinemann.
Cox, T. (1993), *Stress Research and Stress Management: Putting Theory to Work*, Sudbury: HSE Books.
Cox, T. (2003), 'Work stress: nature, history and challenges', *Science in Parliament*, **60**, 10–11.
Cox, T. and A.J. Griffiths (1996), 'The assessment of psychosocial hazards at work', in M.J. Schabracq, J.A.M. Winnubst and C.L. Cooper (eds), *Handbook of Work and Health Psychology*, Chichester: Wiley & Sons.
Cox, T., A. Griffiths and E. Rial-González (2000), *Research on Work-related Stress*, Luxembourg: Office for Official Publications of the European Communities.
Cox, T., R. Randall and A. Griffiths (2002), *Interventions to Control Stress at Work in Hospital Staff*, Sudbury: HSE Books.
Cox, T., A. Griffiths, C. Barlow, R. Randall, T. Thomson and E. Rial-González (2000), *Organizational Interventions for Work Stress: A Risk Management Approach*, Sudbury: HSE Books.
European Commission (1989), 'Council Framework Directive on the Introduction of Measures to Encourage Improvements in the Safety and Health of Workers at Work', 89/391/EEC, *Official Journal of the European Communities*, **32**, no. L183, 1–8.
European Commission (1996), *Guidance on Risk Assessment at Work*, Brussels: European Commission.
Ferguson, E. and T. Cox (1993), 'Exploratory factor analysis: a users' guide', *International Journal of Selection and Assessment*, **1**, 84–94.
Gardell, B. (1982), 'Work participation and autonomy: a multilevel approach to democracy at the workplace', *International Journal of Health Services*, **12**, 31–41.
Goldenhar, L.M., A.D. Lamontange, T. Katz, C. Heaney and P. Landsbergis (2001), 'The intervention research process in occupational safety and health: an overview from the NORA intervention effectiveness research team', *Journal of Occupational and Environmental Medicine*, **43**, 616–22.
Griffiths, A. (1995), 'Organizational interventions: facing the limits of the natural science paradigm', *Scandinavian Journal of Work, Environment and Health*, **25**, 589–96.
Griffiths, A. (1998), 'The psychosocial work environment', in R.C. McCaig and M.J. Harrington (eds), *The Changing Nature of Occupational Health*, Sudbury: HSE Books.
Griffiths, A., R. Randall, A. Santos and T. Cox (2003), 'Senior nurses: interventions to reduce work stress', in M. Dollard, A. Winefield and H. Winefield (eds), *Occupational Stress in the Service Professions*, London: Taylor & Francis.
Health and Safety Commission (1992), *Management of Health and Safety at Work Regulations*, London: HMSO.
Health and Safety Commission (1999), *Management of Health and Safety at Work Regulations: Approved Code of Practice and Guidance*, London: HMSO.
Health and Safety Executive (1990), *A Guide to the Health and Safety at Work etc Act 1974*, Sudbury: HSE Books.
Health and Safety Executive (1995), *Stress at Work: A Guide for Employers*, Sudbury: HSE Books.
Hernberg, S. (1994), 'Editorial: 20th anniversary issue', *Scandinavian Journal of Work, Environment and Health*, **20**, 5–7.
Hodgson, J.T., J.R. Jones, R.C. Elliott and J. Osman (1993), *Self-reported Work-related Illness*, Sudbury: HSE Books.
Hugentobler, M.K., B.A. Israel and S.J. Schurman (1992), 'An action research approach to workplace health: integrating methods', *Health Education Quarterly*, **19**, 55–76.
Hurst, N.W. (1998), *Risk Assessment: The Human Dimension*, Cambridge: Royal Society of Chemistry.
International Labour Office (1986), *Psychosocial Factors at Work: Recognition and Control*, Occupational Safety and Health Series no. 56, Geneva: International Labour Office.
Israel, B.A., A.J. Schulz, E.A. Parker and A.B. Becker (1998), 'Review of community-based research: assessing partnership approaches to improve public health', *Annual Review of Public Health*, **19**, 173–202.
Israel, B.A., E.A. Baker, L.M. Goldenhar, C.A. Heaney and S.J. Schurman (1996), 'Occupational stress, safety and health: conceptual framework and principles for effective preventions', *Journal of Occupational Health Psychology*, **1**, 261–86.
Jex, S.M. and P.E. Spector (1996), 'The impact of negative affectivity on stressor – strain relations: a replication and extension', *Work & Stress*, **10**, 36–45.
Jick, T.D. (1979), 'Mixing qualitative and quantitative methods: triangulation in action', *Administrative Science Quarterly*, **24**, 602–11.
Johnson, J.V. (1996), 'Conceptual and methodological developments in occupational stress research', An introduction to state-of-the-art reviews, I', *Journal of Occupational Health Psychology*, **1**, 6–8.
Jones, J.R., J.T. Hodgson, T.A. Clegg and R.C. Elliot (1998), *Self-reported Work-relate Illness in 1995*, Sudbury: HSE Books.
Kompier, M.A.J. and T.S. Kristensen (2000), 'Organizational work stress interventions in a theoretical, methodological and practical context', in J. Dunham (ed.), *Stress in Occupations: Past, Present and Future*, London: Whurr Publishers.

Kompier, M.A.J., S.A.E. Geurts, R.W.M. Grundemann, P. Vink and P.G.W. Smulders (1998), 'Cases in stress prevention: the success of a participative and stepwise approach', *Stress Medicine*, **14**, 155–68.

Landsbergis, P.A. and E. Vivona-Vaughn (1995), 'Evaluation of an occupational stress intervention in a public agency', *Journal of Organizational Behaviour*, **16**, 29–48.

Leka, S., A. Griffiths and T. Cox (2003), *Work Organisation and Stress*, Geneva: World Health Organization.

Levi, L. (1981), *Preventing Work Stress*, Reading, MA: Addision-Wesley.

Levi, L. (1984), *Stress in Industry: Causes, Effects and Prevention*, Occupational Safety and Health Series no. 51, Geneva: International Labour Office.

Lindström, K. (1995), 'Finnish research in organizational development and job redesign', in L.R. Murphy, J.J. Hurrell, Jr., S.L. Sauter and G. Puryear Keita (eds), *Job Stress Interventions*, Washington, DC: American Psychological Association.

Nytrø, K., P.O. Saksvik, A. Mikkelsen, P. Bohle and M. Quinlan (2000), 'An appraisal of key factors in the implementation of occupational stress interventions', *Work & Stress*, **3**, 213–25.

Parker, S. and T. Wall (1998), *Job and Work Design: Organizing Work to Promote Well-being and Effectiveness*, London: Sage.

Randall, R., A. Griffiths and T. Cox (2001), 'Using the uncontrolled work setting to shape the evaluation of work stress interventions', in C. Weikert, E. Torkelson and J. Pryce (eds), *Occupational Health Psychology: Europe 2001*, Nottingham: I-WHO Publications.

Schurman, S.J. and B.A. Israel (1995), 'Redesigning work systems to reduce stress: a participatory action research approach to creating change', in L.R. Murphy, J.J. Hurrell, Jr., S.L. Sauter and G. Puryear Keita (eds), *Job Stress Interventions*, Washington, DC: American Psychological Association.

Sparks, K., B. Faragher and C. Cooper (2001), 'Well-being and occupational health in the 21st century workplace', *Journal of Occupational and Organizational Psychology*, **74**, 489–509.

Spector, P.E. (1987), 'Interactive effects of perceived control and job stressors on affective reactions and health outcomes for clerical workers', *Work & Stress*, **1**, 155–62.

Stranks, J. (1996), *The Law and Practice of Risk Assessment*, London: Pitman.

Warr, P.B. (1992), 'Job features and excessive stress', in R. Jenkins and N. Coney (eds), *Prevention of Mental Ill Health at Work*, London: HMSO.

World Health Organization (1995), *Health Consequences of the Chernobyl Accident*, Geneva: World Health Organization.

13 Coping with stress through reason
Edwin A. Locke

Stress is actually a form of emotion, an automatized response to the perception of threat. Emotions are the result of automatic, subconscious appraisals of objects or situations (Locke, 1976).

The stress situation
There are five core elements involved in stress.

1. An important value is perceived as threatened. The value may be one's own self-esteem (as could be threatened by the loss of one's job or a personal rejection), one's own physical survival and well-being (as in the case of a soldier in battle) or a valued other person or object (as in the possible loss of one's spouse due to illness or the failure of one's business).
2. There is a perceived need for action to protect or gain the value. If one is fully convinced (including at the subconscious level) that no action is possible, one feels passive resignation and sadness (or depression) rather than stress.
3. There is uncertainty about being able to take the relevant action. One may not know which action to take or may not feel confident in being able to carry it out. There may also be uncertainty about when and where the threat will manifest itself, making action planning difficult. If an individual is *totally* certain that he can take the action needed to deal with the potential threat at hand (for example, give a public talk), there is no stress.
4. Implicit in the experience of stress is an element of conflict. This may be of the form 'I must deal with this [for example, public speaking], but I can't' or 'I must do this, but I do not want to or do not like it.'
5. There is an emotional response (typically anxiety or fear) which may be accompanied by one or more physical symptoms (for example, restlessness, irritability, fatigue, insomnia, depression, increased heart rate and respiration, high blood pressure, tension, obsessive thoughts, change in appetite, difficulty concentrating). Other emotions can be involved as well, such as anger ('I hate the s.o.b. who is putting me through this'), guilt ('I should have acted differently than I did'), or grief ('How will I survive without my loved one?').

Observe that stress is neither solely in the environment nor solely in the person; rather it is a relationship between the person and the situation. A situation that sends one person into a state of high anxiety or even panic may leave a second person indifferent and may positively excite a third person (for example, flying a small plane). The total amount of stress experienced will depend on such factors as the following:

- importance of the value: perceived threats to more important values (for example, self-esteem) cause more intense emotional responses than those to less important values (Locke, 1976);
- degree of threat: values can be threatened to varying degrees (for example, for a soldier, sentry duty near the front is usually less risky than going directly into a battle);
- duration and chronicity of threat: the longer the duration of a threat, the more it taxes people's resources, including their physical well-being and stamina. The more frequent or chronic the threat, the greater the total amount of stress. Dealing with a terrible boss can be tolerated more easily for one day than every day for a year;
- symptoms: the severity of the symptoms that accompany the emotion of stress can exacerbate the stress. Symptoms themselves can be debilitating and a source of anxiety, especially if they are seen to indicate – or cause – real and serious health problems. One can be stressed about one's reactions to stress. Anxiety about one's anxiety is called meta-anxiety;
- self-esteem and self-efficacy: the former concept is a global term referring to one's estimate of one's worthiness and general efficacy to deal with life's challenges (Judge et al., 1997). Self-efficacy refers to perceived task-specific skills (Bandura, 1997). The higher one's self-esteem (assuming it is real and not pseudo self-esteem; see Locke et al., 1996) and task-relevant skills, the less susceptible one is to stress;
- temperament: some people are more emotionally reactive than others owing to innate physiological factors;
- value system: some people's value systems are more rational than those of others. For example, people who seek always to be superior to others will feel chronically threatened, because there will always be somebody out there who has more of some valued trait or commodity than themselves. Similarly people who desperately seek the approval of others will be out of control of their lives and can have no sense of their own identity. People whose value systems are riddled with contradictions and conflicts will be beset by constant stress. Consider a highly religious businessman. Making a profit is selfish – that is, in his own self-interest – but his religion may have taught that selfishness is evil. Thus the more business success he has, the more guilt he will feel. But, if he gives away all his profits, his business will be threatened and his own material well-being will be undermined.

Furthermore there are certain psychological processes that exacerbate or prolong stress. For example, people can get into a rumination cycle in which the thoughts and appraisals that are the immediate causes of stress are recycled over and over and thus maintain and prolong the emotional response. These negative thoughts usually entail self-condemnation (for example, 'I just am no good'; 'I can't do anything right'; 'My life is hopeless; it will never get any better'); such thoughts, in turn, can lead to depression and even suicide. People may also evade identifying the causal factors entailed in the stress situation and thus fail to take any mitigating action, or they may focus on dealing only with the emotional experience itself by taking alcohol or drugs; this allows some temporary symptom relief but does not address the causal elements that will continue to operate.

Stress prevention

It is a mistake to view stress solely from the viewpoint of coping with it after it occurs. People who live more rational lives are much less likely to experience stress in the first place than those who are less rational. Consider the following two examples:

> John and Susan were high school graduates who both worked but did not have very high incomes. They took the highest-paying jobs they could find, at the expense of doing work they really liked, because they had large bills to pay. They could not understand why they did not seem to enjoy going to work each day. They bought a house, with no down payment, costing more than they could really afford, because they wanted to live in a neighborhood that was just as good as that of John's cousin. They bought more expensive cars than they could afford, usually impulsively, in order to impress the neighbors. They had three kids because that is how many most of their friends and relatives had. They had ten credit cards and when one 'maxed out' they used another until they were all maxed out. Then a child got sick, John lost his job owing to a layoff, and Susan's hours were reduced. John started drinking and Susan began to have insomnia, panic attacks and bouts of depression. John and Susan engaged in daily mutual recriminations as they headed toward bankruptcy. The children became increasingly unmanageable as the home situation deteriorated.
>
> When Bob and Carol graduated from high school they both went to work and saved enough money so that when they got married they could afford a reasonable down payment on a house. They spent months looking for a house they liked within their price range before they bought. They agreed to take jobs they really liked rather than trying to maximize earnings. Before buying cars, they looked through consumer magazines to study the car ratings and to find out how to get the best possible prices. They bought good quality, economical cars. They wanted children but decided, given their incomes and dual careers, that it was best to have only one. They limited themselves to two credit cards with low interest rates and saved a fixed percentage of their income each month for retirement and emergencies.

It is obvious that John and Susan are going to experience far more life stress than Bob and Carol. Why? Because their approaches to life are entirely different. John and Susan are focused on status and conforming to the expectations of others; they live beyond their means without calculating what they can afford; they act on impulse and do not plan their lives or consider the long-range consequences of their actions. Bob and Carol are independent thinkers. They choose jobs that they personally enjoy. They focus on what they can afford, they plan their expenditures, and they consider the consequences of what they do. Bob and Carol will not be exposed to as much life stress as John and Susan, because they are basically in control of their lives. They use reason and not emotion and conformity to make their decisions. People who cope well with life do not typically have to cope chronically with stress, because they are not continually confronted with threats that they themselves brought about or made possible. Of course unforeseen circumstances can affect anyone, but people who consistently use rational thinking to make decisions are much less at risk for stress than those who do not.

Coping with stress

Now let us assume that stress has actually occurred. How does one cope? Typically, coping is dichotomized into two types: emotion-focused and action or cause-focused. The issue of social support will be discussed separately.

Emotion-focused coping
Here the individual tries to deal 'directly' with the disturbing emotion. There are many possibilities. One is the use of psychological defense mechanisms to keep the disturbing emotion or the thoughts behind it out of awareness. Repression is a classic example. Another is distraction: taking actions or thinking thoughts about more pleasant topics to fully occupy one's attention. A third is taking alcohol or drugs in order to lower one's level of tension. A fourth is physical exertion, which is known to have a relaxation effect. A fifth is meditation.

Note that none of these procedures attacks stress at the causal level. Nevertheless some actions may be of help in the short run. Certainly anti-anxiety and anti-depression drugs have been life-savers for many people. Stress symptoms can be severe and such drugs enable people to function productively while they work on the causes of their problems. For people who are stressed because of temperament or other physiological factors or because of an irreplaceable loss, long-term prescription drug use may be necessary, especially as an alternative to alcoholism or the use of dangerous, illicit drugs. Defense mechanisms are self-defeating, because they work to prevent any awareness of emotions and/or their causes.

Action-focused coping
Coping here can be either psychological, or coping in terms of action in the world, or both.
Psychological actions These may involve changing beliefs, changing values and/or changing psychological processes such as framing of events, psychological maturity and emotional control. Psychological change can sometimes be achieved on one's own and sometimes it requires professional counseling.

As regards changing perceptions and beliefs, cause-focused coping addresses the mechanisms that cause stress. Let us begin with perceived value threat. People's perceptions and interpretations of events can be mistaken. I recall a student once coming into my office in tears, because he said that, because of the low grade he received on the first psychology exam, his life was ruined. Here is the way his thinking process went: the low exam grade will lead to a low course grade; the low course grade will lead to a low grade point average (GPA); a low GPA will preclude getting into medical school; and that will destroy his life's ambition, which was to be a doctor. I was able to change his reaction by pointing out the flaws in his line of reasoning, especially with regard to the first two points. Many stress reactions are caused by erroneous beliefs, some of which may be held subconsciously. Stress relief can often be achieved by correcting such errors.

Giving new information does not always work immediately, however, because people may have an implicit vested interest in their irrational beliefs. Consider Mr A, a 21-year-old who felt guilty about masturbation. This issue was tied to his view of masculinity which held that a real man can get a girl anytime he wants. This view of masculinity was tied to his self-esteem. Thus reducing his guilt and self-doubt required dealing not just with masturbation *per se* but with his view of what it means to be a man and its link to his self-esteem. When people are asked to give up irrational self-images, they may resist because giving them up threatens their entire identity.

Now consider values. Three factors can cause harm here. The first is the content of one's value system, the second is one's value hierarchy (relative importance) and the third pertains to one's method of choosing one's values. One can hold values that work against one's well-being; examples noted earlier were trying to feel superior to others, trying to be liked by everyone and holding macho self-images.

It is also possible to hold rational values but to order them mistakenly. Consider, for example, moral character and money. If one puts money first, it means any way one can get it is permissible and one is ripe for criminal activity and permanent worry about being caught, not to mention the stress entailed in maintaining an elaborate network of lies and deception to hide one's true nature. Career versus family issues present a potential conflict problem. Valuing one's family and one's work are both rational, and there is no inherently correct hierarchy. The problem is that, to the degree one pursues one of these, it takes time away from the other. If one values both equally highly, one is in a chronic state of conflict. Thus there is a need for clear prioritization.

People may also have value systems that may or may not be fully rational, but the content is not their own. Rather their values are adopted from others (for example, parents) without thinking or processing. When and if they choose to do their own thinking, they may be caught in a conflict because what they want may not be what they are supposed to want. Consider a young man who was brought up to do as his father wishes, to be a loving, dutiful son. His father wants him to run the family real estate business when the father retires. The father loves real estate, but the son does not like it al all. He wants to be an actor. What is he to do? Run a business that makes him miserable or become an actor and face lifelong guilt? Such a conflict can become unbearable unless it is resolved. The son needs to explain to his father the need to follow a profession that he loves, convince himself that he has a right to his own life choices and then act accordingly.

Value change would involve replacing irrational values with healthy ones. For example, a counselor might be needed to show a client why constantly comparing himself to others causes nothing but misery and to teach him to pursue values that are important to him personally (for example, a job that really interests him). It could also involve helping the client to reprioritize his values. For example, is making money too important? Would he enjoy more time with his family if it could be worked out? In contrast, he might need to spend *more* time at work if his failure to upgrade his skills is threatening his employability. And professional help might be needed to help a client become more independent in his choice of values instead of going along with what everyone else tells him to do.

It must be noted that sometimes the most rational thing to do when a value is threatened is to give it up. For example, it is well known that a very substantial proportion of lawyers hate their profession. And some jobs, even in personally valued professions, are so time-consuming that they prevent any other values from being pursued. One way of coping with a career or job that brings stress rather than happiness is to give up that career or job and find a new one. The same can be said for a marriage that is the source of continual conflict. Divorce may be the best solution in such a case.

Sometimes psychological coping needs to involve *reframing*; by this I mean reinterpreting events. Consider Mr B, who lost his job. He may conclude, 'I am just incompetent and no one will ever want to hire me again.' A more rational interpretation might be: 'I lost this job, because I lacked the specific skills I need. I need to look for another job where the skills I have are needed.' Observe that this type of reframing goes *from the general to the specific.* Stress is increased when inappropriate global conclusions are reached from specific incidents (for example, see Beck *et al.*, 1979).

Consider another case. Ms C got in a terrible auto accident and survived but lost one leg. There are two ways she can frame this. One is like this: 'I have only one leg. I can no longer ski, play tennis or dance, and no man will ever want a cripple like me. I am doomed to a lonely, sedentary life.' Or she can frame it as follows: 'It is amazing that I am alive after such a ghastly accident. I have a chance to live when by all rights I should be dead. When I recover, I am going to get an artificial leg and start learning to use it so I can do many of the things I have always done. If a man really loves me, he will not care about my not having a silly leg.' Note that the contrast here is between negative and positive framing. Positive framing is not simply a feel-good gimmick; it is the objectively correct way to frame many negative experiences (with exceptions to be noted below). The reason is as follows: life is a process of goal-directed action, of goal and value achievement. When one stops valuing, one stops living. If one chooses to keep going after a setback or tragedy, the only way to do it is to continue to pursue whatever values one can still attain. Of course, if one has lost a loved one, that value is irreplaceable and one cannot pretend that such a loss did not occur and make a positive event out of it. The same holds if one is diagnosed with a serious disease. However, even in these cases, one can still choose to pursue the values that *are* still possible to one, which still requires a positive focus.

A third type of framing pertains to 'must' versus 'would like'. Let us say Miss D, a 23-year-old graduate student was rejected by John, the man she had been living with and whom she loved dearly. If she holds to the view that 'I must have John or my life is ruined forever', she will continue to be miserable. In fact, however, for most people there are many possible people whom one could be happy with; it is just a matter of taking the initiative to find them. Thus the correct way for Miss D to frame the situation would be: 'I would really like to have had John for life, but it's not the end of the world. I can survive without him. There are other men in the world. Since I can't have John, I'll find someone else – and since I may be a bit too dependent right now, I will try to live on my own for a while before rushing into another relationship.' She could add positive framing to this, namely, 'And maybe someday I'll find someone who is better suited to me than John.'

Another facet of psychological processing pertains to maturity. Mature people are far less prone to stress than immature people. Maturity entails at least three things: context holding, having a long-range time perspective and emotional self-control. Consider context holding first. Ms E is miserable because someone at work whose record is not as good as hers makes $400 more a year than she does. On the other hand, she loves her work, enjoys her colleagues, likes her boss, and thinks the company she works for is an excellent one. Note that the amount that would be added to her paycheck after taxes by another $400 is trivial, and even the symbolic value of $400 is not that great. If Ms E held the full context of her job situation, the $400, at best, would be a minor annoyance. She feels miserable because she focuses only on the money and not on the total picture.

Now consider long-range thinking. Mr F wants the good things in life – a luxury car, a large house with a pool, and resort vacations. (He does not want these out of conformity, but because he would personally enjoy them.) He is stressed, however, because he cannot bear to wait. He is a young lawyer working toward becoming a partner and, although his pay is good now, it will not increase dramatically for some years. A mature attitude would involve being willing to wait and, in the meantime, saving some of his income, acting on the knowledge that wealth accumulation takes time. The values he wants would be put in the 'to be gained later' file, and thus he would not feel stressed at not being able to act to get them right away.

Emotional control is not, in my opinion, an issue of what is popularly known as emotional intelligence, because intelligence refers to one's ability to grasp abstractions. Rather it means not letting emotions run one's life. One aspect of this means not acting on every emotion one feels just because one feels it. Another aspect is making an effort to understand the causes of one's emotions (including stress). One must learn to choose one's actions by a rational process. That does not mean ignoring emotions (which are important motivationally) but rather asking: what is an appropriate action in this context?

Action in the outside world   Sometimes coping is primarily an issue of improving one's psychology, but typically it also entails taking action in the real world, with reason as one's guide, to remove or mitigate the external threat that is causing the stress. Included in this category are actions taken to raise one's self-efficacy and actions taken to reduce or eliminate conflict. Consider the student mentioned earlier who became very upset at his low grade on a test. Correcting his erroneous beliefs about the consequences of his low test grade alone will not do the trick. He also has to improve his grades on subsequent exams. To do this he has to learn what caused the low grade on the first test. In this case the low grade was caused by lack of studying. Furthermore it turned out that this student did not know what real studying was. So he had to learn better study techniques and put more effort into exam preparation using these techniques. Consider some other examples:

- Ms G is highly stressed because her small business is losing customers and money. To cope she would have to find out why she was losing customers and take steps to improve her products or customer service and/or to get new customers through better marketing.
- Mr H is stressed because his job requires him to work unrelentingly long hours, which is causing fatigue, health problems and loss of time with his family. To fix this he would have to convince his boss to let him take steps to reduce his hours or look for a different job.
- Ms I is going through a divorce and has little money, no job and no place to live. Relevant actions that she would need to take would include finding a place to live, finding a job, making sure she has a car and getting a good lawyer. Once she was in control of her life again, she could take steps to repair the psychological trauma of the divorce. Then she could consider starting to date again and hopefully find a mate who is better suited to her than her ex-husband.
- Mr J's house was destroyed by a tornado, though fortunately no one was hurt. Relevant actions here would include contacting one's insurance agent, searching through the rubble for valuables and possessions that could be salvaged, finding a place to live, and making plans to move or rebuild.

(I do not mean to make these action solutions seem facile; taking the needed actions in cases of stress often requires an enormous struggle).

Action is a very critical stress-reducer, because it is the means by which one preserves or regains or replaces the value. It is the most direct means of taking charge of one's life. Here are some action guidelines:

- consider a number of different alternatives before deciding on a course of action; be wary of tunnel vision;
- think outside the square; be creative about solving stress-related problems;
- breakdown big problems into small ones and attack them one at a time; sometimes it is best to start with the most easily solvable problem in order to build confidence;
- if you are not sure of the best action to take but need to act, try *something*, as long as the result of an error is not too serious;
- if there is time, allow ideas to incubate, especially when the issue is complex and long range planning is required;
- be flexible on the means to reach your goal but tenacious about the goal or value itself, if you have decided to pursue it rather than give it up;
- consult other people whom you trust for ideas (more on this below).

If one does not feel confident about taking the actions needed to cope, then one has to take actions that will build *self-efficacy*. Self-efficacy means task-specific self-confidence, and thus the best way to build it is through skill building by means of practice and training (Bandura, 1997). For example, for many people the most feared activity they can imagine is public speaking. The sources of the fear are such factors as fear that one does not know the subject matter, fear that the audience will react negatively, and fear that one will become so paralyzed with fright that one will be unable to give the talk. But these fears can be overcome by preparing the talk carefully, learning as much as possible about the audience and practicing the talk in front of a small audience to prove than one can do it, and getting feedback so that one can further improve one's skills.

When there is stress on the job, the same principle applies. By gaining more skill at the required activities, one can reduce the actual threat if it is due to low confidence. Even in sex, one can reduce stress by developing the various skills, including communication skills, that are involved in the process.

It should be noted here that self-efficacy also applies to psychological skills. For example, a person who knows he is prone to panic in tough situations will feel more stress when things get tough than someone who knows he can remain calm in the face of threat. Self-control skills can be learned just as action skills can be learned. Self-efficacy will not reduce stress, however, if one really dislikes an activity. Consider Ms K, who was a college professor. She was successful and well regarded at her job and got excellent teacher ratings because she was, in fact, a very good teacher. However she discovered that she really hated teaching. The proper solution here was a career change; the old value had to be given up and replaced by a new one. It is very stressful to maintain a job or career, regardless of whether one is good at it or not, if one does not like what one is doing. This sets up a daily conflict: 'I have to go to work, but I don't want to.' By building efficacy and choosing things one loves, one eliminates both types of conflict mentioned earlier: 'I must deal with this, but I can't' and 'I must do this, but I do not like it.'

Stress management issues

Social support
Social support is mentioned frequently in the literature as a method for coping with stress. While others cannot do all the work, they can be helpful. What can other people do to help one cope?

- They can show understanding and empathy. Sometimes people under stress find this valuable, even if it does not involve any proposed solution.
- They can provide, if desired, information of many types, for example, help correct mistaken beliefs, suggest different value hierarchies, suggest ways to get professional help, suggest options for problem solving.
- They can help one reframe the situation in a more productive manner.
- They can provide material support or help.
- They can boost efficacy through persuasive arguments and expressions of confidence.

Which of these types of support is most relevant in a given case depends on the context, including what the stressed person actually wants and the nature and closeness of the relationship with the other person. Some people are so dependent that they rely solely on social support for coping; in addition to alienating friends and relatives, overdependence leaves one unable to take charge of one's destiny.

Do stress and coping involve two types of appraisals?
Lazarus and Folkman (1984) have made the claim that there are two processes involved in stress which they call 'primary and secondary appraisal'. Primary appraisal is the response to the stressor and secondary appraisal is the response based on having assessed one's resources in relation to the threat. I disagree with this distinction. Consider the following example. A pilot and a co-pilot are flying a small plane. The pilot suddenly drops dead of a heart attack. In scenario 1, the co-pilot is an experienced pilot. In scenario 2, the co-pilot is a student on his first flight. In the Lazarus model, the primary appraisals would be the same in both cases: there is a threat because the pilot has died. But the secondary appraisals would be different because one pilot has the skill to land the plane and the other one does not.

I submit, however, that the primary appraisals would be quite different because they would *already include* the co-pilots' perceptions of their skills. The first co-pilot would know he could land the plane (though he might worry about whether the pilot could still be saved) and thus would not experience a high degree of threat to survival and thus of stress. The second co-pilot would undoubtedly be panicked, because he is up in the air with almost no knowledge of how to land the plane. The degree of stress he experienced would be much greater than that of the first co-pilot owing to a radical difference in perceived self-efficacy. In other words, when one confronts a threat, one does so by automatically estimating, using subconsciously stored knowledge, one's capabilities based on prior self-efficacy. One does not start with fear and then say, 'Oh wait, I can fly, so everything is ok.'

Of course there can be subsequent appraisals, made as the situation changes. For example, the plane's engine could fail, which would stress even the first co-pilot. The second co-pilot could contact the tower by radio and be told that there would be no problem talking him down. But these new appraisals would occur because the situation was now different. In fact, there can be a long series of appraisals of any situation but each one will involve an automatic (subconscious) estimate of one's capabilities at that time and in that context.

Definition of coping
Given the preceding discussion, here is how I would define coping with stress: Coping with stress entails identifying the causal elements in the stress situation and then taking psychological action and action in the outside world to modify the causal elements so as to mitigate or eliminate the value threat, including, if necessary, action to directly relieve stress symptoms.

Coping and reason
The main faculty for coping with stress is the same faculty one uses to cope with life, the faculty of reason. It is through reason, based on the evidence provided by the senses, that one identifies the causal elements in the stress situation. This requires both extrospection, looking at the outside world, and introspection, observing the contents and processes of one's own consciousness. It is through reason that one corrects errors in mental content, mental processes and past action. It is through reason that one identifies the future action alternatives and plans a course of action. And it is through reason that one guides and directs one's actions, both short-range and long-range. As Ayn Rand (1964, p. 23) has argued: 'reason is man's basic means of survival' (see also Peikoff, 1991). Furthermore reason is a volitional process (Binswanger, 1991); one must choose to focus one's mind at the conceptual level, else it will drift passively at the level of sense perception like that of the lower animals. If people used reason more often, there would be far fewer stressed-out individuals in the world.

References
Bandura, A. (1997), *Self-efficacy: The Exercise of Control*, New York: Freeman.
Beck, A., A. Rush, B. Shaw and G. Emery (1979), *Cognitive Therapy of Depression*, New York: Guilford.
Binswanger, H. (1991), 'Volition as cognitive self-regulation', *Organizational Behavior and Human Decision Processes*, **50**, 154–78.
Judge, T., E. Locke and C. Durham (1997), 'The dispositional causes of job satisfaction: a core evaluations approach', in L. Cummings and B. Staw (eds), *Research in Organizational Behavior*, vol. 19, Greenwich, CT: JAI Press.
Lazarus, R. and S. Folkman (1984), *Stress, Appraisal and Coping*, New York: Springer.
Locke, E. (1976), 'The nature of causes of job satisfaction', in M. Dunnette (ed.), *Handbook of Industrial & Organizational Psychology*, Chicago: Rand McNally.
Locke, E., K. McClear and D. Knight (1996), 'Self-esteem and work', in C. Cooper and I. Robertson (eds), *International Review of Industrial and Organizational Psychology*, Chichester, UK: Wiley.
Peikoff, L. (1991), *Objectivism: The Philosophy of Ayn Rand*, New York: Dutton.
Rand, A. (1964), *The Virtue of Selfishness*, New York: Signet.

14 An organizational approach to stress management
Valerie J. Sutherland

The topic of stress management in the workplace has assumed a key position in the discipline of work psychology. Ascribed benefits are in terms of business success and the good health and well-being of the workforce. Whilst interest in stress management in the workplace is considerable, it is not without criticism (Briner and Reynolds, 1999). In this chapter we address one of the criticisms of the traditional approach to stress management, namely the preoccupation of industry in focusing on interventions aimed at helping the individual employee to cope with stress, rather than finding ways of eliminating work-related stress.

A traditional approach to stress management
Typically the focus for stress management activities in the workplace has been on the individual employee. The person–environment fit model for understanding stress (Harrison, 1985) describes this approach to stress control, where the state of stress is viewed as a lack of fit between the person and the work environment. To understand the experience of stress it is necessary to consider the employee's subjective perception of the work environment, and his or her perceived ability to meet demand.

Factors such as needs, wants, attitudes, desires, personality, age, gender, education and experience will influence both actual ability and the perceived ability to cope with a demand. When an imbalance or lack of fit exists between perceived demand and the perception of one's ability to meet that demand, the experience is described as 'feeling stressed' (Lazarus, 1996). Successful coping restores the imbalance, whereas unsuccessful coping results in the manifestation of symptoms of exposure to the stressor.

The person–environment fit model has implications for reducing the incidence of occupational stress (Burke, 1993) and can have impact in two ways. The first is defined as 'secondary level stress management'. Such interventions are response-directed, in that they aim to help improve the stress coping process by enhancing or augmenting the strength of the individual. By providing the individual with more resilience, coping resources and competence it is believed that the employee will experience fewer adverse consequences from exposure to occupational stress (ibid.).

The second approach involves minimizing or eliminating the sources and incidence of stress. This is defined as 'primary stress management'. However there seems to be a tendency for organizations to concentrate attention on individual-level strategies. The following list of individual-level coping strategies is grouped into four categories, based on the suggestion of Newman and Beehr (1979):

- *aimed at psychological conditions*: planning ahead; managing one's life, self-awareness, realistic assessment of self and one's aspirations;

- *aimed at physical or physiological conditions*: diet, exercise, sleep, relaxation;
- *aimed at changing one's behaviour*: learning and using relaxation techniques, becoming less Type A in one's style of behaviour, interpersonal skills training, including leadership and management skills, learning and using time management or assertiveness techniques to avoid being aggressive or non-assertive in interaction with other people at work; taking time off for fun and holidays, developing close friendships and social support networks;
- *aimed at changing one's work environment*: changing to a less demanding job, changing to a less demanding organization.

An example of a secondary-level, response-based stress control intervention is the introduction of assertiveness training for personnel working on a customer services help desk. It is used to alleviate the stress of dealing with difficult customers. Training enables the employee to deal with conflict situations and respond in an appropriate manner. While the source of stress remains constant, that is, customers will continue to be distressed, angry or upset because a product is perceived as unsatisfactory, the telephone help-desk operator will learn the skills of reacting effectively to hostile behaviour. Improved competence will have a positive impact on the confidence of the employee, the customer's complaint is more likely to be dealt with in a satisfactory manner, and the potential for stress is minimized for both parties in the interaction.

Evidence for the effectiveness of this type of stress control programme is mixed. Murphy (1987, 1988) suggests that individual-level interventions can make a difference in temporarily reducing adverse responses to stress, but such effects diminish with time (Ganster *et al.* 1982; Murphy, 1988). However this is a criticism of training in general and not of stress management training specifically. Without the opportunity to rehearse, practise and take part in refresher training, skills might be eroded or lost. Also, as Ganster *et al.* (1982) have shown, on a person's return to the organization, and left to face the demands of the work environment alone, the benefits of individual-level interventions quickly disappear. Critics also believe that this approach to stress management is flawed because it places the onus for change on the individual. Employees perceive that they are being blamed for not coping with a situation and are regarded as problems and non-copers. The message is loud and clear. It is saying, 'You do not seem to be able to handle the stress in your job, so we will help you to cope more effectively'. Whilst these aims might be well intentioned and honourable, the underlying message to the employee also implies that 'We (the organization) are not going to change the way we do things here, you must learn to cope with the situation.'

Although there is a place for this type of intervention there are other problems. Secondary-level programmes teach and encourage the employee to cope with stress rather than tackle the problem at source (Ivancevich *et al.*, 1990). The approach is reactive rather than proactive because it seeks to cure the symptoms of exposure to stress rather than to prevent a stress problem from arising. In addition stress management courses are often introduced as a reaction, in response to a perceived problem within the organization (for example, to combat a high level of absenteeism or accidents at work). Other initiatives such as a counselling service or an employee assistance programme (EAP), that aim to cure symptoms of exposure to stress are a necessary part of a stress control programme, but in isolation are not enough. Indeed they are often described as a 'band-aid' approach to stress management. However a more serious problem is the notion of using a strategy that waits for an employee to become a victim of stress before taking action. This is a risky and potentially high-cost strategy for the employee *and* the organization from legal, compensation and insurance perspectives (Earnshaw and Cooper, 1994).

A tripartite model of stress management

Successful stress control requires an organizational approach that embraces both stress prevention strategies and interventions to cure or resolve the problems associated with exposure to stress that cannot be eliminated from the job. This holistic, tripartite approach consists of the following:

- primary-level stress management – to identify, eliminate or minimize stress;
- secondary-level stress control – to educate and train the employee to cope with stress or respond in a way that is not harmful to the individual or the business;
- tertiary-level stress management – to help and treat the symptoms of those employees who have become victims of exposure to stress. This includes, for example, the use of counselling services and career breaks.

Organizations seem willing to use secondary-level stress management strategies and many offer tertiary care. However it is suggested that more organizations should conduct a stress audit to identify stress (Sutherland and Davidson, 1993) and then reduce the number and strength of occupational stressors. In simple terms it is a question of finding ways to remove or minimize the problems that act as barriers to work performance, job satisfaction and well-being in the workplace. In the following section, primary level options are discussed.

Primary-level stress management

The more commonly used term for this type of stress management strategy is 'organization-level interventions' (Burke, 1993). The following are examples of certain primary-level interventions that can be introduced to minimize or eliminate job stress.

Organizational culture and climate as a source of stress

This is often described simply as 'being in the organization' (Cooper and Marshall, 1978) and is concerned with a sense of belonging, the pressure of workplace politics, poor communication, lack of decision-making opportunities or a threat to freedom and autonomy. It is about the way an organization treats its employees. Included in this are certain social stressors that consist of negative work climate, unfair behaviour and social animosities. These may play a role in the development of irritation and subsequent depressive symptoms (Dormann and Zapf, 2002).

Culture is perceived as a set of learned values that take the form of practices interpreted through rules and norms of behaviour. Therefore building a supportive, trusting and open work climate and culture, and ensuring that the style of management and supervision is compatible with the goals and aims of the organization, are important factors in organizational stress control. It means developing a culture that encourages staff to be supportive of each other in order to facilitate team working and good interpersonal relationships in the workplace. An assessment of the organizational culture is used to guide the process of culture change. Likewise the use of psychometric measures to understand the appropriateness of management style as a potential source of stress might be required. While this has implications for selection and recruitment strategies, it could highlight a need for a secondary-level intervention, such as management retraining.

Research evidence on the impact of mergers and acquisitions as a stressor suggests that more action is necessary to avoid the stress conditions often linked to this business venture (Cartwright and Cooper, 1996). For example, Blake and Mouton (1984) used an interface conflict-solving model to facilitate the acquisition process between an American company and an acquired British organization. The top teams of both organizations engaged in meetings during which they shared perceptions about their concerns and questions. From this a successful operating model emerged. Realistic merger previews (also known as 'a communications programme') have also been used to facilitate the merger process and to reduce stress.

Improving perception of worker control Lack of job control is acknowledged as a potent source of stress and perception of control seems to be important for job satisfaction, health and well-being. While the research evidence to support the demand–control model proposed by Karasek (1979) has been inconsistent, there is sufficient evidence to suggest that a high level of work control has beneficial effects on levels of job satisfaction (Dwyer and Ganster, 1991), psychological well-being (Perrewe and Ganster, 1989) and indicators of cardiovascular disease (Karasek *et al.*, 1988). The aim of this type of intervention is for the workforce to be empowered and involved in changes to any system or practice that induces stress at work.

Lack of participation in decision making is a primary cause of stress, and is mediated by one's perceived influence over the situation and the efficacy of communication in the organization. Feeling controlled rather than 'in-control' is associated with a state of stress. Individuals who feel controlled are likely to perceive their job as a strain rather than a challenge and source of motivation. The use of small-group discussions, or focus groups, is recommended to examine how sources of stress might be reduced. Health circles (Kuhn, cited in ILO, 1993) and the development of self-managed teams (Peters and Waterman, 1982; Chaston, 1998) are examples of interventions used to increase worker participation in the decision-making process and an increased sense of job control.

Managing the stress of job demand
Work overload is a key stressor in modern organizations. A high workload leads to long hours of working, either as paid or unpaid overtime, and sometimes job burnout. Some reanalysis of staffing levels and an improved (real) costing of the impact of 'downsizing', and the job and task redesign options that create reductions to staff numbers, are also recommended to help reduce work overload stress. Some organizations have found that their enthusiasm for downsizing has been too zealous, and a subsequent cost–benefit analysis has proved the reinstatement of certain jobs to be the most effective stress control strategy.

In addition an examination of the relationship between job burnout (Maslach, 1982) (that is, emotional exhaustion, depersonalization and reduced personal accomplishment) and job demand is required. Research evidence indicates that adverse psychological and physiological reactions are affected by the combined impact of two structural conditions of the workplace, namely high demands (workload pressures) and low control (skill discretion and decision authority – see above). Conceptually this is known as the job–demand–control model (JDC) (Karasek, 1979). It has been expanded to include the concept of social support (Johnson and Hall, 1988). For example (Rafferty et al., 2001), among a group of 'at-risk from burnout' employees, the expected strong associations were observed between job demand and measures of emotional exhaustion and depersonalization, but the capacity to use a range of skills on the job, and social support from a supervisor, significantly mediated these effects.

When faced with a job overload situation it is important to ensure that employees are not also stressed by the physical conditions at work. In addition to being a source of stress in its own right, it takes up the attention capacity of the individual, and so the employee is more vulnerable to workplace stress. For example, sickness absence is positively associated with exposure to ambient noise (Kryter, 1994), particularly when the employee is performing cognitively demanding tasks (Fried et al., 2002). Thus the work environment must provide satisfying physical conditions, and a clean and orderly place of work is important for both safety and hygiene reasons. Clearly many of the opportunities for the prevention of stress associated with the physical demands of work exist at the design stage and, of course, in the provision of adequate personal protection equipment. However, many places of work have been modified to optimize technological advances and thereby might no longer provide satisfactory conditions for the workforce. Therefore the practice of open discussion about the issues that directly affect working conditions should be encouraged as much as possible.

Managing shift-work stress The need to engage in shift work affects many people at work and creates negative spillover consequences and costs for the family and society itself. Despite considerable research efforts it is difficult to make generalizations regarding optimal shift patterns. Clearly the need to work shifts represents a major source of stress among blue-collar workers and increasingly more service sector staff is required to engage in shift work. It is likely that individuals do become used to shift work and that it becomes physically less stressful with time, but some work patterns might prevent habituation occurring, and so there is a need to follow guidelines for minimizing the negative impact of shift working. Thus it becomes a prudent part of a stress management strategy to minimize the impact of these potential sources of strain and distress that cannot be eliminated from the world of work. There are a number of options:

1. The design of the shift system – this includes, for example, the identification of an optimal shift pattern or rotation, shift start time and the number of days for recovery between shifts and so on (Daus et al., 1998) and the minimization of circadian rhythm disruption (Waterhouse, 1993; Herbert, 1997).
2. Self-selection versus mandatory shift work (Czeisler et al., 1982; Cervinka, 1993).
3. Stress management education to understand the nature of stress and increased vulnerability caused by shift work.
4. Physical interventions such as the use of light therapy and the drug, melatonin (Daus et al., 1998).

Controlling career stress
Fear of job loss and threat of redundancy are common features of modern working life. Perceived or real pay and job status inequity, lack of job security or limited potential for future career development are sources of stress (Ivancevich and Matteson, 1980). In times of instability poor work conditions are tolerated and employees endure long hours and arduous conditions. This does not happen without costs to the employee and the organization. A keen, competitive jobs market can threaten the quality of co-worker relationships at a time when social support is of particular significance. Indeed the stress caused by insecurity that can be alleviated by supportive working relationships may be broken down if the workforce perceives that competition is necessary to retain a job. Personnel may also stay in a job that is unsuitable or disliked because no suitable alternative for change exists. This results in costs to the organization due to poor productivity or performance. Limited career opportunity can be demotivating and frustrating, and results in negative behaviours directed at the organization, the system of authority, colleagues at work or the family. The following steps can minimize this problem.

- Provide realistic and honest job descriptions. Discuss terms and conditions at the recruitment phase so that the individual can make an informed choice about selecting into the work situation.
- Use appraisal interviews to reduce the stress associated with uncertainty and ambiguity about the future and career potential. The appraisal interview process should be kept separate from a pay review discussion since an employee is unlikely to reveal weakness or training needs if it is perceived that this will adversely affect a pending pay award.

Organizations can also reduce stress related to job or career change by offering career development appraisal, a counselling service, retraining opportunities, job-seeking skills and an outplacement service.

Dealing with bullying and stress
Incidents of bullying in the workplace may be increasing. However we cannot be sure if this is the reality of work life in the new millennium, or the fact that people are more willing to report being bullied. Nevertheless oppressive behaviour will have negative impact in terms of reduced well-being, morale, motivation and contribution to the job (Douglas, 1996). While there is no specific health and safety legislation that deals with bullying at work, employers have a general duty of care to protect employees' health and safety. In law it is possible to seek redress for bullying behaviours that generate sufficient emotional distress and unhealthy physical stress (Douglas, 1996). Thus an employer must ensure that the dignity of the employee is upheld. Bullying is described as persistent, offensive, abusive, intimidating, malicious or insulting behaviour, abuse of power or unfair penal sanctions, which makes the recipient feel upset, threatened, humiliated or vulnerable, which undermines their self-confidence and which may cause them to suffer stress (MSF, 1995). As with harassment, bullying is defined largely by the impact of the behaviour on the recipient, not its intention. An authoritarian culture, poor work relationships

and a lack of clear codes of acceptable behaviours are conditions that foster a climate in which bullying is likely to occur.

One of the first steps to eliminate bullying from the work environment is to raise awareness of bullying through the use of newsletters, posters and meetings. All staff must be aware of what constitutes bullying and that the organization will take action against bullying behaviour. A policy on bullying can be part of a health and safety policy. It defines what behaviour is unacceptable and the sanctions if people go beyond these bounds. Employees should also receive guidance on the steps to be taken if they become a victim of bullying.

Managing the stress of job understimulation and boredom at work
The opposite of work overload and burnout is known as 'rust-out'. Prevention of stress associated with rust-out due to boredom and lack of stimulation in the workplace can be achieved by making changes to the micro-work environment (Karasek, cited in ILO, 1993). This includes increasing workers' skills, autonomy in the job and providing more opportunities for decision making. Hackman-Oldham (1976) explains how the core nature of a job influences one's attitudes and behaviour, and the way it affects both personal and work outcomes, such as motivation, job performance, job satisfaction and labour turnover. It is suggested that any job can be described according to five core dimensions.

1. Skill variety: the different activities, skills and talents the job requires; the more varied the skills we use, the more meaningful the job is seen to be.
2. Task identity: the degree to which a job requires completion of a whole, identifiable piece of work; doing a job from beginning to end with a visible result.
3. Task significance describes the job's impact on the lives or work of other people.
4. Autonomy is the degree of freedom, independence and discretion in scheduling the work and in determining procedures and practices.
5. Feedback: provision of direct, clear information about performance effectiveness.

Redesigning or enriching a job, to improve the amount of skill variety, task identity, task significance, autonomy and feedback, can increase motivation, performance and job satisfaction and reduce stress.

A job analysis is required to inform action that might include job rotation, job share, horizontal job enlargement and increasing responsibility for the job (known as 'vertical loading'). The use of semi-autonomous work groups is similar to the process of vertical loading, but is introduced into a team. It means that a group of employees is empowered to make decisions that affect their work activities. Such initiatives help to alleviate the problems associated with boredom, job dissatisfaction and low work motivation. However this type of job redesign rarely occurs in the absence of other changes, such as pay rates and staffing (Wall, 1984, cited in Murchinsky, 1993).

Providing alternative work arrangements as a stress control intervention
In order to meet consumer demand and the internal pressures associated with the management of a more diverse workforce, organizations are now required to find ways of being flexible and responsive to rapidly changing economic and societal norms. As the

proportion of dual-earner families, single-parent families and female-headed families has increased, it has become necessary for organizations to ensure a family-friendly work environment in order to retain staff (Lewis and Cooper, 1995) and to minimize the negative impact of work–family conflict on employee well-being (Grant-Vallone and Donaldson, 2001). Therefore policies and programmes have been introduced to provide employees with flexibility in time and place of work, dependant care, financial aid and/or information on outside services. Such programmes contribute to improving the business bottom line. Also employees are more attached to organizations with family-friendly policies, regardless of the extent to which they might personally benefit, because offering assistance to employees in need symbolizes a concern for employees (Grover and Crooker, 1995).

Specific types of alternative work arrangements include part-time work; job share; leave of absence, telecommuting and other work-at-home arrangements; and flexitime. Flexible work patterns eliminate travel problems and facilitate coping with dependant care. They can provide employees with time during the normal working day to attend to family issues. Often a key stressor is the problem of childcare for older children, before and after school hours, and during school holidays. Flexitime helps to minimize the impact of this strain, in addition to organizational benefits such as after-school clubs, school holiday activity centres or vouchers to contribute towards the costs of childcare. By these means employees gain greater control over their work and family lives, leading to reduced work–family conflict and increased job satisfaction.

Research findings on the impact of flexitime on the profitability of organizations are mixed. Some evidence of a direct impact on productivity and performance is available. Other studies indicate decreases in sickness absence, tardiness, overtime and turnover and these can also have positive effects on an organization's profitability (Dalton and Mesch, 1990). However the benefits of flexitime need to be balanced against administration and management costs. Assessment of need and potential benefits is essential before embarking on this, or any other activities to control workplace stress.

Managing role stress in the workplace
Role ambiguity and role conflict are acknowledged as potent sources of stress in the work environment, associated with a variety of negative attitudinal health and behavioural outcomes (Ivancevich and Matteson, 1980; Breaugh, 1981). Thus role clarification interventions can be used as stress control strategies. For example, Quick (1979) used participative goal setting to reduce role stress amongst employees in an insurance company. Over a 14-month period, executive officers and immediate staff took part in a field study. During training, three dimensions of goal setting were emphasized: task goal properties (difficulty and clarity), supervisory goal behaviours (the quality and quantity of feedback) and subordinate goal behaviour (participation). Measures were collected six months prior to training and at the five- and eight-month post training points, and significant reductions in measures of role conflict and role ambiguity was observed. Considerable reduction in sickness absenteeism levels was recorded five months after training, but the affect was not sustained at the eight-month point.

Supervisors working in a social services agency were trained in role emphasis, and efforts were made to reduce stress by prompting clear, consistent and positive feedback, and clarifying rules, policies and roles. This initiative was effective in reducing burnout among newly hired staff (Burke, 1987).

Role negotiation as a stress control mechanism   Role negotiation as a way of reducing stress is a technique based on an idea described by Harrison (1972). It is a useful way of overcoming the problems that lead to ineffectiveness caused by behaviour that an individual is unwilling to change, because it would mean a loss of power or influence. Harrison believes that this method works because most people prefer a fair negotiated settlement to a state of unresolved conflict. Thus they will be motivated to engage in some action themselves and make concessions in order to achieve this aim. In role negotiation the change effort is focused solely on the working relationships among the people involved. Likes or dislikes for one another are avoided. During role negotiation an imposed structure is created to allow a controlled negotiation to take place. Each person involved discusses and agrees in writing to change certain behaviours in return for changes in behaviour by the other party. All requests and agreements must be in writing and each person must give something in order to get something. If one party reneges on their part of the bargain, the whole contract becomes invalid. Usually an outside facilitator is used for optimal effectiveness and progress follow-up is required to determine whether contracts are being honoured and to assess the effectiveness of the negotiations.

Conclusion
It is desirable for organizations to use proactive, preventive *and* curative approaches to the management of stress, and at the same time operate at more than one level of focus. This is described as a tripartite, integrated approach to stress management, consisting of primary, secondary and tertiary action. Elkin and Rosch (1990) suggest that the best approach is one that recognizes that changing lifelong patterns, those of the individual worker or those of the organization, takes time and commitment. Furthermore, certain issues are crucial to successful stress management in the workplace.

1. Have a clear idea about why you are becoming involved in a stress-management programme. A stress audit will highlight problem areas and the possible ways to overcome these problems.
2. Decide how you are going to evaluate your initiative and measure the benefits.
3. If there are benefits, share these rewards with employees to maintain and sustain a culture and climate that acknowledge the link between employee well-being and business effectiveness.
4. Take time to understand both staff and management attitudes to your stress-management policy and strategy.
5. Define who is to be involved in an initiative. A project must be endorsed at the highest level to ensure that commitment is strong.
6. Communicate intentions clearly.
7. Provide necessary guarantees of confidentiality.
8. Define how the feedback of results of a stress audit or risk assessment will be treated and used.

Stress-related problems are complex and rarely limited solely to a work or a home life domain, so a holistic, integrated, organizational approach to stress management is recommended (Sutherland and Cooper, 2000). In this the organization and all employees should be encouraged to manage actively the stress that is an inevitable part of living and working in the 21st century. Stress control can only be really successful if it is tackled at the level of the individual and the organization (DeFrank and Cooper, 1987); it is a joint responsibility with potential gains to benefit the workforce and the business itself.

References

Blake, R.R. and J.S. Mouton (1984), *Solving Costly Organizational Conflicts*, San Francisco: Josey-Bass.
Breaugh, J.A. (1981), 'Predicting absenteeism from prior absenteeism and work attitudes', *Journal of Applied Psychology*, **36**, 1–18.
Briner, R.B. and S. Reynolds (1999), 'The costs, benefits and limitations of organizational level stress interventions', *Journal of Organizational Behaviour*, **20**, 647–64.
Burke, R.J. (1987), 'Issues and implications for healthcare delivery systems', in J.C. Quick, R.S. Bhagat, J.E. Dalton and J.D. Quick (eds), *Work Stress; Health Care Systems in the Workplace*, New York: Praeger, pp. 27–49.
Burke, R.J. (1993), 'Organisational-level interventions to reduce occupational stressors', *Work & Stress*, **7**(1), 77–87.
Cartwright, S. and C.L. Cooper (1996), *Managing Mergers, Acquisitions and Joint Ventures*, Oxford: Butterworth Heinemann.
Cervinka, R. (1993), 'Night shift dose and stress at work', *Ergonomics*, **361**(1–3), 152–60.
Chaston, T. (1998), 'Self-managed teams: assessing the benefits for small service sector firms', *British Journal of Management*, **9**, 1–12.
Cooper, C.L. and J. Marshall (1978), *Understanding Executive Stress*, London: Macmillan.
Czeisler, C.A., M.C. Moore-Ede and R.C. Coleman (1982), 'Rotating shift work schedules that disrupt sleep are improved by applying circadian principles', *Science*, **217**(30), 460–62.
Dalton, D.R. and D.J. Mesch (1990), 'The impact of flexible scheduling on employee attendance and turnover', *Administrative Science Quarterly*, **35**, 370–87.
Daus, C. S., D.N. Sanders and D.P. Campbell (1998), 'Consequences of alternate work schedules', in C.L. Cooper and I.T. Roberston (eds), *International Review of Industrial & Organizational Psychology*, **13**, 185–223.
DeFrank, R.S. and C.L. Cooper (1987), 'Worksite stress management interventions. Their effectiveness and conceptualisation', *Journal of Managerial Psychology*, **2**(1), 4–10.
Dormann, C. and D. Zapf (2002), 'Social stressors at work, irritation, and depressive symptoms: accounting for unmeasured third variables in a multi-wave study', *Journal of Occupational and Organizational Psychology*, **75**, 33–58.
Douglas, D. (1996), 'Healing the impact of bullying', *Counselling at Work*, Winter, 7–8.
Dwyer, D.J. and D.C. Ganster (1991), 'The effects of job demands and control on employee attendance and satisfaction', *Journal of Organizational Behaviour*, **12**, 595–608.
Earnshaw, J. and C.L. Cooper (1994), 'Employee stress litigation', *Work & Stress*, **8**(4), 287–95.
Elkin, A.J. and P.J. Rosch (1990), 'Promoting mental health at the workplace: the prevention side of stress management', *Occupational Medicine: State of the Art Review*, **5**(4), 739–54.
Fried, Y., S. Melamed and H.A. Ben-David (2002), 'The joint effects of noise, job complexity and gender on employee sickness absence: an exploratory study across 21 organizations – the CORDIS study', *Journal of Occupational and Organizational Psychology*, **75**, 131–44.
Ganster, D.C., B.T. Mayes, W.E. Sime and G.D. Tharp (1982), 'Managing occupational stress: a field experiment', *Journal of Applied Psychology*, **67**, 533–42.
Grant-Vallone, E.J. and S.I. Donaldson (2001), 'Consequences of work–family conflict on employee well-being over time', *Work & Stress*, **15**(3), 214–26.
Grover, S.L. and K.J. Crooker (1995), 'Who appreciates family-responsive human resource policies: the impact of family-friendly policies on the organizational attachment of parents and non-parents', *Personnel Psychology*, **48**, 271–88.
Hackman J.R. and G. R. Oldham (1976), 'Motivation through the design of work: test of a theory', *Organizational Behaviour and Human Performance*, **16**, 250–79.
Harrison, R. (1972), 'When power conflicts trigger team spirit', *European Business*, Spring, 27–65.
Harrison, R.V. (1985), 'The person–environment fit model and the study of job stress', in T.A. Beehr and R.S. Bhagat (eds), *Human Stress and Cognition in Organization*, New York: John Wiley, pp. 23–56.

Herbert, M. (1997), 'Sleep, circadian Rythms and health', in A. Baum, S. Newman, J. Weinman, R. West and C. McManus (eds), *Cambridge Handbook of Psychology, Health and Medicine*, Cambridge: Cambridge University Press, pp. 165–7.

ILO (1993), 'Safety and related issues pertaining to work on offshore petroleum installations', Tripartite Meeting, International Labour Office, Geneva.

Ivancevich, J.M. and M.T. Matteson (1980), *Stress at Work*, Glenview, IL: Foresman, Scott.

Ivancevich, J.M., M.T. Matteson, S.M. Freedman and J.S. Phillips (1990), 'Worksite stress management interventions', *American Psychologist*, **45**, 252–61.

Johnson, J.V. and E.M. Hall (1988), 'Job strain, work place social support and cardiovascular disease: a cross sectional study of a random sample of the Swedish working population', *American Journal of Public Health*, **78**, 1336–42.

Karasek, R.A. (1979), 'Job demands, job decision latitude, and mental strain: implications for job redesign', *Administrative Science Quarterly*, **24**, 285–308.

Karasek, R., T. Theorell, J.E. Schwartz, P.L. Schnall, C.F. Pieper and J.L. Michele (1988), 'Job characteristics in relation to the prevalence of myocardial infarction in the US Health Examination Survey (HES) and the Health and Nutrition Examination Survey (HANES)', *American Journal of Public Health*, **78**, 910–18.

Kryter, K.D. (1994), *The Handbook of Hearing and the Effects of Noise: Physiology, Psychology and Public Health*, New York: Academic Press.

Lazarus, R.S. (1966), *Psychological Stress and the Coping Process*, New York: McGraw-Hill.

Lewis, S. and C.L. Cooper (1995), 'Balancing the home–work interface: a European perspective', *Human Resource Management*, **5**, 289–305.

Maslach, C. (1982), *Burnout: The Cost of Caring*, New York: Prentice-Hall.

MSF (1995), *Bullying at Work: How to Tackle it: A Guide for MSF Representatives and Members*, Bishop Stortford: College Hill Press.

Murchinsky, P.M. (1993), *Psychology Applied to Work. An Introduction to Industrial and Organizational Psychology*, Pacific Grove, CA: Brooks/Cole.

Murphy, L.R. (1987), 'A review of organisational stress management research: methodological considerations', in *Job Stress: From Theory to Suggestion*, Binghamton, NY: Haworth.

Murphy, L.R. (1988), 'Workplace interventions for stress reduction and prevention', in C.L. Cooper and R. Payne (1988), *Causes, Coping and Consequences of Stress at Work*, New York: John Wiley, pp. 301–39.

Newman, J.D. and T. Beehr (1979), 'Personal and organisational strategies for handling job stress: a review of research and opinion', *Personnel Psychology*, **32**, 1–43.

Perrewe, P.L. and D.C. Ganster (1989), 'The impact of job demands and behavioural control on experienced job stress', *Journal of Organizational Behaviour*, **10**, 213–29.

Peters, T.J. and R.H. Waterman (1982), *In Search of Excellence: Lessons from America's Best Run Companies*, New York: Harper Row.

Quick, J.C. (1979), 'Dyadic goal setting and role stress in field study', *Academy of Management Journal*, **22**, 241–52.

Rafferty, Y., R. Friend and P.R. Landbergis (2001), 'The association between job skill discretion, decision authority and burnout', *Work & Stress*, **15**(1), 73–85.

Sutherland, V.J. and C.L. Cooper (2000), *Strategic Stress Management: An Organizational Approach*, London: Macmillan Business.

Sutherland, V.J. and M.J. Davidson (1993), 'Using a stress audit: the construction site manager experience', *Work and Stress*, **7**(3), 273–86.

Waterhouse, J. (1993), 'Circadian rhythms', *British Medical Journal*, **306**, 448–51.

15 Prevention perspectives in occupational health psychology
Lois E. Tetrick, James Campbell Quick and Jonathan D. Quick

People spend a significant proportion of their lives at work and often their jobs bring meaning and structure to their lives (Jahoda, 1982).[1] In fact, work may dominate the lives of many individuals (Cox, 1997). Since work is a central aspect of many people's lives, it generally is recognized that individuals should have a safe and healthy work environment. Employees should not have to worry about injury or illness, and legislation has been introduced in many industrialized countries including the United States, The Netherlands, Sweden and the European Union to help ensure this (Kompier, 1996). The focus of much of the early work on occupational safety and health was on workers' exposure to physical hazards in the work environment. Increasingly, however, the workplace is viewed as the logical, appropriate context for health promotion, not just the prevention of injuries and illness (Cooper and Cartwright, 1994; Cox, 1997). This broader perspective is concerned with healthy people and healthy organizations especially considering the recent changes in the organization of work as well as changes in the people in the workforce (Levi *et al.*, 1999). The purpose of this chapter is to examine the healthy organizations and healthy people dimensions in occupational health psychology and then to explore two prevention models for enhancing healthy workplaces. The chapter ends with a conclusion about the emergent positive psychology.

Healthy organizations
In considering healthy organizations, one must consider the question of healthy for whom? Many definitions of organizational health have focused on the organization itself. For example, Miles (1965) defined a healthy organization as one that survives but also continues to cope adequately over the long haul, continuously developing and expanding its coping abilities. Cooper and Cartwright (1994) extended this by including the health of employees when they described a healthy organization as one that is financially successful and has a healthy workforce. A healthy organization is able to maintain a healthy and satisfying work environment over time even in times of market turbulence and change. Similarly Quick (1999) indicated that high productivity, high employee satisfaction, good safety records, few disability claims and union grievances, low absenteeism, low turnover and the absence of violence characterized a healthy work environment. One could further extend the consideration of organizational health to the community in which the organization is located. Such an extension makes clear the public health perspective of occupational health psychology and its focus on prevention. Prevention programs aimed at improving the health of organizations benefit both the organization and

the people in them because they reflect a value placed on people, human activities and human relationships (Rosen, 1986; Schein, 1990).

Healthy people
Health is a state of complete physical, mental and social well-being, and not merely the absence of disease or infirmity (The World Health Organization, Constitution, 1948). The Ottawa Charter of the World Health Organization in 1986 defined health as a resource for everyday life, not the object of living. Health is a positive concept including social and personal resources as well as physical capabilities (Nutbeam, 1990). It also has been conceptualized as the ability to have and to reach goals, meet personal needs and cope with everyday life (Raphael et al., 1999). The USA is among the countries who set national health objectives for their people, both with regard to health-related behavior and disease prevention, and to health and safety in the workplace (U.S. DHHS–PHS, 1990).

Occupational health psychology
The purpose of occupational health psychology is to develop, maintain and promote the health of employees directly and the health of their families (Tetrick and Quick, 2003). The primary focus of occupational health psychology is the prevention of illness or injury by creating safe and healthy working environments (Quick et al., 1997b; Sauter et al., 1999). Key areas of concern are work organization factors that place individuals at risk of injury, disease and distress. This requires an interdisciplinary, if not transdisciplinary, approach (Maclean et al., 2000) across multiple disciplines within and beyond psychology. For example, such psychology specialties as human factors, industrial and organizational psychology, social psychology, health psychology and clinical psychology bear upon occupational health psychology, as do other disciplines such as public health, preventive medicine and industrial engineering (Schneider et al., 1999). Integration of these disciplines with a primary focus on prevention is the goal of occupational health psychology. Therefore the focus is on organizational interventions rather than individual interventions, such as counseling (Quick, 1999).

The challenge to occupational health psychology in promoting healthy organizations and healthy people is shaped by two sets of change forces, which are changes in the workplace and changes in the workforce. We explore these change forces in depth elsewhere (Tetrick and Quick, 2003). These changes shape the nature of occupational risks to which people are exposed and the context within which they work. Within this context, the public health notion of prevention may be translated and applied in organizations to avert a range of health problems while enhancing health at work.

Prevention and the public health model: a people-centered approach
Safety and health in the workplace are important public health concerns. There are several schools of thought on prevention, of which two major schools are population-based interventions and interventions for individuals at high risk (Weich, 1997). These two schools set up what has been called the 'prevention paradox' (Rose, 1992). Some people view population-based interventions as wasteful of scarce resources. However high-risk interventions require knowledge of the causes or etiology of particular illnesses and may

Prevention and occupational health psychology 211

be too focused to address the problem. Maclean *et al.* (2000) indicated that more illness may be prevented by making minor changes for many people than by making major changes for those few who are at high-risk. Weich suggested that a high-risk approach to prevention on its own is incapable of reducing the prevalence of the common mental disorders to any significant extent (1997, p. 760). However there is some support to the view that individual-level intervention (counseling) had clear benefits on employees' well-being, while an organization-level intervention (increased participation and control) did not (Reynolds, 1997). The public health model actually incorporates both the population-based and at-risk individual-based models of interventions.

The public health model classifies interventions into three categories: primary interventions, secondary interventions and tertiary interventions (Schmidt, 1994). Figure 15.1 presents a prevention and public health model showing health risk factors, asymptomatic disorders and diseases, and symptomatic disorders and diseases with the accompanying points of intervention (Wallace *et al.*, 1998; Winett 1995).

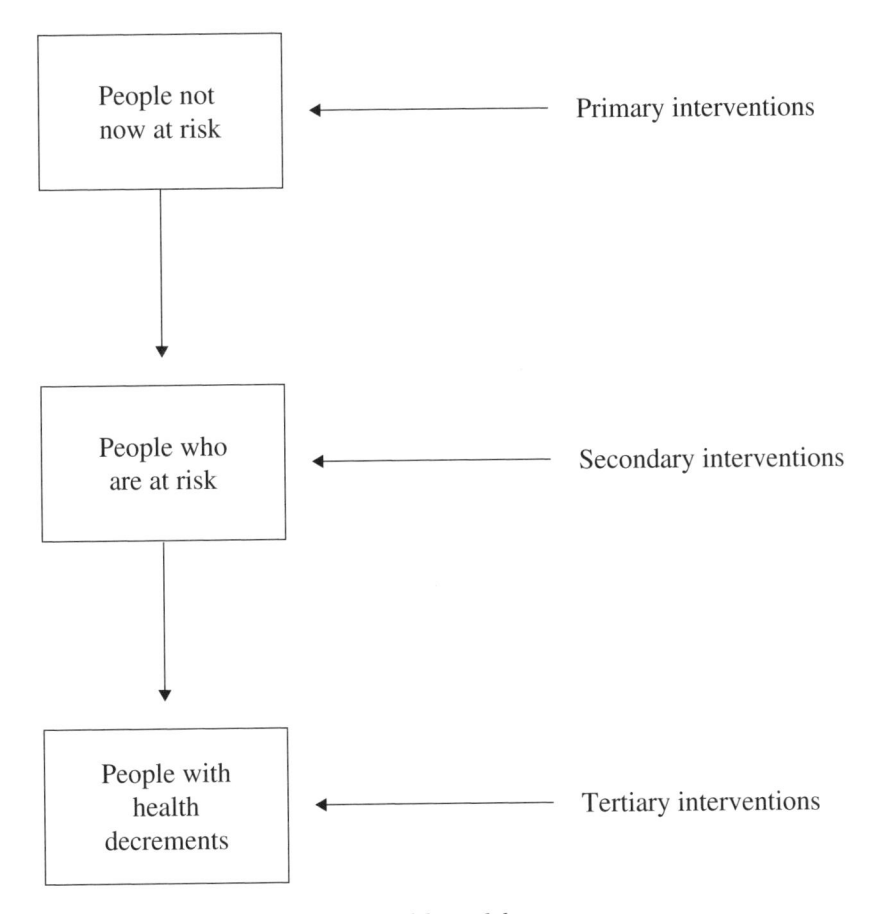

Figure 15.1   A prevention and public health model

Primary interventions focus on prevention among people who are not at risk. This is essentially the population-based model where the intervention is applied to entire populations or groups, although Schmidt (1994) argues that all interventions must have an individual component and therefore need to incorporate psychological theoretical approaches. Primary interventions are frequently used in health promotion and health education campaigns where the message is sent out to everyone, whether they are at risk or not, such as 'infomercials' broadcast on television and radio about the negative health effects of smoking.

Secondary interventions focus on people who are suspected of being at risk for illness or injury. They may be administered to groups or individuals. Staying with the health promotion and health education campaigns example, a secondary intervention would be to aim the message at a particular group of people who are at risk, such as smokers. This would be akin to warning messages on packs of cigarettes.

Lastly, tertiary interventions focus on those who have experienced a loss in their health and attempt to restore them to health. Tertiary interventions are largely therapeutic and curative in nature. These interventions typically are individual-based, although they can be group-based, as with individual therapy and group therapy. A natural progression from our previous example would be the provision of smoking cessation programs to smokers who had experienced loss of lung capacity.

As stated earlier, occupational health psychology focuses on primary interventions and, from a public health and preventive medicine perspective, primary prevention is always the preferred point of intervention (Wallace et al., 1998). A prevention model is highly appropriate in occupational health psychology because it is systemic in nature and recognizes the life history, multifaceted complexity of many health problems (Ilgen, 1990; Quick et al., 1997a; Quick and Tetrick, 2003). These sorts of health problems stand in contrast to the infectious and contagious illnesses for which the traditional public health model was developed, originally to prevent disease epidemics.

Cooper and Cartwright (1994) concluded that healthy organizations will not need secondary and tertiary interventions. However, as Quick (1999) points out, there may be times when secondary or tertiary interventions may be needed because primary prevention was not feasible or individual factors create health concerns for only some people.

Preventive management: a complementary prevention model with a health risk focus
The public health prevention model just elaborated has a clear population, or people, focus, as indicated in Figure 15.1. We would like to elaborate a complementary prevention model that has a focus on health risk factors. This prevention model has been articulated within a theory of preventive management in organizations, translating concepts from public health and preventive medicine to address chronic occupational health problems. Chronic occupational health problems include, for example, stress, workplace violence, suicide and sexual harassment. The preventive management model has been most extensively elaborated in the case of organizational stress and, therefore, we elaborate this prevention model within the context of organizational stress. Here we describe the theory, beginning with the preventive medicine model. Concepts from this model are superimposed on to the stress process in organizations framework, thus effecting the preventive management model for organizational stress. Similar models have been articulated for

workplace violence (Mack *et al.*, 1998) and sexual harassment (Bell, Cycyota and Quick, 2002; Bell, Quick and Cycyota, 2002).

A theory of prevention
The preventive stress management model is based on the translation of the preventive medicine model and its overlay onto the stress process in an organization framework. Using Quick and Quick (1984, p. 13) as a basis, we define preventive management as follows: 'Preventive management is an organizational philosophy and set of principles which employs specific methods for promoting individual and organizational health while preventing individual and organizational disorders, distress and illness.' Two of the central principles of preventive management which bear upon occupational health are that individual and organizational health are interdependent, and that leaders have a responsibility for individual and organizational health.

The preventive medicine model
Preventive medicine is a relatively young branch of medicine aimed at prevention of health problems and disorders, illnesses, diseases and epidemics (Last and Wallace, 1992). Early in the 20th century, Harvard President Charles W. Eliot was instrumental in encouraging Harvard Medical School to be a leader in preventive medicine. A popular result of this effort was a series of lectures during the first decade of that century on sanitation, contagion and other public health topics (Benison *et al.*, 1987, p. 117). The health risks in the early 1900s were primarily acute, such as influenza, as opposed to chronic, such as cardiovascular disease. With the success of the war on acute diseases, the public health and preventive medicine battlefield shifted to the chronic diseases and health promotion (Cohen, 1985; Foss and Rothenberg, 1987).

In contrast to the acute and infectious diseases, chronic diseases do not arise suddenly. Rather chronic diseases develop gradually through a progression of stages, a 'natural life history'. The natural life history of most diseases is one of evolution through stages of susceptibility, early illness and finally advanced or disabling disease. Progress through these three stages may be illustrated with coronary artery disease. At the stage of susceptibility, the individual is healthy, but is exposed to certain health risks or precursors to illness, such as a sedentary life (that is, lack of physical activity and exercise) or cigarette smoking. If these health risks lead to the development of arteriosclerotic plaques in the coronary arteries, the individual is at the stage of early or preclinical disease in which few, if any, symptoms are present. As the disease advances, it becomes symptomatic or clinical disease. Angina pectoris and heart attacks are advanced manifestations of coronary artery disease. This natural life history of a chronic disease is not inevitable and there is growing evidence for natural protective mechanisms and defenses enabling individuals to maintain their health even when exposed to health risks. These natural defenses and homeostatic processes were first discussed by Cannon (1932).

As a means of addressing chronic health problems as well as acute and infectious ones, public health encompasses a broad array of health protection activities inspired by the practice of viewing illnesses within a social context, as President Eliot did (Benison *et al.*, 1987; Ewart, 1991). The predominant diagnostic model in public health involves the interaction between a host (the individual), an agent (health-damaging organism or substance) and the environment. One fundamental concept of preventive medicine is the opportunity for preventive and treatment intervention at each stage in the life history of a disease. Preventive interventions aim to slow, stop or reverse the progression of disease.

The stress process in organizations
Walter B. Cannon was the first to identify the *stress* response, labeling it the 'emergency reaction'. His view of its roots in 'the fighting emotions' set the stage for its identification as the fight-or-flight response (Cannon, 1929). Subsequently Hans Selye's environmental stress investigations found the release of adrenal-gland hormones to be a chief result of stress, normally leading to appropriate adaptation to stressful situations (Selye, 1976a). However the adaptation mechanism may malfunction and cause one or more diseases of maladaptation, such as cardiovascular disease or arthritis. Selye's (1973, 1976b) General Adaptation Syndrome (GAS) included three stages: alarm, resistance and exhaustion. While the alarm stage of the GAS is what Cannon labeled the emergency reaction, it is in the resistance stage of the GAS where an individual struggles, fights and is exposed to health risk and distress. Finally the exhaustion stage is where collapse occurs.

In a shift from this medical framework for stress, Kahn *et al.* (1964) drew attention to the psychology of stress by focusing attention on the psychosocial demands of role conflict and role ambiguity as environmental stressors for people in organizations. They showed how conflict and confusion can lead to individual distress and strain, with their associated organizational costs. Lazarus drew attention to another aspect of the psychology of stress by introducing cognitive appraisal and coping (Lazarus *et al.*, 1985). This line of research identified the role of individual differences in the perceptions of demands and stressors, leading one person to see an opportunity or challenge where another sees a threat.

The translated preventive management model
The preventive management model for chronic occupational health problems, as illustrated with the example of organizational stress, is shown in Figure 15.2 (see Quick *et al.*, 1998 for details). Primary interventions may be used to address organizational demands and stressors that create pressure for people at work. Secondary interventions may be used to address the stress response itself within individuals. While early or preclinical disease begins in the second stage of the *preventive medicine model*, disorder, distress and strain do not begin until the third stage of the *preventive stress management model*. This is an important distinction. While stage two stress responses are basically healthy, they do possess some health risk. Finally, tertiary interventions may be used to address individual and organizational distress. The intervention components of Figures 15.1 and 15.2, which present the public health prevention model and the preventive stress management model, respectively, are essentially the same. Where the two complementary models in these figures differ is the focus and target of the interventions, in the former case it is on population groups and in the latter case it is health-risk factors.

Conclusion
Theory and research are just beginning to fully integrate job and work design with employee health (for example, Parker *et al.*, 2003). Also research directly linking employee

```
┌──────────────┐
│ Demands and  │ ◄─────────────── Primary interventions
│  stressors   │
└──────┬───────┘
       │
       ▼
┌──────────────┐
│  The stress  │ ◄─────────────── Secondary interventions
│   response   │
└──────┬───────┘
       │
       ▼
┌──────────────┐
│ Individual and│
│ organizational│ ◄────────────── Tertiary interventions
│   distress   │
└──────────────┘
```

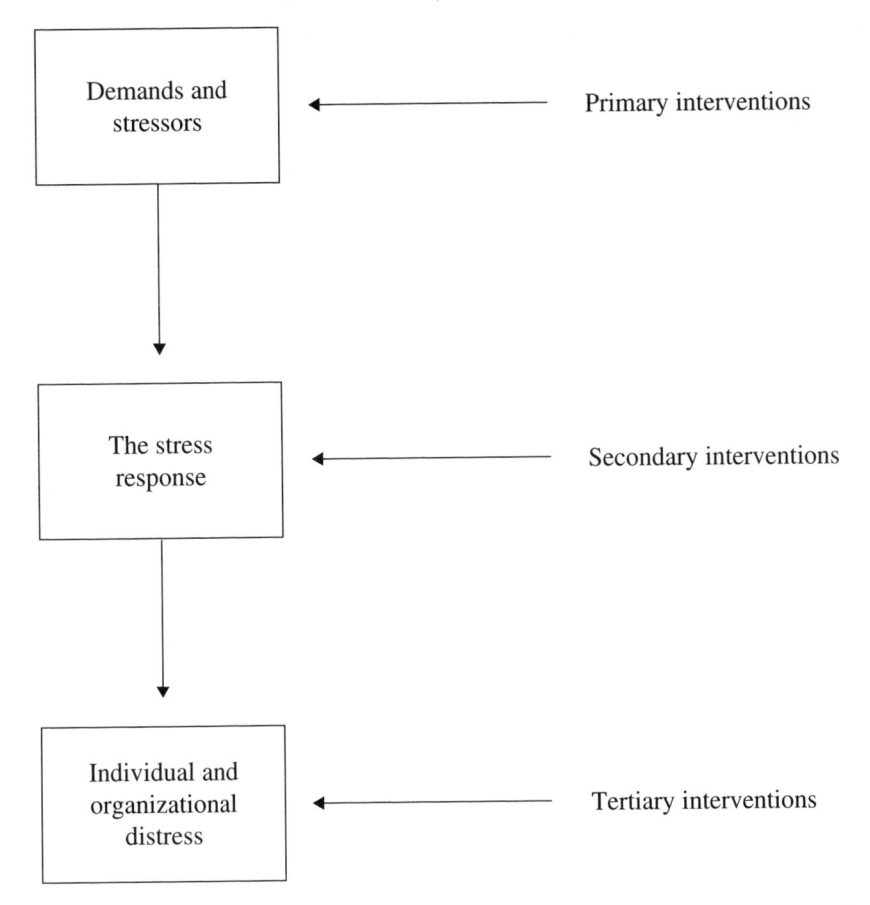

Figure 15.2   A health-risk preventive management model applied to organizational stress

health and organizational health continues to be absent, although research is emerging that at least indirectly links employee health and organizational health (see Tetrick, 2002, for a review). The practice of occupational health psychology requires a sound scientific basis for developing healthy organizations and healthy people. Therefore further research is needed examining the risk factors for individual and organizational health. In addition, more theoretical development and supporting research is needed to refine the definition of health to include, not just the absence of illness, but something more. Perhaps the efforts of positive psychology to understand optimum human functioning and happiness (Seligman and Csikszentmihalyi, 2000) have implications for occupational safety and health and the design of primary interventions to promote health in the workplace. Seligman (1998) chided psychology for focusing on disease to the exclusion of working towards building strength and resilience in people. Occupational health psychology has emerged as a field with its primary focus on primary prevention. As indicated in several of the chapters in the *Handbook of Occupational Health Psychology* (Quick and Tetrick, 2003) there is clear recognition that occupational health psychology is concerned with creating healthy people and healthy organizations, not just the prevention of injury and illness.

Note

1. This chapter is adapted from Chapter 1 ('Prevention at Work: Public Health in Occupational Settings') by Lois E. Tetrick and James Campbell Quick in their *Handbook of Occupational Health Psychology* (Washington, DC: American Psychological Association, 2003), copyright 2003 by the American Psychological Association. Adapted with permission. In addition, we incorporate the prevention perspective reflected in Chapter 12 ('The Theory of Preventive Stress Management in Organizations') by Jonathan D. Quick, James Campbell Quick and Debra L. Nelson in Cary L. Cooper's *Theories of Organizational Stress* (Oxford and New York: Oxford University Press, 1998).

References

Bell, M.P., C. Cycyota and J.C. Quick (2002), 'Affirmative defense: the prevention of sexual harassment', in D.L. Nelson and R. Burke (eds), *Gender, Work Stress and Health: Current Research Issue*, Washington, DC: American Psychological Association, pp. 191–210.
Bell, M.P., J.C. Quick and C. Cycyota (2002), 'Assessment and prevention of sexual harassment: an applied guide to creating healthy organizations', *International Journal of Selection and Assessment*, 10(1/2), 160–67.
Benison, S., A.C. Barger and E.L. Wolfe (1987), *Walter B. Cannon: The Life and Times of a Young Scientist*, Cambridge, MA: Belknap Press.
Cannon, W.B. (1929), *Bodily Changes in Pain, Hunger, Fear and Rage*, New York: D. Appleton-Century (original work published 1915).
Cannon, W.B. (1932), *The Wisdom of the Body*, New York: W.W. Norton.
Cohen, W.S. (1985), 'Health promotion in the workplace: a prescription for good health', *American Psychologist*, 40(2), 213–16.
Cooper, C.L. and S. Cartwright (1994), 'Healthy mind; healthy organization – a proactive approach to occupational stress', *Human Relations*, 47(4), 455.
Cox, T. (1997), 'Workplace health promotion', *Work & Stress*, 11(1), 1–5.
de Vries, M.F.R.K. and K. Balasz (1997), 'The downside of downsizing', *Human Relations*, 50, 11–50.
Ewart, C.K. (1991), 'Social action theory for a public health psychology', *American Psychologist*, 46(9), 931–46.
Foss, L. and K. Rothenberg (1987), *The Second Medical Revolution: From Biomedical to Infomedical*, Boston, MA: New Science Library.
Ilgen, D.R. (1990), 'Health issues at work: opportunities for industrial/organizational psychology', *American Psychologist*, 45, 273–83.
Jahoda, M. (1982), *Employment and Unemployment: A Social Psychological Analysis*, Cambridge: Cambridge University Press.
Kahn, R.L., D.M. Wolfe, R.P. Quinn, J.D. Snoek and R.A. Rosenthal (1964), *Organizational Stress: Studies in Role Conflict and Ambiguity*, New York: Wiley.
Kompier, M.A.J. (1996), 'Job design and well-being', in M.J. Schabracq and J.A.M. Winnubst and C.L. Cooper (eds), *Handbook of Work and Health Psychology*, New York: John Wiley and Sons, pp. 349–68.
Last, J.M. (1988), *A Dictionary of Epidemiology*, 2nd edn, New York: International Epidemiological Association.
Last, J.M. and R.B. Wallace (eds) (1992), *Public Health and Preventive Medicine*, 13th edn, Norwalk, CI: Appleton and Lange.
Lazarus, R.S., A. DeLongis, S. Folkman and R. Gruen (1985), 'Stress and adaptational outcomes: the problem of confounded measures', *American Psychologist*, 40, 770–79.
Levi, L., S.L. Sauter and T. Shimomitsu (1999), 'Work-related stress – it's time to act', *Journal of Occupational Health Psychology*, 4(4), 394–6.
Mack, D.A., C. Shannon, J.D. Quick and J.C. Quick (1998), 'Stress and the preventive management of workplace violence', in R.W. Griffin, A. O'Leary-Kelly and J. Collins (eds), *Dysfunctional Behavior in Organizations – Volume 1: Violent Behavior in Organizations*, Greenwich, CI: JAI Press, pp. 119–41.
Maclean, L.M., R.C. Plotnikoff and A. Moyer (2000), 'Transdisciplinary work with psychology from a population health perspective: an illustration', *Journal of Health Psychology*, 5(2), 173–81.
Miles, M.B. (1965), 'Planned change and organizational health: figure and ground', in F.D. Carver and T.J. Sergiovanni (eds), *Organizations and Human Behavior: Focus on Schools*, New York: McGraw-Hill pp. 375–91.
Nutbeam, D. (1990), 'Health promotion glossary', *Health Promotion International*, 13(4), 349–64.

Parker, S.K., N. Turner and M.A. Griffin (2003), 'Designing health work', in D.A. Hofmann and L.E. Tetrick (eds), *Health and Safety in Organizations: A Multilevel Perspective*, San Francisco: Jossey-Bass, pp. 91–130.
Quick, J.C. (1999), 'Occupational health psychology: the convergence of health and clinical psychology with public health and preventive medicine in an organizational context', *Professional Psychology: Research and Practice*, **30**(2), 123–8.
Quick, J.C. and J. D. Quick (1984), *Organizational Stress and Preventive Management*, New York: McGraw-Hill.
Quick, J.D. and L.E. Tetrick, (eds) (2003), *Handbook of Occupational Health Psychology*, Washington, DC: American Psychological Association.
Quick, J.C., J.D. Quick, D.L. Nelson and J.J. Hurrell Jr (1997a), *Preventive Stress Management in Organization*, Washington, DC: American Psychological Association.
Quick, J.C., W.J. Camara, J.J. Hurrell, J.V. Johnson, C.S. Piotrkowski, S.L. Sauter and C.D. Spielberger (1997b), 'Introduction and historical overview', *Journal of Occupational Health Psychology*, **2**(1), 3–6.
Quick, J.D., J.C. Quick and D.L. Nelson (1998), 'The theory of preventive stress management in organizations', in C.L. Cooper (ed.), *Theories of Organizational Stress*, Oxford and New York: Oxford University Press, pp. 246–68.
Quick, J.C., L.E. Tetrick, J. A. Adkins. and C. Klunder (2002), 'Occupational health psychology', in I. Weiner (ed.), *Comprehensive Handbook of Psychology*, New York: John Wiley & Sons.
Raphael, D., B. Steinmetz, R. Renwick, I. Rootman, I. Brown, H. Sehdev, S. Phillips and T. Smith (1999), 'The community quality of life project: a health promotion approach to understanding communities', *Health Promotion International*, **14**(3), 197–209.
Reynolds, S. (1997), 'Psychological well-being at work: is prevention better than cure?', *Journal of Psychosomatic Research*, **43**(1), 93–102.
Rose, G. (1992), *The Strategy of Preventive Medicine*, Oxford: Oxford University Press.
Rosen, R.H. (1986), *Healthy Companies*, New York: American Management Association.
Sauter, S.L., J.J. Hurrell, H.R. Fox, L.E. Tetrick and J. Barling (1999), 'Occupational health psychology: an emerging discipline', *Industrial Health*, **37**, 199–211.
Schein, E.H. (1990), 'Organizational culture', *American Psychologist*, **45**(2), 109–11.
Schmidt, L.R. (1994), 'A psychological look at public health: contents and methodology', *International Review of Health Psychology*, **3**, 3–36.
Schneider, D.L., W.J. Camara, L.E. Tetrick and C.R. Stenberg (1999), 'Training in occupational health psychology: initial efforts and alternative models', *Professional Psychology: Research and Practice*, **30**(2), 138–42.
Seligman, M.E.P. (1998), 'Building human strength: psychology's forgotten mission', *APA Monitor, President's Column*, retrieved 18 January 2002, from http://www.apa.org/monitor/jan98/pres.html.
Seligman, M.E.P. and M. Csikszentmihalyi (2000), 'Positive psychology: an introduction', *American Psychologist*, **55**, 5–14.
Selye, H. (1973), 'Evolution of the stress concept', *American Scientist*, **61**(6), 692–9.
Selye, H. (1976a), *Stress in Health and Disease*, Boston: Butterworths.
Selye, M. (1976b),*The Stress of life*, 2nd edn, New York: McGraw-Hill (original work published 1956).
Tetrick, L.E. (2002), 'Individual and organizational health', in P. Perrew and D. Ganster (eds), *Historical and Current Perspectives on Stress and Health, Vol. 2*, Stamford, CT: Elsevier Science Ltd, pp. 117–41.
Tetrick, L.E and J.C. Quick (2003), 'Prevention at work: public health in occupation settings', in J. Quick and L. Tetrick (eds), *Handbook of Occupational Health Psychology*, Washington, DC: American Psychological Association, pp. 3–17.
U.S. Department of Health and Human Services (DHHS)–Public Health Service (PHS) (1990), Healthy People 2000: National Health Promotion and Disease Prevention Objectives, Washington, DC: U.S. DHHS–PHS.
Wallace, R.B. and B.N. Doebbeling (1998), *Maxcy–Rosenau–Last Public Health and Preventive Medicine*, 14th edn, Stamford, CT: Appleton and Lange.
Weich, S. (1997), 'Prevention of the common mental disorders: a public health perspective', *Psychological Medicine*, **27**, 757–64.
Winett, R.A. (1995), 'A framework for health promotion and disease prevention and programs', *American Psychologist*, **50**(5), 341–50.

16 Emotional intelligence and coping with occupational stress
Moshe Zeidner

For most people in modern society, work is a major source of self-esteem, life satisfaction and well-being. At the same time, the job environment can also be a major source of personal distress and unhappiness (Cartwright and Cooper, 1996). In fact occupational stress is rapidly becoming one of the most pressing organizational and health concerns in the Western world today. Widespread concern over the implications of stress in the workplace is attested to by the burgeoning literature on job stress and by the proliferation of stress management and training programs. Moreover research has demonstrated highly comparable sources of work stress, levels of stress and personal characteristics that cause workers to be susceptible to stress in various occupational settings across the globe (Mack et al., 1998).

Proponents of emotional intelligence (EI) (Goleman, 1995, 1998; Salovey et al., 1999) have recently claimed that a better understanding and regulation of one's emotions may dramatically enhance personal coping capabilities at the workplace and affect favorably adaptive outcomes. Accordingly EI should be systematically related to individual differences in coping, which, in turn, should confer generally more or less successful outcomes on the individual.

This chapter sets out to portray our current understanding of the role of EI in coping with stress in occupational settings. We begin by briefly discussing sources of occupational stress and strategies for coping with stress at work. We then discuss the possibly pivotal role of EI in coping with stress in occupational settings. We conclude by discussing the implications of EI theory and research for coping with success and adaptive outcomes at the workplace.

Occupational stress, coping and adaptive outcomes
What is occupational stress?
Following the transactional model of stress, Beehr and Newman (1978) view 'job stress' as a condition wherein job-related factors (for example, workload, time pressures, degree of control) interact with the worker's personal resources (skills, expectations, coping skills, dispositions) to change (disrupt/enhance) the worker's physiological or psychological condition, so that the person is forced to deviate from normal functioning. An adaptive response to job stress is a response intended to eliminate, ameliorate or change the stress-producing factors in the job context or to modify the individual's psychological reactions to the stressful job situation. A basic underlying assumption of this model is that a precondition for organizational stress is that there are substantial differences in rewards and costs for meeting versus not meeting organizational demands. According to the demand–control model put forth by Karasek (1989), when the psychological demands of

the job are high and the individual worker's control over the task and decision latitude (that is, authority to make decisions on the job and breadth of skills used) is low, this results in adverse psychological strain.

Organizational stress is a significant problem at the international level (Mack et al., 1998). Research by Schwartz and Stone (1993) reported that, when 112 married couples were asked to rate undesirable problems, work-related problems were the most frequently chosen after personal problems. Furthermore this study showed that about 20 per cent of the most bothersome problems of the day reported by adults, including weekends when respondents did not work, were related to happenings at work, suggesting that work is a significant source of stress in modern life. Negative interactions with people at work accounted for the greatest proportion of work problems (almost 75 per cent), followed by heavy workload (14 per cent). Other categories of specific events such as hiring, firing, criticism and changes at work were reported relatively infrequently. Furthermore a review by Mack et al. (1998) shows highly comparable sources of work stress, levels of stress and personal characteristics that cause workers to be susceptible to stress.

Occupational stress appears to be a growing problem as major organizations increasingly find themselves functioning in rapidly changing environments. Furthermore organizations have become more and more aggressively competitive, fueling endemic fears concerning job security. The extent to which individuals are capable of coping effectively with the stress and strain of work has partial implications for their continued surrounding and for society generally. On the managerial level, the extent to which managers and leaders will embrace or resist change may depend on their ability to cope with emotional elements that are involved with the transition (Mossholder et al., 2000).

As the information society comes of age, information technology (IT) continues to revolutionize the way that business is conducted and the workforce is becoming more diverse and dynamic by the hour. In an environment of rapid organizational change, the individual is required to adapt to the changes in order to accommodate to the needs of the organization. Change requires the employee to function in a different manner and this requires considerable expenditure of emotional resources. Furthermore the nature of stress at work is rapidly changing and has been in a rapid state of flux for over a decade now. Thus organizational change can be extremely stressful because of the feelings of insecurity it evokes and it may severely threaten one's sense of self. A number of the more prevalent types of changes at the worksite (for example, mergers, globalization, privatization, international competition, restructuring, distant working) have the potential to generate considerable degrees of uncertainty, ambiguity and resultant stress in 21st-century occupational settings.

As a response to a struggling economy, intense foreign competition and a need to compete on a global basis, companies have often met challenges by 'downsizing', 'rightsizing', re-engineering and restructuring on a massive scale. As a result, even those individuals who have managed to hold onto their jobs no longer take job security for granted. Some organizations may be characterized as being in a crisis (Gladstein and Reilly, 1985). These organizations are confronted by a threat that is unanticipated and presents a major threat to the survival of the system, with little time to act to solve the crisis. Typically a threat situation may be differentiated along the following features: magnitude of loss, probability of loss and the time associated with the event. Threats lead to less information shared among groups, less information exchanged among channels, and less information used for decision-making purposes.

Job stress and maladaptive outcomes Job-related or occupational stress is rapidly becoming one of the most pressing occupational and health concerns in the country today. This widespread concern over the implications of stress in the workplace is attested to by the burgeoning literature on job stress. Evidence in the medical and health sciences suggests that the influence of stress in organizations may be of epidemic proportions. As pointed out by Schuler (1980), while work can surely be fulfilling and be a major source of life satisfaction and well-being, providing a person with a sense of identity and purpose, the worksite can also be a source of stress for many (Cartwright and Cooper, 1996). For example, in a survey of Oregan school administrators, Gmelch et al. (1982), reported that the majority reported that at least 70 per cent of their total life stress resulted from their jobs.

Overall there is little dispute that stress has a dysfunctional impact on both the individual and the organizational outcomes, with work-related stress being directly responsible for immense human and financial costs (Cartwright and Cooper, 1996). Frequently described as the 'Black Plague' of the post-industrial era, stress has become a major problem of everyday life, threatening individual, organizational and societal health. For example, with US industry losing approximately 550 million working days to absenteeism, it is estimated that 54 per cent of these absences are in some way stress-related (Elkin and Rosch, 1990). The overall total cost of stress to American organizations assessed by absenteeism, reduced productivity, compensation claims, health insurance and direct medical expenses, now adds up to more than 150 billion dollars a year (Karasek and Theorell, 1990). Empirical links have been demonstrated between stress and the incidence of coronary heart disease, certain forms of cancer, mental disease and breakdown, poor health behaviors, family problems, job dissatisfaction and accidents. A large proportion of premature deaths in Western countries is attributed to stress-related illness. Among the diseases most frequently related to stress in organizations are coronary heart disease, high blood pressure and peptic ulcers (Schuler, 1980). Coronary–vascular disease is a major contributing factor to disability and hospital care in the USA. The indirect costs of stress are reflected in the substantial level of substance abuse, and high divorce rates, death and accidents. Indeed stressful encounters at the workplace have been linked to a wide range of negative outcomes that impair the workers' effective functioning. Thus the literature suggests that occupational stress can adversely affect a person's physical and mental health, job satisfaction, performance and labor turnover. Stress may also result in a high incidence of aggressive behaviors and accidents and thefts. The mental and physical health effects of job stress are not only disruptive influences for the individual but also a real cost to the organization, on which many individuals depend. Furthermore work stresses may feed into the family and social life, becoming potential sources of disturbance, pervading the whole quality of life.

Over the past two decades a substantial amount of research on job stress has been conducted, much of it examining the potential consequences of stress on criterion variables such as job satisfaction, job burnout, mental health, the practice of good health behaviors, physical disease, morbidity and mortality. The literature consistently shows that perceived stress on the job is related to employee health and well-being (Beehr and Newman, 1978). The stress process may contribute to a wide range of physical and mental disorders, including infectious disease, chronic respiratory ailments, cardiovascular disease, depression and cancer (House, 1981).

When a worker is under stress he tends to behave in a rigid manner and this may result in narrowing of field of attention, simplification of information codes and reduction in the number of channels used for accessing information (Zeidner, 1998). This is similar to the cognitive closure caused by extreme anxiety (Kruglanski and Jaffe, 1988). Stress impedes the ability to appraise, be receptive and take action along a more promising course. To reverse the effects of this process, emotional intelligence operates to bring emotional intensity to an optimal level. Too much reduction in negative feelings might also bring about stagnation and lack of motivation to change undesirable work conditions. Dissatisfaction with organizational outcomes can arouse uncomfortable feelings, leading to further assessment and learning (Nguyen Huy, 1999). The effects of stressors are likely to be cumulative and each new stress uses up a portion of a psychological safety margin. Strains can be prevented or decreased by controlling stressors or increasing coping capability.

Several major effects of job stress on psychological strain tend to hold across occupations, but particular stresses, as well as the relation between stress and strain, vary from occupation to occupation (Caplan *et al.*, 1975). While the deleterious effect of stress on worker's well-being has been frequently demonstrated, the crippling effect on *job performance* has only been presumed. A study by Westman and Eden (1988) reported that perceived stress was negatively related to job performance at three points of measurement in a sample of 326 officer cadets in combat units.

Specific sources of stress at the workplace Over three decades of systematic study in the area of occupational stress have generated a substantial body of evidence on factors which contribute to stress, and sources of stress (O'Driscoll and Cooper, 1994). Indeed the potential sources of workplace stress are many and various and not easy for the individual or organization to identify or deal with effectively. Research in occupational settings has typically focused on jobs suspected of being high-stress risks, like air-traffic controllers, police, executives, nurses, and working with the critically ill (Cooper and Kelley, 1993).

A wide array of interacting factors might be a source of managerial stress; examples are excessive work demands and pressures, 'downsizing', work overload, lack of worker–job fit, unrealistic expectations, harassment and need for in-service training. Work stress can be caused by factors such as too much or too little work, time pressures and deadlines, having too many decisions, fatigue from the physical strains of work (assembly line), excessive travel, having to cope with frequent changes at the workplace, and errors in making financial decisions (Cooper and Marshall, 1978). Interestingly job requirements to regulate negative emotions and express positive emotions are themselves a frequent source of stress and physical symptoms (Schaubroeck and Jones, 2000). In sum, almost every job description will include factors that for some individuals and at some point will be a source of pressure.

We now discuss some of the major categories of work stress, based on a slightly modified taxonomy suggested by Cartwright and Cooper (1996). The modified taxonomy identifies a number of sources of stress at the worksite.

Factors intrinsic to the job, task or workplace This category includes physical conditions and task-related sources of stress (Schuler, 1980). Sources of stress involving poor physical working conditions which surround the worker include inadequate lighting, noise, pathogenic agents, physical danger, crowded space and lack of privacy. Certain task characteristics such as work overload/underload, lack of autonomy, disruption of work patterns (for example, shift in work load), long and unconventional hours, shift work, extensive travel, high risk, uncertainty and new technology, difficulty and pace have been related to stress (ibid.).

Following French and Caplan (1973), it is useful to differentiate between quantitative overload (too much to do) and qualitative stress (task is too difficult). Research by Cooper and Marshall (1978) suggests that quantitative overload is indeed a major source of stress with important health implications. Both qualitative and quantitative overload produce an array of different symptoms of psychological strain, including job dissatisfaction, tension, low self-esteem, threat, high cholesterol levels, skin resistance and smoking. More chronic and serious consequences include coronary heart disease, escapist drinking and absenteeism.

Role in the organization Among the key dimensions of perceived role-related stress are ambiguity, conflict and powerlessness (Katz *et al.*, 1964). *Role ambiguity* arises when a person suffers from uncertainty when she has inadequate information about the work role or where there is a lack of clarity about work objectives associated with this role, about work colleagues' expectations of the work role, and about scope and responsibilities of the job (Cooper and Marshall, 1978). For example, if newly hired floor managers at a department store do not know what their duties are, what authority they process, how they are to be evaluated and so on, they may hesitate to make decisions and will rely on trial and error in meeting the expectation of the organization. Role ambiguity has been linked to job stress and high levels of anxiety, along with poor productivity (Kottkamp and Travlos, 1986).

Role conflict, a further source of occupational stress, evolves when behaviors expected by an individual and by other others in the organization are inconsistent (Hammer and Tosi, 1974). People with role conflicts in a particular work role are torn by conflicting job demands or when they are engaged in things they really do not want to do (Cooper and Marshall, 1978). For example, a novice high school teacher may perceive incompatible work demands from administrators, parents, fellow teachers and students. Katz and Kahn (1978) reported that role conflict was related to job stress, high job-related tension and lower self-esteem). Kahn *et al.* (1964) found that men who suffered from role conflict had lower job-related tension and research by Cooper suggests this is related to coronary heart disease (CHD), particularly among white-collar workers.

Powerlessness, another major source of job stress, refers to the perception that an individual cannot control outcomes. Powerlessness has been linked to high anxiety, job dissatisfaction, poor job performance, tardiness and low self-esteem (Kottkamp and Travlos, 1986). Kahn *et al.* (1964) found that men who suffered from role ambiguity experienced lower job satisfaction, higher job-related stress and lower self-confidence. Ashford (1988) found that feelings of low personal control and poor ability to tolerate ambiguity were linked with high stress in a sample of 180 AT&T employees who coped with divestiture and transition to an unregulated entity. Furthermore feelings of personal control and tolerance of ambiguity are among the most useful buffers of the transition-related stressors. Newman and Beehr (1979) reported that role conflict and role ambiguity were significantly, but modestly, related to perceived threat on the job in a sample of 61 high-level managers in an executive developmental program. French and Caplan (Caplan *et al.*, 1975; Caplan and Jones, 1975; French and Caplan, 1973) demonstrated that role ambiguity, role conflict, role underload, role overload and role–status incongruency are related to higher stress. What makes role ambiguity so stressful is that it is related to uncertainty. Role characteristics include job security, related to an individual's need for security, recognition and achievement.

Problematic relationships with others at work Another source of stress on the job has to do with the nature of the relationship with one's subordinates and colleagues (Cooper and Marshall, 1978). This includes poor relationships with workers and superiors, customers and clients. Poor relationships between group members are a central factor in poor individual and organizational health. This includes low trust, low supportiveness and low interest in listening to and trying to deal with problems that confront organizational members. Some data suggest that those negative interactions with co-workers and employees and clients and supervisors are the most frequently reported source of work-related problems. This is related to a person's need for acceptance and interpersonal recognition. When these interpersonal relations are not satisfactory to an individual, stress is often a result (Schuler, 1980).

Career development This category includes problems involving career transitions, job loss, underpromotion, demotion and derailing, having reached a career plateau, early retirement or unclear career future. Indeed lack of job security (fear of being redundant, early retirement); status incongruity (under or overpromotion, frustration at having reached one's career ceiling) is a source of fear for many in post-industrial society (Cooper and Marshall, 1978). Transitions and organizational changes are frequently viewed as being extremely disruptive.

Ashford (1988) reviews literature showing that transitions are frequently characterized by uncertainties about procedures and social norms and individuals lack guidelines for acting appropriately in a changing context. Major strategic changes in organizations often generate ambiguity about potential terminations, transfers and need to survive. Transitions also generate worries over future reward contingencies. Transition causes the significant disruption of an individual's work life in that employees must learn new skills and retool, which requires expenditure of resources. Thus the more adjustment it requires, the more stress it provokes. Ashford (1988) found that, among the specific sources of stress during AT&T transitions, were the following key stressors: uncertainty of advancement criteria, uncertainty of performance and perceived disruption. Additional factors that evoke stress include pay compression, job insecurity, feeling boxed in and having little authority. Indeed job insecurity and career development have increasingly become a source of stress during the merger/acquisition boon of the 1980s.

Organizational structure, climate and culture In this category are subsumed stressors related to the particular organizational milieu and culture one belongs to. This may include lack of a person–role fit, inadequate training and skills; inappropriate management style, lack of feedback from co-workers and superiors, and lack of effective consultation; poor communication and ugly office politics. The mismatch and gap between job demands and requisite knowledge, skills and abilities may result in high strain for workers in the new service-based economy. Threat to an individual's freedom, autonomy and identity (for example, no participation in the decision-making process, no sense of belonging, lack of effective consultation, poor communication, office politics, restrictions on behavior) is a source of stress for many. Furthermore personal and sexual harassment has assumed increasing prominence as a source of stress at the worksite. To the extent that the individual must endure such ridicule, strain is likely to result. Human service jobs may pose demands that are different from those of other professions because workers must use themselves as the technology for meeting the needs of clients, who, in turn, do not always express gratitude or appreciation. Stressors associated with organizational climate, including measures of perceived job design, leadership and relationships with co-workers, have been found to be related to worker satisfaction and alienation in studies of human service workers. A variety of sources of job stress (for example, workload, role conflict, poor relationships between workers and their peers, supervisors and subordinates, and lack of subjective fit between person and environment in a number of occupations) have been reported to predict job dissatisfaction, psychological symptoms and various risk factors in coronary heart disease (French and Caplan, 1973). Career stress may be associated with multiple negative outcomes.

Home/work interface Managing the interface between work and home is a potential source of stress, particularly for dual-career couples or those experiencing financial crises. By providing more flexible work arrangements and adopting family-friendly employment policies, this source of stress may be ameliorated.

How do we cope with occupational stress?
There is some research to suggest that most people do not cope well with organizational change and transitions, and consequently suffer long-term adverse mental and physical health. In fact coping with and managing work stress is more complex than dealing with stressful events outside work, because of the inherent constraints within the work environment, which restricts the range of acceptable coping responses and limits individual control.

Researchers have suggested that coping behaviors can minimize the impact of stress and alleviate its negative consequences. Pearlin and Schooler (1978) have identified three major protective functions of coping: (a) avoiding, eliminating or modifying conditions giving rise to problems, (b) perceptually controlling meanings of experience in a manner that neutralizes stress, and (c) keeping emotional consequences of problems within manageable bounds.

Despite a growing volume of studies on occupational stress, relatively few studies have addressed employees' efforts to cope with the stress of the workplace, and the literature is relatively silent about the ways that employees cope with transitions in the workplace. At present we have insufficient data bearing on all the potential sources of stress that are most salient to individuals in different occupational categories and how these stressors are perceived. Thus we need studies that enable people to report events or stressful encounters that are important to them in specific occupational sites. Furthermore research on stress-coping behaviors has not simultaneously explored specific stressors at the worksite and actual responses to these stressors. Although one can hardly imagine a model of occupational stress that does not include coping responses, this particular facet of the stress process remains the least developed and least understood.

One problem in research in this area is that many existing models view stress as a static construct, with interventions offering a one-time fix. Overall the impact of organizational change on employee stress has received little attention. Coping research has been problematic, partly because of the complexity of the phenomena and partly because of the methodology that has been commonly employed. Thus, as noted by Golembiewski and Munzenrider (1988), whereas coping is a *process*, most measures available are *static*. Significant advances must be made in understanding coping if we are to increase the value of stress research significantly. Thus research is needed using a critical incident analysis, in which individuals are asked to describe stressful transactions in terms of three elements: antecedents and circumstances in which stress occurred, responses (own and others') in that situation, and consequences.

It is noted that coping is situation-specific (Zeidner and Saklofske, 1996) and varies with the particular stressors in the job situation and task demands. Thus an adequate treatment would require a discussion of specific forms of coping per occupational setting. Changes contemplated by those presiding over the organization may pose real problems for individuals; while many resist these changes and transitions, others attempt to cope with them (Ashford, 1988).

What do we know about the way individuals cope with job stress? Overall few methods of coping with job stress have been evaluated by rigorous methods (Beehr and Newman, 1978). Organizational strategies to cope with job stress are aimed at changing organizational processes, structures or programs (ibid.). This includes changing selection, placement and training procedures; changing socialization processes; changing organizational structure and using participative decision making changing the reward system. All of the organizational modes for managing job stress are in need of rigorous testing. Personal strategies are aimed at changing one's psychological condition. This category includes planning ahead, psychological or mental withdrawal, philosophy of life reassessment and meditation. Personal strategies are a particularly adaptive strategy when little can be done to change the situation. Other modes of coping include strategies aimed at changing a person's physical conditions (diet), strategies aimed at changing one's behavior (behavior modification), social support, withdrawal, strategies aimed at changing one's work environment, and changing jobs or positions in the organization to work in less stressful environments. All of the personal strategies are in need of rigorous empirical study (Beehr and Newman, 1978).

Research points to a number of individual different coping strategies employees use to cope with job stress. Thus Newman and Beehr reported four individual coping strategies: (a) changing one's work environment, (b) changing one's behavior, (c) changing personal physical conditions (diet, exercise), (d) changing psychological conditions (planning ahead, managing one's life and so on). Latack (1986) provided empirical evidence for three dimensions of coping with job stress: (a) control (both actions and appraisals), (b) escape (actions and thoughts) and (c) symptom management (relaxation and exercise).

Pearlin and Schooler (1978) and Folkman and Lazarus (1980) reported differences in the way work problems are coped with, as compared with family and interpersonal problems. They surveyed the effectiveness of coping in four realms: work, marriage, parenting and household economics. Whereas coping responses were successful in the sense of reducing strain in the first three realms, they had little effect on strain resulting from work. Lazarus and Folkman (1984) found higher levels of problem-focused than emotion-focused coping when negotiating with stressful events on the job. Pearlin and Schooler (1978) reported the opposite pattern of results.

Schwartz and Stone (1993) found that work-related problems and stressors are approached via action-oriented and problem-focused coping efforts rather than distraction or other emotion-focused or avoidance strategies, which distances one from the emotional consequences of stressors. This supports the conclusion of Folkman and Lazarus (1980), that work elicits greater problem-focused coping. This suggests that individuals high in emotional intelligence would be expected to show a preference for problem-focused over other forms of copping. A review of the literature by Cartwright and Cooper (1996) suggests that work-related stress and routine daily work hassles elicit more task-oriented than emotion-focused strategies. This may be so because opportunities to discharge emotions in the workplace are generally restricted.

Research by La Rocco and Jones (1978) suggests that, whereas social support bears a direct main effect on job-related strains, such as job dissatisfaction, it has a buffering effect on health-related variables, including psychological and somatic. Furthermore strain was observed to be related to emotion-focused coping. This suggests either that palliative coping is harmful or that emotion-focused coping is simply a reaction to high levels of job stress (rather than the causes of stress and strain). These authors conclude that little is to be gained by exhorting human service professionals to change their ways of coping, because individual coping has little impact on job strain. Social support is clearly effective in counteracting burnout.

Some research suggests that, whereas individual coping efforts may not be particularly effective in organizational settings, group coping, operationalized as social support, might be particularly effective in group settings. Thus research by Shinn et al. (1984) suggests that, in the workplace, where many influential stress factors are beyond an individual's control, individual coping strategies may be less potent than 'higher level' strategies (involving groups of workers or entire organizations). Job stressors may be among the problems that are not amenable to individual solutions, but depend on highly organized cooperative efforts that transcend those of the individual, no matter how well developed one's personal resources.

Coping as mediator versus moderator of stress
There is currently some confusion over whether coping should be construed as a mediating link between occupational stress and outcomes or as a moderator of the stress–strain relations (O'Driscoll and Cooper, 1994). La Rocco and Jones (1978) found little evidence for the commonly held assumption that social support moderates the impact of occupational stress on adaptive outcomes in a sample of 3725 enlisted Navy personnel. Thus, while the linkage of job stress and negative outcomes has been documented, less attention has been paid to the discovery of factors that might buffer and alleviate stress.

Emotional intelligence and occupational settings

EI refers to the competence to identify and express emotions, understand emotions, assimilate emotions in thought, and regulate both positive and negative emotions in self and others. Emotional intelligence (EI) has recently emerged as a key construct in present-day psychological research, appearing as one of the most widely discussed aspects of intelligence in the current literature. A search for the phrase 'emotional intelligence' (EI) on the Internet search engine Google turns up more than 100 000 documents. Whereas this may not be much compared to 'IQ' (3 360 000), it is quite striking for a psychological term that was introduced to the literature in 1990 and that, before 1995, was the province of a handful of specialists.

Research in this area has prospered, in part, as a result of the increasing personal importance of intelligence for people in modern society. EI has also been claimed to have important implications for success and adaptive outcomes in a wide array of domains, including education (see Zeidner *et al.*, 2002, for a critical review), clinical intervention (see Matthews *et al.*, 2002) and the workplace (see Zeidner *et al.*, in press). The term's popularity can be attributed largely to a single event: the publication of the book *Emotional Intelligence* by Daniel Goleman (1995), which sparked explosive growth in EI research in the late 1990s. Daniel Goleman's book on the topic appeared on the New York Times Best-Sellers List in 1996, the same year in which a *Time Magazine* article was devoted to detailed exposition of the topic. Moreover the last few years have witnessed a plethora of trade texts dealing with self-help and management practices, assessment and other practical applications implicit to the concept of emotional intelligence.

It is generally agreed that EI can be split into components such as those listed, but there is no consensus on the nature of the components. Bar-On (1997), for example, provides a rather different listing that emphasizes components more related to stress research, such as stress tolerance and optimism. Researchers also differ at a more fundamental level, in terms of whether they conceptualize EI as more like a cognitive ability or a personality trait. Another unresolved issue is the extent to which EI can be identified as a cross-cultural universal, or whether it can be defined only with reference to specific cultural norms.

Much of the popular impact of emotional intelligence derives from its potential applications. It is claimed that high EI helps people in their personal lives, in dealing with stressful events and in career success. A subtext here is that the benefits of general (cognitive) intelligence are overstated, and emotional intelligence may often be more important than conventional 'IQ'. It is claimed, too, that EI can be trained, and there is a growing impetus towards the provision of personal and workplace interventions which purport to increase EI. It seems that many people believe that EI exists and personal and societal benefits will follow from investment in programs to increase EI. One of the attractive features of EI research is that it counters the pessimism contained in Charles Murray and Richard Herrnstein's Bell Curve (1994) by offering hope for a more utopian, classless society, unconstrained by genetic heritage.

Popular interest notwithstanding, scientific investigation of a clearly identified construct of emotional intelligence is sparse. Although several measures have been (or are currently being) designed for its assessment, it remains uncertain whether there is anything to emotional intelligence that psychologists working within the fields of applied psychological research do not know already. Moreover the media hype and vast number of trade texts devoted to the topic often subsume findings from these fields in a faddish sort of way, rather than dealing directly with the topic as defined by its chief exponents.

EI and occupational performance
A large array of competencies have been claimed to be critical for success in occupational settings (see review by Zeidner *et al.*, in press). For example, Goleman (1998) lists 25 different competencies necessary for effective performance in various occupational contexts. Thus confidentiality is touted as important for loan officers and priests, while trust and empathy appear vital for psychotherapists, social workers and marriage counselors. Among the specific competencies claimed to be of critical importance in a variety of occupational settings are the following.

1. *Emotional self-awareness.* This competence includes identification of emotion and understanding how emotions are related to one's goal, thoughts, behaviors and accomplishments (Goleman, 1998; Weisinger, 1998).
2. *Regulation of emotions in the self.* This competence involves intentionally eliciting and sustaining pleasant and unpleasant emotions when considered appropriate, effectively channeling negative affect, and restraining negative emotional outbursts and impulses (Boyatzis, 1982; Goleman, 1998).
3. *Social awareness of emotions and empathy*, which includes awareness of others' feelings, needs and concerns, understanding and sympathizing with others' emotions and responding to others' unspoken feelings (Goleman, 1998; Huy, 1999; cf. Salovey and Mayer, 1990; Williams and Sternberg, 1988).[1]
4. *Regulating emotions in others.* This competence incorporates influencing others' effectively communicating with others and managing conflicts (Weisinger, 1998).
5. *Motivational tendencies*, which include such components as internal strivings, attributions and need for achievement (Bar-On, 2000; Boyatzis *et al.*, 2000; Cooper and Sawaf, 1997; Goleman, 1998; Weisinger, 1998).
6. *Character*, which includes trust and integrity (Cooper and Sawaf, 1997; Goleman, 1998; Weisinger, 1998).

EI is claimed to affect a wide array of work behaviors, including employee commitment, teamwork, development of talent, innovation, quality of service and customer loyalty. According to Cooper (1997), research attests that people with high levels of emotional intelligence experience more career success, build stronger personal relationships, lead more effectively and enjoy better health than those with low emotional quotient (EQ). Why is this so?

First, more emotionally intelligent individuals presumably succeed at communicating their ideas, goals and intentions in interesting and assertive ways, thus making others feel better suited to the occupational environment (Goleman, 1998). Second, EI may be related to the social skills needed for teamwork, with high EI individuals particularly adept at designing projects that involve infusing products with feelings and aesthetics (Mayer and Salovey, 1997; Sjoberg, 2001). Third, organizational leaders who are high on EI, in concert with a supportive organizational climate and the human resources team, may affect the relationship in the work setting, which, in turn, has an impact upon group and individual EI and organizational commitment (Cherniss and Goleman, 2001). EI may also be useful for group development since a large part of effective and smooth teamwork is knowing each other's strengths and weaknesses and leveraging strengths whenever possible (Bar-On, 1997). Finally EI is claimed to influence one's ability to succeed in coping with environmental demands and pressures, clearly an important set of behaviors to harness under stressful work conditions.

A recent theoretical model proposed by Jordan *et al.* (in press) implicates EI as a moderator variable that predicts employee emotional and behavioral responses to job insecurity. According to this model, employees low in EI are hypothesized to be more susceptible than employees high in EI to negative emotions resulting from job insecurity. Therefore they are more likely to behave defensively and negatively (for example, hypervigilance, 'copping out', 'buck passing', avoidance), lowering affective commitment and increasing job-related tension in response to their insecurity. These two emotional reactions then lead to negative coping (for example, distancing, wishful thinking) and defensive decision-making behaviors. By contrast, high EI employees are better able to deal emotionally with job insecurity and will be able to ameliorate the effect of job insecurity on their affective commitment. This frequently leads to increased work commitment and effort, positive coping behaviors (problem-focused), and reframing of perceptions of insecurity as an existing challenge. Unfortunately no empirical data were provided in support of this theoretical model and its validity remains to be vindicated.

Several unsubstantiated claims have appeared in the popular literature and the media about the significant role of EI in the workplace. Thus EI has been claimed validly to predict a variety of successful behaviors at work, at a level exceeding that of intelligence (see Cooper and Sawaf, 1997; Goleman, 1998; Hay Group, 2000; Weisinger, 1998). In the *Time Magazine* article which helped popularize EI, Gibbs (1995) wrote, 'In the corporate world IQ gets you hired but EQ gets you promoted' (p. 59). Watkin (2000) suggests, without empirical support that, use of EI for recruitment decisions leads to 90-percentile success rates. He goes on to claim that 'what distinguishes top performers in every field, in every industry sector, is not high IQ or technical expertise, it is EI'. (p. 91). Similarly Goleman (1995) has claimed, from research on over 500 organizations by the Hay Group, that EI (rather than IQ) accounts for over 85 per cent of outstanding performance in top leaders. Of note, however, is that Goleman is unable to cite empirical data supporting any causal link between EI and any of its supposed, positive effects.

To summarize: despite the important role attributed to a wide array of emotional competencies in the workplace, there is currently only a modicum of research supporting the meaningful role attributed to EI (and nested emotional competencies) in determining occupational success. Many of the popular claims presented in the literature regarding the role of EI in determining work success and well-being are rather misleading in that they seem to present scientific studies supporting their claims, while in fact failing to do so. In short, despite some rather fantastic claims to the contrary, the guiding principle appears at present to be *caveat emptor*.

Furthermore, judging by previous reviews (Zeidner *et al.*, in press), there are no convincing empirical data supporting the use of EI measures for purposes of occupational and career assessment. To the best of our knowledge, there is no replicated research, published in peer-review journals, that has reliably demonstrated that EI measures add meaningful incremental variance to the prediction of occupational criteria. That is, EI does not appear to possess incremental validity above (and beyond) that predicted by conventional ability and personality measures. Furthermore, because there is no hard evidence showing that EI bears a differential pattern of validity for various occupational groupings, there is little psychometric justification for their use in specific occupational contexts.

EI and coping with occupational stress
Proponents of EI often see effective coping with stress as central to EI. In fact, current thinking among EI researchers (for example, Salovey *et al.*, 1999) suggests that the way people identify, understand, regulate and repair emotions (in self and others) helps determine coping behaviors and consequent adaptive outcomes.

Coping is a multidimensional construct that has traditionally been defined in the stress literature as the process of managing the external/internal demands that are appraised as taxing or exceeding a person's resources (Lazarus and Folkman, 1984). However some EI researchers have argued that it is not just these demands that a person needs to cope with in a stressful encounter, but rather the emotions evoked by the demands with which a person actually needs to cope. Furthermore, Salovey *et al.* (1999) claim that more emotionally intelligent individuals cope more successfully, because they 'accurately perceive and appraise their emotional states, know how and when to express their feelings, and can effectively regulate their mood states' (p. 161). Similarly Bar-On (1997) includes 'stress management' and 'adaptability' as two major components of EI. Thus some researchers consider stress management and adaptive coping as a major component of EI (for example, Bar-On, 1997). Others (for example, Epstein, 1998; Salovey *et al.*, 1999), however, view EI as a personal antecedent of adaptive coping, working through various causal factors in determining adaptive coping (which we discuss below).

EI researchers (for example, Goleman, 1995; Salovey *et al.*, 1999) would readily embrace the notion of adaptive coping as 'emotional intelligence in action,' supporting mastery of emotions, emotional growth and both cognitive and emotional differentiation, allowing us to evolve in an ever-changing world. Current thinking in the EI literature (Epstein, 1998; Salovey *et al.*, 1999), supported only by a sparse amount of systematic empirical research, points to a number of reasons why emotionally intelligent individuals would be expected to experience less stress. These theorists would also claim that emotionally intelligent individuals cope more adaptively once stress is experienced.

Before discussing the specific role of EI in coping with occupational stress, it would be useful to review briefly the concept of occupational stress. Thus, following a brief overview, we point out some major sources of occupational stress and discuss how individuals cope with this prevalent form of stress.

Mediating factors in the EI–coping with stress relationship
EI may work through a host of personal variables (coping resources, constructive appraisals, effective emotion regulation, effective social skills, flexible coping strategies) to make an impact upon adaptive coping in the workplace. EI researchers claim that successful coping depends on the integrated operation of rational as well as emotional

competencies (Salovey et al., 2000). Accordingly the entire hierarchy of emotional skills (that is, basic perceptual and expressive skills, emotional knowledge and regulation of emotions) must be developed and employed for successful regulation of emotion and coping to take place. According to these researchers, major deficiencies in basic emotional competencies will interfere with the development and implementation of more complex coping. Thus a person who finds it difficult to identify or express her emotions may also find it difficult to seek emotional social support or ventilate feelings.

We turn now to delineate purported mediating mechanisms in the claimed EI–coping relationship appearing in the EI literature.

Avoidance of stressful encounters Emotionally intelligent persons, it is claimed, may create a less stressful environment for themselves by conducting their personal and social lives in ways that produce fewer frustrating or distressing events (Epstein, 1998). Because high EI individuals would not get themselves into stressful situations at the worksite to begin with (for example, agreeing to lead a project doomed to fail), they would not need to deploy as many adaptive resources in coping with stress in their lives. Furthermore emotionally intelligent individuals, it is claimed, may be good at identifying and thus avoiding potentially dangerous or harmful social contexts, owing to more careful and effective monitoring of the emotional cues in social situations (cf. Epstein, 1998). At present, however, there is no hard empirical evidence to support this claim. In addition adaptive success may require engaging with and successfully managing aversive environments. Studies of social anxiety suggest that avoidance of stressful circumstances undermines self-confidence and hinders the acquisition of social skills (Wells, 2000). However even highly emotionally intelligent individuals may not always find it possible to avoid stressful situations.

Richer coping resources Emotionally intelligent individuals, it is claimed, may have richer emotional and social personal coping resources than their less emotionally intelligent counterparts (cf. Epstein, 1998; Salovey et al., 1999). Thus, when emotionally intelligent individuals compare the demands of a stressful encounter at work vis-à-vis their perceived resources and competencies, they tend to assess the encounter as intrinsically less stressful. In particular EI has been hypothesized to work through the social resource of perceived social support in determining adaptive coping (Salovey et al., 1999). Accordingly EI has been claimed to equip the individual with the necessary social skills required to build a solid and supportive social network. Thus individuals high in EI are said to be more likely to have developed adequate social skills, to be better connected socially, and to have greater access to a wide network of social support. Social support at the worksite is then obtained and utilized effectively in times of need, with emotionally intelligent individuals better able to rely on rich social networks to provide them with an emotional buffer against negative life events (Salovey et al., 2000). Hard evidence for the importance of personal resources in mediating the EI–coping interface at work is sparse and in further need of empirical instantiation.

Greater self-efficacy for emotion regulation Persons high in EI, it is claimed, have a greater sense of self-efficacy with respect to regulation of emotions (Salovey et al., 2001).

That is, they believe they have the wherewithal to employ the strategies necessary to repair negative moods following a stressful or traumatic encounter at the worksite, as well as to elicit and maintain positive moods when appropriate. Moreover high self-efficacy is claimed to work through coping strategies to affect outcomes (ibid.). According to this hypothesis, individuals who can clearly perceive their feelings and believe they can repair negative moods turn their attentional resources towards coping and minimize the potentially deleterious impact of stressful events. It is further claimed that the optimistic belief system and constructive thinking patterns of high EI individuals allow them to take on challenges and risks. This follows from the fact they have confidence that things will work out well, and cope instrumentally and adaptively with stressful encounters (Epstein, 1998). Overall there is very little evidence for the above claims and further work is needed to support the purported role of self-efficacy as a mediating variable in the EI–coping relationship, and to show that EI adds anything to existing self-efficacy constructs at the workplace (for example, Bandura, 1997).

More constructive perceptions and situational appraisals   Emotionally intelligent individuals, it is claimed, are characterized by more constructive thought patterns and find it easier to catch and to identify faulty appraisals and correct maladaptive construals (Epstein, 1998). It is said that high EI individuals become aware of their mental responses and the strong influence their cognitions have on their feelings. Therefore they tend to tune in more readily to their stream of consciousness and more faithfully observe the procession of their thoughts. Furthermore high EI individuals tend to interpret stressful conditions at work, if unavoidable, in a more benign and less stressful way, viewing them more as challenges than as threats (cf. Epstein, 1998). It has been further claimed, but not firmly substantiated, that individuals who can make sense out of their feelings show greater rebound from induced negative mood and increased decline in rumination compared to those lower in clarity (Salovey, Stroud *et al.*, in press). Notwithstanding claims in the EI literature, there is very little evidence in support of these claims and the role of appraisals in mediating the EI–coping relationship has not been firmly established and is presently a hypothesis in need of future testing and research.

Adaptive regulation and repairing of emotions   Clarity of emotions and repair of emotions, essential components of EI, are claimed to be essential ingredients for adaptive coping with stress (Salovey *et al.*, 2000). Furthermore high EI individuals are believed to be good emotional copers: not taking minor routine hassles to heart (Epstein, 1998). They are said to be calm, 'centered' and characterized by peace of mind, more effective in dealing with negative feeling and to experience less stress in living than others. In particular they are claimed not to take things personally, are not overly sensitive to disapproval or failure, and do not worry about things that are beyond control (ibid.). Those skilled at regulating their emotions following a stressful encounter at work should be better able to repair their negative emotional states, by engaging in sports, self-help pep talks or pleasant activities as a distraction from negative affect. Strategies that actively manage mood, such as using relaxation techniques and engaging in pleasant activities, appear to be more successful than more passive strategies such as resting or taking drugs or alcohol (Thayer, 1996). Here again future research is needed to investigate whether measures of EI are associated with the use of more effective mood-management strategies.

Emotional skills Emotionally intelligent individuals are claimed to have certain emotional skills that allow them to disclose effectively their past personal traumas at work (Salovey *et al.*, 1999). Research surveyed by Pennebaker (1997) shows that the simple act of disclosing emotional experience in writing improves a person's physical and mental health, including improvement of immune functioning, decreased depression, improved grades in college students and reduced symptoms. 'Cognitive housekeeping' and the disclosure process restructures disturbing experiences, giving them a coherent and meaningful place in the person's life. Emotionally intelligent individuals, it is claimed, are able to strike a healthy balance between pleasant distractions from aversive events and coming to terms with their mood (Salovey *et al.*, 2000). Furthermore high EI individuals can engage reflectively or detach themselves from emotions, depending on utility. Being more adept at directing their thoughts away from negative emotions, they are hypothesized to engage less in dysfunctional worry and excessive rumination. Although the evidence suggests that emotional closure is indeed salutary to one's mental and physical health (Pennebaker, 1997), little research substantiates the proposed nexus of relations between EI, emotional skills (for example, emotional disclosure, handling worry) and effective coping.

Use of effective coping strategies EI researchers claim that emotionally intelligent individuals engage in more active coping responses to stressful occupational situations, whereas those low in emotional intelligence tend to opt for less adaptive emotion-focused or avoidance responses in stressful situations. Thus emotionally intelligent people are said to cope more efficiently with situations at work or elsewhere once they have interpreted them as stressful (Epstein, 1998). Problem-focused coping has been associated with the competencies clearly to perceive, differentiate and repair one's emotions. According to this line of reasoning, people need to perceive their feelings clearly in a stressful situation and believe they are capable of managing their emotions in order for them to cope adaptively.

Competence and flexibility in coping EI might relate both to availability of more effective coping strategies and to more flexible, adaptive selection from among the person's repertoire of strategies. Recent research (Endler *et al.*, 2000) has highlighted the importance of matching coping facets to situational demands. Thus high EI individuals should be able to cope more flexibly and less stereotypically by optimally fitting coping patterns to the cognitive and perceptual styles of the self, as well as the constraints and affordances of the worksite. A body of research (Zeidner and Saklofske, 1996) suggests that, in controllable situations, active and problem-focused coping is more effective and adaptive, whereas, when stressors are uncontrollable, emotion-focused coping may be the only available and feasible coping response. Thus individuals high in EI would be expected to employ problem-focused coping strategies when something can be done to alter the situation. They would also appear to prefer to use emotion-focused coping strategies when there is little that can be done to change the stressful circumstances. High EI is also claimed to lead to more effective emotion regulation which, in turn, leads to less rumination and preoccupation, along with greater clarity and organization of emotions (Salovey et al., 1999).

It is evident that the scope of individual differences in coping linked to EI is very broad. Some of the mediating mechanisms (for example, adaptive regulation and availability of emotional skills) refer directly to coping with emotion itself. Other mechanisms, such as managing exposure to stressors, and more constructive appraisal and coping, are more likely to influence emotion indirectly, depending on the outcome of the encounter. It is uncertain which of these various mechanisms should relate to EI and which to other personality and ability factors, reflecting the conceptual weaknesses of EI described elsewhere (Matthews et al., 2002; Zeidner et al., 2001).

Empirical research

A major weakness in the EI literature is the lack of systematic *empirical* work substantiating the claim that EI plays a pivotal role in adaptive coping in general and at the workplace in particular. Although several causal mechanisms have been proposed to explain the purported link between EI and coping, very few data exist on the magnitude of the relationship between EI and coping. Such evidence as there is suggests a rather modest link and yet authors are prone to taking for granted that EI may be identified with adaptive coping. Furthermore, even assuming that the evidence for a substantial association between EI and coping is forthcoming, there is little evidence for most of the claimed causal mechanisms.

Bar-On (1997) reports that the EQ-i self-report measure correlates moderately with high task-focused coping and low emotion-focused coping. Specifically, Bar-On reports low to moderate positive correlations between EI and problem-focused coping, low to moderate negative correlations between EI and emotion-focused coping, and negligible correlations with avoidance coping. These trends were substantiated by a Lisrel analysis. However, exactly this result would be expected, based on the high correlation between EQ-i and neuroticism, which is similarly related to coping (Endler and Parker, 1990, 1999). Discriminant validity has not been established.

Ciarrochi, Chan and Bajgar (2000) report a study of the Schutte et al. (1998) EI scale in adolescents, that did not address stress directly, but provided some mixed findings. On the positive side, EI was related to perceived social support. The authors also found that a subscale of the EI measure, 'Managing Self-Relevant Emotions', related to emotional content in stories generated by participants, depending on the type of mood previously induced, an effect attributed to use of mood-regulation strategies such as mood repair (negative mood induction) and mood maintenance (positive induction). On the negative side, EI failed to moderate emotional response to negative and positive mood inductions used in the study, so the mood management strategies attributed to EI did not appear to be effective in regulating mood in this context. Results of studies using the Multifactor Emotional Intelligence Scale (MEIS) have been somewhat confusing. Ciarrochi, Chan and Caputi (2000) suggest that the MEIS indexes individual differences in mood management, but the evidence for this claim is somewhat indirect, and EI had no effect on negative mood response.

A recent unpublished study conducted at the University of Cincinnati represents the only study to date to link the MSCEIT to coping and subjective stress response. A sample of 199 college students completed six of the subtests of the MSCEIT (Mayer et al., 2001) submitted, with two subtests each for the Perception, Understanding and Management branches. A principal axis factor analysis identified a general factor explaining 40 per cent of the variance, which was used as an estimate of EI. Participants were then randomly allocated to one of four conditions, a control condition (reading magazines), or one of three stress conditions validated in previous research (for example, Matthews et al., 1999). The stress conditions were intended to elicit fatigue (vigilance task), overload of attention (time-pressured working memory task) or personal failure (impossible nine-letter anagrams). The Dundee Stress State Questionnaire (DSSQ) (Matthews et al., 1999), was administered before and after performance. Results confirmed that the three conditions induced different patterns of subjective stress response, including, in all three conditions, increases in distress of >1 SD, relative to the control condition. After performance, participants completed the Assessment of Life Events scale (ALE) (Ferguson et al., 1999), as a measure of situational threat and challenge appraisal. They also completed the Coping in Task Situations (CITS) questionnaire (Matthews and Campbell, 1998), which assesses use of task-focused, emotion-focused and avoidance strategies in performance settings.

The literature suggests that adaptive coping with occupational stress should lead to positive outcomes, such as heightened job satisfaction, fewer psychosomatic symptoms and decreased anxiety (Latack, 1986). Thus emotional intelligence, which is purportedly related to adaptive coping with stressful situations, should affect positive job outcomes. At present we have no evidence suggesting that coping moderates the effect of stress on job performance.

Summary and conclusions
Overall relatively few studies have addressed employees' efforts to cope with the stress of the workplace and the literature is relatively silent about the ways that employees cope with transitions in the workplace. Furthermore the implications of current research on coping in occupational settings for the role of emotional intelligence are complex (see Matthews et al., 2002). On one hand, theory would suggest that individuals high in emotional intelligence would show a preference for problem-focused over other forms of coping when something can be done to alter the source of stress. However, when little can be done to alter the source of stress, emotion-focused coping should be the most adaptive. Unfortunately there is no published research that bears this out, and further research is needed to test these hypotheses. On the other hand, given the research that suggests that individual coping efforts are not very effective in making a difference at the workplace (see Matthews et al., 2002, for a review), it is highly questionable to what extent coping strategies would be helpful to those emotionally intelligent individuals who apply them.

Overall the role of emotional intelligence in affecting the effectiveness of macro-level interventions would be expected to be minimal. Furthermore there are no peer-reviewed studies in the literature, to our knowledge, that systematically look at the relationship between emotional intelligence, coping and adaptive outcomes in specific occupational settings. Thus we are in urgent need of studies which enable people to report events, or stressful encounters that are important to them in specific occupational sites, how they cope with them and the role of emotional intelligence in coping with occupational stress.

Furthermore, as we pointed out in our review of the EI literature (Matthews et al., 2002), reviews of EI stress reduction programs at work often include, under the rubric of EI interventions and coping with stress programs, worksite programs which have existed and been in place for some time in the past (increasing self-efficacy and work motivation, sensitivity training, human relations and so on). The success of these commonplace and longstanding programs is inappropriately taken as effectiveness of EI programs. At present the effectiveness of EI-based training programs remains unclear.

EI should be conceptualized as an *aptitude* for handling challenging situations, as opposed to an *outcome* variable, that is the successful resolution of emotional challenges. The aptitude increases the likelihood of a successful outcome, but it does not guarantee it, because outcome also depends on situational factors. Furthermore it is important to note that, for EI to have explanatory power, it must be distinguished from stress outcomes, as an aptitude or competencies that controls whether or not a person handles demanding events successfully. In other words, a person's EI should not just tell us about their propensity to experience stress symptoms: it should tell us something about the underlying causes of stress vulnerability and we should be able to measure these causal factors independently of assessments of distress. For example, if the key to emotional intelligence is good self-control (Goleman, 1995), we should be able to assess the person's self-control under non-stressful conditions, and show that self-control predicts lower distress when the person is under pressure.

A major weakness of the expanding body of research on coping with stress and EI is that it tends to neglect the extensive and well-established literature on stress and coping. As discussed by Matthews et al., 2002, we can already measure the person's vulnerability to stress symptoms such as negative emotion and worry with a high degree of validity, by using existing personality scales. The danger, then, is that, in the field of stress, EI research is simply reinventing the wheel in relabeling extant stress vulnerability constructs as 'emotional intelligence.' Alternatively existing stress research may actually have missed something important about individual differences, which is captured by the notion of EI. Given the dearth of empirical work, it becomes important to look at whether the concept of EI as a master faculty for adaptive coping is compatible with existing stress theory.

Note

Mayer et al. (1999) see this construct as a 'shadow variable', one that mimics EI in several respects, but that seems conceptually and ontologically distinct.

References

Ashford, S.J. (1988), 'Individual strategies for coping with stress', *Journal of Applied Behavioral Science*, **24**, 19–36.
Bandura, A. (1997), *Self-efficacy: The exercise of control*, New York: W.H. Freeman & Co.
Bar-On, R. (1997), *EQi: Bar-On Emotional Quotient Inventory*, Toronto: Multi-Health Systems.
Bar-On, R. (2000), 'Emotional and social intelligence: insights from the Emotional Quotient Inventory', in R. Bar-On and J.D.A. Parker (eds), *The Handbook of Emotional Intelligence*, San Francisco: Jossey-Bass, pp. 363–88.
Beehr, T.A. and J.E. Newman (1978), 'Job stress, employee health and organizational effectiveness: a facet analysis, model, and literature review', *Personnel Psychology*, **31**, 665–99.
Boyatzis, R. (1982), *The Competent Manager*, New York: Wiley & Sons.
Boyatzis, R., D. Goleman and K. Rhee (2000), 'Clustering competence in emotional intelligence: insights from the emotional competence inventory', in R. Bar-On and J.D.A. Parker (eds), *The Handbook of Emotional Intelligence*, San Francisco: Jossey-Bass.

Caplan, R.D. and K.W. Jones (1975), 'Effects of work load, role ambiguity, and type A personality on anxiety, depression and heart rate', *Journal of Applied Psychology*, **60**, 713–19.
Caplan, R.D., S. Cobb, J.R.P.J. French, R.V. Harrison and S.R.J.R. Pinneau (1975), *Job Demands and Worker Health*, Washington, DC: US Government Office.
Cartwright, S. and C.L. Cooper (1996), 'Coping in occupational settings', in M. Zeidner and N.S. Endler (eds), *Handbook of Coping*, New York: Wiley, pp. 202–20.
Cherniss, C. and D. Goleman (2001), 'Training for emotional intelligence: a model', in C. Cherniss and D. Goleman (eds), *The Emotionally Intelligent Workplace*, San Francisco: Jossey-Bass, pp.209–33.
Ciarrochi, J., A. Chan and J. Bajgar (2000), 'Measuring emotional intelligence in adolescents', manuscript submitted for publication.
Ciarrochi, J., A. Chan and P. Caputi (2000), 'A critical evaluation of the emotional intelligence construct', *Personality and Individual Differences*, **28**, 539–61.
Cooper, C.L. and M. Kelley (1993), 'Occupational stress in head teachers: a national UK study', *British Journal of Educational Psychology*, **63**, 130–43.
Cooper, C.L. and J. Marshall (1978), 'Sources of managerial and white collar stress', in C.L. Cooper and R. Payne (eds), *Stress at Work*, Chichester: Wiley, pp. 81–105.
Cooper, R.K. (1997), 'Applying emotional intelligence in the workplace', *Training and Development*, **51**, 31–3.
Cooper, R.K. and A. Sawaf (1997), 'Executive EQ: emotional intelligence in leaders and organizations', New York: Grosset/Putnam.
Elkin, A.J. and P.J. Rosch (1990), 'Promoting mental health at the workplace: the prevention side of stress management', *Occupational Medicine: State of the Art Review*, **5**, 739–54.
Endler, N. and J. Parker (1990), 'Multidimensional assessment of coping: a critical review', *Journal of Personality and Social Psychology*, **58**, 844–54.
Endler, N. and J. Parker (1999), *The Coping Inventory for Stressful Situations (CISS)*, 2nd edn, Toronto: Multi-health System.
Endler, N.S., R.L. Speer, J.M. Johnson and G. Flett (2000), 'Controllability, coping, efficacy and distress', *European Journal of Personality*, **14**, 245–64.
Epstein, S. (1998), *Constructive Thinking: The Key to Emotional Intelligence*, New York: Praeger.
Ferguson, E., G. Matthews and T. Cox (1999), 'The Appraisal of Life Events (ALE) scale: reliability and validity', *British Journal of Health Psychology*, **4**, 97–116.
Folkman, S. and R.S. Lazarus (1980), 'An analysis of coping in a middle-aged community sample', *Journal of Health and Social Behavior*, **21**, 219–39.
French, J.R.P. and R.D. Caplan (1973), 'Organizational stress and individual strain', in A.J. Marrow (ed.), *The Failure of Success*, New York: AMAC Com, pp. 30–36.
Gibbs, N. (1995), 'What's your EQ?', *Time*, 2 October, pp.60–68.
Gladstein, D.L. and N.P. Reilly (1985), 'Group decision making under threat: the tycoon game', *Academy of Management Journal*, **28**, 613–27.
Gmelch, W., J. Koch, B. Swent and R. Tung (1982), 'What stresses school administrators and how they cope', paper presented at the AERA, New York, March.
Goleman, D. (1995), *Emotional Intelligence: Why it Can Matter More than IQ*, New York: Bantam Books.
Goleman, D. (1998), *Working with Emotional Intelligence*, New York: Bantam Books.
Golembiewski, R.T. and R.F. Munzenrider (1988), *Phases of Burnout: Developments in Concepts and Applications*, New York: Praeger.
Hammer, W.C. and H.L. Tosi (1974), 'Relationship of role conflict and role ambiguity to job involvement measures', *Journal of Applied Psychology*, **59**, 497–9.
Hay Group (2000), 'Emotional intelligence: a "soft" skill with a hard edge' (<http://ei.haygroup.com/about_ei/>).
House, J.S. (1981), *Work Stress and Social Support*, Reading, MA: Addison-Wesley.
Huy, Q.N. (1999), 'Emotional capability, emotional intelligence and radical change', *Academy of Management Review*, **24**, 325–45.
Jordan, P.J., N.M. Ashkanasy and C.E.J. Hartel (in press), 'Emotional intelligence as a moderator of emotional and behavioral reactions to job insecurity', *Academy of Management Review*.
Kahn, R.L., D.M. Wolfe, R.P. Quinn, J.D. Snoek and R.A. Rosenthal (1964), *Organizational Stress: Studies in Role Conflict and Ambiguity*, New York: Wiley.
Karasek, R. (1989), 'Control in the workplace and its health-related aspects', in S.L. Sauter, J.J. Hurrell and C.L. Cooper (eds), *Job Control and Worker Health*, Chichester: Wiley.
Karasek, R. and T. Theorell (1990), *Healthy work: Stress Productivity and the Reconstruction of Working Life*, New York: Wiley.

Katz, D. and R.L. Kahn (1978), *The Social Psychology of Organizations*, New York: Wiley.
Kottkamp, R.B. and A.L. Travlos (1986), 'Selected job stressors, emotional exhaustion, job satisfaction, and thrust behavior of the high school principal', *The Alberta Journal of Educational Research*, **32**, 234–48.
Kruglanski, A. and Y. Jaffe (1988), 'Curing by knowing: the epistemic approach to cognitive therapy', in L.Y. Abramson (ed.), *Social Cognition and Clinical Psychology: A Synthesis*, New York: The Guilford Press, pp. 254–291.
La Rocco, J.M. and A.P. Jones (1978), 'Co-worker and leader support as moderators of stress–strain relationships in work situations', *Journal of Applied Psychology*, **63**, 629–34.
Latack, J.C. (1986), 'Coping with job stress: measures and future directions for scale development', *Journal of Applied Psychology*, **71**, 377–85.
Lazarus, R. and S. Folkman (1984), *Stress, Appraisal and Coping*, New York: Springer.
Mack, D.A., D.L. Nelson and J.C. Quick (1998), 'The stress of oganisational change: a dynamic process model', *Applied Psychology: An International Review*, **47**, 219–32.
Matthews, G. and S.E. Campbell (1998), 'Task-induced stress and individual differences in coping', *Proceedings of the 42nd Annual Meeting of the Human Factors and Ergonomics Society*, Santa Monica, CA: HFES, pp. 821–5.
Matthews, G., M. Zeidner and R. Roberts (2002), *Emotional Intelligence: Science and Myth*, Cambridge: MIT.
Matthews, G., L. Joyner, K. Gilliland, S.E. Campbell, J. Huggins and S. Falconer (1999), 'Validation of a comprehensive stress state questionnaire: towards a state "Big Three"?', in I. Mervielde, I.J. Deary, F. De Fruyt and F. Ostendorf (eds), *Personality Psychology in Europe,* vol. 7, Tilburg: Tilburg University Press, pp. 335–50.
Mayer, J.D. and P. Salovey (1993), 'The intelligence of emotional intelligence', *Intelligence*, **17**, 433–42.
Mayer, J.D. and P. Salovey (1997), 'What is emotional intelligence?', in P. Salovey and D. Sluyter (eds), *Emotional Development and Emotional Intelligence*, New York: Basic Books, pp. 3–31.
Mayer, J.D., D. Caruso and P. Salovey (1999), 'Emotional intelligence meets traditional standards for an intelligence', *Intelligence*, **27**, 267–98.
Mayer, J.D., P. Salovey, D.R. Caruso and G. Sitarenios (2001), 'Emotional intelligence as a standard intelligence', *Emotion*, **1**, 232–42.
Mossholder, K.W., R.P. Settoon, A.A. Armenakis and S.G. Harris (2000), 'Emotion during organizational transformations: an interactive model of survivor reactions', *Group and Organization Management*, **25**, 220–43.
Newman, J.E. and T.A. Beehr (1979), 'Personal and organizational strategies for handling job stress: a review of research and opinion', *Personnel Psychology*, **32**, 1–43.
Nguyen Huy, Q. (1999), 'Emotional capability, emotional intelligence and radical change', *The Academy of Management Review*, **24**, 325–45.
O'Driscoll, M.P. and C.L. Cooper (1994), 'Coping with work-related stress: a critique of existing measures and proposal for an alternative methodology', *Journal of Occupational and Organizational Psychology*, **67**, 343–54.
Pearlin, L.I. and C. Schooler (1978), 'The structure of coping', *Journal of Health and Social Behavior*, **19**, 2–21.
Pennebaker, J.W. (1997), 'Writing about emotional experiences as a therapeutic process', *Psychological Science*, **8**, 162–6.
Salovey, P. and J.D. Mayer (1990), 'Emotional intelligence', *Imagination, Cognition & Personality*, **9**, 185–211.
Salovey, P., A. Woolery and J.D. Mayer (2001), 'Emotional intelligence: conceptualization and measurement', in G. Fletcher and M.S. Clark (eds), *The Blackwell Handbook of Social Psychology (Volume 2: Interpersonal Processes)*. Oxford: Blackwell Publishers.
Salovey, P., B.T. Bedell, J.B. Detweiler and J.D. Mayer (1999), 'Coping intelligently: emotional intelligence and the coping process', in C.R. Snyder (ed.), *Coping: The Psychology of What Works*, New York: Oxford University Press, pp. 141–64.
Salovey, P., B.T. Bedell, J.B. Detweiler and J.D. Mayer (2000), 'Current directions in emotional intelligence research', in M. Lewis and J.M. Haviland-Jones (eds), *Handbook of Emotions*, New York: Guilford Press.
Schaubroeck, J. and J.R. Jones (2000), 'Antecedents of workplace emotional labor dimensions and moderators of their effects on physical symptoms', *Journal of Organizational Behavior*, **21**, 163–83.
Schuler, R.S. (1980), 'Definition and conceptualization of stress in organizations', *Organizational Behavior and Human Performance*, **25**, 184–215.
Schutte, N.S., J.M. Malouff, L.E. Hall, D.J. Haggerty, J.T. Cooper, C.J. Golden and L. Dornhein (1998), 'Development and validation of a measure of emotional intelligence', *Personality and Individual Differences*, **25**, 167–77.
Schwartz, J.E. and A.A. Stone (1993), 'Coping with daily work problems: contributions of problem content, appraisals and person factors', *Work and Stress*, **7**, 47–62.
Shinn, M., M. Rosario, H. Morch and D.E. Chesnut (1984), 'Coping with job stress and burnout in the human services', *Journal of Personality and Social Psychology*, 864–76.

Sjoberg, L. (2001), 'Emotional intelligence: a psychometric analysis', *European Psychologist*, **6**, 79–95.
Thayer, R.E. (1996), *The Origin of Everyday Moods: Managing Energy, Tension and Stress*, New York: Oxford University Press.
Watkin, C. (2000), 'Developing emotional intelligence', *International Journal of Selection and Assessment*, **2**, 89–92.
Weisinger, H. (1998), *Emotional Intelligence at Work: The Untapped Edge for Success*, San Francisco: Jossey-Bass.
Wells, A. (2000), *Emotional Disorders and Metacognition: Innovative Cognitive Therapy*, Chichester: Wiley.
Westman, M. and D. Eden (1988), 'Job stress and subsequent objective performance', working paper no. 963/88.
Williams, W.M. and R.J. Sternberg (1988), 'Group intelligence: why some groups are better than others', *Intelligence*, **12**, 351–77.
Zeidner, M. (1998), *Test Anxiety: The State of the Art*, New York: Plenum.
Zeidner, M. and D. Saklofske (1996), 'Adaptive and maladaptive coping', in M. Zeidner and N.S. Endler (eds), *Handbook of Coping: Theory, Research, Applications*, New York: John Wiley & Sons, pp. 505–31.
Zeidner, M., G.M. Matthews and R. Roberts (2001), 'Slow down, you move too fast: emotional intelligence remains an "elusive" intelligence', *Emotions*, **1**, 265–75.
Zeidner, M. and R. Roberts (in press), 'Emotional intelligence in the workplace: a crtical review', *Applied Psychology: An International Review*.
Zeidner, M., R. Roberts and G. Matthews (2002), 'Can emotional intelligence be schooled? A critical review', *Educational Psychologist*, **37**, 215–31.

PART III

STRESS IN SPECIFIC GROUPS

17 Study and student counselling in higher education: an incentive towards a practice-relevant vision
Eric Depreeuw

Quality: an economic as well as a human reality
The fact that there have been and still are going on some drastic structural and functional changes in European higher education has been discussed and analysed sufficiently elsewhere. One policy aspect was (and still is) aimed at increasing the scale of the institutions. Another point on the agenda is to promote transparancy and flexibility in higher education, concretized in the so-called 'declaration of Bologna'. It would not be exaggerated to claim that this has had its effect, comparable to a myriad of 'explosions' in what used to be calm waters. The intermittent shocks have not left anything unaffected, setting everything in motion, including the familiar boundaries and structures. These commotions and profound changes require an adaptation process but at the same time they provoke resistance and put, at least temporarily, most of those involved under uncomfortable pressure.

Parallel to these structural changes, another basic evolution can be felt, the societal position of the educational institutions. Fast and thorough changes characterize the world in the new millennium. Each society must, if it does not want to be pushed aside, become 'constantly learning'. The result is the call, even the demand, for schools to abandon their 'educational' approach and reform themselves towards 'learning' organizations (Boekaerts, 1999). School culture has been shaken by the (non-academic) economic approach which does not limit itself to a more stringent financial responsibility, but also concerns the field of education as such and, in doing so, handles non-scientific or didactic terms like 'input', 'output', 'added value', 'flexibility' and 'total quality management'.

Still we know that transitional periods should not always be considered as negative. Predominantly they are a sign of overt or slumbering instabilities and consequently offer chances for renewal, for improvement. An increased concern about the quality of education seems such an opportunity. Rightly the lecturers and the students are the primary agents at the micro level. They should, more than before and disregarding their basic discipline, constantly take further training leading to more professional lecturing. It is almost impossible to keep track of the initiatives and publications in this field (cf. McKeachie, 1994; Boekaerts, 1999). The lecturer has to teach in different ways because the student needs to learn how to study and this too deserves special attention and support (Archer and Scevak, 1998).

Quality improvement at student level: a different point of view
In light of what has been said above, the following question urges itself upon us: does there exist in higher education a need for other forms of study and student counselling apart from the academic contribution from the lecturer? Thanks to the increase in scale, but also under a strong societal pressure, the institutions are forced to consider the question whether the

establishment of additional services is relevant in any way, and, if it is, how this should be filled in concretely. Traditionally the institutions of higher education in general and the universities in particular are almost exclusively oriented towards rationality. Education and research are pre-eminently considered cognitive matters, which do not require or attract attention for any non-rational matter. Still some will stress that higher education also has a responsibility and a duty where the social, cultural and educational formation of its students is concerned. In practice, quite a number of initiatives in this direction have been taken. It is striking that, in the US as well as in Europe, an impressive number of services for extracurricular counselling of students has been set up. Stone and Archer (1990) mention the typology of counselling centres, developed by Whiteley, Mahaffey and Gees, based on the responses of 963 four-year American institutions of higher education, 93.4 per cent of which offer one or another form of student counselling. At the same time their attention was drawn to the diversity of these services, which vary from a strict minimum (15 per cent) to an exclusively psychological approach (29 per cent), on to what they call 'macro-centres' (21 per cent) in which attention is given to different aspects of study, that is career guidance and training of certain skills, alongside psychological care. In Europe too, many services exist and here too, the diversity is striking (Bell et al., 1994). Similarly there is a stronger development in Northern Europe than in Southern Europe, but the diversity of institutions in one and the same region is just as considerable.

Another striking conclusion is that some of these centres are very secure while others are marginal and are sometimes even permanently threatened in their existence. Bell et al. (1994) formulate this as follows: 'Psychological counselling is a poorly recognised profession and its role is not easily understood as a necessary or useful adjunct to the educational process.' According to these authors a large number of these centres were set up in times of economic expansion, as a sort of luxurious giveaway to the students. However recent evolutions in Europe and America are such that financial limits are imposed in this department too, despite the fact that almost all centres for student counselling point out that there has been a substantial increase of all sorts of problems within the student population over recent years and that there is also an increasing tendency towards more serious pathologies (Grayson and Cauley, 1989; Stone and Archer, 1990; Bell, 1996; Bell et al., 1994; Clara, 1997; Hirsch, 2001).

Research by Henderson (1996) indicates that the number of first-year college students reporting themselves as having an educational, social or psychological disability increased from 7 per cent in 1988 to 9 per cent in 1995. The Royal College of Psychiatrists of the UK (2003) concludes in its report that there are no reliable research data demonstrating that the incidence of mental health problems among students has been increasing over the last decade. However, all over the UK, mental health services report an increase, not only in the number of students presenting to them, but also in the severity of the problems. The authors stress that students with mental health problems and disorders are a disadvantaged population, deserving special attention and help.

An attempt at identification of study and student counselling
The current educational culture in higher education, the limited financial resources and the absence of a clear and unequivocal identity of these services for study and student counselling do not make it easier to develop an optimal policy for further development,

let alone to decide which services will or will not be offered. However we find in our own practical experience as well as in reliable publications sufficient inspiration to come to a useful synthesis which we hope will give a framework for discussions on reasonable policy making and on the development of practical projects. In our opinion, study and student counselling moves dynamically in two directions: that of the academic context and that of the individual psychosocial reality of the student. It will have to realize its added values to the advantage of the student as well as to the advantage of the educational institution. We will try to clarify this synthesis further.

The proposition of Kiracofe et al. (1994) throws light on an essential point of view: 'a counselling center must be an integral part of the educational mission of the institution and support it in a variety of ways'. Knigge-Illner (1994) differentiates and characterizes the point of view of the study counsellor as an orientation towards the subjective difficulties of students concerning study and professional orientation, exams, retakes and dropping out (study-related problems and study context problem solving). The circumstances in which these problems arise are situated in the interaction between the individual dispositions of the students and the structural characteristics of the educational institution concerned (at meso level and macro level). The psychological counselling links up quite well with the academic reality but is explicitly aimed at the promotion of emancipation and critical sensitization; counselling and therapy are specific variations within this sole formation process of higher education. As a result of the conference of European 'student counsellors' Rott (1991) tries, not without difficulty, to distil some mutual characteristics from the internal discussions. First of all, he concludes that 'student counsellors' do not concentrate on 'what' students study, but 'how' they do it. The individual acquisition of knowledge and its personal integration are closely linked to subjective experiences which can work (dis)functionally. We are thinking of (de)motivation, (pathological) postponing, fear and more serious personality distortions, among other things. Rott goes on to say that the European student counsellor is concerned about the improvement of the information flow between macro, meso and micro level (cf. study and professional orientation or international exchange programmes). Finally this function contains a peculiar and positive appreciation of the individuality of and (cultural) diversity between students as a source of energy in their development towards autonomy.

Bell et al. (1994) and Hirsch (2001), on the other hand, underline the attention of the student counsellor to psychological and emotional well-being in connection with the developmental psychological stage of the student. Adolescence starts earlier and comes to completion in a normal way, at the somatic level, but psychosocial adulthood (to fill in stable relational and professional roles) is often postponed in a disturbing, and sometimes even disruptive manner (Adams et al., 1992). Meanwhile, quite a number of students find themselves in a new social environment, different from their own families, with different insights and lifestyles. In the environment of higher education, students are expected to take a stand concerning (implicit) values, such as achievement pressure and competition, and repeatedly far-reaching choices have to be made at study level as well as personal level. Specific, to the Belgian situation at least, is that students remain financially dependent. The continued effect from late adolescence in this typical setting of higher education can become more complicated through transitory or permanent individual vulnerabilities (Grayson and Cauley, 1989; Hirsch, 2001). Quite often the student is confronted with disturbed relations within a family and/or between partners (conflict at divorce) (Medalie and Rockwell, 1989), loss of primary bindings because of death or illness, revival of earlier traumas or sustainment of new traumas (cf. possibly sexual harassment on the campus or suicide in the immediate environment). The negative evolution of some prevalence statistics also obscures the distinction between 'normal developmental difficulties' and extraordinary stress factors (cf. increase of suicide, violence or abuse). In addition Clara (1997) remarks that all neurotic and psychotic psychopathologies are evenly spread among the student population.

The foregoing demarcates the sphere of activity of the study and student counsellor. He has to gear himself to a student who participates in academic life. If it turns out that this form of counselling fulfils some significant facilitating functions, educational policies will have to conclude that it is in their own interest to (further) develop similar services. After all, the quality of education in the strict sense of the word can be increased in different ways. In addition these centres can be of irreplaceable value to the dissemination of educational and psychosocial care giving. Naturally, as we will discuss further in this chapter, the concrete situation of each centre compared to each of these dimensions has first to be explicitly discussed and reflected on, taking into account the specific institutional culture and variable social expectations.

Functions of study and student counselling

We give below a short overview of possible functions, tasks and assignments for a centre for study and student counselling. Obviously we cannot in this context study in depth every aspect or go deeper into possible controversies. This is a descriptive list which, moreover, can be extended and improved.

Study support

There is a widespread practice of individual and group counselling that aims at making students more robust in fulfilling their study tasks. The latter can be developed in an interactive and attractive ICT format, such as the CD-ROM MANI (Depreeuw, in print). This includes, among other things, coaching where study skills in the strict sense are concerned, learning what to do with 'unstructured time' (study planning and time management), acquiring still missing skills for writing dissertations or giving lectures, support for career planning and interview skills. It is important that these initiatives remain complementary to the task of the faculty or the department. Similarly it is first of all the task of the tutor and his/her colleagues to provide the student with adequate skills for thorough and efficient handling of study material or producing a dissertation. Only those who do not benefit sufficiently from this integrated approach receive additional care from a central service.

Career counselling

As stated above, the students have to take several, mostly very important, decisions in the course of their career. In most cases they are assisted in this adequately by members of the department and especially by their parents and their friends. Still there are quite a few students who do not manage without some extra help. Among other things, we are thinking of clearing up the causes of study failure and the consequent decision to participate in retakes, to redo the year or to move in another direction. Too many students only get as far as superficial analyses; this often has emotional implications (accepting limited capacities, interference with personal or family difficulties, and so on). The consequences of not dealing with the real difficulties are new failures and study careers that go awry. Even so, at other crucial moments of the student's career, a specialized centre can be of great value (for example when changing subject, choosing specialization or profession, post-academic training or living abroad). Evidently this service is not exclusively meant for first-year students. It is striking that second-year students and graduate students also feel a strong need for specialized study support, especially if sufficient attention is given to student support. This we call 'integral student counselling'.

Student support
From what was said before it is clear that quite a number of centres, in Europe as well as in the US, concentrate on individual or group therapy in the strict sense. The theoretical models and treatment strategies which are hereby applied nevertheless vary (Grayson and Cauley, 1989; Bell et al., 1994; Knigge-Illner, 1994). Some centres are mainly psychoanalitically oriented, others work experientially; still others apply behaviour therapy and quite often the result is a mixed or a so-called 'eclectic' approach. In some centres, especially when behaviour therapy is applied, a pragmatic approach is developed for problems which are directly connected to the common ground of the individual vulnerability and the set study tasks. We are here thinking of training sessions aimed at coping with fear of failure (Depreeuw and De Neve, 1992; Zeidner, 1998) or at strengthening social skills. More recently, special attention is being paid to those who belong to the group of rabid 'study postponers' who in the long term, despite their more than wide intellectual possibilities and an adequate educational culture, during their career as well as at psychosocial level, are damaged seriously (Ferrari et al., 1995; Depreeuw et al., 1997; Schouwenburg and Groenewoud, 2000; Van Horebeek et al., 2004). Another example within this section of psychological assistance is crisis intervention. In situations of serious psychological disturbance, acute suicidal crisis or escalation of violence, the student's environment is often under pressure. It is a relief to them when professional people, partly because of their training and wider experience, offer personal and practical support and settle things so that worse situations can be avoided (Stone and Archer, 1990; Kiracofe et al., 1994; Hirsch, 2001).

Those in favour of this psychotherapeutic approach like to refer explicitly to direct and indirect profit from their interventions (avoiding prolonged study periods, successful career in spite of all, well-being, decrease of medical costs and absenteeism, and so on), but these pleas do not always have the effect intended by the outside world. This can be partly explained by the fact that some of these student psychotherapists have maintained a rather isolated position with regard to 'the educational establishment'(cf. basic principle, Kiracofe et al., 1994). Over recent years, the authorities have in different places reorganized therapy supply in the restrictive sense (for example by cutting the number of mandates, restriction of the number of sessions per student, assistance merely aimed at referring patients, restriction of interventions to strictly study-related problems and/or students who are directly hindered in their studies). We will go further into this controversy later on in the chapter.

Specialized diagnostics
Some centres have a long tradition of specialized diagnostics in different fields related to the academic world. In the case of judicious application, psychodiagnostic methods can be of great value (for example interest, study skills, capacities, memory, motivation, fear of failure). Computers with geared test programs reduce time investment to reasonable proportions so that more attention can be given to the transfer of the student to an adequate counselling programme or to a sound career decision. This diagnostic intervention can also be relevant for other services (admission to extra financial resources for the student, or motivation for a request of renewed enrolment) but, at this level, deontological controversies arise quite easily (see below).

Prevention
A psychosocially oriented service is well placed to set up or support preventive initiatives in cooperation with other bodies. We are thinking here of actions taken at relational level or connected to health-improving behaviour where eating, drinking and intake of pills are concerned, going as far as the problem of study load or as far as the coordination of faculty exam assistance. It is clear that the diversity of techniques and resources will be put to use here. We also want to stress the potential secondary and tertiary preventive effects of curative action during the student period. Quite a lot of psychosocial problems, if not adequately treated, can disturb later personal and professional life, as was illustrated by Depreeuw (2003).

Consultation and training
From the emphasis Stone and Archer (1990) and Kiracofe *et al.* (1994) lay on this aspect of 'counselling centres' we might conclude that more attention is given to this subject in the USA than in Europe. Still we notice that there is an increasing tendency towards appealing to the psychosocial professionalism of the study counsellors. This kind of consultative function of a study counselling centre is circumscribed as each activity which involves a member of staff offering assistance or help or an organized programme within the psychosocial field to a member of the academic world or another well-defined group (department, service, club and so on). These initiatives can be part of the realization of the objectives of an educational institution in the medium term (for example, training of tutors); they can also be connected to the previously mentioned acute crises (for example, campus murder or other traumas). Evidently members of a centre for study and student counselling should assume their responsibilities by participating in policy-making committees in which their expertise can contribute to the creation of a better academic ecology.

Receiving and giving training
The fact that the staff members of the centres, previously mentioned, should not be excluded from the learning society goes without saying. They will not only be expected to keep track continuously of what is happening within their own specific professional domain, but they should also be receptive to innovation. This last point can be connected to the methodology used (cf. information technology) as well as to the diversification of the services offered. Bell (1991) rightly points out that the tasks of a centre should be made explicit because they are of direct importance to the orientation of the training. In addition

to this, some centres are confronted by the demand for training of younger colleagues (second cycle of apprenticeship or postgraduate, specialized training) or they are even invited, on the basis of their specific expertise, to play an important role in professional trainings (for example, training of school psychologists or teachers). International academic and political contacts increasingly result in cooperations and exchange agreements on the subject of training. One of the assets of a centre for study and student counselling is its capability to realize optimal interaction between theory and practice.

Research
In addition to what has already been said, it seems appropriate that these centres should set up projects for applied research at the level of the common grounds between educational and psychosocial prevalences. In order to maintain the quality of this research, cooperation with academic colleagues is advisable. The translation of results into relevant and understandable information, for the authorities or the public, should receive sufficient attention.

Feedback
Despite the fact that centres for study and student counselling are not always confronted by a representative sample of the student population, sufficient attention should be given to the detection function. There is an abundancy of examples, some of which we will give to illustrate what has been said here. It is possible to be confronted by several students in a relatively short period of time, who all believe they have been treated wrongly by a tutor; a department, regularly, can be quite careless when it comes to informing students on subjects crucial to them, or it can be quite 'student-unfriendly'; the competition within a certain faculty can be stimulated to such a degree that several students start to feel isolated and even wish to drop out; the overall study load can grow in such a way that an increase in eating disorders (mainly with female students) or medicine consumption follows (for example, as a consequence of fear of failure or exhaustion). Communicating these signals in a differentiating and sound manner is one of the core tasks of these centres. It would be even better if the policy makers were courageous enough to ask for this information on a regular basis (as is the case in my own university) by appointing so-called 'ombudsmen' at the students' service and as intermediators to the university board.

Prerequisites
A clear policy
Setting up a centre for study and student counselling should preferably happen on the basis of clear options. At the start, some of the functions mentioned above will be less explicit (for example, research or passing on of expertise which in the beginning will be present to a lesser degree). But a clear policy concerning the relation between the study counselling function of the centre and its psychotherapeutic care in the strict sense, among other things, is of great importance. Those professionally involved in a study counselling centre will be continuously confronted by psychosocial problems and they will have to take decisions taking into account the nature and the scope of the services available. They therefore need clear directives. We would like to argue that it is necessary to give explicit attention to the psychotherapeutic care available from each centre. How much can be invested in this is determined by several factors, for example the financial potential and

the relevant regional provisions. Should the authorities decide to take a restrictive stand by concluding that these psychosocial problems in the strict sense should be referred to external services and centres, it has to be checked carefully whether students are cared for professionally and efficiently. A waiting list of several months may be tedious for the average citizen; for a student under pressure or with exams coming up, it can be disastrous. In addition to this, it should not be forgotten that the psychotherapeutic services too should have sufficient expertise at their disposal concerning adolescence problems and educational culture. On the other hand, Stone and Archer (1990) warn against an over-heroic attitude, as if a centre would be able to cope with all the misery or to change the establishment fundamentally. Realism at all levels should prevail: opt for what can be realized qualitatively and which can be maintained in the long term.

Finances
Closely related to what has been said previously is the fact that clear decisions should be taken where the financing of the centre is concerned. Stone and Archer (1990) speak of an 'altruistic model' as opposed to an 'economic model'. The first offers all services free, but often this leads to negligent balancing of the services offered while the clientele gets stuck on long waiting lists. The 'economic model' can reduce waiting periods drastically (the discrepancy vis-à-vis the private services is smaller or people can *not* afford it for financial reasons). Another disadvantage of the latter model is evidently that multi-problem (for example psychosocial and financial) students experience serious obstacles to applying for the necessary help; they are thus more or less excluded from it. In a lot of universities, the evolution is towards mixed formulas (partly paid for by the institution or the authorities and partly by the client). Stone and Archer (1990) stress the fact that the system should be unequivocal for all students, although in our opinion it is defensible that there should be a differentiation based on the financial capacity of the student concerned or his family. There is an increasing group in favour of 'quid pro quo' assistance under contract (for example to departments or external institutions).

Balance
Most of the functions which can be part of a centre's tasks demand a continuous exercise of balance from the members of staff. Not only is there the field of tension between the study-oriented and the psychotherapeutic approach but the division of the time and energy available over direct student care, on the one hand, and the remaining functions, on the other, should be attended to. Kiracofe *et al.* (1994) propose a maximum of 65 per cent for personal care. Individual preferences and qualities can influence the time dedicated to certain activities, but in the long run a lack of explicit steering (for example by means of functioning talks) leads to unbalanced relations which are to the disadvantage of the centre. We should also mention here that it is not always easy to combine a sufficiently wide orientation with specialization.

Integral part of the 'academic society'
Those involved in a centre for study and student counselling should not retreat to a therapeutic island. We have stressed this repeatedly. In the first place, the centre should be student-friendly and it should also have a low, attuned threshold for the target group. The

centre should have a reputation and should be within reasonable reach for the tutors so that exchange of information and consulting is encouraged. Preferably an internal consultative committee on study and student counselling will be set up so that departmental and interdepartmental initiatives can be discussed and mutual needs can be assessed faster and more accurately (for example via training of teaching assistants or those responsible for residences). Finally several authors stress the importance of intense contact with the policy makers on student affairs. They should at a higher level be important, well-informed and motivated defenders of the centre's interests, its functions and its staff.

Location
The assistance discussed here would be best organized, spatially and functionally, at a central level. We have in mind a location which brings together all departments of the same institution or the institutions in the same region which can be reached easily by all students. It is crucial to keep in mind also the psychological threshold which results from being considered a client of such a centre by tutors and fellow students. Furthermore we agree with Stone and Archer (1990) when they say that all the functions mentioned before would preferably be brought together in one centre. In particular, splitting up management of the study and student counselling (for example on the base of different tasks or focuses) leads to artificial allocation of functions and demarcation of working territories, inefficient assignment of potential and regularly faltering service towards the students. A large number of the problems brought up by the students contain personal as well as study aspects and demand integrated expertise in both fields (integral approach). Where this unification has not been realized, for example for historical reasons, a lot of work needs to be done on smooth cooperation, communication and exchange of information.

Auto-evaluation
Not only educational institutions are under pressure because of increasing quality assessment. Care centres, too, increasingly have to account for their client friendliness and the effectiveness of the assistance given. We cannot but welcome this tendency but, at the same time, we would like to make a plea for differentiated and appropriate evaluation methods. A direct and systematic contact with the clientele should be developed (for example writing to those who stay away, or measurement of therapy results) and proper registration can also produce assessing data (for example increase or lack of certain subgroups).

Quality
A good centre for study and student counselling should be able to attune itself completely to criteria concerning care and quality and should stay away from commercial and recruitment activities. This is why it is better to accommodate the external information centre of the institution in another department where different rules and strategies (for example advertising and marketing) can be applied without interfering with the credibility and the deontology of the study counsellors.

Team development
There should be continuous assessment of the size and the quality of the team. Kiracofe et al. (1994) plead for an absolute minimum of two full-time staff members. This seems

insufficient to us with regard to the large number of potential tasks, especially when quality is pursued. The same authors apply a ratio of one member of staff to 1000–1500 students. There should be a neutral, preferably central, implementation with its own reception and administration. Those working there should all receive proper training and support. Generally speaking it is accepted that the staff members should have received a decent psychological basic training with sufficient expertise in the field of communication and psychopathology. To reduce the turnover of personnel to a minimum, their statute should be adequately attractive and variable. New opportunities as well as challenges should prevent burnout. As the problem put forward by the student becomes more serious, more attention should be given to the mutual support and fraternal consultation within the team.

Special groups
Society is constantly in progress and consequently this goes also for higher education. Social studies indicate that the student population will change its constitution in the future. Already we can see a much larger participation of female students in many departments, even in those that used to be considered male bastions. But other groups too can require attention for different needs: foreign students, incomer students with a different cultural and religious background (Martinez *et al.*, 1989), students of a certain age (who may be unemployed) or returning students (Johnson and Schwartz, 1989), students who combine advanced study with a professional artistic or sports career, and students suffering from specific physical disabilities or psychological weaknesses (Arnstein, 1989).

Ethics and deontology
American authors especially stress the development and respecting of a deontological code. Partly because of this, it is important that, despite a noticeable diversity among the centres for study and student counselling, this should bring more clarity to the essential identity. Minimum requirements for basic training of those involved should be established and students should be guaranteed respect and professional secrecy. All aspects should be discussed continually and critically, especially those concerning sharing professional secrecy, holding back and passing on relevant information at crucial moments. Offering assistance and student evaluation should be separated as much as possible (which is easier in big schools than in small ones). Finally there should be an authority within reach and trusted by the clientele to which clients can turn. But, once again, this can only be realized once the professional profile is further elaborated.

Conclusion
Setting up and developing centres for study and student counselling in European higher education has taken its full course and we can only welcome this evolution. It seems important, however, that in this evolution the motives of recruitment and competition do not prevail over those of the quality of formation offered to students in the widest sense of the word. It is our intention that the preceding text will contribute to a meaningful policy towards a more effective practice.

References

Adams, G., T. Gullotta and R. Montemayor (eds) (1992), *Adolescent Identity Formation*, London: Sage.
Archer, J. and J. Scevak (1998), 'Enhancing students' motivation to learn: achievement goals in university classrooms', *Educational Psychology*, **18**, 205–23.
Arnstein, R. (1989), 'Chronically disturbed students', in P. Grayson and K. Cauley (eds), *College Psychotherapy*, New York: Guilford, pp. 29–47.
Bell, E. (1991), 'Counselling methods and concepts', in K. Gavin-Kramer, K. Scholle and U. Strehl (eds), *Ein Jahr davor: Studieren in Europa. Dokumente zur Hochschulreform 72/1991*, Bonn: Hochschulrektorenkonferenz, pp. 306–9.
Bell, E. (1996), *Counselling in Further and Higher Education*, Buckingham and Philadelphia: Open University Press.
Bell, E., C. McDevitt, G. Rott and P. Valerio (eds) (1994), 'Introduction', *Psychological counselling in higher education. A European overview*, Naples: Edizioni Citta del Sole, pp. 11–26.
Boekaerts, M. (1999), 'Self-regulated learning: where we are today', *International Journal of Educational Research*, **31**, 445–57.
Clara, A. (1997), 'Campus psychiatry', in M. Phippen (ed.), *Culture and Psyche in Transition. A European Perspective on Student Psychological Health*, Brighton: Fedora, pp. 14–19.
Depreeuw, E. (2003), 'Procrastination and other significant achievement variables in private companies', lecture for the 3rd Biennial Conference on Counseling the Procrastinator, Ohio State University, Columbus, August.
Depreeuw, E. (in press), 'A virtual study body: the CD-ROM Mani as an informative and training instrument for (future) students, their teachers and counsellors', in G. Rott *et al.* (eds), *Proceedings, Psyche Group*, Lisbon: Fedora.
Depreeuw, E.A. and H. De Neve (1992), 'Test anxiety can harm your health: some conclusions based on a student typology', in D. Forgays, T. Sosnowski and K. Wrzesniewski (eds), *Anxiety, Recent Developments in Cognitive, Psychophysiological and Health Research*, Washington: Hemisphere, pp. 211–28.
Depreeuw, E., B. Dejonghe and W. Van Horebeek (1997), 'Procrastination: Just student laziness and lack of motivation or is the challenge for counsellors more complex?', in M. Phippen (ed.), *Culture and Psyche in Transition. A European Perspective on Student Psychological Health*, Brighton: Fedora, pp. 43–50.
Ferrari, J.R., J.L. Johnson and W.G. McCown (1995), *Procrastination and Task Avoidance: Theory, Research and Treatment*, New York: Plenum Press.
Grayson, P. and K. Cauley (1989), *College Psychotherapy*, New York: Guilford.
Henderson, C. (1996), *Profile of 1996 College Freshmen with Disabilities*, Washington, DC: HEATH Resource Center/American Council on Education.
Hirsch, G. (2001), *Helping College Students Succeed: A Model for Effective Intervention*, Philadelphia: Brunner-Routledge.
Johnson, E. and A. Schwartz (1989), 'Returning students', in P. Grayson and K. Cauley (eds), *College Psychotherapy*, New York: Guilford, pp. 316–31.
Kiracofe, N.M., P.A. Donn *et al.* (1994), 'Accreditation standards for university and college counseling centers', *Journal of Counseling and Development*, **73**, 38–43.
Knigge-Illner, H. (1994), 'Neue Aufgaben psychologischer Studienberatung', in H. Knigge-Illner and O. Kruse (eds), *Studieren met Lust und Methode. Neue Gruppenkonzepte für Beratung und Lehre*, Weinheim: Deutscher Studien Verlag, pp. 13–19.
Martinez, A., K. Huang, S. Johnson and S. Edwards (1989), 'Ethnic and international students', in P. Grayson and K. Cauley (eds), *College Psychotherapy*, New York: Guilford, pp. 298–315.
McKeachie, W.J. (1994), *Teaching Tips. Stagies, Research and Theory for College and University Teachers*, Lexington: Heath and Company.
Medalie, J. and W. Rockwell (1989), 'Family problems', in P. Grayson and K. Cauley (eds), *College psychotherapy*, New York: Guilford, pp. 92–112.
Rott, G. (1991), 'Counselling concepts and methods: the development of professionalism in guidance and counselling at European universities', in K. Gavin-Kramer, K. Scholle and U. Strehl (eds), *Ein Jahr davor: Studieren in Europa. Dokumente zur Hochschulreform 72/1991*, Bonn: Hochschulrektorenkonferenz, pp. 95–100.
Royal College of Psychiatrists (2003), *The Mental Health of Students in Higher Education*, Council report CR 112, London: Royal College of Psychiatrists.
Schouwenburg, H. and J. Groenewoud (2000), 'Study motivation under social temptation: effects of trait procrastination', *Personality and Individual Differences*, **30**, 229–40.
Stone, G.L. and J. Archer (1990), 'College and university counseling centers in the 1990s: Challenges and limits', *The Counseling Psychologist*, **18**, 539–607.
Van Horebeek, W., S. Michielsen, A. Neyskens and E. Depreeuw (2004), 'A cognitive-behavioral approach in group treatment of procrastinators in an academic setting', in H. Schouwenburg, C. Lay, T. Pychyl and J. Ferrari (eds), *Counseling the Procrastinator in Academic Settings*, Washington: American Psychological Association, pp. 105–18.
Zeidner, M. (1998), *Test Anxiety: The State of the Art*, New York: Plenum Press.

18 Stress and unemployment: a comparative review of female and male managers
Sandra L. Fielden and Marilyn J. Davidson

Introduction

In the past, middle and senior managers have tended to emerge unscathed from economic recession, and those who did lose their jobs received substantial payoffs and long notice periods. Until the late 1980s the number of unemployed managers was relatively low, but job loss through economic pressures and structural changes is increasingly affecting this occupational group, especially middle managers. The 1990s saw record levels of organizational 'downsizing' which had a major impact on managers, who have borne the brunt of the cutbacks (Capell, 1992). Much of the work performed by middle management has been eroded by information technology and the drive for efficiency, which has placed many managers under enormous pressure to handle ever-increasing workloads (Malo, 1993). Increasing numbers of managers have been discarded as surplus to requirement because they are unable to perform at the required levels; those who have few or no formal qualifications are particularly susceptible to redundancy (White, 1991).

The number of unemployed managers registered with the Department of Education and Employment (DEE) in August 2002 exceeded 65 000. Over 38 000 men and over 26 000 women had previously held managerial positions, most of whom (72 per cent) were seeking jobs at a similar occupation level (National Statistics, 2002). The DEE have identified two important variables which affect the levels of unemployment experienced by managers: location and age. The latest figures available showed that the highest levels of managerial unemployment were to be found in the south of England (56.7 per cent), followed by the north of England (23.3 per cent) and the Midlands (20 per cent) (National Statistics, 2002). These figures do reflect the general levels of unemployment found in the south of England, where unemployment is three times higher than anywhere else in the country, but not for the north or Midlands. Unemployment levels are higher in the north than in the Midlands but the number of unemployed managers is proportionally less in the north, with the lowest numbers of registered unemployed managers recorded in the DEE Northern Region, an area which includes Newcastle and Sunderland.

The second, and more important, variation is related to the age of unemployed managers. A clear relationship is found between the age of unemployed managers and the levels of unemployment experienced by them, with the proportion of unemployed managers increasing substantially with age. In addition the duration of unemployment experienced by managers also increases with age, with older managers being much more likely than their younger counterparts to experience periods of unemployment in excess of six months.

The greatest social change over the last two decades has been the increase of women in paid employment. In 2001, women accounted for half of the UK workforce and this figure will continue to rise until the year 2006 according to recent government projections (Equal

Opportunities Commission, 2004). Although almost a third of all UK managers are now women, the majority are employed at the lowest levels of the managerial hierarchy and tend to be concentrated in marketing, personnel, catering, retailing and education (Davidson and Burke, 2004).

Employment is important to women both as a source of income and as a defining factor in self-conceptions. Attitudes and social patterns which deny the legitimacy of women's employment persist and ignore the importance that work has come to occupy in the lives of many women (Ratcliff and Brogden, 1988). It has often been proposed that women will actually experience less stress than men during unemployment because the work/family interface, which is a major source of stress for working women, is removed (Newell, 1993). This approach has been used to further devalue the worth of women's employment, but research does not support this view. Studies that have included unemployed women show no significant difference between unemployed men and women in terms of self-esteem, hostility and personal distress. However they have found that unemployment is experienced differently by each sex (Stokes and Cochrane, 1984; Leana and Feldman, 1991). In addition further research has shown that women are faced by additional sources of stress, and the denial of the importance of work in women's lives often results in inadequate social 'support' and an undermining of self-worth (Fielden and Davidson, 2001; Ratcliff and Brogden, 1988).

Stress and unemployment model
Employment, and specifically managerial employment, still appears to be intrinsically linked with masculinity, resulting in few studies of women's unemployment and only one previous study relating to unemployed female managers conducted by the authors (Fielden and Davidson, 1996, 2001). This chapter aims to present a review and comparative research model illustrating sources of stress, moderators of stress and stress outcomes that may affect the experiences of unemployed male and female managers. Figure 18.1 presents the proposed model of stress and unemployment in managers, specifically distinguishing areas in which gender differences are likely to be found. This multivariable approach is the first comprehensive paradigm to consider all aspects of unemployment, personality factors and coping strategies cumulating in a model of stress and unemployment in both male and female managers based upon the findings to date. However it should be noted throughout this review that, as there is limited information available as to the effects of unemployment on women, the findings quoted will, unless otherwise stated, refer to unemployed men. Moreover one must also acknowledge that the majority of research to-date relates to blue-collar workers, with only a minimal number of studies concentrating on white-collar workers or managers.

Sources of stress
The first section of the chapter will concentrate on reviewing the literature delineating sources of stress which have been specifically isolated as having particular relevance to managers, with particular emphasis on gender differences between male and female managers. The following five major sources of unemployment stress will be discussed: job loss and unemployment status; financial effect; social support; activities; and job search (see Figure 18.1).

256   *Stress in specific groups*

Sources of stress outcomes

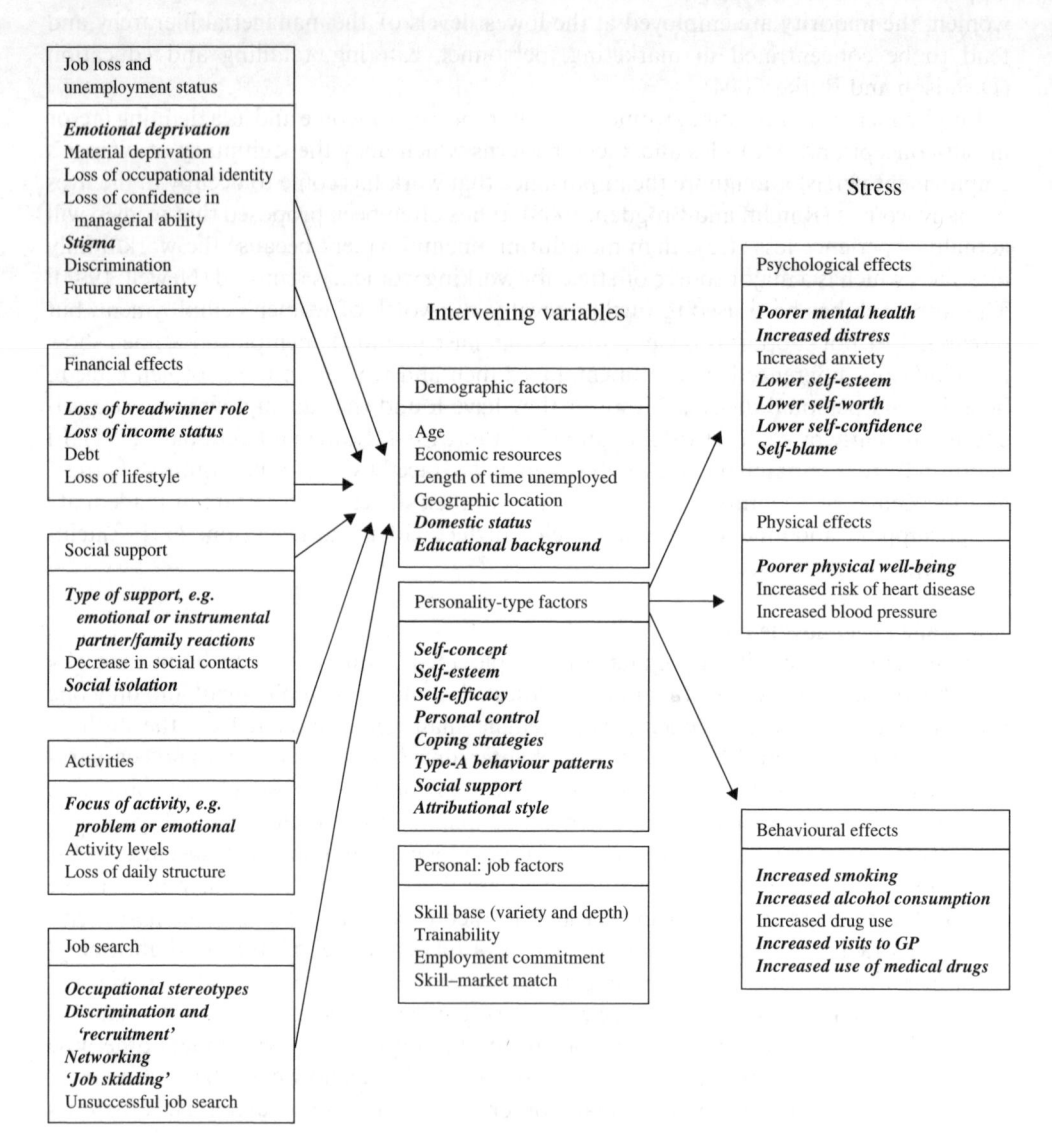

Job loss and unemployment status
- *Emotional deprivation*
- Material deprivation
- Loss of occupational identity
- Loss of confidence in managerial ability
- *Stigma*
- Discrimination
- Future uncertainty

Financial effects
- *Loss of breadwinner role*
- *Loss of income status*
- Debt
- Loss of lifestyle

Social support
- *Type of support, e.g. emotional or instrumental partner/family reactions*
- Decrease in social contacts
- *Social isolation*

Activities
- *Focus of activity, e.g. problem or emotional*
- Activity levels
- Loss of daily structure

Job search
- *Occupational stereotypes*
- *Discrimination and 'recruitment'*
- *Networking*
- *'Job skidding'*
- Unsuccessful job search

Intervening variables

Demographic factors
- Age
- Economic resources
- Length of time unemployed
- Geographic location
- *Domestic status*
- *Educational background*

Personality-type factors
- *Self-concept*
- *Self-esteem*
- *Self-efficacy*
- *Personal control*
- *Coping strategies*
- *Type-A behaviour patterns*
- *Social support*
- *Attributional style*

Personal: job factors
- Skill base (variety and depth)
- Trainability
- Employment commitment
- Skill–market match

Stress

Psychological effects
- *Poorer mental health*
- *Increased distress*
- Increased anxiety
- *Lower self-esteem*
- *Lower self-worth*
- *Lower self-confidence*
- *Self-blame*

Physical effects
- *Poorer physical well-being*
- Increased risk of heart disease
- Increased blood pressure

Behavioural effects
- *Increased smoking*
- *Increased alcohol consumption*
- Increased drug use
- *Increased visits to GP*
- *Increased use of medical drugs*

Note: Bold italics are used to indicate those areas in which gender differences are likely to be found.

Source: Fielden and Davidson (1999).

Figure 18.1   Unemployment: a comparative research model for male and female managers

Job loss and unemployment status

Job loss For the purpose of this review, job loss is defined as *an event that removes paid employment from an individual,* regardless of the motives of the parties involved (Doran et al., 1991; Wanberg and Marchese, 1994). Job loss leads to the loss of both the psychological and practical benefits provided by paid employment, which can create a situation 'replete with intra-psychic and interpersonal turmoil' (Estes, 1973). Research suggests that job loss causes reactions on several levels: on the *emotional* level, anxiety, depression, and/or apathy (Eales, 1988; Melville *et al.*, 1985); on the *cognitive* level, disturbed ability to concentrate, perceive, make decisions and/or be creative (Latack *et al.*, 1995); on the *behavioural* level, abuse of alcohol, tobacco, drugs and/or food (Hammarstrom and Janlert, 1994); and on the *physiological* level, neuroendorine 'stress reactions' (Arnetz *et al.*, 1987; Fleming *et al.*, 1984). Job loss is a key determinant of physical and emotional ill-being for the unemployed person and in some cases these reactions may even lead to increased morbidity and mortality.

The degree to which job loss is experienced as a negative event is dependent upon a number of contextual factors. Kelvin and Jarret (1985), for example, suggest that in times of high unemployment stigmatization of the unemployed is relatively rare, as it is generally assumed that external factors, such as recession, are responsible for unemployment and not individual characteristics. Thus those who do not see unemployment as a personal stigma are more likely to experience better psychological well-being than those who perceive the unemployed as a stigmatized group.

Those who feel that they have no personal control over their job loss experiences are also more likely to experience distress, and are more likely to suffer negative effects during their period of unemployment, than those who feel that they have some degree of personal control over their situation (Fielden and Davidson, 2001; Swinburne, 1981). Individuals who see their job loss resulting from external factors are more likely to perceive themselves as similar to others without jobs, thereby deriving a sense of self-worth from similarity in comparison with other unemployed people (Sheeran *et al.*, 1995). In contrast, those who believe that they are responsible for their own job loss are more likely to perceive themselves as less similar to others without jobs. They generally believe that society also views them as responsible for being unemployed (Breakwell, 1985), thereby stigmatizing themselves by denying the legitimacy of their own unemployment in both social and personal terms. Unemployed managers, who may be more prone to view their own positions as unique or exceptional because of their relatively small numbers, may be more likely to experience self-blame than other unemployed groups. This may be particularly prevalent in unemployed female managers who are even less likely than their male counterparts to have contact with others in a similar position.

Job loss and managers Most unemployment research has been concerned with blue-collar workers, but there are a small number of studies which have looked at the impact of unemployment on male managers and these have produced mixed findings. Fineman (1984) found that male managers showed a significant depreciation in self-esteem, yet Hartley (1980a) found that the self-esteem of male managers ($n = 87$) did not decline during unemployment. Hartley (1980a) proposed that there was no evidence that unemployed managers were any more anxious, tense or apprehensive than employed managers, although this study was conducted during the late 1970s when managerial unemployment was much lower and it might have been much less of a threat to self-esteem. She suggested that, because managers have greater experience in dealing with stressful and pressurized situations, they cope with unemployment by responding in an assertive and resourceful manner. However, in a relatively small study ($n = 20$), Swinburne (1981) reported that male managers did experience the same phasic reaction as blue-collar workers, that is shock, optimism, pessimism and fatalism, although they passed through these phases more slowly. The initial shock of unemployment was the most frequently mentioned emotion experienced by participants, accompanied by fear and uncertainty surrounding the future. Feelings of shame, loss of status and loss of self-respect were reported, but less frequently than anticipated.

Hartley (1980b) proposed that some managers actually welcomed the challenge of job loss and the new opportunities it may have provided, concluding that the responses of unemployed managers were much more complex and varied than those of other unemployed workers, who tend to respond in a more passive way. However there is little support for the idea that managers take such a positive approach to unemployment. Swinburne (1981) found that, although 55 per cent of participants recognize some positive aspects of being out of work, all but a small minority felt that any possible benefits were outweighed by the accompanying fear and uncertainty around the depressed job market. In addition, it is important to note that few of the participants chose to discuss their unemployment voluntarily and this fact was attributed to poor levels of self-disclosure. Where these feelings were disclosed their intensity varied considerably and, while causing distress for some, for some others they were strongly destructive forces (Swinburne, 1981).

To-date only a few studies have been conducted into the effects of unemployment on female managers, and this has produced some interesting results. One qualitative study ($n = 27$), found that the impact of job loss upon female managers was substantial, with unemployed female managers experiencing significant decreases in self-esteem, self-confidence and self-worth (Fielden and Davidson, 1996). The most significant source of stress experienced by unemployed female managers was that faced during job search, with discrimination being encountered at all stages of the recruitment process. The effects of these stressors were minimized by several coping strategies, which included the maintenance of high activity levels, social support and personal control (ibid.). These coping strategies appeared to be extremely successful, with unemployed female managers experiencing similar levels of mental and physical well-being to their employed counterparts. This contrasts with recent research into the personality of unemployed male managers, which has found that they experience greater anxiety than their employed peers (Brindle, 1992).

The number of studies into the effects of unemployment on managers is minimal and the findings of those studies have not been consistent. However the weight of support favours the conclusion that the psychological effects of unemployment for managers are comparable with those for other workers, although the evidence suggests that the experience of unemployment may be qualitatively different. A report produced by the Institute of Management (Duffield, 1994) suggests that the loss of opportunity for skill use is a key factor in the impact of job loss experienced by managers, and that continuing unemployment frequently means that managers lose confidence in their managerial abilities, inhibiting their job search and reducing their chances of success in obtaining suitable employment. Thus the activity that is most likely to benefit them most, job search, is the activity which is also likely to have the greatest negative affect on self-confidence and self-esteem.

Job loss and women The majority of research conducted into the effects of job loss are based upon the male model of work. Thus, in order to compare the effects of job loss on male and female managers, we must first look at the role work has come to occupy in women's lives and how the removal of that role may affect female managers. It is only by gaining an appreciation of women's attitudes towards, work that we can evaluate the possible effects of the removal of the psychological and material benefits of paid employment.

Although the myth that women only work for 'pin money' has been repeatedly exposed, this belief still prevails (Dilnot and Kell, 1988). Yet studies consistently show that women derive both satisfaction and status from work and have an extraordinary attachment to their paid employment, often experiencing an increased sense of self-control and empowerment (Coyle, 1984; Rosenfield, 1989). Pietromonaco *et al.* (1987) found that full-time employment was of particular benefit to those who viewed themselves as career-oriented, reporting significantly higher levels of self-esteem, life satisfaction and well-being than their non-career oriented counterparts. These findings indicate that employment provides women with much more than just a source of income. In addition previous research has also found that women's commitment to work, unlike their male counterparts', is not directly derived from their level of income, but from the degree of satisfaction and sense of belonging they experience at work (Pittman and Orthner, 1988). However, as women enter positions that demand greater investment of time and energy, they can experience increasing conflict between home and work relationships. Thus, although working women, especially those in managerial or professional positions, report high levels of job satisfaction, they also report high levels of stress (Davidson, *et al.*, 1995; Travers and Cooper, 1991).

Working women have many conflicting roles and some observers of women's multiple role involvement have speculated that trying to be worker, wife and mother contributes to greater psychological distress (Muller *et al.*, 1993). Thus it has been suggested that the removal of paid employment from women's lives would reduce this distress. However, although multiple role strain can have an adverse effect on women's mental and physical health, studies have failed to substantiate a consistent relationship (Akabas, 1988). In an alternative approach it has recently been argued that it is the quality of a woman's experience within and across roles, rather than the number of roles, that influences mental health (Piechowski, 1992) with role quality accounting for significant increases in job satisfaction and self-esteem. Findings show that it is not the time investment required to maintain multiple roles that leads to conflict and distress, but the identity derived from those roles that predicts well-being (Carlson *et al.*, 1995). Further to this, it has been suggested that a greater number of roles can actually enhance psychological well-being by providing access to resources and alternative sources of gratification as well as promoting greater social interaction (Thoits, 1986). Thus, rather than having a negative effect on women's health, it would appear that employment actually improves the health of women, married or single, who have a positive attitude towards work (Repetti et al., 1989). This improvement is found to be greatest for women in professional and managerial position for whom employment is often the major identifying role in their lives (Arber et al.,1985).

In general women have learned to cope with the demands of multiple roles by integrating their working and personal lives. However this approach has often been interpreted as a lack of dedication and commitment to work, leading many to believe that employment is a low priority for women. It has been argued that working women are not happier or more satisfied than women who stay at home, and that employment itself bears little relationship to women's well-being (Warr and Parry, 1982). This belief is not supported by previous research, which has clearly shown that unemployed women experience greater stress than working women (Warren, 1980). However the belief that women's employment is relatively unimportant still persists and has resulted in women experiencing greater employment insecurity than men. In times of recession women are the first to be discarded, are most vulnerable to future layoffs and suffer more unemployment than men (Snyder and Nowak, 1984; Rogers, 1980).

Although research has addressed many of the myths about women's attitude to work (Dex, 1988; Billing and Alvesson, 1993) the legitimacy of women's work is still denied by the lack of research in their experiences of job loss and unemployment. This denial is nowhere more evident than in the male-dominated realms of management. Unemployed female managers, unlike employed female managers, seem not only to be considered less valuable than their male counterparts but have continually been disregarded. Unemployed female managers have been treated as an invisible group whose exclusion from previous research highlights how undervalued they and their experiences are.

Unemployment status   Unemployment can be distinguished from job loss by the concept of duration: if an individual does not obtain a new employment immediately, job loss will lead to a period of unemployment. Thus job loss and unemployment form part of a continuum based upon time, with job loss as the precipitating event at one end of the continuum and long-term unemployment at the other. Therefore, in order to understand the full impact of unemployment, we need to consider not just the effects of job loss, but also the effects of continuing unemployment on mental and physical well-being. In assessing these effects we need to consider the consequences of the removal of both latent and manifest benefits, that is financial and psychological deprivation, experienced by both men and women.

The financial effects of unemployment
Most unemployed people experience substantial reductions in their income. Warr and Jackson (1984) found that 66 per cent of people had a total household income between 33 per cent and 50 per cent of their previous employed income. This considerable loss of income, coupled with the meagre level of state unemployment benefits, ensures that the majority of unemployed people live in relative if not absolute poverty (Fryer, 1995). Even those who are initially protected from the effects of reduced income, by either redundancy payments or saving, experience increasing economic deprivation as these resources diminish. Thus economic deprivation is inevitably associated with increasing length of unemployment (Brief et al., 1995), leading to decreases in both physical and

psychological well-being. It is therefore not surprising that findings consistently show that unemployed people experience not only objective financial distress but also significant subjective distress (Fryer, 1995).

Financial stress has been shown to increase the incidence of reported symptoms of illness (Aldwin and Revenson, 1986) and the incidence of mental problems in unemployed populations (Frese and Mohr, 1987), a situation highlighted by a large-scale longitudinal Dutch study, which showed a direct relationship between the level of state benefits and mental well-being, with low levels of financial strain accounting for between 50 per cent and 76 per cent of the psychological distress experienced (Schaufeli and Van Yperen, 1992). The effects of job loss on income levels means that even the 'affluent' unemployed can experience distressing financial deprivation relative to their previous situation (Fryer, 1995). It is important to note that financial hardship is a relative experience, and economic deprivation should not be viewed solely in terms of income change. The degree of deprivation experienced by an individual is based upon their financial position in relationship to self-selected reference groups and the normative expectancies of those groups (Seidman and Rapkin, 1989). Personal identity is increasingly experienced and expressed through spending and consumption, and it has been proposed that we are what we can afford to buy (Fryer, 1995). An inability to spend money on non-essential items, such as entertainment, often leads to a withdrawal from social contact. Thus economic deprivation can result in social isolation, a situation which significantly accentuates the effects of financial stress on mental well-being (Viinamaki et al., 1993).

The performance of many roles is either inhibited or prohibited by poverty, and it has been suggested that men are likely to suffer most from the effects of financial stress because of their inability to fulfil their role as breadwinner. George and Brief (1990) suggest that, whilst there have been dramatic changes in sex roles in the 20th century, there appears to remain an attachment of males to the breadwinner role in many families. Although men are becoming financially more and more dependent upon women, while women are becoming increasingly less financially dependent upon men, conceptions of masculinity still retain the breadwinner role as a defining characteristic. The continuing existence of this role has been reflected in several studies which have found that men's earning have a direct and negative effect on the level of depression they experience, accounting for 67 per cent of the variance of reported life satisfaction, whilst no such link has been found for women (Ross and Huber, 1985; George and Brief, 1990). Thus, while in real terms there may be no difference in the financial responsibilities of unemployed male and female managers, these findings would suggest that the effect of economic deprivation experienced by unemployed male managers may be substantially greater than that experienced by unemployed female managers.

Research into the effects of financial hardship experienced during unemployment are almost solely based upon the income levels of blue-collar workers. Managers potentially earn significantly more than blue-collar workers, hence it would be anticipated that their reduction in income, as a result of job loss, would be much greater than that experienced by other workers. Thus the effects of unemployment in terms of financial strain may be even more traumatic for managers than for blue-collar or non-managerial white-collar workers.

Social support

Employment is an important source of social support, especially for women (Pittman and Orthner, 1988). The loss of this manifest consequence of work through unemployment can lead to feelings of loneliness and social isolation. It is during this time that family and friends can be a valuable source of support, support which can help reduce the general distress, depression and anxiety experienced by unemployed people (Warr et al., 1988). In order to understand the effect family and friends can have on the experiences of unemployed female managers, we must first look at the forms social support can take and their impact on psychological health.

Type of support A well-established social network is a structural prerequisite of feeling socially integrated and emotionally accepted (Veiel and Baumann, 1992). The size of an individual's network, that is the number of friends and family and the frequency of contact with them, is referred to as *social integration*. Studies have found a positive association between the time spent with others and psychological well-being (Bolton and Oatley, 1987; Warr, 1987). However it is not only the number of active social ties which determines the degree of isolation experienced by an individual, but it is also the quality of those ties. *Social support* refers to the perceived quality of relationships, the function of those relationships and the benefits provided by those relationships (Schwarzer et al., 1994). It is important to note that it is not the amount of social support an individual actually receives that moderates the impact of unemployment on well-being, but the perceived availability of that support (Wethington and Kessler, 1986).

The degree to which an individual experiences social integration is an important aspect of most people's lives, but it is close personal relationships, with either family or friends, that for the majority of people are what 'make life meaningful' (Argyle, 1989). These relationships are often the most salient forms of social support, providing both emotional and instrumental support for unemployed individuals (Argyle, 1989). Emotional support is characterized by the actions of caring or listening sympathetically and instrumental support is characterized by rendering tangible assistance, for example in the form of advice or knowledge (Fenlason and Beehr, 1994). It has often been assumed that emotional support is more effective than instrumental support, but research would suggest that the most effective sources of social support are those that provide both types (Kaufmann and Beehr, 1986).

There is considerable evidence that the presence of close relationships helps to stave off depression, certain clinical problems and certain physical ailments by reducing stress (Duck, 1988). Brugha et al. (1990) found that satisfaction with social support accounted for up to 38 per cent of the variance found in patients' recovery from depression.

This is further supported by longitudinal evidence which suggests that unemployed individuals who are unsupported experience significantly higher elevations and more changes in measure of cholesterol, illness symptoms and affective response than those who are supported (Gore, 1978). It has been suggested that, for women, social support is the most important factor in determining mental health during unemployment (Ratcliff and Brogden, 1988). A lack of intimacy has been found to increase significantly the risk of major depression in women and is particularly destructive in those who are unemployed, substantially increasing their risk of depression (Hallstrom, 1986). Research shows that unemployed women actively seek and successfully receive social support from relatives and friends (Retherford *et al.*, 1988). However not all social support is truly supportive and the type of support given appears to be qualitatively different depending upon whether it is given by a partner, a family member or a friend. Research tends to concentrate on these specific sources of support, therefore the literature on each area will be reviewed separately.

Partner's reactions The support offered by a partner during unemployment can be the most crucial variable regarding the well-being of both unemployed men and women. Living with a partner does appear to have beneficial effects, but it is the effective quality of that relationship that is important in determining psychological well-being (Schwartzberg and Dytell, 1989). Support from partners can help to bolster self-esteem and lessen feelings of helplessness and, while the levels of received support appear to be the same for men and women, the type of support given tends to be different (G. Caplan, 1982; Starrin and Larson, 1987). Unemployed men tend to receive emotional support from their spouses rather than any other form of support (Bolton and Oatley, 1987). In contrast, unemployed women tend to receive higher levels of instrumental support, financial or informational, than emotional support, although it does appear to be a crucial form of social support (Starrin and Larson, 1987).

Being in a satisfactory relationship can provide significant benefits, but being married *per se* does not guarantee better psychological well-being and can lead to additional strain where there is a lack of support and understanding. Marital relationships not only act as moderators of the stress response but may also be a source of stress during unemployment. This source of stress appears to be experienced differently by men and women. For example, high rates of unemployment are associated with marital instability and an increased likelihood of divorce for men, but not for women (Sander, 1992). Marital breakdown has negative effects on health regardless of an individual's employment situation, but in conjunction with unemployment can have devastating results on physical and psychological well-being (Taubman and Rosen, 1982). It has been suggested that this difference arises because there is a direct link between loss of male earnings and marital dissatisfaction, but not between loss of female earnings and marital dissatisfaction (Kessler, 1996). This emphasis on male earnings is possibly related to the inability of unemployed men to fulfil their perceived societal role as 'breadwinner', and may be a source of both spousal pressure and self-pressure.

In contrast, unemployed women often find that their partners are unsupportive towards their situation because they actually prefer them to be unemployed (Ratcliff and Brogden, 1988). This can arise from a lack of enthusiasm for their wife working, with some partners deriving satisfaction from their being out of a job. These findings may lead to the conclusion that being married, or living with a partner, may be detrimental to the well-being of unemployed women. However Starrin and Larson (1987) found that unemployed single women experienced greater amounts of depression and higher incidents of physical illness than unemployed wives, suggesting that, even though the emotional support received from the partners of unemployed females is often limited, the instrumental support they receive is of substantial benefit. This is of particular relevance taking into account that female managers are less likely to be married than their male counterparts (Davidson and Cooper, 1992).

Family The reactions of families to an individual's job loss vary considerably and the quality of their experiences within the family can be a crucial moderator of their reaction to unemployment. The social support provided by an individual's family is again subject to gender differences. Unemployed women report that the family environment is an especially potent source of support, but it does not appear to provide the same benefits for men (Holahan and Moos, 1982). Retherford *et al.* (1988) found, in their relatively large study ($n = 216$), that unemployed women were significantly more likely to receive support from their parents than from their partner, other relatives or friends. This support tends to be emotional rather than financial or informational and an individual's reliance on their family members does not usually diminish while they remain unemployed (Jackson, 1988). In contrast, Stokes and Levin (1986) reported that unemployed men are more likely to seek support from friends rather than from their close relations, as they prefer to keep family and work roles separate (Greenglass, 1993a).

While considering the effects of social support on psychological well-being it must be recognized that it is possible for the family environment to exacerbate the effects of unemployment on mental and physical health. Family obligations may carry their own stressors and these may be increased during unemployment, a situation exacerbated by the inability to escape from the family environment (Hibbard and Pope, 1993). The impact of job loss may also be compounded by the negative feedback that unemployed individuals often receive from families. This appears to be particularly relevant for unemployed women, especially those for whom work is a defining factor in their self-concept. Ratcliff and Brogden (1988) suggest that women often experience depressive symptoms because their families are insensitive to the importance the role paid employment has in women's lives. This lack of understanding can lead to feelings of rejection and of worthlessness.

Social contacts Studies have shown that friendships are an important source of social support for both men and women. However gender differences have been consistently found between the quality or nature of friendships sought by men and women (Greenglass, 1993a; Stokes and Levin, 1986). Women have a strong interest in developing close, dyadic relationships, whereas men tend to be more group-oriented, including three or more people. In addition employed men report having more friends and attending more 'get togethers', with significantly greater numbers of friends in an average week than employed women (Stokes and Levin, 1986). Yet men frequently report higher levels of loneliness than women, regardless of their employment status, with the lack of intimacy they experience in their relationships accounting for twice as much variance as for women (Brugha *et al.*, 1990; Stokes and Levin, 1986). This lack of intimacy is exacerbated by the fact that men do not tend to talk to one another as a means of coping, thereby failing to utilize the resources available to them in a constructive or positive way (Greenglass, 1993a).

Work is an important source of close relationships for both men and women, often producing intimate and lasting friendships that individuals frequently do not have access to outside the work environment (Duck, 1988). The social support available at work has a direct effect on psychological well-being, with both working men and women reporting greater levels of social support than those who were either unemployed or non-working (Bolton and Oatley, 1987; Pugliesi, 1988). These social contacts are extremely important to women, with the 'company of others' being cited as the main non-financial reason for working by both employed and unemployed women (Dex, 1988). In contrast, men frequently report financial reasons as their main motivation for working (Pittman and Orthner, 1988), although a large-scale study by Holahan and Moos (1982) suggests that the work environment is a more salient source of social support for men than it is for women; yet it accounts for three times as much of the variance in psychological ill-health of women than of men.

The amount of active social support given by non-family members reduces significantly during unemployment, leaving individuals with smaller networks of social contacts (Jackson, 1988). In addition the quality of social contact frequently changes after job loss, becoming less intimate and more casual (Stokes and Cochrane, 1984). This change may be precipitated by the unemployed person themselves withdrawing from relationships in terms of their disclosure levels about their situation. Avoidance, often from embarrassment, guilt, shame or a lack of money, can rapidly lead to increased social isolation (Stokes and Cochrane, 1984). Thus, at a time when social support is most needed, some of the most beneficial sources of support may be removed (Duck, 1988).

Activities
The loss of employment means a loss of externally imposed structure and enforced activity which gives shape to people's daily lives (Jahoda and Rush, 1980). Activity fulfils three important functions: it maintains mental alertness, it wards off fears and doubts, and provides an objective and a sense of achievement (Swinburne, 1981). Keeping active after job loss becomes increasingly more difficult and the inability to replace the structure and level of meaningful activity can lead to apathy and depression. Two types of inactivity have been identified: not knowing what to do and feeling too depressed to do anything (Swinburne, 1981). The two work together and, once in a state of inactivity, individuals become trapped in a negative circle which is almost impossible to break.

The activities imposed at work range from those of a vacuous nature to those which are highly self-directed and self-structured. Fryer (1986) suggests that unemployment may free people to structure their own time in line with the needs of valued, chosen tasks and their own personal requirements. If this is so, those who were previously employed in repetitive manual positions would be expected to gain more from unemployment than those who had held more self-directed positions. However structuring one's time in a constructive and fulfilling manner may be an ability that the second group are likely to be more proficient at than the first. Those who are characterized by independence, internally developed self-structuring and self-directedness, are more likely to be proactive in unemployment and more able to achieve valued purpose (Fryer, 1986).

The importance of activity during unemployment has been shown in a number of studies which have found that one of the best single predictors of mental health during unemployment was whether or not a man felt his time was occupied, accounting for twice as much variance as the length of time unemployed or age (Hepworth, 1980; Kilpatrick and Trew, 1985). Men initially were able to fill their time with home improvements or gardening but, even though they reported subsequent difficulty in filling their time, they did not engage in domestic or leisure activities (O'Brien, 1986). Once they became locked into a routine of inactivity they reported that they 'just could not be bothered' with anything, even job search (Hepworth, 1980).

The majority of studies which have investigated the effects of activity levels on mental health during unemployment have only included men. The exclusion of women from such research may arise from the view that women's domestic roles provide meaningful and fulfilling activities for all women, and these roles take the place of work roles during unemployment (Warr and Parry, 1982). It has been suggested that, while there is a tendency for unemployed women to fill their time with domestic activities, unemployed female managers frequently reject these roles as they do not provide the self-esteem that women managers need (Duffield, 1994). There is no support for the assumption that women will engage in higher levels of activity during unemployment than men. Wanberg and Marchese (1994) found no gender difference in the activity levels of unemployed men and women, with equal numbers of men and women reporting high, moderate and low levels of time structure. These levels of activity were again associated with mental and physical well-being, and the degree of stress experienced by each group was directly linked to the degree of time structure they maintained.

Although the levels of activity pursued by unemployed men and women appear to be similar, the type of activity they engaged in is gender-oriented. Leana and Feldman (1991) have found gender differences in the focus of activities pursued by men and women. Men are more likely than women to rely on problem-focused activities, that is behaviours that attempt directly to eliminate the source of stress such as job search, retraining and relocation. In contrast, women are more likely to rely on symptom-focused activities, that is behaviours that attempt to eliminate the symptoms of unemployment such as seeking social support. Symptom-focused activities may be more successful in reducing some of the effects of unemployment on mental well-being, such as anxiety and loneliness, but because they do not address the source of the problem (job loss) they may result in longer periods of unemployment.

Job search
The job search activities of the unemployed has received little attention, with few studies considering the difficulties faced by individuals during their search for work. The absence of research is particularly noticeable in regard to unemployed women and managers, with the majority of work that has been conducted concentrating on unemployed men in search of non-managerial positions. Job search is an integral part of the unemployment experience, and unemployed managers are strongly encouraged to use all methods of job search, for example networking, speculative approaches to employers, and employment agencies (Allan, 1989). However the effectiveness of an individual's job search is dependent not only upon their own motivation to gain employment, but upon their approach to job search, their access to alternative methods of job search and the barriers they encounter during their search for employment.

Approaches to job search   Women depend much more upon formal methods of job search than men, reporting more frequent use of public advertisements and private agencies. They are also more likely to find work via the Job Centre, a finding reflected in their tendency to hold more favourable views about the Employment Service than unemployed men. In contrast, men tend to make more speculative approaches to employers, and utilize their personal and business networks more extensively (Daniel, 1990). It has frequently been argued that many of the differences in the experiences of men and women during unemployment arise from the fact that women are not as committed to finding work as men (Sheridan, 1994; Stokes and Cochrane, 1984). This appears to receive support from the finding that, on average, women will spend longer out of work than men. However this generalization conceals major differences between single women, married women without children and married women with children. Single women find jobs more quickly than single men and, while the average duration for married women without dependent children is slightly longer, it is not dissimilar to that for all men. The most striking difference in the duration of unemployment is found in married women with dependent children, who spend significantly longer periods out of work than any other group (Malmberg-Heimonen and Julkunen, 2002). In contrast, the duration of unemployment experienced by men appears to be similar for all groups, regardless of marital status and domestic responsibilities.

Barriers to re-employment   It has been suggested that the most significant barrier faced by unemployed managers in their search for work is their age (Allan, 1989). Previous research with male managers over 40 years of age has shown that, whilst age discrimination is not perceived as an important factor in job loss, it is believed to be the main barrier preventing re-employment (Allan, 1990). Unemployment can be a particularly wrenching experience for older managers, especially those who have had many years' service with one organization (Pittman and Orthner, 1988). The second most important barrier faced by male managers in their search for work appears to be being overqualified (Allan, 1990). These findings have led to the recommendation that unemployed managers, especially those over 40, should expect to be offered jobs at lower levels of responsibility and lower levels of pay than those they had previously held (Allan, 1989; Newman, 1988). Unemployed managers are encouraged to see these jobs as an opportunity to demonstrate their skills and abilities within an organization, enabling them to forge new management careers (Kirkpatrick, 1988). However the recommendation that even a mediocre job is better than no job at all is not supported by previous research, which suggests that individuals employed in jobs perceived to be unsatisfying are just as distressed as those who are unemployed (Winefield *et al.*, 1991).

In addition to age and being overqualified, unemployed male managers have reported five other significant barriers to successful job search (Allan, 1990): the lack of jobs in their area of expertise, the general economic condition, lack of jobs requiring their type of experience, lack of jobs with comparable salaries to their last position, and being unemployed too long. It is anticipated that the barriers encountered by unemployed male managers will also be encountered by unemployed female managers, but in addition they are likely to face barriers that are solely based upon gender discrimination, an issue which warrants separate consideration.

Occupational gender stereotypes   Unemployed female managers have not only to deal with the same financial and psychological consequences as unemployed male managers, they also have to contend with the extra difficulties that the 'think manager, think male' stereotype pose for job search (Sheridan, 1994). Davies and Esseveld (1989) suggest that women's experiences of unemployment and job search are strongly connected to the gender discrimination that they face in the workplace. This discrimination is particularly prevalent in positions that have been traditionally male-dominated, such as management, where women are confronted by additional barriers. These barriers not only have the potential to prevent unemployed women managers from securing employment but also serve to prevent women having access to those positions.

Female managers experience many barriers to advancement when they are employed and it is predicted that they will experience even greater barriers when seeking new employment. The main barrier to unemployed women managers is the perception that 'male = manager' (Sheridan, 1994). The successful manager is aggressive, competitive, independent and self-reliant; he is not feminine. In a survey of 40 organizations, Hirsh and Bevan (1988) found that the phrases most commonly used in management selection to describe the attributes considered necessary to management referred to masculine personality traits. Characteristics such as non-aggression, artistic inclination and concern for the welfare of others are associated with non-related management traits and are seen as weakness that would interfere with effective business processes (Orser, 1994).

Gender segregation in the workplace persists and individual jobs (including management) continue to be highly gender-segregated, with the vast majority of organizational job titles being held by one sex or the other (Davidson, 1996; Jacobs, 1989). Job segregation means that women are frequently inhibited from moving from predominantly female to predominantly male occupations, because of their lack of experience in 'male jobs' (Rosenfeld and Spenner, 1992). However this lack of experience may not necessarily be seen by unemployed female managers as a barrier to their job search activities (Fielden and Davidson, 1996). Although it is anticipated that, in order to avoid many of the barriers, they would have to face applying for male-dominated occupations, their job search activities are more likely to be restricted to predominately female occupations. Consequently this minimizes the risk of rejection and maximizes their chances of successful job search (Fielden and Davidson, 1996).

In addition to prejudice and sex stereotyping, unemployed female managers also have to cope with other specific sources of stress which have been isolated as unique to female managers. These include overt and indirect discrimination from employers and hostile organizational culture, feelings of isolation and being placed in the role of 'token women' (Davidson and Cooper, 1992). It is possible that these barriers to re-employment not only make job search more stressful for unemployed female managers, but may mean that they are less successful in their job search activities than their male counterparts.

Recruitment Employers are under a legal obligation to ensure that their recruitment procedures conform with the Sex Discrimination Act (1975), which states that employers must not discriminate or indicate any hidden intention to discriminate against a potential employee on the grounds of their sex. The very fact that many jobs are still viewed as 'male' or 'female' is often sufficient to prevent the non-dominant group from applying for those positions (Ray, 1990). Recruitment literature often conforms to the typical 'male' manager stereotype. Job search guides often refer to managers as 'he' or 'businessmen' (Dudeney, 1980; Heidrick and Struggles, 1983; Scott and Rochester, 1984). Illustrations used in advertisements frequently portray only men in managerial roles, with women portrayed in supportive non-managerial roles, and job specifications are often worded in terms of 'he/his' (Davidson and Burke, 1994; Ray, 1990). This may not necessarily reflect an intention on the part of the organization openly to discriminate but it is, by implication, indirect discrimination, and illegal. Discrimination of this nature may result in fewer women applying for positions and can be very effective in filtering women out of the recruitment process.

Indirect discrimination may also prevent women from reaching either the interview or short-listing stages, and there is clear evidence that similarly qualified and experienced women receive lower evaluations than men in managerial selection situations (Glick et al., 1988). The reason for this has been explained in terms of sex-role stereotyping and role incongruence. Interviewers frequently hold an image of what they consider to be an 'ideal candidate' and this image is based upon the male model (Stuart, 1992). Thus interviewers often assume that the managerial qualities they are seeking are more likely to be found in a man than in a woman, with qualities such as cooperation and teamwork not being given the same credit as aggression and competitiveness. This means that unemployed female managers are much less likely to be invited to interviews for managerial jobs than their male counterparts, especially for upper middle and senior management positions. As interviews are the most common selection process used by organizations for management selection, and unstructured interviews are shown to be the least valid and reliable selection procedure (Robertson and Iles, 1988), this may pose a significant barrier for unemployed female managers in their search for employment. Those women who are successful in reaching the interview stage face yet further discrimination based on the male model of management, further decreasing their chances of success.

Interviewers tend to make attributions about the candidate based upon their own 'self schema', and generally choose a candidate with whom they can feel comfortable and who they feel will fit into organizational networks, both formal and informal (Duck, 1988). This means that the successful candidate usually reflects the main characteristics of the interviewer, with gender congruence exerting significant influence on decision making (Yoder et al., 1989). As the majority of senior managers, and therefore most interviewers, are male, unemployed female managers are at an obvious disadvantage. Interviewers, as Stephanie Allen, president of The Athena Group, so aptly says, 'tend to pick guys like themselves. If you aren't a guy, it's kind of hard' (Stuart, 1992). Thus, even when women are invited to interviews, they are less likely to succeed than their male counterparts.

The issue of sex discrimination during the recruitment process is widely recognized, yet the protection the Sex Discrimination Act (1975) provides for women is only effective when vacancies are officially advertised. It is estimated that over 50 per cent of all jobs in management are never formally advertised but are filled through personal contacts (Davidson and Cooper, 1992). The vacancies that are formally advertised tend to be with organizations that are committed to equal opportunities, and therefore unlikely to engage in any form of discrimination. This means that, although the legislation is in place, in reality unemployed female managers have little protection against indirect or direct discrimination during job search.

Networking As many vacancies are never formally advertised, the utilization of networks during unemployment is recognized as one of the most important and effective approaches to job search available to managers (Allan, 1989; Moskoff, 1993). Personal contacts function through informal business networks and can provide knowledge, information, support, advice, influence and sponsors (Burke *et al.*, 1995). However the effectiveness of this form of job search depends, not only on an individual's networking skills, but upon the power and influence of those with whom an individual has contact via their network.

The networks of male and female managers are substantially different, in both their composition and their degree of influence. Men's networks mainly consist of men and afford access to those who have influence over critical human resource decisions, such as promotion and recruitment. In contrast, women's networks contain a larger number of women, with less influential members (Burke *et al.*, 1995; Ibarra, 1993). Previous research has consistently shown that managerial women are excluded from the business networks that are available to their male counterparts. This means that, because women managers do not have access to the same informal business networks as their male colleagues, they are denied the same information and assistance (Arroba and James, 1989). Consequently unemployed women managers are likely to be missing out on important job opportunities, as they are excluded from a substantial number of unadvertised managerial positions that are reserved solely for male candidates.

Job skidding   Several large-scale studies have found that, because of financial pressures or lack of job availability, many unemployed individuals take jobs that are of a lower level, in terms of both status and remuneration (Mallinckrodt, 1990; Rosen and College, 1987). This 'job skidding' is experienced by both men and women, but there is considerable evidence that women are more likely to take lower-status jobs and are less likely to obtain a salary commensurate with their previous experience and education than their male counterparts (Levy, 1997; Stroh *et al.*, 1992). This difference in the degree of 'job skidding' encountered by unemployed men and women may arise for a number of reasons.

Firstly, men continue to believe that their adequacy as a provider is indicated by their income level. Pittman and Orthner (1988), in a major study of job commitment, found that a man's perception of income adequacy rested primarily with his own contribution to the family's income, regardless of whether his partner worked full- or part-time. In contrast, women do not report income as their primary reason for entering a career, although salary level does play a significant role in job satisfaction (Kulik, 2001). These findings suggest that a man's commitment to the traditional role of provider may be the driving force during his job search, whereas women may be more influenced by a sense of perceived fit between themselves, their family circumstances and the prospective organization (Pittman and Orthner, 1988).

Secondly, the sense of fit experienced by an individual is considerably affected by the perception of adequate remuneration, or reward equity, for the position in question, and these perceptions are affected by previous experience and market forces (Loscocco and Spitze, 1991). It has been suggested that women have lower pay expectations and are easily satisfied with lower salaries, explaining why salaries in female-dominated occupations tend to be poorer than those in male-dominated occupations (Stevens *et al.*, 1993; Rubery and Fagan, 1993). However the evidence does not consistently support the assumption that women do not value pay as strongly as men. In their large-scale study ($n = 2706$) Loscocco and Spitze (1991) found that organizational pay differentials accounted for twice as much of the variance in the pay satisfaction of women as of men. This indicates that women not only value pay levels but are more likely to be adversely affected by pay differentials in organizations than their male counterparts.

It should also be noted that research indicates that one of the reasons women receive lower salaries is that they have poorer negotiating skills than their male counterparts (Stevens et al., 1993). Therefore a combination of all these factors may lead unemployed female managers to feel undervalued and second-rate, affecting their self-image and self-worth. This may serve to reduce further their self-confidence, resulting in unemployed female managers becoming increasingly unable to pursue jobs at a similar level to those they had previously held.

Unsuccessful job search A major determinant of well-being during unemployment is the experience of job search, an individual's need for a job, and their expectations that job seeking will lead to reemployment (Vinokur and Caplan, 1987). These expectations appear to be influenced by two main factors; an individual's attributional style in dealing with unsuccessful job search and the affirmative support of job-seeking behaviours by significant others, both accounting for 10 per cent of the variance in psychological well-being (Ostell and Divers, 1987; Vinokur and Caplan, 1987) (previously discussed in the social support section, pp. 262–65).

Attribution research focuses on the nature and consequences of casual attributions in terms of the success and failure experienced by individuals, and how those attributions can lead to a state of learned helplessness and depression (Peterson and Seligman, 1987; Weiner, 1986). An individual's attributional style is defined by the way they attribute causality in order to interpret events, and so far three styles have been identified (Peterson et al., 1981). First, there is one external style, where a person tends to attribute the causation of events to external or temporary events, such as social or economic circumstances. There are also two internal styles: a behavioural style which is where an individual attributes an outcome to their own behaviour, and a characterological style which is where an individual attributes outcome to their character rather than their actual actions.

Those who make external or behavioural attributions for negative events, such as unsuccessful job search, generally have better mental health than those who make characterological attributions (Peterson and Seligman, 1987). Female managers tend to make characterological attributions when they are unsuccessful, whereas male managers tend to make behavioural or external attributions to explain their lack of success (Rosenthal et al., 1996; Rothblum and Cole, 1988). This means that unemployed female managers are likely to attribute unsuccessful job search to personality characteristics that are relatively durable and unchanging, whereas unemployed male managers are more likely to attribute unsuccessful job search to actions which could be changed or altered relatively easily to meet the demands of the situation. Thus it would be anticipated that unemployed female managers will suffer greater negative affect, in terms of poorer mental health, from unsuccessful job search than their male counterparts.

As the number of managers chasing the same positions rises, it is inevitable that both unemployed male and female managers will have to deal with increasing levels of unsuccessful job search. Although male and female managers are used to dealing with heavy competition for managerial positions, their reactions to unsuccessful job search in terms of attribution are likely to differ considerably. The research suggests that unemployed female managers are more likely than their male counterparts to suffer poorer mental health as a result of unsuccessful job search, and are less likely to receive effective support.

Intervening variables
Individuals differ in the way they perceive and react to potential stressors. It is therefore important to consider those aspects of an individual's environment or personality that change the likelihood that a stressor or set of stressors will increase the strain they experience. These intervening variables are referred to in the stress literature as 'mediators' and 'moderators', with mediators producing additive effects and moderators producing interactive effects (Parkes, 1994). Mediators relate the stressor to dysfunctioning but, although they are directly and simultaneously related to the outcome measure, they contribute independently to the overall variance. Thus the direct relationship between the stressor and stress outcome breaks down when the mediator is removed. In contrast, moderators change the empirical relationship between independent and dependent variables, altering the magnitude and direction of the effect of one variable on another (Frese and Zapf, 1988). The most important moderators in unemployment stress research are demographic and personality-type factors, for example social support, coping and control. Social support may be viewed as a demographic variable because it relies on the actual availability of family/spousal support. However the majority of research tends to view social support as a personality-type factor, as the need for support and the perception of its availability are rooted in the individual rather than their environment (Ostell and Divers, 1987). People lacking social support tend to show greater stress reactions to unemployment than those with a high degree of social support. By way of contrast, a mediator links directly sources of stress with outcomes; for example stressors which decrease the degree of social support available in turn influence the level of depression experienced during unemployment. The direct relationship between the stressor and depression breaks down when the mediator is removed, or in this case when social support is returned. Mediators include social relationships, age and employment commitment.

Demographic factors
Research into the psychological impact of unemployment has clearly indicated that unemployment has negative consequences for the psychological and physical well-being of most individuals. However it is not a uniform experience and it should be noted that not all individuals react negatively to job loss. Some individuals actually view unemployment as a positive event which provides an opportunity to develop personal interests and to pursue better employment positions (O'Brien, 1986). The effects of unemployment, and the way in which people cope with the unemployment experience, are determined by a complex set of variables that can exacerbate or reduce its impact (Feather, 1992).

Several principal mediating factors have been identified which fall into two broad categories: demographic and personal variables, and environmental factors. Demographic and personal variables include age, gender, social relationships, length of time unemployed, employment commitment and individual coping strategies. Environmental factors include local unemployment levels, availability of social support, opportunities for interpersonal contact, opportunities for skill use and the availability of money (Banks, 1995). Some of these areas are of particular importance and will be given separate consideration.

Age
Numerous studies have linked the age of unemployed people to depressive affects and a curvilinear association between age and mental health during unemployment has been found by several researchers (Hepworth, 1980; Banks, 1995), but the evidence is not conclusive. Rowley and Feather (1987) found that, apart from financial strain, there was little difference between age groups and the psychological affects of unemployment. In contrast, Wooton *et al.* (1994) suggest that age is predictive of a variety of career and employment expectancies, especially relating to re-employment for which age accounts for 51 per cent of the variance, which act as important moderators between age and stress-related effects of job loss. They concluded that the inability to fulfil these expectancies, because of reducing job opportunities, means that increasing age constitutes a substantial risk in terms of mental health. This effect is compounded as reduced expectancies also affect an individual's willingness to participate in the job search process (Wanberg *et al.*, 1996).

Employment commitment
In addition to vocational expectancies, employment commitment has also been found to act as a moderating factor on psychological distress during unemployment. The desire for work is inversely related to psychological well-being: as the desire for employment increases, so affective well-being and self-esteem decreases (Jackson and Warr, 1987; Winefield and Tiggemann, 1994). A strong personal commitment to work in part reflects the need to earn money, but it also reflects non-financial reasons for wanting to work. Pittman and Orthner (1988) found that the employment commitment of men, while influenced by non-financial considerations, was based upon their income needs. In contrast, women's employment commitment is less influenced by financial considerations, but based upon personal needs, accounting for 49 per cent of the variance in employment commitment compared to 37 per cent for men. It is this personal salience which has repeatedly been associated with adverse effects during unemployment: the greater the non-financial commitment, the greater the risks to mental health (Ullah *et al.*, 1985).

Length of time unemployed
Employment commitment, like many other aspects of unemployment, is frequently affected by the length of time an individual has been unemployed. Previous research has shown that the decline in mental and physical well-being experienced by individuals is substantial in the first six months following job loss (Rowley and Feather, 1987; Jackson and Warr, 1987). In the early stages of unemployment uncertainty may lead to high levels of stress, but it has been suggested that the resulting rate of decline reaches a plateau after six months. Unemployed individuals continue to remain less mentally healthy but they experience a much-reduced rate of decline in terms of physical and psychological well-being. This psychological adjustment is attained by individuals establishing new routines at lower levels of activity, by the maintenance of lower levels of expenditure and by the avoidance of threatening situations. This can result in unemployed managers becoming increasingly passive and accepting of their situation and, whilst this may provide some

protection against further decline in psychological well-being, it inhibits job search and their 'rehabilitation' into managerial positions (Duffield, 1994). In contrast, others have predicted that, as the effects of unemployment do decline but are cumulative, and as stress increases, via financial strain, job commitment and so on, the impact on the mental and physical well-being of individuals will be greater, rather than less, as the length of unemployment increases (Fleming et al., 1984).

The length of time an individual is unemployed is dependent upon many factors, but one of the main influences is the prevailing levels of local unemployment (Townsend, 1992). There is a great deal of local and regional variation in levels of unemployment and it has been suggested that high levels of local unemployment are likely to have several beneficial effects (Jackson and Warr, 1987). These levels have been found to moderate the impact of unemployment via Festinge's (1954) social comparison theory. Individuals who live in areas of high unemployment are more likely to perceive greater similarity between themselves and other unemployed people, thereby maintaining self-esteem and self-worth (Sheeran et al., 1995). Individuals also experience less self-blame, as they perceive less personal control over the circumstances surrounding their job loss. However this can have adverse effects if individuals do not feel a sense of control over their future employment prospects.

Personal factors
Self
The impact of job loss and an individual's subsequent experiences of unemployment are moderated by a number of factors, including self-concept, self-esteem, self-efficacy, perceived personal control, and coping strategies. These components have an interactive effect, as well as each exerting a specific influence, on an individual's psychological well-being (Sherer et al., 1982). However, as the psychological effects on unemployed male and female managers are likely to vary substantially with the above factors, the implications of each of these factors will be considered separately.

Self-concept and self-esteem
According to Burns (1980), 'self-concept is a composite image of what we think we are, what we think others think of us and what we would like to be'. An individual's self-concept contains their experiences of their own body, their possessions, their family, their motive structure, drive status, defences and the feelings of pride and shame associated with these facets (Bala and Lakshmi, 1992). Managers tend to view work as more central to their lives than do other workers and are likely to obtain a significant proportion of their self-image, or self-concept, from their work (Kaufman, 1982). The effect of job loss on some managers is 'ego shattering', leading to bitterness, loneliness, helplessness, despondency and a loss of self-respect (Mines, 1979; Fielden and Davidson, 1996), although it has been suggested that the degree of psychological devastation experienced does appear to be connected with the level of prestige associated with an individual's previous position. Research has shown that unemployed male managers, at middle and senior levels, frequently retain their professional identity during unemployment, enabling them to maintain their self-esteem and self-worth (Hartley, 1980a). This contradicts the frequently accepted generalization that unemployment leads to lower self-esteem, but Hartley claims that this assumption may be inaccurate because it fails to take account of individual reactions to unemployment.

As women tend to hold less prestigious management positions than their male counterparts, it is more likely that unemployed female managers will experience greater negative affectivity during unemployment than male managers.

The impact of unemployment on an individual's self-concept results not only from a possible loss of social identity and social status, but also from the identity they gain from being an unemployed person (Rosenberg and Kaplan, 1982). Although the social stigma associated with unemployment has decreased as the number of unemployed white-collar workers has increased, it does still exist. This affects how individuals view themselves and how they feel others view them (Rosenberg and Kaplan, 1982). Research has shown that, compared with unemployed men, unemployed women believe that other people's views of them are significantly more negative and these views, in general, remain constant during unemployment (Sheeran and Abraham, 1994). As working women hold more positive reflected appraisals than working men, the effect of unemployment on their self-concept appears to be substantial (Bala and Lakshmi, 1992). There are several possible reasons why this gender difference may arise:

1. work may be more central to women's self-concept;
2. unemployed women do not have the same status as unemployed men;
3. society does not place the same importance on women's careers, thereby undermining their need to return to work; and/or
4. women's self-concept has or might have a greater degree of *social determination* linked to pressures during socialization, where girls seem to be required to conform to socially acceptable behaviours, norms and so on more than boys are.

Although self-esteem is intrinsically linked to self-concept, its influence on an individual's psychological well-being is to some degree independent of self-concept and therefore warrants separate consideration (Jex *et al.*, 1994). Self-esteem is generally defined as the degree to which we like and value ourselves and may provide a buffer from the negative psychological impact of unemployment. Moreover a loss of self-esteem has frequently been associated with acute psychological distress experienced during unemployment (Kelvin and Jarrett, 1985). Previous research has shown that unemployment frequently results in lower self-esteem and increased stress which places individuals at considerable risk: as unemployment progresses self-esteem tends to decrease, while self-dissatisfaction, self-rejection and self-contempt tend to increase (Kates *et al.*, 1990). However, while previous studies have recognized the importance of individual differences in people's reaction to unemployment, only a few recent studies have identified important gender differences. The evidence suggests that for men self-esteem has no moderating effect between unemployment and anxiety, depression and life-satisfaction (Jex *et al.*, 1994). In contrast, for women unemployment is more strongly associated with anxiety and depression amongst those reporting low levels of self-esteem, accounting for 22 per cent and 21 per cent of the variance, respectively. This difference may arise for a number of reasons:

1. women are more likely to blame themselves for being unemployed;
2. the general tendency of women to attribute failure to internal factors;
3. women value social relationships more than men but doubt their ability to replace those social relationships that may have been lost as a result of unemployment.

Thus women are more likely to suffer lower levels of self-esteem during unemployment, resulting in increased levels of depression and anxiety, than their male counterparts.

The effect of unemployment on the self-esteem of managers may also be subject to these gender differences. Hartley (1980a) found that the self-esteem of male managers, unlike that of male blue-collar workers, does not decline during unemployment, although it can be temporarily depressed by certain events. This may be because the global self-esteem of male managers is strong enough to withstand a decrease of self-esteem in the domain-specific area of employment. This approach appears to buffer the impact of unemployment on male managers who, in comparison with employed managers, do not report high levels of anxiety, tension or apprehension (Hartley, 1980a). In contrast, female managers do experience a decline in self-esteem during unemployment and the associated consequences, that is loss of confidence, loss of self-worth, and feelings of inadequacy (Fielden and Davidson, 1996). This loss of self-esteem appears to affect the global self-esteem of unemployed female managers, as opposed to just the domain-specific self-esteem associated with employment. Thus it is anticipated that unemployed female managers may experience substantially greater negative psychological effects than unemployed male managers, resulting from significantly lower levels of self-esteem.

Self-efficacy
Self-efficacy has been defined as the belief in one's ability to perform a task, or more specifically to execute a specified behaviour, successfully (Bandura, 1982). According to this theory two types of expectancies exert powerful influences on behaviour: outcome expectancy, the belief that certain behaviours will lead to certain outcomes, and self-efficacy expectancy, the belief that one can successfully perform the behaviours in question (Maddux et al., 1982). These expectancies influence the choice of activities people will engage in, the amount of effort they will expend, and how long they will persist in the face of obstacles or aversive experiences. Those with a poor sense of self-efficacy will doubt their own capabilities and as these doubts grow they are likely to reduce their efforts or give up altogether, whereas those with a strong sense of self-efficacy will exert the greatest effort to master the challenges, maintaining high levels of performance (Bandura, 1982). Thus unemployed managers with low levels of self-efficacy are increasingly less likely to engage in job search behaviours, and consequently more likely to experience higher levels of depression and lower levels of self-esteem (Wells-Parker et al., 1990).

Malen and Stroh (1998) found that, for women, outcome expectancies were the main predictors of active or passive coping orientations in relation to occupational roles. This may mean that individuals are reluctant to apply for positions which they feel they are unlikely to attain, a situation especially relevant to unemployed female managers who may perceive many job advertisements as male-oriented. However, in a similar-size study, Vianen and Keizer (1996) found that outcome expectancy was not predictive of an individual's intention to pursue a managerial position, in which self-efficacy plays the central role. They suggest that the more experienced a person is in management tasks the greater their self-efficacy and the greater the motivation to secure a management position. In addition psychological arousal (tension) reduces self-efficacy for management tasks, which prevents an individual from assuming a managerial position. Compared to men, women tend to have less experience of managerial tasks, because their jobs are more task-restricted, they receive less verbal support and they experience greater psychological tension (ibid.). As a consequence their self-efficacy and intention to assume a managerial job is lower than that of their male counterparts. This has significant implications for unemployed female managers who may be less likely to apply for managerial positions that they do not feel fully comply with their previous experience.

Personal control
The way in which individuals perceive their situation and attribute causes of events is dependent upon the degree of personal control they experience. According to Rotter (1966) people have generalized expectancies regarding whether or not their actions will lead to internal or external control of reinforcements. The generalized expectancy of internal control refers to the perception of events, whether positive or negative, as being a consequence of one's own action and thereby potentially under personal control. In contrast, the generalized expectancy of external control refers to the perception of positive or negative events as being unrelated to one's own behaviour and therefore beyond personal control (Lefcourt, 1982). Although people tend to be classified as 'internals' or 'externals' the concept is not dichotomous but of a continuum ranging from highly internal to highly external (Weiten, 1989).

In general, people with an internal locus of control tend to develop fewer psychological disorders than those with an external locus of control (Weiten, 1989). Internals tend to perceive less stress, employ more task-centred coping behaviours and employ fewer emotion-centred behaviours than externals (Anderson, 1977). Previous research has suggested that women are more likely to employ emotion-centred behaviours and report lower levels of internal control, whereas men tend to employ more task-centred behaviours and report higher levels of internal control (Rim, 1987; Vingerhoets and Heck, 1990). This may indicate that women will be more likely to suffer from poorer psychological well-being during unemployment. However Peterson and Seligman (1987) suggest that there are some situations where an external orientation may be more beneficial. Individuals who explain the occurrence of negative events, such as unemployment, in terms of external, unstable and specific causes are less likely to suffer psychological distress than those making internal, stable and global attributions.

Unemployment is often seen as representing an uncontrollable state of affairs and, given the fact that most managers lose their jobs primarily because of factors beyond their control, an external orientation following job loss may protect individuals from the initial effects of unemployment on well-being. However the evidence does not appear to support this view. Swinburne (1981) found that those who perceived some degree of control in regard to their job loss, experienced fewer negative feelings than those who felt that they had no control over what had happened to them. Those who felt least personal control over their job loss experienced more distress and were particularly affected by rejection during job search, they also tended to have lower self-confidence and a decreased receptivity to employment (Baubion-Broye *et al.*, 1989). In contrast, internal locus of control is associated with lower levels of anxiety and depression, and higher levels of self-esteem and life satisfaction (Cvetanovski and Jex, 1994). Previous research has shown that, in general, individuals employed in supervisory and management positions score higher on internal locus of control than those working in non-supervisory positions (Kapalka and

Lachenmeyer, 1988; Mellinger and Erdwins, 1985; St-Yves et al., 1989). Thus it may be anticipated that unemployed managers will perceive relatively higher degrees of personal control and, as a result, will be more intrinsically motivated in their job search, although they may verbalize external causes to explain or defend themselves against actual or expected failures during job search (Rotter, 1966).

Coping strategies
Coping is generally defined as constantly changing cognitive and behavioural efforts to manage the internal and external demands of transactions that tax or exceed a person's resources (Latack et al., 1995). Coping with job loss and unemployment, therefore, refers to cognitive and behavioural efforts to manage the demands faced by an individual as a result of their situation. The process of coping with stressful events, such as unemployment, is complex and highly dynamic and is directed towards moderating the impact of such events on an individual's physical, social and emotional functioning. The coping strategies adopted by an individual are determined by a number of factors, including personality variables (for example personal control and Type A behaviour patterns), demographic factors (for example age and gender), sociodemographic factors (for example education and income) and availability of coping resources (for example self-esteem and experience) (Gist and Mitchell, 1992; Holahan and Moos, 1987).

Vingerhoets and Van Heck (1990) found that men are more inclined to use active problem-focused coping strategies, accounting for 49 per cent of the variance in reported stress levels; they plan and rationalize their actions, they engage in positive thinking, perseverance, self-adaptation and personal growth. In contrast, women prefer emotion-focused solutions, accounting for 44 per cent of the variance in stress levels; they engage in self-blame and wishful thinking, they seek social support and a forum for the expression of their emotions. However women are more likely to engage in active–behavioural coping than men, that is they attempt to deal directly with the problem and its effects by taking positive action (Astor-Dubin and Hammen, 1984). Thus, although unemployed female managers may suffer from increased psychological and psychosomatic symptoms, they are more likely to deal with the problems of unemployment and job search than their male counterparts. Women are more likely to engage in behaviours that involve external recognition, allowing others to label and offer help with their problems, whereas men tend to deal with their problems internally (Omar, 1995). Unemployed female managers, who are most likely to employ emotion-focused coping strategies, will have to deal with expectations and goals of significant others in conjunction with their own objectives. Conflict may arise where these approaches differ and significant others are perceived as unsupportive (Ratcliff and Brogden, 1988). If unemployed female managers cannot deal successfully with this conflict they may be unable to find an effective means of coping with their situation, resulting in poorer psychological well-being, lower self-confidence and lower self-esteem (Holahan and Moos, 1987; Oakland and Ostell, 1996).

Type A behaviour pattern
Unemployed female managers may not only be faced with different sources of stress than their male counterparts, because of their tendency towards emotion-focused coping behaviours, but research suggests that their ability to cope with stress may also be

adversely affected by their tendency towards Type A behaviour patterns (Greenglass, 1993b). Type A behaviour is the overall style of behaviour that is observed in people who are excessively time-conscious, aggressive, competitive, ambitious and hard-driving, and has been found to be a significant predictor of stress-related illness (Edwards *et al.*, 1990; Greenglass, 1993b). It has been reported that Type A behaviour patterns are often elicited by environmental stressors or challenges. Type A individuals are particularly challenged by situations in which their control is threatened, and their primary response in such situations is to struggle to exert and maintain control aggressively over their environment (R.D. Caplan, 1983). This struggle may be exacerbated by unsuccessful job search, which prevents the individual from regaining control of their employment situation. Thus individuals who display Type A behaviour patterns may experience high levels of stress following job loss, which continue to increase as the length of time they are unemployed increases.

The effect of Type A behaviour patterns of psychological and psychosomatic symptoms is strongly influenced by the type of coping strategy employed, accounting for over 10 per cent of the variance (Edwards *et al.*, 1990). Problem-focused coping in conjunction with Type A behaviour results in a decrease in symptoms, whereas emotion-focused coping in conjunction with Type A behaviour results in an increase in symptoms. Although not all studies have found significant gender differences in Type A behaviour, a number of studies have revealed that women managers tend to display higher levels of Type A behaviour than their male counterparts (Davidson and Cooper, 1987; Rees and Cooper, 1992). This behavioural characteristic may mean that unemployed female managers will suffer poorer mental and physical well-being than unemployed male managers, even if they both engage in problem-focused coping strategies.

Stress outcomes: gender similarities and differences in psychological, physical and behavioural stress outcomes

It is widely recognized that the stress of unemployment results in impaired psychological and physical well-being in both men and women, although there is a great deal of conflict in the literature regarding the extent of this impairment experienced by women. This conflict arises from outdated stereotypical views and a lack of understanding surrounding the importance of gender in explaining differences in stress outcomes (Walters, 1993). Jick and Mitz (1985) suggest that women experience psychological stress (for example depression, emotional discomfort) more frequently than men, whereas men experience physiological stress (for example coronary heart disease) more frequently than women. However large-scale research has indicated that this latter belief is unfounded, and the evidence suggests that the link between stress and heart disease is now a major concern for both men and women (Elliott, 1995; Kritz-Silverstein *et al.*, 1992).

One of the most consistent results in mental health surveys is that women report significantly more symptoms than men (Tuosignant *et al.*, 1987). The evidence suggests that this difference may arise for one or more of the following reasons:

1. women are more willing to tell their symptoms to others, because of either greater social acceptance of sickness among women or greater concern for health among women;

2. the 'vocabulary of illness' differs for men and women, women elaborate more about their symptoms, often discussing the psychological effects of their symptoms, not just the physical outcomes;
3. women genuinely experience poorer mental health than men (Tuosignant et al., 1987; Verbrugge, 1985).

Gender differences have frequently been reported in relation to occupational stress and previous research has indicated that female managers react differently from male managers in terms of reported stress outcomes (Davidson et al., 1995). Stress-related illness tends to manifest itself in terms of physical ill-health for male executives, whereas for female executives it is more likely to develop into mental ill-health (Cooper and Melhuish, 1984).

The deleterious behavioural consequences of stress, in terms of smoking and drinking, also differ between men and women. In general, women are more likely to smoke than men regardless of employment status and, whilst unemployment is associated with an overall increase in the smoking levels of both men and women, the increase in the smoking levels of women is significantly higher than that of men during unemployment (Hammarstrom and Janlert, 1994). In contrast, health problems due to drink are more frequently reported amongst unemployed men than their employed counterparts, whereas unemployed women report fewer drinking problems than their employed counterparts (Lahelma et al., 1995).

Stress outcomes and unemployed men
Previous research has consistently identified negative mental and physical outcomes resulting from unemployment. Following job loss individuals frequently experience shame, anger, fear of the future, frustration and disillusionment. Viinamaki et al. (1993) found that continuing unemployment represents a significant risk to mental health and unemployed people are frequently found to experience higher levels of depression, anxiety and distress, in conjunction with lower self-esteem and confidence (Muller et al., 1993; Warr et al., 1988). Several studies have found that the prevalence of depressive illness is significantly higher in unemployed men than in the general population (Eales 1988; Osipow and Fitzgerald, 1993). In some cases this decline in mental well-being is substantial and the rates of suicide and parasuicide have been found to be higher in unemployed men (Platt and Kreitman, 1984; Moser et al., 1984).

The effects of chronic stress experienced as a result of job loss and continuing unemployment, along with symptoms of somatization and minor psychiatric disturbances, frequently lead to a decline in physical well-being (Fleming et al., 1984). Unemployed men have been found to make significantly more visits to their doctor, increase their use of medical drugs and spend more days confined to bed through sickness then employed men (Linn et al., 1985; Layton, 1986). The types of problem presented, for example colds, rashes, respiratory problems and gastrointestinal complaints, support the belief that the illnesses experienced are emotionally derived via the stress response, rather than having an identifiable physical basis (Linn et al., 1985).

The physical repercussions of unemployment may not necessarily be of significance during the period of unemployment, with individuals experiencing merely feelings of being unwell rather than experiencing serious illness. Westcott (1984) found that, although significantly more unemployed men than employed men reported illness, their symptoms were not severe enough to warrant seeking medical advice. However this lack of apparent illness may be disturbingly deceptive, as demonstrated by the findings of the extensive British Regional Heart Study (Shaper and Cook, 1984). This study showed that, regardless of whether or not an individual considered themselves well, unemployed males showed evidence of excessive rates of chronic respiratory disease and ischaemic heart disease. These findings are concurrent with other studies which have found elevated levels of catecholamines in unemployed men. These levels, which increase with the length of unemployment, are linked with interior blood vessel damage, cardiovascular disorders, increased blood pressure and decreases in immune functioning (Fleming et al., 1984).

Stress outcomes and unemployed women
Some studies have proposed that women will be less affected than men by the impact of unemployment, as women are better able to cope with being without paid employment (Kasl and Cobb, 1979). However the limited research that has been conducted does not provide support for these stereotypical views. Several studies have found that unemployed women experience higher levels of psychological distress than employed women who are unable to maintain their mental well-being through domestic roles (Vesalainen and Vuori, 1999; Kulic, 2001). Muller et al. (1993) found that, although work overload did predict poorer psychological well-being for both employed and non-employed women, the interaction between work overload and the lack of challenge perceived by non-employed women in their roles as housewife and/or mother, had a significant impact on their well-being. Without the challenges experienced by female managers in their work roles they may be deprived of 'hardiness', a syndrome of personal beliefs and qualities that influence behaviour, which may protect them from other sources of stress, such as role overload (Kobasa, 1979). Thus, if employment is removed, women may find themselves exposed to additional sources of stress at a time when their ability to cope with those stressors is eroded. This could have a serious effect on women's physical and psychological well-being in addition to the effects of unemployment experienced by men. In addition, the findings of a longitudinal study by Kirtz-Silverstein et al. (1992) suggest that unemployed women suffer poorer physical health and have more unfavourable heart disease risk factors than employed women. Moreover the impact of unemployment on women appears to be so severe that even after re-employment the symptoms of depression do not disappear as they do in men (Dew et al., 1992; Vesalainen and Vuori, 1999). Job loss initiates a distress that is fuelled by uncertainty and insecurity that, for women, cannot be relieved by simply obtaining a new job. Dew et al. (1992) concluded that the experience of job loss not only leads to feelings of depression, apathy and withdrawal in women, it is also more devastating for women than for men. Thus, even though many of the assumptions made about the impact of unemployment on women have no factual basis, they continue to be used to devalue women's experiences of unemployment and have successfully contributed to the underresearching into the experiences of unemployed women.

Comparative stress effects of unemployment on men and women
Few studies have compared the impact of unemployment upon males and females. Those that have are mostly confined to the consequences of unemployment, in terms of physical and psychological well-being, rather than exploring the experiences of men and women

during unemployment in terms of the sources of stress they encounter and how they deal with those stressors. A few relatively small studies claim that unemployment has a significantly greater impact on the well-being of men, who experience higher levels of depressive affect and anxiety than women (Shamir, 1985; Perrucci et al., 1997). Overall findings are inconsistent, with many studies reporting no significant differences in the overall effects of unemployment on the mental and physical well-being of men and women. However, a growing body of literature has acknowledged that certain aspects of unemployment are experienced differently by each sex (Ensminger and Celentano, 1990; Stokes and Cochrane, 1984; Leana and Feldman, 1991). For example, loneliness and disadvantageous consequences are important mediators in the mental health of men, accounting for 25 per cent of the explained variance, whereas network factors are more important for the psychological well-being of women, accounting for 24 per cent of the explained variance (Ensminger and Celentano, 1990; Leeflang et al., 1992; Winefield and Tiggemann, 1985). In addition men and women differ in the way in which they are affected by financial worries. Men tend to be more affected by the indirect consequences of financial deprivation, for example loss of income status, whereas women are most affected by the direct consequences of financial deprivation, for example paying bills (Leeflang et al., 1992).

The main differences found between men and women in their reactions to unemployment have been linked to their domestic circumstance (Daniel, 1990). The greatest disparity found in the impact of unemployment on psychological well-being is between single men and women, with single women suffering poorer mental health than single men, although they find jobs more quickly. This contrasts with the reaction of women who had dependent children who took longer to find work, a situation often attributed to a lack of interest or commitment to work. However, as many women take larger pay cuts in order to return to work, this time delay is more likely to be a product of poor childcare provision provided by employers, the cost and lack of external childcare, and the lack of flexible working patterns offered by employers (Daniel, 1990).

The evidence suggests that there may be some differences in the reaction of men and women to unemployment, which arise from differences in their role configuration rather than from intrinsic gender differences (Ensminger and Celentano, 1990). Further support for this belief comes from research into the impact of job loss on self-concept. Stokes and Cochrane (1984) found that the adverse psychological effects of unemployment were not restricted to a component of self-concept that was solely dependent upon employment status for evaluation, but precipitated a generalized perception of the self. The impact of unemployment on this generalization appears to be much greater for women than it does for men. Employed women hold more positive reflected appraisals than men, whereas unemployed women hold significantly poorer reflected appraisals than unemployed men, believing that other people's views of them are generally negative (Sheeran and Abraham, 1994). This disparity in reflected appraisals may lead to the expectation that unemployed women would experience significantly poorer mental well-being than employed women, whereas a lesser effect would be expected between employed and unemployed men. However, findings contrary to these expectations have been produced by several studies (Perrucci et al., 1997; Snyder and Nowak, 1984). These studies have shown that employed men have lower levels of distress than unemployed men, but there is no significant difference in the levels of distress experienced by employed and unemployed women. These results show that, although the interaction between employment status and psychological well-being may produce the same overall effect, the experience of unemployment is definitely not the same for men and women. These experiences are influenced by factors which have differential effects related to gender, and it is only by exploring these factors and their effects that we can understand the true impact of unemployment on both men and women.

Conclusions

This literature review has identified many potential sources of stress that male and female managers may face during unemployment, and from these findings a research model has been formulated, which will provide a basis for future study (Figure 18.1). The research model illustrates the main sources of stress, moderators of stress and stress outcomes identified by the literature review and indicates areas in which gender differences may be anticipated.

Job loss deprives individuals of both the latent and the manifest consequences of work, adversely affecting physical and mental health. This deprivation can lead to reactions on several levels: emotional, cognitive, behavioural and physiological, and unemployed people have consistently been found to experience higher levels of depression, anxiety and general distress, together with lower self-esteem and confidence. The degree to which unemployment is experienced as a negative event is dependent on a number of factors, including previous experience of unemployment, the relationship between occupational identity and self-identity, perceived stigmatization resulting from interpersonal and intrapersonal comparisons, and perceived responsibility for job loss. It is anticipated that unemployed female managers will experience greater stigmatization and self-blame than their male counterparts, as they are more likely to perceive themselves as unique or exceptional because of their comparatively small numbers.

The financial deprivation experienced during unemployment frequently affects many aspects of an individual's lifestyle, including future planning and the performance of roles. Women tend to be affected by the direct consequences of financial deprivation, whereas men tend to be affected by the indirect consequences such as loss of status and their inability to fulfil their perceived role as 'breadwinner'. This inability is thought to have a substantial effect on self-esteem and for some is the aspect of unemployment which has the single greatest impact on well-being. Thus economic deprivation is likely to have a greater effect on the psychological and physical health of unemployed male managers than on their female counterparts.

Employment is an important source of social support, especially for women, and the loss of this manifest consequence of work through unemployment can lead to feelings of loneliness and isolation. During unemployment men tend to receive emotional support from their partners, whereas women tend to find their partners are 'unsupportive' or they provide only instrumental, that is financial or informational, support. Women tend to rely on their families for emotional support during unemployment and their reliance on family members is maintained throughout their period of unemployment. In contrast, men are more likely to seek support from their friends than from close relations, as they prefer to keep family and work roles separate.

The loss of employment also means a loss of daily structure and enforced activity, and the inability to replace that structure and level of meaningful activity can lead to apathy and depression. Activity maintains mental alertness, wards of fears and doubts and provides a sense of achievement, yet keeping active after job loss becomes increasingly difficult. Several studies have demonstrated the importance of activity levels during unemployment: those who feel their time is fully occupied experience better mental health and are more likely to be successful in their search for work. Although the activity levels of men and women tend to be similar, the type of activity they engage in is gender-oriented. Men are more likely to pursue problem-focused activities, that is behaviours that attempt directly to eliminate the source of stress, whereas women are more likely to engage in emotion-focused activities, that is behaviours that attempt to eliminate the symptoms of unemployment.

It has been suggested that women will be less affected than men by unemployment because they are more influenced by personal rather than financial needs (Warr and Parry, 1982). This view has led to the assumption that women are not as committed to work as men and it has been proposed that, because of the multiple roles women have to deal with, unemployment will actually lead to a reduction in the stress experienced by women. However it appears to be the quality rather than the quantity of roles that is important in determining psychological distress. Thus, compared to their non-managerial counterparts, the removal of the work is likely to increase the psychological distress experienced by unemployed female managers, for whom work may be one of their most rewarding roles (Arber et al., 1985).

In addition, women potentially face discrimination at all stages of the recruitment process, and even though the number of women managers is rising, management is still seen as a male-dominated profession in which women are marginalized by a masculine model of the successful manager. Occupational stereotypes, in conjunction with limited access to formal and informal business networks, mean that female managers are restricted in the number of positions available to them. This also means that they are less likely to obtain a salary commensurate with their previous experience and education. As managers tend to view work as a major component of their self-concept the impact of these barriers upon psychological well-being may be devastating (Fielden and Davidson, 1996).

The effects of unemployment on physical and mental well-being are moderated by a number of factors, including social support, locus of control, demographics, activity levels, job search experiences and coping strategies. These intervening variables are experienced differently by men and women and, although the majority of studies have found no significant difference in the stress outcomes of unemployed men and women, the evidence does suggest that unemployed female managers are more likely to encounter negative factors than their male counterparts (ibid.). For example, women are more likely to receive social support from their parents than from their spouse or friends, but the importance of work in the lives of women is often denied, resulting in non-supportive social 'support'. Where work is central to an individual's self-image, as it is for many female managers, the effects of this denial on psychological well-being can be traumatic, undermining self-confidence and self-worth.

The effect of unemployment on an individual's well-being is strongly influenced by their reaction to job loss and continuing unemployment. A number of gender differences have been identified in the reactions of men and women to their situation and the strategies that they employ in order to cope with the sources of stress they encounter. The self-esteem of male managers does not appear to be affected by unemployment, whereas it is anticipated that unemployed female managers will suffer a significant decrease in self-esteem and self-worth. This decrease arises partly from a perceived loss of personal control, lower self-efficacy and poorer outcome expectancy in terms of job search, and from the tendency of women to use negative emotion-focused coping strategies in contrast to the more positive problem-focused coping strategies generally used by men.

The predictors of mental and physical ill-health are often dissimilar for men and women, and unemployed female managers are likely to be at a greater risk from mental and physical ill-health as a result of the unique stressors they are faced with (for example Billing and Alvesson, 1993; Pittman and Orthner, 1988). Previous research has also suggested that male and female managers react differently in terms of stress outcomes, with stress-related illness being manifest in terms of physical ill-health in men and in terms of mental ill-health in women. However recent studies have suggested that the long-term physical effects of unemployment on the physical well-being of female managers may be greater than those experienced by unemployed male managers.

Gender differences have also been identified in the behavioural consequences of stress, in terms of smoking and drinking. Unemployment is associated with a rise in smoking levels, but this increase is significantly higher for women than for men. In contrast, men are more likely to report drink-related problems during unemployment than their employed counterparts, whereas women tend to report fewer drinking problems than their employed counterparts.

However the proposed research model is limited in its application to unemployed male and female managers, as the current literature focuses mainly on the experiences of unemployed male blue-collar workers. The relationship between stressors, intervening variables and stress outcomes is a complex one and the literature provides a confusing picture, from which few concrete conclusions can be drawn in relation to the possible effects of unemployment on male and female managers. Unfortunately there is little research to-date which explores the comparative effects of unemployment upon male and female managers, and the only conclusions which can be drawn are those which can be summarized from the literature. Further investigation is needed if this relationship is to be fully understood, although work currently being conducted by the authors would suggest that the proposed model has some validity as a tentative analysis of managerial unemployment for both men and women.

Acknowledgment

This amended chapter was originally published as 'Stress and Unemployment: A Comparative Review and Research Model of Female and Male Managers', *British Journal of Management*, **10**, 63–93, 1999, republished with permission from Blackwells Publishers.

References

Akabas, S.H. (1988), 'Women, work and mental health: room for improvement', *Journal of Primary Prevention*, 9(1/2), Fall/Winter, 130–40.

Aldwin, C.M. and T.A. Revenson (1986), 'Vulnerability to economic stress', *American Journal of Community Psychology*, **14**, 161–74.

Allan, P. (1989), 'Tips from the trenches', *Personnel Administrator*, **34**(1), 74–5.

Allan, P. (1990), 'Looking for work after forty: job search experiences of older unemployed managers and professionals', *Journal of Employment Counselling*, **27**, 113–21.
Anderson, C.R. (1977), 'Locus of control, coping behaviours, and performance in a stress setting: a longitudinal study', *Journal of Applied Psychology*, **62**(4), 446–51.
Arber, S., N. Gilbert and A. Dale (1985), 'Paid employment and women's health: a benefit or a source of strain?', *Sociology of Health and Illness*, **7**(3), 375–99.
Argyle, M. (1989), *The Social Psychology of Work*, Harmondsworth: Penguin Books.
Arnetz, B.B., J. Wasserman, B. Petrini, S.O. Brenner, L. Levi, P. Eneroth, H. Salovaara, R. Hielm, L. Salovaara, T. Theorell and L.L. Petterson (1987), 'Immune function in unemployed women', *Psychosomatic Medicine*, **49**(1), 3–12.
Arroba, T. and K. James (1989), 'Are politics palatable to women managers? How women can make wise moves at work', *Women in Management Review*, **3**(5), 123–30.
Astor-Dubin, L. and C. Hammen (1984), 'Cognitive versus behavioural coping responses of men and women: a brief report', *Cognitive Therapy and Research*, **8**, 85–90.
Bala, M. and Lakshmi (1992), 'Perceived self in educated employed and educated unemployed women', *International Journal of Social Psychiatry*, **38**(4), 257–61.
Bandura, A. (1982), 'Self-efficacy mechanism in human agency', *American Psychologist*, **37**(2), 122–47.
Banks, M.H. (1995), 'Psychological effects of prolonged unemployment: relevance to models of work re-entry following injury', *Journal of Occupational Rehabilitation*, **5**(1), 37–53.
Baubion-Broye, A., J.L. Megemont and M. Sellinger (1989), 'Evolution of feelings of control and of information receptivity during periods of unemployment', *Applied Psychology an International Review*, **38**(3), 265–75.
Becker, G.S. (1981), *A Treatise on the Family*, Cambridge, M.A: Harvard University Press.
Billing, Y.D. and M. Alvesson (1993), *Gender, Managers and Organisations*, Berlin: Walter de Gruyter.
Bolton, W. and K. Oatley (1987), 'A longitudinal study of social support and depression in unemployed men', *Psychological Medicine*, **11**, 561–80.
Breakwell, G.M. (1985), 'Abusing the unemployed: an invisible injustice', *Journal of Moral Education*, **14**, 56–62.
Brief, A.P., M.A. Konovsky, R. Goodwin and K. Link (1995), 'Inferring the meaning of work from the effects of unemployment', *Journal of Applied Psychology*, **25**(8), 693–711.
Brindle, L. (1992), 'The redundant executive', *Selection Development Review*, **8**(6), 2–4.
Brugha, T.S., P.E. Bebbington, B. MacCarthy, E. Sturt, T. Wykes and J. Potter (1990), 'Gender, social support and recovery from depressive disorders: a prospective clinical study', *Psychological Medicine*, **20**, 147–56.
Burke, R.J., M.G. Rothstein and J.M. Bristor (1995), 'Interpersonal networks of managerial and professional women and men: descriptive characteristics', *Women in Management Review*, **10**(1), 21–7.
Burns, R.B. (1980), *The Self-Concept Theory*, London: Longman.
Capell, P. (1992), 'Endangered middle managers', *American Demographics*, January, 44–7.
Caplan, G. (1982), 'The family as a support system', in H. McCubbin, E. Cauble and J. Patterson (eds), *Family Stress, Coping and Social Support*, Springfield, IL: Charles C. Thomas.
Caplan, R.D. (1983), 'Person – environment fit: past, present and future', in C.L. Cooper (ed.), *Stress Research*, Chichester: John Wiley & Sons.
Carlson, D.S., K.M. Kacmar and L.P. Stepina (1995), 'An examination of two aspects of work – family conflict: time and identity', *Women in Management Review*, **10**(2), 17–25.
Cooper, C.L. and A. Melhuish (1984), 'Executive stress and health: differences between men and women', *Journal of Occupational Medicine*, **26**(2), 99–103.
Coyle, A. (1984), *Redundant Women*, London: The Women's Press Ltd.
Cvetanovski, J. and S.M. Jex (1994), 'Locus of control of unemployed people and its relationship to psychological and physical well-being', *Work & Stress*, **8**(1), 60–67.
Daniel, W.W. (1990), *The Unemployed Flow*, London: Policy Studies Institute.
Davidson, M.J. and R. Burke (1994), *Women in Management – Current Research Issues*, London: Paul Chapman.
Davidson, M.J. and R. Burke (2004), *Women in Management Worldwide*, London: Ashgate.
Davidson, M.J. and C.L. Cooper (1987), 'Female managers in Britain – a comparative review', *Human Resource Management*, **26**, 217–42.
Davidson, M.J. and C.L. Cooper (1992), *Shattering the Glass Ceiling: The Women Manager*, London: Paul Chapman Publishing.
Davidson, M.J., C.L. Cooper and V. Baldini (1995), 'Occupational stress in female and male graduate managers', *Stress Medicine*, **11**, 157–75.
Davies, K. and J. Esseveld (1989), 'Factory women: redundancy and the search for work: toward a reconceptualization of employment and unemployment', *The Sociological Review*, **37**, 219–52.
Dew, M.A., E.J. Bromet and L. Penkower (1992), 'Mental health effects of job loss in women', *Psychological Medicine*, **22**, 751–64.

Dex, S. (1988), *Women's Attitudes Toward Work*, Basingstoke: Macmillan Press.
Dilnot, A. and M. Kell (1988), 'Male unemployment and women's work', *Fiscal Studies*, **8**(3), 1–16.
Doran, L.I., A.P. Brief, V.K. Stone and J.M. George (1991), 'Behavioral intentions as predictors of job attitudes: the roles of economic choice', *Journal of Applied Psychology*, **76**(1), 40–45.
Duck, S. (1988), *Relating to Others*, Milton Keynes: Open University Press.
Dudeney, C. (1980), *A Guide to Executive Re-employment*, Plymouth: MacDonald & Evans.
Duffield, M. (1994), 'Management development and unemployment', Institute of Management, Bristol, unpublished.
Eales, M.J. (1988), 'Depression and anxiety in unemployed men', *Psychological Medicine*, **18**, 935–45.
Edwards, J.R., A.J. Baglioni and C.L. Cooper (1990), 'Stress, type-a, coping, and psychological and physical symptoms: a multi-sample test of alternative models', *Human Relations*, **43**(10), 919–56.
Elliott, S.J. (1995), 'Psychological stress, women and heart health: a critical review', *Social Science Medicine*, **40**(1), 105–15.
Ensminger, M.E. and D.D. Celentano (1990), 'Gender differences in the effect of unemployment on psychological distress', *Social Science Medicine*, **30**(4), 469–77.
Equal Opportunities Commission (2004), *Facts About Women and Men in Great Britain*, Manchester: EOC.
Estes, R.J. (1973), 'The unemployed professional', doctoral dissertation, University of California at Berkeley; published in S. Fineman (1983), *White Collar Unemployment: Impact and Stress*, Chichester: John Wiley & Sons.
Feather, N.T. (1992), 'Expectancy-value theory and unemployment effects', *Journal of Occupational and Organisational Psychology*, **65**, 315–30.
Fenlason, K.J. and T.A. Beehr (1994), 'Social support and occupational stress: effects of talking to others', *Journal of Organisational Behaviour*, **15**, 157–75.
Festinger, L. (1954), 'A theory of social comparison processes', *Human Relations*, **7**, 117–40.
Fielden, S.L. and M.J. Davidson (1996), 'Sources of stress in unemployed female managers – a pilot study', *International Review of Women and Leadership*, **2**(2), 73–97.
Fielden, S.L. and M.J. Davidson (1999), 'Stress and unemployment: a comparative review and research model of female and male managers', *British Journal of Management*, **10**(1), 63–93.
Fielden, S.L. and M.J. Davidson (2001), 'Stress and gender: unemployed female and male managers', *Applied Psychology: An International Review*, **50**(2), 314–43.
Fineman, S. (1984), *White Collar Unemployment: Impact and Stress*, Chichester: John Wiley & Sons.
Fleming, R., A. Baum, D. Reddy and R.J. Gatchel (1984), 'Behavioural and biochemical effects of job loss and unemployment stress', *Journal of Human Stress*, **10**, 12–17.
Frese, M. and G. Mohr (1987), 'Prolonged unemployment and depression in older workers: a longitudinal study of intervening variables', *Social Science Medicine*, **25**, 173–8.
Frese, M. and D. Zapf (1988), 'Methodological Issues in the Study of Work Stress', in C.L. Cooper and R. Payne (eds), *Causes, Coping and Consequences of Stress at Work*, Chichester: John Wiley & Sons.
Fryer, D.M. (1986), 'Employment deprivation and personal agency during unemployment', *Social Behaviour*, **1**, 3–23.
Fryer, D.M. (1995), 'Labour market disadvantages, deprivation and mental health: benefit agency?', *The Psychologist*, **8**(6), 265–72.
George, J.M. and A.P. Brief (1990), 'The economic instrumentality of work: an examination of the moderating effects of financial requirements and sex on the pay–life satisfaction relationship', *Journal of Vocational Behaviour*, **37**, 357–68.
Gist, M. and T. Mitchell (1992), 'Self-efficacy: a theoretical analysis of its dimensions and malleability', *Academy of Management Review*, **17**, 183–211.
Glick, P., C. Zion and C. Nelson (1988), 'What mediates sex discrimination in living decisions?', *Journal of Personality and Social Psychology*, **55**(2), 178–86.
Gore, S. (1978), 'The effect of social support in moderating the health consequences of unemployment', *Journal of Health and Social Behavior*, **19**, 157–65.
Greenglass, E.R. (1993a), 'The contribution of social support to coping strategies', *Applied Psychology: An International Review*, **42**(4), 323–40.
Greenglass, E.R. (1993b), 'Structural and social–psychological factors associated with job functioning by women managers', *Psychological Reports*, **73**(3), 979–86.
Hallstrom, T. (1986), 'Social origins of major depression: the role of provoking agents and vulnerability factors', *Acta Psychiatrit Scanda*, **73**, 383–9.
Hammarstrom, A. and U. Janlert (1994), 'Unemployment and change of tobacco habits: a study of young people from 16 to 21 years of age', *Addiction*, **89**, 1691–6.
Hartley, J.F. (1980a), 'The impact of unemployment upon the self-esteem of managers', *Journal of Occupational Psychology*, **53**, 147–55.

Hartley, J.F. (1980b), 'The personality of unemployed managers: myths and measurement', *Personnel Review*, **9**(3), 12–8.
Heidrick and Struggles (1983), *The UK Chief Executive and His Outlook*, London: Heidrick & Struggles.
Hepworth, S., (1980), 'Moderating factors of the psychological impact of unemployment', *Journal of Occupational Psychology*, **53**, 139–45.
Hibbard, J.H. and C.R. Pope (1993), 'The quality of social roles as predictors of morbidity and mortality', *Social Science Medicine*, **36**(3), 217–25.
Hirsh, W. and S. Bevan (1988), *What Makes a Manager?*, Brighton: Institute of Manpower Studies.
Holahan, C.J. and R.H. Moos (1982), 'Social support and adjustment: predictive benefits of social climate indices', *American Journal of Community Psychology*, **10**(4), 403–15.
Holahan, C.J. and R.H. Moos (1987), 'Personal and contextual determinants of coping strategies', *Journal of Personality and Social Psychology*, **52**, 946–55.
Ibarra, H. (1993), 'Personal networks of women and minorities in management', *Academy of Management Review*, **18**, 56–87.
Jackson, P.R. (1988), 'Personal networks, support mobilisation and unemployment', *Psychological Medicine*, **18**, 397–404.
Jackson, P.R. and P.B. Warr (1987), 'Mental health of unemployed men in different parts of England and Wales', *British Medical Journal*, **295**, 525–35.
Jacobs, J. (1989), *Revolving Doors: Sex Segregation and Women's Careers*, Stanford, CA: Stanford University Press.
Jahoda, M. and H. Rush (1980), 'Work, employment and unemployment', occasional paper series, Science Policy Research Unit, University of Sussex.
Jex, S.M., J. Cvetanovski and S.J. Allen (1994), 'Self-esteem as a moderator of the impact of unemployment', *Journal of Social Behavior and Personality*, **9**(1), 69–80.
Jick, T.D. and L.F. Mitz (1985), 'Sex differences in work stress', *Academy of Management Review*, **10**, 408–20.
Kapalka, G.M. and J.R. Lachenmeyer (1988), 'Sex-role flexibility, locus of control, and occupational status', *Sex Roles*, **19**(7/8), 417–27.
Kasl, S.V. and S. Cobb (1979), 'Some mental health consequences of plant closing and job loss', in L.A. Ferman and J.P. Gordus (eds), *Mental Health and the Economy*, Kalamazoo, MI: W.E. Upjohn Institute for Employment Research.
Kates, N., B.S. Greiff and D.Q. Hagan (1990), *The Psychological Impact of Job Loss*, Washington, DC: American Psychiatric Association.
Kaufman, H.G. (1982), *Professionals in Search of Work: Coping with the Stress of Job Loss and Unemployment*, New York: Wiley Int.
Kaufmann, G.M. and T.A. Beehr (1986), 'Interactions between job stressors and social support: some counter-intuitive results', *Journal of Applied Psychology*, **71**, 522–6.
Kelvin, P. and J.E. Jarret (1985), *Unemployment: Its Social Psychological Effects*, Cambridge: Cambridge University Press.
Kessler, E. (1996), 'Correlation of marital satisfaction and depression among couples where one spouse has become involuntarily unemployed', *Humanities and Social Sciences*, **57**(2-A), 840–76.
Kilpatrick, R. and K. Trew (1985), 'Life-styles and psychological well-being among unemployed men in Northern Ireland', *Journal of Occupational Psychology*, **58**, 207–16.
Kirkpatrick, D. (1988), 'Smart new ways to use temps', *Fortune*, **112**(9), 51–6.
Kirtz-Silverstein, D., D.L. Wingard and E. Barrett-Connor (1992), 'Employment status and heart disease risk factors in middle-aged women: the Rancho Bernardo study', *American Journal of Public Health*, **82**(2), 215–19.
Kobasa, S.C. (1979), 'Stressful life events, personality and health', *Journal of Personality and Social Psychology*, **37**, 1–11.
Kulik, L. (2001), 'Assessing job search intensity and unemployment-related attitudes among young adults: intergender differences', *Journal of Career Assessment*, **9**(2), 153–67.
Lahelma, E., R. Kangas and K. Manderbacka (1995), 'Drinking and unemployment: contrasting patterns among men and women', *Drug and Alcohol Dependency*, **37**, 71–82.
Latack, J.C., A.J. Kinicki and G.E. Prussia (1995), 'An integrative process model of coping with job loss', *Academy of Management Review*, **20**(2), 311–42.
Layton, C. (1986), 'Employment, unemployment, and responses to the general health questionnaire', *Psychological Reports*, **58**, 807–10.
Leana, C.R. and D.C. Feldman (1991), 'Gender differences in response to unemployment', *Journal of Vocational Behaviour*, **38**, 65–77.
Leeflang, D., D.J. Klien-Hesselink and I.P. Spruit (1992), 'Health effects of unemployment – II: men and women', *Social Science Medicine*, **34**(4), 351–63.
Lefcourt, H.M. (1982), *Locus of Control: Current Trends in Theory and Research*, Hillsdale, NJ: LEA.

Levy, M.L. (1997), 'A model of mental health for reemployed individuals', *The Sciences and Engineering*, **58**(3-B), 1579.
Linn, M.W., R. Sandifer and S. Stein (1985), 'Effects of unemployment on mental and physical health', *American Journal of Public Health*, **75**(5), 502–6.
Loscocco, K.A. and G. Spitze (1991), 'The organisational context of women's and men's pay satisfaction', *Social Science Quarterly*, **72**(1), 3–19.
Maddux, J., M. Sherer and R. Rogers (1982), 'Self-efficacy expectancy and outcome expectancy', *Cognitive Therapy and Research*, **6**, 207–11.
Malen, E.A. and L.K. Stroh (1998), 'The influence of gender on job loss coping behaviour among unemployed managers', *Journal of Employment Counseling*, **35**(1), 26–39.
Mallinckrodt, B. (1990), 'Satisfaction with a new job after unemployment: consequences of job loss for older professionals', *Journal of Counselling Psychology*, **37**, 149–52.
Malmberg-Heimonen, I. and I. Julkunen (2002), 'Equal opportunities, true options or hidden unemployment? A comparative perspective on labour-market marginality', *International Journal of Social Welfare*, **11**(2), 120–31.
Malo, S. (1993), 'Game, set and match to the human jungle', *New Scientist*, July, 45.
Mellinger, S. and P. Erdwins (1985), 'Personality correlates of age and life roles in adult women', *Psychology of Women Quarterly*, **9**, 503–14.
Melville, D.L., D. Hope, D. Bennison and B. Barraclough (1985), 'Depression among men made involuntarily redundant', *Psychological Medicine*, **15**, 789–93.
Mines, H.Y. (1979), 'The unemployed senior executive', *Business Horizon*, **22**(5), 39–40.
Moser, K.A., A.J. Fox and D.R. Jones (1984), 'Unemployment and mortality in the OPCS longitudinal study', *Lancet*, **ii**, 1324–9.
Moskoff, G.R. (1993), 'Four tips for the newly unemployed manager – how to leverage your network and find yourself', *Manage*, **45**, 14–16.
Muller, J., R. Hicks and S. Winocur (1993), 'The effects of employment and unemployment on psychological well-being in Australian clerical workers: gender differences', *Australian Journal of Psychology*, **45**(3), 103–8.
National Statistics (2002), *Labour Market Trends*, **110**(8).
Newell, S. (1993), 'The superwoman syndrome: gender differences in attitudes towards equal opportunities at work and towards domestic responsibilities at home', *Work, Employment & Society*, **7**(2), 275–89.
Newman, K.S. (1988), *Falling from Grace: the Experience of Downward Mobility in the American Middle Class*, New York: Free Press.
Oakland, S. and A. Ostell (1996), 'Measuring coping: a review and critique', *Human Relations*, **49**(2), 133–55.
O'Brien, G.E. (1986), *'Psychology of Work and Unemployment*, Chichester: John Wiley & Sons.
Omar, A.G. (1995), 'Unemployment, coping strategies and gender difference' (estrategias de coping y diferencias debidas al sexo), *Revista Interamericana de Psicologia Ocupacional*, **14**(1), 57–71.
Orser, B. (1994), 'Sex role stereotypes and requisite management characteristics: an international perspective', *Women in Management Review*, **9**(4), 11–19.
Osipow, S.H. and L.F. Fitzgerald (1993), 'Unemployment and mental health: a neglected relationship', *Applied & Preventive Psychology*, **2**(2), 59–63.
Ostell, A. and P. Divers (1987), 'Attributional style, unemployment and mental health', *Journal of Occupational Psychology*, **60**, 333–7.
Parkes, K.R. (1994), 'Personality and coping as moderators of work stress process: models, methods and measures', *Work & Stress*, **8**(2), 110–29.
Perrucci, C.C., R. Perrucci and D.B. Targ (1997), 'Gender differences in the economic, psychological and social effects of plant closings in an expanding economy', *Social Science Journal*, **34**(2), 217–33.
Peterson, C. and M.E. Seligman (1987), 'Explanatory style and illness', *Journal of Personality and Social Psychology*, **55**, 237–65.
Peterson, C., S.M. Schwartz and M.E. Seligman (1981), 'Self-blame and depressive symptoms', *Journal of Personality and Social Psychology*, **41**, 253–9.
Piechowski, L.D. (1992), 'Mental health and women's multiple roles', *Families in Society: The Journal of Contemporary Human Services*, **20**, 131–9.
Pietromonaco, P.R., J. Manis and H. Markus (1987), 'The relationship of employment to self-perception and well-being in women: a cognitive analysis', *Sex Roles*, **17**(7/8), 467–77.
Pittman, J.F. and D.K. Orthner (1988), 'Gender differences in the prediction of job commitment', *Journal of Social Behavior and Personality*, **3**(4), 227–48.
Platt, S. and N. Kreitman (1984), 'Trends in parasuicide and unemployment among men in Edinburgh', *British Medical Journal*, **289**, 1029–32.
Pleck, J.H. (1985), *Working Wives, Working Husbands*, Beverly Hills: Sage.
Pugliesi, K. (1988), 'Employment characteristics, social support and the well-being of women', *Women and Health*, **14**(1), 35–58.

Ratcliff, K.S. and J. Brogden (1988), 'Unemployed women: when "social support" is not supportive', *Social Problems*, **35**(1), 54–63.
Ray, M. (1990), *Recruitment Advertising*, Newton-le-Willows, Lancs.: McCorquodale (Newton) Ltd.
Rees, D. and C.L. Cooper (1992), 'Occupational stress in health service workers in the UK', *Stress Medicine*, **8**, 79–90.
Repetti, R.L, K.A. Matthews and I. Waldron (1989), 'Employment and women's health: effects of paid employment on women's mental and physical health', *American Psychologist*, **44**(11), 1394–1401.
Retherford, P.S., G.J Hildreth and E.B. Goldsmith (1988), 'Social support and resource management of unemployed women', *Journal of Social Behaviour and Personality*, **3**(4), 191–204.
Rim, Y. (1987), 'A comparative study of two taxonomies of coping styles, personality and sex', *Personality & Individual Differences*, **8**(4), 521–6.
Robertson, I.T. and P.A. Iles (1988), 'Approaches to managerial selection', in C.L. Cooper and I.T. Robertson (eds), *International Review of Industrial and Organisational Psychology*, London: John Wiley.
Rogers, B. (1980), *The Domestication of Women*, London: Kogan Page.
Rosen, E.I. and N. College (1987), 'Job displacement among men and women: the crisis of under-employment', *Social Problems*, 31–42.
Rosenberg, M. and H.B. Kaplan (eds), (1982), *Social Psychology of the Self-Concept*, Arlington Heights, IL: Harlan Davidson.
Rosenfeld, R.A and K.I. Spenner (1992), 'Occupational sex segregation and women's early career job shifts', *Work and Occupations*, **19**(4), 424–49.
Rosenfield, S. (1989), 'The effects of women's employment: perceived control and sex differences in mental health', *Journal of Health and Social Behaviour*, **30**, 77–91.
Rosenthal, P., D. Guest and R. Peccei (1996), 'Gender differences in managers' causal explanations for their work performance: a study in two organisations', *Journal of Occupational and Organisational Psychology*, **69**(2), 145–51.
Ross, C.E. and J. Huber (1985), 'Hardship and depression', *Journal of Health and Social Behavior*, **26**, 312–27.
Rothblum, E.D. and E. Cole (1988), *Treating Women's Fear of Failure*, New York: Harrington Park Press.
Rotter, J.B. (1966), 'Generalised expectancies for internal versus external control of reinforcement', *Psychological Monographs*, **80**, Whole Issue No. 609.
Rowley, K.M. and N.T. Feather (1987), 'The impact of unemployment in relation to age and length of unemployment', *Journal of Occupational Psychology*, **60**, 323–32.
Rubery, J. and C. Fagan (1993), *Bulletin on Women and Employment in the EC*, **3**, October.
Sander, W. (1992), 'Unemployment and marital status in Great Britain', *Social Biology*, **39**(3–4), 299–305.
Schaufeli, W.B. and N.W. Van Yperen (1992), 'Unemployment and psychological distress among graduates: a longitudinal study', *Journal of Occupational and Organizational Psychology*, **65**, 291–305.
Schwartzberg, N.S. and R.S. Dytell (1989), 'Family stress and psychological well-being among employed and nonemployed mothers', *Journal of Social Behaviour and Personality*, **3**(4), 175–90.
Schwartzer, R., A. Hahn and R. Fuchs (1994), in G.P. Keita and J.J. Hurrell (eds), *Job Stress in a Changing Workplace*, Washington, DC: American Psychological Association.
Scott, J. and A. Rochester (1984), *Effective Management Skills: What is a Manager?*, Reading: Cox & Wyman.
Seidman, E. and B. Rapkin (1989), 'Economics and psychosocial dysfunction: toward a conceptual framework and prevention strategies', in D. Felner, L.A. Jason, J.N. Moritsugu and S.S. Faber (eds), *Preventative Psychology*, New York: Pergamon Press.
Shamir, B. (1985), 'Sex differences in psychological adjustment to unemployment and reemployment: a question of commitment, alternatives or finance?', *Social Problems*, **33**(1), 67–79.
Shaper, A.G. and D.G. Cook (1984), 'Unemployment and health', *Lancet*, **ii**, 1344–5.
Sheeran, P. and C. Abraham (1994), 'Unemployment and self-conception: a symbolic interactionist analysis', *Journal of Community & Applied Social Psychology*, **4**, 115–29.
Sheeran, P., D. Abrams and S. Orbell (1995), 'Unemployment, self-esteem, and depression: a social comparison theory approach', *Basic and Applied Social Psychology*, **17**(1 & 2), 65–82.
Sherer, M., J.E. Maddux, B. Mercandante, S. Prentice-Dunn, B. Jacobs and R.W. Rogers (1982), 'The self-efficacy scale: construction and validation', *Psychological Reports*, **51**, 663–71.
Sheridan, A. (1994), 'Managers in cartoons – they are still men in the Harvard Business Review', *Women in Management Review*, **9**(4), 20–24.
Snyder, K.A. and T.C. Nowak (1984), 'Job loss and demoralization: do women fare better than men?', *International Journal of Mental Health*, **13**(1–2), 92–106.
Starrin, B. and G. Larson (1987), 'Coping with unemployment – a contribution to the understanding of women's unemployment', *Social Science and Medicine*, **25**, 163–71.

Stevens, C.K., A.G. Bavetta and M.E. Gist (1993), 'Gender differences in the acquisition of salary negotiation skills: the role of goals, self-efficacy, and perceived control', *Journal of Applied Psychology*, **78**(5), 723–35.
Stokes, G. and R. Cochrane (1984), 'A study of the psychological effects of redundancy and unemployment', *Journal of Occupational Psychology*, **57**, 309–22.
Stokes, J. and I. Levin (1986), 'Gender differences in predicting loneliness from social network characteristics', *Journal of Personality and Social Psychology*, **51**(5), 1069–74.
Stroh, L., J. Brett and A. Reilly (1992), 'All the right stuff: a comparison of female and male managers' career progression', *Journal of Applied Psychology*, **77**, 251–60.
Stuart, P. (1992), 'What does the glass ceiling cost you?', *Personnel Journal*, **71**(11), 70–73.
St-Yves, A., F. Contant, M.H. Freeston, J. Huard and B. Lemieux (1989), 'Locus of control in women occupying middle-management and non-management positions', *Psychological Reports*, **65**, 483–6.
Swinburne, P. (1981), 'The psychological impact of unemployment on managers and professional staff', *Journal of Occupational Psychology*, **54**, 47–64.
Taubman, P. and S. Rosen (1982), 'Healthiness: education and marital status', in V.R. Fuchs (ed.), *Economic Aspects of Health*, Chicago:University of Chicago Press.
Thoits, P.A. (1986), 'Multiple identities: examining gender and marital status differences in distress', *American Sociological Review*, **51**, 259–72.
Townsend, A. (1992), 'Regional and local differentials in labour demand', in E. McLaughlin (ed.), *Understanding Unemployment*, London: Routledge.
Travers, C.J. and C.L. Cooper (1991), 'Stress and status in teaching', *Women in Management Review & Abstracts*, **6**(4), 16–23.
Tuosignant, M., R. Brousseau and L. Tremblay (1987), 'Sex biases in mental health scales: do women tend to report less serious symptoms and confide more than men?', *Psychological Medicine*, **17**, 203–15.
Ullah, P., M.H. Banks and P.B. Warr (1985), 'Social support, social pressures and psychological distress during unemployment', *Psychological Medicine*, **15**, 283–95.
Veiel, H.O.F. and U. Baumann (1992), *The Meaning and Measurement of Social Support*, Washington, DC: Hemisphere.
Verbrugge, L.M. (1985), 'Gender and health: an update on hypothesis and evidence', *Journal of Health and Social Behaviour*, **26**, 156–82.
Vesalainen, J. and J. Vuori (1999), 'Job-seeking, adaptation and re-employment experiences of the unemployed: a 3-year follow-up', *Journal of Community & Applied Social Psychology*, **9**(5), 383–94.
Vianen, A.E.M. and W.A.J. Keizer (1996), 'Gender differences in managerial intention', *Gender, Work and Organisation*, **3**(2), 103–14.
Viinamaki, H., K. Koskela, L. Niskanen and R. Arnkill (1993), 'Unemployment, financial stress and mental well-being: a factory closure study', *European Journal of Psychiatry*, **7**(2), 95–102.
Vingerhoets, A.J.M. and G.L. Van Heck (1990), 'Gender, coping and psychosomatic symptoms', *Psychological Medicine*, **20**, 125–35.
Vinokur, A. and R.D. Caplan (1987), 'Attitudes and social support: determinants of job-seeking behaviour and well-being among the unemployed', *Journal of Applied Social Psychology*, **17**(12), 1007–24.
Walters, V. (1993), 'Stress, anxiety and depression: women's accounts of their health problems', *Social Science and Medicine*, **36**(4), 393–402.
Wanberg, C.R. and M.C. Marchese (1994), 'Heterogeneity in the unemployment experience: a cluster analytic investigation', *Journal of Applied Social Psychology*, **24**(6), 473–88.
Wanberg, C.R., J.D. Watt and D.J. Rumsey (1996), 'Individuals without jobs: an empirical study of job-seeking behaviour and reemployment', *Journal of Applied Psychology*, **81**(1), 76–87.
Warr, P.B. (1987), *Work, Unemployment and Mental Health*, Oxford: Oxford University Press.
Warr, P.B. and P.R. Jackson (1984), 'Men without jobs: some correlates of age and length of unemployment', *Journal of Occupational Psychology*, **57**, 77–85.
Warr, P.B. and P.R. Jackson (1987), 'Adapting to the unemployed role: a longitudinal investigation', *Social Science and Medicine*, **16**, 1691–7.
Warr, P.B. and G. Parry (1982), 'Paid employment and women's psychological well-being', *Psychological Bulletin*, **91**, 498–516.
Warr, P.B., P.R. Jackson and M. Banks (1988), 'Unemployment and mental health: some British studies', *Journal of Social Issues*, **44**(4), 47–68.
Warren, R. (1980), 'Stress, primary support systems and the blue collar woman', in P. Jarley (ed.), *Response to Major Layoffs and Plant Closings*, Lansing, MI: Michigan Department of Mental Health.
Weiner, B. (1986), *An Attributional Theory of Motivation and Emotion*, New York: Springer-Verlag.
Weiten, W. (1989), *Psychology Themes and Variations*, Pacific Grove, CA: Brooke/Cole.
Wells-Parker, E., D.I. Miller and J.S. Topping (1990), 'Development of control-of-outcome scales and self-efficacy scales for women in four life roles', *Journal of Personality Assessment*, **54**(3 & 4), 564–75.

Westcott, G. (1984), 'Unemployment and health', *Lancet*, **ii**, 1464.
Wethington, E. and R.C. Kessler (1986), 'Perceived support, received support and adjustment to stressful life events', *Journal of Health and Social Behavior*, **27**, 78–89.
White, M. (1991), *Against Unemployment*, London: Policy Studies Institute.
White, M. (1994), *Unemployment and Public Policy in a Changing Labour Market*, London: Policy Studies Institute.
Winefield, A.H. and M. Tiggemann (1985), 'Psychological correlates of employment and unemployment: effects, predisposing factors, and sex differences', *Journal of Occupational Psychology*, **58**, 229–42.
Winefield, A.H. and M. Tiggemann (1994), 'Affective reactions to employment and unemployment as a function of prior expectations and motivation', *Psychological Reports*, **75**, 243–7.
Winefield, A.H., H.R. Winefield, M. Tiggemann and R.D. Goldney (1991), 'A longitudinal study of the psychological effects of unemployment and unsatisfactory employment on young adults', *Journal of Applied Psychology*, **76**, 424–31.
Wooton, K.C., J.L. Sulzer and J.M. Cornwell (1994), 'The effects of age, financial strain, and vocational expectancies on the stress-related affect of adult job losers', in G.P. Keita and J.J. Hurrell (eds), *Job Stress in a Changing Workplace*, Washington, DC: American Psychological Association.
Yoder, J.D., P.L. Crumpton and J.F. Zipp (1989), 'The power of number in influencing hiring decisions', *Gender and Society*, **3**(2), 269–76.

19 Stress in veterinary surgeons: a review and pilot study
Howard Kahn and Camilla V.J. Nutter

Introduction

The general public's perception of veterinary surgeons is that of an idyllic existence, of benevolent, caring professionals administering to sick animals and offering comfort and support to concerned clients, an altogether low-stress occupation. Indeed, in 1985, a report (Wilby, 1985) was published assessing the stress levels of various jobs on a ten-point scale. Vets were assessed at 4.5 which, when compared with other 'health' workers, was relatively low (for example dentists 7.3, doctors 6.8, opticians 4.0 and pharmacists 4.5). Yet this somehow seems highly incompatible with statistics which show that veterinary surgeons have one of the highest suicide rates among all of the professions. The UK Mental Health Foundation has noted that 'suicide in veterinary surgeons is around three times more common than in the general population and in pharmacists, dentists, farmers and doctors it is around twice as common. Many of these are occupations which provide easy access to both the methods and knowledge about the methods of suicide. Also these occupations may be particularly prone to stress' (Mental Health Foundation, 1997).

Similar reports emanate from the United States: 'Veterinarians have to deal not only with client grief, but also with their own. Veterinarians have one of the highest suicide rates in the country, and in some European countries, the veterinary profession has the highest suicide rate' (Joyner, 2002). A report from Australia notes that 'veterinary surgeons, world wide, share the dubious distinction of being one of the leading professions in suicide rates. Further, the Veterinary Profession has a high level of attrition of young graduates and, in those remaining within the Profession, a high level of marital or partnership breakups. In other words, our Profession has all the characteristics of a profession under stress, a profession in crisis' (Veterinary Surgeons Board of Western Australia, 2001). One explanation for the high suicide rate has been suggested by the United Kingdom Society of Practising Veterinary Surgeons (SPVS): 'Vets have a paradoxical role in society by being carers whilst being money-makers. This is a recipe for stress' (*SPVS Bulletin*, 1998).

Despite the evidence that suggests that the stress levels among UK vets are high, and after a detailed search of the literature, we found few studies of this problem. Thus we developed a small pilot study with which we hoped to answer two main questions: Is stress a problem within the veterinary profession? Could our methodology be used for a large-scale investigation of the stress levels of veterinary surgeons?

The veterinary profession in the United Kingdom

There were 19 226 vets registered in the UK in 2000, and they cover areas such as general practice, veterinary teaching and research, government service, commerce and industry, international organizations and work overseas. This study focused on veterinary surgeons in general practice. The Royal College of Veterinary Surgeons (RCVS) is the governing body of the veterinary profession in the UK. Under the provisions of the Veterinary Surgeons Act 1966 only a registered veterinary surgeon is permitted to diagnose and treat the injuries and ailments of animals. To become registered and a member of the RCVS, a veterinary degree must be taken. Six universities in the UK offer veterinary degrees approved by the RCVS: Bristol, Cambridge, Edinburgh, Glasgow, Liverpool and the Royal Veterinary College, London. The degree course is generally for five years; in Cambridge it is six years. Every veterinary surgeon has an obligation to deal with emergencies in any species at any time. It is a 24-hour service, every day of the year.

The RCVS manpower survey
The Royal College of Veterinary Surgeons commissioned a manpower survey in 2000 to provide factual guidance on the employment status and type of work carried out by veterinary surgeons registered with the RCVS (RCVS, 2000). The findings of the survey relevant to the present study are shown below.

- Of full-time working veterinary surgeons in the UK, 32 per cent were women; 81 per cent of respondents worked in practice, 14 per cent worked in government services, 5 per cent in Universities, 3 per cent in commerce and industry, 3 per cent in charities and trusts, and 2 per cent in other occupations. Some 8 per cent of veterinary surgeons worked in more than one sector; 3 per cent reported that they worked exclusively in a specialist practice, while 6 per cent worked in both a specialist and a general practice.
- Of veterinary surgeons working in practice in the UK, 55 per cent worked in or for a practice owned by a partnership, 33 per cent worked in or for a practice owned by a sole principal and 4 per cent worked for a practice owned by a limited company.
- The average veterinary surgeon in employment worked 47 hours per week in 2000, but 38 per cent of veterinary surgeons worked for 50 hours or more per week. On average, veterinary surgeons in full-time employment in practice spent 23 hours per week on call; that is, available to treat any emergencies outside the practice's normal working hours.

Research into veterinary surgeons and stress
As we noted above, relatively little has been published about the stress that may be faced by veterinary surgeons. What we did find of relevance to our study is summarized as follows. Watson (1997) suggests that the profession has become full of Type A (that is, coronary-prone) achievers and that this is a major problem. He considers that this is because of the high entry grades needed for a place on a veterinary degree course, which brings in the more academic student. (The authors of the present chapter can see no justification for this assumption.) Watson goes on to state that, for all kinds of good reasons, the past two decades have seen a shift towards the selection of highly qualified, academically and scientifically brilliant students. However, in many instances, the real world of veterinary practice falls short of the high expectations these students have. (The authors do agree that this may indeed be a source of stress to veterinary surgeons.)

McCullagh (1998) suggests that many veterinary surgeons have fallen into the trap of doing nothing but work, and that they are overloaded and suffer from burnout. They may not get the support and approval they deserve from their colleagues and this can lead to feelings of anger and resentment. This buried anger can then lead to depression.

Stobbs (2000) suggests that any event which may produce feelings of failure, helplessness, guilt, frustration, anger or sorrow is a potential cause of stress, and that these emotions may well be experienced on a regular basis throughout the working day of the veterinary surgeon. Vets certainly appear to have a number of potential stressors in their working life: long hours, responsibility, life and death scenarios, shift work or on-call situations, and possibly difficult working conditions on farms and so on. Furthermore vets are dealing with the public, who may well be in a state of heightened emotion because of the sickness of their pets, and at the same time perhaps coping with a disgruntled partner or spouse who would like to see more of them than they do. There may also be additional pressure generated by having to reconcile personal beliefs and a professional code of ethics with decisions that have to be made in practice. On top of this is the fact that vets are often confronted with a suffering animal and a distressed client. Stobbs (2000) suggests that it is thus hardly surprising that veterinary surgeons may well be emotionally vulnerable.

Dale (1997) indicates that one cause of stress in the workplace is that veterinary practice is a constantly changing environment. For example, veterinary surgeons have been required to acknowledge and act upon new health and safety legislation and to reconcile the need for a 24-hour service with the pressure from their staff for better working conditions. A recent reduction in UK client disposable income has necessitated the time-consuming production of estimates before any treatment can be carried out and thus often the euthanasia of an animal that could have been saved had the client had insurance cover. Many veterinary surgeons also have to deal with a recently introduced computer system. The rate and progression of changes in an already emotive profession may have produced a parallel increase in stress at work. Dale (1997) summarizes her opinion of the principal causes of stress at work as being (a) lack of control over the way work is organized and paced, and changes introduced, (b) high levels of uncertainty due to unclear job descriptions and worries about job security or career development, and (c) lack of feedback and appreciation of performance.

Trimpop, Austin and Kirkcaldy (2000) have attempted to identify the major predictors of accident factors among veterinary surgeons in Germany. They observed that work-related injuries and accidents experienced during a recent 12-month period were significantly linked to job-related stress and job satisfaction. Veterinarians frequently reported a high level of stress, due to financial and social constraints as well as a high intrinsic workload. In an extension of this German study, Trimpop, Kirkaldy et al. (2000) note that the mean number of hours worked per week by vets was 51.5 hours, and by auxiliary personnel was 33.4 hours. Almost 60 per cent of vets worked more than 48 hours, compared with 7 per cent of the auxiliary personnel. The authors found that both working hours and perceived occupational stress were consistently related to particular accident behaviours. They contend that the findings of their study lend support to the concerns expressed about the long working hours that now characterize many forms of modern employment.

A final example of research relating to the work of veterinary surgeons is that of Jeyaretnam and Jones (2000), who examined the profession in Australia. (It is interesting to note that most of the research we uncovered has been carried out in Australia and New Zealand. The professional bodies in these countries appear to be relatively proactive and take a major interest in the physical and mental health of their members. For example, see Jeyaretnam *et al.*, 2000, and the *Australian Veterinary Journal*, 2002. A study carried out in Finland – Rejula *et al.*, 2003 – has also been reported.) Jeyaretnam and Jones set out to identify the major occupational hazards encountered by veterinarians and their staff in practice in Australia. Among their findings was that trauma is the greatest cause of physical injury to veterinarians and their staff: veterinarians were bitten, kicked, trampled or fallen upon by their patients, and the major injuries sustained were strains, dislocations, bruising, contusions and fractures; the frequency of work-related motor vehicle accidents was directly linked to the distances driven; veterinarians are at risk from assault by drug addicts (because they stock drugs such as pethidine, ketamine, barbiturates and many analgesics); the working environment of a veterinary practice is one of continuous hard physical and mental work; and veterinarians are at risk from injuries caused by the needles, scalpels and other instruments they use, by chemical hazards such as anaesthetic gases, pesticides, chemotherapeutic agents, prostaglandins, formaldehyde and by biological hazards including allergens and zoonotic diseases. The authors also note that younger veterinarians have identified work responsibility, lack of support and difficult cases as contributing to their stress.

Thus, from the few studies that we were able to uncover, there seems little doubt that veterinary surgeons appear to suffer from higher than average levels of stress and this results in physical and mental ill-health and high rates of suicide. This is far removed from the 'idyllic existence' that we noted at the start of this chapter.

The next stage of our investigation was to carry out a small pilot study of the stress problems faced by veterinarians in the United Kingdom.

Methodology
In order to gather the data we needed for our study, questionnaires were sent to randomly selected veterinary practices across the UK. For this pilot study, contact was made with 22 urban-based practices to determine how many staff were employed at each and thus how many questionnaires to send. The questionnaire chosen to gather the required data was the Occupational Stress Indicator (OSI) (Cooper *et al.*, 1988). It provides a comprehensive tool for use in a stress audit and is based upon the model of stress proposed by Cooper and Marshall (1976). Their model suggests that the sources of stress at work (including extraorganizational sources such as family problems, financial difficulties and so on) interact with particular characteristics of the individual (such as their level of anxiety, Type A behaviour pattern and so forth), to produce the symptoms of ill-health (such as increased smoking and drinking, depression and job dissatisfaction) and, ultimately, coronary heart disease and poorer physical and mental health. The organization will also suffer problems such as poor work performance, errors, high staff turnover, and so on.

The OSI is made up of 167 questions divided into seven self-report questionnaires. Each question is scored on a scale of 1 to 6. The questionnaires are as follows.

1. Job satisfaction. This section consists of 22 questions. The higher the score, the more job satisfaction is indicated. While the relationships between job satisfaction and job stress (and mental ill-health) are complex and not fully understood, generally those who are experiencing stress also have negative attitudes towards their work. Most empirical evidence supports a negative relationship between job stress and job satisfaction (Kahn and Byosiere, 1992).
2. Mental health. This inventory consists of 18 questions. The higher the score, the poorer the individual assesses their mental health.
3. Physical health. This section consists of 12 questions. The higher the score, the poorer the individual assesses their physical health. Both the mental health and physical health scales used provide the respondent's subjective perceptions rather than diagnosed ailments.
4. Type A behaviour. This section consists of 14 questions, and higher scores indicate more type A behaviour. Type A behaviour is regarded as a good predictor of cardiovascular disease and other stress-related illnesses (Booth-Kewley and Friedman, 1987).
5. Locus of control. This section consists of 12 questions, the object of which is to indicate how much the respondent feels they can influence and control the events that go on around them. The higher the score, the less control the individual feels they have (they feel externally controlled), and the lower the score, the more in control they feel (they feel internally controlled). Spector (1982) argues that locus of control is related to job motivation, effort, performance, compliance with authority and supervisory style. People with internal locus of control tend to be more satisfied than people with external locus of control. Andrisani and Nestel (1976) found that internals tend to earn more money and have higher job satisfaction than externals.
6. Sources of pressure at work. This section consists of 61 statements describing potentially stressful work-related items. These collapse into six subscales, namely the pressure at work perceived to be due to the job itself (9 questions), due to the job role (11 questions), due to interpersonal relationships (10 questions), due to career and achievement (9 questions), due to the organizational structure and climate (11 questions) and due to the home/work interface (11 questions). Higher scores indicate that more pressure is perceived for each variable.
7. Techniques used to cope with stress. This inventory consists of 28 questions which collapse into six subscales relating to major coping techniques used by individuals, namely the use of social support (4 questions), task strategies (7 questions), logic (3 questions), home and work relationships (4 questions), effective use of time (4 questions), and involvement (6 questions). Higher scores indicate that more use is made of the particular coping technique.

In addition, the OSI captures biographical and demographic information.

Combined data are available from 22 studies which have used the OSI ($n = 7000$–8000) which can be taken with some confidence to represent an approximation of general population data (Cooper *et al.*, 1994). Reliability and validity data for the seven OSI scales above can be found in Cooper *et al.* (1988) and Robertson *et al.* (1990). The OSI has been used in many studies and is available in numerous languages in addition to English (see, for examples, Cooper, 2001).

A total of 50 questionnaires were issued to veterinary surgeons. The OSI was posted to a contact within the 22 practices, who then handed them to staff at both partner and assistant level. The anonymous questionnaires were returned to the researchers in prepaid, addressed envelopes. In all, 35 (70 per cent) usable questionnaires were returned.

Results

The sample consisted of 21 males and 14 females. Of the males, 13 were married, six were single, one was cohabiting and one was separated; nine males were aged between 21 and 36, and 12 were between 37 and 55. Of the females, six were married and eight were single, ten were aged between 21 and 36, and four were between 37 and 55.

Only two of the respondents (one male, one female) smoked and both smoked less than one packet per day. One felt their smoking habit had not changed in the previous three months and the other felt it had increased. Only one of the respondents did not drink alcohol. The two people who smoked also drank heavily and both felt they should cut down on their alcohol intake. The respondent who felt that their smoking habit had recently increased felt the same about their alcohol intake. This person was also the only respondent not to have an interest or hobby. Of those who did have an interest or hobby, nine felt that it was in some way related to work. Sixteen respondents socialized with their work colleagues.

Of the 35 responders, 28 felt that they maintained a desired body weight almost all the time. Of these, five always took planned exercise, 13 usually took planned exercise and three did not usually take any planned exercise. Four respondents felt that they almost never maintained a desired body weight. Only three of the respondents reported that they did not feel fairly healthy. As many as 20 respondents felt that they had encountered major stressful events over the previous few months which had had an important effect on them, either of a positive or a negative nature.

Table 19.1 presents the means and standard deviations of each of the seven questionnaires which constitute the OSI. Scores for both the 35 veterinary surgeons who completed questionnaires and for the combined data (the general population) are shown. The t-statistics shown are the results of comparing the two groups on each variable. As it was predicted from the little background information which was available about veterinary surgeons that they would indicate more of the factors related to stress than the general population, 1-tailed hypotheses were used.

There are a number of statistically significant differences between veterinary surgeons and the general population on the variables examined. Of the 17 variables examined, five show statistically significant differences between the groups. Compared with norm data, veterinary surgeons indicate greater job satisfaction, a more internal sense of control, less stress due to career and achievement and to organizational structure and climate, and more use made of home and work relationships as a method of coping with stress. The remaining four sources of stress at work, factors intrinsic to the job, the management role, relationships with others, and the home-work interface are all seen as more stressful than by the general population, though none significantly so. Examining the techniques used to cope with stress, three of the remaining five, namely social support, task strategies, and the effective use of time, are also used more by veterinary surgeons, though again none significantly so. The two remaining coping strategies, logic and involvement, are used less

Table 19.1 Comparison of veterinary surgeons and the general population

	General population (n = 7000–8000)		Veterinary surgeons (n = 35)		
Variable	x	SD	x	SD	t
Job satisfaction	82.08	16.60	90.80	14.35	−3.58***
Mental health	55.51	12.95	58.77	13.92	−1.38
Physical health	29.88	9.70	30.14	8.85	−0.17
Type A (coronary-prone) behaviour	51.16	7.62	51.15	10.16	0.01
Locus of control	43.05	5.75	40.09	4.15	4.20***
Sources of pressure					
Factors intrinsic to the job	30.22	6.48	31.80	7.37	−1.27
The managerial role	35.55	8.47	35.87	8.59	−0.22
Relationships with other people	30.31	7.71	30.46	8.10	−0.11
Career and achievement	28.40	8.11	23.11	7.25	4.30***
Organizational structure and climate	38.99	9.21	34.86	9.99	2.44**
Home/work interface	30.99	10.26	32.94	11.24	−1.02
Coping with stress					
Social support	15.07	3.26	15.80	4.17	−1.03
Task strategies	25.30	3.74	25.49	4.37	−0.26
Logic	12.46	2.11	12.11	2.59	0.80
Home and work relationships	15.54	3.64	16.71	4.01	−1.72*
Time	14.34	2.14	14.57	2.25	−0.60
Involvement	23.18	3.43	22.77	3.50	0.69

Note: ***$p<0.0005$; **$p<0.01$; *$p<0.05$; 1-tailed tests.

by veterinary surgeons. Both mental health and physical health are assessed by veterinary surgeons as poorer than the general population.

Data were further analysed to reveal any differences between male and female veterinary surgeons. Table 19.2 shows separately the percentage of men and of women who scored above the average for each variable. Notable differences between the sexes are that a greater percentage of women than men indicate poorer mental and physical health, a greater percentage indicate more stress due to four of the six sources of pressure and a greater percentage indicate that they make more use of social support. Fewer women indicate Type A behaviour and less control over their situation.

Discussion

The results of the pilot study indicate that veterinary surgeons do not have a greater tendency towards Type A (coronary-prone) behaviour compared with the general population and thus results do not support Watson's (1997) assertion that there has been a move towards the selection of more typically Type A students into the veterinary colleges, and that this is the reason for the perceived increase in stress in veterinary surgeons.

Dale (1997) has suggested that the changing environment in which veterinary surgeons have to work is a possible reason for their increased susceptibility to stress. She includes

Table 19.2 Comparison of male and female veterinary surgeons

	Males (n = 21)	Females (n = 14)
Variable		
Job satisfaction	52	50
Mental health	48	79
Physical health	38	57
Type A (coronary-prone) behaviour	62	43
Locus of control	38	50
Sources of pressure		
Factors intrinsic to the job	48	64
The managerial role	57	50
Relationships with other people	57	57
Career and achievement	48	50
Organizational structure and climate	52	57
Home/work interface	48	57
Coping with stress		
Social support	38	86
Task strategies	52	29
Logic	57	36
Home and work relationships	48	64
Time	62	43
Involvement	62	43

Note: Figures show the percentages of male and females who scored above the average for veterinary surgeons.

the pressure of managerial responsibilities and, in particular, the need to balance new health and safety legislation with the requirement of a 24 hour per day service. Most veterinary surgeons told us that they receive little, if any, managerial training, but our results suggest that managerial responsibilities are not a major source of stress for veterinary surgeons. Dale has also suggested that a lack of control over workload and high levels of job ambiguity are potential sources of pressure in veterinarians. The results of the current study do not support these suppositions, in that veterinary surgeons indicate significantly more control over their work and indicate that they do not appear particularly stressed by the actual work that they do.

Cooper and Marshall (1976) highlight job satisfaction as an indicator of how stressed an individual perceives themselves to be. On this basis, the results of our research suggest that, as veterinary surgeons have a significantly higher job satisfaction score than the norm, they do not perceive themselves to be particularly stressed. However it may well be that job satisfaction can be high while at the same time the individual is severely stressed; that is they like their work, but it is affecting their health negatively.

Both the mental and physical health of this sample population of veterinary surgeons were poorer than the norm scores, though not significantly so. This could be because, as McCullagh (1998) suggests, many veterinary surgeons have fallen into the trap of focusing almost entirely on work. This leads to overload and general burnout. Physical health, similarly, could be suffering from the results of 'workaholism'.

Our results suggest that veterinary surgeons use stable relationships as a way of coping with any stress. Women seem to use more of the 'softer' coping strategies such as talking about their pressures and relying on their relationships with others to help them through their problems, while men employ more of the 'harder' techniques, such as improved time management and other task strategies.

Managing stress in veterinary surgeons

To manage or prevent occupational stress in veterinary surgeons, there are several interventions that may be implemented in the workplace. Employee assistance programmes may be a useful way of managing stress, allowing the individual access to external and professional counselling. Stress management training (SMT) could teach individuals useful techniques to raise awareness and recognition of stressors and also techniques to reduce stress such as meditation or breathing exercises. SMT is more a preventive than a curative technique and therefore may be particularly useful to veterinary students or new graduates, before any problems become too great. Stressor reduction interventions aim to reduce workplace stressors. They are costly, however, and may be difficult to implement as they require identification of the stressors and then changes to the organizational structure or function, often leading to increased worker autonomy and participation in decision making. As most veterinary practices are formed as partnerships, increased involvement in running the company may not be welcomed.

The value of teamworking has been suggested as a solution to the stress problems faced by those employed in healthcare by Carter and West (1999). They contend that, as workplaces become more complex and demanding, there is good evidence that working in teams enables people to meet the challenges of those tasks more effectively, and that teamwork buffers health professionals against the inevitable stresses associated with the content of their work. To encourage effective teamwork (which depends, of course, on there being a team of people available within the organization), practices should provide the following:

- clear goals for teams,
- organizational rewards for teams,
- training for the job and training for teamwork,
- the necessary process assistance to support the team in its work,
- a supportive organizational climate, and
- supportive relations between teams in the organization.

Veterinary practices may be able to take advantage of some, if not all, of these suggestions. In the US an academic course has been designed for junior veterinary students which is aimed at providing a forum for lecture and discussion of topics such as team building, conflict resolution, stress management and work–life balance (Harvey et al., 2001). This may be a strategy which other academic and training bodies might wish to consider.

Limitations of the study

The OSI is time-consuming to complete (around 45 minutes), and the reliability of the 'Coping' section, the final questionnaire within the OSI, has been questioned. Perhaps respondents become tired and bored, having answered a large number of questions by the time they come to completing this section of the OSI. It is also worth noting that there may be a particular 'type' of person who completes the OSI, either someone with a particular interest in the area of stress or someone who finds it a distraction from work. It may also be that 'stressed' veterinary surgeons would not fill in the questionnaire at all, either because they would have to face their stress problems or because of their 'symptoms', meaning that they felt they did not have the time.

As the OSI is a self-report survey, it is based on how the participant feels at the time they complete the questionnaire. Thus the results may vary according to when and where the individual answered the questions; the same person could answer the same questionnaire in two consecutive weeks and respond differently. One major weakness of our study is the low number of respondents. This makes our results less reliable than might be desired.

Future research

An attempt to state the sources of stress among veterinarians has been presented by Joyner (2002). Among these she lists the death of the (non-human) patient, the suffering of the patient, being the one to deliver medical intervention which itself causes pain or suffering of the patient, the inability to treat, cure or alleviate suffering because the client cannot afford care, or because the veterinarian may be incapable of treating the animal, or because the natural progression of the disease makes it unresponsive to human intervention, or because of the lack of suitable equipment or medical support. Among other potential sources of stress in veterinary surgeons she cites lack of time and experience, the potential for mistakes, sending clients home with incomplete diagnoses or treatment, euthanasia and body disposition decisions and procedures, change or loss of relationship to client and patient, the suffering and grieving process of clients, the financial and business implications of veterinary medicine and the public view of veterinary medicine and animal relationships.

It would appear that the present study cannot, as constituted, determine whether these factors are indeed major sources of stress for veterinary surgeons. The OSI would require to be supplemented by other items which attempt to measure the factors mentioned above, as well as any others seen as relevant to veterinary surgeons.

Areas of future research should include a much wider study of the veterinary profession. It may be useful to conduct one-to-one or group interviews to gain a more in-depth insight into the problem of occupational stress in the profession. It may also be useful to undertake more detailed analysis of data in order to gain more information about, for example, the effects that foot and mouth disease had on the profession, and whether those in farm animal practice are under more pressure than those in companion animal practice.

There may also be advantages in using the new version of the OSI, ASSET, which was made available only after our study was commenced. ASSET is stated to be a successor to the Occupational Stress Indicator, which was unsuitable for using with everyone across an organization. It has already been used with a number of large organizations and can be administered on-line or with paper and pencil. It reports on the individual's stress profile, perception of job, attitude to job, health issues and supplementary issues. A computer-based, interactive questionnaire may be more useful in gathering required data.

Finally the researchers were unable to gain the support of the RCVS, the governing body of the profession in the UK. Their support would undoubtedly increase the credibility of any study, and thus increase the number of respondents participating in the study and returning completed questionnaires.

References

Andrisani, P.J. and G. Nestel (1976), 'Internal–external control as a contributor to an outcome of work experience', *Journal of Applied Psychology*, **61**, 156–65.
Australian Veterinary Journal (2002), 'Survey details stress factors that influence Australian vets', **80**(9), 522, 524.
Booth-Kewley, S. and H.S. Friedman (1987), 'Psychological predictors of heart disease: a quantitative review', *Psychological Bulletin*, **101**, 343–62.
Carter, A.J. and M.A. West (1999), 'Sharing the burden: teamwork in health care settings', in J. Firth-Cozens and R.L. Payne (eds), *Stress in Health Professionals*, London: Wiley.
Cooper, C.L. (2001), *Managerial, Occupational and Organizational Stress Research*, Aldershot: Ashgate.
Cooper, C.L. and J. Marshall (1976), 'Occupational sources of stress: a review of the literature relating to coronary heart disease and mental ill health', *Journal of Occupational Psychology*, **49**, 11–28.
Cooper, C.L., S.J. Sloan and S. Williams (1988), *Occupational Stress Indicator Management Guide*, Windsor: NFER-Nelson.
Cooper, C.L., S.J. Sloan and S. Williams (1994), *Occupational Stress Indicator. Data Supplement*, Windsor: NFER-Nelson.
Dale, C. (1997), 'Recognising stress in yourself and others', *In Practice*, **19**, 4.
Harvey, A., D. Durrance and G. Couger (2001), 'Staff relations and work–life balance: course outline', *Journal of Veterinary Medical Education*, **28**(2), 69–72.
Jeyaretnam, J. and H. Jones (2000), 'Physical, chemical and biological hazards in veterinary practice', *Australian Veterinary Journal*, **78**(11), 751–8.
Jeyaretnam, J., H. Jones and M. Phillips (2000), 'Disease and injury among veterinarians', *Australian Veterinary Journal*, **78**(9), 625–9.
Joyner, L. (2002), 'Managing grief in veterinary medicine', http://www.cvm.ncsu.edu/info/ce/grief1.htm.
Kahn, R.L. and P. Byosiere (1992), 'Stress in organizations', in M.D. Dunnette and L.M. Hough (eds), *Handbook of Industrial and Organizational Psychology*, vol. 3, Palo Alto, CA: Consulting Psychologists Press, pp. 571–650.
McCullagh, M. (1998), 'Thoughts, feelings and action', *The Veterinary Business Journal*, **27**, 38–40.
Mental Health Foundation (1997), 'Mental Health Foundation briefing no.1: suicide and Deliberate Self-harm', (http://www.mentalhealth.org.uk/page.ctm?pagecode = PBBZ0101).
RCVS (2000), 'The UK Veterinary Profession in 2000', http://www.rcvs.org.uk/visitors/pdf/manpower_survey2000.pdf.
Rejula, K., K. Rasaren, M. Hamalainen, K. Juntunen, M.L. Lindbohm, H. Taskinen, B. Bergbohm and M. Rinta-Jouppi (2003), *Work Environment and Occupational Health of Finnish Veterinarians*, **44**(1), 45–57.
Robertson, I.T., C.L. Cooper and J. Williams (1990), 'The validity of the OSI', *Work and Stress*, **4**(1), 29–39.
Spector, P. (1982), 'Behavior in organizations as a function of employees' locus of control', *Psychological Bulletin*, **91**, 482–99.
SPVS Bulletin (1998), November, Veterinary Business Development Ltd, Peterborough.
Stobbs, C. (2000), 'Dealing with emotionally stressful situations in practice', *In Practice*, **22**, March, 485–8.
Trimpop, R., B. Kirkcaldy, J. Athanasou and C.L. Cooper (2000), 'Individual differences in working hours, work perceptions and accident rates in veterinary surgeries', *Work and Stress*, **14**(2), 181–8.
Trimpop, R., E.J. Austin and B.J. Kirkcaldy (2000), 'Determinants of work-related and driving accidents amongst veterinary surgeons', *Stress Medicine*, **16**, 243–57.
Veterinary Surgeons Board of Western Australia (2001), *Current Issues*, Autumn, http://www.vetsurgeonsboardwa.au.com/0301_09currStress.html#manastre.
Watson, D. (1997), 'Of vets and stress and things', *The Veterinary Business Journal*, **20**, 45–8.
Wilby, J. (1985), 'Good Career Guide', *Sunday Times*, London.

N.B. all online periodicals and documents were retrieved September 2002, from source.

20 Structural work change and health: studies of long spells of sick leave and hospitalization among working men and women during a period of marked changes in the Swedish labour market

Gabriel Oxenstierna, Hugo Westerlund, Jane Ferrie, Martin Hyde, Jan Hagberg and Töres Theorell

Background

Structural changes have been common throughout the industrial world during the last three decades. One important element has been 'downsizing'. Sweden is interesting to study from this point of view, for several reasons. The most important reason is that the structural changes have been condensed into a relatively short period (especially when Sweden is compared to several other countries, including the United States, the United Kingdom and some European countries such as Holland). Another important reason is that Sweden has had very good registers and national surveys which make it possible to study many aspects and consequences of these changes.

The most dramatic changes took place from the late 1980s to the end of the 1990s. At first there was downsizing in many sectors, not least in the public sector. In hospitals, for instance, staff numbers were reduced by an average of 20 per cent. In addition, many work organizations were also restructured in other ways, for example by reorganization, centralization, privatization and/or outsourcing. During the first half of this period there was a major recession in the Swedish economy, with a resultant tripling of unemployment rates. This was followed by a recovery: during the latter half of the 1990s the employment rates rose again (although they never reached the high rates of the 1980s). Still today there are about half a million people fewer in the labour force compared with 1990. These processes have been described by several authors (for example, Theorell, 2003; Välfärdsbokslut/S000:3, 2000). The prevalence of work-related mental symptoms showed a pronounced increase from 1997. This coincided with a steep decline in self-reported authority over decisions in Swedish employees. Throughout the decade there was a progressive increase in psychological demands.

The late 1990s and the first years of the new millennium were also characterized by a rising incidence of long spells of sick leave. This has been very expensive for the state, and there has been an intensive public and political debate. A number of explanations for the rising long-term sick leave rates are possible, including demographic changes. The percentage of unemployed and prematurely retired varies throughout the years of study and this may have major effects on the sick leave rates. Finally, of course, the structural changes themselves may lead to mental illness. There is a need to explore the proportion of long-lasting sick leave that could be attributed to the work environment and structural change. A number of questions arise in the analysis of the relationships between structural changes in the labour market, changes in health and changes in sick leave rate. The following questions have been pursued in our project, 'Lean production in the Swedish 1990s'.

If we divide the working population into men and women, into older, middle-aged and younger workers and finally into those in the public and those in the private sectors respectively, how could we describe the development of the psychosocial work environment, mental and physical symptoms and long-term sick leave? To what extent and in what way is the development different in these different subgroups of the working population? In particular we want to describe the development of crucial parameters related to the demand–control–support model (Karasek and Theorell, 1990). The time course and the temporal relationships between work environment changes and health are of particular importance.

In general, downsizing of staff is associated with a deteriorating financial climate for the branch. On the other hand, expansion may reflect an improving financial climate. Particularly in the public sector, expansion may sometimes mean fusion of several units. In some parts of the present study, a differentiation was made between moderate downsizing/expansion and large downsizing/expansion. These concepts were operationally defined as downsizing/expansion reaching at least 18 per cent (large) or 9–18 per cent (moderate) reduction/increase in staff from one year to the next. The question was whether such changes are relevant to subsequent risk of hospitalization or long spells of sick leave during follow-up. Another question is also whether possible associations between changes in number of staff and health could be explained partly or totally by psychosocial work environment factors in these work sites.

Finally sick leave levels may be sensitive to many factors, including labour market fluctuations. We wanted to know whether subjects with increased vulnerability to illness development are more sensitive to labour market fluctuations (downsizing and expansion) than others. The societal discussion has been focused on the possibility that there may be too liberal use of sick leave. Questions dealing with underutilization of sick leave could also create problems, however. 'Sickness presenteeism' (Aronsson et al., 2000) could increase the risk of serious illness development. In one part of our study we could identify male and female subjects who had been found in an epidemiological cardiovascular screening to have a high cardiovascular risk score. We wanted to examine whether, among employees going through downsizing periods, those who had such a risk score are more likely to abstain from long spells of sick leave than others.

Description of time course
Two theoretical models, the demand–control–support (Karasek and Theorell, 1990) and the effort–reward imbalance models (Siegrist, 2002), can be explored in the Swedish Work Environment Surveys. These questionnaire-based surveys have been performed every second year since 1989 with randomly selected working Swedish men and women. Throughout the years, on average 77.8 per cent of the selected men and women have participated.

Throughout the 1990s Sweden experienced a protracted period of economic recession. The impact of this on the working population was twofold, through redundancies and increased workload for those remaining in employment. During the years 1990 to 1993 the number of working people in Sweden decreased by more than 700 000. However the effects of this organizational restructuring were also felt by those who remained in work throughout this period. Not only was the workforce restructured but relations at the workplace were also dramatically transformed. Between 1991 and 1999 the proportion of women who reported insufficient social support at work increased. The largest increase, from 27.5 per cent to 50.9 per cent, was observed among older women employed in the public sector. The proportion of men who reported diminished social support at work also increased, but this increase was smaller. Overall, in the second half of the 1990s, according to national surveys, 36 per cent of the entire workforce reported that they received insufficient support from superiors and 17 per cent from fellow-workers (Arbetsmiljöverket och Statistiska Centralbyrån, 2001). This decline in social support at work has been accompanied by a significant decrease in the amount of control that people can exert over their work. Between 1989 and 1999 there was an increase in the share of the workforce who reported insufficient work control, such as the timing or planning of work (SCB, 2001). The detrimental effects on health of increased demands, decreased control and lack of social support at work may partly explain why sick leave rates increased during the late part of the 1990s. At the end of the decade unemployment rates decreased in Sweden, but they were followed by a steep increase in sickness absence, which in 2002 cost the government SEK 47bn.

Downsizing has in previous studies, as well as in the public debate, been associated with increased sickness absence. However, no studies have looked at the long-term relationship between expansion and morbidity. One of our studies (Westerlund et al., 2004) examined the relationship between exposure to personnel change during 1991–6 and subsequent morbidity. As outcomes, we assessed both long-term (90 days or more during a three-year period) medically certified sickness absence and hospital admission for specified diagnoses, all of which could be assumed to be partly related to psychosocial conditions. The outcome was recorded during 1997–9 and accordingly the study had a longitudinal design. For this study, data from 24 036 participants of the Work Environment Surveys of 1989 to 1999 were used. The selection of cases was such that only people with a complete employment record during the relevant period were selected, resulting in a basically healthy initial population. All the analyses were adjusted for age and social class. The calculations were done both for the sample as a whole and separately for men and women in the private and public sectors, respectively.

The change in odds for *each additional year* of exposure to change in number of staff (from 0 to 6 years) was calculated. Accumulated exposure to large expansion ($\geq$18% per year) was, somewhat surprisingly, shown to be related to an increased risk of long-term sickness absence as well as hospital admission. Moderate expansion ($\geq$8% and <18% per year), on the other hand, was associated with a decreased risk of hospitalization, as could have been expected. The strongest associations between large expansion and increased sickness absence was found among women in the public sector. In this group, there was an almost threefold risk for people with full exposure (all six years) compared to those who had not been exposed in any of the years. Moderate downsizing ($\geq$8% and <18% per year) was, in line with earlier research, associated with an increased risk of long-lasting sickness absence. No effects could be shown for large downsizing, probably because there were too few cases with repeated exposures to major downsizing.

This part of the study provides reasonable evidence that repeated exposure to rapid personnel expansion in workplaces, possibly in connection with centralization, predicts long-term sickness absence and hospital admission, indicating that this exposure should be considered in future studies, policy making and occupational health care practice. In many cases expansion of the number of staff in the public sector during a period of downsizing (the 1990s) corresponds with centralization of work tasks to larger units. The study could indicate the risks for the workers' health of relatively 'uncontrolled' centralization. The study also confirms earlier findings that downsizing is associated with health risks.

Downsizing, high cardiovascular risk score and long sick leave
The objective was to determine whether changes in the number of staff in workplaces (downsizing or expansion) are associated with medium to long-term sick leave among employees with an elevated risk of developing cardiovascular disease (Theorell et al., 2003). Participants in this part of the study were those in the WOLF study of cardiovascular risk factors in working men and women in greater Stockholm during the years 1992–5. The response rate was 76 per cent. From the medical examination a cardiovascular score was calculated for each participant. Psychosocial work environment indices (quantitative demands, intellectual discretion, authority over decisions and social support) were derived for each subject from a self-administered questionnaire.

The WOLF study base was linked to the Statistics Sweden registry of economic and administrative activities. This made it possible to identify work sites with at least an 8 per cent decrease in staff ('downsizing') or a corresponding minimum 8 per cent increase ('expansion') during a 12-month period. Remaining work sites were labelled 'stable'. Sick leave spells lasting for at least 15 days during the calendar year following downsizing/expansion were identified for each subject through linkage with official registers. Complete data were available for 5720 employees aged 18 to 65. Lack of sick leave spells lasting for 15 days or more was used as an outcome variable: medically certified sick leave.

In multiple logistic regression including downsizing, expansion, age and cardiovascular risk score, the findings were significant for women. Increased likelihood of having no medically certified sick leave (15 days or more) was found during the year following both downsizing and expansion. These analyses were adjusted for age, cardiovascular score and interactions between cardiovascular score and downsizing/expansion. As expected a high cardiovascular risk score reduced the likelihood of having no long-term sick leave. However separate analyses were performed of women with and without high cardiovascular score. These showed that downsizing had a more pronounced statistical effect on reduced long-term sick leave among those with high than among those with low cardiovascular score. In men there were no consistent findings. The inclusion of psychosocial work environment variables and social class did not change the results markedly. Thus we found evidence of a reduction of long-term sick leave in women after downsizing. This was particularly evident among those with high cardiovascular score.

The source of support, decision authority and prospective long term sick leave
In some groups (see above) social support deteriorated during the 1990s. This motivated us to study the relationship between two sources of support – from supervisors and from

Table 20.1   Typologies of the social support combinations for the four groups

		Support from workmates	
		High	Low
Support from supervisors	High	Dual support	Supervisor support only
	Low	Workmate support only	Weak support

workmates respectively – and long term sick leave prospectively as well as other health outcomes cross-sectionally.

Four groups were operationalized using the two social support measures in the questionnaire. Respondents were asked, 'Can you receive support and encouragement from superiors when your work becomes heavy?' and 'Can you receive support and encouragement from fellow-workers when your work becomes heavy?'. The response options for each question were the same (Always, Mostly, Mostly not and Never). These were dichotomized into good support (Always and Mostly) and poor support (Mostly not and Never). The four groups were then created on the basis of the amount of support received from supervisors and workmates, respectively. Table 20.1 shows the typologies for the social support combinations (Oxenstierna et al., 2004). Those who reported good support from both supervisors and workmates were labelled 'Dual support'. Those who reported good support from their supervisors but not from their workmates were labelled 'Supervisor support only'. Those who received poor support from their supervisors but good support from their workmates were labelled 'Workmate support only'. Finally those who received poor support from both supervisors and workmates were labelled 'Weak support'.

The additional third dimension decision authority was then added. This was created by the summation of the responses to three questions: 'Is it possible for you to set your own work tempo?', 'Is it possible for you to decide, on your own, when various tasks are to be done (for example, by choosing to work a bit faster some days and taking it easier other days)?' and 'Are you involved in planning your work (for example, what is to be done, how it is to be done, or who is to work with you)?' This created an index with a 0–10 range. The scale was dichotomized at the point when roughly half the sample were in each group (low decision authority coded as six and under and high decision authority coded as greater than six). Each group was then divided into high decision authority and low decision authority, creating a total of eight groups (see Figure 20.1).

The results of the analyses lend support to the model that we introduced. Firstly, although the general trend is for all groups to have significantly increased risks compared to the most privileged group, the different groups have different likelihoods for the different outcomes. The results for conflict at work and bullying are the expected ones. For both sexes subjects in the group with workmate support only with low control are the most likely to be in conflict with their supervisors. The subjects in the weak support group with low control are at the greatest risk of being in conflict with workmates and of being bullied, which is of course expected. The magnitude

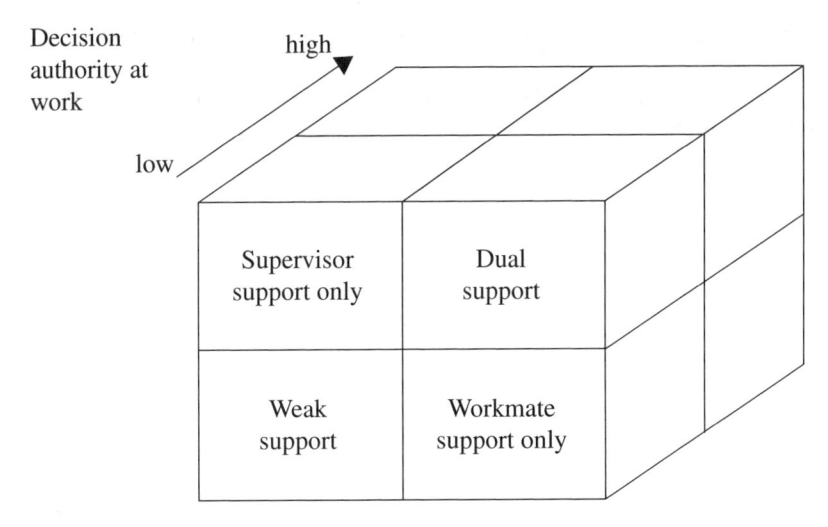

Figure 20.1   Three-dimensional model of the combination of the social support groups and decision authority

of the odds ratios, however, are surprisingly great: subjects in this group were up to eight times more likely than subjects in the reference group to report having been bullied.

The results for both general physical symptoms and pain after work show that all groups have significantly higher risks than the reference group. High decision authority modifies the results for all groups. The highest risk is for the subjects in the weak support group with low control. Although not all the results are significant, all exposed groups apart from the male 'dual support' group with low control have higher likelihood than the reference groups of being on long-term sick leave. The pattern for women again demonstrates the importance of decision authority, while the results for men suggest that support from colleagues might be of greater importance.

The consistent finding for the analyses is that people within each support group with high decision authority have a lower risk than their counterparts with low decision authority. This illustrates the importance of the interaction between social support and decision latitude (job control), although it suggests that job control is the more important of the two. The findings raise interesting questions about the reasons behind conflicts at work. What this suggests is that the job itself is a main cause of conflict with both superiors and workmates. Workers who are unable to control their own work are likely to be subject to greater interference and pressure from their superiors than those who have a certain degree of autonomy in organizing their work. This may also become a source of conflict with fellow-workers, either in one's own work or in the work of the team in which the conditions depend on the efforts of the workmates, or conflict may arise from a general sense of frustration.

We have shown that support and employees' authority over decisions are of great relevance to long-term sick leave pain, physical symptoms, conflicts and bullying. The results suggest that significant improvements can be achieved through a change in the social support structure of the organization and an increase in the employees' authority over decisions.

There is concern about how older workers will fare in the new, harsher, economic environment (Punch and Pearce, 2000).The periods of labour market restructuring through the 1980s and 1990s have created a new set of challenges for older workers. Evidence has shown that, once unemployed, older workers find it difficult to regain employment and often take less skilled and more poorly paid jobs if they are re-employed (Lasko and Phillipson, 1991). Age discrimination also prevents many older people from joining retraining schemes that might help them regain employment or cope with technological change.

Population ageing has been accompanied by decreasing labour market participation amongst older workers (OECD, 2002). Early labour market exit for older workers and the potential problems thereof have been an issue for some time. The economic recessions and subsequent organizational restructuring that occurred throughout Europe in the last decades of the 20th century had a negative impact on the labour market position of older people. In most European countries there are three main ways for older people to 'bridge' the time between early labour market exit and formal retirement, unemployment benefits/income support, disability benefits or early pensions (Carey, 2002). The use of these is different at different periods and for different social groups (Henkens *et al.*, 1996).

It is obviously important to discover what the causal factors are for each of these types of labour market exit and what the consequences are for the people that take (or are forced into) them. Evidence from Denmark, using the population registers, reveals that people who took a disability pension had a high relative mortality risk immediately after retirement, whilst the relative risk of premature mortality for those who took a long-term unemployment pension increased with time since retirement (Quaade *et al.*, 2002). Similar studies in Norway show that early retirement was associated with poor health throughout the 1980s and 1990s (Dahl and Elstad, 2001). However there is evidence that early retirement can have positive effects. In a study of British civil servants aged 54–59 years, mental health functioning was found to have improved amongst the retirees while it deteriorated amongst those who continued working (Mein *et al.*, 2003). Data from US studies show that retirement was associated with increased participation in sports and exercise (Evenson *et al.*, 2002), reduced anxiety, increased positive affect and, conversely, reduced sense of control (Drentea, 2002).

Using the Swedish Work Environment Survey (SWES), we have begun to analyse these issues (Hyde *et al.*, forthcoming). Using pooled cross-sectional data from four waves of the SWES (1991, 1993, 1995 and 1997) we analysed the effect of different types of labour market exit on the risk of hospitalization two years after labour market exit, compared to those who remained in employment, for those aged between 55 and 63 years. Types of labour market exit were derived from the tax and benefit codes collected from the government database and matched to individual cases through their unique social security number. Likewise annual incidence of hospitalization was taken from government registers matched to the individual cases. The advantage of doing this is that it allows us to look at a large, nationally representative sample using an objective measure of morbidity. Our results indicate that labour market exit is a varied process and that certain routes can have detrimental effects on a person's health. Even after controlling for age, social class and prior hospitalization or long-term sick leave, those who are were made unemployed were twice as likely to have been hospitalized following labour market exit than those who stayed in work. Interestingly, however, neither those who took a disability pension nor those who took early retirement had a greater risk of hospitalization. The differences for either route were non-significant.

Certainly the negative health consequences of unemployment are well known and in this respect older people are no different from the rest of the working population. What is concerning is the evidence that older people are more likely to be long-term unemployed and have very little chance of re-employment the longer they remain unemployed (Henkens et al., 1996) which will thus increase their risk of poor health and hospitalization. Regarding the interpretation of the other results, it is plausible that removing someone who already has poor health from potentially dangerous or stressful work environment, through disability pension, reduces their likelihood of hospitalization. Although we are unable to ascertain the degree of volition involved in the decision to take early retirement, the lack of any real difference between this group and those who remain in employment suggests that they are relatively healthy individuals who have chosen not to work rather than been forced out because of ill-health.

Conclusion

The economic crises and subsequent organizational restructuring that took place through the 1990s in Sweden have had a series of effects on the work environment and labour market participation of the Swedish working population. Access to a series of large representative surveys of the working population throughout this period (carried out every two years from 1989) which have been matched to a series of government registers through the participants' unique identification number have allowed us to explore a wide range of work environment issues.

On the one hand the results of the studies thus far undertaken are perhaps unsurprising. In line with many other studies the evidence shows that downsizing has a negative effect on health, that those who have good social support and good control at work have good health and that unemployment poses serious health risks for older people. The finding that women with a high cardiovascular risk score show evidence of sickness presenteeism during a year of follow-up illustrates that 'sick leave behaviour' is not only a matter of potential 'overuse of benefits' but also the result of a complex interaction between individuals and environmental factors. Sometimes these interactions may lead to 'underuse' of the system, which may endanger the health of vulnerable individuals. However they also illustrate the complex and novel issues for work environment research that have emerged throughout this period. For example expansion as well as downsizing has been shown to have detrimental effects on health. In addition the ways in which social support and decision authority at work interact produces a much more varied and complex work environment and new forms of early labour market exit are evolving which may introduce new risks for health. It is therefore apparent that these are important but formative studies the results of which require further attention.

An important extension of the work on the effects of downsizing and expansion might be to analyse why certain firms embark on a downsizing or expansionist strategy and whether this differs by industry or sector and whether the effects are different accordingly. The importance of the interaction between social support and decision authority opens up a potentially fruitful area of inquiry. Although the combined support model presented in this chapter produced interesting results, different and more sophisticated combinations of sources of support and workplace control need to be explored to test the robustness of the idea.

Issues regarding older workers are rapidly becoming a major research area, and what we have been able to do here is only a small part of what needs to be done to fully understand these processes. Future work needs to explore the effects of work environment factors on early labour market exit and the type of exit route taken, as well as assessing the interconnection between these factors and the wider political structure. Alongside taking up these future questions a greater and more rewarding challenge would be to analyse these issues in combination. Obviously the economic recession that precipitated the waves of downsizing, with its effects on health, also encouraged governments to adopt early retirement policies to achieve, relatively conflict-free, headcount reductions in the workforce and to reduce unemployment figures. Hence a possible area for future collaborative work would be to analyse how downsizing or expansion affects labour market participation directly and indirectly through health. Similarly one could argue that the ways in which social support and job control operate might be very different in firms undergoing restructuring than those which are relatively stable.

While it is apparent that there are many interesting and important questions that can still be answered by the data we have, it is also clear that all the studies share some limitations. Firstly all the studies rely on large-scale aggregated data in which general economic trends are translated into individual health outcomes. Hence, although we can show that for instance involuntary labour market exit through unemployment increases the risk of hospitalization, we cannot, with these data, know why that is the case. Accordingly we do not know what goes on during unemployment that causes poor health. The same can be said of downsizing or expansion or work presenteeism. While we, and others (Ferrie et al., 1998), are able to show that organizational restructuring has a negative effect on health, we do not know how it is organized within the workplace and how this affects health.

Much of the recent work environment research has argued for a clearer understanding of the mechanisms through which adverse psychosocial work conditions produce ill-health (Siegrist, 2002). However these studies have largely focused on the psychobiological pathways in order to redress the so-called 'black box' approach. Yet one could argue that the same is needed for all the different levels involved in work environment research. The work on social support and job control shows that processes work at the level of the organization or the firm. The work on older workers demonstrates that social policy and even demographic changes can have an effect on the work environment. Data from Sweden from the 1990s show that work and access to work continue to be important for health. As our research techniques and ideas improve we become more aware of and, we hope, better able to understand the complex ways in which this is the case. The studies presented here reflect a range of research topics which reflect this complexity but also demand that we are both more and less focused in our research.

Future work in these areas should not only try to get 'under the skin' of the statistical associations they find and uncover the processes at work, but should also consider how seemingly different issues might be propelled by shared processes.

References

Arbetsmiljöverket och Statistiska Centralbyrån (National Board of Work Environment and Statistics, Sweden.) (2001), 'Negativ stress och ohälsa' (Negative stress and ill-health), *Information om utbildning och arbetsmarknad* (Information on education and labour market).
Aronsson, G., K. Gustafsson and M. Dallner (2000), 'Sick but yet at work. An empirical study of sickness presenteeism', *Journal of Epidemiol Community Health*, 54, 502–9.
Carey, D. (2002), 'Coping with population ageing in the Netherlands', Economics department working papers, 325, OECD.
Dahl, E. and J.I. Elstad (2001), 'Recent changes in social structure and health inequalities in Norway', *Scandinavian Journal of Public Health*, 29 (Suppl 55), 7–17.
Drentea, P. (2002), 'Retirement and mental health', *Journal of Aging and Health*, 14, 167–94.
Evenson, K.R., W.D. Rosamond, C. Jianwen, A.V. Diez-Roux, and F.L. Brancati (2002), 'Influence of retirement on leisure time physical activity. The Atherosclerosis Risk in Community Study', *American Journal of Epidemiology*, 155, 692–9.
Ferrie, J.E., M.J. Shipley, M.G. Marmot, S. Stansfeld and G. Davey Smith (1998), 'The health effects of major organisational change and job insecurity', *Soc Sci Med*, 46, 243–54.
Henkens, K., M. Sprengers and F. Tazelaar (1996), 'Unemployment and the older worker', *Ageing and Society*, 16, 561–78.
Karasek, R.A. and T. Theorell (1990), *Healthy Work*, New York: Basic Books.
Lasko, F. and C. Phillipson (1991), *Changing Work and Retirement*, Milton Keynes: Open University Press.
Mein, G., P. Martikainen, H. Hemingway, S. Stansfield and M. Marmot (2003), 'Is retirement good or bad for mental and physical health functioning? Whitehall II longitudinal study of civil servants', *Journal of Epidemiology and Community Health*, 57, 46–9.
OECD (2002), 'Increasing employment – the role of later retirement', *Economic Outlook*, 72.
Oxenstierna, G., M. Hyde, H. Westerlund, K. Jeding, J. Ferie and T. Theorell (2004), 'The dual support model and its relationship to poor health', *Scandinavian Journal of Public Health*, (in review).
Punch, A. and D.L. Pearce (2000), 'Europe's population and labour market beyond 2000', *Population studies*, 33.
Quaade, T., G. Engholm, A.M.T. Johansen and H. Møller (2002), 'Mortality in relation to early retirement in Denmark: a population-based study', *Scandinavian Journal of Public Health*, 30, 216–22.
SCB (2001), 'Arbetsmiljön 1999' (The work environment 1999), Statistiska meddelanden AM 68 SM 0001, Stockholm.
Siegrist, J. (2002), 'Effort–reward imbalance at work and health', in P. Perrewe and D. Ganster (eds), *Research in Occupational Stress and Well-being*, vol. 2, *Historical and Current Perspectives on Stress and Health*, Amsterdam: Elsevier, pp. 261–91.
Theorell, T. (2003), 'Democracy at work and its relationship to health', in P. Perrewe and D. Ganster (eds), *Research in Occupational Stress and Well-being*, vol. 3, Amsterdam: Elsevier.
Theorell, T., G. Oxenstierna, H. Westerlund, J. Ferrie, J. Hagberg and L. Alfredsson (2003), 'Downsizing of staff is associated with lowered medically certified sick leave in female employees', *OEM*, 6(9).
Välfärd vid vägskäl (Welfare at the crossroads) (2000), Utvecklingen under 1990-talet (The Development during the 1990s), Commission. Välfärdsbokslut/SOU 2000:3 (Welfare Audit). Stockholm.
Westerlund, H., J. Ferie, J. Hagberg, G. Oxenstierna, K. Jeding and T. Theorell (2004), 'Workplace expansion: an overlooked risks factor for long-term sickness absence and hospital admission', *The Lancet*.

21 Role-related stress experienced by temporary employees
Ellen I. Shupe

During the past several decades, the United States has witnessed a significant restructuring of the workplace environment, with a trend toward the increased use of externally based personnel (Pfeffer and Baron, 1988). Although such externalization has taken several forms, it has been most notably manifested in the use of a contingent workforce, including the reliance on temporary employees to fill positions that traditionally have been occupied by permanent employees (Barling and Gallagher, 1996). Indeed, recent estimates suggest that temporary employees represent about 20 per cent of the US workforce (Caudron, 1994). Furthermore, given the real and perceived structural, political and financial benefits associated with the use of a temporary workforce (Pfeffer and Baron, 1988), the trend is unlikely to change in the near future.

Although psychological and organizational *theory* related to temporary work is beginning to catch up with the externalization trend, actual *empirical* work has lagged further behind, particularly in the area of stress and coping. Indeed, with a few notable exceptions (for example, Bauer and Truxillo, 2000; Chen *et al.*, 1999), there has been a clear absence of research examining stress experienced by temporary employees, in part because of the difficulty inherent in collecting data from this population. Temporary workers are generally employed on a short-term basis or, in the case of 'temp-to-perm' workers, retain their job permanently after passing through an initial probationary period. In either case, it is difficult to gain access to the workers to collect data, either because of the itinerant nature of their work or because of the relatively high incidence of voluntary and involuntary turnover and layoffs.

The relative dearth of stress research on the temporary workforce is particularly unfortunate, as the population represents a potentially very interesting subject situated within a unique historical and organizational context. For a variety of reasons, temporary workers could be expected to experience high levels of stress, particularly role-related stress such as role ambiguity. They are learning and adapting to a new role, while being socialized into a new working environment and culture. In the case of temp-to-perm workers, such as the sample in the current study, this role-related stress may be amplified by the evaluative context of an extended probationary period.

The study reported here extends the literature on temporary workers and organizational stress by examining the stress experienced by temp-to-perm employees working in an engineering products manufacturing firm. Specifically the study compares the levels of role-related stressors for temp-to-perm employees and permanent worker norms, tests for possible psychological and work-related consequences of the stressors and examines the direct and moderating effects of social support on these stress–strain relations, using the literature on work adjustment and stress and coping as a theoretical framework.

Transition-related stress and social support
Although the literature on stress in temporary employees is limited, there is a more substantial body of research on the role-related stress experienced in the context of other organizational transitions. Work-related transitions are stressful largely because of the uncertainty of change and the effects of new demands on the individual (Nelson *et al.*, 1995). For example, individuals in organizations undergoing major reorganization often experience a variety of physical, psychological and behavioral stress-related symptoms as a result of inter-role conflict, role ambiguity and other stressors (Ashford, 1988; O'Neill and Lenn, 1995; Pollard, 2001). A recent longitudinal study on job security in the context of an organizational merger exemplifies this area of research (Probst, 2002). Results of this study indicated that news of an impending merger leads to an increase in job insecurity and accompanying stress-related symptoms, including negative job attitudes, lowered psychological and physical health, and organizational withdrawal.

Similarly, newly hired permanent employees often experience stress and attendant symptoms of strain as they navigate their way through new surroundings, a new set of roles and expectations and a new organizational culture (for example, Katz, 1985; van der Velde, 1995), through a process of socialization. Briefly, organizational socialization is a multi-stage process through which individuals acquire an understanding of organizational values, norms and expectations in order to perform successfully a new role and integrate into an unfamiliar organization (Louis, 1980; Schein, 1978). Literature on work adjustment and organizational socialization suggests that entry and the accompanying socialization processes are stressful, owing to a variety of demands placed on individuals during a period of heightened uncertainty and ambiguity.

Most relevant for temporary workers is the 'encounter' stage of socialization, the period generally spanning the first six months on the job, during which newcomers are suddenly bombarded with a host of new, unfamiliar sensory cues which can lead to an experience of 'reality shock'. During this encounter stage, newcomers are faced with challenges on two major fronts. First, they must work to learn all expectations associated with their new roles within the organization. This role-related information is often acquired indirectly, through observations of relevant role models and monitoring of behavior–outcome contingencies, both of which allow a gradual understanding of the organizational values and the critical behaviors related to those values. In addition to the role-related learning, newcomers must engage in an acculturation process, through which they come to understand and accept the organizational culture. Because the culture consists of norms, expectations and understandings that are collectively held yet rarely communicated explicitly, efforts at learning the culture are also indirect and are fraught with ambiguities and frustrations. In sum, the initial socialization period is often associated with heightened levels of stress, as workers must simultaneously learn about and adjust to a set of new roles, behaviors and norms, form relationships with relevant parties within and outside the organization, and deal with the reality of unmet expectations (see Frese, 1982; Louis, 1980; Schein, 1978).

Role-related stress
According to Kahn's role theory (for example, Kahn and French, 1970; Kahn *et al.*, 1964), employees often feel stress as a direct result of their experiences fulfilling work-related

roles. Specifically, when individuals perceive that they are receiving conflicting demands in the context of a given role, they may experience *role conflict*, a conflict that is objectively based but is experienced psychologically. For example, a supervisor might feel pressure from management to set high production goals but feel a simultaneous pressure from his subordinate workers to relax production expectations (Kahn French, 1970). In addition to this domain-specific intra-role conflict, Kahn also identified inter-role conflict, or the conflict experienced as a result of conflicting demands from participation in different social groups. The literature on inter-role conflict has overwhelmingly focused on the interface between the work and family roles. Stress resulting from this so-called 'work–family conflict' is thought to stem from at least two sources: conflicting time demands and role-specific strains that spill over to and detract from performance in the other domain (Kopelman et al., 1983). As is the case with intra-role conflict, this time and strain-based work–family conflict is experienced as a stressor and is typically accompanied by an array of undesirable psychological and behavioral consequences (for example, Grandey and Cropanzano, 1999; Schuler et al., 1977).

In addition to role conflict, Kahn's theory claims that individuals may experience other stressors as a direct result of fulfilling work-related roles. Most notably, when individuals do not have the appropriate information needed to successfully fulfill a given work role, they may experience *role ambiguity*. Like role conflict, role ambiguity is experienced as a stressor, and often leads to anxiety, dissatisfaction and lowered levels of performance (Kahn et al., 1964).

More recent stress theories also highlight the role of ambiguity, or uncertainty, in work-related stress. For example, in their model based on expectancy theory, Beehr and Bhagat (1985) introduce three general characteristics of a stressful situation that determine the level of stress experienced in decision-making: (1) the perceived uncertainty of the situation, (2) the perceived importance of the outcomes, and (3) the duration of the perceived uncertainty. Similarly, according to person–environment fit (PEF) theories of stress, ambiguity related to the work role will lead to greater stress (for example, Caplan, 1983; Edwards et al., 1998; Harrison, 1978). These theories claim that stress arises from an interaction between factors related to an individual and factors related to the work environment; specifically stress is directly caused by the real or perceived lack of fit between an individual and his or her work environment. The degree of fit is partly determined by the congruence between the perceived demands of the job and the abilities of the individual (Caplan, 1983). In a situation in which the demands are unclear (that is, a situation involving role ambiguity), the person–environment fit is likely to be poor, a state that could lead to the experience of stress.

Temporary employees are likely to experience heightened levels of role conflict, work–family conflict and role ambiguity. As newcomers to an organization, they are faced with a set of new work-related strains and they may be relatively new at the game of managing work and family-related responsibilities and demands. Likewise temporary employees must learn a new set of norms and expectations associated with an unfamiliar culture, and this period of learning and adjustment takes time. Just as arrivals in a new country often experience 'culture shock', as they are overwhelmed by unfamiliar rules, behaviors and expectations, one would expect new temporary employees who must 'learn the ropes' also to experience role-related stress.

The effects of social support

As is the case for other organizational stressors, it is likely that the transition-related role stress and/or its negative effects may be mitigated by the availability of coping resources and the use of effective coping strategies (for example, Folkman *et al.*, 1986; Viswesvaran *et al.*, 1999). The current study examines the specific effects of social support, which has been shown to be effective both at preventing stressors directly and at moderating their impact, and is particularly relevant to the domain of role stressors and adjustment (for example, Carlson and Perrewe, 1999).

Social support, or 'the availability of helping relationships and the quality of those relationships' (Leavy, 1983, p. 5) is one of the most pervasive coping tools and, as such, has been examined extensively in the stress and coping literature. Although the conceptualization of social support and the types of the stressors and strains vary widely across studies, the research is clear in suggesting that social support can be an important resource in the context of stressful situations. This is true in part because social support affects the stressor–strain relation on several levels and thus has an impact on the entire stress process. Specifically social support reduces the psychological and physical outcomes, or strains experienced, reduces the level of stressors experienced and moderates the stressor–strain relation (Viswesvaran *et al.*, 1999). Furthermore, these protective effects of social support apparently occur for a variety of reasons (Pierce *et al.*, 1996), including providing the information and tools needed to help individuals 'solve' current stressors and make them less vulnerable to future stressors, allowing individuals to structure situations so as to avoid stressors, and providing emotional support. Given the weight of research on its effects, social support is expected to benefit the temp-to-perm employees in the face of role-related stress.

In sum, the purpose of the present study was to examine issues of stress and coping in a sample of temp-to-perm employees. Based on the stress and work adjustment literature discussed above, it is expected that temp-to-perm employees will experience elevated levels of role stressors compared to permanent workers, the experience of role-related stress will predict negative psychological and job-related consequences, and these effects will be directly affected or moderated by social support resources.

Method

Participants and procedure

Data were collected from an engineering products manufacturing company which employs approximately 1100 workers. As temporary employees, the participants typically worked as 'affiliate employees' for a 90-day probationary period, during which they were employed by a temporary employment agency. At the end of the probationary period the employees were taken on as permanent employees, retained as temporary employees for a maximum of six months, or let go.

A total of 108 employees were given a survey containing the measures before or after their shift, or during a break approximately 15 days after initial placement in the company. They were asked to complete the survey within 48 hours, put it in the self-addressed envelope provided, and return the sealed envelope by mail to the principal investigator or to a designated member of the temporary employment agency. Employees were given coupons that could be redeemed at local retailers as compensation for completing the questionnaire.

A total of 47 completed surveys were received, resulting in a response rate of 44 per cent. Of the 47 participants, five eventually left the company for personal reasons, 11 were fired for reasons related to performance and/or attendance, nine were laid off and 22 were taken on as permanent employees. The final sample consisted of 26 male respondents and 21 female respondents. The sample was ethnically diverse (including 53 per cent non-Hispanic white, 32 per cent non-Hispanic black and 8 per cent Hispanic) and the vast majority of the participants worked in low-level manufacturing and assembly positions.

Materials
Participants completed survey booklets including measures of role stressors, psychological and work-related outcomes, social support resources and standard demographic variables. All non-demographic variables were assessed with established scales with known psychometric properties, as detailed below. The means, standard deviations and Cronbach alphas for all measures are presented in Table 21.1, and the simple product–moment correlations between the variables represented by the measures are presented in Table 21.2.

Predictor variables
Role conflict and role ambiguity Role conflict and role ambiguity were assessed with scales developed by Rizzo et al., (1970). The role conflict scale asked respondents to indicate the extent to which they felt statements describing situations involving conflicting expectations and organizational demands were true of their experiences at work. The measure of role ambiguity used the same response scale with statements describing ambiguous situations including those involving behavior–outcome contingencies, work-related expectations, policies and duties. Both scales have been shown to have high validity and reliability and have been used extensively in research related to role-related stress (for example, Gonzalez-Roma and Lloret, 1998; Kelloway and Barling, 1990).

Table 21.1 Summary statistics for measures used in regression models

Construct	No. items	Scale mean	SD	α
Role conflict	7	20.7	7.64	0.80
Role ambiguity	6	16.2	5.64	0.77
Work-to-family conflict	6	17.0	6.30	0.77
Family-to-work conflict	4	9.9	3.96	0.68
Psychological distress	2	7.2	2.75	0.63
Life satisfaction	5	20.1	6.59	0.80
Job withdrawal	6	13.5	4.58	0.76
Job satisfaction	9	15.4	8.41	0.88
Social support	18			
Supervisor support	6	18.2	4.34	0.87
Co-worker support	6	17.8	4.24	0.88
Extraorganizational support	6	21.7	3.21	0.88

Table 21.2 Correlations among variables measured

Variable	1	2	3	4	5	6	7	8	9	10
1. Ambiguity	–									
2. Role conflict	0.58**	–								
3. Interrole conflict	0.32*	0.36*	–							
4. Job satisfaction	−0.23	−0.12	−0.25	–						
5. Job withdrawal	0.21	0.12	0.02	−0.42**	–					
6. Distress	0.34*	0.46**	0.40**	−0.15	−0.12	–				
7. Life satisfaction	−0.11	−0.22	−0.26	0.27	0.05	−0.32*	–			
8. Extra-organiz. support	−0.15	−0.33*	−0.32*	0.10	0.15	−0.19	0.26	–		
9. Supervisor support	−0.31*	−0.22	−0.09	0.35*	−0.14	−0.50**	0.24	0.17	–	
10. Co-worker support	−0.05	0.10	−0.05	0.22	0.01	−0.24	0.12	0.03	0.70**	–

Note: *$p < 0.05$. ***$p < 0.01$.

Work–family conflict. The scale used to assess work–family conflict was a composite measure of work-to-family conflict (that is, the conflict experienced when work interferes with family life) and family-to-work conflict (that is, the conflict experienced when family interferes with work life). Work-to-family conflict was assessed with Kopelman *et al.*'s (1983) measure of interrole conflict, and family-to-work conflict was assessed with a version of Kopelman *et al.*'s scale, with wording modified to reflect the different direction of role interference. Respondents were asked to indicate the extent to which they agreed with six work-to-family items (for example, 'After work I come home too tired to do some of the things I'd like to do') and four family-to-work items (for example, 'Family events or appointments often conflict with my work demands') on a seven-point scale.

Criterion variables
Psychological distress Psychological distress was assessed with two items adopted from Grandey and Cropanzano (1999), asking respondents to indicate the extent to which they agreed with statements related to the stressfulness of their life (for example, 'I would say that I have more going on than I can handle').

Life satisfaction Participants' overall life satisfaction was assessed with the Satisfaction with Life Scale (Diener *et al.*, 1985), a five-item scale that asks respondents to indicate the extent to which they agree with statements related to their satisfaction with life in general, on a seven-point Likert-type scale.

Job withdrawal Job withdrawal (behaviors and intentions representing a partial or complete withdrawal from a specific job) was assessed with a shortened version of a scale developed by Hanisch and Hulin (1990, 1991). The scale requires participants to answer six questions related to their thoughts about, and intentions to quit, their jobs (for example, 'How easy or difficult would it be for you to get another job as good as this one?'), on a five-point scale.

Job satisfaction Respondents' work satisfaction was assessed with the work satisfaction facet scale of the Job Descriptive Index (JDI) (Smith *et al.*, 1969; Roznowski, 1989). Participants circled 'yes', 'no' or '?' (don't know) to indicate whether they thought a list of nine adjectives characterized their experiences at work.

Moderator variables
Social support resources Social support was measured with three subscales developed by Caplan *et al.*, (1975). Respondents were asked to indicate the extent to which each of three sets of people ('your immediate supervisor', 'other people at work' and 'your spouse, friends and relatives') provided six different aspects of social support (for example, being willing to listen to personal problems), on a four-point scale.

Results
Comparison of stressors with permanent employee norms
In order to compare the levels of role-related stress experienced by temp-to-perm employees with permanent employee norms, means of normative reference groups were

compared to the temp-to-perm sample using a series of independent sample *t*-tests. The comparisons were made for the two role stressors (role ambiguity and role conflict) for which normative data were available. A total of six samples from a wide range of occupational settings were identified from the stress and coping literature and used as reference groups. Sample 1 consisted of male occupational therapists (Brown, 1998); sample 2 consisted of all levels of nursing personnel; sample 3 consisted of employees from a manufacturing firm; sample 4 consisted of employees from a communications utility firm, sample 5 consisted of food service and janitorial personnel at a southern university hospital; and sample 6 consisted of nursing aides employed at the same hospital (Schuler et al., 1977). While results of *t*-test comparisons for the role ambiguity variable were inconclusive, the results for the role conflict variable were generally inconsistent with predictions (see Tables 21.3 and 21.4). Specifically, although the temp-to-perm sample scored significantly higher than the hospital employees and nursing aides in terms of role ambiguity, they scored either at the same level or significantly lower than the other four samples. Additionally, the temp-to-perm sample scored at the same level or lower than all six samples in terms of role conflict.

Relation of stressors to stress-related outcomes
Hierarchical multiple regression analyses were performed to allow an examination of possible stressor–outcome relations for the temp-to-perm sample. Specifically, relations between the three role-related stressors (role conflict, role ambiguity and work–family conflict) and four potential outcomes (job withdrawal, job satisfaction, life satisfaction and psychological distress) were examined. In the first block of each regression, an outcome variable was regressed onto the three stressors. In the next block, the three social support variables (supervisor support, co-worker support and extraorganizational support) were added to the model. Finally, the social support × stressor interaction terms were added in the third block in order to examine potential moderating effects of the social support variables. For each model, regression diagnostic checks were conducted by examining Cook's distance values, which provide a measure of the change in the regression coefficients achieved by iteratively deleting each case. For each set of regression

Table 21.3 Mean comparisons on role ambiguity for temp-to-perm and permanent employee reference groups

	N	Mean	SD	*t*-statistic
Temp-to-perm sample	43	2.70	0.94	
Sample 1 (occupational therapists)	164	2.40	0.95	−1.86
Sample 2 (nursing employees)	374	2.60	0.96	0.66
Sample 3 (manufacturing employees)	362	3.36	1.26	−4.18***
Sample 4 (public utility employees)	399	3.22	1.03	−3.41***
Sample 5 (hospital employees)	99	1.41	1.18	6.93***
Sample 6 (nursing aides)	70	1.23	1.04	7.75***

Note: *t*-statistics given for mean comparisons between temp-to-perm sample and each permanent employee reference group; ***$p < 0.01$, two-tailed.

Table 21.4 Mean comparisons on role conflict for temp-to-perm and permanent employee reference groups

	N	Mean	SD	t-statistic
Temp-to-perm sample	42	2.96	1.09	
Sample 1 (occupational therapists)	164	4.08	1.16	−5.86***
Sample 2 (nursing employees)	374	3.26	1.05	−1.70*
Sample 3 (manufacturing employees)	362	3.79	1.21	−4.62***
Sample 4 (public utility employees)	399	4.07	0.81	−6.42***
Sample 5 (hospital employees)	99	3.57	1.23	−2.92***
Sample 6 (nursing aides)	70	3.14	1.19	−0.817

Note: t-statistics given for mean comparisons between temp-to-perm sample and each permanent employee reference group; *$p < 0.10$, ***$p < 0.01$, all two-tailed.

analyses, participants with a Cook's distance value that was judged to be exceedingly large relative to the other participants' values, were excluded from the analyses.

Results of these initial analyses indicated a potential problem with multicollinearity between role conflict and role ambiguity and between supervisor support and co-worker support. Specifically, the bivariate correlations were close to 0.7, and in both cases, the F-statistic for the full model was statistically significant, but none of the t-ratios for the regression coefficients for individual predictors were statistically significant. On the basis of this diagnostic information, the likelihood of multicollinearity was perceived to be high (Berry and Feldman, 1985). Accordingly, two adjustments to the models were made. First, supervisor support and co-worker support were combined into a single, more parsimonious, 'work-based support' variable. Two separate sets of regressions were then conducted for the role conflict and ambiguity predictors, in order best to estimate their unique influence on the outcome variables. In all cases, the alpha was set at 0.10; this higher than traditional alpha was deemed appropriate given the early stage of research in this area and the exploratory nature of the study.

Results of regression analyses for both sets of models indicated a significant main effect of the role stressors for psychological distress (see Table 21.5). Examination of the standardized betas indicated that the significant effects were primarily due to role conflict and role ambiguity. In both cases, individuals experiencing higher levels of the role stressors were more likely to experience increased psychological distress. In addition, there was a significant main effect of the role stressors for life satisfaction. Examination of the standardized betas indicated that the significant effect was due primarily to role ambiguity: individuals who experienced higher levels of ambiguity were more likely to experience decreased satisfaction. Finally results indicated a main effect of social support for work satisfaction, due primarily to the specific effects of work-based support; individuals experiencing increased social support from their supervisors and co-workers generally experienced higher levels of job satisfaction.

Although the sample size (and resulting power) was too small to detect a statistically significant effect from any of the social support × stressor interaction terms, the size of the coefficient of determination for several of the terms seemed to warrant a closer

Table 21.5 Summary of hierarchical regression models

Criterion	N	Predictor		Std beta	R^2	ΔR^2	F_{change}
Distress	32	Step 1	Role conflict	0.41**	0.38	0.38	8.81***
			Interrole conflict	0.27			
		Step 2	Work-based support	−0.28*	0.45	0.08	1.86
			Extraorganizational support	0.04			
		Step 3	Conflict × work support	0.58	0.50	0.05	0.55
			Conflict × extraorganiz. support	1.7			
			Interrole × work support	−0.23			
			Interrole × extraorganiz. support	−2.1			
	33	Step 1	Role ambiguity	0.37**	0.31	0.31	6.65**
			Interrole conflict	0.26			
		Step 2	Work-based support	−0.17	0.37	0.06	1.32
			Extraorganizational support	0.18			
		Step 3	Ambiguity × work support	−0.44	0.42	0.05	0.49
			Ambiguity × extraorganiz. support	1.7			
			Interrole × work support	−0.36			
			Interrole × extraorganiz. support	1.3			
Life sat.	33	Step 1	Role conflict	−0.15	0.04	0.04	0.65
			Interrole conflict	−0.07			
		Step 2	Work-based support	0.13	0.07	0.03	0.49
			Extraorganizational support	0.15			

Table 21.5 (continued)

Criterion	N	Predictor	Std beta	R^2	ΔR^2	F_{change}
		Step 3		0.15	0.08	0.54
		Conflict × work support	0.56			
		Conflict × extraorganiz. support	−0.03			
		Interrole × work support	−1.1			
		Interrole × extraorganiz. support	−1.7			
	31	Step 1		0.18	0.18	2.97*
		Role ambiguity	−0.37*			
		Interrole conflict	−0.09			
		Step 2		0.20	0.02	0.38
		Work-based support	0.16			
		Extraorganizational support	0.01			
		Step 3		0.29	0.10	0.75
		Ambiguity × work support	−1.1			
		Ambiguity × extraorganiz. support	−0.27			
		Interrole × work support	−0.83			
		Interrole × extraorganiz. support	−1.1			
Job with.	34	Step 1		0.12	0.12	2.10
		Role conflict	0.40*			
		Interrole conflict	−0.12			
		Step 2		0.13	0.01	0.82
		Work-based support	−0.08			
		Extraorganizational support	0.08			
		Step 3		0.22	0.09	0.59
		Conflict × work support	0.24			
		Conflict × extraorganiz. support	1.98			
		Interrole × work support	−0.45			
		Interrole × extraorganiz. support	−2.52			
	36	Step 1		0.06	0.06	1.14
		Role ambiguity	0.27			
		Interrole conflict	−0.13			

	Step 2				
	Work-based support	−0.06	0.08	0.02	0.73
	Extraorganizational support	0.14	0.20	0.11	0.46
	Step 3				
	Ambiguity × work support	−0.29			
	Ambiguity × extraorganiz. support	−1.99*			
	Interrole × work support	−0.26			
	Interrole × extraorganiz. support	−0.11			
Job sat.	32				
	Step 1				
	Role conflict	−0.35*	0.09	0.09	1.51
	Interrole conflict	0.13			
	Step 2				
	Work-based support	0.38**	0.24	0.15	2.60*
	Extraorganizational support	0.02			
	Step 3				
	Conflict × work support	−0.01	0.28	0.04	0.29
	Conflict × extraorganiz. support	0.06			
	Interrole × work support	−1.20			
	Interrole × extraorganiz. support	2.73			
	35				
	Step 1				
	Role ambiguity	−0.20	0.07	0.07	1.24
	Interrole conflict	−0.10			
	Step 2				
	Work-based support	0.30*	0.16	0.09	1.53
	Extraorganizational support	−0.01			
	Step 3				
	Ambiguity × work support	−1.29	0.24	0.09	0.74
	Ambiguity × extraorganiz. support	0.74			
	Interrole × work support	−0.63			
	Interrole × extraorganiz. support	0.46			

Note: Life sat. = life satisfaction; Job with. = job withdrawal; Job sat. = job satisfaction; †$p < 0.10$ **$p < 0.05$ ***$p < 0.01$.

examination of the data. To accomplish this, the sample was first dichotomized on the basis of individuals' scores on the work-based social support variable and again on the extraorganizational social support (that is, support from spouse, friends and relatives) variable. Then interaction terms that accounted for a large amount of the variance (close to 10 per cent) in the outcome variables were identified (see Table 21.5). For each of these interactions, social support x stressor graphs were created for the specific term or terms that were judged to be particularly important given the relative size of their standardized betas. With a single exception, the graphs suggested that the social support variables moderated the stressor–strain relation as follows: low levels of work-based support and high levels of extraorganizational support resulted in a weaker relation between the role-based stressors and strains. In other words, workers with higher levels of work-based support and lower levels of extraorganizational support tended to experience the worst consequences as a result of role-based stressors. Figures 21.1 and 21.2 illustrate this pattern with role ambiguity and the job satisfaction outcome variable.

Discussion

The purpose of this study was to examine the levels and effects of stress in a sample of temp-to-perm employees. The study compared the levels of role-related stress experienced

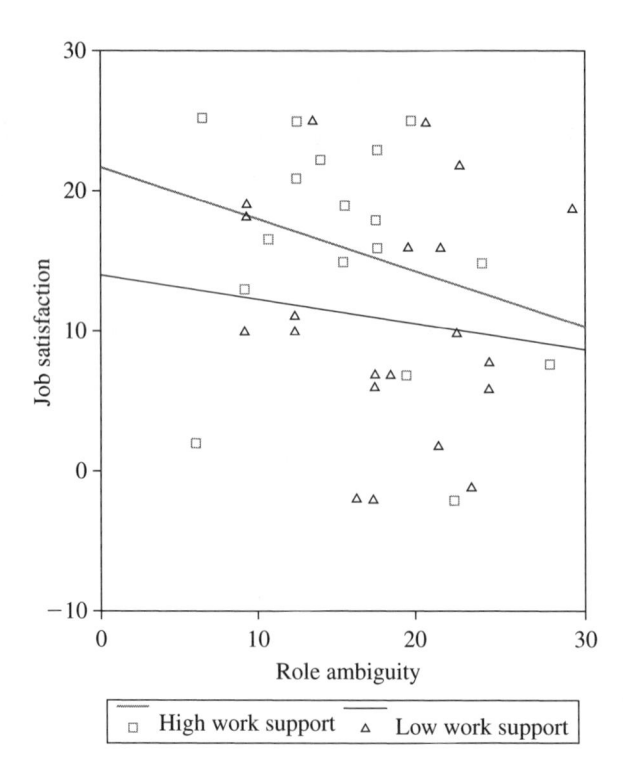

Figure 21.1   Best fitting regression for job satisfaction on role ambiguity for two levels of work-based support.

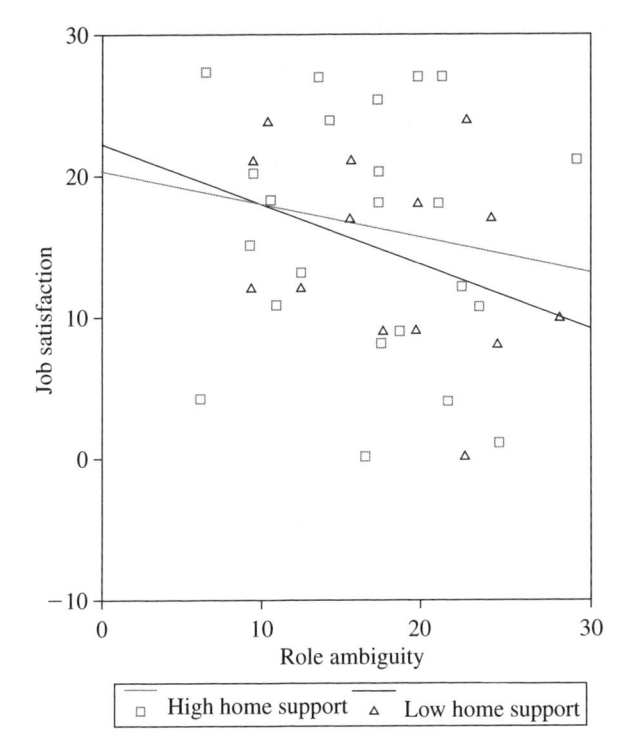

[Figure: scatter plot of Job satisfaction vs Role ambiguity with two regression lines for High home support (squares) and Low home support (triangles).]

Figure 21.2 Best fitting regression for job satisfaction on role ambiguity for two levels of extraorganizational support.

by temp-to-perm employees to six permanent worker samples, examined the relation of the experience of stress to psychological and work-related outcomes and investigated the potential direct and moderating effects of work-based and extraorganizational social support.

Results suggested that the temp-to-perm workers experienced a modest level of role ambiguity and a low level of role conflict relative to the six permanent worker reference groups. Specifically, the level of role ambiguity experienced by the temp-to-perm workers was significantly higher than two of the hospital employee samples, but not significantly different from or significantly lower than the other four samples. Furthermore, contrary to predictions, the level of role conflict experienced was significantly lower than that of all but the nursing aide sample. There are at least two possible explanations for these counter-intuitive results, both of which are related to the timing of data collection. First, it is possible that the first two-week period represents a 'honeymoon' phase, in which the benefits of the job are particularly salient and function to mask or shield the workers from the full magnitude of potential stressors. Second, it is possible that the role conflict is not masked, but rather that the apparent low levels of role conflict are real. Although the two-week mark was chosen for data collection because it was assumed that the stressors related to adjustment would be high at this time, it is possible that the workers cannot fully grasp the complexities of the job this soon after the hire date. The new employees may not yet realize, for example, that they 'have to do things that should be done differently' or 'complete assignments without adequate resources'.

Although the results suggested that temp-to-perm workers generally did not experience higher levels of the role stressors than did permanent worker comparison groups, the workers did experience low to moderate levels of the stressors, which proved to be enough to lead to some undesirable psychological outcomes. Consistent with the literature on the psychological effects of organizational stress in the permanent workforce (for example, Beehr et al., 1990), the experience of role conflict was shown to be related to increased levels of psychological distress. Additionally, the experience of role ambiguity was related both to increased levels of psychological distress and to decreased levels of life satisfaction. Thus, these preliminary results suggest that stress experienced in the first two weeks of the temp-to-perm probationary period do have some very real effects on the workers in terms of their psychological well-being.

Examination of the results for the social support variables revealed several interesting patterns. First, there was a significant direct (main) effect of social support on job satisfaction, with social support accounting for a full 15 per cent of the variance in workers' satisfaction. More specifically, temp-to-perm workers experiencing higher levels of work-based social support tended to be more satisfied with their job. In addition, there were several social support x stressor interactions indicating interesting and potentially important effects. The interactions seemed to suggest that the effects of all three role stressors were moderated by social support, but that the direction of the moderating effect was different for work-based and extraorganizational support. Although *higher* levels of extraorganizational support weakened or buffered the effect of role stressors on job withdrawal, job satisfaction and life satisfaction variables, *lower* levels of work-based support buffered the effect of the role stressors on job satisfaction and life satisfaction variables. In other words, workers with a great deal of extraorganizational support and workers with little work-based support apparently suffered fewer consequences of stress than did their temp-to-perm co-workers. Although the latter result is somewhat counterintuitive, it is not necessarily inconsistent with the literature. Indeed, other researchers have demonstrated that, in some cases, social support has a 'reverse buffering' effect on stress-related outcomes (Beehr, 1976; Chen et al., 1999; Fenlason and Beehr, 1994; Kaufmann and Beehr, 1986). Instead of shielding individuals from the strains that often accompany the experience of stress, social support can actually intensify these strains.

Two possible explanations have been offered for the reverse buffering effect. First, it has been suggested that individuals may mobilize their support resources after encountering the stressors and experiencing the resulting strain (Kaufmann and Beehr, 1986). Given the evidence suggesting that in the majority of cases there is a negative relation between social support and strain (for example, Viswesvaran et al., 1999), it appears that the implied sequence of events does not occur with regularity. An alternative explanation may be more plausible, as it suggests the possibility of both buffering and reverse buffering effects. Specifically, several researchers have suggested that the *content* of the supportive communications may play an important role in determining the nature of the buffering effects (Kaufmann and Beehr, 1986; LaRocco et al., 1980). They suggest that, although communications of a positive nature may lessen the strain experienced, negative supportive communications may function actually to increase the resulting strain. For example, supportive communications from co-workers may convince the stressed workers that things are as bad as or even worse than they seem. Several studies have examined this possibility by analyzing the direct or moderating effects of support on strain, separately for different contents of communication. Although some research suggests that negative communications do not cause the increased experience of strain (Beehr et al., 1990), other research suggests that they do (Chen et al., 1999; Fenlason and Beehr, 1994). Perhaps most relevant to the current research is Chen and colleagues' study that employed a temp-to-perm sample, results of which suggested that negative job-related communications increase levels of the temp-to-perm employees' work-related anxiety. This evidence, together with the obtained pattern of results, suggests that the supportive work-based communications received by participants in the current study were largely negative in content.

Results demonstrating the reverse buffering effect in the current study are consistent with earlier observations in the coping literature suggesting that social support is highly selective in its buffering effects, with the specific effects of support depending on the nature of the strain and the nature and source of the support (for example, Chisholm et al., 1986; Wells, 1982). A more specific hypothesis that represents an extension of this effect suggests that whether social support provides a buffering effect depends on the extent to which there is a *match* between elements of the stress and coping process (for example, Cohen and Wills, 1985). For example, social support might be expected to moderate the effects of a stressor, if the source of the support, the type of stressor and the type of strain represented the same domain. In the current study evidence for this matching hypothesis can be examined for work-based support, stressors and strains, by comparing the buffering effects of work-based support with the effects of extraorganization support, for the job satisfaction and job withdrawal variables. To this end, an examination of the standardized betas for the extraorganizational versus work-based support × stressor interactions suggests that work-based support provides no real benefit beyond the benefit of extraorganizational support. In fact, as mentioned above, work-based support actually appears to heighten the experience of work-related strains. Thus the current study does not provide evidence in support of the matching hypothesis.

Limitations and future directions

Although its results are both promising and interesting, the study is not without limitations. One methodological concern is the study's sole reliance on self-report measures, raising the possibility of spurious relations owing to the lack of method variance. Although the lack of method variance is always a potential problem in research involving self-report data, the pattern of correlations (Table 21.2) suggests that it does not pose a serious threat to the current study. For example, while the role stressors generally were significantly correlated with the strains, that was not always the case (for example, inter-role conflict and job withdrawal correlated at $r = 0.02$). A second, and perhaps more important, methodological consideration is the use of non-experimental, cross-sectional data, leading to the concern of reverse causation. Although available theory suggests the presence of a causal relation between role stressors and strains, it is recognized that cross-sectional, correlational data do not allow for causal inferences and are therefore limited in their scope and implications (for example, Newcomb, 1990). However, it could be argued that the decision to use cross-sectional, rather than longitudinal data in the current study is justifiable given the early stage of research on stress and coping in the temporary workforce. Specifically, cross-sectional data allow a relatively inexpensive and efficient test of the model that is useful before undertaking the much more time-consuming and costly longitudinal research (Markel and Frone, 1998). Thus, although longitudinal research obviously represents an important pursuit for the future, cross-sectional research can also play an important role at this stage of research.

Future work could also provide a more complete illustration of the complexities intrinsic to the role of social support. For example, data from the current study suggest that supportive work-based communications may actually increase the experience of strain. This reverse buffering effect was explained as a possible result of the negative content of the communications. Research providing a direct test of this explanation in the context of a wide range of psychological, work-related and health-related strains would represent an important contribution to the literature. Likewise, a more complete test of the matching hypothesis in the temporary workforce, using measures of a variety of forms and sources of support, and types of stressors and strains, seems warranted.

Conclusions

The increased reliance on an externally based workforce, combined with the already high number of these workers in organizations, suggests a critical need for a greater understanding of the experiences of this unique population. The study reported here represents an initial, exploratory attempt to provide this understanding in the context of stress-related experiences, using a sample of temp-to-perm workers. Results suggested that, although the temp-to-perm employees generally experienced lower levels of role-related stress than did permanent reference groups, the stress they did experience had negative implications in terms of psychological well-being. Furthermore, work-based and extra-organizational social support appears to play a moderating role in the stress–strain relation, in interesting and sometimes counterintuitive ways. Although it is recognized that data collection on the temporary worker population brings unique challenges, the somewhat preliminary yet provocative results of the current study highlight the importance of continuing this line of research.

Acknowledgment

The author thanks Vicki Magley and Bill Rogers for their advice on issues related to research presented in this chapter and for helpful comments on earlier versions.

References

Ashford, S.J. (1988), 'Individual strategies for coping with stress during organizational transitions', *Journal of Applied Behavioral Science*, **24**, 19–36.
Barling, J. and D.G. Gallagher (1996), 'Part-time employment', in C.L. Cooper and I.T. Robertson (eds), *International Review of Industrial and Organizational Psychology*, vol.II, London: Wiley and Sons, pp. 243–77.
Bauer, T.N. and D.M. Truxillo (2000), 'Temp-to-permanent employees: a longitudinal study of stress and selection success', *Journal of Occupational Health Psychology*, **5**, 337–46.
Beehr, T.A. (1976), 'Perceived situational moderators of the relationship between subjective role ambiguity and role strain', *Journal of Applied Psychology*, **61**, 35–40.
Beehr, T.A. and R. Bhagat (1985), *Human Stress and Cognitions in Organizations: An Integrated Perspective*, New York: Wiley.

Beehr, T.A., L.A. King and D.W. King (1990), 'Social support and occupational stress: talking to supervisors', *Journal of Vocational Behavior*, **36**, 61–81.
Berry, W.D. and S. Feldman (1985), *Multiple Regression in Practice*, Newbury Park: Sage.
Brown, G.T. (1998), 'Role strain experienced by male occupational therapists: a descriptive survey', *British Journal of Occupational Therapy*, **61**, 410–17.
Caplan, R.D. (1983), 'Person–environment fit: past, present, and future', in C.L. Cooper (ed.), *Stress Research*, New York: Wiley, pp. 35–78.
Caplan, R.D., S. Cobb and J.R. French (1975), 'Relationship of cessation of smoking with job stress, personality, and social support', *Journal of Applied Psychology*, **60**, 211–19.
Carlson, D.S. and P.L. Perrewe (1999), 'The role of social support in the stressor–strain relationship: an examination of work–family conflict', *Journal of Management*, **25**, 513–40.
Caudron, S. (1994), 'Contingent workforce spurs HR planning', *Personnel Journal*, **73**, 52–60.
Chen, P.Y., P.M. Popovich and M. Kogan (1999), 'Let's talk: patterns and correlates of social support among temporary employees', *Journal of Occupational Health Psychology*, **4**, 55–62.
Chisholm, R.F., S.V. Kasl and L. Mueller (1986), 'The effects of social support on nuclear worker responses to the Three Mile Island accident', *Journal of Occupational Behaviour*, **7**, 179–93.
Cohen, S. and T.A. Wills (1985), 'Stress, social support and the buffering hypothesis', *Psychological Bulletin*, **98**, 310–57.
Diener, E., R.J. Emmons, R.J. Larsen and S. Griffin (1985), 'The satisfaction with life scale', *Journal of Personality Assessment*, **49**, 71–5.
Edwards, J.R., R.D. Caplan and R.V. Harrison (1998), 'Person–environment fit theory: conceptual foundations, empirical evidence and directions for future research', in C.L. Cooper (ed.), *Theories of Organizational Stress*, Oxford: Oxford University Press, pp. 28–67.
Fenlason, K.J. and T.A. Beehr (1994), 'Social support and occupational stress: effects of talking to others', *Journal of Organizational Behavior*, **15**, 157–75.
Folkman, S., R.S. Lazarus, R.J. Gruen and A. DeLongis (1986), ' Appraisal, coping, health status and psychological symptoms', *Journal of Personality and Social Psychology*, **50**, 571–9.
Frese, M. (1982), 'Occupational socialization and psychological development: an underemphasized research perspective in industrial psychology', *Journal of Occupational Psychology*, **55**, 209–24.
Gonzalez-Roma, V. and S. Lloret (1998), 'Construct validity of Rizzo et al.'s (1970) role conflict and ambiguity scales: a multisample study', *Applied Psychology: An International Review*, **47**, 535–45.
Grandey, A.A. and R. Cropanzano (1999), 'The conservation of resources model applied to work–family conflict and strain', *Journal of Vocational Behavior*, **54**, 350–70.
Hanisch, K.A. and C.L. Hulin (1990), 'Job attitudes and organizational withdrawal: an examination of retirement and other voluntary withdrawal behaviors', *Journal of Vocational Behavior*, **37**, 60–78.
Hanisch, K.A. and C.L. Hulin (1991), 'General attitudes and organizational withdrawal: an evaluation of a causal model', *Journal of Vocational Behavior*, **39**, 110–28.
Harrison, R.V. (1978), 'Person-environment fit and job stress', in C.L. Cooper and R. Payne (eds), *Stress at Work*, New York: Wiley, pp. 175–205.
Hughes, E.C. (1958), *Men and their Work*, Glencoe, IL: Free Press.
Kahn, R.L. and J.R.P. French, Jr. (1970), 'Status and conflict: two themes in the study of Stress', in J.E. McGrath (ed.), *Social and Psychological Factors in Stress*, New York: Holt Reinhart.
Kahn, R.L., D.M. Wolfe, R.P. Quinn, J.D. Snoek and R.A. Rosenthal (1964), *Organizational Stress: Studies in Role Conflict and Role Ambiguity*, New York: Wiley.
Katz, R. (1985), 'Organizational stress and early socialization experiences', in T.A. Beehr and R.S. Bhagat (eds), *Human Stress and Cognition in Organization: An Integrated Perspective*, New York: Wiley, pp. 117–39.
Kaufmann, G.M. and T.A. Beehr (1986), 'Interactions between job stressors and social support: some counterintuitive results', *Journal of Applied Psychology*, **71**, 522–6.
Kelloway, E.K. and J. Barling (1990), 'Item content versus item wording: disentangling role conflict and role ambiguity', *Journal of Applied Psychology*, **75**, 738–42.
Kopelman, R.E., J.H. Greenhaus and T.F. Connolly (1983), 'A model of work, family and interrole conflict: a construct validation study', *Organizational Behavior and Human Performance*, **32**, 198–215.
LaRocco, J.M., J.S. House and J.R.P. French, Jr. (1980), 'Social support, occupational stress and health', *Journal of Health and Social Behavior*, **21**, 202–18.
Leavy, R.L. (1983), 'Social support and psychological disorder: a review', *Journal of Community Psychology*, **11**, 3–21.
Louis, M. (1980), 'Surprise and sense making: what newcomers experience in entering unfamiliar organizational settings', *Administrative Science Quarterly*, **25**, 226–51.
Markel, K.S. and M.R. Frone (1998), 'Job characteristics, work–school conflict, and school outcomes among adolescents: testing a structural model', *Journal of Applied Psychology*, **83**, 277–87.

Nelson, D.L., J.C. Quick, M.E. Eakin and P.A.C. Matuszek (1995), 'Beyond organizational entry and newcomer stress: building a self-reliant workforce', *International Journal of Stress Management*, **2**, 1–14.

Newcomb, M.D. (1990), 'What structural equation modeling can tell us about social support', in B.R. Sarason, I.G. Sarason and G.R. Pierce (eds), *Social Support: An Interactional View*, New York: John Wiley & Sons.

O'Neill, H.M. and J. Lenn (1995), 'Voices of survivors: words that downsizing CEOs should hear', *Academy of Management Executives*, **9**, 23–34.

Pfeffer, J. and J.N. Baron (1988), 'Taking the workers back out: recent trends in the structuring of employment', *Research in Organizational Behavior*, **10**, 257–303.

Pierce, G.R., I.G. Sarason and B.R. Sarason (1996), 'Coping and social support', in M. Zeidner and N. Endler (eds), *Handbook of Coping: Theory, Research and Applications*, Oxford: Wiley, pp. 434–51.

Pollard, T.M. (2001), 'Changes in mental well-being, blood pressure and total cholesterol levels during workplace reorganization: the impact of uncertainty', *Work & Stress*, **15**, 14–28.

Probst, T.M. (2002), 'The impact of job insecurity on employee work attitudes, job adaptation and organizational withdrawal behaviors', in J.M. Brett and F. Drawzow (eds), *The psychology of work: Theoretically Based Empirical Research*, Mahwah, NJ: Lawrence Erlbaum Associates, pp.141–68.

Rizzo, J.R., R.J. House and J.I. Lirtzman (1970), 'Role conflict and ambiguity in complex organizations', *Administrative Science Quarterly*, **15**, 150–63.

Roznowski, M. (1989), 'Examination of the measurement properties of the Job Descriptive Index with experimental items', *Journal of Applied Psychology*, **74**, 805–14.

Schein, E.H. (1978), *Career Dynamics: Matching Individual and Organizational Needs*, Reading, MA: Addison-Wesley.

Schuler, R.S., R.J. Aldag and A.P. Brief (1977), 'Role conflict and role ambiguity: a scale analysis', *Organizational Behavior and Human Performance*, **20**, 111–28.

Smith, P.C., L.M. Kendall and C.L. Hulin (1969), *The Measurement of Satisfaction in Work and Retirement: A Strategy for the Study of Attitudes*, Oxford,: Rand McNally.

Van der Velde, M. and M.D. Class (1995), 'The relationship of role conflict and ambiguity to organizational culture', in S. Sauter and L.R. Murphy (eds), *Organizational Risk Factors for Job Stress*, Washington, DC: American Psychological Association, pp. 53–7.

Viswesvaran, C., J.I. Sanchez and J. Fisher (1999), 'The role of social support in the process of work stress: a meta-analysis', *Journal of Vocational Behavior*, **54**, 314–34.

Wells, J.A. (1982), 'Objective job conditions, social support and perceived stress among blue collar workers', *Journal of Occupational Behavior*, **3**, 79–94.

PART IV

STRESS, WELL-BEING AND HEALTH

22 The role of psychosocial factors in the development of periodontal disease

Alexander-Stamatios G. Antoniou, Diamanto Komboli, John Vrotsos and Zacharias Mantzavinos

Introduction

Periodontal diseases constitute infections related to specific pathogenic bacteria, which, in turn, attack and subsequently colonize the subgingival area. Several specific oral bacteria can be considered as representative for periodontal diseases and these include *Actinobasillicus actinomycetemcomitans, Bacteroides forsythus, Porphyromonas gingivalis, Camphylobacter rectus* and *Fusobacterium nucleatum*, all of which are associated with more severe forms of periodontal diseases (Genco *et al.*, 1998). Periodontal diseases are now recognized as the bacterial infections which affect a large proportion of the general adult population of 25–75-year-olds, causing great discomfort, pain and tooth loss (Hugoson and Jordan, 1982; Miller *et al.*, 1987; Brown and Loë, 1993). A very important feature of the disease is that these specific bacteria are capable of colonizing the subgingival area and infecting it in spite of the protective mechanisms of the host (Baker *et al.*, 1961).

The initiation and progression of periodontal diseases is determined and modified by specific local and systemic conditions, which are identified as risk factors. Genco (1996) has divided risk factors into two categories: (a) local risk factors, which are related to an earlier stage of development including dietary factors, osteopenia/osteoporosis, AIDS and stress, and (b) systemic risk factors which can be modified, including factors such as tobacco smoking and diabetes mellitus. The fact that the systemic risk factors can be modified is very important for the management of the disease. Risk factors are considered to be environmental exposures, specific characteristics or behaviors that have been associated with destructive forms of periodontal diseases. We have therefore been led to the intensive study of these risk factors since we first became aware of the potential importance of susceptibility factors, affecting as they do the initiation and progression of the disease.

Epidemiological studies present specific systemic risk factors, which include diabetes mellitus (Nelson *et al.*, 1990; Shlossman *et al.*, 1990; Emrich *et al.*, 1991; Oliver and Tervonen, 1993) and tobacco smoking (Pindborg, 1947; Frandsen and Pindborg, 1949; Solomon *et al.*, 1968; Ismail *et al.*, 1983). Furthermore gender (Norderyd *et al.*, 1993; Grossi *et al.*, 1994, 1995; US Public Health Service, 1965) and age (Marshall-Day *et al.*, 1955; Schei *et al.*, 1959; Russele, 1960; Holm-Pendersen *et al.*, 1975; Abdellatif and Burt, 1987; Beck *et al.*, 1990; Machtei *et al.*, 1994) are related to the increasing predominance and importance of periodontal diseases. Other factors such as AIDS (Felten *et al.*, 1993; Gyorfi *et al.*, 1994) have also been considered. People diagnosed as HIV positive and AIDS victims suffer from periodontal disease, including severe and painful narcotizing forms.

There is a growing body of research and evidence that reveals a link between psychosocial stress and periodontal diseases, although there is not enough evidence to support its influence on the initiation and progression of the disease. Kanterman (1955), on the psychosomatic aspects of periodontitis, stated: 'the psyche, when subjected to emotional conflicts over long periods, becomes an important factor in causing a chain of somatic reactions that result in pathologic changes. Such changes affect neural, vascular and endocrine systems, which play a very important role in maintaining the health of the oral tissues'. This review aims to be a critical evaluation of the existing evidence that supports this correlation, as ascertaining at length to what degree stress affects the periodontium.

Determinants for periodontal disease

Age

It is now common knowledge that the severity of periodontal disease increases with age. In a 10-year retrospective radiographic study (Papapanou, 1996), the author studied 201 individuals of different age groups and assessed the progression of bone loss. Over this period of observation, bone loss remained relatively constant in all groups except the oldest. Studies also report that plaque development and severity of periodontal disease are greater in advanced age compared to younger age groups (Abdellatif and Burt, 1987). Therefore most studies suggest that these older age groups present more severe forms of periodontal disease because of the tissue destruction that takes place over the years and not because of old age.

Gender

According to studies (US Public Health Service, 1965; DeRouen et al., 1991), males seem to be more susceptible to periodontal disease than females. Males usually report fewer dental visits than women, who exhibit better oral hygiene habits. Specific hormonal conditions in women are related to gingival inflammatory conditions (Genco, 1996), such as pregnancy gingivitis. The hormone estrogen in women is likely to be a protective factor against periodontitis and may be a valuable element in determining the small increase of periodontal disease in the male population.

Tobacco use

Smoking remains a great risk factor for periodontal disease. Ismail et al. (1983), found that tobacco use is an important risk factor for periodontitis after adjusting specific variables such as age, socioeconomic status and oral hygiene status. Substantial evidence shows that the periodontal micro flora in the smoking population is different from the micro flora of non-smokers. Moreover the smoking population's healing mechanisms and healing capacity after treatment are far less satisfactory compared to those of non-smokers after therapy. The clinical community, however, in spite of the long history that links tobacco use to periodontal disease, is not yet convinced of this association.

AIDS

Many studies reveal a correlation between acquired immune deficiency syndrome (AIDS) and severe forms of periodontal disease (Greenberg, 1996; Greenspan and Greenspan, 1996; Phelan, 1997). A study by Salvi et al. (1997) suggested that severe forms of periodontal disease in patients suffering from AIDS must be considered in a different light by periodontologists, with respect to prognosis etiology, therapy and risk factors, because of the distinct and special characteristic features of patients diagnosed with AIDS, in terms of host response (Papapanou, 1998).

Socioeconomic status
Studies comparing the population of industrial countries to the population of developing countries suggest that nutritional habits may be associated with periodontal disease, especially in the developing countries (Russell, 1960, 1962). However studies that endeavor to establish correlations between nutritional habits and periodontal disease fail to establish a clear and valid relationship between the two (Waerhaug, 1967; Wertheimer et al., 1967).

Risk assessment and study designs
Beck (1994) has proposed a risk assessment scheme which examines the evidence of each risk factor in order to evalute whether assessment has been performed more than once and in different populations: that valid biological scenarios have been identified in relation to those specific risk factors, that a cross-sectional association is established and, finally, that targeting studies are available.

Assessment of risk in periodontal disease is achieved by gingival scoring methods, usually the measurement of bleeding, clinical attachment levels and loss of alveolar housing using radiographic evidence (Genco, 1996). Several study designs have proved useful for the assessment of the factors affecting periodontitis. Case series reports, anecdote studies and case histories, although they constitute a sufficient basis for the construction of a hypothesis, have not proved to be the strongest line of evidence. Studies which are aimed at a large proportion of the general population, such as longitudinal studies and cross-sectional studies, even though they are often more complicated to assess as regards reliability and validity, provide strong evidence that the risk indicator – a factor associated with the disease and identified by cross-sectional and case control studies – is indeed a true risk factor for the disease.

The randomized controlled trial is an experimental design which has proved to be the most valid and the strongest of all designs, providing strong support for the clinical importance of the risk factor in the progression of the disease. In this design the modification of the risk factor is assigned randomly to a test group, which is then compared to a control group receiving placebo intervention, and at a later stage of the trial the two groups are compared in order to identify any possible differences between them. If differences are evident, other placebo-controlled randomized trials are set up, in which the progression and treatment response are measured along with the modified risk factor.

A cross-sectional study conducted by Grossi *et al.* (1995), attempted to delineate specific risk factors for periodontitis. This study included 1361 participants between 25 and 74 years of age, of which 665 were male and 696 were female. Variables such as clinical attachment loss were utilized as the outcome variable. The association with the number of explanatory variables of periodontal destruction, as measured in an earlier study, was made in respect to alveolar bone loss. These variables were age, gender (male), tobacco use, history of allergies, the presence of *Porphyromonas gingivalis* or *Bacteroides forsythus*, subgingival plaque and education. The odd ratios for more severe alveolar bone loss were greater for the tobacco user and age variables than their counterparts.

What is psychosocial stress?
The term 'stress' is used to describe complex phenomena of a psychological and physical nature that are partially understood (Linden *et al.*, 1996). Stress also refers to the psychophysiological response of living organisms to a perceptive challenge or threat (Kiecolt-Glaser *et al.*, 1984). The presence, intensity or absence of stress response in living organisms depend on the organism's perception of the particular situation, together with the organism's ability to master the situation it is exposed to. The stress response, often regarded as threatening for the organism, is proved to be essential for its survival (Breivik *et al.*, 1996). However stress can become dangerous and threatening to the organism when the organ systems have already been predisposed to pathology or when stress levels are sustained.

Stress can be better explained as part of a complex and dynamic system of interaction between independent people and their environment. Psychological factors, such as mood, personality characteristics and feelings of helplessness, are able to affect the ways in which people respond and deal with stress (McClelland *et al.*, 1980). There are certain life events, such as job loss or the death of a spouse, illness or financial strains, which cause more stress than others.

Thus stress is the way someone reacts to a situation and not the situation itself. Situations of uncertainty, such as lack of specific information and absence or complete loss of control, amongst others, can trigger endocrine changes within the body. On the other hand, the presence of all the above can lead to turning the organism's alarm off and moderate its stress response (Ursin and Olff, 1993). Consequently a variety of diseases including infectious diseases, negative and stressful life events can be considered as important risk factors.

The concept that stress can affect the development of pathology in the periodontal tissue has been in existence for the past two millennia. In a document dating back to 401BC, the great Greek historian Xenophon describes a painful oral condition from which soldiers often suffered, with the distinctive characteristic of being malodorous. The idea that psychological factors can affect the development and progress of a disease has become part of folk wisdom (Plant and Friedman, 1991) and only in the last couple of decades have there been attempts, through research, to establish links and relations between behavior, the nervous system and the immune system (Cohen *et al.*, 1990, 1995; Blalock, 1994; Ader *et al.*, 1995).

Primarily, stress was associated with acute necrotizing ulcerative gingivitis (ANUG), also referred to as 'trench mouth' because of its effect on World War I front line soldiers (Papapanou, 1998). Early studies have identified stress as being a predisposing factor to ANUG (Cohen-Cole *et al.*, 1983; Shore and Harvillia, 1986), while in HIV patients stress has been identified as partly responsible for the increased severity of necrotizing ulcerate gingivitis (NUG) (Horning and Cohen, 1995) and periodontitis as well. Evidence linking ANUG and stress has been established from studies in which individuals were exposed to stressful situations over certain periods of time (Monteiro da Silva *et al.*, 1995).

It is widely acknowledged that there is a certain degree of congruence between the immune system and the central nervous system (CNS). Several characteristics of the response of the immune system are common to the response of the nervous system. Functional interaction between the two systems is accomplished through two basic routes: the connection via the neuroendocrine system (Berczi and Kovacs, 1987) and the nervous system's innervating lymphoid tissues (Felten et al., 1987). The common characteristics between the immune system and the CNS are summarized as follows (Ballieux, 1991): the capacity to store information through a developed memory system, the use of specific messengers which are capable of transferring information between the cells and, based on cell traffic, communication at a distance. A number of studies indicate that damage to specific brain areas can give rise to altered responses of the immune system (Cohen et al., 1995).

Reports strongly support the contention that the mind can influence the body's capacity for healing (Cousins, 1976, 1989). Relatively consistent literature and research suggest the relationship between stressful life events and the increased risks in contracting various diseases such as breast cancer and heart disease. The role of psychosocial stress in periodontal diseases in humans has been proposed by many authors (Dorian et al., 1986; Arnetz et al., 1987). We shall now review the studies that have been conducted in the past and document the correlation between stress and periodontal disease and, subsequently, determine whether stress constitutes a risk factor for periodontal diseases.

Laboratory studies on animals
There have been a number of studies and experimentation on animals in laboratory settings, indicating the important role of stress in periodontal disease, most of which are based on the concept of general adaptation syndrome (Selye, 1946).

The state of learned helplessness, when it is characterized by a high degree of emotional response and a low degree of learning a new response, seems to be able to cause alterations in the immune system and the neuroendocrine system in a negative direction (Shavit et al., 1986; Murison and Overmier, 1993). For many years, this state has been exploited as a human depression model but it also occurs in animals that have been exposed to electric shock which they were incapable of avoiding (Overmier and Seligman, 1967). An important feature and result of this study was that this does not occur in animals that are able to avoid the shock.

Most studies on animals include rats and mice populations. Gupta et al., (1960), created stress conditions for rats and hamsters by employing intermittent ringing of bells and exposure to bright lights over a period of 12 weeks. The authors located changes in the calcified tissue in the hamsters but not in the rats that were used for the experiment.

A study using the subcutaneous model in mice was conducted by Shapira et al. (1999). The main objective of this study was to investigate the effect of stress on host response to *Porphyromonas gingivalis*. Mice were divided into four groups, depending on the treatment and the stimuli they were exposed to. Each group was exposed to particular stress conditions accordingly: controls, isolation stress, cold stress and those caused by injection of corticosterone. On the third day of the experiment, bacteria of *Porphyromonas gingivalis* were injected into the mice chambers. Later, the chambers were sampled and analyzed for tumor necrosis factor-levels (TNF), interferon factor necrosis-levels (IFN) and leukocyte numbers. Results indicated that reduction in the TNF levels caused by stress might have an impact in the pathogenesis of periodontitis in humans who experience emotional stress.

A similar experiment was performed by Cohen et al., (1969), who studied 150 mice, which were subjected to three different stressors for a period of one to four-week intervals. Mice that received daily injections of cortisone demonstrated formation of periodontal pocket, calculus deposition, apical proliferation of epithelial attachment, alveolar bone loss and inflammation. No changes were observed in mice receiving a daily dosage of 0.05mg of adrenaline, while those subjected to cold stress presented minor changes, which were characterized by decreased osteoblastic activity.

Of great interest is the study conducted by Ratcliff (1956), who used rats and induced stress in them by immobilization with the use of adhesive tape. He withheld food from the subjects of the experiment for a period of 68 hours. His observations revealed pathogenic alterations: reduction of cementoblasts and osteoblasts, a split in the gingival crevicular epithelium and a sloughing of the keratinized layers of the gingival epithelium. The findings of this study are indeed very important, but the fact that these changes may have been caused by food deprivation rather than emotional stress should not be overlooked.

Studies on human populations
Periodontologists wished to enhance their clinical observations with research conducted amongst human populations, which would give rise to positive evidence linking psychosocial factors and periodontal diseases. However, human studies are rather limited. Moulton et al., (1952) suggested that, prior to several cases of acute necrotizing ulceral gingivitis, there was an acute phase of anxiety caused by conflicts of independence and sexual needs. Significant links were also established between periodontal disease and factors such as age, marital status, somatization and hysteria as much in psychiatric patients as in the normal population (Baker et al., 1961).

A major and significant risk factor, especially in today's industrial society, is work-related stress. Linden et al. (1996) examined the association between work-related stress and the progression of periodontitis in employed adults who received regular dental care. On the second examination of the study, the authors assessed the risk factor stress using the occupational stress indicator (Cooper et al., 1988), and suggested that work-related stress may in fact be a risk factor for the progression of periodontal disease, together with other factors such as socioeconomic status, age, lower job satisfaction, Type A personality and locus of control. Locus of control, by definition, is the degree to which individuals perceive situations in their lives as controllable or beyond their control, due to powerful others or fate (Lefcourt, 1976). The results of the study indicated that people who felt less in control of their everyday situations presented greater change in attachment.

Marcenes and Sheiham (1992), examined the relationship between oral health status and work-related stress, conducting a correlational study which included 164 workers (male), aged between 35 and 44 years of age. The participants were divided equally into four categories. The examination recorded the number of filled, damaged and missing teeth, periodontal pockets and gingival bleeding on probing. Regression analysis reported a significant association between work-related stress, socioeconomic status and marital quality and periodontal disease. In a later study, Marcenes et al. (1993) suggested that negative life events, such as marital and/or family problems, were significantly associated with acute and chronic oral symptoms.

Important correlation has been established between positive and negative life events and periodontal disease. The first study that systematically related periodontal disease to self-reported life events was made by Green et al. (1986), who investigated somatic symptomatology, gingival and periodontal pathology in relation to stressful life events in 50 male veterans. The researchers found that there was a significant association between stressful life events, that is distress arising from somatic dysfunction, and periodontal status.

Association between negative life events and periodontal disease was found in a recent case–control study by Croucher et al. (1997). This study included 100 dental patients and the same number of healthy periodontal controls, equally matching gender and age. The data collected by the study included tobacco use, sociodemographic variables, oral health habits and negative life events. The results of the study demonstrated associations between negative life events and tobacco use, dental plaque, being unemployed and stressful life events. The study suggested that oral risk factors and psychosocial factors appeared to be significant determinants for periodontal disease.

An additional significant finding in this report was that, while negative life events were associated with periodontal disease, positive life events were associated with better periodontal health and status. According to the authors, these findings give rise to two very important issues: on the one hand, the meaning and desirability of each life event is a determining factor in whether the event will have harmful or positive effects in periodontal status; on the other hand, positive life events may be considered as protective factors for periodontitis, and negative life events as predisposing factors for the development of periodontal disease.

Belting and Gupta (1961), studied 104 psychiatric patients and found that, when bruxism, clenching, calculus and brushing frequency were held constant, the psychiatric patients presented higher periodontal disease scores than their 122 controls, and that the severity of their periodontal disease increased in parallel with the increase of their degree of anxiety.

Emotional stress has also been reported as a significant risk factor for periodontal disease. People who undergo emotional stress tend to engage in unfavorable health behaviors (Breivik et al., 1996). Studies try to establish a relationship between personality factors and periodontal disease. In a study by Freeman and Gross (1993), 40 healthy individuals and 62 patients were formed into two groups. The results of the study demonstrated that there are certain personality factors that tend to be associated with periodontal disease. DeMarco (1976) concluded that 11 Vietnam War veterans, then aged between 22 and 32 years, diagnosed with severe alveolar bone loss, demonstrated emotional stress as a common denominator.

It has been argued that behavioral changes, which occur as coping styles/responses or adaptation to environmental changes, influence the risk of disease. Genco et al. (1999), conducted a cross-sectional study, a large survey, that included 1426 participants, aged between 25 and 74 years: the famous Erie County study. In this study the authors investigated the effects of psychosocial factors on periodontal disease using the following psychosocial instruments: The Life Event Scale, Measures of Chronic Stress, Brief Symptom Inventory (BSI), Coping Styles and Strategies, and Hassles and Uplifts (Cohen et al., 1997).

Potential factors such as age, gender, general health, dental care and smoking were controllable. The authors found that there was a significant association between stress, financial strain, distress and depression, as they seemed to be important factors in higher levels of periodontal disease. Lack of significance was established between financial strain and periodontal disease probably, according to the authors, because of the presence of some uncontrolled extraneous variables measured according to alveolar bone loss and attachment, which may have affected the scores. It could also be argued that this may be due to the fact that each person deals with work-related stress in different ways from others. The authors stressed the importance of adequate coping behaviors in the reduction of the stress levels which are associated with this particular oral disease.

Conclusion

Investigations into the very nature of periodontal diseases started as early as the 1960s. Epidemiological studies were conducted extensively in the United States as well as in other countries, mostly using the Periodontal Disease Index of Ramfjord (1967) and the Periodontal Index of Russell (1967) (Page, 1995).

Even though there is substantial and powerful evidence that stress is a principal factor for periodontal disease and its progression, studies so far are not conclusive enough to validate that psychosomatic factors constitute predisposing factors in the pathogenesis of the disease of the periodontium autonomously (Salvi et al., 1997). However we have ascertained that stress is a factor for periodontal diseases but, from our knowledge so far, only in combination with other factors, which together cause damage to the periodontal tissue. Future studies should focus primarily on trying to secure such conditions that would allow for safe and clear outcomes, implying and proving that stress, as a unique, autonomous and independent risk factor affects periodontal disease.

Future research should focus on stress individually as an important risk factor. Genco, Ho, Kopman, Grossi, Dunford and Tedesco (1998) suggest a series of guidelines for future research in order to evaluate accurately the role of psychosocial stress in the rise and progression of periodontal disease:

1. Periodontal disease should be measured as a unique disease and not as part of a complex of diseases, as so far studied (diseases like ANUG and stomatitis).
2. Appropriate and validated measures should be used for assessing coping behaviors, stress and distress individually.
3. Specific and identified at-risk behaviors such as oral hygiene and dental visits should be measured in parallel with assessment of gingivitis, plaque and other oral diseases.
4. Large longitudinal epidemiological and cross-sectional studies should be conducted in order to assess whether stress, distress and coping behaviors/styles are indeed true risk factors for periodontal diseases.
5. Of significant importance is the study of particular mechanisms in which psychosocial risk factors affect the disease of the periodontium, in order to ascertain the biological background of this relationship.
6. Intervention studies are needed for stress and distress reduction, in order to validate the modification of stress as a method of management for diseases associated with stress.

References

Abdellatif, H.M. and B.A. Burt (1987), 'An epidemiological investigation into the relative importance of age and oral hygiene status as determinants to periodontitis', *Journal of Dental Research*, **66**, 13–18.

Ader, R., N. Cohen and D. Felten (1995), 'Psychoimmunology: interaction between the nervous system and the immune system', *Lancet*, **345**, 99–103.

Arnetz, B.B., J. Wasserman, B. Petrini, S.O. Brenner, L. Levi, P. Eneroth, H. Salvoaara, R. Hjelm, L. Salvoaara, T.R. Theorel and I.L. Patterson (1987), 'Immune function in unemployed women', *Psychosomatic Medicine*, **49**, 3–12.

Baker, E.G., G.H. Crook and E.D. Schwacher (1961), 'Personality correlates of periodontal diseases', *Journal of Dental Research*, **40**, 396–403.

Ballieux, R.E. (1991), 'Impact of mental health on the immune response', *Journal of Clinical Periodontology*, **18**, 427–30.

Beck, J.D. (1994), 'Methods of assessing risk for periodontitis and developing multifactorial models', *Journal of Periodontology*, **65**, 468–78.

Beck, J.D., G.G. Koch, G. Rozier and G.E. Tudor (1990), 'Prevalence and risk indicators for periodontal attachment loss in a population of older community-dwelling blacks and whites', *Journal of Periodontology*, **61**, 521–8.

Belting, C.M. and O.P. Gupta (1961), 'The influence of psychiatric disturbances on the severity of periodontal disease', *Journal of Peridontology*, **32**, 219–26.

Berczi, I. and K. Kovacs (1987), *Hormones and Immunity*, Lancaster: MTP Press Ltd.

Blalock, J.E. (1994), 'The syntax of the immune-endocrine communication', *Immunology Today*, **15**, 504–11.

Breivik, T., P.S. Thrane, R. Murison and P. Gjermo (1996), 'Emotional stress effects on immunity, gingivitis and periodontitis', *European Journal of Oral Science*, **104**, 327–34.

Brown, L.J and H. Löe (1993), 'Prevalence, extent, severity and progression of periodontal disease', *Periodontology, 2000*, **2**, 57–71.

Cohen, M.M., S. Shusterman and G. Shklar (1969), 'The effect of stressor agents on the grey lethal mouse strain periodontium', *Journal of Periodontology*, **40**, 462–6.

Cohen, N., D. Felten and R. Ader (1990), 'Interaction between the brain and the immune system', *Annual Review of Pharmacology and Toxicology*, **30**.

Cohen, N., D. Felten and R. Ader (1995), 'Psychoneuroimmunology: interaction between the nervous and the immune system', *Lancet*, **345**.

Cohen, S., R.C. Kessler and L.U. Gordon (1997), *Measuring Stress: A Guide for Health and Social Scientists*, Oxford: Oxford University Press.

Cohen-Cole, S.A., R.B. Cogen, A.W. Stevens, K. Kirk, E. Gaiton, J. Bird, R. Cooksey and A. Freeman (1983), 'Psychiatric, psychosocial and endocrine correlates of acute necrotizing ulserate gingivitis ("trench mouth"): a preliminary report', *Psychiatric Medicine*, **2**, 215–25.

Cooper, C.L., S.J Sloan and S. Williams (1988), *Occupational Stress Indicator*, Windsor: NFER-Nelson.

Cousins, N. (1976), 'Anatomy of an Illness', *New England Journal of Medicine*, **295**, 1458–63.

Cousins, N. (1989), *Head First: the Biology of Hope*, New York: Dutton.

Croucher, R., W.S. Marcenes, M.C. Torres, F.W. Hughes and A. Sheiham (1997), 'The relationship between life-events and periodontitis', *Journal of Clinical Periodontal*, **24**, 39–43.

DeMarco, T.J. (1976), 'Periodontal emotional stress syndrome', *Journal of Periodontology*, **47**, 67–8.

DeRouen, T.A., L. Mancl and P. Hujoel (1991), 'Measurement of association between periodontal disease using statistical methods for independent data', *Journal of Periodontal Research*, **26**, 218–29.

Dorian, B.J., P.E. Garfinkel, E.C. Keystone, R. Gorczynski and P. Darby (1986), 'Stress, immunity and illness', *Psychosomatic Medicine*, **48**, 304–5.

Emrich, L.J., M. Shlossman and R.J. Genco (1991), 'Periodontal disease in non-insulin-dependent diabetes mellitus', *Journal of Periodontology*, **62**, 123–30.

Felten, D.L., S.Y. Felten, D.L. Bellinger and K.S. Madden (1993), 'Fundamental aspect of neural-immune signals', *Psychotherapy and Psychosomatics*, **60**, 46–56.

Felten, D.L., S.Y. Felten, D.L. Bellinger, S.L. Carlson, K.D. Ackerman, K.S. Madden, J.A. Olschowski and S. Livnat (1987), 'Noradrenergic sympathetic neutral interaction with the immune system: structure and function', *Immunological Reviews*, **100**, 225–60.

Frandsen, A. and J.J. Pindborg (1949), 'Tobacco and gingivitis III: difference in action of cigarettes and pipe smoking', *Journal of Dental Research*, **28**, 464–5.

Freeman, R. and S. Gross (1993), 'Stress measures as predictors of periodontal disease: a preliminary communication', *Community Dentistry Oral Epidemiology*, **21**, 176–7.

Genco, C.A., B.M. Odusanya and J. Potempa (1998), 'A peptide domain on gingipain R which confers immunity against porphyromonas gingivalis infection in mice', *Infection Immunology*, **66**, 4108–14.

Genco, R.J. (1996), 'Current views of risk factors for periodontal diseases', *Journal of Periodontology*, **67**, (suppl.), 1041–9.
Genco, R.J., A.W. Ho, S.G. Gross, R.G. Dunford and L.A. Tedesco (1999), 'Relationship of stress, distress and inadequate coping behaviors to periodontal disease', *Journal of Periodontology*, **70**, 711–23.
Genco, R.J., A.W. Ho, J. Kopman, S.G. Grossi, R.G. Dunford and L.A. Tedesco (1998), 'Models to evaluate the role of stress in periodontal disease', *Annual Periodontology*, **3**(1), 288–302.
Green, W., W. Tryon, B. Marks and J. Huryn (1986), 'Periodontal disease as a function of life events stress', *Journal of Human Stress*, **12**, 32–7.
Greenberg, M.S. (1996), 'HIV-associated lesion', *Dermatologic Clinics*, **14**, 319–26.
Greenspan, D. and J.S. Greenspan (1996), 'HIV-related oral disease', *Lancet*, **348** (9029), 729–33.
Grossi, S.G., R.J. Genco, E.E. Machtei, A.W. Ho, G. Koch, R. Dunford, J.J. Zambon and E. Hausmann (1995), 'Assessment of risk for periodontal disease II: risk indicators for alveolar bone loss', *Journal of Periodontology*, **66**, 23–9.
Grossi, S.G., J.J. Zambon, A.W. Ho, G. Koch, R.G. Dunford, E.E. Machtei, O.M. Norderyd and R.J. Genco (1994), 'Evaluations of risk indicators for periodontal disease', *Journal of Periodontology*, **65**, 260–7.
Gupta, O.P., H. Blechman and S.S. Stahl (1960), 'Effects of stress on the periodontal tissues of young adult male rats and hamsters', *Journal of Periodontology*, **31**, 413–7.
Gyorfi, A., A. Fazekas, Z.S. Suba, C.J. Dalsgaard and O. Ringden (1994), 'Neurogenic component in ligature-induced periodontitis in the rat', *Journal of Clinical Periodontology*, **21**, 601–5.
Holm-Pedersen, P., N. Agerbaek and E. Theilade (1975), 'Experimental gingivitis in young and elderly individuals', *Journal of Clinical Periodontology*, **2**, 14–24.
Horning, G.M. and M.E. Cohen (1995), 'Necrotizing ulcerative gingivitis, periodontitis and stomatitis: clinical staging and predisposing factors', *Journal of Periodontology*, **66**, 990–8.
Hugoson, A. and T. Jordan (1982), 'Frequency distribution of individuals aged 20–70 years according to severity of periodontal disease', *Community Dentistry Oral Epidemiology*, **10**, 187–92.
Ismail, A.L., B.A. Burt and S.A Eklund (1983), 'Epidemiologic patterns of smoking and periodontal disease in the United States', *Journal of the American Dental Association*, **106**, 617–23.
Kanterman, D.B. (1955), 'The psychosomatic aspect of periodontal disease', *Journal of Periodontology*, **26**, 47.
Kiecolt-Glaser, J.K., W. Garner, C. Spiecher, G.M. Penn, J. Holliday and R. Glaser (1984), 'Psychosocial modifiers of immunocompetence in medical students', *Psychosomatic Medicine*, **46**, 7–14.
Lefcourt, H.M. (1976), *Locus of Control: Current Trends in Theory and Research*, Hillsdale: Erlbaum.
Linden, G.J., B.H. Mullally and R. Freeman (1996), 'Stress and the progression of periodontal disease', *Journal of Clinical Periodontology*, **23**, 675–80.
Machtei, E.E., R. Dunford, S.G. Grossi and R.J. Genco (1994), 'Cumulative nature of periodontal attachment loss', *Journal of Periodontal Research*, **29**, 361–4.
Marcenes, W.S. and A. Sheiham (1992), 'The relationship between work stress and oral health status', *Social Science and Medicine*, **35**, 1511–20.
Marcenes, W.S., R. Croucher, A. Sheiham and M. Marmot (1993), 'The relationship between self-reported oral symptoms and life events', *Psychology And Health*, **8**, 123–34.
Marshall-Day, C.D., R.G. Stevens and L.F. Quigley Jr. (1955), 'Periodontal disease prevalence and incidence', *Journal of Periodontology*, **26**, 185–203.
McClelland, D.C., E. Floor, R.J. Davidson and C. Saron (1980), 'Stressed power motivation, sympathetic activation, immune function and immunity', *Journal of Human Stress*, **6**, 11–9.
Miller, A.J., J.A. Brunelle, J.P. Carlos, L.J. Brown H. Löe (1987), 'Oral health of United States adults, national findings', National Institute of Dental Research, Bethesda, MD, NIH Publications no.87, 2868.
Monteiro da Silva, A.M., H.N. Newman and D.A. Oakley (1995), 'Psychosocial factors in inflammatory periodontal diseases: a review', *Journal of Clinical Periodontology*, **22**, 516–26.
Moulton, R., S. Ewen and W. Thieman (1952), 'Emotional factors in periodontal disease', *Oral Surgery*, **5**, 833.
Murison, R. and J.B. Overmier (1993), 'Parallelism among stress effects on ulcer, immuno-suppression and analgesia: commonality of mechanisms?', *Journal of Physiology*, **87**, 253–9.
Nelson, R.G., M. Shlossman and L.M. Budding (1990), 'Periodontal disease in non-insulin-dependent diabetes mellitus in Pima Indians', *Diabetes Care*, **13**, 836–40.
Norderyd, O.M., S.G. Grossi, E.E. Machtei, J.J. Zambon, E. Hausmann, R.G. Dunford and R.J. Genco (1993), 'Periodontal status of women taking postmenopausal estrogen supplementation', *Journal of Periodontology*, **64**, 957–62.
Oliver, R.C. and T. Tervonen (1993), 'Periodontitis and tooth loss: comparing diabetics with the general population', *Journal of American Dental Association*, **124**, 71–6.
Overmier, J.B., M.E.P. Seligman (1967), 'Effects of inescapable shocks upon subsequent escape and avoidance responding', *Journal of Comparative Physiology*, **63**, 28–33.

Page, R.C. (1995), 'Critical issues in periodontal research', *Journal of Dental Research*, **74** (4), 1118–28.
Papapanou, P. (1996), 'Periodontal diseases: epidemiology', *Annual Periodontology*, **1**, 1–36.
Papapanou, P. (1998), 'Risk assessment in the diagnosis and treatment of periodontal diseases', *Journal of Dental Education*, **62**, 10, 829–30.
Phelan, J.A. (1997), 'Oral manifestations of human immunodeficiency virus infection', *Medical Clinics of North America*, **81**, 511–31.
Pindborg, J.J. (1947), 'Tobacco and gingivitis I: statistical examination of the significance of tobacco in the development of ulceromembranous gingivitis and in the formation of calculus', *Journal of Dental Research*, **26**, 261–4.
Plant, S.M. and S.B. Friedman (1991), 'Psychosocial factors in infectious diseases', in R. Ader (ed.), *Psychoneuroimmunology*, Orlando: Academic Press.
Ramfjord, S.P. (1967), 'The periodontal disease index (PDI)', *Journal of Periodontal*, **38** (suppl.), 602–10.
Ratcliff, P.A. (1956), 'The relationship of the general adaptation syndrome to the periodontal tissue in the rat', *Journal of Periodontology*, **27**, 40–3.
Russell, A.L. (1960), 'Geographical distribution and epidemiology of periodontal disease', World Health Organization, Geneva (WHO/DH/33/34).
Russell, A.L. (1962), 'Periodontal disease in well and malnourished populations', *Archives of Environmental Health*, **5**, 153–7.
Russell, A.L. (1967), 'The periodontal index', *Journal of Periodontal*, **38** (II), 585–91.
Salvi, G.E., H.P. Lawrence, S. Offenbacher and J.D. Beck (1997), 'Influence of risk factors on the pathogenesis of periodontitis', *Periodontal 2000*, **14**, 173–210.
Schei, O., J. Waerhaug, A. Lovdal and A. Arno (1959), 'Alveolar bone loss as related to oral hygiene and age', *Journal of Periodontology*, **30**, 7–16.
Selye, H. (1946), 'The general adaptation syndrome and the diseases of adaptation', *Journal of Clinical Endocrinology*, **6**, 117–230.
Shapira, L., Y. Houri-Haddad, I. Flolov, A. Halabi and D. Ben-Nathan (1999), 'The effect of stress on the inflammatory response to porphyromonas gingivalis in a mouse subcutaneous chamber model', *Journal of Periodontology*, **70**, 289–93.
Shavit, Y., J.W. Lewis, G.W. Terman, R.P. Gale and J.C. Liebeskind (1986), 'Stress, oproid peptides and immune function', in B.C.A. Fredrickson, H.C. Hendrie, J.N. Hingtgen and M.H. Aprison, (eds), *Neuroregulation of Autonomic, Endocrine and Immune Systems*, Boston: Martinus Nijhoff, 343–66.
Shlossman, M., W.C. Knowler, D.J. Pettitt and R.J. Genco (1990), 'Type 2 diabetes mellitus and periodontal disease', *Journal of the American Dental Association*, **121**, 532–6.
Shore, R.S. and J. Harvillia (1986), 'Acute necrotizing ulcerate gingivitis: etiology and stress relationships', *International Journal of Psychosomatics*, **83**, 215–25.
Solomon, H.A., R.L. Priore and I.D.J. Bross (1968), 'Cigarette smoking and periodontal disease', *Journal of American Dental Association*, **77**, 1081–4.
Ursin, H. and M. Olff (1993), 'Psychobiology of coping and defense strategies', *Neuropsychobiology*, **28**, 61–71.
US Public Health Service, National Center for Health Statistics (1965), *Periodontal disease in Adults, United States 1960–1969*. PHS Publication no.100, Series 11, no.12, Washington, DC: Government Printing Office.
Waerhaug, J. (1967), 'Prevalence of periodontal disease in Ceylon: association with age, sex, oral hygiene, socio-economic factors, vitamin deficiencies, malnutrition, betel and tobacco consumption and ethnic group: final report', *Acta Odontological Scand.*, **25**, 205–31.
Wertheimer, F.W., R.H. Brewster and C.L. White (1967), 'Periodontal disease and nutrition in Thailand', *Journal of Periodontology*, **38**, 100–4.

23 Work–family conflict and stress
Paula Brough and Michael O'Driscoll

Introduction

Over the past twenty years, increasing attention has been paid by researchers and organizations to the interface between people's work and their family lives. In 1977, Rosabeth Kanter argued that the notion that work and life off the job are separate worlds is a 'myth'. Since then there has been a growing volume of research on the interaction between job or work demands and experiences and family life. The burgeoning literature on this topic can be attributed to a variety of reasons, including changing family structures, with a significant increase in the number of dual-earner families and single-parent families; changing family orientations, with many couples now delaying the onset of children and also reducing the overall number of children; increasing participation of women in the workforce, to the point where in many Western countries, in particular, employed women now outnumber their male colleagues; and finally, a greater desire to achieve some kind of 'balance' between work and family responsibilities, to enhance both individual and family well-being.

In addition to the above trends, other developments within industry and society more generally have also contributed to a sharper focus on the implications of work and employment for family life. In particular, technological developments over the past decade or so (such as laptop computers and mobile phones) have enabled work to be conducted more flexibly in terms of both space and time, which in turn has led to a blurring of boundaries between job and family time. Similarly globalization has in many cases heightened the requirement for organizations to react more flexibly to market demands, and this need for greater flexibility has filtered down to individual employees.

The above concatenation of forces has inevitably created environments where there can be interference or conflict between work and family commitments and responsibilities, and this conflict can incur physical and psychological costs for individuals and their families. Researchers interested in these issues have sought to identify the nature of the work–family interface and to describe the processes which account for the impact of each domain on the other. In this chapter we describe ways in which levels of work–family conflict have been assessed in empirical research, highlight some of the consequences of work–family conflict and discuss some potential mediators and moderators of the relationship between work–family conflict and distress. We conclude the chapter with some observations on practical implications for organizations as they endeavour to assist employee efforts to achieve work–family 'balance' (Frone, 2003; Williams and Alliger, 1994).

Definitions

Perhaps unfortunately, research on the work–family interface has incorporated an array of concepts and has not always defined these concepts consistently. Although there are many theoretical models to draw upon, Greenhaus and Parasuraman's (1986) conceptualization of 'work–nonwork' stress (see Figure 23.1) provides a valuable framework for the present discussion of relationships between work and family issues. In this framework, a variety of events and occurrences at work and in people's off-the-job ('nonwork') lives can function as potential causes of perceived stress, along with the interface between work and nonwork, which is the focus of the present chapter. These stressors create perceived stress and then induce three forms of strain (emotional, behavioural and physiological). Finally strain is postulated to contribute to several outcomes at work and in the nonwork domain, such as decreased job performance, greater absenteeism, physical illness and interpersonal (family) relationship difficulties. Clearly not all of these consequences necessarily result for each person, but there is now substantial evidence (see later in this chapter) that the outcomes identified by Greenhaus and Parasuraman are associated with the interface between the work and nonwork domains. Work–family conflict is viewed as a major stressor in many people's lives, hence one in which researchers and organizations need to pay particular attention.

Most research on this topic has focused on one element of the nonwork domain, namely family. A primary reason for this is that, for many individuals, the family is a major component of their off-the-job life. Typically interference between job and family is referred to as 'work–family conflict'. (Note that, although we will briefly refer to favourable relationships between job and family, often referred to as work–family facilitation or enhancement, the main thrust of this chapter is on the 'dark side' of the work–family interface.) Early research tended not to differentiate the directions of this conflict, whereas more recently researchers have argued that there are two distinct, albeit related, directions: *work-to-family* conflict (WFC) and *family-to-work* conflict (FWC).

In addition Greenhaus and Beutell (1985) described three different forms of WFC and FWC: time-based conflict, strain-based conflict and behaviour-based conflict. Time-based conflict builds upon the 'rational' model (Gutek *et al.*, 1991) or 'utilitarian' model (Lobel, 1991) of work–family relations, which posits that time is a limited resource and that devoting greater time to one area of life (such as one's job) inevitably reduces the amount of time available for another (for example the family). Hence job and family impose demands on a person's time. Strain-based conflict, on the other hand, occurs when there is a spillover of negative emotions from one domain into the other. For instance, negative emotional reactions to workplace stressors can lead to expressions of irritability toward family members or withdrawal from family interaction in order to recuperate (O'Driscoll, 1996). Similarly distress in one's family life might overflow into the job domain, affecting the individual's job satisfaction and ability to perform at expected levels. Finally behaviour-based conflict arises when the norms and role expectations in one area of life are incompatible with those in the other. For example, at work an individual may be expected to be aggressive, ambitious, hard-driving and task-oriented. Successful job performance may be contingent upon demonstration of these behaviours. In contrast, at home being loving, supportive and accommodating may be regarded as essential to developing and fostering a happy and healthy family life. Clearly these opposing expectations may create a tension between work and family behaviours, as well as impeding the transition from one environment to the other.

In sum, interrole conflict explanations of spillover between work and family life have focused on the negative impact of interference between work and family demands, along

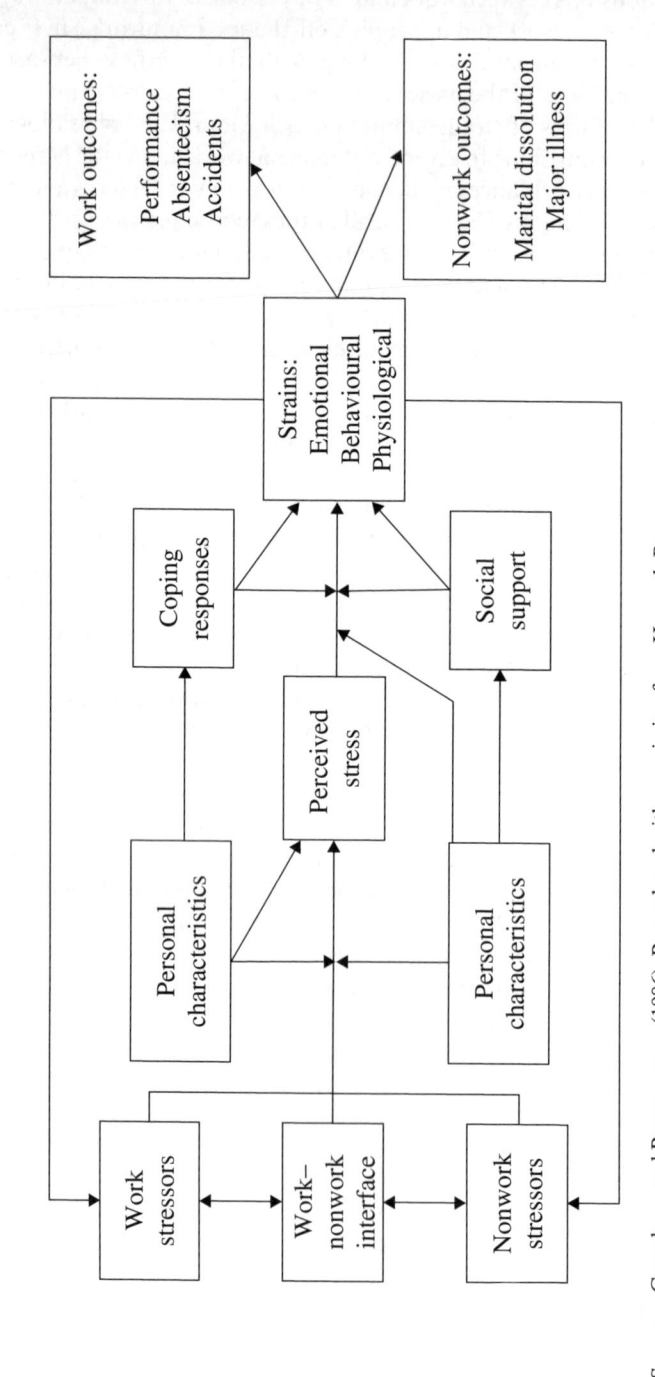

Source: Greenhaus and Parasuraman (1986). Reproduced with permission from Haworth Press.

Figure 23.1 Greenhaus and Parasuraman's (1986) model of the sources and consequences of work and non-work stress

with the transfer of emotional strain (or distress) from one context to the other. Current thinking is that this spillover may occur in both directions (that is, work-to-family and family-to-work), although there is evidence that most people report greater levels of work-to-family than family-to-work conflict. Furthermore individuals may experience three major forms of work–family conflict (time-based, strain-based and behaviour-based), although most research to date has investigated time- and strain-based interrole conflict.

Measurement of interrole conflict
As noted above, recent formulations of work–family conflict have considered this as a bidirectional concept, with the possibility that spillover may occur in both directions. Methodologically this differentiation is important, because it acknowledges that work-to-family conflict and family-to-work conflict are distinct variables and should be assessed separately. Several instruments have been constructed to examine the two directions of conflict, although as yet there would appear to be no 'standard' approach to the measurement of these variables, and there have been no investigations of the comparability of different measures. Examples of instruments which differentiate between WFC and FWC are those constructed by Gutek *et al.* (1991), Frone *et al.* (1992) and Netemeyer *et al.* (1996). All of these measures contain four or five items for each construct, and include items on both time-based and strain-based conflict, but not behaviour-based conflict. In a recent study, however, Major *et al.* (2002) amalgamated some of Netemeyer *et al.*'s items with others developed specifically for their study to investigate just time-based family-to-work conflict (FWC). Other recent investigations, however, have continued to assess work–family conflict non-directionally (for example Carlson and Perrewe, 1999; Noor, 2002; Schwartzberg and Dytell, 1996) or have examined one direction of influence only, typically work-to-family conflict (for example Stephens and Sommer, 1996).

Few researchers have endeavoured to develop measures of work–family conflict that encapsulate Greenhaus and Beutell's (1985) tripartite division of interrole conflict types. Stephens and Sommer (1996) constructed a pool of items addressing time-based, strain-based and behaviour-based conflict, although their focus was solely on work-to-family conflict. A more extensive exploration of the Greenhaus–Beutell conceptualization was reported by Carlson and Kacmar (2000). In addition to including separate assessments of time-based, strain-based and behaviour-based conflict, they also examined work-to-family and family-to-work conflict as separate constructs.

From the above discussion it is clear that further refinement of measurement instruments is required in this area of research. In particular, standardization of work–family conflict measures would enable more consistent comparison across studies. Currently, while there would appear to be some degree of congruence between the various instruments used, their overall comparability has not been determined. Also, while extant studies have illustrated that work-to-family conflict and family-to-work conflict may have differing antecedents and consequences (see discussion below), future research is needed to ascertain whether the three forms of conflict contribute independently to behavioural, psychological and physiological outcomes. If this is the case, clearly researchers will need to ensure separate assessment of these three forms. On the other hand, if it is demonstrated that the contributions of time-based, strain-based and behavior–based conflict are interwoven and indistinguishable, continued refinement of work–family conflict measures may not be a priority.

Consequences of work–family conflict
This section examines two principal outcomes of work–family conflict within the stress process. First the main psychological consequences focusing primarily on well-being will be described, followed by a discussion of potential physical health consequences.

Psychological well-being
Greenhaus and Parasuraman's (1986) model of psychological well-being suggests that accurate measurement is dependent upon the inclusion of both work and family stressors. It seems intuitive to deduce that the total amount of stress experienced (that is both work stress and non-work stress) should have a greater impact on personal outcomes, compared with the contribution of stress from one domain only. Frone *et al.* (1994) support this view and suggest that occupational stress research adopts a 'broad ecological perspective' incorporating both work and nonwork stressors in order to produce accurate estimates of psychological well-being (p. 144). Frone *et al.* evaluated the individual impact of work stressors, family stressors and work–family conflict upon psychological distress, and found that each stressor was positively related to this form of strain. Greenhaus and Parasuraman (2002) also suggested we should focus upon the perceived *conflict* of time allocation to both individual family and work roles, rather than the actual time or demands themselves, when we are estimating outcomes. Thus it is the successful management of various personal roles and responsibilities which influence perceived stress and well-being outcomes (Friedman and Greenhaus, 2000).

Associations between work–family conflict and psychological distress have been widely explored and suggest a strong positive relationship: increased conflict is associated with increased psychological distress (Major *et al.*, 2002; Stephens *et al.*, 2001). Associations between increased interrole conflict and levels of depression have also been demonstrated (MacEwen and Barling, 1994; Noor, 2002). Typically experiences of both types of interdomain conflict produce increased depression levels (Allen *et al.*, 2000; Frone *et al.*, 1996).

The relationships between stressors and their effects across the domains are fairly clear. Work-to-family conflict predicts adverse family domain outcomes and, conversely, family-to-work conflict predicts adverse work outcomes (Brough and Kelling, 2002; Frone, 2003; O'Driscoll *et al.*, 1992; Parasuraman *et al.*, 1992). These family and work outcomes encompass both affective conditions such as dissatisfaction and distress, and behavioural outcomes such as absenteeism, lateness and poor performance (Frone, 2003). In addition to these direct effects, the two pathways of inter-domain conflict have been identified as mediating variables in the work/family demands and psychological distress relationships (Frone *et al.*, 1996; Voydanoff, 2002), although the mediation effect of interrole conflict may be partial only (Hughes and Galinsky, 1994).

The use of longitudinal methodologies, which incorporate modelling or regression techniques, allow the relationships between work–family conflict and various outcomes to be explored in more detail. These methodologies are useful in identifying the direction of causality and the amount of impact which inter-domain conflict has upon different 'outcomes'. For example, Bacharach *et al.* (1991) found that work–family conflict predicted burnout to a similar extent within their two samples of nurses and engineers. In their study, burnout was composed of items of strain from both the work and the home domains. In turn, work–family conflict was predicted by differing amounts of work overload and within-role conflict. Kelloway *et al.* (1999), using cross-lagged analyses, demonstrated that the experience of stress at Time 1 predicted subsequent (Time 2) work–family conflict. Kelloway *et al.* concluded that, as well as predicting strain, inter-domain conflict also appears to be caused by prior stress experiences.

It is pertinent to consider that multiple roles may improve perceptions of well-being and performance across the home and work domains. Thus the benefits gained by parenting, such as increased security, status and enrichment, can have positive consequences for work performance (Kirchmeyer, 1992). Similarly, high perceptions of work role quality can have positive benefits for family life, including reducing the stress of being both a carer and a spouse (Johnson *et al.* 2000). Positive consequences of multiple roles such as high levels of self-esteem, life satisfaction and physical health have also been recorded (Grandey and Cropanzano, 1999; O'Driscoll, 1996). Successful employment outside the home is also associated with a sense of accomplishment and higher levels of self confidence (Aryee *et al.*, 1999; Beatty, 1996). However the focus of this chapter is on the potential negative consequences of engagement in multiple roles (work and family), rather than the benefits.

Physical health
Early research suggested no association existed between work–family conflict and physical health outcomes (for example Klitzman *et al.*, 1990). However recent research suggests a negative association does exist. That is, high levels of work–family conflict may produce adverse physical health (Frone *et al.*, 1997). For example, Bacharach *et al.* (1991) demonstrated an association between work–family conflict and a variety of negative health outcomes, including burnout, while Lee (1997) found that the dual demands of paid employment and caregiving (for elderly parents) were associated with the classic physical stress–strain symptomology: weight loss or gain, headaches, drowsiness and insomnia. The strain imposed by work–family conflict has also been linked to coronary heart disease (Haynes *et al.*, 1984), decreased appetite and energy levels, increased fatigue, nervous tension and anxiety (Allen *et al.*, 2000), as well as increased cholesterol levels and somatic complaints (Thomas and Ganster, 1995).

Alcohol consumption
Interrole conflict and alcohol consumption also appear to be positively linked: increased conflict is associated with increased alcohol consumption (Noor, 2002). Frone *et al.* (1996) measured 'heavy alcohol use', which included the number of alcoholic drinks consumed per day, frequency of drunkenness and the amount of alcohol dependence. They found that only work-to-family and not family-to-work conflict was positively linked to heavy alcohol use. This finding is not surprising, as the occupational stress and coping literature has long recognized the use of alcohol as an escapism coping strategy (Burke, 1998; O'Driscoll and Brough, 2003). Furthermore it is also apparent that alcohol is much more likely to be consumed in the home than at work, regardless of the actual source of the stressor (or conflict). Thus the stronger association with work-to-family, rather than

family-to-work, conflict is perhaps to be expected, and has implications for the measurement criteria commonly utilized here.

Additional consequences
Other consequences of work–family stress include work (and also nonwork/general life) satisfaction. It is notable that job satisfaction can be influenced to a large extent by organizational and/or supervisor support, especially in terms of the perceived support with family demands. This point is discussed in more detail later (under 'Organizational practice implications'). Satisfaction levels are widely included as a criterion in both the home and work domains (Boles *et al.*, 2001; Noor, 2002). Other organizational outcomes include organizational commitment, career satisfaction, turnover, absenteeism, work performance and burnout (Allen *et al.*, 2000; Hammer *et al.*, 2002; Netemeyer *et al.*, 1996; O'Driscoll, 1996).

Consequences within the family domain have been examined less frequently, but include parental performance, destructive parenting behaviours, child behaviours and marital satisfaction (MacEwen and Barling, 1994). The effects of interrole conflict upon individual cognitive abilities have also received some attention, especially in terms of reduced concentration and attention levels (Fryer and Warr, 1984; MacEwen and Barling, 1994). Finally, withdrawal from the work or family domain has received some attention, primarily in the form of absenteeism rates (Goff *et al.*, 1990). It is apparent that high demands in one domain, requiring enhanced levels of attention and energies by the individual, will generally lead to a withdrawal of energies from the second domain, and especially for acute, unplanned demands. Thus a child's sudden illness may produce absenteeism from work, or sudden work deadlines may reduce the amount of family time. MacEwen and Barling's (1994) work–family conflict model is included here as an illustration of the relationships between inter-domain conflict and these more unusual consequences (see Figure 23.2).

Pathways of influence

Above we have reviewed some of the potential outcomes of work–family conflict and have highlighted in particular the psychological distress which can emanate from interference between the work and family domains. Research in this field also suggests that there may be several factors which can influence the interaction between work–family conflict and outcome variables. In this section we identify some of the proposed moderators and mediators of the work–family conflict to distress relationship. Our intention here is not to provide a comprehensive review of research on moderators and mediators, but rather to draw attention to a few salient variables.

Clearly there are many factors which may play an important role in determining the impact of work–family conflict on people's work and family lives. Of these, some which have been explored empirically are gender, parental/family responsibilities, available resources (for example finance, social support), level of involvement in both work and family, and personal variables (such as coping strategies, locus of control and negative affectivity). We focus in particular on gender, coping strategies and the utilization of social support, as these variables have been considered as key factors in the conflict–distress relationship.

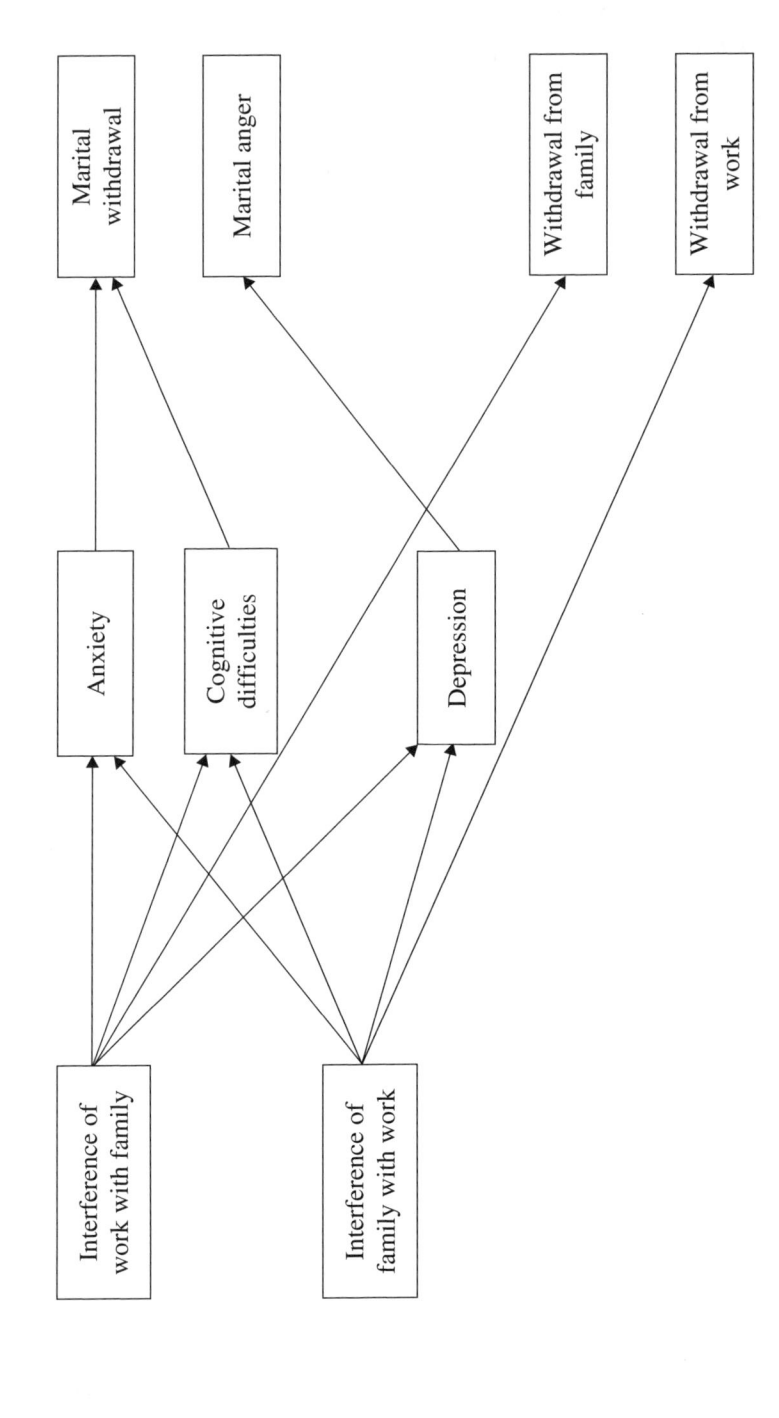

Source: MacEwen and Barling (1994); reproduced with permission.

Figure 23.2 A work–family conflict model

Voydanoff (2002) has noted that there are several pathways of influence between work–family conflict and physical and psychological 'outcomes'. To fully understand the mechanisms by which inter-domain conflict affects individual well-being, we need to examine the prevalence and impact of each of these pathways. Work–family conflict (both WFC and FWC) may have a direct effect on certain outcomes, for example when time demands from work (family) directly prevent a person from attending to family (work) commitments. Most studies of the consequences of work–family conflict have explored these direct effects. However it is also possible that other variables may mediate the relationship between work–family conflict and distress. This mediating pathway can be represented as follows:

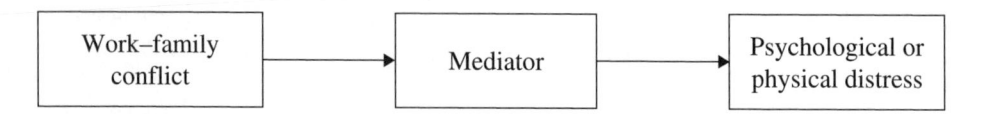

```
[Work–family conflict] → [Mediator] → [Psychological or physical distress]
```

An example of a potential mediating variable would be social support (whose role we discuss in more detail shortly). For instance, when an individual experiences conflict between their work and family, they may elicit practical and emotional support from their spouse/partner. If this support is effective, a decrease in psychological strain may result.

Finally several variables have been posited as potential moderators of the interrole conflict–strain relationship. A moderation effect occurs when the effect of the predictor variable (in this case, work–family conflict) is greater for some groups than for others. Examples of possible moderators include gender, coping and social support, all of which we review briefly below. Diagrammatically, a moderator effect is depicted as follows:

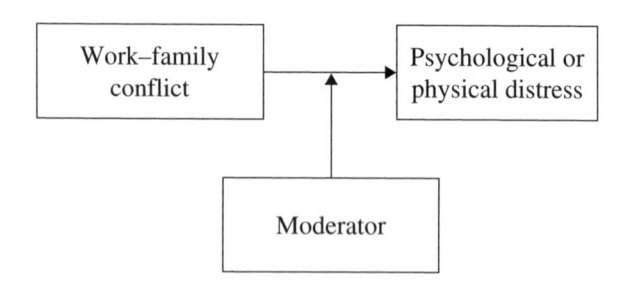

```
[Work–family conflict] → [Psychological or physical distress]
            ↑
       [Moderator]
```

Gender

Numerous comparisons have been conducted of male and female experiences of work–family conflict. It is suggested that social pressures, including sex role socialization, remain a strong influence on the accepted 'normal' values and behaviours for both men and women and that 'deeply ingrained norms' (Major, 1993, p. 150) continue to emphasize a woman's family responsibilities and a man's income-generating responsibilities. Such reasoning is used to explain why interrole conflict is highest for women in the work-to-family direction, while family-to-work conflict is generally stronger for men

(Frone et al., 1996). However other research has begun to challenge this view, coinciding with the change in social expectations of achieving an overall improved quality of life for both women and men. For example, family roles and the quality of family life have been found to be equally important to both men and women (Frone, 2003; Schwartzberg and Dytell, 1996; Thomas and Ganster, 1995). Carr (2002) has suggested that the strategies adopted by both men and women for dealing with work and family responsibilities are beginning to converge, with increasing family responsibilities adopted by each new male generation. Despite this trend, however, female workers continue to shoulder a greater proportion of family responsibilities, particularly through the temporary withdrawal from paid employment.

Research evidence on male/female differences in levels of work–family conflict, as well as on the consequences of conflict, is inconsistent, and several recent studies have found few, if any, gender differences (Voydanoff, 2002). In a review of the relationships between gender, work and family, Barnett and Hyde (2001, p. 784) suggested that 'psychological gender differences are not, in general, large or immutable'. Research supports this conclusion, with studies by Eagle et al. (1997), Frone et al. (1996), Grandey and Cropanzano (1999) and Schwartzberg and Dytell (1996) all demonstrating no significant differences between men and women in overall levels of work–family conflict. It should be noted, however, that some studies have obtained gender differences in specific directions of interrole conflict. For example, Stephens and Sommer (1996) observed that women experienced a greater amount of work-to-family conflict than did their male counterparts. (These researchers did not, however, assess family-to-work conflict, which has often been assumed to be greater for women.)

The moderating effects of gender (on the relationship between conflict and psychological or physical distress) have also been explored in various studies. MacEwen and Barling (1994) developed a comprehensive model of the effects of work-to-family and family-to-work interference (see Figure 23.2) and compared outcomes for men and women. Their research illustrated that, for men, interference of the family with work life predicted anxiety and depression, whereas for women these symptoms of strain were more strongly predicted by the interference of work with family life. These findings suggest that conflict between the work and family domains may have different meanings for men and women, a proposition which is consistent with the notion of 'life role values' explicated by Carlson and Kacmar (2000). These researchers argued that the relative importance of different roles to an individual may influence the extent to which interrole conflict is experienced and its effects on psychological outcomes, such as satisfaction with the job and family. Carlson and Kacmar found that individuals who valued work over family experienced greater family-to-work conflict and reduced family satisfaction, whereas those who valued family over work were more likely to report work-to-family conflict and lower job satisfaction. When both domains were rated as highly important, there was a strong relationship between work–family conflict and both job and life satisfaction. The authors suggested that the 'simultaneous pursuit of roles individuals value may give rise to conflict' (p. 1050). It may be, therefore, that in studies which have found gender differences male and female participants have had different priorities or life role values. Hence gender *per se* is not the critical issue, but rather the relationship between gender and different value patterns.

Dependants
It is clear that the presence of dependants increases interrole conflict, and this is especially relevant for women rather than for men (Noor, 2002). The presence of dependants produces an increase in home demands and generally entails a reduction in paid employment time. Brough and Kelling (2002), for example, compared the work hours of women with and without dependants and found the latter group were employed for significantly fewer hours (40 hours compared to 36 hours per week, respectively). Nordenmark (2002) also found that the number of children in a family was linearly associated with the desire of both parents to reduce their working hours and to spend more time with their children. However it is the total number of hours worked both in paid employment and on household/family tasks which is pertinent to the conflict debate and is associated with decreased health outcomes. Noor (2002) suggested that the total hours worked each week for individuals in family groups (three or more dependants) is 90 for women and 70 for men – an average gender difference of about 2.5 hours per day.

The presence of dependants has been found to increase levels of psychological strain and consistently to reduce work–life balance (Tausig and Fenwick, 2001). Nordenmark (2002) concluded that employed fathers experienced higher levels of psychological strain than employed non-fathers. Similarly Beatty (1996) found that employed mothers had increased levels of work–family conflict and negative health outcomes than employed non-mothers. Additionally mothers who received little spousal support also had higher levels of depression. Brough and Kelling (2002) found that single (female) parents/carers experienced higher levels of psychological strain than carers with a partner. The number and ages of children, particularly the age of the youngest child, are also generally considered to increase parental demands. Having a child of infant or pre-school age produces the highest parental demands (Major *et al.* 2002; Parasuraman and Simmers, 2001).

Coping strategies
Another factor which may be important for understanding the impact of work–family conflict on distress is the type of coping that the individual engages in. Edwards and Rothbard (2000), for example, have commented that some people may utilize role segmentation as a mechanism for minimizing the intrusion of work and family demands into the other domain. Although previous research has generally not supported the notion of segmentation between work and family, typically this research has interpreted a significant correlation between job satisfaction and family satisfaction as evidence that the two domains spill over into each other, and hence are not segmented. Edwards and Rothbard differentiated between intentional and unintentional separation of work and family, illustrating that 'segmentation is now viewed as an active process whereby people maintain a boundary between work and family' (p. 181). A similar point has been raised by Grandey and Cropanzano (1999), who referred to compartmentalization as an active coping strategy for managing the potentially negative impacts of too much spillover between work and family domains.

Despite the presumed importance of coping, there has been relatively little systematic investigation of the ameliorating effects of different strategies for coping with excessive work–family conflict and, as with research on gender differences, the findings have not been conclusive. Matsui *et al.*, (1995) examined the effects of structural role redefinition, which involves changing external role expectations from family or work colleagues, so that they impose less demand on one's time or energy. Contrary to prediction, however, Matsui et al. found that neither work-role redefinition nor family–role definition had a consistent moderating effect on the relationship between work–family conflict and life strain.

Aryee, Luk, Leung and Lo (1999) and Frone et al., (1994) explored the buffering influence of problem-focused or 'active' coping. Logically it would be anticipated that efforts to control the effects of work–family conflict should have positive benefits for individuals trying to balance work and family demands. However active coping displayed no significant buffering effects in either of these studies. One possible explanation for this is that individuals may not have been able to control the demands on their time and energy from both work and family, hence problem-focused coping had minimal impact on an essentially uncontrollable state of affairs.

In summary, although intuitively one would expect coping strategies to have a considerable influence on the relationship between work–family conflict and psychological outcomes, particularly distress, these strategies have not been consistently found to exert a substantial effect. As noted, a potential reason for the lack of significant moderating effects for problem-focused or 'active' coping may be that individuals perceive pressures and demands from the work and family to be uncontrollable. Hence future research needs to explore the level of control which individuals feel they can exert over the work–family interface.

Social support
Another variable which has received considerable attention in research on work–family conflict is the extent of social support which individuals utilize or have available to them. Several studies have investigated the direct, mediating and moderating impact of various forms of social support, including practical assistance, provision of information and socioemotional support. Voydanoff (2002) has commented that social support from one's family (especially one's partner or spouse) should serve to alleviate the negative impact of work–family conflict. Similarly Frone (2003) observed that support from family and work colleagues is a potential resource for the mitigation of interrole conflict.

Research on social support has typically investigated both the direct and the moderating (buffering) effects of this variable. As with coping strategies, however, evidence is varied and inconsistent. There is no doubt that higher levels of social support are associated with reduced psychological, and perhaps even physical, strain or distress (Frone, 2003). However, despite the logical appeal of the buffering hypothesis, moderating effects of social support have not always been demonstrated. Aryee, Fields and Luk (1999) found that support from one's spouse did moderate the relationship between parental role overload and family-to-work conflict, but there was no moderation of work-to-family conflict. A similar finding was reported by Matsui et al. (1995), who found that husband support buffered the relationship between parental demands and work–family conflict, while Noor (2002) demonstrated that support from their husband alleviated the negative effects of excessive work hours and poor quality work experience on levels of work–family conflict among a sample of Malaysian women. Carlson and Perrewe (1999) also found buffering effects of both work and family support on the relationship between work and family demands and interrole conflict. None of these studies, however, examined the potential moderating effect of support on the conflict–distress relationship.

Frone *et al.* (1994) did explore the buffering effects of perceived support on distress, but obtained no significant conflict x support interaction terms in regressions on depression and physical health symptoms. They suggested that a possible reason why social support did not function as a moderator in their research is that individuals either did not value the kinds of support available or did not have the capacity to utilize available supports effectively. Further research should examine both of these possibilities, along with individual differences in support-utilization preferences and capabilities, which may have a major bearing on the impact of support on symptoms of distress.

To summarize, although there is substantial evidence that social support from work colleagues and from family may be directly linked with reduced strain, the presumed buffering effects of this variable have not been conclusively demonstrated. As noted by Frone *et al.* (1994) and Cooper *et al.* (2001), simply analysing the statistical interaction between stressors (such as work–family conflict) and support may not be sufficient to capture adequately the complexities of this construct and its functions.

In this section we have provided a brief overview of some variables which have been posited as having a major role in the process linking work–family conflict to distress. From the evidence presented, it is clear that additional research needs to explore in more depth some of the key functions which are played by variables such as gender, coping and social support. Furthermore, as discussed by Edwards and Rothbard (2000), simple linear models of relationships may be inadequate to test interrelationships between the array of potentially relevant factors in the conflict–distress relationship.

Implications for organizational policies and practices
Interventions to reduce the negative effects of inter-domain conflict can occur at either the individual or the organizational level and typically include a combination of both. In terms of occupational stress theories, these practices can be defined as individual and organizational coping responses, and their use is expected to reduce the impact of work–family conflict (Voydanoff, 2002). A brief exploration of some common organizational interventions is provided here. Individual coping responses have been discussed briefly above.

Part-time and flexible working arrangements
Intuitively it seems logical to assume that flexible working arrangements would function to reduce interrole conflict and subsequently increase both personal and organizational health and performance outcomes. A substantial volume of research suggests this is indeed the case. Flexible working arrangements, including regular shift systems, have been found to significantly lower the perceived experiences of work and family conflicts (Kushner and Harrison, 2002; Thomas and Ganster, 1995). Kropf (2002) described recent investigations conducted by a number of US corporations and universities investigating the issue of work–family conflict and preferred organizational interventions. Kropf concluded that part-time and flexible working arrangements are interventions which significantly reduce work–family conflict. Nordenmark (2002) found that more women (31 per cent) than men (19 per cent) considered reducing their work hours to allow more time for

family responsibilities. This was especially the case for women with both children and a cohabiting partner, and for women in the higher ranks of an organization.

Galinsky et al. (1996) also found that 11 per cent more employed parents would change jobs to gain access to increased flexitime job benefits, as compared to employees without children. This trend is reflected in the increasing numbers of women establishing small businesses. Such businesses are perceived as offering greater flexibility and control over working hours, thus allowing family responsibilities to be more easily addressed (Eagle et al., 1997). Interestingly all of the US organizations on the Working Mother (1999) list of the *100 Best Companies for Working Mothers* offer flexible working arrangements of some kind. Furthermore flexible working arrangements were identified as one of the top interventions (Kropf, 2002).

In addition, owing to the societal changes described previously, especially the recognition that quality of life typically includes a balance between work and family involvement, the demand for part-time jobs is increasing among both men and women. For example, one major international organization recorded a doubling of demand for part-time work from its male employees (Kantrowitz et al., 1989). Similarly another large organization implemented a variety of flexible working options after considerable demand from its engineers. Nearly 4 per cent of the workforce utilized the flexible working options in the first year of operation and the organization retained 100 per cent of these new part-time workers (Thomas and Ganster, 1995; Shellenbarger, 1992). Kropf (2002) also recognizes that a substantial number of employees are likely to use both full and part-time working options at different points in their career and life stages. This contradicts the more popular perception that employees can be wholly categorized as either full or part-time workers (see also Lee, 1997). Interestingly Bohen and Viveros-Long (1981) found that the basic provision of flexible working arrangements can have a substantial impact even among employees without any dependant responsibilities. The option of such flexible working hours is therefore over time likely to support a large number of employees. Part-time work is still, however, heavily associated with lower wages and/or reductions in other employment benefits such as pensions and health entitlements and this is especially the case for non-professional workers (Wenger, 2001) and women (Carr, 2002). Overall the success of flexible working arrangements both for the organization through performance measures and for the individual in terms of satisfaction levels has been acknowledged (Greenhaus and Parasuraman, 1986; Kropf, 2002).

Despite the evidence discussed above, it is also pertinent that some research has failed to demonstrate any positive effects of flexible work hours or of part-time work. Tausig and Fenwick (2001), for example, analysed data collected in 1992 from a national US sample of 3381 employees and found that working non-standard shifts (that is not normal Monday–Friday hours of work) and working part-time increased rather than reduced, levels of work–family conflict. Tausig and Fenwick have suggested that the adverse consequences associated with part-time work, such as financial and career disadvantages, may outweigh any advantages gained, such as more family time. Such adverse consequences in turn appear to increase rather than reduce perceived levels of inter-domain conflict. Major et al., (2002) also found that the association between the number of hours worked and the level of work interference with family life (WFC) was not moderated by any scheduling flexibility. Instead WFC was related directly to the number of hours worked.

Parental leave

Parental leave is perceived as a worthwhile intervention, through both practical aspects of actually helping working parents to cope with childcare demands, and illustrating, in a more generic sense, the flexibility and supportive nature of the organization (Greenhaus and Parasuraman, 1986). Hence the inclusion of such programmes within promotional company literature to attract and retain employees (Voydanoff, 2002). However an employee's accessibility to parental leave is strongly dependent upon both national policies and organizational culture. A number of countries still have no national legislation concerning maternal rights and benefits, while discrimination against pregnant employees, including the actual loss of employment, remains common (Shellenbarger, 1992). Both the existence and the scope of parental leave are therefore often specific to an organisation. Organizations that offer generous leave allowances are often exemplified. For example, Dupont's mid-1980s research on the extent of childcare use amongst its employees and the subsequent introduction of a two month parental leave policy ensures that the organization is often cited within this literature (Kraut, 1990).

Paternal leave is far less common than maternal leave. In Sweden both maternal and paternal leave programmes have been in place over the last few decades. Approximately 44 per cent of Swedish fathers, for example, use parental leave, staying at home an average of 41 days. However, in Sweden and elsewhere, the stigma associated with the taking of parental leave remains much stronger for men as compared to women (Starrels, 1992).

Working at home

The technological advances which have recently allowed employees to work at home constitute a mixed blessing. For some employees this practice is invaluable and assists with childcare responsibilities. Such opportunities again demonstrate the perceived flexibility and consideration of the modern employer (Greenhaus and Parasuraman, 1986). The benefits of working at home include enhanced work–family relationships, perceived quality of life benefits, improved work-related well-being and improved work performance (Standen et al., 1999). However working at home may also have adverse consequences, noticeably the lack of a physical separation between home and work life (boundary setting) and the perception of being continuously available for work, seven days a week. These elements can serve to increase levels of psychological strain (Hammer et al., 2002). Overall the perceived flexibility offered by the ability to work at home, especially in terms of the balancing of home and work demands, illustrates that this method of work will continue to increase.

Child/elder care provision

Thomas and Thomas (1990) found that employer assistance with childcare was associated with organizational outcomes such as increased morale and productivity, reduced accident rates and reduced levels of absenteeism and turnover. Similar effects were found with the employer provision of elder care, primarily through a reduction in strain experienced (Burden and Googins, 1987). Shellenbarger (1992) suggested that approximately two-thirds of US companies offer some form of childcare assistance to their employees, although only about 20 per cent of companies provide actual childcare centres or direct financial help of some kind. The provision of childcare programmes and/or support of some kind by an employer is generally perceived as being more valuable by female than by male employees (Frone and Yardley, 1996).

Supervisor support
Supervisor support is emerging as an important variable in the reduction of work–family conflict. The types of support provided by the supervisor follow those recognized within the stress and coping literature and include emotional, informational, appraisal and instrumental support (Nielson et al., 2001). A supportive supervisor is one who tolerates the family spillover into the work domain, generally through small concessions such as the employee's making and receiving of some family-related telephone calls, approving flexible working arrangements and such like (Greenglass, 2000; Thomas and Ganster, 1995; Voydanoff, 2002). This support is particularly valuable with unexpected incidences such as child/elderly parent sickness, sudden cancellations of carer arrangements and during school holidays. It has been argued that responsible employers should recognize that family demands can unexpectedly increase at certain times. With a degree of flexibility to enable employees to deal with these demands, subsequent conflict and the corresponding strain outcomes will be greatly reduced (Kelloway et al., 1999; Nielson et al., 2001). Shellenbarger (1992) provides an interesting overview of the lack of supervisory and/or organizational support experienced by a cross-section of US employees, especially by those experiencing parenthood for the first time. Shellenbarger suggested that antifamily discrimination remains abundant in the majority of organizations and, for example, serves effectively to perpetuate the glass ceiling.

Research into the consequences of supervisor support has focused upon similarities between the supervisor's and the incumbent's perceptions and values of work–family life. A close value match can positively influence such outcomes as incumbent job satisfaction, periods of leave, work absence and turnover (Nielson et al., 2001; Thompson et al., 2001). The Families and Work Institute (1993) reported how the training of supervisors in family-friendly supportive techniques produced increases in both employees' perceptions of organizational support and employee well-being over a two-year period. The provision of supervisor support is also closely linked to the issue of spouse and family support (see Brough and Kelling, 2002; Voydanoff, 2002, for family-related support implications).

Conclusion
It is apparent that a number of organizational interventions aimed at reducing the experience of work–family conflict are available. Such interventions are often referred to as 'family-friendly policies' or 'family supportive programmes' and an employee's preference and loyalty towards organizations which employ such interventions are generally acknowledged (Hobson et al., 2001; Kushner and Harrison, 2002; Rosin and Korabik, 2002). The use of family-friendly policies can reduce interrole conflict, absenteeism and turnover and increase individual health and satisfaction outcomes (Greenglass, 2000; Lee, 1997; Rosin and Korabik, 2002; Thomas and Ganster, 1995; Vinokur et al., 1999; Voydanoff, 2002) and can reduce perceptions of stress (Galinsky et al., 1996).

The call for organizations to assist employees in reducing their levels of work–family conflict has been made for the last 15 years or so (Greenhaus and Parasuraman, 1986). Organizational intervention is generally self-serving: offering both practical support and creating a positive image as a considerate employer. Most organizational interventions generally occur in large progressive companies, which have both the finances and the flexibility to consider adequate implementation (Frone et al., 1996; Thomas and Ganster, 1995). The reluctance in the widespread uptake and implication of organizational interventions is perhaps due to the classification of work–family conflict as being primarily a woman's problem (Starrels, 1992). However the research reviewed by this chapter illustrates that few gender differences actually exist in either the antecedents or the outcomes of work–family conflict. Furthermore recent social changes suggest that both men and women value their overall quality of life (that is both work and family domains) increasingly more equally (Schwartberg and Dytell, 1996). Therefore the advantages produced by the successful implementation of family-friendly organizational practices can be applicable to both female and male employees.

The successful implementation of family-friendly organizational practices often also depends on the prevailing corporate culture (Frone et al., 1996; Lee, 1997). An encouragement to employees to use such practices, without the implication of any (informal) disadvantages, should obviously occur. This level of encouragement, of course, differs across organizations, which is why some organizational practices are enforced by legislation (for example parental leave in many countries). Most organizational structures and cultures continue to reward continuous full-time employment (Carr, 2002).

Responsible employers should also be aware of a final issue, which is often overlooked. Most family-friendly organizational practices are designed to reduce family-to-work conflict, which as we have seen typically occurs with less intensity and frequency than work-to-family conflict (Frone et al., 1996). Thus interventions designed to reduce the effects of work on family life would be more valuable but currently actually occur far less frequently. Some of the organizational practices described above (for example teleworking) do, of course, address the two inter-domain conflict pathways simultaneously. Further consideration of the bidirectional effects of work–family conflict is required to ensure that individuals, their families and organizations can reap the full benefits of interventions designed to reduce the negative impacts of this potent, and increasingly prevalent, stressor.

References
Allen, T.D., D.E.L. Herst, C.S. Bruck and M. Sutton (2000), 'Consequences associated with work-to-family conflict: a review and agenda for future research', *Journal of Occupational Health Psychology*, **5**, 278–308.
Aryee, S., D. Fields and V. Luk (1999), 'A cross-cultural test of a model of the work–family interface', *Journal of Management*, **25**, 491–511.
Aryee, S.., V. Luk, A. Leung and S. Lo (1991), 'Role stressors, interole conflict and well-being: the modulating influence of spousal support and coping behaviors among employed parents in Hong Kong', *Journal of Vocational Behavior*, **54**, 259–78.
Bacharach, S.B., P. Bamberger and S. Conley (1991), 'Work–home conflict among nurses and engineers: mediating the impact of role stress on burnout and satisfaction at work', *Journal of Organizational Behavior*, **12**, 39–53.
Barnett R.C. and J.S. Hyde (2001), 'Women, men, work and family', *American Psychologist*, **56**, 781–96.
Beatty, C.A. (1996), 'The stress of managerial and professional women: is the price too high?', *Journal of Organizational Behavior*, **17**, 233–51.
Bohen, H.H. and A. Viveros-Long (1981), *Balancing Jobs and Family Life*, Philadelphia: Temple University Press.
Boles, J.S., W.G. Howard and H.H. Donofrio (2001), 'An investigation into the interrelationships of work–family conflict, family–work conflict and work satisfaction', *Journal of Managerial Issues*, **13**, 376–90.
Brough, P. and A. Kelling (2002), 'Women, work and well-being: an analysis of the work–family conflict', *New Zealand Journal of Psychology*, **31**, 29–38.

Burden, D.S. and B. Googins (1987), 'Boston University balancing job and homelife study', Boston University, School of Social Work.
Burke, R.J. (1998), 'Work and non-work stressors and well-being among police officers: the role of coping', *Anxiety, Stress and Coping: An International Journal*, **11**, 345–62.
Carlson, D.S. and K.M. Kacmar (2000), 'Work–family conflict in the organization: do life role values makes a difference?', *Journal of Management*, **26**, 1031–54.
Carlson, D.S. and P.L. Perrewe (1999), 'The role of social support in the stressor–strain relationship: an examination of work–family conflict', *Journal of Management*, **25**, 513–40.
Carr, D. (2002), 'The psychological consequences of work–family trade-offs for three cohorts of men and women', *Social Psychology Quarterly*, **65**, 103–24.
Cooper, C.L., P.J. Dewe and M.P. O'Driscoll (2001), *Organizational Stress: A Review and Critique of Theory, Research and Applications*, Thousand Oaks, CA: Sage Publications.
Eagle, B.W., E.W. Miles and M.L. Icenogle (1997), 'Interrole conflicts and the permeability of the work and family domains: are there gender differences?', *Journal of Vocational Behaviour*, **50**, 168–84.
Edwards, J.R. and N.P. Rothbard (2000), 'Mechanisms linking work and family: clarifying the relationship between work and family constructs', *Academy of Management Review*, **25**, 178–99.
Families and Work Institute, (1993), *An Evaluation of Johnson & Johnson's Work–Family Initiative*, New York: Families and Work Institute.
Friedman, S.D. and J.H. Greenhaus (2000), *Work and Family – Allies or Enemies? What Happens when Business Professionals Confront Life Choices*, Oxford: Oxford University Press.
Frone, M.R. (2003), 'Work–family balance', in J.C. Quick and L.E. Tetrick (eds), *Handbook of Occupational Health Psychology*, Washington, DC: American Psychological Association, pp. 143–62.
Frone, M.R., and J.K. Yardley (1996), 'Workplace family-supportive programmes: predictors of employed parents' importance ratings', *Journal of Occupational and Organizational Psychology*, **69**(4), 351–66.
Frone, M.R., M. Russell and G.M. Barnes (1996), 'Work–family conflict to substance use among employed mothers: the role of negative affect', *Journal of Marriage and the Family*, **56**, 1019–30.
Frone, M.R., M. Russell and M.L. Cooper (1992), 'Antecedents and outcomes of work–family conflict: testing a model of the work–family interface', *Journal of Applied Psychology*, **77**, 65–78.
Frone, M.R., M. Russell and M.L. Cooper (1994), 'Relationship of work and family stressors to psychological distress: the independent moderating influence of social support, mastery, active coping and self-focused attention', in R. Crandall and P.L. Perrewe (eds), *Occupational Stress: A Handbook*, London: Taylor & Francis, pp. 129–50.
Frone, M.R., M. Russell and M.L. Cooper (1997), 'Relation of work–family conflict to health outcomes: a four year longitudinal study of employed parents', *Journal of Occupational & Organizational Psychology*, **70**, 325–35.
Fryer, D. and P. Warr (1984), 'Unemployment and cognitive difficulties', *British Journal of Clinical Psychology*, **23**, 67–88.
Galinsky, E., J.T. Bond and D.E. Friedman (1996), 'The role of employers in addressing the needs of employed parents', *Journal of Social Issues*, **52**, 111–36.
Goff, S.J., M.K. Mount and R.L. Jamison (1990), 'Employer supported child care, work/family conflict and absenteeism: a field study', *Personnel Psychology*, **43**, 793–809.
Grandey, A.A. and R. Cropanzano (1999), 'The conservation of resources model applied to work–family conflict and strain', *Journal of Vocational Behavior*, **54**, 350–70.
Greenglass, E.R. (2000), 'Work, family and psychological functioning: conflict or synergy?', in P. Dewe, M. Leiter and T. Cox (eds), *Coping, Health & Organizations*, London: Taylor & Francis, pp. 87–108.
Greenhaus, J.H. and N.J. Beutell (1985), 'Sources of conflict between work and family roles', *Academy of Management Review*, **10**, 76–88.
Greenhaus, J.H. and S. Parasuraman (1986), 'A work–nonwork interactive perspective of stress and its consequences', *Journal of Organizational Behavior Management*, **8**, 37–60.
Greenhaus, J.H. and S. Parasuraman (2002), 'The allocation of time to work and family roles', in D.L. Nelson and R.J. Burke (eds), *Gender, Work Stress and Health*, Washington, DC: American Psychological Association, pp. 115–28.
Gutek, B., S. Searle and L. Klepa (1991), 'Rational versus gender role explanations for work–family conflict', *Journal of Applied Psychology*, **76**, 560–68.
Hammer, L.B., C.L. Colton, S. Caubet and K.J. Brockwood (2002), 'The unbalanced life: work and family conflict', in L. Thomas and M. Hersen (eds), *Organizational Interventions for Stress and Work–Life Conflict*, Sage Publications.
Haynes, S.G., E.D. Eaker and M. Feinleib (1984), 'The effects of unemployment, family, and job stress on coronary heart disease patterns in women', in E.B. Gold (ed.), *The Changing Risk of Disease in Women: An Epidemiological Approach*, Lexington, MA: Heath, pp. 37–48.

Hobson, C.J., L. Delunas and D. Kesic (2001), 'Compelling evidence of the need for corporate work/life balance initiatives: results from a national survey of stressful life-events', *Journal of Employment Counseling*, **38**, 38–44.
Hughes, D.L. and E. Galinsky (1994), 'Gender, job and family conditions, and psychological symptoms', *Psychology of Women Quarterly*, **18**, 251–70.
Johnson, J.S., L.B. Hammer, M.B. Neal and J.M. McLeod (2000), 'The effects of work–family coping strategies on work–family outcomes', *Proceedings of the 15th Annual Society for Industrial and Organizational Psychology Conference*, New Orleans, 14–16 April.
Kandel, D.B., M. Davies and V.H. Raveis (1985), 'The stressfulness of daily social roles for women: marital, occupational and household roles', *Journal of Health and Social Behaviour*, **26**, 64–78.
Kanter, R.M. (1977), *Work and Family in the United States: A Critical Review and Agenda for Research and Policy*, New York: Russell Sage Foundation.
Kantrowitz, B., P. Wingert and K. Robbins (1989), 'Advocating a "mommy track"', *Newsweek*, 13 March, **113**, 45.
Kelloway, E.K., B.H. Gottlieb and L. Barham (1999), 'The source, nature and direction of work and family conflict: a longitudinal investigation', *Journal of Occupational Health Psychology*, **4**, 337–46.
Kirchmeyer, C. (1992), 'Perceptions of nonwork-to-work spillover: challenging the common view of conflict-ridden domain relationships', *Basic and Applied Social Psychology*, **13**, 231–49.
Klitzman, S., J. House, B.A. Israel and R.P. Mero (1990), 'Work stress, nonwork stress and health', *Journal of Behavioural Medicine*, **13**, 221–43.
Kraut, A.I. (1990), 'Some lessons on organizational research concerning work and family issues', *Human Resource Planning*, **13**, 109–18.
Kropf, M.B. (2002), 'Reduced work arrangements for managers and professionals: a potential solution to conflicting demands', in D.L. Nelson and R.J. Burke (eds), *Gender, Work Stress and Health*, Washington, DC: American Psychological Association, pp. 155–67.
Kushner, K.E. and M.J. Harrison (2002), 'Employed mothers: stress and balance-focused coping', *Canadian Journal of Nursing Research*, **34**, 47–65.
Lee, J.A. (1997), 'Balancing elder care responsibilities and work: two empirical studies', *Journal of Occupational Health Psychology*, **2**, 220–8.
Lobel, S.A. (1991), 'Allocation of investment in work and family roles: alternative theories and implications for research', *Academy of Management Review*, **16**, 507–21.
MacEwen, K.E. and J. Barling (1994), 'Daily consequences of work interference with family and family interference with work', *Work and Stress*, **8**, 244–54.
Major, B. (1993), 'Gender, entitlement and the distinction of family labor', *Journal of Social Issues*, **49**, 141–59.
Major, V.S., K.J. Klein and M.G. Ehrhart (2002), 'Work time, work interference with family, and psychological distress', *Journal of Applied Psychology*, **87**(3), 427–36.
Matsui, T., T. Ohsawa and M.-L. Onglatco (1995), 'Work–family conflict and the stress-buffering effects of husband support and coping behaviour among Japanese married working women', *Journal of Vocational Behavior*, **47**, 178–92.
Netemeyer, R.G., J.S. Boles and R. McMurrian (1996), 'Development and validation of work–family conflict and family–work conflict scales', *Journal of Applied Psychology*, **81**, 400–10.
Nielson, T.R., D.S. Carlson and M.J. Lankau (2001), 'The supportive mentor as a mean of reducing work–family conflict', *Journal of Vocational Behavior*, **59**, 364–81.
Noor, N.M. (2002), 'The moderating effect of spouse support on the relationship between work variables and women's work–family conflict', *Psychologia: An International Journal of Psychology in the Orient*, **45**, 12–23.
Nordenmark, M. (2002), 'Multiple social roles – a resource or a burden: is it possible for men and women to combine paid work with family life in a satisfactory way?', *Gender, Work and Organization*, **9**, 125–45.
O'Driscoll, M. and P.A. Brough (2003), 'Job stress and burnout', in M. O'Driscoll, P. Taylor and T. Kalliath (eds), *Organizational Psychology in Australia and New Zealand*, Oxford: Oxford University Press.
O'Driscoll, M., T. Kalliath and P. Brough (2001), 'Overview of the interface between work and family transactions', *Proceedings of the Annual Conference of the New Zealand Psychological Society*, Auckland, 25–9 August.
O'Driscoll, M.P. (1996), 'The interface between job and off-job roles: enhancement and conflict', in: Cooper, C.L. and I.T. Robertson (eds), *International Review of Industrial and Organizational Psychology*, Chichester: Wiley, 279–306.
O'Driscoll, M.P., D.R. Illgen and K. Hildreth (1992), 'Time devoted to job and off-job activities, interrole conflict and affective experiences', *Journal of Applied Psychology*, **77**, 272–9.
Parasuraman, S. and C. Simmers (2001), 'Type of employment, work–family conflict and well-being: a comparative study', *Journal of Organizational Behavior*, **22**, 551–68.

Parasuraman, S., J.H. Greenhaus and C.S. Granrose (1992), 'Role stressors, social support, and well-being among two-career couples', *Journal of Organizational Behavior*, **13**, 339–56.
Perrewe, P.L. and D.S. Carlson (2002), 'Do men and women benefit from social support equally? Results from a field examination within the work and family context', in D.L. Nelson and R.J. Burke (eds), *Gender, Work Stress and Health*, Washington, DC: American Psychological Association, pp. 101–14.
Rosin, H.M. and K. Korabik (2002), 'Do family-friendly policies fulfill their promise? An investigation of their impact on work–family conflict and work and personal outcomes', in D.L. Nelson and R.J. Burke (eds), *Gender, Work Stress and Health*, Washington DC: American Psychological Association, pp. 211–26.
Schwartzberg, N. and R. Dytell (1996), 'Dual-earner families: the importance of work stress and family stress for psychological well-being', *Journal of Occupational Health Psychology*, **1**, 211–23.
Shellenbarger, S. (1992), 'Lessons from the workplace: how corporate policies and attitudes lag behind workers' changing needs', *Human Resource Management*, **31**, 157–69.
Small, S. and D. Riley (1990), 'Toward a multidimensional assessment of work spillover into family life', *Journal of Marriage and the Family*, **52**, 51–61.
Standen, P., K. Daniels and D. Lamond (1999), 'The home as a workplace: work–family interaction and psychological well-being in telework', *Journal of Occupational Health Psycholgy*, **4**, 368–81.
Starrels, M. (1992), 'The evolution of workplace family policy research', *Journal of Family Issues*, **13**, 259–78.
Stephens, G.K. and S.M. Sommer (1996), 'The measurement of work to family conflict', *Educational and Psychological Measurement*, **56**, 475–86.
Stephens, M.A.P, A.L. Townsend, L.M. Martire and J.A. Druley (2001), 'Balancing parent care with other roles: interrole conflict of adult daughter caregivers', *Journal of Gerontology*, **56B**(1), 24–34.
Tausig, M. and R. Fenwick (2001), 'Unbinding time: alternate work schedules and work–life balance', *Journal of Family and Economic Issues*, **22**(2), 101–19.
Thomas, L.T. and D.C. Ganster (1995), 'Impact of family-supportive work variables on work–family conflict and strain: a control perspective', *Journal of Applied Psychology*, **80**, 6–15.
Thomas, L.T. and J.T. Thomas (1990), 'The ABCs of child care: building blocks of competitive advantage', *Sloan Management Review*, **31**, 31–41.
Thompson, B., A. Kirk-Brown and D. Brown (2001), 'Women police: the impact of work stress on family members', in P.A. Hancock and P.A. Desmond (eds), *Stress, Workload and Fatigue*, London: Lawrence Erlbaum, pp. 200–10.
Vinokur, A.D., P.F. Pierce and C.L. Buck (1999), 'Work–family conflicts of women in the Air Force: their influence on mental health and functioning', *Journal of Organizational Behavior*, **20**, 865–78.
Voydanoff, P. (2002), 'Linkages between the work–family interface and work, family, and individual outcomes: an integrative model, *Journal of Family Issues*, **23**, 138–64.
Wallace, J.E. (1999), 'Work-to-nonwork conflict among married male and female lawyers', *Journal of Organizational Behavior*, **20**, 797–816.
Wenger, J. (2001), 'The continuing problems with part-time jobs' (Economic Policy Institute Issue Brief # 155), The Economic Policy Institute, Washington, DC.
Williams, K.J. and G.M. Alliger (1994), 'Role stressors, mood spillover and perceptions of work–family conflict in employed parents', *Academy of Management Journal*, **37**, 837–68.
Working Mother Magazine (1999), '100 best companies for working mothers', October.
Zapf, D., C. Dormann and M. Frese (1996), 'Longitudinal studies in organizational stress research: a review of the literature with reference to methodological issues', *Journal of Occupational Health Psychology*, **1**, 145–69.

24 Workaholism in organizations: work and well-being consequences[1]
Ronald J. Burke

Although the popular press has paid considerable attention to workaholism (Fassel, 1990; Garfield, 1987; Kiechel, 1989a, 1989b; Killinger, 1991; Klaft and Kleiner, 1988; Machlowitz, 1980; Waddell, 1993), very little research has been undertaken to further our understanding of it. Most writing has been anecdotal and clinical (Fassel, 1990; Killinger, 1991; Oates, 1971; Schaef and Fassel, 1988). Basic questions of definition have not been addressed and measurement concerns have been avoided (Scott *et al.*, 1997).[2]

It should come as no surprise, then, that opinions, observations and conclusions about workaholism are both varied and conflicting. Some writers view workaholism positively from an organizational perspective (Korn *et al.*, 1987; Machlowitz, 1980; Sprankle and Ebel, 1987). Machlowitz (1980) conducted a qualitative interview study of 100 workaholics and found them to be very satisfied and productive. Others view workaholism negatively (Killinger, 1991; Schaef and Fassel, 1988; Oates, 1971). These writers equate workaholism with other addictions and depict workaholics as unhappy, obsessive, tragic figures who are not performing their jobs well and are creating difficulties for their co-workers (Naughton, 1987; Oates, 1971; Porter, 1996). The first group would advocate the encouragement of workaholism; the second would discourage it.

Some researchers have proposed the existence of different types of workaholic behaviour patterns, each having potentially different antecedents and associations with job performance, work and life outcomes (Naughton, 1987; Scott *et al.*, 1997; Spence and Robbins, 1992). Naughton (1987) presents a typology of workaholism based on the dimensions of career commitment and obsession–compulsion, identifying four types of workaholics. Scott *et al.* (1997) propose three types of workaholic behaviour patterns: compulsive–dependent, perfectionist and achievement-oriented. Spence and Robbins (1992) propose three workaholic patterns based on their workaholic triad notion: work addicts, enthusiastic addicts and work enthusiasts.

A compelling case could be made for devoting more research attention to workaholism. The concept has received considerable attention in the popular press. There have also been suggestions that workaholism may be increasing in North America (Schor, 1991; Fassel, 1990). What role does workaholism play in the time famine experienced by many (Perlow, 1997)? In addition, it is not clear whether workaholism has positive or negative organizational consequences (Machlowitz, 1980; Killinger, 1991). There is also debate on the association of workaholic behaviours with a variety of personal well-being indicators such as psychological and physical health and self-esteem. Different types of workaholic behaviour patterns likely exist, each having unique antecedents and outcomes. The question of whether workaholism can, or should, be reduced has also been raised (Porter, 1996; Killinger, 1991; Seybold and Salomone, 1994). Finally it is important to study workaholism among women and examine possible gender differences in prevalence, antecedents and consequences (Doerfler and Kammer, 1986). The few studies that have compared levels of workaholism in samples of women and men have reported few differences (Burke, 1999a; Doerfler and Kammer, 1986; Spence and Robbins, 1992). Women in particular professions may be as prone to exhibit workaholism as are men.

This review examines the literature on workaholism in organizations. Workaholism is acknowledged to be a stable individual characteristic, though how it is distinguished from other chracteristics is often unclear. The review addresses the following areas: types of workaholics, definitions and measures of workaholism, the prevalence of workaholism, validating job behaviours, antecedents of workaholism, work outcome consequences, health consequences, extra-work satisfactions and family functioning, evaluating workaholism components, gender differences, reducing workaholism and future research directions. Research programmes begun by Robinson (1998) and Spence and Robbins (1992), though having different emphases, serve as useful starting points for future research efforts.

Theories of workaholism

Up to the present time the majority of research on workaholism has been atheoretical, with the possible exception of some family systems-based investigations (see Robinson, 1998). McMillan *et al.* (2003) review and apply theoretical perspectives to the concept of workaholism: addiction theory (both medical and psychological), learning theory, trait theory, cognitive theory and family systems theory. Each theory offers its own set of predictions about the development, stability and changeability of workaholism. Unfortunately none of the theories has been tested to determine their usefulness. McMillan *et al.* (2003) conclude that trait and cognitive theories have received preliminary empirical support while learning, addiction and family systems theories, though promising, require empirical confirmation. Workaholism appears to be a personal trait that is activated and then maintained by environmental factors.

Definitions of workaholism

Research on workaholism has been hindered by the absence of acceptable definitions and measures (Scott *et al.*, 1997). It is difficult to understand and research a phenomenon until one can define what it is. Mosier (1983) defined workaholism in terms of hours worked; workaholics were those who worked at least 50 hours per week. Cherrington (1980) sees workaholism as 'an irrational commitment to excessive work. Workaholics are unable to take time off or to comfortably divert their interests' (p. 257). Machlowitz (1980) defines workaholics as people 'who always devote more time and thoughts to their work than the situation demands . . . what sets workaholics apart from other workers is their attitude toward work, not the number of hours they work' (p. 1).

Killinger (1991) defines a workaholic as 'a person who gradually becomes emotionally crippled and addicted to control and power in a compulsive drive to gain approval and success' (p. 6). Robinson (1997) defines workaholism 'as a progressive, potentially fatal disorder, characterized by self-imposed demands, compulsive overworking, inability to regulate work habits and an over-indulgence in work to the exclusion of most other life activities' (p. 81). Oates (1971), generally acknowledged as the first person to use the word 'workaholic' defined it as 'a person whose need for work has become so excessive that it creates noticeable disturbance or interference with his bodily health, personal happiness, and interpersonal relationships, and with his smooth social functioning' (p. 4).

Porter (1996) defines workaholism as 'an excessive involvement with work evidenced by neglect in other areas of life and based on internal motives of behavior maintenance rather than requirements of the job or organization' (p. 71). Most writers use the terms 'excessive work', 'workaholism' and 'work addiction' interchangeably. Scott et al. (1997) used a three-step process to develop what they term 'a reasonable definition' of the construct. They first collected characteristics attributed to workaholics in the practical and clinical literature. They then looked for conceptual similarities among these characteristics. They also differentiated the workaholic concept from similar constructs (for example job involvement) to reduce redundancy. They identified three elements in workaholic behaviour patterns using this process: discretionary time spent in work activities, thinking about work when not working, and working beyond organizational requirements.

Spence and Robbins (1992) were the first researchers to define workaholism. They define the workaholic as a person who 'is highly work involved, feels compelled or driven to work because of inner pressures, and is low in enjoyment at work' (p. 62). Most writers view workaholism as a stable individual characteristic (Scott et al., 1997; Spence and Robbins, 1992).

Measures of workaholism

A number of measures of workaholism have been reported in both the popular and academic literatures. Many of these are listings of behaviours in checklist form, are used once and never validated. Machlowitz (1980) lists ten characteristics (for example, 'Do you get up early, no matter how late you go to bed', in a yes/no format. She writes that, if you answer yes to eight or more questions you may be a workaholic. Killinger (1991) lists 30 items in her workaholic quiz (for example, 'Do you think you are special or different from other people?'), also answered in a yes/no format. She suggests that, if you answer 20 or more yes, most likely you are a workaholic. There is no information about where these items came from nor any psychometric information about the properties of these two scales.

Three other measures of workaholism have been developed and reported, along with information of some of each measure's properties (Haymon, 1993; Robinson, 1998; Spence and Robbins, 1992). Haymon (1993) developed the Workaholic Adjective Checklist (WAC) for his doctoral dissertation and used it in a sample of over 200 college males. It contains 72 items based on attitudinal and behavioural characteristics of individuals thought to be addicted to work. Responses to each item are made on a Likert scale (describes me/does not describe me). Participants in the upper third of the WAC scale score distribution were classified as workaholic, those scoring in the lower third were classified as non-workaholic. Further analyses of WAC scores yielded five factors: anxiety, obsessive–compulsive behaviour, mania, intolerance and self-doubt.

Using one item of the WAC which described characteristics of workaholics as the criterion (18, 17 per cent of the example classifying themselves as workaholics), 15 of 18 (83 per cent) were correctly classified as workaholics in a discriminant function analysis using the five factors of the WAC as predictors. Of those who did not classify themselves as workaholics (N = 89), 79 (89 per cent) were correctly classified.

Robinson and his colleagues developed the Work Addiction Risk Test (WART). The WART contains 25 items drawn from symptoms (characteristics) reported by writers on workaholism (Robinson, 1998). Respondents rate items on a four-point Likert scale (1 = never true, 4 = always true) according to how well each item describes their work habits (for example, 'It's important that I see the concrete results of what I do'). Scores can range from 25 to 100. Robinson states that scores of 25 to 56 indicate that you are not work-addicted, scores from 57 to 66, mildly work-addicted, and scores from 67 to 100, highly work-addicted. Scores above 65 fall greater than one standard deviation above the mean. The items on the WART, based on a review of available literature, were grouped into five categories: overdoing, self-worth, control-perfectionism, intimacy and preoccupation-future reference. No evidence (for example factor analysis) is offered to support this five-factor notion.

Robinson and his colleagues report a number of studies providing psychometric information for the WART. They indicate a test–retest reliability over a two-week period in a sample of 151 university students of 0.83, with a coefficient alpha of 0.85 (Robinson, 1998). Robinson and Post (1995) reported split-half reliabilities in three data sets: 169 college students, 106 graduate students and 194 members of Workaholics Anonymous. Based on 442 respondents, a Spearman-Brown split-half coefficient of 0.85 was obtained.

Face validity was determined by having 50 working adults place each of the 25 WART items into one of the five broader categories (for example, overdoing). On average, the 25 items were correctly allocated to the five umbrella categories by 70 per cent of these graduate students (Robinson and Post, 1994). In a similar study, this time involving 20 marriage and family therapists (Robinson and Phillips, 1995), ten items unrelated to work addiction were included with the 25 WART items. The mean percentage of correctly identified workaholism characteristics was 89.

Robinson (1999) tested the criterion-related validity of the WART, again in sample of students, by correlating WART scores with measures of Type A behaviour and anxiety. Comparing high, medium and low WART scorers showed that students scoring higher on the WART also scored higher on anxiety and some Type A components. These findings are not surprising given the conceptual and content overlap between the WART and the two criterion measures.

Spence and Robbins (1992) report the development of their workaholism measure, providing both reliability and concurrent validity information. Using on their definition of workaholism, developed from a review of the literature, they propose three workaholism components: work involvement, feeling driven to the work and work enjoyment. They developed multi-item measures of these components, each having internal consistency reliabilities greater than 0.67. Data were collected in this study from 368 social workers holding academic appointments. Cluster analysis was performed, resulting in the same six profiles for women and men. Three other studies (Elder and Spence, unpublished manuscript; Kanai et al., 1996; Robbins, 1993), using the same three scales, have produced essentially the same profiles: work addicts score high on work involvement, high on feeling driven to work and low on work enjoyment; work enthusiasts score high on work involvement, low on feeling driven to work and high on work enjoyment; enthusiastic workaholics score high on all three workaholism components. Unengaged workers score low on all three workaholism components; relaxed workers score low on feeling driven to work and work involvement and high on work enjoyment; and disenchanted workers score high on feeling driven to work and low on work involvement and work enjoyment. These researchers then offer a number of hypotheses as to how these three workaholic patterns might differ from each other. Thus workaholics would be more perfectionistic, would experience greater stress and report more physical health symptoms.

Types of workaholics
Scott et al. (1997) suggest three types of workaholic behaviour patterns: compulsive–dependent, perfectionist and achievement-oriented. They hypothesize that compulsive–dependent workaholism will be positively related to levels of anxiety, stress and physical and psychological problems and negatively related to job performance and job and life satisfaction. Perfectionist workaholism will be positively related to levels of stress, physical and psychological problems, hostile interpersonal relationships, low job satisfaction and performance and low voluntary turnover and pro-social behaviours.

Oates (1971) identified five types of workaholics: dyed-in-the-wool workaholics, converted workaholics, situational workaholics, pseudoworkaholics and escapists posing as workaholics. Fassel (1990) described four types of workaholics: compulsive workers, binge workers, closet workers and work anorexics. Robinson (1998) distinguished four types of workaholics: relentless workaholics, bulimic workaholics, attention deficit workaholics and savouring workaholics. The existence of different types of workaholic patterns might help to reconcile contradictory research findings and conclusions cited above.

McMillan, Brady, O'Driscoll and Marsh (2002) undertook an examination of the three dimensions in the workaholism battery developed by Spence and Robbins (1992). Data were collected from 320 employees in a wide variety of occupations. Cluster and factor analyses failed to confirm Spence and Robbins' three component model; the work involvement scale was not reproduced as a separate factor. Kanai et al. (1996) also failed to reproduce the work involvement factor in a large sample of Japanese employees (mostly blue-collar, but including some managers and professionals). These findings have led McMillan and Kanai and their colleagues to use only the feeling driven and work enjoyment scales and to eliminate items from both of these scales.

Our own work has supported the existence of the three workaholism component factors in three different studies (Canadian MBA graduates working in managerial and professional jobs, Australian MA and PhD psychologists, and senior managers and owners of construction companies in Norway). It may be that the three-factor structure (also found by Spence and Robbins, 1992; Elder and Spence, unpublished manuscript, in samples of academic social workers and MBA graduates in managerial and professional jobs) emerges most clearly in homogeneous, high-status jobs which McMillan, Marsh and O'Driscoll (2002) term 'narrow prestigious populations'. It seems premature to change the original Spence and Robbins measures at this time.

Changing the measures makes it impossible to compare levels on the workaholism components across studies. It also results in the idiosyncratic creation of workaholism types using two of the three workaholism components (Kanai et al., 1996), the combination of scores on the feeling driven and work enjoyment scales to form a single group labelled workaholics (McMillan, Marsh and O'Driscoll, 2002), or combining one of Spence and Robbins' workaholism types with their three non-workaholic types (Bonebright et al., 2000).

In spite of these changes to the original Spence and Robbins measures, those who have used revised measures have still reported research findings supportive of many of the suggested hypotheses involving potential antecedents and consequences of workaholism and workaholic types. That is, both the work enjoyment and feeling driven scales have shown significant correlations with job satisfaction, intrinsic job motivation, obsessive compulsiveness, and other measures of workaholism. Interestingly hours worked per week has been shown to be positively and significantly correlated with the workaholism components, but only weakly (around 0.20).

Workaholism, as assessed by a version of the Spence and Robbins measure, was found to be only moderately correlated with obsessive–compulsive personality (McMillan, Marsh and O'Driscoll (2002). Instead workaholism related most strongly to work-specific obsessive compulsiveness, suggesting a behavioural trait rather than a personality disorder. There is sound scientific support for considering workaholism as a distinct and investigable concept (Scott et al., 1997). It is only moderately related to measures of work ethic, leisure ethic, obsessive compulsiveness and Type A behaviour.

Prevalence of workaholism
Not surprisingly, based on the varied and ambiguous nature of workaholism definitions, estimates of the prevalence of workaholics vary. Machlowitz (1980) estimated that 5 per cent of the US population were workaholics. Doerfler and Kammer (1986), using Machlowitz's measure, reported that 23 per cent of their sample of physicians, lawyers and psychiatrists/therapists were workaholics. Kanai et al. (1996), in a large Japanese sample consisting primarily of managers, found that about 21 per cent fell into the Spence and Robbins work addict profile. Spence and Robbins (1992) reported, in a sample of professors of social work, that 8 per cent of men and 13 per cent of women fell into their work addict profile. Elder and Spence (unpublished manuscript), using a sample of US MBA graduates, observed percentages falling into workaholism profiles similar to those noted in the earlier Spence and Robbins study.

Burke (1999b), in a sample of employed MBAs, found fairly similar percentages in the three Spence and Robbins workaholic types: work enthusiasts (19 per cent), work addicts (16 per cent) and enthusiastic addicts (14 per cent). The three workaholic types comprised 49 per cent of the sample. These percentages are a reflection of the ways in which the workaholism types are actually created.

Validating job behaviours
There has been considerable speculation regarding the work behaviours likely to be exhibited by workaholics. This list includes hours worked per week, extra hours worked per week, job involvement, job stress, non-delegation of job responsibilties to others, high (or low) levels of job performance, high levels of interpersonal conflict and of lack of trust. There is empirical research which examines some of these hypothesized relationships.

Both Spence and Robbins (1992) and Burke (1999b) provide evidence of the concurrent validity of the Spence and Robbins workaholism profiles. These studies included the same measures of validating job behaviours (for example, job involvement, job stress, time committed to job, perfectionism, non-delegation) and consistently showed that work addicts exhibited higher levels of these validating job behaviours than did the two other workaholic profiles (work enthusiasts and enthusiastic addicts).

Comparisons of the workaholism types on a number of behavioural manifestations provided considerable support for the hypothesized relationships (Burke, 1999b). First, there were no differences between the three workaholism types on hours worked per week. Second, enthusiastic addicts devoted more psychological time to their job than did work addicts and work enthusiasts. Third, work addicts reported greater job stress than did enthusiastic addict, both reporting greater job stress than did work enthusiasts. Fourth, both work enthusiasts and enthusiast addicts reported greater job involvement than did the work addicts. Fifth, work addicts had greater unwillingness to delegate than did work enthusiasts and enthusiastic addicts. Sixth, enthusiastic addicts were more perfectionistic than were work enthusiasts.

Spence and Robbins (1992) found that work addicts reported higher levels of job stress, perfectionism and unwillingness to delegate job duties to others then did work enthusiasts. Kanai *et al.* (1996), using the Spence and Robbins measures, reported that enthusiastic addicts and work addicts scored higher than work enthusiasts on measures of job stress, perfectionism, non-delegation and time committed to job.

Elder and Spence (unpublished manuscript), in a sample of women and men MBA graduates, report that work addicts and enthusiastic addicts scored higher than work enthusiasts on measures of perfectionism, job stress and non-delegation. In summary, Spence and Robbins work addicts exhibit different job behaviours than those of individuals in their other profiles.

Antecedents of workaholism
Three potential antecedents of workaholism have received some conceptual and research attention. Two of these, family of origin and personal beliefs and fears, are the result of socialization practices within families and society at large. The third, organizational support for work–personal life balance, represents organizational values and priorities.

Family of origin
Robinson (1998) has written about work addiction as a symptom of a diseased family system. Work addiction, similar to other addictive behaviours, is intergenerational, passed on to future generations through family processes and dynamics. In this view, work addiction is seen as a learned addictive response to a dysfunctional family of origin system. Pietropinto (1986) suggests that children of workaholics learn that parental love is contingent on the children's high performance.

Although this was not tested directly (workaholism scores of parents were not obtained independently of workaholism scores of their children, with both workaholism scores coming from the same sources), Robinson and his colleagues equate elevated health symptoms of workaholic fathers with elevated health symptoms of their children (for example anxiety and depression) as support for such a relationship (Robinson and Post, 1995, 1997; Robinson and Kelley, 1998; Robinson, 1998).

Personal beliefs and fears

Burke (1999c) examined the relationship between personal beliefs and fears and workaholism. Beliefs and fears, a reflection of values, thoughts and interpersonal styles, have been shown to be precursors of Type A behaviour (Price, 1982). Three measures of beliefs and fears developed by Lee et al. (1996) were used. One, striving against others, had six items (for example 'There can only be one winner in any situation'). A second, no moral principles, had six items (for example, 'I think that nice guys finish last'). The third, prove yourself, had nine items (for example, 'I worry a great deal about what others think of me'). A total score was obtained by combining these three scales.

Burke (1999c) compared the three Spence and Robbins workaholic profiles on these measures of beliefs and fears. Was there a relationship between cognitions managers and professionals hold about their broader environment and levels of workaholism? Analyses provided evidence of such a relationship. First, all three beliefs and fears were significantly correlated with measures of feeling driven (positively) and work enjoyment (negatively). Second, comparisons of workaholism types showed significant type effects on all three measures of beliefs and fears as well as on their composite.

More specifically, work addicts scored significantly higher then work enthusiasts and enthusiastic addicts on measure of striving against others and no moral principles, as well as on the composite measure. In addition, work addicts scored higher on the need to prove self than did work enthusiasts. Workaholism thus emerges as work behaviours in response to feelings of low self-worth and insecurity. This is best reflected in managers' feelings of being driven to work. Paradoxically these beliefs and fears were also found to be associated with lower levels of work enjoyment.

Organizational values

Burke (1999d) compared perceptions of organization culture values supporting work–personal life balance across the three Spence and Robbins workaholism profiles. Organizational values encouraging work–family balance and imbalance were measured by scales proposed by Kofodimos (1993). Organizational values encouraging balance was measured by nine items (for example, 'Setting limits on hours spent at work'). Organizational values supporting imbalance was measured by eight items (for example; 'Traveling to and from work destinations on weekends'). A total balance score was obtained by combining both scales, reversing the imbalance scores.

There was considerable support for the hypothesized relationships. Work addicts reported lesser balance values than both work enthusiasts and enthusiastic addicts and greater imbalance values than work enthusiasts. In summary, work addicts see their workplaces as less supportive of work–personal life balance.

Work outcomes

The relationship between workaholism and indicators of job and career satisfaction and success is difficult to specify. It is likely that different types of workaholics will report varying work and career satisfactions (Scott et al., 1997).

Burke (1999e) compared levels of work and career satisfaction and success among the workaholism profiles observed by Spence and Robbins (1992). Four work outcomes, all significantly intercorrelated, were used. Intent to quit was measured by two items (for

374   *Stress, well-being and health*

example, 'Are you currently looking for a different job in a different organization?'). This scale had been used previously by Burke (1991). Work satisfaction was measured by a seven-item scale developed by Kofodimos (1993). One item was 'I feel challenged by my work.' Career satisfaction was measured by a five-item scale developed by Greenhaus *et al.* (1990). One item was 'I am satisfied with the success I have achieved in my career.' Future career prospects was measured by a three-item scale developed by Greenhaus *et al.* (1990). One item was 'I expect to advance in my career to senior levels of management.'

Work enthusiasts and enthusiastic addicts scored higher than work addicts on both job satisfaction and career satisfaction. In addition, work enthusiasts and enthusiastic addicts scored higher than work addicts on the measure of career prospects. Finally work enthusiasts scored lower than work addicts on the intent to quit measure. In summary work addicts scored lower than work enthusiasts and enthusiastic addicts on job satisfaction, career satisfaction and future career prospects and higher than work enthusiasts on intent to quit. Interestingly all three workaholic types worked the same number of hours per week.

Psychological well-being
There is considerable consensus in the workaholism literature on the association of workaholism and poorer psychological physical well-being. In fact, some definitions of workaholism incorporate aspects of diminished health as central elements. It is not surprising that this relationship has received research attention.

Burke (1999f) compared workaholism types identified by Spence and Robbins (1992) on three indicators of psychological and physical well-being. Data were obtained from 530 employed women and men MBAs using questionnaires. Psychosomatic symptoms was measured by 19 items developed by Quinn and Shepard (1974). Respondents indicated how often they experienced each physical condition (for example, 'headaches') in the past year. Lifestyle behaviours was measured by five items developed by Kofodimos (1993). One item was 'I participate in a regular exercise program.' Emotional well-being was measured by six items developed by Kofodimos (1993). One item was 'I actively seek to understand and improve my emotional well-being.'

The comparisons of the workaholism types on the three measures of psychological and physical well-being provided considerable support for the hypothesized relationships. Thus work enthusiasts and enthusiastic addicts had fewer psychosomatic symptoms than work addicts. In addition, work enthusiasts had more positive lifestyle behaviours than work addicts. Finally, work enthusiasts had more favourable emotional well-being than work addicts; enthusiastic addicts also had more favourable emotional well-being than work addicts. In summary, work addicts had more psychosomatic symptoms than both work enthusiasts and enthusiastic addicts and poorer physical and emotional well-being than work enthusiasts.

Haymon (1993), in a study of 253 male college students, found that students scoring higher on the Workaholic Addictive Checklist (WAC) also had significantly higher scores on depression, anxiety and anger than those scoring lower on the WAC. Kanai *et al.* (1996), using the workaholism triad components developed by Spence and Robbins in a sample of 1072 Japanese workers from ten companies, found that both work addicts and enthusiastic addicts reported more health complaints than did work enthusiasts. There were no differences between these three groups on measures of smoking, alcohol consumption and serious illness, however.

Spence and Robbins (1992), in a sample of men and women social work professors, noted that work addicts indicated more health complaints than did individuals in their other profiles. Elder and Spence (unpublished manuscript), in their study of women and men MBA graduates, observed that work addicts and enthusiastic addicts indicated more health complaints than did work enthusiasts. They also reported that work addicts were less satisfied with their jobs and lives than were enthusiastic addicts and work enthusiasts.

Extra-work satisfactions and family functioning
A number of writers have hypothesized that workaholism is likely to have a negative impact on family functioning (Killinger, 1991; Porter, 2001; Robinson, 2001). Empirical examinations of this hypothesis are unfortunately few. Robinson and Post (1997) report data from a sample of 107 self-identified workaholics (members of Workaholics Anonymous chapters in North America) who completed the WART and a family assessment instrument. Three levels of WART scores were compared. High scores differed from low and medium scores on six of the seven family assessment scales, indicating lower (poorer) family functioning in all cases.

Robinson (1998) also reviews the literature on children of workaholics. Robinson and Kelley (1998) asked 211 young adults (college students) to think back to their childhoods and rate the workaholism of their parents on the WART. Participants also completed measures of depression, anxiety, self-concept and locus of control. College students who perceived their parents as workaholics scored higher on depression and external locus of control. Children of workaholic fathers scored higher on anxiety than did children of non-workaholic fathers. Interestingly mothers' workaholism had no effect on these outcomes. Post and Robinson (1998) and Robinson and Rhoden (1998) attribute the distress of children of workaholic fathers to the presence of a diseased family system, more evidence that work addiction contributes to family dysfunction (Pietropinto, 1986).

Burke (1999g) considered the relationship of workaholism types identified by Spence and Robbins (1992) and extra-work satisfactions. Data were obtained from 530 employed women and men MBAs. Three aspects of life or extra-work satisfaction were included. Family satisfaction was measured by a seven-item scale developed by Kofodimos (1993). One item was 'I have a good relationships with my family members.' Friends satisfaction was measured by three items developed by Kofodimos (1993). One item was 'My friends and I do enjoyable things together.' Community satisfaction was measured by four items also developed by Kofodimos. A sample item was 'I contribute and give back to my community.'

The comparisons of the workaholism types on the three measures of life or extra-work satisfactions provided moderate support for the hypothesized relationships. First, work addicts reported less family satisfaction than did the two other workaholic types; second, work addicts reported less friend satisfaction than did work enthusiasts; third, work enthusiasts reported greater community satisfaction than did work addicts and enthusiastic addicts. Work addicts reported less satisfaction on all three measures than did work enthusiasts and less satisfaction on one (family) than did enthusiastic addicts.

Evaluating workaholism components

The three workaholism measures used in one or more research studies (that is, Haymon, Robinson, Spence and Robbins) all contain components or factors. Do each of these factors have similar and independent relationships with particular outcomes? Or might they have opposite relationships with some outcomes and no relationship with others?

Burke (1999h) considered the question of whether the workaholism triad components had different consequences. A research model was developed to guide both variable selection and analysis strategy. There have been suggestions that both personal and work-setting factors are antecedents of workaholic behaviours (Scott et al., 1997; Schaef and Fassel, 1988). Thus both individual difference characteristics and organizational factors were included for study. Five panels of predictor variables were considered. The first consisted of individual demographic characteristics (for example, age, gender, marital status). The second consisted of three measures of personal beliefs and fears (Lee et al., 1996). The third consisted of work situation demographic factors (for example, years with present employer, size of organization). The fourth included measures of perceived organizational values supporting work–life balance (Kofodimos, 1993). The fifth included the workaholism triad components (work involvement, feeling driven to work, work enjoyment). The important questions were whether the workaholism triad components would add significant increments in explained variance on particular work and personal well-being measures and, if they did, which of the workaholism triad components accounted for these increments.

Outcome measures included aspects of work satisfaction (for example, job satisfaction, career satisfaction, future career prospects, intent to quit), psychological well-being (psychosomatic symptoms, emotional well-being, lifestyle behaviours) and elements of life satisfaction (for example, family satisfaction, friends satisfaction, community satisfaction).

Though significantly intercorrelated, the three workaholism components had only moderate interrelationships, none of these correlations exceeding 0.25. The three workaholism components, considered together, almost always accounted for significant increments in explained variance on outcome measures, controlling for a number of personal and work-setting factors. The magnitude of these effects was larger on job behaviours and work outcomes likely to be evidenced by work addicts and smaller on psychological well-being and extra-work satisfactions. It is likely that the latter would be affected by a wider array of work and life experience, workaholism being only one of them.

An examination of the relationships among specific workaholism components and the various types of outcome variables revealed an interesting and complex pattern of findings. First, work enjoyment and feeling driven to work were significantly related to all seven job behaviour validation measures, while work involvement was significantly related to three of the seven. Respondents scoring higher on the workaholism components also scored higher on job behaviours reflecting workaholism, with one exception – difficulty in delegating. In this instance, respondents scoring higher on work involvement and feeling driven to work and lower on work enjoyment reported greater difficulty in delegating.

Second, joy in work was the only workaholism component related to work outcomes. Respondents reporting greater work enjoyment also reported more job satisfaction, more optimistic future career prospects and more career satisfaction to date. Third, both work enjoyment and feeling driven to work were related to indicators of psychological well-being, but in opposite directions. Respondents reporting greater work enjoyment and lesser feelings of being driven to work indicated more positive psychological well-being. Finally workaholism components had significant effects on only one of the three measures of extra-work satisfactions. Respondents reporting greater work involvement and lesser feelings of being driven to work reported greater community satisfaction.

Although work enjoyment and feeling driven to work had consistent and similar effects on job behaviours reflecting workaholism, these two workaholism components had different effects on work outcomes and psychological well-being. One, work enjoyment, was associated with positive outcomes; the other, feeling driven to work, was associated with negative outcomes. Finally none of the workaholism components showed consistent relationships with measures of extra-work satisfactions.

Gender differences
Spence and Robbins (1992) compared men and women social workers in academic positions on their workaholism triad (work involvement, feeling driven to work, work enjoyment), behavioural correlates (for example, perfectionism, non-delegation) and health complaints. In this sample, women scored significantly higher than men on feeling driven to work, work enjoyment, job stress, job involvement and time commitment scales; no differences were found on work involvement, perfectionism and nondelegation scales. Women also reported more health complaints.

Elder and Spence (unpublished manuscript) reported comparisons of men and women MBA graduates on these measures, along with a few others. Few differences were found. Men did score significantly higher than women on job involvement. There were also similar though not identical relationships among the measures for both genders. The three workaholism triad measures were significantly correlated for men; the feeling driven to work and work enjoyment scales were uncorrelated for women.

Doerfler and Kammer (1986) examined the relationships of levels of workaholism with both sex and sex role orientation (masculine, feminine, androgynous). They collected data from attorneys, physicians and psychologists. Workaholism was measured by the ten characteristics proposed by Machlowitz (1980). They reported that 23 per cent of their respondents were workaholics, consistent across the two sexes and three professional groups. Interestingly a majority of single workaholics were female, and female workaholics reported more masculine and androgynous characteristics than feminine characteristics.

Burke (1999a) compared responses of 277 men and 251 women in his study of workaholism. He first compared the prevalence of Spence and Robbins workaholism types separately in men and women. There were no significant gender differences in these distributions. Women and men fell into each of the six workaholism types to a similar degree. He then compared responses of these men and women on the three workaholism components and on a number of validating job behaviours. It is important first to examine gender differences on personal and situational characteristics before considering gender differences on the workaholism measures to put the latter into a larger context. Females and males were similar on a minority of the items: organizational level, organizational size and the proportion having worked part-time at some point in their careers. However there were considerably more statistically significant female–male differences on these demographic items. Males were older, more likely to be married, to be in longer marriages, more likely to have children, to have more children, had completed their MBA degrees earlier, were less likely to have gaps in their careers, earned higher incomes in 1995 and 1996, and had been in their present jobs and with their present employers a longer period of time. It should be noted that many of these demographic characteristics were themselves significantly correlated and the sample sizes of both female and males were large.

Female–male comparisons were undertaken on the three workaholism components as well as on the seven job behaviour validation measures. Significant differences were present on six of the ten measures. Females were less work-involved, devoted less time to their jobs, worked fewer hours and worked fewer extra hours but reported greater job stress and greater perfectionism than males. Females and males reported similar levels of work enjoyment, feeling driven to work, job involvement and difficulties in delegating.

Implications for our understanding of workaholism
The Spence and Robbins measures of workaholism components (work involvement, feeling driven to work, work enjoyment) were found to be reliable. In addition, factor analyses of the original 25 items generally reproduced the three factors identified by Spence and Robbins (1992), particularly in homogeneous samples of educated managerial and professional employees.

In addition the three workaholism types were found to differ from each other in predicted ways, providing support for this typology. There is more than one type of workaholic. Hours of work is one hallmark of a workaholic; the three workaholism types worked more hours, and more extra hours than did the three non-workaholic types. But the three workaholic types worked the same number of hours. Personal and work situation characteristics did not distinguish the three workaholism types. Workaholics come in all ages, marital and parental statuses, organizational levels and both genders. When differences among the three workaholism types were present, work addicts indicated the poorest outcomes and the most distress, work enthusiasts the best outcomes and the least distress. Work addicts resemble the traditional stereotype of the workaholic as first described by Oates (1971).

The workaholism triad components had different relationships, with different consequences. Feeling driven was generally negatively related to health outcomes; work enjoyment, not surprisingly, was related positively to work outcomes.

Although research on workaholism is on the increase, it is still a relatively underresearched area of study. Few studies have been undertaken outside of North America, a situation that is slowly being remedied, so the generalizability of North American findings must be determined.

Future research directions
Future research on workaholism must move beyond self-report questionnaires. It is also important not to make value judgments about workaholism (workaholism produces negative outcomes). A wider range of variables needs to be studied (extra-work experiences, lifestyle behaviours and other work responses). More innovative data collection strategies using time diaries, triangulated data sources (self-reports, spouse and co-worker reports) and objective measures of work and non-work performance (performance data, salary increases) need to be incorporated in our research programmes. There is also a need for more research to be undertaken in non-North American countries.

McMillan et al. (2001) propose four research design strategies to increase our understanding of workaholism: contrasted group designs, alternating treatment designs, longitudinal studies and broad sampling techniques. Contrasted group designs would provide information on how workaholic behaviour differs from non-workaholic behaviour at work and outside work. Alternating treatment designs would offer the possibility of determining how different treatments or interventions affect workaholism. Such before and after designs would indicate how different conditions affect workaholism. Longitudinal studies would allow researchers to chart the course of workaholism over time. Finally comparisons across organizations, professions, cultures and countries would provide data on prevalence rates among different populations and economies.

Treating workaholism

Although some writers address the treatment of workaholism, we believe that such writing may be premature. Our sense is that the treatment literature merely takes the same techniques and approaches used earlier to address other difficulties (for example, alcoholism, marital difficulties) and applies them to workaholism. More research is needed on workaholism before one can come to grips with what needs to be treated and how this might be undertaken.

It is also important to consider both statistical and practical significance of the differences reported between workaholism types (or workaholics and non-workaholics). A small statistically significant difference may have practical consequences. Thus a 5 per cent difference in poorer health or a 1 per cent difference in relationship satisfaction between work addicts and work enthusiasts (or workaholics and non-workaholics) may represent important differences in people's quality of life.

Notes

1. This research was supported in part by the School of Business, York University. I thank Janet Spence for making her measures available to me. Graeme Macdermid assisted with data collection and analysis; Louise Coutu prepared the manuscript.
2. Owing to space constraints the measures will not be described. Interested readers can find a detailed description of all measures used in this study in my publications, listed in the references.

References

Burke, R.J. (1991), 'Early work and career experiences of female and male managers: reasons for optimism?', *Canadian Journal of Administrative Sciences*, **8**, 224–30.
Burke, R.J. (1999a), 'Workaholism in organizations: gender differences', *Sex Roles*, **41**, 333–45.
Burke, R.J. (1999b), 'Workaholism in organizations: measurement validation and replication', *International Journal of Stress Management*, **6**, 45–55.
Burke, R.J. (1999c), 'Workaholism in organizations: the role of personal beliefs and fears', *Anxiety, Stress and Coping*, **14**, 1–12.
Burke, R.J. (1999d), 'Workaholism in organizations: the role of organizational values', *Personnel Review*, **30**, 637–45.
Burke, R.J. (1999e), 'Are workaholics job satisfied and successful in their careers?', *Career Development International*, **26**, 149–58.
Burke, R.J. (1999f), 'Workaholism in organizations: psychological and physical well-being consequences', *Stress Medicine*, **16**, 11–16.
Burke, R.J. (1999g), 'Workaholism and extra-work satisfactions', International Journal of Organizational Analysis, **7**, 352–64.
Burke, R.J. (1999h), 'It's not how hard you work but how you work hard: evaluating workaholism components', *International Journal of Stress Management*, **6**, 225–39.

Bonebright, C.A., D.L. Clay and R.D. Ankenmann (2000), 'The relationship of workaholism with work–life conflict, life satisfaction, and purpose in life', *Journal of Counseling Psychology*, **47**, 469–77.
Cherrington, D.J. (1980), *The Work Ethic*, New York: American Management Association.
Doerfler, M.C. and P.P. Kammer (1986), 'Workaholism; sex and sex role sterotyping among female professionals', *Sex Roles*, **14**, 551–60.
Elder, E.D. and J.T. Spence, 'Workaholism in the business world: work addiction versus work-enthusiasm in MBAs', unpublished manuscript, Department of Psychology, University of Texas at Austin.
Fassel, D. (1990), *Working Ourselves to Death: The High Costs of Workaholism, the Rewards of Recovery*, San Francisco, CA: Harper Collins.
Garfield, C.A. (1987), *Peak Performers: The New Heroes of American Business*, New York: William Morrow.
Greenhaus, J.H., S. Parasuraman and W. Wormley (1990), 'Organizational experiences and career success of black and white managers', *Academy of Management Journal*, **33**, 64–86.
Haymon, S. (1993), 'The relationship of work addiction and depression, anxiety, and anger in college males', doctoral dissertation, Florida State University, *Dissertation Abstracts International* **53**, 5401–B.
Kanai, A., M. Wakabayashi and S. Fling (1996), 'Workaholism among employees in Japanese corporations: an examination based on the Japanese version of the workaholism scales', Japanese Psychological Research, **38**, 192–203.
Kiechel, W. (1989a), 'The workaholic generation', *Fortune*, 10 April, 50–62.
Kiechel, W. (1989b), 'Workaholics anonymous', *Fortune*, 14 August, 117–18.
Killinger, B. (1991), *Workaholics: The Respectable Addicts*, New York: Simon & Schuster.
Klaft, R.P. and B.H. Kleiner, (1988), 'Understanding workaholics', *Business*, **33**, 37–40.
Kofodimos, J. (1993), *Balancing Act*, San Francisco, CA: Jossey-Bass.
Korn, E.R., G.J. Pratt and P.T. Lambrou, (1987), *Hyper-performance; The A.I.M. Strategy for Releasing your Business Potential* New York: John Wiley.
Lee, C., L.F. Jamieson and P.C. Earley (1996), 'Beliefs and fears and Type A behavior: implications for academic performance and psychiatric health disorder symptoms', *Journal of Organizational Behavior*, **17**, 151–78.
Machlowitz, M. (1980), *Workaholics: Living with them, Working with them*, Reading, MA: Addison-Wesley.
McMillan, L.H.W., N.V. Marsh and M.P. O'Driscoll (2002), 'Workaholism and obsessive compulsiveness: where does the boundary lie?', unpublished manuscript, Department of Psychology, University of Waikato, New Zealand.
McMillan, L.H.W., M.P. O'Driscoll and R.J. Burke (2003), 'Workaholism in organizations: a review of theory, research and future direction', in C.L. Cooper and I.T. Robertson (eds), *International Review of Industrial and Organizational Psychology*, New York: John Wiley, pp. 167–90.
McMillan, L.H.W., E.C. Brady, M.P. O'Driscoll and N.V. Marsh (2002), 'A multifaceted validation study of Spence and Robbins' (1992) workaholism battery', *Journal of Occupational and Organizational Psychology*, **75**, 357–68.
McMillan, L.W.H., M.P. O'Driscoll, N.V. Marsh and E.C. Brady (2001), 'Understanding workaholism: data synthesis, theoretical critique, and future design strategies', *International Journal of Stress Management*, **8**, 69–92.
Mosier, S.K. (1983), 'Workaholics: an analysis of their stress, success and priorities', unpublished masters thesis, University of Texas at Austin.
Naughton, T.J. (1987), 'A conceptual view of workaholism and implications for career counseling and research', *The Career Development Quarterly*, **14**, 180–87.
Oates, W. (1971), *Confessions of a Workaholic: The Facts about Work Addiction*, New York: World.
Perlow, L.A. (1997), *Finding Time: How Corporations, Individuals, and Families can Benefit from New Work Practices*, Ithaca, NY: Cornell University Press.
Pietropinto, A. (1986), 'The workaholic spouse', *Medical Aspects of Human Sexuality*, **20**, 89–96.
Porter, G. (1996), 'Organizational impact of workaholism: suggestions for researching the negative outcomes of excessive work', *Journal of Occupational Health Psychology*, **1**, 70–84.
Porter, G. (2001), 'Workaholics as high-performance employees: the intersection of workplace and family relationship problems', in B.E. Robinson and N. Chase (eds), *High-performing Families: Causes, Consequences and Clinical solutions*, New York: John Wiley, pp. 43–69.
Post, P. and B.E. Robinson (1998), 'School-age children of alcoholics and non-alcoholics: their anxiety, self-esteem and locus of control', *Professional School Counselling*, **1**, 36–40.
Price, V.A. (1982), 'What is Type A behavior? A cognitive social learning model', *Journal of Occupational Behavior*, **3**, 109–30.
Quinn, R.P. and L.J. Shepard (1974), *The 1972–73 Quality of Employment Survey*, Ann Arbor, MI: Institute of Social Research, University of Michigan.
Robbins, A.S. (1993), 'Patterns of workaholism in developmental psychologists', unpublished manuscript, Department of Psychology, University of Texas at Austin.

Robinson, B.E. (1997), 'Work addiction and the family: conceptual and research considerations', *Early Child Development and Care*, **137**, 77–92.
Robinson, B.E. (1998), *Chained to the Desk: a Guidebook for Workaholics, Their Partners and Children and the Clinicians who Treat them*, New York: New York University Press.
Robinson, B.E. (1999), 'Spouses of workaholics: clinical implications for psychotherapy', *Psychotherapy*, **35**, 260–68.
Robinson, B.E. (2001), 'Workaholism and family functioning: a profile of familial relationships, psychological outcomes and research considerations', *Contemporary Family Therapy*, **23**, 123–35.
Robinson, B.E. and L. Kelley (1998), 'Adult children of workaholics: self-concept, anxiety, depression, and locus of control', *American Journal of Family Therapy*, **26**, 35–50.
Robinson, B.E. and B. Phillips (1995), 'Measuring workaholism: content validity of the Work Addiction Risk Test', *Psychological Reports*, **77**, 657–8.
Robinson, B.E. and P. Post (1994), 'Validity of the Work Addiction Risk Test', *Perceptual and Motor Skills*, **78**, 337–8.
Robinson, B.E. and P. Post (1997), 'Risk of work addiction to family functioning', *Psychological Reports*, **81**, 91–5.
Robinson, B.E. and L. Rhoden (1998), *Working with Children of Alcoholics: the Practitioner's Handbook*, 2 ed, Beverly Hills, CA: Sage Publications.
Schaef, A.W. and D. Fassel (1988), *The Addictive Organization*, San Francisco, CA: Harper Row.
Schor, J.B. (1991), *The Overworked American*, New York: Basic Books.
Scott, K.S., K.S. Moore and M.P. Miceli (1997), 'An exploration of the meaning and consequences of workaholism', *Human Relations*, **50**, 287–314.
Seybold, K.C. and P.R. Salomone (1994), 'Understanding workaholism: a view of causes and counseling approaches', *Journal of Counseling and Development*, **73**, 4–9.
Spence, J.T. and A.S. Robbins (1992), 'Workaholism: definition, measurement, and preliminary results', *Journal of Personality Assessment*, **58**, 160–78.
Sprankle, J.K. and H. Ebel (1987), *The Workaholic Syndrome.* New York: Walker Publishing.
Waddell, J.R. (1993), 'The grindstone', *Supervision*, **26**, 11–13.

25 The healthy organization
Jane Henry

Introduction
Positive psychology
The recent positive psychology movement (Seligman and Csikszentmihalyi, 2000) argues that psychologists need to give attention to studying success and excellence, to balance the essentially negative orientation of studying failure and fixing deficiency, which permeates much of psychology. To date positive psychologists have focused primarily on positive strengths and experiences at the individual level (through studies of optimism, resilience, self-efficacy, positive affect, satisfaction and meaning, for example) and positive approaches to community development. The author believes there is an equal case for focusing on positive approaches at the group and organizational levels.

In organizational psychology, as with the discipline more generally, much theory is framed negatively with a view to fixing deficiency and failure. For example the traditional management role is reactive: managers solve problems and trouble shoot; most organizations now work from a competency framework that orients much of their training to inputting missing skills, and empirical work often majors on the negative, addressing problems of stress, burnout, glass ceilings and lack of career development opportunities, for example. In contrast much of the organization consultants' rhetoric (like the self-help literature) takes a positive orientation, advising organisations to adopt vision and mission statements (language borrowed from spiritual discourse), to adopt win–win negotiation, model best practice and encourage managers to forgive mistakes and seek partnership with erstwhile competitors. So, though there is a negative orientation in organizational psychology and organizational rhetoric, it is not nearly as all-encompassing as in other areas of applied psychology such as clinical, educational and health psychology.

Well-being at work
Given that full-time workers can spend around half their waking hours at work, it becomes an important avenue for health. Work is known to play a large part in people's sense of well-being. Flow, a state of mind associated with well-being, is characterized by activities involving challenging skills (Csikszentmihalyi and Csikszentmihalyi, 1988), and found in work and leisure situations, though more frequently at work among professional and craftsmen than white-collar workers (Delle Fave, 2001). With the exception of the voluntarily retired with sufficient funds, those in work tend to rate their well-being, in terms of life satisfaction, higher than those who are unemployed (Haworth, 1997). Jahoda (1982) argued that work was one, if not the main, avenue for social identity, time structuring, collective purpose, social relations and social support, and that together these were key constituents of well-being.

Life satisfaction measures have changed little since the 1950s, though GDP has gone up threefold over the same period (Myers, 2000). It seems that, above a certain basic minimum level of comfort, satisfaction is not related to income. Other factors are more important, these include the amount of coherence between one's values, goals and activities and the amount of control one has over one's activities.

Traditional working practices can seem somewhat inhuman in that command and control systems offer staff little control over their working lives and humans are known to be less stressed when in control of their own destiny. Control over one's life is positively related to well-being. However over the last 50 years, working practices have changed considerably. In particular there has been a shift to more participatory working practices that would appear to offer employees greater control and therefore one might expect that well-being would be enhanced as a consequence.

In a series of studies, Warr (1987, 1999) has shown that well-being at work is influenced by a series of individual and situational variables. Disposition is an important individual factor. Indeed Straw *et al.* (1986) found that affective disposition in junior high school was a moderately good predictor of satisfaction at work in middle age, with a correlation over 0.3. As regards environmental variables influence on well-being, Warr (1987) cites nine factors: opportunity for control, environmental clarity (including feedback and predictability), opportunity for skill use, externally generated goals, variety, opportunity for interpersonal contact, valued social position, availability of money and physical security.

The relationship between these environmental factors and well-being is not necessarily linear as the effects can vary according to the degree to which the variables are present. For example, while some opportunity for control and skill use generally improves well-being, too much can be experienced as coercion, with a corresponding decline in the sense of well-being. Just such a mechanism may be a contributory factor in the recent decline in some measures of satisfaction at work (White, 2001). It is assumed that people are reacting against heavy workloads, enhanced levels of control or scrutiny brought about by the widespread adoption of quality systems in the private sector and performance measures in the public sector, coupled with a perceived decrease in the level of job security, and, in some areas, less opportunity for promotion as a result of to middle management 'downsizing'.

In considering factors that might contribute to a healthy organization in this chapter we look at certain individual, group, organization and interorganizational variables.

Individual

A healthy organization might be expected to respect its employees, offer reasonable remuneration and conditions, and some prospects for development. Interventions designed to improve the psychological health of the employees and through them the organization as a whole include attempts to enrich jobs, improve and align motivation, build in feedback and recognition, increase participation and responsibility and offer opportunities for personal and professional development. Whether a happy worker is an effective one is open to question. The Human Relations school of management had hoped that a satisfied worker would be an efficient one, but Judge *et al.*'s (2001) major meta-analysis suggests that the correlation between job satisfaction and performance is only around 0.3.

Personal development

One area that appears to suggest a healthy approach is the current emphasis on personal and professional development. Many organizations and professional groups require staff to undertake a small amount of CPD (continuing professional development) each year, often around five days. The introduction of IIP (Investors in People) has drawn attention to the importance of individualized development needs, and a statement of an individual's personal needs are now often included in their annual appraisal/coaching session. This may give the employee some control over the training and development they get to take.

Though professional development may be concerned with acquiring skills, competencies and technical expertise, a lot of personal development training tends to relate to ways of understanding the self and developing more sophisticated ways of relating to others. Given that activities in organizations usually involve groups, this emphasis on people is not so surprising.

Existing management training devotes quite a lot of time to what could be classed as teaching the rudiments of wisdom (characterized by Lao Tsu millennia ago as understanding yourself and others). Managers are often offered courses in self-awareness and self-development alongside personal and interpersonal skills. Almost invariably training includes the completion of one or more personality inventories (for example NEO, MBTI, LSI) designed to acquaint staff with their and their colleagues' cognitive style, personality type and role preference and to familiarize them with the consequences for preferred ways of communicating, working, problem solving, decision taking, leadership and the like. Generally such training is done in groups so participants get the chance to contrast their style with their colleagues'. This '360 degree training' offers an individual the opportunity to see whether peers, subordinates and superior staff rate their characteristics and abilities as they would themselves.

This kind of development training not only enables people to understand and communicate with colleagues more appropriately but can also lead to a healthy tolerance of diversity and acceptance of self.

Organizations are also often quick to try new approaches. One example is the speed with which emotional intelligence has been taken up (Salovey and Mayer, 1990). In discussing emotional intelligence, Goleman (1995) highlights the importance of self-awareness, self-regulation, motivation, empathy and social skill in management capability, an emphasis which serves to draw attention to previously somewhat neglected non-cognitive aspects of relating.

Alongside the acceptance of the need for an element of individualized development, the move to targets and performance indicators pushes in the opposite direction to a standardized system. Nowadays training is often fitted into a competency framework. If the system is a rigid one staff may be required to go through certain courses whether or not they feel the need to, and be sent on courses to input competencies they are deemed to need or lack rather than necessarily those that appeal to them.

Building on strengths
Positive psychology has challenged the essentially negative orientation to development present in much applied psychology and epitomized in the use of competency training. It champions the opposite approach of building on strengths. Gallup for instance, identify 34 possible strengths and talents, which can be grouped under four themes: relating, for example communication, empathy; thinking, for example analytical, strategic; striving,

for example adaptability, focus; and impact, for example positivity, command (Coffman and Gonzalez-Molina, 2002). Their advice to individuals is to concentrate on jobs where they can exploit their five or six major strengths and worry less about trying to learn skills in areas where they have little natural talent. The appeal is not so much the specified talents which are similar to traits and capabilities managers are familiar with but the idea of building on strengths rather than focusing on trying to make good deficiencies. Work on the 'Big Five' personality factors – sociability, agreeableness, conscientiousness, openness and neuroticism (Goldberg, 1993) – supports the idea that certain personality variables may be at least partly genetically underpinned. If so it may be far easier, more satisfying and effective for staff to exploit their strengths rather than try to learn to work in ways that are not in accord with their natural forte.

A possible critique of the strengths approach is that it pays little attention to the downside inherent in almost any trait: humour may be fun but it can also get people into trouble. One of the advantages of the most widely used personality inventory in business, the MBTI (Myers Briggs Type Indicator), is that it is a measure of style and each style is framed as having strengths and weaknesses (Bayne, 1994). For example, those with a moderate to high judging preference on the MBTI (high conscientiousness on the 'Big Five') may be focused, well organized and good at meeting deadlines but adaptability may come less readily. In contrast, those with a moderate to high perceiving preference on the MBTI (low conscientiousness on the 'Big Five') may maintain a number of diverse interests and be late handing over material, but are usually good at adapting to change (Hirsch, 1985). A framework such as this, that leads people to understand and value difference, seems very healthy and it is one that seems to help build respect and tolerance.

Confidence and forgiveness
One of the key variables positive psychology has examined is self-efficacy or confidence in one's ability to do a task Bandura (2000). Bandura has shown how positive feedback on progress, modelling success and mastery experiences at work all serve to develop confidence. The importance of confidence and morale is generally well appreciated in organizations. Managers are encouraged to recognize good work individually and collectively, both verbally, via public recognition and through financial and other awards.

Another variable positive psychology has begun to examine is forgiveness (McCullough and Witvliet, 2002). Innovation researchers have long known that experimentation entails the risk of mishap and management gurus have been encouraging managers to forgive mistakes as a means of encouraging creativity (Handy, 1993). In reality forgiving errors can be hard, whether one is inside or outside an organization, and managers do not always manage 'to walk the talk'; nevertheless people in organizations appreciate the need to do so.

Similarly it is rarely easy to be kind, considerate and relate skilfully with everyone we meet, whether in or out of work. The emphasis on personal development and interpersonal skills in most organizations suggests a certain psychological maturity that aims to help individuals to deal with each other in a healthier manner than they might otherwise have done. This is more likely if management sets a good example in this respect. Kanter (1997) has suggested employees are now attracted to organizations that share their values. Commitment is much easier if there such is a match.

Group

A healthy group could be characterized as one that respects its members, takes time to listen to their views, tolerates different styles and aims for win–win solutions (where all parties benefit) where possible.

Team building

There is an appreciation in organizations that groups are central to most of their endeavours; also that teams take time to bond and may need a little nurturing. Indeed organizations often build in time for valued new groups to build teams by paying for the team to go offsite for a weekend for example and the canny manager arranges social get-togethers with a similar end in view.

Feeling you belong to a team is central to most people's sense of well-being. Bonded teams offer members social support and can satisfy a need to belong. Team working has been shown to enhance the well-being of members (Sonnetag, 1996). People working in teams have also been shown to report better psychological health than those working alone (Carter and West, 1999).

Training

Group training generally exhibits a healthy stress on identifying, accepting and working with diversity: for example, showing that group members with different cognitive styles may work and communicate in different ways but that all are valuable, and that, though group members may favour different work roles, successful groups are more likely to contain a mix of personality types (Belbin, 1981; Margerison and McCann, 1990).

Groups are recognized as central to most organizational endeavour and most large organizations have in place training that should enable staff to appreciate group processes and help develop communication skills designed to deal with difficult situations. Though present in the literature, the effects of group dynamics are perhaps less well known at grassroots level (Bion, 1961). It may be that a wider appreciation of the effects of psychodynamics would alert staff to power issues and defensiveness that, if appreciated, would lead workgroups to psychologically healthier ways of relating and smarter communication, as Argyris (1994) has argued.

Creative thinking

Healthy organizations should be open to creative challenges from members. Recently organizations have attempted to draw out the creativity in their staff through attempts to open their culture and introduce various participatory initiatives such as focus groups, alongside suggestion schemes and the like (Henry, 2001).

Psychologists know that people are more likely to explore new territory if they feel safe. Fredrikson's (2002) broaden and build theory shows how experiences of positive emotion tend to broaden the search strategies available to the mind and how a sense of threat can narrow the options considered. Amabile (1983) is one of those who has highlighted the importance of allowing staff to follow their intrinsic motivation if they are to be creative (Mitchell, 1991). Companies such as 3M have allowed their scientific staff a proportion of work-time (15 per cent) for projects of their own choosing. *Post-it* pads came from such a project (Nayak and Ketteringham, 1986). Creativity normally takes persistence and this is easier if one cares about the area. Creativity training encourages staff to reframe negative beliefs positively, for example through the 'yes and' technique, which encourages people to focus on how they can advance an issue despite constraints, and so maintain a more optimistic outlook.

It seems a certain openness and flexibility at work is better placed to enhance organizational creativity and many individuals' sense of well-being than excessive caution and rules.

Organization

One would hope a healthy organization would at a minimum offer reasonable working conditions, be considerate of its employees and open to challenge.

Satisfaction and control

One variable associated with health is control over one's own life. Traditional 'command and control' organizations seem to grant staff little control. The manager determines what staff do and when and employs sanctions if they fail to comply. This lack of delegated authority effectively treats staff as children who needed to be told what to do. It does not seem to be very healthy as it promotes passivity and offers workers little control over their lives. Lack of control over one's activities is generally associated with higher levels of stress and lower levels of satisfaction.

Over the last 50 years, organizational practice has shifted. Bureaucratic chains of command are generally slow and less well-placed to meet the fast response often required in today's competitive environment. Many organizations have attempted to engage and empower workers to varying degrees, partly to be in a position to react more quickly to market demand.

Project-based management where temporary multidisciplinary teams come together for particular projects is increasingly common. Organizations increasingly allow an element of flexi-time, where staff have some flexibility over when they work, and tele-work, where staff have the chance to work at home or on the move rather than in the office for some of their work time. ICT (information and communication technologies) such as e-mail, cell/mobile phones, laptop computers and the Internet mean the office is less central to work than previously in many sectors. In short, there has been a shift to more participatory and in some ways more flexible forms of organization and towards transformational leadership. In countries such as the UK, this has taken place alongside long working hours and an increase in some forms of employee scrutiny introduced through quality and performance management systems. There is also greater job insecurity. One might expect the increase in participatory forms of working to have increased job satisfaction, but this is not universally so. As explained earlier, increases in perceived workload, scrutiny and insecurity seem largely to account for the decline in job satisfaction (Taylor, 2002).

Management fads

Organizations devote considerable effort towards making themselves more efficient and happy places to work in. Indeed the last 50 years have been characterized by a succession of management fads often claiming to fix organizational ills. Managers can be criticized for an almost too eager adoption of these many cure-alls, from management by objectives, through quality and re-engineering to knowledge management and the learning organization. Whilst fads such as re-engineering came to be discredited, not least through an association with 'downsizing', fads like enterprise cultures, empowerment, the learning organization (Senge, 1991), emotional intelligence (Goleman, 1995), and the appreciation of the role of tacit knowledge (Nonaka and Takeuchi, 1995) have probably played their part in humanizing practice in large organizations.

Open culture
The need to survive in an increasingly competitive and global market-place has enhanced interest in open enterprise cultures that appeared to thrive when others floundered. Open cultures are associated with sustained creativity and innovation in organizations. These offer an organizational culture or climate where staff feel free to challenge the status quo and mistakes are forgiven (for example Ekvall, 1997). As with any form of organization, there are swings and roundabouts to open cultures. Jelinek and Schoonhaven (1991) describe how these more open climates typically entail more meetings and more open disagreement, which takes time and is not to everyone's taste.

It must be added that it is a mistake to assume that there is one single type of healthy organization. Some evidence suggest, that different personality types favour different types of organizational culture. For example, Ekvall (1997) contrasted the culture favoured by adaptors, who tend to prefer working in tried and tested ways and improving existing practice, and innovators, who like to challenge existing practice and do things differently. He found production workers, who tended to have more adaptive personalities, favoured the former whereas those in research departments, who tended to be more innovative, preferred more open climates.

Equally, different national cultures have different norms for favoured ways of relating (Hofstede, 1984). For example, Smith and Bond (1993) showed differences in Anglo-Saxon and Chinese approaches to dealing with a team member facing personal difficulties. The considerate supervisor in Japan and Hong Kong would discuss matters indirectly with other members of the team in the individual's absence, whereas in the USA and the UK the same behaviour was seen as most inconsiderate and direct communication was seen as more appropriate. Equally the open culture championed in Anglo-Saxon quarters may fair less well or need considerable adaption to fit cultures in parts of India, Africa, South-east Asia and South America, where high power distance is the norm. So the healthy organization needs to change its flavour as it moves around the world.

Self-organization
Some organizations have moved considerably further down the empowerment road, allowing staff effectively to 'self-organize': for example, to set their own hours, appraise bosses, buy equipment, select and hire staff, deal directly with customers, adopt open accounting (which allows staff access to company finances), limit memo length, claim expenses and even in some cases set their own share of the profits and wages and abolish corporate departments such as personnel and quality. Dutton, a small British engineering company, Oticon, a small-to-medium Danish hearing aid company and Semco a medium-sized Brazilian pump manufacturer are three exponents of this shift. Staff satisfaction in companies that have abolished red tape in this way appears to be very high

(Semler, 1994; Lewis and Lytton, 1995). Organizational defensiveness also seems much less problematic in organizations that have truly empowered staff. However these companies tend to be small or medium in size; larger companies need to coordinate their efforts and it remains to be seen how far self-organization can be applied in such settings.

Nevertheless there is a long-term trend towards more participatory working practices and more open cultures that one would expect to produce healthier organizations, provided the workload is not too onerous and staff have sufficient freedom on how they set about their work. As against these positive steps towards healthy organization, there are plenty of reports of work–life balance problems, staff complaining of stress, long hours, inappropriate targets, unhelpful and increased paper work and in some sectors poor morale, which suggests anything but healthy organization.

In addition politics and vested interests remain part of any organization or grouping. It is argued here that the healthier organization can cope with being open about differences of opinion and is seen to treat differences fairly. Other helpful practices include being seen to reward people for performance, not position or influence, and treating errors and failure as an opportunity for learning. One measure of a healthy organization is a relatively low level of absenteeism and sickness and, in many cases, low staff turnover. Another is the number of suggestions offered by employees.

Interorganization
Increasingly the boundaries of organizations are becoming more fluid and relations across organizations can become as important as those within it.

Partnerships
In the 21st century attention has turned to cross-organizational systems, such as partnerships between competitors, relationships across the supply chain and networking by employees outside the organization. Partnerships between car manufacturers such as Ford and Fiat have enabled them to develop cars jointly, subsequently badged under their separate labels, with considerable savings on development costs. In the private sector, many organizations have found it beneficial to adopt the Japanese system of establishing long-term relationships with a group of suppliers rather than accepting the lowest tender. A long-term relationship makes it more likely that the supplier can invest in staff and resources appropriate to the buyer's requirements. Lewis and Lytton (1995) claim these relationship are easier where there is a match of culture between the organization and its supplier(s).

Networking
Historically we have concentrated on health inside the head of the employee (as in guarding against stress, allowing time for individuals to develop a sense of ownership and encouraging organizational climates where employees feel able to challenge the status quo). Complexity theory's meta-perspective on system dynamics suggests that a lot of the attempts to manage and control organizational dynamics are misguided and unhelpful. The theory points out that agents in any adaptive system, including people in organizations, are naturally creative if left to their own devices, but that it is very difficult to predict what form that creativity will take; and, further, that an element of redundancy tends to

be associated with more robust and therefore healthier systems. Lean approaches may be efficient in the short run but are rarely optimal in the longer term. From this perspective the manager's job changes to one more concerned with facilitating individual networking within, outside and across organizations, minimizing interference and helping to provide resources when required, rather than planning activities in advance and policing others' work (Stacy, 1996). This seems reminiscent of the approach taken in companies who have adopted self-organization:

> Now I look carefully at how a workplace organizes its relationships . . . the time I formerly spent on detailed planning and analysis I now use to look at structures that might facilitate relationships. I have come to expect that something useful occurs if I link up people, units, tasks even though I cannot determine the precise outcomes. I realize more and more that the universe will not co-operate with my desire for determinism. (Wheatley, 1994, p. 43–4)

Community involvement
Perhaps another measure of healthy organizations is the extent to which they engage with their community. Organizations such as The Body Shop, Whitbread and GE Plastics have programmes that involve staff in some form of community involvement: teaching the underprivileged, renovating buildings or helping in some other way. Companies who have adopted this kind of scheme claim that such opportunities are valued by staff, enhance motivation, act as good development training and are excellent vehicles for team building.

Conclusion
A large proportion of the population spends a significant percentage of its life working for organizations, and work often acts as a major source of individual well-being. Healthy organizations can enhance that experience through humane working practices such as democratizing the environment and adopting participatory working practices. Much personal, interpersonal and group training already encourages healthy relationships; moves to more flexible working environments offer further hope of healthier working environments, provided pressure of work and the policing of targets do not become too intrusive. Self-organized companies show considerable promise as a model of healthy organization. Positive approaches to individual, group and organisational development have much, largely untapped potential.

The perennial challenge in organizations is to allow as much freedom as possible while coordinating activities effectively. The new challenge is to maintain healthy organizational practices and thrive in today's changeable and competitive market-place. Healthy organizations need to find the right balance for their particular situation, sector and culture. Globally the trend seems to be moving towards more openness and transparency, which psychology would suggest is a healthy direction to be heading in. Nevertheless further research into organizational practices that lead to positive work experiences is required, as many of us spend a lot of time in organizations we view as far from healthy and feel that work encroaches on personal life in an unhealthy way.

References
Amabile, T. (1983), *The Social Psychology of Creativity*, New York: Springer Verlag.
Argyris, C. (1994), 'Communication that blocks learning', *Harvard Business Review*, July/August, 77–85.

Bandura, A. (2000), 'Cultivate self-efficacy for personal and organisational effectiveness', in E.A. Locke (ed.), *Blackwell Handbook of Principles of Organisational Behaviour*, Oxford: Blackwell, pp. 120–36.
Bayne, R. (1994), 'The Big Five versus the Myers-Biggs', *Psychologist*, January, 14–16.
Belbin, R.M. (1981), *Management Teams: Why They Succeed or Fail*, Oxford: Heinemann.
Bion, W. (1961), *Experiences in Groups*, London: Tavistock.
Carter, A.J. and M.A. West (1999), 'Sharing the burden: teamwork in health-care settings', in R.L. Payne and J. Firth-Cozens (eds), *Stress in Health Care Professionals*, Chichester: Wiley, pp. 191–202.
Coffman, C. and G. Gonzalez-Molina (2002), *Follow this Path*, New York: Gallup.
Csikszentmihalyi, M. and I. Csikszentmihalyi, (1988), *Optimal Experience: Psychological Studies in the Flow of Consciousness*, New York: Cambridge University Press.
Deiner, E., E.M. Suh, R.E. Lucas and H.L. Smith (1999), 'Subjective well-being: Three decades of progress', *Psychological Bulletin*, **125**, 276–302.
Delle Fave, A. (2001), 'Flow and optimal experience', presentation to ESRC Individual and Situational Determinants of Well-being Seminar 3: Work and well-being, Manchester Metropolitan University.
Ekvall, G. (1997), 'Organisational conditions and level of creativity', *Creativity and Innovation Management*, **6**, 195–205.
Fredrikson, B. (2002), 'Positive emotions', in C.R. Synder and J. Lopez (eds), *Handbook of Positive Psychology*, Oxford: Oxford University Press, pp. 120–34.
Goldberg, L.R. (1993), 'The structure of phenotypic personality traits', *American Psychologist*, **48**, 26–43.
Goleman, D. (1995), *Emotional Intelligence*, New York: Bantam.
Handy, C. (1993), 'Trust', *Harvard Business Review*, 40–50.
Haworth, J. (1997), *Work, Leisure and Well-being*, London: Routledge.
Henry, J. (2001a), *Creativity and Perception in Management*, London: Sage.
Henry, J. (2001b), *Creative Management*, 2nd edn, London: Sage.
Henry, J. and D.T. Mayle (2002), *Managing Innovation and Change*, London: Sage.
Henry, J. and D. Walker (eds) (1991), *Managing Innovation*, London: Sage.
Hirsch, S.K. (1985), *Using the Myers-Briggs Type Indicator in Organisations*, Oxford: Oxford Psychologists Press.
Hofstede, G. (1984), *Cultures Consequences: International Differences in Work-related Values*, Beverly Hills, CA: Sage.
Jahoda, M. (1982), *Employment and Unemployment: A Social Psychological Analysis*, Cambridge: Cambridge University Press.
Jelinek, M. and C.B. Schoonhaven (1991), 'Strong culture and its consequences', in J. Henry and D. Walker (eds), *Managing Innovation*, London: Sage.
Judge, T.A., C.J. Thoresen, J.E. Bono and G.K. Patton (2001), 'The job satisfaction – job performance relationship: a qualitative and quantitative review', *Psychological Bulletin*, **127**(3), 376–407.
Kanter, R.M. (1997), 'Restoring people to the heart of the organization', in F. Hesselebein, M. Goldsmith and R. Beckhard (eds), *The Organization of the Future*, Drucker Foundation.
Lewis, K. and S. Lytton (1995), *How to Transform your Company and Enjoy It*, Oxford: Management Books.
Margerison, C. and D. McCann (1990), *Team Management*, London: Mercury.
McCullough, M.E. and C.V. Witvliet (2002), 'The psychology of forgiveness', in C.R. Synder and J. Lopez (eds), *Handbook of Positive Psychology*, Oxford: Oxford University Press, pp. 446–58.
Mitchell, R. (1991), 'Masters of innovation: how 3M keeps its products coming', in J. Henry and D. Walker (eds), *Managing Innovation*, London: Sage.
Myers, D. (2000), 'The funds, friends and faith of happy people', *American Psychologist*, **55**(1), 56–67.
Nayak, R.M. and J. Ketteringham (1986), '3M's little yellow post-it pads: never mind I'll do it myself', in R.M. Nayak and J. Ketteringham, *Breakthroughs*, New York: Arthur Little.
Nonaka, I. and H. Takeuchi (1995), *The Knowledge-Creating Company*, Oxford: Oxford University Press.
Seligman, M. and M. Csikszentmihalyi (2000), 'Positive Psychology Special Issue', *American Psychologist*, January.
Semler, R. (1994), *Maverick*, London: Arrow.
Senge, P. (1991), *The Fifth Discipline: The Art and Practice of the Learning Organisation*, London: Century.
Smith, P.B. and M.H. Bond (1993), *Psychology across Cultures, Analysis and Perspectives*, London: Harvester Wheatsheaf.
Sonnetag, S. (1996), 'Work group factors and individual well-being', in M.A. West (ed.), *The Handbook of Work-Group Psychology*, Chichester: Wiley, pp. 346–67.
Stacy, R. (1996), *Complexity and Creativity in Organisations*, San Francisco, CA: Brett-Koehler.
Straw, B.M., N.E. Bell and J.A. Clausen (1986), 'The dispositional approach to job satisfaction', *Administrative Science Quarterly*, March.
Taylor, R. (2002) *The Future of Work–life Balance*, London: ESRC.

Warr, P. (1987), *Work, Unemployment and Mental Health*, Oxford: Clarendon Press.
Warr, P. (1999), 'Well-being and the workplace', in D. Kahneman, E. Deiner and N. Schwartz (eds), *Well-being: The Foundations of Hedonic Psychology*, New York: Russell, pp. 392–412.
Wheatley, M. (1994), *Leadership and the New Science*, San Francisco, CA: Brett-Koehler.
White, M. (2001), 'The changing face of employment: conditions for active well-being in working life', presentation to ESRC Work and Well-being Seminar, Manchester Metropolitan University, 18 December.

26 Health care and subjective well-being in nations
Bruce Kirkcaldy, Adrian Furnham and Ruut Veenhoven

The issue

With the ever-increasing costs incurred by medical health care in the majority of the industrialized nations of the world, attempts have been made to identify and rectify the deficiencies in the health industry and improve quality management assessment. A central question for politicians and researchers is, to what extent does a country's health care system influence the subjective well-being in its citizens?

The *World Health Report 2000* has been published in an attempt to evaluate diverse health services across the world with a view to comparing performance, and enabling policy makers to appreciate better the complexity of health care. Consequently, in 'unprecedented degree it takes account of the role of people as providers and consumers of health services, as financial contributors to health systems, as workers within them, and as citizens engaged in their responsible management, or stewardship' (WHO, 2001).

It has been reported that only four of the 191 member nations of the World Health Organisation spend in excess of 10 per cent of the GDP on health services. These are the USA, Germany, Lebanon and Switzerland. The *World Health Report* suggests that the expenditure is not reflected in superior quality health service, with nations such as the USA being placed 37th, Germany 25th and Switzerland 20th. The nations ranked amongst the top ten in terms of overall health performance are France (1), Italy (2), San Marino (3), Andorra (4), Malta (5), Singapore (6), Spain (7), Oman (8), Austria (9) and Japan (10).

Several reasons account for the enormous health care expenditures in many of the Western industrialized nations. One factor is related to size and structure of the population (demographic data such as size, age and gender), with, for example, increasingly large numbers of older citizens, and rising public expectations concerning quality of medical health care. Another important source of escalating costs is the increasing innovations in health care technology. They enhance prevention and treatment of ailments and consequently increase the duration and quality of life:

> Technology innovation for health care promotes the industrial sector and has tremendous potential to reduce costs. However, health care technology resources are not always deployed in an optimal fashion: wasteful provision and utilisation by those who provide and utilise health care technology is often attributed to a lack of cost-consciousness. New health care technology is frequently acquired and utilised without clear evidence that it provides a better and cheaper or more cost effective alternative to existing technologies. (Jakubowski and Busse, 1998)

In commenting about what constitutes an effective health system, the *World Health Report* notes:

> it is not always satisfactory to protect or improve the average health of the population, if at the same time inequality worsens or remains high because the gain accrues disproportionately to

those already enjoying better health. The health system also has the responsibility to try to reduce inequalities by improving the health of the worse-off, wherever these inequalities are caused by conditions amenable to intervention. The objective of a good health system is really efficacy at two factors: the best attainable average level – *goodness* – and the smallest feasible differences among individuals and groups – *fairness*. A gain in either one of these, with no change in the other, constitutes an improvement, but the two may be in conflict. (*World Health Report*, p. 26).

In other words a good health system needs to be measured objectively in terms of its effectiveness and equity and subjectively in terms of the well-being of its consumers.

McKee (2001) argues that the WHO study has attempted some innovative work in comparative health care system evaluation, by introducing the construct of stewardship (associated with active involvement in health promotion) and a conceptual framework to target goals of health care, as well as attempting to explore the impact of input variables such as medical health care costs on physical health outcome variables. He cautions, however, that, whilst the health report highlights the many diverse activities that may enhance or restore health, these are not necessarily incorporated in the national health accounts. Furthermore health improvements may be attained through implementation of social policies such as reduction of accident through vehicle safety measures, or other determinants such as a nations' established dietary patterns. Moreover a growing interest has developed in agricultural policies and the development of consumer concerns frequently opposing industrial interests. Finally the data may be fragmentary and thus unreliable in instances where countries do not have adequate information concerning population size, education and health expenditure.

Comparative studies on mental health and psychological well-being
There is also an interesting and important empirical literature on cross national differences in subjective well-being (Diener *et al*, 1995; Kirkcaldy *et al*., 1997; Veenhoven, 2000). Studies attempt to establish empirically the correlates of national well-being, such as economic affluence and political democracy. Some of these studies considered national care systems. For instance, Veenhoven (2000) compared social security systems and found that people are roughly as happy in countries with lavish welfare as in equally affluent countries where provision is more modest. This suggests health care has only a modest impact on self-reported happiness. The health care system, so far, has not been considered in that way.

At the individual level, well-being researchers have noted that health and happiness are closely linked (Arygle, 2001; Myers, 1993). However this relationship is complex and reciprocal with many different hypothesized moderator and intervening variables. Some researchers have argued that health is a necessary predeterminant for subjective well-being. In that view well-being is likely to depend partly on the effectiveness of the national health care systems as well as private care, the individual's ability to pay for it, as well as the acuity and chronicity of their illnesses. Others have argued that subjective well-being is more powerfully determined by individual difference factors, in particular by personality traits such as perceived fate control and extraversion, the latter of which may be biologically determined. In that perspective, the national health care system will hardly affect subjective well-being.

The sociological and psychological explanations are not in conflict, though they differ in three major ways: first the amount of variance they believe specific factors contribute to individual/national happiness/well-being; second the extent to which they believe it is possible to influence well-being/happiness through social policy implications, and third, the mechanisms and processes by which the two factors are reciprocally interactive. By and large economists and sociologists, more than psychologists and psychiatrists believe happiness may be significantly influenced by social policy decisions.

Various studies have reported cross-national analyses of socioeconomic data (for instance, Furnham et al., 1994, 1996). Kirkcaldy et al. (1997) explored the relationship between national differences in personality, socioeconomic situation and work-related attitudes. They showed that a substantial proportion of the variance in *subjective well-being* was explained by economic measures, particularly gross domestic product, suggesting a moderate relationship between happiness and wealth of a nation. It was the relationship with the work-related attitudes rather than personality factors that was most related to wealth:

> nations high in psychological well-being were less competitive and attached less importance to money ... subjective well-being represents an ongoing state of psychological wellness (Diener, 1984) which as such would appear to bear little logical association with hard-driving and materially oriented traits such as competitiveness and evaluation of money. The results suggest that individuals with instrumental beliefs and commitment as well as achievement orientation, but who are cooperative and not exclusively materially oriented, have a higher well-being. (Kirkcaldy et al., 1997)

One of the most conspicuous findings was the relationship between cooperativeness (the obverse of competitiveness) and quality of life (assessed by the human development index). The argument is that initially social and economic competitiveness has a positive driving effect on quality of life, but once a particular level is reached a plateau occurs, and further competitiveness (as in industrial countries) starts to become counterproductive.

As yet research has not attempted to verify whether the ratings of medical health systems across nations in any way relate to other health outcome variables, particularly in the domain of psychological health. The purpose of this study was to address this shortcoming. Figures for the United States in 1996 indicate that, of the $943billion expenditure in health care, 7 per cent went into mental health care. Estimates of the indirect costs of all mental disorders to the US economy are around $79billion, most of which derives from morbidity and decrease in productivity due to illness. It has been calculated that mental disorders account for more than 15 per cent of the burden of disease in the economy, with some of the main ten causes being bipolar disorders, depression, schizophrenia and obsessional – compulsive disorders.

In a Dutch study, Meerding et al., (1998) reported that a substantial proportion of health costs was attributable to mental disorders. Mental retardation is ranked first, dementia third, depression and anxiety fifteenth, schizophrenia twenty-third, drug and alcohol misuse thirty-first, and a non-differentiated group of mental ailments ranked fourth. They further reported that mental disorders are responsible for almost one-third (28.4%) of the budget that could be assigned to diagnostic groups.

The World Health Organisation appears at present to neglect (a) inclusion of subjective reports of health outcome variables, (b) measures of mental health, and (c) salient, relevant intervening variables. Several reasons invite considering outcomes in subjective well-being. One is that well-being may decline when we grow too old, even when free of disability. A second reason is that we may live better with physical limitations than with mental problems and that investment in mental health is thus more productive. Thirdly, effective health care may be detrimental to well-being, for instance when it enforces a joyless lifestyle.

Life expectancy has frequently been used as one of the variables which reflects the medical health efficacy of a nation. The problem remains as to whether success in lengthening life is not achieved at the cost of overall life satisfaction. More specifically, adhering to a healthy lifestyle may not imply an intrinsically enjoyable one, since it forbids many of the mundane pleasures of life, enforcing a more rigid diet and increasing nutritional awareness. Another interesting hypothesis is related to whether there is a natural limit to mental capacity and vitality. Finally success in reducing physical disabilities as measured by DALYS ('disability adjusted life years', a measure of the burden of disability and premature death resulting from illness) may not be the key to successful health care because it may not be associated with superior psychological health.

This study will be in the psychometric tradition: multivariate analysis of national data to explore health–well-being patterns. It was the primary goal to test hypotheses predicting plausible relationships between the health efficacy of a nation and various specific variables of subjective well-being and health behaviour. As yet few attempts have been made to relate these World Health expert ratings to other existent cross-cultural data bases which specifically monitor health outcome variables. Despite obvious methodological deficiencies inherent in such attempts at cross-cultural comparison (Van der Vliert *et al.*, 2000), this form of health evaluative research is creative and provides insight for future social policy making. It not only allows for direct hypothesis testing but further provides correlational evidence of the relationship between macroeconomic variables.

This study will marry various data bases to the *World Health Report* data to explore correlates of the efficiency of health systems. It will follow the methodology of the above-mentioned studies (for example Furnham *et al.*, 1994, 1996; Kirkcaldy *et al.*, 1997). Several tentative hypotheses are formulated below. Essentially, there will be significant differences between those nations who enjoy superior health systems and those who exhibit inferior health systems (as defined by the rankings in the *World Health Report*) in terms of positive and negative affect as well as other behavioural indicators of psychological well-being. A number of specific questions will be focused on, using the various cross-cultural data bases. These include the following:

- Do national health care systems really differ in terms of physical health outcome?
- Does good health care result in enhanced psychological health such as happiness for a greater number of the population (and a more equitable distribution)?
- Is it plausible that investment in mental health will be more conducive to happiness and, in turn, mental well-being?
- Are medical health and socioeconomic factors independent, compensatory or complementary in their role as contributors to mental health (psychological well-being)?

Method
Several data bases were incorporated in the study, including the following:

1. Veenhoven's (2001) World Database of Happiness, which lists research findings on satisfaction with life as a whole. A subset from this database contains the distribution of responses to single questions about this matter in general population surveys all over the world (catalogue of happiness in nations). From this collection we use average happiness in nations (means), dispersion or inequality of happiness (standard deviations) and happiness adjusted life years (a combination of average happiness and life expectancy, analogous to disability-adjusted life years).
    Attempts will also be made to explore 'inequalities in life outcome measures' which correspond to distribution and fairness in psychological health (and so presumably are related to the WHO measures of equality and distribution of health care). For this purpose variation in the outcome variables will be assessed using SD (standard deviations) for happiness and subjective health.
2. Eysenck's trait 'neuroticism' (national means for neuroticism were taken from Barrett and Eysenck's (1984) original 24-country normative data base).
3. Diener's database of 'subjective well-being' (SWB) in nations (Diener *et al.*, 1995; Oishi *et al.*, 1999). The authors reported mean scores on subjective well-being for 55 nations. Their scores of average SWB in nations are partly based on the general population surveys that figure also in Veenhoven's list of happiness in nations (above). They added nations to that list where happiness was only assessed in student samples. From these student samples they also derive estimates of 'negative' and 'positive' affect.
4. Suicide rate: (national rates for accidents and suicides International Classification of Disease (ICD) E950–E959; deaths by suicide or resulting from self-inflicted injury were expressed as cases per 100 000 inhabitants for the years 1987–1995; taken from Eurostat and United Nations *Demographic and Accounts Statistics Yearbook*).
5. WHO statistics of 'Health indicators' incorporating the following:

    –   *DALE* (disability-adjusted life expectancy) is estimated from the fraction of the population surviving to each age, calculated from the birth and death rates, incidence of each disability at each age, and the weight assigned to each disability);
    –   distribution of responsiveness (in fulfilling the population's expectations);
    –   two factors of responsiveness (autonomy, confidentiality, choice or provider or facility, dignity, quality of basic amenities, access to social support networks, respect of persons, and client orientation), goal level and goal distribution,
    –   fairness (this refers to the risk each household faces that to whether the costs of the health system are related more to an individual's ability to pay than to their level of illness. A fair system ensures that low-income individuals are not forced into poverty as a result of their illness);
    –   overall goal;
    –   expenditure (costs incurred for the health system);
    –   health level;
    –   overall health; overall attainment is an absolute measure, but it provides little insight about how the outcome was attained compared to the resources of a

Table 26.1 Sociopsychological and economic variables

Intervening variables	
Wealth and development	
GNP	GNP per capita
Growth	Economic growth
Outcome variables	
Well-being	
Life satisfaction	Average self-reported life satisfaction
Work satisfaction	Average reports of work satisfaction
Positive affect	Population aggregate of positive affectivity
Happiness	Average self-report for happiness
Negative affect	Negative affect
Suicide	Suicide rates per 100 000
Accident	Accident rate
Health system indicators	
Subjective health rating	
DALE	Disability-adjusted life expectancy
Health level	Performance of level of health
Overall health	Overall ranking in health attainment
Input system variables	
Distribution	Distribution of costs within health care
Goal level	Responsiveness (goal level)
Goal distribution	Equality of goal distribution
Fairness	Risk each household faces from health costs
Overall goal	Overall goals set
Expenditure	Costs incurred by the health costs of a nation

nation: hence achievement relative to resources was used as the critical index of a health system's performance (*World Health Report 2000*).

6. The economic variables used in this study include GDP (gross domestic product), HDI (human development index, a combined score indicating national development) and economic growth. The research data were reported in *The Economist* (1995) and generally refer to national statistics for the year ending 1993; they are available for several years for approximately one hundred nations.

Major variables to be used in this project are listed in Table 26.1 above.

Results
The first task was to determine how the various countries cluster according to the data collected. Initially we performed cluster analysis as a multivariate statistical procedure for detecting natural groups in the data set using the eight health indicator variables. The technique of cluster analysis 'resembles discriminant analysis, in which the researcher seeks to classify a set of objects into subgroups although neither the number of subgroups nor the members of the subgroups are known' (Wilkinson, 1988, p. 375). In this instance,

we adopted K Means clustering involving a splitting method, not necessarily hierarchical, to partition the objects (countries) into a selected number of groups (dichotomized into two groups on this occasion) by maximizing between-cluster relative to within-cluster variation, hence similar to performing a one-way analysis of variance where the groups are unknown and the largest F-value is sought by reassigning members of each group' (ibid.). The clustering technique implements algorithms which are outlined by Hartigan (1975).

Country groupings Essentially two distinct clusters were extracted (Table 26.2) based on profile similarity on the health indicator subscales, the first comprising 21 nations,

Table 26.2   Results of the cluster analysis and the differences between cluster

Case distance		Case distance	
Bangladesh	150.12	Argentina	99.57
Brazil	98.56	Australia	30.17
Bulgaria	140.29	Austria	44.74
China	101.12	Belgium	38.75
Egypt	86.15	Canada	33.93
Hungary	124.48	Chile	164.66
India	112.48	Columbia	124.89
Iraq	81.55	CSSR	77.05
Jordan	90.10	Denmark	51.80
Lithuania	109.35	Finland	33.28
Mexico	119.34	France	52.73
Nigeria	223.39	Germany	41.36
Romania	73.98	Greece	40.52
Russia	97.56	Holland	36.23
South Africa	161.66	Iceland	32.16
Sri Lanka	79.16	Ireland	34.99
Syria	50.27	Israel	19.41
Turkey	107.75	Italy	48.06
Uganda	195.50	Japan	57.47
Venezuela	116.34	Korea	93.88
Yugoslavia	85.77	Luxembourg	47.46
		New Zealand	51.37
		Norway	47.85
		Poland	148.47
		Portugal	57.60
		Singapore	75.98
		Spain	44.74
		Sweden	43.92
		Switzerland	40.61
		UAE	65.06
		UK	40.91
		USA	53.92

Table 26.3 A comparison of means (rankings) between clusters across all health indicators

	Cluster mean I	Cluster mean II	F(1,52)	P
Output variables				
DALE	99.32	22.50	98.88	0.001***
Health level	92.23	36.09	33.20	0.001***
Overall health	103.05	24.75	113.83	0.001***
System variables				
Goal level	102.14	22.38	108.90	0.001***
Goal distribution	95.50	14.94	67.63	0.001***
Fairness	118.14	36.03	43.65	0.001***
Overall goal	103.55	19.38	141.67	0.001***
Expenditure	103.55	20.63	135.08	0.001***

Note: Let *** represent $p < 0.001$.

including such countries as Roumania, Iraq, Sri Lanka, Yugoslavia and Egypt. In contrast, there were the 32 nations which constituted the second cluster, and included diverse nations such as Israel, Canada, Australia, Finland, Switzerland, the United Kingdom, Greece and Germany. Subsequently a series of univariate F-tests verified that these two clusters were substantially different on all nine health indicators, in particular overall goal attainment, expenditure, distribution and goal level, and, not unexpectedly, overall health performance.

The indicators 'overall goal attainment', 'distribution' and 'expenditure' emerge as very good discriminators between nations. From the two clusters that were generated on the basis of their work attitude profile, the first cluster displayed lower rankings on the DALE index, distribution, goal level, goal distribution, fairness, overall goal, expenditure, health level and overall health performance scores compared to the second cluster nations (for example Australia, Belgium, Canada, USA).

A series of univariate F-tests were computed to determine whether these clusters of nations differed in their economic profiles. The first cluster of low health care nations did not differ significantly in terms of inflation rate ($F(1,48) = 1.82$, $p > 0.05$) compared to the superior health care nations, nor were there significant differences reported in economic growth ($F(1,48) = 1.39$, n.s.). The nations of the second cluster yielding higher scores on a variety of health system indicators were, however, significantly richer in terms of GDP (cluster I: M = 1647 SD 1266.31, cluster II: M = 17780.69 SD 9368.56; $F(1,48) = 52.37$, $p < 0.001$), and these were in fact the countries which had significantly greater expenditure on their health care systems.

Psychological health and subjective well-being The second phase applied univariate F-tests to analyse whether the subjective reports of well-being profiles were statistically different. If this empirical dichotomization based solely on health evaluation variables has anything meaningful to say about other real-life data in a country, for example psychological well-being (state of happiness, subjective well-being, neuroticism, positive and neg-

Table 26.4 *A comparison of subjective well-being between nations which are highly developed or underdeveloped in terms of their health effectiveness (happiness scores for n = 40 nations)*

Subjective well-being	Cluster I (low health effectiveness)	Cluster II (high health effectiveness)	F-test
Satisfaction home-life	7.27 (0.60)	8.06 (0.47)	17.24***
Job satisfaction	6.92 (0.64)	7.63 (0.45)	13.75***
Happiness years	46.71 (4.72)	60.48 (4.10)	88.72***
Subjective well-being	−0.81 (0.65)	0.26 (0.72)	19.95***
Positive affect	2.39 (0.43)	2.61 (0.65)	1.03
Negative affect	1.37 (0.47)	1.11 (0.29)	3.78
Trait neuroticism	14.30 (2.03)	14.29 (2.35)	0.00
Objective well-being			
Accident rate	85.57 (64.29)	45.50 (20.28)	6.60*
Suicide incidence	21.00 (29.70)	14.73 (9.14)	1.05

Note: Let * $p < 0.05$ and *** $p < 0.001$.

ative affect) then using these groups should be useful in predicting health-related variables, for example accident rates, suicide and criminal activity. This is an example of an external validation significant test of the cluster solution (Aldenderfer and Blashfield, 1984).

Of the eight variables selected (all of which had been collated from often quite distinct cross-cultural data bases using comprehensive questionnaires to assess the constructs involved) five emerged as statistically significant at the level of $p < 0.02$. They are happiness ($F(1,37) = 20.53$, $p < 0.001$), satisfaction with home life ($F(1,31) = 15.25$, $p < 0.001$), work satisfaction ($F(1,31) = 13.75$, $p < 0.001$), subjective well-being ($F(1,35) = 27.17$, $p < 0.001$) and accident rate ($F(1,32) = 7.39$, $p < 0.02$). There was no evidence of differences being observed on negative affect, suicide rate, neuroticism or criminal rate.

Correlations between variables
Correlational analyses are reported in Table 26.5. Happiness, subjective well-being and life satisfaction show the most consistent and highest correlations (correlations with health level and overall health ratings ranged between −0.50 and −0.59). Nations with low ratings in health level care and effectiveness of overall health care were more likely to exhibit high accident and suicide rates (correlation coefficients ranging between +0.44 and +0.60). Inferior psychological well-being, as measured by trait neuroticism and negative affect, was unrelated to a nation's health performance ratings. This suggests that good care in the domain for physical health does not necessarily add to national mental health.

A total of n = 41 completed nation scores for the first column correlations. It was not possible to control adequately for the extraneous effects of differences in material affluence using non-parametric statistics across all variables because nations were nearly always ranked. Some distinct parametric statistics were subsequently conducted using partial correlations controlling for the potentially confounding effects of differences in GDP, and the significant effects persisted. More specifically, the correlation between

Table 26.5 Non-parametric correlations between health variables and specific dimensions of psychological health and behaviour.

Health indices	Psychological well-being						Negative health				
	Happiness 2	Work sat.	Life sat.	Well-being	Positive affect	Inequality in nation's happiness	Neuroticism	Negative affect	Accident rate	Suicide
DALE	−0.79c	−0.37a	−0.52c	−0.49b	−0.18	+0.59c	−0.09	+0.35(a)	+0.34(a)	+0.02
Distribution	−0.62c	−0.39a	−0.38a	−0.40a	−0.18	+0.55c	−0.09	+0.13	+0.28	+0.07
Goal level	−0.85c	−0.60c	−0.60c	−0.62c	−0.38a	+0.56c	−0.03	+0.26	+0.34a	−0.47a
Goal distribution	−0.69c	−0.26	−0.42a	−0.58c	−0.28	+0.50b	−0.13	+0.30	+0.15	−0.10
Fairness	−0.69c	−0.37a	−0.54b	−0.58c	−0.23	+0.53c	+0.08	+0.31	+0.23	−0.31
Overall goal	−0.84c	−0.46b	−0.55c	−0.62c	−0.29	+0.62c	−0.07	+0.26	+0.27	−0.35
Expenditure	−0.84c	−0.51b	−0.68c	−0.70c	−0.39a	+0.56c	−0.11	+0.26	+0.22	−0.50a
Health level	−0.64c	−0.20	−0.44b	−0.35a	−0.10	+0.41a	−0.11	+0.30	+0.48b	−0.25
Over. health	−0.67c	−0.27	−0.43a	−0.47b	−0.05	+0.62c	−0.09	+0.36a	+0.35a	+0.14

Note: (Let $a = p < 0.05$, $b = p < 0.01$, and $c = p < 0.001$) Low health rate scores correspond to high rankings (for example overall health rankings that were numerically low imply superior overall health systems).

Table 26.6 Determinants of psychological well-being (outcome variables)

	beta	t	R = 0.90, adj. R² = 0.80	F(2,38) = 82.80***
Happiness				
Goal level	−0.61	−6.60	0.001***	
Health level	−0.38	−4.10	0.001***	
			R = 0.59, adj. R² = 0.33	F(1,32) = 16.91***
Accidents				
Health level	+0.59	+0.41	0.001***	

Note: Let*** represent $p < 0.001$.

health efficacy and happiness was attenuated when the effects of GDP were controlled, but the correlation was still highly statistically significant ($r = -0.58$, $p < 0.001$) as was the correlation between health expenditure and happiness ($r = -0.54$, $p < 0.001$). Hence the superior subjective well-being reported by the better 'health-provided' nations could not be explained by GDP alone; that is, it *cannot* be due to superior health-ranked nations simply being richer. On the other hand, the expenditure on health care remains significantly associated with well-being.

Owing to the interrelatedness of the various health indicator scales, further statistical analysis was confined to those scales of subjective and objective well-being (happiness and accident rate) which had displayed the highest overall correlation with the health indices. Stepwise multiple regression analyses were subsequently computed to identify the specific determinants of well-being outcome variables. The two health performance variables, goal and health level (beta coefficients of −0.61 and −0.38 respectively), explained approximately two-thirds of the total variance observed in subjective well-being across nations, and health level emerged as the single significant predictor of accident rates, explaining one-third of the variance (Table 26.6).

The scattergram below (Figure 26.1) reveals the relationship between happiness and health level. Scattergrams provide additional information to bivariate statistics because (1) they visualize the degree of relationship, that is, concentration of the cases around a regression line, (2) they allow a view on the shape, for instance you can see whether the relation is linear or not, (3) they bring possible outliers to the attention, and (4) they show how the cases (countries) fit the pattern which helps to generate explanations. Dispersion of happiness (or health) in a country is a measure of inequality. Inequality in society is mostly measured by input, such as income or access to medical care. Dispersion of happiness/health measures equality of output in society.

Clearly those nations with favourable rankings (closer to 1), and thus superior health levels, also displayed the highest happiness scores ($r = -0.64$, $p < 0.001$).

When dispersion in happiness scores are plotted as a function of health level rankings (Figure 26.2), a similar linear relationship is found, but on this occasion the correlation is positive, suggesting that nations with inferior health care systems (high rankings in health level) were more likely to exhibit high inequality in their happiness ratings.

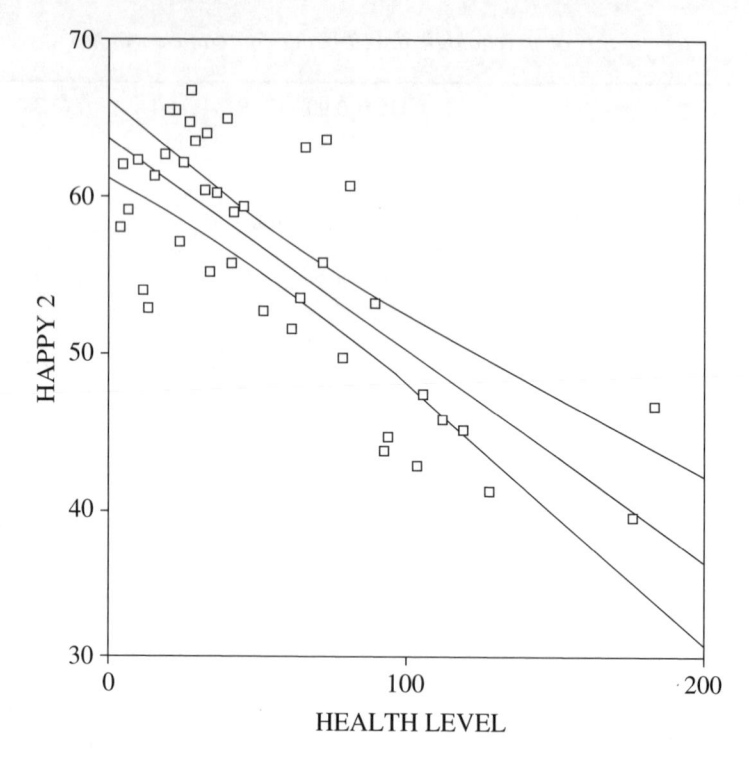

Note: High health level rankings imply inferior health levels. Low rankings mean superior health.

Figure 26.1 Happiness (Happy 2) as a function of rankings of the health level of nations

Figure 26.3 illustrates that the relationship between fairness in health care and happiness was of a similar magnitude of effect to that reported between health level and happiness (cf. Figure 27.1) (r = −0.69, p < 0.001). Nations with greater fairness (financial protection against ill-health) in their health care costs are more likely to show superior subjective well-being, as reflected in the happiness scores.

Finally, countries who were fairer in cost distribution of health care exhibited significantly less dispersion in their happiness scores (more equality in population's happiness ratings); see Figure 26.4.

Discussion

The *World Health Report* was an attempt to explore the strengths and weaknesses of diverse health care systems and to enable cross-culture comparisons to extract specific determinants of health care performance. It is argued that the three desirable goals of health care systems are improvement in the health of the population and reduction of inequalities in health, financial protection regarding the costs of contribution to health care, and enhancing responses to the expectation of the population.

Despite inherent weaknesses and methodological deficiencies it represents a mammoth

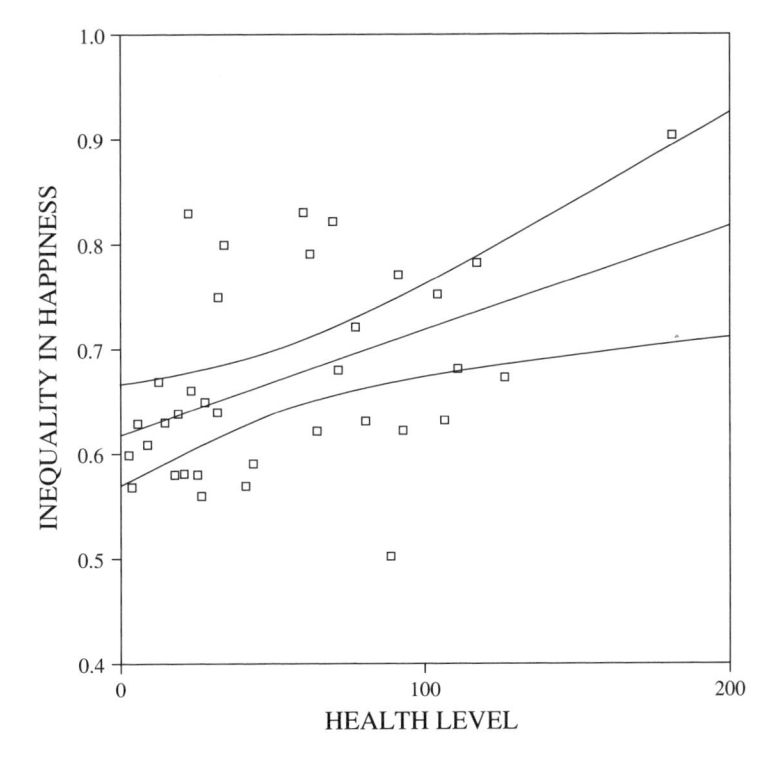

Health care and subjective well-being in nations 405

Note: Low fairness rankings are associated with superior health fairness scores.

Figure 26.2 Inequality (dispersion) of happiness for various health level rankings of nations

task in sociometric and econometric analysis of medical care services. Much can be learned from international comparisons of medical health care, in exploring both similarities and differences in the development and structure of health care systems. The strategy in this study was to try and identify whether, and to what extent, the measures of health care effectiveness relate to other variables to do with general health, more specifically psychological health and/or subjective well-being.

National health care systems and physical health outcome
The major findings using the cluster analysis suggest that two clear groups of nations are generated, one encompassing those countries with highly developed medical health care systems (including the majority of Western European and Nordic countries, as well as nations such as the USA, Australia, UAE and Israel, and Pacific Rim countries such as Singapore, Korea and Japan), and the other cluster representing nations in the process of developing or that are underdeveloped (including Eastern European nations and 'Third World' countries). When these groups were compared in terms of specific health indicators, the magnitude of the effect size was highest for the health *system* variables 'overall goal', 'health expenditure', 'distribution' and 'goal level', and the *outcome* variable, 'overall health performance'.

406   Stress, well-being and health

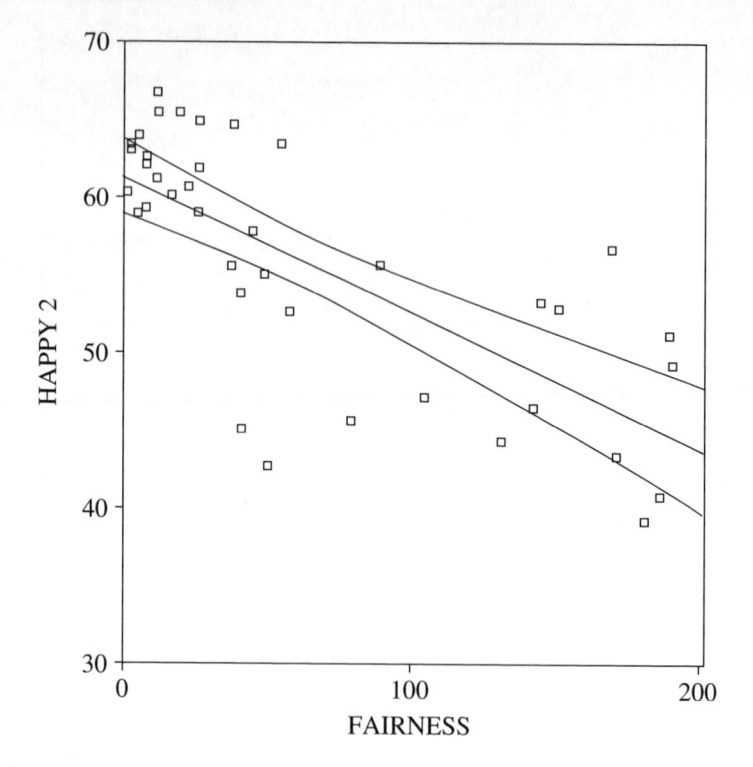

Note: Low fairness rankings are associated with superior health fairness scores.

Figure 26.3   The relationship between fairness in health systems and happiness scores

Clearly these differences are in part due to socioeconomic differences between nations, and some would argue, with Avery:

> World leaders, especially of the G8, should review the globalisation of the world economies with a view to removing unpayable debts, providing targeted economic aid directed towards sustainable development . . . International agencies should accelerate the development of health and social welfare plans, provide grants for education and training, and encourage research into the most efficient and effective ways of improving health . . . National governments should increase aid directed towards tackling major diseases, improving education, primary health care, and health education promotion, and encouraging sustainable development in agriculture. (Avery, 2002)

But clearly the differences observed in health care system performance are not limited to expenditure, as those nations with the highest expenditure on health care are not necessarily ranked as the most efficient in their performance. On the other hand, in order to secure comparatively good medical health care, a minimum health expenditure programme is required, and nations investing beyond that level may not necessarily be reaping the benefits in terms of increased efficiency. At a correlational level, we may observe clear significant correlations between health efficacy and expenditure across

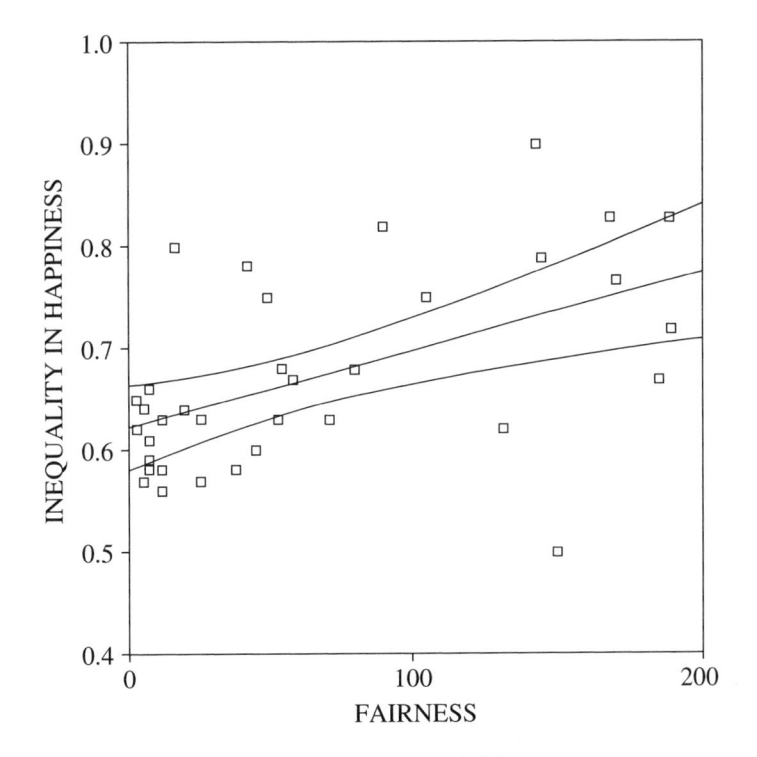

Note: Low fairness rankings are associated with superior health fairness scores.

Figure 26.4 Dispersion in happiness scores and its relationship to a nation's fairness rating in health care

nations, but this relationship may attenuate when doing cross-cultural comparisons between wealthy, industrialized nations.

Health care performance and psychological health (quality and equity)
Furthermore, as shown in Table 26.4, some intriguing patterns emerge: individuals in high health-effective countries appear to report better psychological well-being in terms of being more satisfied both in life and with work, and experiencing higher subjective well-being and happiness, although there was no evidence that they were more psychologically stable (in terms of trait neuroticism), nor were there significant differences reported on negative affect or suicide rate. At the more objective outcome variable level, nations assigned as having superior health care performance ratings did at the same time reveal lower rates of accidents per 100 000 inhabitants. This finding appears consistent with those of previous statistics (*The Economist*, 2001) in which accident rates as measured by deaths per 100 000 inhabitants due to injuries and poisons reveal that the rates were highest for Russia (203.4), Lithuania (142.6), Hungary (92.3), Finland (73.5) and Poland (72.4), and lowest for Sweden (38.6), Greece (39.1), Ireland (39.8), Norway (42.5) and Austria (42.5). Moreover there was a tendency for nations with well-developed health

care systems to report fewer suicides, although the difference did not emerge as statistically significant, probably because of the greater dispersion in suicide rate observed among the less well-developed nations.

Happiness emerged as the single variable which consistently and significantly correlated with each and every one of the health variables. The mean correlation coefficient was 0.74. Moreover, when we analysed the interrelationships between health systems and *dispersion* in happiness (using standard deviations of happiness), there was evidence that the nations with superior health care systems including 'fairness' within their health care were also those which exhibited least inequality in their happiness data.

The linear regression analysis revealed that two of the eight health variables were significant determinants of happiness, explaining approximately two-thirds of the variance observed. Again it was interesting that health expenditure did not emerge as one of the major predictors of happiness. Nations with more favourable rankings in their health care system with respect to goal level and health level were likely to exhibit higher happiness scores. Moreover health level emerged as the single significant predictor of accident rate, with nations with inferior health systems displaying a higher incidence of accidents. It is possible that such countries invest more in time and money educating its citizens about the risks of accidents and their prevention as well as making efforts to ensure that accidents are prevented.

Health expenditure and mental health conducive to happiness
In another study, Kirkcaldy and Furnham (2000) explored the incidence rates of accidents, deaths due to suicide and self-inflicted injuries, as well as deaths resulting from car accidents. They found no evidence of any relationship between negative affect and the outcome variables. Conversely subjective well-being was significantly negatively correlated with incidence of accidents as well as deaths resulting from motor (driving) accidents.

Two central issues arise from this study. Firstly, why is there no link with measures more closely associated with mental health such as neuroticism and negative affect? One methodological explanation may be that this is an artefact due to limited cases, in which case the data may not be truly representative. This kind of explanation is supported by the fact that health care quality does relate to subjective well-being, while mental health and subjective well-being are typically closely linked. Alternatively, a substantive explanation

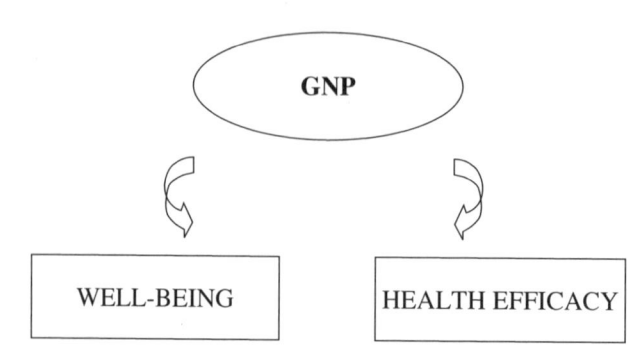

Figure 26.5   A model of the relationship between well-being, health effectiveness and GNP

would be that investment in physical care may be at the cost of mental heath care. There is evidence that, although mental disorders represent a substantial proportion of the illnesses witnessed in Western industrialized countries, only about 6 per cent of the expenditure in medical health care is directed towards mental health. In other words, somatizing cultures would be more inclined to push investments in physical health care.

Secondly, why is health care (quality/fairness) linked to subjective well-being (level/dispersion)? There are several explanations here. It may be that the effects of good care improve physical health, which in turn quite plausibly makes people feel happier. In addition, it may be that the effects of well-being on producing happier citizens may lead them to vote more for investment in public health care.

So the question that remains is, does health effectiveness lead to satisfaction or vice versa? More importantly, what are the other variables that may moderate this relationship? Or is it that macro economic variables are intervening? Our analysis showed that GNP was highly significantly related to both well-being (r = 0.82) and health efficacy (r = 0.70).

Thus variables such as weather, natural resources and stable (democratic) governments may affect GDP, which in turn predicts both subjective well-being and health efficacy, even though the variables themselves may be loosely related (see Figure 26.6). This is extremely important given that so much is spent on health care in an attempt to improve subjective well-being, which may or may not be effective.

Added to this, the analysis is correlational, and we have no details of causal relationships. What did emerge was that subjective well-being and health effectiveness were significantly correlated even after controlling for potentially confounding effects of socioeconomic data (GNP and economic growth), which suggests that economic factors in themselves are not sufficient to explain the differences, although nations with more money to spend on health care overall clearly experienced superior physical and psychological well-being.

Other more complex multidimensional models listed below involving socioeconomic–psychological variables intimately interrelated are probably more accurate representations of the underlining causal mechanisms involved.

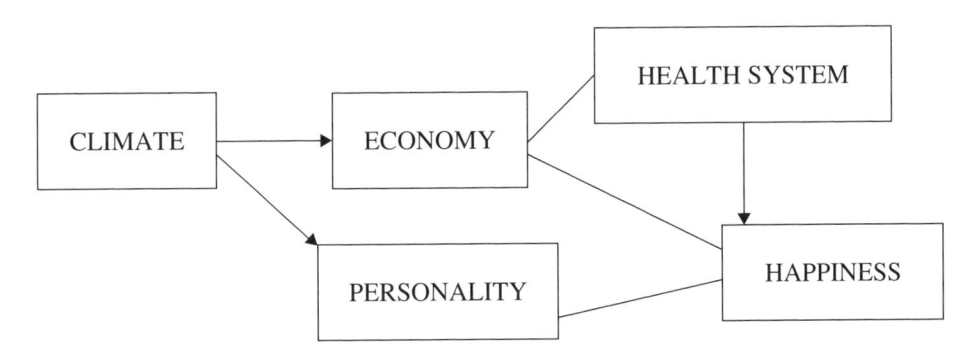

Figure 26.6 A multidimensional causal model of the relationship between geographical, economic and psychological variables and health care and psychological well-being

When we make comparisons between different countries, it may be useful to further distinguish between how satisfied the recipients or consumers of the health systems (patients and clients) and the providers (medical and allied personnel) are. Some European studies have looked at this issue. Mossialos (1996) examined public perception of various European health care systems in terms of the degree of satisfaction in the 15 EU states. Dissatisfaction from a 'consumer' viewpoint was highest for Italy (59.4 per cent being either fairly or very dissatisfied), followed by Portugal (59.3 per cent), Greece (53.90 per cent), the UK (42.9 per cent) and Ireland (29.1 per cent). In contrast, satisfaction was highest for Denmark (90.0 per cent being either very or fairly satisfied), Finland (86.4 per cent), Netherlands (72.8 per cent), Luxembourg (70.1 per cent), Sweden (67.3 per cent) and Germany (66.0 per cent). This is interesting because these nations correspond to those European nations ranked intermediate in our listing (rankings between 9 and 18 of 26 EU nations). Public expectations of resources in medical health care have been supposed to have major health policy consequences, which will have an impact on the investment in health care and scrutinizing of health care reform.

On the other hand, others (for example BMJ Survey, 2001) have examined a league table of unhappiness among the providers (medical doctors) themselves as a function of country. Among the least satisfied European countries were the UK (over two-thirds were either very unhappy or unhappy) followed by Spain (66.7 per cent), Belgium (64.3 per cent), Greece (58.3 per cent), Italy (57.7 per cent) and Ireland (52.4 per cent). Certainly there may be some discrepancies between what consumers perceive as satisfactory and how suppliers, that is the medical profession, evaluate their work.

Certainly, the finding that positive affect, but not negative affect, may be associated with health performance of a nation demands discussion. Future research may try to gain measures of the magnitude of investment in psychological health care, and then correlate these economic measures with mental well-being outcome variables.

Some critical remarks about the study concern the absence of psychological well-being data for those nations with vastly inferior health care listed among the approximately 190 countries in the World Health report (Angola, 181; Central African Republic, 189; Chad, 178; Ethiopia 180; Guinea-Bissau, 176; Lesotho, 183; Liberia, 186; Malawi, 185; Mozambique, 184; Myanmar, 190; Nigeria, 187; Sierra Leone, 191; Somalia, 179; Swaziland, 177; Zambia, 182.) In contrast, our data did include comprehensive data for the majority of the most highly rated nations (France (1), Italy (2), San Marino (3), Andorra (4), Malta (5), Singapore (6), Spain (7), Oman (8), Austria (9), Japan (10), Norway (11), Portugal (12), Monaco (13), Greece (14), Iceland (15) and Luxembourg (16)). Consequently the worst of our data base's health system nations do not correspond with the world's lowest values in health care. This would have the net effect of attenuating any differences between groups.

Criticisms of the psychometrics of the measures include rank-ordering, frequent reliance on single-item scales, and item overlap. Furthermore it is likely that there are curvilinear relationships between such variables as financial and economic factors: 'cost of health care', and psychological health, with increments in health being most noticeably observed among those nations with relatively scarce economic reserves for health care. As we approach the more developed, and financially costly, health care systems, a plateau is probably attained in which little observable change is witnessed with increases in health care expenditure.

Another important point is that the assumption that the efficiency of a health care system (in terms of physical health 'disability-adjusted life expectancy' and cost effectiveness) necessarily relates to better (more intensive and comprehensive 'psychological') care may be invalid. We have no knowledge of what percentage of the health care costs actually goes into counselling or therapy, thus affecting psychological well-being. Alternatively it could be argued that nations who enjoy better physical health will more likely exhibit improved psychological well-being. This issue may be resolved by looking at the magnitude of the correlation coefficients between aspects of psychological well-being and 'expenditure' (cost of health care) as opposed to 'overall goal attainment' (efficacy of health care). Presumably differences should be observed. Our table reveals no such difference, with the exception of 'suicide' and 'accident rates': here we found that, although these behavioural variables were not significantly related to cost of health, they were indeed significantly related to health attainment.

Nord (2000) provides a succinct analysis of the method of data collation in the WHO report:

> Decision makers who, in spite of the above criticisms, are inclined to regard the summary indices of the World Health Report as useful, should be aware that the assignment of weights to different aspects of responsiveness and overall goal attainment is difficult and may be culturally dependent. No country should uncritically accept the weights suggested by the WHO as being scientific or objective or correct. Every country should judge carefully whether the WHO weights fit with the country's own values, and thereby judge the relevance of the various indicators and indices for its own policy making.

Certainly, notwithstanding the interesting results of our study, health care cannot be completely divorced from other socioeconomic factors such as (1) basic infrastructure (for example roads, schools, water supply, electricity and lighting), (2) law, order and corruption, (3) family size and number of inhabitants per household, and (4) the economic prosperity of the country.

Despite all the above-mentioned methodological shortcomings, it is however important to do this research to examine empirically these relationships. Too much ideology and not enough empirical research has been prevalent. Health is a political battlefield, and we need more dispassionate research to explore causal relationships in this domain. If there are errors of measurement, the relationships we have observed between health performance effectiveness and subjective well-being, whilst being statistically significant, are likely to be an underrepresentation of the true magnitude of the association.

Acknowledgments

We would like to express our thanks to Priv. Doz. Dr Georg Siefen, Medical Director of the Westfalia Clinic for Child and Adolescent Psychiatry and Psychosomatic, Marl-Sinsen, who kindly read one of the earlier draft versions of this text and made suggestions for improvement.

References

Aldenderfer, M.S. and R.K. Blashfield (1984), *Cluster Analysis: Quantitative Applications in the Social Sciences*, London & Bevely Hills: Sage.
Argyle, M. (2001), *The Psychology of Happiness*, London: Routledge.
Avery, G. (2002), 'Comparative efficiency of national health systems', *British Medical Journal*, **324**, 48.

Barrett, P. and S.B.G. Eysenck (1984), 'The assessment of personality factors across 25 countries', *Personality and Individual Differences*, **5**, 615–32.
British Medical Journal (2001), 'Analysis of satisfaction among European doctors survey', BMJ website.
Diener, E. (1984), 'Subjective well-being', *Psychological Bulletin*, **95**, 545–75.
Diener, E., M. Diener and C. Diener (1995), 'Factors predicting the subjective well-being of nations', *Journal of Personality and Social Psychology*, **69**, 851–64.
Furnham, A., B.D. Kirkcaldy and R. Lynn (1994), 'National attitudes, competitiveness, money and work: First, Second and Third World differences', *Human Relations*, **47**, (1), 119–32.
Furnham, A., B.D. Kirkcaldy, and R. Lynn (1996), 'Attitudinal correlates of national wealth', *Personality and Individual Differences*, **21** (3), 345–53.
Jakubowski, E. and C.R. Busse (1998), 'Health care system in the EU: a comparative study'. Directorate General for Research, working paper, Public Health and Consumer Policy Service, European Parliament, SACO 101 EN, 11–1198.
Hartigan, J. (1975), *Clustering Algorithms*, New York: John Wiley.
Kirkcaldy, B.D. and A.F. Furnham (2000), 'Positive affectivity, psychological well-being, accident- and traffic-deaths, and suicide: an international comparison', *Studia Psychologica*, **42**, (1–2), 97–104.
Kirkcaldy, B.D., A. Furnham and T. Martin (1997), National differences in personality, socioeconomic and work-related variables', *European Psychologist*, **3**(4), 255–62.
McKee, M. (2001), 'Measuring the efficiency of health systems. The World Health report sets the agenda but there's still a long way to go', *British Medical Journal*, **323**, 295–6.
Meerding, W.J., L. Bonneaux, J.J. Polder, M.A. Koopmanschap and P.J. van der Meas (1998), 'Demographic and epidemiological determinants of health care costs in the Netherlands: cost of illness study', *British Medical Journal*, **317**, 111–5.
Mossialos, A. (1996), *Satisfaction in Health Care Systems*, Brussels: European Union.
Myers, D. (1993), *The Pursuit of Happiness*, New York: Avon Books.
Nord, E. (2000), *World Health Report 2000. A Brief, Critical Consumer Guide, Oslo:* National Institute of Public Health.
Oishi, S., E.F. Diener, R.E. Lucas and E.M. Suh (1999), 'Cross-cultural variations in predictors of life satisfaction: perspectives from needs and values', *Personality and Social Psychology Bulletin*, **25** (8), 980–90.
The Economist (1995), *Pocket World in Figures*, Harmondsworth: Penguin.
The Economist (2001), *Pocket Europe in Figures: Facts and figures about 48 countries that make up Europe today*, London: Profile Books.
Van de Vliert, E., E.S. Kluwer and R. Lynn (2000), 'Citizens of warmer countries are more competitive and poorer: culture or chance' *Journal of Economic Psychology*, **21**, 143–65.
Veenhoven, R. (2000), 'Well-being in the welfare state: level not higher not more equitable', *Journal of Comparative Policy Analysis: Research and Practice*, **2**, 91–125.
Veenhoven, R. (2001), 'State of nations: world database of happiness', Erasmus University of Rottodam, Faculty of Social Sciences.
WHO (2001), *The World Health Report 2000*, Geneva.
Willinson, L. (1988), *Systat: The System for Statistics*, Evarnston: Systat Inc.

27 New technology, the global economy and organizational environments: effects on employee stress, health and well-being
Janice Langan-Fox

The global economy and restructuring
Demands from the economy, market competition and the political arena have led to restructuring and change in the workplace. New strategies have been introduced by organizations to gain a competitive edge, including 'downsizing', restructuring, new production and work processes, multi-skilling and subcontracting. Many of these new practices have been influenced not only by global market forces, but by changing technology and organizational philosophies.

However organizational strategies have resulted in effects on productivity and workers' physical and mental health. Often leaner production has intensified the work pace and demands, and organizations have failed to take into account the human factors involved with the introduction of change and which can have negative effects that outweigh potential productivity increments (Landsbergis et al., 1999). In this new economic environment, globalization has meant that individual economies are more exposed to events taking place in other countries. Negative reactions to change, especially reactions to imposed change, include stress in the form of anxiety and depression, resulting in decreased job satisfaction, reduced job performance, voluntary resignations and absenteeism (Collins, 1998).

Key issues and questions
Several key issues arise from the current organizational environment in considering the work–health relationship. First, there is the influence of the global economy which has brought about dramatic changes in employment participation trends. Second, huge technological advances have accompanied organizational restructures (Langan-Fox, 2001) and have influenced how work is experienced. Third, change may have had a negative effect on autonomy and other aspects of control over work processes. Fourth, increased dependence on technology may have increased responsibility amongst workers but may also have contributed to deskilling, and poor employment prospects for those who cannot keep up with the pace of change. Finally, change in the nature and quality of work has affected health and there are flow-on effects to other areas of life such as the family. These issues and relevant relationships are represented diagrammatically in Figure 27.1.

The present chapter examines these questions and attempts to illuminate research avenues which would provide an agenda for future research. In what follows we examine, first, the effects of downsizing and restructures; second, the requirement of workforce flexibility; third, the effect of unemployment and technology; and, finally, the broad issues involved in the work–health relationship and the attendant risks associated with

414   *Stress, well-being and health*

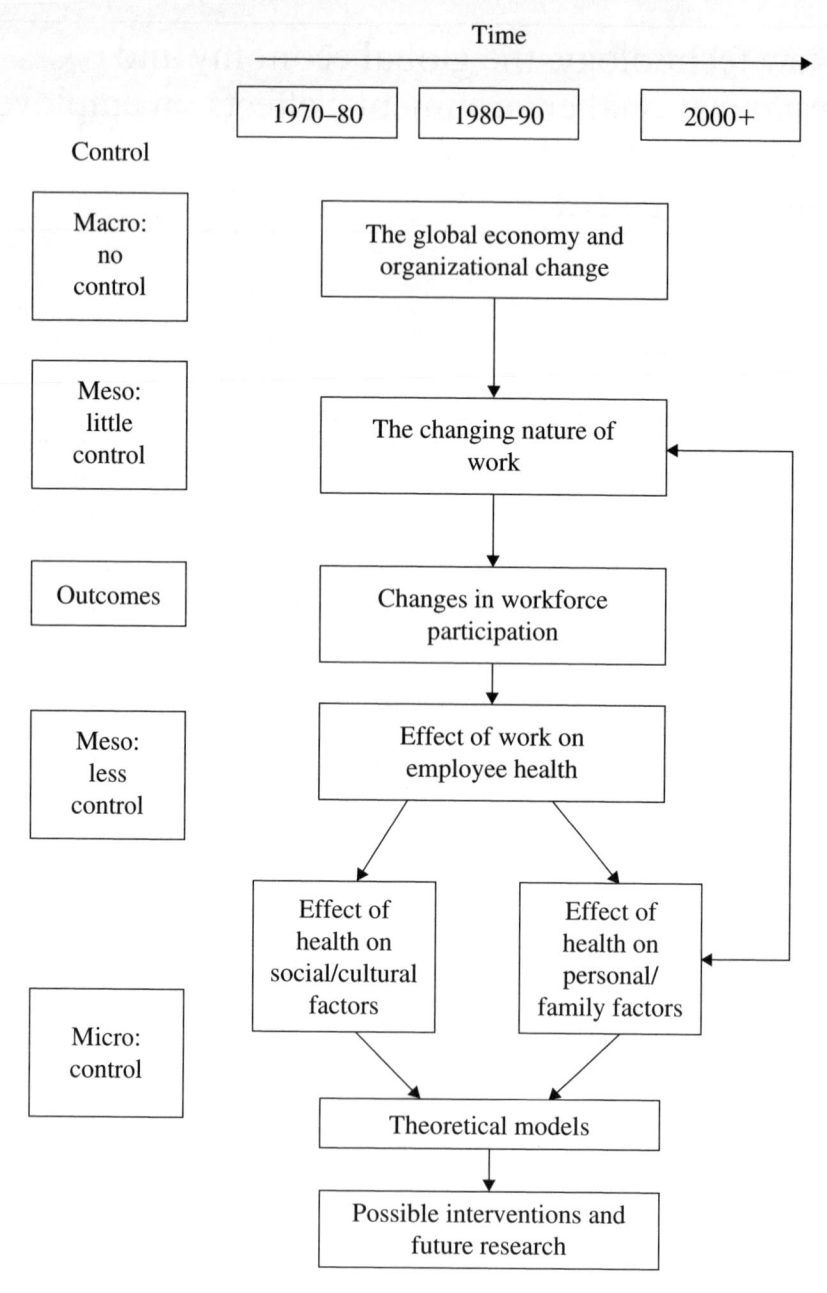

Figure 27.1   Diagrammatic representation of factors in the economy–employee health relationship

employment, and whether interventions and health promotion and prevention programmes have worked, and will work, and how research can provide answers to the various issues presented above.

The economy, employment and changing experiences of workers
Organizational restructuring and downsizing
Downsizing often leads to both systemic (organizational) and negative individual consequences. At the organizational level, one might detect palpable anxiety, diminished morale or uneven job performance of previously high-performing employees. At the individual level one might see manifestations of hypervigilance, anger or guilt in response to being spared from job termination (Schonberg and Lee, 1996). However few studies have examined the impact of new systems of work organization on occupational injuries or illnesses or on job characteristics related to job strain, which have been linked to hypertension and cardiovascular disease. On the other hand there appears to be precious little evidence to support the hypothesis that lean production 'empowers' workers, at least in the automotive industry. In fact studies in this industry suggest that lean production creates intensified work pace and demands (Landsbergis *et al.*, 1999).

Downsizing is likely to continue into the future, yet research evidence suggests that most downsizing efforts do not achieve their objectives (Burke and Nelson, 1999). Two-thirds of firms that downsize repeat the process a year later. Unintended consequences include falls in quality, productivity and customer service. Judge *et al.* (1999) found that two factors, positive self-concept and risk tolerance, predicted coping with organizational change. Downsizing also affects the sense of job security of many workers. Mauno and Kinnumen (1999) showed that perceived job insecurity in 1995 decreased the quality of human relations in organizations and hence perceived efficiency within organizations in 1996.

Downsizing has also been found to be a risk to employee health, but the risk varies by age, socioeconomic status and health, and factors related to place of work, such as size and age of staff (Kivimaeki *et al.*, 1998). These authors found a significant association between downsizing and medically certified sick leave and the rate of absenteeism was 2.3 times greater after major downsizing than after minor downsizing. When the proportion of employees who were older than 50 was high, downsizing increased the individual risk of absence because of ill-health by 3.2 to 14 times.

Flexibility of the workforce
Shiftwork and unusual work hours   With increasing emphasis on employment flexibility, work schedules continue to be a potential health hazard and there is a work schedule–age interaction in the effects of shiftwork. Age strongly influences the negative effects of shiftwork. Kaliterna *et al.* (1995) found that more health complaints were reported by older shiftworkers and also those with longer shiftwork experience. Furthermore, for those in the 40 to 50 age bracket, Haermae (1996) reported that health risks and sleep disturbances in shiftwork increase; older shiftworkers show more night sleep disturbances. Fitness appears to increase shiftwork tolerance, sleep length and night-time alertness. Sleep impairment was mostly linked to shift and strain due to schedules among female hospital workers (Estryn *et al.*, 1990). Women shift crane operators have been found to experience

more sleep disturbances than men and suffer more frequently from drowsiness during work, especially during the morning shift. Women generally suffered more than men from symptoms specific to an 'intolerance syndrome', that is psychoneurotic, digestive, circulatory and chronic fatigue. However, after passing the 'critical decade' of 40–50 years, their subjective health generally improved, whereas older males' health deteriorated more (Oginska et al., 1993).

At a more general (organizational) level, it has been shown by Schecter et al. (1997) that, in a large organizational restructure which also involved downsizing, shift workers reported higher levels of stress than did non-shift workers. Employees on non-standard shifts experience higher job stress and lower job satisfaction, and are able to spend less leisure time with their families than those on standard day shifts (Jamal and Badawi, 1995).

Besides shiftwork, changing schedules also come in the form of 'temporary' or 'permanent part-time', 'casual' and many other variations of this nature.

Temporary and casual work   There appear to be limits to the growth of national and global economies, as there is a shrinking supply of paid work compared to the growing numbers of people seeking it. For some time, traditionally defined full-time and permanent jobs have been understood to be available for all who 'really' want them (APS, 2000). As a consequence, underemployment has received little attention in terms of social and physical consequences and associated causes (Prouse and Dooley, 1997). Both over and underemployment can have negative effects on health. Sokejima and Kagamimori (1998) found that men who worked 11 hours a day had around 2.5 times greater risk of heart attack than men working an eight-hour day, while men working fewer than six hours a day had nearly three times the risk of a heart attack compared to those working an eight-hour day. Therefore underemployment (like unemployment) brings its own stresses and health problems.

The effect of unemployment
In the late 1990s in Australia, 20 per cent of the long-term unemployed reported being either too young or too old as a principal reason for their being unable to obtain a job. A second common reason was lack of skill or education (McLennan, 1999), yet Pryor and Schaffer (1999) contend that jobs for less educated workers have increased faster while, simultaneously, jobs for more educated workers have increased slowly and, as a consequence, university graduates are taking high school-level jobs. Hammarstrom (1994) suggested that there are consistent relationships that can be found between unemployment and minor psychological disorders, with few studies examining somatic health. But results to date indicate increased physiological illness, especially amongst unemployed girls. Also the mortality rate is significantly higher among unemployed young men and women, particularly through suicide and accident. For young people, unsatisfactory employment seems no better than unemployment. Social consequences include increased risk of alienation, lack of financial resources, criminality and future exclusion from the labour market (Hammarstrom, 1994).

During the industrial revolution, the introduction of the 'machine age' was feared for its potential to put workers out of jobs. Today the implementation of technology is hardly questioned, and indeed is welcomed in most industries. However the *way* in which new technology is introduced, and the lack of foresight regarding the effects of working with new technology, have not yet been properly planned or understood by those responsible for managing such implementations. These are the New Age problems of modern workplaces: 'technology implementation and infusion'.

The effect of technology
Rapid technological advances have made dramatic changes to the world of work. Technological advances have introduced computers, telecommunications systems, robotics and flexible manufacturing operations. Routine tasks are increasingly automated, meaning employees' skills are becoming obsolete more quickly, which indicates an increasing need for continuing training and education. The Internet offers new ways of doing business; bypassing intermediaries, there is greater communication between customer and producer, and new distribution chains are created along with added stress for employees (Drucker et al., 1997). Notwithstanding these changes, research examining the effects of technology on workers has been minimal (see, for example, Langan-Fox, 1996, 2001).

Parcel et al. (1988) investigated the effects of organizational change and working conditions on workers employed by an ultra-high-technology firm and found differences among computer and non-computing professionals which indicated increased stress amongst the former group, attributable to pressures of knowledge upgrades, and effects synonymous with machine-paced work. These effects are often not considered by managers who tend only to consider the physical health risks involved in occupational stress when introducing new technology (Langan-Fox, 2001).

Psychosocial aspects of using video display terminals (VDTs) have been recognized as contributors to employees' mental and physical health problems for more than 15 years (LeGrande, 1999), yet little has been done by employers to change work organization conditions to improve this aspect for VDT users. Smith (1997) found that psychosocial aspects of work are one of the main sources of problems. Factors associated with ill-health include lack of employee skill use, monotonous tasks, high job demands and work pressure, a lack of control over the job, poor supervisory relations, fear of job loss and unreliable technology. Amick and Celentano (1991) illustrated that technology is indirectly associated with job satisfaction and psychosomatic symptoms by how it structured the job. A machine-paced technological system of work was associated with greater job demands, less control in the job, and less co-worker support, but not with supervisor support. Arnetz and Wilholm (1997) suggest that employees in modern office environments more often report suffering from psychosomatic symptoms and believe that the introduction of information technologies constitute potential stressors which overly challenge employees' cognitive resources, especially when faced with factors highlighted by Smith (1997).

It is obvious, then, that the health of employees is affected by change, by restructures, reorganizations, new technology and the like. Some of the effects of these changes have been referred to in the foregoing. What follows is a more broad-ranging discussion of the way workers' health is affected by these changes.

Global work/health trends and costs: changing patterns of work and health
American workers are working harder and longer than in the last two decades just to maintain the same living standards (McGuire, 1999). It is believed that a quarter to a third of workers have high job stress and report feeling drained at the end of the day. In the space

of a generation, American workers' hours worked per week have gone up by 8 per cent to an average of 47 hours, and 20 per cent of the American workforce is working more than 49 hours a week; this increase in work is coupled with a greater fear of being fired. This has led to social and family disruptions.

Some people suggest that economic policies that encourage downsizing and wage imbalances are the source of the problem. In fact, many companies that have eliminated jobs have experienced increased health care costs, lower morale and lower productivity (Landsbergis et al., 1999). This has implications for the changing nature of the field of occupational and safety health. There has been growing public awareness in America about the costs of occupational stress and the need for preventative action.

Impact of work tasks on physiological health
Job tasks have a profound impact on employee health; for instance, Krause et al. (1997) report results that show that heavy work, work in uncomfortable positions, long work hours, noise at work, physical job strain, musculoskeletal strain, repetitive or continuous muscle strain mental job strain and job dissatisfaction were all significantly associated with the incidence of disability retirement.

High job demands have been found to relate to neck and shoulder symptoms and the tendency to become overworked (Skov et al., 1996), whilst lack of variation in the job, low control over time and high competition have been related to neck symptoms. Ahlberg-Hulten et al. (1995) found that psychological demands, authority over decisions, skill utilization and support at work had a significant effect on lower back symptoms. In the United States, annual productivity losses per worker due to chronic backache were approximately $28 billion (Rizzo et al., 1998). Factors correlated with lower back pain include heavy physical work, static or postural effort, dynamic workload and exposure to whole-body vibration (Halpern, 1992). Bru et al. (1997) suggest that perceived stress and effort are positively correlated with back pain.

So-called 'light industry', or the 'high-tech' industries, also have their negative effects on health. Data entry visual display terminal (VDT) workers report the highest rates of cumulative trauma musculoskeletal pain, followed by technical, clerical and professional workers (LeGrande, 1999). Further, Conway (1999) reports results of research into workers using video terminals and found that psychological stress was related to visual difficulties and musculoskeletal discomfort. Jacobsen and Petterson (1993) investigated occupation-related health complaints among dental technologists and reported that half of the employees had experienced some kind of job-related health problem: musculoskeletal and dermal reactions were common.

It has been estimated that 2.2 per cent of deaths worldwide are attributable to occupation-related injuries or disease (Murray and Lopez, 1996). Of those aged 15 years or more who reported a condition due to an accident, incident or exposure, 42 per cent reported that the condition was work-related. Even minor complaints can be costly to business. For example, Hu et al. (1999) have found that migraines cost American employers about $13 billion a year because of missed workdays and impaired work function; close to $8 billion was directly due to missed workdays. Salminem (1993) predicts that work processes will speed up further; the number of older workers will increase, perhaps leading to an increased accident risk for older employees.

Impact of work on mental health
In Australia, although occupational stress may have reached its peak as a cause of workplace injury and illness, the costs associated with such injuries remain high; work by Mackay and Cooper (1987) revealed that Australians of all demographic groups are feeling more stressed than they had in the past (see also Code and Langan-Fox, 2002; Langan-Fox, 1997; Langan-Fox and Poole, 1995). Many social factors may have influenced this increase, including changing sex-role expectations, technological transformations and new social attitudes to institutions and authority. Demands for greater employee efficiency have led to increased workload and occupational stress.

Occupational stress affects all levels of employees across all occupations. Murphy *et al.* (1995) suggest that reported job stress in the US workforce is on the increase. Financial costs of stress in the US are estimated to be $150 billion per year. However most of the costs of occupational stress are hidden and show up in absenteeism, poor work performance, work flow interference and the need for employee replacement and retraining. Medical authorities estimate stress is costing Australian businesses $1.2 billion dollars annually in compensation payouts, dented productivity, impaired performance and accidents (Johns, 1995). This figure was partly attributed to poor management, downsizing, cost cutting, heavy workloads, abusive customers, conflict and lack of employee consultation.

Job-related stress incidents have remained a relatively constant proportion of the total injury and illness cases resulting in work absences (Bergman and Webster, 1999). In 1996, job-related stress accounted for almost two-thirds of all anxiety disorders resulting in lost workdays and, between 1992 and 1996, job-related stress consistently resulted in lengthy absences with a median duration ranging from 10 to 33 days (Armstrong-Strasson, 1997; Buttner, 1992; Cavanaugh *et al.*, 2000). Managerial and professional specialities, and technical, sales and administrative support occupations, had a higher proportion of neurotic reactions to stress.

The largest increase in stress appears to be at the milder levels of vocational discontent and adjustment stress reactions and there have also been increases in personality–person–job-fit problems (Appay, 1998; Arney, 1988). At a general level, these increases can be attributed to the changing nature of work: increased pace of change, structural reform processes, changing work practices, adapting to new technologies, competing situational demands, multiskilling, flattening organizational structures and loss of job security.

There is growing recognition that effective strategies for managing occupational stress and injury must be implemented.

Intervention and prevention: tackling health problems in the workplace
During the 19th and early 20th centuries, workers struggled to secure shorter working weeks. However, during the latter part of the 20th century, work became more highly valued than leisure for its ability to provide 'the good life' through the provision of consumer goods and services. Today 49 per cent of Americans believe too much importance is given to work and not enough to time away from work. Work time stabilized in the USA at around 40 hours per week, but now appears to be lengthening. Paid and unpaid work time in all jobs is longer today than it was 20 years ago, rising from 43.6 hours in 1977 to 47.1 hours in 1997 per week (Swanberg *et al.*, 1999).

Instead of viewing progress as transcending work, necessity and economic concerns, Americans now tend to view work as an end in itself, the ultimate measure of progress and definition of progress. Something like a theology of work has ensued. Americans tend to answer traditional religious questions (who am I? where am I going?) in terms of work instead of formal religion. The result is an age of seriousness 'the world of total work'. The idea of a 'job for life' and 'marriage for life' are no longer taken as given in Western society, and many individuals need to adapt to changing circumstances and multiple sources of stress at varying times in their lives. The realms of family and work are being seen as open and interactive systems that are complex and dynamic and the increasing involvement in the workforce of women has raised issues related to the balancing of work and family demands (Hurrell and Murphy, 1991).

Changes in the workforce, greater availability of cars, the shift of jobs to urban locations have increased commuting by car. In the USA, the volume of cars on the road rose by 90 per cent between 1970 and 1989, with only a 4 per cent increase in urban road capacity. In this same period there was decline in the use of public transport for the purpose of getting to work. Whatever means of transport used, travelling to work is a part of the working day and often a source of stress. Factors associated with travelling, including air pollution, lack of comfort, noise, weather and crowding, are chronic, potentially causing strain and health problems. Possible governmental and organizational preventative strategies include incentives to use mass-transport, technology and company methods such as relocation, working from home and flexible working hours (Koslowsky *et al.*, 1995).

Employee assistance programs, health promotion and prevention
It is a fact that workplace health promotion programs have grown exponentially over the past 20 years. Contents include fitness programs, smoking cessation courses, reduction in alcohol consumption, eating habits, hypertension courses, and lower back pain courses. While limited research has been done on integrated health programs, early evidence suggests positive benefits for the employee and the organization (Schreurs *et al.*, 1996). Strategies for reducing work-related stress include making working conditions less stressful, helping individuals adapt by teaching them better coping strategies, and identifying the stressful relationship between the individual or group and the work setting (Long, 1995).

Research investigating the effectiveness of employee assistance programmes (EAP) and counselling interventions has been mixed. Interventions can be grouped into four categories: first, job design to improve working conditions; second, surveillance of psychological disorders and risk factors; third, information dissemination and training; fourth, enrichment of psychological health services for workers (Ross and Altmeier, 1994). Ramanathan (1992) has suggested that, although personal stress and employee productivity are related, EAP interventions may improve employee productivity without reducing employee stress. Bayer (1991) suggests that client-centred EAPs provide the highest quality services, as measured by high client satisfaction, minimal referral needs, elimination or alleviation of work performance problems, and low or no relapse to maladaptive behaviours such as addiction or insubordination; and client-centred EAPs show a cost advantage, as evidenced by outcome data.

However, French *et al.* (1997) argue that underlying the credible integration of EAPs into worksite culture is the positive and robust relationship between employee trust and confidence in the EAP and actual use. Interventions should address multiple risk factors, address a variety of health behaviours and use a number of intervention strategies without adversely affecting productivity. Structural and organizational changes to the wider worksite environment should be made to promote healthier choices and encourage a health-promoting culture at work (Oldenburg and Harris, 1996).

Iwi *et al.* (1998) investigated self-reported well-being of employees facing organizational change, and the effect of an intervention, and suggested that adverse effects on staff facing organizational change may be ameliorated by improved management practice. In a study comparing two types of stress intervention, Reynolds (1997) suggested that counselling has clear benefits for employees' psychological well-being and that organizational intervention does not. Neither intervention had any impact on perceptions of work characteristics, physical symptoms or absenteeism.

A brief nap during post-lunch rest is helpful for maintaining subsequent alertness and performance even under prior sleep deficit, particularly around the afternoon dip, and humour and play can have instrumental value in work settings (Moore and Cooper, 1996; Morreal, 1991). Specifically humour can benefit workers' mental and physical health by reducing pathogenic stress; promoting mental flexibility which involves divergent thinking, creative problem solving, risk taking and tolerance for ambiguity and change, by encouraging disengagement and objectivity; and increasing effective job interactions by building teamwork and morale. Also telling jokes may reduce boredom and defuse hostile situations (Morreal, 1991).

The most efficient strategies for reducing distress in work settings, it seems, are those which increase the distance between the worker and the problem, or those which are emotion-focused or palliative (Murphy, 1985). Optimal support should match the type of stressful event. Controllable stressors are best solved by instrumental and esteem support. Uncontrollable stressors are best satisfied by emotional support. Macro structures of organizations that affect social support systems are difficult to influence with intervention programmes. Nonetheless, less profound change can be implemented in the meso and micro systems through group and individual counselling. Although a work environment without stress is an impossible goal, much can be done to reduce the risk of stress, strain and burnout, and much of that risk has to do with social support, organizational support, organizational structure and organizational culture (Murphy, 1985). Schierhout *et al.* (1995) found that ergonomic stress could be reduced with simple surveillance methods, and educational programmes in the workplace. And interventions to reduce the stress of computer technology have included improved technology implementation approaches and increased employee participation in implementation, with for example, proper ergonomic conditions, increased organizational support, improved job content, proper workload to decrease work pressure and enhanced opportunities for social support (Smith *et al.*, 1999).

Programs offered in many organizations are 'curative' in nature. Thus the strategies introduced in worksites are aimed at curing problems *after* workers experience the negative effects of stress. A better approach to managing stress would include interventions that are 'preventive'. Both the individual and the organization need to be the target for intervention.

Research directions for improving employee health and well-being

The globalization of economies has prompted major changes in the nature of work. People in a wide range of occupations are coping with greater uncertainty and more intense demands for increased productivity (Leiter and Harvie, 1997). One cause of this is the move from an industry-based economy to an information-based economy. The diffusion of information technology has made some jobs obsolete and redesigned others, which has led to an increased demand for decision-making skills and training. Generally training methods have lagged behind constantly evolving technology, therefore not meeting the needs of complex situations which call for novel solutions. Thus there is a move towards training workers in self-directed problem-solving skills that allow them to tackle novel situations. Computer-based training is also becoming an option, although it can be very expensive (Coovert and Craiger, 1997). Waterman et al. (1994) suggest that, to meet the challenge, competition and chaos in the world of work, a career-resilient, self-reliant workforce is needed.

Summers et al. (1995) identified the following trends in the industrial structure of rural labour markets in the USA: (1) sectoral shifts in the rural economy and increased global competition; (2) shift of labour out of agriculture and into the service sector; (3) increasing rural unemployment and unemployment rates in the 1980s (higher than those found in urban areas); (4) lower household and family income in rural regions than in urban areas; and (5) increasing and greater rates of part-time employment in rural than in urban areas.

Labour and manual work are giving way to knowledge and technology as the basis for work. Manufacturing is in decline and services are growing. Hierarchies and bureaucracies are going out and networks and partnerships are coming in. The career in an organization is being replaced by job mobility and career changes. Greater attention needs to be paid to work conducted outside or at the margins of the regulated workforce, for example, voluntary work, small businesses and home workers (Waterman et al., 1994).

Attention to psychosocial hazards in work environments should also become an increasingly important component of occupational safety and health interventions. Research findings have linked a number of measurable psychosocial characteristics to negative psychological and physiological consequences. Several economic trends indicate that more jobs will be created with high levels of psychosocial hazards. These economic trends include a decline in wages, a move away from a manufacturing base, increased hours of work, a decline in unionization rates and poorly implemented technological changes (Cahill, 1996).

Growth has occurred in the service sector and there are fewer jobs in manufacturing and production. Longer hours are being performed by full-time workers. Greater numbers of workers are performing flexible casual and part-time work, and knowledge and responsibility required by workers has increased. Less job security and more job changes are entering people's lives, along with more subcontracting by firms. Women are participating more in the paid workforce. The balance of work is shifting from production of goods to the provision of business and community services. This implies a devaluing of skills traditionally favoured in production of goods in favour of interpersonal and cognitive skills, with widespread personal, social and geographical implications. This is seen to be associated with a stronger labour market position for women than men, concentration of work at both ends of the hours distribution, with a small proportion working very long hours and a large number with few hours per week, and the increasing division of families and neighbourhoods into the work-rich and the work-poor. So how can this be dealt with?

Firstly, prevention of the premature decline of physical capacities and adaptability of the worker could be addressed by health promotion and continuing job training. Secondly, some measures for adjusting work demands in accordance with functional capacities of the individual are needed. Thirdly, employers and fellow workers should be educated on the strengths of the ageing worker, and the capacity of such workers to continue contributing because of their experience, motivation and skills. If implemented, these measures would ensure a path towards productive ageing (Chan and Koh, 1997).

Sachs and Shatz (1994) suggest that internationalization has contributed to falling manufacturing employment, especially in low-skilled sectors, and their findings also show increasing income inequality between low-skilled and high-skilled manufacturing workers. The changes in trade from 1978 to 1990 are associated with a 7.2 per cent decline of generally lower-skilled production jobs and a 2.1 per cent decline of non-production jobs.

Employees need training to optimize use of technology including basic skills. Technical training (installation and maintenance of technology) and skill training (use of technology and software) are critical. In high-performance work systems machines perform all the repetitive mental and physical tasks, and people spend their time deploying machine capabilities to produce variety and customize products and services. This requires workers who can transfer knowledge and prior experience to handle a continuous stream of exceptions. Skills for managing this challenge are crucial; they include deciding the importance of information, understanding the meaning of information and utilizing the information appropriately (Waterman *et al.*, 1994). The new economy will require a much more skilled workforce. Employees need training to optimize use of technology, for example technical training and skill training. In high-performance work systems machines perform all the repetitive mental and physical tasks, and people spend their time deploying machine capabilities to produce variety and customize products and services. This requires workers who can transfer knowledge and use prior experience to handle a continuous stream of exceptions. Employers need to build high-performance systems and design technologies to utilize worker skills (Carnevale, 1995).

Downsizing and delayering do not automatically mean increased productivity. Negative attitudes between workers and overworked managers are more likely unless a more democratic approach is taken, with workers helping to redesign their own work (James, 1996). Parker *et al.* (1997) findings from a four-year longitudinal study of strategic downsizing suggest that introducing deliberate work organization and change management strategies can combat the negative effects of reduced head count. Results showed that there was no overall decrease in well-being from before to after downsizing for the employees remaining in the organization, despite an increase in work demands. The potential detrimental effect of demands appears to have been offset by improvement in work characteristics arising from initiatives introduced as part of the downsizing strategy. To improve the effects of downsizing, managers need to focus closely on the controllable aspects of initiation, implementation and institutionalization (Burke and Nelson, 1998). Good management, employee involvement and understanding of human factors are essential for successful change to be implemented. This can include training workers to be adaptive and able to cope with change, but ideally focuses on the source of problems in the work and production processes.

Menaghan (1994) argues that the sociological study of stress must move still further – beyond individual mental health consequences – and consider the multiple social and intergenerational consequences of adults' socially structured stressors. In particular, the study of work stressors must consider their impact on workers' intimate marital relationships, on their parenting activities and on their children's emotional well-being. Cooper and Payne (1991) suggest that there is an intuitive link between personality variables and stress. Future research, in addition to looking at the relationships between personality variables, needs to examine the relationships between personality factors, as well as with other sociodemographic variables, to shed light on the causal relationships between these factors and stress.

Simon (1997) suggests that some meanings of role identities are associated with symptoms and are involved in gender differences in distress. These and other findings suggest that stress researchers should incorporate the meanings that individuals attach to their role identities and devote greater attention to men's and women's perceptions of both the positive and the negative aspects of their role involvement. There is also a need to develop measures of cognitive abilities that are capable of assessing individual differences in dealing with real-world problems, for instance properly developed measures of practical intelligence. The stress literature has tended to avoid doing studies which recognize that stress is a process that takes place over time. Issues of problem solving style and capacity are interrelated and important for understanding the stress process (Payne, 1991). There is also a need for research into coping flexibility and consistency (Parkes, 1994).

It has been suggested that managerial strategies for creating healthy work environments involve two key principles. These are that (a) individual and organizational health are interdependent, and (b) management has a responsibility for individual and organizational health. Organizational culture and management support are recognized as essential aspects for supporting health and safety in the workplace. In low-safety organizations, production was valued over employee welfare, inadequate resources were provided for the safety effort, safety values were espoused, rather than actual, employees were blamed for their injuries and the workforce was demoralized (Quick, 1998).

Work is a major determinant of well-being, with major implications for social, economic and personal prosperity. Currently work is undergoing a fundamental redefinition caused by factors such as intensified global competition, access to new and developing markets, fluctuating demographics, rising expectations of the labour force and the rapid advancement of computerized technology (Donaldson *et al.*, 1999). A shift can be observed in the manner in which work and income security are acquired. In the future the careers of an increasing number of people will comprised shorter, successive or simultaneous work relationships in either part- or full-time contexts. As a result, less time will be spent in one function and/or one company. New systems of work organization have been introduced by employers throughout the industrialized world in order to improve productivity, product quality and profitability; for example: lean production, total quality management (TQM), quality circles, 'just-in-time' (JIT) inventory systems, cellular or modular manufacturing, re-engineering and high-performance work organizations. They have been extolled as reforms of Taylorism and the traditional assembly-line approach to job design, but little research has assessed their effects on workers' physical and mental health (Landsbergis et al., 1999).

Traditionally the significance of work in human life has related to economic survival and professional identity. In the future, work identity will need to be seen as competence in assigning work and employment a meaningful place in one's life, and in formulating a plan of action about work and employment (Stern, 1993). Vallas (1989) argues that the introduction of information technologies has caused a historic shift in the role of the worker's body within the production process. The demand for new 'intellective' skills will affect both workers and management. Organizations need to empower employees to adopt the role of change agent and encourage them to take action to solve the problems that stress them. To help employees cope with change, organizations can pursue strategies related to communication, leadership, job-related tasks and stress management programmes (Callan, 1993). Suggestions for restoring employee strength and morale during downsizing and restructuring programmes include the following: stabilize key people, clarify the change message, emphasizing the goals and vision for the future, communicate, invest in survivors, drive out fear and build in trust, and keep the spirit of change alive (Peixotto, 1998).

Conclusion
The future of work points towards even greater unemployment (ABS, 1994; International Labour Office, 1986). The major trend is not so much towards the 'end of work' but to strategic expansion, through economic concentration and the externalization of labour. As a result of fierce competition, different forms of labour organization are appearing, as well as new costs for society. Today's 'cascading subcontracting' is related, not only to the externalization of labour costs, but also to the externalization of risks and responsibilities and, consequently, could be said to contradict more and more the basic principles of democracy (Appay, 1998). Parkes (1996) suggests that, in the future, work will be organized into larger units of production, and workers will be expected to assume greater decision-making responsibilities in planning and performing the work to be done.

New forms of work organization which may emerge in the coming decade include the fading distinction between blue- and white-collar work as occupational status is defined more in terms of skills and knowledge, and multi-skilling breaks down barriers between skilled and unskilled work, trades and professions. Self-employment and contract employment are predicted to increase, and retraining will become a constant requirement to ensure that skills remain relevant as people change occupations.

As organizations require greater information about competitors, markets, customers and other external factors, many knowledge-intensive jobs will expand, including those of contractors, experts, consultants, part-timers, joint-venture partners and so on. These workers are more likely to identify with their knowledge than with the organizations that employ them. Increasing mobility for highly demanded, outsourced, knowledge-based workers is likely to occur (Landsbury, 1994). Major questions for the future include how to lead the organizations that create and nurture knowledge; when to rely on machines for decision making and how to maintain an individual and organizational attitude of continual learning and sense of control over the production process (Drucker et al., 1997).

Acknowledgment
Grateful thanks to Kathy Armstrong and Jeromy Anglin, who assisted with literature reviews.

References
ABS (1994), *1995–2011 Labour Force Projections Australia*, Australian Bureau of Statistics, catalogue 6290.0.
Ahlberg-Hulten, G.K., T. Theorell and F. Sigala (1995), 'Social support, job strain and musculoskeletal pain among female health care personnel', *Scandinavian Journal of Work, Environment and Health*, **21** (6), 435–9.
Amick, B.C. and D.D. Celentano (1991), 'Structural determinants of the psychosocial work environment: introducing technology in the work stress framework', *Ergonomics*, **34**(5), 625–46.
Appay, B. (1998), 'Economic concentration and the externalization of labour', *Economic and Industrial Democracy*, **19**, 161–84.
APS (2000), 'The psychology of work and unemployment in Australia today', A discussion paper of the Australian Psychological Society, Carlton, Victoria, Australia.
Armstrong-Strassen, M. (1997), 'The effect of repeated downsizing and surplus designation on remaining managers: an exploratory study', *Anxiety, Stress and Coping: An International Journal*, **10** (4), 377–84.
Arnetz, B.B. and C. Wilhom (1997), 'Technological stress: psychophysiological symptoms in modern offices', *Journal of Psychosomatic Research*, **43**, 35–42.
Arney, L.K. (1988), 'Effects of personality–environment fit on job stress', *Educational and Psychological Research*, **8**, 1–18.
Bayer, D.L. (1991), 'Client-centered employee assistance services', paper presented at the Annual Professional Development Institute of the Employee Assistance Society of America, Atlantic City, NJ, 9–12 June.
Bru, E., S. Svebak, R.J. Mykletun and J.P. Gitlesen (1997), 'Back pain, dysphoric versus euphoric moods and the experience of stress and effort in female hospital staff', *Personality and Individual Differences*, **22** (4), 565–73.
Burke, R.J. and D. Nelson (1998), 'Mergers and acquistions, downsizing and privatisation: a North American perspective', in M. Gowing and J.D. Kraft (eds), *The New Organisational Reality: Downsizing, Restructuring and Revitalisation*, Washington, DC: APA, pp. 21–54.
Buttner, E.H. (1992), 'Entrepreneurial stress: is it hazardous to your health?', *Journal of Managerial Issues*, **4** (2), 223–40.
Cahill, J. (1996), 'Psychosocial aspects of interventions in occupational safety and health', *American Journal of Industrial Medicine*, **29**(4), 308–13.
Callan, V.J. (1993), 'Individual and organizational strategies for coping with organizational change', *Work and Stress*, **7**, 63–75.
Cavanaugh, M.A., W.R. Boswell, M.V. Roehling and J.W. Boudreau (2000), 'An empirical examination of self-reported work stress among U.S. managers', *Journal of Applied Psychology*, **85**(1), 65–74.
Chan, G.V. and D.S. Koh (1997), 'The ageing worker', *Ann. Acad. Medicine Singapore*.
Code, S. and J. Langan-Fox (2001), 'Motivation, cognitions and traits: predicting occupational health, well-being and performance', *Stress and Health*, **17**, 159–74.
Collins, D. (1998), *Organisational Change: Sociological Perspectives*, London: Routledge.
Conway, F.T. (1999), 'Psychological mood state, psychosocial aspects of work and musculoskeletal discomfort in intensive video display terminal (VDT) work', *International Journal of Human–Computer Interaction*, **11**(2), 95–107.
Cooper C.L. and R. Payne (1991), 'Introduction', in C.L. Cooper and R. Payne (eds), *Personality and Stress: Individual Differences in the Stress Process*, Chichester: John Wiley and Sons, pp.1–4.
Coovert, M. and J.P. Craiger (1997), 'Performance modeling for training effectiveness', in J.K. Ford (ed.), *Improving Training Effectiveness in Work Organizations*, Mahwah, NJ: Lawrence Erlbaum Associates, pp. 47–71.
Donaldson, S.I., S. Sussman and C.W. Dent (1999), 'Health behaviour, quality of work life, and organisational effectiveness in the lumber industry, *Health Education Behaviour*, **26**(4), 579–91.
Drucker, P.F., E. Dyson, C. Handy, P. Saffo and P. Senge (1997), 'Looking ahead: implications of the present', *Harvard Business Review*, **75**(5),18–20, 30, 32.
Estryn, B.M., M. Kaniski, E. Peigne, N. Bonnet, E. Vaichere, C. Gozlan, S. Azoulay and M. Giorgi (1990), 'Stress at work and mental health status among female hospital workers', *British Journal of Industrial Medicine*, **15**, 14–32.
French, M.T., P.M. Roman, L.J. Dunlap and P.D. Steele (1997), 'Factors that influence the use and perceptions of employee assistance programs at six worksites', *Journal of Occupational Health Psychology*, **2** (4), 312–24.
Haermae, M. (1996), 'Ageing, physical fitness and shiftwork tolerance', *Applied Ergonomics*, **27** (1), 25–9.
Halpern, M. (1992), 'Prevention of low back pain: basic ergonomics in the workplace and the clinic', *Baillieres Clinical Rheumatol*, **6**(3), 705–30.

Hammarstrom, A. (1994), 'Health consequences of youth unemployment – review from a gender perspective', *Social Science Medicine*, **38** (5), 699–709.
Hu, X.H., L.E. Markson, R.B. Lipton, W.F. Stewart and M.L. Berger (1999), 'Burden of migraine in the United States: disability and economic costs', *Archives of International Medicine*, **159**(8), 813–18.
Hurrell, J.J. Jr and L.R. Murphy (1991), 'Locus of control, job demands, and health', in C.L. Cooper and R. Payne (eds) *Personality and Stress: Individual Differences in the Stress Process*, Chichester: John Wiley and Sons, pp. 133–49.
International Labour Office (1986), *Economically Active Population: Estimates and Projections 1950–2025*, vol. 4, Geneva: International Labour Office.
Iverson, R.D., M. Olekalns and P.J. Erwin (1998), 'Affectivity, organizational stressors and absenteeism: a causal model of burnout and its consequences', *Journal of Vocational Behavior*, **52**, 1–23.
Jacobsen, N. and A.H. Pettersen (1993), 'Self-reported occupation-related health complaints among dental laboratory technicians', *Quintessence Int.*, **24**(6), 409–15.
Jamal, M. and J.A. Badawi (1995), 'Nonstandard work schedules and work and nonwork experiences of Muslim immigrants: a study of a minority in the majority', *Journal of Social Behavior and Personality*, **10**(2), 395–408.
James, D. (1996), 'Forget downsizing, now it's participative redesign', *Business Review Weekly (Aust)*, **18**(46), 70–72.
Johns, G. (1995), 'Occupational stress and well-being at work', in P. Cotton (ed.), *Psychological Health in the Workplace: Understanding and Managing Occupational Stress*, Carlton, Victoria, Australia: Australian Psychological Society.
Judge, T.A., C.J. Thoresen, V. Pucik and T.M. Welbourne (1999), 'Managerial coping with organisational change: a dispositional perspective', *Journal of Applied Psychology*, **84**(1), 107–22.
Kaliterna, L., S. Vidacek, Z. Prizmic and V.B. Radosevic (1995), 'Is tolerance to shift work predictable from individual difference measures?', *Work and Stress*, **9**, 140–47.
Kivimaeki, M., J. Vahtera, M. Koskenvuo, A. Uutela and J. Pentti (1998), 'Response of hostile individuals to stressful changes in their working lives: test of a psychosocial vulnerability model', *Psychological Medicine*, **28**(4), 903–13.
Koslowsky, M., A. Kluger and M. Reich (1995), *Commuting Stress: Causes, Effects and Methods of Coping*, New York: Plenum Press.
Krause, N., J. Lynch, G.A. Kaplan, R.D. Cohen, D.E. Goldberg and J.T. Salonen (1997), 'Predictors of disability retirement', *Scandinavian Journal of Work and Environmental Health*, **23**(6), 403–13.
Landsbergis, P.A., J. Cahill and P. Schnall (1999), 'The impact of production and related new systems of work organization on worker health,' *Journal of Occupational Health Psychology*, **4**(2), 108–30.
Landsbury, R.D. (1994), 'The workforce of the future: implications for industrial relations, education and training', *Economic and Labour Relations Review*, **5**, 104–16.
Langan-Fox, J. (1996), 'Validity and reliability of measures of occupational and role stress using samples of Australian managers and professionals', *Stress Medicine*, **12**, 211–25.
Langan-Fox, J. (2001), 'Communication in organisations: speed, diversity, networks and influence on organisational effectiveness. human health and relationships', in N. Anderson, D.S. Ones, H.K. Sinangil, C. Vswesvaren (eds), *International Handbook of Work and Organizational Psychology*, vol. 2, London: Sage, 188–205.
Langan-Fox, J. and M.E. Poole (1995), 'Occupational stress in Australian business and professional women', *Stress Medicine*, **11**(2), 113–22.
LeGrande, H. (1999), 'Generating ideas with divergent thinking tools in the development of instructional strategies: a case study', *Dissertation Abstracts International Section A: Humanities and Social Sciences*, **59**(7-A), 2343.
Leiter, M.P. and P. Harvie (1997), 'Correspondence of supervisor and subordinate perspectives during major organizational change', *Journal of Occupational Health Psychology*, **2**(4), 343–52.
Long, B.C. (1995), *Stress in the Work Place: ERIC Digest*, Greensboro, NC: Canadian Guidance and Counselling Foundation.
Mackay, C.J. and C.L. Cooper (1987), 'Occupational stress and health: some current issues', in C.L. Cooper and I.T. Robertson (eds), *International Review of Industrial and Organisational Psychology*, Chichester: John Wiley, pp. 167–79.
Mauno, S. and U. Kunnunnen (1999), 'Job insecurity and well-being: a longitudinal study among male and female employees in Finland', *Community Work and Family*, **12**(2), 147–71.
McGuire, P.A. (1999), 'Worker stress, health reaching critical point', *APA Monitor*, **30**(5), 1, 27.
McLennan, W. (1999), *1999 Year Book Australia*, vol. 81, Canberra: Australian Bureau of Statistics.
Menaghan, E.G. (1994), 'The daily grind: work stressors, family patterns and intergenerational outcomes', in W.R. Avison and I.A. Gotlieb (eds), *Stress and Mental Health: Contemporary Issues and Prospects for the Future*, New York: Plenum Press, pp. 115–47.

Moore, K.A. and C.L. Cooper (1996), 'Stress in mental health professionals: a theoretical overview', *The International Journal of Social Psychiatry*, **42**(2), 82–9.
Morreal, J. (1991), 'Humor and Work', *Humor*, **4**, 359–73.
Murphy, L.R. (1985), Individual coping strategies', in C.L. Cooper and M.J. Smith (eds), *Job Stress and Blue Collar Work*, Chichester: Wiley.
Murphy, L.R., J.J. Hurrell, Jr., S.L. Sauter and G.P. Keita (1995), *Job Stress Interventions*, Washington: American Psychological Association.
Murray, C.J.L. and A.D. Lopez (eds) (1996), *The Global Burden of Disease: A Comprehensive Assessment of Mortality and Disability from Diseases, Injuries and Risk Factors in 1990 and Projected to 2020*, Boston, Harvard University Press.
Oginska, H., J. Pokorski and A. Oginski (1993), 'Gender, ageing, and shiftwork intolerance', *Ergonomics*, **36**, 161–8.
Parcel, T.L., M. Wallace, R. Kaufman and D. Grant (1988), 'Looking Forward Again: Occupational Variation in Worker Response to Employment within an Ultra-High Technology Firm', *Work and Stress*, **15**, 22–35.
Parker, S.K., N. Chmiel and T.D. Wall (1997), 'Work characteristics and employee well-being within a context of strategic downsizing', *Journal of Occupational Health Psychology*, **2**(4), 289–303.
Parkes, K.R. (1994), 'Personality and coping as moderators of work stress processes: models, methods and measures', *Work and Stress*, **8**, 110–29.
Parkes, K.R. (1998), 'Psychosocial aspects of stress, health and safety on North Sea installations', *Scandinavian Journal of Work, Environment and Health*, **24**(5), 321–33.
Payne, R. (1991), 'Individual differences in cognition and the stress process', in C.I. Cooper and R. Payne (eds), *Personality and Stress: Individual Differences in the Stress Process*, Chichester: John Wiley and Sons, pp. 181–201.
Prouse, J. and D. Dooley (1997), 'Effects of underemployment on school-leavers' self-esteem', *Journal of Adolescence*, **20**(3), 243–60.
Pryor, F.L. and D.L. Schaffer (1999), *Who's Not Working and Why: employment, Cognitive Skills, Wages and the Changing U.S. Labor Market*, Cambridge: Cambridge University Press.
Quick, J.C. (1998), 'Introduction to the measurement of stress at work', *Journal of Occupational Health Psychology*, **3**(4), 291–3.
Ramanathan, C.S. (1992), 'EAP's response to personal stress and productivity: implications for occupational social work', *Social Work*, **37**(3), 234–9.
Reynolds, S. (1997), 'Psychological well-being at work: is prevention better than cure?', *Journal of Psychosomatic Research*, **43**, 93–102.
Rizzo, J.A., T.A. Abbot and M.L. Berger (1998), 'The labor productivity effects of chronic backache in the United States', *Medical Care*, **36**(10), 1471–88.
Ross, R. and E. Altmaier (1994), *Intervention in Occupational Stress: A Handbook of Counselling for Stress at Work*, London: Sage.
Sachs, J.D. and H.J. Shatz (1994), 'Trade and jobs in U.S. manufacturing', *Brookings Papers on Economic Activity*, **2**(1), 1–69.
Salminem, S. (1993), 'The specific accident factor of older employees', *Accident Analysis and Prevention*, **25**, 99–102.
Schecter, J., L.W. Green, L. Olsen, K. Kruse and M. Cargo (1997), 'Application of Karasek's demand/control model in a Canadian occupational setting including shift workers during a period of reorganization and downsizing', *American Journal of Health Promotion*, **11** (6), 394–9.
Schierhout, G.H., J.E. Meyers and R.S. Bridger (1995), 'Work-related musculoskeletal disorders and ergonomic stressors in the South African workforce', *Occupational and Environmental Medicine*, **52**, 46–50.
Schonberg, S.E. and S.S. Lee (1996), 'Identifying the real EAP client: ensuring ethical dilemmas', *Ethics and behaviour*, **6**(3), 203–12.
Schwartzberg, N.S. and R.S. Dytell (1996), 'Dual-earner families: the importance of work stress and family stress for psychological well-being', *Journal of Occupational Health Psychology*, **1**(2), 211–23.
Simon, R.W. (1997), 'The meanings individuals attach to role identities and their implications for mental health', *Journal of Health and Social Behavior*, **38**(3), 256–74.
Skov, T., V. Borg, and E. Orhede (1996), 'Psychosocial and physical risk factors for musculoskeletal disorders of the neck, shoulders and lower back in salespeople', *Occupational and Environmental Medicine*, **53**(5), 351–6.
Smith, M.J. (1997), 'Psychosocial aspects of working with video display terminals (VDTs) and employee physical and mental health', *Ergonomics*, **40**(10), 1002–15.
Smith, M.J., F.T. Conway and B.T. Karesh (1999), 'Occupational stress in human–computer interaction', *Industrial Health*, **37**(2), 157–73.
Stern, E. (1993), 'The transformation of work-related development in a rapidly changing world: exploring how to learn from each other', *Journal of Career Development*, **20**, 91–7.

Summers, G.F., F. Horton and C. Gringeri (1995), 'Understanding trends in rural labor markets', in E.N. Emery (ed.), *The Changing American Countryside: Rural People and Places*, Lawrence, KS: University Press of Kansas, pp. 197–10.

Waterman, R.H., J.A. Waterman and B.A. Collard (1994), 'Toward a career resilient workforce', *Harvard Business Review*, **72**(4), 87–94.

28 The effects of effort–reward imbalance at work on health

Johannes Siegrist, Bianca Falck and Ljiljana Joksimovic

Introduction

The importance of work for health goes beyond traditional occupational diseases. Given the far-reaching changes in the nature of work in advanced societies, health-adverse psychosocial work environments are becoming more prevalent. These psychosocial work environments are characterized by work pressure, frequent interruptions, information overload and a low level of task control or autonomy. Irregular working hours, shift work and exposure to noise may aggravate adversity, as is the case with threats of job instability and redundancy, forced mobility and the prospects of involuntary retirement. As will be discussed, these psychosocial work factors affect people's health and well-being, and this needs to be considered under the purview of occupational health.

Why is work so important for human well-being? How does work contribute to the burden of stress and its adverse effects on health? In all advanced societies work and occupation in adult life are accorded primacy for the following reasons. First, having a job is often a prerequisite for continuous income and, thus, for independence from traditional support systems (family, community welfare and so on). Moreover level of income determines a wide range of life' opportunities. Secondly, training for a job and achieving an appropriate occupational status are important parts of socialization. It is through education, job training and status acquisition that personal growth and development are realized, a core social identity outside the family is acquired, and goal-directed activity in human life is shaped. Furthermore occupation defines an important criterion of social stratification. Finally, occupational settings produce the most pervasive and continuous demands during one's lifetime. They take up the largest amount of active time in mid-life, thus providing a source of recurrent negative and positive cognitions, emotions and related behaviors.

Because adverse psychosocial work environments cannot be identified by direct physical or chemical measurements, theoretical models are needed to analyze them. A theoretical model is best understood as a heuristic device that selectively reduces complex reality to meaningful components. Two such theoretical models have received special attention in recent years: the demand–control and the effort–reward imbalance models.

The demand–control model is based on the premise that strain occurs when there is high psychological work demand in combination with a low degree of task control (Karasek and Theorell, 1990). Low control at work is defined in terms of low level of decision latitude (authority over decisions) and a low level of skill utilization. While high demand/low control jobs are assumed to produce strain in those exposed ('job strain') this two-dimensional model offers a 'salutogenic' in addition to a 'pathogenic' perspective: jobs defined by high demands and a high level of decision latitude and skill utilization ('active jobs') promote personal growth and feelings of mastery or self-efficacy. These concepts are rooted in research on stress physiology and health psychology (Skinner, 1996; Spector, 1998; Steptoe and Appels, 1989). More recently the two-dimensional demand–control model was modified to include a third dimension, social support at work. The instrumental, cognitive and emotional support at work was shown to buffer strain reactions (House, 1981; Johnson and Hall, 1988). Accordingly, highest level of strain (and strongest effects on health) are expected in jobs defined by high demands, low control and low social support (Karasek and Theorell, 1990).

Demand–control theory offers a sociological conceptualization of work stress that is restricted to the situational aspects of the psychosocial work environment that does not take aspects of individual coping into account. In terms of policy implications, this has the advantage of pointing to the structural levels where change may be initiated (see below).

A complementary model – effort–reward imbalance – views work stress within a distributive justice framework, focusing on the reciprocity of the work contract (Siegrist, 1996, see also Cosmides and Tooby, 1992). This model assumes that effort at work is spent for the rewards of money, esteem and career opportunities including job security. The model of effort–reward imbalance claims that lack of reciprocity between costs and gains (that is high 'cost'/low 'gain' conditions) elicits sustained strain reactions. For instance, having a demanding but unstable job or expending continuously high effort without being offered any prospects for promotion cause high cost/low gain conditions. The emphasis on occupational rewards (including job security) reflects changes in the global economy and labour market with the growing importance of fragmented careers, job instability, underemployment, redundancy, forced occupational mobility and their resultant financial consequences.

According to this model, strain reactions from high cost/low gain conditions are most intense and long-lasting in the following circumstances: (a) lack of alternatives in the labor market that prevent people from giving up even unfavorable jobs, as the anticipated costs of disengagement (for example the risk of being laid off) outweigh costs of accepting inadequate benefits; (b) unfair job arrangements that may be accepted for a certain period of time for the strategic purposes of improving their chances for career promotion at a later stage; (c) a specific personal pattern of coping with demands and eliciting rewards characterized by overcommitment, which may prevent people from accurately assessing cost–gain relations. 'Overcommitment' defines a set of attitudes, behaviors and emotions reflecting excessive striving in combination with a strong desire for approval and esteem (Siegrist, 1996). At the psychological level, experience of effort–reward imbalance is often paralleled by feelings of impaired self-esteem, whereas experiencing a balance is assumed to promote 'salutogenic' feelings of satisfaction, enhanced self-worth and success.

While specific individual coping characteristics (overcommitment) are included in this model it nevertheless offers a clear distinction of the extrinsic and intrinsic components both at the conceptual and at the operational levels.

Empirical evidence
Over the past 15 years a substantial body of evidence has been obtained that documents the explanatory power of the two work stress models with regard to a variety of diseases and conditions of ill-health in different occupational groups. Many studies testing the demand–control model have been summarized in several recent reviews (Schnall et al., 2000; Karasek et al., 1998; Hemingway and Marmot, 1999; Stansfeld and Marmot, 2002).

Although a number of investigations showed no association between demand–control and health, the majority showed a positive association for the model or its components. Roughly, in summarizing the evidence, a doubling of the risk of disease was observed in employees exposed to job strain, and the magnitude of the population-attributable risk of job strain for prevalent diseases such as coronary heart diseases was estimated to be around 10 per cent (Schnall et al., 2000).

In the recent past, there has been a rapid growth of evidence demonstrating a similar contribution of the effort–reward imbalance model (Marmot et al., 2002; Schnall et al., 2000; Siegrist, 2002). This evidence with regard to cardiovascular and other disease is presented here in greater detail. The review first summarizes available evidence for the model with regard to cardiovascular risk and disease, mainly coronary heart disease (CHD) (see Table 28.1), and then provides an overview of study results for other health indicators (see Table 28.2).

In relation to CHD and its major risk factors, three prospective observational studies, a follow-up study and three cross-sectional or case-control studies have reported findings

Table 28.1 Studies of effort–reward imbalance and cardiovascular risk (overview)

First author (year)	Type of study	Cardiovascular outcome*	High effort/low reward (ERI) and/or overcommitment (OC)	Relative risks of disease**
Siegrist (1990)	prospective	acute MI, SCD, subclinical CHD	ERI + OC	3.4–4.5
Bosma (1998)	prospective	newly reported CHD	ERI + OC***	2.2
Kuper (2002)	prospective	CHD	ERI + OC***	1.3
Kivimäki (2002)	prospective	cardiovascular mortality	ERI +OC***	2.4
Peter (1998)	cross-sectional	Prevalence of hypertension, prevalence of high LDL cholesterol	ERI only OC only	male: 1.6 female: 1.3
Peter (2002)	case-control	acute MI versus healthy control (men)	ERI only	1.7
Siegrist (1997)	cross-sectional	prevalence of high LDL cholesterol	ERI only	3.5
Joksimovic (1999)	follow-up	coronary restenosis following CHD	OC only	2.8

Notes: *CHD = coronary heart disease, LDL = low density lipoprotein cholesterol, MI = myocardial infarction, SCD = sudden cardiac death; **proxy measures of the original effort–reward imbalance scale; ***Depending on the type of statistical analysis, the relative increase of risk of disease was calculated in terms of odds ratios, hazard ratios or risk ratios.

Source: Adapted from Siegrist (2002), pp. 262–91.

Table 28.2 Studies of effort–reward imbalance and other health outcomes (overview)

First author (year)	Type of study	Health outcome	High effort/ low reward (ERI) and / or overcommitment (OC)	Relative risk of disease *
Stansfeld (1998)	prospective	functioning: physical (I), mental (II), social (III)	ERI + OC **	I II III male: 1.4 1.7 1.6 female: 2.0 2.3 1.8
Stansfeld (1999)	prospective	psychiatric disorder	ERI + OC**	male: 2.5 female: 1.6
Stansfeld (2000)	prospective	alcohol dependence (men)	ERI + OC**	1.9
Kuper (2002)	prospective	physical functioning, mental functioning	ERI + OC** ERI + OC**	1.4 2.2
Tsutsumi, Kayaba et al. (2001)	cross-sectional	depression	ERI OC	3.7 3.1
Pikhart (2001)	cross-sectional	self-rated health	ERI	2.6
Rugulies (2000)	cross-sectional	back pain psychosomatic symptoms, self-rated health	ERI	1.9–3.6
Killmer (1999)	cross-sectional	burnout: exhaustion (I), depersonalization (II)	ERI OC	I II 3.6 2.0 1.8 2.3
Joksimovic (2002)	cross-sectional	musculoskeletal pain	ERI OC	1.9–4.3
Larisch (2003)	cross-sectional	depression	ERI OC	5.9 5.9

Note: *the relative increase of risk of disease was calculated in terms of odds ratios; **proxy measures of the original effort–reward imbalance scale.

Source: Adapted from Siegrist (2002) pp. 262–91.

with partial or full confirmation of the model's basic hypotheses (see Table 28.1). A German study of blue-collar workers, covering some 2000 person-years (Siegrist *et al.*, 1990), and the Whitehall II study of British civil servants based on an original sample of 10 308 men and women were followed over a mean 5.3 years (Bosma *et al.*, 1998) are prospective investigations. Interestingly the findings derived from this latter study have recently been replicated for a period of 11 years where effort–reward imbalance at work still predicted incident CHD in a significant way (Kuper et al., 2002). More recently a cohort of some 821 industrial employees in Finland was followed over a period of 25 years, and cardiovascular mortality was analyzed as a function of exposure of work stress (Kivimaeki et al., 2002). Although a Swedish cohort study of some 5720 healthy employed men and women is also prospective, baseline data only are currently available (Peter et al., 1998). Two further studies are of a cross-sectional nature, one representing a large case-control study of 951 male and female CHD patients and 1147 healthy controls (Peter et al., 2002) and one analyzing associations of psychosocial work stress with cardiovascular risk factors in a group of 179 male middle-managers (Siegrist et al., 1997). A follow-up study of 106 coronary patients who underwent coronary angioplasty was conducted to explore the role of effort–reward imbalance in predicting coronary restenosis following coronary angioplasty (Joksimovic et al., 1999).

It should be noted that the original questionnaire measuring effort–reward imbalance was not available at baseline screening of two of the studies reported. Therefore proxy measures have been constructed to measure the model. As can be seen from Table 28.1, effort–reward imbalance (or its main components) was associated with an increased risk of CHD in all instances. This excess risk could not be explained by established biomedical or behavioural risk factors, as these variables were taken into account in multivariate statistical analysis (see Table 28.1). Adjusting for major cardiovascular risk factors in multivariate statistical models, such as hypertension, hyperlipidemia or elevated fibrinogen, might, in fact, result in 'overadjustment' as these risk factors are partly influenced by stress-induced sustained activation of the autonomic nervous system as well. Indeed several cross-sectional investigations have documented associations of effort–reward imbalance and the prevalence of hypertension, hyperlipidemia or a co-manifestation of these two cardiovascular risk factors (Peter et al., 1998; Marmot et al., 2002).

Additional evidence not reported in Table 28.1 is available from a Finnish prospective study that did not provide an explicit measure of the model, but documented a significantly elevated risk hazard (RH) of cardiovascular mortality (RH: 2.3) among men whose work was defined by a combination of high demands with low income, a finding that the authors interpreted in the framework of the effort–reward imbalance model (Lynch, Krause, Kaplan, Tuomilehto, Salonen, et al., 1997). In the same study it was also found that progression of carotid atherosclerosis, as established by ultrasound technique, was most advanced in the subgroup of workers exposed to high demands and low economic rewards (Lynch, Krause, Kaplan, Salonen, Salonen, et al., 1997).

Overall, evidence supports the theory that high cost/low gain conditions at work are associated with an increased risk of cardiovascular disease. Results further illustrate that a combination of information on perceived structural conditions and on personal coping characteristics has more explanatory power than an approach that is restricted to only one of these two model components.

Additional health outcomes were explored in the Whitehall II study and other investigations (see Table 28.2). Mild-to-moderate psychiatric disorders, subjective health functioning and alcohol dependence were all significantly associated with effort–reward imbalance in the Whitehall II study (Stansfeld et al., 1998, 1999, 2000, Kuper et al., 2002).

Another investigation was conducted into 190 male and female employees of a small Japanese plant during a time of economic hardship. After adjustment for age, gender, occupational status and job type, effort–reward imbalance was associated with a 3.7-fold increased risk of depression. A similarly increased risk was observed for overcommitment (Tsutsumi, Kayaba, Theorell, Siegrist, 2001). In a study conducted in four post-communist countries in Central and Eastern Europe with a total of 3941 working subjects, a 2.6-fold increased risk of poor self-rated health was observed in those suffering from effort–reward imbalance at work (Pikhart et al., 2001).

In the US, a study of 258 room cleaners in four large hotels reported increased risks of low back pain, upper back pain, severe bodily pain, psychosomatic symptoms and poor self-rated health when exposed to effort–reward imbalance at work (Rugulies and Krause, 2000). Similarly, in a group of 316 male and female employees of a public transport enterprise in Germany, scoring high on overcommitment was associated with musculoskeletal pain in the neck, in the hip and in lower extremities (Joksimovic et al., 2002).

Emotional exhaustion and burnout were two health indicators determined to be associated with effort–reward imbalance in a study of 202 nurses in a German university hospital. Moreover feeling burnout was more frequent in nurses with a high level of overcommitment, and affects were particularly strong in overcommitted nurses who suffered from effort–reward imbalance (Bakker et al., 2000; Killmer, 1999). Two additional large-scale studies reinforced this latter notion that an interaction of overcommitment with effort–reward imbalance is associated with the relatively strongest effects on health. One was a representative cross-section survey of some 11 175 employed Dutch men and women (Jonge et al., 2000) and the other was the above-mentioned Whitehall II study (Kuper et al., 2002).

In summary, both the extrinsic and the intrinsic components of the effort–reward imbalance model are now considered significant risk factors for the development of stress-related diseases and ill-health, in particular CHD, depressive symptoms, alcohol dependence and poor self-rated health. Current evidence indicates that adverse effects on health are prevalent among men and women in mid-life and early old life, and that these effects are not restricted to modern Western societies.

A case study testing reward components
As was shown, the model of effort–reward imbalance combines the three dimensions of occupational rewards (salary/occupational standing, esteem/recognition, job security) into a single summary measure entering the equation of reciprocity/non-reciprocity between costs and gains. Yet for theoretical and practical reasons, it is important to understand what is the relevance of each single reward component for well-being and health. For instance, one could argue that increasing salary is the easiest way of resolving or reducing the burden of stress at work and that more troublesome issues such as improving leadership skills, creating a climate of mutual appreciation, introducing non-monetary incentives or modifying established schemes of job promotion or status hierarchy could simply be ignored. Alternatively one could stick to an exclusive human relations approach of intervention, disregarding the relevant dimensions of adequate pay, occupational standing and job security. In other words, type of reward may matter if the theoretical model is to be useful for the design of intervention measures.

In an attempt to explore this notion of relative importance for health of each one of the three reward dimensions we have undertaken a reanalysis of data available from a recent investigation conducted in our group (Falck, 2002; Siegrist et al., 2002). This was a cross-sectional study of a sample of 316 middle-aged male and female employees of a public transport enterprise in Germany, mostly bus and subway drivers, repair personnel and employees working in the administration. It was the aim of the study to test associations of effort–reward imbalance at work with three indicators of self-reported health: depressive symptoms, musculoskeletal symptoms and anginal complaints.

The following measures were applied: Effort–reward imbalance at work was measured by a standardized psychometric questionnaire containing 23 Likert-scaled items (Siegrist et al., 2004; Tsutsumi, Kayaba, Theorell, Siegrist, 2001). The dimension of extrinsic effort is measured by a unidimensional scale containing six items; the dimension of reward is measured of a scale composed of 11 items where, in a second-order factor analysis, three factors loading on one latent factor 'reward' were identified: 'salary/occupational standing' (four items), 'esteem' (five items) and 'job security' (two items). Three ratios were computed: (a) a ratio between effort and salary/occupational standing, (b) a ratio between effort and esteem, and (c) a ratio between effort and job security. After introducing a correction factor for unequal number of items in the nominator and denominator values > 1.10 indicate an imbalance between (high) effort and (low) reward. The intrinsic component of the model was assessed by the unidimensional scale 'overcommitment' (six items) (for detailed psychometric information, see Falck, 2002; Siegrist et al., 2002).

Depressive symptoms were measured by the validated German version of the CES-D scale (15 items, Hautzinger and Bailer 1993; see also Larisch et al., 2003). Musculoskeletal symptoms were assessed by a standardized questionnaire measuring frequency of pain at different locations (Berger-Schmitt et al., 1996) and information on anginal complaints was obtained from the Rose Angina Questionnaire (Rose et al., 1977).

Using univariate and bivariate analyses of the variables under study we performed multivariate logistic regression analysis. Variables entering the models were dichotomized as follows: effort–reward imbalance: values >1.10 versus remaining values; depressive symptoms: values in the upper tertile versus remaining values; musculoskeletal symptoms: subjects indicating pain during last 12 months and last seven days with an intensity of at least 6 on a scale from 1 (low) to 10 (high) were scored at risk; anginal complaints: subjects fulfilling all four criteria of anginal complaints were scored at risk.

In the first model, the predicting variables were included and respective odds ratios of the three health indicators, with 95 per cent confidence intervals, were calculated, adjusting for the effects of age and gender. In the second model, level of education and income, measuring the respondent's socioeconomic status, were additionally introduced as confounders. In view of the relatively small sample size a level of significance $p < 0.05$ was considered appropriate. In Table 28.3 the results of this analysis are displayed. In this sample of male and female public transport employees, all three components of occupational rewards were associated with the three health indicators under study. In other words, the finding of an association of effort–reward imbalance with reduced health at the level of a summary measure is replicated at the level of the three single, more specific measures estimating this imbalance. Moreover, comparing the relative strength of the associations, esteem reward exceeds the two remaining indicators with respect to depressive

Table 28.3 *Associations of three components of effort–reward imbalance at work with three indicators of self-reported health*

	\multicolumn{2}{c}{Ratio between effort and salary/occup. standing}	\multicolumn{2}{c}{Ratio between effort and esteem}	\multicolumn{2}{c}{Ratio between effort and job security}
	OR	CI	OR	CI	OR	CI

Depressive Symptoms

	OR	CI	OR	CI	OR	CI
model 1*	10.53	(4.29/25.85)	10.78	(4.42/26.28)	3.84	(2.16/6.84)
model 2**	9.74	(3.93/24.11)	12.42	(4.82/32.00)	4.00	(2.19/7.31)

Musculoskeletal Symptoms

| model 1* | 3.36 | (1.43/7.88) | 3.67 | (1.61/8.37) | 2.82 | (1.46/5.43) |
| model 2** | 3.60 | (1.48/8.76) | 4.13 | (1.75/9.75) | 2.90 | (1.48/5.71) |

Anginal Complaints

| model 1* | 3.49 | (1.42/8.59) | 3.88 | (1.58/9.55) | 4.79 | (2.03/11.31) |
| model 2** | 3.68 | (1.48/9.16) | 4.19 | (1.68/10.56) | 5.35 | (2.21/12.94) |

Notes: *model 1, effects are adjusted for gender and age; **model 2, effects are adjusted additionally for income and education; OR = odds ratios, CI = 95% confidence intervals; n = 316 public transport employees.

symptoms and musculoskeletal pain. On the other hand, reward related to job security was found to be more important than the other two components with respect to anginal complaints. When adjusting for the confounding effects of age, gender and socioeconomic status, the odds ratios in these analyses were not reduced.

In conclusion, this case study documents consistent associations of an imbalance between effort and reward at work, based on the three separate reward components as weighted against effort. Interestingly odds ratios of depressive symptoms and musculoskeletal pain were particularly strong in public transport employees who suffer from a reward deficiency in terms of esteem and recognition.

Findings need to be interpreted with caution in view of the fact that the study was cross-sectional, the sample size was limited and all measures were based on self-reported data. However it is important to mention that the relative contribution of single reward components can be estimated when analyzing associations of work-related stress with health. An independent recent study confirmed the relevance of distinguishing the three reward components in assessing their association with health (Vegchel *et al.*, 2002). Thus this additional information may be helpful in the design of tailored measures of worksite health promotion.

Implications for worksite health promotion
What are the policy implications of this new information? First, it is possible to identify dimensions of work-related stress in a wide range of occupations using standardized,

well-tested questionnaires. These questionnaires measuring the effort–reward imbalance model as well as the demand–control model are now available in a number of languages for use in international studies. Thus further scientific evidence is obtained demonstrating associations between adverse psychosocial work environments and health indicators in working populations. Moreover it is possible to use these measures to evaluate the amount of work-related stress in specific businesses or occupational groups. Information can then be fed back to those concerned, for instance to serve as a basis of monitoring activities or stress prevention programs.

The design and implementation of worksite stress prevention and health promotion programs are considered a crucial implication of the new evidence discussed above. Both approaches, the effort–reward imbalance model and the demand–control model, offer specific suggestions in this respect. Whereas propositions derived from the demand–control model are related to measures of job redesign, job enlargement, job enrichment, skill training and enhanced participation (Karasek and Theorell, 1990; Karasek, 1992), the focus of the effort–reward imbalance model is on adequate terms of exchange between efforts and rewards. Examples of such measures include the development of compensatory wage systems, the provision of models of gain sharing and the strengthening of non-monetary gratifications. Moreover ways of improving promotional opportunities and job security need to be explored. As was shown in this contribution, improvement of esteem and recognition seems to be a particularly important dimension of worksite health promotion. Emphasis on improved leadership skills, enhanced vertical and horizontal information flow, appropriate feedback to co-workers, subordinates and superiors and the development of a culture of recognition and non-monetary gratifications is well justified. Several models of guided group work and counseling can be adapted to this aim. Finally, in addition to structural and interpersonal measures, increased individual competence in stress management is useful. In particular, inadequate ways of coping with workload can be identified and changed, such as attitudes of an excessive overcommitment to the working life. Employees suffering from overcommitment may become aware of the salutogenic potentials of relaxation and strong socioemotional support (Aust et al., 1997; Puls et al., 2002).

Theory-guided research on work-related stress and health is not restricted to an exclusive scientific activity. Rather it has far-reaching practical implications for the prevention or reduction of the burden of stress at work and the promotion of health. In view of the psychosocial and economic costs produced by work-related stress and in view of the substantial challenges of a globalized economy, these practical implications need to be considered with high priority. Several strategies of implementing this new knowledge are available. Among these, social marketing approaches, improved legislation, the creation of conclusive evidence of cost effectiveness of stress prevention at work and the formation of cooperative networks of scientists and decision makers hold special promise.

References

Aust, B., R. Peter and J. Siegrist (1997), 'Stress management in bus drivers: a pilot study based on the model of effort–reward imbalance', *International Journal of Stress Management*, **4**, 297–305.
Bakker, A.B., C. Killmer, J. Siegrist and W.B. Schaufeli (2000), 'Effort–reward imbalance and burnout among nurses', *Journal of Advanced Nursing*, **31**, 884–91.
Berger-Schmitt, R., T. Kohlmann and H. Raspe (1996), 'Rückenschmerzen in Ost- und Westdeutschland', *Gesundheitswesen*, **58**, 519–24.

Bosma, H., R. Peter, J. Siegrist and M. Marmot (1998), 'Two alternative job stress models and the risk of coronary heart disease', *American Journal of Public Health*, **88**, 68–74.
Cosmides, L. and J. Tooby (1992), 'Cognitive adaptations for social exchange', in J.H. Barkow, L. Cosmides and J. Tooby (eds), *The Adapted Mind: Evolutionary Psychology and the Generation of Culture*, New York: Oxford University Press, pp.163–228.
Falck, B. (2002), 'Die Bedeutung der Mehrdimensionalität beruflicher Gratifikationen für die Gesundheit – eine explorative Studie', Masters thesis, University of Duesseldorf.
Hautzinger, M. and M. Bailer (1993), 'Allgemeine Depressionsskala', Beltz Test, Weinheim.
Hemingway, H. and M. Marmot (1999), 'Psychosocial factors in the aetiology and prognosis of coronary heart disease: systematic review of prospective cohort studies', *British Medical Journal*, 318, 1460–7.
House, J. (1981), *Work, Stress and Social Support*, Reading, MA: Addison-Wesley.
Johnson, J.V. and E. Hall (1988), 'Job strain, work place, social support and cardiovascular disease', *American Journal of Public Health*, 78, 1336–42.
Joksimovic, L., D. Starke, O.v.d. Knesebeck and J. Siegrist (2002), 'Perceived work stress, overcommitment and self-reported musculoskeletal pain: a cross-sectional investigation', *International Journal of Behavioral Medicine*, 9, 122–38.
Joksimovic, L., J. Siegrist, M. Meyer-Hammer, R. Peter, B. Franke, W. Klimek, M. Heintzen and B.E. Strauer (1999), 'Overcommitment predicts restenosis after coronary angioplasty in cardiac patients', *International Journal of Behavioral Medicine*, 6, 356–69.
Jonge, J. de, H. Bosma, R. Peter and J. Siegrist (2000), 'Job strain, effort–reward imbalance and employee well-being: a large-scale cross-sectional study', *Social Science & Medicine*, 50, 1317–27.
Karasek, R. (1992), 'Stress prevention through work reorganization: a summary of 19 international case studies', *Conditions of Work Digest*, 11, 23–41.
Karasek, R., C. Brisson, N. Kawakami, I. Houtman, P. Bongers and B. Amick (1998), 'The job content questionnaire (JCQ): an instrument for internationally comparative assessments of psychosocial job characteristics', *Journal of Occupational Health Psychology*, 4, 322–55.
Karasek, R.A. and T. Theorell (1990), *Healthy Work. Stress, Productivity and the Reconstruction of Working Life*, New York: Basic Books.
Killmer, C. (1999), *Burnout bei Krankenschwestern*, Münster: LIT-Verlag.
Kivimaeki, M., P. Leino-Arjas, R. Luukkonen, H. Riihikäki, J. Vahtera and J. Kirjonen (2002), 'Work stress and risk of cardiovascular mortality: prospective cohort study of industrial employees', *British Medical Journal*, 325, 857–60.
Kuper, H., A. Singh-Manoux, J. Siegrist and M. Marmot (2002), 'When reciprocity fails: effort–reward imbalance in relation to CHD and health functioning within the Whitehall II study', *Occupational and Environmental Medicine*, 59, 777–84.
Larisch, M., L. Joksimovic, O.v.d Knesebeck, D. Starke and J. Siegrist (2003), 'Berufliche Gratifikationskrisen und depressive Symptome', *Psychotherapie, Psychosomatik und Medizinische Psychologie*, 53, 223–8.
Lynch, J., N. Krause, G.A. Kaplan, R. Salonen and J.P. Salonen (1997), 'Work place demands, economic reward, and progression of carotid atherosclerosis', *Circulation*, 96, 302–7.
Lynch, J., N. Krause, G.A. Kaplan, J. Tuomilehto and J.T. Salonen (1997), 'Work place conditions, socioeconomic status, and the risk of mortality and acute myocardial infarction: the Kuopio ischemic heart disease risk factor study', *American Journal of Public Health*, 87, 617–22.
Marmot, M., J. Siegrist and T. Theorell (2002), 'Work and coronary heart disease', in S.A. Stansfeld and M. Marmot (eds), *Stress and the Heart*, London: BMJ Books, pp.50–71.
Peter, R., L. Alfredson, N. Hammar, J. Siegrist, T. Theorell and P. Westerholm (1998), 'High effort, low reward, and cardiovascular risk factors in employed Swedish men and women: baseline results from the WOLF Study', *Journal of Epidemiology and Community Health*, 52, 540–7.
Peter, R., J. Siegrist, J. Hallqvist, C. Reuterwall and T. Theorell, SHEEP Study Group (2002), 'Psychosocial work environment and myocardial infarction: improving risk estimation by combining two alternative job stress models in the SHEEP study', *Journal of Epidemiology and Community Health*, 56, 294–300.
Pikhart, H., M. Bobak, J. Siegrist, A. Pajak, S. Rywik, J. Kyshegyi, A. Gostautas, Z. Skodova and M. Marmot (2001), 'Psychosocial work characteristics and self-rated health in four post-communist countries', *Journal of Epidemiology Community Health*, 55, 624–30.
Puls, W., M.L. Inhester and H. Wienold (2002), 'Stress management trainings as a component of workplace prevention of substance use disorders', *Sucht*, 48, 271–83.
Rose, G., P. McCartney and D. Wright (1977), 'Self-administration of a questionnaire on chest pain and intermittent claudication', *British Journal of Preventive and Social Medicine*, 31, 42–8.
Rugulies, R. and N. Krause (2000), 'The impact of job stress on musculoskeletal disorders, psychosomatic symptoms and general health in hotel room cleaners', *International Journal of Behavioral Medicine*, 7, 16.

Schnall, P.L., K. Belkic, P. Landsbergis and D. Baker (2000), 'The workplace and cardiovascular disease', *Occupatational Medicine State of the Art Reviews*, **15**, 1–374.

Siegrist, J. (1996), 'Adverse health effects of high effort–low reward conditions at work', *Journal of Occupational Health Psychology*, **1**, 27–43.

Siegrist, J. (2002), 'Effort–reward imbalance at work and health', in P. Perrewe and D. Ganster (eds), *Historical and Current Perspectives on Stress and Health*, vol.2, Amsterdam: JAI, pp.262–91.

Siegrist, J., R. Peter, P. Cremer and D. Seidel (1997), 'Chronic work stress is associated with atherogenic lipids and elevated fibrinogen in middle-aged men', *Journal of Internal Medicine*, **242**, 149–56.

Siegrist, J., R. Peter, A. Junge, P. Cremer and D. Seidel (1990), 'Low status control, high effort at work and ischemic heart disease, prospective evidence from blue-collar men', *Social Science & Medicine*, **31**, 1129–36.

Siegrist, J., D. Starke, O.v.d. Knesebeck, L. Joksimovic, N. Dragnao and M. Larisch (2002), 'Soziale Reziprozität und Gesundheit – eine explorative Studie zu beruflichen und ausserberuflichen Gratifikationskrisen' (Social reciprocity and health – an exploratory study on effort–reward imbalance), unpublished research report, Department of Medical Sociology, University of Duesseldorf.

Siegrist, J., D. Starke, T. Chandola, I. Godin, M. Marmot, I. Niedhammer and R. Peter (2004), 'The measurement of effort–reward imbalance at work: European comparisons', *Social Science & Medicine*, **58**, 1483–99.

Skinner, E.A. (1996), 'A guide to constructs of control', *Journal of Personality and Social Psychology*, **71**, 549–70.

Spector, P.E. (1998), 'A control theory of job stress process', in C.E. Cooper (ed.), *Theories of Organizational Stress*, Oxford: Oxford University Press, pp.153–69.

Stansfeld, S. and M. Marmot (eds) (2002), *Stress and the Heart, Psychosocial Pathways to Coronary Heart Disease*, London: BMJ Books.

Stansfeld, S., J. Head and M. Marmot (2000), *Work-related Factors and Ill Health: the Whitehall II Study*, London: HSE Books.

Stansfeld, S., H. Bosma, H. Hemingway and M. Marmot (1998), 'Psychosocial work characteristics and social support as predictors of SF-36 functioning: the Whitehall II Study', *Psychosomatic Medicine*, **60**, 247–55.

Stansfeld, S., R. Fuhrer, M.J. Shipley and M.G. Marmot (1999), 'Work characteristics predict psychiatric disorder: prospective results from the Whitehall II study', *Occupational and Environmental Medicine*, **56**, 302–7.

Steptoe, A. and A. Appels (eds) (1989), *Stress, Personal Control and Health*, Chichester: Wiley.

Tsutsumi, A., K. Kayaba, T. Theorell and J. Siegrist (2001), 'Association between job stress and depression among Japanese employees threatened by job loss in comparison between two complementary job stress models', *Scandinavian Journal of Work and Environment Health*, **27**, 146–53.

Tsutsumi, A., T. Ishitake, R. Peter, J. Siegrist and T. Matoba (2001), 'The Japanese version of the effort–reward imbalance questionnaire: a study in dental technicians', *Work & Stress*, **15**, 86–96.

Vegchel, N. van, J. de Jonge, A.B. Bakker and W.B. Schaufeli (2002), 'Testing global and specific indicators of rewards in the effort–reward imbalance model: does it make any difference', *European Journal of Work and Organizational Psychology*, **11**, 403–21.

29 Occupational stress and health
Charles D. Spielberger and Eric C. Reheiser

In a recent publication of the World Health Organization (WHO), entitled 'Global Strategy on Occupational Health for All', it was noted that 'occupational health and the well-being of working people are crucial prerequisites for productivity and are of utmost importance for overall socioeconomic and sustainable development' (WHO, 2000, p. 2). The significant impact of health hazards in the workplace has also clearly influenced other global agencies, such as the United Nations and the International Labour Organization. According to the WHO (ibid., p. 6), 'every citizen of the world has a right to healthy and safe work and to a work environment that enables him or her to live a socially and economically productive life'.

Hazards in the workplace have had negative effects on the health and well-being of workers throughout human history. The phrase, 'mad as a hatter', came into the English language long before anyone knew that mercury in the materials used in making hats affected the central nervous system (Kahn, 1981). In the 19th century, descriptions of the 'black lung' disease of coal miners recognized a causal link between the specific characteristics of a hazardous work environment and a particular physical disorder. While exposure to hazardous physical, chemical or biological substances continue to affect health and working capacity negatively, the WHO estimates that 'an equal number [30–50 per cent] of working people report psychological overload at work resulting in stress symptoms' (WHO, 2000, p. 3).

Research has shown that the psychological demands of a job can have pervasive and profound emotional and physical effects on the lives of workers (Kahn, 1981; Karasek and Theorell, 1990; Matteson and Ivancevich, 1982). In a nationwide study of occupational stress (Northwestern National Life, 1991), the proportion of workers who reported 'feeling highly stressed' more than doubled from 1985 to 1990, and those reporting multiple stress-related illnesses increased from 13 per cent to 25 per cent. Moreover 69 per cent of the 600 workers who where surveyed in this study reported that their productivity was reduced because of high stress levels, and 'one in three say job stress is the single greatest stress in their lives' (ibid., p. 2). Of the study participants, 17 per cent also reported missing one or more days of work each year because of high stress levels, and 14 per cent indicated that stress had caused them to quit or change jobs during the preceding two years.

In a follow-up study by Northwestern National Life (1992) of more than 1200 full-time, private-sector employees, 40 per cent reported that their jobs were 'very' or 'extremely' stressful. Compared with workers reporting lower levels of occupational stress, the employees who perceived their jobs as highly stressful were also twice as likely to work overtime frequently (62 per cent v. 34 per cent), think about quitting their job (59 per cent v. 26 per cent), experience burnout on the job (50 per cent v. 19 per cent), and suffer stress-related medical problems (55 per cent v. 21 per cent). Consequently it is not surprising that many organizations now recognize that overworked and stressed employees do not perform as well and experience more health-related problems than those who enjoy their jobs and have time to relax (Fraser, 2001).

Rapid change is now a fundamental characteristic of modern working life, with greater demands to learn new skills in order to adapt to increasingly complex types of work. A recent study conducted by the Princeton Survey Research Associates (1997) found that 75 per cent of employees believed that they experience more on-the-job stress than workers did a generation ago. The most important challenges for occupational health in the 21st century, according to the WHO (2000), will include the impact of psychosocial stressors, such as new information technologies, automation, psychological overload and pressure for higher productivity. These challenges will continue to result in increased stress in the workforce, and require that more attention be given to the psychosocial aspects of work. Greater attention must also be given to an ageing population of workers, as well as the special needs of the chronically ill and handicapped (ibid.).

The explosive increase in research on occupational stress, especially during the last decade (for example, Cooper and Cartwright, 1994; Quick et al., 1997; Spielberger and Reheiser, 1994; Spielberger et al., 2002), has clearly established that job-related stress has an adverse impact on productivity, absenteeism, worker turnover and employee health. In addition to these severe consequences of stress-related problems in the workplace, reduced productivity and diminished customer services are hidden costs that often result from 'exhausted or depressed employees [who] are not energetic, accurate, or innovative at work' (Karasek and Theorell, 1990, p. 167). According to Matteson and Ivancevich (1982), costs in the US economy relating to reduced productivity, absenteeism and worker turnover have continued to escalate as a function of measured occupational stress.

Financial compensation of workers for stress-related problems has also increased markedly in recent years (Grippa and Durbin, 1986), as reflected most clearly in a dramatic rise in the occupational claims of employees seeking compensation for stress-induced psychological dysfunctions (Lowman, 1993). In the US alone, according to Sauter (1992, p. 14), 'nearly 600,000 workers are disabled for reasons of psychological disorders', costing $5.5 billion in annual payments to individuals and their families. The combined costs of occupational stress to US business and industry is estimated to be 'between $150 billion and $180 billion a year' (Wright and Smye, 1996, p. 7).

Growing recognition of the adverse consequences of stress in the workplace for employee health and well-being is clearly reflected in an increasing number of studies of occupational stress published in the medical and psychological literature during the past quarter-century. The number of publications cited in PsychInfo over the past 30 years in which job, work or occupational stress was included in the title, is compared in Figure 29.1 with studies of family stress. Since 1970, studies of stress in the workplace have increased more than 17 fold, whereas research on family stress has received considerably less attention. Consistent with these results, a study conducted by the St. Paul Fire and Marine Insurance Company (1992) found that problems at work were more strongly associated with health complaints than were any other life stressor events, including family problems.

It is readily apparent that increased concerns about job stress have stimulated numerous studies that have helped to identify important sources of stress in the workplace (Quick et al., 1997). It should be noted, however, that the theories that guided this research have differed from study to study, resulting in diverse goals of investigation, conceptual

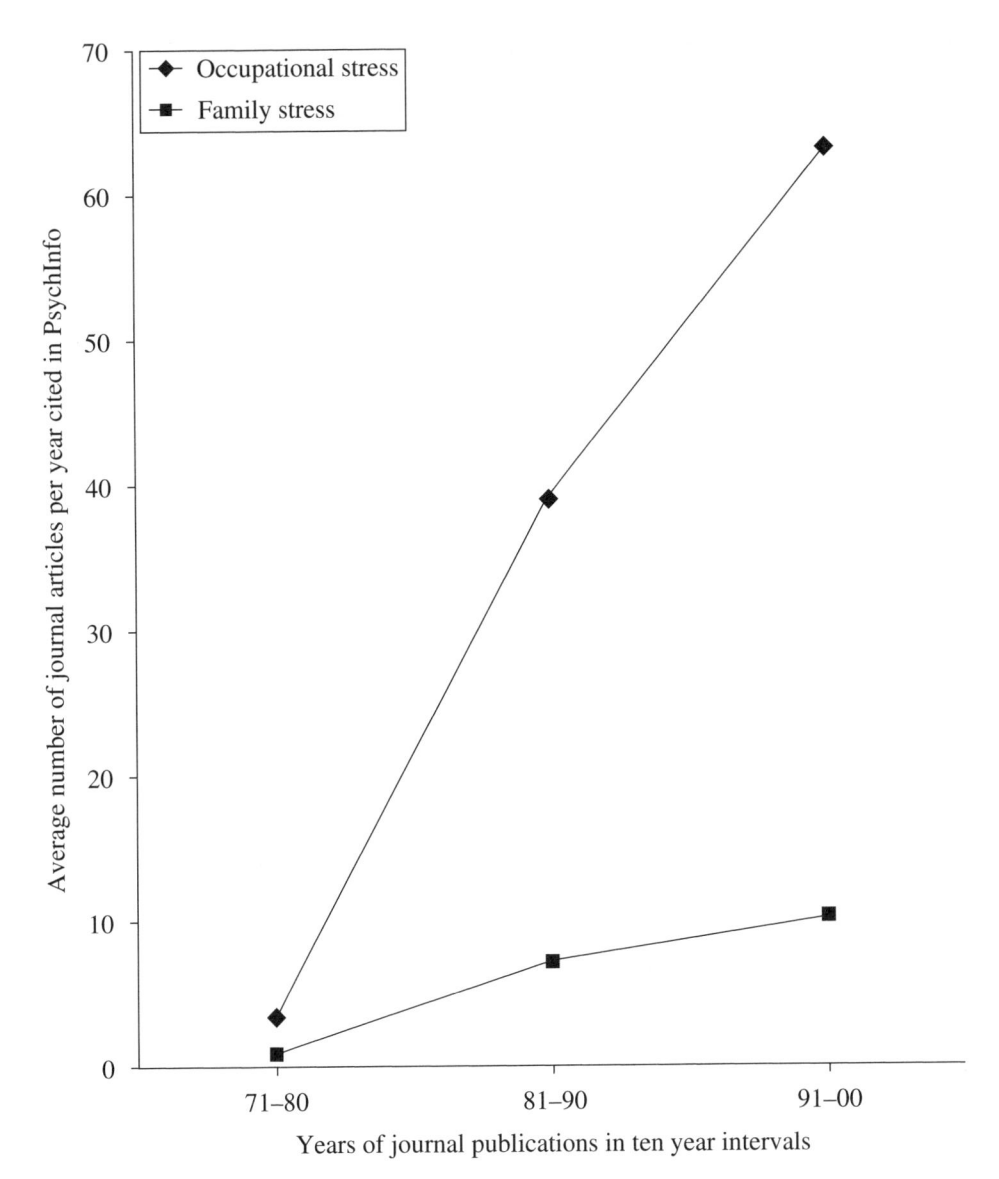

Figure 29.1 Mean number of publications per year listed in PsychInfo for each decade from 1971 to 2000 in which 'occupational stress' or 'family stress' was included in the title

confusion and inconsistent and often conflicting research findings (Kasl, 1978; Schuler, 1980). Kahn and Byosiere (1992) have reviewed and evaluated the most influential models of occupational stress and summarized the empirical findings relating to these models. While some investigators have focused on the pressures of a particular job, others have been concerned primarily with the behavioral and health consequences of work-related stress (Schuler, 1991). These diverse models of occupational stress have also stimulated the construction of a variety of job stress measures. Consequently, in order to clarify and interpret research findings on occupational stress, it is essential to understand the conceptual models that have guided this research, and the measures that have been developed to assess stress and strain in the workplace.

Models and theories of occupational stress

More than a half-century ago, Kurt Lewin (1951) observed that the characteristics of a person interact with environmental stressors to determine how much strain is experienced by an individual, and the effects of strain on behavior and health. French, Caplan, Kahn and their colleagues (French and Caplan, 1972; French et al., 1982; French and Kahn, 1962; Kahn et al., 1964) subsequently incorporated Lewin's concepts of stress and strain in their Person – Environment Fit (PE-Fit) theory, which is widely accepted as a major conceptual framework for research on occupational stress (Chemers et al., 1985; Edwards and Cooper, 1990). In the context of this theoretical orientation, occupational stress is defined in terms of job characteristics that pose a threat to the individual resulting from a poor match between the abilities of the employee and the demands of the job (French and Caplan, 1972). The workplace stress that occurs as a result of incompatible person–environment fit produces psychological strain that may contribute to stress-related physical disorders (French et al., 1982).

Guided by PE-Fit theory, research on occupational stress has investigated organizational demands, job duties and requirements, employee skills and abilities, job satisfaction and individual differences in attitudes, personality traits and health status (for example, Beehr and Newman, 1978; Cooper et al., 1994; Cooper and Marshall, 1976; Marshall and Cooper, 1979). PE-Fit concepts, especially role ambiguity and role conflict (Caplan, 1987; French et al., 1982; Kahn et al., 1964), have been examined in numerous studies (for example, Fisher and Gitelson, 1983; Hamner and Tosi, 1974; Keenan and Newton, 1984). When job demands and pressures in the work environment exceed the skills and abilities of the employee, or when these demands conflict with the employee's goals and values, this lack of fit contributes to work overload, role ambiguity and conflicting role demands (Kahn and Byosiere, 1992). The resulting psychological and physical strain may then lead to adverse behavioral consequences, such as lower productivity, absenteeism, employee burnout, turnover and health-related problems.

Although the PE-Fit model appropriately emphasizes the interaction of the skills and abilities of the worker with the pressures and demands of the work environment, this model has been criticized because it lacks specificity, gives insufficient attention to specific sources of stress in the workplace (Edwards and Cooper, 1990), and 'has not yielded a highly focused approach' (Chemers et al., 1985, p. 628). The adequacy of the PE-Fit model has also been questioned because it is 'repeatedly plagued with serious theoretical and methodological problems' (Edwards and Cooper, 1990, p. 294), fails to identify important person and environmental variables (Schuler, 1980) and does not distinguish between different forms and types of fit (Edwards and Cooper, 1990; Eulberg et al., 1988; Ganster et al., 1986).

Cooper and Marshall's (1976; Marshall and Cooper, 1979) Stress at Work model is similar to PE-Fit theory, but is more specific in identifying five major categories of job pressure and lack of organizational support in the workplace that contribute to occupational stress: (1) pressures intrinsic to the job; (2) the employee's role in the organization; (3) interpersonal relationships at work; (4) limitations in career development; and (5) organizational structure and climate. Pressures intrinsic to the job include difficult working conditions, such as time pressures and work overload. Lack of clarity regarding the employee's organizational role and responsibilities contributes to role conflict and ambiguity. Stressful interpersonal relations at work result from difficulties with supervisors, co-workers and subordinates. Limitations in career development lead to concerns about job tenure and opportunity for advancement. Stressors related to organizational structure and climate include failure to recognize an employee's contributions and lack of participation in decision making. The Stress at Work model also takes into account the personal characteristics of employees, and the effects on occupational stress of life crises and family problems. A possible shortcoming of this model is that it gives relatively little attention to the role of employee perception and cognitive appraisal of stress in the workplace (Kahn and Byosiere, 1992).

Karasek's (1979) Demand–Control model focuses on interactions between the objective demands of the work environment and the decision latitude of employees in meeting these demands (Karasek and Theorell, 1990). According to this model, 'the greatest risk to physical and mental health from stress occurs to workers facing high psychological workload demands or pressures combined with low control or decision latitude in meeting those demands' (Schnall, 1998, p. 1). The combination of high job demands with relatively little control contributes to lowered productivity and a greater risk of health-related problems (Theorell and Karasek, 1996). The Demand–Control model also recognizes the beneficial effects of social support from supervisors and co-workers (Karasek et al., 1982; Schnall, 1998). According to Karasek et al. (1998, p. 325), 'jobs which are high in demand, low in control, and also low in social support at work carry the highest risk of illness'. However control latitude is difficult to measure, as noted by Sauter and Hurrell (1989, p. xvi), who observed that 'fundamental questions remain concerning the conceptualization and operationalization of the [control] construct'. Similarly Fletcher and Jones (1993) concluded that the Demand–Control model, 'despite its popularity and intuitive appeal, has proved difficult to validate in the workplace' (p. 320).

The PE-Fit, Stress at Work and Demand–Control models of occupational stress focus on interactions of job pressures with the skills, abilities and decision latitude of workers. While recognizing the importance of identifying specific sources of stress in the workplace, Kahn and Byosiere (1992) noted that these models do not give adequate consideration to the critical role of cognitive appraisal in mediating the effects of stressful working conditions on the emotional reactions of the worker. Edwards and Rothbard (1999) have also pointed out that the PE-Fit model needs to give greater attention to the way employees' values, goals and desires influence their appraisal of specific sources of job-related stress.

Lazarus' (1966) Transactional Process model of psychological stress and coping conceptualizes stress as a process that involves a complex transaction between a person and her/his environment (Lazarus and Folkman, 1984). In applying this model to occupational stress, Lazarus (1991) emphasizes the distinction between sources of stress ('stressors') in the workplace and the emotional reactions that are evoked when a particular stressor is cognitively appraised as threatening. Three types of appraisal mediate the effects of stressors on emotional reactions. Primary appraisal occurs when a stressor is evaluated in terms of its immediate impact on a person's well-being. Secondary appraisal takes into account the resources of the employee for coping with the stressor. The third type, reappraisal, incorporates new information resulting from the worker's appraisal of the effectiveness of her/his efforts to cope with a particular stressor. Lazarus clearly recognizes the importance of the way workers' abilities match environmental demands, but gives greater emphasis to the individual's appraisal of stressful situations and coping skills. When threatening job demands exceed the person's ability to deal effectively with them, strain is experienced in the form of negative emotions, for example, anxiety, anger and depression.

The P-E Fit, Stress at Work and Demand–Control models, and Lazarus' Transactional Process conception of occupational stress have both strengths and limitations. Moreover, these theories appear to be overlapping and complementary, rather than contradictory frameworks for understanding stress in the workplace. The P-E Fit, Stress at Work and Demand–Control models focus on general working conditions that produce job strain (work demands), stressful interpersonal relations at work, organizational structure and support, and the skills and degree of control available to the worker. In contrast, Lazarus' Transactional Process model focuses on how an employee's appraisal of a particular stressor event is markedly influenced by the worker's personality and coping skills.

The National Institute for Occupational Safety and Health (NIOSH) defines job stress in terms of 'the harmful physical and emotional responses that occur when the requirements of the job do not match the capabilities, resources, or needs of the worker' (NIOSH, 2002). This definition of job stress, as well as the resulting model developed by NIOSH, was primarily influenced by PE-Fit theory. The primary difference between the NIOSH and PE-Fit, Stress at Work and Demand–Control models is in the relative emphasis placed on worker characteristics versus working conditions. The NIOSH model explicitly recognizes that exposure to stressful working conditions plays a primary role in causing job stress and influencing worker safety and health, while 'individual and other situational factors can intervene to strengthen or weaken this influence' (ibid., p. 6). However, the NIOSH model gives little attention to the significant influence of the employee's cognitive appraisal of sources of stress in the workplace.

Spielberger's State–Trait Process (STP) model of occupational stress focuses on the perceived severity and frequency of occurrence of two major categories of stressor events, job pressures and lack of support (Spielberger et al., 2002). The STP model builds on the PE-Fit and Transactional Process models by endeavoring to integrate these models with the conception of anxiety, anger and depression as emotional states and personality traits (Spielberger, 1972; Spielberger et al., 1983; Spielberger et al., 1988). The STP model gives greater emphasis than other models to the effects of individual differences in personality traits in determining how workplace stressors are perceived and appraised. Consistent with Quick et al.'s (1997, p. 10) definition of occupational stress as 'the mind body arousal resulting from the physical and/or psychological demands associated with the job', the immediate perception and appraisal of a stressor as dangerous or threatening leads to the emotional arousal of anxiety and anger, and the associated activation of the autonomic nervous system. If severe and persistent, the resulting psychological and physical strain may cause adverse behavioral consequences, such as employee burnout and health-related problems (Spielberger and Vagg, 1999; Vagg and Spielberger, 1998).

The PE-Fit, Stress at Work, Demand–Control, Transactional Process, NIOSH and STP models have stimulated and guided the construction of a number of measures of occupational stress, which have been reviewed and evaluated by Murphy (1995), Quick *et al.* (1997) and Hurrell *et al.* (1998). Jackson and Schuler (1985, p. 47) recommend that research on occupational stress focus on 'the development of good diagnostic tools for pinpointing specific aspects about one's job that are ambiguous or conflicting'. In a similar vein, Murphy and Hurrell (1987) call for the construction of generic questionnaires with core sets of questions to facilitate the comparison of stress levels in various occupational groups.

Measurement of occupational stress

Models of stress in the workplace have stimulated the development of a number of psychometric measures of occupational stress, and guided research that has contributed to the clarification and refinement of the underlying theoretical constructs. Most measures of occupational stress evaluate working conditions that produce job strain, how specific stressor events are perceived and appraised, and the coping skills of the individual worker. Eight of the more widely used job stress measures are briefly described below in the approximate chronological order of their publication. Each measure is considered within the context of the model(s) of occupational stress that stimulated its development.

PE-Fit theory guided Insel and Moos' (1974) development of the Work Environment Scale (WES), which was designed to measure organizational climate. The WES includes subscales that assess work pressures, employee relationships and supervisory support (Moos, 1981). PE-Fit theory and role stress theory (Kahn *et al.*, 1964) contributed to Ivancevich and Matteson's (1976, 1980) construction of the Stress Diagnostic Survey (SDS), an empirically developed, comprehensive self-report inventory. A revised and expanded version of the SDS has been used to assess the frequency with which specific sources of stress are experienced by managers, flight attendants, computer operators and employees in a variety of work settings (Ivancevich *et al.*, 1990).

Karasek's (1979) Demand–Control model provides the conceptual framework for developing the Job Content Questionnaire (JCQ), which is widely used in research on job demands, decision latitude, skill utilization and job satisfaction (Karasek *et al.*, 1998; Karasek *et al.*, 1995). The JCQ has been used extensively to assess supervisor and co-worker support, and physical and mental health problems (Hurrell *et al.*, 1998). Research with the JCQ has also established a 'clear relationship between adverse job conditions (particularly low decision latitude) and coronary heart disease' (Theorell and Karasek, 1996, p. 23).

Osipow and his colleagues (Osipow, 1998; Osipow and Davis, 1988; Osipow *et al.*, 1985; Osipow and Spokane, 1980, 1987) developed the Occupational Stress Inventory (OSInv) to evaluate three major categories of PE-Fit variables: occupational role stress, psychological and physical strain, and coping resources. The seven specific scales that are included in the OSInv assess role overload, role ambiguity, vocational strain, interpersonal strain, physical strain, self-care and social support. The OSInv has been used extensively to examine and compare the stress levels of a number of different occupational groups (Forney, 1982; Pelletier, 1983; Rayburn et al., 1982) and to evaluate the effectiveness of stress management programs (Higgins, 1986).

Cooper and Marshall's (1976) Stress at Work model, along with aspects of the PE-Fit, Demand–Control and Transactional Process models, guided the construction and validation of the Occupational Stress Indicator (OSInd) (Cooper et al., 1988). Six major dimensions of occupational stress are assessed by the OSInd: job pressures, job pressure control, job satisfaction, Type-A personality, coping strategies, and physical and mental health problems. Recently revised and shortened by Williams and Cooper (1998), the OSInd was renamed the Pressure Management Indicator (PMI), which provides profiles on specific sources of job pressure, employee characteristics and the effects of occupational stress on individual employees.

Spielberger's STP model provided the conceptual framework for the development of the Police Stress Survey (PSS) to assess work-related stressors experienced by law enforcement officers (Spielberger et al., 1980; Spielberger et al., 1981). The 60 stressor events assessed by the PSS were identified in focused discussion groups with police officers. Of these, 39 were found to be equally appropriate for high school teachers by simply substituting the words 'teacher' and 'school' for 'police officer' and 'department' (Grier, 1982). In subsequent research, 30 of these 39 stressor events were found to describe generic, job-related stressors that were commonly experienced by managerial, professional and clerical employees in a variety of business, industrial and educational settings (Spielberger, 1991). Following Murphy and Hurrell's (1987) recommendation that measures of occupational stress include a core set of items, these 30 stressor events were selected for the Job Stress Survey (JSS) (Spielberger, 1991; Spielberger and Vagg, 1999). According to Kasl (1998, p. 393), the empirically based method for identifying the 30 generic sources of stress assessed by the JSS is 'phenomenologically faithful to the experience of workers'.

The JSS assesses the perceived severity ('intensity') of 30 specific sources of occupational stress, and how often each of these stressors was experienced in the work environment during the previous six months. Factor analyses of the frequency ratings of the 30 JSS items for a large sample of managers and professionals identified five first-order factors; job pressure and lack of support emerged as higher order factors (Wasala, 2001). The higher-order job pressure factor was associated with two of the first-order factors: work-related conditions and requirements, and job duties and responsibilities. The higher-order lack of support factor was related to the remaining three first-order factors, which were defined by JSS items with content related to lack of support from supervisors, lack of support from co-workers and lack of perceived organizational support. The first and higher-order JSS factors are graphically presented in Figure 29.2 as antecedent conditions in the application of the State–Trait Process model to the study of occupational stress (Spielberger et al., 2002). As hypothesized by the STP model, the effects of the job-related stressor events assessed by the JSS on the psychological and physical strains and adverse behavioral consequences are mediated by the employees' perception and appraisal of these stressors.

Motowidlo et al. (1986) have developed a self-report questionnaire that assesses the intensity and frequency of stressful work events experienced by nurses working in a hospital setting. Their findings confirmed that ratings of subjective intensity and frequency

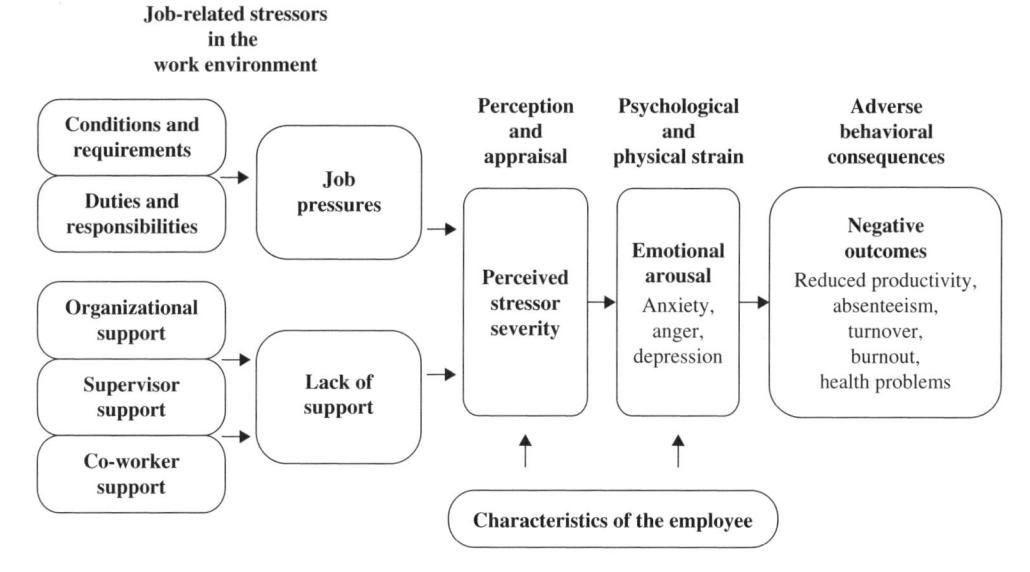

Figure 29.2 The expanded State–Trait Process Model for the study of occupational stressors and work-related stress

of occurrence were associated with decrements in job performance. The intensity and frequency of occurrence of stressor events are also assessed by the Work Stress Inventory (WSI) (Barone, 1994; Barone et al., 1988), which consists of separate scales for measuring organizational stress and job risk. The Organizational Stress scale of the WSI assesses job pressures and lack of support, but does not distinguish between these concepts. The WSI Job Risk scale assesses aspects of the work environment that involve safety, exertion and hazardous physical conditions.

On the basis of a comprehensive review of the job stress literature, researchers at the US National Institute for Occupational Safety and Health (NIOSH) developed the Generic Job Stress Questionnaire (GJSQ) (Hurrell and McLaney, 1988). Influenced primarily by PE-Fit and Demand–Control theory, the GJSQ consists of 13 scales that were either adapted from other widely used occupational stress measures or constructed to assess dimensions of job stress for which no valid measures were available (Hurrell et al., 1998). Role conflict and ambiguity, job responsibilities, workload, skill utilization, job demands and control, job dissatisfaction, somatic problems, depression and other sources of distress in the workplace are assessed by the GJSQ.

In summary, measures of occupational stress provide information about physical and psychological strain, social support and individual differences in ability, personality and coping skills, which contribute to understanding the nature and impact of stress in the workplace. However, the omnibus nature of most job stress measures is both a source of strength and a significant concern (Hurrell et al., 1998; Kasl, 1998). Moreover, as noted by Williams and Cooper (1998), a number of job stress measures include items that inquire about group reactions, rather than the stress experienced by a particular respondent. The perceived severity of a particular stressor also tends to be confounded with how often the stressor was experienced (Hurrell et al., 1998). As observed by Dewe (1989, p. 993): 'When measuring work stressors, more attention should be given to such facets as intensity, frequency and the meaning individuals attribute to events.' Clearly it is important to identify and assess the perceived severity and frequency of occurrence of sources of occupational stress.

Occupational stress and health in the workplace
The information obtained with the JSS provides a detailed analysis of the perceived severity of 30 generic sources of stress that occur in most work environments, along with the frequency of occurrence of each stressor event. It should be noted, however, that the JSS does not directly assess the emotional states and personality traits that may also contribute to health-related problems. Consequently, in evaluating the effects of occupational stress, it is essential to measure the employees' feelings and personality characteristics, along with the perceived severity and frequency of occurrence of sources of stress in the workplace. It is also essential to evaluate the physical condition of the worker and the emotional states that are activated by workplace stressor events.

In medical examinations, physicians routinely measure vital signs such as pulse rate, blood pressure and temperature, which provide essential information about physical health. When a physician detects an abnormal pulse during a physical examination, this signals a potentially significant problem in the functioning of the cardiovascular system. Running a high fever may indicate that the immune system is not protecting the person from harmful viruses. Intense anxiety and anger are analogous to elevations in pulse rate and blood pressure, while the presence of a fever, as indicated by abnormally high body temperature, may be considered as roughly analogous to depression. Elevations in temperature that define a fever are interpreted by physicians as a strong indication of the presence of an infection or metabolic problem that requires immediate attention (Guyton, 1977). Similarly symptoms of depression often indicate the presence of pervasive unresolved conflicts that result in an emotional fever.

Anxiety, anger and depression, the psychological vital signs that are the most critical indicators of an individual's well-being, often reflect the impact of occupational strain. Consequently the assessment of variations in the intensity and duration of these emotional states should be included in the evaluation of occupational stress. The State–Trait Personality Inventory (STPI) (Spielberger, 1979; Spielberger et al., 1995), which assesses anxiety, anger and depression, provides essential information about a person's mental health. Elevated scores on these STPI scales can help to identify negative emotional reactions to workplace stressor events, and reveal long-standing personality conflicts that may affect an individual's working life. Assessing emotional vital signs can also provide meaningful feedback to enhance employees' awareness and understanding of their feelings, and help them to cope more effectively with occupational stressors.

Symptoms of anxiety are typically found in almost all emotional disorders. Recent research findings, as well as observations of daily life, suggest that problems with anger are also ubiquitous, and that individuals high in anger as a personality trait frequently experience angry feelings across a wide range of situations (Deffenbacher, 1992; Deffenbacher et al., 1986; Deffenbacher et al., 1987; Hogg and Deffenbacher, 1986). Depression has been described as 'the common cold of mental health problems that strikes the rich and poor as well as the young and the old' (Rosenfeld, 1999, p. 10). Therefore, as with anxiety and anger, the assessment of depression is essential in the assessment of psychological well-being.

Curiosity, which is also measured by the STPI, motivates exploratory behavior and contributes to successful adaptation to environmental stimuli. Thus curiosity which research has shown to be inversely related to anxiety, anger and depression may be considered as a positive vital sign and a strong indicator of an individual's psychological well-being. The utilization of the STPI in the assessment of psychological vital signs can provide essential information regarding an individual's feelings of anxiety, anger, depression and curiosity, which may be directly influenced by the occupational stressors that are assessed with the JSS.

References

Barone, D.F. (ed.) (1994), *Developing a Transactional Psychology of Work Stress*, New York: Taylor & Francis.
Barone, D.F., G.R. Caddy, A.D. Katell, F.B. Roselione and R.A. Hamilton (1988), 'The work stress inventory: organizational stress and job risk', *Educational and Psychological Measurement*, **48**, 141–54.
Beehr, T.A. and J.E. Newman (1978), 'Job stress, employee health, and organizational effectiveness: a facet analysis, model and literature review', *Personnel Psychology*, **31**, 665–99.
Caplan, R.D. (1987), 'Person–environment fit theory and organizations: commensurate dimensions, time perspectives, and mechanisms', *Journal of Vocational Behavior*, **31**, 248–67.
Chemers, M.M., R.B. Hays, F. Rhodewalt and J. Wysocki (1985), 'A person–environment analysis of job stress: a contingency model explanation', *Journal of Personality and Social Psychology*, **49**, 628–35.
Cooper, C.L. and S. Cartwright (1994), 'Healthy mind: healthy organization – a proactive approach to occupational stress', *Human Relations*, **47**, 455–70.
Cooper, C.L. and J. Marshall (1976), 'Occupational sources of stress: a review of the literature relating to coronary heart disease and mental ill health', *Journal of Occupational Psychology*, **49**, 11–28.
Cooper, C.L., B.D. Kirkcaldy and J. Brown (1994), 'A model of job stress and physical health: the role of individual differences', *Personality and Individual Differences*, **16**, 653–5.
Cooper, C.L., S.J. Sloan and S. Williams (1988), *The Occupational Stress Indicator (OSI)*, Windsor: NFER Nelson.
Deffenbacher, J.L. (1992), 'Trait anger: theory, findings, and implications', in C.D. Spielberger and J.N. Butcher (eds), *Advances in Personality Assessment*, vol.9, Hillsdale, NJ: Lawrence Erlbaum Associates, pp. 177–201.
Deffenbacher, J.L., P.M. Demm and A.D. Brandon (1986), 'High general anger: correlates and treatment', *Behavior Research and Therapy*, **24**, 480–9.
Deffenbacher, J.L., D.A. Story, R.S. Stark, J.A. Hogg and A.D. Brandon (1987), 'Cognitive-relaxation and social skills interventions in the treatment of general anger', *Journal of Counseling Psychology*, **34**, 171–6.
Dewe, P.J. (1989), 'Examining the nature of work stress: individual evaluations of stressful experiences and coping', *Human Relations*, **42**(11), 993–1013.
Edwards, J.R. and C.L. Cooper (1990), 'The person–environment fit approach to stress: recurring problems and some suggested solutions', *Journal of Organizational Behavior*, **11**, 293–307.
Edwards, J.R. and N.P. Rothbard (1999), 'Work and family stress and well-being: an examination of person–environment fit in the work and family domains', *Organizational Behavior and Human Decision Processes*, **77**(2), 85–129.
Eulberg, J.R., J.A. Weekley and R.S. Bhagat (1988), 'Models of stress in organizational research: a metatheoretical perspective', *Human Relations*, **41**, 331–50.
Fisher, C.D. and R. Gitelson (1983), 'A meta-analysis of the correlates of role conflict and ambiguity', *Journal of Applied Psychology*, **68**, 320–33.
Fletcher, B.C. and F. Jones (1993), 'A refutation of Karasek's demand–discretion model of occupational stress with a range of dependent measures', *Journal of Organizational Behavior*, **14**, 319–30.
Forney, D.S. (1982), 'Sex and age and the incidence of reported stress, strain and burnout among career development professionals', unpublished master's, University of Maryland.
Fraser, J.A. (2001), *White-collar Sweatshop: The Deterioration of Work and Its Rewards in Corporate America*, New York: W.W. Norton & Co.
French, J.R.P., Jr. and R.D. Caplan (1972), 'Occupational stress and individual strain', in A.J. Marrow (ed.), *The Failure of Success*, New York: Amacom, pp. 30–66.
French, J.R.P., Jr. and R.L. Kahn (1962), 'A programmatic approach to studying the industrial environment and mental health', *Journal of Social Issues*, **18**(3), 1–47.

French, J.R.P., Jr., R.D. Caplan and R.V. Harrison (1982), *The Mechanisms of Job Stress and Strain*, London: Wiley.
Ganster, D., M.R. Fusilier and B.T. Mayes (1986), 'Role of social support in the experience of stress at work', *Journal of Applied Psychology*, **71**(1), 102–10.
Grier, K.S. (1982), 'A comparison of job stress in law enforcement and teaching' (Doctoral dissertation, University of South Florida, 1981), *Dissertation Abstracts International*, **43**, 870B.
Grippa, A.I. and D. Durbin (1986), 'Worker's compensation occupational disease claims', *National Council Compensation Insurance Digest*, **1**, 5–23
Guyton, A.C. (1977), *Basic Human Physiology: Normal Function and Mechanism of Disease*, Philadelphia: W.B. Saunders.
Hamner, W.C. and H.L. Tosi (1974), 'Relationship of role conflict and role ambiguity to job involvement measures', *Journal of Applied Psychology*, **59**, 497–9.
Higgins, N. (1986), 'Occupational stress and working women: the effectiveness of two stress-reduction programs', *Journal of Vocational Behavior*, **29**, 66–78.
Hogg, J.A. and J.L. Deffenbacher (1986), 'Irrational beliefs, depression and anger in college students', *Journal of College Student Personnel*, **27**, 349–53.
Hurrell, J.J. and A.M. McLaney (1988), 'Exposure to job stress: a new psychometric instrument', *Scandinavian Journal of Work Environment and Health*, **14**(Supplement 1), 27–8.
Hurrell, J.J., D.L. Nelson and B.L. Simmons (1998), 'Measuring job stressors and strains: where we have been, where we are, and where we need to go', *Journal of Occupational Health Psychology*, **3**(4), 368–89.
Insel, P.M. and R.H. Moos (1974), *Work Environment Scale, Form R*, Palo Alto, CA: Consulting Psychologists Press.
Ivancevich, J.M. and M.T. Matteson (1976), *Stress Diagnostic Survey (SDS): Comments and Psychometric Properties of a Multidimensional Self-report Inventory*, Houston, TX: FD Associates.
Ivancevich, J.M. and M.T. Matteson (1980), *Stress and Work, A Managerial Perspective*, Glenview, IL: Scott, Foresman and Company.
Ivancevich, J.M., M.T. Matteson and F.P. Dorin (1990), *Stress Diagnostic Survey (SDS)*, Houston, TX: FD Associates.
Jackson, S.E. and R.S. Schuler (1985), 'A meta-analysis and conceptual critique of research on role ambiguity and role conflict in work settings', *Organizational Behavior and Human Decision Process*, **36**, 16–78.
Kahn, R.L. (1981), *Work and Health*, New York: Wiley.
Kahn, R.L. and P. Byosiere (1992), 'Stress in organizations', in M.D. Dunnette and L.M. Hough (eds), *Handbook of Industrial and Organizational Psychology*, vol. 3, Palo Alto, CA: Consulting Psychologists Press, pp. 571–650.
Kahn, R.L., D.M. Wolfe, R.P. Quinn, J.D. Snoeck and R.A. Rosenthal (1964), *Organizational Stress: Studies in Role Conflict and Ambiguity*, New York: Wiley.
Karasek, R.A. (1979), 'Job demands, job decision latitude, and mental strain: implications for job redesign', *Administrative Science Quarterly*, **24**, 285–307.
Karasek, R.A. and T. Theorell (1990), *Healthy Work: Stress, Productivity, and the Reconstruction of Working Life*, New York: Basic Books.
Karasek, R.A., K. Hulbert and B. Simmerman (1995), 'JCQ user's project summary: 10 years of job content questionnaire use', unpublished manuscript, University of Massachusetts.
Karasek, R.A., K.P. Triantis and S.S. Chaudhry (1982), 'Coworker and supervisor support as moderators of associations between task characteristics and mental strain', *Journal of Occupational Behaviour*, **3**(2), 181–200.
Karasek, R.A., C. Brisson, N. Kawakami, I. Hourman, P. Bongers and B. Amick (1998), 'The Job Content Questionnaire (JCQ): an instrument for internationally comparative assessments of psychosocial job characteristics', *Journal of Occupational Health Psychology*, **3**, 322–55.
Kasl, S.V. (1978), 'Epidemiological contributions to the study of work stress', in C.L. Cooper and R.L. Payne (eds), *Stress at Work*, New York: Wiley, pp. 3–38.
Kasl, S.V. (1998), 'Measuring job stressors and studying the health impact of the work environment: an epidemiologic commentary', *Journal of Occupational Health Psychology*, **3**(4), 390–401.
Keenan, A. and T.J. Newton (1984), 'Frustration in organizations: relationships to role stress, climate, and psychological strain', *Journal of Occupational Psychology*, **57**, 57–65.
Lazarus, R.S. (1966), *Psychological Stress and the Coping Process*, New York: McGraw-Hill.
Lazarus, R.S. (1991), 'Psychological stress in the workplace', *Journal of Social Behavior and Personality*, **6**, 1–13.
Lazarus, R.S. and S. Folkman (1984), *Stress, Appraisal, and Coping*, New York: Springer.
Lewin, K. (1951), *Field Theory in Social Science*, New York: Harper.
Lowman, R.L. (1993), *Counseling and Psychotherapy of Work Dysfunctions*, Washington, DC: American Psychological Association.

Marshall, J. and C. Cooper (1979), 'Work experiences of middle and senior managers: the pressure and satisfaction', *International Management Review*, **19**, 81–96.
Matteson, M.T. and J.M. Ivancevich (1982), *Managing Job Stress and Health: The Intelligent Person's Guide*, New York: Free Press.
Moos, R.H. (1981), *Work Environment Scale Manual*, Palo Alto, CA: Consulting Psychologists Press.
Motowidlo, S.J., J.S. Packard and M.R. Manning (1986), 'Occupational stress: its causes and consequences for job performance', *Journal of Applied Psychology*, **71**(4), 618–29.
Murphy, J.R. and J.J. Hurrell (eds) (1987), *Stress Measurement and Management in Organizations: Development and Current Status*, New York: Praiger.
Murphy, L.R. (1995), 'Occupational stress management: current status and future directions', in C.L. Cooper and D.M. Rousseau (eds), *Trends in Organizational Behavior*, vol. 2, Chichester: John Wiley & Sons, pp. 1–14.
NIOSH (2002), (URL) www.cdc.gov/niosh/stresswk.htm.
Northwestern National Life, (1991), *Employee Burnout: America's Newest Epidemic*, Minneapolis, MN: Northwestern National Life.
Northwestern National Life, (1992), *Employee Burnout: Causes and Cures*, Minneapolis, MN: Northwestern National Life.
Osipow, S.H. (1998), *Occupational Stress Inventory – Revised: Professional Manual*, Odessa, FL: Psychological Assessment Resources.
Osipow, S.H. and A.S. Davis (1988), 'The relationship of coping resources to occupational stress and strain', *Journal of Vocational Behavior*, **32**, 1–15.
Osipow, S.H. and A.R. Spokane (1980), *The Occupational Environment Scales, Personal Strain Questionnaire and Personal Resources Questionnaire, Form E-1*, Columbus, OH: Marathon Consulting & Press.
Osipow, S.H. and A.R. Spokane (1987), *Occupational Stress Inventory*, Odessa, FL: Psychological Assessment Resources.
Osipow, S.H., R.E. Doty and A.R. Spokane (1985), 'Occupational stress, strain, and coping across the life span', *Journal of Vocational Behavior*, **27**, 98–108.
Pelletier, D.M. (1983), 'Career officers pass stress test', *College Placement Council Spotlight*, **6**(1–2), 98–108.
Princeton Survey Research Associates (1997), *Labor Day Survey: State of Workers*, Princeton, NJ: Princeton Survey Research Associates.
Quick, J.C., J.D. Quick, D.L. Nelson and J.J.J. Hurrell (1997), *Preventive Stress Management in Organizations*, Washington, DC: American Psychological Association.
Rayburn, C.A., L.J. and L. Rogers (1982), 'Women, men, and religion: stress within sanctuary walls', *Journal of Pastoral Counseling*, **17**, 75–83.
Rosenfeld, I. (1999), 'When the sadness won't go away', *Parade Magazine*, 19 September, 10.
St. Paul Fire and Marine Insurance Company (1992), *American Workers under Pressure Technical Report*, St. Paul, MN: St. Paul Fire and Marine Insurance Company.
Sauter, S.L. (1992), 'Introduction to the NIOSH proposed national strategy', in G.P. Keita and S.L. Sauter (eds), *Work and Well-being: An Agenda for the 1990s*, Washington, DC: American Psychological Association, pp.11–16.
Sauter, S.L. and J.J. Hurrell, Jr (eds) (1989), 'Introduction', in S.L. Sauter, J.J. Hurrell and C.L. Cooper (eds), *Job Control and Worker Health*. Chichester: Wiley.
Schnall, P. (1998) (URL) www.workhealth.org/strain/briefintro.html/.
Schuler, R.S. (1980), 'Definition and conceptualization of stress in organizations' *Organizational Behavior and Human Performance*, **25**, 184–215.
Schuler, R.S. (ed.) (1991), 'Foreword', in P.L. Parrewe (ed.), *Handbook on Job Stress*, Corte Madera, CA: Select Press.
Spielberger, C.D. (ed.) (1972), *Anxiety as an Emotional State*, vol.1, New York: Academic Press.
Spielberger, C.D. (1979), 'Preliminary manual for the State–Trait Personality Inventory (STPI)', unpublished manuscript, University of South Florida.
Spielberger, C.D. (1991), *Preliminary Test Manual for the Job Stress Survey (JSS)*, Odessa, FL: Psychological Assessment Resources.
Spielberger, C.D. and E.C. Reheiser (1994), 'Job stress in university, corporate and military personnel', *International Journal of Stress Management*, **1**, 19–31.
Spielberger, C.D. and P.R. Vagg (1999), *Job Stress Survey – Professional Manual*, Odessa FL: Psychological Assessment Resources.
Spielberger, C.D., K.S. Grier and J.M. Pate (1980), 'The Florida Police Stress Survey', *Florida Fraternal Order of Police Journal* (Winter), 66–7.
Spielberger, C.D., S.S. Krasner and E.P. Solomon (eds) (1988), *The Experience, Expression, and Control of Anger*, New York: Springer Verlag Publishers.
Spielberger, C.D., P.R. Vagg and C.F. Wasala (2002), 'Occupational stress: job pressures and lack of support',

in J.C. Quick and L. Tetrick (eds), *Handbook of Occupational Health Psychology*, Washington, DC: American Psychological Association, pp. 185–200.

Spielberger, C.D., G. Jacobs, S. Russsell and R.S. Crane (eds) (1983), 'Assessment of Anger: The State–Trait Anger Scale', in J.N. Butcher and C.D. Spielberger (eds), *Advances in Personality Assessment*, vol. 2, Hillsdale, NJ: LEA, pp. 159–87.

Spielberger, C.D., L.G. Westberry, K.S. Grier and G. Greenfield (1981), 'The Police Stress Survey: sources of stress in law enforcement', *Human Resources Institute Monograph Series, University of South Florida*, **3**(6).

Spielberger, C.D., L.M. Ritterband, S.J. Sydeman, E.C. Reheiser and K.K. Unger (1995), 'Assessment of emotional states and personality traits: measuring psychological vital signs', in J.N. Butcher (ed.), *Clinical Personality Assessment: Practical Approaches*, New York: Oxford University Press, pp. 42–58.

Theorell, T. and R.A. Karasek (1996), 'Current issues relating to psychosocial job strain and cardiovascular disease research', *Journal of Occupational Health Psychology*, **1**, 9–26.

Vagg, P.R. and C.D. Spielberger (1998), 'Occupational stress: measuring job pressure and organizational support in the workplace', *Journal of Occupational Health Psychology*, 3(4), 294–305.

Wasala, D.F. (2001), 'Organizational stressors and work-related stress', unpublished master's thesis, University of South Florida.

WHO, (2000) (URL) www.who.int/oeh/OCHweb/OCHweb/OSHpages/OSHdocuments/Global/Strategy/GlobalStrategyonOccupationalHealth.htm.

Williams, S. and C.L. Cooper (1998), *Pressure Management Indicator (PMI)*, Harrogate: RAD Ltd.

Wright, L.A. and M.D. Smye (1996), *Corporate Abuse: How Lean and Mean Robs People and Profits*, New York: Macmillan.

30 The role of emotions in cardiovascular disorders
Juan José Miguel-Tobal and Héctor González-Ordi

Emotions and health

In the mid-19th century, three-fifths of deaths occurring in developed countries were due to infectious diseases. Since then, the improvements in sanitary conditions, life habits, medical developments, water and food care treatments, public programmes for immunization, prevention and environmental control and so on have provided a considerable decrease in such deaths (Terris, 1980). However other diseases have replaced them, occupying the top rankings of mortality causes. These diseases are the cardiovascular diseases, cancer and, more recently, immune and chronic degenerative diseases, which can be considered as diseases related to behaviour and individual life style.

During the 1960s health professionals became aware of the importance of prevention in such diseases and the need to transform the traditional medical view with the biopsychosocial model, which takes into account, in addition to biological factors, psychological and social factors in the onset and maintenance of diseases. Regardless of the model used, the commonly named 'negative' emotions, such as anxiety, stress, anger or depression, have undoubtedly reached the level of core variables to be researched, treated or controlled in the new concept of health. Additionally the role of negative emotions as risk factors in the development and maintenance of these diseases is becoming well established (Martínez Sánchez and Fernández Castro, 1994; Matthews *et al.*, 1998; Miguel-Tobal, 2000; Miguel-Tobal and Casado, 1994, 1999; Suinn, 2001).

Emotional reactions such as anxiety, anger or sadness present physiological correlates as a result of complex mechanisms. Under the influence of the nervous system, these mechanisms affect gland secretions, organs, tissues, muscles and blood. Indeed there is an increasing volume of studies which demonstrate the relationship between emotional factors and cardiovascular, gastrointestinal and cancer disorders.

One of the best fields of study of this relationship has been, and still is, the classically named 'psychosomatic disorders', currently conceptualized as psychophysiological disorders. Psychophysiological disorders have been traditionally defined as those that present a clear evidence of organic disease and, at the same time, a significant proportion of psychological determinants (Maher, 1978). Therefore such disorders present physical symptoms or organic dysfunctions that are closely related to psychological factors (Gatchel *et al.*, 1989).

In spite of their twofold character (physical and psychological) such kinds of disorders have been treated almost exclusively from a medical point of view. However, with the rise of disciplines such as psychosomatic medicine, behavioural medicine and health psychology, several psychological variables become relevant. Both medicine and psychology have searched for the etiology of such disorders and, over the years, different factors have been taken into account as possible explanations. It is now known that the real etiology is based on multi-causality, with combinations of several factors. This multi-causality, based on the simultaneous consideration of genetic, environmental and psychological factors, and mainly focused on the interaction between these factors as an individual's predisposition to suffer a certain disease, is the major contribution of psychological research in this field. This enabled psychophysiological disorders to be understood, not as specific or distinctive diseases, but as those physical alterations that are brought about, exacerbated or maintained by psychological factors.

The genesis, development and maintenance of psychophysiological disorders are currently related to several agents such as anxiety, anger/hostility, environmental factors, life style, stress endurance, genetic factors, personality characteristics, cognitive factors and coping styles. As mentioned, the most relevant emotions regarding psychophysiological disorders include anxiety, stress and anger. We now consider these in more detail.

Anxiety

Anxiety is one of the most common and universal emotions. This emotional reaction to the perception of threatening or dangerous stimuli will be present during an individual's lifetime. In fact, anxiety elicited by stimuli or situations such as animals, physical danger and separation entails an early biological acquisition as it protects children from potential dangers. In this sense, there is no doubt that anxiety must be considered as an essential value in the preservation of individuals and species.

In different ways, anxiety has enjoyed outstanding status in psychology literature since the early decades of the 20th century. Undoubtedly anxiety is the best understood and most studied emotional reaction. As an example, it should be noted that, in the decade from 1988 to 1998, the PsycLIT international database registered 21 486 scientific contributions (Miguel-Tobal and Cano-Vindel, 2002). This considerable volume of works is due to several reasons. First of all, anxiety is a paradigmatic *emotional reaction*, and it allows studies on emotion based upon this specific emotion. Secondly, since the 1950s, anxiety has been studied as one of the core characteristics of personality. Several studies focused on the *trait anxiety* concept as a relatively stable tendency to interpret situations as threatening or dangerous, and to react to them with more or less intense or durable *anxiety states*. Finally, the increase in knowledge about anxiety has benefited the development of practical applications, owing to its implications in the development of a great number of psychological and psychophysiological disorders, and its well-known relationship with performance in academic, work and sport settings.

From a personality perspective, trait anxiety has evolved from a unitary conceptualization (Spielberger, 1966, 1972) to a multidimensional approach (Endler, 1975, 1980). Since the seminal works of Cattell or Spielberger in the 1960s, the differenciation between state and trait anxiety has become classical. State anxiety is defined as a transitory emotional reaction to the individual's perception of a threatening or dangerous situation. On the other hand, trait anxiety must be addressed as a relatively stable tendency to interpret situations as threatening or dangerous, and to react to them with anxiety states. Later works of Endler and his colleagues put forward the multidimensional nature of trait anxiety, remarking the existence of different facets (social evaluation, physical danger and so on) closely related to specific situations (Endler and Flett, 2001; Endler and Kocovski, 2003).

From an emotions perspective, anxiety has been conceptualized as a universal emotion, common to all members of a species. This emotion appears when an individual perceives a situation as threatening or dangerous, regardless of the real threat, by facilitating an individual's response to threat or danger by preparing him for defensive action or avoidance. This implies a great adaptive value. Until the late 1960s, this reaction was believed to be based on a unitary arousal process; however the works of Lacey (1967) and Lang (1968) revealed that an anxiety reaction involves different response systems (cognitive, physiological and motor), usually discordant with each other. In this sense, anxiety is a combination of responses, including cognitive, physiological and behavioural (motor) reactions. These responses are provoked by identifiable cognitive–subjective, physiological or environmental stimuli. In spite of the fact that there is not an accurate explanation regarding the contents of each system, and that there are some disagreements among authors on what should be understood by the cognitive system's responses or, in lesser degree, by the physiological system's responses (Cone and Hawkins, 1977; Fernández-Ballesteros, 1983), this classification of the different anxiety responses in three systems is widely used and acknowledged.

The main manifestations of state anxiety or anxiety reactions can be seen in Table 30.1 (Miguel-Tobal, 1996). With the aim of integrating the above-mentioned aspects, anxiety must be considered as an emotional response, or pattern of responses, which includes unpleasant cognitive aspects, physiological aspects characterized by a high arousal of the autonomous nervous system, and inaccurate and less adaptive motor or behavioural reactions. Anxiety response may be provoked both by situational–external and internal stimuli such as thoughts, ideas, images and so on, perceived by the individual as threatening or dangerous. Such kinds of anxiety-eliciting stimuli (external or internal) will be mainly determined by subjects' characteristics; in this sense, there are remarkable individual

Table 30.1   Main manifestations of anxiety

Cognitive (subjective thoughts, ideas or images, and their influence on individual functioning)	
Worries	Negative thoughts: inferiority, unable to act and so on
Insecurity	Difficulties in taking options
Fear	Anticipation of threat and danger
Apprehension	Lack of concentration
General sense of disorganization and lack of control of the environment; unclear thinking.	
Physiological (consequences of the activity of different physiological systems)	
Cardiovascular symptoms: heartbeat, tachycardia, high blood pressure, heat flows	
Respiratory symptoms: sense of suffocation, dyspnea, increased breathing, chest pain	
Gastrointestinal symptoms: nauseas, vomiting, diarrhoea and digestive disturbances	
Genitourinary symptoms: enuresis, premature ejaculation, frigidity, erectile impotence	
Neuromuscular symptoms: muscle tension, trembling, headaches, fatigue, cramps	
Neurovegetative symptoms: dry mouth, excessive sweating, dizziness, faintness	
Motor (overt behaviours as a consequence of cognitive and physiological activity)	
Hyperactivity	Uncoordinated movements
Motor inhibition	Stutter and other verbal disturbances
Repetitive movements	Avoidance behaviour

Source: Miguel-Tobal (1996).

differences related to the tendency to manifest anxiety reactions in different situations (Miguel-Tobal, 1990).

So far, we have considered anxiety as a normal, adaptive and common emotional response of individuals to different threatening or dangerous situations or circumstances. However, when its frequency, intensity and duration are excessive, producing serious limitations in different facets of the individual's life and reducing their adaptability to the environment, we must talk about pathological anxiety.

Anxiety is closely related to anxiety disorders, depression, the traditionally labelled 'neurotic' disorders, many psychotic disorders and a wide variety of psychophysiological disorders such as cardiovascular disorders, peptic ulcers, headaches, premenstrual syndrome, asthma, skin disorders and so on. It is also involved in addictive behaviour and eating and sexual disorders; recent findings even relate anxiety to weaknesses of the immune system (Miguel-Tobal and González-Ordi, 2003).

Due to the wide variety of problems in which this emotion plays an important role, anxiety must be considered a central core in psychopathology and health psychology. In fact, thousands of people with anxiety problems seek help in hospitals, health centres and so on, causing important economic costs to public health services. Anxiety and stress are often used as interchangeable terms, even in the specialized literature, owing to the fact that they have many elements in common. As Endler (1988) pointed out, the concepts overlap each other, presenting many coincident aspects.

Stress

One of the first relevant figures in studying and publishing specific proposals on stress was Claude Bernard (1878). The eminent 19th-century French physiologist defined stress as an adaptive response to external stimuli. He also introduced the basic principle of *homeostasis*.

Subsequently Walter B. Cannon (1929, 1932) devoted special interest to studying homeostasis. He contributed definitively in establishing its importance in the process of stress up until now. Homeostasis is the process by which the normal balance of metabolic processes, or a relatively constant internal environment in the body, is maintained (Kolb and Whishaw, 2001). Organisms tend to react to environmental pressures with coordinated patterns of physiological activity (and behaviour), or oscillations and systematic rhythms of change in physiological variables which play an important role in stability and adaptation (Giardino et al., 2000). Cannon (1932) proposed that each organism possesses constant levels of physiological components, and there is an optimal level for each organism regarding the number of physiological components. Therefore homeostasis consists of a process that maintains adequate levels of physiological components when an oscillation occurs.

The other big contribution of Walter B. Cannon to the study of stress was to identify a specific type of stress response: the 'fight or flight' response to stress. This response is an emergency mechanism elicited by the organism, activated in a few seconds, which prepares it to respond adequately and efficiently to a threatening or dangerous stimulus. This may consist of a confronting or fight response, or an avoiding or flight strategy, depending on what is more adaptive for the organism and the species (Miguel-Tobal, 2000). This response is mainly composed of several physiological changes mediated by the sympathetic nervous system of the spinal cord which facilitates the fast release of hormones such as adrenaline and noradrenaline. This release directly affects organs innervated by the sympathetic nervous system as well as target organs activated in the process. There is also an activation of the somatic system with increases in respiratory rate and muscle tone. All changes such as increases in respiratory rate, heart rate, muscle tone and oxygen flow prepare the body for a sudden burst of activity, increasing attention, performance and perceptual skills, in order to respond with a fight or flight response.

The current perspective on the study of stress was first delineated by the physiologist Hans Selye in the mid-1930s. Selye extended the concept of homeostasis by including the hypothalamic–pituitary–adrenocortical axis mediated responses in the process of stress. Selye (1936, 1956) further developed a generalized model of stress response including consequences of long-term exposure to stressors. He defined his model as a General Adaptation Syndrome (GAS). It includes several general reactions which conform to a similar pattern of bodily response in order to improve the adaptation and survival of the organism. The General Adaptation Syndrome consists of three stages, related to different activation levels.

Alarm reaction stage   This is the first response in the stress response pattern, and describes the first actions of the organism exposed to stressful conditions. There are two elements: a first shock reaction similar to 'fight or flight' response proposed by Cannon, characterized by a sympathoadrenal hyperreactivity; and a reaction that mobilizes the organism to recover homeostasis.

Resistance stage   This appears because the organism is unable to maintain the arousal levels fostered in the alarm reaction stage in the continuous presence of stressful stimuli. This stage is characterized by high arousal levels (but lower than in the alarm stage) because the organism must be adapted to the stressful conditions. In this stage the hypothalamic–pituitary–adrenocortical axis is mainly involved, saving and maintaining the organism's energy, and suppressing some functions, such as sexual or reproductive behaviours.

Exhaustion stage   There is a breakdown of the organism in this stage, owing to a lack of resources and energy to respond to the continuous environmental demands that provide arousal levels and pseudo-balance that the organism exhibited in the resistance stage. This will generate physiological and psychological disturbances, which Selye named 'adaptation disorders'. Such disorders will break down organisms' homeostasis and provoke irreversible noxious, even lethal, effects.

Selye consequently defined stress as the state that accompanies General Adaptation Syndrome. He focused especially on the physiological responses of this process, as well as on the effects on health. In addition to physiological stress responses, there are emotional consequences which facilitate responses such as anxiety, anger or depression. In any case, there are negative physiological, cognitive and behavioural effects to stress, especially at the resistance and exhaustion stages, as can be seen in Table 30.2.

In view of the aim of this chapter, it should be especially noted that there is a close relationship between stress and cardiovascular responses (Hjemdahl, 2000). Using a

Table 30.2 *Negative effects of the resistance and exhauston stages*

Cognitive	Physiological	Behavioural
Lack of concentration	Increased level of catecholamines, corticoesteroids and glucose	Increased number of accidents
Unable to take decisions		
Lack of memory	Increased heart rate and blood pressure	Drugs consumption: alcohol, tobacco, caffeine etc
Low self-esteem		
High sensitivity to criticisms	Increased sweating	Hyperactivity
	Pupil dilation	Impulsivity

stimulus–response scheme for cardiovascular responses to psychological stress, Hjemdahl argued that:

> the perception of 'stress' is modified by multiple factors, which reinforce or attenuate the arousal evoked by the stimulus. The cardiovascular response is mediated by neurohormonal activation. Several factors may modify the neurohormonal activation as well as responses to the mediating neurohormones. Finally, the cardiovascular responses may be buffered by baroreflexes aimed at maintaining blood pressure at prestimulus levels, but the efficiency of the baroreflex is attenuated during stress. (p. 391)

Hjemdahl's model can be seen in Figure 30.1.

Anger
Anger can be defined as a negative emotion that includes irritation, angry feelings and rage. Such feelings are the subjective components of anger. Additionally it is accompanied by a physiological pattern characterized by increasing levels of arousal of the sympathetic nervous system and endocrine system, increases in muscle tension and a motor response that implies different facial expressions and aggressive behaviour. This emotion is mainly elicited during interpersonal situations appraised by the subject as an intentional and unjustified violation of his/her expectations or personal territory. Fight response used to be the prior coping mechanism chosen in these situations.

Anger, like anxiety, is initially studied as a personality characteristic highlighting the distinction between trait anger and state anger (Spielberger *et al.*, 1983). However literature reviews on anger and hostility show that anger expression and experience tends to be confounded with situational determinants of anger reactions. Indeed the first assessment instruments draw a complex and heterogeneous phenomenon, confounding three closely related concepts: anger, hostility and aggression. Therefore a coherent theoretical model which differentiates these three concepts and, at the same time, explicitly recognizes the state–trait distinction is necessary in order to develop and validate a psychometric assessment instrument on anger.

So, in addition to clarifying and integrating an explicit definition of anger, it is also necessary to differentiate it from other similar terms and to study all the elements involved in the anger phenomenon. Spielberger *et al.* (1983) delineated a classical distinction between the three concepts:

Source: Adapted from Hjemdahl (2000).

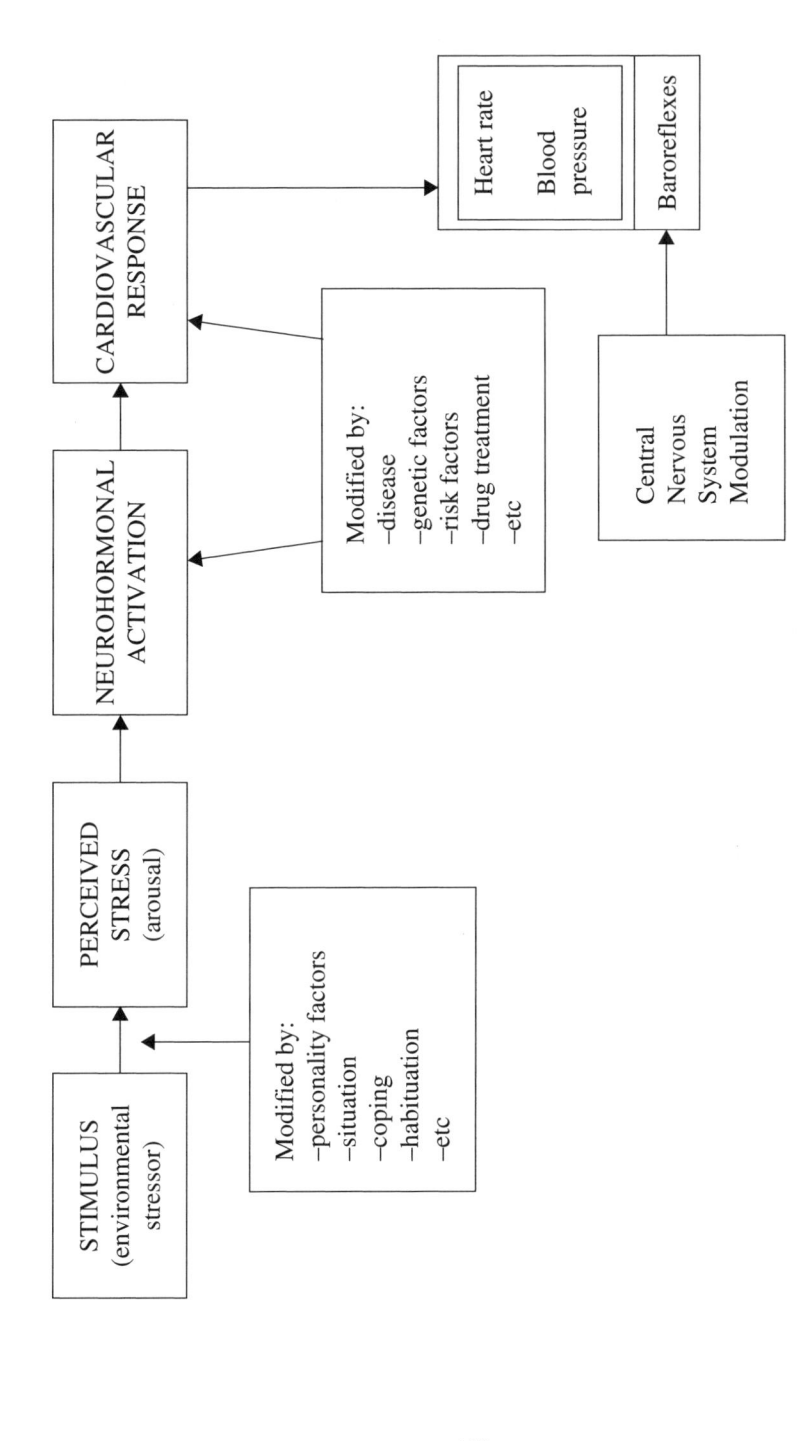

Figure 30.1 Relationship between stress and cardiovascular responses

1. *anger* refers to an emotional state characterized by angry feelings of variable intensity (irritation, annoyance and anger),
2. *hostility* refers to a persistent negative appraisal attitude towards others,
3. *aggression*: a goal-directed behaviour to damage things or injury persons.

Spielberger *et al.* (1983) point out that anger is a simpler concept than hostility and aggression. Basically, hostility is an attitude that usually involves angry feelings and promotes or motivates goal-directed aggressive behaviours including object destruction, insulting others or damaging people and surrounding objects. While anger and hostility mainly refer to feelings and attitudes, aggression goes further, in the sense that it involves destructive or punitive behaviours directed against other people or objects.

Undoubtedly these three concepts are often intermingled. Hostility implies angry feelings and, at the same time, promotes attitudes that motivate aggressive behaviours. Similarly, although anger is considered simpler than aggression, it also includes aggressive behaviours, both physical and verbal. The distinction between hostile and instrumental aggression must also been taken into account. Hostile aggression refers to goal-directed behaviours due to anger, while instrumental aggression refers to the aggressive behaviours used to overcome the obstacles that are hindering the attainment of a goal.

Owing to the conceptual definition overlaps between anger, hostility and aggression, and to the wide variety of procedures used to assess such constructs, a new concept appeared: the AHA (Anger–Hostility–Aggression) Syndrome (Spielberger *et al.*, 1985; Spielberger *et al.*, 1988). Although we have tried to differentiate the three concepts, it is clear that they often appear close together in a certain emotional reaction. Therefore we will refer to AHA syndrome when we delineate the relationship between anger and cardiovascular disorders. In this context, AHA syndrome is truly highlighted and, at the same time, helps to delimit and clarify more accurately the concept of anger.

Cardiovascular disease
According to Davidson (1994), the term 'cardiovascular disease' refers to any disorder of the heart and blood vessels, including hypertension, coronary artery disease (CAD), cardiac dysrhythmias, cerebrovascular disease, valvular heart disease, cardiomyopathies, peripheral vascular disease and congenital cardiac abnormalities.

Although it is not currently possible to determine the exact main causes underlying cardiovascular disorders, there are several factors interacting with each other, which increase the risk of cardiovascular disease. In this sense, the interaction of coronary risk factors means that an individual may suffer more than one of these factors simultaneously, hence increasing the probability to develop a cardiovascular disorder. Taking into account the overall amount of research, coronary risk factors can be classified as follows:

Inherent risk factors
Genetic or physical factors are non-modifiable by means of behavioural strategies. However their risk potential may be reduced by the application of adequate patterns of behaviour.

- *Age*: aging increases the probability of cardiovascular death due to multiple causes;
- *Family antecedents*: relatives diagnosed with cardiovascular disease;

- *Gender*: death rates are more significant in mid-adult males;
- *Race*: black Americans present a 40 per cent higher mortality rate than white Americans. This higher risk of Blacks can also be due to social, economic and behavioural factors;
- *Diabetes*: diabetes increases the probability of coronary death, as it exacerbates other risk factors and neutralizes the protective action of endogenous estrogens in pre-menopausal women.

Physiological factors

- *Hypertension*: hypertension is the condition of sustained elevated arterial blood pressure. Consequences of hypertension are related to atherosclerosis, which increases the probability of dying of coronary disease, myocardial infarction, sudden stroke and atherothrombotic brain infarction;
- *Obesity*: obesity is closely related to and predicts hypertension;
- *Cholesterol levels*: cholesterol is found in the cardiovascular system in the form of low density lipoproteins (LDL) or high density lipoproteins (HDL). While LDL improve cardiovascular disorders, HDL reduce its risk. This is especially clear in young and mid-adults, but less in olders people;
- *Uric acid*: some researches relate uric acid with the risk of developing coronary disease.

Behavioural factors

- *Diet*: diet can increase or decrease the probability of cardiovascular disorders to a greater degree than being overweight. While a highly saturated fat diet increases the risk of suffering these types of diseases, a diet rich in vitamins (antioxidants, vitamin E, selenium and so on) or fibre reduces it;
- *Physical exercise*: although there is no evidence of the relationship between physical exercise and coronary disease incidence reduction, its practice reduces body weight and blood pressure, and improves lipid profile. These outcomes suggest possible benefits in reducing cardiovascular disease;
- *Tobacco consumption*: this is the most relevant behavioural risk factor. Smokers have a two or threefold predisposition to cardiovascular death than non-smokers. Passive smoking increases by 20 per cent the risk of developing cardiovascular disease. Carbon monoxide, rather than nicotine, is the most dangerous component in the genesis of atherosclerosis;
- *Coffee consumption*: caffeine produces tachycardia, increasing transient blood pressure. Although there is contradictory scientific evidence, caffeine can produce arrythmias, triggering a coronary disease established earlier.

Psychosocial factors

- *Marriage and social networks*: low social support is related to an increasing risk of coronary disease. Researches found that, six months after myocardial infarction,

people who lived alone showed twofold probability of re-experiencing coronary disease. Social support reduces risk of cardiovascular death in the case that friends and relatives encourage patients to keep on an adequate life style and carry on with medical prescriptions and so on;
- *Low economic and education level*: subjects with low economic resources or educational level have fewer probabilities of receiving medical assistance and they are more prone to suffering such kinds of disorders;
- *High levels of anxiety and stress*: chronic stress is implicated in cardiovascular disease, increasing blood pressure that can produce atherosclerotic plaque rupture;
- *Type A behaviour pattern*: TABP is characterized by excessive competitive drive, impatience, hostility and vigorous speech characteristics. After a period of increase and enthusiasm in the study of TABP and cardiovascular disorders, several studies began to criticize such relationships, in the sense that TABP is not a unitary phenomenon and it is possible that not all of its characteristics (competitiveness, time urgency, hostility and so on) contribute equally to coronary risk. Therefore studies have tried to identify the components of TABP that are most strongly associated with cardiovascular disorders. Hostility and anger are the most significant components;
- *Hostility*: hostility predicts mostly coronary artery disease. Hostility refers to a negative appraisal persistent attitude to others, promoting aggressive behaviour;
- *Anger* is an emotional state characterized by angry feelings of variable intensity (irritation, annoyance, anger). Anger experience may not be implicated in the cardiovascular system, but anger expression is closely related to cardiovascular disease. In this sense, anger-in or anger repression is a harmful aspect of cardiovascular disorders. With the onset of cardiovascular disease, both anger experience and expression exacerbate it.

Cardiovascular disorders are of enormous interest in current scientific literature, together with the role of emotional variables like anxiety, stress, hostility and anger in the onset, development and maintenance of such disorders. Let us consider now how the panorama is delineated for scientific psychology literature. In this sense, Fernández-López and Miguel-Tobal (2002) reviewed the evolution of publications in psychology on this matter, using international computerized databases. Results are summarized in Figures 30.2 and 30.3.

Figure 30.2 shows the number of psychology publications including two of the most important cardiovascular disorders: hypertension and myocardial infarction, indexed by three-year intervals. As can be seen, there is a significant increase in the publications devoted to all the key words indexed ('cardiovascular', 'hypertension' and 'myocardial infarction'), in a period ranging from 1966 to 2001. The term 'cardiovascular' is the most referred to in publications, regardless of the year consulted. Indeed, in the period 1999–2001, 'cardiovascular' accounts for 1328 publications, while 'hypertension' and 'myocardial infarction' only account for 438 and 192 publications, respectively, over the same period. This evident difference may be due to the fact that 'cardiovascular' is a more general term, while 'hypertension' and 'myocardial infarction' are more specific. In any case, all terms show a considerable increase, especially from the 1980s. It should also be noted that, while 'hypertension' and 'cardiovascular' terms have a continuous increasing

Source: Fernández-López and Miguel-Tobal (2002).

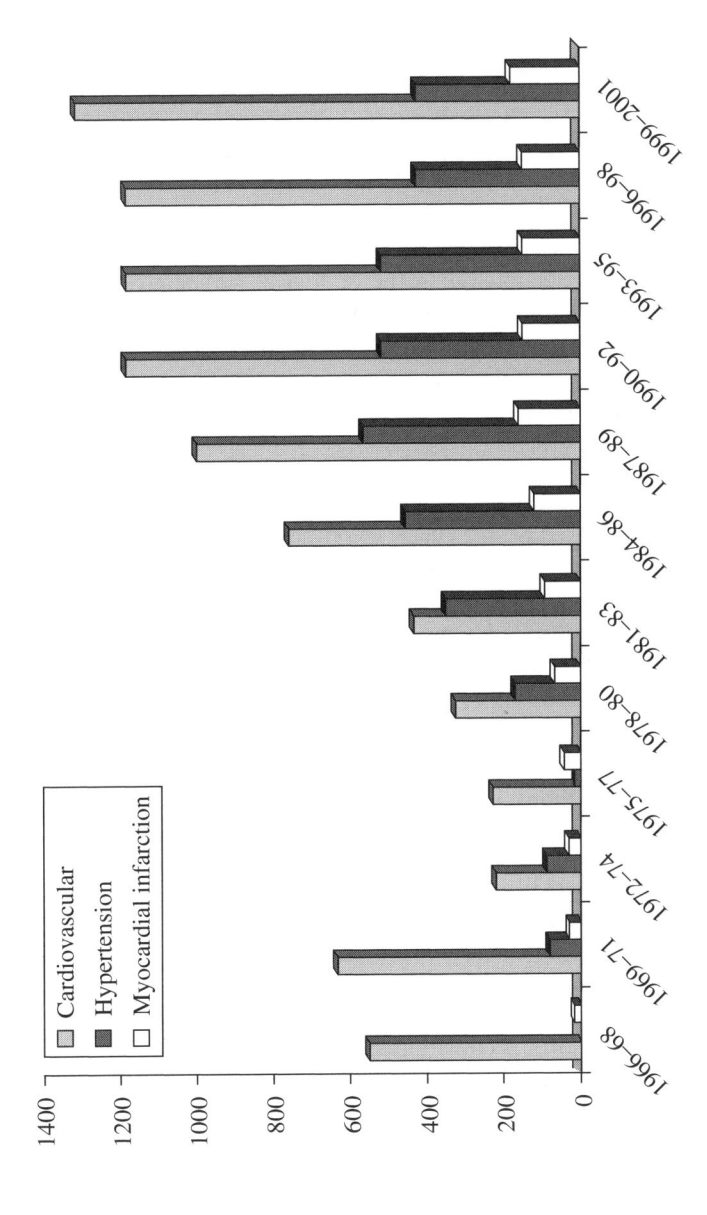

Figure 30.2 Evolution of psychological literature regarding the key words 'cardiovascular', 'hypertension' and 'myocardial infarction'

rate, 'cardiovascular' registered an important decrease during the 1970s. The amount of 637 publications in the late 1960s were not reached and surpassed until the mid-1980s; in the meantime, an average of 270 publications appeared for every three-year interval.

Figure 30.3 shows the evolution of psychology publications regarding the key word 'cardiovascular' associated with 'stress', 'anxiety' and 'anger', respectively, indexed in three-year intervals. In the period from 1966 to 2001, stress is the term most cited, followed by 'anxiety' and 'anger'. Once again, the number of publications mentioning 'cardiovascular' and the mentioned emotional variables increased from the mid-1980s, especially in relation to 'stress' and 'anxiety'. Regarding 'anxiety', a remarkable increase in research began as early as the mid-1970s. This increase could be due to the changes that occurred regarding its conceptualization during that decade. Before the 1970s, anxiety was mainly conceptualized as a personality trait or characteristic, but in the late 1970s, the study of anxiety from the three response systems' (cognitive, physiological and motor) point of view facilitated a broader scope, including the biological perspective in addition to the psychological one. Finally it should be noted that in the late 1990s there is a spectacular increase in publications on the relationship between 'heart' and emotional variables.

Taking Figures 30.2 and 30.3 together, it can be seen that the number of psychology publications on cardiovascular disorders and their relationship with emotional variables such as stress, anxiety and anger has increased considerably, especially since the 1980s.

For decades, cardiovascular disease has been the leading cause of mortality in industrialized countries (Uemura and Pisa, 1988; Davidson, 1994) and its prevalence is increasing in the developing world (Reddy and Yusuf, 1998), accounting for more than 45 per cent of the deaths in 1997, according to the World Health Organization. Additionally, and taking into account that psychological and medical research indicated a strong relationship between several psychological variables and suffering cardiovascular diseases, it is not surprising that cardiovascular disorders are placed in the top rank of health psychology study. As Gatchel, Baum and Krantz pointed out some time ago, 'cardiovascular disorders, including coronary heart disease, high blood pressure, and stroke, are widely studied topics in health psychology' (Gatchel et al., 1989, p. 97). Moreover, in recent decades an increasing volume of literature on this topic has been witnessed (Fernández-López and Miguel-Tobal, 2002).

Cardiovascular disorders in Spain are also the first cause of death both for males (31.6 per cent) and for females (39.1 per cent), followed by cancer (30.6 per cent for males and 24.4 per cent for females) and, at a considerably lower rate, by respiratory illness (11.8 per cent for males and 8.0 per cent for females) (Ministerio de Sanidad y Consumo, 2001). Among cardiovascular disorders, hypertension and coronary artery disease (and its closely related pathology, myocardial infarction) received special attention from health psychology, because both disorders contributed largely to cardiac failure, and emotional variables such as anxiety and anger are closely related to their onset or exacerbation (Mittleman et al., 1995; Suinn, 2001).

Hypertension or high blood pressure is the most common cardiovascular disease, and its prevalence exceeds 20 per cent in developed countries (Davidson, 1991). Hypertension and coronary artery disease are recognized as the leading causes of heart failure in the general population both in Europe and in the USA (Kannel, 2000). Indeed hypertension is a well-recognized risk factor for stroke, myocardial infarction and congestive heart

Source: As for Figure 30.2.

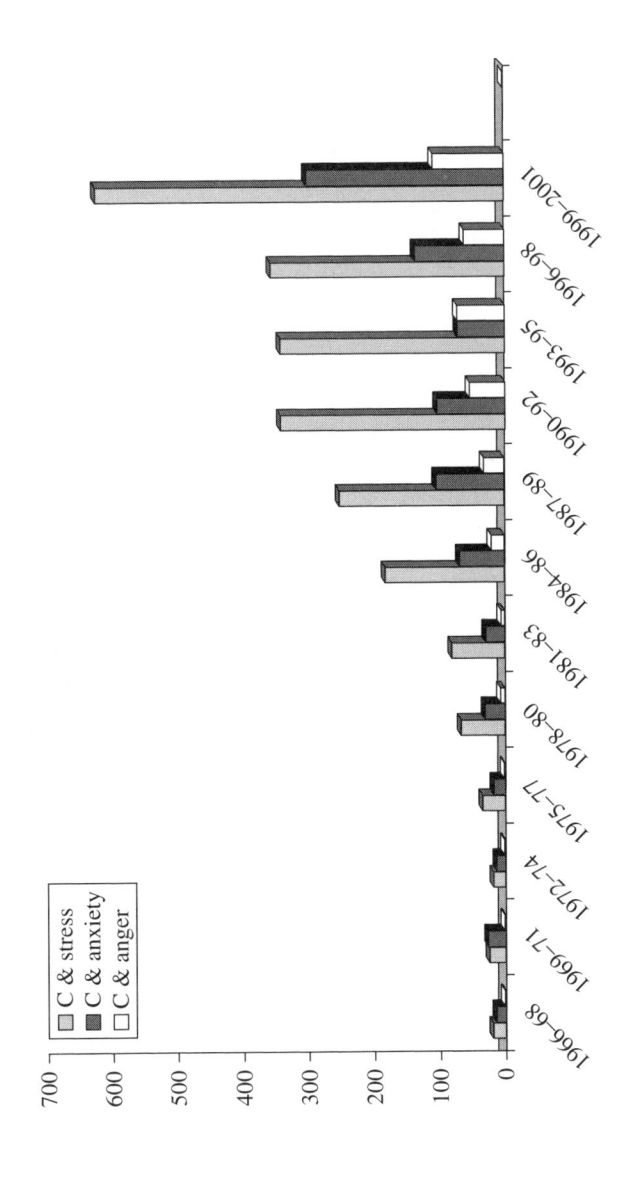

Figure 30.3 Evolution of psychological literature regarding the key word 'cardiovascular', in combination with 'stress', 'anxiety' and 'anger'

failure (Rosen *et al.*, 1993). Prevalence of hypertension is related to age, race and gender. Hypertension incidence is higher in Blacks than in Whites, particularly in the United States. In young to middle-aged adults, prevalence is much greater in males than in females, while incidence increases quite dramatically in women after the menopause (Sherwood and Carels, 2000).

Mortality rates vary considerably from one country to another as regards coronary artery disease. There are markedly higher rates in countries such as Northern Ireland, Scotland and Finland, while there are much lower rates (three or four times less) in countries around Mediterranean Europe (Spain, Italy, Greece and France). Japan is the country with the lowest rates, where deaths caused by coronary artery disease are ten times fewer than in the first mentioned countries (Davidson, 1991). Myocardial infarction is the most frequent specific pathology related to coronary artery disease and, according to the Framingham study, has a large hazard ratio and subsequent high attributable risk for cardiac failure, accounting for 34 per cent and 13 per cent of the cases in men and women, respectively (Kannel, 2000).

Anger, anxiety and stress in cardiovascular disorders
Multiple-factor conception research on cardiovascular disease identified anger and anxiety as two of the risk factors when considering its prediction and explanation. In the words of Suinn (2001), 'these "terrible twos" increase vulnerability to illness, especially upper respiratory illness, compromise the immune system, increase lipid levels, exacerbate pain and increase the risk of death from cardiovascular disease and from all sources of death' (p. 34).

Regarding anger, the development of the Type A Behavior Pattern (TABP) in the 1950s by the cardiologists Friedman and Rosenman contributed considerably to this fact. TABP is characterized by excessive competitive drive, impatience, hostility and vigorous speech characteristics. After a period of rise and enthusiasm in the study of TABP and cardiovascular disorders, several studies began to doubt this relationship in the sense that TABP is not a unitary phenomenon and it is possible that not all of its characteristics (competitiveness, time urgency, hostility and so on) contribute equally to coronary risk. Therefore studies have tried to identify the components of TABP that are most strongly associated with cardiovascular disorders.

Anger and hostility came to be seen as among the outstanding components of TABC regarding predictive value in the onset and maintenance of cardiovascular diseases. Shumaker and Czajkowski (1994) consider anger as the most stable component of TABC, showing the strongest association with hypertension, coronary artery disease and other cardiovascular diseases, for example triggering the onset of acute myocardial infarction (Mittleman *et al.*, 1995).

Miller *et al.* (1996) also concluded, from a meta-analysis of 45 studies, that hostility is an independent risk factor of coronary heart disease. Matthews *et al.* (1998) conducted a prospective study of 200 healthy women after measuring their levels of hostility and anxiety. Ten years later, measures of atherosclerosis were obtained, and results showed a significant relationship between the earlier measures of anxiety and hostility and current levels of atherosclerotic disease symptoms. Barefoot *et al.* (1983) found in a prospective study that there is a significant association between hostility and cardiovascular incidence and deaths.

Smith and Christensen (1992) suggested that hostility-prone people manifest episodes of anger more frequently and are more vigilant regarding their surroundings. Therefore there is a close relationship between anger and vigilance that influences cardiovascular and endocrine responses, and contributes to the development of related diseases. Suarez and Williams (1990) considered that individuals with high hostility and livelihood of manifesting anger-out have a greater risk of developing coronary diseases, while individuals who suppress anger expression have a greater risk of suffering hypertension. Indeed Haynes *et al.* (1980) have already found in a prospective study a significant relationship between coronary disease and anger-in.

Regarding anxiety and stress, it is known that 'mental stress' elicits a cardiovascular response pattern typical of the 'defence reaction', with increases in heart rate and cardiac output and redistribution of blood flow to different organs in both animal and humans. Blood pressure increases despite a net decrease in systemic vascular resistance, which is related to vasodilatation in large tissues, notably skeletal muscle and adipose tissue, whereas vasoconstriction occurs in the kidneys, splanchnic organs and skin. Stress is involved in the pathogenesis of several cardiovascular diseases such as hypertension and myocardial infarction, and in sudden death (Hjemdahl, 2000; Sherwood and Carels, 2000).

Baker *et al.* (2000) argued that 'current models of the effects of acute physical and mental stress on cardiac pathophysiology suggest that activation of the autonomic nervous system induced by behavioural factors may increase the risk of cardiovascular events' (p. 327). In this sense, these authors proposed a model which illustrates pathways through which acute mental stress is linked to myocardial ischemia and clinical coronary events such as heart attack or sudden death. These links are thought to exist in individuals with pre-existing coronary artery disease or dysfunction, prior myocardial infarction or poor cardiac function, who are therefore at higher risk of these clinical events. Baker *et al.*'s model can be seen in Figure 30.4.

Suinn (2001) proposed four mechanisms probably involved with the incontrovertible evidence that both anxiety and anger are hazardous to health, especially cardiovascular disease:

1. anxiety–anger leads to vigilance and scanning, which, along with the emotional arousal itself, involves activation of the sympathetic nervous system (SNS) (Smith *et al.*, 2000; Williams *et al.*, 1985). Activation of SNS mediates other bodily functions such as the cardiovascular system the immune system and the endocrine system (Dimsdale *et al.*, 1983; Niaura *et al.*, 1992; Stoney and West, 1997);
2. anxiety–anger leads to poor health behaviours, including unhealthy life styles such as alcohol and tobacco consumption, unhealthy diet, disturbed sleep patterns, poor compliance with medical prescriptions, lack of exercise and so on (Leiker and Hailey, 1988; Cohen and Williamson, 1991; Siegler *et al.*, 1992; Smith and Christensen, 1992);
3. anxiety–anger is associated with psychosocial characteristics affecting vulnerability, such as low social support and high interpersonal conflicts (Krantz *et al.*, 1988; Smith and Pope, 1990; Suarez and Williams, 1989);
4. anxiety–anger is an expression of underlying constitutional or biological factors such as hyperresponsive nervous system or even alterations in serotonin levels (Krantz and Durel, 1983; Plomin *et al.*, 1990).

Source: Adapted from Baker et al. (2000).

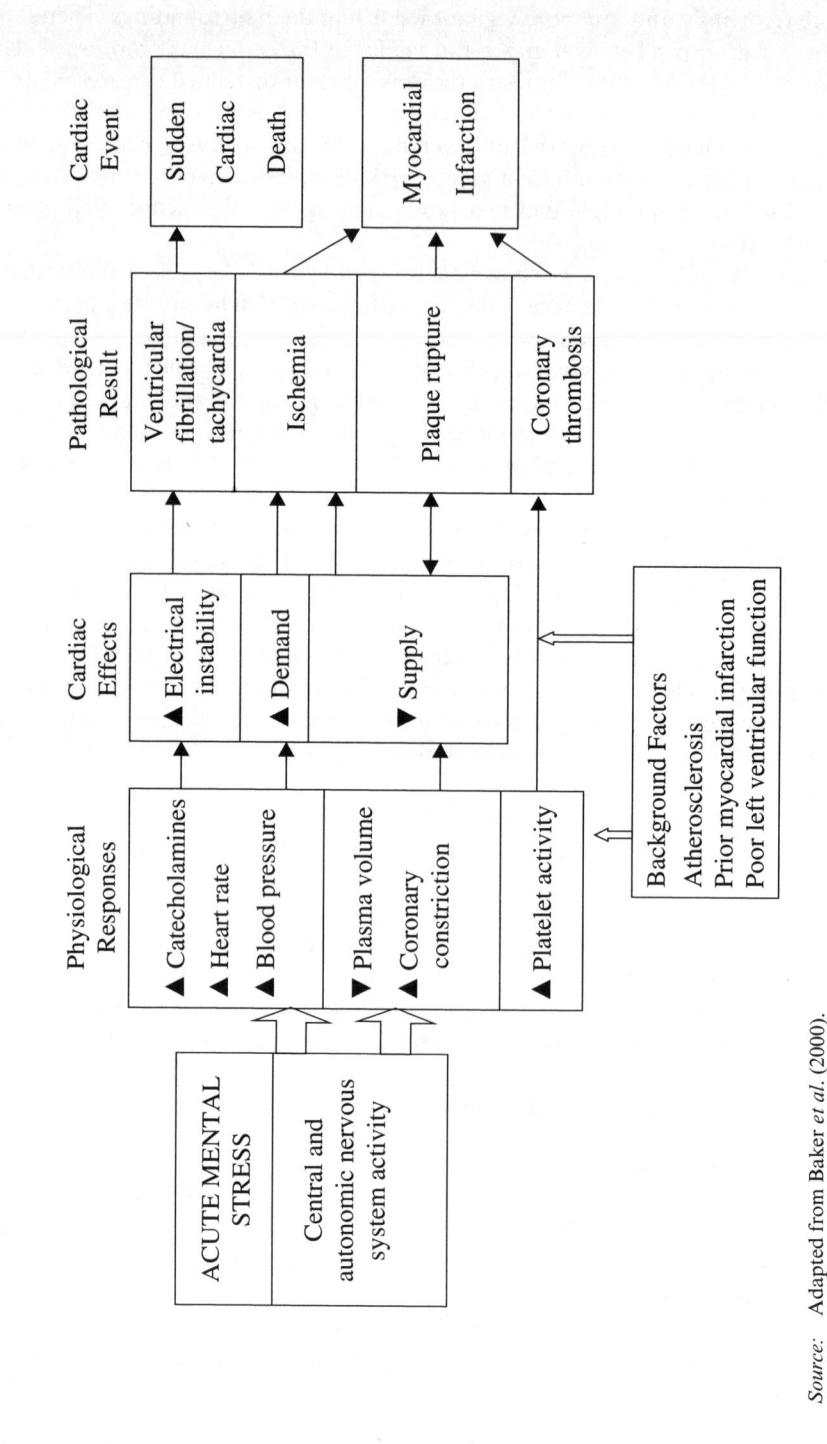

Figure 30.4 Effects of acute mental stress on cardiac pathophysiology

These four mechanisms are not mutually exclusive; all of them suggest very interesting points of view and future research lines on the role of anxiety and anger in cardiovascular disease.

Finally, according to Leventhal (2000), negative emotions may precede illness and reduce endurance or increase vulnerability to different disorders; at the same time, emotional negative states such as anxiety, stress and anger can appear as consequence of illness. Therefore there is a bidirectional relationship between negative emotionality and illness.

Anger, anxiety and hypertension
Hypertension is the condition of sustained elevated arterial blood pressure. According to Steptoe (2000), the criteria for defining hypertension are somewhat arbitrary, as the distribution of blood pressure level in the population is continuous. The American Heart Association defines hypertension as a systolic blood pressure at rest $\geq$ 140mmHg and/or a diastolic blood pressure $\geq$ 90mmHg. In other countries, the systolic blood pressure cutoff is 150 or 160mmHg, whereas the diastolic criterion is 95 or 100mmHg. Risk of coronary heart disease and stroke is directly related to blood pressure level, so hypertension defines those individuals who are at an especially elevated risk (Steptoe, 2000).

The prevalence of hypertension according to the 140/90mmHg criterion is approximately 25 per cent among adults in the United States (ibid.). Using the criterion of 160/95mmHg, recent data in the United Kingdom revealed that 23 per cent of men and 22 per cent of women are hypertensive. Between one-third and one-half of hypertensives are not diagnosed and are unaware of their condition, owing to the fact that hypertension is not consistently associated with symptoms. The number of diagnosed hypertensives who are not treated is substantial, while as many as 50 per cent of patients who are prescribed antihypertensive medication do not have their blood pressure controlled adequately.

Most cases of hypertension, between 90 and 95 per cent, are regarded as essential or primary hypertension (Sherwood and Carels, 2000). Although the etiopathogenic mechanism is not well established yet, there is overwhelming evidence that the sympathetic nervous system is frequently implicated in the early stages of hypertension and, consequently, stress may be involved in the etiology of hypertension.

It is well known that, even in normotensive individuals, a wide variety of environmental stimuli that provoke a moderate or intense emotional reaction may trigger transient increases in blood pressure. This cardiovascular reactivity is higher in hypertensive patients or in people with family antecedents of hypertension (Ditto and Miller, 1989). These facts lead to theories that include psychosocial factors in the pathogenesis of hypertension. Firstly, the early considerations of Alexander (1939), who, from a psychodynamic point of view, drew attention to the fact that hypertensive patients were unable to express angry feelings, generating a maintained state of resentment, must be taken into account.

Current research is mainly focused on detecting hypertensive subjects' characteristic personality traits in two lines of investigation. The first is to study the incidence of hypertension in psychiatric populations. This research line has received much criticism because of the difficulty of generalizing results to the hypertension general population, and it is difficult to know whether hypertension arises before or after the onset of the 'psychiatric disorder'.

Another and more suitable research line is the use of objective instruments for the measurement of psychological variables in samples of normotensive and hypertensive subjects in order to establish comparisons between the two groups. Correlational methodology is commonly used in this research line. Therefore research outcomes must be cautious in order to avoid erroneous cause–effect conclusions on the relationship between personality characteristics and development of hypertension. Some contradictory results that appear in this field are due to the samples used. In this sense, both clinical and normal samples must be matched in variables such as age, gender and education level.

Regardless of these methodological considerations, studies have drawn attention to the importance of anxiety and anger in the maintenance of hypertension. Harburg et al. (1979) stressed the importance of anger suppression as a variable that contributes to increase blood pressure and influences hypertension. Baer et al. (1979) found that hypertensive subjects scored higher than normotensive in anger activation, anxiety and resentment. Schalling and Svensson (1984) studied the relationship between personality traits and blood pressure in soldiers of the Swedish Army. They found that hypertensive individuals scored higher than normotensives in anxiety, tension, neuroticism and aggression-inhibition scales. Consistent with the earlier view of Alexander (1939) and contrary to the TABP concept, authors describe the hypertensive subject profile as an anxious individual, with lack of assertiveness, who inhibits or represses his/her anger.

Van der Ploeg et al. (1985), by using the State–Trait Anger Expression Inventory (Spielberger et al., 1983; Spielberger, 1988, 1991) in samples of hypertensive patients and normotensive subjects, found that the first scored higher in anger-state and anger-expression than the second sample. Comparisons by gender showed that hypertensive males scored significantly higher in anger-state and anger-trait than normotensive males; however there were no significant differences between hypertensive and normotensive females.

Thailer et al. (1985) argued that hypertensive patients with high plasmatic rennin showed higher levels of suppressed anger, susceptibility, paranoidism, depression and anxiety. Dimsdale et al. (1986) confirmed the relationship between irritation feelings and suppressed anger, and essential hypertension. Boutelle et al. (1987) concluded that hypertensive subjects are more prone to feel anger but also show higher scores in avoiding anger expression. In this sense, Goldstein et al. (1988) found that normotensives used to express angry feelings more easily than hypertensive subjects. Pagotto et al. (1992) indicated that hypertensive subjects showed higher levels of anxiety than normal subjects.

Miller (1992) examined the influence of trait anxiety in cardiovascular response of normotensive subjects (PH−), and normotensive subjects with family antecedents of hypertension (PH+). PH+ subjects with high trait anxiety showed higher increases in the forearm heart rate and blood volume in the presence of certain stresssors, and lower levels of vascular resistance than PH+ subjects with low trait anxiety and PH− subjects. There were no differences between PH+ subjects with low trait anxiety and PH− subjects regarding cardiovascular response. Miller suggested that anxiety could be a moderating factor for the individual cardiovascular response and, by extension, a risk factor for hypertension.

Miguel-Tobal (1993) carried out a pilot research in order to study the relationship between anxiety and anger, and essential hypertension by using the Inventory of Situations and Responses of Anxiety (ISRA) and the Spanish version of the State–Trait

Anger Expression Inventory (STAXI). The sample was of 105 subjects classified into two groups according to their blood pressure levels: normotensives and hypertensives. The groups were matched in age and gender. Results revealed a profile for hypertensive subjects characterized by higher levels of anxiety in all ISRA scales (general trait, systems of response and specific traits). Additionally hypertensives showed more disposition to express anger when criticized or treated unfairly by other individuals (angry reaction), a higher frequency with which angry feelings are held in or suppressed (anger-in), and lower frequency in expressing anger states by means of aggressive behaviours (anger-out) than normotensive subjects.

More recently, Miguel-Tobal et al. (1997) carried out a study with similar measures, including ISRA and STAXI. The sample was of 202 subjects (34 per cent males and 66 per cent females, aged between 19 and 77 years). There were two groups: normal subjects ($n = 109$) and hypertensive subjects ($n = 93$), matched in age and gender. The hypertensive group showed significantly higher levels in all anxiety measures than the normals (trait anxiety; cognitive, physiological, motor anxiety; test, interpersonal, phobic and daily life anxiety). Additionally hypertensives also showed significantly higher levels in the frequency with which angry feelings were held in or suppressed (anger-in) than the normal group.

As in the pilot study of Miguel-Tobal (1993), all anxiety measures were significantly higher for hypertensive than for normals. However, regarding anger, previous results are not confirmed, owing to the fact that the hypertensive subject does not appear to show a higher tendency to express anger than the normal subject; nevertheless differences appear to be related to the way in which this anger is expressed. In later studies (Casado, 1994; Miguel-Tobal et al., 1997) hypertensive subjects showed more anger-in. In other words, when the hypertensive subject feels angry, he or she tends to hold in or suppress his/her angry feelings. This higher score in anger-in obtained by hypertensives than normotensives has also been found in the development and validation of the Spanish version of the State–Trait Anger Expression Inventory, STAXI-2 (Miguel-Tobal et al., 2001).

Finally Miguel-Tobal et al. (1997) addressed another study related to myocardial infarction using the same measures (ISRA for anxiety and STAXI for anger) as in the hypertension study. The sample was of 88 male subjects aged between 38 and 76 years. Two groups were matched by age, one by one: the normal group ($n = 44$) and the myocardial infarction group ($n = 44$). Results showed that there were no differences regarding anxiety measures. Anger results revealed that there were highly significant differences regarding anger-in, in the sense that myocardial infarction patients showed a considerably higher tendency to hold in or suppress their angry feelings than the normal group. Comparing results with the hypertension group, anger-in is the most relevant anger measure again, but in a greater degree for myocardial infarction patients. In addition, myocardial infarction patients showed lower levels of state-anger, which measures the intensity of angry feelings at a particular time, than the normal group. The fact that myocardial infarction patients do not report higher levels of anxiety than normal subjects, but show higher scores in anger-in and low self-reported state-anger, offers support to the hypothesis of an excessive control of emotional expression or a repressive response style, characterized by repression and/or denial of self-reported anxiety.

Some authors have pointed out that a denial or suppression symptom may be used as a coping mechanism to reduce anxiety and β-adrenergic-related stimulation. This can increase survival rates. However, this same fact could have a negative effect before infarction as it delays the search for medical assistance. On the other hand, it is also interesting to consider the fact that infarcted subjects' answers to self-report instruments could be influenced by medical counselling, as they tend to be in agreement with it. In this sense, most patients have probably heard advice such as 'be calm', 'it is not advisable for you to be stressed', 'you must relax', among others, several times.

It is desirable that the increasing amount of research in this area should clarify, in the coming years, the multiple interrelations between emotions and cardiovascular disorders, from both a general and a specific point of view, enabling a deeper knowledge of the mechanisms involved in the onset, development and maintenance of such disorders. Undoubtedly this would assume an important advance in psychological treatments in dealing efficiently with the main cause of death in developed countries.

References

Alexander, F. (1939), 'Emotional factors in essential hypertension', *Psychosomatic Medicine*, **1**, 175–9.
Baer, P.E., F.H. Collins, G.C. Bourenoff, and M.F. Ketchel, (1979), 'Assessing personality factors in essential hypertension with a brief self-report instrument', *Psychosomatic Medicine*, **41**, 721–30.
Baker, G.J., S. Suchday and D.S. Krantz (2000), 'Heart disease/attack', in G. Fink (ed.), *Encyclopedia of Stress*, vol. 2, San Diego, CA: Academic Press, pp. 326–33.
Barefoot, J.C., G. Dahlstrom and R.B. Williams, (1983), 'Hostility, CHD incidence, and total mortality: a 25 years follow-up of 255 physicians', *Psychosomatic Medicine*, **45**, 59–63.
Bernard, C. (1878), *Les phénomènes de la vie*, vol. 1, Paris: Librairie J-B Baillière et Fils.
Boutelle, R., S. Epstein and M. Ruddy (1987), 'The relation of essential hypertension to feelings of anxiety, depression, and anger', *Psychiatry*, **50**, 206–17.
Cannon, W.B. (1929), 'Organization for physiological homeostasis', *Physiology Reviews*, **9**, 399–431.
Cannon, W.B. (1932), *The Wisdom of the Body*, New York: Norton.
Casado, M.I. (1994), 'Ansiedad, estrés y trastornos psicofisiológicos' (Anxiety, stress and psychoplysiological disorders), doctoral dissertation, Complutense University of Madrid.
Cohen, S. and G. Williamson (1991), 'Stress and infectious disease in humans', *Psychological Bulletin*, **109**, 5–24.
Cone, J.D. and R.P Hawkins (1977), *Behavioural Assessment: New Directions in Clinical Psychology*, New York: Brunner-Mazel.
Davidson, D.M. (1991), *Preventive Cardiology*, Baltimore, MD: Wlliams & Wilkins.
Davidson, D.M. (1994), 'An introduction to cardiovascular disease', in S.A. Shumaker and S.M. Czajkowski (eds), *Social Support and Cardiovascular Disease*, New York: Plenum Press, pp. 3–19.
Dimsdale, J.E., A. Herd and L. Hartley (1983), 'Epinephrine mediated increases in plasma cholesterol', *Psychosomatic Medicine*, **45**, 227–32.
Dimsdale, J.E., C.H. Pierce and D. Schoenfeld (1986), 'Suppressed anger and blood pressure. The effects of race, social class, obesity and age', *Psychosomatic Medicine*, **48**, 430–36.
Ditto, B. and S.B. Miller (1989), 'Forearm blood flow responses of offspring of hypertensives to an extended stress task', *Hypertension*, **13**, 181–7.
Endler, N.S. (1975), 'A person–situation interaction model for anxiety', in C.D. Spielberger and I.G. Sarason (eds), *Stress and Anxiety*, vol. 1, Washington, DC: Hemisphere Publishing, pp. 145–64.
Endler, N.S. (1980), 'Person–situation interaction and anxiety', in I.L. Kutash and L.B. Schlesinger (eds), *Handbook on Stress and Anxiety*, Contemporary Knowledge, Theory and Treatment, San Francisco: Jossey-Bass, pp. 249–66.
Endler, N.S. and G.L. Flatt (2001), *Endler Multidimensional Anxiety Scales – Social Anxiety Scales. Manual*, Los Angeles, CA: Western Psychological Services.
Endler, N.S. and N.L. Kocovski (2003), 'Anxiety assessment', in R. Fernández-Ballesteros (ed.), *Encyclopedia of Psychological Assessment*, vol. 1, London: Sage Publication, pp. 35–40.
Fernández-Ballesteros, R. (1983), *Psicodiagnóstico* (Psychodiagnostic), Madrid: UNED.
Fernández-López, V. and J.J. Miguel-Tobal (2002), 'Actividad cardiovascular y variables psicológicas. Una revisión de la literatura de los últimos treinta y cinco años' (Cardiovascular activity and psychological factors. A literature review of the last 35 years), paper presented at the IV Congreso Internacional de la Sociedad Española para el Estudio de la Ansiedad y el Estrés (SEAS), Benidorm, 19–21 September.

Gatchel, R.J., A. Baum and D.S. Krantz (1989), *An Introduction to Health Psychology*, 2nd edn, New York: McGraw-Hill.
Giardino, N.D., P.M. Lehrer and J.M. Feldman (2000), 'The role of oscillations in self-regulation: their contribution to homeostasis', in D.T. Kenny, J.G. Carlson, F.J. McGuigan and J.L. Sheppard (eds), *Stress and Health: Research and Clinical Applications*, Amsterdam: Arwood Academic Publishers, pp. 27–51.
Goldstein, H.S., D. Med, R. Eldelbarg, C.F. Meier and L. Davis (1988), 'Relationship of resting blood pressure and heart rate to experienced anger and expressed anger', *Psychosomatic Medicine*, **50**, 321–9.
Harburg, E., E.H. Blakekock and P.J. Roeper (1979), 'Resentful and reflective coping with arbitrary authority and blood pressure: Detroit', *Psychosomatic Medicine*, **41**, 189–202.
Haynes, S.G., M. Feinleib and W.B. Kannel (1980), 'The relationship of psychosocial factors to coronary heart disease in the Framingham Study. III: eight year incidence of coronary heart disease', *American Journal of Epidemiology*, **111**, 37–58.
Hjemdahl, P. (2000), 'Cardiovascular system and stress', in G. Fink (ed.), *Encyclopedia of Stress*, vol. 1, San Diego, CA: Academic Press, pp. 389–403.
Kannel, W.B. (2000), 'Vital epidemiologic clues in heart failure', *Journal of Clinical Epidemiology*, **53**, 229–35.
Kolb, B and I.Q. Whishaw (2001), *An Introduction to Brain and Behaviour*, New York: Worth.
Krantz, D. and L. Durel (1983), 'Psychobiological substrates of the Type A behavior pattern', *Health Psychology*, **2**, 393–411.
Krantz, D., R. Contrada, R. Hill and E. Friedler (1988), 'Environmental stress and biobehavioral antecedents of coronary heart disease', *Journal of Consulting and Clinical Psychology*, **56**, 333–41.
Lacey, J.I. (1967), 'Somatic responses patterning and stress: some revisions of the activation theory', in M.H. Appley and R. Trumbull (eds), *Psychological Stress: Issues in Research*. New York: Appleton-Century-Crofts, pp. 14–42.
Lang, P.J. (1968), 'Fear reduction and fear behavior: problems in treating a construct', in J.M. Shilen (ed), *Research in Psychotherapy*, vol. III, Washington, DC: American Psychological Association, pp. 90–103.
Leiker, M. and B. Hailey (1988), 'A link between hostility and disease: poor health habits?', *Behavioural Medicine*, **3**, 129–33.
Leventhal, H. (2000), 'Emotions: structure and adaptative functions', in G. Fink (ed), *Encyclopedia of Stress*, vol. 2, San Diego, CA: Academic Press, pp. 34–47.
Maher, B.A. (1978), *Principios de psicopatología* (Principles of Psychopathology), México: McGraw-Hill.
Martínez Sánchez, F. and J. Fernández Castro (1994), 'Emoción y salud. Desarrollos en Psicología Básica y Aplicada. Presentación del monográfico' (Emotion and health developments in general and applied psychology), *Anales de Psicología*, **10**, 101–10.
Matthews, K., J. Owens, L. Kuller, K. Sutton-Tyrrell and L. Jansen-McWilliams (1998), 'Are hostility and anxiety associated with carotid atherosclerosis in healthy postmenopausal women?', *Psychosomatic Medicine*, **60**, 633–8.
Miguel-Tobal, J.J. (1990), 'La ansiedad' (Anxiety), in J. Mayor and J.L. Pinillos (eds), *Tratado de Psicología General* (Handbook of General Psychology), vol. 8: *Motivación y Emoción* (Motivation and Emotion), Madrid: Alhambra, pp. 309–44.
Miguel-Tobal. J.J. (1993), '*Ansiedad y trastornos cardiovasculares*' (Anxiety and cardiovascular disorders), paper presented at the III 'Latini Dies' Congress, Toulouse.
Miguel-Tobal, J.J. (1996*)*, *La Ansiedad* (Anxiety), Madrid: Aguilar.
Miguel-Tobal, J.J. (2000), 'Emociones y salud: principios y aplicaciones' (Emotions and health: principles and applications), in J.M. Peiró and P. Valcárcel (eds), *Psicología y Sociedad* (Psychology and Society), Valencia: Real Sociedad Económica de Amigos del Pais, pp. 79–108.
Miguel-Tobal, J.J. and A. Cano-Vindel (2002), 'Emoción y clínica: psicopatología de las emociones' (Emotion and clinical practice: psychopathology of emotions), in F. Palmero, E.G. Fernández-Abascal, F. Martínez and M. Choliz (eds), *Psicología de la motivación y la emoción* (Psychology of motivation and emotion), Madrid: McGraw-Hill, pp. 571–81.
Miguel-Tobal, J.J. and M.I Casado (1994), 'Emociones y trastornos psicofisiológicos' (Emotions and psychophysiological disorders), *Ansiedad y Estrés*, **0**, 1–13.
Miguel-Tobal, J.J. and M.I. Casado (1999), 'Ansiedad: aspectos básicos y de intervención' (Anxiety: basic and treatment principles), in E.G. Fernández-Abascal and F. Palmero (eds), *Emociones y salud* (Emotions and health), Barcelona: Ariel, pp. 91–123.
Miguel-Tobal, J.J., M.I. Casado, A. Cano-Vindel and C.D. Spielberger (1997), 'El estudio de la ira en los trastornos cardiovasculares mediante el empleo del Inventario de Expresión de Ira Estado-Rasgo – STAXI' (The study of anger in cardiovascular disorders by using the State–Trait Anger Expression Inventory – STAXI), *Ansiedad y Estrés*, **3**, 5–20.
Miguel-Tobal, J.J., M.I. Casado, A. Cano-Vindel and C.D. Spielberger (2001), *Inventario de Expresión de Ira Estado-Rasgo – STAXI-2. Manual* (State–Trait Anger Expression Inventory – STAXI-2. Manual), Madrid: TEA Ediciones.

Miguel-Tobal, J.J and H. González-Ordi (2003), 'Anxiety disorders assessment', in R. Fernández-Ballesteros (ed.), Encyclopedia of Psychological Assessment, vol. 1, London: Sage publication, pp. 40–45.
Miller, S.B. (1992), 'Affective moderators of the cardiovascular response to stress in offspring of hypertensives', *Journal of Psychosomatic Research*, **36**, 149–57.
Miller, T., T. Smith, C. Turner, M. Guijarro and A. Hallet (1996), 'A meta-analytic review of research on hostility and physical health', *Psychological Bulletin*, **119**, 322–48.
Ministerio de Sanidad y Consumo (2001), 'Mortalidad en España en 1998' (Mortality in Spain in 1998), *Boletín Epidemiológico (Centro Nacional de Epidemiología)*, **9**, 241–8.
Mittleman, M.A., M. Maclure, J.B. Sherwood, R.P. Mulry, G.H. Tofler, S.C. Jacobs, R. Friedman, H. Benson and J.E. Muller (1995), 'Triggering of acute myocardial infarction onset by episodes of anger', *Circulation*, **92**, 1720–25.
Niaura, R., C. Stoney and P. Herbert (1992), 'Lipids in psychological research: the last decade', *Biological Psychology*, **34**, 1–43.
Pagotto, U., F. Fallo and G. Fava (1992), 'Anxiety and sensitivity in essential hypertension', *Stress Medicine*, **8**, 113–15.
Plomin, R., H. Chipuer and J. Loehlin (1990), 'Behavioral genetics and personality', in L. Pervin (ed.), *Handbook of Personality: Theory and Research*, New York: Guilford Press, pp. 225–43.
Reddy, K.S., and S. Yusuf (1998), 'Emerging epidemic of cardiovascular disease in developing countries', *Circulation*, **97**, 596–601.
Rosen, R.C., E. Brondolo and J.B. Kostis (1993), 'Nonpharmacological treatment of essential hypertension: research and clinical applications', in R.J. Gatchel and E.B. Blanchard (eds), *Psychophysiological Disorders: Research and Clinical Applications*, Washington, DC: American Psychological Association, pp. 63–110.
Schalling, D. and J. Svensson (1984), 'Blood pressure and personality', *Personality and Individual Differences*, **6**, 151–60.
Selye, H. (1936), 'A syndrome produced by diverse nocuous agents', *Nature*, **138**, 32.
Selye, H. (1956), *The Stress of Life*, New York: McGraw-Hill.
Sherwood, A. and R.A. Carels (2000), 'Blood pressure', in G. Fink (ed.), *Encyclopedia of Stress*, vol. 1, San Diego, CA: Academic Press, pp. 331–8.
Shumaker, S.A. and S.M. Czajkowski (eds) (1994), *Social Support and Cardiovascular Disease*, New York: Plenum Press.
Siegler, I., B. Peterson, J. Barefoot and R. Williams, Jr (1992), 'Hostility during late adolescence predicts coronary risk factors at mid-life', *American Journal of Epidemiology*, **136**, 146–54.
Smith, T. and A. Christensen (1992), 'Hostility, health, and social contexts', in H. Friedman (ed.), *Hostility, coping and health*, Washington, DC: American Psychological Association, pp. 33–48.
Smith, T. and M. Pope (1990), 'Cynical hostility as a health risk: current status and future directions', *Journal of Social Behaviour and Personality*, **5**, 77–88.
Smith, T., J. Ruiz and B. Uchino (2000), 'Vigilance, active coping, and cardiovascular reactivity during social interaction in young men', *Health Psychology*, **19**, 382–92.
Spielberger, C.D. (1966), *Anxiety and Behaviour*, New York: Academic Press.
Spielberger, C.D. (ed.) (1972), *Anxiety: Current Trends in Theory and Research*, vol. 1, New York: Academic Press.
Spielberger, C.D. (1988), *State–Trait Anger Expression Inventory*, Odessa, FL: Psychological Assessment Resources.
Spielberger, C.D. (1991), *Manual for the State-Trait Anger Expression Inventory (STAXI)*, rev. research edn, odessa, FL: Psychological Assessment Resources.
Spielberger, C.D., S. Krasner and E. Solomon (1988), 'The experience, expression and control of anger', in M.P. Janisse (ed), *Individual Differences, Stress and Health Psychology*, New York: Springer-Verlag, pp. 89–108.
Spielberger, C.D., G. Jacobs, S.F. Russell and R.S. Crane (1983), 'Assessment of anger: the State–Trait Anger Scale', in J.N. Butcher and C.D. Spielberger (eds), *Advances in Personality Assessment*, vol. 2, Hillsdale, NJ: LEA.
Spielberger, C.D., E.H. Johnson, S.F. Russell, R.S. Crane, G. Jacobs and T.J. Worden (1985), 'The experience and expression of anger. Construction and validation of the Anger Expression Scale', in M.A. Chesney and R.H. Rosenman (eds), *Anger and Hostility in Cardiovascular and Behavioural Disorders*, New York: Hemisphere/McGraw-Hill.
Steptoe, A. (2000), 'Hypertension', in G. Fink (ed.), *Encyclopedia of Stress*, vol. 2, San Diego, CA: Academic Press, pp. 425–31.
Stoney, C. and S. West (1997), 'Lipids, personality and stress: Mechanisms and modulators', in M. Hillbrand and R. Spitz (eds), *Lipids and Human Behaviour*, Washington, DC: American Psychological Association, pp. 47–66.
Suarez, E. and R. Williams (1989), 'Situational determinants of cardiovascular and emotional reactivity in high and low hostile men', *Psychosomatic Medicine*, **51**, 404–18.

Suarez, E. and R. Williams (1990), 'The relationship between dimensions of hostility and cardiovascular reactivity as a function of task characteristics', *Psychosomatic Medicine*, **52**, 558–70.
Suinn, R.M. (2001), 'The terrible twos – anger and anxiety', *American Psychologist*, **56**, 27–36.
Terris, M. (1980), 'Epidemiology as a guide to health policy', *Annual Review of Public Health*, **1**, 323–44.
Thailer, S.A., R. Friedman, G.A. Harsfield and T.G. Pickering (1985), 'Psychological differences between high-normal and low-rennin hypertension', *Psychosomatic Medicine*, **47**, 294–7.
Uemura, K. and Z. Pisa (1988), 'Trends in cardiovascular disease mortality in industrialized countries since 1950', *World Health Statistics Quarterly*, **41**, 155–78.
Van der Ploeg, H.M., E.T. Van Buuren and P. Van Brummelen (1985), 'The role of anger in hypertension', *Psychotherapy Psychosomatic*, **43**, 186–93.
Williams, R., Jr., J. Barefoot and R. Shekelle (1985), 'The health consequences of hostility', in M. Chesney and R. Roseman (eds), *Anger and Hostility in Cardiovascular and Behavioural Disorders*, Washington, DC: Hemisphere, pp. 173–85.

31 The impact of short business travels on the individual, the family and the organization
Mina Westman

Rapid growth, globalization and economic forces have eroded national borders, facilitating the transfer of goods and services from one country to another. In this global economy, short business trips have become common.[1] Managers' presence in the setting of organizations other than their own not only serves to initiate or enhance relationships with customers and suppliers, but also increases the visibility of their organization. Organizations see the economic benefits of travel, among them establishing new contracts and retaining existing customers. However some researchers believe that, in addition to financial costs, business travel incurs potential human costs such as deterioration in well-being and performance of the traveling employees and their organization. Whereas the literature on expatriates is very rich and thorough, there is very sparse research on short business travels and on their impact on the traveler, the family and the organization. Most researchers on business travel regard such trips as a source of stress to the travelers (for example, DeFrank *et al.*, 2000; Dimberg *et al.*, 2002) and their families (Espino *et al.*, 2002; Dimberg *et al.*, 2002). Only one study demonstrated positive effects of business trips (Westman and Etzion, 2002). Business travel seems to be a dual experience, consisting of hassles and uplifts, losses and gains, all affecting travelers' well being. These contradicting effects suggest that research must also focus on variables that determine the perception of the trip as a negative or a positive experience.

The present chapter examines the effects of business trips on the traveler's personal life, family life and success in accomplishing organizational goals. It will highlight the costs and benefits of such trips to the traveler, his/her family and the organization. In addition, this chapter will identify variables that have an impact upon the experience and consequences of the trip. Finally, theoretical and practical implications will be proposed.

Travel stressors
DeFrank *et al.*, (2000, p. 59) define travel stress as the 'perceptual, emotional, behavioral and physical responses made by an individual to the various problems faced during one or more of the phases of travel'.[2] They identify specific travel stressors for three phases of the trip: pre-trip stressors, trip stressors and post-trip stressors.[3]

Pre-trip stressors include trip planning (for example, flights, hotels, appointment arrangement) and work arrangements (for example, leaving the office in good order, delegating work to subordinates, dealing with unanswered mail). According to DeFrank *et al.* (2000) some executives push themselves to tie as many loose ends as possible prior to departure, which may result in frustration and, ultimately, stress. As regards home and family issues, a high percentage (around 70 per cent) of business travelers are married, and most find extended absences from home to be difficult. Before the trip, travelers work to make the absence as painless as possible (for example, planning for unexpected emergencies, completing chores).

Trip stressors include characteristics of the travel (for example, duration and intensity, unexpected complications) and the air travel itself (anxiety during flight, turbulence, uncomfortable seating, flight delays or cancellations, lost luggage and so on) and travel logistics (for example, quality of accommodations and of communications infrastructure). When a functional communications infrastructure is not available and e-mail and voice-mail communication are not possible on a consistent basis, travel stress will increase and make effective performance more difficult. Other trip stressors are job-related factors (for example, complex job assignments, worry about the work accumulating at the home office) and cultural differences (for example culture shock). According to DeFrank *et al.* (2000), unmet expectations and the need for rapid cultural adjustment can result in stress.

Post-trip stressors may include job demands (for example, problems faced and decisions made in the traveler's absence, new projects developed and staffed without their input, overload) and family demands (for example unfinished household chores, guilt over missing important events, dealing with the needs of a spouse).

DeFrank *et al.* (2000) concluded that these stressors caused by business travel disturb the efficient functioning of the traveler and, as a result, decrease organizational success. Leider (1991) discussed the travel stressors on the family, and claimed that the temporary separation can – and does – place a strain on family relationships. He argued that all three phases of the trip affect the family. Therefore the longer the trip, the more intense is the stress at each point. He labeled the three stress points letting go, separation and re-entry.

Stress point 1: letting go
The period leading up to departure is a time of stress for the traveler and the family, as both parties anticipate the upcoming separation. The family often busies itself as a coping strategy to reduce the discomfort of their anticipated loss. To illustrate, one spouse says, 'Friends ask me, "Is she going again?" I say "yes" and they ask, "where to now?" Often I'm not clear about where she is going now, almost as if not paying too much attention will soften the blow.'

Stress point 2: separation
Chronic travel separation brings out deeply held feelings of loneliness. It is a painful trade-off of the traveling life. Being away, travelers cannot deal with their children's normal ups and downs, and children learn to live without them. As the stressful realities of travel become apparent, separation blues and loneliness often set in. Long-distance contact with office and home assures people that they are still important and needed.

Stress point 3: re-entry
Re-entry is triggered by the stresses of coming home, a point at which the implications of having been absent become clear. For some, both work and home life have continued smoothly in their absence, while others face disruptions on one or both fronts upon re-entry. Some travelers develop fantasies of what homecoming will be like: 'Return of the Hero'. In reality, they often find that each family member has been living out his or her own journey in their absence. One traveler admits, 'Things don't stop just because I'm

home. The hero's re-entry lasts about five minutes. In fact, with my teenagers, they are likely to be busy just when I'm free.' Leider (1991) concluded that, for many chronic travelers, the processes of letting go, separating and re-entering never seems to stop. The traveler feels as though he or she is in a revolving door, coming home from one trip or leaving on another one. Leider (1991) suggests that, even when families claim to understand the traveler's job needs, they often have suppressed feelings toward him or her. Such feelings leave their mark on family relationships.

Liese (2000) also relates to stressors in different phases of the trip and claims that the hardest part of business travel seems to be the phase of coming home labeled also 'travel hangover'. Short business travels are time-intensive and render employees temporarily unavailable to fulfill their personal and family roles. Thus a person may come directly to the office after a long flight, feeling tired and jetlagged, and hence somewhat irritable. The desk is piled with unopened mail that needs attention, the e-mail box overflowing with queries waiting for answers. Upon returning home after the day's work, the person must pay bills and tend to household chores, while the family, which has kept on with its life in the absence of the traveler, expresses little or no interest in the trip.

Striker et al. (1999), who investigated 498 staff of the World Bank, found that more than a third reported high to very high travel stress. Furthermore they found that social, job and emotional concerns such as impact of travel on the family, workload upon return and sense of isolation contributed to most of this stress.

The literature reviewed thus far has focused on the various stressors that might emerge as a consequence of traveling. The following section deals with findings concerning the outcomes of such stressors.

Consequences of short business trips

Physical and psychological strains were identified as affecting travelers who take short business trips. Employees of the World Bank who travel abroad as part of their job were the subjects of several such studies.

Striker et al. (1999) found that the rate of medical insurance claims made by World Bank travelers was 80 per cent higher for men and 18 per cent higher for women travelers than it was for their non-traveling counterparts. Dimberg et al. (2002), investigating the impact of business trips on employees of the World Bank, found that the demands of business trips result in a high level of stress for many travelers, and tend to correlate with seeking psychological treatment. Furthermore they found that psychological disorders increased linearly with the number of missions traveled. For men the ratio tripled with two or more missions. For women the same pattern was found but the increase was less pronounced. The increase in stress-related psychological disorders was similar in men and women who traveled four or more missions a year and were almost three times those of non-travelers. Among disorders found were anxiety, acute reaction to stress and adjustment disorders. These figures relate to objective data, claims filed for visits with a mental health provider (psychologist or psychiatrist).

While some researchers focused on either physical or psychological strains, Rogers (1998) investigated both kinds of strains in a study of 140 traveling employees. The researcher found that 76 per cent of the travelers had travel-related physical health problems, 92 per cent suffered from travel-related psychological health problems (travel worries) and 73 per cent described a negative impact on their family life. Problem areas in work and cultural environment were identified by 96 per cent of the respondents. Rogers' conclusion was that international business travelers are at risk for health, family and work problems.

Leider (1991) exemplifies problems with traveling life illustrated by a competent management consultant who flew 90 000 miles in one recent year: 'You start losing touch with things,' she says. She complains about being chronically tired and feels overwhelmed by the increasing number of demands placed on her. The quality of her life outside of work has suffered. Many once-important friendships have vanished. The things she used to like to do around the house no longer get done. She feels she has lost control and needs to take charge. Earlier in her career, she says, there was some magic in telling someone, 'I've been asked to speak in San Francisco next month.' She adds, 'I feel as though I'm always going somewhere, never being anywhere.'

The impact of marital status
Family stress affects the traveler differently at various stages of life. Some researchers claim that business trips are more difficult for single people, as they have no spouse to help them care for their domestic responsibilities and personal obligations while they are away (Fisher, 1998), whereas a family might also serve as a support mechanism for the traveler, helping to take care of affairs in his/her absence. This can reduce the stress level, especially once returning from the trip. However, for most people, having a family, especially with young children, makes the traveling experience a more stressful one. Fisher (1998) found that business trips are most difficult for travelers with young families. This difficulty can stem from the traveler's stress on missing special family events (such as birthdays or a child's sports events), the traveler's concern for the well-being of the spouse and the children, or from fear of disappointing the children and of complaints from the spouse.

According to DeFrank *et al.* (2000), family stressors are most prominent before and after the trip. At the pre-trip phase, these stressors can result from inability to spend time with the family because of heavy workload, and at the post-trip phase they can result from conflicting needs of the tired and overloaded traveler and the family's demands. Dennis (1997) reports that about 82 per cent of surveyed business travelers had missed family events while away on business. As much as travelers try to maintain frequent communication with the family, even to the point of daily phone calls and help with the children's homework via fax, it hardly ever seems to be enough and to compensate for the physical distance from home. Thus balancing work and family life has become a very serious issue for many business travelers.

The impact of traveling on the family
Research on expatriates indicates that the satisfaction of the employee's family is positively related to the expatriate's success on the job. However there is little empirical research on the work–family interface for business travelers. Employees who travel frequently have continually to adjust to and switch between resident and traveling roles. Furthermore their families may evolve two separate routines – one for when the employee is present, and one for when the employee is absent. Thus traveling affects not only the traveler but also the spouse and children.

Liese's (2000) findings demonstrate that the business traveler's experience of increased psychological disorders is mirrored in the family. The two sources of psychological strain experienced by the family are the difficulties caused by frequent absences of the spouse and a crossover of the traveler's stress and strain to his/her spouse. Crossover is defined as stress experienced in the workplace leading to stress being experienced by the spouse at home (Westman, 2001). Accordingly the stress and strain of the traveler cross over to the spouse either via empathy or via a conflictual interaction process (Westman and Vinokur, 1998).

Rogers (1998) demonstrated the impact of traveling on the family. In a study of 140 traveling employees she found that 73 per cent of them said that their business trips had a negative impact on their family life. Dimberg *et al.* (2002) found that the travelers' spouses (males and females) filed claims for medical treatment at a rate about 16 per cent higher than spouses of non-travelers. For psychological disorders, the rate of insurance claims was about twice as high for the spouses of travelers as compared with spouses of non-travelers. Furthermore, for stress-related psychological diagnosis, the rates were three times higher in both male and female spouses of travelers than in spouses of non-travelers. In general their study demonstrated that the physical and psychological impact on the traveler's family is substantial. This is especially true for situations in which the traveling is frequent, as this prevents easy adaptation and setting in to new routines.

Similarly Espino *et al.* (2002) investigated the negative effect of short business trips on the whole family among spouses of travelers from the World Bank group. Their findings indicate that frequent travels increase the strain on the family and, as a by-product, contribute significantly to the stress of the travelers. This is a kind of loss spiral, with the family suffering from the long absences and exhibiting strain, which acts as a stressor for the traveler. This finding may also be a product of crossover of stress and strain. In the context of business travel this can happen as the stress of the traveler crosses over to the spouse and affects his/her well-being, resulting in deteriorated physical and emotional health and effectiveness.

As business travel often increases work–family conflict, this might lead to marital distress. Work–family conflict is affected by the structural characteristics of the two roles, including the person's marital status, the presence, number and ages of children, social support received from the spouse, the spouse's employment status and the social support given by supervisors and co-workers. Work-related travel renders the traveler temporarily unavailable to fulfill his/her family-related roles (Roehling and Bultman, 2002). This can increase work–family conflict, spillover, crossover and marital distress.

The reviewed literature suggests that business trips have negative effects on the traveler and the family. However, if it affects the traveler and his/her family, it is very likely that it also affects the workplace through processes of spillover and crossover.

The positive impact of short business trips
The previous sections reviewed the literature on travel stress and its maladaptive outcomes. However, in the work and family contexts, experiences that are only negative or positive are very rare and most situations include a combination of positive and negative ingredients. Therefore, next, I will examine the positive outcomes of short business trips. As all the reviewed research of business travels focuses on stress and strain, this

examination will begin with theories and research pertaining to positive effects in general, such as positive psychology, conservation of resources (COR) theory and subjective well-being.

DeFrank *et al.* (2000), who performed a thorough review of all the stressors and strains that short business travel entails, devote only a few sentences to the possible positive outcomes of such travels: 'For many, travel can be very educational, providing exposure to new places and cultures, and even giving insight into new business practices and product ideas. It can lead to individual growth, broadening one's awareness of domestic and global issues and enhancing one's sensitivity to the concerns of other populations' (p. 59). The proportion of negative versus positive effects in their review is typical of stress research, which focuses mainly on negative outcomes. The positive impact of short business trips, such as exposure to new places and cultures, insight into new business practices and product ideas, individual growth, and enhancing visibility of organization in general, has rarely been studied. However, in recent years, the issue of positive psychology, including positive affects, has been extensively studied, demonstrating very promising findings. Positive psychology is the scientific study of human strength and optimal functioning. An essential question is, 'Under what conditions may work foster human strength and optimal functioning?' and it is the intent of this chapter to address this question, using a salutogenic paradigm proposing to explain well-being and benefits resulting from short business trips. Business trips are likely to evoke negative feelings because of overload and other demands but also present opportunities to experience positive emotions because of a sense of accomplishment and a kind of time off.

Business travel research will be addressed here as a special case of respite research and, therefore, we develop ideas concerning business travel based on principles of respite research. Vacation and respite research have dealt with the impact of respite on psychological outcomes (for example, burnout, satisfaction) and behavioral outcomes (for example, absenteeism, performance). According to Westman and Eden (1997), 'a respite from work may be a day off, a weekend, a vacation, or some other form of absence from the work setting when the everyday regular pressures of the job are absent' (p. 516). Accordingly business travel could be considered a special case of respite, as the traveler is away from the regular work setting and experiences a kind of detachment from it. Respite studies have demonstrated affective consequences of respite: job and life satisfaction (Lounsbury and Hoopes, 1986), decreased stress and burnout (Etzion, 2003; Etzion *et al.*, 1998; Westman and Eden, 1997; Westman and Etzion, 2002).

Westman and Etzion (2002) were the first to focus on business travels from the angle of respite. They investigated the impact of overseas business trips on job stress and burnout among 57 employees of Israeli high-tech firms whose jobs include overseas travel. Participants completed questionnaires on three occasions, ten days prior to going abroad (pre-trip), once during their stay abroad (trip) and one week after returning to their regular workplace (post-trip). A significant decline in stress was detected immediately after the trip. Job stress was lower after returning to the permanent worksite than it was before the trip and during it. Similarly burnout was lower after returning from the trip than it was prior to departure. Burnout was also lower upon returning from the trip than during the stay abroad, but the difference was not significant. Both the anticipation of the overseas journey and the work abroad itself may have been stressful for these employees.

Only upon returning to their routine jobs did the level of burnout decrease. Westman and Etzion concluded that the decrease in job stress and burnout might be evidence of a delayed respite. Though these travelers experienced a heavy workload and ambiguity during the trip, they also enjoyed the physical detachment from their office and their families. Furthermore they had a chance to experience new things and to feel personal accomplishment. This is in accord with Leider's (1991) observation that immediately after 'letting go', the travelers may find their morale elevated because of the change of scenery and their high expectations of the trip.

Psychological detachment from work
The benefit of detachment as an aspect of respite was explored by Etzion *et al.* (1998), who studied civilian engineers serving brief stints of active reserve military service in the Israel Defense Forces. They showed that even a respite that is not a time of leisure has the same impact as vacation. Defining detachment from work as the individual's sense of being away from the work situation, they found that, the greater the detachment during respite, the greater the reduction in burnout. The same mechanism may apply to business travelers. Though they are in constant contact with the home office, the resource gain during business trips may result from the temporary respite from worksite, as the travel allows for a sense of detachment from the workplace. In terms of conservation of resources theory (COR), such detachment prevents the loss of resources resulting from the chronic job demands.

Embedding business travel research in the conservation of resources theory
One way to enrich business travel research is by embedding it in Hobfoll's (1989) COR theory. The main tenet of COR theory is that stress occurs when individuals are either threatened with resource loss, actually lose resources or fail to gain resources following resource investment. Resources include objects, personal characteristics, conditions and energies. Resource gain can prevent, offset or forestall resource loss. Accordingly a gain cycle generates its own positive energy because resource accretion means that more resources can be invested in obtaining further gains, and resource surpluses promote well-being. Westman and Eden (1997) were the first to embed respite research within the COR theory. Following this conceptualization, viewing business trips as a special case of respite, such trips could be considered one of the mechanisms that might offset the cycle of loss and start a cycle of gain and enable travelers to replenish their resources.

Despite the dominant role of resource loss, resource gain may help in buffering the ameliorating effect of resource loss. In order to resist stress, according to COR theory, business trips can interrupt loss spirals and create gain spirals. By leaving the regular working atmosphere and distancing oneself from the daily demands (of work and home), the traveler might not only stop the loss of resources, resulting from job pressure and family demands, but also gain new resources (new friends, increased sense of self-efficacy, new cultural experiences, rest, pleasant experiences and so on). Hence one beneficial outcome of business trips may be a balance of resources that is more positive. As Hobfoll and Shirom suggested (1993), a relaxation period between stress episodes allows for resource gain, and the time away from the work setting, even on a business trip, can be regarded as such a period.

Hobfoll and Lilly (1993) demonstrated that gains become important only in the context of a sequence of losses. Business travel may be a source of resource loss for the traveler, starting at the pre-trip phase with trip planning and job demands, through the trip phase with physical and psychological demands and ending at the post-trip phase which can be characterized by overload. Against these resource losses, the resources gained during the business trip have a strong positive emotional effect on the traveler. In a similar vein, Presser and Hermsen (1996) maintain that business travels may be regarded as a valued resource because of the autonomy and status they entail. During the business trip the traveler acts as a representative of the firm with minimal supervision, allowing for autonomous scheduling of work and meetings. Furthermore some travels have additional positive consequences such as enhancing job mobility and expanding one's personal horizons. The authors conclude that the effect of business travel on personal growth is extremely positive.

Subjective well-being
A related concept that can shed light on the possible potential consequences of short business travel is subjective well-being (SWB), which, according to Shmotkin (1998), refers to the overall evaluation that people make of the quality of their life. This is in accord with Hobfoll's (1989) note: 'when people develop resource surpluses, they are likely to experience positive well-being (eustress)' (p. 517). Lewinson et al. (1991) concluded that general well-being relates to situation-based variables (for example, positive change and pleasant social experiences) as well as to personal characteristics (for example, social abilities, self-esteem and belief in one's ability to cope with stressful situations) and it seems that these variables can also be applied to an examination of business travel. Many characteristics of business travel contribute to personal well-being as defined by Lewinson et al. (1991). Positive effects resulting from experience include improvement in the ability to cope with new situations, self-confidence, feelings of psychological and philosophical enrichment, a wider perspective and appreciation of life, new insights, feeling as if one is a more well-rounded person, improved ability to communicate with others, deeper and more profound thinking, feeling more relaxed, and so forth. A specific area of self-growth is a result of experiencing a new and different culture, which gives travelers a different perspective on themselves and their lives and makes them more tolerant toward other people.

According to SWB literature, well-being is advanced when individuals are able to pursue their personal goals in ways that are intrinsically valued and autonomously chosen (Diener, 1984). Accordingly respite from the physical work setting and/or the family may improve well-being through (a) improving individuals' control over their activities, a unique opportunity to follow one's own goals, and (b) through resources accumulation that facilitates goals fulfillment.

The coping process
Moos and Schaefer (1993) conceptualize the coping process using a framework that emphasizes both personal and situational factors as influencing the coping efforts. According to their model: (a) the process of coping with stressful situations can increase the well-being of the individual; (b) there is a dynamic feedback process between coping responses and personal resources: the better a person copes with a situation, the more

personal and social resources (self-confidence, support from others) he/she gains, and the larger the resources at one's disposal the better one can cope with future situations. In the context of business travel this can be seen as creating a spiral of resource gain: general well-being can improve the personal and work results of the business trip, and these results increase the resources with which the individual can cope on the next trip. In this sense, the more experience a person gains in business trips, the higher the chance that he/she will experience such trips as positive events that increase well-being.

Gaining resources during business travel occurs not only through passively experiencing the positive effects of the trip but also through proactive behavior. The different ways in which people cope with business travel experiences are examples of this proactive behavior, and result in minimizing the resource loss and increasing the resource gain resulting from a trip. Coping can also be seen as successful adaptation to the new situation, adaptation that generates new resources, which replenish lost resources, and stops the loss spiral and starts a gain spiral.

Change of attitude can transform what used to be a negative, stressful experience into an enjoyable experience that increases the person's well-being. Folkman and Moskowitz (2000) describe the mechanisms that allow for positive coping with stressful experiences to occur. These mechanisms are positive reappraisal (through which the meaning of the situation is changed in a way that allows the person to experience positive emotions and psychological well-being), problem-focused coping (possible even in situations with very little personal control) and creation of positive events (infusion of ordinary events with positive meaning or finding humor in otherwise stressful situations). Use of these mechanisms can explain how people can not only survive the stress of business trips but even change it into an experience that increases their personal resource balance and their well-being.

Positive and negative aspects of business trips: a conceptual model
Based on positive psychology, respite and business travel literature, and on 28 interviews conducted in Israel, Sweden and the USA (Westman and Shraga, 2003), the following meta-model is proposed for outlining the relationships between the various facets of the business travel process. The proposed model integrates business trip research into a COR theory and anchors it in respite research. Important elements in the proposed model are gains and losses at each phase of the trip. A basic assumption of the model is that business trips are part of a job and not the job itself. Another assumption is that business trips are job events that occur over time, therefore suggesting that each business trip is an unfolding experience consisting of four phases[3]: pre-trip, journey (for example flight), stay and post-trip. This means relating to these trips as events where each phase has its gains and losses. Furthermore business trips are viewed as a cycle where experiences from previous trips have an impact upon the experiences and outcomes of the following trips. The model can guide research to determine how experiences and processes in the work and family domain are linked and how the business trips' effects are likely to vary for workers characterized by different personality attributes and by different family status and level of organizational support.

Figure 31.1 distinguishes between nine facets and constructs: job demands, family demands, business trips' gains and losses, coping, time, personal characteristics, family

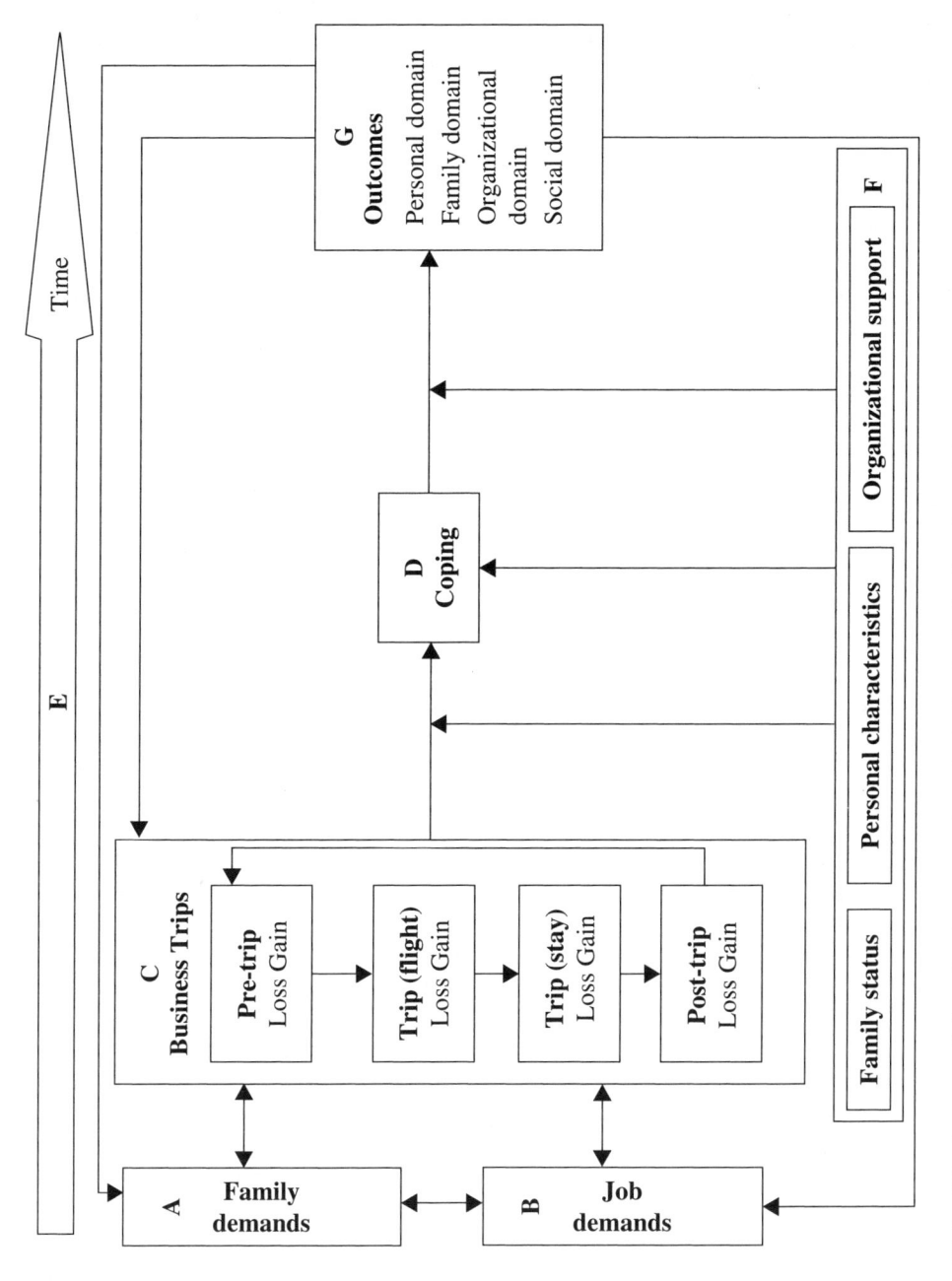

Figure 31.1 The impact of short business travel on the individual, the family and the organization

status, organizational support and outcomes. The model delineates a bidirectional relationship between Box A and Box B, indicating that job demands and family demands are interrelated. Furthermore job and family demands may cause losses and gains at different phases of the trip (arrow from A and B to C) whereas the gains and losses of the trip affect job and family demands (arrows from C to A and B). Each phase of the trip (Box C) has unique but also similar negative and positive events, losses and gains. To illustrate, in the pre-trip phase there is overload, excitement and expectation to gain; in the second phase good or bad flight conditions; in the third phase while being away there is overload, loneliness and a feeling of being a VIP; and in the fourth phase overload, success or failure. Gains and losses in various phases of the trip affect the next pre-trip phase. The model also indicates the importance of time (Box E), as each phase of trip affects the others and each event unfolds and affects other trips and other facets at different times. The losses and gains spirals affect the coping process (Box D) which in turn affects (arrow from D to G), the psychological, physical and behavioral consequences for the individual and the family, and the performance consequences for the organization. Box F includes personal characteristics (age, gender, previous experience, self-esteem), family status (married, children, spouse's job status) and organizational support, which affect the coping process and moderate the relationship between coping and outcomes. The outcomes facet (G) affects facets A, B and C via feedback loops (arrows from G to A, B and C). Some of the linkages in the model are well supported empirically (arrows from A and B to C), whereas others require further support, and several of the variables have not yet been investigated in business trips research. Thus this is a dynamic model consisting of feedback loops between constructs and across time.

Theoretical implications
Respite research and short business travel research both address the contrast between individuals' well-being on their regular job and off it. Thus these two lines of research could be mutually enriching. Following Eden (2001), it is suggested that studying business travelers and contrasting their stresses and strains to those of similar persons in the organization who are not traveling as part of their job (or to themselves before they started traveling as part of their job) could shed light on some of the same issues that respite research evolved to explore. However the main difference between short business trips and other respites is that people on respite from their job (for example vacation) can be completely disengaged from their jobs, whereas business travelers can only be detached from the physical job environment. They may experience a change in venue but not in overload and responsibility. We could broaden the scope of respite research by comparing patterns of business travel to learn how different degrees of disengagement (for example frequent to no communication with home office, having a spouse join the trip, having a vacation after completing the overseas job) relate to indices of stress and strain. This would be a natural extension that would shed light on many of the same issues dealt with by respite research.

Moreover business travel has a dual effect: while some individuals bloom and find travel exhilarating, others may be almost incapacitated by the same trip. Learning what makes business trips a positive experience might help us counsel business travelers on how to benefit more from their time away from the regular job. However there are still many moderators to be studied before we know enough to predict who will benefit from what kind of respite. There has been comparatively little research on the effect of employees' frequent absences on their work and family lives. Such research on frequent travelers is timely, given the recent impetus of companies to globalize.

Practical implications

DeFrank *et al.* (2000) indicate that problems caused by business travel can severely disrupt an executive's ability to perform effectively for the organization while being away, and can even influence performance negatively after return to the office. These difficulties have major implications for the success of the organization and for the physical and emotional health of employees and their families. Therefore it is important for the organization to take care of the traveler's well-being.

Korn (1999) recommends two approaches to dealing with travel stress – attempting to reduce stressors before they occur and counteracting their effects once they have occurred – recommendations which are consistent with Quick *et al.*'s (1997) primary and secondary prevention model maintaining that 'Preventive stress management helps one convert stress from a threat into opportunity for health and achievement' (p. 304). They describe three phases of prevention: primary, secondary and tertiary. Primary prevention attempts to modify the stressors to which people are subject in the work environment. This can include environmental interventions to remove stressors either in the workplace or elsewhere. Secondary prevention tries to change the way in which individuals and organizations respond to work demands. This involves reducing the severity of the symptoms before they lead to more serious problems. The impact of travel, like that of other job-related events, varies considerably from one individual to the other. Therefore one of the tools for preventing stress and strain of potential travelers should be adequate recruitment and selection of employees for positions that require extensive foreign travel. The candidates for positions that require frequent business trips should have a large reservoir of personal and social resources (emotional stability, open-mindedness, tolerance to ambiguity, relationship skills and so on), and the selection process should be constructed to identify these attributes alongside professional capabilities.

Furthermore, in order to minimize the problems that can occur as a result of adjustment to the host culture, it is recommended that knowledge and understanding of the other culture be enhanced. The organization can also improve the traveler's ability to cope by providing cultural knowledge and practical support to both the travelers and their families. An additional option is help the traveler meet people who have already been to the countries they travel to and discussing their experiences and ways of coping with the foreign culture. While he or she is on the trip, the organization can make sure that the traveler's needs are met.

Other ways of minimizing traveling stress concern the trip itself. As much as possible night flights should be avoided and traveling should be made as easy and as comfortable as possible. Trips should not be planned too closely to each other, and the number of weekends away should be minimized. Notification of any travel should be given as far in advance as possible.

According to Striker *et al.* (1999), the organization should provide more support for maintaining balance between work and home demands. Thus legitimized time off might also help relieve stress by giving travelers more of a sense of control, providing an option of a day off, whether it is actually taken by the traveler or not. Without the official support of the organization, travelers who try to resolve the work–family conflict by themselves (for example by taking a day off upon returning from a business trip) may be perceived as less committed and may feel a conflict between their needs and the needs of their family and the expectations of their managers. Allowing the travelers to take their spouses with them once every few trips can also be beneficial for the traveler and the family. Another way of dealing with travel stress is by maximizing the positive effects of the trip. For example, cultural preparation can change the experience of the trip from a confusing one to one of pleasure and excitement.

Reducing stressors before they occur, counteracting the effects of stressors after they occur and maximizing the effect of travels can be facilitated by the traveler, his/her family and the organization. A major application will be in offering data which will assist organizational policy makers in formulating strategies which will enable employees and their families to contribute to the organizations' globalization needs while still having successful and fulfilling family lives. Executives must recognize the work–family concerns of their 'frequent travelers'. They have an obligation to consider the inherent stresses associated with frequent and sometimes lengthy separations of employees and their families. The extent to which an organization transforms procedures in recognizing the strain that business travel places on their employees will affect the success or failure of their international operations.

Notes

1. This chapter relates only to short business trip–travels, and not to expatriation.
2. A detailed description of these stressors can be found in DeFrank *et al.* (2000).
3. Several researchers refer to three phases. However, I find it important to differentiate between the journey itself (phase 2) and the stay abroad (phase 3).

References

DeFrank R.S., R. Konopaske and J.M. Ivancevich (2000), 'Executive travel stress: perils of the road warrior', *Academy of Management Executive*, **14**(2), 58–71.
Dennis, A. (1997), 'The life of a road warrior', *Journal of Accountancy*, **184**(4), 89–91.
Diener, E. (1984), 'Subjective well-being', *Psychological Bulletin*, **95**, 542–75.
Dimberg, L.A, J. Srtiker, C. Nordanlycke-Yoo, L. Nagy, K.A. Mundt and S.I. Sulsky (2002), 'Mental health insurance claims among spouses of frequent business travelers', *Occupational and Environmental Medicine*, **59**, 175–81.
Eden, D. (2001), 'Job stress and respite relief: overcoming high-tech tethers', in P.L. Perrewé and D.C. Ganster (eds), *Research in Occupational Stress and Well-being: Exploring Theoretical Mechanisms and Perspectives*, vol. 1, New York: JAI, pp. 143–94.
Espino, C.M., S.M. Sundstorm, H.L. Frick, M. Jacobs and M. Peters (2002), 'International business travel: impact on families and travelers', *Occupational and Environmental Medicine*, **59**, 309–22.
Etzion, D. (2003), 'Annual vacation: duration of relief from job stressors and burnout', *Stress Anxiety and Coping*, **16**, 213–26.
Etzion, D., D. Eden and Y. Lapidot (1998), 'Relief from job stressors and burnout. Reserve service as a respite', *Journal of Applied Psychology*, **83**, 577–85.
Fisher, C. (1998), 'Business on the road', *American Demographics*, **20**, 44–9.
Folkman, S. and J.T. Moskowitz (2000), 'Stress, positive emotion and coping', *Current Directions in Psychological Science*, **9**, 115–18.
Hobfoll, S.E. (1989), 'Conservation of resources: a new attempt at conceptualizing stress', *American Psychologist*, **44**, 513–24.

Hobfoll, S.E. (2002), 'Social and psychological resources and adaptation', *Review of General Psychology*, **6**, 307–24.
Hobfoll, S.E. and R.S. Lilly (1993), 'Resource conservation as a strategy for community psychology', *Journal of Community Psychology*, **21**, 128–48.
Hobfoll, S.E. and A. Shirom (1993), 'Stress and burnout in the workplace: conservation of resources', in T. Golombiewski (ed.), *Handbook of Organizational Behavior*, New York: Marcel Dekker.
Korn, I. (1999), 'Stress test', *Successful Meetings*, **48**, 42–4.
Leider, R.J. (1991), 'Till travel do us part (stress caused by family separation resulting from business travel)', *Training and Development*, **45**, 46–51.
Lewinson, P.M., J.E. Redner and J.R. Seeley (1991), 'The relationship between life satisfaction and psychosocial variables: new perspectives', in F. Strack, M. Argyle and N. Schwarz (eds), *Subjective Well Being: an Interdisciplinary Perspective*, Oxford: Pergamon, pp. 141–69.
Liese, B. (2000), 'International business travel and stress: common ground for the individual and the organization', paper presented at the International Travel health Symposium on Stress, the Business Traveler and Corporate Health, The World Bank, Washington, DC, April.
Lounsbury, J.W. and L.L. Hoopes (1986), 'A vacation from work: changes in work and nonwork outcomes', *Journal of Applied Psychology*, **71**, 392–401.
Moos, R.H. and J.A. Schaefer (1993), 'Coping resources and processes: current concepts and measures', in L. Goldberger and S. Breznitz (eds), *Handbook of Stress: Theoretical and Clinical Aspects*, New York: Free Press, pp. 234–57.
Presser, H. and J. Hermsen, (1996), 'Gender differences in the determinants of work-related overnight travel among employed Americans', *Work and Occupation*, **23**, 87–115.
Quick, J.C., J.P. Quick, D.L. Nelson and J.J. Hurrel (1997), *Preventive Stress Management in Organizations*, Washington, DC: American Psychological Association.
Roehling, P.V. and M. Bultman (2002), 'Does absence make the heart grow fonder? Work-related travel and marital satisfaction', *Sex Rolls*, **46**, 279–93.
Rogers, H.L. (1998), 'A survey of the travel health experiences of international business travelers', thesis submitted to the Faculty of Graduate Studies of Nursing, Calgary, Alberta.
Shmotkin, D. (1998), 'Declarative and differential aspects of subjective well-being and its implications for mental health in later life', in J. Lomranz (ed.), *Handbook of Aging and Mental Health: an Integrative Approach*, New York: Plenum Press, pp. 15–43.
Striker, J., R.S. Luippold, L. Nagy, B. Liese, C. Bigelow and K.A. Mundt (1999), 'Risk factors for psychological stress among international business travelers', *Occupational and Environmental Medicine*, **56**, 245–52.
Westman, M. (2001), 'Stress and strain crossover', *Human Relations*, **54**, 557–91.
Westman, M. and D. Eden (1997), 'Effects of vacation on job stress and burnout: relief and fade-out', *Journal of Applied Psychology*, **82**, 516–27.
Westman, M. and D. Etzion (2002), 'The impact of short overseas business trips on job stress and burnout', *Applied Psychology: An International Review*, **51**, 582–92.
Westman, M. and O. Shraga (2003), 'The effects of international business travels', working paper no. 5/2003, The Israel Institute of Business Research, Tel Aviv University.
Westman, M. and A.D. Vinokur, (1998), 'Unraveling the relationship of distress levels within couples: common stressors, emphatic reactions or crossover via social interaction?', *Human Relations*, **51**, 137–56.

PART V

PROFESSIONAL BURNOUT

32 Burnout and emotions: an underresearched issue in search of a theory
Dirk Enzmann

Since the early 1970s, burnout research has developed from a science derogatively classified as 'pop-psychology' into an important branch of stress research in occupational and organizational psychology. Whereas 25 years ago anecdotic reports on burned out cases and efforts to clarify the definition and concept of burnout prevailed, nowadays the practical and scientific relevance of burnout research is generally acknowledged. This is mainly the consequence of two developments.

For one thing, the question of how to define burnout has been settled quite easily by the establishment of the Maslach Burnout Inventory (MBI) (Maslach and Jackson, 1981a; Maslach et al., 1996) as the most widely used instrument to measure burnout, that is emotional exhaustion (feelings of fatigue and of being drained by one's work), depersonalization (a negative attitude towards and a dehumanizing treatment of clients) and reduced personal accomplishment (lack of feelings of competence and achievements in one's work with people). The MBI was basically designed to assess burnout in 'helping' professions, hence the name, MBI–Human Services Survey (MBI–HSS). To assess burnout within occupations that are not people-oriented, a general version of MBI, the MBI–General Survey (MBI–GS) (Maslach et al., 1996) has been developed. Similar to the MBI–HSS, its three components are denoted as exhaustion, cynicism and efficacy at work. Based upon the MBI and its inductive operationalization of burnout, the MBI–GS extends and generalizes the construct 'burnout'.

Secondly, the burnout phenomenon was taken up by occupational and organizational psychologists, who placed the construct of burnout into the framework of stress theory (Cherniss, 1980b; Leiter, 1991; Cox et al., 1993; Hobfoll and Shirom, 1993) and who conducted (almost exclusively with the MBI) empirical studies concerning the relationship between working conditions, burnout and its concomitants (see Lee and Ashforth, 1996; Schaufeli and Enzmann, 1998). Ever since burnout research has entered its empirical stage and situational and personal conditions of burnout were thoroughly examined, the theoretical framework of burnout research has been significantly expanded, during the 1990s especially, by analysing and emphasizing the importance of interaction between situation and person (see Maslach et al., 2001). This was accompanied by further extensions of the construct, for instance the reinterpretation of burnout as an erosion of professional engagement (Maslach and Leiter, 1997) or as comprising different levels of activation and pleasure in one's work (Schaufeli et al., 2002). A recent development is the growing interest in the relevance of emotion work and the regulation of emotions at work for the development of burnout (see Zapf, 2002).

By accentuating emotion work and regulation of emotions as central themes, the focus of attention lies again on an aspect which had already been of special interest at the very beginning of burnout research, but which had moved into the background during the development of burnout into a scientific concept. In the early stages of burnout research, the prevailing perspective was to explain burnout as being caused by emotionally demanding interactions with other people, which were phenomenologically characterized by negative attitudes and emotions towards people and towards the job. In describing her early thinking about burnout, Maslach reports, 'The implication was that working with other people, particularly in a caregiving relationship, was at the heart of the burnout phenomenon.' (Maslach, 1993, p. 23). She defined burnout as a syndrome characterized (among others) by 'feelings of being emotionally overextended and depleted of one's emotional resources' (p. 21). Accordingly the dominant dimension of the MBI was termed *emotional* exhaustion. Similarly, Pines *et al.*, authors of the popular book, 'Burnout–From Tedium to Personal Growth' (Pines *et al.*, 1981) defined burnout as a syndrome of physical, *emotional* and mental exhaustion. Meanwhile, however, the concept of burnout is expanded into a reaction that can occur in any profession and the 'emotional' component of exhaustion has been dropped, at least conceptually. The MBI–GS, the new variant of the MBI, 'defines burnout as a crisis in one's relationship with work, not necessarily as a crisis in one's relationship with people at work' (Maslach *et al.*, 1996, p. 20). It is constructed to measure a continuum from engagement to burnout: 'Engagement is an energetic state in which one is dedicated to excellent performance of work and confident of one's effectiveness. In contrast, burnout is a state of exhaustion in which one is cynical about one's occupation and doubtful of one's capacity to perform.' (ibid.).

The following will address the issue of the role of emotions in the development of burnout. In doing so, the main problem will be to determine whether the present operationalization of burnout in the MBI–HSS and MBI–GS really taps the primal aspect of the phenomenon and how to evaluate the results of previous studies (which were rather based upon a stress theory approach) against the background of the original idea of putting emotionally demanding interactions at the heart of the burnout phenomenon. Finally future directions of burnout research which could advance this early concept will be sketched.

Emotionally demanding interactions and burnout
To answer the question whether emotionally demanding interactions with clients are at the heart of the burnout phenomenon, Schaufeli and Enzmann (1998) reviewed 16 empirical studies that employed the three burnout dimensions of the MBI–HSS as criteria and measures of job and client-related stressors as predictors. Common job-related stressors such as work overload and time pressure should have minor effects on burnout compared to stressors resulting from the interaction with clients, such as emotionally demanding clients or confrontation with death and dying. However, contrary to expectations, in most studies common job-related stressors (workload, time pressure, role conflicts) correlated more strongly with burnout than client-related stressors (contact with terminally ill patients and conflicts in interactions). The authors concluded, 'Hence, it seems that, on empirical grounds, the assertion that burnout is particularly related to emotionally charged interactions with clients has to be refuted' (p. 84).

Reviewing results with respect to caseload and burnout, Koeske and Koeske (1989) did point to the necessity to distinguish between the number of client contacts (quantity) and the type of client contact (quality): because heavy caseload also implies workload and time pressure, the number of client contacts might be confounded with problems in interacting with clients. The ratio of negative to positive contacts might be a better indicator of emotionally demanding interactions.

With regard to the three dimensions of the MBI, meta-analyses showed that emotional exhaustion is best predicted by job demands; the best predictors are workload and time pressure (Lee and Ashforth, 1996; Schaufeli and Enzmann, 1998). The relationships to depersonalization are much weaker, the weakest that with personal accomplishment.

One objection to the results presented could be that nearly all studies included in the meta-analyses are based on cross-sectional studies that cannot distinguish between causes and effects. Moreover, because burnout is likely to be a long-term reaction, cross-sectional studies cannot reveal the factors responsible for the development of burnout. However, the main result that quantitative demands such as time pressure play a more important role than qualitative demands such as confrontation with death and dying, especially with respect to emotional exhaustion, was also found in a one-year longitudinal study (Enzmann, 1995).

Although validation studies showed that assessments of respondents' degree of burnout made independently by others or by component profiles of those who declare themselves to be burnt out validated only the emotional exhaustion scale of the MBI (see Cox *et al.*, 1993), at the same time results of numerous studies confirm the notion of Maslach (1993, p. 27) that 'emotional exhaustion is the closest to an orthodox stress variable'. It is noteworthy that especially *emotional* exhaustion is related to quantitative workload rather than qualitative demands that result from interacting with difficult clients or dealing with emotionally demanding situations. Apart from the conclusion that burnout is unrelated to emotional demands (which seems to be rather unlikely), there are at least two possible ways to interpret this result: the MBI does not measure burnout but something else, and emotional demands have not been properly investigated or operationalized, therefore individual processing of demands (coping and emotion regulation processes) deserve closer attention.

Burnout and the MBI: problems of operationalization
It is important to recognize that the MBI was not developed deductively by applying a validated theory of burnout. Instead, the initial research was very exploratory, the items of the MBI being drawn from interviews, other questionnaire surveys and observations. Exploratory factor analyses of, initially, 47 items resulted in the three factors currently known as emotional exhaustion (EE), depersonalization (DP) and personal accomplishment (PA), plus a fourth factor, involvement, that was dropped later (Maslach and Jackson, 1981b). It is quite conceivable that another pool of items could have resulted in different dimensions of burnout, for example a much stronger factor of involvement or other items to assess emotional exhaustion. It is likely that this would have led to a different definition of burnout and it could have changed the course of research on burnout considerably. Because the MBI has been developed inductively, a replication of the factorial structure of the current MBI in different populations, or the correlation of its subscales with a range of possible causes, concomitants or consequences, is not necessarily an appropriate means to establish the validity of the construct as such and to develop a conclusive theory of burnout.

With respect to the factorial structure of the MBI, a close examination of the loadings shows that especially those items that tap interactions with clients have the lowest loadings on the subscale EE or tend to have common error variances with items of the subscale DP (Enzmann, 1995). This is a first indication that EE might not assess emotional exhaustion as it has been paraphrased and interpreted in the early publications (that is *emotional exhaustion as a reaction to emotionally demanding interactions* with other people).

The close relationship of emotional exhaustion (EE) as measured by the MBI with time pressure indicates that EE is rather a general measure of fatigue or general exhaustion. The frequency of situations characterized by time pressure (one of the strongest predictors of EE) is essentially a quantitative demand, for which fatigue is a characteristic reaction (Hacker and Richter, 1984). In contrast, emotionally demanding interactions, the assumed primal cause of burnout, are essentially a qualitative demand. In general, time pressure should correlate rather negatively with burnout because it forces professionals to reduce intense emotional involvement with their clients. This is in line with the results of a longitudinal study that showed that the effect of empathic distress on personal accomplishment (PA) is buffered by time pressure (Enzmann, 1995). The negative effect of empathic distress on burnout in terms of PA was less when time pressure was high. Thus EE as measured by the MBI seems to be a symptom of prolonged fatigue rather than burnout. This view is supported by a validity study that compared the psychometric properties of six fatigue questionnaires including EE in a sample of working people (De Vries et al., 2003). A one-factor solution of all six measures was found with a high loading of EE (0.82). A secondary analysis with two factors employed by the author found EE to have the highest loading on the strongest factor (0.96), together with 'need for recovery' and measures of physical fatigue.

The items of the subscale depersonalization (DP) have special problems as well. Conceptually DP is the most interesting subscale because it links stressful and 'bad' situations of the job to unprofessional and dehumanizing behaviour of 'good people' towards their clients or people in need. However it is difficult to assess emotional hardening and cynical attitudes if the respondents have developed a high degree of depersonalization in its original sense. For example, a person who endorses the statement, 'I worry that this job is hardening me emotionally', cannot be completely depersonalized. In contrast, an affirmative answer can be interpreted as an indication that the respondent is *not* (yet) dehumanized or emotionally hardened. The fact, that DP correlates positively with EE is no counter argument, because it is likely that tired professionals happen to treat their clients in a callous manner. High scores on the subscale DP might indicate that the respondent is able to recognize this problem. Additionally this subscale suffers most from social desirable responding ($r = -0.31, p < 0.001, 95\%$ CI $= -0.38$ to -0.24) (Enzmann, 1995, p. 143).

To evaluate possible problems of the subscale personal accomplishment (PA) is more difficult. On the one hand, this scale shows the weakest correlations with the other subscales and with measures of stress that are typically included in research on stress and burnout. On the other hand, there are some results that fit the proposition that PA is a genuine burnout dimension. A study on emotion work and its effects on burnout (Zapf et al., 2001) showed that although weakly related or unrelated to common job stressors (uncertainty, organizational problems, time pressure), PA correlated positively with the necessity to display positive emotions in interacting with clients and with the requirement to pay attention to their feelings. In terms of explained variance, emotion work had the strongest effect on PA after controlling for gender, age, support and other job characteristics. Similarly a longitudinal study on the relationship between empathy and burnout (Enzmann, 1995) showed that PA was the only burnout dimension that was affected by interaction effects of empathy (perspective taking and empathic distress) with job stress (time pressure and confrontation with death and dying). Thus, with respect to emotional demands at work and emotional responding (empathy), the results fit better the notion of PA as a dimension of burnout that is affected by interpersonal emotions than EE and DP. Earlier research did not show this, probably because the studies used rather indirect indicators of emotional demands or emotional responding.

Alternatives of conceptualizing burnout and *emotional* exhaustion
Despite numerous attempts to develop theoretical models that explain burnout, only a few have tried to redefine the construct as such and the way to measure it. With the exception of the MBI–GB and the notion that burnout is a bipolar construct ranging from engagement to burnout (see above), none of the most prominent models (see Schaufeli and Enzmann, 1998), for example the 'disturbed action pattern' model (Burisch, 1989), the 'conservation of resources' model (Hobfoll and Shirom, 1993), the 'existential' model of burnout (Pines, 1993), the 'social competence' model (Harrison, 1983), the model of emotional overload (Maslach, 1982), Leiter's process model of burnout (Leiter, 1993), the 'dual level social exchange model' (Schaufeli *et al.*, 1996), the 'reality shock' model (Cherniss, 1980a) or the 'environmental' model of burnout (Golembiewski and Munzenrider, 1988), challenges the way to *measure* burnout.

The most pronounced criticism of the prevailing definition of burnout has been elaborated by Cherniss (1986). Criticizing the metaphor of burnout as rooted in a mechanistic stress terminology, Cherniss proposes to conceptualize burnout as a 'symptom of the loss of social commitment' (p. 219), thereby rejecting the idea that burnout is a response to 'overcommitment'. Instead, burnout is thought to be caused by a weakening of the moral–religious paradigm and could be prevented if the work of professionals were based on a 'belief in a transcendent body of ideas and a strong identification with a group, institution, or method that is based on those ideas' (p. 219). With respect to the phenomenology of burnout, Cherniss expects the truly committed to feel very energetic, whereas professionals feel drained and exhausted if social commitment is lacking.

Another reconceptualization has been proposed recently by Schaufeli and his colleagues, who characterize burnout as low levels of activation and pleasure and the opposite of burnout as engagement, 'as a persistent, positive affective–motivational state of fulfillment in employees that is characterized by vigor, dedication, and absorption' (Maslach *et al.*, 2001, p. 417). To measure engagement, a questionnaire has been developed that showed a high correlation between engagement and the efficacy dimension of the MBI–GS (see Schaufeli *et al.*, 2002). Whereas burnout as measured by the MBI correlates more strongly with job demands, engagement is more strongly related to job resources. However the idea that emotions at work and the regulation of emotions might be the most significant precursor of burnout has been abandoned.

Despite the prevailing claim since the beginning of burnout research that emotional exhaustion is a central characteristic of burnout, there is still no clear conceptual definition of *emotional* exhaustion. The line of argument has always been rather fuzzy: because the professionals become exhausted owing to excessive *emotional* demands, the exhaustion is *emotional*; alternatively, because the emotions towards clients or the job change and become more negative, or because the professionals harden emotionally, the engagement is reduced; because the result of less engagement is accompanied by more negative *emotions* or more *callous* interactions, it is termed *emotional* exhaustion.

But is it really possible at all to become emotionally exhausted in analogy to physical exhaustion where increased efforts can compensate a depletion of energy? An answer from a functionalist perspective on emotions is 'One cannot really elicit emotion at will; one can only work oneself into it, to some extent. Also, one cannot really abolish emotion at will; one can only work oneself out of it, to some extent, for some duration' (Frijda, 1986, p. 468). That means that emotional exhaustion is rather a surface phenomenon; emotional exhaustion, in the sense that it becomes more difficult to feel, is not possible because it is impossible to feel at will. However it is possible to promote conditions at will that generate or facilitate the experience and expression of certain emotions, and this capacity may become exhausted.

What can cause the exhaustion of the capacity to regulate one's emotions indirectly? And what is the effect of a state of low energy or physical fatigue that is often encountered among people who were subjected to prolonged stress and excessive demands? On the one hand, physical exhaustion and a state of low energy is likely to contribute to the diminished capacity to regulate one's emotions at will by creating situations or cognitions that facilitate the experience or expression of emotions that in turn help to regulate interpersonal behaviour. On the other hand, physical exhaustion does not necessarily imply a reduction of emotional responsiveness. Some emotional responses are 'a function of exhaustion, prolonged stress, or illness. We refer here to the complex of enhanced irritability, anxiousness, and sentimentality, of enhanced startle responses and diminished concentration and pain tolerance' (ibid., p. 406). Thus a state of low energy should not be equated with emotional exhaustion in the sense of reduced emotional responsiveness.

There are several ways to regulate one's emotion experiences and emotional expressions indirectly. One can change (or leave) emotion-inducing situations, one can change the attention to situational aspects that are linked to certain emotional responses; one can change the meaning of such situational aspects (reappraisal); and finally one can try to modulate one's emotional responses if they occur (suppression) (Gross and John, 2003). Perhaps it is the capacity and the way to regulate one's emotional experiences and expressions indirectly that distinguishes experienced and efficient professionals that show no signs of burnout from inexperienced burned-out professionals. This might explain why training in psychosocial interventions that include (among others) engagement skills, mood assessment, training of coping strategies and expression of emotions may have pronounced effects on reducing burnout, especially with regard to depersonalization and personal accomplishment (for example, Ewers *et al.*, 2002).

Future directions of research on burnout and emotions
The emotional 'components' of exhaustion, especially the emotional consequences of demands at work, deserve more attention. If the lack of capacity to regulate one's own emotional experiences and expressions that influence interactions with other people

positively is at the heart of burnout in its original sense, one should try to find means to assess (changes in) this capacity. To explain burnout one has to explain how it happens that this capacity diminishes. This comes close to the beginning of Maslach's research on burnout: 'the research did not even begin with a focus on burnout at all. Instead, my interest was in emotion and in the general question of how people "know" what they are feeling' (Maslach, 1993, p. 21). Thus, burnout research in this sense would return to its roots and become a theory of the situations that allow and suppress the capacity to regulate one's own and others' emotions, respectively the social, attitudinal and emotional consequences of factors that inhibit professionals' emotion work. Recent research has shown that the way in which people try to regulate their emotions has important consequences for their affect, their relationships and their well-being. Gross and John (2003) showed that attempts to suppress the experience or the expression of positive or negative emotions are more costly and have more negative consequences than antecedent-focused emotion regulation that aims at emotion-eliciting situations or its meanings.

This line of research would complement recent approaches that began to investigate the relationship of emotion work and emotional well-being (see Zapf, 2002). In this line of research job requirements with respect to expressing and sensing emotions, as well as emotion work strategies (automatic emotion regulation, deep acting, surface acting, emotional deviance, sensing emotions) are investigated. Classical burnout research in the orthodox paradigm of work stress has contributed enormously to our knowledge of organizational and task-related working conditions and personality factors that contribute to exhaustion, cynicism and feelings of inefficacy, including its consequences for clients or the organization. To supplement this research with the focus on emotions, emotional demands and emotion regulation at work seems to be promising. It is doubtful, however, whether the prevailing conceptualization of burnout and the current way to measure it will suffice for this task.

References

Burisch, M. (1989), *Das Burnout-Syndrom. Theorie der inneren Erschöpfung* (The Burnout Syndrome: A Theory of Internal Exhaustion), Berlin: Springer.
Cherniss, C. (1980a), *Professional Burnout in the Social Service Organizations,* New York: Praeger.
Cherniss, C. (1980b), *Staff Burnout. Job Stress in the Human Services,* Beverly Hills, CA: Sage.
Cherniss, C. (1986), 'Different ways of thinking about burnout', in E. Seidman and J. Rappaport (eds), *Redefining Social Problems,* New York: Plenum Press, pp. 217–29
Cox, T., G. Kuk and M.P. Leiter (1993), 'Burnout, health, work stress, and organizational healthiness', in W.B. Schaufeli, C. Maslach and T. Marek (eds), *Professional Burnout: Recent Developments in Theory and Research,* Washington, DC: Taylor & Francis, pp. 177–93.
De Vries, J., H.J. Michielsen and G.L. Van Heck (2003), 'Assessment of fatigue among working people: a comparison of six questionnaires', *Occupational and Environmental Medicine,* **60**(Suppl.1), i10–i15.
Enzmann, D. (1995), *Gestresst, erschöpft oder ausgebrannt? Einflüsse von Arbeitssituation, Empathie und Coping auf den Burnoutprozess* (Stressed, exhausted, or burned out? Effects of working conditions, empathy and coping on the development of burnout), Munich: Profil.
Ewers, P., T. Bradshaw, J. McGovern and B. Ewers (2002), 'Does training in psychosocial interventions reduce burnout rates in forensic nurses?', *Journal of Advanced Nursing,* **37**, 470–76.
Frijda, N. (1986), *The Emotions,* Cambridge: Cambridge University Press.
Golembiewski, R.T. and R.F. Munzenrider (1988). *Phases of Burnout: Developments in Concepts and Applications,* New York: Praeger.
Gross, J.J. and O.P. John (2003), 'Individual differences in two emotion regulation processes: implications for affect, relationships and well-being', *Journal of Personality and Social Psychology,* **85**, 348–62.

Hacker, W. and P. Richter (1984), *Psychische Fehlbeanspruchung. Psychische Ermüdung, Monotonie, Sättigung und Stress* (Psychological excessive demands. Psychological fatigue, monotony, saturation and stress), 2nd edn, Berlin: Springer.

Harrison, W.D. (1983), 'A social competence model of burnout,' in B.A. Farber (ed.), *Stress and Burnout in the Human Service Professions*, New York: Pergamon, pp. 29–39.

Hobfoll, S.E. and A. Shirom, (1993), 'Stress and burnout in the workplace: conservation of resources', in R.T. Golembiewski (ed.), *Handbook of Organizational Behavior*, New York: M. Dekker, pp. 41–60.

Koeske, G.F. and R.D. Koeske (1989), 'Construct validity of the Maslach Burnout Inventory: a critical view and reconceptualization', *Journal of Applied Behavioral Sciences*, **25**, 131–44.

Lee, R.T. and B.E. Ashforth (1996), 'A meta-analytic examination of the correlates of the three dimensions of job burnout', *Journal of Applied Psychology*, **81**(2), 123–33.

Leiter, M.P. (1991), 'Coping patterns as predictors of burnout: the function of control and escapist coping patterns', *Journal of Organizational Behavior*, **12**(2), 123–44.

Leiter, M.P. (1993), 'Burnout as a developmental process: consideration of models', in W.B. Schaufeli, C. Maslach and T. Marek (eds), *Professional Burnout: Recent Developments in Theory and Research*, Washington, DC: Taylor & Francis, pp. 237–50.

Maslach, C. (1982), 'Burnout: a social psychological analysis', in J.W. Jones (ed.), *The Burnout Syndrome*, Park Ridge, IL: London House, pp. 30–53.

Maslach, C. (1993), 'Burnout: a multidimensional perspective,' in W.B. Schaufeli, C. Maslach and T. Marek (eds), *Professional Burnout: Recent Developments in Theory and Research*, Washington, DC: Taylor & Francis, pp. 19–113.

Maslach, C. and S.E. Jackson (1981a), *Maslach Burnout Inventory. Research Edition*, Palo Alto, CA: Consulting Psychologists Press.

Maslach, C. and S.E. Jackson (1981b), 'The measurement of experienced burnout', *Journal of Occupational Behaviour*, **2**, 99–113.

Maslach, C. and M.P. Leiter (1997), *The Truth About Burnout: How Organizations Cause Personal Stress and What to Do About It*, San Francisco, CA: Jossey-Bass.

Maslach, C., S.E. Jackson and M. Leiter (1996), *Maslach Burnout Inventory. Manual*, 3rd ed, Palo Alto, CA: Consulting Psychologists Press.

Maslach, C., W.B. Schaufeli and M.P. Leiter (2001), 'Job burnout', *Annual Review of Psychology*, **52**, 397–422.

Pines, A.M. (1993), 'Burnout: an existential perspective', in W.B. Schaufeli, C. Maslach and T. Marek (eds), *Professional Burnout: Recent Developments in Theory and Research*, Washington, DC: Taylor & Francis, pp. 33–51.

Pines, A.M., E. Aronson and D. Kafry (1981), *Burnout: From Tedium to Personal Growth*, New York: Free Press.

Schaufeli, W.B. and D. Enzmann (1998), *The Burnout Companion to Study and Practice: A Critical Analysis*, London: Taylor & Francis.

Schaufeli, W.B., D. Van Dierendonck and K. Van Gorp (1996), 'Burnout and reciprocity: towards a dual-level social exchange model', *Work & Stress*, **3**, 225–37.

Schaufeli, W.B., I.M. Martinez, A.M. Pinto, M. Salanova and A.B. Bakker (2002), 'Burnout and engagement in university students – a cross-national study', *Journal of Cross-Cultural Psychology*, **33**, 464–81.

Zapf, D. (2002), 'Emotion work and psychological well-being. A review of the literature and some conceptual considerations', *Human Resource Management Review*, **12**, 237–68.

Zapf, D., C. Seifert, B. Schmutte, H. Mertini and M. Holz (2001), 'Emotion work and job stressors and their effects on burnout', *Psychology and Health*, **16**, 527–45.

33 Proactive coping, resources and burnout: implications for occupational stress
Esther R. Greenglass

In recent years considerable research has focused on occupational stress. This is to be expected, given its deleterious effects. Stress on the job has been linked to a host of psychological and physical symptoms. For example, Spector (1987) reports significant positive correlations between excessive workload and anxiety, frustration and job dissatisfaction, as well as health symptoms. Work stress may also trigger anger feelings, which can result in higher levels of anxiety. The disruptive effects of stress can be seen as well in organizational functioning and in interpersonal relationships. Stress and burnout are major factors that have been linked to the development of both physical and psychological illness (McGrath *et al.*, 1989). Burnout may be defined as a state of physical, emotional and mental exhaustion that results from long-term involvement in work situations that are emotionally demanding (Maslach and Jackson, 1986). Burnout is also related to self-reported measures of personal distress (Belcastro and Gold, 1983; Greenglass, 1991; Greenglass *et al.*, 1990; Schaufeli and Enzmann, 1998). Burnout in teachers correlates positively with depression, anxiety and somatization (Greenglass *et al.*, 1990; Bakker *et al.*, 2000).

At the same time, individuals vary in their reactions to workplace distress. Research supports the idea that personal resources can affect people's reactions to stress and burnout. Individuals who are affluent, healthy, capable and optimistic are resourceful and thus are less vulnerable to work stress. When confronting stress, perceived competence, labeled as perceived self-efficacy or optimistic self-beliefs, is crucial. Perceived self-efficacy and optimism are seen as prerequisites for coping with stresses including job loss and work overload. Perceived self-efficacy, as a personal resource, reflects the person's optimistic self-beliefs about being able to deal with critical demands by means of adaptive actions. It can also be regarded as an optimistic view of one's capacity to deal with stress. Low self-efficacy is a central factor in the etiology of burnout (Cherniss, 1990). For Leiter (1991), burnout is inconsistent with a sense of self-determination or self-efficacy; burnout diminishes the potential for subsequent effectiveness.

Research attention has focused on coping strategies and the ways in which they can alleviate stress levels and promote a higher quality of life at work. Coping strategies and behaviors at work involving mastery or problem solving are associated with more positive outcomes and decreased distress than are escape or more passive forms of coping (Leiter, 1991; Armstrong-Stassen, 1994). Research with nurses experiencing hospital 'downsizing' showed that individual skills, particularly coping ability, were related to their feelings about professional accomplishments as well as their depression and anxiety. Nurses with higher professional efficacy may be more likely to engage in control-oriented coping than those who are lower on professional efficacy (Greenglass and Burke, 2000).

Perceived self-efficacy, as a personal resource, reflects the person's optimistic self-beliefs about being able to deal with critical demands by means of adaptive actions. It can also be regarded as an optimistic view of one's capacity to deal with stress. In nurses, high self-efficacy is associated with lower emotional exhaustion, less cynicism, less depression and anxiety, greater job satisfaction and higher levels of professional efficacy (ibid.).

Coping, resources and outcomes
Discussion of factors that increase professional efficacy and decrease burnout, and the demonstration that control coping measures the extent to which the individual takes the initiative in coping efforts and self-efficacy contribute to higher feelings of professional competence, coincide with notions emphasizing positive psychology and the need to study their determinants and effects (Seligman and Csikszentmihalyi, 2000). Optimism, a sense of personal control and the ability to find meaning in one's life experiences are useful and important psychological resources long believed to be associated with the promotion of mental health (Seligman, 1998). There are several reasons for believing that positive beliefs might influence the course of illness. For example, positive beliefs may lead to higher levels of physical health by promoting better health practices. Individuals who have a positive sense of self-worth and believe in their own ability to exert control may be more likely to practice conscientious health habits. Positive emotional states are associated with good social relationships. Self-confident and optimistic individuals may have more social support and/or they may be more effective in mobilizing social support when they experience high levels of stress (Taylor and Brown, 1994). Also there is reason to believe that individuals who have well-developed psychosocial resources, including a sense of personal control, high self-esteem and optimism, are more likely to cope proactively with respect to health, which may minimize the effects of stress (Aspinwall and Taylor, 1997).

Proactive coping
While, in the past, coping was seen mainly as reactive, a strategy to be used once stress had been experienced, more recently coping is being seen as something one can do *before* stress occurs. Increasingly, coping is seen as having multiple positive functions. Proactive coping is a coping strategy that is multidimensional and forward-looking. Proactive coping combines autonomous goal setting with self-regulatory goal attainment cognitions. Proactive coping integrates processes of personal quality of life management with those of self-regulatory goal attainment (Greenglass, Schwarzer, Jakubiec, Fiksenbaum and Taubert, 1999; Greenglass, Schwarzer and Taubert, 1999).

Proactive coping differs from traditional, reactive conceptions of coping (Schwarzer, 2000) in that proactive coping is more future-oriented, while reactive coping deals with stressful events that have occurred. Proactive coping is regarded as goal management, where people have a vision and see demands as opportunities. In reactive coping, people perceive difficult situations as threats or losses.

Proactive coping involves processes through which people anticipate potential stressors and act in advance to prevent them. To the extent that individuals offset, eliminate, reduce or modify impending stressful events, such proactive behavior can eliminate a great deal of stress before it occurs. The skills associated with this behavior include planning, goal setting, organization and mental simulation (Aspinwall and Taylor, 1997).

The Proactive Coping Inventory (PCI) is multidimensional and consists of six subscales that were developed to assess the various aspects of proactive coping (Greenglass, Schwarzer, Jakubiec, Fiksenbaum and Taubert, 1999; Greenglass, Schwarzer and Taubert, 1999). The subscales of the PCI assess proactive coping, strategic planning, reflective coping, preventive coping and instrumental and emotional support seeking. Greenglass (2002a) reports acceptable psychometrics for the scales, including their cross-cultural validity.

The proactive coping subscale of the PCI has been found to be highly correlated positively with scores on an internal control scale in Canadian and Polish–Canadian students (Greenglass, 2002a). An essential aspect of proactive coping is perceived control. Research reports that situational appraisals of control have been linked to performance of active problem-solving coping strategies. Employees who believe that they have little control over work domains are less likely to engage in active problem-solving coping and are more likely to employ emotion-focused strategies (Folkman, 1984). In this context, perceived control refers to the belief that one can influence the environment. Control strategies reflect a 'take charge' approach often involving making a plan of action, focusing efforts on solving the problem at hand and taking direct action. Research indicates that perceived control is associated with decreased stress levels and improved worker health. Perceived control also buffers the potentially deleterious effects of stress on mental and physical health. Additional research suggests that individuals high on self-efficacy are more likely to feel they are able to control challenging environmental demands by taking adaptive action (Bandura, 1992). If one feels confident enough to be able to control challenges or threats, successful action is more likely (Schwarzer, 1993). Individuals who hold beliefs that outcomes are within their own control are more likely to employ control coping strategies than those who see outcomes resulting by chance (Schwarzer, 1992, 1993; Folkman, 1984; Bandura, 1992).

Occupational stress and burnout
Individuals vary both in the amount of stress they experience at work and in the extent of coping they use. Burnout may also be seen as a work-related syndrome stemming from the individual's perception of a significant gap between expectations of successful professional performance and an observed, far less satisfying, reality (Friedman, 2000).

Burnout is inconsistent with a sense of self-determination or self-efficacy; it diminishes the potential for subsequent effectiveness. A great deal of research has been devoted to the understanding of factors contributing to burnout and its consequences for individuals. For example, research shows that burnout is correlated with numerous self-reported measures of personal distress (Greenglass, 1991; Schaufeli and Enzmann, 1998).

Burnout and proactive coping
Proactive coping consists of efforts to build up general resources that facilitate the achievement of challenging goals and promote personal growth. Since burnout represents a depletion of resources including self-efficacy, effective coping strategies and social support, high proactive coping should be associated with lower burnout since a proactive coper is also able to utilize resources to offset stress and burnout. In a study of burnout in German teachers, the relationship between proactive coping and burnout was examined (Schwarzer and

Taubert, 2002). It was hypothesized that proactive coping would be associated with lower levels of burnout. In this study, 316 German teachers were surveyed and job burnout was defined three-dimensionally in terms of emotional exhaustion, depersonalization and lack of personal accomplishment (Maslach et al., 1996). Emotional exhaustion was defined as the depletion of energy; those who are exhausted feel overextended, drained and unable to recover. Depersonalization was defined as the tendency to treat one's clients, students or patients as objects. Lack of personal accomplishment referred to a lack of feelings of accomplishment in one's work. To illustrate the relationship between proactive coping and burnout, the sample was subdivided into low, medium and high proactive teachers who were plotted against the three dimensions of burnout. Results showed a significant pattern of decreasing burnout with increasing levels of proactive coping. High proactive teachers reported less emotional exhaustion, less depersonalization and more personal accomplishment than low proactive teachers.

The study also included short scales to assess the three stress appraisal dimensions of challenge, threat and loss (Jerusalem and Schwarzer, 1992). It was expected that high proactive coping would be associated with higher challenge appraisals, whereas low proactive coping would be linked to higher threat and higher loss appraisals. The data confirmed this hypothesis. Proactive teachers perceived their stress as more challenging, and less threatening and loss-based, than their less proactive counterparts. To summarize, proactive teachers, in this study, experienced less job burnout, perceived more challenges and less threat and loss, and displayed more professional engagement than their reactive counterparts (Schwarzer and Taubert, 2002).

Study 1

A study is reported here in which work stress and burnout are examined in a sample of 178 respondents. Both direct and indirect relationships between proactive coping and distress are examined. The sample consisted of respondents who were employed in a variety of mainly while-collar occupations in a large Canadian city. Sixty per cent were women, approximately two-thirds were non-university-educated and 57 per cent were married and living with their spouse/partner. They filled out an anonymous self-report questionnaire consisting of various psychological measures.

In this study, burnout comprised three different dimensions: emotional exhaustion, cynicism and reduced professional efficacy (Schaufeli et al., 1996). Emotional exhaustion refers to feelings of being emotionally overextended, while cynicism reflects indifference or a distant attitude towards one's work. Professional efficacy refers to satisfaction with past and present accomplishments at work. Burnout was measured with the MBI–General Survey (Schaufeli et al., 1996) which yields measures on the three burnout components. The validity of the MBI–General Survey is reported in a series of principal component analyses in which emotional exhaustion was associated with mental and physical strain, work overload and role conflict of clients (Schaufeli et al., 1996). Proactive coping was assessed using the 14-item proactive coping subscale of the Proactive Coping Inventory (PCI) (Greenglass, Schwarzer and Taubert, 1999).

The relationship between proactive coping and burnout was examined using structural equation modeling. The theoretical model put forth hypothesized that proactive coping would lead to higher levels of professional efficacy and to lower levels of emotional

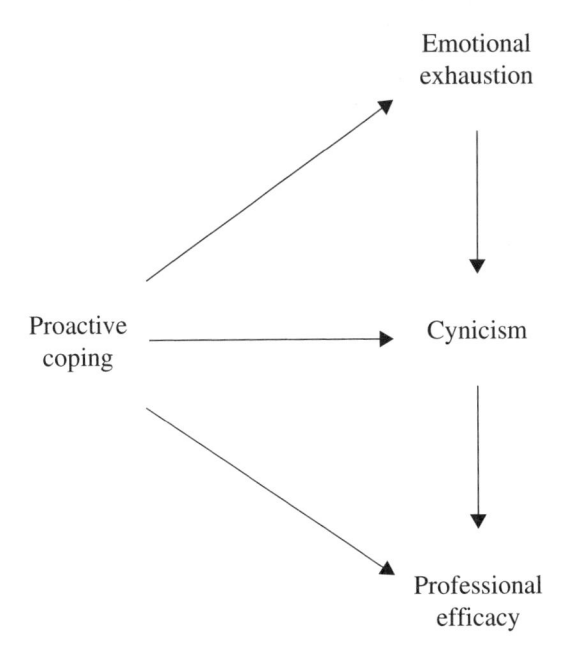

Figure 33.1 Theoretical model relating proactive coping to emotional exhaustion, cynicism and professional efficacy

exhaustion and cynicism (see Figure 33.1). It was expected that emotional exhaustion would lead to cynicism and that cynicism would lead to lower levels of professional efficacy. Parallel results were reported in teachers where emotional exhaustion led to depersonalization and depersonalization led to lower levels of personal accomplishment (Greenglass *et al.*, 1998).

Structural equation analysis was used to test the theoretical model presented in Figure 33.1. All analyses were conducted using AMOS version 4.0 (Arbuckle and Wothke, 1999). The maximum likelihood method of parameter estimation was utilized. The analysis was performed on 176 respondents (cases with missing data were excluded from analyses). The independence model that tests the hypothesis that the variables are uncorrelated with one another was rejected ($\chi^2(6, N= 176) = 136.089, p = 0.000$), thus the data were suitable for SEM analyses. The goodness of fit test ($\chi^2(1) = 3.98\ p = 0.046$) and the chi-square/df ratio (c/min=3.98) failed to support the theoretical model. However other fit indices were highly satisfactory (GFI=0.989; AFGI=0.889; NFI=0.971; IFI=0.978; CFI=0.977), except for the RMSEA=0.043 and the TLI=0.862.

The path, as indicated in the theoretical model, from cynicism to professional efficacy, was not significant and subsequently was removed. The analysis was rerun. In an attempt to develop a better-fitting, more parsimonious model, post hoc modification indices were performed. A modification index suggested a negative correlation between cynicism and professional efficacy. This modification provided an improved fit of the data to the model ($\chi^2(1) = 0.275, p = 0.600$, GFI = 0.999; AFGI = 0.992, NFI = 0.998, IFI = 1.00, CFI = 1.00 and RMSEA=0.000). The final model is presented in Figure 33.2.

Proactive coping had a negative impact on emotional exhaustion ($\beta = -0.25$) and cynicism ($\beta = -0.17$). Proactive coping directly increased the level of professional efficacy ($\beta = 0.29$). Emotional exhaustion had a direct impact on cynicism ($\beta = 0.61$). Proactive coping had an indirect effect on cynicism through emotional exhaustion ($\beta = -0.25 * 0.61$).

As expected, proactive coping contributed positively to professional efficacy. This is because proactive coping focuses on accumulating resources and setting goals for improvement, efforts which contribute positively to a sense of professional accomplishment and competence, that is, professional efficacy. Thus, to the extent that individuals employ at work coping strategies based on proactivity, they are more likely to experience a higher sense of professional efficacy in their jobs.

The findings that emotional exhaustion led to cynicism, and that cynicism and professional efficacy are reciprocally determined, parallel previous findings that the burnout components are related to each other (Greenglass *et al.*, 1998). Proactive coping would appear to be a useful tool in managing work-related stress and burnout and in promoting a higher level of professional competence at work. The results of the study point to the importance of integrating individual coping activity, in particular proactive coping, with work-related factors, in predicting levels of burnout at work. Individuals who employed proactive coping strategies were less likely to experience emotional exhaustion and cynicism, probably owing to their perception that they possessed greater resources to cope with stress, including the ability to plan, reflect and utilize social resources.

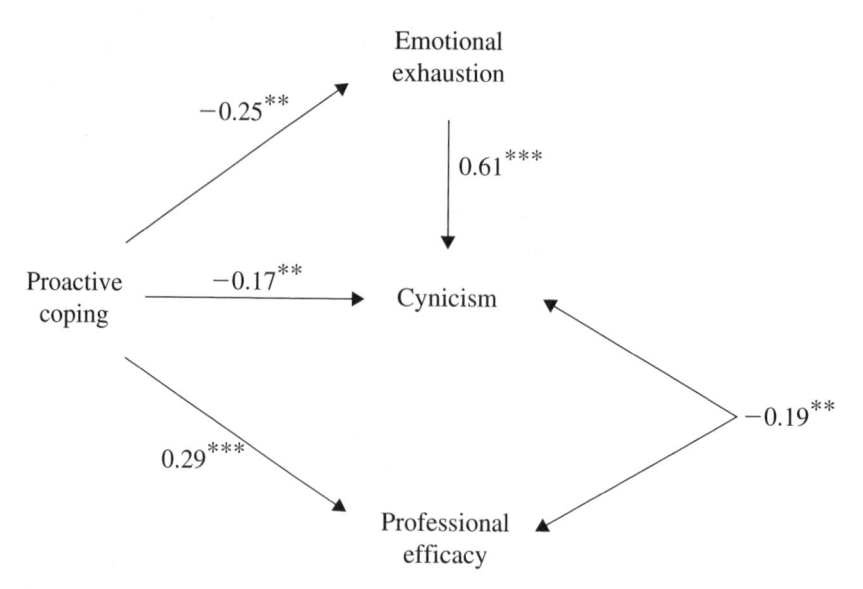

Note: $**p < 0.01$; $***p < 0.001$.

Figure 33.2 *Structural model relating proactive coping to emotional exhaustion, cynicism and professional efficacy*

Work stress, anger and proactive coping

Work stress can lead to feelings of anger that, in turn, may trigger higher levels of anxiety. In addition to its disruptive effects on organizational functioning and interpersonal relationships, the frequent experience of angry feelings has deleterious effects on health. Research has established a significant relationship between anger/hostility and coronary heart disease (CHD) incidence and mortality (Barefoot et al., 1983; Shekelle et al., 1983). The management of anger and hostility necessitates a conceptual integration of the dynamics of anger experience with the process of coping.

Perceived unfair treatment at work has been cited as a precipitant of anger and distress (Thomas, 1993; Schaufeli and Enzmann, 1998). According to Equity Theory, people pursue reciprocity in their interpersonal and organizational relationships (Rousseau, 1989). What they invest and gain from a relationship should be proportional to the investments and gains of the other party in the relationship. When they perceive that relationships are inequitable, they feel distressed and are motivated to restore equity (Schaufeli and Enzmann, 1998). Unfair treatment at work involves lack of equity and therefore should lead to the experience of anger. Thus, with the perception of unfair treatment at work, there should be an increase in anger, due to the perception of a broken psychological contract.

Additional data indicate that anger is also significantly related to depression (Kopper and Epperson, 1996). Weiner (1982) argues that anger (directed toward the self) results in depression. According to Beck's (1967) cognitive theory of psychopathology, depression can be precipitated by stressful situations that overtax the individual. Frequent contributors to depression include situations that lower an individual's self-esteem as well as those that thwart achievement of important goals. Beck argues that, when individuals are exposed to such stressors, they respond with ideas of personal deficiency, self-blame and pessimism. In depression, these ideas or schemas, according to Beck, consist of negative conceptions of the person's own worth, of his/her personal performance and nihilistic expectations.

Research suggests that the use of disclosure and active coping techniques, including access to and use of social support resources, should lead to communicative non-threatening expression of anger and hostility (Stoney and Engebretson, 1994). In this way, anger-provoking situations may be redefined or restructured so as to be less threatening, thereby leading to lower levels of anger and, as a result, lower depression. Additional research has shown that respondents who displayed health benefits following disclosure demonstrated increased insight and cognitive restructuring over time, compared with those who did not display improved health (Pennebaker, 1993). Social sharing or talking about feelings, including anger, is aimed at solving problems or lessening emotional distress.

The processes through which people anticipate potential stressors and act in advance to prevent them can be seen as proactive behavior. To the extent that individuals offset, eliminate, reduce or modify impending frustrating events, proactive behavior can eliminate a great deal of anger and depression before it occurs. The negative relationship between proactive coping and depression has been reported in Turkish Canadians (Uskul and Greenglass, 2000), in Polish Canadians (Greenglass, 2002a), in elderly Canadians (Greenglass, 2002b), and in Polish university students (Pasikowski et al., 2002). Proactive coping has also been reported to be negatively associated with scores on several other measures of distress, including emotional exhaustion and depersonalization. Moreover, since proactive coping has been associated with lower threat and fewer loss appraisals (Schwarzer and Taubert, 2002), it should lead directly to lower levels of depression.

Study 2

In a second study reported here, the relationship between perception of fair treatment, proactive coping, anger and depression was examined in the same sample of employed adults as described in Study 1. Proactive coping was assessed using the 14-item proactive coping subscale of the Proactive Coping Inventory (PCI) (Greenglass, Schwarzer and Taubert, 1999). Outcomes include state anger, a subscale of The State-Trait Anger Expression Inventory (STAXI) scales (Spielberger, 1988), depression, using a subscale of the Hopkins Symptom Checklist (HSCL) (Derogatis et al., 1979) and perception of fair treatment at work using a five-item measure (Greenglass, 2000). Reliabilities of composite variables for most scales were above 0.75.

A theoretical model was put forth that examined the relationship between proactive coping, fair treatment, anger and depression (see Figure 33.3). It was expected that proactive coping would lead to the perception of greater fairness at work since individuals who use proactive coping feel confident they have the inner resources to cope with work demands, may be less likely to perceive treatment at work as a threat and thereby more likely to perceive that they are being treated fairly at work. Perception of fair treatment at work should lead to less anger and, as a result, less depression. Further, to the extent that individuals use coping techniques based on proactivity, they should be less likely to experience depression. And higher fair treatment should lead to lower levels of depression.

Structural equation modeling was used to explore the relationship between proactive coping, fair treatment, depression and state anger. AMOS version 4.0 (Arbuckle and Wothke, 1999) was used to provide path coefficients and tests of the overall goodness of fit of the theoretical model that is presented in Figure 33.3. The maximum likelihood method of parameter estimation was utilized. The analysis was performed on 173 respondents (cases with missing data were excluded from analyses).

The independence model, that tests the hypothesis that the variables are uncorrelated with one another, was rejected (χ^2 (6, N = 173)=162.765, p = 0.001), thus the data were suitable for SEM analyses. The χ^2 goodness of fit statistics (χ^2 (1) = 1.223, p = 0.269) and the chi-square/df ratio (c/min = 1.223) indicated that the model provided an adequate fit to the data. Other indices provided by AMOS also showed good fit. The goodness of fit index, the adjusted goodness of fit index, the normed fit index and the incremental fit index were respectively 0.996, 0.965, 0.992, and 0.999. No post hoc modifications were required.

Further results showed that proactive coping had a direct impact on fair treatment (β = 0.32) and a negative impact on depression (β = −0.19). Fair treatment had a negative impact on state anger (β = −0.51), as well as on depression (β = −0.14). State anger had a direct effect on depression (β = 0.49). Proactive coping exerted an indirect effect on depression through fair treatment and state anger (β = 0.32 * β = −0.51 * β = 0.49) and through fair treatment alone(β = 0.32 * β = −0.14). The total effect of proactive coping on depression was β = −0.31 (see Figure 33.4).

Taken together, these results demonstrate that, to the extent that individuals employ at work coping strategies based on proactivity, they are more likely to perceive fair treatment

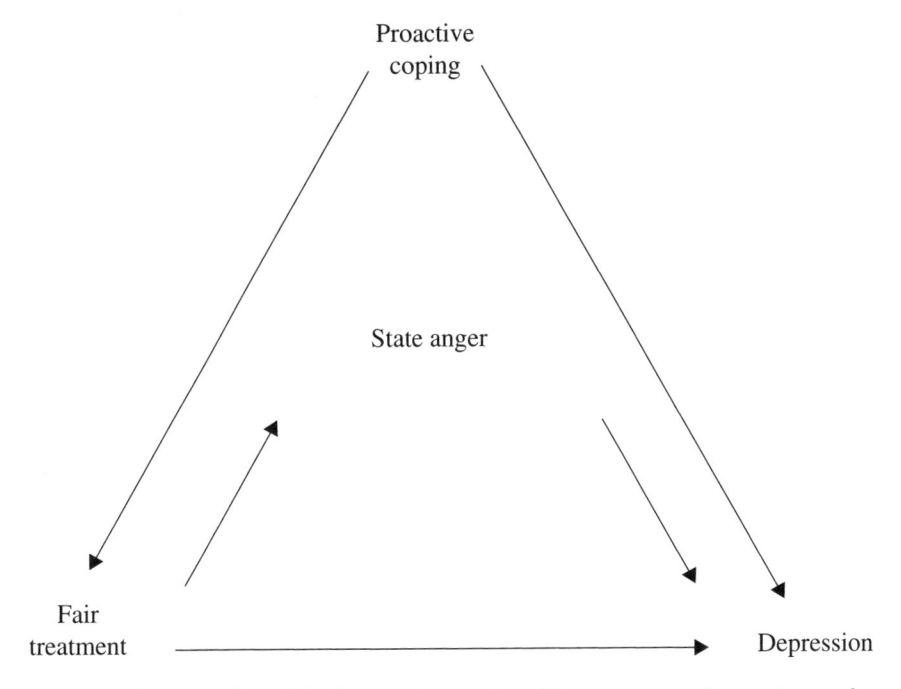

```
              Proactive
               coping
                 /\
                /  \
               /    \
              /      \
             /        \
            /          \
           /  State anger \
          /              \
         /                \
        ▼                  ▼
      Fair                 Depression
    treatment ──────────►
```

Figure 33.3 Theoretical model of proactive coping, fair treatment, depression and anger

at work and, as a result, experience less anger. Results further showed that state anger contributed directly to depression. These findings parallel previous results showing that anger at work is a significant predictor of depression (Greenglass, 2000). Anger is also significantly related to depression in college students (Kopper and Epperson, 1996). Additional data showed that proactive coping led to significantly lower depression. Thus, taken together, the data suggest that proactive coping is incompatible with depression.

A theoretical model of proactive coping, resources and outcomes
Figure 33.5 presents a schematic representation of the theoretical relationship between proactive coping, internal and external resources and various outcomes, both positive and negative. As can been seen in this diagram, proactive coping mediates between resources and outcomes. Internal resources may include optimism and self-efficacy beliefs and represent affective and cognitive elements, respectively, that define felt competency to handle a stressful situation. External resources are found in the social context within which individual coping develops and include different types of support such as information, practical help and/or emotional sustenance. Social support can serve a variety of functions. For example, to the extent that an individual draws on informational support, the perception of the meaningful aspects of a stressful situation can be modified. The sharing of feelings and affect that can occur in an emotionally supportive relationship can also result in changes in the meaning of a stressful situation for an individual. Thus cognitive changes may occur in one's perception of a stressful situation as a result of affective support.

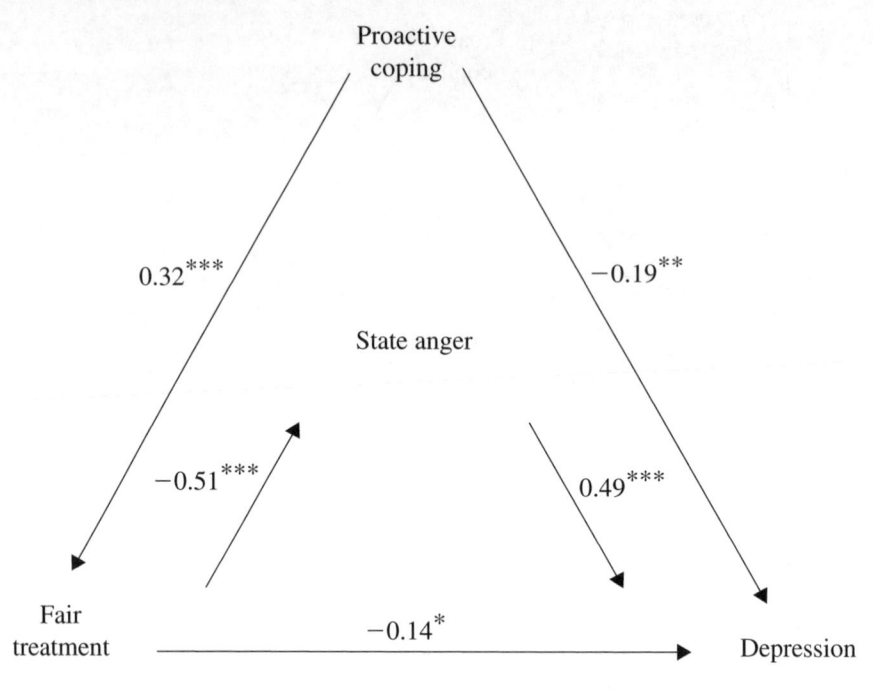

Notes: **p < 0.05; **p < 0.01; ***p < 0.001.

Figure 33.4 Structural model of proactive coping, fair treatment, depression and anger

At the same time, self-efficacy and social support are positively related to each other; to the extent that individuals possess self-efficacy, they also tend to report significantly more support from those around them. People with a high sense of social efficacy create social support for themselves. Perceived self-efficacy reduces vulnerability to depression through the cultivation of socially supportive networks (Holahan and Holahan, 1987a, 1987b) and social support enhances perceived self-efficacy. This in turn fosters successful adaptation and reduces stress and depression. Thus a strong sense of self-efficacy facilitates development of socially supportive relationships and, reciprocally, social support enhances perceived self-efficacy (Bandura, 1992). Proactive coping is seen as directly reducing negative outcomes, including depression and burnout, especially emotional exhaustion, depersonalization and cynicism, as well as anger. Because proactive coping is a positive strategy that is seen as promoting self-growth, professional efficacy and life satisfaction may be seen to increase with this kind of coping.

Summary and conclusions

In this chapter we have demonstrated that coping theory and research may be applied to the area of occupational stress and burnout. In particular, the concept of coping employed here is a broader one than the one that has been traditionally used and applied in the literature. In this context, proactive coping refers to positive striving, benefit finding and search for meaning. By extending coping behavior to goal pursuit, by referring to

```
┌─────────────────────────┐                              ┌─────────────────────────┐
│ Resources: Internal     │                              │ Outcomes: positive      │
│                         │                              │                         │
│   Self-efficacy         │                              │   Life satisfaction     │
│   Optimism              │                              │   Fair treatment        │
│                         │                              │   Professional efficacy │
└─────────────────────────┘                              └─────────────────────────┘
            ▲                      ┌───────────┐                      ▲
            │                      │ Proactive │                      │
            │                      │  Coping   │                      │
            ▼                      └───────────┘                      ▼
┌─────────────────────────┐                              ┌─────────────────────────┐
│ Resources: External     │                              │ Outcomes: negative      │
│                         │                              │                         │
│  Social support:        │                              │   Depression            │
│  information,           │                              │   Burnout               │
│  practical, emotional   │                              │   Anger                 │
│  support                │                              │                         │
└─────────────────────────┘                              └─────────────────────────┘
```

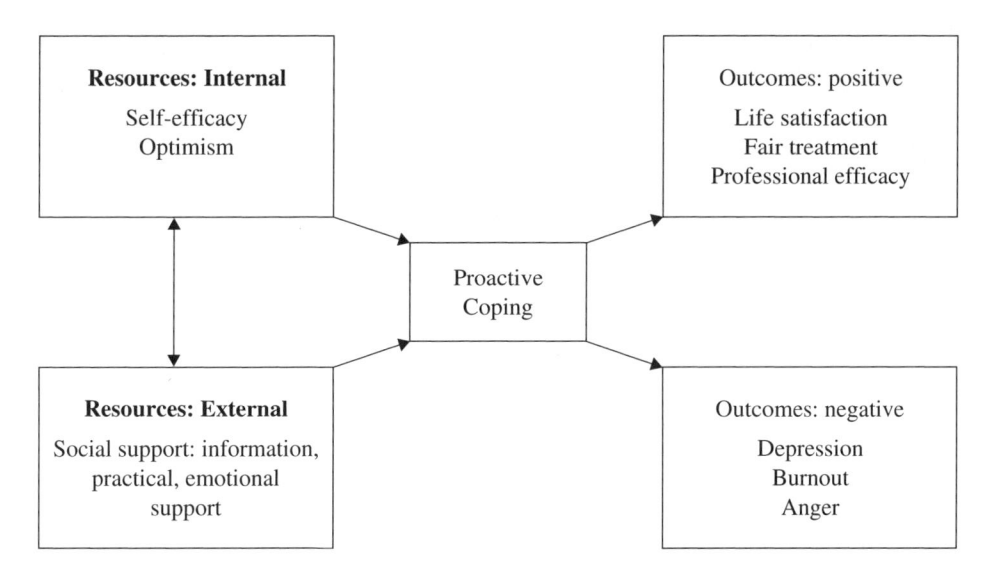

Figure 33.5   Theoretical model: resources, proactive coping and outcomes

coping as preparatory and preventive, and by considering intentionality as an important dimension of coping theory and behavior, coping is broadened to cover positive striving rather than simply reacting to stressors that have already occurred. These notions are particularly applicable to the work setting where assessment includes evaluation not only of the ability to meet demands and goals but also of the capacity to deal effectively with day-to-day work stressors. Proactive coping directly reduces stress at work and contributes to increased efficacy at work. Thus, by integrating coping theory with research on stress and burnout, we can suggest ways in which individuals can reduce their work stress and improve their quality of life at work.

References

Arbuckle, J.L. and W. Wothke (1999), *Amos 4.0 User's Guide*, Chicago: SPSS.
Armstrong-Stassen, M. (1994), 'Coping with transition: a study of layoff survivors', *Journal of Organizational Behaviour*, **15**, 597–621.
Aspinwall, L.G. and S.E. Taylor (1997), 'A stitch in time: self-regulation and proactive coping', *Psychological Bulletin*, **121**, 417–36.
Bakker, A.B., W.B. Schaufeli, E. Demerouti, P.M.P. Janssen, R. Van der Hulst and J. Brouwer (2000), 'Using equity theory to examine the difference between burnout and depression', *Anxiety, Stress and Coping*, **13**, 247–68.
Bandura, A. (1992), 'Exercise of personal agency through the self-efficacy mechanism', in R. Schwarzer (ed.), *Self-efficacy: Thought Control of Action*, Washington, DC: Hemisphere Publishing, pp. 3–38.
Barefoot, J.C., W.G. Dahlstrom and R.B. Williams, Jr. (1983), 'Hostility, CHD incidence and total mortality. A 25-year follow-up study of 255 physicians', *Psychosomatic Medicine*, **45**, 59–63.
Beck, A.T. (1967), *Depression: Causes and Treatment*, Philadelphia: University of Pennsylvania Press.
Belcastro, P.A. and R.S. Gold (1983), 'Teacher stress and burnout: implications for school health personnel', *Journal of School Health*, **53**, 404–7.
Cherniss, C. (1990), 'The human side of corporate competitiveness', In D.B. Fishman and C. Cherniss (eds), *The Human Side of Corporate Competitiveness*, Newbury Park, CA: Sage Publications.
Derogatis, L.R., R.S. Lipman, K. Rickels, E.H. Uhlenhuth and L. Cori (1979), 'The Hopkins Symptom Checklist (HSCL): a self-report symptom inventory', *Behavioural Science*, **19**, 1–15.

Folkman, S. (1984), 'Personal control and stress and coping processes: a theoretical analysis', *Journal of Personality and Social Psychology*, **46**, 839–52.
Friedman, I.A. (2000), 'Burnout in teachers: shattered dreams of impeccable professional performance', *Journal of Clinical Psychology*, **56**, 595–606.
Greenglass, E.R. (1991), 'Burnout and gender: theoretical and organizational implications', *Canadian Psychology*, **32**, 562–72.
Greenglass, E.R. (2000), 'Work rage and its psychological implications', paper presented at the 21st International STAR Conference, Bratislava, Slovakia, 20–22 July.
Greenglass, E.R. (2002a), 'Proactive coping', in E. Frydenberg (ed.), *Beyond Coping: Meeting Goals, Vision and Challenges*, London: Oxford University Press, pp. 37–62.
Greenglass, E.R. (2002b), 'Proactive coping, stress and social support: psychological implications', address at the XXV International Congress of Applied Psychology (IAAP), Singapore, 7–12 July.
Greenglass, E.R. and R.J. Burke (2000), 'Hospital downsizing, individual resources and occupational stressors in nurses', *Anxiety, Stress and Coping*, **13**, 371–90.
Greenglass, E.R., R.J. Burke and R. Konarski (1998), 'Components of burnout, resources and gender-related differences', *Journal of Applied Social Psychology*, **28**, 1088–1106.
Greenglass, E.R., R.J. Burke and M. Ondrack (1990), 'A gender-role perspective of coping and burnout', *Applied Psychology: An International Review*, **39**, 5–27.
Greenglass, E.R., R. Schwarzer and S. Taubert (1999), *The Proactive Coping Inventory (PCI): A multidimensional research instrument* (on-line publication, available at http://www.psych.yorku.ca/greenglass/).
Greenglass, E.R., R. Schwarzer, D. Jakubiec, L. Fiksenbaum and S. Taubert (1999), 'The Proactive Coping Inventory (PCI): A Multidimensional Research Instrument', paper presented at the 20th International Conference of the Stress and Anxiety Research Society (STAR), Cracow, Poland, 12–14 July.
Holahan, C.K. and C.J. Holahan (1987a), 'Self-efficacy, social support and depression in aging: a longitudinal analysis', *Journal of Gerontology*, **42**, 65–8.
Holahan, C.K. and C.J. Holahan (1987b), 'Life stress, hassles and self-efficacy in aging: a replication and extension', *Journal of Applied Social Psychology*, **17**, 574–92.
Jerusalem, M. and R. Schwarzer (1992), 'Self-efficacy as a resource factor in stress appraisal processes', in R. Schwarzer (eds), *Self-efficacy: Thought Control of Action*, Washington, DC: Hemisphere Publishing, pp. 195–213.
Kopper, B.A. and D.L. Epperson (1996), 'The experience and expression of anger: relationships with gender, gender role socialization, depression and mental health functioning', *Journal of Counseling Psychology*, **43**, 158–65.
Leiter, M.P. (1991), 'Coping patterns as predictors of burnout: the function of control and escapist coping patterns', *Journal of Organizational Behaviour*, **12**, 123–44.
Maslach, C. and S.E. Jackson (1986), *Maslach Burnout Inventory Manual*, 2nd edn, Palo Alto, CA: Consulting Psychologists Press.
Maslach, C., S.E. Jackson and M.P. Leiter (1996), *Maslach Burnout Inventory Manual*, 3rd edn, Palo Alto, CA: Consulting Psychologists Press.
McGrath, A., D. Houghton and N. Reid (1989), 'Occupational stress, and teachers in Northern Ireland', *Work and Stress*, **3**, 359–68.
Pasikowski, T., H. Sek, E.R. Greenglass and S. Taubert (2002), 'The Proactive Coping Inventory–Polish Adaptation', *Polish Psychological Bulletin*, **33**, 41–6.
Pennebaker, J.W. (1993), 'Putting stress into words: health, linguistic and therapeutic implications', *Behaviour Research and Therapy*, **31**, 539–48.
Rousseau, D.M. (1989), 'Psychological and implied contracts in organizations', *Employee Responsibilities and Rights Journal*, **2**, 212–39.
Schaufeli, W.B. and D. Enzmann (1998), *The Burnout Companion to Study and Practice: A Critical Analysis*, London: Taylor & Francis.
Schaufeli, W.B., M.P. Leiter, C. Maslach and S.E. Jackson (1996), 'The Maslach Burnout Inventory – General Survey (MBI–GS) 1996', in C. Maslach, S.E. Jackson and M.P. Leiter (1996), *Maslach Burnout Inventory Manual*, 3rd edn, Palo Alto, CA: Consulting Psychologists Press.
Schwarzer, R. (1992), *Self-efficacy: Thought Control of Action*, New York: Hemisphere Publishing.
Schwarzer, R. (1993), 'Measurement of perceived self-efficacy', unpublished manuscript, Free University of Berlin.
Schwarzer, R. (2000), 'Manage stress at work through preventive and proactive coping', in E.A. Locke (ed.), *The Blackwell Handbook of Principles of Organizational Behaviour*, Oxford: Blackwell, pp. 342–55.
Schwarzer, R. and S. Taubert (2002), 'Tenacious goal pursuits and striving toward personal growth: proactive coping', in E. Frydenberg (ed.), *Beyond Coping: Meeting Goals, Visions and Challenges*, London: Oxford University Press, pp. 19–35.

Seligman, M.E.P. (1998), 'Positive social science', *APA Monitor*, **29**(2), 5.
Seligman, M.E.P. and M. Csikszentmihalyi (2000), 'Positive psychology: an introduction, Special Issue on happiness, excellence and optimal human functioning', *American Psychologist*, **55**, 5–14.
Shekelle, R.B., M. Gale, A.M. Ostfeld and O. Paul (1983), 'Hostility, risk of coronary heart disease, and mortality', *Psychosomatic Medicine*, **45**, 109–14.
Spector, P.E. (1987), 'Interactive effects of perceived control and job stressors on affective reactions and health outcomes for clerical workers', *Work and Stress*, **1**, 155–62.
Spielberger, C.D. (1988), *State–Trait Anger Expression Inventory*, Tampa, FL: Psychological Assessment Resources.
Stoney, C.M. and T.O. Engebretson (1994), 'Anger and hostility: potential mediators of the gender difference in coronary heart disease', in A.W. Siegman and T.W. Smith (eds), *Anger, Hostility and the Heart*, Hillsdale, NJ: Lawrence Erlbaum Associates, pp. 215–37.
Taylor, S.E. and J.D. Brown (1994), 'Positive illusions and well being revisited: separating fact from fiction', *Psychological Bulletin*, **116**, 21–7.
Thomas, S.P. (1993), *Women and Anger*, New York: Springer Publication Company.
Uskul, A.K. and E.R. Greenglass (2000), 'Proactive coping and psychological well being among Turkish immigrants in Canada', paper presented at the 21st International STAR (Stress and Anxiety Research Society) Conference, Bratislava, Slovakia, 20–22 July.
Weiner, H. (1982), 'The prospects for psychosomatic medicine: selected topics', *Psychosomatic Medicine*, **44**, 491–517.

34 Burnout and wornout: concepts and data from a national survey
Lennart Hallsten

Introduction

In recent years, burnout has attracted wide attention both in research and in the mass media. The concept 'burnout' is not new, however, and it has been applied in research for nearly 30 years. At first, burnout was met with skepticism, but with the establishment of standardized instruments (Maslach and Jackson, 1981; Pines *et al.*, 1981) and well-designed studies, the concept has won wider acceptance. Numerous papers and books, around 6000 (Schaufeli and Enzmann, 1998), have been published on this topic.

Another reason for the growing interest is that the concept may serve as an expressive metaphor for facets of the changed ill-health panorama in Western countries. Some decades ago, industrial mental health problems typically referred to monotony, isolation, meaninglessness and lack of commitment, but with the changes in work intensity and content, in professionalization and in management and supervision strategies, the ill-health character also appears to be altered. Work assignments are nowadays often perceived as more meaningful and evolving, but they entail hazards of cognitive and emotional overload rather than underload, which may result in fatigue, exhaustion and in feelings of inefficiency and depression. Concerns about serious clinical consequences of burnout have been articulated in Sweden, and the label 'burnout' has been used as a diagnosis in medical certificates. People with stress-related exhaustion symptoms have also been found at risk for very long sickness absences (National Social Insurance Board, 2002).

Some Swedish data from national work environment surveys and surveys on work-related ill-health are indicative of these changes. The number of people reporting high demands in their jobs increased by some 10 per cent from 1991 to 1999 (SWEA, 2001) and the increase was especially marked for women and public employees. Self-reported ill-health problems have also increased, especially milder mental health symptoms. Ten to 15 per cent of the female employees stated in 1991 that they had sleeping problems every week. In 1999, these figures were doubled, and male employees showed similar trends. Weekly feelings of uneasiness and dissatisfaction at the eve of the working day have also become more common. Work-related stress reactions and psychic strains were more than doubled for women, from around 6 per cent to about 15 per cent. For men, the corresponding increase was from 3 to 6 per cent. Fatigue and inability to relax also grew among employees during the 1990s (Bejerot and Aronsson, 2001) and employees unable to relax from work increased from 34 to 43 per cent among men and from 44 to 51 per cent among women from 1989 to 1997. Increasing psychic symptoms, however, afflicted not only employees. Unemployed people showed similar increases in anxiety to those of employed people, although from a higher absolute level (Hallsten and Isaksson, 2001). An overview of the Swedish work and health situation during the 1990s is presented by Marklund (2001).

These ill-health changes match the presumed symptoms of burnout and the work-related changes also correspond to generally assumed causes of burnout. To date, however, the job burnout literature has mainly confirmed associations between burnout and more permanent job characteristics, such as high or conflicting demands, low control or support, lack of rewards and client contact (Lee and Ashforth, 1996; Maslach et al., 2001; Schaufeli and Enzmann, 1998). Connections with organizational and job-related changes have seldom been studied in relation to burnout, and it has only in exceptional cases been confirmed that lay-offs and 'downsizing' increase the risk of burnout (Burke, 2002; Kalimo, 2000). Empirical support is also largely lacking for the rather widespread assumption (Maslach, 1982; Maslach et al., 2001) that burnout should be more common among occupations with high mental and emotional demands.

During the last two decades burnout has mainly been regarded as a work-related stress reaction or crisis. The foremost representatives of such a view have been Christina Maslach, Wilmar Schaufeli and Michael Leiter, who have created what have become the standard instruments for assessing burnout, the Maslach Burnout Inventories (MBI–HS and MBI–GS) (Maslach and Jackson, 1981; Maslach et al., 1996). The view of burnout as an exclusively job-related phenomenon is, however, not generally supported, and other standpoints have been formulated (Hallsten, 1993; Pines, 1996; Pines et al., 1981). Pines and Hallsten have understood burnout as a generic, existential process that may occur in any setting, not just among employers and employees. Instruments have also been developed from a context-free perspective on burnout, for example the Burnout Measure (BM) (Pines et al., 1981) and the Copenhagen Burnout Inventory (Borritz and Kristensen, 2000). Since the development of the MBIs proceeded from a deliberately contextualized view on burnout, the issue of the job-restrictedness of burnout is more of a conceptual than an empirical question. Still it should be noted that the job-relatedness of burnout has not received any careful empirical examination, and the MBIs cannot be utilized for such a purpose since these instruments just address people with a job. Another typical feature of burnout research is that practically all studies have been case studies, mainly within 'people jobs' such as in health care, schools and social work, and hitherto only Kalimo (1999) has published burnout data from a representative sample. Since she used a version of the MBIs, only occupationally active people were included in the sample. A representative population study of burnout, with both employed and non-employed individuals, has been lacking.

The study to be presented here is, however, a national survey of burnout. The study was carried out from a decontextualized perspective on burnout and included people both inside and outside the labor market. Another point of departure for the study was that ordinary assessments of burnout by the MBIs or the BM tend to become overinclusive (Hallsten, 1993) and that these instruments capture groups that should be differentiated from each other. A process view of burnout may facilitate such a distinction.

Burnout as a phase in a generic crisis process
The MBIs imply an idea of burnout as a multidimensional state or syndrome consisting of three dimensions: emotional exhaustion, cynicism and reduced professional efficacy. Emotional exhaustion is often regarded as the core dimension of burnout, although it is the least specific aspect of MBI with obvious similarities to mental strain and low mental

health (Schaufeli and van Dierendonck, 1993). Earlier it was postulated that burnout might only occur in 'people work', but today it is assumed that burnout may happen in any job context. By linking burnout to the occupational sector, the concept gains in precision, but this aim may be achieved by other means. Here the job-restricted standpoint is relaxed and burnout is regarded as a generic phenomenon which may arise in any setting. If so desired, contextualized burnout processes may be specified by labels such as 'job burnout', 'education burnout', 'family burnout' and so on.

Elsewhere (Hallsten, 1993) a process model for burnout has been presented where burnout is conceived as a late phase in a process of burning out. This process may take place in the context of work, family, education, intensive job search and so on. The initial phase of the process was called 'absorbing commitment', characterized by high involvement and engagement but also by signs of concern and anxiety. This phase may turn over into 'frustrated strivings' and eventually into 'burnout' in the case of exposure to recurring or chronic stressors. The coping efforts during 'frustrated strivings' may be quite demanding and 'burnout' is assumed to occur after experiences of defeat or of reduced functional capacity. The burnout process is seen as one route to crisis and strain occurring when enactment of a self-definitional role is threatened or hindered. But, as in other crises, positive resolutions are attainable.

It is assumed that traditional measures of burnout capture a rather heterogeneous group and a multitude of processes are presumed to result in crises and strain expressed by emotional exhaustion, cynicism and low efficiency. Therefore it is important to try to distinguish the process of burning out from similar, yet different, courses. The idea has been to assess motives and drives behind 'absorbing commitment', motives that may be relatively unaffected by the process. Earlier interviews had suggested that those vulnerable to burnout processes seemed to endorse a script, 'I am my achievements'; that is their self-esteem was contingent on how well they performed in roles of central value for their self-realization. I have called this contingent self-esteem (see for example Crocker and Wolfe, 2001; Johnson, 1997) 'performance-based self-esteem'. Data on this motive in combination with data from traditional burnout inventories have been used in an attempt to assess the process of burning out.

According to this view, states of exhaustion, strain and negative attitudes are not regarded as indications of burnout unless traces of performance-based self-esteem can be observed. High BM scores, as well as high emotional exhaustion, are assumed primarily to express exhaustion and psychological strain, and at least two high-strain subgroups may be isolated, 'burnout' and 'wornout'. High scores on the BM together with low performance-based self-esteem are here seen as an indication of wornout rather than burnout. 'Wornout' is used as an umbrella term for strain states not influenced by exhausting attempts to create or to maintain self-esteem (for somewhat different uses of the term, see Cox *et al.*, 1993; Fischer, 1983). Most people do not have or develop an attitude of absorbing commitment towards their jobs, studies or activities. Some have low expectations and engagement, others have more balanced attitudes and less demanding coping patterns, but may still become exhausted, cynical and strained in some circumstances. In general it is assumed that the burnouts are or have been more involved in and committed to their activities than the wornouts. Presumably the burnout group has lived in environments with higher demands and their values, expectations and personal agency beliefs have probably deviated from those of the wornout group. Hence the burnouts are expected to have shown more intensive striving than the wornouts, both in relation to ordinary work or daily tasks and in coping attempts to change job or non-job conditions. Individuals high in performance-based self-esteem are presumably more hesitant than those low in performance-based self-esteem to accept relief and rest from a demanding activity to avoid risks of blows to their self-esteem.

The assumption made here is that it is fruitful to differentiate different strain or crisis developments. Such a distinction based on an etiology of burnout makes the construct more precise, and the job-restrictedness may appear arbitrary from a psychological point of view. Presumably this process conceptualization of burnout will also be more in line with the old informal connotation of the concept – see Hallsten (2001) – used by authors and artists more than a century ago to describe crisis states occurring after intense preoccupation and striving in vastly different settings. By taking motives and drives into consideration, the process view also brings the concept into line with descriptions of burnout as a motivational phenomenon. For instance, in their integrative model of burnout, Schaufeli and Enzmann (1998) maintain that 'strong motivation' has a crucial role in the development of burnout, and Freudenberger (1974) assumed that burnout primarily occurred among overcommitted individuals. Assessments established on a process view may also demonstrate less ambiguous relations to certain assumed antecedents of burnout, such as occupation and organizational changes and events.

In this process perspective, burnout denotes a certain strain and contingent self-esteem profile or pattern. By combining strain data from Pines' BM scale and self-esteem data from a scale for performance-based self-esteem (PBS), four strain/contingent self-esteem patterns are obtained: see Table 34.1. 'Burnout' refers here to a combination of high strain and high performance-based self-esteem, while 'wornout' corresponds to high strain and low performance-based self-esteem. Two low-strain profiles are also distinguished, a 'relaxed' group and a group of 'well-adapted strivers'. This strain/contingent self-esteem classification is used in the present study.

Relations to various background, occupational, job and family variables for burnout and wornout

The prevalence of the four strain/contingent self-esteem profiles will be related to a selection of background, occupational, job and family variables with the main purpose of

Table 34.1 Four strain/contingent self-esteem patterns

	Low scores on performance-based self-esteem	High scores on performance-based self-esteem
Low scores on traditional burnout scales such as the BM ('low-strain')	'Relaxed'	'Well-adapted strivers'
High scores on traditional burnout scales such as the BM ('high strain')	'Wornout'	'Burnout'

examining whether wornout and burnout had similar associations to these variables. Three dichotomic contrast variables, 'burnout', 'wornout' and 'burnout–wornout' were constructed for this aim. The first two variables contrast the low strain groups to the burnout and the wornout groups, respectively, while the third variable contrasts the two high-strain groups.

Guidance for predictions was obtained from overviews of the relations between burnout and various background, occupational, organizational and job variables (Hallsten et al., 2002; Lee and Ashforth, 1996; Schaufeli and Enzmann, 1998). Practically all studies referred to have utilized the MBIs, and most of the significant relations have been observed for emotional exhaustion. It is assumed that variables showing rather consistent significant relations to the MBIs, and especially to emotional exhaustion, mainly influence psychological strain. Hence it is predicted that these variables will have similar relations to wornout and burnout. Examples of such variables are gender, marital status and various job conditions such as low job control and low supervisory support. An exception is high job demands that quite invariably have shown positive relations to emotional exhaustion. High job demands are, however, presumed to readily initiate self-esteem concerns and to be more closely related to burnout than to wornout. Some variables not usually incorporated in burnout studies, immigrant, employment status, family demands and family relations, are also assumed to show similar and significant associations to both burnout and wornout. This is based on data from indices of general well-being, for example from the General Health Questionnaire, which correlate substantially with emotional exhaustion (Golembiewski et al., 1992; Kalimo, 1999). High family demands are not expected to bring about as many self-esteem concerns and strivings as high job demands may do in the present sample.

Events and conditions that may trigger preoccupation with self-evaluation and achievement, as well as more intense strivings and coping, are assumed to show stronger relations to burnout than to wornout. Possible instances of such events and conditions are recent vocational change, notices of lay-off or termination, high job demands and strict personal responsibility for job tasks. The burnout–wornout variable will be used for these examinations.

This variable is also utilized to examine whether burnout and wornout show opposite relations to certain variables. It is generally assumed that the directions in the associations with most variables are the same for wornout and burnout, but some plausible exceptions to this pattern may be outlined. One such variable is age. It is assumed that burnout is more common among younger people than among older ones, since it is sensible to believe that concerns about self-evaluation are more common among younger individuals than among older ones. Hence the opposite pattern would be the case for wornout. Another variable expected to show opposite patterns with wornout and burnout is social status. Internal and external demands to achieve and perform are probably stronger for higher than for lower social status groups, and higher prevalences of burnout might then occur among high social status groups than among low status groups. In contrast, wornout would be more frequent among low status groups than among high status groups. This would also have consequences for the relations with occupations and occupational types. It is predicted that the associations between wornout and burnout should be negative over occupations. Furthermore burnout would be more frequent among 'paper' and 'people' jobs than among 'things' jobs, while wornout would be more frequent in 'things' jobs. Labor market sectors would also show dissimilar relations since social status groups are unevenly distributed over these sectors. The highest prevalence of burnout would be found among government employees, while wornout should be most common in the private and municipal sectors.

Aim and questions
The major aim of the present study was to carry out an epidemiological examination of the prevalence of burnout and wornout for groups inside and outside the labor market in Sweden, and to relate burnout and wornout to various labor market, occupational, job and family variables. The following questions are focused upon:

- How frequent were burnout and wornout among Swedes in different demographic and occupational groups? For example, were burnout and wornout more frequent among women than among men? Were burnout and wornout observed among groups outside the labor market, such as students and unemployed people?
- Had burnout and wornout similar and significant relations to gender, marital status, immigrant, employment status, low job control, low supervisory support, family demands and family relations?
- Had burnout stronger relations than wornout to certain event variables, such as recent vocational change and notices of termination, and to job condition variables indicating high job demands and strict personal responsibility for job assignments?
- Did burnout and wornout show opposite trends in relation to age, social status and occupation?

Methods
The study was based on postal questionnaires in the year 2000 sent out to a national sample of 7056 people aged 18–64 years, living in Sweden. A follow-up was carried out one year later, but the current data were derived from the first wave. Statistics Sweden administrated the surveys. The questionnaires included items about demographics, labor market position, occupation, organizational changes, work conditions, sickness absence, family situation and conditions, economy, general health as well as burnout and self-esteem. In general, the items used in the questionnaire were of a standardized nature and had been tested in other studies.

Variables and indices
Background variables Five background variables were used: gender, age, marital status, immigrant and socioeconomic status (SES). These variables were treated as categorical ones and mostly dichotomized (gender: men (46 per cent), women (54 per cent); age: below 40 years (44 per cent), 40 years and more (56 per cent); marital status: single (31 per cent), married/cohabiting (69 per cent); immigrant: non-immigrant (88 per cent), immigrant (12 per cent); SES: blue-collar (45 per cent), low/middle-level white collar (41 per cent), and high-level white-collar (15 per cent). The percentages refer to the proportions of those with data on both the BM and the PBS scales.

Labor market position and employment status Labor market positions were classified into eight categories: employed, self-employed, home-worker (care of own children), unemployed, student, contract pensioner, disability pensioner and year-long sick. The last category often included formally employed people, but in the analyses they were regarded as non-employed, since work had not constituted their environment for long. A variable named 'employment status' was obtained by classifying the labor market positions into employment (employee, self-employed) and non-employment (home-worker, unemployed, student, contract pensioner, disability pensioner and year-long sick). Seventy-four per cent of the responders were employed and 26 per cent non-employed.

Occupation and occupational type Twenty occupations or occupational groups with more than 30 members were selected for the analyses. The occupations were derived from the ISCO 88 classification of ILO, and are seen in Figure 34.5. All occupations were also categorized into three occupational types: 'People jobs' (39 per cent), 'Paper jobs' (32 per cent) and 'Things jobs' (30 per cent), according to a method applied in Sweden (Härenstam et al., 2000). Another variable used was 'vocational change', referring to a vocational change during the last six months. Six per cent of the employed group had changed their employment.

Organizational and job variables Burnout has in general shown strong associations with organizational and job conditions such as demands, control and support, and the relations between some such conditions and burnout and wornout will be presented. Variables referring to 'conflicting demands', 'control of work pace' and 'supervisory support' were retrieved from standard survey instruments used in Sweden. The first two variables had six response alternatives varying from 'not at all' to 'almost all the time', while the last variable had four response alternatives with 'never' and 'always' as endpoints. In addition, it was of interest to study the associations for burnout and wornout with certain organizational events and conditions that may influence strivings and efforts. One such variable was 'notice of termination', which designated notices of termination in the organization during the last year, and to which the employees responded with 'yes' or 'no'. Another item was 'sickness substitution', that is how large a part of the job assignments employees had to make up for after sickness absence. The four response alternatives varied between 'not at all' and 'all or nearly all'. To simplify interpretations, all responses to the organizational and job items were dichotomized into a 'high' and a 'low' level.

Family or non-job variables Family and non-job variables are seldom included in burnout studies, and if such variables are utilized they nearly always refer to support aspects, but not to demands. Here, however, the associations for burnout and wornout with perceived family or non-job demands are studied. One item was 'I have tasks at home that use up all my energy' and another was 'How have your relations been with the persons close to you over the last year?' To the first item, four response alternatives were offered (from totally disagree to totally agree) while there were five response alternatives (from bad to good) for the second variable. The responses to these items were dichotomized.

Burnout and wornout Inspired by the burnout model presented above, the burnout and wornout categories were derived from two scales, the Pines' Burnout Measure (BM) (Pines *et al.*, 1981) and a scale for performance-based self-esteem (PBS). The context-free BM was chosen to allow persons outside the labor market to respond to the scale. The BM consists of 21 items about feelings and attitudes (for example, How often over the last year have you had the following experiences: 'Being tired', 'Feeling depressed', 'Being emotionally exhausted', and so on) with seven response alternatives, from 'Never' to 'Always'. Next to the MBI scales, the BM is probably the most applied burnout inventory and it has a high internal consistency (here: $\alpha = 0.90$). The BM is highly correlated with the exhaustion dimension in the MBIs. As in most other studies, the BM is here treated as a unidimensional scale, although three dimensions (demoralization, tiredness and loss of motive) have often been extracted from factor analyses (Enzmann *et al.*, 1998; Schaufeli *et al.*, 2001). For each individual an arithmetic mean for the BM was calculated according to a formula presented by Pines (Pines *et al.*, 1981). The total sample mean was 2.97 (SD = 0.93, N = 4822).

Performance-based self-esteem (PBS) was measured by a scale with four items ($\alpha = 0.85$). The PBS scale included the following items:

1. I think that I sometimes try to prove my worth by being competent;
2. At times, I have to be better than others to be good enough myself;
3. My self-esteem is far too dependent on my daily achievements;
4. Occasionally I feel obsessed with accomplishing something of value.

Five response alternatives with the two verbal anchors, 'Fully disagree' and 'Fully agree' were presented. An arithmetic mean was calculated from the responses for each person and the sample mean was 2.79 (SD = 1.11; N = 4845). The stability of the scale over one year as measured in the present study was $r = 0.69$. The PBS scale was positively related to the BM ($r = 0.43$). This correlation suggests that performance-based self-esteem either acts as a vulnerability factor for strain and exhaustion or that performance-based self-esteem is a strain-dependent attitude. The PBS scores correlated substantially with a tendency to exert oneself ($r = 0.54$) and with problems saying 'no' to expectations from others ($r = 0.36$). High PBS scorers also testified to more voluntary overtime ($r = 0.18$) and reduced lunch-breaks ($r = 0.20$) than those with low PBS scores, and this was true as well for sickness presenteeism ($r = 0.20$); that is, working although one is sick (Aronsson *et al.*, 2000). These relations indicate a convergent validity of the PBS. Women reported higher PBS scores than men, and high PBS scores were more common among younger and highly educated people than, respectively, among older and less educated people (see Hallsten *et al.*, 2002).

Those with high scores both on the PBS and on traditional burnout scales such as the BM are classified as (on the verge of) 'burnout'. Here cut-off levels on both scales were based on empirical data. It was found that, at a BM score ≥ 4.0, the prevalences of stress-related medium to long sickness absence (an accumulated absence of one month or more per year) steeply increased, and the cut-off point for high and low BM scores was then set at ≥ 4.0. Fourteen per cent belonged to the high BM group. The PBS scale was weakly and linearly related to sickness absence, and another criterion was used to obtain a reasonable cut-off value. When analyzing the stability of the combined Pines–PBS categories over one year, a cut-off value just above the PBS scale midpoint (3.0) optimized the stability

(70 per cent). Thus the cut-off value for high and low PBS scorers was set to >3.0, and with this criterion 39 per cent of the sample had high PBS scores.

People with PBS-values > 3.0 and BM-values ≥ 4.0 were regarded as (on the verge of) 'burnout'. Individuals with low PBS scores and high BM scores were classified as 'wornout' who expressed exhaustion and distress to a similar degree to the burnouts, but with a lower inclination to validate and attain self-esteem through achievements and accomplishments. The two remaining groups were the well-adapted strivers (low BM–high PBS) and the relaxed individuals (low BM–low PBS). Three dichotomic contrast variables were created to compare the relative prevalences of burnout and wornout. Two of them, 'burnout' ('burnout–low strain') and 'wornout' ('wornout–low strain'), were created to compare burnout and wornout with the combined low-strain groups, the relaxed group and the well-adapted strivers. The third variable, 'burnout–wornout', was derived from the high-strain subgroup and this variable consisted of just the burnouts and the wornouts.

Statistical analyses
χ^2 tests were applied to study the associations between the variables. The relations to the background, labor market, occupational, organizational, job and family variables were analyzed for all burnout and wornout variables. This was made for the four strain-contingent self-esteem categories and for the contrast variables 'burnout', 'wornout' and 'burnout–wornout'.

Response rates
In 2000, 4878 individuals of the population sample of 7056 responded to the questionnaire. Hence the response rate was 69.1 per cent, which is about normal for studies of the kind handled by Statistics Sweden. The response rate was not randomly distributed over the background and occupational variables, and somewhat higher rates were seen for women and more established groups in society. For instance, of the responders with BM and PBS data, 54 per cent were women and 46 per cent men. The background and employment position six months before the survey was known. Seventy-one per cent of the employed group and 61 per cent of the non-employed group responded to the survey. Younger, less educated and single people tended to respond to a slightly less degree than, respectively, older, well educated and married/cohabiting people.

Results
Total sample
Data on the strain-contingent self-esteem categories were obtained from 4810 individuals. The most frequent category was the relaxed group (55.7 per cent) followed by the well-adapted strivers (30.1 per cent). Over 9 per cent (9.3 per cent) were classified as burnout and almost 5 per cent as wornout (4.9 per cent). Hence burnout became a more frequent category than wornout.

Associations with background variables
The distributions of the four strain-contingent self-esteem categories for gender are presented in Figure 34.1. Relatively more men than women belonged to the relaxed group, while more women than men appeared in the two high-strain groups, the burnout and

Figure 34.1 Prevalence of the four strain-contingent self-esteem categories for men and women (per cent)

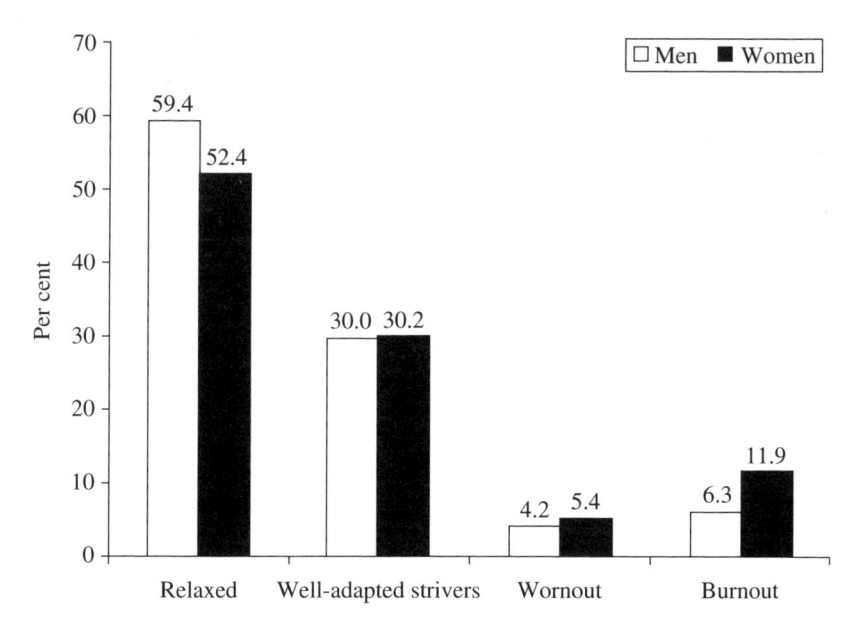

Note: N = 2218 and 2592, respectively.

wornout groups. Nearly twice as many women as men belonged to the burnout group, while the gender difference in wornout was smaller. The outcomes of significance tests of the associations are presented in Table 34.2, and it can be seen that the prevalences of the four strain-contingent self-esteem categories were significantly different for men and women. The same was true for both the burnout and the wornout contrast variable. In spite of this, the reciprocal contrast variable, burnout–wornout, indicated that high-strain women and men were differently divided into burnout and wornout. Forty per cent of these men and 31 per cent of these women were classified as wornout, while 60 per cent of the high-strain men and 69 per cent of the high-strain women were burnout. This different division into burnout and wornout was not in agreement with the prior assumption.

Although the relative burnout and wornout proportions were dissimilar, both indices ranked the genders consistently. According to both the burnout and wornout variables, women were worse off than men. Such consistent rankings were seen for two other background variables, marital status and immigrant. Singles had higher prevalences of burnout and wornout (12.4 and 5.7 per cent) than married or cohabiting individuals (8.0 and 4.5 per cent, respectively). The burnout and wornout proportions for immigrants were 15.5 and 6.8 per cent and for non-immigrants 8.5 and 4.6 per cent. Thus the burnout prevalence was almost twice as high for immigrants as for non-immigrants. In line with the assumption, there were no significant differences in the associations for burnout and wornout with marital status and immigrants (Table 34.2).

Table 34.2 χ^2 tests of different prevalences of strain/contingent self-esteem groups, burnout and wornout for some demographic, occupational, job and family variables

Variable	Four strain/self-esteem groups N	df	χ^2	Contrast: burnout–low strain N	df	χ^2	Contrast: wornout–low strain N	df	χ^2	Contrast: burnout–wornout N	df	χ^2
Demographic variables												
Gender	4810	3	53,9***	4575	1	46,0***	4362	1	5,8*	683	1	5,2*
Age	4810	3	54,7***	4575	1	0,1	4362	1	2,8+	683	1	2,5
Marital status	4810	3	36,6***	4575	1	25,4***	4362	1	4,7+	683	1	1,5
Immigrant	4809	3	48,1***	4574	1	32,4**	4362	1	7,5*	682	1	1,1
Social status	3697	6	27,6***	3526	2	3,0	3382	2	7,0*	486	2	10,5**
Labor market, occupation												
Labor market position	4714	21	247,9***	4486	7	170,7***	4277	7	82,7***	665	7	12,4+
Employment	4714	3	74,8***	4486	1	61,6***	4277	1	15,6***	665	1	2,0
Labor market sector	3404	9	28,3*	3261	3	19,5***	3159	3	6,6+	388	3	8,7*
Occupational type	3375	6	25,9***	3232	2	7,4*	3131	2	5,6+	387	2	11,8**
Occupation	3366	57	101,9***	3224	19	30,3*	3126	19	25,6	382	19	36,8**
Vocational change	3292	3	16,7**	3148	1	9,4**	3048	1	0,2	388	1	3,9*
Organization, job												
Notice of termination	2883	3	22,9***	2774	1	15,9***	2691	1	0,5	301	1	2,9+
Conflicting demands	3448	3	133,2***	3303	1	98,5***	3195	1	17,8***	398	1	5,0*
Control work pace	3473	3	87,5***	3326	1	51,8***	3216	1	30,1***	404	1	0,0
Supervisory support	3210	3	131,4***	3072	1	70,8***	2971	1	60,8***	377	1	1,1
Sickness substitution	3313	3	46,2***	3167	1	15,4***	3069	1	0,2	390	1	7,5**
Family												
High home demands	4653	3	72,0***	3261	1	21,6***	3153	1	18,7***	390	1	0,3
Bad family relations	4796	3	559,4***	3345	1	212,6***	3235	1	132,5***	404	1	0,0

Note: + p < 0.10; * p < 0.05; ** p < 0.01; *** p < 0.001.

Age was expected to show opposite patterns for burnout and wornout, but age had a non-significant relation to burnout. Burnout was as frequent among young (<40 years: 9.5 per cent) as among old (≥40 years: 9.2 per cent) people. There was a weak and just marginally significant difference for wornout (4.3 and 5.4 per cent, respectively) in the expected direction. The low-strain categories were related to age, however. The younger group had fewer people in the relaxed category than the older group (51 per cent and 60 per cent, respectively), while the reverse was true for the well-adjusted strivers (36 per cent versus 26 per cent). For socioeconomic status (SES), the burnout and wornout indices ranked the three SES categories in opposite directions as expected: see Figure 34.2. Wornout tended to decrease with SES level, while burnout demonstrated an opposite trend. The blue-collar group had a larger proportion in the relaxed category (60 per cent) than the low and high white-collar groups (54 per cent for both groups). An opposite trend was seen for the well-adjusted strivers (27 per cent, 33 per cent and 34 per cent for the three SES-groups). The high-strain SES groups showed different burnout and wornout prevalences. Of the high-strain blue-collar group, 44 per cent were wornout and 56 per cent burnout, while the corresponding proportions for the high white-collar group were 24 and 76 per cent. Thus the high-strain SES groups had dissimilar compositions of burnout and wornout (Table 34.2).

All associations between the four strain–self–esteem categories and the background variables, as well as all for other variables, were clearly significant (Table 34.2). The burnout–low strain prevalences were significantly different for gender, marital status and immigrant. The associations with wornout were generally lower than for burnout, but the relations with gender, marital status, immigrant and social status were statistically

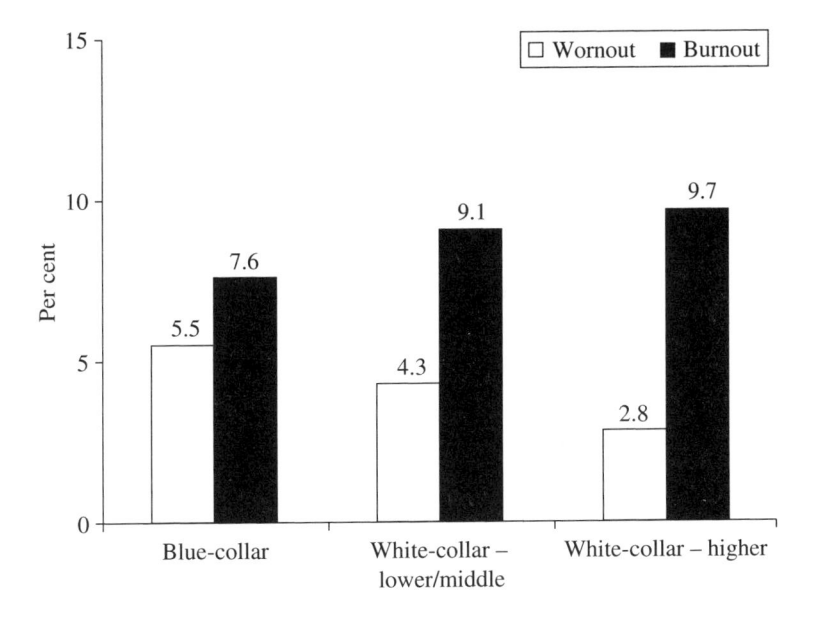

Note: N = 1663, 1498 and 563.

Figure 34.2 Prevalence of wornout and burnout for the three SES categories (per cent)

528 Professional burnout

significant (p < 0.05). Corresponding analyses on the associations with the background variables for the employed subsample showed similar results as for the total sample, and the statistical tests showed only marginally different outcomes.

Associations with labor market and occupational variables
According to the job restriction view, burnout may only occur among those active in the labor market. Here a context-free instrument was used to measure burnout and wornout and those people outside the labor market were allowed to respond to the instrument. The results indicated that both burnout and wornout were more frequent among the non-employed group than among the employed group (see Figure 34.3). Twice as many non-employed as employed individuals were classified as burnout (14.7 per cent and 7.4 per cent respectively), while the corresponding proportions for wornout were 6.6 per cent and 4.2 per cent. Both differences were significant, which was less surprising since the year-long sick and the disability pensioners were included in the non-employed group. All non-employed groups, however, with the exception of contract pensioners, had higher prevalences of burnout than the employed and self-employed groups. An exceptionally high level of burnout (39.6 per cent) was observed for those who had been continuously sick-listed for a year or more. Both students and the unemployed had

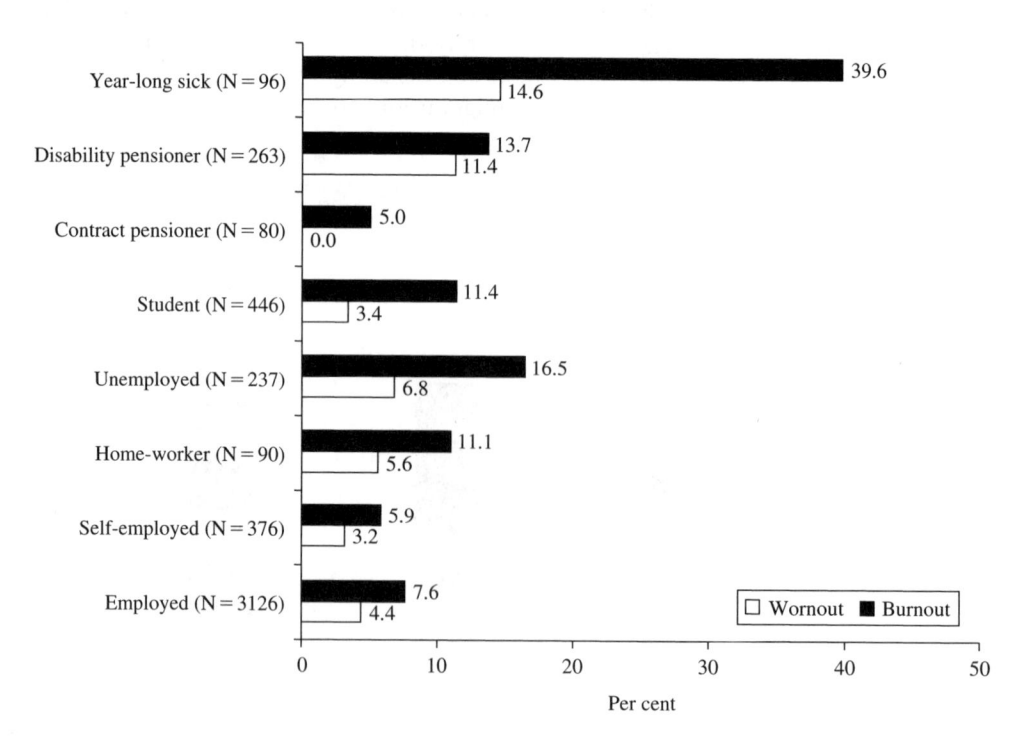

Group	Burnout	Wornout
Year-long sick (N = 96)	39.6	14.6
Disability pensioner (N = 263)	13.7	11.4
Contract pensioner (N = 80)	5.0	0.0
Student (N = 446)	11.4	3.4
Unemployed (N = 237)	16.5	6.8
Home-worker (N = 90)	11.1	5.6
Self-employed (N = 376)	5.9	3.2
Employed (N = 3126)	7.6	4.4

Note: N = 4714.

Figure 34.3 Prevalence of burnout and wornout among eight labor market positions (*per cent*)

significantly higher levels of burnout than employees. The difference between the last two groups remained significant ($OR = 2.12$, $p < 0.01$) in a multivariate logistic regression analysis after control for the background variables, while the difference between students and employees became non-significant in a multivariate logistic regression analysis. The students and unemployed did not differ significantly from the employees in terms of wornout. As expected, burnout and wornout did not show any significantly different distributions over employment status and employment positions (see Table 34.2).

Four labor market sectors were distinguished, the governmental, the municipal (local government), the county council and the private sector. Burnout was more common in the government sector (14.3 per cent) than in the other three sectors (6.2 to 6.8 per cent), while the prevalence for wornout varied much less (3.8 to 5.7 per cent) with the highest level among municipal employees. As expected, the presence of burnout and wornout among high-strain employees differed significantly for the labor market sectors (Table 34.2).

Prevalences of burnout and wornout for three occupational types are presented in Figure 34.4. Burnout was most frequent in 'Paper work', which also had the lowest level of wornout. The prevalences of burnout and wornout among high-strain employees were significantly different from each other (Table 34.2) as predicted, and the occupational types were differently ranked by the burnout and wornout indices.

Twenty occupational groups and their burnout and wornout proportions are described in Figure 34.5. The occupations are listed in order of their burnout prevalences, with the highest proportion for teachers and the lowest for stationary plant operators. A significant difference between the occupations was found for burnout, but not for wornout, and the

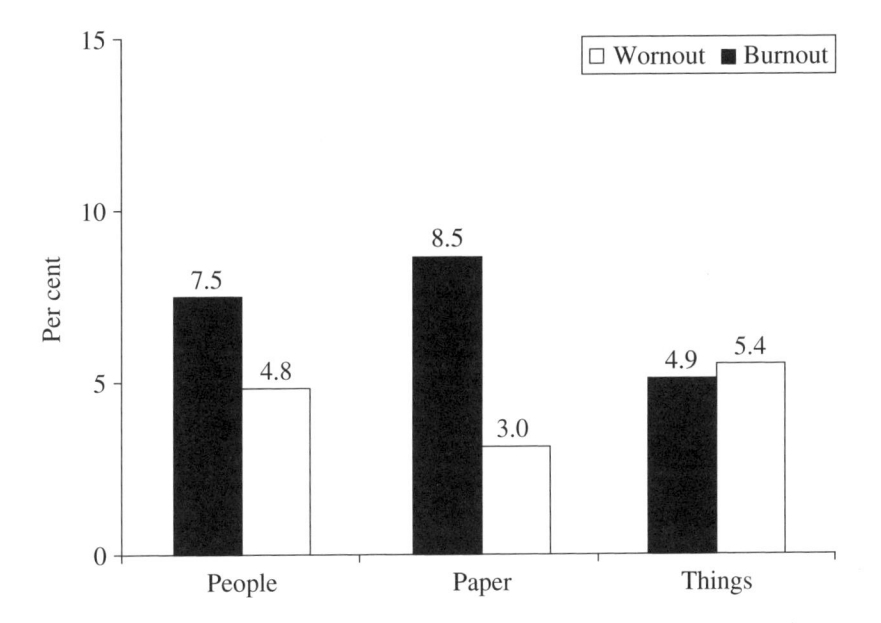

Note: N = 1252, 999 and 1124.

Figure 34.4 Prevalence of burnout and wornout in three occupational types (per cent)

Note: The number in front of the occupation label refers to the ISCO code; total N = 3366.

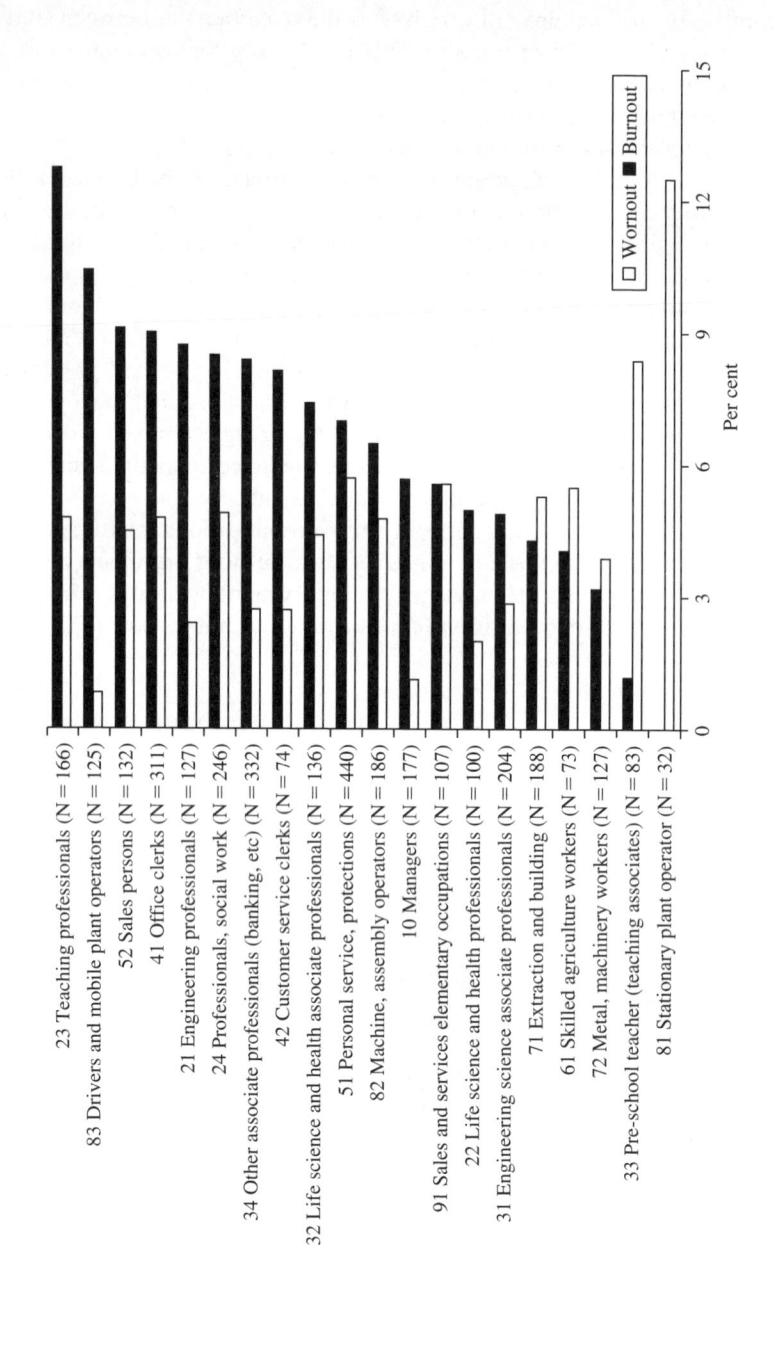

Figure 34.5   Prevalence of burnout and wornout in 20 occupational groups (per cent)

prevalence differences in burnout and wornout for high-strain employees were clearly significant. There was a clear negative rank correlation between burnout and wornout over the occupations (rho = −0.58, $p < 0.01$); that is occupations with high prevalences of burnout tended to have low levels of wornout and vice versa. It is interesting to note that some occupations seldom attended to in burnout studies, such as drivers, sales persons and office clerks, had relatively high prevalences of burnout, while groups such as health professionals and pre-school teachers had relative low prevalences. It should be observed, however, that the differences between the non-extreme occupations were not significant.

Recent vocational changes were presumed to influence wornout and burnout differently. Some support for such a view was found, in that burnout was relatively more common among those that had recently changed vocation as compared to those that had not (13.0 per cent and 7.1 per cent, respectively). Recent vocational change was not related to wornout (Table 34.2).

Organization and job conditions
It was assumed that both burnout and wornout should be clearly and similarly related to control and support in the job. Those with low control over work pace and low supervisory support indicated higher prevalences of burnout and wornout than those with high control and high support. Slightly more than 10 per cent (10.1 per cent) of those with low control were classified as burnout as compared to 3.9 per cent of the high control group, and the corresponding figures for employees with low and high support were 12.0 and 4.5 per cent. The wornout proportions were 5.8 and 2.3 per cent for the low and high control employees and 7.6 and 2.2 per cent for the low and high support employees. For these two variables, high-strain employees were similarly divided into burnout and wornout (Table 34.2), suggesting that job control and supervisory support were as likely to create burnout as wornout.

Job demands were assumed to be more closely related to burnout than to wornout and this prediction was confirmed (see Table 34.2). Employees with frequent conflicting demands reported higher prevalences of burnout and wornout than those with lower frequencies. Over 17 per cent (17.1 per cent) was classified as burnout among employees who often met conflicting demands in their jobs, as compared to 5.5 per cent who perceived such demands less often. The corresponding wornout proportions, 6.9 and 3.7 per cent, differed less and, consequently, conflicting job demands had dissimilar relations to burnout and wornout. Job conditions indicating strict personal responsibility were also presumed to affect burnout and wornout differently. One such aspect may be illustrated by the variable 'sickness substitution', which measures the degree to which job assignments had to be made up for after sickness absences. For those who had to make up for all or nearly all tasks not done (35 per cent) 9.8 per cent were burnout as compared to 6.1 per cent who did not have to make up to a similar degree. Wornout was approximately equally common in these two groups (4.1 and 4.6 per cent, respectively), and the difference in relative prevalences of burnout and wornout was clearly significant (Table 34.2).

Organizational events such as notices of termination seemed also to have differential influences on burnout and wornout, as presumed. Burnout was more common among those who during the previous year had experienced a notice of termination in their organization than among the ones that had not (10.6 per cent and 5.8 per cent, respectively). The corresponding prevalences for wornout were not significantly different from each other (4.1 per cent and 3.7 per cent). There was a marginally significantly different division of burnout and wornout among high-strain individuals with and without experiences of notices of termination.

Family or non-job demands
Presumed influences of family or non-job demands on wornout and burnout were examined for the two variables 'High home demands' and 'Bad family relations'. Those agreeing with the statement that home assignments consumed all energy had higher levels of burnout and wornout than the ones that disagreed with the statement. The burnout prevalences were 12.4 and 7.3 per cent and the wornout prevalences 6.5 and 3.9 per cent, respectively. Bad relations within the family or with close friends had very strong effects on both burnout and wornout. Individuals stating that they had rather bad or bad relations or relations varying in quality during the previous year (23 per cent) had much higher burnout and wornout proportions than the ones stating that they had rather good or good relations. Of the latter group, 5.3 per cent were classified as burnout as compared to 23.0 per cent of the ones with worse family relations. The corresponding wornout proportions were 2.8 and 11.9 per cent. In line with the assumption, the relative prevalences of burnout and wornout did not differ significantly among high-strain individuals (Table 34.2).

The relations to the family or non-job demands were similar for the employed and self-employed subgroup. Burnout was reported by 10.1 per cent of those with high home demands, as compared to 5.9 per cent for the ones with fewer family demands. The wornout prevalences were 6.1 and 3.2 per cent. Among employees with bad family relations, 18.7 per cent were burnout as compared to 4.2 per cent of the ones with good relations. Corresponding wornout prevalences were 10.7 and 2.4 per cent.

Discussion and conclusions
The present study of burnout and wornout differs from most other burnout studies in two respects, in definition of burnout and in scope. In contrast to practically all earlier burnout studies, the current one is not a case study but a representative population study. As such it gives an overview of the burnout landscape with rare data, for example of burnout prevalences in several occupations, in work sectors and in different labor market positions. The other deviation concerns definition. Burnout was conceptualized as a phase in a generic process of burning out, not as a job-restricted mental state or syndrome as implied by the sole use of burnout instruments such as the MBIs. In the present study, two scales, an ordinary burnout instrument, the BM, and the PBS scale were applied to capture burnout, and burnout was operationalized as a certain exhaustion–distress/contingent self-esteem profile. Thus, compared to the state view, it in a sense entails a stricter definition of burnout, and it distinguishes two high exhaustion–strain phases, burnout and wornout. In another sense, however, the process view of burnout denotes a wider phenomenon, in not being restricted to work or to any other setting, and individuals outside the labor market were included in the sample. Thanks to these departures from ordinary conceptualizations and study designs, new comparisons and data were obtainable and burnout individuals were given a somewhat different portrayal.

However the process approach involved some additional assumptions and considerations. It was presumed that a scale for performance-based self-esteem (PBS) used jointly with an ordinary burnout instrument would adequately seize phases of the burning out process, and such an assumption entails uncertainty even if the PBS scale seems to have substantial validity. A complication arises in connection with profile specification and the choice of reasonable cut-off points on the BM and the PBS scales. Sensitivity analyses may give some evidence on the consequences of selection of other cut-off values, and some such analyses have been carried out. For instance, if the cut-off value on the PBS scale is increased to ≥ 3.5, the proportions of burnout and wornout become equally large, around 7 per cent. The associations with other variables were, however, just marginally influenced by such a change, and the significance tests showed largely the same outcomes as the ones presented in Table 34.2. The higher the cut-off point is set on the PBS scale, the larger the difference in denotation between the process and state-defined concepts of burnout. Here reliability considerations influenced the cut off-points for the PBS scale, resulting in burnout as a more common category than wornout. The plausibility of such a difference is worth considering, but possible causes of such a difference are readily obtained from viewing performance-based self-esteem either as a vulnerability factor for strain and exhaustion in face of troublesome conditions, or as a more or less strain-dependent attitude. Data from longitudinal studies including the PBS and BM scales as well as antecedent variables may indicate the reasonableness of these two interpretations. Anyhow, the estimated proportion of burnout among employees (7.4 per cent) happened to be nearly identical with the prevalence of 'serious burnout' (7.2 per cent) in Kalimo's study (Kalimo, 1999).

Fourteen per cent of employees had high values on the BM (≥ 4.0) with an increased risk (over nine times the risk for those with lower BM values) for stress-induced, accumulated sickness absences over a month. This seems to be a high proportion of high-strain individuals, but it may be a slight underestimation. Analyses of the response rates to the second wave showed that those with high BM values responded somewhat, although not significantly, less (84 per cent) than the ones with lower BM values (87 per cent).

An important finding of the study was that wornout and burnout in a largely predictable way exhibited similar and dissimilar associations to a number of possible antecedent factors. Equally essential was that variables plausibly related to burnout such as organizational events as well as to certain job conditions and occupational groups were found to be associated with burnout.

As predicted, burnout and wornout were similarly and significantly related to marital status, immigrant, employment status, labor market position, job control, supervisory support, family demands and family relations. The predictions just failed for gender. Still more appealing was that wornout and burnout in a predictable way were differentially related to vocational and organizational changes and to variables connected to high job demands and personal responsibility at work (sickness substitution). Burnout showed stronger associations with these variables, indicating greater exposure to these factors for the burnout group than for the wornout group. These outcomes are in agreement with Kalimo's finding of increased job burnout among employees given notice of lay-off (ibid.). Thus an empirical link has been discerned between burnout and some widespread work-related changes and events seen during the last decade. The view of burnout as a more job demand-induced phenomenon than wornout received some verification in that burnout were more closely related to frequent conflicting job demands than wornout. Many organizational conditions and events in present-day work life may contribute to conflicting demands, but a common feature may be that they easily produce self-esteem threats and efforts to cope with the situation. The similar and significant relations of high home demands to burnout and wornout demonstrate that, for this sample, home demands were quite strenuous and fatiguing but not as closely connected to self-esteem preoccupations and strivings as job demands. The presence of exclusive personal and non-transferable job assignments have probably grown with the increase in professionalization and individualized jobs, and the negative relation between sickness substitution and burnout may be an indication that burnout also is related to such occupational tendencies. A general conclusion seems to be that burnout was more closely correlated to recent organizational trends than wornout.

The finding that wornout and burnout showed opposite trends in relation to social status, occupation and labor market sector as expected is also of considerable significance. Wornout was more prevalent in the lower social status groups while burnout was more frequent in the highest social status groups (the professionals). Higher relative frequencies of burnout were found for 'paper' and 'people' jobs than for 'things' jobs, while the opposite was true for wornout. The clear difference in burnout between jobs in the governmental sector and in the other sectors is in accordance with this trend. These results suggest that the often presumed risk of burnout among professionals and semi-professionals, and among those with mentally and emotionally demanding jobs, may be seized by this process view on burnout. Kalimo (ibid.) did not find similar trends in her representative sample with her state assessment of burnout. Some deviant outcomes from this general pattern were, however, observed, for example the high occurrence of burnout among drivers and mobile plant operators, and the low prevalence of burnout among pre-school teachers. Whether or not these prevalences may be attributed to random factors cannot at present be settled.

The clear negative relations between burnout and wornout over the 20 occupational groups were conspicuous, and this suggests that individuals in various occupations differ in their inclinations to self-focused attention and to striving when confronted by troublesome conditions and events. Still it should be emphasized that the occupational differences in wornout and burnout were rather modest, which is in agreement both with Kalimo's (2000) data and with Swedish national data on stress and mental strain at work (SWEA, 2000). It should be remembered, however, that occupational differences in burnout, as measured exclusively with the BM, were still smaller. Part of the occupational differences in burnout and wornout may also be ascribed to different demographic characteristics among the occupational members. If control was exerted for the five background variables in a multivariate logistic regression analysis, the occupational differences in burnout and wornout became non-significant. This might be interpreted as that the occupational differences were only caused by different personal characteristics among the occupational members. However such a conclusion is questionable, given a quite probable self-selection in the occupations.

In light of the usual job restriction notion of burnout, it may be surprising to find burnout to be more prevalent in positions outside the labor market. With the definition applied here, burnout appears mainly to be a non-employment phenomenon, although it should not be concluded that burnout was only caused by non-employment factors for these groups. Earlier studies of mental health assessed by scales such as the General Health Questionnaire (GHQ) (Murphy and Athanasou, 1999; Winefield, 1995), have almost invariably shown that unemployed people have worse mental health than employed ones. The GHQ, the BM and the emotional exhaustion scale of the MBI are closely related (Kalimo, 1999), and from such a viewpoint the present outcome for the unemployed group becomes less striking. It is also likely that the perceived demands actively to seek and find a job are high for those in a work-oriented society such as Sweden. Considerable increases in low mental health among both employed and unemployed groups during the 1990s were also observed in Sweden (Hallsten and Isaksson, 2001). The very high prevalence of burnout among the year-long sick-listed also suggests that burnout processes may lead to extended sickness absences and perhaps to clinical forms of burnout. This is now examined with data from the second wave of this survey. Burnout and wornout were also positively related to non-work or family demands, and the association with bad relations within the family was very clear. This was also true for employed groups and, in a multiple logistic regression analysis, it was found that family and non-job factors contributed to burnout even after control for a large number of background, employment, organizational and coping factors (Hallsten et al., 2002). Whether or not family and non-job demands also influence job burnout, as measured by the MBIs, should be examined. Anyhow researchers interested in burnout should not neglect groups and possible antecedents outside the labor market.

Although some problems were noted with the present process view of burnout, it appears to have some advantages as compared to the usual state conception, from both theoretical and empirical perspectives. The process view is more theory-based since it is based on a certain process and it seems to be more in line with very old connotations of the concept used by authors and artists. Burnout also in a sense becomes a more precise concept since it is based on profile data from two scales that distinguish two high exhaustion–strain phenomena, burnout and wornout. More important, however, was that this conceptualization of burnout and wornout created differential relations to certain variables. One consequence of this finding is that the distinction between burnout and wornout may resolve deviant outcomes from different studies, in that wornout processes may have been dominating in some studies and burnout processes in others. Another consequence is that this process conception of burnout may be a tool in detecting more specific causes and consequences of strain and exhaustion, thereby being an asset in prevention and cure. In organizations, as in other settings, it would be of value to discuss and reflect on causes and contributions to performance-based self-esteem and possible ways to manage or reduce it.

References

Aronsson, G., K. Gustafsson and M. Dallner (2000), 'Sick but yet at work. An empirical study of sickness presenteeism', *Journal of Epidemiology and Community Health*, **54**(7), 502–9.

Bejerot, E. and G. Aronsson (2001), 'Mentally and physically fatiguing work–trends in the 1990s', in S. Marklund (ed.), *Worklife and Health in Sweden 2000*, Stockholm: Swedish Work Environment Authority & National Institute for Working Life, pp. 175–87.

Borritz, M. and T.S. Kristensen (2000), *Copenhagen Burnout Inventory. Normative Data from a Representative Danish Population on Personal Burnout*, Copenhagen: National Institute of Occupational Health.

Burke, R.J. (2002), 'Work experiences and psychological well-being of former hospital-based nurses now employed elsewhere', *Psychological Reports*, **91**(3, pt2), 1059–64.

Cox, T., G. Kuk and M.P. Leiter (1993), 'Burnout, health, work stress and organizational healthiness', in W.B. Schaufeli, C. Maslach and T. Marek (eds), *Professional Burnout. Recent Developments in Theory and Research*, Washington, DC: Taylor & Francis, pp. 177–93.

Crocker, J. and C.T. Wolfe (2001), 'Contingencies of self-worth', *Psychological Review*, **108**(3), 593–623.
Enzmann, D., W.B. Schaufeli, P. Janssen and A. Rozeman (1998), 'Dimensionality and validity of the Burnout Measure', *Journal of Occupational and Organizational Psychology*, **71**, 331–51.
Fischer, H.J.A. (1983), 'A psychoanalytic view of burnout', in B.A. Farber (ed.), *Stress and Burnout in the Human Service Professions*, New York: Pergamon Press, pp. 40–45.
Freudenberger, H.J. (1974), 'Staff burnout', *Journal of Social Issues*, **30**(1), 159–65.
Golembiewski, R.T., R.F. Munzenrider, K. Scherb and W. Billingsey (1992), 'Burnout and psychiatric "cases": early evidences of an association', *Anxiety, Stress and Coping: An International Journal*, **5**(1), 69–78.
Hallsten, L. (1993), 'Burning out: a framework', in W. Schaufeli, C. Maslach and T. Marek (eds), *Professional Burnout: Recent Developments in Theory and Research*, Washington, DC: Taylor & Francis, pp. 95–113.
Hallsten, L. (2001), 'Utbränning – en processmodell' (Burnout – a process model), *Svensk Rehabilitering*, **3**, 26–35.
Hallsten, L. and K. Isaksson (2001), 'Unemployment, precarious employment and psychological ill-health', in S. Marklund (ed.), *Worklife and Health in Sweden 2000*, Stockholm: Swedish Work Environment Authority & National Institute for Working Life.
Hallsten, L., K. Bellaagh and K. Gustafsson (2002), 'Utbränning i Sverige – en populationsstudie' (Burnout in Sweden – a population study), *Arbete och Hälsa*, **6**.
Härenstam, A., H. Westberg, L. Karlqvist, O. Leijon, A. Rydbeck, K. Waldenström, P. Wiklund, G. Nise and C. Jansson (2000), *Hur kan könsskillnader i arbets – och livsvillkor förstås?* (How to understand gender differences in work and life conditions?), Report No. 2000:16, Stockholm: National Institute for Working Life.
Johnson, M. (1997), 'On the dynamics of self-esteem. Empirical validation of basic self-esteem and earning self-esteem', unpublished PhD thesis, Stockholm University.
Kalimo, R. (1999), *Psychosocial Resources and Burnout of Women*, Report No. 1999:20, Helsinki: Finnish Institute of Occupational Health.
Kalimo, R. (2000), 'The challenge of changing work and stress for human resources. The case of Finland', *Journal of Tokyo Medical University*, **58**(3), 349–56.
Lee, R. and B. Ashforth (1996), 'A meta-analytic examination of the correlates of the three dimensions of job burnout', *Journal of Applied Psychology*, **81**, 123–33.
Marklund, S. (ed.) (2001), *Worklife and Health in Sweden 2000*, Stockholm: Swedish Work Environment Authority & National Institute for Working Life.
Maslach, C. (1976), 'Burned-out', *Human Behavior*, **5**(9), 16–22.
Maslach, C. (1982), *Burnout: The Cost of Caring*, Englewood Cliffs, NJ: Prentice-Hall.
Maslach, C. and S.E. Jackson (1981), 'The measurement of experienced burnout', *Occupational Behavior*, **2**, 99–113.
Maslach, C., S.E. Jackson and M.P. Leiter (1996), *Maslach Burnout Inventory Manual*, 3rd edn, Palo Alto: Consulting Psychologists Press.
Maslach, C., W.B. Schaufeli and M.P. Leiter (2001), 'Job burnout', *Annual Review of Psychology*, **52**, 397–422.
Murphy, G.C. and J.A. Athanasou (1999), 'The effect of unemployment on mental health', *Journal of Occupational and Organizational Psychology*, **72**(1), 83–99.
The National Social Insurance Board (2002), *Långtidssjukskrivningar för psykisk sjukdom och utbrändhet* (Long-term sickness absence for psychic illness and burnout), Report No. 2002:4, Stockholm: The National Social Insurance Board.
Pines, A.M. (1996), *Couple Burnout. Causes and Cures*, New York: Routledge.
Pines, A.M., E. Aronson and D. Kafry (1981), *Burnout: From Tedium to Personal Growth*, New York: The Free Press.
Schaufeli, W. and D. Enzmann (1998), *The Burnout Companion to Study and Practice: a Critical Analysis*, London: Taylor & Francis.
Schaufeli, W. and D. van Dierendonck (1993), 'The construct validity of two burnout measures', *Journal of Organizational Behavior*, **14**, 631–47.
Schaufeli, W.B., A.B. Bakker, K. Hoogduin, C. Schaap and A. Kladler (2001), 'On the clinical validity of the Maslach Burnout Inventory and the Burnout Measure', *Psychology and Health*, **16**, 565–82.
SWEA (The Swedish Work Environment Authority) (2000), *Work-related Health Problems 2000*, Stockholm: The Swedish Work Environment Authority, Statistics Sweden.
SWEA (The Swedish Work Environment Authority) (2001), *Negativ stress och ohälsa* (Negative stress and ill health), Stockholm: The Swedish Work Environment Authority, Statistics Sweden.
Winefield, A.H. (1995), 'Unemployment: its psychological costs', in C.L. Cooper and I.T. Robertson (eds), *International Review of Industrial and Organizational Psychology 1995*, vol. 10, Chichester: John Wiley & Sons, pp. 169–212.

35 'Burning in' – 'burning out' in public: aspects of the burnout process in community-based psychiatric services
Thomas Hyphantis and Venetsanos Mavreas

Burnout has been defined as a mental process and experience leading to work-related behavior. Its main components, emotional exhaustion, depersonalization and decreased sense of personal accomplishment (Maslach and Jackson, 1986), refer to mental experiences and symptoms similar to those of the well-known negative style of thinking which is common in depressive disorders (Beck *et al.*, 1979).

All definitions of the burnout process (Pines, 1983; Farber, 1983; Lee and Ashforth, 1990; Kuremyr *et al.*, 1994; Bendow, 1998; Iacovides *et al.*, 2003) underline the fact that burnout commonly appears in emotionally demanding situations and that it is especially common in the staff of human service workers, acknowledging 'the unique pressures of utilizing one's self as the "tool" in face to face work with the needy, demanding and often troubled clients' (Farber, 1983). This holds especially true for professionals working in the mental health services.

Psychoanalytic (Fischer, 1983), cybernetic (Heifetz and Bersani, 1983) or social competence models (Harrison, 1983) have been applied in order to clarify the nature of burnout. It is worth pointing out that Farber (1983) described burnout as 'the result of being stressed and having no "out" ', while Harrison (1983) suggested that burnout will be developed by 'persons who highly value their work but are unable to achieve the desired goals rather than accomplish a sense of competence'.

Thinking according to the psychoanalytical process, that is by employing 'free associations', words and phrases that cross one's mind along with 'burnout' are burn with desire, burn the candle at both ends, burn to the ground, burn out a fuse, burn to ashes. All these associations are characterized by an intense, strong and loud condition, which is always present *before* 'burn-out': desire, passion, challenging the 'borders', claiming victory. It seems that 'burnout' is usually preceded by a 'burnin'.

A relatively recent review on personal traits and professional burnout in heath professionals (Antoniou, 1999) stressed that heath professionals are more often individual-oriented persons, with a tendency of devotion towards their patients and an idealistic view. In particular, professionals who have decided to work with mental patients are, obviously, fond of this kind of job. It is common among professionals who work in community and rehabilitation psychiatric services to have quit or changed their previous job or position, which was probably quiet, safe and less difficult and demanding compared to the present one. It is worth pointing out that working in the aforementioned fields is characterized by a huge personal investment and frequent frustrations. Pines (1986) stressed that the most committed workers tend to burn out severely. In his opinion, the cause of burnout is existential and rests in the human need to ascribe meaning to life.

When work does not make this possible, burnout is inevitable (Pines and Aronson, 1989).

A huge personal investment results in a huge 'burn-in'. This is probably the first state that needs to be dealt with, before switching to 'burn-out'. Indeed discussion about the important interaction between the two could lead to the avoidance of 'burn-out' through understanding 'burn-in'. Interestingly, a large body of literature has shown that professionals in the mental heath services seem to be more vulnerable to the 'burn-in'–'burn-out' process. Findings from related studies contribute to the aforementioned points of our concept.

A sophisticated and relatively recent longitudinal study in the UK (Prosser et al., 1999) showed that, while staff were not becoming increasingly 'burnt out' over time, being based in the community was associated with poorer mental health over the three year-period studied, in comparison to general hospitals' psychiatric staff. Clinical mental health staff from three adult mental health sectors in inner South London participated in the study with a response rate ranging from 60 per cent to 76 per cent. The 12-item General Health Questionnaire (GHQ-12) (Goldberg and Williams, 1988), the Maslach Burnout Inventory (Maslach and Jackson, 1986) and the general job satisfaction item from the Job Diagnostic Survey (Hackman and Oldham, 1975) were used. Overall, staff had relatively high scores for 'emotional exhaustion' and poor psychological well-being. 'Overload' was significantly higher when based in the community, while nurses and social workers were found to be significantly more stressed and less satisfied than others on the basis of the combined outcome measure.

Psychiatrists working in community care seem to suffer often from burnout. Onyett et al. (1997) found psychiatrists to have some of the highest 'emotional exhaustion' scores amongst staff sampled from 57 community mental health groups. Livianos-Aldana et al. (1999), in a sample of psychiatrists attending the National Congress of Psychiatry held in Valencia, Spain, found unexpectedly higher rates in all three subscales of the Maslach Burnout Inventory than those published to date.

Another recent, carefully designed, study in Finland reported similar results (Korkeila et al., 2003). In all, 3133 licenced physicians participated in this study, with a response rate of 74 per cent. Psychiatrists and child psychiatrists reported burnout, threat of severe burnout, depression and mental disorder more commonly than other physicians. Moreover psychiatrists and child psychiatrists reported less often 'good' or 'rather good' self-perceived health. Depression had a moderate positive correlation with the overall Maslach Burnout Inventory score, indicating that emotional exhaustion, as a symptom of burnout, was common among psychiatrists, especially those working in community care.

It is interesting that the majority of the factors that were found contributing to burnout refer to a kind of closure and deprivation: lack of possibilities to consult a colleague, lack of supervision at work, lack of self-confidence, together with introversion and depression, were significantly associated with overall burnout level and emotional exhaustion (Korkeila et al., 2003). Thus a shutting-down in the communication between inside and outside, that reflects a complete splitting between 'burn-in' and 'burn-out', could be the key concept in the understanding of professional and emotional exhaustion.

Nowadays this splitting is characteristic of a particular and widespread perception that reality is experienced as split, in many and varied ways. We refer, for instance, to the split between body and soul, sensible and conceivable, inner and outer. In each case, the familiar area of reality is considered as more familiar and real while the other is downgraded to a more alien and less real state. Man usually lives in this split area: floundering around between the two sides and trying to find a solution, he is caught in the mesh of this division. But, as the Greek Nobellaureate poet Odysseas Elytis says: 'the world hasn't got two elements – it cannot be divided; and joy and sorrow look alike on man's brow'.

It could be that man, caught in this split world, avoiding and fighting with the 'other' side, is not essentially in a position to recognize and accept it. Regarding 'Burnout', according to such a division, some professionals burn out, some not. It seems that we ignore the fact that 'burn-out' in itself incorporates 'burn-in', and vice versa. Acceptance of such a division ostracizes the other side, the undesirable; it puts up a fight against it, whose result is to rule out any possibility of understanding it. But as we furiously fight against any undesirable side (that is 'burn-out'), denying essentially its reason for existence (the desirable 'burn-in'), we rule out any effort to converse with it, and hence to integrate it in our working life.

Benbow and Jolley (2002) investigated the relationship between work patterns, burnout and stress in 145 consultant old age psychiatrists, using a workload questionnaire, the Stress Checklist (Breakwell, 1990) and the Maslach Burnout Inventory. The whole group scored highly on emotional exhaustion, which was particularly intense in those who were younger and in those who spent less time on research and study.

Although a number of hypotheses for the greater degree of burnout in younger psychiatrists have been suggested (Maslach, 1982; Agius *et al.*, 1996; Moore and Cooper, 1996; Schaufeli, 1999), none has adequately interpreted this surprising finding. Taking into consideration the great enthusiasm regarding clinical practice that many of the younger professionals show, along with the 'shutting-down' of any other interest within work, such us research and study, we could suggest that an explanation for the greater burnout in younger psychiatrists lies in the aforementioned 'splitting' between 'in' and 'out'.

This splitting and isolation runs through most studies as a risk factor of burnout in psychiatric services, either as an employee's personality factor or as a workplace and organizational characteristic. A cross-sectional study, for example, in Sweden, which examined 1051 psychiatrists and mental health nurses, confirms that organizational characteristics are more important than individual ones in predicting exhaustion and professional fulfillment in mental health professionals, indicating that the psychosocial work environment and well-being of mental health professionals can be improved by concentrating on organizational factors such as efficiency, personal development and goal quality (Thomsen *et al.*, 1999).

Similar findings were reported from another study, in the United States, in which 58 per cent of the responder physicians reported high emotional exhaustion, while organizational measures were the strongest predictors of this exhaustion (Deckard *et al.*, 1994). These results permit the authors to suggest the need for organizations to examine the impact of their structures, policies and procedures on physician stress and quality of work-life.

On the other hand, research conducted among consultant psychiatrists has repeatedly shown that personality traits (for example openness, agreeableness) as well as work-related variables (for example psychiatrists versus trainees, high versus low job satisfaction) have been considered as factors of high risk for emotional exhaustion, while burnout was more likely to occur among psychiatrists than among other medical practitioners.

In agreement with the above-mentioned findings are the results of Deary *et al.*'s (1996) study. They compared a randomly selected group of consultant psychiatrists with a combined group of physicians and surgeons on several stress-related variables. According to the results, psychiatrists reported fewer clinical work demands and differed significantly from physicians and surgeons by being high in neuroticism, openness and agreeableness as well as low in conscientiousness. In addition, psychiatrists were more depressed and emotionally exhausted than other physicians. However they did not report more work-related stress than physicians and surgeons. Within the group of psychiatrists, high correlations with stress-related variables were obtained, suggesting that there might be a disposition to experience negative emotions in some individuals. Moreover, this study, in addition to our introductory comments regarding the personal and emotional investment underlying the choice of community psychiatry as a career, suggests that particular personality characteristics might dispose some people toward their choice of profession.

Additional research in this area concerned the impact of work-related variables on consultants' mental health and indicated risk factors for burnout. Ramirez *et al.* (1996) examined the relationship between mental health and job stress and satisfaction, as well as job and demographic characteristics among four specialist groups in the UK, including consultants. Results indicated that there were non-significant differences between the four groups regarding psychiatric morbidity. It seemed that job satisfaction significantly protected consultants' mental health against job stress. Both burnout and psychiatric morbidity were associated with stress-related factors, involving feeling overloaded and the effect overload has on home life, feeling poorly managed and resourced as well as dealing with patients' suffering. Burnout was also associated with low satisfaction when relationships with patients, relatives and staff, professional status/esteem and intellectual stimulation were taken into account. In addition, results indicated that being aged 55 years or under and being single were independent risk factors for burnout. Burnout was also found to be more prevalent among consultants who felt insufficiently trained in communication and management skills. The authors concluded that consultants' mental health is likely to be protected against the high demands of medical practice in terms of maintaining or enhancing job satisfaction by providing training in communication and management skills.

The risk of 'burning-out' among young trainees in psychiatry should not be overlooked. On these grounds, an important topic of research might involve studying job-related variables within the group of psychiatrists and their impact on burnout occurrence. Indeed, in a study carried out by Amstutz *et al.* (2001), potentially burnout-related variables (for example demographic characteristics, work, leisure activities and personality) were assessed for three subgroups of psychiatrists: residents, psychiatrists working as staff members or in leading positions in psychiatric institutions and psychiatrists working in private practice. Results indicated that psychiatric residents reported significantly higher emotional exhaustion. They also obtained higher scores on neuroticism and lower scores on frustration tolerance on the Munich Personality Test. As far as work-related variables were concerned, they turned out to be of slight importance only, whereas no influence could be demonstrated for participating in different leisure activities.

Such findings were in accordance with the ones that Greenfeld (1985) ended up with, after reviewing the existing literature on the distressing or painful aspects of the psychotherapeutic role. He indicated that a failure to cope adequately with distress generated during the training period might lead to continued distress and distortion of the psychotherapeutic role. In terms of prevention, the author suggested that an open discussion of the distressing aspects of the psychotherapeutic role, an increased focus on the problems dealt with during the training period as well as practical suggestions for reducing the intensity of this distress may progressively reduce or correct these painful aspects of training and practice.

At this point it might be important to underline once again that young therapists are the ones that are usually susceptible to emotional exhaustion and that display great enthusiasm regarding clinical practice. It is such openness as well as the acceptance of, or even the adjustment to, these difficulties that mainly contribute to emotional exhaustion.

With regard to other findings concerning personality involvement in burnout, one realizes that the role of such 'closeness' as was previously reported remains central. According to a prospective study conducted by McCranie and Brandsma (1988), physicians that appeared to have low self-esteem, expressed feelings of inadequacy, dysphoria and obsessive worry, passivity, social anxiety as well as withdrawal from others, shortly before entering the medical school, were more likely to display emotional exhaustion. In other words, those who seem withdrawn and 'closed up' appear to be at great risk of burning.

Other findings concerning coping strategies that are engaged against distress have been on the same lines. In particular they underline the role of certain personality features, such as sociability and sense of humor, as being of great importance (Scheiber, 1987). They additionally stress the role of talking to others and employing coping methods other than avoidance (Cushway, 1992). These results confirm the role of openness and communication between inside and outside, in the prevention of burnout.

The focus of the present chapter is to lay emphasis on aspects of burnout in community-based psychiatric employees underlying the greater corpus of recent research on the topic. It has been apparent that the understanding of a syndrome such as 'burnout' could not be complete without taking into account the other side of the condition, the commitment, investment, urge and drive towards being employed in meaningful work, which sometimes turns a motive, a stimulus and a fire-raising factor into a destroyer, a devastator and an arsonist. Acceptance and recognition of such a relation between the two opposite aspects of the condition could lead to a better understanding of the nature of 'burning' in work, avoiding divisions that are concentrated only on 'burning out', ignoring the urge of 'burning in'.

The division between inside and outside only substantiates the non-acceptance of the otherness. Besides, in this division probably lies the root of an atmosphere of false intimacy, pseudo-collusion and symbiosis we often find in the intermediate community psychiatric structures (Simpson, 1989; Van Humbeeck et al., 2001), indicating a loss of distance from the other side and an absence of a sense of non-intimacy, absolutely necessary in our view, since otherness is indeed inaccessible and non-intimate.

All the above-mentioned studies showed that the more closed the community mental health personnel is, the greater the risk of emotional exhaustion, and that the more closed the organization is, the higher the risk of burnout. The openness and exchange between the two opposites could permit an understanding of burnout as illness and not as 'dis-ease', that is a kind of comfort deprivation.

Burnout can be seen as a reminder that the inhabitants of the system have reached their limits, even if they are no longer the limits of a weak man before omnipotence, but respect before something that is far beyond. The well-known psychotherapeutic practice leads our minds to Faust, who preferred burning eternally, in order to live in flames: 'the air is now is so full of phantoms that no-one can avoid them'.

References

Agius, R.M., H. Blenkin, I.J. Deary, H.E. Zealley and R.A. Wood (1996), 'Survey of perceived stress and work demands of consultant doctors', *Journal of Occupational and Environmental Medicine*, **53**, 217–24.
Amstutz, M.C., M. Neuenschwander and J. Modestin (2001), 'Burnout in psychiatric physicians. Results of an empirical study', *Psychiatrische Praxis*, **28**(4), 163–7.
Antoniou, A-.S. (1999), 'Personal Traits and Professional Burnout in Health Professionals', *Archives of Hellenic Medicine*, **16**(1), 20–28.
Beck, A.T., A.J. Rush, B.F. Shaw and G. Emery (1979), *Cognitive Therapy of Depression*, New York: Guilford.
Benbow, S. (1998), 'Burnout: current knowledge and relevance to old age psychiatry', *International Journal of Geriatric Psychiatry*, **13**, 520–26.
Benbow, S.M. and D.J. Jolley (2002), 'Burnout and stress amongst old age psychiatrists', *International Journal of Geriatric Psychiatry*, **17**(8), 710–4.
Breakwell, G.M. (1990), 'Are you stressed out?', *American Journal of Nursing*, **90**, 31–3.
Cushway, D. (1992), 'Stress in clinical psychology trainees', *British Journal of Clinical Psychology*, **31**(2), 169–79.
Deary, I.J., R.M. Agius and A. Sadler (1996), 'Personality and stress in consultant psychiatrists', *International Journal of Social Psychiatry*, **42**(2), 112–23.
Deckard, G., M. Meterko and D. Field (1994), 'Physician burnout: an examination of personal, professional, and organizational relationships', *Medical Care*, **32**(7), 745–54.
Farber, B.A. (1983), 'Introduction: a critical perspective on burnout', in B.A. Farber (ed.), *Stress and Burnout in the Human Service Professions*, Oxford: Pergamon.
Fischer, H.J. (1983), 'A psychoanalytic view of burnout', in B.A. Farber (ed.), *Stress and Burnout in the Human Service Professions*, Oxford: Pergamon.
Goldberg, D. and P. Williams (1988), *A Users' Guide to the General Health Questionnaire*, Windsor: NFER-Nelson.
Greenfeld, D. (1985), 'Stresses of the psychotherapeutic role', *Hillside Journal of Clinical Psychiatry*, **7**(2), 165–83.
Hackman, J.R. and G.R. Oldham (1975), 'Development of the Job Diagnostic Survey', *Journal of Applied Psychology*, **60**, 159–70.
Harrison, W.D. (1983), 'A social competence model of burnout', in B.A. Farber (ed.), *Stress and Burnout in the Human Service Professions*, Oxford: Pergamon.
Heifetz, L.J. and H.A. Bersani (1983), 'Disrupting the cybernetics of personal growth: toward a unified theory of burnout in the human services', in B.A. Farber (ed.), *Stress and Burnout in the Human Service Professions*, Oxford: Pergamon.
Iacovides, A., K.N. Fountoulakis, S. Kaprinis and G. Kaprinis (2003), 'The relationship between job stress, burnout and clinical depression', *Journal of Affective Disorders*, **75**(3), 209–21.
Korkeila, J.A., S. Toyry, K. Kumpulainen, J.M. Toivola, K. Rasanen and R. Kalimo (2003), 'Burnout and self-perceived health among Finnish psychiatrists and child psychiatrists: a national survey', *Scandinavian Journal of Public Health*, **31**(2), 85–91.
Kuremyr, D., M. Kihlgren, A. Norberg, S. Astrom and I. Karlsson (1994), 'Emotional experiences, empathy and burnout among staff caring for demented patients at a collective living unit and a nursing home', *Journal of Advanced Nursing*, **19**, 670–9.
Lee, R.T. and B.E. Ashforth (1990), 'On the meaning of Maslach's three dimensions of burnout', *Journal of Applied Psychology*, **75**, 743.
Livianos-Aldana, L., C. De Las Cuevas Castresana, L. Rojo Moreno (1999), 'Psychiatrist's burnout: a survey', *Actas Españolas Psiquiatria*, **27**(5), 305–9.
Maslach, C. (1982), *Burnout – the Cost of Caring*, New York: Prentice-Hall.
Maslach, C. and S. Jackson (1986), *Maslach Burnout Inventory Manual*, Palo Alto, CA: Consulting Psychologists Press.

McCranie, E.W. and J.M. Brandsma (1988), 'Personality antecedents of burnout among middle-aged physicians', *Behavioral Medicine*, **14**(1), 30–36.

Moore, K.A. and C.L. Cooper (1996), 'Stress in mental health professionals: a theoretical overview', *International Journal of Social Psychiatry*, **42**, 82–9.

Onyett, S., T. Pillenger and M. Muijen (1997), 'Job satisfaction and burnout among members of community mental health teams', *Journal of Mental Health*, **6**, 55–66.

Pines, A. and E. Aronson (1989), *Career Burnout: Causes and Cures*, New York: The Free Press, p. xii.

Pines, A.M. (1986), 'Who is to blame for helper's burnout? Environmental impact', in C.D. Scott and K. Hawk (eds), *Heal Thyself: The Health of Health Care Professionals*, New York: Brunner/Mazel.

Pines, A.P. (1983), 'On burnout and the buffering effects of social support', in B.A. Farber (ed.), *Stress and Burnout in the Human Service Professions*, Oxford: Pergamon.

Prosser, D., S. Johnson, E. Kuipers, G. Dunn, G. Szmukler, Y. Reid, P. Bebbington and G. Thornicroft (1999), 'Mental health, "burnout" and job satisfaction in a longitudinal study of mental health staff', *Social Psychiatry and Psychiatric Epidemiology*, **34**(6), 295–300.

Ramirez, A.J., J. Graham, M.A. Richards, A. Cull and W.M. Gregory (1996), 'Mental health of hospital consultants: the effects of stress and satisfaction at work', *Lancet*, **16**, 347(9003), 724–8.

Schaufeli, W. (1999), 'Burnout', in J. Firth-Cozens and R.L. Payne (eds), *Stress in Health Professionals: Psychological and Organisational Causes and Interventions*, Chichester: Wiley, pp. 17–32.

Scheiber, S.C. (1987), 'Stress in physicians', in R. Payne and J. Firth-Cozens (eds), *Stress in Health Professionals*, Chichester: Wiley.

Simpson, R.B.C. (1989), 'Expressed emotion and nursing the schizophrenic patient', *Journal of Advanced Nursing*, **14**, 459–66.

Thomsen, S., J. Soares, P. Nolan, J. Dallender and B. Arnetz (1999), 'Feelings of professional fulfilment and exhaustion in mental health personnel: the importance of organisational and individual factors', *Psychother Psychosom*, **68**(3), 157–64.

Van, Humbeeck G., Ch. Van Audenhove, G. Pieters, M. De Hert, G. Storms, H. Vertommen, J. Peuskens and J. Heyman (2001), 'Expressed emotion in staff–client relationships: the professionals' and residents' perspectives', *Soc Psychiatry Psychiatr Epidemiol*, **36**, 486–92.

36 A mediation model of job burnout
Michael P. Leiter and Christina Maslach

A mediation model of job burnout

Job stress has been recognized as a significant occupational hazard which can impair both health and work performance (for example Sauter and Murphy, 1995). The worker's internal experience of stress is assumed to play a mediating role between the impact of external job demands (stressors) and work-related outcomes (such as absenteeism or illness). This basic model should be especially true of the stress phenomenon known as 'job burnout', which involves a prolonged response to chronic interpersonal job conditions (Maslach, 1993). Our research in this area leads us to propose that organizational conditions influence a worker's experience of burnout (or of its positive opposite of job engagement). The level of burnout or engagement will then determine how well the worker does the job, and how he or she feels about the larger organization. For example, assessments of employees' level of experienced burnout or engagement have predicted clients' evaluation of service quality (Leiter et al., 1998) and employees' evaluation of organizational change (Leiter and Harvie, 1998).

Two decades of research on burnout have identified the three key dimensions of this phenomenon (exhaustion, cynicism and a lack of effectiveness), a plethora of organizational risk factors across many occupations in various countries, and some work-related outcomes (see Maslach et al., 2001; Schaufeli and Enzmann, 1998). However there has not yet been much research that directly tests the proposed mediation model by including measures of all three model components: experienced burnout organizational factors and work-related outcomes. The current study was designed as a first approximation of such a test.

Experienced burnout

Burnout is a syndrome of exhaustion, cynicism and inefficacy experienced by people in their worklife (Maslach et al., 1996). Burnout describes the endpoint of a three-dimensional continuum of energy, involvement, and efficacy. At the opposite end of this continuum is engagement with work, characterized by feeling energetic, involved in one's work, and efficacious. An individual's position on the continuum from burnout to engagement has direct implications for quality of life and indirect implications for health and performance. Burnout has been the focus of a considerable scope of applied research since the mid 1970s (Schaufeli and Enzmann, 1998).

Organizational factors

Our greatest challenge was to devise a measure of organizational factors. In reviewing the proliferation of organizational correlates in many studies of burnout and job stress, we had identified six key domains: workload, control, reward, community, fairness and values (Maslach and Leiter, 1997; Leiter and Maslach, 1999; Leiter and Maslach, 2004). The first two areas are reflected in the Demand–Control model of job stress (Karasek and

Theorell, 1990), and 'reward' refers to the power of reinforcements to shape behavior. 'Community' captures all of the work on social support and role conflict, while 'fairness' emerges from the literature on equity and social justice. Finally, the area of values picks up the cognitive–emotional power of job goals and expectations.

A consistent theme throughout this research literature is the problematic relationship between the individual and the situation, which is often described in terms of imbalance or misalignment or misfit: for example, the demands of the job exceed the capacity of the individual to cope effectively. Some of the earliest models of organizational stress focused on this notion of job–person fit, and subsequent theorizing continued to highlight the importance of both individual and contextual factors (see Kahn and Byosiere, 1992). The general concept of person–job fit has had a long history of trying to address variations in people's reaction to the workplace by considering the congruence between personal and organizational characteristics (for more recent examples, see Finnegan, 2000; Lauver and Kristof-Brown, 2001; O'Reilly et al., 1999; Schneider, 2001). In addition to its theoretical significance, this notion of congruence has an applied relevance, as we have found that employees consider it meaningful to describe their work experience in these terms.

Our goal, then, was to develop a measure that would apply this basic idea of congruence to the assessment of the six key areas of work life. In addition, we wanted this measure to have a generic format that could be utilized easily by a wide range of employees in a variety of organizations. We chose to focus on people's judgment of the congruence itself, and not on the two component parts of person and of job. In this regard, we adopted the Lewinian analysis as described by Schneider (2001) which argues for the greater value of assessing the person and the job together as a total constellation, rather than assessing them separately and computing their 'fit' post hoc. Thus our new measure asks respondents to rate their level of experienced congruence with the job within the six domains of work life. It is not designed to test directly any theory of person–job fit. This new measure, the Areas of Worklife Scale, has the potential to provide useful diagnostic information to organizations interested in interventions to deal with burnout (Leiter and Maslach, 2000).

Six areas of worklife The basic hypothesis in our mediation model is that, the greater the perceived incongruence between the person and the job in these six areas, the greater the likelihood of burnout; conversely, the greater the perceived congruence, the greater the likelihood of engagement with work. This would suggest a simple additive model, in which incongruence in each of the six areas would contribute separately to greater burnout. However the research literature suggests the possibility of more complex interrelationships between the six areas, and the current study provides the opportunity to test that possibility.

Studies have consistently found workload to be a strong and distinct predictor of the exhaustion dimension of burnout (Cordes and Dougherty, 1993; Maslach et al., 2001; Schaufeli and Enzmann, 1998). Structural models of burnout have shown that exhaustion then mediates the relationship of workload to the other two dimensions of burnout (Lee and Ashforth, 1996; Leiter and Harvie, 1998). This association reflects the relationship of work demands to occupational stress in the stress and coping literature (Cox et al., 1993).

The Demand–Control theory of job stress (Karasek and Theorell, 1990) has made the case for the enabling role of control. This area includes employees' perceived capacity to influence decisions that affect their work, to exercise professional autonomy and to gain access to the resources necessary to do an effective job. A sense of control indicates that individuals feel they have sufficient authority to perform effectively, yet are not overwhelmed by excessive responsibility at work. Because control is so central to employees' ability to influence the people and processes that determine the quality of worklife, we propose that it serves as the starting point in our mediation model and will influence the extent to which people can attain congruence in the other areas, especially workload, reward, fairness and community. In contrast to the interaction of demand and control predicted by the Karasek and Theorell model, we proposed a series of main effects such that insufficient control and excessive workload will each aggravate burnout and sufficient control and manageable workload will promote engagement with work. Control derives its pivotal position in the model from its implication of agency: control reflects employees' sense of having the freedom and capacity to make consequential choices. Although excessive workload may constrain employees' options, it does not in itself determine employees' professional autonomy or administrative authority. In contrast employees view work that they have chosen differently from work that others or circumstances impose upon them.

The reward area of worklife addresses the extent to which rewards – monetary, social and intrinsic – are consistent with expectations. Fairness is the extent to which decisions at work are perceived as being fair and people are treated with respect. It reflects employees' experience of institutional justice at work (Tyler, 1990). Community is the overall quality of social interaction at work, including issues of conflict, mutual support, closeness and the capacity to work as a team. This area encompasses the extensive research on social support and burnout (see Greenglass *et al.*, 1994).

The area of values plays an integrating role in the model, reflecting the overall consistency in the other areas of worklife. Consequently it mediates the relationship of the other areas with the psychological experience of burnout or engagement. Congruence in values indicates that the organization's central values are consistent with those of the employee. The individual embraces the organization's mission as a personal mission whose fulfillment is consistent with personal aspirations. When values are incongruent, employees perceive the organization's mission to be incompatible with their own well-being and that of the larger community.

Work-related outcome
To test our mediation model across multiple samples, we needed to identify a more generic work-related outcome that would be relevant and significant for all respondents. The ideal measure – an independently assessed behavioral indicator – is rarely available from participating organizations. We decided to measure employees' evaluation of the general change within the organization: whether they saw things getting better or worse within the workplace. A positive perception of change is a central outcome in post-industrial organizations that emphasize quality of service and must continually adapt to volatile conditions.

Organizational change is best viewed as a continuous process shaped by strategic decisions, in contrast with a model of rigidity disrupted on occasion by change agents (Weick and Quinn, 1999). The relevant question from the perspective of continuous change is the extent to which employees perceive the organization as changing for better or for worse, not whether they perceive any change at all. Especially important to employees' capacity to function in a productive and fulfilling fashion are high-performance management practices that pertain to job security, decision making, training, hiring, compensation, communication and reduced status distinctions (Pfeffer, 1998). Employees' evaluation of the direction of continuous change in these practices is an informative indicator of their overall relationship with their work and, as such, a central outcome measure. The measure has a temporal dimension as it is based on employees' perceptions of developments over the previous months. This assessment holds implications for employees' views of their organization's future to the extent that the measure reflects an overall trajectory of improvement or deterioration. Evaluation of organizational change is highly appropriate as an outcome measure when specific behavioral indicators are unavailable as it reflects the extent to which employees view their organization as a secure, appropriate and attractive focus for their creative energies.

Hypotheses
Prior research has concentrated primarily on the impact of the work environment with experienced burnout. There has been less consideration of the role of burnout in mediating the relationship of the work environment with important outcomes, and little that has explored pathways among the six areas of the work environment. The study to be reported here explores a more complete model, including both direct and mediated pathways.

Our analysis leads to the following hypotheses. The first set proposes the replication of the standard pathways among the three dimensions of burnout: exhaustion predicts cynicism that in turn negatively predicts efficacy. Second, all three dimensions are proposed to predict the outcome of evaluation of change. The third set of hypotheses concerns the relationship of the six areas of worklife to the three dimensions of burnout. As discussed earlier, workload is predicted to have a direct path to exhaustion. 'Values' is predicted to mediate the relationship of all areas (except workload) with the three dimensions of burnout. The integrating role of values is consistent with its definition as a relatively abstract area of worklife. In contrast the other five areas of worklife have an explicit basis in employees' day-to-day interactions with people, tasks and events at work. 'Values' is conceived and measured to reflect employees' overall assessment of the extent to which the basic quality of these interactions indicates that the organization furthers what is important and valuable to employees. In this model, employees' specific interactions with the workplace are the basis of their evaluation of the workplace in contrast to a trait-based perspective that employees' attitudes determine their interactions. While this research does not explicitly contrast trait and situational models, it is important to acknowledge the situational nature of the model that guides these hypotheses. Control is predicted to be related to the other areas of workload, reward, fairness and community.

The combined set of hypotheses forms the Mediation Model depicted in Figure 36.1. The viability of this model will be tested in several steps, each of which focuses on a distinct aspect of the model. The objective of these contrasts is not to pit one theory against another, but to consider the extent to which each element of the model contributes to the overall fit. Without such contrasts, a model with a good overall fit may include elements

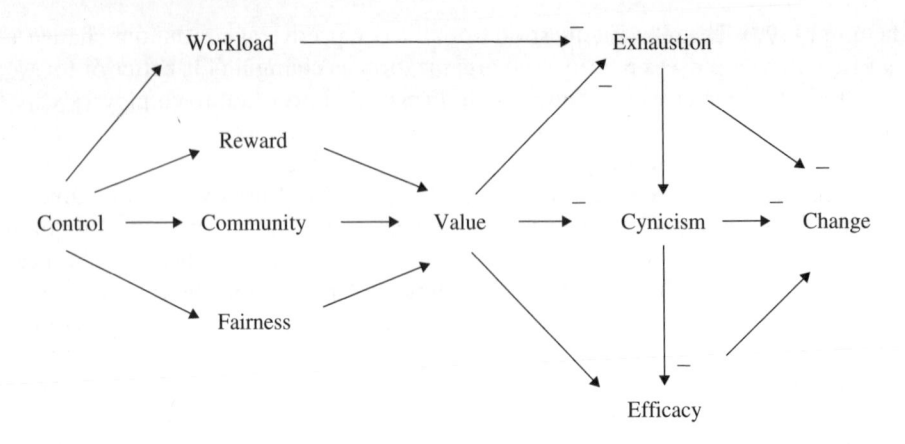

Figure 36.1   Hypothesized model

of little consequence. The Mediation Model will be contrasted with two baseline models: first, an Independence Model (no factor loadings and no paths among the latent variables) and, second, a Structural Null Model (factor loadings but no paths among the latent variables). Thirdly, the Mediation Model will be contrasted with a Burnout Null Model (including the paths from exhaustion to cynicism and from cynicism to efficacy only). The Burnout Null Model is a meaningful contrast point, as the Mediation Model is meant to improve the prediction beyond the paths among the three dimensions of burnout.

The fourth contrast will be with a Burnout Predictor Model, which includes (1) the paths from burnout to the outcome of change, and (2) the paths from both workload and values to burnout. This model comprises the basic components of the mediation model, but does not include any of the relationships among the six areas of worklife. Note that the path from workload to exhaustion is negative because workload, consistent with the other five areas of worklife, is measured in terms of congruence, with a higher score indicating a more manageable workload.

The analysis will then add the paths among these six areas in two steps. Thus the fifth contrast will be the Values Model, which adds the paths of reward, community and fairness with values, consistent with the role of values as summarizing a person's view of a work setting. The full Mediation Model will add the paths of control to the other areas, consistent with the proposed role of control noted in the introduction. Finally the analysis will test the mediation hypothesis by assessing whether there is additional explanatory power in an Alternative Model, which adds a direct path from values to evaluation of change. This last test contrasts the mediation role of burnout with a model in which worklife directly affects outcomes without shaping a person's levels of exhaustion, cynicism or efficacy.

Method

A survey was administered to the entire workforce of two organizations. The assessment was carried out as an organizational check-up on institutional well-being, utilizing a check-up survey process developed by the authors in their prior research (Leiter and Maslach, 2000). In both samples, there was an interest in assessing the current organizational climate (although the reasons for doing so were quite different). In each organization, the process of administering the survey to all employees was overseen by a check-up survey team that was selected to be (1) representative of the constituencies within the organization, (2) explicitly supported by senior management, and (3) highly collaborative through all levels and departments of the larger organization. This process is designed to produce a high level of employee participation within the organization, with a minimum goal of a 70 per cent response rate (see Leiter and Maslach, 2000 for details of this organizational check-up process). The authors guided each organization through the process and provided participants with a comprehensive report. In both samples, the assessment process included measures of the three key components of the model: the six domains of worklife, experienced job burnout and evaluation of organizational change.

Participants
A test of the new measure and of the full model required a large sample of employees who worked within a common organizational setting. Two such organizational samples were obtained, in order to test the viability of the model in two distinct work environments, as well as across a range of occupations.

University sample A university was facing a number of critical issues involving staff morale and performance. Within the student services division of that university, the Human Resources office took a fresh new look at human resources management and organizational development. As a result, several initiatives surfaced. One was to assess the quality of work life through the eyes of the staff. A proposal was made to senior management which requested that staff be surveyed. The results of the survey would enable this organization to further enhance the quality of work life by implementing new initiatives and programs.

The organization distributed surveys to all 905 staff members in the various settings that provided student services; this division of the university did not include academic staff. The researchers received 740 completed surveys for a response rate of 81.8 per cent. The sample for this analysis consisted of only the 602 full-time employees. Of the respondents, 65.3 per cent were female, and 34.7 per cent were male. Participants had worked at the organization for varying lengths of time: 3.8 per cent had worked at the organization for more than 25 years, 13.1 per cent for 16 to 25 years, 35 per cent for six to 15 years, 34.7 per cent for one to five years, and 13.4 per cent for less than one year. Their occupations included student service professionals (139), administrative and clerical (134), facilities maintenance (98), operations (86), food services (83), senior management (34), computing and technical (34) and communications (16).

Hospital sample Three health care institutions in a large city were undergoing a merger that had been mandated by the provincial government. One of the sites was a major research hospital that covered a wide range of tertiary health specialties. The other two sites had distinct focus areas defined by patient population in one site and type of disorder in the other site. The senior management of the newly merged institution initiated a survey of all staff members to provide an information flow that would facilitate the success of the merger. The differences in history and focus of the three sites as well as staff members' initial reactions to the merger suggested that the institution faced a major challenge in integrating the values and operations of the three sites. The sites differed in the relative importance that they placed on clinical research, education and patient care. The primary operational challenge faced by the two smaller institutions upon integration was to function as a large-scale institution rather than as a moderately small stand-alone facility. The dynamics of this challenge were evident in comments by managers and front-line staff members, which disparaged the other settings and expressed skepticism about the potential to integrate services. On the basis of anecdotal observations of a divisive organizational culture, management contracted for a detailed assessment of the employees' response to their work situation.

The organization distributed surveys to all 3500 staff members in the various settings. The researchers received 2633 completed surveys for a response rate of 75.2 per cent. The sample for this analysis was the 2009 full-time employees within these responses. Of the respondents, 82.1 per cent were female. Participants had worked at the organization for varying lengths of time: 12.6 per cent had worked at the organization for more than 21 years, 33.1 per cent for 11 to 20 years, 24.8 per cent for 6 to 10 years, 19.8 per cent for 1 to 5 years, and 9.7 per cent for less than one year. Occupational groups included nurses (30.7 per cent), other health professionals (23.1 per cent), service workers (9.0 per cent), researchers (3.1 per cent), clerical workers (14.1 per cent), corporate support (4.7 per cent), management (7.2 per cent) and other (8.2 per cent). Physicians declined to participate in the survey as they were not employees of the hospital, but utilized the facilities as independent professionals.

Measures

Three measures assessed the primary elements of the study: the six areas of worklife, the three dimensions of burnout and people's evaluation of change. In each of the two settings these measures were sections of larger questionnaires that addressed other issues of concern to the respective organizations.

Burnout The Maslach Burnout Inventory–General Scale (MBI–GS) (Schaufeli *et al.*, 1996) measures the three dimensions of the burnout–engagement continuum: exhaustion–energy, cynicism–involvement and inefficacy–efficacy. The items are framed as statements of job-related feelings (for example 'I feel burned out from my work', 'I feel confident that I am effective at getting things done') and are rated on a six-point frequency scale (ranging from 'never' to 'daily'). Burnout is reflected in higher scores on exhaustion and cynicism, and lower scores on efficacy, while the opposite pattern reflects greater engagement. Developed from the original MBI (Maslach and Jackson, 1981), which was designed for human service occupations, the MBI–GS is a 16-item measure that evaluates burnout among people in all occupations. Thus the MBI–GS was appropriate for all employees within the participating organizations, providing comparative data among units and occupational groups.

Six areas of worklife The Areas of Worklife Scale (AWS) measure (Leiter and Maslach, 2000) comprises 29 items that produce distinct scores for each of the six areas of worklife: workload (6), control (3), reward (4), community (5), fairness (6) and values (5). The items were worded as statements of perceived congruence or incongruence between oneself and the job. Thus each subscale includes positively worded items of congruence, for example, 'I have enough time to do what's important in my job' (workload) and negatively worded items of incongruence, for example, 'Working here forces me to compromise my values' (values). Respondents indicate their degree of agreement with these statements on a five-point Likert-type scale ranging from one (strongly disagree), through three (hard to decide), to five (strongly agree). The scoring for the negatively worded items is reversed. For each of the six subscales, the AWS measure defines congruence as a high score (greater then 3.00), indicating a higher degree of perceived alignment between the workplace and the respondent's preferences. Conversely it defines incongruence as a low score (less than 3.00), indicating more perceived misalignment or misfit between the worker and the workplace. The AWS items were developed from a series of staff surveys conducted by the Centre for Organizational Research & Development (Leiter and Harvie, 1998; Maslach and Leiter, 1997) as a means of assessing the constructs underlying our analysis of the six areas of worklife. The scale has yielded a consistent factor structure across samples and has shown consistently high correlations with the MBI–GS (Leiter and Maslach, 1999).

Evidence for the validity of the items was provided by examining the correspondence of scores on the Areas of Worklife measure with written comments provided by participants in the hospital study. The overwhelming proportion of the comments submitted by 1443 participants contained complaints. A qualitative analysis assigned comments from individuals to nodes, many of which were relevant to the six areas of worklife. Table 36.1 displays correlations of scores on the six areas of worklife with a binary indicator of whether an individual wrote a complaint within the various categories listed in the first column. The second column indicates the area of worklife most directly relevant to each node. The pattern of correlations in Table 36.1 indicates that complaints were most strongly correlated with scores on the area of worklife which was most directly relevant.

Further evidence of the AWS validity is evident in the correspondence of participants' ratings of control with their supervisory role within the organizations. In the university sample, those with supervisory responsibility rated control more highly ($M = 3.69$, $SD = 0.80$, $N = 183$) than those with no supervisory responsibilities ($M = 3.48$, $SD = 0.90$, $N = 104$) or those who supervised only student employees ($M = 3.46$, $SD = 0.96$, $N = 284$) ($F_{(2, 568)} = 3.81$, $p < 0.05$). In the hospital, senior managers scored highest on control ($M = 3.78$, $SD = 0.70$, $N = 16$), followed by directors ($M = 3.40$, $SD = 0.87$, $N = 37$) and supervisors ($M = 3.24$, $SD = 0.79$, $N = 309$), and front-line staff ($M = 2.91$, $SD = 0.81$, $N = 1514$) ($F_{(3, 1872)} = 22.44$, $p < 0.001$). These patterns support the discriminant and convergent validity of the AWS.

Evaluation of change Evaluation of change was assessed by 11 items in the hospital sample and 12 items in the university sample, of which the first three items were used in the model testing. This measure has served as an outcome measure in previous research (Leiter and Harvie, 1998). Participants rated items on a five-point Likert-type scale from one (much worse) through three (no change) to five (much better), in response to an introductory sentence: 'How do you perceive changes over the past six months in the following?' As explained below, the causal model analysis limited each latent variable to three indicators. The three items used in the model testing referred to 'services you provide',

Table 36.1 Correspondence with qualitative analysis

Category	Area of worklife	Workload	Control	Rewards	Community	Fairness	Values
Workload on wards	Workload	**−0.14**	0.02	−0.05	0.00	−0.02	0.02
Workload (administrative)	Workload	**−0.13**	−0.06	−0.02	−0.05	−0.03	−0.01
Patient care concerns	Workload	**−0.09**	−0.05	−0.06	−0.07	−0.04	−0.04
Number of staff	Workload	**−0.06**	−0.04	−0.04	−0.03	−0.06	0.01
Clerical support	Workload	**−0.08**	0.07	0.01	0.02	−0.02	0.04
Distribution of workload	Workload	**−0.06**	−0.04	−0.06	−0.06	−0.04	−0.04
Timing of amalgamation	Workload	**−0.10**	0.00	0.00	0.01	−0.03	−0.02
Excessive/ unproductive meetings	Control	−0.04	**0.08**	0.06	0.00	0.05	0.05
Professional autonomy/ control	Control	−0.06	**−0.08**	−0.05	−0.03	−0.07	0.00
Flexible work times and place	Control	0.02	**−0.06**	−0.01	−0.01	−0.03	0.00
Positive feedback and appreciation	Reward	−0.03	−0.02	**−0.07**	0.01	−0.03	−0.01
Appreciation	Reward	−0.05	−0.08	**−0.11**	−0.03	−0.02	−0.07
Accountability for work	Community	−0.07	−0.02	−0.04	**−0.10**	−0.05	−0.01
Fairness	Fairness	0.00	−0.05	−0.12	−0.07	**−0.14**	−0.07
Educational opportunities	Fairness	−0.04	−0.03	−0.06	0.01	**−0.08**	−0.06
Trust	Fairness	0.01	−0.06	−0.06	−0.04	**−0.11**	0.03
Working relationships	Fairness	−0.07	−0.06	−0.07	−0.05	**−0.10**	−0.03
Respect	Fairness	−0.05	−0.04	−0.11	**−0.07**	**−0.07**	−0.03
Fair distribution of rewards	Fairness	−0.03	−0.07	**−0.08**	−0.06	**−0.08**	−0.02
Staff involvement/input	Values	−0.03	−0.01	−0.03	−0.04	−0.09	**−0.09**
Social get-togethers/ functions	Values	−0.02	0.01	0.05	0.03	−0.02	**0.08**

Note: **Bold** type indicates largest correlation in a row.

'your involvement in decisions that affect your work' and 'your job security'. All three issues – services, decision making and job security – have been issues of concern in burnout research (Schaufeli and Enzmann, 1998) and were identified as critical challenges in the participating organizations. Pfeffer (1998) identified job security and decentralized decision making as basic conditions for employees' positive evaluation of organizational change. Although the scale assesses a wide range of issues, the measure focuses on respondents' general assessment of progress within the organization, as evident in the relatively high level of inter-item consistency across the scale items (alpha = 0.95). This pattern is consistent with that of a causal construct (Bollen and Lennox, 1991) in which responses on diverse items are determined by an underlying construct. The timeframe of six months was consistent with that of the MBI–GS, as well as with a reasonable span for employees to consider when evaluating their work settings. Further, it provided a consistent metric across the two samples. The overall variable of evaluation of change is computed as the average rating across all of the change items.

Results
Descriptive statistics
Tables 36.2 and 36.3 display the descriptive statistics and means for the variables for the university sample and the hospital sample, respectively. In regard to the mean scores for the areas of worklife, a rating of 3.00 is neutral, with means above 3.00 indicating a positive perception of the experienced congruence with that area of work life, and means below 3.00 indicating a negative perception of a greater incongruence. In the university sample, the most positive rating within the six areas is control (3.53) followed by community (3.32), values (3.28), and reward (3.21). The most negative rating was within fairness (2.63). Evaluation of change received a slightly positive rating of 3.06. In the hospital sample, the most positive rating within the six areas is values (3.60) followed by community (3.31). The most negative rating was within workload (2.56) followed by fairness (2.68). Evaluation of change received a slightly negative rating of 2.85. For both samples, scores on the three dimensions of job burnout were in the normative range reported for various occupational groups (Maslach et al., 1996). The correlations were in the expected direction, and all were statistically significant except for the correlation of workload with efficacy in the university sample.

Model testing
The hypothesized model was tested against data from each of the two samples using a structural equation modeling program (EQS) (Bentler, 1995). This analysis was structured to consider (1) the overall fit of the model, and (2) whether all of the paths in Figure 36.1 are statistically significant. It also provided a confirmatory factor analysis for all of the measures in the model. The analysis also considered the extent to which the burnout–engagement continuum mediates the relationship of the six areas of worklife with the outcome of evaluation of change. In this analysis only three indicators were used as indicators of each of the latent variables: the three dimensions of burnout, the six areas of worklife and perception of change. Limiting the number of indicators to three focuses the analysis mainly on the structural equation model, which is the primarily focus of this study. This approach differs from one in which scale reliability is considered solely in reference to

Table 36.2 *Descriptive statistics and correlations, university sample*

Variable	Mean	Std. deviation	alpha	Cynicism	Efficacy	Workload	Control	Reward	Community	Fairness	Values	Change
Exhaustion	2.72	1.50	0.90	0.57	−0.19	0.57	−0.40	−0.45	−0.34	−0.38	−0.33	−0.47
Cynicism	1.96	1.46	0.82		−0.38	0.19	−0.42	−0.49	−0.44	−0.42	−0.43	−0.47
Efficacy	4.61	0.92	0.72			−0.04	0.22	0.23	0.22	0.14	0.25	0.26
Workload	3.11	0.88	0.73				−0.18	−0.21	−0.10	−0.15	−0.08	−0.22
Control	3.53	0.90	0.64					0.53	0.44	0.51	0.38	0.55
Reward	3.21	1.06	0.87						0.55	0.59	0.44	0.57
Community	3.32	0.90	0.85							0.50	0.44	0.49
Fairness	2.63	0.94	0.87								0.57	0.61
Values	3.28	0.77	0.76									0.45
Change	3.06	0.68	0.89									

Note: $N = 602$; all correlations except for Workload with Efficacy significant, $p < 0.01$.

Table 36.3 Descriptive statistics and correlations, hospital sample

Variable	Mean	Std. deviation	alpha	Cynicism	Efficacy	Workload	Control	Reward	Community	Fairness	Values	Change
Exhaustion	3.02	1.55	0.92	0.51	−0.07	−0.62	−0.37	−0.37	−0.30	−0.37	−0.23	−0.36
Cynicism	1.84	1.36	0.82		−0.31	−0.19	−0.35	−0.40	−0.33	−0.37	−0.38	−0.40
Efficacy	4.46	1.00	0.75			0.00	0.18	0.20	0.17	0.11	0.24	0.19
Workload	2.56	0.81	0.80				0.29	0.24	0.17	0.29	0.11	0.31
Control	2.98	0.82	0.75					0.46	0.38	0.48	0.28	0.38
Reward	3.02	0.95	0.85						0.38	0.47	0.28	0.39
Community	3.31	0.83	0.85							0.40	0.28	0.37
Fairness	2.68	0.80	0.83								0.36	0.51
Values	3.60	0.65	0.70									0.35
Change	2.85	0.60	0.89									

Note: $N = 2009$; all correlations except for Workload with Efficacy significant, $p < 0.01$.

overall inter-item consistency among the items. In contrast, structural equation analysis considers, in addition to high inter-correlations among the items within a latent construct, the consistency in the correlations of each indicator within that latent construct with the indicators within the model's other latent constructs (Bentler and Chou, 1987; Hayduk, 1987; Jaccard and Wan, 1996).

Whereas each indicator added to the causal model makes a distinct demand on the predictive power of the model, a limit of three indicators for each construct yields the most parsimonious perspective on the structural model. A limit of three indicators also brings a rigor to measurement construction in that it requires that every item maintain a strong level of inter-item correlation with the other two items, and that all three items maintain a consistent pattern relative to the other constructs in the model. It is necessary to have at least three indicators for the analysis to calculate the underlying consistency among the items. Similarly three items are necessary to compute Cronbach's alpha. One pair of items produces only one correlation, while three items produce three correlations, the commonality of which determines the inter-item consistency among the items. Single-item indicators rarely meet the distribution specifications of a causal modeling analysis and provide no basis for determining commonality among indicators. Selecting the first three indicators of each scale, rather than searching for the most auspicious items, emphasizes their strong inter-item consistency. The factor loadings of these indicators for the two samples are displayed in Figure 36.2 and 36.3; these are the coefficients in the context of the causal model analysis described below.

The goodness of fit analyses presented in Table 36.4 and Table 36.5 present the model contrasts for each of the two samples. For both samples the Structural Null, comprising only the factor loadings and no structural relationships, constituted a major improvement over the Independence Model. In turn, the Burnout Null Model provided another improvement in both samples, but with goodness of fit indices short of the criterion level of 0.90 (see Table 36.4 and Table 36.5). For the university sample, the Mediation model improves the goodness of fit (χ^2 difference $_{(13\,df)}$ = 2184.24 − 953.40 = 1230.74 ($p < 0.0001$)) over the Burnout Null Model. The additional model contrasts differentiated this improvement in fit. First, the Burnout Predictor Model improved the fit over the Burnout Null Model (χ^2 difference $_{(7\,df)}$ = 2184.14 − 1921.23 = 262.91 ($p < 0.0001$)). This difference indicates that the Mediation model fits the data considerably better than a model that includes only the relationships among the three dimensions of burnout. Second, the Value Model improved the fit over the Burnout Predictor Model (χ^2 difference $_{(2\,df)}$ = 1921.23 − 1584.44 = 336.79 ($p < 0.0001$)). Third, the Mediation Model improved the fit over the Value Model (χ^2 difference $_{(5\,df)}$ = 1584.44 − 953.40 = 631.04 ($p < 0.0001$)).

For the hospital sample, the Mediation Model also improves the goodness of fit (χ^2 difference $_{(15\,df)}$ = 4802.31 − 2043.21 = 2759.10 ($p < 0.0001$)) over the Burnout Null Model. The additional model contrasts differentiated this improvement in fit. First, the Burnout Predictor Model improved the fit over the Burnout Null Model (χ^2 difference $_{(7\,df)}$ = 4802.31 − 3528.29 = 1274.02 ($p < 0.0001$)). Second, the Value Model improved the fit over the Burnout Predictor Model (χ^2 difference $_{(2\,df)}$ = 3528.29 − 3325.62 = 202.67 ($p < 0.0001$)). Third, the Mediation Model improved the fit over the Value Model (χ^2 difference $_{(5\,df)}$ = 3325.62 − 2043.21 = 1282.41 ($p < 0.0001$)).

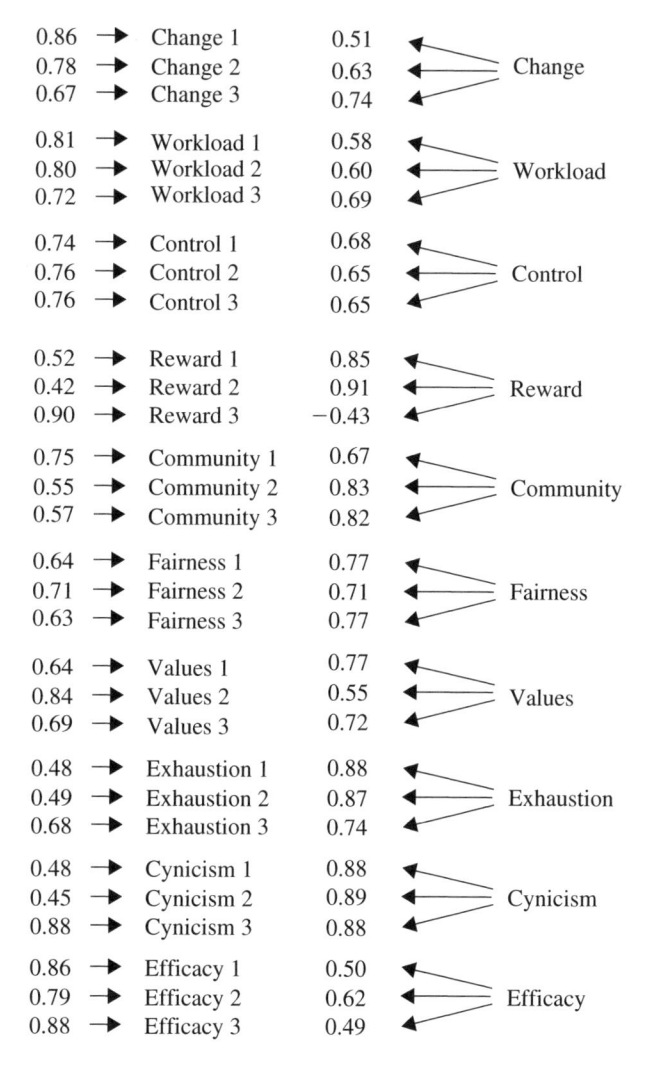

Figure 36.2   Factor loadings, university sample

Unlike the chi square, the Bentler–Bonett Non-Normed Fit Index and the Comparative Fit Index are independent of sample size, providing a basis for assessing the relative fit of the model to the two samples. An examination of the fit indices in the two samples suggests that the model is equally applicable to both.

The mediating role of job burnout was tested by an Alternative Model that had a direct path from values to evaluation of change. In the university sample this addition resulted in a significant increase in the model fit (χ^2 difference $_{(1\,df)}$= 1020.85 − 1008.65 = 12.20 ($p < 0.01$)), but not in the hospital sample (χ^2 difference $_{(1\,df)}$= 2958.46 − 2964.75 = −6.29 (*n. s.*)). This finding acknowledges that the mediating role of burnout is not complete in every sample, but confirms that mediation is the consistent theme across settings.

558 Professional burnout

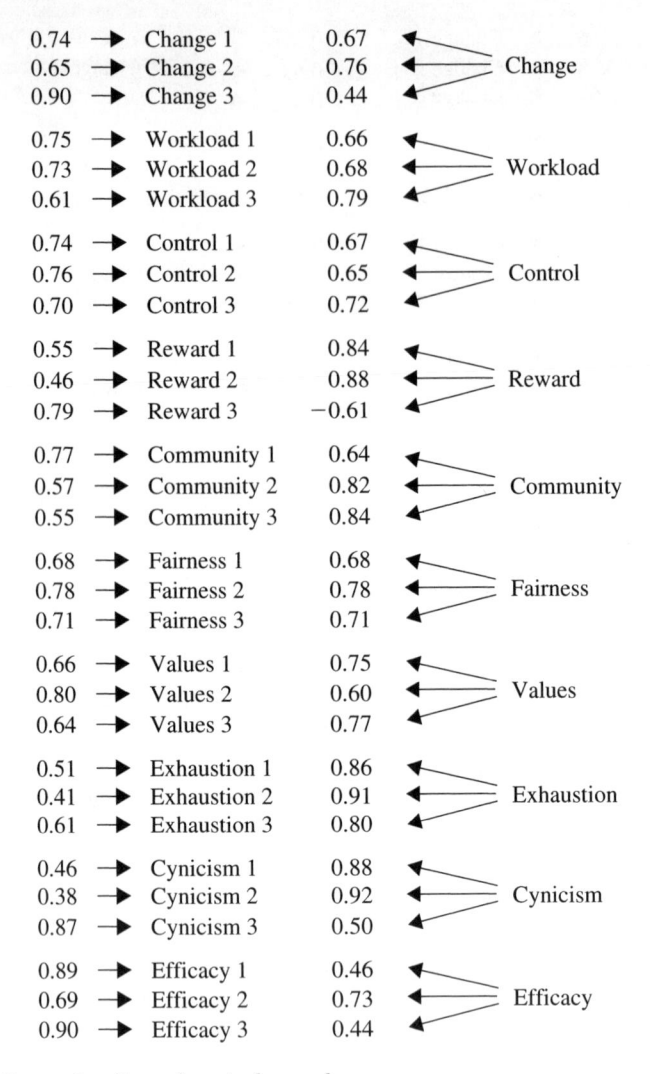

```
0.74 → Change 1       0.67 ←⎫
0.65 → Change 2       0.76 ←── Change
0.90 → Change 3       0.44 ←⎭

0.75 → Workload 1     0.66 ←⎫
0.73 → Workload 2     0.68 ←── Workload
0.61 → Workload 3     0.79 ←⎭

0.74 → Control 1      0.67 ←⎫
0.76 → Control 2      0.65 ←── Control
0.70 → Control 3      0.72 ←⎭

0.55 → Reward 1       0.84 ←⎫
0.46 → Reward 2       0.88 ←── Reward
0.79 → Reward 3      −0.61 ←⎭

0.77 → Community 1    0.64 ←⎫
0.57 → Community 2    0.82 ←── Community
0.55 → Community 3    0.84 ←⎭

0.68 → Fairness 1     0.68 ←⎫
0.78 → Fairness 2     0.78 ←── Fairness
0.71 → Fairness 3     0.71 ←⎭

0.66 → Values 1       0.75 ←⎫
0.80 → Values 2       0.60 ←── Values
0.64 → Values 3       0.77 ←⎭

0.51 → Exhaustion 1   0.86 ←⎫
0.41 → Exhaustion 2   0.91 ←── Exhaustion
0.61 → Exhaustion 3   0.80 ←⎭

0.46 → Cynicism 1     0.88 ←⎫
0.38 → Cynicism 2     0.92 ←── Cynicism
0.87 → Cynicism 3     0.50 ←⎭

0.89 → Efficacy 1     0.46 ←⎫
0.69 → Efficacy 2     0.73 ←── Efficacy
0.90 → Efficacy 3     0.44 ←⎭
```

Figure 36.3   Factor loadings, hospital sample

Figures 36.4 and 36.5 display the coefficients for the various paths in the model for the university sample and the hospital sample, respectively. The analyses confirmed that all of the proposed paths in both samples were statistically significant ($p < 0.05$). All components of the hypothesized model were confirmed.

Direct and indirect effects
The direct and indirect effects for the university sample are displayed in Table 36.6; those of the hospital sample are displayed in Table 36.7. The two analyses are largely consistent with one another. Both analyses confirm the pivotal role of control in the model: in addition to its strong direct paths to workload, reward, community and fairness, control

Table 36.4 Model contrasts university sample

Model	Degrees of freedom	Chi square	Bentler–Bonett non-normed fit index	Comparative fit index	LISREL adjusted goodness of fit	Root mean square residual
Independence	435	6900.28				
Structural Null	405	2349.79	0.688	0.709	0.676	0.405
Burnout Null	403	2184.14	0.703	0.725	0.700	0.349
Burnout Predictor	396	1921.23	0.741	0.754	0.748	0.327
Value	393	1584.44	0.756	0.780	0.766	0.283
Mediation	389	953.40	0.902	0.913	0.885	0.161

Table 36.5 Model contrasts hospital sample

Model	Degrees of freedom	Chi square	Bentler–Bonett non-normed fit index	Comparative fit index	LISREL adjusted goodness of fit	Root mean square residual
Independence	435	20817.38				
Structural Null	405	5334.14	0.740	0.758	0.739	0.324
Burnout Null	403	4802.31	0.767	0.784	0.772	0.277
Burnout Predictor	396	3528.29	0.831	0.846	0.830	0.236
Value	393	3325.62	0.841	0.856	0.841	0.145
Mediation	389	2043.21	0.909	0.919	0.911	0.121

makes a major indirect contribution to predicting all of the other variables in the study. This pattern is especially striking with the prediction of values, in which the indirect contribution of control is greater than the direct contribution of any of the three areas of worklife with a direct path to values. In the hospital sample, control's indirect contribution to predicting exhaustion is larger than the direct path from values to exhaustion, mediated through the direct path from workload to exhaustion. In the university sample, the direct path from values to exhaustion was larger than the indirect path from control. In both samples workload made a large indirect contribution on assessment of change and on cynicism through its direct path to exhaustion.

Discussion

The findings from this study provide support for the proposed mediation model. The experience of burnout or engagement is the link between the organizational context and

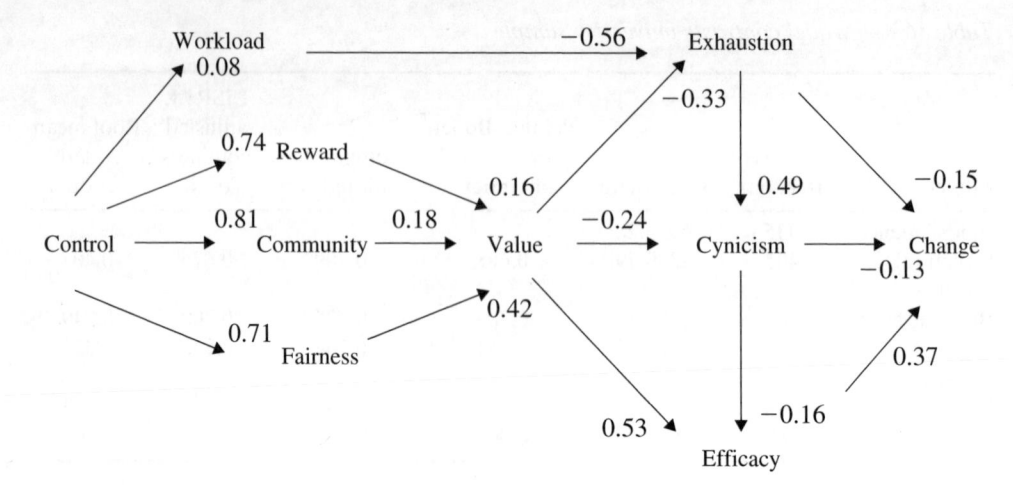

Figure 36.4   Causal model coefficients, university sample

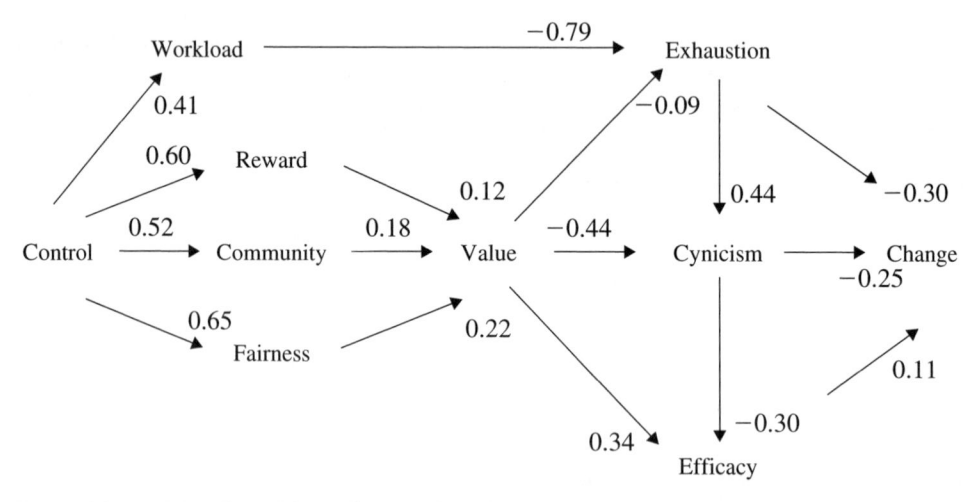

Figure 36.5   Causal model coefficients, hospital sample

work-related outcomes. It is not simply that burnout is an important psychological outcome in its own right, but that it is related to people's commitment to their job and their evaluation of organizational change. The clear implication is that the burnout experience should be predictive of other job-related outcomes, such as work behaviors, and this should be the focus of future research.

A striking aspect of the findings is the complex way in which the six areas of worklife predicted burnout. Workload and control each played critical roles (thus replicating conceptually the Demand–Control model) but were not sufficient. Reward, community and fairness added further power to predict values, which in turn was the critical predictor of

Table 36.6 Direct and indirect effects, university sample

Outcome	Workload	Control	Reward	Community	Fairness	Value	Exhaustion	Cynicism	Efficacy
Change Values	0.217	0.267	0.057	0.069	0.181	0.399			
		0.311	**0.123**	**0.184**	**0.217**				
Exhaustion	**−0.569**	−0.309	−0.048	−0.059	−0.154	**−0.340**			
Cynicism	−0.264	−0.311	−0.065	−0.079	−0.208	**−0.459**	**−0.382**		
Efficacy	0.084	0.321	0.077	0.095	0.248	**0.547**	**0.464**	**−0.318**	**0.432**
							−0.148	**−0.319**	

Note: **Bold** indicates direct effects.

Table 36.7 Direct and indirect effects, hospital sample

Outcome	Workload	Control	Reward	Community	Fairness	Value	Exhaustion	Cynicism	Efficacy
Change Values	0.298	0.173	0.021	0.031	0.037	0.170			
		0.311	**0.123**	**0.184**	**0.217**				
Exhaustion	**−0.786**	−0.345	−0.012	−0.017	−0.020	**−0.094**			
Cynicism	−0.345	−0.233	−0.037	−0.056	−0.066	**−0.305**	**−0.380**		
Efficacy	0.103	0.175	0.053	0.079	0.093	**0.428**	**0.439**	**−0.188**	**0.251**
							−0.131	**−0.298**	

Note: **Bold** indicates direct effects.

the three dimensions of burnout. The results revealed that this was not a simple additive model, but a more complicated mediation model in its own right. The strong pathways from control to reward, community and fairness acknowledge the role of autonomy and participative decision making to empower people to shape other key areas of working life. The subsequent pathways from these three areas to values are consistent with people integrating their work experiences on various fronts into a coherent perspective on their working life. Through these complex relationships, the mediation model takes a step towards reflecting the processes through which people make sense of their work experience, and the resulting conceptual framework constitutes a major advance over simple listings of organizational characteristics.

It is especially noteworthy that this complex pattern was replicated so strongly in two very different organizations, each with very heterogeneous workforces. There was a remarkable consistency in factor structures and EQS models across these two large and diverse samples. These results provide impressive support for the power of the six areas construct and the new measure of them. These findings suggest a research agenda for burnout based on a structured perspective of workplaces. The set of organizational correlates of burnout has grown so diverse that its further adumbration does not appear constructive in itself. The mediation model identifies six distinct dimensions of work settings that encompass a large scope of burnout's organizational correlates while remaining sufficiently focused to be manageable. The structure of their relationships in the mediation model – including the pivotal role of control, the relative independence of workload and the pervasive influence of values – defines a psychological environment in which people perceive and experience the world of work. Underlying the model and the measures is the concept of a person's experienced congruence or incongruence with the job environment. Rather than proposing an ideal job or the ideal employee, the model accepts a wide range of functional job environments and a wide range of personal aspirations and inclinations that shape the way people work. The focus of the research is examining the interactions of these two dynamic and complex entities.

The interpretation of these results must be tempered, of course, by the fact that they are based on self-report data in a cross-sectional research design. We have proposed a causal sequence, but the EQS analyses cannot provide a definitive test of those causal relationships. Subsequent phases of our research program will include longitudinal studies in which other, non-self-report, sources of data will provide a broader context for the subjective assessments reflected in the check-up survey responses (see Leiter and Maslach, 2004, for an initial set of longitudinal analyses).

Nevertheless the self-report format of the check-up survey has proved to be a powerful tool for mobilizing organizational self-reflection and change. The process of the organizational check-up is designed to inspire the full participation of all the employees, as indicated by the strikingly high response rates in both samples. The main intent of the survey is to generate a comprehensive profile of the organization's workforce, which can be used to inform decisions about intervention. However the participative nature of the check-up process can be viewed as an intervention in itself, which engages all employees in an organizational dialogue and prepares them to get involved in future change. Longitudinal studies assessing the impact of interventions will be the basis of assessing the extent to which this potential can be fulfilled.

We have implemented this check-up process in several organizations, in addition to the two utilized in the current study. All of them have used the check-up information to plan change initiatives with the intention of follow-up surveys at approximately two-year intervals. As this information base evolves it will provide a perspective on, not only the theoretical implications of our mediation model, but the model's practical implications as well.

References

Bentler, P.M. (1995), *EQS: Structural equations program manual*, Encino, CA: Multivariate Software.
Bentler, P.M. and C.P. Chou (1987), 'Practical issues in structural modeling', *Sociological Methods and Research*, **16**, 78–117.
Bollen, K.A. and R. Lennox (1991), 'Conventional wisdom on measurement: a structural equation perspective', *Psychological Bulletin*, **110**, 305–14.
Cordes, C.L. and T.W. Dougherty (1993), 'A review and an integration of research on job burnout', *Academy of Management Review*, **18**, 621–56.
Cox, T., G. Kuk and M.P. Leiter (1993), 'Burnout, health, workstress and organizational healthiness', in W. Schaufeli, C. Maslach and T. Marek (eds), *Professional Burnout: Recent Developments in Theory and Research*, Washington: Taylor & Francis, pp. 177–93.
Finnegan, J.E. (2000), 'The impact of person and organizational values on organizational commitment', *Journal of Occupational & Organizational Psychology*, **73**(2), 149–69.
Greenglass, E.R., L. Fiksenbaum and R.J. Burke (1994), 'The relationship between social support and burnout over time in teachers', *Journal of Social Behavior and Personality*, **9**, 219–30.
Hayduk, L. (1987), *Structural Equation Modeling with LISREL*, Baltimore, MD: Johns Hopkins University Press.
Jaccard, J.R. and C.K. Wan (1996), *LISREL Approaches to Interaction Effects in Multiple Regression*, Thousand Oaks, CA: Sage.
Kahn, R.L. and P. Byosiere (1992), 'Stress in organizations', in M.D. Dunnette and L.M. Hough (eds), *Handbook of Industrial and Organizational Psychology*, vol. 3, Palo Alto, CA: Consulting Psychologists Press, pp. 571–650.
Karasek, R. and T. Theorell (1990), *Stress, Productivity, and the Reconstruction of Working Life*, New York: Basic Books.
Lauver, K.J. and A. Kristof-Brown (2001), 'Distinguishing between employees' perceptions of person–job and person–organization fit', *Journal of Vocational Behavior*, **59**, 454–70.
Lee, R.T. and B.E. Ashforth (1996), 'A meta-analytic examination of the correlates of the three dimensions of job burnout', *Journal of Applied Psychology*, **8**, 123–33.
Leiter, M.P. and P. Harvie (1998), 'Conditions for staff acceptance of organizational change: burnout as a mediating construct', *Anxiety, Stress & Coping*, **11**, 1–25.
Leiter, M.P. and C. Maslach (1999), 'Six areas of worklife: a model of the organizational context of burnout', *Journal of Health and Human Services Administration*, **21**, 472–89.
Leiter, M.P. and C. Maslach (2000), *Preventing Burnout and Building Engagement: A Complete Program for Organizational Renewal*, San Francisco: Jossey-Bass.
Leiter, M.P. and C. Maslach (2004), 'Areas of worklife: a structured approach to organizational predictors of job burnout', in P.L. Perrewe and D.C. Ganster (eds), *Research in Occupational Stress and Well Being: Emotional and Psysiological Processes and Positive Intervention Strategies*, Oxford: JAI Press/Elsevier, pp. 91–134.
Leiter, M.P., P. Harvie and C. Frizzell (1998), 'The correspondence of patient satisfaction and nurse burnout', *Social Science & Medicine*, **47**, 1611–17.
Maslach, C. (1993), 'Burnout: a multidimensional perspective', in W.B. Schaufeli, C. Maslach and T. Marek (eds), *Professional Burnout: Recent Developments in Theory and Research*, Washington, DC: Taylor & Francis, pp. 19–32.
Maslach, C. and S.E. Jackson (1981), 'The measurement of experienced burnout', *Journal of Occupational Behavior*, **2**, 99–113.
Maslach, C. and M.P. Leiter (1997), *The Truth about Burnout*, San Francisco: Jossey-Bass.
Maslach, C., S.E. Jackson and M.P. Leiter (1996), *Maslach Burnout Inventory Manual*, 3rd edn, Palo Alto, CA: Consulting Psychologists Press.
Maslach, D., W.B. Schaufeli and M.P. Leiter (2001), 'Job burnout', *Annual Review of Psychology*, **52**, 397–422.
O'Reilly, C.A., J.A. Chatman and D.F. Caldwell (1999), 'Managerial personality and performance: a semi-idiographic approach', *Journal of Research in Personality*, **33**, 514–45.

Pfeffer, J. (1998), *The Human Equation*, Boston: Harvard Business School.
Sauter, S.L. and L.R. Murphy (eds) (1995), *Organizational Risk Factors for Job Stress*, Washington, DC: American Psychological Association.
Schaufeli, W.B. and D. Enzmann (1998), *The Burnout Companion to Study and Practice: A Critical Analysis*, London: Taylor & Francis.
Schaufeli, W.B., M.P. Leiter, C. Maslach and S.E. Jackson (1996), 'The Maslach Burnout Inventory–General Survey', in C. Maslach, S.E. Jackson and M.P. Leiter (eds), *MBI Manual*, 3rd edn, Palo Alto, CA: Consulting Psychologists Press.
Schneider, B. (2001), 'Fits about fit', *Applied Psychology: An International Review*, **50**, 141–52.
Tyler, T.R. (1990), *Why People Obey the Law*, New Haven, CT: Yale University Press.
Weick, K.E. and R.E. Quinn (1999), 'Organizational change and development', *Annual Review of Psychology*, **50**, 361–86.

37 Love and work: the relationships between their unconscious choices and burnout
Ayala Malach Pines

'One can live magnificently in this world if one knows how to work and how to love,' wrote Tolstoy in a letter to a friend in 1856. Freud is alleged to have also written that the abilities to love and to work are the evidence for psychological well-being. People's choice of a career and an intimate partner tell us a great deal about who they are and have a major impact on their lives.

The importance of both work and love for healthy functioning has been well documented empirically (for example Barnett, 1993; Baruch *et al.*, 1983; Hazan and Shaver, 1990; Lee and Kanungo, 1984), yet studies of love generally ignore its relationship to work and studies of work ignore its relationship to love (Hazan and Shaver, 1990), adhering to what Kanter termed the 'myth of separate worlds' (Kanter, 1977).

The relationship between work and love was noted in studies documenting the spillover of work stress to the family (for example Boles *et al.*, 1997; Eckenrode and Gore, 1990; Golembiewski, 2000; Hochschild, 1999; Kanter, 1977; Kinnunen and Mauno, 1998; Pensa, 1999; Valtinson, 1998; Zedeck, 1992). It seems that satisfaction in one sphere of life is associated with satisfaction in the other and stress in one sphere is associated with stress in the other (Hazan and Shaver, 1990). An important question that seems worthy of an in-depth discussion is the reason for this relationship.

The current chapter addresses this question in the context of the relationship between career and couple burnout. It argues, on the basis of a psychoanalytic–existential perspective, that the underlying causes of career and couple burnout are similar. They are related on the one hand to the original, in part unconscious, reasons for their choice – an attempt to resolve similar childhood issues through either a career or an intimate relationship. In addition, both career and couple burnout are related to a similar sense of failure in an existential quest to find meaning in life through either work or love. With the psychoanalytic–existential perspective, a certain correlation between career and couple burnout can be expected. Before discussing this proposition in greater detail, a brief introduction seems in order on career and couple burnout and the psychoanalytic–existential perspective on burnout.[1]

Career and couple burnout: a psychoanalytic–existential perspective
Burnout, experienced as a state of physical, emotional and mental exhaustion (Pines and Aronson, 1988) as well as depersonalization and reduced personal accomplishment (Maslach, 1982, 1993), is the end result of a process of attrition in which highly motivated and committed individuals lose their spirit (for example Freudenberger, 1980, p. 13; Maslach, 1982, p. 3; Pines, 1993, p. 386; Pines and Aronson, 1988 p. 9). You cannot

'burn out' unless you were 'on fire' to begin with. The person who reaches the burnout stage says in one way or another: 'I've had it. I can't take it anymore.'

Burnout has become a frequent topic of research since the mid-1970s, with close to 2000 studies published in the last decade alone. Studies documented the existence of burnout in a wide range of occupations, its varied physical, emotional, cognitive and behavioral symptoms and its high cost for individuals, organizations and society at large (for example Maslach and Leiter, 1997; Schaufeli *et al.*, 1993).

The vast majority of these studies focused on career burnout in the human services, despite repeated calls for research that expands the narrow occupational focus pursued (for example Burke, 1986) and examines burnout in relationships other than professional provider–recipient (Maslach, 1993). Few studies addressed burnout outside the work sphere in general and in marriage in particular (for example Leaman, 1983; Pines, 1996). More research addressed the spillover of career burnout to marriage (for example Bulka, 1984; Jackson and Maslach, 1982; Jayaratne *et al.*, 1986; Westman and Etzion, 1995; Westman, 2002).

Different theories attempted to explain burnout, such as psychoanalytic theory (Fischer, 1983; Freudenberger, 1980), Jungian theory (Garden, 1989, 1995), social comparison theory (Buunk *et al.*, 1994), social exchange theory (Schaufeli *et al.*, 1996; VanYperen *et al.*, 1992), equity theory (Van Dierendonck *et al.*, 1994) the job demands–controls model (Landsbergis, 1988) and, more recently, the pysychoanalytic existential perspective (Pines, 2000a, 2000b).

According to the existential perspective, burnout originates in people's need to find significance in their life and their sense that they failed in this quest. The answer to the question why people choose a particular way to obtain significance is based on the psychoanalytic notion that people choose to replicate significant childhood experiences.

For the existential perspective, the root cause of burnout lies in people's need to believe that their lives are meaningful, that the things they do are useful and important. Ernest Becker (1973), on the basis of Otto Rank's work, argued that people's need to believe that the things they do are meaningful is their way of coping with the angst caused by facing their own mortality. In order to be able to deny death we need to feel heroic, to know that our lives are meaningful, that we matter in the larger 'cosmic' scheme of things. According to Becker and Otto Rank, people choose to become 'heroes' according to their culture-prescribed 'hero system'. One of the most frequently chosen answers to the existential quest is work. The other is love. People who expect to derive a sense of existential significance either from their work or from their intimate relationship enter with high hopes, idealistic and motivated. When they feel that they have failed, that their life is insignificant, that they make no difference in the world, they start feeling helpless and hopeless and eventually burn out.

If we accept the premise that some people try to derive a sense of existential significance from their work, the next question we need to address is why they choose to do it through the particular occupation that they have chosen (Pines, 2002; 2003). Many attempts were made to answer this question. Most of these attempts included such factors as aptitudes, abilities, interests, resources and limitations (for example Parsons, 1909; Swanson, 1996). Psychoanalytic theory makes a significant contribution to this body of research and practice by adding the dimension of unconscious career choices (for example Kets de Vries *et al.*, 1991; Obholzer and Roberts, 1997).

The unconscious determinants of any vocational choice reflect the individual's personal and familial history. People choose an occupation that enables them to replicate significant childhood experiences (Pines and Yanai, 2001).

When the choice of a career involves such significant issues, people enter it with very high hopes, ego involvement and passion. The greatest passion is typically located where some unresolved childhood issue ('metaphor wound') lies, fueled by the hope of resolving it. Success helps heal childhood wounds. But when work repeats the childhood trauma rather than healing it, the result is career burnout (Pines, 2002; 2003).

Like career burnout, couple burnout is a painful state of physical emotional and mental exhaustion that afflicts people who expected romantic love to give meaning to their lives. It occurs when they realize that, despite all their efforts, their intimate relationship does not and will not provide that. In its extreme form, burnout marks the breaking point – the 'I've had it' – of a relationship (Pines, 1996).

According to existential psychologists (for example Yalom,1980), if self-actualization in the sphere of work helps us fend off our fear of death, an intimate relationship, the merging with another person, helps us fend off our fear of life. Becker (1973) (once again using the work of Otto Rank) argues that romantic love enables us to bond with something (represented in someone) we adore and see as larger than ourselves.

If we accept the premise that some people try to derive a sense of existential significance from their intimate relationships, the next question that we need to address is why they choose to do it by falling in love with a particular person (Pines, 2001). Once again, many attempts have been made to answer this question. Psychoanalytic theory makes a significant contribution to this body of theory and research by adding the dimension of unconscious romantic choices that reflect the individual's personal and familial history (for example Bowen, 1978; Dicks, 1967; Freud, 1917; Mittelman, 1944). We choose a romantic partner who enables us to replicate significant childhood experiences and gratify ungratified childhood needs (Pines, 2001).

When a romantic relationship involves such significant issues, it is not surprising that people enter it with very high hopes, ego involvement and passion. The greatest passion is typically located where some unresolved childhood issue lies, fueled by the hope of resolving and healing it. A loving relationship helps heal childhood wounds. But when people feel that they failed, when their intimate relationship repeats the childhood trauma rather than healing it, the result is couple burnout (Pines, 1996).

The relationship between career and couple burnout
It seems that the existential–psychoanalytic perspective can explain the etiology of both career and couple burnout. And if indeed people's choices of both their career and love relationships are motivated by the need to replicate and thus heal the same childhood trauma, it can be expected that there will be a relationship between them. Ample clinical evidence supports this notion. Here are some examples.

A psychologist whose father was a Narcissist with depressive tendencies felt 'unseen' by him. The career choice to become a therapist and specialize in work with depressed Narcissists and the choice of romantic partners who also had similar personality characteristics was motivated by an unconscious desire to heal this childhood trauma. The burnout, in both career and marriage, was related to the psychologist's painful realization of repeating in both cases the childhood trauma, rather than healing it.

A nurse, who was sexually abused and felt totally helpless as a child, tried unconsciously to heal this childhood trauma by choosing an occupation that is characterized by the professional's great control and the patient's great helplessness, and by marrying a drug-dependent partner. Her career and marriage burnout were both caused by a feeling of helplessness and a sense that she was repeating her childhood trauma rather than healing it in her inability to heal her patients, her husband or herself.

An accountant whose father was temperamental, with frequent angry outbursts, and a mother who was flat emotionally felt criticized by the mother for being 'just like father'. The choice to become an accountant and the choice of a romantic partner with whom the relationship was a very dispassionate 'brother/sister' relationship were both motivated by a desire not to be 'like father'. Her career and marriage burnout were both related to the painful realization that work and love without passion were death-like.

In addition to such clinical evidence, a number of studies found a relationship between burnout on the job and the quality of the marriage. Three studies involving 1187 professionals who described their work, marriage and burnout discovered that people who were stressed at work but felt supported by their partner were able to cope with work situations that were otherwise intolerable (Pines, 1996, pp. 80–81). A bad relationship, on the other hand, was found to have a negative effect on the work sphere as well.

Interestingly findings of the three studies comparing career and marriage burnout revealed that overall burnout was related more to marital problems than it was to job stress. Apparently the overall quality of people's life is more affected by the quality of their marriage than by the quality of their work. This is an important finding considering that most people concentrate their best energies on their jobs, perhaps in the belief that they have to work at their jobs, while their relationships will somehow take care of themselves. Participants in the three studies described their marriages not only as more important to them but also as more satisfying emotionally and as less pressured than their work.

A comparison of the levels of burnout on the job and in marriage showed striking similarities. In a combined sample of 960 men and women the average score of couple burnout was 3.3. This score was identical to the average score of job burnout obtained in a sample of 3916 men and women. Similarly the average couple burnout score in a study of 200 Israelis was 2.8. This score was identical to the job burnout score obtained in a combined sample of 393 Israelis (Pines and Aronson, 1988). (Those readers who are curious about their own scores of couple burnout and job burnout are invited to respond to the short version of the Burnout Measure at the end of the chapter.)

Judging by the similarity in people's levels of burnout on the job and in couple relationships, one can assume that there is a parallel not only in the intensity but also in the subjective experience of both. Indeed, just as in job burnout, people experience couple burnout as a state of physical, emotional and mental exhaustion, caused by long involvement in emotionally demanding situations. People burn out in their marriages for the same reason that they burn out in their jobs: their experiences do not match their romantic ideals. Workers burn out because they cannot achieve what they expected in their work, and couples burn out because the relationship is not what they imagined.

Not surprisingly, the process leading to couple burnout is very similar to the process leading to job burnout. We can see this similarity in the career burnout and couple burnout models presented in Figures 37.1 and 37.2. Just as couple burnout can happen only to couples who started their relationship in love, career burnout can happen only to idealistic and highly motivated individuals. Like couples in love, who expect the love to give meaning to their life, idealistic people work hard because they expect their work to give their life a sense of significance.

When people have such high expectations of either their work or their marriage and they can reach those expectations, they reach peak performance in their work, or in the case of marriage a relationship with roots and wings. But if they cannot achieve those expectations, no matter how hard they try, the result is burnout.

Job and couple burnout not only parallel each other, they also affect each other. It is very difficult to isolate the experience of burnout, either at work or in marriage. When people start burning out on their jobs, typically they pull back from co-workers and begin to feel isolated. They think they are not getting enough appreciation for their work. Consequently they start putting increasing demands on their mates for professional appreciation and challenge. Such demands are both unfair and unrealistic, since the mate in most cases is not well enough informed or qualified to fulfill them. Yet the atmosphere of disappointment and regret becomes associated with the marriage. Burnout can work the other way as well, spilling over from home into work. Most of this involves people who escape marital problems by totally investing themselves in their work. People like that usually come to work very early, leave very late, and take work home with them so as to avoid the danger of having to talk to their mates.

Similar findings were reported in studies on the spillover of career burnout to marriage (for example Bulka, 1984; Jackson and Maslach, 1982; Jayaratne et al., 1986; Westman, 2002; Westman and Etzion, 1995) and in studies on the spillover of work stress to the family (for example Jones and Fletcher, 1993; Rook et al., 1991; Vinokur and Westman, 1998).

A very small part of the research on the spillover of work stress and burnout to the family addressed the influence of culture (for example Gatmon, 1999). No research has addressed directly the relationship between career burnout and couple burnout. Both these aspects were addressed in a cross-cultural study that focused on the relationship between career burnout and couple burnout. Before describing the results of this study, a brief introduction on culture and cross-cultural studies of burnout seems in order.

On culture and cross-cultural studies of burnout
As noted earlier, the vast majority of studies on burnout focused on documenting its existence within certain occupational groups. The assumption underlying these studies is that burnout is a universal phenomenon that can be explained by the requirements and stresses of a particular occupation. This assumption can be challenged on both theoretical grounds (for example Bond, 1988) and empirical grounds (for example Schaufeli and Van-Dierendonck, 1996). Furthermore this assumption has rarely been tested directly. Very few studies examined burnout cross-culturally (only about 20 out of close to 2000 published in the last decade). Among the studies that did so, many studied burnout in one culture (for example Baba et al., 1999; Abu Hilal, 1995). Few (for example Golembiewski

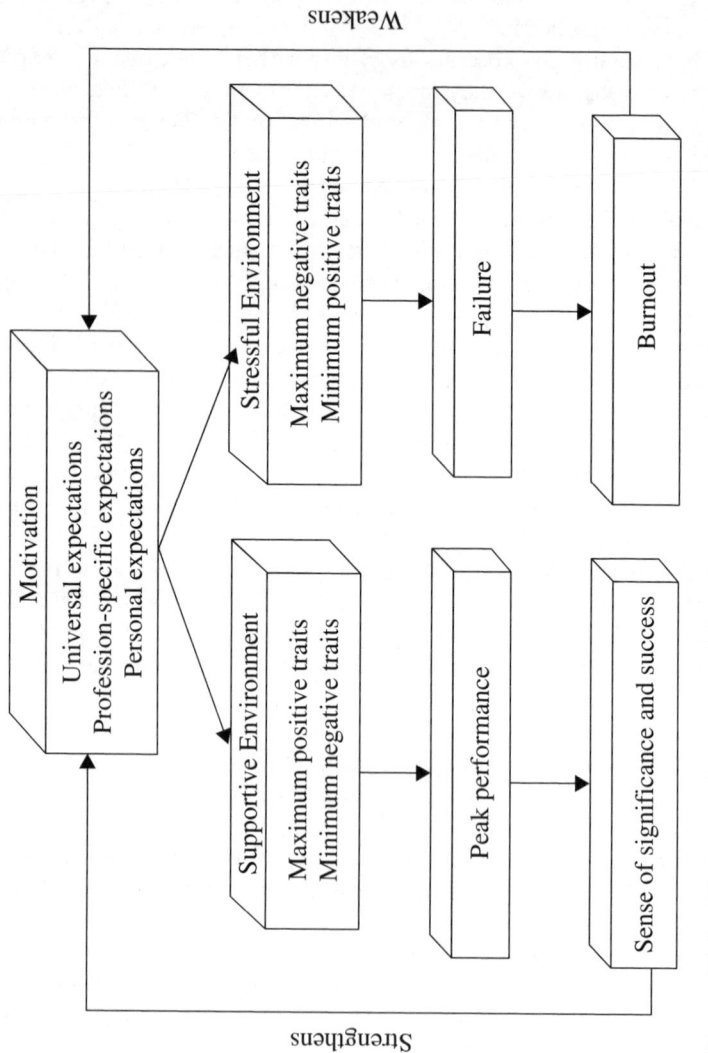

Figure 37.1 The career burnout model

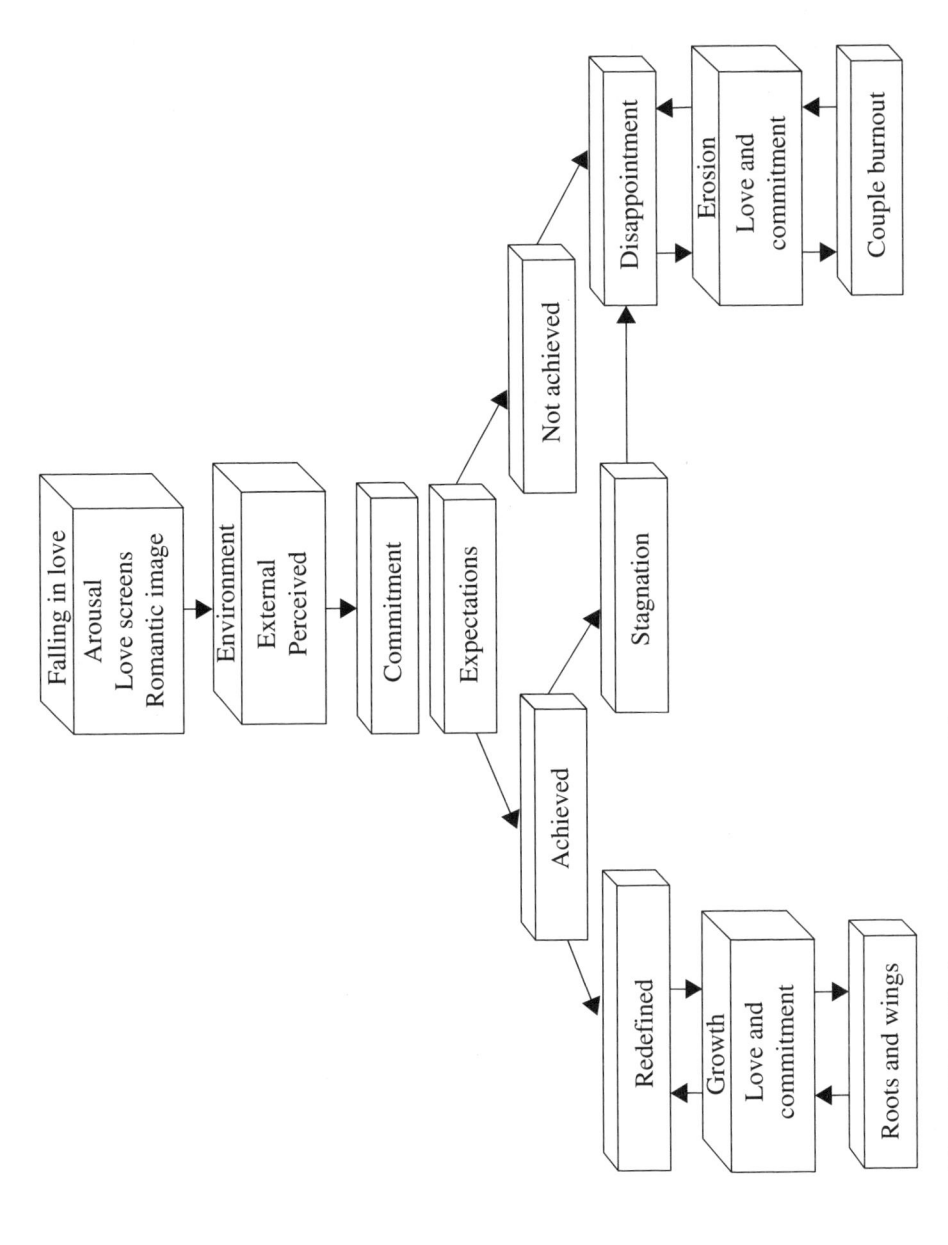

Figure 37.2   The love and burnout model

et al., 1996; Green *et al.*, 1991, Schaufeli & Van-Dierendonck, 1996) attempted to document its universality.

What is culture? There is no single best definition of culture or way of studying cultural effects. Rather, as Peng *et al.* (2000) note, 'research psychologists highlight various aspects of culture, adopting invariably imperfect but workable assumptions about what culture is' (p. 171). Peng and his colleagues describe three dominant traditions that arrange cultures by their value systems, by their conceptions of selfhood and by their implicit folk theories: the value, the self and the theory traditions.

The dominant figure in the 'value' tradition is Hofstede, who defines culture as 'the collective programming of the mind which distinguishes the members of the group or category of people from another' (Hofstede, 1991, p. 5). Culture consists of the abstract values, beliefs and perceptions of the world that underlie and are reflected in people's behavior (Haviland, 1993). Smith and Peterson (1996), who elaborated on Hofstede's work, defined culture more concisely as a system of shared meaning.

Hofstede (1991, 1993) suggests four criteria for distinguishing between cultures: individualism v. collectivism, power distance, uncertainty avoidance and masuclinity v. femininity. A regards Individualism v. Collectivism, a collectivist society is one in which the interest of the group prevails over the interest of the individual. The opposite is true in an individualistic society. The USA and Great Britain are characterized by strong individualism, Finland is moderately individualistic, Israel and Spain are on the border and Portugal is collectivist. Power distance refers to differences in power and authority or inequality among people, from relatively equal (small power distance), to extremely unequal (large power distance). Portugal and Spain have moderate power distance, the USA, Great Britain and Finland a below moderate power distance, while is Israel an extremely small power distance. The degree to which people in a country prefer structured over unstructured situations indicates uncertainty avoidance. Portugal has a very strong uncertainty avoidance, Spain and Israel strong, Finland moderate, the USA and Great Britain a relatively weak uncertainty avoidance. As for masculinity v. femininity, a masculine culture is characterized by assertiveness and competitiveness and stresses achievement and material success, whereas a feminine culture puts family before work (Hofstede, 1998) and is characterized by warmth and collaboration and stresses harmony and relationships quality. Great Britain and the USA are masculine, Israel relatively masculine, whereas Spain, and more so Portugal and Finland, are relatively feminine.

In the 'self' tradition, Markus and Kitayama (1991) believe that self-conceptions are at the very heart of what culture is. They describe two types of culturally driven ways of 'being' a self: independent and interdependent. An independent construal of self, seen in the USA, Great Britain and Israel, is characterized by a sense of autonomy and being relatively distinct from others. An interdependent construal of self, seen in Eastern cultures and to a lesser degree Latin ones, is characterized by an emphasis on the inter-relatedness of the individual to others.

Researchers in the 'theory' tradition believe that people in particular cultures have in common implicit theories about the world. Different attitudes towards work and family were found to characterize the Spanish culture (Aram and Walochik, 1996/7; Crow, 1985; Lenero, 1977, 1983; Pines and Guendelman, 1995; Madariaga, 1969; Lewis *et al.*, 1999) as compared to the American, British or Israeli cultures (Horowitz and Lissak, 1989; Ohana, 1998), reflecting different implicit theories about their relative importance. In the former, the emphasis is on the family, in the latter on work.

All three traditions are relevant to work–home conflict and its manifestation in a relationship between career and couple burnout. In the 'value' tradition, of Hofstede's four criteria, masculinity–femininity (Hofstede, 1998) seems most relevant. As noted by Rosalind Barnett (1993), in most cultures, career is considered the masculine 'core role' and motherhood is the feminine 'core role'. Thus it can be expected that the more masculine a culture, the more dominant work will be, and the more feminine a culture, the more dominant the family. The more masculine the culture, the more it can be expected that work will interfere in the home sphere, resulting in a higher correlation between career and couple burnout.

In the 'self' tradition, following Markus and Kitayama (1991), an independent construal of self can be expected to be associated with emphasis on personal autonomy and striving for career success even at the expense of the family, whereas an interdependent construal of self can be expected to be associated with greater commitment to the family.

With the 'theory' tradition, it can be expected that the relative importance of work and family will be a significant part of the implicit theories about the world which people in a particular culture will have in common.

On the basis of all three traditions, it can be expected that different cultures will put different emphases on work as compared to family, a difference that will manifest itself in different correlations between career and couple burnout. Using the psychoanalytic–existential perspective, on the other hand, a similar correlation can be expected between career and marriage burnout no matter what the culture, as long as people in that culture are free to choose both their career and their intimate partner. The reason is that the correlation between career and couple burnout reflects similar unresolved issues that underlie the original choice of both.

The first cross-cultural study that investigated the relationship between career and couple burnout has done so among six cultures that seem rather different according to all three traditions: the USA, Great Britain, Israel, Finland, Portugal and Spain (Pines and Nunes, 2003). Despite their differences, all six countries are Western countries in which one (especially if one is a graduate student) is relatively free to choose both a career and a family. According to the value, the self and the theory traditions, different correlations between career and couple burnout were expected. From the existential–psychoanalytic perspective, a significant correlation was expected between career burnout and couple burnout in all six samples. But since people's lives are influenced by many more external variables than childhood experiences, it was expected that the correlations would be moderate.

A total of 109 Israelis, 838 Portuguese, 317 Spaniards, 144 British, 54 Americans and 110 Finns, all of them graduate social science students, participated in the study. The choice of graduate students was to ensure as much as possible similar homogeneous samples with a similar education and socioeconomic status (that allows freedom of both romantic and occupational choice), that are old enough to have both a family and a career. The Portuguese, Spanish and British data were collected by Renato Nunes, the Finn data was collected by Timo and Tuula Laes, the American data were collected by Dale Larsen and the Israeli data were collected by Ayala Malach-Pines.

Translated versions of the Burnout Measure short version (BMS) (Pines, 2005) and the Couple Burnout Measure (CBM) (Pines, 1996) were used. Results showed that, despite numerous differences between the samples studied (in culture, size, age, percentage of men and women and years of marriage), Pearson correlation analyses show similar significant moderate correlations (around $r = 0.30$) between career and couple burnout in all six samples, thus confirming the study's main hypothesis.

The finding that in six samples, from six Western countries different in their value systems, conceptions of selfhood and implicit folk theories, a similar (moderate yet significant) correlation is found between career and couple burnout seems to suggest that the correlation has more to do with an inherent relationship between these two life experiences than with cultural influences. It is possible, of course, that the consistent correlation found between career and couple burnout is not the result of a true relationship between the two but an artifact, the result of using a similar measure for studying both. Clinical evidence of the type presented earlier suggests that this is probably not the case. In addition, observations of respondents' reactions to the two measures suggest that they have no problem differentiating between their experience of burnout in the spheres of work and love. Furthermore, F tests comparing their responses to the two measures suggest significantly different patterns of response. All this evidence seems to suggest that burnout is an identifiable experience that can occur at work, in marriage or in both.

The alternative to the artifact explanation is that the correlation between career and couple burnout is due to people's attempt to derive a sense of existential significance through both love and work and their sense that they have failed similarly in this request in both spheres. The results of a recent study that show a modest positive correlation between work commitment and family commitment (Marks and MacDermid, 1996) seem to support this interpretation. They suggest that people bring a similar drive and sense of commitment to their work and their family life. The underlying reason for this similarity, according to psychoanalytic theory, is assumed to be the similar childhood experiences that influence both love choice and career choice. This alternative explanation offers tentative support for the existential–psychoanalytic perspective on both career and couple burnout.

The findings also demonstrate the importance of studying burnout cross-culturally, despite the fact that cross-cultural research is notoriously difficult to conduct. Future research will need to use more sophisticated methodologies and larger, more representative, samples of participants. At a more substantive level, future research will also need to explore further the causes, correlates and consequences of the relationship between career and couple burnout. See Figure 37.3.

Implications for career and couple counseling
In the introduction to this chapter it was noted that knowing people's career and love choices provides a wealth of information about them. At a deeper level, that information is an outside reflection of the inner workings of people's psyche. A curious phenomenon, noted in counseling with people who come because of either career or couple burnout, is their tendency to confuse the two. A person may come complaining about career burnout, only to realize after a brief exploration that the real problem is the marriage or, alternatively, may come for counseling because of a supposed problem of marriage burnout only to discover that the real problem is the work.

Please use the following scale to answer the following ten questions:

1	2	3	4	5	6	7
never	almost never	rarely	sometimes	often	very often	always

When you think about your work/intimate relationship, how often do you feel the following?

Tired __
Disappointed with people/your partner __
Hopeless __
Trapped __
Helpless __
Depressed __
Weak/sickly __
Insecure/like a failure __
Difficulties sleeping __
'I've had it' __

Note: *This is a short (ten-item) version of the 21-item Burnout Measure (Pines and Aronson, 1988) and Couple Burnout Measure (Pines, 1996).

*Figure 37.3   Short version (BMS) (Pines, 2005)**

The most important implication for both career and couple counseling of the relationship between career and couple burnout is the value of addressing this very relationship: whether people come for counseling complaining about one or the other. Addressing this relationship helps shift the focus to the underlying cause, which in most cases is an unresolved childhood issue responsible for the original choice of both.

Note

1. This chapter is based on an article entitled 'The relationship between career and couple burnout: implication for career and couple counseling' published in 2003 in the *Journal of Employment Counseling.*

References

Abu Hilal, M.M. (1995), 'Dimensionality of burnout: testing for invariance across Jordanian and Emirati teachers', *Psychological Reports*, **77**, 1367–75.
Aram, J.D. and K. Walochik (1996), 'Improvisation and the Spanish manager', *International Studies of Management & Organization*, **26**, 73–89.
Baba, V., B.L. Galperin and T.R.Lituchy (1999), 'Occupational mental health: a study of work related depression among nurses in the Caribbean', *International Journal of Nursing Studies*, **36**, 163–9.
Barnett, R.C. (1993), 'Multiple roles, gender and psychological distress', in L. Goldberger and S. Breznitz (eds), *Handbook of Stress*, 2nd edn, New York: Free Press, 427–49.
Baruch, G., R.C. Barnett and C. Rivers (1983), *Lifeprints: New Patterns of Life and Work for Today's Women*, New York: McGraw-Hill.
Becker, E. (1973), *The Denial of Death*, New York: Free Press.

Boles, J., M.W. Johnston and J.F. Hair (1997), 'Role stress, work–family conflict and emotional exhaustion: inter-relationships and effects on some role related consequences', *Journal of Personal Selling and Sales Management*, **17**, 17–28.

Bond, M.H. (ed.)(1988), *The Cross Cultural Challenge to Social Psychology*, New York: Sage.

Bowen, M. (1978), *Family Therapy in Clinical Practice*, New York: Jason Aronson.

Bulka, R.P. (1984), 'Logotherapy as an answer to burnout', *International Forum for Logotherapy*, **7**, 8–17.

Burke, R.J. (1986), 'The present and future of stress research', *Journal of Organizational Behavior Management*, **8**, 249–67.

Buunk, B.P., W.B. Schaufeli and J.F. Ybema (1994), 'Burnout, uncertainty, and the desire for social comparison among nurses', *Journal of Applied Social Psychology*, **24**, 1701–18.

Crow, J.A. (1985), *Spain, the Root and the Flower: An Interpretation of Spain and Spanish People*, Berkeley: University of California Press.

Dicks, H.V. (1967), *Marital Tensions*, New York: Basic Books.

Eckenrode, J. and S. Gore (eds) (1990), *Stress Between Work and Family*, New York: Plenum.

Etzion, D. and A.M. Pines (1986), 'Sex and culture in burnout and coping among human service professionals', *Journal of Cross Cultural Psychology*, **17**, 191–209.

Fischer, H.A (1983), 'Psychoanalytic view of burnout', in B. Farber (ed.), *Stress and Burnout in the Human Service Professions*, New York: Pergammon, pp. 40–45.

Freud, S. (1917/1963), *Introduction Lectures on Psychoanalysis*, pt III, London: Hogarth Press.

Freudenberger, H.J. (1980), *Burn-out: The High Cost of High Achievement*, Garden City, New York: Doubleday.

Garden, A.M. (1989), 'Burnout: the effect of psychological type on research', *Journal of Occupational Psychology*, **62**, 223–34.

Garden, A.M. (1995), 'The purpose of burnout: a Jungian interpretation', in R. Crandall and P.L. Perrewe (eds), *Occupational Stress: A Handbook. Series in Health Psychology and Behavioral Medicine*, Philadelphia, PA: Taylor & Francis, pp. 207–22.

Gatmon, D.N. (1999), 'Cultural and parental role models for combining work and family roles in Sweden and the United States', *Dissertation Abstracts International*, B, **59**, 5165.

Golembiewski, R.T. (2000), 'Family and work: an integrating design', in R.T. Golembiewski (ed.), *Handbook of Organizational Consultation*, 2nd edn, New York: Marcel Dekker.

Golembiewski, R.T., R.A. Boudreau, R.E. Munzenrider and L. Huaping (1996), *Global Burnout: A Worldwide Pandemic Explored by the Phase Model*, Greenwich, CT: JAI Press.

Green, D.E., F.H. Walkey and A. Taylor (1991), 'The three factor structure of the burnout inventory: a multicultural, multinational confirmatory study', *Journal of Social Behavior and Personality*, **6**, 453–72.

Haviland, W. (1993), *Cultural Anthropology*, Philadelphia: Harcourt Brace Jovanovich College Publishers.

Hazan, C. and P.R. Shaver (1990), 'Love and work: an attachment-theoretical perspective', *Journal of Personality and Social Psychology*, **59**, 270–80.

Hochschild, A.R. (1999), *The Time Bind: When Work becomes Home and Home becomes Work*, New York: Henry Holt.

Hofstede, G. (1991), *Cultures and Organizations: Software of the Mind*, London: McGraw Hill.

Hofstede, G. (1993), 'Cultural constraints in management theories', *Academy of Management Executive*, **7**, 81–7.

Hofstede, G. (ed.) (1998), *Masculinity and Femininity: The Taboo Dimension of National Cultures*, Thousand Oaks, CA: Sage Publications.

Horowitz, D. and M. Lissak (1989), *Trouble in Utopia: The Overburdened Polity of Israel*, Chicago: University of Chicago Press.

Jackson, S.E. and C. Maslach (1982), 'After-effects of job-related stress: families as victims', *Journal of Occupational Behavior*, **3**, 63–77.

Jayaratne, S., W.A. Chess and D.A. Knukel (1986), 'Burnout: its impact on child welfare workers and their spouses', *Social Work*, **31**, 53–9.

Jones, E. and B. Fletcher (1993), 'An empirical study of occupational stress transmission in working couples', *Human Relations*, **46**, 881–902.

Kanter, R. (1977), *Work and Family in the United States: A Critical Review and Agenda for Policy*, New York: Sage.

Kets de Vries, M.F.R. and Associates (1991), *Organizations on the Couch*, San Francisco: Jossey-Bass.

Kinnunen, U. and S. Mauno (1998), 'Antecedents and outcomes of work–family conflict among women and men in Finland', *Human Relations*, **51**, 157–77.

Laes, T. and T. Laes (2001), 'Career burnout and its relationship to couple burnout in Finland: a pilot study', paper presented at a symposium entitled 'The Relationship between Career and Couple Burnout: A Cross-Cultural Perspective', held at the Annual Convention of The American Psychological Association, San Francisco, California.

Landsbergis, P.A. (1988), 'Occupational stress among health care workers: a test of the job demands–control model', *Journal of Organizational Behavior*, **9**, 217–39.
Leaman, D.R. (1983), 'Needs assessment: a technique to reverse marital burnout', *Journal of Psychology and Christianity*, **2**, 47–51.
Lee, M.D. and R.N. Kanungo (eds) (1984), *Management of work and personal life*, New York: Praeger.
Lenero, O.L. (ed.) (1977), *Beyond the Nuclear Family Model: Cross Cultural Perspective*, London: Sage-ISA.
Lenero, O.L. (1983), *El fenomeno Familiar en Mexico*, Mexico City: Instituto Mexicano De Estudio Sociales.
Lewis, S., J. Smithson and J. Brannen (1999), 'Young European's orientation to families and work', *Annals of the Academy of Political and Social Science*, **562**, 83–97.
Madariaga, S. de (1969), *Englishmen, Frenchmen, Spaniards*, New York: Hill and Wang.
Marks, S.R. and S.M. MacDermid (1996), 'Multiple roles and the self: a theory of role balance', *Journal of Marriage and the Family*, **61**, 476–90.
Markus, H.R. and S. Kitayama (1991), 'Cultural variation in the self concept. Culture and self: implications for cognition, emotion and motivation', *Psychological Review*, **98**, 224–53.
Maslach, C. (1982), *Burnout – The Cost of Caring*, Englewood Cliffs, NJ: Prentice-Hall.
Maslach, C. (1993), 'Burnout: a multidimensional perspective', in W. Schaufeli, C. Maslach and T. Marek (eds), *Professional Burnout: Recent Developments in Theory and Research*, Washington, DC: Taylor & Francis, pp. 19–32.
Maslach, C. and M.P. Leiter (1997), *The Truth about Burnout: How Organizations Cause Personal Stress and What to Do about it*, San Francisco: Jossey-Bass.
Mittelman, B. (1944), 'Complementary neurotic reactions in intimate relationships', *Psychoanalytic Quarterly*, **13**, 479–91.
Obholzer, A. and V.Z. Roberts (1997), *The Unconscious at Work*, London/New York: Routledge.
Ohana, D. (1998), *The Last Israelis*, Tel-Aviv: Hakibutz Hameuchad, (Hebrew).
Parsons, F. (1909/1989), *Choosing a Vocation*, Boston: Houghton Mifflin.
Peng, K., D. Ames and E. Knowles (2000), 'Culture and human inference: perspectives from three traditions', in David Matsumoto (ed.), *Handbook of Cross-cultural Psychology*, Oxford: Oxford University Press, pp. 171–97.
Pensa, E. (1999), 'Family and professional choices: conflict or complicity?' in U. Gielen and L. Anna Comunian (eds), *International Approaches to the Family and Family Therapy*, series on international and cross cultural psychology, Padua, Italy: Unipress, pp. 273–89.
Pines, A.M. (1993), 'Burnout – an existential perspective', in W. Schaufeli, C. Maslach and T. Marek (eds), *Professional Burnout: Developments in Theory and Research*, Washington, DC: Taylor & Francis, pp.33–52.
Pines, A.M. (1996), *Couple Burnout*, New York/London: Routledge.
Pines, A.M. (2000a), 'Treating career burnout: an existential perspective', *Journal of Clinical Psychology. In Session: Psychotherapy in Practice*, **56**, 1–10.
Pines, A.M. (2000b), 'Nurses' burnout: an existential psychodynamic perspective', *Journal of Psychosocial Nursing*, **38**(2) 1–9.
Pines, A.M. (2001), *Falling in Love: Why we Choose the Lovers we Choose*, New York/London: Routledge.
Pines, A.M. (2002), 'A psychoathalytic existential approach to burnout: demonstrated in the cases of a nurse, a teacher and a manger', *Psychotherapy: Thory / research / Pratice / Training*, **39**, 103–13.
Pines, A.M. (2003), 'Unconscious influences on career choice: entrepener vs manager', *Australian Journal of Career Development*, **12**(2), 7–18.
Pines, A.M. (2005), 'The burnout measure: short version (BMS)', *International Journal of Stress Management*, (in press).
Pines, A.M. and E. Aronson (1988), *Career Burnout: Causes and Cures*, New York: Free Press.
Pines, A.M. and S. Guendelman (1995), 'Exploring the relevance of burnout to Mexican blue collar women', *Journal of Vocational Behavior*, **47**, 1–20.
Pines, A.M. and R. Nunes (2003), 'The relationship between career and couple burnout: implication for career and couple counseling', *Journal of Employment Counseling*, **40**, 50–64.
Pines, A.M. and O. Yanai (2001), 'Unconscious determinants of career choice and burnout: theoretical model and counseling strategy', *Journal of Employment Counseling*, **38**, 170–84.
Rook, S.K., D. Dooley and R. Catalano (1991), 'Stress transmission: the effects of husband's job stressors on emotional health of their wives', *Journal of Marriage and the Family*, **53**, 165–77.
Schaufeli, W.B. and D. Van Dierendonck (1996), 'A cautionary note about the cross-national and clinical validity of cut-off points for the Maslach Burnout Inventory', *Psychological Reports*, **76**, 1083–90.
Schaufeli, W.B., C. Maslach and T. Marek (eds) (1993), *Professional Burnout: Recent Developments in Theory and Research*, Washington, DC: Taylor & Francis.
Schaufeli, W.B., D. Van-Dierendonck and K. Van Gorp (1996), 'Burnout and reciprocity: toward a dual-level social exchange model', *Work and Stress*, **10**, 225–37.

Smith, P.B. and M.F. Peterson (1996), 'In search of the "Euro-manager": convergences and divergences in event management', in G.M. Breakwell and E. Lyons (eds), *Changing European Identities: Social Psychological Analyses of Social Change*, International Series in Social Psychology, Woburn, MA: Butterworth-Heinemann, pp.371–9.

Swanson, J. (1996), 'The theory is the pratice: trait and factor/person–environment fit counseling', in M.L. Savickas and B.W. Wash (eds), *Handbook of Career Counseling: Theory and Pratice*, Palo Alto, CA: Davies-Blank Publishing, pp. 93–108.

Tolstoy, L. (1856), 'A letter to Valerya Aresenyev', 9 November.

Valtinson, G.R. (1998), 'A multi-sample confirmatory analysis of work–family conflict', *Dissertation Abstract International*, **59**, (3-B), 1401.

Van Dierendonck, D., W. Schaufeli and H.J. Sixma (1994), 'Burnout among general practitioners: a perspective from equity theory', *Journal of Social and Clinical Psychology*, **13**, 86–100.

VanYperen, N.W., B.P. Buunk and W.B. Schaufeli (1992), 'Communal orientation and the burnout syndrome among nurses', *Journal of Applied Social Psychology*, **22**, 173–89.

Vinokur, A.D. and M. Westman (1998), 'Unraveling the relationship of distress levels within couples: common stressors, empathic reactions, or crossover via social interaction?', *Human Relations*, **51**, 137–57.

Westman, M. (2002), 'Crossover or stress and strain in the family and workplace', *Historical and Current Perspectives on Stress and Health*, **2**, 143–81.

Westman, M. and D. Etzion (1995), 'Crossover of stress, strain and resources from one spouse to another', *Journal of Organizational Behavior*, **16**, 169–81.

Yalom, I.D. (1980), *Existential Psychotherapy*, New York: Basic Books.

Zedeck, S. (ed.) (1992), *Work, Families and Organizations*, San Francisco: Jossey-Bass.

38 Unconscious influences on the choice of a career and their relationship to burnout: a psychoanalytic existential approach
Ayala Malach Pines

Burnout is the end result of a process in which highly motivated and committed individuals lose their spirit (for example Freudenberger, 1980; Maslach, 1982; Pines and Aronson, 1988). It characterizes people who entered their careers with high hopes, ideals and ego involvement and is experienced as a state of physical, emotional and mental exhaustion (Pines and Aronson, 1988), lowered sense of accomplishment and depersonalization (Maslach, 1982).

Different conceptual formulations were offered in an attempt to explain the etiology of burnout, including psychoanalytic theory (Fischer, 1983; Freudenberger, 1980), Jungian theory (Garden, 1989; 1995), social comparison theory (Buunk et al., 1994), social exchange theory (Schaufeli et al., 1996), equity theory (Van Dierendonck et al., 1994). The present chapter proposes a psychoanalytic existential perspective that can both explain the etiology of burnout and serve as a foundation for an effective approach to treat it (Pines, 2000a).

According to the existential perspective, the root cause of burnout lies in people's need to believe that their lives are meaningful, that the things they do are useful, important, even 'heroic' (for example Pines, 1993). This perspective is based on such noted theorists as Victor Frankl (1976), who believed that 'the striving to find meaning in one's life is the primary motivational force in man' (p. 154). Ernest Becker (1973), in his Pulitzer prize-winning book *The Denial of Death*, wrote that people's need to believe that the things they do are meaningful is their way of coping with the angst caused by facing their own mortality. In order to be able to deny death, people need to feel heroic, to know that their lives are meaningful, that they matter in the larger scheme of things. Today, in most Western countries, one of the frequently chosen answers to the existential quest, among those who can afford it, is work. People who choose this option try to derive from their work a sense of meaning for their entire life. This is why they often enter it with very high hopes, goals and expectations, idealistic and motivated. And this is why many relate to their work as a calling.

When these highly motivated and highly committed individuals (Cherniss, 1995) feel that their work is insignificant, that they make no difference to the world, they start feeling helpless and hopeless and eventually burn out (Pines, 1993).

If one accepts the premise that people try to derive a sense of existential significance from work, the next question one needs to address is why they choose to do it via the particular career that they have chosen. Why does one person choose to achieve existential significance by being a psychologist and another by being a nurse, a teacher, a manager or an entrepreneur? The choice of a career is a complex and multifaceted process that includes all the spheres of a person's life (Hall, 1996). Since the turn of the 20th century, many scholars have attempted to identify the factors that influence this process. They have identified such factors as aptitudes, interests, resources, limitations, requirements and opportunities (for example, Parsons, 1909; Ginzberg, 1951; Super, 1953, 1957; Swanson, 1996). A different perspective is offered by psychoanalytic theory (for example, Bratcher, 1982; Kets de Vries, 1995, 1996; Kets de Vries and Associates, 1991; McKelvie and Friedland, 1978; Obholzer and Roberts, 1997; Pines and Yanai, 2000; Pruyser, 1980). The psychoanalytic vantage point assumes that 'the work that any person undertakes in almost any environment, excepting only the extremes of slavery and imprisonment, is to some extent determined by personal choice, made at several levels of consciousness' (Pruyser, 1980, p. 61).

According to the psychoanalytic perspective, the unconscious determinants of any vocational choice reflect the individual's personal and familial history. People choose an occupation that enables them to replicate significant childhood experiences, gratify needs that were ungratified in their childhood and actualize occupational dreams passed on to them by their familial heritage (Pines and Yanai, 2000).

At times individuals are influenced by familial forces and legacies that are outside their awareness or with which they have not been able to deal satisfactorily in the past. These forces are also operating when they make their career decision (Bratcher, 1982). McKelvie and Friedland (1978) describe the familial influences on career choices, linking people's behavior and feelings about themselves to the existential need to find and assure a place of belonging. They show how people's career interests have been influenced by the values, roles and family constellation patterns in their families of origin.

The tendency to choose a particular occupation, the internal permission to choose according to this preference and to function successfully as a professional are all assumed to depend on the relationships with key people, especially the parents, during childhood and those people's own career choices.

Psychoanalytic theory was also used to explain career burnout (Fischer, 1983; Freudenberger, 1980). Freudenberger believed that the most overly committed and excessively dedicated professionals, who use their job as a substitute for social life and believe that they are indispensable, are most likely to burn out. The reason is that these people attribute an inordinate sense of importance to their work, which they then take to be a demonstration of their own importance. When they are subject to extraordinarily demanding situations, they burn out. Fischer (1983) adds to this conceptualization the idea that people who burn out tend to suffer from 'the illusion of grandiosity' (p. 43). In the course of normal development, the direct manifestations of this megalomania become subdued and covert, ultimately reappearing in the formation of one's ideals. The confirmation of this 'illusion of grandiosity' serves to sustain one's basic sense of self-esteem. The disconfirmation of the illusion by a failure causes burnout.

The current chapter suggests an integration of the psychoanalytic and existential ideas as a way to understand the etiology of burnout. According to the existential approach, the choice of a career involves deeply significant issues and thus people enter it with very high goals and expectations, ego involvement and passion. According to the psychoanalytic approach, the greatest passion and ego involvement are located where an unresolved childhood issue or 'metaphoric wound' lies, fueled by the hope of resolving the issue or 'healing the wound'. Success helps heal childhood wounds. However, when people feel that they have failed, when the work experience repeats the childhood trauma rather than healing it, the result is burnout.

On the basis of the psychodynamic perspective, it can be assumed that people choose different occupations to overcome different unresolved childhood issues, which is to say that the unresolved issues that propel one person to become a teacher are different from the issues that propel another person to become a manager or a nurse. Still using the psychodynamic perspective, it can be further assumed that the reasons for burnout in different occupations are related in one way or another, consciously or unconsciously, to a failure to heal such childhood wounds.

In combination, the psychoanalytic and existential perspectives suggest that an occupational choice is influenced by psychodynamic reasons that tend to be similar for people who choose a particular occupation and different for people in different occupations. These reasons make people enter their chosen profession with high goals and expectations. The goals and expectations reflect at a deeper level people's hopes to derive from their work a sense of existential significance. When the goals and expectations do not materialize, the result is burnout (Pines, 2002a; 2003).

The present chapter attempts to demonstrate the utility of the integrated psychoanalytic existential perspective for the understanding and treatment of burnout, using four examples, of a nurse, a teacher, a manager and an entrepreneur.[1]

Method
The participants, nurse, teacher, manager and entrepreneur, all came seeking therapy because of a problem of burnout. The clinical work, using a psychoanalytic existential approach, involved between 12 and 24 sessions lasting 50 minutes, that included exploration of childhood in general, traumatic childhood experiences, parents' occupations and occupational dreams, relationships with parents and family of origin dynamic; the relationship between these childhood variables and the person's occupational choice, occupational history and professional goals; and the three-way relationship between the childhood variables, the occupational goals and the experience of burnout.

The four cases and the way they were treated will be described briefly after a presentation of the research on burnout in each profession.

Nurses' burnout
Ever since the introduction of burnout into the scientific literature in the mid-1970s, nurses' burnout has received extensive and continuous research attention. In a review of 15 years of burnout research, Enzmann and Kleiber (1990) counted 144 studies of nurses' burnout. Duquette *et al.* (1994) in their literature review analyzed 300 documents related to burnout in nurses. The reason for all this attention seems obvious: nurses are considered to be particularly susceptible to the danger of burnout because of the very stressful nature of their work. Indeed nurses' burnout was found to be related to such work features as high workload (Caldwell and Weiner, 1982; Duquette *et al.*, 1994; Landsbergis, 1988), poor social support (Cronin-Stubbs and Rooks, 1985; Duquette *et al.*, 1994; Firth *et al.*, 1986; Makoto and Masao, 1994; Robinson *et al.*, 1991), a perceived imbalance between investments and outcomes in relationships with patients (Schaufeli and Janczur, 1994) and a reduced sense of personal accomplishment (McGrath *et al.*, 1989).

According to the existential perspective, nurses' burnout is caused by experiencing work as insignificant and making no difference to the patients. Most of the findings reported in the literature can be understood from this perspective. For example, why does overload cause burnout in nurses? Because it prevents nurses from doing their work the way they think it should be done, and thus prevents their experiencing success and significance in their work. Perceived imbalance between investments and outcomes in relationships with patients is a cause of burnout for the same reason: it prevents nurses from experiencing success and significance in their work. Reduced sense of personal accomplishment expresses the very essence of the failure to derive existential significance from work. The findings of other studies on nurses' burnout can also be understood from this perspective.

If one accepts the premise that nurses are trying to derive a sense of existential significance from their work, the next question that still remains to be answered is why they choose to do it via nursing. When nurses are asked why they chose a career in nursing, their answer invariably includes a reference to helping the sick and the dying (Pines, 2000b). The idealized image of nursing implied by these answers – a Florence Nightingale who holds in her arms a sick or dying patient – seems to imply tremendous control. After all, what other human relationship involves as much control as the control exercised by a nurse over her incapacitated patient? In support of this notion, research (for example Ellis and Miller, 1993) also shows that the need for control, consciously or unconsciously, plays a major role in the decision to become a nurse.

My own work with nurses often reveals a traumatic experience related to lack of control (Pines, 2000b). In one case, a nurse's realization of how little control she had over her fate was caused by a traumatic experience at age 12 of being run over by a cab while walking on a sidewalk, resulting in her being hospitalized for many months. In a second nurse's case, there was a trauma of being moved away from a home in the country, where she felt like 'a flower in a greenhouse' surrounded by open fields and many close friends, to the city where there were walls instead of trees and she was 'all alone'. She cried and pleaded with her parents. Being unable to change their mind made her feel 'helpless and powerless'. In a third case there was powerlessness of a daughter against a domineering father who forced her to go to a religious school she hated: 'I cried and cried but nothing helped. I was powerless. It was awful.' In another case a childhood sexual abuse was the root of the need for control, and in another being tormented by a father who threw his daughter into a pile of snow and stood laughing. Ilene is also an example.

Ilene

Ilene was born to a medical family. One of her grandmothers was a dentist, the other an anesthesiologist. Her mother wanted to be a physician but was not accepted by the medical school and felt very frustrated in her work as a medical technician. The mother, who was very domineering, wanted desperately for Ilene to become a physician, but Ilene wanted to be a nurse because 'Nurses have more control. A nurse is in direct contact with the patient. She controls the patient's situation and reports it to the physician. The physician's contact with the patient is less direct and immediate. Consequently, as a physician you have less control over the patient's life.'

Why is control so important to Ilene? The answer, according to psychoanalytic theory, probably has to do with a traumatic childhood experience or a series of such experiences.

When asked to recall a difficult experience in her childhood, Ilene talked about being a sickly child and being forced by her mother to wear heavy clothes even when the weather was hot. 'I would beg her to let me wear lighter clothes. I told her that all the other girls were wearing nylons and that the kids at school were making fun of me for wearing heavy wool stockings. But no amount of begging and no arguments could ever change her mind. At the end she always won. I felt helpless and powerless. Mother always had the upper hand.' As a nurse, Ilene reverses roles. The patient is helpless (the way she was) and she is the kind and understanding nurse who helps (by providing the understanding she so desperately wanted but never received as a child). She is in control (the way she never felt as a child).

What caused Ilene's burnout? As is often the case (Freudenberger, 1980; Maslach, 1982; Pines and Aronson, 1988) Ilene's burnout was caused primarily by feeling that she could not do her work the way she thought it should be done, especially because of the interference of the head nurse in her department. She felt unable to respond to the needs of her patients because of a big patient load and was pained by the suffering of people there was no way to help. She felt powerless in her dealings with the head nurse, certain physicians and the administration. Especially difficult to handle were 'not having enough control over patient care' and her 'limited authority'.

Once a connection was made between the psychodynamic reasons for her choice of a nursing career and her need for control in order to derive a sense of existential significance from her work, Ilene applied for a position as a head nurse in her unit. When she received it, she felt a renewed excitement about her work.

Teachers' burnout
Teacher burnout has also received extensive and continuous research attention (for example Blase, 1982; Byrne, 1994; Cedoline, 1982; Farber, 1984, 1991, Friedman, 1992, 2000; Pines, 2002b; Schaufeli, 1998; Shirom, 1986; Van Horn et al., 1999). Much of this research documented the existence of teachers' burnout and attempted to identify its causes. Different studies have suggested that the best predictors of teacher burnout are managing disruptive students, student violence and apathy, and a poor relationship between teacher and students, followed by administrative insensitivity and lack of support in dealing with discipline problems, bureaucratic incompetence and lack of voice in organizational decision making (Farber, 1991; Friedman and Lotan, 1985; Sakharov and Farber, 1983). Other variables identified as causing teacher burnout are class size, overload and lack of feedback from colleagues and the administration (Brenner and Bentall, 1984; Cedoline, 1982; Ursprung, 1986; Malanowski and Wood, 1984). But the problem of student discipline ranks at or near the top of almost all teacher stress surveys: 'Nothing gets teachers so worked up and so ready to leave the profession as this issue' (Farber, 1991 p. 53).

According to the existential perspective, the reason for this seems obvious: disruptive students make it impossible for teachers to teach the rest of the class and thus make it impossible for them to derive a sense of existential significance from their work. An obvious lack of interest in learning on the part of students and lack of attention in class are powerful causes of teacher burnout because they let teachers know that they are insignificant. The reason large classes are difficult for teachers is that in large classes teachers spend too much time restraining and disciplining their students and not enough time educating them – the activity that contributes most to their sense of significance. Overload causes burnout because teachers feel that they cannot do their work the way it should be done. Lack of feedback from colleagues and the administration causes burnout because it makes teachers feel that their work is not important enough to justify another teacher's or the administration's attention.

Why do teachers choose a career in teaching? When asked this question, most teachers respond with such reasons as a desire to educate students, to shape their minds, to inspire them. Some mention an inspirational teacher they had, read about or saw in a movie (such as the teacher from the movie, *To Sir, with love*) (Pines, 2002b).

The idealized image that emerges from these expectations is of a teacher who stands alone in front of an attentive class, educating students and inspiring them. What psychodynamic reasons can explain the choice of such an ideal?

Work with teachers suggests that a frequent traumatic childhood experience they mention has to do with feeling alone in the world and either being laughed at, humiliated and insulted, or else in great danger (Pines, 2002b). For example: 'When I was a young girl my mother cut my hair very short because I had psoriasis on my skull. I was too embarrassed to leave the house.' 'Children in my neighborhood mocked me because I wore glasses, they called me Abu Arba (four eyes). I felt humiliated and ugly. I couldn't handle it. I ran home.' 'A big kid in my neighborhood hit me. I felt all alone, helpless and humiliated. The only thing I could do was cry.' 'A dog bit my cheek when I was ten. I felt very scared. I was bleeding a lot. I worried how my parents will [*sic*] respond. I didn't know what response to expect. I was afraid they will [*sic*] mock me and call me a baby. I just continued running with my bleeding cheek.' 'The most traumatic experience was a tonsils operation I had after an illness and a long period of pain. I was terrified of the operation. The anesthetization was done in a primitive and terrifying way. They held me down on the lap of a male nurse in the operating room and stuffed a piece of gauze with anesthetics in my face. When I woke up from the operation I didn't stop vomiting and bleeding. I refused all the ice cream they offered me.'

When these themes are compared to the identifying characteristics of teaching, the connection seems apparent. The teacher who educates, inspires and influences students is healing a childhood trauma of insult, humiliation and anxiety. The teacher who stands alone in front of an attentive class and provides students with knowledge and values, shapes their personalities and influences their future is healing a childhood trauma of feeling alone in the world, helpless and fearful in the face of great danger.

What happens when a teacher's hopes (both conscious and unconscious) are not fulfilled? The teacher who has to face discipline problems without support from the administration repeats a childhood trauma of feeling alone in the world and in great danger. A teacher who feels unappreciated by students, parents and the administration repeats a childhood trauma of inferiority, insult and humiliation. The teacher who is threatened by students and afraid of them repeats a childhood trauma of fear, anxiety and helplessness. Mary is an example.

Mary
Mary came to therapy because, after 18 years, she felt burned out in her work as a teacher. The thing that was most difficult for her to handle was her students' 'apathy and total lack

of interest and motivation'. She remembered herself as a high-school student, adoring her charismatic teacher. He was the reason why she went into teaching. And she managed to do it successfully and happily for a long time, but now she has had it. She could not handle it anymore.

Mary's parents were poor, uneducated emigrants who could hardly speak the language. They were anxious and insecure and Mary was ashamed of them. She was a skinny, shy, anxious and rather unattractive girl who rarely dared speak up in class. Her admiration of her teacher enabled her to identify with a charismatic role model. 'I saw a teacher as someone who is worthy of respect, an admired educational figure, someone students look up to. The idea of becoming a teacher appealed to me very much. I was attracted to the daily contact between the teacher and the students, The teacher seemed to me to be someone who knows everything, the final authority, someone with wide areas of knowledge.'

This romantic image of teaching filled Mary with high hopes. Her work as a teacher enabled her to fulfill these hopes. Now she was the one everyone had to listen to, the one who was worthy of respect. Her success as a teacher gave her a sense of meaning and helped heal her childhood trauma.

Her difficulties started when 'the status of teaching started eroding'. She felt that the new generation of students had no respect for education or for her as a teacher. She was convinced that the parents, the school administration and society at large were also to blame. Cases of vandalism against teachers made her anxious. Disruptive students, and the apathy with which their misconduct was received by other students as well as the parents and the school administration, made her feel worthless. She no longer wanted to be a teacher.

Once a connection was made between Mary's childhood experiences as a shy, anxious, insecure girl and her choice of a teaching career; once she understood what aspects of work gave her a sense of meaning and why she burned out when she no longer had these aspects in her work, Mary was able to make a career change. She went back to school and got an MA in Educational Management, then she asked for and received a highly rewarding position as the Assistant Manager in her school.

Managers' burnout
Management is defined as an 'executive action that transforms external reality consistently with the personal inner theatre of the leader' (Lapierre, 1991, p. 71). Managers have been the focus of a great deal of research (over 6000 studies in the last decade alone); however, their burnout has been the focus of much smaller research attention (less than 1 per cent, or 50 articles, in the same period of time). What attracted more attention was the psychological make-up of managers (Zaleznik, 1990, 1991; Zaleznik and Kets De Vries, 1975; Kets De Vries, 1989, 1991, 1995; Lapierre, 1991; Levinson, 1982) and the 'internal theatre' (the inner life and unconscious forces) that propel the choice of a management career.

The characteristic traits of a high-ranking manager are self-confidence, a need for admiring attention and an intense need for power and influence that can at times become addictive (Kets de Vries and Associates, 1991). The high need for power is seen as the result of childhood experiences of uncertainty and lack of power, control and information. A frequent experience is the lack of a father who is present, attentive and provides solid emotional certainty. The experienced absence of a father can be the result of the father's actual death or, more frequently, the father's frequent travels abroad or a highly demanding career, or else the father's emotional absence. A high percentage of the fathers of successful managers were themselves successful managers and were distant fathers that did not have an intimate relationship with either their sons or their wives. To be a successful manager means psychologically to raise yourself in a better way than your real father did, with more power and far better control of your life and its uncertainties. Zaleznik (1991) described the essence of this experience as being 'twice born'. Individuals who are unconsciously propelled to be leaders and are successful in their quest are 'born' again, becoming 'their own father'. Their reflexive longing is to be in charge, in control, to be the father. The need for a corrective emotional experience of power is dominant in the internal theatre of high-ranking managers.

When asked what were their goals and expectations at the start of their career, most managers mention having a significant impact on the organization, having resources, doing their own thing, being number one, being a success, making the organization the best that it can be, being appreciated and recognized, and having the power and status to do something significant (Pines and Aronson, 1988, ch. 3).

The ideal image of management that is revealed in these goals and expectations is of being the head of a pyramid, the father of the organization who leads it to success and is acknowledged and rewarded for it. Given this ideal image, that is expected to give the manager a sense of existential significance and heal a childhood trauma of fatherlessness and powerlessness, it is not surprising that the main causes of burnout for managers are not having enough power to have a real impact, inadequate resources, political, administrative and bureaucratic interference, inability to do things the way they should be done, inadequate recognition and lack of opportunities for advancement and rewards (ibid.).

If the goal that is expected to give your life a sense of meaning is to have a significant impact on the organization and make it the best that it can be, your burnout is likely to be caused by not having enough power and resources to have a real impact. If your goal is to be number one and to be appreciated and recognized, you are likely to burn out because of inadequate recognition and opportunities for advancement. If you expect to do your own thing, political, administrative and bureaucratic interference that prevent you from doing things the way you think they should be done are likely to be very difficult and burnout conducive for you.

How are the reasons for managers' burnout related to the reasons that propel them towards a career in management? The results of a study that compared the childhood family dynamic of managers and entrepreneurs (Pines et al., 2002) suggest certain differences, especially regarding the relationship with father between these two 'leaders of the organizational theatre'. Managers, the study shows, perceive themselves as far more similar to their fathers in a number of positive traits including love of management and of challenge, commitment, being a dreamer as well as a realist, self-confidence and creativity. Managers also describe their mothers more positively and themselves as more similar to them than entrepreneurs, and they describe a better relationship with both parents. It is also significant that the life satisfaction and disappointment of managers (but not of entrepreneurs) are both correlated to the life satisfaction and disappointment of their fathers. All in all, the results suggest much better relationships between managers and their parents. While both may have a 'father issue' as a result of the absence of a father in their childhood, for the managers (but not the entrepreneurs) the father is someone they identify with and want to get approval from (Pines *et al.*, 2002). Dan is an example (Pines, 2000a).

Dan
Dan, a high-ranking manager in his mid-forties, came to therapy complaining about burnout. When he started his career in management Dan was convinced that he would make a major contribution to society. When he realized that his contribution was far smaller than he had hoped, he started feeling empty and disillusioned, aware of his mortality and the passage of time. These feelings eventually led to his burnout.

Both of Dan's parents were Holocaust survivors. His mother lost most of her family in a concentration camp. She herself survived the horrible ordeal, but it left her very anxious. Her anxieties focused on food and her love (that was at times suffocating) was expressed primarily through food. His father's experiences during the war left him closed and hardened. Dan's father became a successful contractor. Because of his work-related travels, he was often absent from home. As a child Dan remembers sitting on the grass waiting for his father, anxious that he might never come back (like his father's father, who disappeared during the war). Dan experienced his father as distant, dominant and critical, and his love as contingent on Dan's success. Because of his need for his father's approval, Dan worked very hard to gain it by succeeding in sports, school, the army and work. But the approval never came.

Dan became the managing coordinator between a food processing company and a food marketing company. The heads of both companies were powerful directors that Dan admired and loved. While the managerial position meant following in his father's footsteps, the content of his occupation – food – was related to Dan's mother's preoccupation with food. Given his parents' reasonably happy marriage, Dan was able to combine successfully both his father's and his mother's vocational legacies.

But there was something else Dan needed desperately from his work: he needed approval from a father figure, the kind of approval he was unable to receive from his own father. Receiving such parental approval would have given Dan a sense of success and existential significance. Instead, he found himself torn between the conflicting demands of these two powerful 'fathers' and failing, just as he failed to achieve his father's recognition. This failure was the major impetus for his burnout. After seven years in his position as a coordinating manager, Dan felt tired, discouraged and disillusioned. He felt he was not contributing anything significant and decided it was time to quit.

After Dan worked through his father issue in therapy, he was able to talk to his father and discovered that his father was very proud of him and that what Dan considered 'criticisms' were his father's misguided attempts to be helpful. The big change in Dan's relationship with his father caused a change in what he wanted in a career. He still wanted to manage (like his father) and he wanted to be involved in the food industry (his mother's legacy) but he no longer needed a father figure to give him approval. He wanted to build companies (like his father built buildings) and, once finished, move on. Dan decided to help heal companies in financial trouble. He saw in this the kind of challenge that would give him a sense of existential significance. It did.

Entrepreneurs' burnout

An entrepreneur is an individual who is 'instrumental to the conception of the idea of an enterprise and its implementation' (Kets de Vries, 1996, p. 856) and is 'a puzzling figure to large segments of the population in many societies' (Kets de Vries, 1980, p. 43). As long as 70 years ago, Joseph Schumpeter described the entrepreneur as an innovator and a catalyst of change who continuously does things that have not been done before and do not fit established societal patterns (Schumpeter, 1934, 1965).

Despite controversy (Shaver, 1995), most studies agree that entrepreneurs have distinct personality traits (Aldridge, 1997; Bonnett and Furnham, 1991; Brandstaetter, 1997; Cooper and Gimeno-Gascón, 1992; Fraboni and Saltstone, 1990; Frese *et al.*, 2000; Holler *et al.*, 1992; Kets de Vries 1980, 1985, 1996; Lynn, 1969; McLelland, 1987; Nicholson, 1988; Plant, 1996; Solomon and Winslow, 1988; Winslow and Solomon, 1987, 1989). Among the traits mentioned most often are high achievement motivation, need for control, internal locus of control, autonomy, distrust, independence, assertiveness, initiative, self-confidence, optimism, imagination, persistence in problem solving, single-mindedness, leadership, decisiveness, competitiveness, desire for applause and risk taking.

Several studies investigated the effect of culture, gender, education and family background on entrepreneurs (for example Cooper, 1986; Cooper and Gimeno-Gascón, 1992; Mulholland, 1996; Vega, 1996). They showed that they tend to be first-born (Hisrich and Brush, 1986), from ethnic and religious minority groups (Kasdan, 1965), have substantial formal education (Cooper, 1986) tend to grow up in families where the father was self-employed (for example Cromie *et al.*, 1992; Cooper and Gimeno-Gascón, 1992; Sayigh, 1962) and the family supported early start-up activities (Dyer and Handler, 1994; Carroll and Mosakowski, 1987).

Psychoanalysis with entrepreneurs helps explain the family dynamic that shapes their personality. These clinical studies suggest that the childhood of entrepreneurs often involves deprivation and turmoil, with such themes as 'escape from poverty' and 'the parent who went away' dominating their life stories. Father is portrayed as absent, remote, unpredictable and rejecting, mother as strong, controlling and assuming part of the father's traditional role. The early experiences of rejection, parental inconsistencies and control are assumed to result in considerable controlled rage, hostility, guilt and suspiciousness of people in position of authority (Kets de Vries, 1976, 1977, 1980, 1996).

Entrepreneurs and managers compared

While psychoanalytic writings on managers tend not to mention entrepreneurs and those written about entrepreneurs tend not to mention managers, their respective descriptions suggest a number of significant points of comparison. One is the relationship with the father. While both the fathers of entrepreneurs and managers are described as absent, the father of entrepreneurs is described as rejecting, unpredictable and remote; the fathers of managers, successful managers themselves, are absent because of a highly demanding career. This difference may be critical for the psychological development of their sons. In the entrepreneur, the childhood experiences of deprivation and turmoil and the father's rejection are likely to result in negative feelings towards the father and towards people and structures that symbolize the father: people in authority and hierarchical organizations. In the manager, the childhood absence of an admired father is likely to result in identification with the father and with people and institutions that symbolize the father: people in authority and hierarchical organizations.

On this reasoning, it could be expected that entrepreneurs and managers will have different feelings toward their fathers and toward authority, hierarchy and structure in general; feelings that will be manifested in their different career choices and different expectations from their careers: expectations that, if not realized, may lead to burnout.

Avner, the entrepreneur to be described next, and Dan, the manager who has just been described, in addition to being Israeli and born in Israel, have other things in common: both are in their mid-forties, tall and handsome. Both of them are highly successful professionally, married, and are committed husbands and fathers. Both of them are also second-generation Holocaust survivors. And, most importantly, both of them came to therapy complaining about burnout.

Avner

Avner, 43 years old, tall and handsome with dark hair and skin, came to therapy complaining about depression and burnout. After 20 years as the head of an electronics company he built, he felt depressed and discouraged. The company was not taking off and he was no longer excited about his work. Maybe it was time to quit.

Avner is married and has three children ranging in age from high school to kindergarten. He is not too close to his children and blames in part his wife's overinvolvement with them that left him out. Avner fell in love with his wife because she was bright, sharp, direct, outspoken and a giving person. He knew right away that she was the one he wanted to build a family with. After 18 years of marriage he still feels they have a good marriage, based on deep friendship, but is distressed by his wife's overinvolvement and lack of boundaries with their children and by her lack of tact and sensitivity towards him. These stresses are clearly related to the things he found at first most attractive about her (Pines, 1996, 1999).

Avner's father is a Holocaust survivor. He was born in Poland to a very wealthy family. His father was a successful businessman who traded automobile parts. His mother was a housewife and their home was elegant and full of art treasures. The war started when he was 13 and his safe and comfortable world was shattered. His parents were killed by the Nazis and he survived the war by hiding his Jewish identity. After the establishment of the state of Israel in 1948, he came to Israel and started working as a mechanic for a public company. He never talked about his experiences during the war. Avner describes him as a difficult man, intelligent but closed, ascetic, unhappy and nervous, with dark moods, a father who never showed love.

His mother, the middle one of three children, came from a much more humble background. Her parents managed to escape from Poland to what was then Palestine before the Holocaust. Her father was a laborer and her mother a housewife. She herself was born during the war, a period of financial stresses and anxiety in Israel. When she grew up she became an accountant. Avner describes her as very picky and a 'nag'.

Avner is the older of two sons. His brother is two years younger and works with Avner in his company. Avner describes a very difficult and stormy relationship with his father in his childhood. As a result of it, he left his home at 14 to go to a boarding school. 'I just came to them and said that this is what I'm going to do. They didn't object. I think that my father was actually relieved.'

Avner's parents met in Israel and have had a stormy and rather unhappy marriage. The boys were cared for, but did not feel loved. Avner describes his father as a 'bad father' with whom he never had a real conversation. 'He never cared about or appreciated anything I did, was always angry and cared more about the shine on his car than about me.' Avner did not respect his father as a child and does not respect him as an adult. Despite his engineering skills, which he attributes to his father, Avner does not feel that he received anything else from his depressed, closed and critical father. After leaving home at 14, he never came back, and even now has difficulty coming to his parents for a visit or talking to them, especially to his father.

Right after his army service Avner started his business, which manufactures electronic equipment that is now sold all around the globe. Avner does not like the managerial aspect of his work: 'It bores me to death', he says. Some aspects of managing people are particularly difficult. After analyzing those difficulties Avner realized that he has great difficulty with employees who reminded him of his father. Two of these 'father figures' gave him difficulty for years, drained his energy and caused havoc in the organization. His difficulties with them were a major contributor to his burnout.

The first question addressed in Avner's therapy was why he chose his career and how he expected to derive from it a sense of existential significance. This question was addressed with the help of a vocational genogram (Dagley, 1984).

Given his skills in electronics, it seemed natural for Avner to choose a career in this area. His grandfather's 'occupational genes' may have contributed to an interest in a business. The choice of entrepreneurship can be explained by the negative relationship with his father that made him feel like a psychological orphan (Kets de Vries, 1989; Pines *et al.*, 2002) Given his parents' rather unhappy marriage, Avner was not able to combine his father's (mechanics) and mother's (book keeping) vocational legacy. He had to choose, and he chose to follow his grandfather's (business selling parts) and father's (mechanics) legacy. But there was something else Avner needed from his work, something that propelled him unconsciously. He needed to repeat his frustrating childhood experience with a father figure to whom he will be able to prove something he was unable to prove to his father – that he is right and worthy of respect. That would have given him a sense of significance.

The second question Avner addressed was why he felt a sense of failure in his existential quest, and how this sense of failure was related to his burnout.

The way Avner chose to receive the acknowledgment he so desperately needed was guaranteed to help him relive his childhood trauma rather than heal it. Avner was extremely considerate towards his frustrating 'father figures', investing in them endless hours and energy that he now sees would have been better spent with his family. But rather than being impressed and convinced, they became a major cause of stress and problems in the organization. It is worth adding that anxiety and depression such as Avner's are frequent among second-generation Holocaust survivors.

The last issue addressed in Avner's therapy concerned the changes that needed to take place for him to be able again to derive existential significance from his work.

Given Avner's unresolved issues with his father, it seemed clear that this should be the focus of his therapy. At first Avner had no childhood memories of his father, but as therapy progressed he started having extremely painful memories and was able to talk about his father and his frustration, pain and anger as a child and an adolescent. Avner was not able to approach his father and have more personal conversations with him. The painful memories were too much of an obstacle.

However Avner was able to master his depression and anxiety and was very excited about the changes he was making in his life. He still feels he wants to make a significant change in his career. He now knows he does not want to manage. He wants to be an entrepreneur. A big international company approached Avner and suggested taking over his company. He is considering this offer seriously, but wants to make sure the change will offer him the kind of challenge that would give him a sense of existential significance, rather than make him a manager of some one else's company. 'When I started building my company I couldn't wait for the morning to break. I want to get back this enthusiasm. I now realize that I pushed the company into new projects because I needed the change and not because the company needed it. A company needs time to integrate, but I keep pushing it to grow because this is more exciting for me. The problem is that, if I sell the company, they will want me to remain, and I could never imagine myself as an employee. I need the challenge of an entrepreneurial project to feel alive.'

Avner, who is still very attached to his wife and admires her intellect, felt that she was insensitive to his feelings (the way his parents were). In therapy he came to understand how he was replicating in his marriage his unresolved childhood issues (Pines, 1999). The realization enabled a change in his relationship with his children and his wife, so the two of them were now 'closer than they have ever been before.'

Discussion
The four clinical cases described seem to support the psychoanalytic–existential approach to burnout. They suggest that people's career choices are influenced by unconscious forces that propel them to re-enact and overcome challenging childhood experiences. The goals and expectations they have when they enter their career are related to these unconscious forces and are expected to provide existential significance for their lives. When they fail to achieve them they burn out.

Different psychodynamic reasons seem to propel people to choose a career in nursing, management and teaching. Nurses often reveal a traumatic experience related to lack of control. This may explain, at least in part, the professional choice of a career that is characterized by immense control over patients who are anesthetized, paralyzed or otherwise incapacitated. Teachers often reveal a traumatic experience related to being the center of negative attention: humiliation, anxiety, isolation. This may account, at least in part, for the choice of a career in which one expects to stand in front of a class of adoring students that can be educated, inspired, shaped and molded. Managers often reveal a traumatic experience related to the absence of an admired father – whether real or psychological. The desire to be a manager expresses an unconscious desire for power and influence (become a father) and for the recognition of the organization (a metaphoric father). Entrepreneurs also reveal a traumatic experience related to their fathers, but not admired fathers, rather fathers they do not identify with. Their desire to create something new that will prove existing structures wrong can be understood in light of the desire to prove their fathers wrong.

As a result, the causes of burnout also tend to be occupation-specific. For nurses, the most frequent cause of burnout involves witnessing human suffering without being able to help. For teachers it is discipline problems and students being unmotivated, inattentive, indifferent, impertinent and disparaging. For managers it is not having power and resources to have real impact. For entrepreneurs, it is the inability to create something new and successful.

In all four cases presented, the primary cause of burnout was not hard work, but rather the things that made it impossible for the professionals to derive a sense of existential significance from their work. In all four cases, there seems to be a relationship between the primary causes of burnout and the goals and expectations (on the conscious, rather than unconscious, level) that the professionals reported that they had when they entered their career.

For nurses, the most important declared goal was to help people in pain; consequently the greatest cause of their burnout is witnessing human pain without being able to help. For teachers, the most important declared goal was to educate students, influence and inspire them, shape their personalities and influence their future. Consequently the major causes of their burnout are those aspects of their work (such as discipline problems and students being disruptive, impertinent and disparaging) that make it obvious that they have failed. For managers, the most important goal was to have a significant impact on the organization, making it the best that it can be, doing it their own way and being a success. Consequently their most powerful cause of burnout is not having enough power and resources to have a real impact and do things the way they should be done. For entrepreneurs, the most important goal was to create something new that will be a great success and will prove everyone else wrong. Their most powerful cause of burnout was not being able to accomplish that.

The relationship between the goals and expectations professionals reported they had when they entered their career and the stresses that they said eventually caused their burnout supports the existential perspective on burnout.

The observation that people who enter teaching, nursing, management or entrepreneursip have similar reasons for the choice of their particular career, and have similar goals and expectations at the start of their career, provides indirect support for the psychodynamic perspective. It suggests that there are deeper, mostly unconscious, reasons that are responsible for the choice of a career.

This chapter has focused on nurses, teachers, managers and entrepreneurs, but a similar analysis can be made of the causes of burnout among most professional groups, including psychologists, physicians, insurance agents, dentists, police officers and secret service agents (to mention just a few examples). Secret service agents, who frequently recount a childhood trauma in which they felt all alone in the world with no one to trust, enter in their work a world in which no one can be trusted (including themselves) and eventually burn out for that very reason. Psychologists, who as children failed to help a parent master a psychological problem (such as depression) and entered psychology hoping to help others where they had failed (specializing in work with depressed patients) burn out when they realize that, like their parents, their patients are either unwilling or unable to benefit from their help.

For physicians, who hoped that conquering death would give their life a sense of meaning, because they felt helpless witnessing death in their childhood, a major cause of burnout is confronting the limitations of medicine and being unable to prevent illness, pain and death. For insurance agents, who went into the field of insurance because of a childhood experience of a family's financial devastation, hoping to protect themselves and others from such dire events, a major cause of burnout is a failure to provide this protection. Dentists, who dreamed about being in the medical profession but failed to enter medicine, go into dentistry hoping it will give them the importance they did not experience as children. They burn out when their professional work is unappreciated. Entrepreneurs, who tend to be 'psychological orphans', are propelled by the need to do their own thing and prove to the world that they are right, but burn out when they cannot do what they think is right or when they are proved wrong. Police officers, who as children were often on the other side of the law or felt weak against the lawless, enter the police force in the hope of being strong and right. They burn out when they realize that being a police officer or being righteous or lawful does not make you strong.

Making the connection between the unconscious reasons for the choice of a career and the particular significance expected to be derived from it, and making the connection between the failure to derive existential significance from work and burnout, besides having a theoretical significance, have a very concrete implication. They can be translated to a treatment approach for career burnout (Pines, 2000a). The treatment approach includes three steps:

1. identifying the conscious and unconscious reasons for the individual's career choice and how the chosen career was expected to provide a sense of existential significance;
2. identifying the reasons for the individual's failure to derive a sense of existential significance from the work and how this sense of failure is related to burnout;
3. identifying changes that will enable the individual to derive a sense of existential significance from work.

Identifying the conscious and unconscious reasons for the individual's career choice requires a detailed exploration of childhood experiences, including role in the family, relationships with each one of the parents as well as the relationship between the parents, the parents' jobs, hobbies, occupational dreams and satisfaction from life. Traumatic childhood experiences of the person and the parents need to be examined in terms of their influence on the career choice. How the chosen career was expected to provide a sense of existential significance can be examined by an exploration of the relationship between the childhood experiences and the occupational choice as well as the goals and expectations at the start of the career.

Identifying the reasons for the individual's failure to derive a sense of existential significance from the work requires a detailed examination of the reasons for the dissatisfaction and burnout at work. This examination also provides the connection between the person's failed existential quest and burnout.

Identifying changes that will enable the individual to derive a sense of existential significance from work requires making the connection between the childhood experiences, the frustrated occupational goals and the experience of burnout. Once these connections are made, it is possible to examine various options that will enable the person to derive new existential significance from work.

This treatment approach was used, successfully, in the cases of the nurse the teacher and the manager presented in this chapter. It was also used successfully with people suffering from burnout in the other occupations mentioned briefly. It was used cross-culturally (in both Israel and the USA) and in a group context as well as in individual therapy. This is not meant to imply that it is the only or necessarily the best approach for treating burnout, just as the chapter is not meant to imply that the psychoanalytic existential perspective is the best or most parsimonious explanation for the etiology of burnout. It is, however, meant to offer it as an effective approach.

There are a number of other noteworthy qualifications. First, the paper focuses on people who choose their occupations, when most of the earth's population has little or no choice in the work they pursue. Indeed a study of Mexican blue-collar women shows that the antecedents of burnout were different in them than in American human service professionals. The blue-collar women experienced burnout when work did not enable them to escape conditions of poverty, while the white-collar human service professionals experienced burnout when they felt unable to have significant impact on people's lives (Pines and Guendelman, 1995).

Second, the psychoanalytic existential perspective is not meant as an essentialist 'one size fits all' explanation for the internal motivations of people in various occupations. Obviously people in different occupations constitute a variegated population with a multiplicity of personalities, personal histories, views and values. Individual and within-group differences may be larger than any cross-occupation differences of the type discussed in this chapter. Thus, for example, not all nurses are driven to nursing because of a desire to seek control. Some nurses were 'parentified' children who had taken care of parents and younger siblings, and were drawn to the profession for defensive reasons. That is, they were too terrified to allow anyone to take care of them, much as they might long for such a thing, so they engaged in the defense of reaction formation and kept taking care of others until they exhausted themselves.

Individual differences are more important than modal personalities or central tendencies if one is working with a single individual. Furthermore, despite the psychoanalytic notion that the choice of a career is determined by a deeply enacted choice made at various levels of consciousness, people are not static but dynamic and ever-changing. At times, when people actually experience the texture of the work they have dreamt about since childhood, they experience a disconnection between the internal vision and the external reality which makes them abandon that occupational dream.

In the future, systematic research will need to prove the efficacy of the psychoanalytic existential approach for the treatment of burnout using different occupational groups (such as psychologists, physicians, dentists and police officers). In addition future research will also need to compare its efficacy to the efficacy of other treatment approaches that can and have been derived from other theoretical approaches to burnout.

Note

1. The cases of the nurse, the teacher and the manager are described in Pines (2002); the case of the entrepreneur is described in Pines (2003).

References

Aldridge, J.H. (1997), 'An occupational personality profile of the male entrepreneur as assessed by the 16PF fifth edition', *Dissertation Abstracts International*, **58**(5-B), 2728.
Becker, E. (1973), *The Denial of Death*, New York: Free Press.
Blase, I.J. (1982), 'A social psychological grounded theory of teacher stress and burnout', *Educational Administration Quarterly*, **18**, 93–113.
Bonnett, C. and A. Furnham (1991), 'Who wants to be an entrepreneur? A study of adolescents interested in a Young Enterprise scheme', *Journal of Economic Psychology*, **12**, 465–78.
Brandstaetter, H. (1997), 'Becoming an entrepreneur: a question of personality structure?', *Journal of Economic Psychology*, 18, 157–77.
Bratcher, W.E. (1982), 'The influence of the family on career selection: a family systems perspective', *The Personnel & Guidance Journal*, **61**, 87–91.
Brenner, S.O. and R. Bentall (1984), 'The teacher stress process: a cross cultural analysis', *Journal of Occupational Behavior*, **5**, 183–96.
Buunk, B.P., W.B. Schaufeli and J.F. Ybema (1994), 'Burnout, uncertainty, and the desire for social comparison among nurses', *Journal of Applied Social Psychology*, **24**, 1701–18.
Byrne, B.M. (1994), 'Burnout: testing for the validity, replication, and invariance of causal structure across elementary, intermediate, and secondary teachers', *American Journal of Social Behavior and Personality*, **1**, 107–12.
Caldwell, T. and M.F. Weiner (1982), 'Stresses and coping in ICU nursing', *General Hospital Psychiatry*, **3**, 119–27.
Carroll, G.R. and E. Mosakowski (1987), 'The career dynamics of self employment', *Administrative Science Quarterly*, **32**, 570–89.
Cedoline, A.J. (1982), 'Job Burnout in Public Education', Teachers College, Columbia University, New York.
Cherniss, C. (1995), *Beyond Burnout*, New York: Routledge.
Cooper, A.C. (1986), 'Entrepreneurship and high technology', in D.L. Sexton and R.W. Smilor (eds), *The Art and Science of Entrepreneurship*, Cambridge, MA: Ballinger, pp. 153–68.
Cooper, A.C. and F.J. Gimeno-Gascón (1992), 'Entrepreneurs, processes of founding, and new firm performance', in D.L. Sexton and J.D. Kasarda (eds), *The State of the Art of Entrepreneurship*, Boston: Kent Publishing Co., pp. 301–40.
Cromie, S., I. Callaghan and M. Jansen (1992), 'The entrepreneurial tendencies of managers: a research note', *British Journal of Management*, **3**, 1–5.
Cronin-Stubbs, D. and C.A. Rooks (1985), 'The stress, social support and burnout of critical care nurses', *Heart & Lung*, **14**, 31–9.
Dagley, J. (1984), *A Vocational Genogram*, Athens: GA: University of Georgia.
Duquette, A., S. Kerouac, B. Sandhu and L. Beaudet (1994), 'Factors relating to nursing burnout: a review of empirical knowledge', *Issues in Mental Health Nursing*, **15**, 337–58.
Dyer, W.G. and W. Handler (1994), 'Entrepreneurship and family business: exploring the connection', *Entrepreneurship Theory and Practice*, **19**, 71–83.
Ellis, B.H. and K.I. Miller (1993), 'The role of assertiveness, personal control, and participation in the prediction of nurse burnout', *Journal of Applied Communication Research*, **21**, 327–42.
Enzmann, D. and D. Kleiber (1990), *Burnout: 15 Years of Research: An International Bibliography*, Gottingen: Hogrefe.
Farber, B.A. (1984), 'Teacher burnout: assumptions, myths and issues', *Teachers College Record*, **86**, 321–38.
Farber, B.A. (1991), *Crisis in Education: Stress and Burnout in the American Teacher*, San Francisco, CA: Jossey Bass.
Firth, H., J. McIntee, P. McKeown and P. Britton (1986), 'Interpersonal support amongst nurses at work', *Journal of Advanced Nursing*, **11**, 273–82.
Fischer, H. (1983), 'A psychoanalytic view of burnout', in B. Farber (ed.) (1983), *Stress and Burnout in the Human Service Professions*, New York: Pergamon, pp. 40–5.
Fraboni, M. and R. Saltstone (1990), 'First and second generation entrepreneur typologies: dimensions of personality', *Journal of Social Behavior and Personality*, **5**, 105–13.
Frankl, V.E. (1976), *Man's Search for Meaning*, New York: Pocket Book.
Frese, M., E. Chell and H. Klandt (2000), 'Psychological approaches to entrepreneurship. Introduction', *European Journal of Work and Organizational Psychology*, **9**(1), 3–6.
Freudenberger, H.J. (1980), *Burn-out: The High Cost of High Achievement*, Garden City, New York: Doubleday.
Friedman, I.A. (1992), 'High – and low – burnout schools: school culture aspects of teacher burnout', *Journal of Educational Research*, **84**, 325–33.
Friedman, I.A. (2000), 'Burnout in teachers: shattered dreams of impeccable professional performance', *Journal of Clinical Psychology. In Session. Psychotherapy in Practice*, 595–606.

Friedman, I.A. and A. Lotan (1985), '*The burnout of the teacher in Israel*', The Henrietta Szold Institute, Jerusalem, publication no.268, (Hebrew).
Garden, A.M. (1989), 'Burnout: the effect of psychological type on research', *Journal of Occupational Psychology*, **62**, 223–34.
Garden, A.M. (1995), 'The purpose of burnout: a Jungian interpretation', in R. Crandall and P.L. Perrewé (eds), *Occupational Stress: A Handbook. Series in Health Psychology and Behavioral Medicine*, Philadelphia, PA: Taylor & Francis, pp. 207–22.
Ginzberg, E. (1951), *Occupational Choice*, New York: Columbia University Press.
Hall, D.T. (1996), 'Long live the career', in D.T. Hall and Associates (eds), *The Career is Dead – Long Live the Career*, San Francisco: Jossey-Bass, pp. 1–12.
Hisrich, R.D. and C. Brush (1986), 'Characteristics of the minority entrepreneur', *Journal of Small Business Management*, **24**, 1–8.
Holler, M.J., V. Host and K. Kristensen (1992), 'Decision on strategic markets: an experimental study', *Scandinavian Journal of Management*, **8**, 133–46.
Kasdan, (1965), 'Family structure, migration and the entrepreneur', *Comparative Study of Society*, 7(4).
Kets de Vries, M.F.R. (1976), 'What makes entrepreneurs entrepreneurial?', *Business and Society Review*, **17**, 18–23.
Kets de Vries, M.F.R. (1977), 'The entrepreneurial personality: a person at the cross-roads', *Journal of Management Studies*, **14**, 34–58.
Kets de Vries, M.F.R. (1980), 'Stress and the entrepreneur', in C.L. Cooper and R. Payne (eds), *Current Concerns in Occupational Stress*, New York: John Wiley and Sons.
Kets de Vries, M.F.R. (1985), 'The dark side of entrepreneurship', *Harvard Business Review*, November–December, 160–168.
Kets de Vries, M.F.R. (1989), *Prisoners of Leadership*, New York: Wiley.
Kets de Vries, M.F.R. (1991), 'On becoming a CEO', in M.F.R Kets de Vries *et al.* (eds), *Organizations of the Couch: Clinical Perspectives on Organizational Behavior and Change*, San-Francisco: Jossey-Bass, pp. 120–39.
Kets de Vries, M.F.R. (1995), *Life and Death in the Executive Fast Lane*, San-Francisco: Jossey-Bass.
Kets de Vries, M.F.R. (1996), 'The anatomy of the entrepreneur', *Human Relations*, **49**, 853–83.
Kets de Vries, M.F.R. and Associates (1991), *Organizations on the Couch*, San Francisco: Jossey-Bass.
Landsbergis, P.A. (1998), 'Occupational stress among health care workers: a test of the job demands–control model', *Journal of Organizational Behavior*, **9**, 217–39.
Lapierre, L. (1991), 'Exploring the dynamics of leadership', in M.F.R Kets de Vries *et al.* (eds), *Organizations of the Couch: Clinical Perspectives on Organizational Behavior and Change*, San-Francisco, CA: Jossey-Bass, pp. 69–93.
Levinson, H. (1982), *Executive: The Guide to Responsive Management*, Cambridge MA: Harvard University Press.
Lynn, R. (1969), 'Personality characteristics of a group of entrepreneurs', *Occupational Psychology*, **43**, 151–2.
Makoto, K. and T. Masao (1994), 'Burnout among nurses: the relationship between stresses and burnout', *Japanese Journal of Experimental Social psychology*, **34**, 33–4.
Malanowski, J.R. and P.H. Wood (1984), 'Burnout and self-actualization in public school teachers', *Journal of Psychology*, **117**, 23–6.
Maslach, C. (1982), *Burnout – The Cost of Caring*, Englewood Cliffs, NJ: Prentice Hall.
McGrath, A., N. Reid and J. Boor (1989), 'Occupational stress in nursing', *International Journal of Nursing Studies*, **3**, 3–31.
McKelvie, W.H. and B.U. Friedland (1978), 'The life style and career counseling', in L. Baruth and D. Ekstein (eds), *Life Style: Theory, Practice and Research*, Dubuque, I: Kendal/Hunt.
McLelland, D.C. (1987), 'Characteristics of successful entrepreneurs', *Journal of Creative Behavior*, **21**, 219–33.
Mulholland, K. (1996), 'Entrepreneurialism, masculinity and the self-made man', in D.L. Collinson and J. Hearn (eds), *Men as Managers, Managers as Men: Critical Perspectives on Men, Masculinity and Management*, London: Sage, pp. 123–49.
Nicholson, N. (1988), 'Personality and entrepreneurial leadership: a study of the heads of the UK's most successful independent companies', *European management Journal*, **16**, 529–39.
Obholzer, A. and V.Z. Roberts (1997), *The Unconscious at Work*, London/New York: Routledge.
Parsons, F. (1909), *Choosing a Vocation*, Garrett Park, MD: Garrett Park Press.
Pines, A.M. (1993), 'Burnout – an existential perspective', in W. Schaufeli, C. Maslach and T. Marek (eds), *Professional Burnout: Developments in Theory and Research*, Washington, DC: Taylor & Francis, pp. 33–52.
Pines, A.M. (1996), *Couple Burnout: Causes and Cures*, New York: Routledge.
Pines, A.M. (1999), *Falling in Love: How we Choose the Lovers we Choose*, New York: Routledge.

Pines, A.M. (2000a), 'Treating career burnout: an existential perspective', *Journal of Clinical Psychology. In Session: Psychotherapy in Practice*, **56**, 1–10.
Pines, A.M. (2000b), 'Nurses' burnout: an existential psychodynamic perspective', *Journal of Psychosocial Nursing*, **38**(2), 1–9.
Pines, A.M. (2002a), 'A psychoanalytic existential approach to burnout: demonstrated in the cases of a nurse, a teacher and a manager', *Psychotherapy: Theory/Research/Practice/Training*, **39**, 103–13.
Pines, A.M. (2002b), 'Teacher burnout: a psychodynamic existential perspective', *Teacher and Teaching: Theory and Practice*, **8**, 121–40.
Pines, A.M. (2002c), 'The female entrepreneur: burnout treated using a psychodynamic existential approach', *Clinical Case Studies*, **1**, 171–81.
Pines, A.M. (2003), 'Unconscious influences on career choice: entrepreneur vs. manager', *Australian Journal of Career Development*, **12**(2) 7–18.
Pines, A.M. and E. Aronson (1988), *Career Burnout: Causes and Cures*, New York: Free Press.
Pines, A.M. and S. Guendelman (1995), 'Exploring the relevance of burnout to Mexican blue collar women', *Journal of Occupational Behavior*, **47**, 1–20.
Pines, A.M. and O. Yanai (2000), 'Unconscious influences on the choice of a career: implications for organizational consultation', *Journal of Health and Human Services Administration*, **21**(4), 502–11.
Pines, A.M., A. Sadeh, D. Dvir and O. Yafe-Yanai (2002), 'Entrepreneurs and managers: similar yet different', *International Journal of Organizational Analysis*, **10**(2) 172–90.
Plant, P. (1996), 'Work values and counseling: careerist, wage earner and entrepreneur', *International Journal for the Advancement of Counseling*, **19**, 373–7.
Pruyser, P.W. (1980), 'Work: curse or blessing?', *Bulletin of the Menninger Clinic*, **44**, 59–73.
Robinson, S.E., S.L. Roth, J. Keim and M. Levenson (1991), 'Nurse burnout: work related and demographic factors as culprits', *Research in Nursing and Health*, **14**, 223–8.
Sakharov, M. and B.A. Farber (1983), 'A critical study of burnout in teachers', in B.A. Farber (ed.), *Stress and Burnout in Human Service Professions*, New York: Pergamon Press.
Sayigh, Y.A. (1962), *Entrepreneurs of Lebanon*, Cambridge MA: Harvard University Press.
Schaufeli, W.B. (1998), 'Burnout and lack of reciprocity among teachers', paper presented at a symposium on teacher burnout held at the annual meeting of the American Psychological Association, San Francisco, California, August.
Schaufeli, W.B. and B. Janczur (1994), 'Burnout among nurses. a Polish–dutch comparison', *Journal of Cross Cultural Psychology*, **25**, 95–113.
Schaufeli, W.B., D. Van Dierendonck and K. Van Gorp (1996), 'Burnout and reciprocity: toward a dual-level social exchange model', *Work & Stress*, **3**, 225–37.
Schumpeter, J.A. (1934), *The Theory of Economic Development*, Cambridge, MA: Harvard University Press.
Schumpeter, J.A. (1965), 'Economic theory and entrepreneurial history', in E.C.J. Aiken (ed.), *Explorations in Enterprise* Cambridge, MA: Harvard University Press.
Shaver, K. (1995), 'The entrepreneurial personality myth', *Business and Economic Review*, **41**, 20–3.
Shirom, A. (1986), 'Does stress lead to affective strain or vice versa? A structural regression test', paper presented at the Congress of the International Association of Applied Psychology, Jerusalem, Israel.
Solomon, G.T. and E.K. Winslow (1988), 'Toward a descriptive profile of the entrepreneur', *Journal of Creative Behavior*, **22**, 162–71.
Super, D.E. (1953), 'A theory of vocational development', *American Psychologist*, **8**, 185–90.
Super, D.E. (1957), *The psychology of careers*, New York: Harper & Row.
Swanson, J. (1996), 'The theory is the practice: trait and factor/person–environment fit counseling', in M.L. Savickas and B.W. Walsh (eds), *Handbook of Career Counseling: Theory and Practice*, Palo Alto, CA: Daviesblack, publishing, pp. 93–108.
Ursprung, A.W. (1986), 'Burnout in the human services: a review of the literature', *Rehabilitation Counseling Bulletin*, **29**, 190–99.
Van Dierendonck, D., W. Schaufeli and H.J. Sixma (1994), 'Burnout among general practitioners: a perspective from equity theory', *Journal of Social and Clinical Psychology*, **13**, 86–100.
Van Horn, J.E., W.B. Schaufeli and D. Enzmann (1999), 'Teacher burnout and lack of reciprocity', *Journal of Applied Social Psychology*, **29**, 91–108.
Vega, G. (1996), 'Letting go: when entrepreneurs turn into managers', *Dissertation Abstracts International*, **56**(9-A), 3654.
Winslow, E.K. and G.T. Solomon (1987), 'Entrepreneurs are more than non conformists: they are mildly sociopathic', *Journal of Creative Behavior*, **21**, 202–13.
Winslow, E.K. and G.T. Solomon (1989), 'Further development of a descriptive profile of entrepreneurs', *Journal of Creative Behavior*, **23**, 149–61.
Yalom, I. (1980), *Existential Psychotherapy*, New York: Basic Books.

Zaleznik, A. (1990), *Executive's Guide to Motivating People*, Chicago: Bonus.
Zaleznik, A. (1991), 'Leading and managing: understanding the difference', in M.F.R. Kets de Vries *et al.* (eds), *Organizations of the Couch: Clinical Perspectives on Organizational Behavior and Change*, San-Francisco: Jossey-Bass, pp. 97–119.
Zaleznik, A. and M.F.R. Kets De Vries (1975/1980), *Power and the Corporate Mind*, Boston: Houghton Mifflin.

39 Does burnout affect physical health? A review of the evidence

Arie Shirom and Samuel Melamed

Burnout has received increased research attention in recent years. During the period 1995–2002, annually about 150 articles that concerned burnout appeared in journals covered by PsychInfo. As is evident, burnout has been a major focus of researchers' efforts. A recent review of the area of burnout (Schaufeli and Enzmann, 1998) found about 5500 entries with 'burnout' as a key word between 1975 and 1995. Notwithstanding this large number of studies, the relationships between burnout and physical health, including physiological risk factors and physical disease states, have hardly been explored. The literature on burnout and well-being or mental health is substantial, but has not been reviewed with sufficient attention to the instruments used to gauge burnout and their respective construct validity. The objectives of this chapter are to review current knowledge on the above issues and to provide a perspective on future directions of research into burnout–health linkages.

We start out by discussing the conceptual meaning of burnout. Burnout is viewed as an affective reaction to ongoing stress. We contend that core content of this affective reaction is the gradual depletion over time of individuals' intrinsic energetic resources, leading to feelings of emotional exhaustion, physical fatigue and cognitive weariness (Shirom, 1989). Given the multidimensionality of the construct and the controversy over its operational definition (Maslach *et al.*, 2001), this conceptual analysis is essential for understanding the possible health consequences of burnout. We seek in this chapter to propose mechanisms that link burnout and health (cf. Schaufeli and Greenglass, 2001). The following sections cover the empirical literature on burnout's linkages with mental and physical health, respectively.

Typically, empirical studies on the health consequences of burnout are based on a cross-sectional study design and measure burnout, and also mental health, by asking respondents to complete a self-report questionnaire. In this review, the emphasis is on longitudinal studies on burnout's impact on health since they give more credence to cause and effect statements. The voluminous empirical research on burnout has already been reviewed by several by meta-analytic studies (Collins, 1999; Lee and Ashforth, 1996; Schaufeli and Enzmann, 1998). Most of this research has measured burnout with the Maslach Burnout Inventory (MBI). In references made to this body of studies, we will focus on results reported for the emotional exhaustion scale.

This review covers burnout of employees in work organizations, excluding research that deals exclusively with non-employment settings (for example, athletes' burnout: Dale and Weinberg, 1990). Also excluded is research that deals with burnout in life domains other than work, such as crossover of burnout among marital partners (for example, Pines, 1996; Westman and Etzion, 1995).

The conceptual basis of burnout

During the 1980s and early 1990s, research on burnout, regardless of the conceptual approach employed, dealt almost exclusively with people-oriented professionals (for example, teachers, nurses, doctors, social workers and police). People-oriented professionals often enter their mostly public sector profession with service-oriented idealistic goals. They typically work under norms that expect them to continuously invest emotional, cognitive and even physical energy in service recipients. In most of today's advanced market economies, the public sector has to adjust to consumers' growing demands for quality service, 'downsizing' and budgetary retrenchments. Inevitably such a context of overloading and conflicting demands is a fertile ground for creating a process of emotional exhaustion, mental weariness and physical fatigue that Freudenberger, who pioneered in scientifically investigating this phenomenon, labeled 'burnout'.

Freudenberger (1974, 1980), pioneering clinically oriented work on burnout, inspired three different conceptual approaches to burnout, each with its distinct measure. We refer to the conceptual schemes and measures of Maslach and her colleagues (Maslach, 1982; Maslach and Leiter, 1997), of Pines and her colleagues (Pines and Aronson, 1988; Pines et al., 1981) and of Shirom and Melamed (Shirom, 1989; Hobfoll and Shirom, 1993, 2000; Melamed et al., 1992). In this review, we will emphasize issues related to the validity of the first conceptual approach to burnout, including the measurement instrument constructed by Maslach and her colleagues, the Maslach Burnout Inventory (MBI)(Maslach et al., 1996). The reason for this focus is that the MBI was one of the very first scientifically validated burnout measurement instruments, and it has been the most widely used in scholarly research (Schaufeli and Enzmann, 1998). The first version of the MBI reflected the field's preoccupation with professionals in people-oriented occupations. Subsequently the construction of newer versions of the popular MBI, applicable to other occupational groups (Maslach et al., 1996) extended the study of burnout to other categories of employees.

The Maslach Burnout Model and Inventory

According to this conceptualization (Maslach and Jackson, 1981; Maslach, 1982; Maslach and Leiter, 1997), burnout is viewed as a syndrome that consists of three dimensions: emotional exhaustion, depersonalization and reduced personal accomplishment. Emotional exhaustion, which refers to feelings of being depleted of one's emotional resources, is regarded as the basic individual stress component of the syndrome (Maslach et al., 2001). Depersonalization, referring to negative, cynical or excessively detached responses to other people at work, represents the interpersonal component of burnout. Reduced personal accomplishment, referring to feelings of decline in one's competence and productivity and to one's lowered sense of self-efficacy, represents the self-evaluation component of burnout (Maslach, 1998, p. 69). The three dimensions were not deducted theoretically but resulted from labeling exploratory factor-analyzed items initially collected to reflect the range of experiences associated with the phenomenon of burnout (Maslach, 1998, p. 68; Schaufeli and Enzmann, 1998, p. 51).

Subsequently Maslach and her colleagues modified the original definition of the latter two dimensions (cf. Maslach et al., 2001, p. 399). Depersonalization was renamed 'cynicism', though it still referred to the same cluster of symptoms involving other people at work rather than service recipients. However the new label for this dimension of the syndrome poses new problems. As an emerging new concept in psychology and organizational behavior, the term 'cynicism' is used to refer to negative attitudes involving frustration from, disillusionment with and distrust of organizations, persons, groups or objects (Andersson and Bateman, 1997; Dean *et al.*, 1998). Abraham (2000) has suggested that work cynicism, one of the forms of cynicism that she had identified in her research, tends to be closely related to burnout. Garden (1987) has argued that this dimension of the syndrome of burnout gauges several distinct attitudes, including distancing, hostility, rejection and unconcern. It follows that the discriminant validity of this component of burnout, relative to the current conceptualizations of employee or work cynicism or relative to the other distinct attitudinal concepts noted by Garden (1987), has yet to be established.

The third dimension was relabeled 'reduced efficacy' or 'ineffectiveness', depicted to include the self-assessments of low self-efficacy, lack of accomplishment, lack of productivity and incompetence (Leiter and Maslach, 2001). Each of these concepts, self-efficacy, accomplishment or achievement, personal productivity or performance, and personal competence, represents a distinct field of research in the behavioral sciences and the authors of the MBI have yet to clarify on what theoretical grounds they can be grouped together to represent a single conceptual entity. Does reduced efficacy refer to one's confidence in one's capability to execute successfully courses of action required to deal with prospective tasks, as self-efficacy is customarily defined (for example, Lee and Bobko, 1994; Stajkovic and Luthans, 1998)? Does the third dimension of burnout reflect one's belief in one's knowledge and skills, as competence is often conceptualized (Foschi, 2000; Sandberg, 2000)? As an additional alternative, does it relate to self-assessed job performance or performance expectations (for example, Stajkovic and Luthans, 1998)? It appears that each of the second and third dimensions of the MBI, as currently defined, probably represents several multifaceted constructs, each having different theoretical implications with regard to the emotional exhaustion component of burnout suggested by the authors of the MBI (cf. Moore, 2000, p. 341).

Clearly the conceptualization of burnout as tapped by the MBI relates to it as a multidimensional construct. A construct is multidimensional when it refers to several distinct but related dimensions that are viewed as a single theoretical construct (Law *et al.*, 1998). The proponents of this multidimensional view of burnout (for example, Maslach, 1998) argue that it provides a holistic representation of a complex phenomenon, broadly conceived as referring to the process of wear and tear or continuous encroachment upon employees' resources. However they have yet to provide convincing theoretical arguments as to why the three different clusters of symptoms that comprise their conceptualization of burnout should 'hang together' (cf. Maslach *et al.*, 2001). They further argue that their conceptualization allows researchers to use broadly conceived types of stress in both the work and the family domains as potential antecedents of burnout, thus increasing its explained variance. However there is a paucity of evidence that there are specific antecedent variables or mechanisms leading to all of the three clusters of symptoms included in the MBI (Collins, 1999; Lee and Ashforth, 1996; Schaufeli and Enzmann, 1998). A case in point is the phase model of burnout, developed by Golembiewski and his colleagues and tested in a series of studies (see, for example, Golembiewski and Boss, 1992; Golembiewski *et al.*, 1986; Golembiewski and Munzenrider, 1988). One of the theoretical assumptions upon which this model was based was that individuals experiencing burnout on the dimension of emotional exhaustion do not necessarily experience either of the other two clusters of symptoms. Indeed Golembiewski and his colleagues (Golembiewski *et al.*, 1986; Golembiewski and Munzenrider, 1988; Golembiewski and Boss, 1992) have provided the notion that each phase or dimension of burnout may develop independently of each other.

Maslach (1998, p. 70) has argued that adding the dimensions of cynicism and reduced personal efficacy to the core dimension of emotional exhaustion was justified in that they add the interpersonal aspect of burnout to the conceptualization of the phenomenon. However the emotional exhaustion scale of the MBI already includes items that tap interpersonal aspects of work, such as 'working with people all day is really a strain for me', and 'Working with people directly puts too much stress on me' (Maslach and Jackson, 1981). Conceptually, therefore, the view of burnout as a syndrome consisting of three clusters of symptoms lacks theoretical underpinnings, has not been supported by evidence demonstrating a common etiology for the three dimensions, and includes two clusters of symptoms, cynicism and reduced personal effectiveness, that appear to be too heterogeneous for advancing our knowledge on burnout.

In sum, the MBI, the measurement scale whose process of construction has led inductively to the above conceptualization, has been the most popular instrument for measuring burnout in empirical research (for reviews of studies using it, see Collins, 1999; Lee and Ashforth, 1996; Schaufeli and Enzmann, 1998). It contains items purportedly assessing each of the three clusters of symptoms included in the syndrome view of burnout, namely emotional exhaustion, cynicism or depersonalization, and reduced effectiveness or lowered professional efficacy. It asks respondents to indicate the frequency over the work year with which they have experienced each feeling on a seven-point scale ranging from zero (never) to six (every day). Three indices are usually constructed relating to each of the above dimensions (for a recent psychometric critique, see Barnett *et al.*, 1999). The factorial validity of the MBI has been extensively studied (Byrne, 1994; Handy, 1988; Lee and Ashforth, 1996; Schaufeli and Dierendonck, 1993; Schaufeli and Buunk, 1996). Most of the researchers examining this aspect of MBI validity have reported that a three-factor solution better fits their data than does a two-dimensional or a one-dimensional structure (for recent examples, see Boles *et al.*, 2000; Schutte *et al.*, 2000). Researchers using the MBI have most often constructed three different indices corresponding to the three dimensions of emotional exhaustion, cynicism and reduced personal effectiveness. Several studies have argued, on both theoretical and psychometric grounds, that the use of a total score to represent total burnout should be avoided (for example, Moore, 2000; Kalliath *et al.*, 2000; Koeske and Koeske, 1989). The emotional exhaustion dimension has been consistently viewed as the core component of the MBI (for example, Moore, 2000; Cordes *et al.*, 1997; Burke and Greenglass, 1995). Most studies have shown it to be the most internally consistent and stable of the three components (Schaufeli and Enzmann, 1998). In meta-analytic reviews, it has been shown to be the most responsive to the nature and intensity of work-related stress (Lee and Ashforth, 1996; Schaufeli and Enzmann, 1998).

Pines' Burnout Model and Measure
Pines and her colleagues define burnout as the state of physical, emotional and mental exhaustion caused by long–term involvement in emotionally demanding situations (Pines

and Aronson, 1988, p. 9). This view does not restrict the application of the term 'burnout' to the helping professions, as was initially the case with the first version of the MBI (Winnubst, 1993). Indeed Pines and her colleagues have applied it not only to employment relationships (Pines et al., 1981) and organizational careers (Pines and Aronson, 1988), but also to marital relationships (Pines, 1988, 1996) and to the aftermath of political conflicts (Pines, 1993).

Much like the case of the MBI, the Pines et al. conceptualization and measure of burnout, the BM (Burnout Measure) emerged from clinical experience and case studies. In the process of actually constructing the BM, Pines and her colleagues moved away from their original conceptualization to an empirical definition that regards burnout as a syndrome of co-occurring symptoms that include helplessness, hopelessness, entrapment, decreased enthusiasm, irritability and a sense of lowered self-esteem (cf. Pines, 1993). None of these symptoms is anchored in the context of work or employment relationships. The BM is considered a one-dimensional measure yielding a single composite burnout score. As we have noted, the overlap between the conceptual definition and the operational definition of the BM is minimal (cf. Schaufeli and Enzmann, 1998, p. 48). In addition, the discriminant validity of the BM, relative to depression, anxiety and self-esteem, is in doubt (cf. Shirom and Ezrachi, 2003). This has led researchers to describe the BM as a general index of psychological distress that encompasses physical fatigue, emotional exhaustion, depression, anxiety and reduced self-esteem (for example, Schaufeli and Dierendonck, 1993, p. 645; Shirom and Ezrachi, 2003). Therefore it appears irrelevant to assess the linkage between burnout and indicators of mental health like depression or anxiety using questionnaire measures, since the overlap between the items used to gauge burnout by the BM and depression or anxiety is considerable (Shirom and Ezrachi, 2003). As we were unable to find any evidence linking the BM to disease end states or to physiological risk factors for physical disease, we have not included studies that have used it in this review.

Shirom–Melamed Burnout Model and Measure (SMBM)
The conceptualization of burnout that underlies the Shirom–Melamed Burnout Measure (SMBM) was inspired by the work of Maslach and her colleagues and Pines and her colleagues, and views burnout as an affective state characterized by one's feelings of being depleted of one's physical, emotional and cognitive energies. Burnout follows prolonged exposure to chronic stress. Relative to chronic stress, event-based conceptualizations of stress, like those that relate to critical life events or acute stress and to episodic stress or hassles, derive from different theoretical approaches (Derogatis and Coons, 1993) and have been found to be differently related to physiological risk factors in coronary heart disease (Kahn and Byosiere, 1992).

Theoretically the SMBM was based on Hobfoll's (1989, 1998) Conservation of Resources (COR) theory. COR theory's fundamental tenets are that people have a basic motivation to obtain, retain and protect that which they value, including material, social and energetic resources. According to COR theory (Hobfoll, 1989, 1998) stress at work occurs when individuals are either threatened with resource loss, lose resources or fail to regain resources following resource investment. One of the corollaries of COR theory is that stress does not occur as a single event, but rather represents an unfolding process, wherein those who lack a strong resource pool are more likely to experience cycles of resource loss. The affective state of burnout is likely to exist when individuals experience a cycle of resource loss over a period of time at work (Hobfoll and Freedy, 1993). For example, a reference librarian who comes to work every morning to face yet another line of students impatiently awaiting her help, lacking opportunities to replenish her resources, is likely to cycle into a forceful spiral of resource loss and as a result feel burned out at work.

The conceptualization of burnout formulated by Shirom (1989) based on COR theory (Hobfoll and Shirom, 1993, 2000) relates to energetic resources only, and covers physical, emotional and cognitive energies. Burnout thus represents a combination of physical fatigue, emotional exhaustion and cognitive weariness, three closely interrelated factors (Hobfoll and Shirom, 2000) that can be represented by a single score of burnout. Physical fatigue refers to feelings of tiredness and low levels of energy in carrying out daily tasks at work, like getting up in the morning to go to work. Emotional exhaustion refers to feeling too weak to display empathy to clients or co-workers and lacking the energy needed to invest in relationships with other people at work. Cognitive weariness refers to feelings of slow thinking and reduced mental agility. Each component of burnout covers the draining and depletion of energetic resources in a particular domain.

There are three reasons for the focus on the combination of physical fatigue, emotional exhaustion and cognitive weariness in the conceptualization of burnout that has led to the construction of the SMBM. First, these forms of energy are individually possessed, and theoretically are expected to be closely interrelated. COR theory postulates that personal resources affect each other and exist as a resource pool, and that lacking one is often associated with lacking the other (ibid.). Empirical research conducted with the SMBM has supported the linkage among physical fatigue, emotional exhaustion and cognitive weariness (for example Melamed et al., 1992; Shirom et al., 1997). Second, the three forms of individually possessed energy included in the SMBM represent a coherent set that does not overlap any other established behavioral science concept, like depression and anxiety or like aspects of the self-concept such as self-esteem and self-efficacy. Third, the conceptualization of the SMBM clearly differentiates burnout from stress appraisals anteceding burnout, from coping behaviors that individuals may engage in to ameliorate the negative aspects of burnout such as distancing themselves from client recipients, and from probable consequences of burnout such as performance decrements. This stands in contrast to the two other conceptualizations of burnout outlined above.

A series of studies that confirmed expected relationships between the SMBM and physiological variables have lent support to its construct validity. In these studies, respondents' total score on the SMBM was used to predict risk factors for cardiovascular disease (Melamed et al., 1992; Shirom et al., 1997), quasi-inflammatory factors in the blood (Lerman et al., 1999), salivary cortisol levels (Melamed et al., 1999) and upper respiratory infections (Kushnir and Melamed, 1992). These studies are covered in more detail below. However the convergent validity of the SMBM relative to the MBI and the BM has yet to be established, as has its discriminant validity relative to other types of possible emotional reactions to chronic stress at work, such as anger, hostility, anxiety and depressive symptomatology. The factorial validity of the SMBM needs to be investigated in additional occupational categories. Also there is a paucity of evidence with regard to the possibility that different types of stress may have varying effects on physical fatigue, emotional exhaustion and cognitive weariness, thus casting doubt on the use of a single composite score of the SMBM to represent burnout. There is some indirect evidence suggesting that each of the three components of the SMBM may be related to a different coping style (Vingerhoets, 1985).

Models of burnout and health

Past reviews of the burnout literature (Burke and Richardson, 2000; Cordes and Dougherty, 1993; Moore, 2000; Schaufeli and Enzmann, 1998; Hobfoll and Shirom, 2000; Shirom, 1989) view burnout as a consequence of one's exposure to chronic job stress. The chronic stresses that may lead to burnout include qualitative and quantitative overload, role conflict and ambiguity, lack of participation and lack of social support. Burnout has been shown to be more job-related and situation-specific relative to emotional distress such as depression (Maslach et al., 2001). Among the major theoretical approaches to burnout reviewed in Cooper (1998), none focuses on the burnout–health relationship.

Our theoretical view of stress and burnout is based on Hobfoll's COR theory (Hobfoll and Shirom, 1993, 2000). Hereafter, we will link this theoretical view to burnout's relations with mental and physical health. According to COR theory (Hobfoll, 1989, 1998), when individuals experience loss of resources they respond by attempting to limit the loss and maximizing the gain of resources. To achieve this, they usually employ other resources. When circumstances at work or otherwise threaten people's obtaining or maintaining resources, stress ensues. As indicated, COR theory postulates that stress occurs under one of three conditions: when resources are threatened, when resources are lost, and when individuals invest resources and do not reap the anticipated return. Insofar as COR theory (ibid.) further postulates that, because individuals strive to protect themselves from resource loss, loss is more salient than gain, in a work situation employees are more sensitive to workplace stresses that threaten their resources. Thus for teachers, for example, having to discipline students and face negative feedback from their supervisors will be more salient than any rewards that they might receive. The stress of interpersonal conflict has been shown to be particularly salient in the burnout phenomenon (Leiter and Maslach, 1988).

A meta-analysis by Lee and Ashforth (1996) examined how demand and resource correlates and behavioral and attitudinal correlates were related to each of the three scales that comprise the MBI. In agreement with the COR theory-based view of stress and burnout outlined above, these authors found that both the demand and the resource correlates were more strongly related to emotional exhaustion than to either depersonalization or personal accomplishment. These investigators also found that, consistent with COR theory of stress, emotional exhaustion was more strongly related to the demand correlates than to the resource correlates, suggesting that workers may have been sensitive to the possibility of resource loss. These meta-analytic results were subsequently reconfirmed by additional studies, such as Demerouti et al. (2000) who used a burnout scale that focused on energy depletion.

Applying these notions to the relations of burnout with mental health, we argue that individuals feel burned out when they perceive a continuous net loss, which cannot be replenished, of the physical, emotional or cognitive energy that they possess. This feeling of continuing net loss of any combination of physical vigorousness, emotional robustness and cognitive agility represents an emotional response to the experienced stresses. Moreover expanding other resources, borrowing or gaining additional resources by investing in existing resources cannot compensate for the net loss. Indeed burned-out individuals risk entering an escalating spiral of losses (Hobfoll and Shirom, 2000), culminating in an advanced stage of burnout, in which depression may become the predominant emotion. They may even reach advanced stages of burnout that are manifested by symptoms of psychological withdrawal such as acting with cynicism toward and dehumanizing their customers or clients. As noted by Schaufeli and Enzmann (1998), longitudinal studies to date have not supported the notion of a time lag between the stress experience and the feelings of burnout. It could be that stress and burnout affect each other simultaneously, which could explain the failure of the eight longitudinal studies examined by Schaufeli and Enzmann (1998) to reproduce the effects of stress on burnout found in most cross-sectional studies.

This theoretical perspective has direct implications with regard to the linkages among burnout, anxiety and depression. COR theory implies that during its early stages burnout will be characterized by a process of depletion of energy resources directed at coping with the threatening demands, that is with work-related stresses. During this stage of coping, burnout may occur concomitantly with a high level of anxiety, due to the direct and active coping behaviors that usually entail a high level of arousal. When and if these coping behaviors prove ineffective, the individual may give up, and resort to emotional detachment and defensive behaviors that may lead to depressive symptoms (cf. Shirom and Ezrahi, 2003). Cherniss (1980a, 1980b) has found that in the later stages of burnout individuals behave defensively and hence display cynicism toward clients, withdrawal and emotional detachment (for empirical support, see Burke and Greenglass, 1989, 1995). These attempts at coping have limited effectiveness and often cycle to heighten burnout and problems for both the individuals and the organizations in which they work. The unique core of burnout, as posited above, is distinctive in content and nomological network from either depression or anxiety (Corrigan et al., 1994; Leiter and Durup, 1994). Measures of depression, such as the Beck Depression Inventory (Beck et al., 1961) include items that gauge passivity and relative incapacity for purposeful action. In addition, as proposed above, later phases of burnout may be accompanied by depressive symptomatology. These two considerations may explain the often-reported high positive correlation between burnout and measures of depression (for example, Meier, 1984; Schaufeli and Enzmann, 1998). On the basis of these theoretical arguments, we expect burnout to be conceptually distinct from depression. Depressive symptomatology is affectively complex, and includes lack of pleasurable experience, anger, guilt, apprehension and physiological symptoms of distress. Moreover cognitive views of depression regard it as related primarily to pessimism about the self, capabilities and the future (Fisher, 1984).

This theoretical position may be exemplified by burnout among people-oriented professionals, such as teachers, social workers and nurses. When faced with overload and interpersonal stress on the job on a continuing basis, the key issue for these individuals is the amount of emotional energy they need to meet the job demands. When they feel emotionally exhausted, direct or problem-focused coping, which invariably requires that they invest emotional energy, is no longer a viable option. Presumably they employ emotion-focused coping in an effort to ameliorate their feelings of emotional exhaustion, and attempt to distance themselves from their service recipients, psychologically withdraw from their job tasks or limit their exposure to their clients. This may explain the often found linkage between emotional exhaustion and cynicism (Lee and Ashforth, 1996). In a recent study of the process of burnout among general practitioners, a study that used a five-year longitudinal design, Bakker and his colleagues (Bakker, Schaufeli, Sixma et al., 2000) found that repeated confrontation with demanding patients over a long period of time depleted the GPs' emotional resources, with perceptions of inequity or lack of reciprocity mediating the process. This study also reported that emotional exhaustion evoked a cynical attitude towards patients. However the linkage of emotional exhaustion and cynicism does not mean that emotional exhaustion is necessarily followed by cynical attitudes or indirect coping styles like distancing. Nor does it necessarily follow from this linkage that burnout's core meaning and ways of coping with advanced stages of it belong to the same conceptual space (cf. Maslach et al., 2001, p. 403).

The health consequences of burnout: mental health
Burnout has been linked to several negative organizational outcomes, including increased turnover and absenteeism (for example, Jackson et al., 1986; Parker and Kulik, 1995), lower organizational commitment (Maslach and Leiter, 1997), increase in suicidal feelings (Samuelson et al., 1997) and the self-reported use of violence by police against civilians (Kop et al., 1999). Indicators of mental health whose linkages with burnout were investigated include depression symptoms, anxiety and somatic complaints. Somatic complaints refer to subjectively reported health-related problems reported by individuals, including circulatory and heart problems, musuloskeletal pains, excessive sweating and gastrointestinal problems. Depression symptomatology, as distinct from the clinical state of depression, includes feelings of sadness, emptiness, hopelessness, helplessness, dysphoric feelings and low energy. It is the latter component of depressive symptomatology that gave rise to the conjecture that burnout may overlap with depression (Schaufeli and Buunk, 2003).

Theoretically the two constructs are different each from the other. Depression signifies a generalized distress encompassing all life domains, whereas burnout is context-specific in that it refers to the depletion of individuals' energetic resources at work (the SMBM) or to a set of work-related attitudes (the BMI). Empirically factor-analytic studies of all items measuring burnout and depression (for references, see Schaufeli and Enzmann, 1998, and also Nadaoka et al., 1997) have generally found each construct to load on different factors, indicating that these measures probably tap different conceptual domains. Two theoretical considerations support the hypothesis that burnout and depression share a significant amount of their respective variance. First, these two conceptual entities share some antecedent variables: chronic stress influences both burnout and depression. Second, depressive symptomatology is regarded as being a component of one of the 'Big Five' personality factors, neuroticism (McCrae and John, 1992), and this personality trait has been shown to be closely related to burnout (Zellars et al., 2000). Third, Leiter and Durup (1994) argued that the MBI's emotional exhaustion overlaps the lowered energy and chronic fatigue symptoms, regarded as symptoms of depression (dysthymic disorder).

Especially noteworthy is Glass and McKnight's (1996) review of 18 studies that measured depression and burnout. Only one out of the 18 studies used the BM to measure burnout, and therefore the conclusions are relevant to burnout as gauged by the BMI. Glass and McKnight's review suggested that depressive affect and burnout may have a common etiology, and that their shared variance may be due to their concurrent development. Glass and McKnight concluded that burnout and depressive symptomatology are not mutually redundant and that their shared variance does not indicate complete isomorphism. Schaufeli and Enzmann (1998) quantitatively reviewed 12 studies (including the above six) and concluded that burnout and depression, while sharing appreciable variance, do not represent mutually redundant concepts denoting the same underlying dysphoric state. This meta-analytic study reported that the emotional exhaustion component of the MBI and depression shared on average 28 per cent of their variance, while depersonalization and reduced personal accomplishment shared on average 13 per cent and 9 per cent, respectively, of their variance with depression.

Several studies have compared the construct validity of burnout and depression. A study of hospital nurses (Glass et al., 1993) found that, under certain conditions, burnout may develop into depression. However McKnight and Glass (1995) found that burnout and depression were reciprocally related rather than one being causally related to the other. In a recent study (Bakker, Schaufeli, Demerouti et al., 2000) in which burnout and depression among school teachers was investigated, lack of reciprocity in relations with students was found to predict burnout but not depression, whereas lack of reciprocity in relations with one's partner was found to predict depression but not burnout. Therefore, while burnout and depression share some dysphoric symptoms, including low energy, fatigue and inability to concentrate, and consequently have been found to be empirically related each to the other, the evidence summarized above supports the conclusion that they are two distinct and separable constructs.

It may also be possible that negative emotions, including anxiety, depression and burnout, reinforce each other, particularly in people who are susceptible to emotional stimuli (cf. Bakker and Schaufeli, 2000). The discriminant validity of burnout measures in relation to anxiety has been investigated in several studies (Bakker and Schaufeli, 2000; Brenninkmeyer et al., 2001; Leiter and Durup, 1994). Burnout may overlap with anxiety, since high levels of emotional exhaustion may raise individuals' level of anxiety in stressful situations and weaken their ability to cope with anxiety (Winnubst, 1993). Richardson et al.'s (1992) study assessed the extent to which trait anxiety predicted each of the MBI components, and concluded that it may function as a relatively stable individual difference in the burnout process. Likewise Turnipseed (1998), using both trait and state anxiety scales to predict each of the MBI components, suggested that both are significant contributors to burnout, especially the emotional exhaustion component of the MBI. Several studies have found burnout to be associated with a variety of somatic symptoms, including sleep disturbances, recurrent headaches and gastrointestinal problems (for example, Kahill, 1988; Gorter et al., 2000). Such somatic symptoms may merely reflect a personal disposition of negative affectivity (Watson and Pennebaker, 1989) rather than poor physical health. In sum, as could be expected on the basis of the above theoretical arguments, burnout, depression, anxiety and somatic complaints were found to be significantly associated (Schaufeli and Buunk, 2003; Schaufeli and Enzmann, 1998). However there is hardly any support for the contention that the construct of burnout is mutually redundant with any of the other indicators of poor mental health, including depression, anxiety and somatic complaints.

The health consequences of burnout: physical health
Researchers that have used the BMI (for example, Schaufeli and Enzmann, 1998, p. 87) have made the claim that burnout does not reflect the type of psychophysiological arousal that can lead to health problems and that it is not likely to be a precursor of disease states such as high blood pressure or diabetes. As we will show in this section, the bulk of available evidence does not support this view. The wear and tear of energetic resources, considered to be the core dimension of burnout, is implicated in several health problems via other etiological pathways, including the immune system and inflammatory processes. The research literature strongly suggests that chronic exposure to work and life stress may negatively affect physical health. A wide range of physical morbidity manifests this: cardiovascular disease, infectious illness, cancer, diabetes, rheumatoid arthritis and musculoskeletal disorders (Dougall and Baum, 2001; Shirom, 2003). Several reviews have suggested possible mechanisms that underlie stress and disease associations (including Bairey Merz *et al.*, 2002; Baum and Posluszny, 1999; Steptoe, 1991; and Kelly *et al.*, 1997). As noted above, there is evidence suggesting that burnout results from ineffective coping with work and life stresses and may well be chronic, lasting over long periods of time. Therefore it seems logical to assume that burnout will also be associated with degraded physical health and psychological well-being, as suggested by reviewers of the burnout literature (Burke and Richardson, 2000; Cordes and Dougherty, 1993).

Burnout has been linked to self-reported ill-health or disease states. One study found small but significant associations between the MBI and self-reported episodes of cold or flu, but failed to find a significant correlation with cholesterol ratio (Hendrix *et al.*, 1991). Appels and his colleagues (for example, Appels and Mulder, 1989) pioneered in the first systematic research in this area using objective indicators of physical morbidity. The predictor variable in their series of studies was vital exhaustion (VE), representing a construct that to some extent overlaps burnout. VE, as assessed by the Maastrict Questionnaire, was defined to include unusual fatigue, increased irritability and feelings of demoralization (Appels and Mulder, 1988), and was shown to be distinct from depression (van Diest and Appels, 1991). In a series of studies, Appels and his colleagues found that VE was associated with sleep disturbances (van Diest, 1990; van Diest and Appels, 1994) and cardiac symptoms (angina pectoris and unstable angina) (Appels and Mulder, 1989). Moreover it was predictive of future myocardial infarction (MI) in men and women, independent of the classic risk factors (Appels and Mulder, 1988, 1989; Appels *et al.*, 1993). To illustrate, in 4.2 years of follow-up of healthy men, VE was predictive of future MI, even after controlling for blood pressure, smoking, cholesterol levels, age and the use of anti-hypertensive drugs (Appels and Mulder, 1988). In a case-control study of women with first MI there was found a relative risk of 2.75 for MI associated with VE after adjusting for several potent confound variables (Appels *et al.*, 1993). In another study, VE was also found to be a precursor of sudden cardiac death (Appels and Otten, 1992). Using data from the prospective study of healthy men mentioned above, Appels and Schouten (1991a) found that a single question measuring burnout, 'Have you ever been burned out?'

was found to be predictive of MI risk [RR (relative risk) = 2.13, $p<0.01$]. To the best of our knowledge, the relationships between the VE measure and either of the burnout measures have never been explored. Nonetheless this last finding suggests that not only VE, but burnout too, may be a risk factor for coronary heart disease (CHD).

Our program of research started in the early 1990s to explore the association between burnout and physical health (Shirom, 2002). In this programmatic research effort, performed among white- and blue-collar workers, burnout was assessed by the SMBM. The findings provided the first evidence that burnout, as assessed by one of the measures specifically constructed to gauge it, may have a negative influence on physical health. In a study of 104 disease-free male employees of a high-tech company, Melamed et al. (1992) found burnout to be associated with elevated risk factors for cardiovascular disease. Specifically this study reported that the combination of high burnout and tension was significantly associated with increased total cholesterol, low-density lipoprotein (LDL), triglycerides and uric acid, and marginally with ECG abnormality. No association was found for systolic and diastolic blood pressure. In addition, in that study, consistent with findings of other studies (for example, Gorter et al., 2000), a high level of burnout was also associated with poor health habits, including smoking and lack of participation in leisure physical activities. In another prospective study of healthy male and female employees (Shirom et al., 1997), emotional exhaustion (as measured by the SMBM) in men was found to be predictive of cholesterol changes, evidenced two to three years later. Among female employees emotional exhaustion was positively correlated with cholesterol and triglycerides levels, whereas the correlation with physical fatigue was negative (Shirom et al., 1997).

Type 2 diabetes mellitus (DM) is a complex disorder characterized by impaired secretion of insulin and increased resistance to insulin, and associated with increased risk of coronary heart disease, peripheral vascular disease, renal failure and blindness (Bailey, 2002; Beckman et al., 2002). The past two decades have witnessed an explosive increase in the number of people diagnosed with diabetes worldwide (Seidell, 2000; Zimmet et al., 2001), primarily type 2 DM (Zimmet et al., 2001). In the USA nearly ten million people are affected with type 2 DM and the prevalence is increasing (Nelson et al., 1988). It is argued that diabetes is now becoming one of the main threats to human health in the 21st century (Zimmet et al., 2001).

The most important risk factor in the onset of type 2 diabetes is obesity, in particular abdominal obesity, and obesity is on the rise worldwide (Visscher and Seidell, 2001). The correlation of increased diabetes with increased obesity has led to the adoption of the term 'diabesity' (Zimmet et al., 2001). Other established risk factors for type 2 DM include age and family history of diabetes. Additional factors found to be associated with this condition are alcohol intake, smoking, reduced physical activity, diets with a high glycaemic load and a low cereal fiber content (Rimm et al., 1995; Pan et al., 1997; Nakanishi et al., 2000; Salmeron et al., 1997; Stagnaro et al. 2002). Furthermore certain risk factors for coronary heart disease, such as hypertension and dyslipidemia, are also known to be associated with risk of type 2 DM (Jacobsen et al., 2002; Beckman et al., 2002).

It is believed that stress plays a significant role in the etiology of type 2 DM, but only a few studies have systematically tested this hypothesis (Feldman and Steptoe, 2003; Surwit and Schneider, 1993). Some studies have shown that the risk of developing type 2

DM is higher in certain occupations, for instance among air traffic controllers and transport workers (Cobb and Rose, 1973; Morikawa et al., 1997). Other studies, focusing on working hours, have yielded conflicting results (Kawakami et al., 1999; Nakanishi et al., 2001). There is a paucity of prospective studies directly linking work-related stress and clinically diagnosed type 2 DM. Several studies, however, have examined the association with glycosylated hemoglobin A1c (Hb A1c) which is not used in the diagnosis of diabetes but provides a measure of chronic glycemia and is also used to assess the effectiveness of therapies provided to those inflicted with DM (Barr et al., 2002). Hb A1c appears to be a marker of the increased risk of developing atherosclerosis, MI, strokes, cataracts and loss of the elasticity of arteries, joints and lungs (Kelly et al., 1997). The results have shown that greater job strain and lower social support at the workplace may be associated with increased concentrations of Hb A1c (Kawakami et al., 2000). Thus it is still unclear whether psychosocial stress is causally implicated in the onset of diabetes. A recent study on burnout and type 2 DM risk (Melamed et al., 2003) provides initial support for such a possibility. This study was conducted among primarily white-collar Israeli workers. After excluding those who had a history of diabetes mellitus or other chronic diseases, 633 workers were followed up for a period of three to five years. During this period there were 17 new cases of treated type 2 DM. Burnout, as measured by the SMBM, was found to be associated with increased risk of type 2 DM (OR=1.83, 95 per cent CI 1.20–2.77), even after controlling for age, sex, body mass index, smoking, period of follow-up and job category. Thus this finding suggests that burnout might be a risk factor for type 2 DM in Israeli workers.

Findings from a study of blue-collar workers (Melamed et al., 1999) provided evidence supporting the notion that burnout is associated with increased somatic and physiological hyper-arousal. Among those reporting higher levels of burnout, there was a higher prevalence of unpleasant sensations of tension and restlessness at work, post-work irritability, sleep disturbances, complaints of waking up exhausted and higher cortisol levels during the workday (Melamed et al., 1999). These findings suggest that burned-out individuals may have an inability to unwind after working hours. Furthermore these people may suffer from insomnia and non-refreshing sleep. This may explain in part, the chronic fatigue experienced by those who are burned-out. Insomnia in general (Carney et al., 1990; van Diest, 1990) and waking up exhausted in particular (Appels and Schouten, 1991b), were found to be risk indicators of future MI. Therefore the findings of this study suggest an additional pathway by which burnout may be associated with increased risk of cardiovascular disease (CVD).

Taken together, the findings of the above studies suggest that burnout may be associated with CVD risk through multiple pathways: increased biochemical risk factors, development of diabetes (conceived to be an independent risk factor of CVD: Visscher and Seidell, 2001) and sleep disturbances.

In recent years, following the findings that the classical risk factors (hypertension, poor lipids profile, smoking, lack of physical exercise and being overweight) explain only in part the incidence (new cases) of MI, research efforts have been directed toward identifying new risk factors for CVD. One such risk factor is inflammation, which accumulating evidence indicates is linked to atherosclerosis and acute coronary syndromes (Libby et al., 2002; Rose, 1999; Koenig, 2000). There is also evidence that chronic inflammation may play an important role in linking diabetes and CVD as well as evidence supporting the relationships between markers of inflammation, abnormalities of glucose metabolism and CVD endpoints (Resnick and Howard, 2002). Findings from the study by Lerman et al. (1999), suggesting that burnout may be associated with inflammation condition, revealed a close association between burnout and leukocyte adhesiveness/aggregation (LAA).

LAA is a sensitive marker that detects inflammation and assesses its intensity (Rotstein et al., 2002). The adoption of LAA as a marker of inflammation was based on the notion that white blood cells get activated and sticky during the inflammatory response (Frenetto and Wagner, 1996a, 1996b). LAA probably represents both enhanced expression of cell adhesion molecules during cell activation, as well as the appearance of plasmatic adhesive proteins during the acute phase response (Rotstein et al., 2002). Additional evidence indicates that there is a high correlation between LAA and erythrocyte aggregation (Shapira et al., 2001), and there is also evidence regarding red blood cell aggregation in patients with hyperlipidemia, diabetes mellitus, hypertension and acute MI (Berliner et al., 2001; Shapira et al., 2001). Thus, by implication, burnout may be associated with CVD risk through the presence of smoldering inflammation, though this hypothesis awaits further research and confirmation.

Research on the health implications of the burnout syndrome suggests that the adverse effect on health may go beyond diabetes and the cardiovascular system. Accumulating evidence points to the association between stress, immunity and susceptibility to infectious disease (Marsland et al., 2001). Following this evidence, new studies have been initiated to explore the effect of burnout on the immune system and its possible association with infectious disease.

In a study of office workers, one of the dimensions that form burnout as assessed by the MBI, namely depersonalization, was found to be associated with reduced cellular immunity (lower natural killer (NK) cell activity and lower proportionality of CD57+CD16 to total lymphocytes. This was independent of health behaviors (for example, smoking, alcohol use, obesity) or work stress (Nakamura et al., 1999). In a study conducted during the first Gulf War it was found that prewar burnout (measured by the SMBM) was associated with wartime threat appraisal (worry) and upper respiratory infections (Kushnir and Melamed, 1992). These findings suggest that burned-out people may be at risk of reduced immunocompetence and may be potentially prone to a variety of infectious diseases such as upper respiratory infections and different types of viral infections. Again this may be an important venue for future research.

There is yet an additional domain of human health that may be influenced by burnout, that of male infertility. Research findings have supported the hypothesis that stress has a negative impact on semen quality (for example, Harrison et al., 1987; Clarke et al., 1999; Giblin et al., 1988). Based on this set of findings, a case-control study was recently initiated to explore the possibility that burnout will also have negative repercussions on male fertility. The results confirmed this suspicion. Males with infertility problems (based on combined criteria of sperm concentration, quantity and quality of motility) were found to have significantly higher burnout scores (on the SMBM) compared with controls (Sheiner et al., 2002). This finding, if replicated, will point to yet another research frontier concerning the relationship of burnout to health impairments.

Summary and conclusions

Research on the implications of burnout for physical health is relatively new, yet the accumulating evidence suggests that chronic burnout may harm physical health through different pathways. These include adoption of negative health habits and failure to engage in health-promoting behaviors. Additional important pathways include increased biochemical and hematological risk factors for CVD, diabetes (as an independent risk factor for CVD), sleep disturbances, exacerbation of the inflammation process and impairment of the immune system. This can result in various forms of physical morbidity: CVD, cardiac death, type 2 DM and its complications, infectious diseases and impairment of sperm quality.

It seems that future research aimed at clarifying the possible effects of stress on health may benefit from including as an additional predictor variable. Burnout may become a proxy variable reflecting the combined influence of chronic stresses, critical life events and hassles, at work and in other life domains. Furthermore, as indicated, burnout may also reflect the use of ineffective ways of coping with a variety of stresses. Therefore including burnout in future studies may lead to the identification of individuals chronically exposed to various forms of stress and to their major types of depleted coping resources. The lines of research summarized above suggest that these individuals run the highest risk of impaired health.

Organizational implications

The set of findings presented in this review reinforces the need to search for preventive measures to combat stress and burnout. Earlier organization studies provide sufficient reasons to combat burnout as part of the preventive effort aiming at ameliorating low morale, reduced motivation, increased absenteeism and reduced performance effectiveness. The new data suggest that effective measures to prevent burnout may also prove to be protective of health and beneficial to physical well-being, and may result in reduced disability, lowered health care costs, prevention of early retirement and perhaps even prevention of premature death.

Adverse organizational conditions have been shown to be more significant in the etiology of burnout than personality factors (Schaufeli and Enzmann, 1998). The lesson for burnout researchers is that it is plausible that individual traits predisposing employees to burnout interact with organizational features that contribute to the development of burnout. As an example, when a major economic slump moves management to require that all employees increase their input of available personal energy and time to ensure the organization's survival, those employees who possess high self-esteem are less likely to experience burnout as a result (Cordes and Dougherty, 1993).

Senior management has a role to play in instituting preventive measures, including training programs designed to promote effective stress management techniques and on-site recreational facilities. Organizational interventions to reduce burnout have great potential, but are complex to implement and costly in terms of resources required. The changing nature of employment relationships, including the transient and dynamic nature of the employee–employer psychological contract, entails putting more emphasis on individual-oriented approaches to combat burnout. The role of individual coping resources, including self-efficacy, hardiness and social support from friends and family, may become more important in future interventions.

Interventions to reduce burnout
It has been argued that workplace-based interventions aimed at reducing stress and modifying some of the maladaptive responses to stress often have little or no effect (Briner and Reynolds, 1999). Is this conclusion relevant to interventions designed to ameliorate burnout? Most of the burnout interventions reported in the literature are individual-oriented and provide treatment, not prevention, much like other stress interventions (Nelson et al., 2001). There are hardly any reports on interventions that were based on a systematic audit of the structural sources of workplace burnout with the objectives of alleviating or eliminating the stresses leading to burnout.

An intervention frequently used by organizations attempting to ameliorate burnout amongst their employees is peer support groups. The theoretical perspective offered in this chapter may explain the focus of many interventions on enriching and strengthening the social support available to or utilized by burned-out employees. According to the predictions of COR theory, the depletion of one's energetic resources and impoverished social support are closely related (Hobfoll, 1989, 1998). Those lacking a strong resource pool, including those with impoverished social support, are more likely to become burned out, or to go through cycles of resource loss when they cope with work-related stress. Additionally people with depleted energetic resources, who complain of physical fatigue, emotional exhaustion and cognitive weariness, may appear to their significant others at work as less attractive and therefore less likely to have access to social support. The literature contains considerable support for these arguments. In a review of the area of social support and stress, Curtona and Russell (1990) integrated four studies that had investigated the effects of social support on burnout among public school teachers, hospital nurses, therapists and critical care nurses, respectively. In all four studies, negative associations between social support and burnout were found. For reasons explained above, these negative relationships may be reciprocal.

The peer social support intervention is particularly popular in educational institutions (for example, Travers and Cooper, 1996; Cooley and Yavanoff, 1996; Vandenberghe and Huberman, 1999). Such peer-based support groups provide their members with informational and emotional support, and in some cases instrumental support too (Burke and Richardson, 2000). Since social support is a major potential route to resources that are beyond those that individuals possess directly, it is a critical resource in many employment-related stressful situations (Hobfoll and Shirom, 2000) and may help them to replenish their depleted energetic resources. However how social support is actually used is dependent on several factors, including one's sense of mastery and environmental control.

In a longitudinal study of burnout among teachers, Brouwers and Tomic (2000) found that emotional exhaustion had a negative effect on self-efficacy beliefs and that this effect occurred simultaneously rather than over time. Brouwers and Tomic reasoned that interventions that incorporate enactive mastery experiences, the most important source of self-efficacy beliefs, were likely to have an ameliorative effect on teachers' emotional exhaustion. An example would be having teachers learn and experiment with skills to cope with disruptive student behaviors. In the same vein, the environmental sense of control is an important stress management resource (cf. Fisher, 1984). Those with a high sense of control tend to use their resources judiciously, relying on themselves when this is deemed most appropriate and using available social support when that is the more effective coping route (Hobfoll and Shirom, 2000). Therefore interventions that combine both social support and bolstering of control may be more efficacious in reducing burnout in organizations. For example, a multifaceted intervention that combined peer social support and bolstering of professional self-efficacy was found to reduce burnout (measured by the SMBM) relative to a control group of non-participants (Rabin et al., 2000). Yet another example is the study of Freedy and Hobfoll (1994), who enhanced nurses' coping skills by teaching them how to use their social support and individual mastery resources and found a significant reduction in emotional exhaustion in the experimental group relative to the non-treated control group.

Directions for future research
An important area for future research is the discriminating validity of burnout, according to either of its different operational definitions, and other types of emotional distress, particularly anxiety and depression. We have argued that burnout, anxiety and depression are conceptually distinct emotional reactions to stress, citing studies that support this contention (for example, Schaufeli and Dierendonck, 1993). Still the overlap found in several studies (Schaufeli and Enzmann, 1998; Cherniss, 1995) between depression and the emotional exhaustion scale of the MBI, the most robust and reliable out of the three scales that comprise the MBI, is a cause for concern. The propositions that early stages of burnout are more likely to be accompanied by heightened anxiety than the more progressive stages that may be linked to depressive symptomatology need to be tested in longitudinal research.

The plausibility of the proposition that burnout, as conceptualized here in terms of its core meaning, will overlap to some extent with the disease state of Chronic Fatigue Syndrome (CFS) or with its immediate precursor, chronic fatigue, has yet to be tested. In future investigations, individuals who score highest on burnout measures should be followed up for possible development of CFS.

An important area of research concerns the possibility that there are situational and personality mediators of the relationships between burnout and health, in particular burnout as a possible precursor of cardiovascular disease. One of the predictions of COR theory is that individuals who lack strong resources are more likely to experience cycles of resource losses. When not replenished, such cycles are likely to result in chronic depletion of energy, namely progressive burnout. Cherniss (1995) posited that the advance of burnout is contingent upon individuals' level of self-efficacy, and there is some support for this contention (Brouwers and Tomic, 2000). Lower levels of burnout will be expected in work situations that allow employees to experience success and thus feel efficacious, namely under job and organizational conditions that provide opportunities to experience challenge, control, feedback of results and support from supervisors and coworkers (cf. Schaufeli and Buunk, 1996; Brouwers and Tomic, 2000). Thus Chang and his colleagues (Chang et al., 2000) found, in a study of working college students, that optimism was a potent predictor of the emotional exhaustion scale of the BMI even after the effects of stress were controlled. Chang et al. (2000) concluded that concrete affirmations of job accomplishments, such as with merit awards, and increasing employees' optimistic expectancies may lower their risk of job burnout. The possibility that these job features and work characteristics may exert a moderating effect on the burnout–health relationship needs to be explored in future research.

The role of personality factors in the etiological processes leading from burnout to physical health is complex and multifaceted, and probably hardly explored (Kahill, 1988). Garden (1989, 1991) concluded that certain personality types self-select into specific occupations and that these individuals interact with stressful occupational environments that produce the experience of burnout and ill-health. Other possible paths of influence of personality characteristics on burnout relationships with health may exist. Several studies have reported a positive association of the Type A behavior pattern with emotional exhaustion (Schaufeli and Enzmann, 1998). Neuroticism may lead people to report higher levels of burnout regardless of the situation (cf. Watson and Clark, 1984). Burnout may also exacerbate certain personality traits. It appears that the complex interactions between personality traits and burnout have yet to be described and understood, and it follows that future research should look for moderators and mediators of stress–burnout relationships.

Conclusions

We claim that this review is timely and important in light of the sharp increase in recent years in the incidence of stress-related workers' compensation claims, covered by the relevant workers' compensation laws, in several advanced market economies, like the USA, the Netherlands and the UK (cf. Schaufeli and Enzmann, 1998). Given the data provided on the prevalence of burnout in advanced market economies, improving our understanding of the complex relationships between burnout and health is critical for informing prevention, intervention and public policy efforts. Advances in our knowledge are unlikely to result from research employing fuzzy concepts and relying upon instruments whose construct validity is in doubt, which is the reason for our selective focus, in this review, on certain theoretical and conceptual issues in burnout research.

Burnout is likely to represent a pressing social problem in the years to come. Competitive pressures in manufacturing industries that originate in the global market, the continuing process of consumer empowerment in service industries, and the rise and decline of the high-tech industry are among the factors likely to affect employees' levels of burnout in different industries. In addition employees in many advanced market economies are experiencing heightened job insecurity, demands for excessive work hours, the need for continuous retraining entailed by the accelerating pace of change in informational technologies, and the blurring of the line separating work and home life. In many European countries, employers are enjoined by governmental regulations on occupational health to implement preventive interventions that concern job stress and burnout. For this reason, we submit that continuous research efforts aimed at improving our understanding of the pathways leading from burnout to health are of crucial importance.

References

Abraham, R. (2000), 'Organizational cynicism: bases and consequences', *Genetic, Social and General Psychology Monographs*, **126**, 269–92.

Andersson, L.M. and T.S. Bateman (1997), 'Cynicism in the workplace: some causes and effects', *Journal of Organizational Behavior*, **18**, 449–65.

Appels, A and P. Mulder (1988), 'Excess fatigue as a precursor of myocardial infarction', *European Heart Journal*, **9**, 758–64.
Appels, A. and P. Mulder (1989) 'Fatigue and heart disease: the association between "vital exhaustion" and past, present and future coronary heart disease', *Journal of Psychosomatic Research*, **33**, 727–38.
Appels, A. and F. Otten (1992), 'Exhaustion as a precursor of cardiac death', *British Jornal of Clinical Psychology*, **31**, 351–56.
Appels, A. and E. Schouten (1991a), 'Burnout as a risk factor for coronary heart disease', *Behavioral Medicine*, **17**, 53–9.
Appels, A. and E. Schouten (1991b), 'Waking up exhausted as a risk indicator of myocardial infarction', *Psychosomatic Medicine*, **68**, 395–8.
Appels, A., P.R.J. Falger and E.G.W. Schouten (1993), 'Vital exhaustion as a risk indicator for myocardial infarction in women', *Journal of Psychosomatic Research*, **37**, 881–90.
Bailey, B.K. (2002), 'Diabetes mellitus and its chronic complications', *AORN Journal*, **76**, 266–76, 278–82.
Bairey Merz, C.N., J. Dwyer, C.K. Nordstrom, K.G. Walton, J.W. Salerno and R.H. Schneider (2002), 'Psychosocial stress and cardiovascular disease: pathophysiological links', *Behavioral Medicine*, **27**, 141–7.
Bakker, A.B. and W.B. Schaufeli (2000), 'Burnout contagion processes among teachers', *Journal of Applied Social Psychology*, **30**, 2289–308.
Bakker, A.B., W.B. Schaufeli, H.J. Sixma, W. Bosveld and D. Van Dierendonck (2000), 'Patient demands, lack of reciprocity, and burnout: a five-year longitudinal study among general practioners', *Journal of Organizational Behavior*, **21**, 425–41.
Bakker, A.B., W.B. Schaufeli, E. Demerouti, P.P.M. Janssen, R.V.D. Hulst and J. Brouwer (2000), 'Using equity theory to examine the difference between burnout and depression', *Anxiety, Stress, and Coping*, **13**, 247–68.
Barnett, R.C., R.T. Brennan and K.C. Careis (1999), 'A closer look at the measurement of burnout', *Journal of Applied Biobehavioral Research*, **4**, 65–78.
Barr, R.G., D.M. Nathan, J.B. Meigs and D.E. Singer (2002), 'Tests of glycemia for the diagnosis of type 2 diabetes mellitus', *Annals of Internal Medicine*, **137**, 263–72.
Baum, A. and D.M. Posluszny (1999), 'Health psychology: Mapping biobehavioral contributions to health and illness', *Annual Review of Psychology*, **50**, 137–63.
Beck, A.T., C.H. Ward, M. Mendelson, J. Mock and J. Erbaugh (1961), 'An inventory for measuring depression', *Archives of General Psychiatry*, **4**, 561–71.
Beckman, J.A., M.A. Creager and P. Libby (2002), 'Diabetes and atherosclerosis', *Journal of the American Medical Association*, **287**, 2570–581.
Berliner, S., D. Zeltser, R. Rotstein, R. Fusman, I. Shapira (2001), 'A leukocyte and erythrocyte adhesiveness/aggregation test to reveal the presence of smoldering inflammation and risk factors for atherosclerosis', *Medical Hypotheses*, **57**, 207–9.
Boles, J.S., D.H. Dean, J.M. Ricks, J.C. Short and G.P. Wang (2000), 'The dimensionality of the Maslach Burnout Inventory across small business owners and educators', *Journal of Vocational Behavior*, **56**, 12–34.
Brenninkmeyer, V., N.W. Van Yperen and B.P. Buunk (2001), 'Burnout and depression are not identical twins: is decline of superiority a distinguishing feature?', *Personality and Individual Differences*, **30**, 873–80.
Briner, R.B. and S. Reynolds (1999), 'The costs, benefits, and limitations of organizational level stress interventions', *Journal of Organizational Behavior*, **20**, 647–64.
Brouwers, A. and W. Tomic (2000), 'A longitudinal study of teacher burnout and perceived self-efficacy in classroom management', *Teaching and Teacher Education*, **16**, 239–53.
Burke, R.J. and E.R. Greenglass (1989), 'Psychological burnout among men and women in teaching: an examination of the Cherniss model', *Human Relations*, **42**, 261–73.
Burke, R.J. and E. Greenglass (1995), 'A longitudinal study of psychological burnout in teachers', *Human Relations*, **48**, 187–203.
Burke, R.J. and A.M. Richardson (2000), 'Psychological burnout in organizations', in R.T. Golembiewski (ed.), *Handbook of Organizational Behavior*, 2nd edn, New York: Marcel Dekker, pp. 327–68.
Byrne, B.M. (1994), 'Burnout: testing for validity, replication, and invariance of causal structure cross elementary, intermediate, and secondary teachers', *American Educational Research Journal*, **31**, 645–73.
Carney, R.M., K.E. Freedland and A.S. Jaffee (1990), 'Insomnia and depression prior to myocardial infarction', *Psychosomatic Medicine*, **52**, 603–9.
Chang, E., K.L. Rand and D.R. Strunk (2000), 'Optimism and risk for job burnout among working college students', *Personality and Individual Differences*, **29**, 255–63.
Cherniss, C. (1980a), *Staff Burnout: Job Stress in the Human Services*, Beverly Hills, CA: Sage.
Cherniss, C. (1980b), *Professional Burnout in Human Service Organizations*, New York: Praeger.
Cherniss, C. (1995), *Beyond Burnout*, New York and London: Routledge.
Clarke, R.N., S.C. Klock, A. Geoghegan, D.E. Travassos (1999), 'Relationship between psychological stress and semen quality among in-vitro fertilization patients', *Human Reproduction*, **14**, 753–8.

Cobb, S. and R.M. Rose (1973), 'Hypertension, peptic ulcer and diabetes in air traffic controllers', *Journal of the American Medical Association*, **224**, 489–92.
Collins, V.A. (1999), 'A meta-analysis of burnout and occupational stress', unpublished doctoral dissertation, University of North Texas; University Microfilm Accession Number: AAT 9945794.
Cooley, E. and P. Yavanoff (1996), 'Supporting professionals-at-risk: interventions to reduce burnout and improve retention of special educators', *Exceptional Childern*, **62**, 336–55.
Cooper, C.L. (ed.) (1998), *Theories of organizational stress*, New York: Oxford University Press.
Cordes, C.L. and T.W. Dougherty (1993), 'A review and integration of research on job burnout', *Academy of Management Review*, **18**, 621–56.
Cordes, C.L., T.W. Dougherty and M. Blum (1997), 'Patterns of burnout among managers and professionals: a comparison of models', *Journal of Organizational Behavior*, **18**, 685–701.
Corrigan, P.W., E.P. Holmes, D. Luchins, B. Buican, A. Basit and J.J. Parkes (1994), 'Staff burnout in a psychiatric hospital: a cross-lagged panel design', *Journal of Organizational Behavior*, **15**, 65–74.
Curtona, C.E. and D.W. Russell (1990), 'Type of social support and specific stress: toward a theory of optimal matching', in B.R. Sarason, I.G. Sarason and G.R. Pierce (eds), *Social Support: An Interactional View*, New York: Wiley, pp. 319–61.
Dale, J. and R. Weinberg (1990), 'Burnout in sport: a review and critique', *Applied Sport Psychology*, **2**, 67–83.
Dean, J.W., P. Brandes and R. Dharwadkar (1998), 'Organizational cynicism', *Academy of Management Review*, **23**, 341–52.
Demerouti, E., A.B. Bakker, F. Nachreiner and W.B. Schaufeli (2000), 'A model of burnout and life satisfaction amonst nurses', *Journal of Advanced Nursing*, **32**, 454–64.
Derogatis, L.R. and M.L. Coons (1993), 'Self-report measures of stress', in L. Goldberger and S. Breznitz (eds), *Handbook of stress*, 2nd edn, New York: The Free Press, pp. 200–34.
Dougall, A.L. and A. Baum (2001), 'Stress, health and illness', in A. Baum, T.A. Revenson and J.E. Singer (eds), *Handbook of Health Psychology*, Mahweh, NJ: Lawrence Erlbaum Associates, pp. 321–37.
Feldman, P.J. and A. Steptoe (2003), 'Psychosocial and socioeconomic factor associated with glycated hemoglobin in nondiabetic middle-age men and women', *Health Psychology*, **22**, 398–405.
Fisher, S. (1984), *Stress and the Perception of Control*, London: Lawrence Erlbaum.
Foschi, M. (2000), 'Double standards for competence: theory and research', *Annual Review of Sociology*, **26**, 21–42.
Freedy, J.R. and S.E. Hobfoll (1994), 'Stress inoculation for reduction of burnout: a conservation of resources approach', *Anxiety, Stress and Coping*, **6**, 311–25.
Frenetto, P.S. and D.D. Wagner (1996a), 'Adhesion molecules – Part 1', *New England Journal of Medicine*, **334**, 1526–9.
Frenetto, P.S. and D.D. Wagner (1996b), 'Adhesion molecules – Part 2: blood vessels and blood cells', *New England Journal of Medicine*, **335**, 43–5.
Freudenberger, H.J. (1974), 'Staff bumout', *Journal of Social Issues*, **30**, 159–64.
Freudenberger, H.J. (1980), *Burnout: The High Costs of High Achievement*, New York: Anchor Press.
Garden, A.M. (1987), 'Depersonalization: a valid dimension of burnout?', *Human Relations*, **40**, 545–60.
Garden, A.M. (1989), 'Burnout: the effects of psychological types on research findings', *Journal of Occupational Psychology*, **62**, 223–34.
Garden, A.M. (1991), 'The purpose of burnout: a Jungian interpretation', *Journal of Social Behavior and Personality*, **6**, 73–93.
Giblin, P.T., M.L. Poland, K.S. Moghissi, J.W. Ager and J.M. Olson (1988), 'Effect of stress and characteristic adaptability on semen quality in healthy men', *Fertility and Sterility*, **49**, 127–32.
Glass, D.C. and J.D. McKnight (1996), 'Perceived control, depressive symptomatology, and professional burnout: a review of the evidence', *Psychology and Health*, **11**, 23–48.
Glass, D.C., J. D. McKnight and H. Valdimarsdotter (1993), 'Depression, burnout, and perceptions of control in hospital nurses', *Journal of Consulting and Clinical Psychology*, **61**, 147–55.
Golembiewski, R.T. and W. Boss (1992), 'Phases of burnout in diagnosis and intervention', *Research in Organizational Change and Development*, **6**, 115–52.
Golembiewski, R.T. and R. Munzenrider (1988), *Phases of Burnout: Developments in Concepts and Applications*, New York: Praeger.
Golembiewski, R.T., R. Munzenrider and J. Stevenson (1986), *Stress in organizations*, New York: Praeger.
Gorter, R.C., M.A.J. Eijkman and J. Hoogstraten (2000), 'Burnout and health among Dutch dentists', *European Journal of Oral Sciences*, **108**, 261–7.
Handy, J.A. (1988), 'Theoretical and methodological problems within occupational stress and burnout research', *Human Relations*, **41**, 351–65.
Harrison, K.L., V.J. Callan and J.F. Hennessey (1987), 'Stress and semen quality in an in-vitro fertilization program', *Fertility and Sterility*, **48**, 633–6.

Hendrix, W.H., R.P. Steel, T.C. Leap and T.P. Summers (1991), 'Development of a stress-related health promotion model: antecedents and organizational effectiveness outcomes', *Journal of Social Behavior and Personality*, **6**, 141–62.
Hobfoll, S.E. (1988), *The Ecology of Stress*, Washington, DC: Hemisphere Publishing Co.
Hobfoll, S.E. (1989), 'Conservation of resources: a new attempt at conceptualizing stress', *American Psychologist*, **44**, 513–24.
Hobfoll, S. E. (1998), *The Psychology and Philosophy of Stress, Culture and Community*, New York: Plenum.
Hobfoll, S.E. and J. Freedy (1993), 'Conservation of resources: a general theory applied to burnout', in W.B. Schaufeli, C. Maslach and T. Marek (eds), *Professional Burnout: Recent Developments in Theory and Research*, New York: Taylor and Francis, pp. 115–35.
Hobfoll, S.E. and A. Shirom (1993), 'Stress and burnout in work organizations', in R.T. Golembiewski (ed.), *Handbook of organization behavior*, New York: Dekker pp. 41–61.
Hobfoll, S.E. and A. Shirom (2000), 'Conservation of resources theory: applications to stress and management in the workplace', in R.T. Golembiewski (ed.), *Handbook of Organization Behavior*, 2nd rev. edn, New York: Dekker, pp. 57–81.
Jackson, S.E., R.L. Schwab and R.S. Schuler (1986), 'Toward an understanding of the burnout phenomenon', *Journal of Applied Psychology*, **71**, 630–40.
Jacobsen, B.K., K.H. Bonan and I. Njolstad (2002), 'Cardiovascular risk factors, change in risk factors over 7 years, and the risk of clinical diabetes mellitus type 2. The Tromso study', *Journal of Clinical Epidemiology*, **55**, 647–53.
Kahill, S. (1988), 'Symptoms of professional burnout: a review of the empirical evidence', *Canadian Psychology*, **29**, 284–97.
Kahn, R.L. and P. Byosiere (1992), 'Stress in organizations', in M.D. Dunnette and L.M. Hough (eds), *Handbook of Industrial and Organizational Psychology*, vol. 3, Palo Alto, CA: Consulting Psychology Press, pp. 571–651.
Kalliath, T.J., M.P. O'Driscoll, D.F. Gillespie and A.G. Bluedorn (2000), 'A test of the Maslach Burnout Inventory in 3 samples of healthcare professionals', *Work & Stress*, **14**, 35–50.
Kawakami, N., K. Akachi, H. Shimizu, et al. (2000), 'Job strain, social support in the workplace, and haemoglobin A1c in Japanese men', *Occupational and Environmental Medicine*, **57**, 805–9.
Kawakami, N., S. Araki, N. Takasuka, H. Shimizu and H. Shibashi (1999), 'Overtime, psychosocial working conditions, and occurrence of non-insulin dependent diabetes mellitus in Japanese men', *Journal of Epidemiology and Community Health*, **53**, 359–63.
Kelly, S., C. Hertzman and M. Daniels (1997), 'Searching for the biological pathways between stress and health', *Annual Review of Public Health*, **18**, 437–62.
Koenig, W. (2000), 'Inflammation and coronary heart disease: an overview', *Cardiology in Review*, **9**, 31–5.
Koeske, C.F. and R.D. Koeske (1989), 'Construct validity of the Maslach Burnout Inventory: a critical review', *Journal of Applied Behavioral Science*, **25**, 131–44.
Kop, N., M. Euwema and W. Schaufeli (1999), 'Burnout, job stress, and violent behaviour among Dutch police officers', *Work and Stress*, **13**, 326–40.
Kushnir, T. and S. Melamed (1992), 'The Gulf War and burnout', *Psychological Medicine*, **22**, 987–95.
Law, K.S., C.S. Wong and W.H. Mobley (1998), 'Toward a taxonomy of multidimensional constructs', *Academy of Management Review*, **23**, 741–5.
Lee, C. and P. Bobko (1994), 'Self-efficacy beliefs: comparison of five measures', *Journal of Applied Psychology*, **79**, 364–9.
Lee, R. and B.E. Ashforth (1996), 'A meta-analytic examination of the correlates of the three dimensions of job burnout', *Journal of Applied Psychology*, **81**, 123–33.
Leiter, M.P. and J. Durup (1994), 'The discriminant validity of burnout and depression: a confirmatory factor analytic study', *Anxiety, Stress, and Coping*, **7**, 357–73.
Leiter, M.P. and C. Maslach (1988), 'The impact of interpersonal environment on burnout and organizational commitment', *Journal of Organizational Behavior*, **9**, 297–308.
Leiter, M.P. and C. Maslach (2001), 'Burnout and health', in A. Baum, T.A. Revenson and J.E. Singer (eds), *Handbook of health psychology*, New Jersey: Erlbaum pp. 415–22.
Lerman, Y., S. Melamed, Y. Shargin, T. Kushnir, Y. Rotgoltz, A. Shirom and M. Aronoson (1999), 'The association between burnout at work and leukocyte adhesiveness/aggregation', *Psychosomatic Medicine*, **61**, 828–33.
Libby, P., P.M. Ridker and A. Maseri (2002), 'Inflammation and atherosclerosis', *Circulation*, **105**, 1135–43.
Marsland, A.L., E.A. Buchen, S. Cohen and S.B. Manuck (2001), in A. Baum, T.A. Revenson and J.E. Singer (eds), *Handbook of Health Psychology*, Mahweh, NJ: Lawrence Erlbaum Associates, pp. 683–95.
Maslach, C. (1982), *Burnout: The Cost of Caring*, Englewood Cliffs, NJ: Prentice-Hall.
Maslach, C. (1998), 'A multidimensional theory of burnout', in C.L. Cooper (ed.), *Theories of Organizational Stress*, Oxford: Oxford University Press, pp. 68–85.

Maslach, D. and S. Jackson (1981), 'The measurement of experienced burnout', *Journal of Occuaptional Behavior*, **2**, 99–115.
Maslach, C. and M.P. Leiter (1997), *The Truth about Burnout*, San Francisco: Jossey-Bass.
Maslach, C., W.B. Schaufeli and M.P. Leiter (2001), 'Job burnout', *Annual Review of Psychology*, **52**, 397–422.
Maslach, C., S.E. Jackson and M.P. Leiter (1996), *Maslach Burnout Inventory Manual*, 3rd edn, Palo Alto, CA: Consulting Psychologists Press.
McCrae, R.R. and O.D. John (1992), 'An introduction to the Five Factor model and its applications', *Journal of Personality*, **60**, 175–215.
McKnight, J.D. and D.C. Glass (1995), 'Perceptions of control, burnout and depressive symptomatology: a replication and extension', *Journal of Consulting and Clinical Psychology*, **63**, 490–4.
Meier, S.T. (1984), 'The construct validity of burnout', *Journal of Occupational Psychology*, **57**, 211–9.
Melamed, S., T. Kushnir and A. Shirom (1992), 'Burnout and risk factors for Cardiovascular disease', *Behavioral Medicine*, **18**, 53–61.
Melamed, S., A. Shirom and P. Froom (2003), 'Burnout and risk of type 2 diabetes mellitus (DM) in Israeli workers', paper presented at the Work, Stress and Health Conference, Toronto, Ontario, Canada, 20–2, March.
Melamed, S., U. Ugarten, A. Shirom, L. Kahana, Y. Lerman and P. Froom (1999), 'Chronic burnout, somatic arousal and elevated cortisol levels', *Journal of Psychosomatic Research*, **46**, 591–8.
Moore, J.E. (2000), 'Why is this happening? A causal attribution approach to work exhaustion consequences', *Academy of Management Review*, **25**, 335–49.
Morikawa, Y., H. Nakagawa, M. Ishizaki and M. Tabata (1997), 'Ten-year follow-up study on the relation between the development of non-insulin-dependent diabetes mellitus and occupation', *American Journal of Industrial Medicine*, **31**, 80–4.
Nadaoka, T., M. Kashiwakura, A. Oiji, Y. Morioka and S. Totsuka (1997), 'Stress and psychiatric disorders in local government officials in Japan, in relation to their occupational level', *Acta Psychiatrica Scandinavica*, **96**, 176–83.
Nakamura, H., H. Nagase, M. Yoshida and K. Ogino (1999), *Journal of Psychosomatic Research*, **6**, 569–78.
Nakanishi, N., K. Nakamura, Y. Matsuo and M. Yoshida (2000), 'Cigarette smoking and risk for impaired fasting glucose and type 2 diabetes in middle-aged Japanese men', *Annals of Internal Medicine*, **133**, 183–91.
Nakanishi, N., K. Nishina, H. Yoshida and K. Matsuo (2001), 'Hours of work and the risk of developing impaired fasting glucose or type 2 diabetes mellitus in Japanese male office workers', *Occupational and Environmental Medicine*, **58**, 569–74.
Nelson, D.L., J.C. Quick and B.L. Simmons (2001), 'Preventive management of work stress: current themes and future challenges', in A. Baum, T.A. Revenson and J.E. Singer (eds), *Handbook of Health Psychology*, Mahawah, NJ: Erlbaum, pp. 349–64.
Nelson, R.G., J.E. Everhart, W.C. Knowler and P.H. Bennett (1988), 'Incidence, prevalence and risk factors for non-insulin-dependent diabetes mellitus', *Primary Care*, **15**, 227–50.
Pan, X.R., G.W. Li, Y.H. Hu, et al. (1997), 'Effects of diet and exercise in preventing NIDDM in people with impaired glucose tolerance. The Da Quing IGT and diabetes study', *Diabetes Care*, **20**, 537–44.
Parker, P.A. and J.A. Kulik (1995), 'Burnout, self- and supervisor-related job performance, and absenteeism among nurses', *Journal of Behavioral Medicine*, **18**, 581–99.
Pines, A. (1988), *Keeping the Spark Alive: Preventing Burnout in Love and Marriage*, New York: St Martin's Press.
Pines, A. (1993), 'Burnout', in L. Goldberger and S. Breznitz (eds), *Handbook of stress* (2nd edn, New York: The Free Press, pp. 386–403.
Pines, A. (1996), *Couple Burnout*, New York and London: Routledge.
Pines, A. and E. Aronson (1988), *Career Burnout: Causes and Cures*, New York: Free Press.
Pines, A., E. Aronson and D. Kafry (1981), *Burnout: From Tedium to Personal Growth*, New York: The Free Press.
Rabin, S., M. Saffer, E. Weisberg, T. Kornitzer-Enav, I. Peled and J. Ribak (2000), 'A multifaceted mental health training program in reducing burnout among occupational social workers', *Israel Journal of Psychiatry and Related Science*, **37**, 12–9.
Resnick, H.E., B.V. Howard (2002), 'Diabetes and cardiovascular disease, *Annual Review of Medicine*, **53**, 245–67.
Richardson, A.M., R.J. Burke and M.P. Leiter (1992), 'Occupational demands, psychological burnout, and anxiety among hospital personnel in Norway', *Anxiety, Stress, and coping*, **5**, 55–68.
Rimm, E.B., J. Chan, M.J. Stampfer, G.A. Colditz and W.C. Willett (1995), 'Prospective study of cigarette smoking, alcohol use, and the risk of diabetes in men', *British Medical Journal*, **310**, 555–9.
Rose, R. (1999), 'Atherosclerosis: an inflammatory disease', *New England Journal of Medicine*, **340**, 115–26.
Rotstein, R., D. Mardi, D. Justo, et al. (2002), 'The leukocyte adhesiveness/aggregation test (LAAT) conveys information of biological relevance and is not a result of chance collision. Something more than another hypothesis', *Medical Hypotheses*, **59**, 341–3.

Salmeron, J., J.E. Manson, M.J. Stampfer, G.A. Colditz, A.L. Wing and W.C. Willett (1997), 'Dietary fiber, glycemic load, and risk of non-insulin-dependent diabetes mellitus in women', *Journal of the American Medical Association (JAMA)*, **277**, 472–7.

Samuelson, M., J.P. Gustavsson, I.L. Petterson, B. Arentz and M. Asberg (1997), 'Suicidal feelings and work environment in psychiatric nursing personnel', *Social Psychiatry and Psychiatric Epidemiology*, **32**, 391–7.

Sandberg, J. (2000), 'Understanding human competence at work: an integrative approach', *Academy of Management Journal*, **43**, 9–25.

Schaufeli, W.B. and B.P. Buunk (1996), 'Professional burnout', in M.J. Schabracq, J.A.M. Winnust and C.L. Cooper (eds), *Handbook of Work and Health Psychology*, New York: Wiley, pp. 311–46.

Schaufeli, W.B. and B.P. Buunk (2003), 'Burnout: an overview of 25 years of research and thoerizing', in M.J. Schabracq, J.A.M. Winnubst and C.L. Cooper (eds), *The handbook of work and health psychology*, 2nd edn, Chichester Wiley, pp. 383–429.

Schaufeli, W.B. and D. Van Dierendonck (1993), 'The construct validity of two burnoutmeasures', *Journal of Organizational Behavior*, **14**, 631–47.

Schaufeli, W.B. and D. Enzmann (1998), *The Burnout Companion to Sand Practice: A Critical Analysis*, Washington, DC: Taylor & Francis.

Schaufeli, W.B. and E.R. Greenglass (2001), 'Introduction to special issue on burnout and health', *Psychology and Health*, **16**, 501–10.

Schutte, N., S. Toppinen, R. Kalimo and W. Schaufeli (2000), 'The factorial validity of the Maslach Burnout Inventory–General Survey (MBI–GS) across occupational groups and nations', *Journal of Occupational and Organizational Psychology*, **73**, 53–66.

Seidell, J.C. (2000), 'Obesity, insulin resistance and diabetes – a worldwide epidemic', *British Journal of Nutrition*, **83**, Suppl.1, S5–S8.

Shapira, I., R. Rotstein, R. Fusman and B. Gluzman (2001), 'Combined leukocyte and erythrocyte aggregation in patients with acute myocardial infarction', *International Journal of Cardiology*, **78**, 299–305.

Sheiner, E., E. Sheiner, R. Carel, G. Potashnik and I. Shohan-Vardi (2002), 'Potential association between male infertility and occupational psychological stress', *Journal of Occupational and Environmental Medicine*, **44**(12), 1–7.

Shirom, A. (1989), 'Burnout in work organizations', in C.L. Cooper and I. Robertson (eds), *International Review of Industrial and Organizational Psychology*, New York: Wiley, pp. 26–48.

Shirom, A. (2002), 'Job-related burnout: a review', in J.C. Quick and L.E. Tetrick (eds), *Handbook of Occupational Health Psychology*, Washington, DC: American Psychological Association, pp. 245–65.

Shirom, A. (2003), 'The effects of work-related stress on health', in M.J. Schabrag, J.A.M. Winnbust and L.L. Cooper (eds), *Handbook of Work and Health Psychology*, 2nd edn, New York: Wiley pp. 63–83.

Shirom, A. and J. Ezrachi (2003), 'On the discriminant validity of burnout, depression and anxiety', *Anxiety, Coping, and Stress*, **16**, 83–99.

Shirom, A., M. Westman, O. Shamai and R.S. Carel (1997), 'The effects of work overload and burnout on cholesterol and triglycerides levels: the moderating effects of emotional reactivity among male and female employees', *Journal of Occupational Health Psychology*, **2**, 275–88.

Stagnaro, S., P.J. West, F.B. Hu, J.P. Manson and W.C. Willett (2002), 'Diet and risk of Type 2 diabetes', *New England Journal of Medicine*, **346**, 297–8.

Stajkovic, A.D. and F. Luthans (1998), 'Self-efficacy and work-related performance: a meta-analysis', *Psychological Bulletin*, **124**, 240–61.

Steptoe, A. (1991), 'The links between stress and illness', *Journal of Psychosomatic Research*, **35**, 633–44.

Surwit, R.S. and M.S. Schneider (1993), 'Role of stress in the etiology and treatment of diabetes mellitus', *Psychosomatic Medicine*, **55**, 380–93.

Travers, C. and C. Cooper (eds) (1996), *Teachers under Pressure: Stress in the Teaching Profession*, London: Routledge.

Turnipseed, D.L. (1998), 'Anxiety and burnout in the health care work environment', *Psychological Reports*, **82**, 627–42.

Vandenberghe, R. and A.M. Huberman (eds) (1999), *Understanding and Preventing Teacher Burnout: A Source book of International Research and Practice*, New York: Cambridge University Press.

van Diest, R. (1990), 'Subjective sleep characteristics as coronary risk factors, their association with Type A behavior and vital exhaustion', *Journal of Psychosomatic Research*, **34**, 415–26.

van Diest, R. and A. Appels (1991), 'Vital exhaustion and depression: a conceptual study', *Journal of Psychosomatic Research*, **35**, 535–44.

van Diest, R. and A. Appels (1994), 'Sleep physiological characteristics of exhausted men', *Psychosomatic Medicine*, **52**, 28–35.

Vingerhoets, A.J.J.M. (1985), *Psychosocial Stress: An Experimental Approach*, Lisse, Switzerland: Swets & Zeitlinger.

Visscher, T.L.S. and J.C. Seidel (2001), 'The public health impact of obesity', *Annual Review of Public Health*, **22**, 355–75.
Watson, D. and L.A. Clark (1984), 'Negative effectivity: the disposition to experience aversive emotional states', *Psychological Bulletin*, **96**, 465–90.
Watson, D. and J.W. Pennebaker (1989), 'Health complaints, stress and distress: exploring the central role of negative affectivity', *Psychology Review*, **96**, 234–54.
Westman, M. and D. Etzion (1995), 'Crossover of stress, strain and resources from one spouse to another', *Journal of Organizational Behavior*, **16**, 169–81.
Winnubst, J. (1993), 'Organizational structure, social support, and burnout', in W. Schaufeli, C. Maslach and T. Marek (eds), *Professional Burnout: Recent Developments in Theory and Research*, Washington, DC: Taylor & Francis, pp. 151–62.
Zellars, K.L., P.L. Perrewe and W.A. Hochwarter (2000), 'Burnout in health care: the role of the five factors of personality', *Journal of Applied Social Psychology*, **30**, 1570–98.
Zimmet, P., K.G.M.M. Alberti and J. Show (2001), 'Global and societal implications of the diabetes epidemic', *Nature*, **114**, 782–7.

40 Rediscovering meaning and purpose at work: the transpersonal psychology background of a burnout prevention programme
Dirk van Dierendonck, Bert Garssen and Adriaan Visser

'Our need to believe that the things we do are meaningful is our way of dealing with the fear caused by facing up to our mortality. To avoid and deny death we need to feel heroic, to know that our lives are meaningful, that we matter in the large "cosmic" scheme of things' (Bekker, 1973).

As work becomes more dynamic and decentralized, organizations frequently change their structure, and the only constant factor seems to be change itself, with the consequence that employees become more and more physically, emotionally and spiritually exhausted. There is an increasing recognition of the organizational costs and the negative consequences for the employees and the organizations of stressful workplaces (Paoli, 1997). Consequences include high turnover, absenteeism and poor performance, both in terms of productivity and in the quality of work. It is, therefore, not surprising that a number of intervention and prevention programmes have been developed. Until now, most stress management and burnout prevention programmes have been limited to a cognitive–behavioural focus, aiming at cognitive restructuring, didactic stress management and relaxation (Pines and Aronson, 1988).

Burnout is generally viewed as a long-term stress reaction specific to those individuals who have been working under unrelieved stressful conditions for too long. The term 'burnout' is a metaphor that refers to the draining of energy; that is, more energy is lost than replenished, comparable to a car battery, which will run empty if not enough energy is generated from the dynamo. Individuals most vulnerable to burnout are often those who are strongly motivated and involved in their work (Schaufeli and Enzmann, 1998). For these individuals, work is the main reason for their existence, their main source from which to derive meaning. With religion no longer providing the necessary answers, some of us seek it in our work. However work can never fulfil those high expectations. If these individuals no longer find meaning, burnout is a likely end result. Burnout can thus be defined as 'a state of fatigue or frustration brought about by devotion to a cause, way of life, or relationship that failed to produce the expected reward' (Freudenberger and Richelson, 1990).

The process of burning out is conceptualized here in line with above-mentioned definition, as the end result of a gradual process of disillusionment in the quest to derive existential significance from work (Pines, 1993). The importance of meaning in people's efforts to handle difficult and disappointing events, both in the work context and in life in general, was also stressed by Park and Folkman (1997). According to their model, meaning plays a crucial role in the coping process. In this process, meaning refers to people's enduring belief and valued goals, to their assumptions about order and to their life goals and purpose. Meaning influences not only the appraisal of events as potentially stressful, for example when they obstruct valued goals, but meaning also influences attempts to alleviate distress resulting from experiencing such stressful events. For example, the reappraisal of meaning can help people achieve reconciliation with a changed situation. It is, therefore, not surprising that finding meaningful work has been described as the key antidote to burnout (Cherniss, 1995). According to Cherniss, rewarding and meaningful work is characterized by the ability to make a significant impact on the lives of other people, by providing an intellectual challenge and by the continuing possibilities for professional growth.

This chapter describes a burnout prevention programme that was developed from a transpersonal psychology point of view. The reason for choosing this approach is that the desire to finding meaning and purpose and to make a difference is ultimately expressed in the search for spiritual fulfilment (Neck and Milliman, 1994). Transpersonal psychology provides tools to give implicit and explicit attention to spirituality within such a programme. Its approach to personal growth and learning helps people to enhance their sense of global meaning, as well as their sense of work-related meaning. The purpose of this chapter is to show how and in what way, within an organizational setting, transpersonal psychology can be useful for enhancing personal growth and reducing stress and burnout. It describes the background of the programme and illustrates this with findings and quotations from interviews with participants.

Transpersonal psychology and psychosynthesis
The first use of the word 'transpersonal' can be traced to William James in 1905. In the late 1960s, with the establishment of the Transpersonal Institute and the introduction of a new journal, the *Journal of Transpersonal Psychology*, transpersonal psychology became a new field of interest for psychologists (Chinen, 1996). Transpersonal psychology was labelled the 'fourth force' psychology by Maslow (1968), after the psychoanalytic, behavioural and humanistic traditions in psychology. It takes into account the psychological principles of these earlier traditions, and also includes transpersonal experiences.

The practical application of transpersonal psychology principles within psychotherapy has been most strongly influenced by Roberto Assagioli (see Battista, 1996). Assagioli (1965) conceptualized healthy human adult development in two distinct stages: personal psychosynthesis and spiritual psychosynthesis. Personal psychosynthesis involves exploring the structure of one's own psyche and becoming familiar with the contents of one's personal unconscious. After discovering the elements that make up our personality, it is important to gain control over them. The guiding principle here is that 'we are dominated by everything with which our self becomes identified. We can dominate and control everything from which we disidentify ourselves' (Assagioli, 1965, p. 22). The purpose of personal psychosynthesis is to help integrate, to synthesize, the individual around the personal self. Spiritual psychosynthesis consists of the integration of the personality around a deeper centre, the spiritual self, of which the integrated personality becomes an instrument. The acknowledgment of the spiritual dimension recognizes that there is a connectedness that goes beyond the personal level and that this spiritual dimension is essential for (re)discovering meaning and purpose in life.

In comparing psychosynthesis with other approaches it is helpful to realize that it differs from psychoanalysis in that the emphasis is on synthesis and not on analysis.

According to psychosynthesis, analysis – the separation of the whole into components – is not enough for achieving lasting change in our feelings, in our attitudes and in our behaviour. It is important to take our analytic understanding and integrate these components into a harmonious, integrated whole: physical, emotional, mental and spiritual (Gerard, 1964). In developing psychosynthesis, Assagioli was influenced by ideas from eastern spiritual disciplines like yoga and Buddhism (Battista, 1996). Within Western psychology, the psychosynthesis approach to human development is most strongly related to Jungian psychology. Both emphasize the need to develop oneself as a person first, before commencing on a path towards spiritual development. The acknowledgment of the spiritual dimension recognizes that there is a connectedness that goes beyond the personal level and that this spiritual dimension is essential for (re)discovering meaning and purpose in life. Two essential elements in the transpersonal counselling process are self-acceptance and uncovering the beliefs (for example, personal, familial, cultural) that create someone's reality (Strohl, 1998). The fundamental assumption underlying this perspective is that individuals have the innate wisdom and knowledge to find their own personal responses to the questions and distresses that life can confront them with.

'The challenge to inner mastership'
The project was called 'The Challenge to Inner Mastership'. It combined training and research. The training consisted of ten full days in a conference centre located away from work, spread over three months. Participants were recruited from three major industrial concerns in The Netherlands. In all, 38 people, most of them with a background in engineering, followed the programme. The participants were divided into four groups, with the size of the groups ranging from 8 to 11 people. Two psychosynthesis counsellors, a man and a woman, guided all four groups.

The programme
The training started with a two-day meeting, followed by six separate days, each held bi-weekly. It was completed with another two-day meeting. All meetings were held in a resort in the countryside. Three months later, a follow-up meeting of one morning finished the training. The participants were encouraged to keep a diary during the training and to write an emotional autobiography. Both were strictly for personal use. Writing helps participants to review and reflect on their life. It facilitates an enhanced self-awareness, supports the commitment to make changes and helps to clarify problems in order to open oneself up to solutions (Whitmore, 1991).

Each day focused on a specific theme. The days were semi-structured. A typical day would start with a short meditation, followed by a session in which participants reflected on the two weeks since the last meeting. Next guided imagery techniques were used to focus on the theme of the day. During the rest of the day the theme was further explored in several ways, including drawing the images that came up in the guided imagery, discussions in small groups and in the whole group. Each day closed with an assignment for the participants, to focus on the next theme over the 14 days to the next meeting.

The themes of the first two-day meeting were body consciousness, emotions and the mind. Visualizations focused on the relation with one's body, one's emotions and desires, and one's mind. The last exercise of the meeting was the well-known self-identification exercise (Ferrucci, 1993). This exercise helps to obtain an overview of one's personality and experience the self as pure conciousness, as the most elementary and distinctive part of our being. In psychosynthesis, the self is defined as the only part of us that remains forever the same, no matter what emotions we experience or whatever happens in our life. In the exercise, one is asked to identify and disidentify with one's body, feelings, desires and thoughts, respectively. Regular practice makes it possible to observe, regulate, direct or transcend the different aspects of our consciousness. What is left is an enhanced awareness of the observer, the self, and a greater freedom to choose which part of our personality we want to express. This exercise was also recommended as daily homework.

The third day explored aspects of the personality known within psychosynthesis as 'subpersonalities'. Subpersonalities are the different elements in our personality, elements that are expressed in the different roles we play in our life. A subpersonality can be viewed as a synthesis of habits, characteristics and other psychological elements (Whitmore, 1991). It acknowledges that we are one individual with different qualities for different situations. The identification with a subpersonality is often an unconscious process. In specific situations, we experience that we are the subpersonality that is dominant in that context. The recognition of different subpersonalities and their relevance in the different areas of our life opens a window towards a greater freedom to choose alternative behaviour.

On day four, attention was given to supportive and critical influences and 'heroes'. The outer and inner authorities were the subject of day five. Both days focused on the people in our lives that influenced us, now and in the past (for example, our parents). Days six and seven focused on love and will, and on autonomy and interconnectedness, respectively. Day eight was entitled 'the spiritual autobiography'. Participants were invited to share the most touching moment in their lives. This day, together with day three on subpersonalities, was in the opinion of the participants the most effective and insightful. The concluding two-day meeting finished the training by focusing on love for oneself, personal values and the personal mission. Throughout the training, themes were illustrated by inspirational quotations from, for example, *The Prophet* by Kabir and the *Upanishads*.

Success factors
The evaluation
The programme was evaluated with a combination of surveys and interviews. A total of 34 people completed the surveys three times: pre-programme, post-programme and at the follow-up six months later. They were also interviewed six months after finishing the programme. This group consisted of 27 male and seven female participants, with a mean age of 40 years and an average employment record within their company of 14 years. A comparison group, consisting of colleagues who matched the participants on demographic variables, was included in the study. In an earlier paper (Van Dierendonck *et al.*, 2005), we reported on the quantitative results of the evaluation. These results showed that this programme can be an effective tool to provide people with the necessary resources to meet the challenges at work. It reduced burnout, enhanced emotional intelligence and feelings of spirituality, and improved the style of coping. The programme encouraged the bending back of ongoing loss into an upward, gain spiral.

Some of the most salient outcomes of the interviews are used here to illustrate the main elements of the intervention and how they affected the participants. Qualitative data are a valuable source of information in that they present results in a way that is more holistic, values experience and emphasizes meaning over measurement (Chamberlain et al., 1997). The central effect of the programme mentioned in all interviews was an enhanced insight into oneself. The self-esteem of several participants had increased. The second effect was a greater understanding of their social environment, most notably their spouse and colleagues. Most participants also mentioned their increased ability to say 'no'. Their improved insight into themselves helped them to stay within the limits of their capabilities. They were better able to distance themselves from things that happened at work and at home. As a whole the participants indicated improvement in their general outlook on life. They had become more positive, more relaxed, more open to others, more assertive, more energetic, more emphatic, and/or experienced more self-acceptance.

Spiritual exercises
The participants indicated in the interviews that three factors contributed strongly to the success of the programme. The first factor was the regular use of spiritual exercises: guided imagery techniques and meditation. Guided imagery techniques have several functions (Crampton, 1992). They can help a person to see more clearly what his problems are and what his growth potential is; they also encourage a dialogue between the conscious and the unconscious. Drawing and discussing the images that arise in a visualization facilitate an enhanced self-knowledge. One's dormant potential can be awakened and strengthened. An additional advantage is that visualizations can easily be done at home. This fosters the participant's personal development and growth. Several participants said that the exercises had helped them to listen better to their inner voice or intuition. They experienced more from the inside and became more creative in finding solutions for difficult situations. Examples of exercises that were used can be found in Assagioli (1965) and Ferrucci (1993).

Meditation was new for almost everybody. The trainers introduced it in a low-key manner, as sitting in silence. Although some were very cynical about meditating beforehand, looking back they considered these moments of 'just sitting' as important in the whole process. It helped to bring personal issues to the surface. After a few sessions, almost everyone was enjoying those moments of silence and awareness of what was happening inside.

Before the training, most participants felt a certain unrest regarding their work and their lives. They were unhappy but unsure where these feelings originated. In the interviews, they mentioned that the meditations and the guided visualizations had encouraged an enhanced insight in themselves and had helped them to find more inner peace. If a situation could not be changed, these exercises encouraged acceptance (that is, reappraisal of meaning); on the other hand, if change was possible, the exercises encouraged taking charge of a situation and starting to make changes (that is, active coping).

The group process
The second success factor was the group process. The group process can be an important instrument to encourage personal growth. Our approach in facilitating this group process was inspired by Yeomans (1995), who developed a particular kind of group work, called 'the Corona Process'. According to Yeomans, working within what he calls a spiritual context means taking into account three interdependent dimensions of a human being's

inner experience: personal, psychical and spiritual. These dimensions together influence the group process. A group has a personality consisting of the identifications and relationships of its members. Like an individual, a group also has a psyche consisting of the collective unconsciousness of the members. In addition a group has a spiritual dimension, which is the organizing principle of the group. In a way similar to individuals whom we try to help express their deepest identity, we also help the group to contact and express its true nature. Through the Corona Process, members of a group start to bring more harmony into their interrelations. The group starts to reorganize its personality and psyche to express more truly and deeply its spiritual force. Deeper-level issues can be resolved, which will lead eventually to an enhanced insight and resolution, to an ability to express oneself in new and creative ways.

Most participants in our programme commented on the close bonds between all group members. The atmosphere was experienced as safe and open. Sharing different points of view, for example between men and women, was very enlightening and instructive. People were never judged for who they were, what they had done with their life, or on their worldview. It was seen as important that everyone conducted himself or herself in a way characterized by the utmost care and honesty.

The group had an important role in facilitating the recognition of similarity between one's own experience and that of others. These similarities were experienced as pleasurable. One felt less alone. Talking, listening and asking one another questions were the active ingredients. They encouraged a process of reflection on one's own situation. In the beginning this was a scary experience for some participants, but after some time it became enjoyable. The men especially became more comfortable with listening to feelings and showing emotions. Everyone saw the fact that the groups consisted of both men and women as relevant. Men and women differed in their views on important issues like work and family. Exchanging these different viewpoints was a valuable experience.

'Well, I think that everyone in our group was very open and was very amenable to the others. We tried to do the best we could, really looking at things that happened in the group, but also looking at oneself. It felt strange in the beginning, but it went along by itself after one or two sessions. Nobody kept things for him or herself. I experienced very much openness in the group.'

Yeomans (1995) formulated a set of guidelines to support the Corona Process. Important elements are the following: work within a circle; slow down and take time to listen to yourself and others; breathe fully; allow for and accept silence in the group; be truthful at all times; listen deeply; do not judge yourself or others; and be patient. According to Yeomans, working within these guidelines will create an energy field that will grow stronger and more coherent as the process unfolds.

The psychosynthesis counsellors
The counsellors were the third key factor in the programme. An essential function of the psychosynthesis counsellors was encouraging a process within the participants that leads to the uncovering of beliefs that create one's reality. Vital elements in the training were teaching the participants self-acceptance, responsibility for one's life and trust in one's inner wisdom. To achieve this, and to facilitate the Corona Process, the counsellors had to focus more on being than on doing (ibid.).

All participants were of the opinion that the success of this programme depended to a great extent on the skills of the counsellors. They were described as patient, empathic, relaxed, flexible, open and sincere, vigorous and charismatic. Their wisdom and insight into human nature inspired trust and a sense of security in the group. Their non-forcing attitude reflected the basic assumption that individuals have the innate wisdom and knowledge to find their own personal responses. It was greatly appreciated that the counsellors respected the personal boundaries of the participants. Sharing of personal stuff with the group was absolutely voluntary.

'Their role was to encourage processes and trains of thought in a non-forcing, non-authoritative way. They created a free rein where processes came into being as if by themselves. It was non-directive. There was room for everybody's viewpoint, for finding one's own explanation and meaning.'

Important characteristics of the style of psychosynthesis counsellors who aspire to work with the Corona Process are practising presence, being vulnerable, welcoming the experiences of all members, withholding judgment, working with a beginner's mind, initiating structure when needed and being willing to let go if possible, being sensitive to the group field and keeping the group within it (for a more elaborate description, see Yeomans, 1995).

Conclusion

'Throughout the training I have gained an improved insight in myself on several areas. I know better how things function, I am better able to cope with issues that confront me.' This chapter has described a burnout prevention programme that was developed from a transpersonal psychology point of view. By encouraging personal growth, it achieved reduced feelings of burnout and an enhanced sense of well-being among the participants. On the whole, the combined results of the survey and interview data lead us to conclude that our programme shows promise as an additional approach to the more traditionally used programmes. One concrete example of the benefits of following this programme was that several participants indicated an improved ability to handle critical remarks on their work, which resulted in a reduced feeling of stress. This improvement existed not only in the minds of the participants, given that the survey data showed a drop in burned-out cases of 55 per cent (Van Dierendonck et al., 2005).

The spiritual dimension played an essential part in the programme. Spirituality can be viewed as the ultimate context of giving meaning to life. The participants experienced a greater sense of worth, hope and reason for living. Their feeling of inner strength was enhanced and their capacity for transcendence had increased. They had a greater ability to step back from their lives and gain a new perspective.

Although most participants were unfamiliar with the psychosynthesis approach beforehand, and some of them were downright sceptical, all were enthusiastic afterwards. This is illustrated by the fact that nobody dropped out of this quite intensive programme. Only a small group said that the training had only a little effect. These people were of the opinion that they were already feeling good about themselves and their work before participating in the programme. The quantitative results (Van Dierendonck et al., 2005) showed that strongest improvements were found among those participants who experienced less meaning and less inner strength beforehand.

To conclude, we have described a transpersonal approach that has the potential of becoming a valuable addition to our already existing programmes to encourage personal growth and prevent burnout.

References

Assagioli, R. (1965), *Psychosynthesis: a Manual of Principles and Techniques*, New York: The Viking Press.
Battista, J.R. (1996), 'Abraham Maslow and Roberto Assagioli: pioneers of transpersonal psychology', in B.W. Scotton, A.B. Chinen and J.R. Battista, *Textbook of Transpersonal Psychiatry and Psychology*, New York: Basic Books, pp. 52–61.
Bekker, E. (1973), *The Denial of Death*, New York: Free Press.
Chamberlain, K., C. Stephens and A.C. Lyons (1997), 'Encompassing experience: meanings and methods in health psychology', *Psychology and Health*, **12**, 691–709.
Cherniss, C. (1995), *Beyond Burnout*, London: Routledge.
Chinen, A.B. (1996), 'The emergence of transpersonal psychiatry', in B.W. Scotton, A.B. Chinen and J.R. Battista, *Textbook of Transpersonal Psychiatry and Psychology*, New York: Basic Book, pp. 9–18.
Crampton, M. (1992), *The Use of Mental Imagery in Psychosynthesis*, Amsterdam: Instituut voor Psychosynthese.
Ferrucci, P. (1993), *What We May Be: Techniques for Psychological and Spiritual Growth Through Psychosynthesis*, New York: J.P. Tarcher.
Freudenberger, H.J. with G. Richelson (1990), *Burnout: How to Beat the High Cost of Success*, New York: Bantam Books.
Gerard, R. (1964), *Psychosynthesis: a Psychotherapy for the Whole Man*, New York: Psychosynthesis Research Foundation.
Maslow, A. (1968), *Toward a Psychology of Being*, New York: VanNostrand/Reinhold.
Neck, C.P. and J.F. Milliman (1994), 'Thought self-leadership. Finding spiritual fulfilment in organizational life', *Journal of Managerial Psychology*, **9**(6), 9–16.
Paoli, P. (1997), *Second European survey on the work environment, 1995*, Dublin: European Foundation for the Improvement of Living and Working Conditions, Loughlinstown House.
Park, C.L. and S. Folkman (1997), 'Meaning in the context of stress and coping', *Review of General Psychology*, **1**, 115–44.
Pines, A.M. (1993), 'Burnout: an existential perspective', in W.B. Schaufeli, C. Maslach and T. Marek (eds), *Professional Burnout, Recent Developments in Theory and Research*, Washington, DC: Taylor & Francis, pp. 33–51.
Pines, A.M. and E. Aronson (1988), *Career Burnout: Causes and Cures*, New York: Free Press.
Schaufeli, W.B. and D. Enzmann (1998), *The Burnout Companion to Research and Practice: a Critical Analysis*, Washington, DC: Taylor & Francis.
Strohl, J.E. (1998), 'Transpersonalism: ego meets soul', *Journal of Counseling and Development*, **76**, 397–403.
Van Dierendonck, D., B. Garssen and A. Visser (2005), 'Burnout prevention through personal growth', *International Journal of Stress Management* (in press).
Whitmore, D. (1991), *Psychosynthesis Counselling in Action*, London: Sage Publications.
Yeomans, T. (1995), *The Corona Process: Group Work in a Spiritual Context*, Concord, MA: The Concord Institute.

PART VI

EMOTIONAL INTELLIGENCE

AT WORK

41 Emotional intelligence and transformational leadership
Alexander-Stamatios G. Antoniou

Introduction

> If those who are now called leaders do not acquire authentic and adequate philosophical education and ... if both political power and philosophical mind do not characterize the same individual ... then there will be no end of misfortunes for the cities. (Plato, *Republic* E, 473–4)

Over recent decades effective leadership perceptions and study results have shifted interest towards interpersonal skills (Palmer *et al.*, 2001) and the leader's ability to motivate subordinates, create and maintain a sense of contribution to the organization as a whole, contrary to the previous perceptions of inspecting, controlling and planning leaders. Current research focuses on identifying traits and/or aspects of behaviour that constitute the fundamental elements for contemporary effective leadership roles, as much in order to enhance the development of effective leaders as to identify and recruit them successfully (Pratch and Jacobowitz, 1998). Emotional intelligence is a relatively new concept, which is receiving a lot of attention, with vast applicability in many organizational areas, including job satisfaction, commitment and performance (Cooper and Sawaf, 1997; Wright and Staw, 1999).

Recently in-depth study of leadership within organizations has addressed the concept of effective leadership. Furthermore, certain research groups claim that the notion of emotional intelligence applies to the largest proportion of effectiveness in leader behaviour (Hay Group, 2000). There are various leadership models that aim to create the conceptual basis of leader behaviour and the interaction between the leader–member dyad, with the transactional leadership model as one of the most influential. However, during the last decade, transformational leadership has been well established as the most effective leadership behaviour as it is primarily related to and based upon emotions and emotion-based interaction (Palmer *et al.*, 2001). This chapter aims to establish that transformational leadership behaviours constitute an emotion-based approach, which is directed towards broadening and elevating subordinate interests beyond the self. This approach is concerned with the accomplishment of group tasks and the common mission, generating subordinates' acceptance and awareness (Yammering and Bass, 1990; Hartog *et al.*, 1997).

Emotions and emotional intelligence

Emotions constitute the highest form of the sensory relationship between humans and the objects and facts of reality; this relationship is characterized by relative stability, generality and correlation between needs and values which have been developed throughout an individual's personal development. Emotions are distinguished from psychic circumstantial excitation and are directed towards phenomena which are of constant importance and which, moreover, are responsible for the direction of the individual's activity. They appear as a specific and subjective form of human existence, emphasizing those elements which are important for the individual and which drive his/her actions towards the satisfaction of their needs (Karpenko et al., 1998).

The formation of stable emotional relationships is the most important presupposition of personality development. It constitutes the main aim and ultimate result of the individual's learning ability. The conscious knowledge of motives, models and behavioural stipulations alone is not enough to guide the individual's existence within society. On the contrary, only when the individual becomes possessed of stable emotions is this knowledge shaped and formed into behaviour. During the process of personality formation, emotions are organized into a hierarchical system in which some of those emotions maintain their original position in less dynamic levels of self-actualization, while others move on to a more powerful position. (Viliounas and Gippenreiter, 1984).

Every aspect of human activity is accompanied by a variety of emotions. The importance of emotional management has led to the designation and study of emotional intelligence and its abilities, especially in organizational settings. The intense and competitive challenges of the international economy are accompanied by changes in managing and organizing modern organizations and individual organizational behaviour and their adaptation to the ever-growing demands of the workplace. The increased competition favours individuals who possess personal motives, show initiative, have the inner tendency to surpass themselves and their personal limits, and are optimistic enough to use constructively any obstacle they meet on the way.

Psychological assessment has proved to be of great value and significance, since organizational performance and effectiveness directly depend on placing the right person in the right position. Work-related demands presuppose appropriate abilities and capabilities, which result from the careful analysis of profession and position requirements. The appropriate and valid analysis of demands relative to an organizational position depends on the correct choice of psychometric tools. Research indicates that there is a close relationship between organizational productivity and the choice of the appropriate psychometric tool for candidate recruitment (Anastasi, 1982).

Research conducted during recent decades in order to identify the factors related to eminent occupational performance has widely questioned the fact that occupational success is related to intellectual intelligence. At the very dawn of psychological theorizing and research on intellectual intelligence (IQ), psychologists focused on the cognitive aspects of intelligence such as memory and problem solving. Quite early, though, they recognized aspects in intelligence that were non-cognitive and equally important, such as social and affective factors. Wechsler (1943) suggested that there are some 'non-intellective' factors (p. 103), which determine intelligence, while Thorndike (1920), suggested there must be multiple intelligences and that measuring intra- and interpersonal intelligence is as important as measuring intellectual intelligence with the IQ test.

The notion of emotional intelligence was built on the long tradition of theory and research on the non-cognitive factors which are related to people's success as much in life as in the workplace, and is a term coined by Salovey and Mayer (1990), who described emotional intelligence as 'a form of social intelligence that involves the ability to monitor one's own and other's feelings and emotions, to discriminate among them, and to use this information to guide one's thinking and action'.

Emotional intelligence (EQ) is the term which refers to those other non-intellective factors that lead to healthy relationships and success in life and career (McMullen, 2003). It is also the ability to manage emotions, linked and not opposed to intellectual intelligence (McMullen, 2002).

Emotional intelligence refers to the ability to know when and how to express emotion as well as being able to control it. Barsade (1998) conducted an experiment at Yale University which included volunteers instructed to play the role of managers, allocating bonuses to their subordinates. Among them, a trained actor was instructed always to talk first; he was enthusiastic and cheerful within some groups, hostile and depressed in others. The results of the experiment were twofold: on the one hand, the actor proved to be capable of 'infecting' group feelings and emotions. On the other, positive emotions resulted in improved inner group cooperation and fairness in distributing the bonuses to their 'subordinates'.

Another important element of emotional intelligence in the workplace is the ability to manage stress. This emotional competence is linked to success. In a retail store chain, the most successful store managers were those who were able to manage stressful situations, while their success was based on sales per employee, sales per square foot and net profits (Luscha and Serpkeuci, 1990). This aspect of EQ is closely connected to Seligman's (1990) notion of 'learned optimism'.

This construct refers to the causal attributions made by individuals when confronted with failure: pessimists tend to attribute internally, globally and permanently, while, on the contrary, optimists tend to attribute externally, specifically and temporarily (Cherniss, 2000); optimism leads to increased productivity. New salesmen at Met Life, who scored high on the 'learned optimism' scale, sold 37 per cent more life insurance policies than those who scored high on 'pessimism' in their two first years in the organization (Seligman, 1990).

As research studies reveal, IQ has not proved to be a very good predictor of organizational performance (Poon Teng Fatt, 2002). The results of a study of 80 PhD science candidates who, when they were students at Berkeley University in the 1950s, undertook a series of personality tests, IQ tests and interviews, showed that, 40 years later, when monitored on their success by experts in their own field and based on their résumés, emotional and social abilities were four times more important in determining professional success than their IQ scores (Cherniss, 2000).

Although cognitive ability has been demonstrated to play a less important and/or a more limited role in determining professional success, there are a number of studies which stress the fact that cognitive and non-cognitive abilities are interlinked, suggesting mutual cooperation between the IQ and the EQ (Dulewicz and Higgs, 2000). The most famous example is the 'marshmallow' experiment which was conducted during the 1960s at a nursery school, on the Stanford University campus (Shoda et al., 1990). Psychologists interviewed four-year-old children individually and offered them the following choice: they would either be given one marshmallow or, if they waited for 15–20 minutes until the experimenter came back into the room, they would be given two. Some children found ways to distract themselves and wait until the experimenter came back, while other children impulsively grabbed the marshmallow as soon as the experimenter had left the room.

When, 14 years later, those same children were tracked down and interviewed, those who had waited were more motivated and capable of coping with life's frustrations, while their ability to delay gratification contributed to their intellectual potential (Goleman, 1996).

Approaches to emotional intelligence

Emotions are becoming recognized as an important element of organizational life and good conduct. Emotional intelligence theorists (Gardner, 1983; Bar-On, 1988, 2000; Salovey and Mayer, 1990; Goleman, 1995, 1998a, 2001; Rozell et al., 2002) have proposed many ideas, drawing on psychoanalytic, behavioural and brain research, which illustrate that emotional intelligence can become a loyal organizational servant (Gabriel and Griffiths, 2002). The most significant of these ideas is that the majority of modern organizations depend on emotional skills such as empathy, self-awareness and sensitivity.

Furthermore, unlike intellectual intelligence, emotional intelligence is capable of developing and improving through types of training. According to Bar-On (1997), IQ reaches its highest peak at about 21 years of age, while emotional intelligence develops from an individual's childhood experiences to his late adulthood. Dulewicz and Higgs (1999) suggest that emotional intelligence consists of seven components. These fall into two categories: (a) learned and developed skills of emotional intelligence, such as coaching, and (b) skills and aspects which are related to the individuals' personality. There are many approaches that attempt to explain the value of emotion throughout various aspects of human life; three of the most important are briefly discussed below.

Social constructionist approach to emotional intelligence

One of the most interesting approaches to emotional intelligence is the social constructionist approach. According to this approach, emotions are social phenomena which help to make sense of social situations and enable individuals to respond and function effectively in them (Fineman, 1993, 1997; Mangham, 1998). The quality of each emotion – pleasant or disturbing – depends on the individual's interpretation of each situation, which is tested through the individual's relationship with others. Emotions are shaped by culture; culture provides the background and the unwritten rules which refer the appropriateness of each emotion to a given situation and audience: emotions are situation-specific. Moreover, according to social constructionists, emotions preserve individual values and signal the individual's needs for change (Lazarus, 1991).

Applied in the workplace, the individual's adopted emotional responses are not a simple expression of emotional intelligence, but a form of compliance with higher-status individuals within the organization (Ackroyd and Thompson, 1999). This form of compliance, according to this approach, occasionally leads to the individual feeling alienated, and is capable of causing burnout. Fineman and Gabriel (2000) have put forward the following ideas, which are the most significant in the social constructionist approaches to emotion:

- emotions constitute social phenomena,
- emotions are situation-specific,
- emotions have practical use,
- emotions are described through the use of language and are enacted in the presence

of an audience,
- emotions reconcile social aspects of emotions with personal feelings.

Psychoanalytic approach to emotional intelligence
Like the social constructionist approach, psychoanalysis places emotion at the centre of human affairs, dismissing the view that emotions can be deployed according to self-interest and quantified within one category, such as emotional intelligence. Psychoanalysis can be a useful tool for unravelling an organization's emotional life. According to psychoanalysis, emotions belong to pre-social, pre-linguistic and primitive levels of human existence (Craib, 1998). The unconscious is viewed as the arena, which is both a source of emotions and ideas threatening mental functioning and a territory of defensive mechanisms protecting the individual's equilibrium from painful and dangerous thoughts. Organizations are viewed as much as a source of creativity and excitement for the individual as a source of discontent and illusion (Gabriel and Carr, 2002).

Emotions are seen as a coping mechanism which enables the individual to adapt to different circumstances every time. Emotions and rationality are viewed as conflicting principles which drive our motivation (Antonacopoulou and Gabriel, 2001). Psychoanalysis recognizes the complexity of our motivations. Human motivation is driven by the unconscious and, even though there are often conscious explanations for certain actions or thoughts, psychoanalysis will examine the chance of unconscious factors affecting that particular human action.

Therefore, while for some people work is a mere necessity, for others it constitutes an arena in which to enhance their super-ego and/or build their self-esteem (Smelser, 1998; Obholzer, 1999). Psychoanalysis has been widely criticized but, no matter how problematic, it can offer valuable insights on organizational life and conduct.

Philosophical approach to emotional intelligence
Boyatzis *et al.* (2000) suggested that, since an individual's operating philosophy surpasses any social environment, the missing link between values and behaviour is philosophy; philosophy would therefore seem important in explaining individual behaviour, as it is related to the individual's values and beliefs. Conceptually values are individual beliefs about one or multiple theories; they are conditional and/or instrumental (Rokeach, 1973) and expressive (Hetcher, 1993). According to Rokeach (1973), values are combined into systems, while they are organizations of beliefs and a continuum of relevant importance for the individual, which concerns 'end states' or the individual's preferred conduct (p. 5).

Boyatzis *et al.* (2000) argue that, in order to find the link between individuals' values and behaviour, a close and thorough examination of an individual's operating philosophy may prove to be the key. Work preferences and interests are closely related to the values and value system of every individual. The authors based their study upon three major operating philosophies which appear to influence the beliefs and thoughts of individuals in different ways: the pragmatic, intellectual and human operating philosophy.

1. Based on major philosophies such as pragmatism (Pierce, 1931; Rorty, 1991), instrumentalism (Dewey, 1917), consequentialism (Pettit, 1993) and utilitarianism (Mill, 1991), this operating philosophy stresses the importance of worth. The individual

acts and behaves in ways that promote and maximize benefit. According to the moral personality which is shaped by rational enquiry and the community in which the individuals live (Singer, 1995), individuals acting on pragmatic operating philosophy value money because it applies to all aspects of human conduct, and not because money is the ultimate end of their lives.

2. Based on rationalism (Descartes, 1955; Spinoza, 1985) and philosophical structuralism (Levi-Strauss, 1967) as well as postmodernism (Nietzsche, 1968), individuals acting according to intellectual operating philosophy assess their actions and activities in terms of their consistency with particular sets of rules or guidelines. In a way closely related to the social constructionist approach, the individual constructs an image of the world and how it works. This construction provides emotional security for the individual. Truth is based on what is known and what is known is based on reason; what is known is a social construction and, therefore, contextually relative.

3. Finally, the individual with human operating philosophy, based on humanism (Sellars, 1933), collectivism (Chamberlin, 1937) and hermeneutics (Gadamer, 1977), views personal bonds in people and relationships as the ultimate meaning of life. Faithfulness to human values and loyalty are the basic traits of these individuals, while they believe that the value of an activity is based on its impact on the people to whom they relate.

Compared to earlier constructs (Kluckhohn, 1951; Allport et al., 1960; Kluckhohn and Strodtbeck, 1961; Holland, 1985, 1996; Schwartz, 1992; Kahle, 1996), the conceptual approach to operating philosophies provides a more fundamental personality structure (Boyatzis et al., 1999). According to the authors, a person's operating philosophy does not easily change over any period time, if ever.

Emotional intelligence frameworks
H. Gardner (1983), a Harvard psychologist and one of the most influential theorists of Intelligence, introduced a widely acknowledged model of 'multiple intelligences'; he is now recognized as the pioneer in distinguishing between intellectual and emotional capacities. Gardner stressed the importance of culture and brain structure in relation to seven proposed intelligences: parallel to cognitive, verbal and mathematical abilities, he recognized two types of 'personal intelligences', which referred to knowing oneself and one's social relationships.

Less than a decade later, Bar-On's (1988) work was considered to be the first attempt to evaluate and measure emotional intelligence. Based on a 19-year research, the Bar-On Emotional Quotient Inventory is designed to measure constructs which are related to EQ as a better predictor of occupational success than the traditional measures of intellectual intelligence (IQ) (Boyatzis and Van Oosten, 2002; Cavallo and Brienza, 2003).

The Mayer and Salovey framework of emotional intelligence
A complete framework of emotional intelligence was suggested by Salovey and Mayer (1990), who defined EQ as an individual's ability to control and appraise his/her emotions and the emotions of others, the ability to distinguish between emotions and to use them in such ways that they direct the individual's thought and actions. The authors put great

emphasis on the cognitive dimension of EQ, in which ability is based on complex and interactive psychological processes between emotion and cognition (Mayer and Salovey, 1997). Their framework is divided into four components:

1. *Perception, appraisal and expression of emotions*: the individual's ability to identify emotions and their content, to express their emotional needs and to be able to distinguish false emotions through careful inner evaluation.
2. *Emotion's facilitation of thinking*: this component involves the individual's ability to recognize different emotions and differentiate between them accordingly. From birth, emotions indicate environmental and personal changes which can be generated on demand so that they are better understood.
3. *Understanding and analysing emotions; employing emotional knowledge*: the individual's understanding of emotions and the ability to use them. This understanding will also enable the individual to recognize contradictory emotions and their combination.
4. *Reflective regulation of emotions to promote emotional and intellectual growth*: this component involves the individual's ability to elaborate on effective strategies which may be used as an aid to achieving goals. This component promotes the individual's intellectual and emotional growth.

Goleman's framework of emotional competencies
Model no. 1 (Goleman, 1998b) Drawing on the Mayer and Salovey (1997) model on EQ, Goleman (1998b) developed his emotional competency framework which can be applied to organizational settings. According to Goleman, emotional intelligence is related to motivation: the ability to manage emotions in relationships, motivating oneself and recognizing personal and others' feelings and emotions; this element was not included in the Mayer and Salovey framework. Goleman's model includes five basic components and 25 emotional and social abilities (Table 41.1):

1. *Self-awareness*: the individual's ability to acknowledge his/her emotions at any given moment and to be able to use them as a guide to decision making, realistically evaluating his/her abilities and values.
2. *Self-regulation*: the individual's ability to handle emotions in such a way as not to interfere with given tasks (Mischel et al., 1990).
3. *Motivation*: the individual's emotional tendency that leads him/her towards the achievement of goals.
4. *Empathy*: the individual's ability to 'read' the non-verbal expression of others' needs, to be aware of their feelings and to be able to consider others' perspectives.
5. *Social skills*: this component involves the individual's accurate reading of social situations and the effective handling of relationships. This person will be better able to interact and lead in teamwork and generally in organizations.

Model no. 2 (Goleman, 2000) Following a number of studies carried out in order to test the best way of adapting this model to the new statistical data, Goleman (2000) corrected his model of emotional competency by reducing it to four components and 20 emotional

Table 41.1 Goleman's framework of emotional competencies

a (1998)	b (2000)
Self-awareness	**Self-awareness**
emotional awareness	emotional awareness
accurate self-assessment	accurate self-assessment
self-confidence	self-confidence
Self-regulation	**Self-management**
self-control	self-control
trustworthiness	trustworthiness
conscientiousness	conscientiousness
adaptability	adaptability
innovativeness	achievement orientation
Self-motivation	initiative
achievement	**Social-awareness**
commitment	insight
initiative	service orientation
optimism	organizational awareness
Empathy	**Relationship management**
empathy	influence
service orientation	communication
developing others	leadership
leveraging diversity	change catalyst
political awareness	conflict management
Social skills	building bonds
influence	collaboration and cooperation
communication	team capabilities
leadership	
change catalyst	
conflict management	
building bonds	
collaboration and cooperation	
team capabilities	

and social abilities (Table 41.1):

1. *Self-awareness*: the individual's ability to acknowledge his/her inner psychic state, preferences and personal resources.
2. *Self-management*: the individual's ability to manage his/her emotions and impulses.
3. *Social-awareness*: the individual's ability to acknowledge his/her social environment. As with 'social skills', the individual who possesses this ability is able to interact better with others around him/her and lead teams and organizations in general.
4. *Relationship management*: the individual's ability to manage relationships and effectively read the social situations in which he/she is an active member.

Table 41.2   Measures of emotional intelligence

---
1. Work Profile Questionnaire – emotional intelligence version (WPQ EI)
2. Emotional Competence Inventory 360° (ECI 360°) (Boyatzis *et al.*, 1999)
3. Multifactoral Emotional Intelligence Scale (MEIS™) (Mayer and Salovey, 1997)
4. Bar-On Emotional Quotient Inventory (Bar-On EQ-I) (Bar-On, 1997)

Based on these frameworks, especially designed psychometric tools have been constructed to measure the dimensions of emotional intelligence, which vary according to the model on which they are based and collaborated form (Table 41.2). Each questionnaire bases its validity directly on the definition and dimensions defined by its authors. More research is needed in order for future conclusions to be based on more objective results and in order to avoid simple description of personality characteristics when referring to dimensions of emotional intelligence, which may not actually refer to the subject studied.

Emotional intelligence and leadership

In modern organizations, which are more service-oriented (Perrella, 1999) the old inspecting, controlling and plan-oriented image of leaders has evolved into leadership roles which are more inspiring and motivation-oriented, aiming to give a sense of importance and individual contribution to the employees of the organization (Hogan *et al.*, 1994). Authors argue that the effective management of organizations is facing continual challenges: organization downsizing, a plethora of information available, and so on (Luthans, 1998).

Leadership skills, which have become the most important asset of effective managers (Messmer, 1999), are based on interpersonal skills and need to be appropriate and decisive according to the situation (Cacioppe, 1997). Studies indicate that there are six specific traits that distinguish leaders from non-leaders: the ambition and desire to lead, task-relevant knowledge and self-confidence, intelligence, integrity, honesty and high levels of energy (Kilpatrick and Locke, 1991).

But what are the characteristics of a leader? This question still generates a lot of debate but, nevertheless, theorists argue that there are specific traits shared by all leaders (Bennis, 1994) (Table 41.3):

1. Leaders have a vision; a clear idea about their pursuits, regardless of setbacks and obstacles.
2. Leaders have passion; they are able to inspire, motivate and communicate their passion to others.
3. Leaders are characterized by integrity, honesty, maturity and self-knowledge.
4. Leaders have passion for learning and exploring new horizons.
5. Leaders are daring and willing to take risks.

The major themes that emerge in the literature relative to leadership theory, which is power-oriented (McClelland and Boyatzis, 1982), are transformational and transactional leadership (Robbins *et al.*, 1994; Hartog *et al.*, 1997). Bennis' (1994) description applies to transformational leadership qualities. Leaders have emotional intelligence and their

Table 41.3 Bennis' list of differences between a manager and a leader (Bennis, 1994)

a Manager	a Leader
Administers	Innovates
Is a copy	Is an original
Maintains	Develops
Focuses on systems and structure	Focuses on people
Relies on control	Inspires trust
Has a short–range view	Has a long–range
Asks how and when	Asks what and why
Has his eye on the bottom line	Has his eye on the horizon
Imitates	Originates
Accepts the status quo	Challenges it
Is the classic good soldier	Is his own person
Does things right	Does the right thing

responsibility is to implement an organization at all levels, by creating a work environment where individuals are responsible for their performance, where individual competencies are developed, where individuals are challenged to learn new things and where ownership is transferred from work itself to those who do the work (Belasco and Stayer, 1993). Although this chapter will focus on transformational leadership and its relation to emotional intelligence, contrasting it to the transactional model – both continually emerge in research – it will analyse the relationship of this particular type of leadership and EQ.

Transactional versus transformational leadership
Transactional leadership is largely based on the exchange between the leader and the subordinates. The major goal of the transactional leader is to motivate and guide followers in the direction of the desired goal. Originally the transactional leadership theory was based on two distinct behaviours: contingent rewards and passive management (Yukl, 1998). The transactional leader uses rewards in order to influence followers' motivation and punishments in response to deviation from the standards set by him/her, relative to acceptable performance.

On revision of the theory, Bass and Avolio (1990) added two more categories to the transactional leadership model: active management by exception and laissez-faire leadership. The former describes the leader as correcting the subordinates' actions in order to achieve the desired result, while the latter, laissez-faire leadership, refers to the leader's passive indifference, not only to the task at hand but also to the individual follower.

According to Bass (1998), the transactional relationship between the leader and the follower entails an exchange between the two: the follower acts accordingly in response to or in anticipation of rewards and support from the leader. When the organizational environment or even the very nature of the job has failed to provide the subordinate with the necessary motivation and satisfaction, the leader will compensate for this deficiency through his/her action and behaviour (Hartog et al., 1997). Examples of the transactional leadership approach are the situational leadership theory (Cacioppe, 1997), the vertical dyad theory (Graen and Scandura, 1987) and the path–goal theory (House and Mitchell, 1974; Indvink, 1986). A variety of transactional theories have been tested and some of them in particular have received considerable support.

Transformational leaders have the ability to lead their followers' actions in favour of the organization, often by stressing their followers' individual importance to the organization and the independence of their individual effort (Yukl and Fleet, 1992), inspiring them to do more than expected. Research indicates that transformational leaders motivate their followers and encourage them to go beyond their personal interests and act in favour of the group, generating acceptance for the mission of the group (Yammering and Bass, 1990).

Transformational leaders stimulate their followers' intellect, paying attention to individual differences and creating a realistic vision of the future. The original theory on transformational leadership included three types of behaviour (Bass, 1985) descriptive of the transformational leader: individual consideration (providing support and encouragement), charisma (arousing followers' emotions and providing the fertile ground for identification with the leader) and intellectual stimulation (inspiring followers to view situations and problems from new perspectives).

The revision of the theory (Bass and Avolio, 1990) added a fourth category, inspirational motivation, which referred to the leader's ability to communicate a vision to followers and to model appropriate behaviours according to the circumstances. The ability to promote integrity between people and systems within the organization, so that it is directed towards a vision, is another aspect of effective transformational leadership (Hughes et al., 1994).

Finally, transformational leaders are able to inspire followers to pursue high values and, even though they might leave the organizational environment, followers will continue their efforts to achieve the original vision (Pitcher, 1999). Another dimension should be added at this point: the dimension of pseudo-transformational leaders (Bass, 1998). Pseudo-transformational leaders act like transformational leaders but in fact are not concerned with sacrificing their own self-interests either for the organization or for the common goal or good (Avolio, 1999) (Table 41.4).

A number of studies have been conducted with the aim of establishing whether subordinates can differentiate between transactional and transformational leadership behaviours, giving diverse results: some studies indicate that subordinates seem to be able to differentiate between the two leadership behaviours (Atwater and Yammering, 1993; Yammering and Dubinsky, 1994), while other studies (Scandura and Schriesheim, 1994) indicate that even though the two leadership behaviours seem to be distinct from each other subordinates may not be able to differentiate between them (Fields and Herold, 1997).

And, while the two theories of leadership may be distinct (Kakabadse and Kakabadse, 1999) (Table 41.5), authors argue (Burns, 1978; Hater and Bass, 1988) that this does not imply that they are not related, but rather that they are the two opposite ends of the same continuum. This suggestion could indicate that a leader could be both transactional and transformational at the same time (Bryman, 1992) since both are active leadership styles

Table 41.4 Examples of pseudo-transformational and transformational leaders (Avolio, 1999) (extracts)

Pseudo-transformational leaders	Transformational leaders
Idi Amin	Andrew Carnegie
Nicolae Ceausescu	Mahatma Gandhi
Adolf Hitler	Marshal Tito
Joseph Goebbels	Bishop Desmond Tutu

Distinguishing characteristics

Pseudo-transformational leaders	Transformational leaders
self-aggrandizing	envisions a more desirable future
dominating	seeks consensus and is sympathetic
exploitative of others	respects differences and develops independent followers
manipulative	unites through internalization of mission and values
unites through fear/compliance	is self-sacrificing and trustworthy

and behaviours. Thite (1999), who examined the leadership styles of technical project teams, found that successful team leaders were those who were more transformational but also those who were rated as active transactional leaders.

Nevertheless laissez-faire leadership, which applies to the transactional leadership model, contrasts with transformational leadership since it constitutes a passive and inactive type of leadership behaviour (Yammering et al., 1993); its passive and inactive element could, justifiably, indicate the absence of leadership. But, as Hartog et al. (1997) argue, this more passive leader behaviour may empower subordinates, making it a useful component of the transformational style of leadership.

Many research efforts have been made to determine whether leadership and subordinates' evaluation of leaders are related to gender differences and gender stereotypes. Eagly and Johnston (1990), in their meta-analytic review, found that male leaders were more task-oriented, autocratic and directive than female leaders who were more interpersonally oriented, democratic (Carless, 1998), showed more collaboration and shared decision making with others within the group (Eagly et al., 1991; Kakabadse and Kakabadse, 1999).

Studies also suggest that female leaders are more transformational than male leaders in organizational settings (Bass and Avolio, 1992), but also in more non-organizational and more non-traditional settings (Druskat, 1994). Since the literature indicates that women use more transformational leadership styles and, therefore, may actually be more effective and accepted by subordinates (Maher, 1997), why is it that, throughout history, the greatest leaders were male?

Table 41.5 Distinguishing transformational from transactional leadership (Karabadse and Karabadse, 1999)

Attributes	Transformational leader	Transactional leader
Approach	innovate (creates opportunity, imagines new areas to explore)	balance of operations
Interaction	personal in their orientation to group members	role-bounded
Focus	focus on vision, values, expectations and context	focus on control, production and results
Influence	within and outside the construct of structure and their immediate jurisdiction	within the designated group
Motivates through	volitional activity (emotion, offering, suggestions)	formal-authority mechanisms
Uses	influence (power)	control
Values	cooperation, unity, equality, justice and fairness in addition to efficiency and effectiveness	coordination, efficiency and effectiveness
Communicates	indirectly and directly, gives overlapping and ambiguous assignment	directly, giving clear directions, solitary assignment
Represents	direction in history	process
Oriented towards	ends	means
Is	philosopher	technologist
Has	transforming impact	transactional impact
Role	discretionary	prescribed
Main tasks	defines and communicates goals, motivates	implements goals, referees, coaches
Thinking time frame	futuristic (tomorrow and the day after)	current (yesterday's output, today's problem)
Thinking context	global	local
Main direction	renewal	maintenance

Gender stereotypes and the perceptions that surround these stereotypes is the answer. The study of gender stereotypes in leader effectiveness is especially important, given the fact that it is directly related to subsequent subordinate behaviour (Darley and Fazio, 1980; Lord and Maher, 1990). Deaux and Major (1987) suggested that, when gender stereotypes in leadership are activated, subordinates' actions are consistent with those stereotypes. Women do not fit well traditional leader stereotypes, while men are expected to be efficient leaders. Eagly *et al.* (1992) found that subordinate biases towards leader gender were the main reason for gender differences relative to leadership.

Emotional intelligence and transformational leadership

Recently scholars have begun to give emphasis to leaders' emotional intelligence when considering organizational improvement (Hesselbein *et al.*, 1996; Cooper, 1997; Harrison, 1997), which is closely related to transformational leadership, as established earlier in this chapter. Transformational leadership has been identified as a significant factor of effectiveness in a variety of organizational contexts (Patterson *et al.*, 1995; Barling *et al.*, 1996; Lowe *et al.*, 1996; Geyer and Steyrer, 1998).

Emotional intelligence, as a milestone of effective transformational leadership, has been shown to enhance leader commitment to the organization (Abraham, 2000), positive emotions towards organizational commitment (George, 2000) and good organizational performance (Watkin, 2000). The effectiveness of transformational leadership has raised questions of how it is developed (Zacharatos *et al.*, 2000) and which factors may predispose individuals to use this particular leadership behaviour (Turner and Barling, 2000).

According to Goleman (1998b), emotional intelligence is a significant element in leader effectiveness. Barling, Slater and Kelloway (2000) argue that emotional intelligent individuals are more likely to exhibit transformational leadership behaviour, for a number of reasons. On the one hand, transformational leaders have the capability (individualized consideration) to understand their followers' needs, empathize and, therefore, interact more effectively and, as a result, manage relationships in a positive manner. The empathy element of transformational leaders seems to be a pre-requisite to the developing and mentoring of others (Bass, 1998). On the other hand, being able to delay gratification and the ability to manage their own emotions can enhance followers' trust and respect. This will promote positive follower impact and capacity for self-knowledge (Greenspan, 1989).

Butler *et al.* (1999) examined the relationship of transformational leadership to greater trust and job satisfaction of 78 members of self-directed work teams. The authors found that both job satisfaction and greater trust are related to transformational leadership behaviour. Transformational leadership was, moreover, associated with subordinate and leaders' job satisfaction, while it was proved to promote trust between leaders and subordinates, with positive correlation to job satisfaction. These findings are consistent with previous ones of Podsakoff *et al.* (1990), who identified six leadership behaviours which may influence employee job satisfaction and citizenship behaviour:

1. *Articulating a vision*: demonstrating competency, consistency and integrity.
2. *Providing model behaviour*: serving as a role model; a fundamental condition for trust.
3. *Fostering the acceptance of group goals*: showing that everyone, including leaders, is moving in the same direction in order to achieve a goal.
4. *High performance expectations*: anticipating the best possible performance, stressing the leader's expectations of subordinates, showing consistency between values and behaviour.
5. *Individual support*: reassuring subordinates of the leader's loyalty to every individual member while providing support (closely related to trust).
6. *Intellectual stimulation*: providing fertile ground for exploring new horizons.

Gardner and Stough (2002) examined the relationship between leadership style and emotional intelligence in 110 senior level managers. They found that transformational leadership was strongly related to emotional intelligence, in contrast to transactional leadership. Consistent with other research findings, the authors demonstrated that transformational leaders were able to motivate and shift subordinate organizational emphasis from self to collective organizational interests.

Leaders who used more transformational than transactional behaviours reported being more effective in controlling and managing their emotions, were more understanding of others' emotions and were able to use their emotional knowledge in solving problems. Again recognizing previous research (Barling, Moutinho and Kelloway, 2000; Palmer *et al.*, 2001), found that contingent rewards, even though a transactional leadership component, were positively related to emotional intelligence, clarity of leader expectations and rewards for subordinate performance.

A similar study (Barling, Slater and Kelloway, 2000) investigating the relationship between emotional intelligence and transformational leadership concluded that there is an association between three aspects of transformational leadership – inspirational motivation, individualized consideration and idealized influence – with a transactional leadership component: contingent rewards and emotional intelligence. The authors argued that confirmatory factor analysis (Carless, 1998) showed that contingent rewards fit more with transformational rather with transactional leadership. Furthermore they established that laissez-faire leadership is not related to emotional intelligence, as it is a non-active and non-leadership form of behaviour.

Transformational leadership, apart from being related to subordinate motivation and productivity, is also related to the leader's ability to empower norms, which are associated with common assumptions and basic values that give emphasis to the individual subordinate's role and his/her feelings about power and autonomy (Conger and Kanungo, 1988; Nanus, 1992). Masi and Cooke (2000) examined the effects of transformational leadership on subordinate motivation, empowering norms and organizational productivity. Empowering norms were closely related to the self-image of the leader. Transferring from organizational settings to leadership politics, Glad and Blanton (1997) examined the leadership behaviours and personal characteristics of Nelson Mandela and F.W. de Klerk, in South Africa. The authors found that charisma is the element that determines the effectiveness of a leader.

Farranda (1999) suggests that leading an organization through major changes is a mission and business practice. The author says that a transformational leader is the person who has the ability to relieve subordinates of their fears of the unknown, who makes subordinates feel responsible for their work, achieving common goals and overcoming obstacles, and, finally, is exceptional in using analytic thinking combined with emotionality in order to bring out the best in people.

Transformational leaders have the emotional background to face up to dilemmas and critical decisions, while acknowledging the fact that common values and beliefs are of great importance for an organization, being able to identify individuals who do not share the values of the organization and make the appropriate changes accordingly (Grubbs, 1999).

Transformational leadership is distinguished from effective managerial practices (Table 41.3) (Bennis, 1994; Tracey and Hinkin, 1998). Tracey and Hinkin (1998) found that, unlike managers, transformational leaders are more prone to critical analysis, evaluation, problem solving and decision making, factors that are consistent with the element of intellectual stimulation. Furthermore the two additional elements of transformational leadership, idealized influence and individual consideration, were found to emphasize facilitation for performance improvement and self-development. This study is consistent with Cavallo and Brienza's (2003) findings in examining emotional competence and leadership excellence at Johnson and Johnson. The author found that, in 358 managers across the Johnson Consumer & Personal Care Group (JJC & PC Group), high performance managers were more significantly correlated with emotional intelligence aspects, self-management, self-awareness and social skills, than average performance managers.

Emotional management and self-awareness have been established as significant elements of effective leadership. In their book *Primal Leadership*, Goleman *et al.* (2002) propose that a leader's emotional duty, to him/herself and to subordinates, is genuine and primal; in other words, the leader's emotional duty is essential and the most important characteristic of effective/resonant leadership. Ekman (2003) found that negative emotions cannot be hidden and are reflected and communicated through facial muscles.

Leading subordinates' emotions in a positive direction is termed by the authors 'coordination and harmony', while leading subordinates' emotions in a negative direction is termed 'dis-coordination and disharmony'. Effective leaders in the 11th September crisis at the World Trade Centre were calming and visible, being constantly able to communicate what was known as much as what was not known, giving hope and optimism through being realistic (American Psychological Association, 2003; Boyatzis, 2003).

Goleman *et al.* (2002), suggested the theoretical framework of primal leadership, which is the hormonal and neural basis of explaining the positive effects and outcomes of transformational leadership, while establishing that the leadership style is linked to brain function, and hormones and competencies linked to emotional intelligence. The development of the model is based upon neurological brain functions which lead to effective leadership. The key element of this model is that it is based on emotions, as regards both the leader's emotions towards subordinates and the respect for others' emotions which are the guiding power of individuals' everyday conduct.

Primal emotions such as fear or anger are filtered in the human brain, as it is designed to 'survive' emergency situations, through the prefrontal brain area, securing more effective reactions by keeping emotions under control and promoting balance between emotions and cognition. The authors argue that elevated cognitive and emotional abilities characterize primal leadership. The neuronic system is responsible for cognitive abilities and emotions, which are separate within the brain but still maintain a close connection.

The connection and collaboration between cognition and emotions is the basis of emotional intelligence and the neural basis of primal leadership. The authors maintain that emotional competencies are not inherent but are the result of learning processes; therefore, they can be taught. Each emotional competency can contribute uniquely to effective and harmonic leadership. Based on the theory of productivity, which brings forward the connection between the neurological bases of emotional intelligence and emotional competencies, the primary argument is that primal leadership has the best results possible through emotional intelligent leaders. On the basis of previous work about emotional competencies, Goleman *et al.* suggest that the most effective leaders so far have exhibited only two of the four competencies established and that there is no specific way towards primal leadership, since it largely depends upon different personal styles.

Concluding remarks on emotional intelligence and transformational leadership
When considering leadership effectiveness, transformational leadership behaviours and emotional intelligence are emphasized (Sosik and Megerian, 1999). It has been well established through the literature (Bass, 1985; Bass and Avolio, 1990; Avolio, 1999) that transformational leadership is related to positive organizational outcomes, job satisfaction of both leaders and subordinates (Hater and Bass, 1988; Koh et al., 1995), active organizational commitment (Bycio et al., 1995; Barling et al., 1996) and reduced stress levels (Sosik and Godshalk, 2000) both in field experiments (Howell and Avolio, 1993) and in laboratory studies (Kilpatrick and Locke, 1996).

Goleman et al. (2002), using their hormonal and neural theory to explain the effectiveness of emotional intelligence, maintain that transformational leaders are effective because they create a sense of direction beyond day-to-day task completion, create vision for the future and possess the art of good managing relationships through authenticity and honesty. The authors suggest that the most effective leadership training programmes are those that are associated with culture and competencies and are directed towards learning and its maintenance. These programmes include the following elements:

1. direct connection with the organizational culture, or its change;
2. seminars which are directed towards the theory and practice of personal change;
3. learning skills, which are based equally on emotional intelligence competencies and the development of organizational skills;
4. dynamic and creative learning experiences, which are accompanied by clear objectives;
5. the creation of such relationships, which promote learning: counselling and learning groups.

The extensive research in this field has suggested, on the one hand, that we know little about training effective transformational leaders (Gordon, 1985) and, on the other hand, that, in training attempts, there has rarely been any evaluation against organizational criteria (Burke and Day, 1986) (also keeping in mind that 'leadership' is a term which is poorly defined (Barker, 1997)). In addition, it has been suggested that, although learning skills can contribute to the development of emotional intelligence, this is impossible to achieve in one course only.

What organizations need is to focus on broader aspects of organizational behaviour and organizational change and, on the other hand, to provide continuing support and a compelling reason for individuals to change. Recent studies suggest that organizations can either train transformational leaders or recruit them according to the particular competencies determined and set by the organization (Bamberger and Meshoulam, 2000).

Following, and subsequently extending, the study by Kelloway et al. (2000) assessing leader effectiveness through training, Kelloway and Barling (2000) assessed leadership training interventions by using two types of measures: interventions would be perceived as successful when, on the one hand, subordinates could identify transformational leadership behaviours and, on the other hand, leadership behaviours could be related to positive organizational outcomes. Using these two measures of leadership effectiveness, the authors concluded that small changes and their maintenance have beneficial effects on subordinate behavioural outcomes, because they affect leaders' integrity, build respect and enhance the element of idealized influence. Inspirational motivation enhances subordinate self-efficiency and inspires individuals to put more effort into accomplishing a common task in pursuit of a common vision.

Finally, individualized consideration helps consider and assess every individual through subordinates' needs while, through intellectual stimulation, subordinates are inspired to use new ways of thinking. Even though the findings and suggestions of the literature and research findings are essential and important, future research should focus on investigating the relationship between transformational leadership and emotional intelligence as regards trust and job satisfaction, and also on the process by which transformational leaders exert their power and influence over subordinates.

Acknowledgments

I would like to express my sincere thanks to Professor Richard Boyatzis for his useful and constructive comments on a previous version of this chapter.

References

Abraham, R. (2000), 'The role of job control as a moderator of emotional dissonance and emotional intelligence–outcome relationships', *The Journal of Psychology*, **134**, 169–84.
Ackroyd, S. and P. Thompson (1999), *Organizational Misbehaviour*, London: Sage.
Allport, G.W., P.E. Vernon and G. Lindzey (1960), *Study of Values*, Boston: Houghton Mifflin.
American Psychological Association (2003), 'Task force on workplace violence: "Responses to workplace violence post 9/11: What can organizations do?"', http://www.apa.org/pubinfo/post911workplace.html.
Anastasi, A. (1982), *Psychological Assessment*, New York: Macmillan Publishing Company.
Antonacopoulou, E.P. and Y. Gabriel (2001), 'Emotion, learning and organisational change: towards an integration of psychoanalytic and other perspectives', *Journal of Organizational Change Management*, **14**(5), 435–51.
Atwater, L.E. and E.J. Yammering (1993), 'Personal attributes as predictors of superiors' and subordinates' perceptions of military academy leadership', *Human Relations*, **46**, 645–68.
Avolio, B.J. (1999), *Full Leadership Development: Building the Vital Forces in Organizations*, Thousand Oaks: Sage Publications.
Bamberger, P. and I. Meshoulam (2000), *Human Resource Strategy: Formulation, Implementation and Impact*, Thousand Oaks: Sage Publications.
Barker, R.A. (1997), 'How can we train leaders if we do not know what leadership is?', *Human Relations*, **50**(4), 343–62.
Bar-On, R. (1988), 'The development of an operational concept of psychological well being', unpublished doctoral dissertation, Rhodes University, South Africa.
Bar-On, R. (1997), *Bar-On Emotional Quotient Inventory: Technical manual*, New York: Multi-Health Systems.
Bar-On, R. (2000), 'Emotional and social intelligence', in R. Bar-On and J.D.A. Parker (eds), *The Handbook of Emotional Intelligence*, San Francisco, CA: Jossey-Bass.
Barling, J., S. Moutinho and E.K. Kelloway (2000), 'Transformational leadership and group performance: the mediating role of affective commitment', Queen's University, Kingston, Ontario.
Barling, J., F. Slater and E.K Kelloway (2000), 'Transformational leadership and emotional intelligence: an exploratory study', *Leadership and Organization Development Journal*, **21**(3), 157–61.
Barling, J., T. Weber and E.K. Kelloway (1996), 'Effects of transformational leadership training on attitudinal and fiscal outcomes: a field experiment', *Journal of Applied Psychology*, **81**, 827–32.
Barsade, S. (1998), 'The ripple effect: emotional contagion in groups', working paper, Yale University School of Management.
Bass, B.M. (1985), 'Leadership and performance beyond expectations', New York: Free Press.
Bass, B.M. (1998), *Transformational Leadership*, Hillsdale, NJ: Erlbaum.

Bass, B.M. and B.J. Avolio (1990), 'Developing transformational leadership: 1992 and beyond', *Journal of European Industrial Training*, **14**, 21–7.
Bass, B.M. and B.J. Avolio (1992), 'Multifactor leadership questionnaire, Form SX', Center for Leadership Studies, State University of New York at Binghampton.
Belasco, J.A. and R.C. Stayer (1993), *Flight of the Buffalo*, New York: Warner Books.
Bennis, W. (1994), 'On becoming a leader', New York: Addison Wesley.
Boyatzis, R.E., D. Goleman and K. Rhee (1999), 'Clustering competence in emotional intelligence: insights from the Emotional Competence Inventory', in R. Bar-On and D.A. Parker, *Handbook of Emotional Intelligence*, San Francisco: Jossey-Bass.
Boyatzis, R.E., A.J. Murphy and J.V. Wheeler (2000), 'Philosophy as the missing link between values and behavior', Case Western Reserve University, Cleveland.
Boyatzis, R.E. (2003), 'Effective leadership in a crisis: using emotional intelligence to inspire resilience', unpublished report.
Boyatzis, R.E. and E. Van Oosten (2002), 'Developing emotionally intelligent organizations', in R. Millar (eds), *International Executive Development Programmes*, 7th edn, London: Kogan Page Publishers.
Bryman, A. (1992), *Charisma and Leadership in Organisations*, London: Sage.
Burke, M.J. and R.M. Day (1986), 'A cumulative study of training', *Journal of Applied Psychology*, **71**, 232–65.
Burns, J.M. (1978), *Leadership*, New York: Harper & Row.
Butler, J.K., S.R. Cantrell Jr. and R.J. Flick (1999), 'Transformational leadership behaviors, upward trust and satisfaction in self managed work teams', *Organizational Development Journal*, **17**(1), 13.
Bycio, P., R.D. Hackett and J.S. Allen (1995), 'Further assessment of Bass's (1985), conceptualisation of transactional and transformational leadership', *Journal of Applied Psychology*, **80**, 468–78.
Cacioppe, R. (1997), 'Leadership moment by moment', *Leadership and Organizational Development Journal*, **18**(7), 335–45.
Carless, S.A. (1998), 'Assessing the discriminant validity of transformational leader behaviour, as measured by the MLQ', *Journal of Occupational and Organizational Psychology*, **71**, 353–8.
Cavallo, K. and D. Brienza (2003), 'Emotional competence and leadership excellence at Johnson & Johnson: the emotional intelligence and leadership study', Consortium for Research on Emotional Intelligence in Organizations (www.eiconsortium.org).
Chamberlin, W.H (1937), *Collectivism, a False Utopia*, New York: Macmillan Company.
Cherniss, C. (2000), 'Emotional intelligence: what it is and why it matters', paper presented at the Annual Meeting of the Society for Industrial and Organizational Psychology, New Orleans.
Conger, J.A. and R.N. Kanungo (1988), 'Training charismatic leadership: a risky and critical task', in J.A. Conger and R.N. Kanungo (eds), *Charismatic Leadership*, San Francisco: Jossey-Bass.
Cooper, R.K (1997), 'Applying emotional intelligence in the workplace' *Training and Development*, **51**, 31–8.
Cooper, R.K. and A. Sawaf (1997), *Executive EQ: Emotional Intelligence in Leadership and Organizations*, New York: Grosset/ Putname.
Craib, I. (1998), *Experiencing Identity*, London: Sage.
Darley, J. and R. Fazio (1980), 'Expectancy confirmation process arising in the social interaction sequence', *American Psychologist*, **35**, 867–81.
Deaux, K. and B. Major (1987), 'Putting gender into context: an interactive model of gender related behaviour', *Psychological Review*, **94**, 369–89.
Descartes, R. (1955), *The Philosophical Works of Descartes*, vols 1–2, trans. and ed. S. Haldane and G.R.T. Ross, New York: Dover.
Dewey, J. (1917), *Creative Intelligence: Essays in the Pragmatic Attitude*, New York: Holt.
Druskat, V.U. (1994), 'Gender and leadership style: transformational and transactional leadership in the Roman Catholic Church', *Leadership Quarterly*, **5**, 99–119.
Dulewicz, V. and M. Higgs (1999), 'Can emotional intelligence be measured and developed?', *Leadership and Organizational Development Journal*, **20**, 242–52.
Dulewicz, V. and M. Higgs (2000), 'Emotional intelligence: a review and evaluation study', *Journal of Managerial Psychology*, **15**(4), 341–72.
Eagly, A.H. and B.T. Johnston (1990), 'Gender and leadership style: a meta-analysis, *Psychological Bulletin*, **108**(2), 233–56.
Eagly, A.H., M.G. Makhijani and B.G. Klonsky (1992), 'Gender and the evaluation of leaders: a meta-analysis', *Psychological Bulletin*, **111**, 3–22.
Eagly A.H., R.D. Ashomore, M.G. Makhijiami and L.C. Longo (1991), 'What is beautiful is good . . . A meta-analytic review of research on the physical attractiveness stereotype', *Psychological Bulletin*, **111**, 109–23.
Ekman, P. (2003), *Gripped by Emotion*, New York: Times Books, Henry Holt.
Farranda, T. (1999), 'Transformational leaders', *Incentive*, **172**(10), 14–15.

Fields, D.L. and D.M. Herold (1997), 'Using the leadership practice inventory to measure the transformational and transactional leadership', *Educational and Psychological Measurement*, **57**(4), 569–79.
Fineman, S. (1993), 'Organizations as emotional arenas', *Emotions in Organizations*, London: Sage.
Fineman, S. (1997), 'Emotion and management learning', *Management Learning*, **28**(1), 13–25.
Fineman, S. and Y. Gabriel (2000), 'The study of organizational emotions: psychoanalytic and social constructionist perspectives', paper presented at the Annual Symposium of the International Society for the Psychoanalytic Study of Organizations, London.
Gabriel, Y. and A. Carr (2002), 'Organizations, management and psychoanalysis: an overview', *Journal of Managerial Psychology*, **17**(5), 348–65.
Gabriel, Y. and D.S. Griffiths (2002), 'Emotions, learning, organizing', *The Learning Organization*, **9**(5), 214–21.
Gadamer, H.G. (1977), *Philosophical Hermeneutics*, trans. and ed. D.E. Linge, Berkeley: University of California Press.
Gardner, H. (1983), *Frames of Mind, the Theory of Multiple Intelligences*, New York: Basic Books.
Gardner, L. and C. Stough (2002), 'Examining the relationship between leadership and emotional intelligence in senior level managers', *Leadership and Organization Development Journal*, **23**(2), 68–78.
George, J.M. (2000), 'Emotions and leadership: the role of emotional intelligence', *Human Relations*, **53**, 1027–41.
Geyer, A.L.J. and J.M. Steyrer (1998), 'Transformational leadership and objective performance in banks', *Applied Psychology: An International Review*, **47**, 397–420.
Gibson, C. (1995), 'An understanding of gender differences in leadership across four countries', *Journal of International Business Studies*, second quarter, 225–79.
Glad, B. and R. Blanton (1997), 'F.W. de Klerk and Nelson Mandela: a study of cooperative transformational leadership', *Presidential Studies Quarterly*, **27**(3), 565–90.
Goleman, D. (1995), *Emotional Intelligence*, New York: Bantam Books.
Goleman, D. (1996), *Emotional Intelligence*, London: Bloomsbury.
Goleman, D. (1998a), 'What makes a leader?', *Harvard Business Review*, 93–102.
Goleman, D. (1998b), 'The emotional intelligence of leaders', *Leader to Leader*, 20–26.
Goleman, D. (2000), 'Intelligent leadership', *Executive Excellence*, **3**, 17.
Goleman, D. (2001), 'What makes a leader?', in J. Henry (ed.), *Creative Management*, London: Sage.
Goleman, D., R. Boyatzis and A. McKee (2002), *Primal Leadership*, Boston, MA: Harvard Business School Press.
Gordon, J. (1985), 'Games managers play', *Training*, 30–45.
Graen, G. and T. Scandura (1987), 'Toward a psychology of dyadic organizing', in L.L. Cummings and B. Staw (eds), *Research in Organizational Behaviour*, New York: JAI Press, pp. 175–208.
Greenspan, S.I. (1989), 'Emotional intelligence', in K. Field, B.J. Cohler and G. Wool (eds), *Learning and Education: Psychoanalytic Perspectives*, Madison: International University Press.
Grubbs, J.R. (1999), 'The transformational leader', *Occupational Health and Safety*, **68**(3), 22–6.
Harrison, R. (1997), 'Why your firm needs emotional intelligence', *People Management*, **3**, 1–41.
Hartog, D.N., J.J. Van Muijen and P.L. Koopman (1997), 'Transactional versus transformational leadership: an analysis of the MLQ', *Journal of Occupational and Organisational Psychology*, **70**, 19–34.
Hater, J.J. and B.M. Bass (1988), 'Superiors' evaluation and subordinates' perceptions of transformational and transactional leadership', *Journal of Applied Psychology*, **73**, 695–702.
Hay Group (2000), *Emotional Intelligence*, London: Bloomsbury Publishing.
Hechter, M. (1993), 'Values research in the social and behavioural sciences', in M. Hetcher, L. Nadel and R.E. Michod (eds), *The Origin of Values*, New York: Aldine de Gruyter.
Hesselbein, F., M. Goldsmith and R. Beckhard (1996), *The Leader of the Future*, San Francisco: Jossey-Bass.
Hogan, R., G. Curphy and J. Hogan (1994), 'What we know about leadership effectiveness and personality', *American Psychologist*, **49**, 493–504.
Holland, J.L. (1985), 'Making vocational choices: a theory of vocational personalities and work environments', Psychological Assessment Resources, Odessa, Florida.
Holland, J.L. (1996), 'Exploring careers with a typology: what we have learned and some new directions', *America Psychologist*, **51**(4), 397–406.
House, R.J. and T.R. Mitchell (1974), 'The Path–Goal theory of leadership', *Contemporary Business*, **3**, 81–98.
Howell, J.M. and B.J. Avolio (1993), 'Transformational leadership, transactional leadership, locus of control and support for innovation: key predictors of consolidated-business-unit performance', *Journal of Applied Psychology*, **78**, 891–902.
Hughes, R., L.R.C. Ginnett and G.C. Curphy (1994), *Leadership, Enhancing the Lessons of Experience*, Boston: Irwin McGraw-Hill.
Indvink, J. (1986), 'Path–Goal theory of leadership: a meta-analysis', *Proceedings*, Chicago: Academy of Management.

Kahle, L.R. (1996), 'Social values and consumer behaviour: research from the List of Values', in C. Seligman, J.M. Olson and M.P. Zanna (eds), *The Psychology of Values: the Ontario Symposium*, vol. 8, Hillsdale, NJ: Lawrence Erlbaum Associates.

KaKabadse, A. and N. Kakabadse (1999), *Essence of Leadership*, London: International Thompson Business Press.

Karpenko, L.A., A.B. Petrovsky and M.G. Yaroshevsky (1998), *Kratky Psychologichesky Slovar*, Rostov-na-Donu: Fenix.

Kelloway, E.K. and J. Barling (2000), 'What we have learnt about developing transformational leaders', *Leadership and Organization Development Journal*, **21**(7), 355–62.

Kelloway, E.K., J. Barling and J. Helleur (2000), 'Enhancing transformational leadership: the roles of training and feedback', *Leadership and Organization Development Journal*, **21**(3), 145–9.

Kilpatrick, S.A. and E.A. Locke (1991), 'Leadership: do traits matter?', *Academy of Management Executive*, May, 48–60.

Kilpatrick, S.A. and E.A. Locke (1996), 'Direct and indirect effects of three core charismatic leadership components on performance and attitudes', *Journal of Applied Psychology*, **81**, 36–51.

Kluckhohn, C. (1951), 'Values and value-orientations in the theory of action', in T. Parson and E.A. Shils (eds), *Toward a General Theory of Action*, Cambridge, MA: Harvard University Press.

Kluckhohn, C. and F. Strodtbeck (1961), *Variations in Value Orientations*, Evanston, IL: Row, Paterson and Co.

Koh, W.L., R.M. Steers and J.R. Terborg (1995), 'The effects of transformational leadership on teacher attitudes and student performance in Singapore', *Journal of Organizational Behaviour*, **16**, 319–33.

Lazarus, R. (1991), *Emotions and Adaptation*, Oxford: Oxford University Press.

Levi-Strauss, C. (1967), *Structural Anthropology*, trans. C. Jacobson and B.G. Schoepf. New York: Doubleday.

Lord, R. and K.J. Maher (1990), 'Leadership perceptions and leadership performance: two distinct but interrelated processes', in J. Carroll (ed.), *Applied Social Psychology and Organizational Settings*, Hillsdale, NJ: Erlbaum.

Lowe, K.B., K.G. Kroeck and N. Sivasubramanium (1996), 'Effectiveness correlates of transformational and transactional leadership: a meta-analytic review', *Leadership Quarterly*, **7**, 385–425.

Lusch, R.F. and R.R. Serpkeuci (1990), 'Personal differences, job tension, job outcomes and store performance: a study of retail managers', *Journal of Marketing*, **54**(1), 85–101.

Luthans, F. (1998), *Organizational Behaviour*, Boston, MA: McGraw-Hill.

Maher, K.J. (1997), 'Gender-related stereotypes of transformational and transactional leadership', *Sex Roles*, **37**(3/4), 209–25.

Mangham, I. (1998), 'Emotional discourse in organizations', in D. Grant and T. Keenoy (eds), *Discourse and Organization*, London: Sage.

Masi, R.J. and R.A. Cooke (2000), 'Effects of transformational leadership on subordinate motivation, empowering norms and organizational productivity', *International Journal of Organizational Analysis*, **8**(1), 16–47.

Mayer, J.D. and P. Salovey (1997), 'What is emotional intelligence?', in P. Salovey and D.J. Sluyter (eds), *Emotional Development and Emotional Intelligence*, New York: Basic Books.

McClelland, D. C. and R.E. Boyatzis (1982), 'Leadership motive pattern and long-term success in management', *Journal of Applied Psychology*, **67**(9), 737–43

McMullen, B. (2002), 'Cognitive intelligence', *BMJ*, 325(suppl.): S193.

McMullen, B. (2003), 'Spiritual intelligence', *BMJ*, 326: S51.

Messmer, M. (1999), 'Building leadership skills', *Strategic Finance*, **81**(1), 10–12.

Mill, J.S. (1991), *On Liberty and Other Essays*, ed. J. Gray, New York: Oxford University Press.

Mischel, W., P.K. Peake and Y. Shoda (1990), 'Predicting adolescent cognitive and self–regulatory competencies from pre-school delay of gratification', *Development Psychology*, 25–33.

Nanus, B. (1992), *Visionary Leadership: Creating a Compelling Sense of Direction for Your Organization*, San Francisco: Jossey-Bass.

Nietzsche, F. (1968), *Basic Writings of Nietzsche*, trans. and ed. W. Kaufman, New York: Modern Library.

Obholzer, A. (1999), 'Managing the unconscious at work', in R. French and R. Vince (eds), *Group Relations, Management and Organization*, Oxford: Oxford University Press.

Palmer, B., M. Walls, Z. Burgess and C. Stough (2001), 'Emotional intelligence and effective leadership', *Leadership and Organization Development*, **22**, 1–7.

Patterson, C., J.B. Fuller, K. Kester and D.Y. Stringer (1995), 'A meta-analytic examination of leadership style and selected compliance outcomes', paper presented at the Society for Industrial and Organizational Psychology, Orlando, Florida.

Perrella, J.E. (1999), *The Importance of Working Together: Individuals Add; Team Players Multiply. Vital Speeches of the Day*, New York: City News Publishing Company.

Pettit, P. (1993), *Consequentialism*, Brookfield: Dartmouth Publishing Co.

Pierce, C.S. (1931), *Collected Papers of Charles Sanders Pierce*, vol.1, ed. C. Hartshorne and P. Weiss, Cambridge, MA: Harvard University Press.
Pitcher, P. (1999), 'Artists, Craftsmen and Technocrats', *Training and Development*, 30–33.
Podsakoff, P.M., S.B. McKenzie, R.H. Moorman and R. Fetter (1990), 'Transformational leader behaviors and their effects on members' trust in leader, satisfaction and organizational citizenship behaviors', *Leadership Quarterly*, **1**, 107–42.
Poon Teng Fatt, J. (2002), 'Emotional intelligence: for human resource managers', *Management Research News*, **25**(11), 57–74.
Pratch, L. and J. Jacobowitz (1998), 'Integrative capacity and the evaluation of leadership', *Journal of Applied Behavioral Science*, **34**, 180–82.
Robbins, T., R. Waters-March, R. Cacioppe and B. Millet (1994), *Organizational Behaviour*, Prentice-Hall.
Rokeach, M. (1973), *The Nature of Human Values*, New York: Free Press.
Rorty, R. (1991), *Objectivity, Relativism and Truth*, Cambridge: Cambridge University Press.
Rozell, E.J., C.E. Pettitjohn and S.R. Parker (2002), 'An empirical evaluation of emotional intelligence: the impact on management development', *The Journal of Management Development*, **21**(4), 272–89.
Salovey, P. and J.D. Mayer (1990), 'Emotional intelligence', *Imagination, Cognition and Personality*, **9**, 185–211.
Scandura, T.A. and C.A. Schriesheim (1994), 'Leader–member exchange and supervisor career mentoring as complementary constructs in leadership research', *Academy of Management Journal*, **37**(6), 1588–1602.
Schwartz, S.H (1992), 'Universals in the content and structure of values: theoretical advances and empirical tests in 20 countries', *Advances in Experimental Social Psychology*, **25**, 1–65.
Seligman, M.E.P. (1990), *Learned Optimism*, New York: Knopf.
Sellars, R.W. (1933), 'A humanist manifesto', *The Humanist*, 58–61.
Shoda, Y., W. Mischel and P.K. Peak (1990), 'Predicting adolescent cognitive and self-regulatory competencies from pre-school delay of gratification: identifying diagnostic conditions', *Developmental Psychology*, **26**(6), 978–86.
Singer, P. (1995), *A Companion to Ethics*, London: Blackwell Publishing.
Smelser, N.J. (1998), 'The rational and the ambivalent in the social sciences', in N.J. Smelser (ed.), *The Social Edges of Psychoanalysis*, Berkeley: University of California Press.
Sosik, J.J. and V.M. Godshalk (2000), 'Leadership styles, mentoring functions and job related stress: a conceptual model and preliminary study', *Journal of Organizational Behavior*, **21**, 365–90.
Sosik, J. and J. Megerian (1999), 'Understanding leader emotional intelligence and performance', *Group and Organization Management*, **24**, 367–91.
Spinoza, B. de (1985), *The Collected Works of Spinoza*, vol. 1, trans. E. Curley, Princeton, NJ: Princeton, University Press.
Thite, M. (1999), 'Relationship between leadership and information technology project sources', in B.J. Avolio (ed.), *Full Leadership Development: Building the Vital Forces in Organizations*, Thousand Oaks: Sage Publications.
Thorndike, E.L. (1920), 'Intelligence and its uses', *Harper's Magazine*, **140**, 227–35.
Tracey, B.J. and T.R. Hinkin (1998), 'Transformational leadership or effective managerial practices?', *Group and Organizational Management*, **23**(3), 220–36.
Triandis, H.C. (1993), 'Cross cultural industrial and organizational psychology', in H.C. Triandis, M. Dunnette and L. Hough (eds), *Handbook of Industrial and Organizational Psychology*, vol. 4, Palo Acts, CA: Psychologists Press.
Turner, N. and J. Barling (2000), 'Moral reasoning and transformational leadership: an exploratory study', School of Business, Queen's University, Kingston, Ontario.
Villiounas, V.K and N. Gippenreiter (1984), *The Psychology of Emotions*, Moscow: MGY.
Watkin, C. (2000), 'Developing emotional intelligence', *International Journal of Selection and Assessment*, **8**, 89–92.
Wechsler, D. (1943), 'Non-intellective factors in general intelligence', *Psychological Bulletin*, **37**, 444–5.
Wright, T.A. and B.M. Staw (1999), 'Affect and favourable work outcomes: two longitudinal tests of the happy productive worker thesis', *Journal of Organizational Behaviour*, **20**, 1–23.
Yammering, F.J. and B.M. Bass (1990), 'Long-term forecasting of transformational leadership and its effects among naval officers', in K.E. Clark and M.B. Clark (eds), *Measures of leadership*, Greenboro: Centre for creative Leadership.
Yammering, F.J. and A.J. Dubinsky (1994), 'Transformational leadership theory: using levels of analysis to determine boundary conditions', *Personnel Psychology*, **47**, 787–811.
Yammering, F.J., W.D. Spangler and B.M. Bass (1993), 'Transformational leadership and performance: longitudinal investigation', *Leadership Quarterly*, **4**, 81–102.
Yukl, G. (1998), *Leadership in Organisations*, 4th edn, Englewood Ceiffs, NJ: Prentice-Hall.

Yukl, G. and D. van Fleet (1992), 'Theory and research on leadership in organizations', in M.D. Dunnette and L.M. Hough (eds), *Handbook of Industrial and Organizational Psychology*, vol. 3, 2nd edn, Palo Alto, CA: Psychologists Press.

Zacharatos, A., J. Barling and E.K. Kelloway (2000), 'Development and effects of transformational leadership in adolescents', *Leadership Quarterly*.

42 Developing leadership through emotional intelligence
Richard E. Boyatzis

Elena was upset. She was snapping at people and felt out of sorts. She had not slept well the night before. Even though she was chief financial office (CFO) of a large corporation in Moscow, something in the previous day's seminar bothered her. She had been considering how to improve her leadership style through developing more emotional intelligence. The instructor had explained that such efforts were short-lived if not anchored in a personal vision. Some time after lunch, it dawned on Elena what was so troubling. She did not know what she wanted out of life. She does not dream about the future, and so found it difficult if not impossible to conceive of a personal vision.

It certainly was not because she did not have a bright future: she was among the elite in her country. But she had trained and entered corporate life in Russia 20 years earlier, under a regime with different assumptions about possibilities in life and a career. Her subordinates were also frustrated. Elena had trouble creating excitement about a future for the organization. She had learned not to dream about the future, but to react to things as they occurred. It had shaped her approach to leadership. This reactive style was not working well.

There are millions of Elenas working in organizations throughout the world. They want to be better managers and leaders, but are puzzled as to how to reach that elusive goal. With the best of intentions, they attend training programs, get MBAs and hire consultants and coaches to help. And yet the degree of change is often small. They feel compelled to throw more resources into training, or slowly develop a belief that great managers and leaders are born, not made. True, management of our organizations seems better than it was decades ago. But it is a sobering observation that the return on this massive investment in management and leadership development is small. If the outcomes were subjected to a rigorous utility analysis, a prudent business person would liquidate or divest the effort.

The most common mistake is to think that acquiring more knowledge will make you a better manager or leader. To be an effective manager or leader, a person needs the ability to use their knowledge and to make things happen. These can be called competencies, which Boyatzis (1982) defined as 'the underlying characteristics of a person that lead to or cause effective and outstanding performance'. Whether direct empirical research is reviewed (Bray et al., 1974; Boyatzis, 1982; Kotter, 1982; Thornton and Byham, 1982; Luthans et al., 1988; Howard and Bray, 1988) or meta-analytic syntheses are used (Campbell et al., 1970; Spencer and Spencer, 1993; Goleman, 1998), there are a set of competencies that have been shown to cause or predict outstanding manager or leader performance. Regardless of author or study, they tend to include abilities from three clusters: (1) cognitive or intellectual ability, such as systems thinking; (2) self-management or intrapersonal abilities, such as adaptability; and (3) relationship management or interpersonal abilities, such as networking. The latter two clusters make up what we call 'emotional intelligence competencies' (Goleman, 1998; Goleman *et al.*, 2002).

Beyond knowledge and competencies, the additional ingredient necessary to outstanding performance appears to be the desire to use one's talent. This seems driven by a person's values, philosophy, sense of calling or mission, unconscious motives and traits. These three domains of capability (knowledge, competencies and motivational drivers) help us to understand 'what a person needs to do' (knowledge), 'how a person needs to do it' (competencies) and 'why a person will do it' (values, motives and unconscious dispositions).

The assumption for too long has been that these abilities, or competencies, are characteristics with which you are born. This deterministic view has led to a focus on selection and placement rather than development. But these competencies, and in particular the ones called emotional intelligence, can be developed.

A growing body of research has helped us to discover a process that yields sustained behavioral change. These improvements provide hope and evidence that people can develop as managers and leaders. They can develop the abilities, or competencies, that matter the most to outstanding performance – the ones we call emotional intelligence. Although the process appears to be common sense, it is not common practice.

Can a person develop their talent?
Decades of research on the effects of psychotherapy (Hubble *et al.*, 1999), self-help programs (Kanfer and Goldstein, 1991), cognitive behavior therapy (Barlow, 1988), training programs (Morrow *et al.*, 1997) and education (Pascarella and Terenzini, 1991; Winter *et al.*, 1981) have shown that people can change their behavior, moods and self-image. But most of the studies focused on a single characteristic, such as maintenance of sobriety, reduction in a specific anxiety or a set of characteristics often determined by the assessment instrument, such as the scales of the Minnesota Multiphasic Personality Inventory (MMPI). For example, the impact of achievement motivation training was a dramatic increase in small business success, with people creating more new jobs, starting more new businesses and paying more taxes than comparison groups (McClelland and Winter, 1969; Miron and McClelland, 1979). The impact of power motivation training was improved maintenance of sobriety (Cutter *et al.*, 1977). But there are few studies showing sustained improvements in the sets of desirable behavior that lead to outstanding performance.

The 'honeymoon effect' of typical training programs might start with improvement immediately following the program, but within months it drops precipitously (Campbell *et al.*, 1970). Only 15 programs were found in a global search of the literature by the Consortium on Research on Emotional Intelligence in Organizations to improve emotional intelligence. Most of them showed an impact on job outcomes, such as number of new businesses started, or life outcomes, such as finding a job or satisfaction (Cherniss and Adler, 2000), which are the ultimate purpose of development efforts. But showing an impact on outcomes, while desired, may also blur *how* the change actually occurs. Furthermore, when a change has been noted, a question about the sustainability of the changes is raised because of the relatively short time periods studied.

The few published studies examining improvement of more than one of these competencies show an overall improvement of about 10 per cent in emotional intelligence abilities three to 18 months after training (Noe and Schmitt, 1986; Hand *et al.*, 1973; Wexley and Memeroff, 1975; Latham and Saari, 1979; Young and Dixon, 1996). More recent meta-analytic studies and utility analyses confirm that significant changes can and do occur, but not with the impact that the level of investment would lead us to expect, nor with many types of training (Morrow *et al.*, 1997; Baldwin and Ford 1988; Burke and Day, 1986). There are, undoubtedly, other studies which were not found and reviewed, or not available through journals and books and, therefore, overlooked. We do not claim this is an exhaustive review, but one suggestive of the percentage improvement as a rough approximation of the real impact. This approximation is offered to help in the comparison of relative impact of management training, management education and self-directed learning.

The results appear no better than from standard MBA programs, where there is no attempt to enhance emotional intelligence abilities. The best data here come from a research project by the American Assembly of Collegiate Schools of Business which found that the behavior of graduating students from two highly ranked business schools, compared to their levels when they began their MBA training, showed only improvements of 2 per cent in the skills of emotional intelligence (DDI, 1985). In fact, when students from four other high-ranking MBA programs were assessed on a range of tests and direct behavioral measures, they showed a gain of 4 per cent in self-awareness and self-management abilities, but a *decrease* of 3 per cent in social awareness and relationship management (Boyatzis and Sokol, 1982; Boyatzis, Renio-McKee and Thompson, 1995).

A series of longitudinal studies under way at the Weatherhead School of Management of Case Western Reserve University have shown that people can change on this complex set of competencies that we call emotional intelligence that distinguish outstanding performers in management and professions. The improvement lasted for years. A visual comparison of the percentage improvement in behavioral measures of emotional intelligence from different samples is shown in Figure 42.1.

MBA students, averaging 27 years of age at entry into the program, showed dramatic changes on videotaped and audiotaped behavioral samples and questionnaire measures of these competencies as a result of the competency-based, outcome-oriented MBA program implemented in 1990 (Boyatzis, Baker *et al.*, 1995; Boyatzis, Leonard, Rhee and Wheeler, 1996; Boyatzis *et al.*, 2002).

Four cadres of full-time MBA students graduating in 1992, 1993, 1994 and 1995 showed 47 per cent improvement on self-awareness competencies like self-confidence and on self-management competencies such as the drive to achieve and adaptability in the one to two years to graduation, compared to performance when they first entered. When it came to social awareness and relationship management skills, improvements were even greater: 75 per cent on competencies such as empathy and team leadership.

Meanwhile, with the part-time MBA students graduating in 1994, 1995 and 1996, the dramatic improvement was found again in these students who typically take three to five years to graduate. These groups showed a 67 per cent improvement in self-awareness and self-management competencies and a 40 per cent improvement in social awareness and social skills competencies by the end of their MBA program.

That is not all. Jane Wheeler tracked down groups of these part-timers two years after they had graduated. Even then, they still showed improvements in the same range: 63 per cent on the self-awareness and self-management competencies, and 45 per cent on

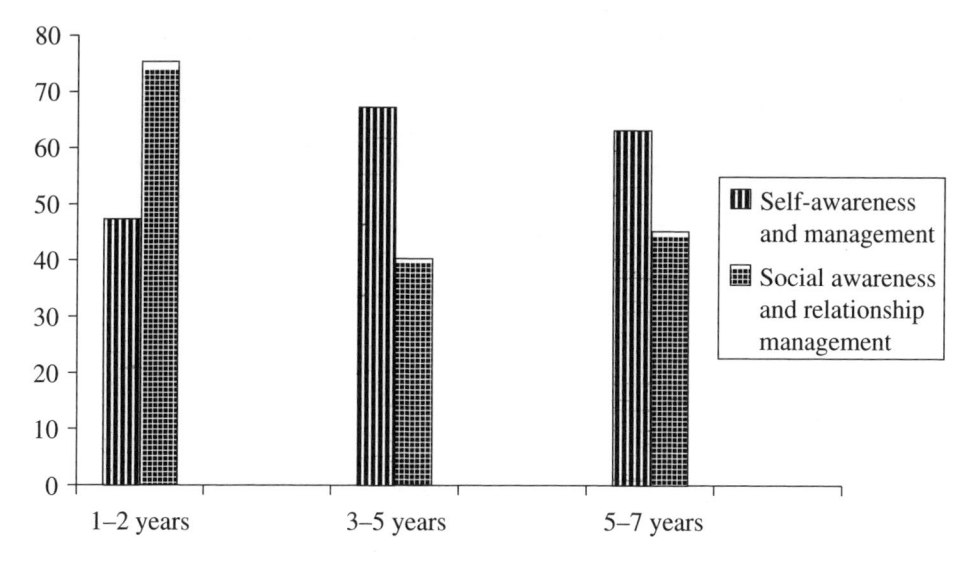

Figure 42.1 Percentage improvement of emotional intelligence competencies of different groups of MBA graduates taking the self-directed learning course

the social awareness and relationship management competencies. This is in contrast to MBA graduates of the Weatherhead School of Management (WSOM) of the 1988 and 1989 traditional full-time and part-time program who showed improvement in substantially fewer of the competencies.

The positive effects of this program were not limited to MBAs. In a longitudinal study of four classes completing the Professional Fellows Program (an executive education program at the Weatherhead School of Management), Ballou et al. (1999) showed that these 45–55-year-old professionals and executives improved on self-confidence, leadership, helping, goal setting and action skills. These were 67 per cent of the emotional intelligence competencies assessed in this study.

Self-directed learning
What the studies referred to above have shown is that adults learn what they want to learn. Other things, even if acquired temporarily (for example, for a test), are soon forgotten (Specht and Sandlin, 1991). Students, children, patients, clients and subordinates may act as if they care about learning something and go through the motions, but they proceed to disregard it or forget it, unless it is something which they want to learn. This does not include changes induced, willingly or not, by chemical or hormonal changes in one's body. But even in such situations, the interpretation of the changes and behavioral comportment following it will be affected by the person's will, values and motivations.

In this way it appears that most, if not all, sustainable behavioral change is intentional. Self-directed change is an intentional change in an aspect of who you are (the real) or who you want to be (the ideal), or both. Self-directed learning is self-directed change in which you are aware of the change and understand the process of change.

The process of self-directed learning is shown graphically in Figure 42.2 (Boyatzis, 1999; Boyatzis, 2001; Goleman *et al.*, 2002). This is an enhancement of the earlier models developed by Kolb *et al.* (1968), Boyatzis and Kolb (1969), Kolb and Boyatzis (1970a, 1970b) and Kolb (1971).

The description and explanation of the process in this chapter is organized around five points of discontinuity. A person might begin self-directed learning at any point in the process, but it will often begin when the person experiences a discontinuity, the associated epiphany or a moment of awareness and a sense of urgency.

This model describes the process as designed into a required course and the elements of the MBA and executive programs implemented in 1990 at the Weatherhead School of Management. Experimentation and research into the various components have resulted in refinement of these components and the model as discussed in this chapter. For a detailed description of the course, read Boyatzis (1994, 1995).

The first discontinuity: catching your dreams, engaging your passion
Franklin is wrestling with redirecting his career for an old reason. He has been executive director of a foundation for ten years. Donors, program recipients and policy makers consider him a distinctive success within the foundation world. His emotional intelligence is considered a model to be emulated by others, as is his incisive intellect. And yet he is restless. During a coaching session that was part of an assessment and development program, he identified two possible career paths for the future: he could leverage his expertise and join a larger, global foundation as executive director or he could become an executive for a company. The attraction of corporate life would be higher compensation.

When asked if he was feeling pressure from his family about money, Franklin said, 'Not at all.' Asked why he considered leaving the arena he felt passionate about with a deep sense of social mission, and whether there were any challenges a company can give him that he did not feel in a foundation, he looked toward the ceiling and shook his head. He realized that he was reacting to frustrations of his current situation. Once free of considering 'doing time' or 'paying his dues' in a company as a desirable option, he began to brainstorm ideas for adding to his personal income while leading foundations. He thought of expanding his writing to include books and giving speeches as ways to supplement his income.

Franklin was having trouble identifying his ideal work for the future. His deep, inner commitment to the not-for-profit world was ignored in considering the attractiveness of the private sector. But these attractions were things others found desirable, not Franklin. The first discontinuity and potential starting point for the process of self-directed learning is the discovery of who you want to be. Our ideal self is an image of the person we want to be. It emerges from our ego ideal, dreams and aspirations. Sometimes this appears as a wake-up call, alerting us to the observation that we have lost the enthusiasm or passion we once had for what we are doing and how we are living (Boyatzis, McKee and Goleman, 2002).

The last 20 years have revealed literature supporting the power of positive imaging or visioning in sports psychology, meditation and biofeedback research, and other psychophysiological research. It is believed that the potency of focusing one's thoughts on a specific desired state is driven by the emotional components of the brain (Goleman, 1995).

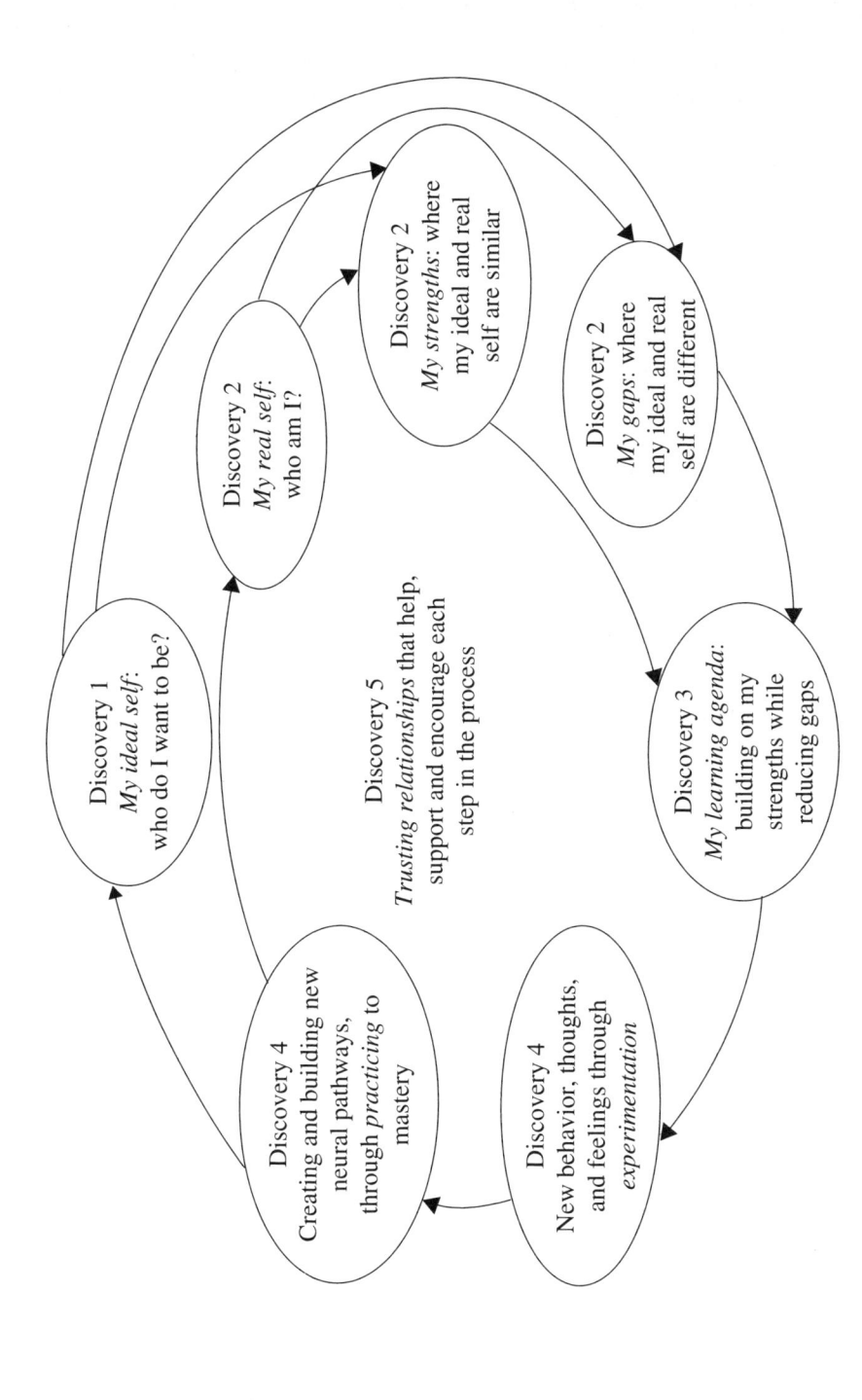

Figure 42.2 Boyatzis' theory of self-directed learning

This research indicates that we can gain access to and engage deep emotional commitment and psychic energy if we engage our passions and conceptually catch our dreams in our ideal self-image. It is an anomaly that we know the importance of consideration of the ideal self and yet, often, when engaged in a change or learning process, we skip over the clear formulation or articulation of our ideal self image. If a parent, spouse, boss or teacher indicates something that should be different, they are telling us about the person *they* want us to be. As adults, we often allow ourselves to be anesthetized to our dreams and lose sight of our deeply felt ideal self.

The second discontinuity: am I a boiling frog?
Joe started a doctoral program to propel him into his new life. His friends and family thought he was crazy. He owned and ran three health care companies, a nursing home, a temporary service agency specializing in health workers and a small consulting practice. The nursing home had some problems, including cash flow and a quarrelsome partner. It was not clear who was the antagonist between the two partners, but the relationship felt like a bad marriage staying together 'for the children'. Joe began teaching management part-time at a local university and loved it. The university made him a full-time faculty member. He was pursuing an executive doctorate in management to refine his research and writing skills. This is a doctoral program designed for scholar-practitioners with, typically, 20 or more years of work experience of which at least ten are in management or leadership positions.

He loved the program but was running himself ragged with all of the responsibilities. When Richard Boyatzis asked him, 'Joe, what do you most want to be doing in five to ten years?' Joe did not hesitate: 'I love teaching. I would like to contribute through writing. I can translate complex concepts into language that people understand. I would love to do some research and test my ideas. But mostly, I love teaching.'

'Why are you keeping all these businesses?'

He turned with a questioning look, 'What do you mean?'

Pointing to the draft of his essay on his desired future, Professor Boyatzis clarified: 'You are a full-time faculty member. You want to be a full-time faculty member. You want to spend more time writing and doing some research. You are currently in a doctoral program. And yet you are still involved in running three businesses. Don't you think this is too much? Haven't you made a choice already as to which you want? So why the ambivalence?'

Joe listed the contractual complications and financial implications leading to his conclusion that he must continue all three businesses. But then he added, 'I have considered handing the temporary services business to my son, letting the consulting business drop away to nothing by just not taking any new projects.' Once provoked in this way, he started to consider speeding up time frame. He brainstormed a few steps that would remove him from running the nursing home within a year, and from ownership of the nursing home within two years. Nodding his head with a growing smile, Joe said, 'This could work. This could really work! Boy oh boy, do I look forward to two years from now!'

Joe had changed but was confusing his old self with the person he had become. Joe knew that he was not as exciting a leader in his businesses as he had been in the past, while, in the classroom, he engaged students using his humor and playfulness. Facing his real self, looking in the mirror, was difficult.

The awareness of the current self, the person that others see and with whom they interact, is elusive. For normal reasons, the human psyche protects itself from the automatic 'intake' and conscious realization of all information about ourselves. These ego-defense mechanisms serve to protect us. They also conspire to delude us into an image of who we are that feeds on itself, becomes self-perpetuating and eventually may become dysfunctional (Goleman, 1985).

The greatest challenge to an accurate current self-image (that is, seeing yourself as others see you, and consistent with other internal states, beliefs, emotions and so forth) is the 'boiling frog' syndrome. It is said that dropping a frog into a pot of boiling water will result in it immediately jumping out. But place a frog in a pot of cool water, and gradually raise the temperature to boiling, and the frog will remain in the water until it is cooked.

Certain factors contribute to our becoming boiling frogs. First, people around you may not let you see a change. They may not give you feedback or information about how they see it. Also they may be victims of the boiling frog syndrome themselves, as they adjust their perception on a daily basis. Second, enablers, those forgiving the change, frightened of it, or who do not care, may allow it to pass unnoticed.

To truly consider changing a part of yourself, you must have a sense of what you value and want to keep. These areas in which your real self and ideal self are consistent or congruent can be considered strengths. Likewise, to consider what you want to preserve about yourself involves admitting aspects of yourself that you wish to change or adapt in some manner. Areas where your real self and ideal self are not consistent can be considered gaps.

All too often, people explore growth or development by focusing on the 'gaps' or deficiencies. Organizational training programs and managers conducting annual reviews often make the same mistake. There is an assumption that we can 'leave well enough alone' and get to the areas that need work. It is no wonder that many of these programs or procedures intended to help a person develop result in the individual feeling battered, beleaguered and bruised, not helped, encouraged, motivated or guided.

There are four major 'learning points' from the first two discontinuities in the self-directed learning process: (1) engage your passion and create your dreams; (2) Know thyself; (3) identify or articulate both your strengths (those aspects of yourself you want to preserve) and the gaps or discrepancies in your real and ideal selves (those aspects of yourself you want to adapt or change); and (4) keep your attention on both characteristics, forces or factors – do not let one become the preoccupation.

All of these learning points can be achieved by finding and using multiple sources for feedback about your ideal self, real self, strengths and gaps. The sources of insight into your real self can include systematically collecting information from others, such as 360 degree feedback, currently considered fashionable in organizations. Other sources of insight into your real self, strengths and gaps may come from behavioral feedback through videotaped or audiotaped interactions, such as are collected in assessment centers. Various psychological tests can help you determine or make explicit inner aspects of your real self, such as values, philosophy, traits and motives.

Sources for insight into your ideal self are more personal and more elusive than those for the real self. Various exercises and tests can help by making explicit various dreams or aspirations you have for the future. Talking with close friends or mentors can help. Allowing yourself to think about your desired future, not merely your prediction of your most likely future, is the biggest obstacle. These conversations and explorations must take place in psychologically safe surroundings.

The third discontinuity: mindfulness through a learning agenda

Karen was describing her career goals during an MBA class. At 27, she was energetic, poised and ready to take on the world. She identified her long-term career goal as to buy or open an art gallery in Chicago or a big mid-western city. When asked why an art gallery, she embarrassingly admitted she loved art but could not paint or sculpt. Karen explained that she would approach her career goal by working for a large bank for a number of years to learn more about finance, not to mention making some money. Others in class thought this made sense, until the professor said, 'So in order to learn to be an entrepreneur in the arts, you want to work in a large, bureaucratic organization that values conformity, where most people wear gray or blue suits with red ties or scarves and managers demand adherence to policies, rules and regulations? In this environment, you might extinguish the entrepreneurial spirit and confidence that you have and need to run an art gallery successfully.'

Karen's original draft of her learning plan would not have led to her desired future. She had absorbed an image from her reference group of fellow students and her general image of business: she thought she needed to master finance to be an entrepreneur. MBA mythology has ranked banks as one of the best places to work to master finance. So Karen had written her original plan, to work in an organization that was not of interest to her. Later conversations with her professor resulted in a learning plan more directly aimed at a future toward which she had passionate commitment.

The third discontinuity in self-directed learning is development of an agenda and focussing on the desired future. While performance at work or happiness in life may be the eventual consequence of our efforts, a learning agenda focuses on development. A learning orientation arouses a positive belief in one's capability and the hope of improvement. This results in people setting personal standards of performance, rather than 'normative' standards that merely mimic what others have done (Beaubien and Payne, 1999). Meanwhile, a performance orientation evokes anxiety and doubts about whether or not we can change (Chen et al., 2000).

As part of one of the longitudinal studies at the Weatherhead School of Management, Leonard (1996) showed that MBAs who set goals desiring change in certain competencies, changed significantly in those competencies as compared to other MBAs. Previous goal-setting literature had shown how goals affected certain changes in specific competencies (Locke and Latham, 1990), but had not established evidence of behavioral change in a comprehensive set of competencies that constitute emotional intelligence.

The major learning point from this section, crucial in self-directed learning, is *create your own, personal learning agenda.* A major threat to effective goal setting and planning is that people are already busy and cannot add anything else to their lives. In such cases, the only success with self-directed change and learning occurs if people can determine what to say 'no' to and stop some current activities in their lives to make room for new activities.

Another potential challenge or threat is the development of a plan that calls for a person to engage in activities different from their preferred learning style or learning flexibility (Kolb, 1984; Boyatzis, 1994). In such cases a person commits himself to activities or action steps in a plan that require a learning style which is not their preference or not within their range of competencies. When this occurs, a person becomes demotivated and often stops the activities, or becomes impatient and decides that the goals are not worth the effort.

The fourth discontinuity: metamorphosis
Bob wanted to build a portfolio of manufacturing companies in which he would have significant ownership, together with meaningful involvement in the management. A passive approach to providing venture capital was not enough. But Bob knew he was often impatient and not as sensitive to others as he would like. He wanted to develop a style that was collaborative with others, not managing them. Too many companies acquired by venture capitalists languish from inattention or falter from too much 'help'. Bob said, 'An owner will be reluctant to sell his or her business to someone with whom they have a poor rapport, and the envisioned "advisory group" will become dysfunctional.' So he wanted to build his empathy and patience with others as a stepping stone to a more collaborative leadership style.

To experiment with this enhanced or new talent in understanding others, he decided to start with an opportunity closer to home – actually at home. Bob's relationship with two of his children, in particular his two daughters, should be more fun and more supportive than it had been recently. He saw a way to work on his leadership style while rebuilding family relationships. He declared a learning goal to 'identify an activity of mutual interest that I can do with my daughters on a routine basis (that is, two or three times a month)'. He knew they had expressed interest in two sports, golf and horseback riding. Bob talked to his daughters; more importantly, he opened up the possibility and listened to their responses. They then set up a schedule to go riding and golfing on a monthly basis. He committed himself to watching movies with them that they wanted to see and even watched MTV with them.

The fourth discontinuity is to experiment and practice desired changes. Acting on the plan and toward the goals involves numerous activities. These often take place in the context of experimenting with new behavior. Typically following a period of experimentation, the person practices the new behaviors in actual settings within which they wish to use them, such as at work or at home. During this part of the process, self-directed change and learning begins to look like a 'continuous improvement' process.

To develop or learn new behavior, the person must find ways to learn more from on-going experiences. That is, the experimentation and practice does not always require attending 'courses' or a new activity. It may involve trying something different in a current setting, reflecting on what occurs, and experimenting further in this setting. Sometimes this part of the process requires finding and using opportunities to learn and change. People may not even think they have changed until they have tried new behavior in a work or 'real world' setting.

Dreyfus (1990) studied managers of scientists and engineers who were considered superior performers. Once she had documented that they used considerably more of certain abilities than their less effective counterparts, she pursued the ways in which they developed some of those abilities. One of the distinguishing abilities was group management, also called team building. She found that many of these middle-aged managers had first experimented with team-building skills in high school and college, in sports, clubs and living groups. Later, when they became 'bench scientists and engineers' working on problems in relative isolation, they still pursued use and practicing of this ability in activities outside work. They practiced team building and group management in social and community organizations, such as Boy Scouts, and professional associations in planning conferences and such.

The experimentation and practice are most effective when they occur in conditions in which the person feels safe (Kolb and Boyatzis, 1970b). This sense of psychological safety creates an atmosphere in which the person can try new behavior, perceptions and thoughts with relatively less risk of shame, embarrassment or serious consequences of failure.

The fifth discontinuity: relationships that enable us to learn
Our relationships are an essential part of our environment. The most crucial relationships are often a part of groups that have particular importance to us. These relationships and groups give us a sense of identity, guide us as to what is appropriate and 'good' behavior and provide feedback on our behavior. In sociology, they are called 'reference' groups. These relationships create a 'context' within which we interpret our progress on desired changes, the utility of new learning, and even contribute significant input to formulation of the ideal (Kram, 1996).

In this sense, our relationships are mediators, moderators, interpreters, sources of feedback, sources of support and permission for change and learning. They may also be the most important source of protection from relapses or returning to our earlier forms of behavior. Wheeler (1999) analyzed the extent to which the MBA graduates worked on their goals in multiple 'life spheres' (work, family, recreational groups and so on). In a two-year follow-up study of two of the graduating classes of part-time MBA students, she found that those who worked on their goals and plans in multiple sets of relationships improved the most, and more than those working on goals in only one setting, such as at work or within one relationship.

In a study of the impact of the year-long executive development program for doctors, lawyers, professors, engineers and other professionals mentioned earlier, Ballou *et al.* (1999) found that participants gained self-confidence during the program. Even at the beginning of the program others would say that these participants were very high in self-confidence. It was a curious finding. The best explanation came from follow-up questions put to the graduates of the program. They explained the evident increase in self-confidence as an increase in the confidence to change. Their existing reference groups (that is, family, groups at work, professional groups, community groups) all had an investment in their staying the same; meanwhile the person wanted to change. The Professional Fellows Program allowed them to develop a new reference group that encouraged change.

Based on social identity, reference group, and now relational theories, our relationships both meditate and moderate our sense of who we are and who we want to be. We develop or elaborate our ideal self from these contexts; we label and interpret our real self from these contexts; we interpret and value strengths (that is, aspects considered our core that we wish to preserve) from these contexts; we interpret and value gaps (that is, aspects considered weaknesses or things we wish to change) from these contexts.

The major learning points from the fourth and fifth discontinuities critical in self-directed learning process are (1) experiment and practice and try to learn more from your experiences; (2) find settings in which you feel psychologically safe, within which to experiment and practice; and (3) develop and use your relationships as part of your change and learning process.

Concluding thought

Adults can develop leadership and emotional intelligence. As leaders, we can only create environments in which others want to use their capabilities and emotional intelligence if we are authentic and consistent in our own demonstration of these behaviors. Through the self-directed learning process, we have the opportunity to truly make a difference. Whether applied in universities or companies, government agencies or not-for-profits, this process can help us coach each other to create the social environments we want and find so conducive to making a difference.

References

Baldwin, Timothy and J. Kevin Ford (1988), 'Transfer of training: a review and directions for future research', *Personnel Psychology*, **41**, 63–105.

Ballou, R., D. Bowers, R.E. Boyatzis and D.A. Kolb (1999), 'Fellowship in lifelong learning: an executive development program for advanced professionals', *Journal of Management Education*, **23**(4), pp. 338–54.

Barlow, D.H. (1988), *Anxiety and Disorders: The Nature and Treatment of Anxiety and Panic*, New York: The Guilford Press.

Boyatzis, R.E. (1982), *The Competent Manager: A Model for Effective Performance*, New York: John Wiley & Sons.

Boyatzis, R.E. (1994), 'Stimulating self-directed change: a required MBA course called Managerial Assessment and Development', *Journal of Management Education*, **18**(3), 304–23.

Boyatzis, R.E. (1995), 'Cornerstones of change: building a path for self-directed learning', in R.E. Boyatzis, S.C. Cowen and D.A. Kolb (1995), *Innovation in Professional Education: Steps on a Journey from Teaching to Learning*, San Francisco: Jossey-Bass, pp. 50–94.

Boyatzis, R.E. (1999), 'Self-directed change and learning as a necessary meta-competency for success and effectiveness in the 21st century', in R. Sims and J.G. Veres (eds), *Keys to Employee Success in the Coming Decades*, Westport, CN: Greenwood Publishing.

Boyatzis, R.E. (2001), 'How and why individuals are able to develop emotional intelligence', in C. Cherniss and D. Goleman (eds), *The Emotionally Intelligent Workplace: How to Select for, Measure and Improve Emotional Intelligence in Individuals, Groups and Organizations*, San Francisco: Jossey-Bass.

Boyatzis, R.E. and D.A. Kolb (1969), 'Feedback and self-directed behavior change', unpublished working paper 394-69, Sloan School of Management, MIT.

Boyatzis, R.E. and M. Sokol (1982), 'A pilot project to assess the feasibility of assessing skills and personal characteristics of students in collegiate business programs', Report to the AACSB (St. Louis, MO).

Boyatzis, R.E., A. McKee and D. Goleman (2002), 'Reawakening your passion for work', *Harvard Business Review*, **80**(4), 86–94.

Boyatzis, R.E., A. Renio-McKee and L. Thompson (1995), 'Past accomplishments: establishing the impact and baseline of earlier programs', in R.E. Boyatzis, S.S. Cowen and D.A. Kolb (eds), *Innovation in Professional Education: Steps on a Journey from Teaching to Learning*, San Francisco: Jossey-Bass.

Boyatzis, R.E., E. Stubbs and S.N. Taylor (2002), 'Learning cognitive and emotional intelligence competencies through graduate management education', *Academy of Management Journal on Learning and Education*, **1**(2), 150–62.

Boyatzis, R.E., J. Wheeler and R. Wright (in press), 'Competency development in graduate education: a longitudinal perspective', *Proceedings of the First World Conference on Self-Directed Learning*, GIRAT, Montreal.

Boyatzis, R.E., D. Leonard, K. Rhee and J.V. Wheeler (1996), 'Competencies can be developed, but not the way we thought', *Capability*, **2**(2), 25–41.

Boyatzis, R.E., A. Baker, D. Leonard, K. Rhee and L. Thompson (1995), 'Will it make a difference? Assessing a value-based, outcome-oriented, competency-based professional program', in R.E. Boyatzis, S.S. Cowen and D.A. Kolb (eds), *Innovating in Professional Education: Steps on a Journey from Teaching to Learning*, San Francisco: Jossey-Bass.

Bray, D.W., R.J. Campbell and D.L. Grant (1974), *Formative Years in Business: A Long Term AT&T Study of Managerial Lives*, New York: John Wiley & Sons.

Burke, M.J. and R.R. Day (1986), 'A cumulative study of the effectiveness of managerial training', *Journal of Applied Psychology*, **71**(2), 232–45.
Campbell, J.P., M.D. Dunnette, E.E. Lawler and K.E. Weick (1970), *Managerial Behavior, Performance, and Effectiveness*, New York: McGraw-Hill.
Chen, G., S.M. Gully, J.A. Whiteman and R.N. Kilcullen (2000), 'Examination of relationships among trait-like individual differences, state-like individual differences, and learning performance', *Journal of Applied Psychology*, **85**(6), 835–47.
Cherniss, C. and M. Adler (2000), *Promoting Emotional Intelligence in Organizations: Make Training in Emotional Intelligence Effective*, Washington, DC: American Society of Training and Development.
Cutter, H., R.E. Boyatzis and D. Clancy (1977), 'The effectiveness of power motivation training for rehabilitating alcoholics', *Journal of Studies on Alcohol*, **38**(1).
Development Dimensions International (DDI) (1985), 'Final report: phase III', report to the AACSB, St. Louis, MO.
Dreyfus, C. (1990), 'The characteristics of high performing managers of scientists and engineers', unpublished doctoral dissertation, Case Western Reserve University.
Goleman, D. (1985), *Vital Lies, Simple Truths: The Psychology of Self-deception*, New York: Simon & Schuster.
Goleman, D. (1995), *Emotional Intelligence*, New York: Bantam Books.
Goleman, D. (1998), *Working with Emotional Intelligence*, New York: Bantam Books.
Goleman, D., R.E. Boyatzis and A. McKee (2002), *Primal Leadership: Realizing the Power of Emotional Intelligence*, Boston, MA: Harvard Business School Press.
Hand, H.H., M.D. Richards and J.W. Slocum Jr. (1973), 'Organizational climate and the effectiveness of a human relations training program', *Academy of Management Journal*, **16**(2), 185–246.
Howard, A. and D. Bray (1988), *Managerial Lives in Transition: Advancing Age and Changing Times*, New York: Guilford Press.
Hubble, M.A., B.L. Duncan and S.D. Miller (eds) (1999), *The Heart and Soul of Change: What Works in Therapy*, Washington, DC: American Psychological Association.
Kanfer, F.H. and A.P. Goldstein (eds) (1991), *Helping People Change: A Textbook of Methods*, 4th edn, Boston: Allyn and Bacon.
Kolb, D.A. (1971), 'A cybernetic model of human change and growth', unpublished working paper, 526–71, Sloan School of Management, MIT.
Kolb, D.A. (1984), *Experiential Learning: Experience as the Source of Learning and Development*, Englewood Cliffs, NJ: Prentice-Hall.
Kolb, D.A. and R.E. Boyatzis (1970a), 'On the dynamics of the helping relationship', *Journal of Applied Behavioral Science*, **6**(3), 267–89.
Kolb, D.A. and R.E. Boyatzis (1970b), 'Goal-setting and self-directed behavior change', *Human Relations*, **23**(5), 439–57.
Kolb, D.A., S.K. Winter and D.E. Berlew (1968), 'Self-directed change: two studies', *Journal of Applied Behavioral Science*, **6**(3), 453–71.
Kotter, J.P. (1982), *The General Managers*, New York: Free Press.
Kram, K.E. (1996), 'A relational approach to careers', in D.T. Hall (ed.), *The Career is Dead: Long Live the Career*, San Francisco, CA: Jossey-Bass Publishers, pp. 132–57.
Latham, G.P. and L.M. Saari (1979), 'Application of social-learning theory to training supervisors through behavioral modeling', *Journal of Applied Psychology*, **64**(3), 239–46.
Leonard, D. (1996), 'The impact of learning goals on self-directed change in management development and education', doctoral dissertation, Case Western Reserve University.
Locke, E.A. and G.P. Latham (1990), *A Theory of Goal Setting and Task Performance*, Englewood Cliffs, NJ: Prentice-Hall.
Luthans, F., R.M. Hodgetts and S.A. Rosenkrantz (1988), *Real managers*, Cambridge, MA: Ballinger Press.
McClelland, D.C. and D.G. Winter (1969), *Motivating Economic Achievement*, New York: Free Press.
Miron, D. and D.C. McClelland (1979), 'The impact of achievement motivation training on small business', *California Management Review*, **21**(4), 13–28.
Morrow, C.C., M.Q. Jarrett and M.T. Rupinski (1997), 'An investigation of the effect and economic utility of corporate-wide training', *Personnel Psychology*, **50**, 91–119.
Noe, R.A. and N. Schmitt (1986), 'The influence of trainee attitudes on training effectiveness: test of a model', *Personnel Psychology*, **39**, 497–523.
Pascarella, E.T. and P.T. Terenzini (1991), *How College Affects Students: Findings and Insights from Twenty Years of Research*, San Francisco: Jossey-Bass.
Specht, L. and P. Sandlin (1991), 'The differential effects of experiential learning activities and traditional lecture classes in accounting', *Simulations and Gaming*, **22**(2), 196–210.
Spencer, L.M. Jr. and S.M. Spencer (1993), *Competence at Work: Models for Superior Performance*, New York: John Wiley & Sons.

Thornton, G.C. and W.C. Byham (1982), *Assessment Centers and Managerial Performance*, New York: Academic Press.
Wexley, K.N. and W.F. Memeroff (1975), 'Effectiveness of positive reinforcement and goal setting as methods of management development', *Journal of Applied Psychology*, **60**(4), 446–50.
Wheeler, J.V. (1999), 'The impact of social environments on self-directed change and learning', unpublished doctoral dissertation, Case Western Reserve University.
Winter, D.G., D.C. McClelland and A.J. Stewart (1981), *A New Case for the Liberal Arts: Assessing Institutional Goals and Student Development*, San Francisco: Jossey-Bass.
Young D.P. and N.M. Dixon (1996), *Helping Leaders Take Effective Action: A Program Evaluation*, Greensboro, NC: Center for Creative Leadership.

Index

ability, gap between job demands and 224
absenteeism 29, 94
   by occupational group 116
   due to illness or injury 111–12
   due to stress 442
   see also sick leave
absorbing commitment 518
accidents
   health care study 401, 402, 403, 408
   job-related stress 295
acculturation 93–4
accumulation 42
acetylcholine 73, 74
Actinobasillicus actinomycetemcomitans 335
action learning 130
action planning, risk reduction 183–4
action-focused coping 191–5, 226, 357
activation, burnout as low level of 499
active jobs 32
active learning
   future research 144–8
   and strain 143–4
   work characteristics
      knowledge concerning 133–9
      temporal effects of 139–43
active management by exception 642
active-passive dimensions of work, activity participation 24–5
activities
   during unemployment 265–6
   participation in 24–5
ACTU *see* Australian Council of Trade Unions
acute necrotizing ulcerative gingivitis 338
acute stress disorder 48, 49
adaptive regulation, of emotions 232–3
addiction
   and anxiety 458
   mobile phone use 154
   vulnerability to 81
adenosine triphosphate 74
adopted values 192
adrenal medulla 71, 74, 79
adrenal suppression 81
adrenaline (epinephrine) 73, 459
advanced manufacturing technology (AMT) 155–6
aetiology, stress research 66–7

age
   barrier to re-employment 267
   burnout and wornout 520, 526, 527, 539
   cardiovascular disease 462
   hypertension 468
   negative effects of shiftwork 415
   periodontal disease 336
   unemployment and stress 273
aggression 462
AHA *see* Anger-Hostility-Aggression Syndrome
AIDS, periodontal disease 335, 336–7
air traffic controllers, stress research 105–06
alarm reaction stage, GAS 459
alcohol dependence 434, 435
alcohol withdrawal 81
alcoholism 81
ALE *see* Assessment of Life Events scale
alienation
   between labour and capital 39–40, 40–41
   and stress 123–5
altruistic model, financing counselling centres 250
American Psychological Association (APA) 65
AMT *see* advanced manufacturing technology
amygdala 73–4
anergia 81
anger 460–62
   assessment of 450
   cardiovascular disease 464, 467, 468–71
   depression 509
   hypertension 471–4
   proactive coping 510–11, 512
   workaholism 374
Anger-Hostility-Aggression (AHA) Syndrome 462
angina 437, 609
angiotensin II 72
animal studies, periodontal diseases 339–40
anorexia nervosa 81
anti-depression drugs 191
ANUG *see* acute necrotizing ulcerative gingivitis
anxiety
   assessment of 450
   cardiovascular disease 464, 467, 468–71
   effect on information processing 143
   hypertension 471–4

long-term stress 112
  psychophysiological disorders 456–8
  self-reported 120
  unemployment 257, 275, 516
  workaholism 374, 375
APA *see* American Psychological Association
appetite, increased 81
appraisals
  controlling career stress 203
  stress and coping 196–7
aptitude, emotional intelligence as an 236
arcuate proopiomelanocortin neurons 74
Areas of Worklife Scale (AWS) 550–51
arginine-vasopressin 70, 71, 72
Aristotle 102, 122
ASD *see* acute stress disorder
assertiveness training 199
Assessment of Life Events scale (ALE) 235
atherosclerosis 80, 95, 434, 463, 468
ATP *see* adenosine triphosphate
attribution research, unsuccessful job search 271
atypical depression 81
Australian Council of Trade Unions (ACTU) 44
auto-evaluation, study and student counselling 251
autoimmune disease 82
automation
  changes in mental states 25
  emotional labour 157
autonomic nervous system 70, 74, 79, 469
autonomy 46, 204, 485
Avner 589–91
avoidance behaviour 44, 166, 231, 572
AVP *see* arginine-vasopressin
AWS *see* Areas of Worklife Scale

back pain 59, 418, 435
Bacteroides forsythus 335, 337
banking, automated procedures 157
Bar-On Emotional Quotient Inventory 638
Beck Depression Inventory 606
behavioural adaptations, during stress 71
behavioural disengagement 96–7
behavioural reactions, job loss 257
beliefs
  changing 191
  workaholism 373
Bernard, Claude 458
biological basis, stress-related diseases 70–83
blood pressure 94, 95, 220, 450, 466, 469, 610
blue-collar workers 202, 276, 433, 527, 611
BM *see* Burnout Measure
bodily pain 435

body systems, responses to stress 75–9
'boiling frog' syndrome 662–4
boredom at work 204
brain circuits, stress response 70, 72
brain function, leadership style 648
brain stem 70
brain systems, activated by stress system 73–4
British Household Panel Survey (1995) 114
British Regional Heart Study 281
buffers
  illness and stress 103, 357
  see also reverse buffering effect
'Building Better Health' programme 169
bullying 203–4
burn-in 538–9
burnout
  business travel 483–4
  career choice 579–94
  community-based psychiatric services 537–42
  conceptual basis 600–607
    alternatives 499–500
  definitions 495, 496, 537
  effort-reward imbalance 435
  emotionally demanding interactions 496–7
  growing interest in 516
  health consequences
    interventions to reduce 614–15
    mental health 607–9
    organizational implications 613–14
    physical health 609–12
  models 600–607
    see also Burnout Measure; Maslach Burnout Inventory; mediation model
  national survey
    aims and questions 521
    discussion and conclusions 532–5
    four strain/contingent self-esteem patterns 519–21
    methods 521–4
    process perspective 517–19
    results 524–32
  occupational stress 505–8
  overcommitment 435
  research 495–6, 517, 566, 599
    future 500–501, 615–16
  work–family conflict 351
  see also career and couple burnout; job burnout
Burnout Measure (BM) 517, 518, 523, 535, 602–3
Burnout Null Model 548, 556, 559
Burnout Predictor Model 548, 556, 559
burnout prevention programme 623–30

call centres 156–7
Camphylobacter rectus 335
cancer 609
Cannon, Walter B. 214, 458
capacity for flow 103
Capital 41
cardiac symptoms 609
cardiovascular disease 455
  anxiety, anger and stress 468–71
  behavioural factors 463
  burnout 609, 610, 611
  defined 462
  inherent risk factors 462–3
  long-term stress 112
  mortality and prevalence 466–8
  occupational stress 220
  physiological factors 463
  psychosocial factors 463–4
  publications 464–6
  relationship between stress and 461
  risk
    downsizing 307–11
    effort-reward imbalance 432–4
  social support 33
career changes, burnout and wornout 531
career choice
  and burnout 579–94
    existential-psychoanalytic perspective study
      method 581
      nurses' burnout 581–3
      teachers' burnout 583–5
    entrepreneurs' burnout 588
    managers' burnout 585–7
      comparison of managers and entrepreneurs 588–91
      discussion 591–4
    unconscious determinants 567
career counselling 246–7
career and couple burnout 565–75
  culture and cross-cultural studies 569–74
  implications for counselling 574–5
  psychoanalytic-existential perspective 565–7
  relationship between 567–9
career development
  organizational change 3
  psychosocial hazards 179
  work-related stress 223
career satisfaction, workaholism 373–4
career stress, controlling 203
carotid atherosclerosis 95, 434
caseload, and burnout 496–7
caseness 94–5
casual work 416

cataracts 611
catecholaminergic activity 81, 82, 281
causality
  interpretation of events 271
  stress research 66–7
cause-focused coping 191
cellular immunity, reduced 612
Census surveys, measuring ethnicity 88
central arousal sympathetic systems 73
central nervous system 339
CFS *see* chronic fatigue syndrome
challenge, lack of 124
challenge appraisals 105
Challenge to Inner Mastership
  conclusion 629–30
  programme 625–6
  success factors 626–9
change management studies 4
  conclusion 15–16
  introduction of
    information system in state government department 12–13
    multi-disciplinary work teams in midwifery hospitals 9–12
    new pay scheme in a corporatized public utility 7–9
  organizational context and sample 13–15
  stress and coping approach 4–7
character 228
CHD *see* coronary heart disease
chemical hazards 296
chest pains 94
childcare 205, 360–61
childhood sexual abuse 81
childhood trauma
  career choice and burnout 567, 580–81
    case studies 582–3, 584, 585, 586, 590
  romantic choice and couple burnout 567
children
  self-reported anxiety 120
  of workaholics 375
cholesterol levels 463, 610
cholinergic activity 82
chronic diseases 213
chronic fatigue syndrome 81, 615
chronic heart disease 164
chronic respiratory disease 281
chronic stress 80–81, 464
citizenship behaviour, transformational leadership 646
CITS *see* Coping in Task Situations
class *see* social class
climacteric depression 81
CNS *see* central nervous system

co-workers, supportive communication 319, 328–9
coffee consumption 463
cognitive appraisal theory 104–5
cognitive disengagement 96–7
cognitive housekeeping 233
cognitive intelligence 167
cognitive reactions, job loss 257
cognitive-phenomenological model, stress and coping 4–16
colds 609
collective training programme, shared leadership 129
collectivism, and culture 572
Commission for Racial Equality (CRE) 90
commitment
    active learning hypothesis 134–7
    as moderating factor 273
    multiple roles and lack of 260
    see also overcommitment; reduced commitment
communication, job-related 328–9
Communication Workers Union (CWU) 94
community, mediation model, burnout 552, 554, 555, 557, 558, 560, 561
community involvement, healthy organizations 390
community-based psychiatric services, burnout 537–42
compartmentalization, work and family 356
compensation claims
    interactive justice 31
    occupational stress 39, 48, 442
competence
    in coping 233–4
    learning process 134
competencies
    defined 656
    emotional 639–41
complementary prevention model 212–14
confidence 385
confound model, negative affectivity 23
congestive heart failure 466–8
conservation of resources (COR) theory
    business travel research 484–5
    conceptualization of burnout 603–4, 605–6
constructive thought patterns 232
consultation, counselling centres 248
consumer-company gap 157
contingent rewards 642, 647
contingent self-esteem 518, 519–21
continuing professional development (CPD) 384
continuous net loss, and burnout 605–6

control 33–7
    bolstering sense of 614–15
    mediation model, burnout 552, 554, 555, 557, 558, 559, 560, 561
    need for, career choice 582, 583
    psychosocial hazards 179
    see also emotional control; job-demand control model; self-control; workplace control
control strategies 505
controllability awareness 34
cooperation, organizational 125–6
cooperativeness, and quality of life 395
coping
    change management 4–16
    defining 197
    discrepancy reduction behaviour 38–9
    emotional intelligence 218, 230–35
    occupational stress 26–8, 224–6
    and reason 197
    research 503
    resources and outcomes 504–5
    see also action-focused coping; emotion-focused coping; stress and coping study
coping process
    business travel 485–6
    importance of meaning in 623–4
coping strategies 96–7
    individual-level 198–9
    occupational stress indicator 297
    stress and strain relationship 168–9
    unemployment and stress 258, 278
    veterinary surgeons 298–9, 300, 301
    work–family conflict 356–7
coping style, risk of periodontal disease 341
Coping in Task Situations (CITS) questionnaire 235
COR see conservation of resources theory
Corona Process 627–8
coronary artery disease 213, 466
coronary heart disease 35, 95, 220, 279, 432–4, 509, 610
corporate culture, family-friendly practices 362
correlation, stress research 64
corticotrophin-releasing hormone (CRH) 70, 71, 72–3, 74, 75, 80, 81
cortisol 74, 80, 81, 105–6
costs see financial costs; health costs
Council Framework Directive on the Introduction of Measures to Encourage Improvements in the Safety and Health of Workers at Work 176

counselling
   career and couple burnout 574–5
   psychological well-being 421
   see also psychosynthesis counsellors; study and student counselling
couple burnout *see* career and couple burnout
courage 103
CPD *see* continuing professional development
CRE *see* Commission for Racial Equality
creative thinking 386–7
CRH *see* corticotrophin-releasing hormone
crisis intervention, student support 247
critical incident analysis 225
cross-cultural studies, career and couple burnout 573–4
cross-sectional studies
   active learning and JDC model 138, 144
   design pitfalls 64
   periodontal disease 337–8
cultural knowledge, business travel 489
culture
   and burnout 569–73
   see also corporate culture; organizational culture; school culture
culture shock, temporary employees 316
curiosity 451
Cushing syndrome 79, 81
CWU *see* Communication Workers Union
cybernetics, occupational stress 37–40
cynicism
   later stages of burnout 606
   Maslach Burnout Model 600–601, 602
   mediation model, burnout 554, 555, 557, 558, 560, 561
   proactive coping and emotional exhaustion 507, 508, 512
cytokines 72, 74, 75, 77, 78

DALYS 396
Dan 587–8
data collection, risk management 184
decision authority, long-term sick leave 307–11
decision making
   burnout 553
   involvement of employees in 4
   shared leadership 130
   stress
      due to lack of participation 201
      involved in 316
declaration of Bologna 243
defense mechanisms 27, 191, 469
defensive behaviour 229
degree courses, veterinary 294
demand-control *see* job-demand control model

demographic factors
   burnout and wornout 526
   psychological impacts of stress 272–4
demoralization 609
denial 473–4
The Denial of Death 579
dentists, career choice and burnout 593
deontology, study and student counselling 252
dependants, work–family conflict 356
depersonalization 497, 498, 506, 600
depression
   and anger 509
   assessment of 450–51
   attribution research 271
   and burnout 606, 607–8
   effort-reward imbalance 436–7
   and learning 143
   long-term stress 112
   proactive coping 510–11, 512
   stress response 79, 80, 81, 94
   and unemployment 257, 261, 263, 275, 280
   work–family conflict 356
   workaholism 374
diabetes mellitus (DM) 81, 335, 463, 609, 610–11, 612
diagnostic model, in public health 213–14
diet 463
disclosure 233, 509
discourses, stress 20, 43–5
discrepancy, feedback mechanisms 38
discrepancy reduction behaviour 38–9
discrimination, and stress 90–91, 92–3
disease
   deaths from 418
   vulnerability to 81
   see also cardiovascular disease; chronic diseases; infectious diseases; periodontal diseases; stress-related diseases
disengagement 96–7
   see also engagement
disposition, well-being at work 383
disruptive students, teachers' burnout 583
distraction 191
distributive justice 29, 30
double bind situation, burnout as 29
downsizing
   Swedish study 304–12
      description of time course 305–7
      cardiovascular risk and sick leave 307–11
      conclusion 311–12
   work–health relationship 415, 423–4

drinking
  as coping mechanism 191
  excessive 94
  unemployment and stress 280
  veterinary profession 298
  work–family conflict 351–2
  see also alcohol dependence; alcoholism
drug addicts, assault on veterinarians 296
drug taking 191
DSSQ *see* Dundee Stress State Questionnaire
Dundee Stress State Questionnaire (DSSQ) 235
dynamic equilibrium theory 24, 35–7
dyslipidemia 79

eating disorders 458
ecological view, of humans 21
economic climate, change in psychological contract 30
economic model, financing counselling centres 250
Economic and Philosophical Manuscripts of 1844 41
economic recession, Sweden 305–6
educational aspects, business travel 483
educational attainment, cardiovascular disease 464
effective coping strategies 233
effective health care systems 393–4, 396
effective leadership 633
  training programmes 649
efficacy
  active learning 137
  mediation model, burnout 554, 555, 557, 558, 560, 561
  proactive coping, emotional exhaustion and 507, 508, 513
  see also ineffectiveness; self-efficacy
effort–reward imbalance model 34–5
  effect on health 430–38
    case study testing reward components 435–7
    empirical evidence 431–5
    implications for worksite health promotion 437–8
    Swedish Work Environment Surveys 305
eicosanoids 77
elder care, work–family conflict 360–61
electronic performance monitoring (EPM) 154
email 154, 155
emotion-focused coping 191, 278
emotional closure 233
emotional competencies 639–41
emotional control 194

emotional exhaustion 435, 497, 498, 499–500, 600
  job demands 520
  proactive coping and cynicism 506–8, 512
Emotional Intelligence 227
emotional intelligence
  approaches to 636–8
  coping capabilities 218
  and emotions 633–6
  frameworks 638–41
  leadership *see* leadership
  occupational settings 227–35
  personal development 384
  stress reduction programmes 236
  stress and strain relationship 166–7
emotional intelligence-coping relationship 230–35
emotional labour 157
emotional management 634
emotional reactions, job loss 257
emotional regulation 228, 231–2, 232–3, 500, 640
emotional skills 233
emotional stress, periodontal diseases 341
emotional support 262, 421
emotions
  and burnout 496–7
  and emotional intelligence 633–6
  and health 455–62
  regulation of 228, 231, 232–3, 500, 640
empathy 228, 384, 639, 640
employee assistance programmes 301
employee functioning, work control 157
employee support systems, audits 182
employees
  organizational change
    change management strategies 4–16
    experience of uncertainty 3–4
    participation in decision-making 4
    strategies for maintaining control over work 154–5
  see also temporary employees; work–health relationship
employer responsibility, health and safety 176–7
employment
  changing nature of 59–60
  commitment *see* commitment
  importance to women 255
  see also paid employment; precarious employment; unemployment
employment assistance programs (EAPs) 420–21
employment status, and burnout 522, 529

enactive mastery 6, 614
encounter stage, socialization 315
endocrine dysfunction 33
energetic resources, depleted 614
engagement 499
  see also disengagement
entrepreneurs
  career choice and burnout 588, 591, 592, 593
  compared with managers 588–91
environment
  alienation 124
  mediating factors 272–3
  organizational attunement to 125
  psychosocial hazards 179
  stability in 22
  and well-being 383
  see also work environments
epinephrine see adrenaline
EPM see electronic performance monitoring
EQ see emotional intelligence
EQ-i self report measure 234
equal opportunity policies 90
equipment, psychosocial hazards 179
equity theory 509
  occupational stress 29–30
ergonomic stress 421
ERI see effort–reward imbalance model
Erie County Study 341
erroneous beliefs 191
ethics, study and student counselling 252
ethnic discrimination, stress 92–3
ethnic disparities, historical approaches to 90–91
ethnic identity, and experience of stress 97
ethnic minorities, proneness to stress 91–2
ethnic minority workers, prevalence of 89–90
ethnic self-identification 88
ethnicity
  and coping 97
  and health 95–6
  measuring 88–9
  terminology and definitions 87–8
eudaemonia 102
European Foundation for the Improvement of Living and Working Conditions 59
European Foundation survey (1996) 175
European framework directive, health and safety at work 62
European Parliament, work-related stress 62
Eustress 104–6
  experiences of nurses 106–8
  implications for practice 108–9
  implications for research 109

event characteristics, employee adjustment to change 3–16
everyday reality
  good leadership 126
  maintaining 122–3
executive stress, myth of 114–17
exercise see physical exercise; spiritual exercises
exhaustion, mediation model, burnout 557, 558, 559, 560, 561
exhaustion stage, GAS 459–60
existential perspective, burnout 566, 567, 579
  managers 586
  nurses 582
  teachers 583
expansion (organizational), and health 305, 306, 307
expectations, and burnout 592
expenditure, health care 393, 408–11
experience, secondary alienation 124
experimental studies, need for 67
expert judgements, risk assessments 182
exploding the myth of executive stress 111
exposure to hazards 179
expression of emotions 635
external attributions, interpretation of events 271
external locus of control 165–6, 277
external resources 511
extra-work satisfactions, workaholism 375
extraversion 22, 26, 35

fair treatment, proactive coping 510–11, 512
fairness, mediation model, burnout 552, 553, 554, 555, 557, 558, 560, 561
family
  impact of business travels 481–2, 487
  see also work–family conflict
family antecedents, cardiovascular disease 462
family dynamics, entrepreneurial personality 588
family functioning, workaholism 375
family of origin, workaholism 372
family support, unemployment 264
family variables, burnout and wornout 522, 526, 532, 535
family-friendly policies 205
family-friendly practices 362
family-to-work conflict (FWC) 347, 349, 352, 354
father issues, career choice and burnout 586, 587
fatigue 40–41, 59, 81, 516, 609
fears, workaholism 373

feedback
  cybernetic theory 37–8
  learning motivation 137–8
  performance effectiveness 204
  study and student counselling 249
feedback loops 37–8
'feeling driven to work' 373, 376
female leaders 644
female managers
  exclusion from business networks 270
  indirect discrimination, recruitment 269
  mental health 95–6
  performance pressures 93
  unemployed
    coping strategies 278
    effects of 258
    gender discrimination 267–8
    importance of social support 262–3
    job loss 259–60
    mental health symptoms 279–80
    partner support 263
    personality 278–9
    self-efficacy 276
    self-esteem 275–6
    stress effects, compared with men 281–3
    stress outcomes 281
    unsuccessful job search 271
female veterinarians 300
feminine culture 572
fever 450
fibromyalgia 81
fight–flight response 124, 214, 458–9
finances, study and student counselling 250
financial costs, stress 94, 220, 419, 442
financial deprivation, unemployment 260–61, 282, 283
financial stress, illness 261
first-order change 38
fitness, shiftwork tolerance 415
flexibility, in coping 233–4
flexible working 205
  work–family conflict 358–9
  work–health relationship 415–16
flow, capacity for 103
flu 609
focus groups, stress reduction 201
force field analysis 129
forgiveness 385
Fourth National Survey of Ethnic Minorities 88
friendships 264
Frustrated strivings 518
functional communication model 31
Fusobacterium nucleatum 335

G-protein-coupled receptors 73
GABA *see* γ-amino-butyric acid
Gardner's multiple intelligences 638
GAS *see* General Adaptation Syndrome
gastrointestinal problems 608
gender
  cardiovascular disease 463
  hypertension 468
  periodontal disease 336
  unemployment *see* unemployed managers
  work–family conflict 354–5
  see also men; women
gender differences
  burnout and wornout 525, 526
  coping 96
  distress 424
  veterinary surgeons 300
  workaholism 377–8
gender discrimination
  impact on health 93
  in workplace 267–8
gender segregation, in workplace 268
gender stereotypes
  leader effectiveness 645
  occupational 267–8
General Adaptation Syndrome (GAS) theory 91, 214, 459–60
General Health Questionnaire (GHQ–12) 111, 114, 115, 520, 534, 538
general models, work-related stress 63–4
Generic Job Stress Questionnaire (GJSQ) 449
GHQ–12 *see* General Health Questionnaire
gingival scoring methods 337
global economy
  restructuring 413
  work–health relationship 413
Global Strategy on Occupational Health for All 441
glucocorticoids 71, 73, 74, 75, 79
glycemia 611
goal acceptance 6
goal setting 125, 205
goals
  and burnout 592
  shared leadership 130
Goleman's framework, emotional competencies 639–41
gonadal growth, interactions of HPA axis with 75, 76
good leadership 125–6
government sector, burnout and wornout 529
group process, burnout prevention programme 627–8

group programmes, implementing shared leadership 129
group training 386
groups, healthy 386–7
growth hormone, stress response 75
Guidance on Risk Assessment at Work (EC) 180
guided imagery techniques 625, 627

halo effects, risk assessments 183
happiness, and health care 394, 401, 402, 403, 407, 408–11
hardiness 103–4, 167
harm, assessment of 181–2
harm/loss appraisals 105
Harvard Medical School 213
Hashimoto's thyroiditis 82
hazard identification 181
hazards *see* occupational hazards
headaches 608
health
  and burnout *see* burnout
  defined 210
  and emotions 455–62
  impact of stress on 94–6
  job characteristics 67
  long-term stress 112
  organizational factors 178
  positive organizational behaviour 103–4
  positive psychology 102–3
  racial and gender discrimination 93
  structural change 304–12
  see also mental health; physical health; work–health relationship
health care, and subjective well-being 393–411
health costs
  health care 393, 395
  stress 94–5
health promotion 209
  effort–reward imbalance model 437–8
  workplace programmes 420–21
health and safety
  legislation 62, 176–7
  policies 204
Health and Safety at Work etc Act (1974) 176
healthy organizations 209–10, 382–90
  group variables 386–7
  healthy people 210
  individual variables 383–5
  interorganizational variables 389–90
  occupational health psychology 210
  organizational variables 387–9
healthy people 210
hepatic gluconeogenesis 79
heroes 566

high strain jobs 32
high-density lipoproteins (HDL) 463
high-risk interventions 210–11
high-tech industries, effect on health 418
higher education, counselling in 243–52
hippocampus 74
HIV 335, 338
home, working at 360
home health care, eustress and attitudes at work 107–8
home–work interface
  psychosocial hazards 179
  work-related stress 224
homeostasis 70, 458, 459
honeymoon effect, training programmes 657
honeymoon phase, temporary employment 327
hope 108–9
hospital nurses, eustress and attitudes at work 107–8
hospitalization, labour market exit 310
hostile aggression 462
hostile organizational culture 268
hostility 462, 464, 468, 469
hours of work
  dependants 356
  and health 415–16
  levels of strain 119
  US managers 119–20
  work–health relationship 419, 423
'how' questions, stress research 67
human interaction, mass production of 156–7
human operating philosophy 638
human population studies, periodontal diseases 340–43
Human Relations School 41
humans, ecological view 21
humour 421
husband support 357
hyperactivation, stress system 80–81
hypercortisolism 79, 81
hyperlipidemia 434, 612
hyperphagia 81
hypertension
  anger, anxiety and 471–4
  cardiovascular disease 463
  disease due to 466–7
  effort–reward imbalance 35, 434
  ethnic groups 96
  psychological publications 464–6
  red blood cell aggregation 612
  stress-related vulnerability 95
hyperthyroidism 81
hypoactivation, stress system 81

hypothalamic-pituitary-adrenal (HPA) axis 71
  activation 72, 73
  glucocorticoids 74
  influence of metabolism 79
  interactions
    with gonadal growth and thyroid axes 75–7
    with immune system 77–9
  stress response research 459
hypothalamus 70, 71
hypothyroidism 81

IIP *see* Investors in People
Ilene 582–3
illness
  absence due to 111–12
  self-reported 516
  vulnerability to 166
  see also mental illness; physical illness
immigrants, burnout and wornout 525, 526, 527
immune system
  common characteristics between CNS and 339
  interactions of HPS axis with 76, 77–9
  social support 33
Independence Model 548, 556, 559
indirect discrimination, recruitment of women 269
individual factors, healthy organizations 383–5
individual-level coping strategies 198–9
individual-level intervention 211
individualism 572
individuals
  characteristics
    stress and health 61–2
    stress-strain relationship 163–71
  costs of stress 94–5
  differences
    coping and emotional intelligence 234
    risk assessments 183
  impact of short business travel 487
industrial occupations, job satisfaction 115
industrial relations difficulties 94
ineffectiveness 601
infectious diseases 81, 82, 338, 609, 612
infertility, and burnout 612
inflammation, diabetes and CVD 611–12
inflammatory cytokines 75, 77–8
inflammatory disease 81
inflammatory stimuli, HPA axis response 81–2

information provision
  during organizational change 4
  readiness for change 7
    case studies 7–15
  self-efficacy 6
    case studies 7–15
information sources, perception of self-efficacy 6
inhibitory neuronal pathways 73
injuries
  absence due to 111–12
  deaths from 418
  failure to return to work after 39
  veterinary practice 296
insomnia 611
institutional discrimination 92–3
insulin resistance 79
insurance agents, career choice and burnout 593
insurance claims, business travel 480, 482
integral student counselling 247
intellective skills, demand for 425
intellectual intelligence, occupational success 634
intellectual operating philosophy 638
intelligence quotient 229
intenneurons 74
intentionality 513
interactive justice 30, 31, 40
interleukin 1β 77
interleukin IL–6 77
internal attributions, interpretation of events 271
internal cues, self-efficacy 6
internal locus of control 165, 166, 277
internal resources 511
interorganizational variables, healthy organizations 389–90
interpersonal conflict, and burnout 29
interpersonal constructions, occupational stress 28–31
interpersonal relationships
  occupational stress 223
  psychosocial hazards 179
interrole conflict *see* work–family conflict
interventions
  evaluations, risk management 184–5
  health and safety 422
  preventive management model 210–12, 214
  role clarification 205
  to reduce burnout 614–15
  stress research 68
  work–family conflict 361–2
  work–health relationship 419–20

see also crisis intervention; stress management
interviewers, in recruitment 269
intolerance syndrome 416
intrapersonal constructions, occupational stress 21–8
introversion 22
Inventory of Situations and Responses of Anxiety (ISRA) 472–3
Investors in People (IIP) 384
irritability 94, 609, 611
ischaemic heart disease 281
ISRA *see* Inventory of Situations and Responses of Anxiety

JCQ *see* Job Content Questionnaire
JDC *see* job demand–control model
job analysis 204
job burnout
  mediation model *see* mediation model
  occupational stress 28–9
job challenge, active learning 137
job characteristics
  active learning
    future research 144–8
    knowledge concerning 133–9
    temporal effects 139–43
  affect on personality 24–5
  health status 67
job conditions, burnout 522, 531–2
job content, psychosocial hazards 179
Job Content Questionnaire (JCQ) 447
job control
  active learning 140–41
    distinguishing specific effects 147
  burnout 531
  healthy organizations 387
  improving perceptions of 201
  social support and 309
job demand–control model 32–3, 445
  active learning hypothesis
    current knowledge 133–9
    temporal effects on learning 139–43
  four quadrants 132–3
  health promotion measures 438
  mediation model, burnout 546
  Swedish Work Environment surveys 305
job demands
  active learning 140–41
    distinguishing specific effects 147
  burnout and wornout 531
  emotional exhaustion 497, 520
  gap between knowledge and 224
  managing stress of 201–2
job descriptions 203

job dissatisfaction 115–16
job insecurity 47, 60, 168, 229
job involvement 134–7
job loss
  experience of 257, 274, 281, 283, 284
  managers 257–9
  women 259–60, 281
job overload 202
job satisfaction
  active learning hypothesis 134–7
  burnout 29, 540
  enjoyment of work 376
  health care 401
  health variables 402
  healthy organizations 387
  low demand and high control 32
  negative affectivity 23
  occupational groups 113–14, 115–16
  occupational stress indicator 297
  procedural justice 30
  salary level 270
  technology 417
  temporary employees 319, 320, 325, 328
  transformational leadership 646
  veterinary surgeons 298, 299, 300
  work–family conflict 352
  workaholism 373–4
job search 266
  approaches to 266–7
  personal contacts 269–70
  unsuccessful 271–2
job security
  burnout 553
  effort-reward imbalance 437
job simplification 156, 157
job skidding 270–71
job stress, business travel 483
Job Stress Survey (JSS) 448, 450
job turnover 29, 30
job understimulation 204
job withdrawal 319, 320, 324–5, 328
jobs, core dimensions 204
joke telling 421
JSS *see* Job Stress Survey
justice theory 30–31, 40

knowledge
  construction of reality 44
  gap between job demands and 224
  post-structuralist theory 43–4

labour power, valorization 41–2
labour process analysis, occupational stress 40–48

labour market exit, older people 310
labour market position, burnout and wornout 522, 526, 528–9, 534
labour turnover 94
laissez-faire leadership 642, 644, 647
latent deprivation model 23–4
LC-NE *see* locus ceruleus-norepinephrine
leaders
  characteristics of 641
  female 644
  pseudo-transformational 644
  qualities and abilities of ideal 126–7
leadership
  defining good 125–6
  emotional intelligence 641–2
    developing through 656–67
  see also effective leadership; shared leadership; transactional leadership; transformational leadership
learned helplessness 271, 339
learned optimism 635
learning *see* self-directed learning
learning organizations 243
learning-by-doing 130
legislation, work-related stress 62–3, 176–7
leisure activities, participation in 24–5
length of time unemployed, and stress 273–4
letting go, travel stress point 479
leukocyte adhesiveness/aggression 612
LHRH *see* luteinizing hormone-releasing hormone
life events
  periodontal diseases 341
  psychological well-being 36
life expectancy, medical health efficacy 396
life satisfaction
  career-oriented women 259
  health care 401, 402
  life expectancy 396
  measures 382–3
  temporary employees 319, 320, 323–4, 328
lipid mediators 72, 74
LOC *see* locus of control
location, study and student counselling 251
locus ceruleus-norepinephrine (LC-NE) system 70, 73, 74
locus of control (LOC)
  occupational stress indicator 297
  stress and strain relationship 165–6
  unemployment and stress 277
  veterinary surgeons 299, 300
long-range thinking 193–4
long-term sick leave, downsizing 307–11
long-term stress, and health 112

longitudinal research
  active learning 144–5
  work–family conflict 350–51
  work-related stress 66
love, existential quest 566, 567
love and burnout model 571
low strain jobs 32, 33
low-density lipoproteins (LDL) 463, 610
low-level jobs/occupations, strain and illness 113, 115
Luddites 152
luteinizing hormone-releasing hormone (LHRH) 75

Macpherson Report 90
maladaptive coping 168–9
maladaptive outcomes, occupational stress 220–21
male unemployed managers
  activities 265
  barriers to re-employment 267
  financial stress and depression 261
  job search approaches 266, 267
  self-esteem 274, 276
  stress effects, compared with women 281–3
  stress outcomes 280–81
male veterinarians 300
malnutrition 81
management control
  audits 182
  of labor process 43, 44
management fads 387–8
Management of Health and Safety at Work Regulations (1992) 176
management training 384
managerial jobs, internal LOC 166
managerial prerogative 43
managerial strategies, healthy environments 424
managers
  burnout 585–6, 591, 592
    compared with entrepreneurs 588–91
  differences between leaders and 642
  job satisfaction 115
  see also senior managers; unemployed managers
'Managing Pressure' programme 169
Managing Self Relevant Emotions 234
manpower survey, veterinary surgeons 294
manual workers, nervous strain 113
manufacturing occupations, job satisfaction 115
marital relationships, moderators of stress 263

marital status
  burnout and wornout 525, 526, 527
  short business travels 481
marriage, cardiovascular disease 463–4
'marshmallow' experiment 635–6
Marxist perspective, labour process 40–43
Mary 584–5
masculine culture 572
Maslach Burnout Inventory – Education Survey (MBI-ES) 141
Maslach Burnout Inventory – General Survey (MBI-GS) 495, 550
Maslach Burnout Inventory – Human Services Survey (MBI-HSS) 495, 496
Maslach Burnout Inventory (MBI) 29, 495, 497–9, 600–602
mass production, of human interaction 156–7
mastery 134, 137, 141
maternal leave 360
maturing, coping with stress 193–4
Mayer and Salovey framework, emotional intelligence 638–9
MBI see Maslach Burnout Inventory
MBI-ES see Maslach Burnout Inventory – Education Survey
MBI-GS see Maslach Burnout Inventory – General Survey
MBI-HSS see Maslach Burnout Inventory – Human Services Survey
MBTI see Myers Briggs Type Indicator
meaning, importance in coping process 623–4
meaningfulness 108–9, 566
measurement, of active learning 145
mediating factors
  coping 226
  unemployment and stress 272–9
  work–family conflict 352–8
mediation model, job burnout 544
  areas of worklife 545–6
  discussion 559–63
  experienced burnout 544
  hypotheses 547–8
  method 548–53
  organizational factors 544–5
  results 553–9
  work-related outcome 546–7
medical examinations 450
medical insurance claims, business travel 480, 482
medicine, preventive 213–14
meditation 191, 627
MEIS see Multifactor Emotional Intelligence Scale
melancholic depression 79, 80, 81

men
  infertility, burnout 612
  TABP and CHD 164
  work–family conflict 355
  see also husband support; male unemployed managers; male veterinarians
mental health
  activity levels during unemployment 266
  consequences of burnout 607–9
  female managers 95–6
  health care
    expenditure and happiness 408–11
    performance 407–8
  impact of work 419
  multiple roles 259
  occupational stress indicator 297
  perceived control 34
  subjective well-being 394–404
  unemployment 535
  veterinary surgeons 299, 300–301
  see also psychological distress; psychological well-being
mental illness
  buffers 103, 357
  effort-reward imbalance 434
  health costs 395
  prevalence of minor 111
  students 244
  unemployment 261, 279–80, 416
mental stress, cardiac physiology 469–71
mesocortical dopamine system 73
mesolimbic dopamine system 73
metabolism, influence of HPA axis 79
methodological issues, stress research 64–5
mice studies, periodontal disease and stress 339–40
micro-processes, stress research 67
migration, stress 93–4
military, relationship between work and hardiness 103–4
mind, influence on healing 339
miners' nystagmus 45
mobile phones 153–4
moderating factors
  coping 226
  emotional intelligence 229
  temporary employees 320
  unemployment and stress 272–9
  work–family conflict 352–8
monopoly capitalism 42
mood management strategies 232, 234
morale, positive work experiences 36
mortality
  cardiovascular disease 466, 468

occupational-related injuries and disease 418
stress-related disease 220, 509
mortality ratios, by causes and class
  (1970–72) 112
  (1991–93) 117
motivation 384, 519, 639, 640
motivational tendencies 228
MSCEIT 234–5
multi-causality, psychophysiological disorders 455–6
Multifactor Emotional Intelligence Scale (MEIS) 234
multiple intelligences 638
multiple roles
  commitment to work 260
  and well-being 259, 351
municipal employees, burnout and wornout 529
musculoskeletal disorders 609
musculoskeletal pain 418, 435, 436, 437
Myers Briggs Type Indicator (MBTI) 385
myocardial infarction 464, 465, 466, 473, 609, 612

NA *see* negative affectivity
naps, post-lunch 421
narcotic withdrawal 81
national cultures 388
national health care systems, physical health 405–7
National Institute for Occupational Safety and Health (NIOSH) 21, 446, 449
neck and shoulder symptoms 418
negative affectivity (NA) 23, 167
negative appraisals 105
negative coping 229
negative feedback 38
negative learning 140
negative life events, periodontal diseases 341
negotiation, work conditions 43
neoplastic diseases 81
nervous strain 113
networking
  health organizations 389–90
  unemployed managers 269–70
neural connections, stress system 73
neuropeptides 74
neuroticism 22–3, 26, 29, 36, 401, 402
neurotransmitters 73
new technology 152–8
  changes in the workplace 152–3
  defined 151
  struggle for workplace control 153–7
newspaper production 152–3, 158

nicotine withdrawal 81
night flights, business travel 489
NIOSH *see* National Institute for Occupational Safety and Health
nitric oxide 74
non-delegation 372
non-job demands, burnout and wornout 532
non-manual workers, nervous strain 113
NORA (National Occupational Research Agenda) 68
noradrenaline (norepinephrine) 73, 74, 459
notices of termination, burnout and wornout 531–2
Nottingham approach, work-related stress 174–85
nucleus accumbens 73
nurses
  burnout 435, 581–3, 591, 592
  experiences of eustress 106–8
  stress-related illness 94

obesity 79, 463, 610
objective knowledge 44
obsessive-compulsive disorder 81, 371
occupational gender stereotypes 267–8
occupational groups
  absence from work 116
  burnout and wornout 520–21, 522, 526, 527, 529–31, 534
  executive stress 115
  job satisfaction 113–14, 115–16
occupational hazards
  negative effects on health 441
  veterinarians 296
  see also physical hazards; psychosocial hazards
occupational health psychology 210
occupational safety, work intensity and job insecurity 47
occupational stress
  anger and proactive coping 509–11
  burnout *see* burnout
  concept of 20
  coping with 224–6
  cybernetics and systems theory 37–40
  definitions 21, 218–20
  emotional intelligence and coping 230
  interpersonal constructions 28–31
  intrapersonal constructions 21–8
  labour process analysis 40–48
  maladaptive outcomes 220–21
  measurement of 447–50
  models and theories 31–3, 49–51, 444–7
  organizational variables 20–21

psychomedical model 20
research 442–3
specific sources of 221–4
synthesis of constructions 48–51
in the workplace 450–51
see also work stress; work-related stress
Occupational Stress Indicator (OSInd) 296–7, 302, 448
Occupational Stress Inventory (OSInv) 447–8
occupational success, intellectual intelligence 634
older workers, structural change 310
open culture 388
opioid peptides 73
optimism 26, 103, 167, 504, 615–16
organizational change
　employees
　　change management strategies 4–16
　　experience of uncertainty 3–4
　　participation in decision-making 4
　mediation model, burnout 546–7, 551–3, 554, 555, 557, 558, 560
　occupational stress 219
　perception of job control 33
　role of information provision 4
　work–health relationship 413
organizational climate
　coping and well-being 27
　occupational stress 24, 223–4
　psychological wellbeing 36–7
　as a source of stress 200–201
organizational culture
　health and safety 424
　occupational stress 223–4
　personality type 388
　psychosocial hazards 179
　as a source of stress 200–201
　women's experience of hostile 268
organizational factors
　burnout and wornout 522, 526, 531–2
　occupational stress 20–21
　poor health 178
　psychological distress and morale 36
organizational justice theory 30–31, 40
organizational learning, risk management 184–5
organizational policies, work–family conflict 358–61
organizational psychology 382
organizational restructuring
　work–health relationship 415
　see also downsizing
organizational socialization 315

organizational strategies, coping with job stress 225
organizational stress, health-risk preventive management 215
organizational structure, occupational stress 223–4
organizational theory, occupational stress 31–3
organizational values, workaholism 373
organizations
　appeal of new technology 152
　impact of short business travel 487
　see also healthy organizations; work environments
OSInd *see* Occupational Stress Indicator
OSInv *see* Occupational Stress Inventory
osteoporosis 80
Ottawa Charter of the World Health Organization 210
outside world, taking action in 194–5
overcommitment 35, 435, 519
overemployment, employee health 416
overqualification, barrier to re-employment 267

paid employment, numbers of women in 254–5
panic disorder 81
paperwork, burnout and burnout 520, 529, 534
paradigms, occupational stress 49–50
paraventricular nuclei (PVN) 70, 74
parental leave, work–family conflict 359
part-time working, work–family conflict 358–9
partner support 263, 357
partnerships 389
parvocellular CRH 70
passive jobs 32, 140
passive management 642
paternal issues, and burnout 586, 587
paternal leave 360
path analysis 65
pay differentials 270–71
pay satisfaction 29
PCI *see* Proactive Coping Inventory
peer support groups 614
people, healthy 210
'people' jobs, burnout and wornout 520–21, 529, 534
people-centred approach, prevention 210–12
peptic ulcers 220
peptidergic activity 82
perceived conflict of time 350
perceived control 34, 505
perceived inequity 29–30
perceived self-efficacy 504, 512
perceived stress, levels of 117–19

perceived support 358
perceived threat 191, 223
perceptions
   changing 191
   reliability, validity and accuracy 182–3
   of well-being 351
perfect acculturation 94
perfectionism 370, 372
performance, emotional intelligence 228–30
performance-based self-esteem 523
periodontal diseases 335–42
   bacteria related to 335
   determinants 336–7
   epidemiological studies 335, 342
   future research 342
   human population studies 340–43
   initiation and progression of 335
   laboratory studies on animals 339–40
   risk assessments and study designs 337–8
person–environment fit model 32, 444
   coping with stress 198
   role ambiguity 316
personal accomplishment 498–9
   reduced 582, 600
personal contacts, job search 269–70
personal control
   as psychological resource 504
   unemployment and stress 277–8
personal development 383–4
personal factors, stress and unemployment 274–9
personal harassment 224
personal identity, economic deprivation 261
personal learning agendas 664–5
personal and protective occupations, job satisfaction 115
personal psychosynthesis 624
personality
   burnout and health 537, 615
   development, stable relationships 634
   entrepreneurs 588
   job characteristics and learning 147
   occupational stress 22–6
   teacher stress 96
   see also Type A behaviour pattern
phase model, of burnout 601–2
philosophical approach, emotional intelligence 637–8
physical exercise
   cardiovascular disease 463
   excessive 81
   veterinarians 298
physical exertion 191
physical hazards 178, 179, 296

physical health
   consequences of burnout 609–12
   impact of work tasks 418
   national health care systems 405–7
   occupational stress indicator 297
   and perceived control 34
   veterinary surgeons 299, 300–301
   work intensity and job insecurity 47
   work–family conflict 351
physical illness
   buffers 103, 357
   financial stress 261
   unemployment 280
physicians, career choice and burnout 592–3
physiological adaptations, during stress 71
Pines' Burnout Model and Measure 517, 518, 523, 535, 602–3
platelet-activating factor 77
play 421
pleasure, burnout as low level of 499
POB *see* positive organizational behaviour
Police Stress Survey (PSS) 448
policies
   equal opportunity 90
   family-friendly 205
   health and safety 204
   study and student counselling 249–50
   work–family conflict 358–61
political activities, participation in 24–5
population-based interventions 210
Porphyromonas gingivalis 335, 337, 339
positive appraisals 105
positive feedback 38
positive framing 193
positive organizational behaviour (POB) 103–4
positive psychology 102–3, 382, 384, 385, 483
post-structuralist theory 43–4
post-traumatic stress disorder 48–9, 81
post-trip stressors 479
postganglionic neurons 74
postpartum depression 81
power distance, and culture 572
powerlessness 222–3
pragmatic operating philosophy 637–8
pre-trip stressors 478–9
precarious employment 47
prefrontal cortex 73
preganglionic neurons 74
premature deaths 220
premenstrual tension 81
presenteeism 35
pressure at work
   occupational stress indicator 297
   veterinarians 299, 300

prevalence, stress research 67–8
prevention
    complementary model 212–14
    initiatives, study and student counselling 248
    public health model 210–12
    of stress 190
    stress research 68
prevention paradox 210–11
preventive measures, burnout 613
prewar burnout, wartime threat appraisal 612
Primal Leadership 648
primary alienation 123
primary appraisal 5
primary intervention 211, 212, 214
primary prevention, business travel 489
primary stress management 198
primary-level stress management 200–206
Princeton Survey Research Associates 442
proactive coping 504–5
    and burnout 505–6
        study 506–8
    resources and outcomes 511–12
    self-efficacy 513
    work stress and anger 509–10
        study 510–11
Proactive Coping Inventory (PCI) 505
problem-focused coping 226, 233, 278, 279, 357
problematic relationships 223
procedural justice 29, 30
process model, of burnout 517–19
productivity
    burnout 29
    psychometric tools of recruitment 634
    reduced through stress 441, 442
professional development 384
professionals
    burnout and wornout 534, 537
    job satisfaction 115
    nervous strain 113
pseudo-transformational leaders 644
PSS *see* Police Stress Survey
psychiatric patients, periodontal diseases 341
psychiatric services, burnout in 537–52
psychoanalytic approach, emotional intelligence 637
psychoanalytic perspective
    burnout 537, 566
    career choice 580
psychodynamic reasons, career choice 581
psychological actions, coping 191–4
psychological contract, changes in 30, 157–8
psychological counselling 244
psychological defense mechanisms 27, 191
psychological distress
    high demand and low control 32
    temporary workers 319, 320, 323
    work experiences 36
psychological morbidity, prevalence of minor 111
psychological processes
    changing 192–4
    exacerbating stress 189
psychological symptoms, TABP 279
psychological well-being
    comparative studies 394–404
    counselling 421
    dynamic equilibrium theory 35–6
    impact of unemployment 282
    self-esteem 275
    social support 264
    work experiences 27
    work intensity and job insecurity 47
    work–family conflict 350–51
    workaholism 374–5
psychology
    misuse of methodology 65
    see also occupational health psychology; positive psychology; transpersonal psychology
psychomedical model
    basic assumptions 38
    occupational stress 20
psychophysiological disorders 455–6
    relevant emotions 456–62
psychosis 96
psychosocial adulthood 245
psychosocial factors
    cardiovascular disease 463–4
    work-related stress 59–68
psychosocial hazards
    health and safety interventions 422
    work-related stress 177–80
psychosocial stress, defined 338–9
psychosomatic symptoms 279, 435
psychosynthesis 624–5
psychosynthesis counsellors 628–9
psychotherapy, student support 247
psychotic disorders 458
PsycLIT 456
PTSD *see* post-traumatic stress disorder
public health model, prevention 210–12
pulse rates, abnormal 450
PVN *see* paraventricular nuclei

qualitative overload 222
quality
    as economic and human reality 243
    student counselling 251

quality control, poor 94
quality improvement, at student level 243–4
quality of life, and cooperativeness 395
quality of work, work–health relationship 413
quantitative overload 222

race
  cardiovascular disease 463
  hypertension 468
Race Relations Act (1965) 90
Race Relations Act (1976) 90
Race Relations (Amendment) Act (2000) 90
racial discrimination, impact on health 93
racism 92
raised blood pressure 94, 95, 220, 466, 469
randomized controlled trials, periodontal disease 337
rat studies, periodontal disease and stress 340
rational values, wrongly ordered 192
rationalism 638
RCVS *see* Royal College of Veterinary Surgeons
re-employment, barriers to 267
re-entry, travel stress point 479–80
readiness for change 6–7
  case studies 7–15
reality
  knowledge discourses 44
  see also everyday reality
reason, and coping 197
reciprocal effects, stress research 67
reciprocity 509
recruitment, unemployed managers 268–9
red blood cell aggregation 612
reduced cellular immunity 612
reduced commitment, job burnout 29
reduced efficacy, MBI 601
reduced personal accomplishment 582, 600
reframing 192–3
regulation *see* emotional regulation
relationship management 640
relationships
  couple burnout 567
  personality development and stable 634
  self-directed learning 666–7
  and stress 223
  see also interpersonal relationships; marital relationships; work–health relationship
relax, inability to 516
relaxed group, burnout study 519, 524, 527
repair, of emotions 232–3
repetitive strain injury (RSI) 45, 46

repression 191
research
  active learning 138–9, 144–8
  burnout 495–6, 517, 566, 599
    future 500–501, 615–16
  coping 225, 503
  emotional intelligence 227–8, 234–5
  ethnicity and health 97
  eustress 109
  occupational stress 442–3
  periodontal disease 342
  study and student counselling 249
  temporary employees 314
  work–family conflict 346
  work–health relationship 422–5
  work-related stress
    future direction 66–8
    general models 63–4
    methodological issues 64–5
  workaholism 366–7, 378–9
  see also longitudinal research
research designs
  cross-sectional studies 64
  periodontal disease 337–8
residual risk, drawing conclusions about 182
resigned satisfaction 137
resistance stage, GAS 459, 460
respite research, business travel 483–4
response-based approach, to stress 91
restlessness at work 611
retirement, effects 310
reverse buffering effect 328–9
rewards, mediation model, burnout 546, 552, 554, 555, 557, 558, 560, 561
rheumatoid arthritis 81, 82, 609
richer coping resources 231
risk assessments
  definition of 180
  inclusion of physical hazards 179
  key principles 181
  periodontal disease 337–8
  stepwise process 181–2
  in terms of the law 177
risk avoidance 44
risk discourses 44–5
risk estimation 183
risk factors
  cardiovascular disease 462–4
  identification of likely 182
  periodontal diseases 335
  stress research 68
  work-related stress 60–61
risk imposition 45

risk management model
  work-related stress
    adapting for 177
    evaluation and organizational learning 184–5
    psychosocial and organizational characteristics 178
    risk assessment cycle 180–83
    risk reduction cycle 183–4
    suggested use 175–6
risk reduction 183–4
role ambiguity
  measuring 117, 118
  organizational change 3
  psychosocial hazards 179
  as source of stress 205, 222, 223
  temporary employees 316, 318, 319, 327, 328
role conflict
  measuring 117, 118
  organizational change 3
  psychosocial hazards 179
  as source of stress 205, 222, 223
  temporary employees 316, 318, 319, 327
role negotiation 206
role overload 3, 117, 223
role underload 223
role-related stress 222–3
  managing 205–6
  temporary employees 315–30
romantic choices, unconscious 567
Royal College of Veterinary Surgeons (RCVS) 294
RSI *see* repetitive strain injury
rust-out 204

safety *see* health and safety; occupational safety
salary
  effort-reward imbalance 437
  level, job satisfaction 270
  see also pay differentials; pay satisfaction
schizophrenia 96
school culture 243
scientific management *see* Taylorism
seasonal depression 81
second-order change 38
secondary alienation 123–4
secondary appraisal 5
secondary interventions 211, 212, 214
secondary prevention, business travel 489
secondary-level stress control 199, 200
segmentation, work and family 356
self tradition, culture 572, 573
self-acceptance 628

self-awareness 228, 384, 639, 640, 648
self-blame 166, 278
self-concept 274–6
self-control 194, 236
self-directed learning 659–60
  creating a personal agenda 664–5
  developing and using relationships 666–7
  discovering who we want to be 660–62
  experimenting and practicing changes 665–6
  knowing oneself 662–4
self-efficacy
  building 195
  change-related 5–6
    case studies 7–15
  emotional intelligence 231–2
  perceived 504
  social support 512
  stress-strain relationship 167
  unemployment and stress 276–7
self-esteem 167, 259, 274–6, 436–7
  see also contingent self-esteem; performance-based self-esteem
self-identification
  ethnic 88
  techniques 625–6
self-importance 154
self-managed teams 201
self-management 640
self-motivation 640
self-organization 388–9
self-regulation 228, 384, 639, 640
self-regulatory processes, job characteristics and learning 147–8
self-report questionnaire, occupational stress 448–9
self-reports, job demand-control 33
Sely, Hans 214, 459
senior managers
  emotional intelligence and leadership style 646–7
  preventive measures, burnout 613
separation, travel stress point 479
serotonergic activity 82
serotonin 73, 77
sex discrimination, during recruitment 269
Sex Discrimination Act (1975) 268, 269
sex roles 261
sex-role socialization 354
sexism, impact on health 93
sexual disorders 458
sexual harassment 224
shared leadership 127
  advantages 127–8

disadvantages 128
implementation 128–30
shiftwork
  employee health 415–16
  managing stress 202
Shirom-Melamed Burnout Model and Measure (SMBM) 603–5
short business travels 478–90
  consequences of 480–84
  psychological detachment from work 484–90
  stressors 478–80
sick leave
  ambient noise 202
  burnout and year-long sick 528, 535
  downsizing 306, 307–11
  levels 305
  statistics 94
sickness presenteeism 305
single unemployed men, impact on psychological well-being 282
single unemployed women
  depression 263
  impact on psychological well-being 282
  job search 267
situational appraisals 5, 232
situational factors
  job burnout 29
  stress and strain relationship 167–8
situational mediators, burnout and health 615
skill training 423
skill variety 204
skills
  emotional 233
  gap between job demands and 224
skills use, unemployment 258–9
sleep impairment 415–16, 608, 611
small group discussions, stress reduction 201
SMBM see Shirom-Melamed Burnout Model and Measure
SMI see stress management intervention
smoking
  burnout 610
  cardiovascular disease 463
  periodontal disease 336
  unemployment and stress 280
  veterinary profession 298
SMT see stress management training
social awareness 228, 640
social class
  absence due to illness or injury 111–12
  prevalence of minor psychiatric morbidity 111
  standardized mortality ratios 112, 117
  and stress 46

social commitment, burnout as loss of 499
social comparison information 38
social conditions, personality changes 25
social connectedness 120
social constructionist approach, emotional intelligence 636–7
social contacts, unemployment 264–5
social desirability effects, risk assessments 183
social integration 262
social interaction, via email 155
social isolation, economic deprivation 261
social networks 262, 463–4
social problem, burnout as future 616
social process, occupational stress as a 45–8
social skills 639, 640
social support
  coping with stress 196
  as job characteristic 146–7
  long-term sick leave 307–9
  self-efficacy 512
  stress-strain relationship 168
  temporary employees 317, 320, 328–9
  unemployed managers 262–5, 283
  and well-being 33, 264
  work–family conflict 357–8
social systems theory 37
socialization period, stress levels 315
Society of Practising Veterinary Surgeons (SPVS) 293
socioeconomic status
  burnout and wornout 520, 526, 527, 534
  cardiovascular disease 464
  periodontal disease 337, 340
  subjective well-being 395
somatic symptoms 608
somatomedin C 75
somatostatin 74
Spain, cardiovascular disease 466
special groups, study and student counselling 252
specialized diagnostics, higher education 248
spillover effect, active learning hypothesis 134
spiritual autobiographies 626
spiritual exercises 627
spiritual psychosynthesis 624
splitting, between burn-in and burn-out 538–9
SPVS see Society of Practising Veterinary Surgeons
stability, in well-being and the environment 22
stable relationships, personality development 634
State-Trait Anger Expression Inventory (STAXI) 472–3

State-Trait Personality Inventory (STPI) 450, 451
State-Trait Process (STP) model 446–7, 449
statistical analyses 64–5
statistical associations 64
statistical inference 65
statistical packages 65
status, business travel 485
status incongruency 223
STAXI *see* State-Trait Anger Expression Inventory
stimulatory neuronal pathways 73
stimulus-based approach, to stress 91
STP *see* State-Trait Process
STPI *see* State-Trait Personality Inventory
strain, and active learning 139, 143–4
strain hypothesis, JDC model 133
strengths, building on 384–5
stress
  and alienation 123–5
  appraisals 196–7
  body's response to 75–9
  cardiovascular disease 461, 464, 468–71
  change management 4–16
  concept of 70
  coping with 190–95
  core elements involved in 188
  defining 91–2
  diabetes 610–11
  ethnic discrimination 92–3
  ethnic identity and experience of 97
  ethnic-specific causes 92
  factors contributing to
    the amount experienced 188–9
    the prolongation of 189
  impact on health 94–6
  migration and acculturation 93–4
  organizational culture and climate 200–201
  periodontal diseases 335–42
  prevention *see* prevention
  psychophysiological disorders 458–9
  social support 196
  unemployment *see* unemployed managers
  veterinary surgeons 293–303
  work–family conflict 346–62
  see also Eustress; executive stress; occupational stress; perceived stress; psychosocial stress; role-related stress; work-related stress
Stress at Work model 444–5
stress epidemic 45–6, 48, 220
stress management
  coping strategies 169
  emotional intelligence 167, 635
  locus of control 166
  preventive 213, 489
  primary level 200–206
  situational factors 168
  social support 168
  traditional approach to 198–200
  tripartite model 200
  type A behaviour pattern 165
  veterinary surgeons 301
stress management intervention (SMI) reports 96
stress management training (SMT) programmes 169–70, 301
stress response 70–4, 214, 338
stress system
  pathophysiology 79–82
  physiology 70–4
stress-related diseases, biological basis 70–83
stress–strain relationship, individual factors 163–71
stressful encounters, avoidance of 231
stressors
  travel 478–80
  veterinary practice 295
  in the workplace 117–18
strikes 27
stroke 96, 466, 611
structural changes
  and health 304–12
  higher education 243
  work–health relationship 413, 415
structural equation modelling
  change management study 8
  organizational climate and morale 36
  personality and job stress 24
  stress research 65
Structural Null Model 548, 556, 559
student support 247
students
  anger and depression 511
  burnout 528–9
  self-reported anxiety 120
  and teacher burnout 583
study failure 246–7
study and student counselling 243–52
  functions of 246–9
  identification of 244–6
  need for additional services 243–4
  prerequisites 249–52
study support 246
subgroups analysis 66–7
subjective well-being
  business travel 485
  comparative studies 394–404

subpersonalities 626
suicide rates
  health care 401, 402, 407
  veterinary surgeons 293
supervisor support
  temporary employees 319
  work–family conflict 361
support *see* social support; student support
supportive communication, from co-workers 328–9
surplus value 42
surveillance mechanisms, stress research 68
Swedish labour market, structural health and change 304–12
sympathetic nervous system 74, 459
sympathetic/adrenomedullary system 71, 74, 79
systemic risk factors, periodontal diseases 335
systems theory, occupational stress 37–40

T-helper–1 suppression 81, 82
TABP *see* Type A behaviour pattern
talent
  desire to use 657
  development of 657–9
task identity 204
task performance 6
task significance 204
task-related sources, of stress 222
Taylorism 25, 40, 41, 43, 156, 425
Teacherline 94
teachers
  burnout 534, 583–5, 591, 592
  job control, efficacy and learning 141
  stress and personality 96
  stress-related illness 94
team building 386
team development, study and student counselling 251–2
teamworking 103, 301
technical training 423
technology
  work–health relationship 413, 416–17
  see also new technology
teleworking/telecommuting 155
temporary employees 314–30
  numbers 314
  research 314
  role-related stress 315–17
    organizational transitions 315
    social support 317
  stress and coping study
    method 317–20
    results 320–26

discussion 326–9
limitations and future direction 329–30
temporary work, employee health 416
tension 276, 611
tertiary interventions 211, 212, 214
tertiary-level stress control 200
theft 30
theology of work 420
theories
  occupational stress 31–3, 49–51, 444–7
  work-related stress 61
theory tradition, culture 572–3
'thing' jobs, burnout and wornout 521, 529, 534
threat appraisal 105, 612
threats
  organizational 219–20
  perceived 191, 223
thyroid axes, interactions of HPA with 75, 76, 77
thyroid stimulating hormone (TSH) 75, 82
time off, business travel 489–90
time path, implementing shared leadership 129
time wasting 33
training
  emotional intelligence 636
  honeymoon effect 657
  need for 423
  study and student counselling 248–9
  see also assertiveness training; group training; management training; stress management training
trait anxiety 120
transactional leadership 642–3
  distinguished from transformational 645
transactional model, of stress 91, 163
Transactional Process model, psychological stress 445–6
transactional theory, occupational stress 31–3
transformational leadership 103, 633, 643–4
  distinguished from transactional leadership 645
  emotional intelligence 646–9
  concluding remarks 649–50
transition-related stress, social support 315
transitions, occupational stress 223
translation process, in risk reduction 183–4
transpersonal psychology 624
trauma
  injuries to veterinary surgeons 296
  see also childhood trauma
travelling to work
  and stress 420
  see also short business travels

treatment approach, to burnout 593–4
trench mouth 338
triangulation
  risk assessments 183
  stress research 67
triglycerides 610
trip stressors 479
tripartite model, stress management 200
trust, transformational leadership 646
TSH see thyroid stimulating hormone
tumor necrosis factor-α 77, 340
tumors 81, 82
Type 2 diabetes mellitus 610–11
Type A behaviour pattern (TABP)
  cardiovascular disease 464, 468
  controversiality of 25–6
  coronary behaviours 95
  emotional exhaustion 616
  occupational stress indicator 297
  original motivation of research into 25
  stress management 165
  stress and strain-related outcomes 164–5
  unemployment and stress 278–9
  veterinary surgeons 294, 299, 300

ulcers 112
uncertainty avoidance 572
unconscious processes
  career choice 567
  impact on behaviour and adaptation 27
underemployment, employee health 416
unemployed managers, and stress 254–85
  comparative research model 256
  conclusions 283–6
  demographic factors 272–4
  gender differences 279–83
  intervening variables 272
  personal factors 274–9
  sources of 255–72
unemployment
  anxiety 516
  burnout and wornout 528, 534
  financial effects 260–61
  mental health 535
  older workers 310
  rates, UK ethnic minorities 90
  risk, work-related stress 60
  work–health relationship 416–17
unemployment status 260
uric acid 463, 610

valorization, labour power 41–2
value tradition, of cultures 572

values
  changing 191–2
  mediation model, burnout 546, 552, 554, 555, 557, 558, 560, 561
  work preferences 637
  see also organizational values
vasoconstriction 469
vasodilation 469
verbal persuasion, self-efficacy 6
veterinary degrees 294
veterinary surgeons
  numbers in UK 293–4
  paradoxical role 293
  public perception of 293
  stress management 301
  stress research 294–6
    methodology 296–8
    results 298–9
      discussion 299–301
      limitations of study 302
      future research 302–3
  suicide rates 293
Veterinary Surgeons Act (1966) 294
video display terminals 417, 418
violence 179
vision, shared leadership 129
visual difficulties 418
visual display terminals 154–5
visualizations 625, 627
vital exhaustion 609, 610
volunteers, SMT 170
vulnerability, to disease and illness 81, 166
vulnerability model, negative affectivity 23

WAC see Workaholic Adjective Checklist
WART see Work Addiction Risk Test
weight gain 81
well-adjusted strivers, burnout study 519, 524, 527
well-being
  at work 382–3
  career-oriented women 259
  latent deprivation model 23–4
  social support 33
  stability 22
  see also psychological well-being
WERS see Workplace Employment Relations Survey
WES see Work Environment Scale
Western Australia Workers Compensation and Rehabilitation Bill (1993) 31
Western Collaborative Group 164
white blood cell activation 612
white collar workers 527

Whitehall studies 25, 31, 433–4
Wilson, Harold 152
wishful thinking 278
withdrawal behaviours 36, 37, 81, 319, 320, 324–5, 328
WOLF study 307–11
women
  importance of employment to 255
  importance of social contacts 264–5
  intolerance syndrome 416
  job search approaches 266, 267
  long-term sick leave after downsizing 307–8
  numbers in paid employment 254–5
  pay differentials 270–71
  preferred coping strategies 96
  stress-related illness 95–6
  work–family conflict 355
  see also female managers; female veterinarians
work
  changing nature of 59–60
  experiences
    morale 36
    psychological distress 36
    well-being 27
  organization, new forms 424–5
  preferences, and values 637
  well-being at 382–3
  see also employment; hours of work; jobs; pressure of work; theology of work
Work Addiction Risk Test (WART) 369, 375
Work Adjustment Theory 22
work arrangements, alternative 204–5
work behaviours, workaholism 371–2
work conditions
  negotiation 43
  personality changes 25
work enjoyment 373, 376
work enthusiasts 372, 373
Work Environment Scale (WES) 447
Work Environment Surveys (Swedish) 305, 306, 516
work environments
  change and stress 295, 299–300
  effect of ethnicity in 89
  family–friendly 205
  psychosocial 67–8
  stress prevention 202
work groups, semi-autonomous 204
work pace 179
work redesign 103
work schedule 179
work stress, ethnicity and 87–97
Work Stress Inventory (WSI) 449

work–family conflict 346–62
  business travels 482
  consequences 350–52
  definitions 346–9
  interventions to reduce 361–2
  measurement of interrole conflict 349–50
  mediators and moderators of 352–8
  organizational policies and practices 358–61
  research 346
  temporary employees 316, 319, 320
work–health relationship
  changes in workforce participation 417–18
  EAPs, health promotion and prevention 420–21
  effect of
    technology 417
    unemployment 416–17
  flexible working 415–16
  global economy and restructuring 413
  impact of work
    on mental health 419
    on physiological health 418
  intervention and prevention 419–20
  key issues 413–15
  research directions 422–5
  restructuring and downsizing 415
  temporary and casual work 416
work-related stress 59–68
  current knowledge 59–63
  evidence for 174–5
  future research 63–8
  legislation 176–7
  major challenge to health and safety 174
  oral health 340–41
  psychosocial hazards 177–80
  risk management model
    adapting 177
    evaluation and organizational learning 184–5
    psychosocial and organizational characteristics 178
    risk assessment cycle 180–83
    risk reduction cycle 183–4
    suggested use 175–6
  see also occupational stress
Workaholic Adjective Checklist (WAC) 368, 374
workaholics, types of 370–71
workaholism
  antecedents of 372–8
  implications for understanding 378
  definitions 367–8
  evaluating components of 376–7
  measures of 368–70

prevalence of 371
research 366–7
   future 378–9
theories of 367
treating 379
work behaviours 371–2
worker fatigue 40–41
workforce participation, changes 417–18
workload
   mediation model, burnout 545, 552, 553, 554, 555, 557, 558, 559, 560, 561
   psychosocial hazards 179
workplace
   changes in 152–3
   emotional intelligence in 636
   hazards *see* occupational hazards
   stress *see* stress

workplace control
   effective employee functioning 157
   new technology 153–7
   struggle for 152–3
Workplace Employment Relations Survey (WERS) 93
World Health Report (2000) 393–4, 404
wornout 518, 523–4, 525, 531–2
WSI *see* Work Stress Inventory

Xenophon 338

Y
γ-amino-butyric acid (GABA) 73
year-long sick, burnout 528, 535